✓ Y0-AGG-152

# LINN'S WORLD STAMP ALMANAC

## A HANDBOOK FOR STAMP COLLECTORS

### Compiled and Edited by
### the Staff of Linn's Stamp News

## FOURTH EDITION

Published by Amos Press Inc., Post Office Box 29, Sidney, Ohio 45367. Publishers of Linn's Stamp News, the world's largest and most informative weekly stamp newspaper; Stamp World, a monthly publication for stamp collectors; Coin World, a weekly newspaper for the entire numismatic field; and Cars & Parts Magazine, a monthly magazine for the auto enthusiast.
Copyright 1982 by Amos Press Inc.

# Foreword

This volume is designed to fill a long-standing gap in philatelic literature, by providing an extensive and comprehensive compendium of the factual materials most essential for a full understanding and appreciation of stamp collecting.

With this work the collector is able to determine at a glance the meaning of a philatelic term in a German auction catalog, or the country issuing a stamp bearing mysterious inscriptions. What is the law affecting philatelic activities? To whom should one write with a stampic complaint or question? The answers are all here in the "Linn's World Stamp Almanac."

Here also are such materials as lists of stamp journals and reference books, of museums and libraries with stamp holdings, and of the large and small clubs and societies which make possible personal interaction in the hobby.

The almanac was compiled with the cooperation of persons throughout the philatelic field. The editors now have need of continuing cooperation from our readers. Comments and suggestions, especially ideas for additional material that users would like to see in future editions, are most welcome.

It is the hope of Linn's Stamp News that the almanac will be a research companion for the stamp collector in all of his day-to-day hobby activities, and a source of information which can add greatly to his participation in and enjoyment of the many facets of philately.

# Staff

**Publisher**
Wayne Lawrence

**Co-publisher**
William T. Amos

**Editor**
Edwin O. Neuce

**Managing Editor**
Jeanne D. Mears

**Staff Contributors:**
Elaine Boughner, Joseph Brockert
Laura Gahagan, Dort Getrost,
Susan Hughes, William A. Jones,
Jeannette Lunsford, Denise McCarty,
Donna O'Keefe, Fran Pfeiffer,
John Sicker.

**Other Contributors:**
John Apfelbaum, Renee Bowden,
James H. Bruns, D. Larry Crumbley,
Tony Crumbley, Frederick S. Dickson,
Belmont Faries, Herman (Pat) Herst,
Ernest A. Kehr, Mark Kellner,
Milton Mitchell, R.P. Odenweller,
Stan Showalter, various
representatives of the collector
and dealer groups, and others.

**Almanac Coordinators**
Jeanne D. Mears and Donna O'Keefe

**Art and Layout Coordinators**
Phil Miller and J. Skinn

**Cover Art**
Mike Lindsay

**Marketing/Sales**
Claude deLorraine

# Contents

(Chapter numbers are shown on left of each chapter title. Bold face numbers to right indicate first page of chapter, while smaller light face numbers indicate page within a chapter dealing with a subject of specific importance to that chapter.)

# Philately's Role in History 1

## History of World Postal Communications

Postal communications have been part of our everyday lives for so long that it is sometimes difficult to remember the long history of slow development in the world's postal services. The posts originated with the ancient empires, for with the introduction of written records, government over extensive territories, the concentration of populations in cities, and the specialization of occupations, came the need for the efficient transmission of messages.

### The Early Empires

The word "post" comes from the Latin term for a fixed station or position. The early empires set up series of stations dedicated to relaying official correspondence or to speeding messengers on their way with fresh transport. With time the systems were refined sufficiently to permit the conveyance of officials on public business along with the correspondence.

Examples of these services are found as early as the 19th century B.C., in clay tablets discovered at the early Assyrian business community of Kanesh in Cappadocia. The tablets were enclosed in clay envelopes and apparently enjoyed efficient and safe transport.

The Bible provides a reference to the early Middle Eastern communications systems. A passage in 2 Chronicles 30 notes that "Hezekiah sent to all Israel and Judah, and wrote letters also to Ephraim and Manasseh, that they should come to the house of the Lord at Jerusalem, to keep the passover to the Lord the God of Israel . . . So couriers went throughout all Israel and Judah with letters from the king and his princes, as the king had commanded . . . So the couriers went from city to city through the country of Ephraim and Manasseh, and as far as Zebulun."

Another early system developed in Egypt, after the 2400 B.C. introduction of papyrus, a paper-like substance composed of wetted and pressed strips of plant material, and the development of a corresponding quick and easy-to-form script. The scribe had a specialized and highly enviable occupation in a society where the norm was still hard manual labor.

Noted posts of a somewhat later date were those of China and Persia. In the former nation, "I Chan" or post-stages were instituted during the Chou Dynasty (1122-255 B.C.). In the 14th century A.D., Marco Polo found 10,000 stations utilizing 200,000 horses. By the 20th century the Ch'ing Dynasty had 15,000 stations for routing correspondence by foot couriers, and 1,600 with horses or boats for priority materials.

### The Persian Posts

Perhaps the most efficient of the early posts was that of Persia, in the 5th and 6th centuries B.C. The Greek historian Herodotus described the outstanding system of roads and highly organized communications in Book V of "The Persian Wars" (edited by Francis R.B. Godolphin in 1942).

"Now the true account of the road in question is the following: Royal stations exist along its whole length, and excellent caravanserais; and throughout, it traverses an inhabited tract, and is free from danger.

"In Lydia and Phrygia there are twenty stations within a distance of ninety-four and one-half parasangs (a parasang originally representing an hour's journey). On leaving Phrygia the Halys has to be crossed, and here are gates through which you must pass before you can traverse the stream. A strong force guards this post.

"When you have made the passage, and are come into Cappadocia, twenty-eight stations and 104 parasangs bring you to the borders of Cilicia, where the road passes through two sets of gates, at each of which there is a guard posted.

"Leaving these behind, you go on through Cilicia, where you find three stations in a distance of fifteen and one-half parasangs. The boundary between Cilicia and Armenia is the river Euphrates, which it is necessary to cross in boats. In Armenia the resting-places are fifteen in number, and the distance fifty-six and one-half parasangs . . ."

The Persian posts are also described in the Biblical book of Esther, chapter 3: "Then the king's secretaries were summoned on the thirteenth day of the first month, and an edict, according to all that Haman commanded, was written to the king's satraps and to the governors over all the provinces and to the princes of all the peoples, to every province in its own script and every people in its own language; it was written in the name of King Ahasuerus and sealed with the king's ring.

"Letters were sent by couriers to all the king's provinces . . . The couriers went in haste by order of the king . . .

"Letters were sent by mounted couriers riding on swift horses (some translations add mules and camels) that were used in the king's service, bred from the royal stud." (8, 10)

This Persian system contributed the main features of those used in the Greek and Roman empires, where a common language helped simplify postal communications. Facilities were maintained by the local communities, and were restricted to official business. As the empires grew in size the postal systems grew with them, and were essential to successful administration.

## Posts for Private Correspondence

It was during this period, in the first few centuries A.D., that substantial private organizations for commercial and personal mail began to develop. Individuals were becoming more and more mobile, and were no longer as tied to their local communities.

Such private services were frequently quite slow to appear and grow. In China, despite the antiquity of the postal system as a whole, min-hsin chu or people's letter offices did not appear until about the 15th century. They were managed by firms which needed transport for their own business messages and permitted others to make use of the routes for a moderate fee. In this same period Ming Emperor Yung Lo opened the imperial mails to private use.

In general, European postal development was retarded by the absence of real central authority with the decline of the Roman empire, and by the accompanying reduction in commerce and literacy. This situation began to change in the 11th century, with the efforts of religious and educational institutions. Parchment came largely to replace papyrus, and paper, best suited of all for correspondence, made its appearance.

Italian cities became the centers of commercial development, and established the necessary postal routes for business documents. Amadeo Tasso's 15th-century system in Venice became the famed Thurn and Taxis service for the Holy Roman Empire, a postal empire which remained in operation into the 19th century.

The Thurn and Taxis postal system was operated by a single family, with a contribution from the government and fees from private users. The revolutions of the 19th century established at least temporarily the primacy of individual nation states, and the expanding activities and responsibilities of the new administrations made government monopolies of the posts an apparent necessity. In most areas these postal trends had been developing slowly for generations.

## Reforms and Innovations

For the future development of worldwide communications, some of the most important events of postal history took place in Great Britain in the middle of the 19th century. The country had had both official and private posts, but a state monopoly on domestic and foreign correspondence was claimed as early as the 17th century. Postage rates were high, for the fees were regarded as a tax.

In 1840, Rowland Hill succeeded in a campaign to establish a low, uniform rate for postage throughout the country, and to have the administration sell indicia indicating that postage had been paid. This did away with a complex system of distance computations and the collection of fees from addressees. It also created a precedent which was soon accepted throughout much of the Western world.

Following the introduction of Britain's "Penny Black" adhesive postage stamp in 1840, the City Despatch Post in New York issued stamps in 1842. Geneva, Zurich, and Brazil followed the next year, Basle and the U.S. Postmasters' Provisionals in 1845, and Mauritius, Trinidad, and the U.S. government itself in 1847.

Later in the 19th century came another important reform, the agreement among the world's postal systems mutually to regulate and facilitate the exchange of mails and the collection of international postal revenues. The General Postal Union, now known as the Universal Postal Union, was formed in 1874. The confusing arrangements that had grown up over the centuries were simplified and modernized.

The British Empire went even further in the realms of uniformity and low fees at the turn of the century, when the Imperial Penny Postage system was established. Anomalies in the rate structures had at times made it possible for other European countries to offer lower postage to British colonies than did Britain herself; under the new arrangement, however, letters could be sent throughout much of the empire at a rate of one penny.

This was an especially great mark of the increasingly accepted view of the post office as a public service. Such colonies as Canada, East Africa, and Australia had attracted many settlers from Great Britain herself, and these individuals were frequently without substantial funds and unable to pay high postal charges. The Post Office was still registering a profit on overall transactions, but was willing, under some pressure from certain colonies, to forego this profit in the interests of improved communications. There was also the distinct possibility that increased volume would ultimately restore the profit.

The posts would effectively bind together the far-flung components of the empire, accomplishing on a personal and commercial basis the same function as they had performed for official communications in the ancient empires.

On Oct. 1, 1908, Great Britain and the United States entered into a special agreement establishing a penny post between the two great English-speaking nations.

The Imperial Penny Post agreements are now gone: two world wars, rising costs, and the decline of the British Empire have definitely seen to that. This period remains, however, as a monument to some of the highest motives in the administration of postal communications.

## New Transport and Technology

The two great themes of the 20th century have been increasing technology and the resulting introduction of new methods of communication, and the regular introduction of higher and higher postal rates. Until recently mail volume had increased steadily, a mark of the lasting demand for this essential service. In the past few years, however, many nations have begun to experience an unfavorable reaction to rising costs and reduced services.

Part of the difficulties are made up by the use of new methods and techniques. While the first mails were carried by runners and mounted couriers, and those of a later date by horse-drawn vehicles, in the 1800s the railroad came into its own as a new way of speedy carriage. The first such transport came in 1830 in England, and was soon a great success. Another innovation was the pneumatic tube, carrying messages beneath city streets without regard for weather or traffic. This has now become a casu-

alty of overwhelming mail volume and the development of motor vehicle transport.

The 19th century also saw the revolutionary impact of steam-powered vessels carrying mail by water routes. Earlier services had been maintained by sailing ships, and could be quite unpredictable depending upon prevailing winds. The famed Cunard line of Great Britain began operations in 1840, and the Pacific Mail Steamship Company became active for the United States in the 1860s.

This same period saw the growing usage of iron for ship construction, creating vessels much better adapted for hard employment than the familiar wooden composition.

Airmail began in earnest during the 1870-71 Prussian siege of Paris, when vast quantities of materials were brought out by balloon over the lines. Heavier-than-air craft were in operation by the first decade of the 20th century, with what is accepted as the world's first official mail carriage by an airplane taking place in India in 1911.

Airmail is one area where the costs of postage have decreased significantly since the first introduction of the service. In the early years the airplane was a novelty, and any carriage of mail was a souvenir or experimental arrangement. Even when the carriage of messages by air was reasonably well established costs kept the fees relatively high. Increased volume, the profitability of air transport as a whole, and the influence of the Universal Postal Union agreements have in recent decades kept international airmail at a cost within the reach of most correspondents.

## Modern Communications

In 1970 the "Mailgram" service, which permits the transmission of messages by microwave network, went into operation. The orbiting of the Westar communications satellite in 1974 made this vehicle available for the Mailgrams, and more recent innovations have included the provision of paid reply forms and other special services.

Mailgram messages are designed to be moved speedily from sender to the recipient's post office, where they are to be given priority delivery in the normal mail stream. Western Union states that "electronic mail has finally eliminated distance as a factor in the time it takes to move messages."

More earthbound mail has also enjoyed the application of much new technology since the traditional hand sorting and dispatch. Mail cancellation was mechanized in the late 19th century. Many postal administrations are today experimenting with or generally applying such innovations as imprinted address codes, optical tagging, and machines which actually read handwritten letters and numbers.

It seems clear that this is only the beginning of the new postal technology, for improved methodology is one clear necessity in dealing with the vast volume of worldwide mails.

While the Mailgram system is probably the electronic system most familiar to many mail users, the transmission of data between persons and computers has generally become an active and complex field. Many of these systems became known to businessmen during the U.S. postal strike of 1970, when it was necessary to find alternatives to standard postal delivery.

One very new idea is the International Telephone and Telegraph Corporation's glass optical fibers, which can carry vast amounts of information through the use of laser beams. The firm notes that if the promise of current experiments is realized, a flexible cable of fibers about the thickness of a pencil would be able to transmit the entire Bible in one tenth of a second.

High capacity is also demonstrated by the Xerox Corporation 800 model communicating electronic typing system, which it is stated can transmit up to 120 characters a second over ordinary telephone circuits. This works out to more than two pages of double spaced text per minute.

Xerox Office Systems Division president Dr. Robert J. Potter describes the system as "a viable alternative to mail service, particularly when utilizing low-cost evening or night telephone rates."

Other corporations are also working on solutions to the problems of our ever-increasing communications, and these specific examples are only singled out to show some of the directions in which the overall science is moving.

Generally, the tendency in the area of alternatives to the mail service has been to enhance direct communications between individuals and businesses, increasing the speed of transmission and decreasing the cost. Some possibilities utilize pre-existing linkages and improve capabilities for senders and receivers; others create new connections with improved possibilities in the transmission itself.

All of this is of extreme importance, for just as the ancient empires were dependent upon efficient communications for continued government and commerce, so modern relations, both national and international, require easy channels of information exchange. The ever-growing complexity of the material which must be known, and the sobering potential consequences of poor communications in a crisis, place a greater premium on new methodology and technology than ever before.

In many developing countries the mail service continues to have a genuine mystique, providing a link with the outside world and offering an influential avenue for information of outstanding personal importance.

Postal communications will have to rise to the challenge of this varied situation, or they will be replaced by alternatives which will provide the needed services.

# Stamp Issuing Entities

Since Great Britain issued the Penny Black and Two-Pence Blue in 1840, over 700 governments have issued postage stamps. This has produced an array of stamps that may bewilder the beginning stamp collector, especially the collector whose study of history has somehow not included such areas as Alaouites or Trebizond.

In the following listing, we have attempted to provide a compilation of the nations, provinces, cities, armies, etc., which have, at some point, issued postage stamps.

For the purposes of this listing, we have limited our stamp issuing entities to those authorities exercising de facto political control of an area or territory, which have issued stamps for other than strictly local use. We have thus omitted the listing of issues by purely municipal and private individuals.

We have attempted to provide brief geographical and historical sketches for each of these entities, so that the reader may obtain a general idea of where the country issuing a given stamp is located and what the general circumstances might be surrounding its use.

We have not attempted to give complete philatelic background of all stamp issuing entities. The dates in the parentheses following the name of the country indicate the period of time during which stamps were, or are still being issued. A perusal of any of the leading catalogs will supply additional information.

— A —

**ABU DHABI (1964-72)**

A sheikdom in the former Trucial States in eastern Arabia, bordering on the Persian Gulf.

Under British protection 1862-1971, Abu Dhabi joined with the other Trucial States to form the independent United Arab Emirates on December 2, 1971.

Long undeveloped, with few resources, Abu Dhabi's medieval existence began to change dramatically with the discovery of oil in 1958. By the 1970s, it had become a major oil exporter and enjoyed one of the highest per capita incomes in the world.

## ADEN (1937-65)

Former British colony and protectorate in southwest Arabia. The colony of Aden was attached to India 1839-1937, and Indian stamps were used.

Stamps of the colony were first issued in 1937, being used in most of the Aden protectorate area, as well as within the Aden colony itself.

In 1963, the two districts, except for the eastern Kathiri and Qu'aiti states, united to form the Federation of South Arabia.

Aden stamps were replaced by those of the Federation on April 1, 1965.

## AEGEAN ISLANDS (Individual Islands' Issues) (1912-32)

A number of Italian issues were overprinted with names of the various Aegean islands including Calchi, Calino, Caso, Coo, Fero, Fisso, Nisiro, Patmo, Piscopi, Rhodes (Rodi), Scarpanto, Simi and Stampalia.

AEGEAN ISLANDS

## AEGEAN ISLANDS (DODECANESE) (1912-47)

A group of twelve islands in the southeastern Aegean Sea.

Under Turkish rule since the early 16th century, the islands declared their independence in 1912, during the Italo-Turkish War, but were soon occupied by Italy. Greece recognized Italian control of the islands in 1920, and Turkey formally ceded them to Italy in 1923.

Occupied by Germany after the Italian collapse in 1943, they were liberated by the British in 1945.

Italy issued a large number of stamps for use in the islands from 1912-43, while the Germans overprinted a few issues from 1943-45.

During 1945-47, stamps of the British Middle East Forces were used. In 1947, specially overprinted Greek stamps were used. Regular Greek issues have been used since 1947, when the islands were annexed by Greece.

## AFARS AND ISSAS, FRENCH TERRITORY OF THE (1967-1977)

A French overseas territory in northeast Africa bordering on the Gulf of Aden. Formerly the French Somali Coast.

On June 27, 1977, on the occasion of this territory becoming independent, the name was changed to Djibouti.

## AFGHANISTAN (1871-)

A republic in central Asia. Long divided and ruled by neighboring states, Afghanistan's history as a unified nation began in 1747, when Afghanistan was freed and established a large empire in east Persia and northwest India.

During the 19th century, Afghani power declined, and during 1881-1919, the country was dominated by the British.

After 1919, Afghanistan broke away from British influence. In 1973, the monarchy was replaced by a republican government.

The republic was overthrown in a pro-Soviet coup in 1978. The new regime was unable to unify the country or to quell conservative resistance in the countryside.

In December 1979, the U.S.S.R. invaded Afghanistan, establishing what it hoped would be a more effective government. During 1980-81, the 60,000-100,000 Soviet troops and the regular Afghan army were unable to defeat the rebels, who remained in control of much of the country.

## AGUERA, LA (1920-24)

District in the western Sahara on the Atlantic coast. A Spanish possession, La Aguera issued its own stamps until 1924, when it was attached to the Spanish Sahara.

## AITUTAKI (1903-32, 1972-)

One of the Cook Islands in the South Pacific Ocean, northeast of New Zealand. Aitutaki issued its own stamps until 1932, when these were replaced by those of the Cook Islands. In August 1972, Aitutaki resumed issuing its own stamps.

## AJMAN (1964-72)

One of the Trucial States in eastern Arabia. A sheikdom under British protection from 1892-1971, Ajman joined the independent United Arab Emirates on Dec. 2, 1971.

UAE issues replaced those of Ajman in 1972. Subsequent Ajman issues came on to the philatelic market after 1972, but these were not recognized as valid by the government.

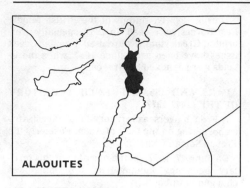

ALAOUITES

## ALAOUITES (1925-30)

A district of Syria, bordering on the Mediterranean Sea. Alaouites was under Turkish rule until 1918, when it was occupied by French.

During 1920-41, it was ruled by France under mandate from the League of Nations.

In 1930, the name of the province was changed to Latakia, and stamps so inscribed came into use. In 1941, Latakia was annexed by Syria, and its issues were replaced by Syrian stamps.

## ALBANIA (1913-)

A republic in southeast Europe, bordering on the Adriatic Sea. Under Turkish rule from 1478-1912, Albania became independent after the first Balkan War.

Overrun by German, Serbian, Montenegrin, Greek, Bulgarian, Italian, French and Austrian troops during World War I, foreign forces remained in Albania until 1921.

In 1939, the country was occupied by Italy, and later, Germany. In 1944, British-supported Communist guerrillas drove the Germans from the country and established a provisional government.

In 1946, a Communist people's republic was proclaimed. At first it appeared that Albania would become a satellite of Yugoslavia, but it has stubbornly maintained its independence. In 1960, because of the Soviet Union's de-Stalinization campaign, Albania broke with the U.S.S.R. and aligned its foreign policy with that of the People's Republic of China. In 1978 China's liberalization brought a break between that country and Albania.

Albania is the most economically undeveloped of the Eastern European nations.

## ALEDSCHEN (ALSEDZIAI) (1941)

A city in Lithuania. In 1941, the local German military commander overprinted Russian stamps "Laisvi/Alsedziai/24-VI-41" for use in the area.

## ALEXANDERSTADT (BOLSCHAJA ALEXANDROWKA) (1941-42)

A city in the Ukraine. During 1941-42, the local German military authorities issued Russian

stamps surcharged "16.8.41"/Swastika/ "B.ALEX." and new values for use in the district.

ALEXANDRETTA

## ALEXANDRETTA (1938)

A district of southern Turkey, bordering on the Mediterranean Sea. Alexandretta was part of the Ottoman Turkish Empire for several hundred years, until its occupation by the French in 1918.

It was administered as part of the French mandate of Syria until 1938, when it became autonomous from Syria, its name being changed to Hatay.

Stamps of Hatay replaced those of Alexandretta. In 1939, the territory was returned to Turkey, and Turkish stamps have since been in use.

## ALEXANDRIA (1899-1931)

An Egyptian port on the Mediterranean Sea.

The French Post Office in Alexandria operated from 1830 through March 31, 1931. Regular French issues were used until 1899, when separate issues were begun for Alexandria.

## ALGERIA (1924-58, 1962-)

A republic in Northern Africa. Under Turkish rule from 1518-1830, Algeria was occupied by France after 1830.

During World War II, it was under the pro-Nazi Vichy regime until 1943, when it was occupied by U.S.-Free French forces.

In 1958, Algeria became an integral part of France, and French stamps replaced those of the colony. In 1962, Algeria became independent and resumed issuing its own stamps.

During 1967-74, Algeria maintained close ties with the U.S.S.R., but in recent years, it has moved into a more neutral position.

Despite oil earnings and attempts at land reform and industrialization, Algeria is plagued by endemic poverty and unemployment.

## ALLENSTEIN (1920)

A district of East Prussia, Allenstein was one of those territories administered by the Allies until 1920, when a local plebiscite resulted in the area's return to Germany.

German stamps overprinted for Allenstein were used during the plebiscite period. Since the end of World War II, this area has been a part of Poland.

## ALSACE AND LORRAINE (1870-72, 1940-41)

Two districts lying between France and Germany. Long disputed, these areas were annexed by Germany in 1871, retaken by France in 1918, retaken by Germany in 1939, and finally reoccupied by France in 1945.

German occupation issues for Alsace and Lorraine were used throughout occupied France from 1870-71 and in the two provinces from 1870-72.

Individual overprints on German stamps were issued for Alsace and Lorraine in 1940. On Jan. 1, 1942, they were replaced by regular German stamps.

## ALWAR (1877-1902)

A former feudatory state in Northern India, southwest of Delhi. Separate issues were used until 1902, after which they were replaced by Indian stamps.

## AMIENS (1909)

A city in northern France. During May 13-19, 1909, local provisionals were issued by the Chamber of Commerce during a strike by postal employees.

## AMUR PROVINCE (1920)

Between February and April 1920, a People's Revolutionary Committee ruled at Blagoveschensk, in southeastern Siberia. The Amur Province was absorbed by the Far Eastern Republic, when that state was formed on April 6, 1920.

## ANDAMAN AND NICOBAR ISLANDS (1942)

Located in the Indian Ocean, these islands were first settled by the British in 1789. Subsequently, they fell under the administration of the governor-general of India and now form part of the Indian republic.

During World War II, the islands were occupied by the Japanese. At this time, contemporary British Indian stamps were crudely surcharged for use in the islands.

## ANDORRA (1928-)

An autonomous enclave in the Pyrenees Mountains, jointly administered by France and the Spanish bishop of Urgel. Stamps are issued by both France and Spain for use in the principality.

## ANGOLA (1870-)

A former Portuguese colony in southwestern Africa. The Angolan coast came under Portuguese control in the 16th century, while the interior was conquered during the late 19th century.

Angolan nationalist groups waged a guerrilla war against the Portuguese during 1961-74. In 1974 Portugal agreed to the independence of the country, and on Nov. 11, 1975, Angola became an independent nation.

With the withdrawal of Portugal, the three largest of the nationalists groups quickly fell out over the composition of the new government.

The ensuing civil war caused most of the whites remaining in Angola to emigrate and brought the economic collapse of the country.

Massive Soviet aid and the intervention of Cuban troops on the side of the Marxist faction brought a pro-Soviet regime to power in 1976.

Angolan support for the SWAPO guerrillas, whose raids into Namibia have often originated from bases within Angola, has brought a number of retalitory South African strikes into Angola. Some 25,000 Soviet, Cuban, East German, and Portuguese communist troops and advisors remain in the country.

## ANGRA (1892-1906)

An administrative district of the Azores, in the central Atlantic. Angra's stamps were replaced by those of the Azores in 1906. Since 1931 regular Portuguese stamps have been used in the district.

## ANGUILLA (1967-)

A small island in the Caribbean, formerly attached to St. Kitts-Nevis-Anguilla. In September 1967, Anguilla declared its independence from both that state and Great Britain. In 1971 direct British control was reestablished.

## ANJOUAN (1892-1914)

One of the Comoro Islands in the Indian Ocean near Madagascar. The sultanate of Anjouan came under French protection in 1886, and separate stamp issues began in 1892. Stamps of Anjouan were replaced by those of Madagascar in 1914. In 1950, issues of the Comoro Islands came into use.

## ANNAM AND TONKIN (1888-92)

Roughly, the area of Tonkin and Annam Protectorates corresponds with modern Vietnam. From 1892, regular issues of French Indo-China were used, although in 1936, Indo-China issued a separate set for Annam.

Since 1945, stamps of the People's Democratic Republic of Vietnam have been used in the north, while those of the republic of Vietnam were used in the south from 1954-75.

## ANTEQUERA (1936)

A city in the province of Malaga, in southern Spain.

Contemporary Spanish stamps were overprinted for local use on the authority of the Falangist military commander in October 1936.

## ANTIGUA (1862-)

A state in association with Great Britain, comprising the island of Antigua and several smaller islands in the eastern Caribbean, southeast of Puerto Rico.

Under British rule since 1632, Antigua became a separate colony in 1956. In 1967 Antigua became self-governing and became the independent state of Antigua-Barbuda in 1981.

Stamp-issuing dependencies of Antigua are Barbuda and Redonda.

## ARAD (1919)

A district of pre-World War I Hungary, occupied by France in 1919, at which time overprinted Hungarian stamps were issued. The district is now a part of Romania.

## ARBE (RAB) (1920)

An island in the Mali Kvarner, off the northwestern coast of Yugoslavia. During d'Annunzio's occupation of Fiume, issues were overprinted for Arbe.

## ARGENTINA (1858-)

A republic in southern South America. Independent from Spain in 1816, Argentina was torn by regional separationism through much of the 19th century. This is reflected in the issuing of separate stamps by several Argentine provinces during 1858-80.

Large-scale European immigration and investment after the 1880s made Argentina the most economically advanced nation in South America.

Since 1930, Argentina has, more often than not, been ruled by authoritarian military regimes. During World War II, the government was sympathetic to the Axis, and after the war a large number of ex-Nazis found sanctuary in Argentina.

In 1946, Juan Domingo Peron was elected president, and he dominated the country's political life until his death in 1974, although he was in exile 1955-73.

Chronic, unresolved economic and social tensions erupted into virtual civil war during 1976-80. Both leftist guerrillas, and the military government used terror and violence to further their ends. Thousands died in the conflict.

Although the government suppressed the radical terrorists and restored some semblance of order, Argentina's economy had deteriorated badly. High unemployment and spiraling inflation have provoked intense popular dissatisfaction with the ruling junta. Argentina's seizure of the Falkland Islands in early April 1982, was, at least in part, an attempt to unify the nation behind the regime.

## ARGYROKASTRON (GJINOKASTER) (1914)

A city in Southern Albania. Turkish stamps were surcharged for use during the area's occupation by Greece.

## ARMAVIR (1920)

A city in northern Caucasus, Russia. Two Russian stamps were surcharged by the local authorities.

## ARMENIA (1919-23)

The westernmost area of the Caucasus. Long under a vague Turkish suzerainty, Armenia was conquered by the Russians during the 19th century.

During World War I, Armenia was occupied by Turco-German forces. Between May 1918, and December 1920, and again between February and April 1921, it existed as an independent republic, issuing its own stamps.

In 1923, it joined the Transcaucasian Federation of Soviet Republics. Transcaucasian issues were soon superseded by those of the Soviet Union.

## ARMY OF THE NORTH (1919)

During 1919, the Army of the North, under Gen. Rodzianko, fought against the Soviet forces in the Petrograd (Leningrad) area. This army was subsequently incorporated into Gen. Nikolai N. Yudenitch's Army of the Northwest.

## ARMY OF THE NORTHWEST (1919)

An anti-Bolshevik force under the command of General Yudenitch, which operated in northwestern Russia around the city of Pskov. Between June and November 1919, this army threatened the Soviets in Petrograd (Leningrad). In November it was defeated by the Red Army and dissolved.

## ARMY OF THE WEST (1919)

The Western Army was formed in Courland in 1919 to maintain German influence in the Baltic States. It was primarily an instrument of the German High Command, which was forbidden to operate directly in the region.

The Army of the West was concerned less with the threat of the Bolsheviks in Russia than with restoring the domination of German land-holders in the area, and so refused to cooperate with Yudenitch in fighting the Russians.

In November 1919, the army attacked Riga, but was thrown back by an Anglo-Latvian counter-offensive which brought about the force's dissolution.

## ASCENSION (1922-)

An island in the South Atlantic Ocean. Occupied by the British in 1815, Ascension was attached to the crown colony of St. Helena in 1922.

## ASCH (1938)

A city in the Sudetenland (Czechoslovakia). Local authorities overprinted Czech stamps in 1938, upon the area's cession to Germany.

## AUNUS (1919)

Aunus, the Finnish name for Olonets, a Russian town, was occupied by Finnish forces in 1919. Finnish stamps overprinted with the town name were used during the occupation.

## AUSTRALIA (1902-)

An island continent between the Pacific and Indian oceans, southeast of Asia. British settlement began in the late 18th century, with six colonies developing — New South Wales, Victoria, Queensland, South Australia, Western Australia and Tasmania.

These colonies united to form the Commonwealth of Australia on Jan. 1, 1901, although they continued to issue their own stamps for a number of years.

Australia has rich natural resources and since World War II has developed into the major economic power of the region. It has maintained close ties with the United States since 1945, although in recent years, Japan has replaced the U.S. as Australia's major economic partner.

Australia administers a number of island groups in the South Pacific and plays a leading role in the region.

## AUSTRALIAN ANTARCTIC TERRITORY (1957-)

A large portion of Antarctica is claimed by Australia, which maintains scientific research stations in the area. Stamps of the Australian Antarctic Territory are also valid for postage in Australia.

## AUSTRIA (1850-)

A republic in central Europe. The center of the Hapsburg Empire, which during the 16th-19th centuries controlled (at one time or another) Hungary, Czechoslovakia, Belgium, The Netherlands, and large portions of Yugoslavia, Poland, Romania, Italy and Germany.

After 1815, Austrian power declined with the growth of nationalism among its subjects. In 1867, the Austro-Hungarian dual monarchy was created to appease Hungarian nationalists, but the government resisted similar concessions to other national groups.

The assassination of the Archduke Francis Ferdinand, heir to the Austro-Hungarian throne, in Sarajevo, Bosnia, on June 28, 1914, began the series of events that quickly led to World War I.

During World War I, Austrian troops were active in the Balkans, Romania, Poland, Russia and Italy, but by October 1918, Austria's armies were routed, and the monarchy collapsed.

The empire dissolved rapidly, and Austria emerged much reduced in size, representing the German-speaking area of the empire. In 1918 the republic of "German Austria" was formed, and there was considerable sentiment for annexation by Germany.

By the Treaty of St. Germain (1922), Austria was expressly forbidden to unite with Germany and the country's name became simply "Austria."

During the 1930s, an Austrian fascist regime attempted to maintain independence, but in March 1938, Germany invaded and quickly occupied the country, merging it into the Third Reich with only a token protest from the Allies.

In 1945, the Allies liberated Austria, and the republic was reestablished.

In 1955, foreign troops were withdrawn, and Austria proclaimed its political neutrality.

Austria maintains close economic ties with much of western Europe.

## AUSTRIAN OFFICES IN CRETE (1903-14)

Like several other European nations, Austria maintained its own post offices in Crete, using stamps valued in French centimes and francs.

Although intended for use in Crete, these issues were available for use at Austrian post offices throughout the Turkish Empire.

## AUSTRIAN OFFICES IN THE TURKISH EMPIRE (1867-1914)

Austria began using special stamps for its offices in the Turkish Empire in 1867, having previously used its issues for Lombardy-Venetia for these offices.

Austrian post offices in the Turkish Empire were closed Dec. 15, 1914.

## AVILA (1937)

The capital city of the province of the same name, in central Spain.

A Nationalist overprint was applied to contemporary Spanish stamps by the local authorities.

## AZERBAIJAN (IRANIAN) (1945-46)

A province in northwestern Iran. Occupied by Soviet forces during World War II, a puppet government was established in May 1945, at which time contemporary Iranian stamps were overprinted for use.

In March 1946, Soviet troops withdrew, and Azerbaijan became an "autonomous" government. In December 1946, full Iranian administration was restored.

## AZERBAIJAN (RUSSIAN) (1919-24)

The eastern portion of the Caucasus. Occupied by Russia in the 19th century, Azerbaijan declared its independence in 1917, after the Russian Revolution. Turkish and British occupation was followed by the establishment of a Communist regime in 1920.

Azerbaijan was incorporated into the Transcaucasian Federated Republic in 1923. Soviet stamps have been used since 1924.

## AZORES (1868-1931, 1980-)

A group of islands in the North Atlantic. The islands used Portuguese stamps until 1868, when overprinted stamps came into use.

Separate Azores issues were replaced by regular Portuguese stamps in 1931. In 1980 Portugal again began to issue separate stamps for the Azores.

— B —

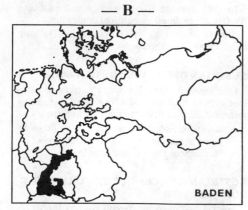

BADEN

## BADEN (1851-71, 1905, 1946-49)

A former grand duchy in southwestern Germany on the Rhine River. In 1870, it joined the German Empire.

After World War II, Baden was included in the French zone of occupation and separate issues were again in use from 1945-49, with some issues valid for use in the German Federal Republic until March 31, 1950.

## BAENA (1937)

A city in the province of Cordoba in southern Spain.

In July 1937, contemporary Spanish stamps were overprinted to commemorate the anniversary of the Nationalist landing at Cadiz and the Nationalist occupation of Baena.

## BAHAMAS (1859-)

A scattered group of some 700 islands and 2,000 islets in the Atlantic Ocean, east of Florida.

One of the Bahamian islands (San Salvador, now Watling Island) was the site of Columbus' first landfall in the New World. The Bahamas were largely bypassed by Europeans, however, until British settlement began in 1647. In 1783, the Bahamas became a British colony.

The Bahamas became self-governing in 1964 and fully independent in 1973. International banking and tourism are the country's major industries.

## BAHAWALPUR (1945-50)

A state of Pakistan. In 1947, the Moslem amir declared independence from India and joined Bahawalpur to Pakistan.

## BAHRAIN (1933-)

An archipelago in the Persian Gulf. Under British protection 1861-1971, Bahrain used a variety of stamps: unoverprinted Indian stamps from 1884 to 1933; overprinted Indian issues 1933-48; overprinted British issues 1948-60; and its own designs from 1960.

Oil was first discovered in 1932 and has become, with international banking, the economic mainstay of a very prosperous Bahrain.

Tensions between the Sunnite majority (60 per cent) and Shi'ite minority (40 per cent) have grown since the establishment of the fundamentalist Shi'ite regime in Iran.

## BAMRA (1888-94)

A feudatory state in eastern India. Bamra issued separate stamps until 1894, when its issues were replaced by those of India.

## BANAT BACSKA (1919)

A district of south central Europe, formerly under Hungarian rule. In 1919, postal authorities at Temesvar overprinted Hungarian stamps, which were used largely to pay the salaries of postal workers.

The area is now divided between Yugoslavia and Romania.

## BANGKOK (1882-85)

The capital of Thailand. During 1855-85, Britain exercised extraterritorial privileges in Bangkok, which included the right to use her own stamps.

Straits Settlements stamps overprinted "B" were used until July 1, 1885.

## BANGLADESH (1971-)

A republic in the Bengal region of south Asia. Formerly East Pakistan, Bangladesh declared its independence in April 1971.

After a bitter civil war, Pakistan was defeated by India and the rebels, and Bangladesh independence was recognized in December 1971.

Since independence, Bangladesh has suffered continuing economic problems and political instability. In foreign affairs, it is closely linked to India and the Soviet Union.

Before the issue of Bangladesh's first definitive set (and for some time thereafter), existing stocks of Pakistani stamps were overprinted locally, creating so many varieties that, at this time, no general catalog has attempted to list them.

## BANJA LUKA (1941)

A city in northern Bosnia (Yugoslavia). During World War II, two Yugoslavian stamps were overprinted by the local partisans for use in the area.

## BARANYA (1919)

A Hungarian district briefly occupied by Serbia after World War I.

## BARBADOS (1852-)

An island in the West Indies. A British colony from 1628-1966. On Nov. 30, 1966, Barbados became an independent state within the British Commonwealth.

## BARBUDA (1922, 1968-)

A small island in the Leeward group in the West Indies. A dependency of Antigua.

## BARWANI (1921-48)

A former feudatory state in western India. Barwani stamps were replaced by those of India on July 1, 1948.

### BASE ATLANTICA (1943-44)

During World War II, the Supreme Commander of Italian submarine forces authorized the overprinting of a number of Italian stamps for use by Italian military personnel stationed in Bordeaux, France.

### BASEL (1845)

Capital of the canton of the same name, in northern Switzerland. Basel is situated on the Rhine and borders on both France and Germany. In 1845 the famous "Basel Dove" was issued. Since regarded as one of the most beautiful of the classic issues, it was not popular among the townspeople and was soon withdrawn.

### BASUTOLAND (1933-66)

A former British crown colony surrounded by South Africa. Under British control after 1871, Basutoland became the independent state of Lesotho on Oct. 4, 1966.

Stamps of the Cape of Good Hope were used 1871-1910, and those of the Union of South Africa 1910-33, when the colony began to use its own issues.

### BATUM (1919-20)

A Georgian port on the Black Sea, Batum was annexed by Russia from Turkey in 1878 and became a major Russian naval base.

During World War I, it was occupied by the Germans and the Turks, and in December 1918, Batum was occupied by British forces. The port was evacuated by the British in July 1920.

During the British occupation, three series of lithographed stamps (two overprinted "British Occupation"), as well as a number of Russian stamps overprinted and surcharged, were in use.

After the British evacuation, stamps of Georgia were used, these being replaced by Russian stamps in 1923.

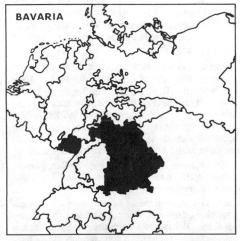

### BAVARIA (1849-1920)

Former kingdom in southern Germany. Bavaria joined the German Empire in 1870, retaining its own monarchy. The country was briefly independent following World War I.

Bavarian stamps were replaced by German issues in 1920.

### BECHUANALAND PROTECTORATE (1888-1966)

District in south central Africa, directly north of the Republic of South Africa. A British protectorate was established over the region in 1885, ending with the area becoming independent as the Republic of Botswana in 1966.

### BEIRUT (1909-14)

The capital of Lebanon. Prior to World War I, a number of European nations maintained their own postal systems in Beirut.

The Russian post office used stamps of the Russian Levant overprinted "Beyrouth" after 1909. In January 1905, the French authorities overprinted a contemporary French Offices in Turkey stamp for provisional use in Beirut. In July 1906, a similar provisional was used by the British authorities in Beirut. Both are scarce.

### BEJUMA (1854)

A small town near Valencia, Venezuela. In 1854, the postmaster issued local stamps to frank mail to Valencia.

### BELGIAN CONGO (1886-1960)

A former Belgian colony in central Africa. In 1885, the Congo Free State was established under the personal rule of Leopold II.

In 1908, the Belgian government assumed control of the area, withdrawing after the establishment of the independent Republic of the Congo in 1960.

### BELGIUM (1849-)

A constitutional monarchy in northwest Europe, bordering on the English Channel.

Conquered by Julius Caesar in the 1st century B.C., Belgium was ruled by a succession of foreign nations for nearly 2,000 years. In 1830, Belgium became independent from the last of these foreign rulers, the Dutch. Because of its strategic position, Belgian independence and neutrality was guaranteed by the major European powers.

In 1914, Germany occupied most of the country, although Belgium's spirited resistance throughout the war earned worldwide respect. Germany again occupied Belgium during World War II.

Since 1945, Belgium has aligned itself with the West and is a member of both NATO and the Common Market.

### BELIZE (1973-)

A former British colony in Central America.

Formerly known as British Honduras, the name "Belize" was adopted in 1973. Belize became independent on Sept. 20, 1981.

A total of 1,800 British troops remain stationed in Belize to protect the country from Guatemala, which has long exerted a rather dubious claim to the territory.

## BENIN (1892-99, 1976-)

The coastal area of Dahomey, on the Gulf of Guinea, Benin was occupied by the French in the 19th century.

Separate stamps were issued from 1892. In 1895, the area was grouped with recently conquered inland territories to form the French colony of Dahomey.

In November 1975, Dahomey changed its name to the People's Republic of Benin.

## BERGEDORF (1861-68)

A town in northern Germany, originally owned by Hamburg and the Free City of Lubeck (1420-1867). In 1867, it passed into the sole possession of Hamburg.

Bergedorf began issuing stamps in 1861, these being replaced by those of the North German Confederation in 1868.

## BERLIN (1945-46, 1948-)

The capital of Prussia and after 1871, of Germany. Surrounded by the Soviet Zone of Occupation, Berlin was divided into U.S., British, French and Soviet zones in 1945.

In 1948, political tension brought the creation of the zones of West (Allied) Berlin and East (Soviet) Berlin.

In 1949, East Berlin became the capital of the German Democratic Republic.

## BERMUDA (1848-)

A group of islands in the west central Atlantic Ocean. A British colony since 1609, Bermuda was granted internal self-government in 1968.

## BHOPAL (1876-1950)

A former feudatory state in central India. Bhopal issued separate stamps for ordinary use until 1908, when they were replaced by Indian stamps.

Bhopal continued to issue its own official stamps until 1950, when these, too, were replaced by Indian issues.

## BHUTAN (1955-)

Kingdom in the eastern Himalayas between India and Tibet.

Bhutan was under British influence during the 19th century and was a British protectorate after 1910. In 1949 it became independent, although it is guided in foreign relations by India, with whom it carries on 99 per cent of its commerce.

Since 1966 Bhutan has issued large numbers of attractive (and philatelically inspired) stamps. Among the novel forms these issues have taken are: gold, silver and steel foil, designs printed on silk, 3-D plastic stamps and souvenir sheets, miniature plastic records, plastic bas-relief, and designs printed on rose-scented paper.

## BHOR (1879-1902)

A former feudatory state in western India. Bhor issues were replaced by those of India in 1902.

## BIAFRA (1968-70)

The eastern region of Nigeria, in which is concentrated the Ibo tribe. On May 30, 1967, the Ibos proclaimed the independent Republic of Biafra, and on Feb. 5, 1968, the first Biafran postage stamps were issued.

On Jan. 9, 1970, after a bitter civil war, Biafra surrendered to armies of the central government. Since that time, stamps of Nigeria have been in use.

During 1968-70, some 68 major varieties were issued, as well as several overprinted sets that appeared on the market after Biafra's defeat. These latter sets were not issued for postal use and so are excluded from most major catalogs.

## BIALYSTOK (1916)

A city and province in northeastern Poland. In 1916, the local German military commander issued stamps for use in the area.

## BIJAWAR (1935-39)

A former feudatory state in central India. Bijawar issued stamps from 1935-39, after which they were replaced by Indian stamps.

## BILBAO (1937)

The major port of northern Spain, located on the Bay of Biscay.

Spanish stamps were overprinted in July 1937, to celebrate the occupation of the city by Franco's Nationalist forces.

## BOHEMIA AND MORAVIA (1939-45)

A German puppet-state created from the western provinces of Czechoslovakia prior to World War II. Bohemia and Moravia were reincorporated into Czechoslovakia following the war.

## BOLIVIA (1867-)

A land-locked republic in South America, Bolivia was part of the Inca empire during the 13th-16th centuries. It was conquered by Spain in the 1530s and, as the Presidency of Charcas, was attached to the vice-royalty of Rio de la Plata. Notable primarily for its rich silver mines, which were exploited and depleted by the Spanish, Bolivia was an imperial backwater for three centuries.

In 1825, the Spanish were expelled, and Bolivia, taking its name from the Great Liberator Simon Bolivar, became independent.

Bolivia has been beset by numerous wars and revolutions. In the first hundred years of its independence, Bolivia lost territory to Chile, Brazil and Paraguay, three of its four neighbors. Its only coastal territory was lost to Chile in the War of the Pacific (1879-84).

Chronic internal instability has given Bolivia one of the lowest standards of living in Latin America. Its government has been a bewildering succession of military dictatorships.

Because of frequent shortages of regular postal issues, one often finds revenues, postage dues and bisects used provisionally by Bolivian post offices.

BOSNIA ▇ HERZEGOVINA ░░░░

### BOSNIA AND HERZEGOVINA (1879-1918)

Located in southwestern Yugoslavia, the provinces of Bosnia and Herzegovina were placed under Austria protection in 1878, and a year later, their first separate stamps appeared.

Formally Ottoman provinces, Bosnia and Herzegovina were only nominally under Turkish rule after this, and in 1908, Austria-Hungary annexed the area.

In 1914, the Austrian Archduke Ferdinand, heir to the aging Austrian emperor, was assassinated at Sarajevo, the capital, setting the series of events that culminated in World War I.

Since 1918, Bosnia and Herzegovina have formed part of Yugoslavia.

### BOTSWANA (1966-)

A republic in central southern Africa, directly north of the Republic of South Africa. Formerly the British Bechuanaland Protectorate, the republic became independent as Botswana on Sept. 30, 1966.

Many Botswanans are migrant workers in South Africa, with which Botswana is closely linked.

### BRAC (BRAZZA) (1944)

An island in the Adriatic Sea, off the coast of Yugoslavia. In 1944, Yugoslavian stamps were overprinted by the German military authorities for use in the island.

### BRAZIL (1843-)

A large republic, occupying nearly half of South America. Brazil was discovered by Europeans in 1500, and Portugal soon began colonizing the coastal areas. During 1808-21, after Napoleon had occupied Portugal, Brazil was the seat of the Portuguese empire. In 1821, the Portuguese king returned to Lisbon, leaving his son, Dom Pedro, to act as regent in Brazil.

In 1822, Dom Pedro declared the independence of the Empire of Brazil. Although Dom Pedro and his son, Dom Pedro II, were popular, the feeling grew that an American monarchy was an anachronism, and in 1889 a bloodless coup established the republic.

Since 1930, except for the period 1956-64, Brazil has been ruled by a succession of military regimes. During the 1970s, the government eased repressive policies and since 1979, has liberalized political conditions considerably.

Ambitious industrial and agricultural programs since 1930 have capitalized on the country's enormous natural resources, and Brazil has become the leading industrial nation of Latin America. Economic growth has been slowed in recent years by the enormous increases in prices for petroleum, which Brazil must import.

### BREMEN (1855-68)

A major German seaport in northwestern Germany. Bremen was a free city and a member of the German and, later, the North German Confederations, joining the German Empire in 1870.

Bremen used its own stamps from 1855-68, after which issues of the North German Confederation came into use.

### BRITISH ANTARCTIC TERRITORY (1963-)

A British territory in the south Atlantic Ocean, forming part of the Falkland Islands Dependencies.

### BRITISH BECHUANALAND (1886-98)

Located in southern Africa, British Bechuanaland was a British crown colony until 1895, when it was annexed to Cape Colony. It is now part of the Republic of South Africa.

Overprinted stamps of Cape Colony were in use from 1886 to 1898, when they were replaced by regular Cape Colony stamps.

Since 1910, stamps of South Africa have been used, although most Cape Colony stamps remained valid until 1937.

### BRITISH CENTRAL AFRICA (1891-1908)

A former British territory in central Africa. In 1907, British Central Africa adopted the name Nyasaland Protectorate, which subsequently became independent as the Republic of Malawi.

### BRITISH COLUMBIA AND VANCOUVER ISLAND (1860-71)

A Canadian province on the northwest coast of North America, bordering on the Pacific Ocean. The two British colonies of Vancouver (established 1849) and British Columbia (established 1858) united in 1866 and joined the Canadian Confederation in 1871.

### BRITISH EAST AFRICA (1890-1903)

Territories originally under control of the British East Africa Co., after 1895 directly under British administration.

In 1903, the area was reformed as the East Africa and Uganda protectorates.

During 1895-1903, this area used overprinted stamps of Britain, India and Zanzibar, as well as its own issues. In 1903, East Africa and Uganda issues came into use.

### BRITISH GUIANA (1850-1966)

A former colony on the northern coast of South America, British Guiana became an independent republic in 1966, assuming the name Guyana.

Early issues of British Guiana include a number of major rarities, among them "The World's Most Valuable Stamp," the 1-cent black on magenta of 1856. This stamp is unique and has passed through the hands of some of the giants of philately.

### BRITISH HONDURAS (1866-1973)

Located in Central America on the Caribbean Sea, this area was contested by the British and Spanish until 1798, when British authority was secured.

In 1862, it became a British colony under Jamaican administration, and in 1884 became a separate colony. In 1973, British Honduras changed its name to Belize.

### BRITISH INDIAN OCEAN TERRITORY (1968-80)

A group of British-owned islands in the Indian Ocean. Formerly dependencies of Mauritius and the Seychelles, these islands were organized as a crown colony on Nov. 8, 1965. In 1980, the name of the colony was changed to Zil Eloigne Sesel (later changed to Zil Elwagne Sesel).

### BRITISH OFFICES IN CHINA (1917-30)

Britain long maintained post offices in various Chinese cities. Stamps of Hong Kong were used in these offices until Dec. 31, 1916, after which Hong Kong stamps overprinted "China" were used.

On Nov. 30, 1922, all British post offices in China were closed, except in the leased territory of Wei-hai-wei, which used British Offices in China issues until Sept. 30, 1930.

### BRITISH OFFICES IN MOROCCO (1898-1957)

British post offices in Morocco used overprinted contemporary stamps of Gibraltar (1898-1906) and Britain.

Separate issues were used in the Spanish Zone, the French Zone, and Tangier, as well as the general issues used throughout the country.

Regular British stamps were also often used.

### BRITISH OFFICES IN THE TURKISH EMPIRE (1885-1914, 1919-23)

Until 1885, regular British stamps were used by British post offices in the Ottoman Empire. After that date, British stamps surcharged in Turkish currency or overprinted "LEVANT" were used.

British post offices in the area were closed Oct. 1, 1914, reopened March 1919, and finally closed Sept. 27, 1923.

### BRITISH VIRGIN ISLANDS (1866-)

A group of islands in the West Indies, southeast of Puerto Rico. The western portion of the Virgin Islands were under Danish rule until 1917, and under the United States since. The 30 eastern islands, which comprise the British Virgin Islands, were under Dutch control until 1666, when they passed to Britain.

Until 1956 they were administered as part of the Leeward Islands colony. In 1956 the British Virgin Islands became a separate crown colony and in 1967 became an Associated State, with Britain retaining control of foreign affairs and defense.

### BRUNEI (1906-)

A sultanate on the northwest coast of Borneo, situated between the Malaysian states of Sabah and Sarawak. Under British protection since 1888, Brunei secured full self-government in 1971. Britain retains control of foreign affairs. Complete independence is targeted for 1983.

### BRUNSWICK (BRAUNSCHWEIG) (1852-68)

A former duchy in northern Germany, joining the German Empire in 1870. Brunswick's issues were used from 1852-68, when they were replaced by those of the North German Confederation.

**BUENOS AIRES**

### BUENOS AIRES (1858-64)

Buenos Aires, long the chief port and commercial center of Argentina, was at various times in the 19th century independent from the rest of the country.

Since 1862, however, it has formed a province of Argentina, whose stamps have been in use since 1864. A British post office in the city used regular British stamps (canceled "B-32") from 1860 to 1873.

### BULGARIA (1879-)

A communist People's Republic in southeastern Europe.

During the 10th and 12th centuries, the Bulgars ruled much of the Balkan peninsula but subsequently declined in power, falling under Turkish control in 1396. In 1878 Bulgaria became an autonomous principality, under nominal Turkish rule. In fact, Bulgaria was independent — more closely aligned with Russia than with Turkey — and this independence was formalized in 1908.

The Treaty of San Stefano (1878) established a "Greater Bulgaria," which included all Bulgars and encompassed territory which now forms parts of Yugoslavia, Greece, Romania and Turkey. The powers, fearing the expansion of Russian influence in the Balkans through such a large client-state, overturned that treaty at the Congress of Berlin, later in the year. Bulgaria's foreign policy from 1878 through 1944 was based on the creation of this Greater Bulgaria.

In 1885, Bulgaria absorbed Eastern Rumelia, and in the Balkan Wars (1912-13) further expanded its borders. Its defeat by the Allies in World War I cost Bulgaria its Aegean coastline, and its defeat in World War II brought the overthrow of the monarchy and the establishment of the communist regime.

Bulgaria is one of the most reliable of the Soviet satellites in eastern Europe.

**BUNDI (1894-1948)**

A former feudatory state in northwestern India, Bundi issued stamps from 1894 to 1902 and from 1915 to 1948. During 1902-15 and after 1950 stamps of India were used. From 1948-50, stamps of Rajasthan were in use.

**BURGOS (1936-38)**

A province in north central Spain.

Burgos was occupied by the Nationalists early in the Spanish Civil War, and a large number of overprinted Spanish postage and fiscal stamps were used in the province during this period.

**BURMA (1937-)**

A republic in southeast Asia. Burma was a part of British India until 1937, when it became a separate territory under Britain.

Occupied by Japan, 1942-45, Burma was reoccupied by Britain, which granted independence on Jan. 4, 1948.

Burma maintains a staunch nationalist socialism and keeps relations with other countries to a minimum. In 1978, government repression drove 150,000 Moslem Burmese to flee the country, settling in neighboring Bangladesh.

**BURUNDI (1962-)**

A republic in Central Africa. As Urundi, it was administered by Belgium, under a United Nations mandate, until it became an independent kingdom in 1962. In 1966, the monarchy was overthrown by a military coup.

Traditionally, Burundi has been ruled by the Tutsi (Watusi) tribe, which comprises only 14 per cent of the population. In 1972-73, the Bantu Hutus, who make up 85 per cent of Burundi's population, revolted, sparking a genocidal civil war in which 100,000 Hutsi and 10,000 Tutsi were killed. Another 100,000 Hutsi fled to Tanzania and Zaire. The government is presently at-

tempting to undo the effects of this struggle and is committed to a policy of ethnic reconciliation.

**BUSHIRE (1915)**

An Iranian port on the Persian Gulf. Bushire was occupied by British forces from Aug. 8, 1915, to Oct. 16, 1915.

**BUSSAHIR (BASHAHR) (1895-1901)**

A former feudatory state in northern India, Bussahir stamps were replaced by those of India. With the closing of the state post office, large numbers of remainders and reprints were released to the philatelic market. These exist both unused and canceled "19 MA 1900."

## — C —

**CABO GRACIAS A DIOS (1904-12)**

A cape and seaport in the extreme northeast of Nicaragua. The circulation of two radically different currencies in the country necessitated the overprinting of Nicaraguan stamps for use in the province.

**CADIZ (1936-37)**

A major Spanish port on the Atlantic Ocean, located in Southern Spain.

Contemporary Spanish stamps were overprinted by the Nationalist local authorities during the Spanish Civil War.

**CALIMNO (1912-32)**

One of the Turkish Dodecanese Islands in the eastern Aegean Sea. Occupied by Italy in 1912, Italian stamps overprinted "Calimno" were used from 1912-29, when they were replaced by the Aegean Island's general issues.

Sets overprinted with the island's name were released in 1930 and 1932.

**CAMBODIA (1951-)**

A communist republic in southeast Asia. It lies in Indo-China and borders Vietnam, Laos and Thailand.

During the 9th-13th centuries, Cambodia was the center of the Khmer empire, which ruled Thailand, Cambodia, Laos and southern Vietnam. By the 19th century, Khmer power had long been declining, and in 1863, a French protectorate was established over Cambodia.

A constitutional monarchy was established in 1941. In 1951, Cambodia became a separate member of the French Union, and in 1955, it became fully independent.

During the Vietnamese War, Cambodia attempted to maintain its independence and neutrality. In 1965, relations were broken with the United States, after ARVN forces attacked Viet-Cong bases in Cambodia. By 1969, the Viet-Cong-supported Khmer Rouge rebels posed such a threat that relations were restored.

In 1970, the monarchy was deposed, and a pro-western republic was established. In 1971, the name Khmer Republic was adopted.

There followed several years of intense fighting between the North Vietnamese and Khmer Rouge and the U.S.-backed forces of the republic. More than 100,000 died during 1971-75. The communists quickly defeated government forces after the U.S. withdrawal from South Vietnam.

There followed one of the more bizarre and horrifying episodes in recent history. The Khmer Rouge broke with the Vietnamese allies and began a systematic reign of terror that claimed one million lives during 1975-78. During this period (1977-78), Cambodia was renamed Democratic Kampuchea.

In 1978, border skirmishes with Vietnam erupted into war, and in January 1979, a Vietnamese-backed regime was established. Continuing civil war and widespread famine during 1979-80, following three years of Khmer Rouge atrocities, have left the country devastated.

## CAMEROUN (1897-)

A republic in West Africa. Cameroun was a German protectorate until 1915, when it was occupied by the British and French.

In 1922, it was mandated to these countries by the League of Nations. The French portion became the independent State of Cameroun in 1960, with the southern portion of the British mandate joining it in 1961.

The northern portion of the British mandate joined Nigeria. In 1972, Cameroun changed its official designation to the United Republic of Cameroon.

Politically stable, Cameroon has enjoyed considerable development in agriculture and transportation since independence.

## CAMPECHE (1876)

A Mexican state occupying the western part of the Yucatan peninsula.

## CAMPIONE D'ITALIA (1944-52)

A small Italian enclave in Switzerland, which for a time issued stamps valid for postage to Switzerland and Italy.

These issues were used during the period when northern Italy was controlled by the Italian Social Republic, while Campione remained loyal to the royalist government, from which it was unable to secure supplies of stamps.

## CANADA (1851-)

An independent state within the British Commonwealth, occupying the northern portion of North America.

Under French rule until 1763, when it was transferred to Britain, modern Canada was formed with the union of the various individual British colonies in North America in 1867. British Columbia and Vancouver Island were added in 1871, Prince Edward Island in 1873, and Newfoundland in 1949.

Canada possesses rich natural resources, but her harsh climate and small population have slowed development.

Canada has encouraged the differences among its people, socially and politically so that rather than a melting pot, the country more resembles a patchwork quilt. This has produced a richness and variety among the various ethnic groups in Canada.

It has also encouraged the development of regionalism and separatism: the western provinces are largely Conservative, while the East is largely Liberal; the majority of the population is English-speaking and of British descent, while in Quebec, 80 per cent are of French descent.

## CANAL ZONE (1904-79)

A strip of land 10 miles wide lying on either side of the Panama Canal, from the Atlantic to Pacific oceans, dividing the Republic of Panama into two parts.

Thwarted by Colombia from building the Panama Canal through its territory, the U.S. supported the Panamanian revolution of 1903, and almost immediately received a perpetual lease to the territory.

In 1978, the United States and Panama agreed to a revised treaty, allowing for the gradual transfer of control of the Canal to Panama by the end of the century. On Sept. 30, 1979, the U.S. Canal Zone Postal Service ceased operation, and on Oct. 1, the Panamanian Postal Service took charge.

## CANARY ISLANDS (1936-39)

A group of islands in the Atlantic Ocean, located off the northwestern coast of Africa.

Under Spanish rule since the 15th century, the Canary Islands have normally used regular Spanish issues.

During the Spanish Civil War, however, a large number of overprinted stamps were used on mail carried by a provisional airline service linking Las Palmas with Seville, where it was linked to the rest of Europe. These issues were in use until the reestablishment of the Spanish state service in May 1938.

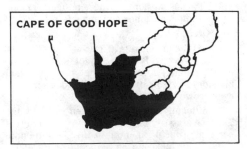

CAPE OF GOOD HOPE

## CAPE OF GOOD HOPE (1853-1910)

Located at the southern tip of Africa, the Cape of Good Hope was originally a Dutch colony, passing to the British after the Napoleonic Wars.

Conflict between English immigrants and established Dutch settlers (Boers) led to the withdrawal of the Boers into the interior after 1836.

These tensions, intensified by the discovery of rich diamond and gold deposits, increasing English immigration and Britain's imperialistic policy, resulted in the Boer War of 1899-1902, which ended with British occupation of the formerly independent Boer republics.

In 1910, Cape Colony joined with Natal, Transvaal and the Orange River Colony to form the Union of South Africa.

During the Boer War, a number of provisionals appeared, the most famous of which were issued at Mafeking, where the defending British force was commanded by Gen. Robert S.S. Baden-Powell, who later established the Boy Scouts.

## CAPE JUBY (1916-48)

A Spanish possession in the western Sahara on the Atlantic coast, opposite the Canary Islands. Secured by agreement with France, Spanish troops occupied Cape Juby in 1916, at which time overprinted stamps of Rio de Oro were issued.

From 1916 to 1919, stamps of Rio de Oro and Spanish Morocco were used in the area. In January 1919, overprinted stamps again appeared, and these remained in use until 1948, when they were replaced by those of the Spanish Sahara.

## CAPE VERDE (1877-)

A group of islands in the Atlantic Ocean, west of Senegal.

Uninhabited when first discovered by the Portuguese in 1456 or 1460, the first Portuguese settlers arrived in 1462, and black slaves were introduced soon thereafter. The modern Cape Verdeans are descendents of the two groups.

In 1975, Cape Verde became independent, with close ties to Guinea-Bissau (the former Portuguese Guinea). Drought and famine in recent years have created major difficulties for this already impoverished nation.

## CAROLINE ISLANDS (1900-14)

A large group of islands in the western Pacific Ocean. The Carolines were purchased by Germany from Spain in 1899. They were captured by Japan in 1914 and subsequently administered by the Japanese under a mandate from the League of Nations.

In 1944 they were occupied by the United States and since 1947 have been administered by the United States, under a mandate from the United Nations, as part of the Pacific Islands Trusteeship.

Japanese stamps were used from 1914 to 1944, and U.S. issues since 1944.

## CARPATHO-UKRAINE (1939, 1944-45)

The easternmost province of pre-Munich Czechoslovakia. It was created as an autonomous state in 1938 and annexed by Hungary in 1939.

With the Axis withdrawal in 1944, the area became independent for a brief time, reverting to Hungary in 1945. In 1949, it was annexed by the U.S.S.R.

## CARCHI (1912-32)

One of the Turkish Dodecanese Islands in the eastern Aegean Sea. Carchi was occupied by Italy in 1912.

Italian stamps overprinted "Karki," "Calchi," or "Carchi" were used until 1929, when the general Aegean Islands' issues came into use. Two sets overprinted with the island's name were issued in 1930 and 1932.

## CARUPANO (1902-03)

A port of Venezuela, near Trinidad. During the Anglo-German-Italian occupation of La Guaira, Carupano was isolated and soon ran out of stamps, necessitating the issue of provisional issues, until regular stocks could be obtained.

## CASO (1912-32)

One of the Turkish Dodecanese Islands in the eastern Aegean Sea. Caso was occupied by Italy in 1912, at which time Italian issues overprinted "Caso" were placed in use. These were replaced in 1929 by the general Aegean Islands' issues, although two sets overprinted for the island were issued in 1930 and 1932.

## CASTELLORIZO (1920-32)

Small island in the Mediterranean off the southwest coast of Turkey. Occupied by France in 1915, Castellorizo was transferred to Italy in 1920. After World War II, the island, along with the rest of the Dodecanese Islands, passed to Greece.

## CATTARO (1944)

A Yugoslavian province on the Adriatic, occupied by the Italians from 1941-43, and Germans, 1943-45, during World War II.

In 1944, Italian and Yugoslavia issues were overprinted for use in Cattaro by the German Occupation Authorities.

## CAVALLA (1893-1914)

A town in northern Greece. The French post office in Cavalla used unoverprinted French stamps (canceled "5156" within a diamond-shaped grid of dots) after 1874. During 1893-1914, it used stamps overprinted or inscribed "Cavalle."

Seized by Bulgaria from Turkey in 1912, Cavalla was taken by the Greeks in 1913. Bulgarian stamps overprinted by the Greek occupation authorities were used pending the arrival of regular Greek stocks.

## CAYMAN ISLANDS (1901-)

Three islands in the Caribbean Sea, northwest of Jamaica. The Cayman Islands have been a British colony since its settlement in the 18th century.

During the 1970s, the Caymans became a tax-free haven for banking, and many Western banks have branches in the colony.

## CENTRAL AFRICAN REPUBLIC (1959-)

A landlocked nation in central Africa, surrounded by Chad, Cameroon, Congo, Zaire, and the Sudan.

Formerly the French colony of Ubangi-Shari, the Central African Republic was established Dec. 1, 1958, and became fully independent Aug. 13, 1960.

Although possessed of substantial mineral resources, the country has been unable to develop economically and has been politically unstable since independence.

During 1960-65 the CAR was a center of Chinese influence in Africa. In 1965 the pro-Chinese regime was overthrown, and Jean-Bedel Bokassa came to power. On Dec. 4, 1976, Bokassa proclaimed the country the Central African Empire, with himself as Emperor Bokassa I.

Bokassa's rule was marked by almost unrelenting cruelty and barbarism, characterized by rumors that the emperor himself practiced cannibalism.

On Sept. 20, 1979, Bokassa was overthrown in a bloodless coup supported by 800-1,000 French troops, flown in from bases in Gabon and Chad. A republic was reestablished under David Dacko, who had been president of the country 1960-66.

## CENTRAL ALBANIA (1915)

During World War I, Albania was overrun by various foreign armies. From January 1914 to February 1916, the central portion of the country was controlled by a provisional regime under Essad Pasha. Essad was supplanted by the Austrians in 1916.

## CENTRAL CHINA (1949-50)

The Communist Central Chinese Liberation Area included the provinces of Honan, Hupeh, Hunan and Kiangsi. Separate issues for the region were used after the occupation of Hankow from the Nationalists.

## CENTRAL LITHUANIA (1920-22)

Historically a part of Lithuania, this territory was under Russian rule until 1915, when it was occupied by the Germans.

German stamps overprinted for Lithuania were used until December 1918, when regular Lithuanian stamps were issued. In October 1920, the area was occupied by Polish forces, who established an autonomous state, which issued its own stamps during 1920-22.

In 1922, it was annexed by Poland, but in 1939, it was occupied by Soviet forces and returned to Lithuania.

Central Lithuania was soon occupied by the Germans in 1941 and was held until 1945. Since World War II, Soviet stamps have been in use.

## CEPHALONIA AND ITHACA (1941)

Two of the Ionian Islands, off the western coast of Greece. The islands were occupied by Italian forces in 1941, when Greek stamps were overprinted for use in the two islands by the local Italian military authorities.

These were soon superseded by the general occupation issues for the Ionian Islands.

## CEYLON (1857-1972)

Island in the Indian Ocean, off the southeast coast of India. Much of the island was under Portugal during the 16th and 17th centuries, succeeded by the Dutch.

From 1795-1815, the British ruled Ceylon. In 1948, Ceylon became a self-governing dominion and in 1972, it became independent as the Republic of Sri Lanka.

## CHAD (1922-36, 1959-)

A republic in central Africa. A former dependency of Ubangi-Shari, Chad was occupied by the French during 1897-1914, after defeating fierce native resistance.

In 1920, Chad became a separate colony, joining in French Equatorial Africa in 1934. In 1958 the Chad Republic became an independent state in the French Union, and in 1960 it became fully independent.

Following independence, Chad retained close ties with France, which provided economic aid and support in the government's civil war with Libyan-backed Arab guerrillas after 1966.

In 1981, Libyan forces occupied Chad at the request of a coalition government. Libya's efforts to merge the two nations, however, alarmed even the pro-Libyan elements of the regime, and international pressure brought a rapid Libyan withdrawal. The political situation remains tense, and renewed civil war is likely.

## CHAMBA (1886-1950)

A state in northern India, Chamba became independent of Kashmir in 1846. In 1886, its postal service was joined to that of India, and overprinted Indian stamps came into use.

These overprinted issues were replaced by Indian stamps April 1, 1950, although they continued to be postally valid until Jan. 1, 1951.

## CHARKARI (CHARKHARI) (1894-1950)

A former feudatory state in north-central India, Charkari's stamps were replaced by those of India on May 1, 1950.

## CHECINY (1919)

A city in southern Poland. Local stamps were issued in 1919 under the authority of the municipal authorities.

## CHELYABINSK (1920-22)

A city in southwestern Siberia. Russian stamps were overprinted for local use by the municipal authorities during 1920-22.

### CHIAPAS (1866)

A state of southern Mexico, bordering on Guatemala and the Pacific Ocean.

### CHIHUAHUA (1872)

The capital city of the State of Chihuahua in northern Mexico.

### CHILE (1853-)

A republic in southwest South America. Chile was settled by Spain as early as 1540, although Indian resistance in the south was not overcome until the late 19th century. During 1817-18, Chile secured its independence, with the aid of Argentine forces under San Martin.

During the 19th century, Chile aggressively expanded its borders, acquiring nitrate-rich northern districts from Peru and Bolivia during the War of the Pacific, 1879-84, and subduing Indian resistance in the south.

After 1891, Chile was a liberal republic, but economic problems in recent years have produced social unrest and radical regimes, both Leftist and Rightist.

### CHIMARRA (HIMERA) (1914, 1920)

A city in the southern coast of Albania. Philatelically inspired issues were released during the Greek occupation of the port.

### CHINA (1878-)

An ancient country occupying a large area in eastern Asia, between Turkestan and the China Sea and stretching from Siberia to Indo-China. Chinese civilization appeared in the 3rd millennium B.C., producing one of the earliest sophisticated cultures. China was long divided into numerous states, within a feudal system.

China was unified under the Chin and Han dynasties (255 B.C.-220 A.D.), but again broke into contending states after the fall of the Hans.

Unification was achieved under the Sui and T'ang dynasties (589-907), but internal division again appeared.

In the early 13th century, the Mongols overran China, establishing the Yuan dynasty, which at its height (circa 1300) ruled China, Turkestan, Korea and Indo-China.

In 1368, the Ming dynasty expelled the Yuan and inaugurated a period of dynamic growth. In 1644, the Manchu dynasty overthrew the Ming and created a vast and powerful empire.

During 1840-1900, China was defeated in a series of wars, which secured for the European powers numerous concessions within the Chinese empire.

In 1892, Dr. Sun Yat-sen founded the Regenerate China Society which began to foment revolution. In 1911, the empress-dowager was deposed, and a republic proclaimed.

A period of civil war and internal division under local warlords ensued, until Chiang Kaishek, commanding the Nationalist armies, was able to reestablish some unity during the 1920s.

In 1927, Chiang moved against Soviet influence in the Nationalist government, and the Communists split with the regime, launching a guerrilla war against the central government.

In 1931, Japan occupied Manchuria and began to expand into China, openly invading the country in 1937. The Nationalists and Communists maintained an uneasy truce during World War II, but with the defeat of Japan and the occupation of Manchuria by the Soviets, the civil war began in earnest.

By 1949, the Nationalists had been defeated and driven to the island of Formosa (Taiwan). Since that time, the Chinese People's Republic on the mainland and the Republic of China on Taiwan have both claimed to represent the rightful government of China.

The Chinese People's Republic was closely linked with the U.S.S.R. during the 1950s, but by the 1960s this relationship had deteriorated. Conflicting nationalisms became identified with ideological differences, and the two nations have each come to regard the other as its principal enemy.

U.S. relations with the mainland regime, broken in 1950, have become increasingly close since 1971. On Dec. 15, 1978, the U.S. formally recognized the People's Republic as the sole legal government of China.

The Nationalist regime on Taiwan has been politically isolated in recent years. In 1971, it was expelled from the United Nations, in favor of the People's Republic, and in 1978, the United States, its principal ally and supporter, severed formal diplomatic relations. Taiwan has been able, however, to maintain extensive informal contacts abroad through its active international commercial operations.

### CHINA EXPEDITIONARY FORCES (1900-21)

Stamps of British India overprinted "C.E.F." were used by the British Expeditionary Force in China in 1900, 1904, 1909 and 1913-21.

### CHINESE TREATY PORTS (1865-97)

Before the establishment of the imperial posts in 1897, a number of Chinese treaty ports issued local stamps. These include Chungking (1894), Foochow (1895), Hankow (1893), Ichang (1895), Kewkiang (1894), Nanking (1896), Wuhu (1894) and Shanghai (1865).

### CHIOS (1913)

Island in the Aegean Sea. Chios was captured by Greece from Turkey in 1912. In 1913, an overprinted Greek stamp was issued. Stamps of Greece have since been used.

### CHRISTMAS ISLAND (1958-)

An island in the Indian Ocean. Under the British colony of Singapore from 1900-58, Christmas Island was transferred to Australian administration in 1958.

CILICIA

## CILICIA (1919-21)

A district of southern Turkey, northwest of Syria. Cilicia was occupied by the British and French from Turkey in 1918.

In 1919, France assumed sole control and in 1920 received the territory as a mandate from the League of Nations. In 1921, however, Turkish forces expelled the French, and in 1923, France gave up its claims to the area.

During 1919, Cilicia used Palestinian stamps, and during 1919-21, the French regime issued overprinted stamps of Turkey and France.

## COAMO (1898)

A city in Puerto Rico. U.S. forces issued a stamp for provisional use in August-September 1898 after Coamo's occupation from Spain.

## COCHIN (1892-1949)

Early a center of foreign traders, the Portuguese established a trading station at Cochin, a port city in southern India, in 1502. The British followed in 1635, but along with the Portuguese, were expelled by the Dutch in 1663. In 1795, the area passed to the British.

Cochin issued its own stamps until 1949, when it joined with Travancore and the coastal towns of Tangasseri and Anjengo to form the United State of Travancore-Cochin, whose issues then came into use. Indian stamps replaced these issues on April 1, 1951.

## COCHIN CHINA (1886-92)

The southernmost area of Vietnam. Occupied by France from 1863-67, Cochin China served as the base for French expansion in the region.

In 1887, Cochin China was incorporated into French Indo-China, whose stamps were used after 1892.

## COCOS ISLANDS (KEELING ISLANDS) (1963-)

A group of tiny islands in the Indian Ocean under Australian administration. Stamps of the Cocos Islands are also valid in Australia.

## COLOMBIA (1859-)

A republic in northwest South America. The seat of the Spanish viceroyalty of New Granada after 1718, Colombia declared its independence in 1810, finally ousting the Spanish in 1824.

Colombia, Venezuela and Ecuador comprised the State of Greater Colombia until 1830 when the three nations separated.

In 1903 the northern province of Panama broke away from Colombia and, with U.S. support, became independent.

Colombia is one of the few democracies in Latin America, although it has been plagued by chronic violence and disorder. "La Violencia" of 1948-58 claimed 200,000 lives, and political violence, albeit much abated, continues.

Colombia has been officially named the Republic of New Granada (1831-58), the Grenadine Confederation (1858-61), the United States of New Granada (1861), the United States of Colombia (1861-85), and the Republic of Colombia (since 1885).

## COLOMBIA-STATES' ISSUES (1863-1904)

Until 1885, the various Colombia states were sovereign, possessing the right to issue their own stamps.

In 1886, a national convention abolished most of the states' rights, transferring sovereignty to the central government. The states, however, retained the right to issue stamps, and did so as late as 1904.

The states which used their own stamps, along with national issues, were Antioquia, Bolivar, Boyaca, Canca, Cundinamarca, Panama, Santander, the city of Cucuta and Tolima.

## COMORO ISLANDS (1950-)

A group of islands in the Mozambique Channel between Mozambique and Madagascar. Under French rule since the 19th century, the Comoros were attached to Madagascar from 1911-46, being reorganized as an Overseas Territory in 1946. Since 1950, the Comoros have issued their own stamps.

The Comoros became independent in 1975, except for Mayotte, which voted to remain French. A coup soon after independence placed a leftist regime in power, but its increasingly eccentric rule brought another coup in 1978, which replaced it with a pro-French government.

## CONGO DEMOCRATIC REPUBLIC (1960-71)

In January 1960, Belgium agreed to grant independence to the Belgian Congo, and general elections were held May 31. On June 30, the country became independent.

The Congo was immediately torn by domestic violence, causing most whites to flee and two of the richest regions, Katanga and South Kasai, to secede. In August, Belgian troops were replaced by United Nations forces, which gradually restored order and suppressed the independence movements in the south.

In 1963 Katanga was reunited with the Congo, and on June 30, 1964, its president, Moise Tshombe, became president of the Congo.

Within months of the U.N. withdrawal (June '64), yet another separatist movement broke out, when leftists proclaimed a people's republic in Stanleyville. The central government suppressed this uprising, with the support of Belgian and white mercenary troops.

In 1965, General Joseph D. Mobutu became president. He began an Africanization program, wherein all Congolese with Christian names were required to adopt African names (he became Mobutu Sese Seko), Congolese place names were changed, and in 1971, the Congo itself was renamed the Republic of Zaire.

## CONGO PEOPLE'S REPUBLIC (1959-)

A republic on the north bank of the Congo River, in west central Africa. The former French colony of Middle Congo, the Congo became a member state in the French community in 1958 and gained independence in 1960.

After 1963, the Congo adopted a Marxist-Leninist stance, with ties to both the U.S.S.R. and China. U.S. relations, severed in 1965, were restored in 1977.

While French economic ties remain strong, the Congo is politically aligned with the U.S.S.R. with whom a treaty of friendship and cooperation was signed in May 1981.

## CONFEDERATE STATES OF AMERICA (1861-65)

The southern states of the United States, seceded from the Union in 1861 and attempted to establish an independent confederation.

After initial successes against the U.S. forces, the Confederacy was on the defensive after 1863. By early 1865, the rebellious areas had been overrun, and the states were reincorporated within the U.S.

## CONFEDERATE STATES OF AMERICA-PROVISIONAL ISSUES (1861)

In the early months of the Civil War, many southern post offices were without regular stocks of stamps. U.S. stamps in rebel territory were demonitized after June 1, 1861, and general Confederate issues were not available until October 1861.

During the interim, many local postmasters issued provisional stamps and postal stationery. Occasionally, such provisionals appeared later during the war, when regular Confederate stamps were unavailable.

## CONSTANTINOPLE (1909-14, 1921-23)

The capital of the Ottoman Empire, situated on the Hellespont between the Black Sea and the Aegean Sea.

During 1873-81, Turkish stamps were overprinted for local use within the city, and a number of private posts issued stamps.

Italian stamps overprinted "Constantinopoli" were used by the Italian post in the city from 1909-14. These issues were again used from 1921-23 by the Italian garrison in Constantinople.

Stamps of the Russian Levant overprinted with the name of the city were used by the Russian postal service in Constantinople from 1909-14. During 1919, Romanian forces in the city used contemporary Romanian stamps overprinted "Posta Romana Constantinopl" with the emblem of the Romanian PTT.

## COOK ISLANDS (1892-)

A group of islands in the South Pacific Ocean, northeast of New Zealand. In 1901, the Cook Islands became a dependency of New Zealand, gaining internal self-government in 1965.

## CORDOBA (1858-65)

A province in central Argentina, Cordoba issued its own stamps from 1858 to 1865, when they were replaced by the issues of the central government.

## CORFU (1923, 1941)

The major island of the Ionian Islands, off the western coast of Greece in the Ionian Sea. Corfu, under Greek control since 1864, was occupied by Italy in 1923 and 1941-43.

Stamps of Italy and Greece were overprinted by the Italians for use on the island.

## CORRIENTES (1856-80)

The northeast province of Argentina, Corrientes issued its own stamps until 1880, when they were replaced by regular Argentine issues.

## COS (1912-32)

One of the Turkish Dodecanese Islands in the eastern Aegean Sea. Cos was occupied by Italy in 1912, at which time overprinted Italian stamps were issued.

These were superseded by the general Aegean Islands' issues in 1929, although two sets overprinted "Coo" were issued in 1930 and 1932.

## COSTA RICA (1863-)

A republic in Central America, located between Nicaragua and Panama. Under Spain until 1821, Costa Rica's subsequent history has been mostly peaceful enabling it to develop a relatively high standard of living. Still chiefly an agricultural country, individual ownership of land is common.

## COUDEKERQUE (1940)

A city in northern France, near Dunkerque. For a time after the German occupation in World War II, overprinted French stamps were used in the city.

## COURLAND (1945)

In October 1944, German forces in the Courland peninsula were cut off from Germany by the advancing Soviet army. In April 1945, the local German commander overprinted four German stamps for use in the area.

## CRETE (1898-1910, 1944)

A large island in the Aegean Sea, Crete was originally a province of Turkey. Continuous religious civil strife between the Christian and Moslem natives brought the intervention of the Great Powers in 1898.

In 1899, the island was declared an autonomy under Prince George of Greece. In 1908, the Cretan Assembly voted for union with Greece, which finally occurred in 1913.

Crete used Turkish stamps until 1899. Stamps of Crete were used until 1913, when Greek stamps came into use. During 1898-1914, various stamps were issued by the Powers for use in their districts of Crete, including Britain (1898-99), Russia (1899), Austria (1903-14), France (1903-13) and Italy (1900-12).

During World War II, German military air parcel post stamps were overprinted "Inselpost" for use by German troops on Crete and nearby islands, after their isolation following the German withdrawal from Greece.

## CRIMEA (1919)

A large peninsula on the Black Sea, south of the Ukraine. From the Crimea, the Krim Tatars ruled a powerful state during the 15th-17th centuries. They later came under Turkish rule, which was supplanted by Russian rule in 1783.

During World War I, the Crimea was occupied by the Germans, who in June 1918, set up a Tatar government in the area. With the German withdrawal in November, a provisional government was established and several stamps were issued. The Crimea was subsequently occupied by the French, the Bolsheviks, General Denikin's Volunteer Army, and finally by the Bolsheviks a second (and final) time.

During World War II, the Crimea was again occupied by the Germans and was included in the Ukraine administrative district.

CROATIA

## CROATIA (1941-45)

A district of northern Yugoslavia, bordering on the Adriatic Sea. Croatia was a province of Hungary until 1918, when it became a part of Yugoslavia.

In 1941, a German puppet state was created in Croatia. Nominally a kingdom under an Italian prince, in fact the state was ruled by the Croat fascist party.

Croatia was overrun by Russian and Yugoslavian partisan forces in 1945 and reincorporated into Yugoslavia.

## CUAUTLA (1867)

A town in the State of Morelos central Mexico.

## CUBA (1855-)

The largest island of the West Indies, located south of Florida.

Under Spanish rule from 1511-1898, Cuba was the scene of intense revolutionary activity after 1868. In 1898, the sinking of the USS Maine in Havana harbor precipitated the Spanish-American War, which ended with the U.S. assuming trusteeship of the island.

In 1902, the Cuban republic became independent, although the U.S. actively intervened in Cuban affairs until the 1930s.

In 1959 a liberal guerrilla movement, led by Fidel Castro, overthrew the repressive government of Fulgencio Batista, who had ruled Cuba since 1952. Castro, influenced by his brother Raul and Che Guevera, soon began to purge the revolution of its non-Marxist elements.

The regime nationalized foreign holdings and began the program of collectivization that has since taken most agricultural sectors out of private hands. A large number of Cubans preferred exile to the new order, and many hundreds of thousands have fled the island, most settling in the United States.

Castro linked Cuban policy closely with that of the U.S.S.R., which soon established a strong military presence on the island. U.S.-Cuban relations deteriorated rapidly. In 1961, the U.S. backed an abortive invasion by a Cuban exile force, and in 1962, the discovery of nuclear missiles at Soviet bases in Cuba brought the U.S. and the U.S.S.R. to the brink of war. The United States imposed a total trade embargo on Cuba in 1962, which was supported by the Organization of American States in 1963.

In the years since, the Castro regime has improved the standard of living in Cuba and has largely overcome illiteracy. The Cuban economy is dependent on massive Soviet aid, however.

Since 1975, Cuban troops and advisors have actively supported pro-Soviet factions in Africa and, more recently, in Central America.

The U.S. Treasury Department prohibits the importation of Cuban postage stamps into the United States through the mail.

## CUERNAVACA (1867)

The capital city of the State of Morelos in central Mexico.

## CYPRUS (1880-)

A large island in the eastern Mediterranean. Long ruled by foreigners, Cyprus was a Turkish possession from 1571-1878.

In 1878, the British occupied the island, formally annexing it in 1914. In 1960, the British withdrew and Cyprus became an independent republic.

Tension between Greek and Turkish elements, each of which seeks union with the respective mother country, led to a Turkish invasion of northeast Cyprus in 1974.

Since that time, Greek and Turkish regimes have maintained an uneasy truce, dividing the island between them.

## CYRENAICA (1923-35, 1950-51)

A district of north Africa, west of Egypt. Cyrenaica was under Turkish control until 1912, when it was ceded to Italy and incorporated with Tripolitania to form the colony of Libia. In 1942, it was occupied by the British, becoming part of the independent kingdom of Libya in 1951.

## CZECHOSLOVAK LEGION POST (1918-20)

During World War I, many Czech nationalists fought against Austria on the Russian front. After the Russian Revolution, these units attempted to move to the western front to continue fighting, but clashes with the Bolsheviks en route to Vladivostok led to the Czechs' involvement in the Russian Civil War.

The Czechs achieved notable successes, for a time holding large areas along the Trans-Siberian Railroad. News of these successes created sympathy for the cause of Czechoslovak independence.

During this period, the Czech Legion issued a number of stamps for use by its forces in Russia.

## CZECHOSLOVAKIA (1918-)

A republic in central Europe. The medieval kingdom of Bohemia, long a power in central Europe, passed to the Hapsburgs of Austria in 1526.

Nationalism grew in strength throughout the 19th century, and in 1918, Czechoslovakia became independent. In 1938, Czechoslovakia lost border territories to Germany, Hungary and Poland, and in 1939, the balance of the country was occupied by Germany.

In 1945, the country was liberated by Allied forces and the Czechoslovak republic was reestablished. In February 1948, the Communists seized power and by September had effectively suppressed opposition. There followed a long period of violent repression and purges of liberal party leaders.

In January 1968, Alexander Dubeck replaced Antonin Novotny as party leader and launched a program aimed at establishing a democratic Communist system. The Soviet Union feared that the success of such reforms would weaken its control over its Eastern European satellites, and relations between the two governments became increasingly cool. In August, Soviet, Polish, East German, Hungarian and Bulgarian forces invaded Czechoslovakia and put an end to the liberalization. Nearly a third of the Czechoslovak Communist Party members were expelled, and some 40,000 Czechs fled the country. The government has since maintained a repressive, staunchly pro-Soviet policy.

## — D —

## DAHOMEY (1899-1945, 1960-76)

A former republic on the Gulf of Guinea in West Africa.

During 1863-92 France occupied the area, consolidating its holdings as the colony of Dahomey in 1899.

In 1958 Dahomey became an autonomous republic within the French Community, and in 1960 it became an independent republic.

After a series of coups following independence, the present government assumed power in 1972. In 1974, it announced the formation of a Marxist-Leninist socialist state, and in November 1975, changed the name of the country to the People's Republic of Benin.

## DALMATIA (1919-22)

Area on the coast 'of Yugoslavia around the port of Zara. Dalmatia was occupied by Italy in 1918 and became part of Yugoslavia after World War II.

## DANISH WEST INDIES (1855-1917)

A small group of islands east of Puerto Rico. Having passed through the hands of Spain, France, The Netherlands, Great Britain, the Knights of Malta and Brandenburg (Prussia), the islands finally came under Danish rule in 1733 and 1754 (St. Thomas).

In 1916 the colony was sold to the United States, which took possession on April 1, 1917. They were renamed the U.S. Virgin Islands, and U.S. stamps replaced those of the colony.

## DANUBE STEAM NAVIGATION COMPANY (1866-80)

This company carried mail along the Danube, serving all countries through which the river passed, as well as the Russian port of Odessa on the Black Sea.

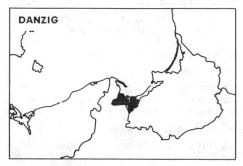

## DANZIG (1920-39)

A port on the Baltic Sea. Part of Prussia until after World War I, Danzig and adjacent territory was made a "Free City and State" under the protection of the League of Nations in 1920.

In 1939, the district was occupied by Germany and in 1945, was annexed by Poland.

**DARDANELLES (1904-14)**

A port on the strait of the same name between the Aegean and Mamara Seas. Issues of the Russian Levant were overprinted for use at its post office at Dardanelles.

**DEBRECEN (1919-20)**

A Hungarian district occupied by Romania after World War I, but later returned to Hungary.

**DEDEAGATCH (1893-1914)**

A seaport in northern Greece. The French post office in Dedeagatch used unoverprinted French issues (canceled "5155" in a diamond-shaped grid of dots) from 1874-93 and stamps overprinted or inscribed "Dedeagh" from 1893 until August 1914.

During the first Balkan War (1912), Dedeagatch was occupied by Bulgaria from Turkey. In 1913, Greece occupied the city from Bulgaria, and overprinted Bulgarian stamps, along with a type-set provisional issue, were used pending the arrival of regular Greek stamps.

**DENMARK (1851-)**

A kingdom in northwestern Europe, located strategically between the North Sea and the Baltic Sea.

Denmark was one of the chief Viking centers and for centuries was one of the leading powers in northern Europe. At one time or another during the Middle Ages, Denmark ruled Norway, Sweden, Finland, Iceland and England.

During the 17th-19th centuries, Danish power declined, and defeats by Sweden, Britain and Prussia forced it back to, roughly, its present boundaries.

After 1815, Denmark adopted a policy of neutrality, which it maintained for 130 years.

This policy was abandoned after World War II, during which the country was occupied by Germany. Denmark was a charter member of NATO and joined the Common Market in 1960.

A rich country agriculturally, Denmark has undergone an industrial boom since 1945. A long tradition of democracy and social cooperation mark the country's political life.

**DHAR (1897-1901)**

A former feudatory state in west-central India, Dhar issues were replaced by those of India on April 1, 1901.

**DIEGO-SUAREZ (1890-96)**

A port at the north end of Madagascar, Diego Suarez was a French colony from 1885 to 1896, when it was attached to Madagascar.

**DJIBOUTI (1977-)**

The former French overseas territory of Afars and Issas in northeast Africa, became independent on June 17, 1977.

Djibouti is supported by French aid, and a French garrison remains in the country.

**DOBRUDJA (1916-18)**

A Romanian territory on the Black Sea, comprising the area south of the Danube River. Dobrudja was occupied by Bulgaria during World War I, during which time overprinted Bulgarian stamps were used in the district.

**DODECANESE ISLANDS (1947)**

The former Italian Aegean Islands, occupied by Greece after World War II. Overprinted Greek stamps were used until their replacement by regular Greek issues.

**DOMINICA (1874-)**

An island in the Caribbean southeast of Puerto Rico. Dominica was a British Crown Colony 1833-1968 and an Associate State 1968-78. On Nov. 3, 1978, it became independent.

**DOMINICAN REPUBLIC (1865-)**

A republic occupying the eastern two-thirds of the island of Hispaniola in the West Indies. The Dominican Republic was ruled by Spain until c.1800, thereafter falling under periods of Spanish, French and Haitian rule until 1844.

In 1861-65, the republic was again occupied by Spain. A Dominican request for annexation by the U.S. was rejected in 1865.

The first stamps used in the country were Spanish colonial issues for Cuba and Puerto Rico. After the Spanish withdrawal, the Dominican Republic began issuing its own stamps.

The rest of the 19th century was marked by political instability. From 1916 to 1922, the country was under U.S. military administration, and U.S. troops remained until 1924. In 1930 General Rafael Trujillo Molina came to power and ruled the country for the next three decades. Trujillo maintained order (at the expense of individual liberties) and brought a degree of economic development. Increasing popular dissatisfaction with Trujillo's repressive regime brought his assassination in 1961 and the fall of his designated successor the following year.

Free elections were held in 1962, but the president was deposed in 1963. In 1965 the ousted leader's followers staged a revolt, bringing U.S. intervention. U.S. troops, along with small contingents from five South American countries, remained as a peacekeeping force until September 1966, presiding over new elections. Since that time, the country has enjoyed relative stability and economic progress.

**DON COSSACK GOVERNMENT (1918-19)**

On June 5, 1918, the Don Cossacks established a republic at Rostov, in southern Russia. Allied with General Denikin's Volunteer Army, the government fell to the Soviets, after Denikin's withdrawal from Rostov in February 1920.

**DUBAI (1963-72)**

A sheikdom in the Trucial States in east Arabia in the Persian Gulf. Dubai was under British protection from 1892-1971 when it became a part of the independent United Arab Emirates.

## DUNKERQUE (1940)

A French port on the English Channel. During July 1-Aug. 9, 1940, French stamps overprinted locally by the German military authorities were in use in the area around Dunkerque.

## DURANGO (1937)

A city in the province of Vizcaya in northern Spain. A 16-value set was overprinted by local authorities in 1937 to commemorate the occupation of the city by the Nationalists.

## DURAZZO (1909-11, 1916-18)

An Albanian port. Italian stamps overprinted "Durazzo" and surcharged in Turkish currency were used by the Italian post office in the city from February 1909 to 1911.

## DUTTIA (DATIA) (1893-1921)

A former feudatory state in north-central India, Duttia's stamps were replaced by Indian issues in 1921.

## — E —

## EAST AFRICA FORCES (1943-50)

British stamps were overprinted "E.A.F." or "Somalia" for use in Italian Somalia under the British occupation.

## EAST AFRICA AND UGANDA PROTECTORATES (1903-21)

A former British administrative unit in eastern Africa, comprising Kenya and Uganda.

## EAST CHINA (1938-50)

The Communist East China Liberation Area included the provinces of Shantung, Kiangsu, Chekiang, Anhwei and Fukien. Fourteen postal districts within East China issued stamps during 1938-49.

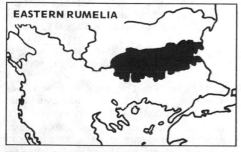

EASTERN RUMELIA

## EASTERN RUMELIA (1880-85)

A Bulgarian district in the southeast Balkan Peninsula. After Turkey's defeat by Russia in 1877-78, Eastern Rumelia became autonomous.

In 1885, a coup overthrew the vestiges of Turkish control and South Bulgaria was established.

## EASTERN SILESIA (1920)

A former Austrian territory in central Europe. After World War I, it was disputed between Czechoslovakia and Poland, being divided between the two countries in 1920.

## ECUADOR (1865-)

Republic on the western coast of South America. Ecuador was the site of a number of early Indian cultures and was the center of the northern Inca empire at the time of its conquest by Spain (1533).

In 1822, Ecuador became independent as part of Bolivar's Great Colombia. In 1830, it withdrew to form a separate nation.

Despite substantial petroleum deposits (it is an OPEC member), Ecuador remains an underdeveloped nation.

A series of military and civilian regimes have alternated control in recent years. Since 1979, a democratic civilian government has ruled the country.

A long-standing border dispute between Ecuador and Peru remains unresolved. Armed hostilities occasionally erupt between the two countries, most recently in January/February 1981.

## EGYPT (1866-)

A republic in northeast Africa. Egypt was one of the centers of the development of western civilization.

The dominant power in the region for 3,500 years, Egypt passed through periods of strength and weakness until 330 B.C., after which it was ruled by foreign states and dynasties until modern times.

After 1517, Egypt was under Turkish control. In 1882, Britain occupied Egypt, although a nominal Turkish suzerainty remained until 1914.

Egypt was under a British protectorate until 1922, after which time, it was virtually independent. British troops remained until 1951, when Egypt became completely independent.

The corruption and extravagance of the monarchy brought the overthrow of King Farouk in 1952 and the establishment of a republic in 1953. In 1954, Lt. Col. Gamel Abdel Nasser, one of the leaders in the 1952 coup, came to power and ruled until his death in 1970.

Nasser pursued a pan-Arab policy and attempted to unite the Arab world under his leadership. The United Arab Republic joined Egypt and Syria 1958-61, but attempts to maintain the union or to include Iraq and Yemen during this period failed.

Nasser's foreign policy, technically neutral, was in most instances aligned with that of the U.S.S.R., and by the time of his death, thousands of Soviet advisors were in Egypt.

Nasser was succeeded by Anwar Sadat, who expelled Soviet advisors in 1971 and who pursued an increasingly pro-Western policy after 1974. Egypt has fought wars with Israel in 1948, 1956, 1967 and 1973. In each instance, Israel won.

In 1979, Egypt and Israel signed a formal peace treaty, establishing formal diplomatic relations, setting a timetable for Israeli withdrawal from Egyptian territory occupied since 1967, and providing for an as yet undetermined Palestinian state.

Egypt's attempt to make peace with Israel brought its ostracism by other Arab nations. Although the issue of a Palestinian state remains a major point of dispute, Egypt has, however, continued to work within the framework of its 1979 treaty with Israel.

In October 1981, Sadat was assassinated. He was quickly succeeded by his vice president, Hosni Mubarak, who has continued Sadat's peace initiative with Israel while working toward restoring normal relations with other Arab states.

Mubarak's firm support of Iraq in its war with Iran, which has included the dispatch of several hundred key Egyptian military personnel to the front, has done much to bring Egypt back into the Arab fold.

## ELOBEY, ANNOBON AND CORISCO (1903-09)

A group of islands near the Guinea coast off west Africa. Acquired by Spain in 1778, stamps of Fernando Po were used from 1868-1903.

In 1909, the islands were attached to Spanish Guinea, now the Republic of Equatorial Guinea.

## ELWA (1941)

A city in Estonia. Russian stamps were provisionally overprinted "Eesti"/"Post" by the German military authorities for use in the city.

## EPIRUS (1914-16)

A region in southeast Albania. Inhabitants set up a provisional government in February 1914, and were united with Greece in December 1914.

In 1916, Franco-Italian forces occupied the area, giving it to Albania after World War I.

## EQUATORIAL GUINEA (1968-)

A republic in the Gulf of Guinea, in West Africa, comprising the former Spanish colonies of Fernando Po and Rio Muni. Equatorial Guinea became independent Oct. 12, 1968.

In 1972 Masie Ngeuma Biyogo became president for life. He ruled by terror, reviving slavery, killing some 50,000 people, and driving tens of thousands more into exile.

The U.S. suspended relations with the Biyogo government in 1976. The U.S.S.R., China, and North Korea maintained close relations, and Cuba maintained a military advisory mission in the country.

On Aug. 5, 1979, Masie was overthrown, and a junta assumed power. The coup does appear to have halted, at least temporarily, the vast numbers of brightly-colored stamps (perfs, imperfs, souvenir sheets, gold-foil sheets, etc.) that have been issued by Equatorial Guinea since the early 1970s.

## ERITREA (1892-1937, 1948-52)

A district in northeast Africa, bordering on the Red Sea. Long under general Ethiopian domination, the area was occupied by Italy during 1870-85. In 1890, Italian possessions in the region were consolidated into Eritrea.

In 1936, the colony was absorbed into Italian East Africa. It was occupied by the British in 1941, after which overprinted British stamps were used. In 1950, Eritrea became an autonomous part of Ethiopia, whose issues have been in use since 1952. Eritrea has not willingly accepted Ethiopian rule and since 1970 has waged a guerilla war, aided by Arab states.

## ERSEKA (1914)

A city in southeastern Albania, occupied by Greece in 1914. During the Greek occupation, the local authorities issued a set of seven stamps for use in the area.

## ESTONIA (1918-40)

A district in northern Europe bordering on the Baltic Sea and the Gulf of Finland. Estonia declared independence from Russia in 1917.

In 1939, Soviet forces occupied the country, absorbing it in 1940. Occupied by Germany from 1941-44 and administered as part of Ostland, Estonia was reoccupied by the U.S.S.R. after World War II.

## ETHIOPIA (ABYSSINIA) (1894-1938, 1942-)

A republic in northeast Africa. Ethiopia was an ancient empire, isolated from the rest of the Christian world after the Moslem conquests of the 7th century.

During the 19th century, the country was again united out of the petty states into which it had disintegrated. An Italian invasion was crushed in 1896, but many outlying areas were gradually lost to the British, French and Italians.

In 1935-36, Ethiopia was defeated by Italy and in 1936, with Eritrea and Italian Somaliland, incorporated into the colony of Italian East Africa.

In 1941, Ethiopia was liberated with the help of British forces and independence was restored.

In 1975, the Emperor Haile Selassie I, who had reigned since 1922, was deposed, and a socialist military regime assumed power.

In 1978 Soviet advisors and 20,000 Cuban troops helped Ethiopia defeat Somalia in a border war in the Ogaden. Ethiopia is the center of Soviet influence in northern Africa.

## EUPEN AND MALMEDY (1920-25)

Two towns in western Germany annexed by Belgium after World War I. Overprinted stamps of Belgium were used until 1925, when regular Belgian issues came into use.

## — F —

## FALKLAND ISLANDS (1878-)

The Falkland Islands (with its dependencies)

comprise some 200 islands off the southeastern coast of South America. Only the two main islands, East and West Falkland, are inhabited. Ninety-eight per cent of the Falklanders are of British descent and have British nationality.

The Falklands were discovered by the British in 1592 but were uninhabited until a French settlement was established in 1764 and a British settlement in 1765. The two countries disputed sovereignty until 1770 when France sold her claim to Spain. Spain and Britain disputed ownership of the islands until 1806, when the Spanish withdrew their settlement.

Although Spain ceased pressing its claim at that time, the newly independent United Provinces of Rio de la Plata claimed the Falklands after 1816. A settlement was maintained 1820-33, when the British reoccupied the islands and peacefully expelled the Argentine garrison.

Argentina has maintained its claim to the Falklands and on April 2, 1982, seized the islands. A British fleet was immediately dispatched to oust the Argentines, and successfully recaptured the islands.

## FALKLAND ISLANDS DEPENDENCIES (1946-63)

Several island groups in the South Atlantic Ocean and the British sector of Antarctica. In 1944, Graham Land, South Georgia, the South Orkneys and South Shetlands received separate sets, overprinted on Falkland issues, and in 1946, general issues for the territory began. In 1962 this area was reorganized as the British Antarctic Territory, with South Georgia remaining attached to the Falklands.

## FAR EASTERN REPUBLIC (1920-22)

The Far Eastern Republic, comprising eastern Siberia from Lake Baikal to the Pacific Ocean, was formed on April 6, 1920, to act as a buffer between the Soviet Union and Japan. The state was immediately beset by intrigues between pro- and anti- Bolshevik factions, with the former finally gaining the upper hand. Japanese forces were forced to withdraw from Vladivostock in November 1922, and soon thereafter the Far Eastern Republic joined the Soviet Union.

## FARIDKOT (1879-1901)

A former principality in the Punjab area of India. Faridkot issued stamps and maintained its own postal system until Jan. 1, 1887, when it signed a postal convention uniting its postal system to that of India.

Overprinted Indian stamps were used until March 31, 1901, when they were replaced by regular Indian issues.

## FAROE ISLANDS (1919, 1940-41, 1975-)

A group of islands in the North Atlantic Ocean. The Faroe Islands, long a Danish possession are now a self-governing part of the kingdom of Denmark. The islands were occupied by Britain during World War II, after Denmark's occupation by Germany.

## FERNANDO PO (1868-1909, 1929, 1960-68)

An island in the Gulf of Guinea, off the west coast of Africa. Fernando Po was acquired by Spain in 1778 and was incorporated into Spanish Guinea in 1909.

In 1960, it became an overseas province of Spain, but in 1968 united with Rio Muni to form the independent republic of Equatorial Guinea.

## FEZZAN-GHADAMES (1943-51)

Districts in the interior of Libya, occupied by French forces during 1942-43. The districts were transferred to the kingdom of Libya in December 1951.

## FIJI (1870-)

A group of islands in the South Pacific Ocean. Fiji was a British colony from 1874-1970 when it became an independent dominion within the British Commonwealth.

## FINLAND (1856-)

A republic in northern Europe. Under Swedish rule from 1187-1809, Finland became a grand duchy with the Russian tsar as grand duke in 1809.

In 1899, Finland was incorporated into the Russian Empire, but in July 1917, the Finnish Diet proclaimed independence. After several years of warfare, Russia accepted Finnish independence in 1919.

In 1939, Finland was invaded by the U.S.S.R. and in 1940, was compelled to cede extensive eastern territories to the Soviets. Finland subsequently allied herself with Germany in an attempt to regain these territories, but her defeat cost even further concessions.

Although economically and culturally oriented toward the West, Finland has since World War II pursued a policy of acquiescence to Soviet power and proximity.

## FIUME (1918-24)

A city on the Adriatic Sea. A former Hungarian port, Fiume was disputed by Italy and Yugoslavia after World War I.

An Italian private army occupied the city in 1919, and a free state was subsequently established during 1920-22. A fascist coup brought Italian occupation in 1922.

In 1924, Fiume was annexed to Italy while adjacent territory was annexed to Yugoslavia.

In May 1945, Fiume was occupied by Yugoslav partisans, and Italian stamps were overprinted for use in the area during 1945-46, after which regular Yugoslavian issues came into use.

## FRANCE (1849-)

A republic in western Europe. France was overrun by the German Franks in the 5th century. During the 8th century, the Frankish kingdom stopped the Arab advance into Europe and by c.800 A.D., the Frankish Empire, under Charlemagne, ruled most of western and central Europe.

In 843, the empire was partitioned, and the western kingdom became the foundation of modern France. During the Middle Ages, France lacked any strong central government, being divided among numerous feudal states.

The English dominated much of the area during the 11th-15th centuries, but they were finally expelled after 1453.

The French Revolution (1789) began a series of wars in Europe that lasted until the final defeat of Napoleon Bonaparte in 1815.

During the second half of the 19th century, France built a far-flung overseas empire.

During World War I, France suffered greatly, and most of the bitterest fighting was on French soil. France emerged from the war the preeminent power on the continent, but in the 1930s it lost ground to a reemerging Germany.

France quickly crumbled before Germany's invasion in May and June 1940. The northern and western portions of the country were occupied by Germany, and a German puppet regime was established in the south. A Free French government, based in Africa, continued to war against the Axis overseas.

Following World War II, France rapidly rebuilt its economy and again played a major role in world affairs. During 1958-70, Gen. Charles de Gaulle's policies of economic and technological development and independence in foreign affairs were aimed at reestablishing France's greatness. De Gaulle disengaged France from its colonial commitments, and during 1958-62 most of French Africa became independent. France, however, retains close economic and political ties with many of its former colonies.

## FRENCH COLONIES
### (1859-1906, 1944-45)

During 1859-92, general French colonial issues were used in French possessions not issuing their own stamps. General postage dues were in use until 1906 and during 1944-45.

The French colonial semipostal issues of 1943-44 were intended for use in the colonies, but were actually used in parts of France occupied by the Free French.

## FRENCH CONGO (1891-1906)

The territory occupied by France, north of the Congo River, at times including Gabon, Ubangi and Chad, as well as the area now included in the Congo People's Republic.

The French Congo issued stamps from 1891 until 1906 when the administrative area was broken up into the separate colonies of Gabon and Middle Congo.

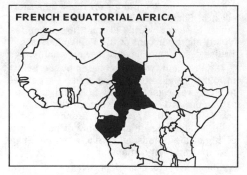

FRENCH EQUATORIAL AFRICA

## FRENCH EQUATORIAL AFRICA (1936-58)

The French possessions north of the Congo River, formerly included in the French Congo. Stamps inscribed French Equatorial Africa were used from 1936 to 1958, when the area was divided into four republics — Chad, Congo, Gabon and Central African Republic, which have since issued their own stamps.

## FRENCH GUIANA (1886-1946)

A former French colony on the northeastern coast of South America, north of Brazil. Separate issues were used in French Guiana from 1886 until 1946, when the area became an overseas department of France, using regular French issues.

## FRENCH GUINEA (1892-1944)

A former French colony on the western coast of Africa. During 1892-1944, French Guinea used its own stamps. In 1944, these were replaced by those of French West Africa.

In 1958, the colony became independent as the republic of Guinea, and again began issuing its own stamps.

## FRENCH INDIA (1892-1954)

Several French enclaves on the east coast of India, dating from the period of French domination of the region in the 18th century.

Separate stamp issues were in use from 1892 until 1954, when the last of the French holdings were transferred to India, and Indian stamps came into use.

## FRENCH MOROCCO (1891-1956)

Former French protectorate in northwest Africa. The French assumed a protectorate over the greater part of Morocco in 1912.

In 1956, the French and Spanish zones were united as the independent kingdom of Morocco.

## FRENCH OFFICES IN CHINA (1894-1922)

Until Dec. 31, 1922, France maintained an extensive postal system in China. In addition to a general series of stamps for these offices, individual issues were used at French post offices in Canton, Hoi Hao, Mongtsen, Pakhoi, Tch'ong K'ing (Chunking), and Yunnan Fou (Kunming).

In addition, stamps were issued for

Kwangchowan, a leased territory administered by French Indo-China.

**FRENCH OFFICES IN CRETE (1902-14)**

France issued two series of stamps for use in its post offices in Crete during the period of that country's autonomous regime.

**FRENCH OFFICES IN EGYPT (1899-1931)**

Until April 1, 1931, France maintained post offices in Alexandria and Port Said, issuing stamps for use in both cities.

**FRENCH OFFICES IN TURKEY (1885-1914, 1921-23)**

Like many other European nations, France maintained its own postal services within the Ottoman Empire. Aside from a general issue, individual issues were used in Cavalle (Cavalla), Dedeagh (Dedeagatch), Port Lagos and Vathy (Samos).

**FRENCH OFFICES IN ZANZIBAR (1894-1906)**

During the late 19th century, France competed with England for influence in East Africa, including Zanzibar.

French post offices in Zanzibar were closed in 1906 when Britain assumed direct control over the sultanate.

**FRENCH POLYNESIA (1892-)**

After 1842, France expanded its holdings in the South Pacific, consolidating these into the Oceanic Settlements in 1885. This group was renamed the French Oceanic Settlements in 1903.

In 1957 the colony was renamed French Polynesia and in the following year became an Overseas Territory of the French Republic.

**FRENCH SOUTHERN AND ANTARCTIC TERRITORIES (1955-)**

The French overseas territory comprising its holdings in the Antarctic area. Formerly dependencies of Madagascar, this administrative unit was established in 1955 to strengthen France's claims in the region.

**FRENCH SUDAN (1894-1943)**

Former French colony in northwest Africa. Separate issues were in use from 1894-1943, when they were replaced by those of French West Africa. In 1959, this area joined with Senegal to form the independent republic of Mali.

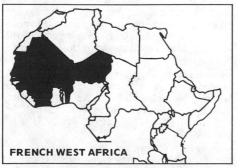

**FRENCH WEST AFRICA**

**FRENCH WEST AFRICA (1943-59)**

Former French administrative unit comprising the African colonies of Senegal, French Guinea, Ivory Coast, Dahomey, French Sudan, Mauritania, Niger and Upper Volta.

Although French West Africa was formed in 1895 as an administrative unit, the various colonies continued to issue their own stamps until 1943, when French West African issues came into use. These, in turn, were replaced by the separate issues of the territories as they became republics during 1958-59.

**FUJEIRA (1964-72)**

Sheikdom in the Trucial States in southeast Arabia, in the Persian Gulf. Fujeira was under British protection from 1892-1971 when it became a member of the independent United Arab Emirates.

**FUNCHAL (1892-1905)**

A city in the Madeira island group in the eastern Atlantic Ocean. Funchal issues were replaced by those of the Azores in 1905. Since 1931, regular Portuguese stamps have been in use.

# — G —

**GABON (1886-1936, 1959-)**

Republic in western Equatorial Africa, north of the Congo region. Gabon was one of the four French colonies comprising French Equatorial Africa. In 1958, Gabon became a republic and in 1960, gained independence from France.

Gabon possesses abundant natural resources and through foreign aid and government development, it has become one of the most prosperous Black African nations.

**GALAPAGOS ISLANDS (1957-59)**

A group of islands in the eastern South Pacific Ocean. Ecuador issued stamps for this province from 1957-59. Although intended for use in the Galapagos, these issues were commonly used throughout Ecuador.

**GAMBIA (1869-)**

Republic in West Africa. British influence was dominant on the coast after the early 17th century, with the inland area occupied in 1902.

In 1965, Gambia became independent and in 1970, it became a republic. It is one of the few African states to remain truly democratic.

Early in 1982 Gambia formed a federation, Sene-Gambia, with Senegal, which, except for a small length of coastline, surrounds it.

**GENEVA (1843-50)**

A canton of Switzerland, almost surrounded by France. Geneva issued several stamps, which were used until the issue of national Swiss stamps in 1850.

**GEORGIA (1919-20)**

A region in the western Caucasus, south of Russia and north of Turkey. Long under Turkish influence, Georgia was conquered by Russia during 1810-78.

In May 1918, following the withdrawal of German forces that had occupied the area during World War I, Georgia declared its independence. Georgia was recognized by the League of Nations, but on Feb. 25, 1921, it was occupied by Soviet forces. The Georgian Soviet Republic was merged into the Transcaucasian Federation of Soviet Republics in March 1922, and issues of the federation replaced those of Georgia on Oct. 1, 1923.

Georgian nationalist sentiment remains strong, provoking strong repression and massive purges since 1972. Despite this, illegal private enterprise and nationalism remain potent forces.

## GERMAN EAST AFRICA (1893-1916)

A former German colony in eastern Africa, on the Indian Ocean. Long dominated by the Arab Sultanate of Zanzibar, German influence in the area was recognized after 1886.

Stamps for the colony were in use from 1893-1916. After World War I, the colony was divided into Tanganyika (British), Ruanda-Urundi (Belgian) and Kionga (Portuguese).

## GERMAN NEW GUINEA (1888-1914)

A former German protectorate, comprising the northeastern portion of New Guinea and the adjacent islands. Regular German stamps were used from 1888-98 when they were replaced by separate issues.

In 1914, the area was occupied by Australian forces and stamps of New Guinea replaced those of the German administration.

## GERMAN SOUTH-WEST AFRICA (1897-1915)

A former German colony on the southwestern coast of Africa. Regular German stamps were used from 1888-97, and stamps of the colony from 1897-1915.

In 1915, South African forces occupied the area, and stamps of the Union of South Africa came into use. In 1919, South Africa was granted a mandate over the territory. Since 1923, stamps of South-West Africa have been used.

## GERMANY (1872-)

State in central Europe. Traditionally divided into numerous petty sovereignties, German unification began with the growth of Prussian power in the 18th century.

French occupation during the Napoleonic Wars brought the dissolution of many of the tinier states and stimulated German nationalism, which looked more and more to Prussia for leadership.

The German Confederation (1815-66) and North German Confederation (1867-71) paved the way for unification. The Franco-Prussian War of 1870-71 brought the German states (except Austria) together to defeat France, and the German victory saw the creation of the German Empire with the Prussian king as emperor.

Germany quickly emerged as the dominant military power on the continent.

In August 1914, after many years of tension, war between the major powers finally erupted, with the Central Powers (Germany and Austria-Hungary; later Bulgaria and Turkey) pitted against the Allies (Britain, France, and Russia, later joined by many other nations, including the United States and Japan). Both sides anticipated a short war and quick victory, but stalemates arose on all major fronts, and both sides settled in for years of trench warfare. During 1916-17, the Central Powers advanced in Russia, and the Russian front collapsed. The Treaty of Brest-Litovsk (March 3, 1918) gave Germany large areas of European Russia and much of the country's industry and mineral resources.

The Central Powers were less successful elsewhere: during the fall of 1918, Turkey surrendered to advancing British and Arab forces, Bulgaria surrendered, and Austria-Hungary collapsed. By this point, Germany itself was near economic collapse. The Kaiser abdicated in November 1918, and a republic was established, soon after which Germany surrendered unconditionally.

The Treaty of Versailles (1919) stripped Germany of its overseas empire and transferred German European territories to France, Belgium, Poland and, after plebscites, to Denmark and Lithuania. The harshness of the treaty's terms and the economic dislocation following the war provided fertile ground for political extremism, which culminated in the naming of Adolph Hitler as Chancellor in 1933.

Hitler's National Socialist German Workers' Party quickly suppressed all political freedoms and began openly to rearm. In 1936 Germany remilitarized the Rhineland, and in 1938 Austria and the Sudetenland (German-speaking Czechoslovakia) were annexed.

In 1939, Germany signed a nonaggression pact with the U.S.S.R., and on Sept. 1, German forces invaded Poland, precipitating World War II. Through 1942, Germany enjoyed an almost unbroken string of military successes. The entry of the United States into the war, however, gradually began to tell, and during 1944-45, Germany was on the retreat. In April 1945, soon after Hitler's suicide, Germany surrendered unconditionally.

Germany lost all territory acquired after 1919, as well as much of that which had been left to her after her defeat in World War I. The country was divided into four zones of occupation, administered by the U.S., Great Britain, France and U.S.S.R.

In 1949 the German Federal Republic was formed from the three western zones, and the

German Democratic Republic was created out of the Soviet zone. The German Federal Republic became fully independent in 1955.

During the 1950s and 1960s, West Germany underwent a major economic boom, which has continued at a slower pace. West Germany now ranks as the 4th greatest economic power in the world and leads most other nations in worker participation in industry.

During the 1970s, West Germany normalized relations with its communist neighbors and has dramatically expanded its trade with Eastern Europe.

## GERMAN DEMOCRATIC REPUBLIC (1949-)

During 1945-49, the U.S.S.R. occupied the eastern zone of Germany, which included the provinces of Saxony-Anhalt, Saxony, Brandenburg, Mecklenburg and Thuringia. On Oct. 7, 1949, the Russian zone was united as the German Democratic Republic. Although East Germany became fully independent in 1954, some 400,000 Soviet troops remain in the country.

The East German economy was held back by heavy-handed central planning until the mid-1960s. A relaxation of controls brought rapid industrialization, and by the early 1970s, East Germany was the ninth ranked economic power in the world.

## GERMANY (SOVIET ZONE LOCAL ISSUES) (1945-46)

During 1945-46, the Soviet occupation postal authorities authorized issues for a number of localities — Berlin-Brandenburg (Berlin Postal Administration); Mecklenburg-Western Pomerania (Mecklenburg-Vorpommern); Saxony (Hall Postal Administration); East Saxony (Dresden Postal Administration); Thuringia (Erfurt Postal Administration); and Western Saxony (Leipzig Postal Administration).

## GERMAN OFFICES IN CHINA (1898-1917)

Germany maintained post offices in various Chinese cities after 1886, with specially overprinted German stamps in use from 1898 to 1917.

## GERMAN OFFICES IN MOROCCO (1899-1919)

German post offices in Morocco began using overprinted German stamps in 1899. In 1914, these offices were closed in the French zone and in 1919, were closed in the Spanish zone.

## GERMAN OFFICES IN TURKEY (1870-1914)

German post offices began operating in Turkish cities in 1870, using unoverprinted stamps of the North German Postal District.

In 1872, these were replaced by regular German issues, and in 1884, overprinted German stamps came into use.

## GHANA (1957-)

A republic in west Africa, on the Gulf of Guinea. Formed from the former British colony of the Gold Coast and the mandated territory of British Togoland in 1957, Ghana became fully independent in 1960.

During 1957-66, Ghana was ruled by Kwame Nkrumah, one of the leaders of its independence movement. Nkrumah launched major economic projects but, in the process, built up a huge foreign debt. His economic mismanagement and repression of political opposition created popular dissatisfaction, and in 1966, he was overthrown in a military coup.

The new regime expelled Chinese and East German advisors, and in 1969, civilian government was restored.

Political instability — the military has ousted civilian governments in 1972, 1978, 1979 and 1982 — and economic stagnation make Ghana's future uncertain.

## GIBRALTAR (1886-)

A fortified promontory on the European side of the Strait of Gibraltar. Strategically located, Gibraltar has passed under a number of rulers.

Britain occupied the area in 1704 and has held it since, although Spain maintains its claim to the colony.

## GILBERT ISLANDS (1976-79)

A group of islands in the Pacific Ocean northeast of Australia. Formerly part of the Gilbert and Ellice Islands, the Gilberts became a separate British crown colony in 1976. The Gilbert Islands became the independent Republic of Kiribati on July 12, 1979.

## GILBERT AND ELLICE ISLANDS (1911-75)

Two groups of islands in the Pacific Ocean northeast of Australia. A British colony after 1915, the groups were separated in 1975, the Ellice Islands renaming themselves Tuvalu.

## GOLD COAST (1875-1957)

Former British colony in Africa on the Gulf of Guinea. Originally held by a variety of European powers, control of the coastal area was consolidated by Great Britain by 1871. The interior was conquered by 1901. In 1957, the Gold Coast became the independent state of Ghana.

The first separate stamps for the Gold Coast were issued in 1875. Gold Coast issues continued in use until their replacement by Ghanan stamps in 1957.

## GRANADA (1936)

A city and province in southern Spain.

During the siege of Granada in July 1936, the Nationalist administration issued a stamp for local use. After the siege was lifted, this stamp was used in other parts of Spain occupied by the Nationalists.

## GRAND COMORO (1897-1911)

One of the Comoro Islands in the Mozambique Channel near Madagascar. In 1911, it was attached to the French colony of Madagascar, whose stamps were used until 1947 when the

Comoro Islands were separated, issuing their own stamps in 1950.

## GREAT BRITAIN (1840-)

Kingdom in northwest Europe comprised of England, Wales, Scotland and Northern Ireland.

After the accession of the Tudor dynasty (1485), Britain became unified and began to develop into a world power. British overseas expansion began in the late 16th century, and in the following 200 years, Britain emerged as the dominant European naval and colonial power, supplanting the Spanish and Dutch.

After her victory in the Napoleonic wars, Britain emerged as the dominant world power, building an empire that, by 1900, included large areas throughout the world.

Although victorious in World War I, Britain suffered severe losses in manpower and resources. The post war period saw the loss of Ireland (1921) and the development of nationalism in India.

During World War II, Britain again suffered. For a year following the fall of France (June 1940), Britain was the only major power to stand against Germany. After Germany's invasion of Russia (June 1941) and Japan's attack on Pearl Harbor (December 1941), she gained powerful allies but continued to bear the brunt of German air attacks.

Britain emerged from World War II victorious, but battered and exhausted. Industrial growth has continued, although she has lost her former predominant economic position. The two decades following World War II saw the dissolution of the empire, and Britain's overseas dominion today is mostly comprised of small scattered island possessions in the West Indies and in the Atlantic, Indian and Pacific oceans.

One major result of this process has been the redirection of Britain's focus from the Commonwealth to Europe. In 1973 Britain joined the Common Market.

Britain issued the first regular adhesive postage stamp in 1840.

## GREAT BRITAIN-REGIONALS (1958-)

In 1958, Britain began issuing regional definitive issues for various areas within the country. Such regionals are sold only at the post offices within the respective regions, but are valid for postage throughout the country.

Regional issues have been released for Guernsey (1958-69); Jersey (1958-69); Isle of Man (1958-73); Northern Ireland (1958-); Scotland (1958-); and Wales and Monmouthshire (1958-).

## GREECE (1861-)

Republic in southeastern Europe. Greece was the center of the Minoan civilization of Crete during the 2nd millennium B.C., and of the Hellenic civilization after c. 800 B.C.

After the 7th and 8th centuries B.C., Greek colonies were established throughout the Mediterranean, producing a civilization that greatly influenced subsequent European development.

The conquests of Alexander the Great spread Greek culture throughout western Asia, and Alexandrine successor states maintained Greek cultural dominance in the Middle East and northern India for two centuries.

After 146 B.C., Greece was conquered by Rome, although the Romans soon became thoroughly Hellenized and so perpetuated Greece's cultural influence.

Greece remained under the Eastern Roman Empire until it was occupied by the French and Italian crusaders. In 1456, the country was conquered by the Turks.

Greek nationalism began to emerge in the late 18th century, culminating in revolution in 1821. By 1832, Greece had become an independent kingdom.

Greece has since expanded to include Greek-speaking territories in the southern Balkans, as well as Crete and the Aegean Islands. The period 1912-19 saw the rapid expansion of Greece's borders, producing many occupation issues.

Greece successfully resisted an Italian invasion in 1940, but German intervention in 1941 brought the country's rapid defeat and occupation by Germany, Italy and Bulgaria. Communist elements, defeated by the royalist government and Britain in 1944-45, waged a guerrilla war against the regime during 1947-49. The communists were suppressed, with U.S. assistance.

In the postwar years, Greece experienced rapid economic growth. Increasing tension between liberal and conservative factions, however, brought a military coup in 1967. After unsuccessfully attempting to moderate the harshness of the regime, King Constantine and the royal family fled the country.

In 1973, this government was overthrown in a second military coup. The new government, in turn, was overthrown in 1974, and democratic civilian government was restored.

## GREENLAND (1905-)

The world's largest island, located in the Arctic, northeast of Canada. Greenland was occupied by the Norsemen during the 10th-15th centuries, but the deteriorating climate and increasingly aggressive Eskimo inroads finally wiped out the European settlements.

In 1721, Denmark again began colonization. In 1953, the colony became an integral part of the kingdom of Denmark.

In 1979, home-rule was extended to Greenland, and a socialist-dominated legislature was elected. Native place names have come into use, and the official name for Greenland is now Nalatdlit Nunat.

Greenland was a U.S. protectorate from 1940-45, during the German occupation of Denmark.

**GRENADA (1861-)**

An island in the West Indies. A British colony since the 18th century, Grenada became an independent state in 1974.

**GRENADA-GRENADINES (1973-)**

A small group of islands in the West Indies administered by Grenada.

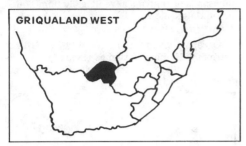

GRIQUALAND WEST

**GRIQUALAND WEST (1874-80)**

Located in South Africa, north of the Orange River, this territory was occupied by the British in 1871, and established as a British crown colony in 1873.

It was annexed to Cape Colony in 1880 and since 1910 has been part of South Africa.

Griqualand West issued one provisional at Kimberley in 1874 and many varieties of the overprint "G" on various Cape Colony stamps during 1877-78. From 1871-77 and after 1880, Cape Colony stamps were in use.

**GRODNO (1919)**

A city in the White Russian Soviet Socialist Republic (U.S.S.R.), formerly part of Poland. After World War I, the German military commander issued stamps overprinted on Ukrainian and Russian stamps.

**GUADALAJARA (1867-68)**

The capital of the state of Jalisco in northwestern Mexico. Guadalajara is one of the major cities of the country and during the war against the French-supported Emperor Maximilian, issued a large number of provisional postage stamps.

**GUADELOUPE (1884-1947)**

An island in the West Indies, under French rule since 1635. From 1775 to 1946, Guadeloupe was a French colony and since 1946 has been an overseas department of France. French stamps replaced those of Guadeloupe in 1947.

**GUAM (1899-1901, 1930-31)**

The largest of the Mariana Islands in the western Pacific, Guam was ceded to the U.S. by Spain in 1898, after its capture by U.S. forces during the Spanish-American War.

Occupied by the Japanese in 1941, the island was recaptured and served as a base for U.S. bomber attacks on Japan during the last months of World War II. Guam is now administered by the U.S. Department of the Interior.

U.S. stamps overprinted "GUAM" were used from 1899 to 1901, when they were replaced by regular U.S. stamps, although the overprinted stamps remained in use for several years.

During 1930-31, Philippine stamps overprinted "GUAM GUARD MAIL" were used by the local military forces.

**GUANACASTE (1885-91)**

A province of Costa Rica. During 1885-91, the government granted a substantially larger discount on stamps purchased by this province, in order to encourage additional sales to offset the high transportation costs to the area.

Stamps used in the province during this period were overprinted to prevent their purchase in Guanacaste and resale elsewhere.

**GUATEMALA (1871-)**

Republic in Central America on the southern border of Mexico. The center of the Maya-Quiche Indian civilization, Guatemala was conquered by the Spanish in the early 16th century.

The center of the Audiencia of Guatemala, which included all of Central America and the Mexican state of Chiapas, Guatemala remained under Spanish rule until 1821 when it declared its independence.

During 1822-23, it was under Mexico, and during 1823-39, it formed part of the Republic of the United States of Central America. Since 1839, Guatemala has been completely independent.

Guatemala's economy is land-based, with ownership concentrated in the hands of a relatively small Spanish-descended oligarchy. Most menial labor is done by Indian laborers. The standard of living is very low for most Guatemalans, and illiteracy is high.

Since independence, Guatemala has been ruled by an almost unbroken succession of military dictatorships. For the past two decades, the country has been wracked by terrorism from both left and right-wing elements.

**GUAYANA (1903)**

A state in eastern Venezuela. In 1903, a revolutionary group issued stamps for use in the area.

**GUERNSEY (1941-45, 1958-)**

An island in the English Channel. A bailiwick under the British crown, Guernsey was occupied by Germany from 1940-45, during which time bisected British issues and locally printed stamps were used.

During 1958-69, regional issues, valid throughout Britain but sold only in Guernsey, were in use along with regular British stamps.

On Oct. 1, 1969, the Guernsey postal administration was separated from that of Britain and the bailiwick has issued its own stamps since that time.

**GUIDIZZOLO (1945)**

A city in northern Italy. Overprinted Italian

stamps were used provisionally, following the collapse of the Italian Social Republic.

### GUINEA (1959-)

Republic in West Africa. Formerly the colony of French Guinea, Guinea became independent on Sept. 28, 1958.

### GUINEA-BISSAU (1974-)

Independent republic on the coast of Africa, bordered by Senegal and Guinea.

Guinea-Bissau was formerly Portuguese Guinea, becoming independent Sept. 10, 1974. The country's independence movement was led by Cape Verdeans, and the two countries are committed to eventual union.

### GUTDORF (MOISAKULA) (1941)

A city in Estonia. Overprinted Russian and Estonian stamps were used for a time during the German occupation in World War II.

### GUYANA (1966-)

A republic on the northeast coast of South America. Formerly the colony of British Guiana, which became independent in 1966. The republic was established in 1970. Guyana's boundaries with Venezuela (which claims half of the country) and Surinam are in dispute.

### GWALIOR (1885-1950)

A state in north central India, Gwalior united its postal system with that of India through a postal convention. Overprinted Indian stamps were used 1885-1950 when they were replaced by regular Indian issues.

## — H —

### HAITI (1881-)

A republic occupying the western third of the island of Hispaniola in the West Indies. The Spanish occupied the island after its discovery by Columbus in 1492, enslaving the Indian population, which was soon exterminated.

In time, the Spanish partially abandoned the island, and the western portion became a base for pirates. This area gradually came under French control, which was recognized by Spain in 1697.

Under the French, African slaves were imported to work the sugar plantations, which were the mainstay of the colony's economy, and in 1804 the descendants of these slaves expelled their French masters.

The Republic of Haiti split into two parts in 1811, but in 1820, it was reunited and enlarged by the conquest of the eastern portion of the island (lost in 1844).

During the 19th century, anarchy and foreign indebtedness increased, finally bringing U.S. occupation in 1915. U.S. troops withdrew in 1934, and the last U.S. controls ended in 1941.

Since 1957, Haiti has been ruled by the Duvaliers, first by Dr. Francois Duvalier ("Papa

Doc") and, since his death in 1971, by his son, Jean-Claude ("Baby Doc").

Haiti is a miserably poor country, the result of years of civil disorder and dictatorial rule. Although Jean-Claude's rule has been less oppressive than that of his father, economic conditions have shown little improvement. In recent years, thousands of Haitians have illegally immigrated to the United States.

### HAMBURG (1859-67)

A seaport and former Free City in northern Germany. Hamburg's stamps (1859-67) were replaced by those of the North German Confederation on Jan. 1, 1868.

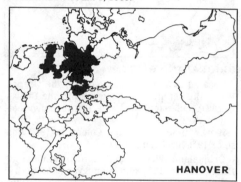

HANOVER

### HANOVER (1850-1866)

A former kingdom in northern Germany. United with Britain from 1714-1837 through a common monarch, Hanover supported Austria in the Austro-Prussian War (1866) and was annexed by Prussia.

Hanover's stamps were first issued in 1850, being replaced by those of Prussia in 1866.

### HATAY (1939)

A semiautonomous district of Syria under French mandate, this area issued stamps as Alexandretta. In 1938, it was renamed Hatay and in 1939, it was absorbed by Turkey.

### HAWAII (1851-1900)

An island group in the north central Pacific, Hawaii became a united kingdom in the late 18th century. After a period of constitutional unrest, the native monarchy was overthrown in 1893.

The provisional government, unsuccessful in securing annexation by the U.S., proclaimed Hawaii a republic. In 1898, the area was annexed by the U.S., and the Territory of Hawaii was established in 1900. In 1959, Hawaii became the 50th state of the U.S.

Hawaiian stamps continued in use after the islands' annexation being finally replaced by regular U.S. stamps in 1900.

### HELIGOLAND (1867-90)

A strategically located island in the North Sea, Heligoland was ceded to Great Britain by Denmark in 1807. Britain transferred the island to Germany in 1890, in exchange for some German claims in East Africa.

The Germans built a major naval base on the island, which was destroyed by the British after World War II. Heligoland was returned to Germany in 1952.

Stamps of Hamburg were used in Heligoland from 1859 to 1867, when separate issues came into use. Among the most attractive of British colonial issues, the plates used in printing Heligoland's stamps passed into private hands and many reprintings were made.

Since 1890, German stamps have been used on the island.

### HEJAZ (1916-25)

Located on the western coast of the Arabian Peninsula, Hejaz includes the Moslem holy cities of Mecca and Medina. In 1916, the grand sherif of Mecca proclaimed the Hejaz independent of Turkish rule and joined the British against Turkey in World War I.

After World War I, the independence of the Kingdom of the Hejaz was confirmed. In 1924, Nejd invaded the Hejaz and in 1926 annexed the country. In 1932, the united kingdoms were renamed Saudi Arabia.

### HELA (1945)

A peninsula on the Gulf of Danzig in northern Europe. German forces on the peninsula were cut off by the advancing Russians and issued a provisional stamp for use on mail to be carried back to Germany proper.

This "U-Boat" stamp was used briefly, although it never actually became necessary to use U-boats to carry this mail.

### HELSINGFORS (HELSINKI) (1866-91)

The capital of Finland. Stamps were issued by the local postmaster and were valid throughout the district.

### HONAN (1941-42)

A province in central China. Overprinted Chinese stamps were issued by the Japanese during World War II.

### HONDURAS (1866-)

Republic in Central America. Originally dominated by the Mayas, Honduras was conquered by Spain in the early 16th century, and until 1838, its history follows that of Guatemala. In 1838, it became independent.

Honduras' chief export is bananas, and the country has been the stereotypical "banana republic" since the last century. In 1975, General Oswaldo Lopez Arellano, president since 1963, was ousted by the Army over charges of widespread bribery. Since that time, the Honduran government has pursued a number of ambitious social programs, and free elections were held in 1981.

In recent years, tensions have increased between Honduras and El Salvador over the presence of some 300,000 Salvadoreans in Honduras. A brief war was fought in 1969, and border clashes occurred in 1970 and 1976.

### HONG KONG (1862-)

A peninsula and island at the mouth of the Canton River in southeast China. Hong Kong has been a British possession since 1841, except for its occupation by Japan from 1941-45.

Hong Kong is highly industrialized, and its annual exports of $9 billion plus are led by textiles, clothing and electronics.

### HOPEI (1941-42)

A province in northern China, surrounding Peking and Tientsin. Regular Chinese stamps were overprinted by occupying Japanese forces during World War II.

### HORTA (1892-1905)

A district of the Azores. From 1868 to 1892 and from 1905-31, stamps of the Azores were used. Since 1931, regular Portuguese stamps have been in use.

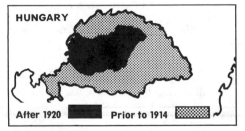

HUNGARY

After 1920 ■    Prior to 1914 ▨

### HUNGARY (1871-)

A people's republic in East Central Europe. This area of flat plains and grasslands, bisected by the Danube River, was a favorite route of eastern tribes invading southern and western Europe. From the 4th-9th centuries, succeeding immigrations of Germans, Huns, Avars and other peoples passed through the region.

Toward the end of the 9th century, Hungary was settled by the Magyars, who for nearly a century raided throughout central Europe. Under Stephen I (977-1038), the Magyars were converted to Christianity and thereafter served as Europe's eastern bulwark against the Asian tribes.

In the early 16th century, the Ottoman Turks destroyed Hungarian power. Most of the country was conquered by the Turks, and the remaining northern and western fringe came under the rule of Hapsburg Austria. During 1686-1718, the Austrians expelled the Turks from Hungary.

Austria completely dominated Hungary until the mid-19th century. Magyar nationalism forced the creation of the Austro-Hungarian Monarchy in 1867, after which Hungary was an equal partner with Austria. Having achieved its own nationalist goals, Hungary denied similar nationalist ambitions among its subject peoples.

The Dual Monarchy's defeat in World War I brought the disintegration of the empire and of the Kingdom of Hungary. During 1918-20, the country was overrun by Serbian, French and Romanian armies and was torn by civil war between royalist and bolshevik factions. Hungary emerged in 1920 as a nationalist state, having lost 50 per cent of its population and 75 per cent of its territory to Yugoslavia, Romania and Czechoslovakia.

In 1938 Hungary participated in the dismemberment of Czechoslovakia and during World War II joined the Axis, regaining much of its former territory. In 1944-45 it was defeated by the U.S.S.R. and reduced to its pre-1938 boundaries. On Feb. 1, 1946, a republic was established, but in 1947 the communists ousted the president and purged noncommunist elements from the government.

Demonstrations in October 1956, turned into open revolt against the regime. In early November, some 200,000 Soviet troops crushed the uprising, and a hard-line regime was reestablished. Some 40,000 Soviet troops remained in Hungary, and Hungarian forces participated in the 1968 Warsaw Pact invasion of Czechoslovakia.

The present Hungarian government has pursued cautiously liberal internal policies since 1968. Elements of small private enterprise and a degree of cultural freedom have been restored, without provoking Soviet reaction.

## HVAR (LESINA) (1944)

An island in the Adriatic Sea, off the coast of Yugoslavia. In 1944, Yugoslavian stamps were overprinted for use on the island by the German military commander of the Dalmatian Province.

## HYDERABAD (1869-1950)

The largest of the princely states, Hyderabad (Deccan) was the most powerful of the native states in southern India. Hyderabad became independent from the Mogul Empire in the early 18th century and allied itself to Britain after c.1760.

After Britain's withdrawal from the subcontinent in 1947, the Moslem rulers of the state resisted domination by Hindu India, but Indian authority was firmly established in September 1948. Hyderabad maintained separate stamp issues until April 1, 1950, since which time Indian stamps have been used.

— I —

## ICARIA (NICARIA) (1912-13)

An island in the Aegean Sea. In July 1912, Icaria declared its independence from Turkey. In November the island was occupied by Greece, and Icarian issues were replaced by overprinted Greek stamps, which, in turn, were replaced by regular Greek stamps.

## ICELAND (1873-)

A large island in the North Atlantic. Iceland was colonized from Norway after c. 870, and after 1380 was under Danish rule.

In 1918, Iceland became independent, united with Denmark only in the person of the Danish monarch. In 1944, Iceland severed this last tie with Denmark and became a republic.

Since 1949, Iceland has been a member of NATO, and the U.S. maintains a sizable base on the island.

## IDAR (1939-44)

A former feudatory state in western India.

## IFNI (1941-1969)

A Spanish enclave on the western coast of Morocco. Ceded to Spain in 1860, Ifni was occupied in 1934. In 1969, Spain returned the area to Morocco, whose stamps replaced those of the colony.

## ILI REPUBLIC (1945- 49)

A short-lived state established by the Uighurs in northwestern Sinkiang. At the end of 1949, the state was integrated into the Chinese People's Republic.

## INDIA (1854-)

Republic in south central Asia, occupying the greater part of the Indian subcontinent between the Himalaya Mountains and the Indian Ocean.

One of the world's earliest civilizations was located in the Indus valley after c. 4000 B.C. This culture was overrun by the Aryans who conquered India 2400-1500 B.C.

During most of its history, India has been divided into many independent, frequently warring states.

In 1498, the Portuguese reached India and quickly began building a commercial empire that dominated the coast areas for a century.

The Portuguese were supplanted by the Dutch in the early 17th century, who in turn were succeeded by the British in the late 17th century.

Anglo-French rivalry for influence over the local princes was intense until Britain's military defeat of the French forces in 1760.

During the next 100 years, the British East India Co. constantly expanded Britain's holdings in the subcontinent.

In 1857, the British government took over the governing of India directly. In 1877, the empire of India was proclaimed with Queen Victoria as empress.

In the early 20th century, Indian nationalism became an increasingly powerful force. After World War I, Mohandas K. Gandhi organized the All-India Congress Party, which assumed the leadership of the Indian independence movement. Later, the Moslem nationalists withdrew from the predominantly Hindu Congress Party to form the Moslem League under Mohammed Ali Jinnah.

After years of agitation and negotiation, the British gave up control of India on Aug. 15, 1947, and the country was partitioned into Hindu (India) and Moslem (Pakistan) states.

Religious riots and war between the two nations began almost immediately. Settled only with great difficulty, war has erupted several times since, most recently in 1971-72.

India absorbed the remaining French holdings in 1956 and seized Portugal's Indian territory in 1961. In 1962, Communist Chinese forces occupied disputed areas in the north.

### INDIA-CONVENTION STATES (1884-1950)

During 1864-86, six Indian states joined their postal services to that of British India, using overprinted Indian stamps. The states entering into such postal conventions were Chamba, Faridkot, Gwalior, Jhind, Nabha and Patiala.

The stamps of the convention states were valid throughout India. They were replaced by those of the Republic of India on Jan. 1, 1951.

### INDIA-FEUDATORY STATES (1864-1951)

After 1862, many rulers of the semiautonomous native princely states began to establish modern public postal systems, utilizing their own stamps.

These systems existed alongside that of British India, with the stamps normally valid only within the state where they were issued.

The Indian feudatory states issuing their own stamps were Alwar (1877-1902); Bamra (1888-94); Barwani (1921-48); Bhopal (1876-1950); Bhor (1879-1902); Bijawar (1935-39); Bundi (1894-1920, 1940-48); Bussahir (1895-1901);

Charkhari (1894-1950); Cochin (1892-1949); Dhar (1897-1901); Duttia (1893-1921); Hyderabad (1869-1950); Idar (1939-44); Indore (1886-1950); Jaipur (1904-49); Jammu and Kashmir (1866-94); Jasdan (1942-50); Jhalawar (1887-1900);

Jind (1874-85); Kishangarh (1899-1949); Las Bela (1897-1907); Morvi (1931-50); Nandgaon (1892-95); Nawanagar (1875-95); Orchha (1913-50); Poonch (1876-94); Rajasthan (1948-50);

Rajpeepla (1880-86); Saurashtra (1864-1950); Sirmoor (1879-1902); Travancore (1888-1949); Travancore-Cochin (1949-51); and Wadhwan (1888-95).

### INDIAN EXPEDITIONARY FORCES (1914-22)

During and after World War I, Indian forces fighting with the Allies used stamps of British India overprinted "I.E.F."

### INDO-CHINA (1889-1949)

Former French administrative unit in southeast Asia, comprising Cochin-China, Cambodia, Annam and Tonkin, and Kwangchowan.

The area broke up in 1949 to form the states of Cambodia, Laos and Vietnam, within the French Union, with the issues of the separate states replacing those of Indo-China.

### INDONESIA (1945-)

A republic occupying the great part of the Malay Archipelago in southeastern Asia; formerly the Netherlands East Indies.

Portugal dominated the area during the 16th century but was supplanted by the Dutch after 1595. Except for a period of British occupation during the Napoleonic wars (1811-16), the area remained under Dutch control until its occupation by Japan in 1942.

After the surrender of Japan in August 1945, Indonesian nationalists under Achmed Sukarno proclaimed the independent Republic of Indonesia in central Java and throughout most of Sumatra.

The ensuing civil war was finally ended by the withdrawal of the Dutch in December 1949. In 1950, Indonesia was unified as a republic.

In 1963 Western New Guinea (West Irian) was absorbed by Indonesia.

During the early 1960s, Indonesia was aligned with the U.S.S.R., but an abortive communist uprising in 1965 brought massive retaliation by the military. President Sukarno, who had ruled as a dictator since 1960, was deposed, and some 300,000 communists executed.

The new regime, under General Suharto, restored peaceful relations with Indonesia's neighbors, restored popular elections and has actively promoted economic development.

In 1976 the former Portuguese Timor was annexed by Indonesia.

### INDORE (HOLKAR) (1886-1949)

A former feudatory state in west-central India. Indore used its own stamps from 1886 to 1949. With its merger into Rajasthan, stamps of that state were used from 1949 to April 1, 1950. Stamps of India are now in use.

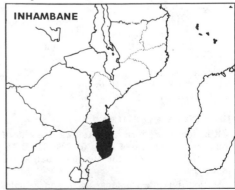

### INHAMBANE (1895-1914)

A district of southern Mozambique. Its stamps were superseded by those of Mozambique.

ININI

## ININI (1932-46)

The interior of French Guiana, on the northeastern coast of South America. During 1930-46, this area was separated from French Guiana, being reunited when the area was absorbed by France.

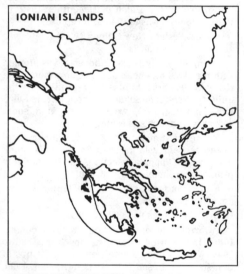

IONIAN ISLANDS

## IONIAN ISLANDS (1859-64, 1941-43)

A group of islands off the western coast of Greece. Occupied at various times by the Greeks, Romans, Byzantines, Venetians, Turks, French and British, the islands were united with Greece in 1864.

Stamps were issued by the British (1859-64), and during World War II, by the occupying Italian forces (1941-43).

## IRAN (PERSIA until 1935) (1870-)

Kingdom in western Asia. Iran was the seat of the ancient kingdom of Elam (c. 3000-640 B.C.), which competed with the Mesopotamian states to its west.

Settled by the Iranians, an Aryan people, c.1800 B.C., from whom arose the Medes, Persians and Parthians. At various times from the 7th century B.C. to the 7th century A.D., Persian states dominated the Middle East, at times ruling territory from Egypt and Thrace to India.

Debilitating wars with Rome weakened Persia, making it easy prey to the Arabs in the 7th century. With the decline of the caliphate after 1040, Persia was torn by centuries of war and anarchy, complicated by Turkish immigration and Mongol invasions (13th-15th centuries).

National unity was reestablished under the Safawid dynasty (1502-1722).

After the mid-18th century, Persia declined, losing its outlying provinces (Afghanistan, the Caucasus, etc.) and falling under European influence.

Russia and Britain carved out spheres of influence in the 19th century and occupied portions of the country in World War I and World War II.

In 1921, Riza Pahlavi, a military chief, led a coup and assumed virtual control of the government, becoming shah in 1925. He began to radically modernize Persia, a program continued by his son and successor, Mohammed Riza Pahlavi.

Mohammed Riza Pahlavi attempted to modernize Iran rapidly and used the country's substantial oil revenues toward this end. While his policies brought a social and economic transformation of Iran, the shah ruled absolutely, and political opposition was suppressed.

Increasing dissatisfaction with the regime brought the coalition of many disparate elements in Iranian society. Anti-government riots brought martial law in September 1978, but the government's position deteriorated rapidly. On Jan. 16, 1979, the shah left Iran, and in mid-February, the caretaker regime of Shahpur Baktiar, a long-time opponent of the shah, was overthrown amid popular demonstrations by supporters of Ayatollah Ruhollah Khomeini. On April 1 the Ayatollah declared Iran an Islamic republic and immediately set about creating a theocratic regime, reflecting staunchly conservative Islamic values.

Khomeini accused the United States, which had strongly supported the shah, of fomenting most of the country's problems. Relations between the two countries quickly deteriorated, and in November 1979, student demonstrators seized U.S. embassy personnel in Teheran. The embassy staff was held hostage, pending the return of the shah to Iran, where he was to be tried by revolutionary courts. The death of the shah in July 1980, did not bring a resolution of the problem, which continued until the captives' release in January 1981.

In September 1980, Iraq attacked Iran, beginning a bitter war that has drained the resources of both nations.

Political and economic instability have become the norm in Iran. Political terrorism and government repression, as bad or worse than under the shah, are everyday occurrences.

## IRAQ (1923-)

A republic in western Asia, occupying the Tigris and Euphrates valley, north of Arabia. Occupied from Turkey by British forces during World War I, Iraq became a British mandated territory in 1920.

In 1921, a kingdom was established under Faisal I, son of King Hussein of Hejaz and leader of the Arab Army in World War I.

Britain withdrew from Iraq in 1932, although it intervened during World War II to overthrow a pro-Axis ministry. In 1958, the monarchy was deposed and a pan-Arab, pro-Soviet republic was established. The new regime nationalized most Iraqi industry and broke up large land holdings.

Iraq has maintained close ties with Syria, which is ruled by another branch of the same Baathist political party. A number of national disputes have come between the two countries.

In 1978, Iraq executed a number of communists and has since expanded trade with the West.

In September 1980, Iraq, prompted by a longstanding border dispute and by the new Iranian regime's attempts to foment revolution among Iraq's Shi'ite minority, invaded Iran. Strong Iranian resistance soon brought the war to a standstill, despite periodic heavy fighting. Although both nations are on the verge of bankruptcy because of the war, no negotiated settlement appears likely.

## IRELAND (1922-)

An island in northwestern Europe, west of Britain. Long restive under British rule, Ireland revolted in 1916, securing independence as a dominion.

In 1949, the Irish Free State became the independent Republic of Ireland. The northern counties where the Protestants are in the majority remain under British rule, although they are claimed by the republic.

## ISRAEL (1948-)

Republic in western Asia, occupying Palestine and (since 1967) border areas of Syria and Egypt.

Under the British mandate, Jewish and Arab elements in Palestine came into bitter conflict over the future of the nation, the Jews wishing to create a homeland for their people while the Arabs advocated the creation of a secular Palestinian state in which the rights of the Jewish minority would be respected.

On May 14, 1948, British troops were withdrawn from Palestine, and the Jewish National Council immediately proclaimed the state of Israel in areas of the country under Jewish control.

Israel was immediately attacked by its Arab neighbors but defeated their forces, emerging from the 1949 cease-fire with its territory approximately 50 per cent larger than that initially allocated for it by the U.N. partition plan.

In 1956, Egypt nationalized the Suez Canal and barred Israeli shipping. Israel invaded Egypt and occupied Gaza and the Sinai. After U.N. intervention, Israel withdrew.

In 1967, after a year of Arab guerrilla raids from Jordan and bombardment of Israeli settlements from Syria, war again broke out.

Israel defeated Egypt, Syria and Jordan in the Six-Day War, occupying the West Bank from Jordan, the Golan Heights from Syria, and Sinai and Gaza from Egypt.

On Oct. 6, 1973, after several years of failure to negotiate a settlement, Arab forces attacked Israel again, reoccupying some lost territory in the Sinai. After initial Arab gains, Israel counterattacked quickly, occupying territory on the west bank of the Suez Canal and advancing in Syria. A cease-fire was negotiated Oct. 24.

Peace negotiations proceeded very slowly during 1973-77, but began to move rapidly after November 1977, when Egyptian President Anwar Sadat visited Jerusalem in an attempt to break the deadlock.

On March 26, 1979, Egypt and Israel signed a formal peace treaty, ending hostilities and establishing diplomatic relations.

Under the terms of the peace treaty, Israel has returned the Sinai to Egypt. Continuing hostility between Israel and the Palestine Liberation Organization make real peace unlikely in the foreseeable future.

## ISTRIA-SLOVENE COAST (1945-47)

Former Italian provinces on the Adriatic Sea, occupied by Yugoslavia after World War II.

## ITALIAN COLONIES (1932-34)

General issues released for all Italian colonies.

## ITALIAN EAST AFRICA (1938-41)

A former Italian colony in East Africa, formed from Eritrea, Italian Somaliland, and Ethiopia. It was occupied by the British in 1941 and after World War II was dissolved.

## ITALIAN OFFICES ABROAD (1861-1923)

Italy maintained many post offices abroad, utilizing a general overprint on Italian stamps (1874-90), overprints for specific cities or territories, and unoverprinted stamps distinguishable only by their cancellations.

Italian post offices were maintained in Egypt, Tunisia, Tripolitania, Eritrea, China, Crete, and many cities in the Turkish Empire and Albania.

## ITALIAN OFFICES IN ALBANIA (1902-09)

During the 19th century, Italy operated her own post offices in a number of Albanian cities, using regular Italian stamps.

In 1883, the Turkish government suppressed

these offices, but in 1902, they were reopened using Italian stamps overprinted "Albania" and surcharged in Turkish currency.

In 1909, these issues were replaced by those of the various cities where Italian post offices were in operation.

## ITALIAN OFFICES IN CHINA (1917-22)

During 1901-17, Italian troops in China, as well as legation and consular personnel, were permitted to use unoverprinted Italian stamps. From September 1917, to Dec. 31, 1922, Italian stamps overprinted for Peking and Tientsin were used.

## ITALIAN SOCIAL REPUBLIC (1943-45)

The Italian puppet state under Mussolini which nominally ruled those areas under German occupation during the final days of World War II.

## ITALY (1862-)

A republic in western Europe. Italy was the center of the Roman Empire, which until the 5th century ruled southern and western Europe, North Africa and much of the Middle East.

After the collapse of Rome, Italy was ruled by a succession of foreign powers: Ostrogoths, Lombards, Franks, Arabs, Normans, Germans, Spanish, Byzantines, and French. By 1815, the country was roughly divided into several spheres: the Sardinian kingdom, which ruled the island of Sardinia and northwestern Italy; the Lombardo-Venetian Kingdom, which was ruled by Austria, in the north; the Papal States, which controlled the central portion of the peninsula; and the Kingdom of the Two Sicilies in the south.

During the 19th century, Italian nationalism grew in strength, and there was increasing sentiment for unification.

During 1859-61, nationalist uprisings deposed local rulers and united most of Italy with Sardina. On March 17, 1861, the united Kingdom of Italy was proclaimed under the House of Savoy.

Italy acquired several African colonies during the late 19th century and in the Italo-Turkish War (1911-12) and World War I acquired territory from Turkey and Austria.

Domestic unrest after World War I brought the Fascist party to power in 1922, although the monarchy was retained. The Fascists, under Benito Mussolini, built up Italy's military forces and pursued an aggressive foreign policy, conquering Ethiopia (1935) and Albania (1939).

Italy entered World War II in 1940 as an ally of Germany, but military reverses brought German domination and in 1943, the invasion of Italy by the Allies.

Mussolini was deposed in 1943, although he was put in charge of the northern Italian Social Republic, a German puppet-state, until its collapse in 1945.

The royalist government, in the meantime, de-clared war on Germany and fought with the Allies to free Italy from German occupation.

In 1946, the monarchy was abolished, and Italy became a republic.

Since World War II, Italy has enjoyed dynamic industrial growth, and its standard of living has improved greatly. The huge increase in petroleum prices during the 1970s has caused serious economic upsets in recent years.

## IVORY COAST (1892-1944, 1959-)

A republic in West Africa, bordering on the Gulf of Guinea. French influence was strong along the coast from 1700 and after 1842, France began to occupy territory in the area.

The boundaries of the colony were fixed between 1892 and 1898, and native resistance was crushed by 1919. During World War II, the Ivory Coast remained under control of the Vichy regime until November 1942.

After 1944, it used stamps of French West Africa. In 1958, the Ivory Coast became a republic, achieving independence in 1960.

The Ivory Coast is the most prosperous of the tropical African nations and is the leader of the pro-Western bloc in Africa.

# — J —

## JAFFA (1909-14)

Israeli port on the Mediterranean Sea. Prior to World War I, a number of European nations maintained their own postal systems in the city.

After 1909, the Russian post used stamps of the Russian Levant overprinted "Jaffa."

## JAIPUR (1904-49)

A former feudatory state in north central India. Jaipur merged into the United State of Rajasthan in 1948. Jaipur's issues were replaced by those of Rajasthan in 1949, which were in turn replaced by those of India on April 1, 1950.

## JAMAICA (1860-)

A republic occupying the island of Jamaica in the West Indies, south of Cuba. Jamaica was discovered by Columbus in 1494 and was occupied by Spain until 1655, after which it became a British possession.

The original Arawak inhabitants soon died out under the Spanish who began the importation of African slaves to work the sugar plantations.

Jamaica became an independent republic on Aug. 6, 1962.

Economic dissatisfaction brought a socialist regime to power 1972-80. Attempts to expand Jamaican ownership in bauxite mining operations and to expand welfare programs failed to improve the economy, and a pro-Western government was elected in 1980. Jamaica has since moved away from Cuba and toward the West.

## JAMMU AND KASHMIR (1866-94)

These north Indian states were united in 1846.

From 1866-1878, each state issued its own stamps with the common issues beginning in 1878.

From 1894-1948, Indian issues were used. Since Indian independence, this predominantly Moslem area has been disputed between India and Pakistan, and stamps of these nations have been used in the territories under their control.

## JANINA (1909-11, 1913-14)

A city in northwest Greece. Janina was part of the Turkish province of Albania until occupied by Greece in 1913. During 1909-11 and 1913, an Italian post office, utilizing overprinted Italian stamps, operated in the city.

## JAPAN (1871-)

A group of islands off the eastern coast of Asia. Japan pursued an isolationist policy until 1854 when a U.S. fleet forced it to admit limited foreign trade.

In 1867, internal dissension caused the restoration of imperial power and centralization within the country. Japan embarked on a program of rapid modernization and by the early 20th century was a world power.

During 1871-1910, Japan expanded her territory through an aggressive imperialistic foreign policy, gaining Formosa, Korea, etc.

Her victory over Russia in 1905 established her as a major military power and encouraged the growth of nationalism throughout Asia.

During World War I, Japan sided with the Allies, acquiring former German Pacific holdings after the war. During 1918-25, Japan occupied portions of Russian Siberia and Sakhalin and in the 1930s began to aggressively expand at the expense of China, which was invaded in 1937.

In 1940, Japan joined the Axis and invaded French Indo-China, and in 1941, attacked British and U.S. territories in the Pacific.

After initial successes, the tide turned against Japan in 1943, ending with her defeat in 1945. All territory, except the home islands, was taken from her by the Allies, who occupied Japan itself until 1952.

Since World War II, Japan has enjoyed an economic boom, making it the World's third greatest industrial power.

## JAPANESE OFFICES IN CHINA (1900-22)

Unoverprinted Japanese stamps were used at a number of Japanese post offices in China from 1876 to 1900. From Jan. 1, 1900, through Dec. 31, 1922, overprinted Japanese stamps were used.

## JAPANESE OFFICE IN KOREA (1900-01)

For a short time, Japanese post offices in Korea used overprinted Japanese stamps. These were withdrawn in April 1901.

## JASDAN (1942-50)

A former feudatory state in western India. Indian stamps replaced those of Jasdan in 1950.

## JERSEY (1941-45, 1958-)

An island in the English Channel united with the British Commonwealth. Local issues were used during the World War II German occupation, regional issues from 1958-69, and issues of the independent Jersey Postal Administration since Oct. 1, 1969.

## JERUSALEM (1909-14, 1948)

The capital of Palestine and a holy city of Judaism, Christianity and Islam. Prior to World War I, a number of European nations maintained their own postal systems in Jerusalem.

Separate issues were made for their posts in the city by Italy (1909-11) and Russia (1909-14).

In 1948, the French consulate operated a postal service in Jerusalem, utilizing overprinted French Consular Service stamps.

## JHALAWAR (1887-90)

A former princely state in western India. Jhalawar's stamps were replaced by regular Indian issues on Nov. 1, 1900.

## JHIND (1874-1950)

A former feudatory state in the northern Punjab of India. Jhind issued stamps from 1874 to 1885, when a postal convention united its postal system to that of India.

From July 1885-April 1, 1950, overprinted Indian stamps were used. Regular Indian issues replaced these overprinted issues on April 1, 1950, although the overprinted stamps remained valid until Jan. 1, 1951.

## JOHORE (1876-)

A former non-federated British Malay state. Johore was under British protection from 1914-57. The area joined the Federation of Malaya in 1957.

## JORDAN (1920-)

A kingdom occupying the territory east of the Jordan River in western Asia. Under Turkish control from 1516-1918, the area was occupied from 1918-46 by Great Britain.

Abdullah, second son of King Hussein of Hejaz, became amir of the Trans-Jordan in 1921 and king when the area became independent in 1946.

Jordan seized a large territory on the western bank of the Jordan River in 1948, but the area was occupied by Israel in 1967.

By 1970, the growing power of Palestinian guerrillas in Jordan provoked a reaction by King Hussein and his Beduoin supporters. After a bitter campaign, Palestinian strength in the country was broken by mid-1971.

King Hussein's government is supported by subsidies from the Arab oil states. Because of this, and because of his opposition to the 1979 Israeli-Egyptian peace treaty, Hussein has moved away from Jordan's traditional pro-Western posture to adopt a nonaligned position. He has warmly supported Iraq in its war with Iran.

— **K** —

**KAMPUCHEA (1977-)**

Cambodia's name was officially changed to Kampuchea in 1977.

**KARELIA (1922, 1941-43)**

A Soviet district east of Finland. During 1921-22, an autonomous government briefly issued stamps until its suppression by the Soviets.

During 1941-43, the area was occupied by Finland at which time overprinted Finnish issues and one semipostal were used.

**KARLSBAD (1938)**

A city in the Sudetenland (Czechoslovakia). In 1938 the local authorities overprinted a large number of Czechoslovakian stamps to commemorate the area's cession to Germany.

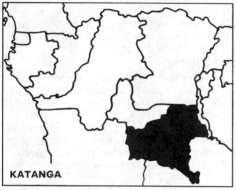

**KATANGA**

**KATANGA (1960-63)**

The southernmost province of Zaire. When Belgium granted independence to the Belgian Congo in 1960, Katanga seceded from the new state. After a bitter struggle, the Katangan regime was crushed by the central government with U.N. support.

In early 1977, Katangan forces based in Angola launched an invasion of the province. After a rapid initial advance, the Katangese were defeated by forces of the Zairean government, with the support of Moroccan troops and aid from the U.S. and other Western powers.

**KEDAH (1912-)**

A sultanate in southwest Malayan peninsula. Kedah was under British protection from 1909-42, Japanese occupation 1942-43, Siamese occupation 1943-45, British administration 1945-57. Since 1948, Kedah has been a member of the Federation of Malaya.

**KELANTAN (1911-)**

A sultanate in northeast Malaya peninsula. The area was under British protection after 1909 and was occupied by Japan (1942-43) and Siam (1943-45) during World War II.

**KENYA (1963-)**

Republic in East Africa. Formerly a British protectorate, the inroads of European settlers provoked the nationalist Mau Mau movement in 1952.

After years of fighting, Great Britain agreed to grant Kenyan independence which was declared Dec. 12, 1963. During 1968-72, the government mounted a campaign against Asians with British passports, who controlled the commerce of the nation, and many were forced to leave the country.

Kenya has shown steady economic growth since independence and enjoys a relatively free political life.

A 1980 military and economic aid accord gives the United States access to Kenyan air and naval bases.

**KENYA AND UGANDA (1922-35)**

The postal union comprising the colony of Kenya (coastal area), the protectorate of Kenya (inland) and Uganda, all British colonial territories.

**KENYA, UGANDA AND TANGANYIKA (1935-64)**

Postal union of Kenya, Uganda and the mandated territory of Tanganyika, British possessions in East Africa. The area was renamed Kenya, Uganda and Tanzania, after Tanganyika and Zanzibar merged to form Tanzania in 1964.

**KERASSUNDE (1909-14)**

A Turkish port on the Black Sea, now Giresun. The Russian post office in Kerassunde used stamps of the Russian Levant overprinted with the name of the city after 1909.

**KHOR FAKKAN (1965-69)**

A dependency of the sheikdom of Sharjah in the Trucial States of eastern Arabia.

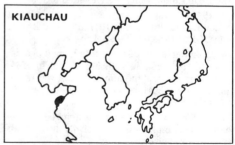

**KIAUCHAU**

**KIAUCHAU (1900-14)**

Former German colony on the southern side of the Shantung peninsula in China. The area was seized by Germany in 1897 and subsequently leased to Germany by China. It was occupied by Japan in 1914 and returned to China in 1922.

**KIEV (1918, 1920)**

Capital of the Ukraine. Kiev issued stamps during the confused period of the Russian Civil War. In 1918, Russian stamps were overprinted with the trident device of the Ukraine, and in 1920, Kievan authorities issued surcharged Russian savings stamps for provisional postage use.

## KILIS (1921)

A city in southern Turkey. After World War I, this area was included in the French-occupied territory of Syria. It was restored to Turkey in 1923.

In 1921, a shortage of regular stamps necessitated a provisional issue.

## KING EDWARD VII LAND (1908)

In 1908, Sir Ernest Henry Shackleton led a British expedition to explore King Edward VII Land in Antarctica. A contemporary New Zealand stamp was overprinted for use by the members of the expedition.

## KIONGA (1916)

A small area in northern Mozambique in the Indian Ocean. Kionga was part of German East Africa until World War I, when it was occupied by Portuguese forces from Mozambique, to which it was joined by the Treaty of Versailles.

## KIRIBATI (1979-)

The British protectorate of the Gilbert Islands became the independent republic of Kiribati on July 12, 1979.

## KIRIN AND HEILUNGCHANG (1927-31)

A district of Manchuria. After 1927, Chinese stamps were overprinted for sale in the area. These issues were replaced by those of Manchukuo in 1931, after Japanese forces overran Manchuria.

## KISHANGARH (1899-1949)

A former princely state in northwestern India. In 1948, it joined Rajasthan, whose stamps were used from 1949-50. Since 1950, Indian issues have been used.

## KONSTANTINSBAD (1938)

A city in the Sudetenland (Czechoslovakia). In 1938 the municipal authorities overprinted a number of Czechoslovakian stamps to commemorate union with Germany.

## KORCE (KORYTSA, also KORYTZA, KORCA, KORITSA OR CORITSA) (1914-18)

The center of the short-lived Eastern Albanian Republic during World War I. Supported by French troops, the republic collapsed upon their withdrawal in 1918.

During its existence, however, the Korce regime issued a number of stamps which are listed under "Albania" in the standard U.S. catalogs.

Forgeries of the 1917-18 issues abound, and collectors should use caution when buying them.

## KOREA, DEMOCRATIC PEOPLE'S REPUBLIC OF (NORTH KOREA) (1946-)

A Communist state occupying the northern half of the Korean peninsula.

After World War II, Korea was occupied from Japan, with U.S. forces holding the southern half of the country and Soviet troops in the north.

In 1948, this partition was made permanent, and separate regimes were established in the two zones. The Democratic People's Republic of Korea was established on May 1, 1948, under the leadership of Kim Il Sung.

In 1950, North Korea attacked South Korea, but three years of fighting, with U.S.,U.N. and Chinese intervention, ended with a cease-fire that left the boundary between the two Koreas essentially unchanged.

The greatest part of Korea's resources and pre-war industry were in the north, and the North Korean government has actively developed these into a substantial industrial plant.

North Korea is a totalitarian state, built upon a personality cult centered around Kim Il Sung. It maintains ties with both China and the U.S.S.R. and has remained neutral in their ideological disputes.

North Korean stamp issues are subject to U.S. Treasury Department restrictions and cannot be imported through the mail.

## KOREA, REPUBLIC OF (SOUTH KOREA)(1946-)

After the establishment of the Democratic People's Republic of Korea in 1948, the Republic of Korea was established in the southern portion of the peninsula occupied by the U.S. The regime in the south was recognized as the legal government of Korea on Dec. 12, 1948.

On June 25, 1950, North Korea attacked South Korea, quickly pushing the South Korean forces back to a small pocket of resistance in the southeast.

Massive U.N. intervention brought a North Korean rout, but the invasion of the North by Communist China brought the retreat of the U.N. forces to below the 38th parallel.

On July 10, 1951, after renewed U.N. advances, peace talks began, and on July 27, 1953, an armistice was achieved.

From 1948 to 1960, Dr. Syngman Rhee was president of South Korea. The corruption of the regime alienated many South Koreans, and in 1960 Rhee was forced to resign. In the following year, a military coup brought Gen. Park Chung Hee to power. Park expanded his power and ruled dictatorially, until his assassination.

A technical state of war continues between the two Koreas, and a large number of U.S. forces remain in the south.

## KOREA (1884-85, 1895-1905, 1946-)

A peninsula in east Asia, surrounded on three sides by the Sea of Japan and the Yellow Sea and bounded on the north by Manchuria and the U.S.S.R.

Korea was under Chinese control until 1895, when it passed under Japanese influence. In 1910, Japan annexed Korea, ruling it until 1945.

After World War II, Korea was divided at the 38th parallel into two zones of occupation — the north under the Soviets and the south under the U.S. In 1948, separate regimes were established in the two zones.

## KUBAN COSSACK GOVERNMENT (1918-20)

In late 1917, the Kuban Cossacks in southern Russia established a republic, which in the spring of 1918 declared its independence. They were recognized by the White Russian government of General Denikin, but after his withdrawal from the area in March 1920, the republic was quickly occupied by the Red Army.

A number of surcharged Russian stamps were issued by this regime.

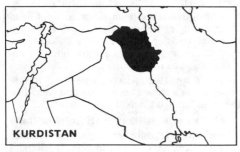

KURDISTAN

## KURDISTAN (1923)

The region of western Asia occupied by the Kurds, divided between Iraq, Iran and Turkey. In 1923, stamps were issued by rebel forces in northern Iraq.

## KURLAND (1945)

Four German stamps were overprinted for use in Kurzeme in April 1945, by German forces cut off by the Soviet advance.

## KUSTANAI (1920)

A city in the Kazakh Soviet Socialist Republic. In 1920, the local authorities overprinted Russian stamps for use in the area.

## KUWAIT (1923-)

A sheikdom at the northern end of the Persian Gulf. Kuwait was under British protection from 1899-1961, becoming independent June 19, 1961.

Kuwait is rich in oil and is one of the more active members of OPEC. During the 1970s, Kuwait has led the push for increasing petroleum prices and has become extremely wealthy.

Education, medical care and social security are free to Kuwaiti citizens, and internal taxation has been abolished.

## KWANGCHOWAN (1906-44)

A Chinese port south of Canton leased by France from 1898-1945. Kwangchowan was administered as part of French Indo-China. Occupied by Japan during World War II, the city was reoccupied by the Chinese after the war.

## KWANGTUNG (1942-50)

A province in southern China, centered around its capital, Canton. Japanese forces oc-

cupying Kwangtung overprinted Chinese stamps for use in the province from 1942-45.

Regular Chinese (Nationalist) issues were used during 1945-49. In October 1949, Canton, which had briefly become the Nationalist capital, fell to the Communists, and Communist issues for South China came into use, to be replaced by national issues in 1950.

## — L —

## LABUAN (1879-1906)

An island off the northwest coast of Borneo. Labuan was ceded by Brunei to Britain in 1848 and administered by the British North Borneo Co. from 1890-1906.

In 1907, Labuan was attached to the Straits Settlements, and since 1945, has been part of British North Borneo (Sabah).

## LAGOS (1874-1906)

A territory in south Nigeria. Lagos was occupied by Great Britain in 1861 and during 1886-1906 was a separate protectorate.

The territory merged with the Southern Nigerian Protectorate in 1906.

## LAOS (1951-)

A state in northwestern Indo-China. Formerly a kingdom of some influence, by the early 19th century Laos was under Siamese rule. In 1893 Siam renounced its claims, and in 1899 Laos became a French protectorate.

During 1941-45, Laos was occupied by Japan. After World War II, Laos was reestablished as a kingdom (1947), under French protection. In 1953 it became independent within the French Union, and in 1956 it became fully independent.

During the Vietnamese War, Laos maintained a precarious neutrality, with troops of both sides active within the country. With the U.S. withdrawal from Indo-China, the neutralist regime collapsed. In May 1975, the Lao Democratic People's Republic, a Vietnamese satellite, was established.

## LAS BELA (1897-1907)

A former feudatory state of India, now a part of Pakistan.

## LATAKIA (1931-37)

This area, orginally called Alaouites, was a district of western Syria under French mandate. Its stamps were replaced by those of Syria in 1937, after its merger with Syria in December 1936.

## LATVIA (1918-41)

A former republic on the Baltic and the Gulf of Riga. Although the majority of Latvians are Slavic, the area was long dominated by a German land-owning class, descendants of the Knights of the Tuetonic Order, who conquered the region during the Middle Ages. Latvia was ruled by Poland and Sweden until Russia occupied the territory in the 18th century.

During 1917-18, Latvia was occupied by Germany, and in 1918 it declared its independence from Russia. During 1919 the Latvian government fought both the Red Army, which sought to reestablish Russian control, and the Army of the West, which sought to maintain German influence. By the end of 1919, Latvia was able to secure its independence.

In 1939, as part of the Soviet-German Non-Aggression Pact, the U.S.S.R. established military bases in Latvia. In June 1940, Soviet forces seized the country, and in July it was absorbed into the Soviet Union.

In July 1941, Germany occupied the country, and many cities overprinted their stocks of Russian stamps for provisional use. In November, German "Ostland" issues were introduced, replacing the many local issues.

During 1944-45, Soviet forces again occupied Latvia, and ordinary Russian stamps were again placed into use.

## LEBANON (1924-)

A republic in western Asia, bordering on the Mediterranean Sea. Under Turkish rule until 1918, Lebanon was occupied by the French after World War I under a League of Nations mandate. It was declared independent in 1941, and in 1944, its independence was implemented.

Lebanon's population is 57 per cent Moslem and 40 per cent Christian, and from 1943 the two groups co-existed through a constitutional apportioning of key government posts. During 1969-75, Palestinian commando groups became increasingly powerful in Lebanon, which they used as a base for raids against Israel.

Efforts of the government to restrain Palestinian activities, with which many Lebanese Moslems sympathized, and after 1970, Israel counterattacks against Palestinian bases in southern Lebanon, brought a destabilization of the Lebanese government.

During 1965-76, these tensions erupted in civil war. Generally, Arab nations supported the Palestinians and leftist Moslem factions, while Israel supported the various Christian groups. In 1976, Syria intervened, suppressed PLO activity, and attempted to mediate the conflict. Although sporadic clashes continue, the presence of foreign troops has prevented the resumption of full-scale civil war.

## LEEWARD ISLANDS (1890-1956)

A group of islands in the West Indies, southeast of Puerto Rico. The Leeward Islands was a former administrative unit of British island possessions in the Caribbean — Antigua, Montserrat, St. Kitts, Nevis and Anguilla, British Virgin Islands, and Dominica (until 1940).

Leeward issues were used throughout the colony, while the issues of the individual presidencies were valid only within their own territories.

## LEMNOS (1912-13)

A Greek island in the Aegean Sea. Lemnos utilized overprinted Greek stamps after its occupation from Turkey.

## LEROS (1912-32)

One of the Dodecanese Islands in the eastern Aegean Sea. Leros was claimed from Turkey by Italy in 1912, at which time Italian stamps overprinted "Leros" were issued.

In 1929, these were superseded by general issues for the Aegean Islands, although two sets overprinted "Lero" were released in 1930 and 1932.

## LESOTHO (1966-)

A kingdom in southern Africa, surrounded by the Republic of South Africa. Until it became independent as Lesotho in 1966, this territory was the British crown colony of Basutoland.

Lesotho is completely surrounded by South Africa, and the majority of its work force is employed in that country.

## LIBERIA (1860-)

A republic on the west coast of Africa, which after 1822 was colonized by freed slaves from the United States. In 1847, Liberia was proclaimed independent.

Liberian political and economic life has been dominated by the descendants of these freed slaves, who constitute less than 3 per cent of the country's population.

In April 1980, a coup deposed the constitutional government. Although the leaders of the new regime seem oriented toward the improvement of the position of the native majority, their exact political and economic goals are as yet unclear.

## LIBYA (1912-)

A republic in northern Africa, bordering on the Mediterranean Sea. Occupied until 1912 by Turkey, the area that is now Libya passed to Italy after its victory in the Turko-Italian War of 1912.

The colonies of Tripolitania and Cyrenaica were united into Libya in 1934. During World War II, the colony was occupied by the Allies with Tripolitania and Cyrenaica under British administration, using "M.E.F." stamps (Middle Eastern Forces), while Fezzan-Ghadames was under French administration, using its own issues.

On Dec. 24, 1951, the independent Kingdom of Libya was established. In September 1969, the monarchy was deposed and the Libyan Arab Republic was established.

The Libyan Arab Republic is ruled by a military junta headed by Col. Muammar al-Qadhafi. Qadhafi's policies are a blend of socialism, fundamentalist Islam and ardent pan-Arabism. Libya has led the movement within OPEC for constantly higher petroleum prices and has used its huge oil income for sweeping social programs and to support radical movements throughout the world.

Libya has actively funded and trained leftist movements, including the Japanese "Red Army," the Irish Republican Army, Black September (the radical arm of the PLO), Philippine Moslem terrorists and others. Since 1975, Libya has been closely linked with the U.S.S.R.

Qadhafi's long-range goal is to assume leadership of the Arab world, and his ambitions have brought problems with a number of Libya's neighbors. In 1976 he was accused of attempting the overthrow of the Sudanese government. In 1977 Libya and Egypt fought several battles on their common border. During 1977-79, Libyan troops supported Arab guerrillas in their attempt to transfer northern Chad to Libyan control. In 1979, Libya attempted to overthrow the government of Tunisia.

### LIECHTENSTEIN (1912- )

A principality in central Europe between Switzerland and Austria. Liechtenstein, founded in 1719, became a sovereign in 1806, and became independent in 1866. Until 1918, it retained close ties with Austria, which until 1920 operated the Liechtenstein postal service.

Since 1920, it has been associated with Switzerland, its post office having been under Swiss administration since 1921.

In 1868, Liechtenstein abolished its army and has since remained free of foreign entanglements. It remains the only European nation denying women the right to vote.

Liechtenstein is one of the major tax havens of the world, and many international corporations have headquarters there. The country's major exports include postage stamps and plastic postage stamp mounts.

### LIPSO (1912-32)

One of the Dodecanese Islands in the eastern Aegean Sea. Lipso was occupied from Turkey by Italy in 1912 at which time Italian stamps overprinted "Lipso" were issued.

In 1929, Lipso's issues were superseded by the general issues for the Aegean Islands, although two sets overprinted "Lisso" or "Lipso" were released in 1930 and 1932.

### LITHUANIA (1918-40)

A country of eastern Europe, northeast of Poland and south of Latvia.

Lithuania ruled a large empire in the later Middle Ages, stretching from the Baltic to the Black Seas. In 1385 it was united with the Kingdom of Poland. Initially the dominant partner, Lithuania was gradually eclipsed by Poland. It was absorbed by Russia in 1793 and remained under Russian control until World War I.

In 1915 the country was occupied by Germany, which supported its declaration of independence from Russia in 1918. German troops re-

mained in Lithuania until the end of 1919. In 1920 the border district of Central Lithuania was lost to Poland, but this was somewhat offset by Lithuania's seizure of the German port of Memel from the Allies in 1923.

In October 1939, Lithuania reoccupied Central Lithuania, in return for which she allowed the Soviet Union to establish military bases. In June 1940, Lithuania was seized by Soviet forces and in July was annexed to the U.S.S.R.

In June 1941, German forces occupied the country, and a number of local overprints on Russian stamps were used, as well as general overprints for Lithuania as a whole. From November 1941 to 1944, German issues overprinted "Ostland" were used.

In 1944, the U.S.S.R. reoccupied Lithuania, and Soviet issues have since been used.

### LIVORNO (1930)

A city in Liguria, Italy. On May 11, 1930, Mussolini visited Livorno, and a local stamp, valid only on that day, was issued by the municipal authorities to commemorate Il Duce's visit.

### LJADY (1942)

A Russian city near Leningrad. The German military commander issued surcharged stamps of Germany and Ostland for use in the area.

### LJUBLJANA (LUBIANA, LAIBACH) (1941-45)

Western Slovenia, separated and established as an Italo-German puppet state during World War II.

### LODZ (1944)

A city in central Poland. During the German occupation, stamps were issued for use in the Jewish Ghetto of the city.

### LOGRONO (1937)

The capital of the province of Logrono in north central Spain. In 1937 a set of stamps was issued by the local Nationalist authorities.

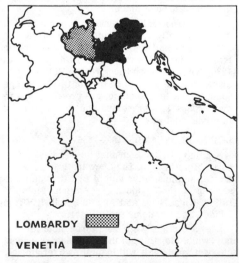

LOMBARDY ▨

VENETIA ▬

## LOMBARDY-VENETIA (1850-66)

The Lombardo-Venetian Kingdom was created in 1815, comprising northeastern Italy, under the Austrian emperor. In 1859, Milan was conquered by Sardinia, and in 1866, Austria relinquished Venetia to the Kingdom of Italy.

The Austrian administration issued separate stamps for this kingdom, inscribed in Italian currency, which were also used in Austrian post offices in the Ottoman Empire.

Since 1866, Italian stamps have been in use.

## LONG ISLAND (1916)

An island (Cheustan or Makronsi) in the Gulf of Smyrna. Long Island was occupied by British forces in 1916, at which time the British commander issued Turkish fiscal stamps overprinted "G.R.I. Postage" and provisional typewritten stamps, used until the British withdrawal from the island.

## LORIENT (1944)

In December 1944, French stamps were overprinted by the German military authorities for local use.

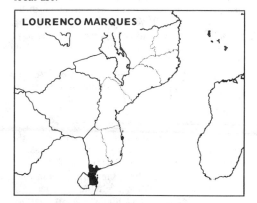

## LOURENCO MARQUES (1895-1920)

A district of southern Mozambique. Its stamps were replaced by those of Mozambique in 1920.

## LUBECK (1859-68)

A former Free City and State in northern Germany on the Baltic Sea. Lubeck's stamps were replaced by those of the North German Confederation.

## LUBOML (1919)

A city in southern Poland. The local authorities issued a series of stamps during the German occupation.

This issue was very speculative and may be found with many "errors."

## LUGA (1941)

A city in northwestern Russia, south of Leningrad. Surcharged Russian stamps were issued by the German military commander.

## LUXEMBOURG (1852-)

A grand duchy in western Europe, strategically located between Germany, France and Belgium.

Until 1890, Luxembourg was ruled by a succession of foreign powers, although from 1815, it was technically independent, joined in personal union with The Netherlands. With the death of William III, king of The Netherlands and grand duke of Luxembourg, the country became completely independent.

Luxembourg was occupied by Germany in both world wars. In 1949, it abandoned its traditional neutrality to become a charter member of NATO. It is a member of the Common Market and is an enthusiastic promoter of European cooperation.

Luxembourg is a prosperous, highly industrialized nation.

# — M —

## MACAO (1884-)

A Chinese port occupied by Portugal since 1557. In 1849, Portugal assumed full sovereignty over the territory, which includes two small, adjacent islands.

## MACEDONIA (1944)

A region in the central Balkans, Macedonia became part of Serbia after 1913, and so became part of Yugoslavia when Serbia merged into that nation.

Bulgaria annexed the territory in 1941. On Sept. 8, 1944, Macedonia declared its independence from Bulgaria. After withdrawal of German troops in November 1944, the area was returned to Yugoslavia.

Overprinted Bulgarian stamps were in use for a few weeks before the collapse of the German puppet government.

## MADAGASCAR (MALAGASY REPUBLIC) (1889-)

A large island in the Indian Ocean off the southeast coast of Africa. During the 19th century, most of the island was united under the Hova tribe which was placed under French protectorate in 1885.

In 1896, the native monarchy was abolished and Madagascar became a French colony, at times administering French island possessions in the area.

In 1958, Madagascar, renamed the Malagasy Republic, became autonomous within the French Union. In 1960 it became fully independent.

French influence remained strong until a 1972 coup brought a socialist regime to power. The new government nationalized French holdings, closed down French military bases and a U.S. space-tracking station, and obtained Chinese aid. France and the U.S. remain the country's chief trading partners.

## MADEIRA (1868-98, 1928-29, 1980-)

A group of islands in the Atlantic Ocean northwest of Africa. Madeira's stamps were replaced by those of Portugal in 1898.

In 1928-29, a special series of stamps was issued for use on certain days, when their use was obligatory.

On Jan. 2, 1980, separate issues again appeared for Madeira.

## MAFIA (1915-18)

A small island off the coast of German East Africa, occupied by the British in December 1914. In January 1915, captured East African stamps were overprinted for use on the island.

Later, German fiscal stamps and Indian issues overprinted "I.E.F." were overprinted "Mafia" or "G.R.I.-Mafia" for local use.

In August 1918, the island was transferred to Tanganyikan administration, and issues of Tanganyika (Tanzania) have since been used.

## MAHRA (1967)

A sultanate in the Aden Protectorate in southwest Arabia. Mahra briefly issued stamps before its absorption into the People's Republic of Southern Yemen.

## MAJORCA (1936-37)

The largest of the Balearic Islands, in the western Mediterranean Sea.

Two sets of overprinted Spanish stamps were issued in 1936 and 1937 under the authority of the Nationalist Civil Governor of the Balearic Islands.

## MAJUJGA (1895)

Province and seaport on the coast of Madagascar. Stamps of France provisionally surcharged were used briefly in February 1895.

## MALACCA (1948-)

Formerly part of the British colony of Straits Settlements. Malacca was under British control since the early 19th century, except for Japanese occupation from 1942-45.

The area is now a part of Malaya within the Malaysian Federation.

## MALAGA (1937)

A province of southern Spain, located on the Mediterranean Sea.

Two sets of stamps, overprinted on Spanish issues, were issued by the Nationalist Civil Governor in 1937.

## MALAWI (1964-)

A republic in south central Africa. Until it became independent on July 6, 1964, Malawi was the British Nyasaland Protectorate. Generally pro-Western, Malawi is closely linked economically with Zimbabwe and South Africa.

## MALAYA, FEDERATION (1957-63)

A formerly independent federation comprising the Malayan states in the southern part of the Malayan Peninsula. The federation merged with Singapore, Sarawak and Sabah to form Malaysia in 1963.

## MALAYA-FEDERATED MALAY STATES (1900-35)

A group of native states in the south portion of the Malayan Peninsula in southeast Asia, under British protection.

The federated states were Perak, Selangor, Negri Sembilan and Pahang.

In 1935, the federation issues were replaced by those of the individual states. In 1945, the Federated Malay States were incorporated into the Malayan Union.

## MALAYSIA (1963-)

Federation within the British Commonwealth. Malaysia was formed Sept. 16, 1963, with the union of the former British territories of the Federation of Malaya, Singapore (until 1965), Sarawak and Sabah (North Borneo).

Malaysia is rich in natural resources and has enjoyed substantial industrial development since independence.

## MALDIVE ISLANDS (1906-)

A group of islands in the Indian Ocean, southwest of Ceylon. The Maldives came under British protection in 1887 and were attached to the Ceylon colony until 1948.

During 1948-64, the islands were closely associated with Great Britain, becoming completely independent July 1965.

In 1968, the 800-year-old sultanate was abolished, and a republic was established. In recent years, the Maldives have maintained close ties with India and the U.S.S.R.

## MALI (1959-)

A republic in West Africa. Formerly the French Sudan, Mali joined Senegal in 1959 to form the independent Federation of Mali.

Senegal withdrew from the federation in 1960, and Mali, which called itself the Sudanese Republic during its union with Senegal, proclaimed its independence as the Republic of Mali.

Mali maintained a carefully neutralist policy until 1968, accepting economic aid from both the Western and Communist blocs.

Since 1968, however, conservative elements have been purged, and Mali has strengthened her ties with Red China.

Since 1973, Mali has suffered terribly from drought and famine.

## MALTA (1860-)

A group of islands in the central Mediterranean Sea, south of Sicily. Strategically located, Malta has been ruled by a long succession of foreign powers, from the Phoenicians through the British, who occupied the islands during the Napoleonic Wars.

Malta became independent in 1964 and a republic in 1974. In 1979 the last British military personnel were withdrawn. Malta maintains a nonaligned foreign policy and receives economic aid from both the Eastern and Western blocs.

## MAN, ISLE OF (1973-)

An island in the Irish Sea, west of Britain. A self-governing crown possession, the Isle of Man used British stamps, along with its own regional issues after 1958, until July 5, 1973, when its postal administration separated from that of Britain.

## MANAMA (1966-72)

A dependency of the sheikdom of Ajman in the Trucial States of eastern Arabia.

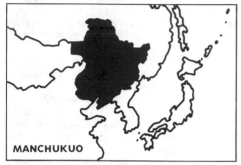

MANCHUKUO

## MANCHUKUO (1932-45)

A former Japanese satellite, comprising Manchuria and Jehol. Established in 1932 under Henry Pu-yi, who as Hsuan Tung had been the last Manchu emperor of China.

In 1934, Pu-yi became Emperor Kang Teh of Manchukuo. The area was occupied by the Soviets in July 1945, and was turned over to the Chinese Communist regime in May 1946.

Nationalist forces held the southern portion of Manchukuo until November 1948, and during 1946-48 issued stamps for this area (North-Eastern Provinces).

## MARIANA ISLANDS (1899-1914)

A group of islands in the western Pacific. Under Spanish rule from 1668-1898, when, except for Guam, they were sold to Germany.

Japan occupied the Marianas in 1914, and Japanese stamps replaced those of the German colony. In 1945, U.S. forces occupied the islands. and U.S. stamps have since been in use.

## MARIENWERDER (1920)

A former Prussian district, which was occupied by the Allies after World War I. A plebiscite in 1920 returned the area to Germany. It was occupied by Poland after World War II.

## MARINO (1930)

A district of northeastern Venezuela, which was controlled by a revolutionary group for a short time during 1903.

## MARSHALL ISLANDS (1889-1914)

Two chains of islands in the western Pacific, occupied by Germany in 1885. In 1914, the islands were occupied by Japan, and Japanese stamps were used until the islands' occupation by the U.S. in 1945.

## MARTINIQUE (1886-1947)

A former French island colony in the West Indies, southeast of Puerto Rico. The island became an integral part of the French republic on Jan. 1, 1947. French stamps are now used.

## MATURIN (1903)

The capital of the state of Monagas in northeastern Venezuela. A revolutionary group in control of the region issued stamps for a short time during 1903.

## MAURITANIA (1906-44, 1960-)

A republic in northwestern Africa, bordering on the Atlantic Ocean. A former French colony, Mauritania was part of French West Africa from 1904 to 1958 and used French West African stamps 1945-49.

In 1958, Mauritania, as the Islamic Republic of Mauritania, became autonomous within the French Union, and in 1960 it became fully independent.

At one time, the territory of Mauritania was ruled by Morocco, and Morocco claimed the area until 1970. In 1976 the mineral-rich Spanish Sahara was divided between the two countries.

In 1980, Mauritania, after four years of war with the Polsario Front, renounced its share of the former Spanish Sahara, which was then occupied by Morocco.

## MAURITIUS (1847-)

An island in the Indian Ocean. Mauritius was a British colony after 1810 and became independent in 1968.

Mauritius enjoys a free political life and a high literacy rate. The economic life of the country has expanded during the past decade.

## MAYOTTE (1892-1914)

One of the Comoro Islands, Mayotte was occupied by France in 1841 and attached to the colony of Madagascar in 1911.

The Comoros were separated from Madagascar in 1947 and began issuing their own stamps in 1950.

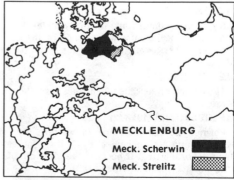

MECKLENBURG

Meck. Scherwin

Meck. Strelitz

## MECKLENBURG-SCHWERIN (1856-67)

A former grand duchy in northern Germany, bordering the Baltic Sea. In 1868, issues of the North German Confederation came into use.

## MECKLENBURG-STRELITZ (1864-67)

A former grand duchy in northern Germany, divided into two parts by Mecklenburg-Schwerin, with which it was joined until 1701.

Its stamps were replaced by those of the North German Confederation in 1868.

## MELILLA (1936)

A port in northern Morocco. Occupied by Spain since 1470, Melilla was a military stronghold administered separately from Spanish Morocco, which was not occupied by Spain until the late 19th and early 20th centuries.

Melilla, along with Cueta, remains a part of Metropolitan Spain.

In 1936 the military authorities in Melilla overprinted two Spanish stamps for local use.

## MEMEL (1920-24, 1939)

A district in northern Europe, on the Baltic Sea. German until after World War I, when the area was occupied by the French. In 1923, frustrated by the League of Nations' failure to decide the disposition of sovereignty over the area, Lithuania seized Memel.

In 1924, this was approved by the League of Nations.

In 1939, Germany reoccupied Memel, and briefly, Lithuanian stamps overprinted "Memelland"/"Ist"/"frei" were used. After World War II, the area was reincorporated in the Lithuanian Soviet Socialist Republic.

## MENG CHIANG (INNER MONGOLIA) (1941-45)

Regular Chinese stamps were overprinted by the Japanese in 1941, and separate issues for this area continued until the end of World War II.

This area was held by the Communist forces at the end of the war and was included in the North China postal district, which issued stamps from 1946 to 1949.

Regular issues of the central government came into use after 1950.

## MERANO (1918)

A city in northern Italy, formerly under Austrian rule. Local stamps were issued by the authorities in 1918, while the area was still a part of Austria.

## MERIDA (1916)

The capital of the state of Yucatan in southern Mexico.

## MESOPOTAMIA (1917-22)

Former Turkish province in western Asia. Mesopotamia was occupied by British forces during World War I. It became the kingdom of Iraq under British mandate in 1921.

## MEXICO (1856-)

A republic in North America, situated between the U.S. and Central America, bordering on the Caribbean Sea and the Pacific Ocean.

Mexico was the center of a number of Indian cultures dating from c. 800 B.C. By the 15th century, the central portion of the country was ruled by the Aztec Empire, which was conquered by the Spanish in 1519-21.

Mexico, as the viceroyalty of New Spain, was the center of Spain's North American Empire for 300 years.

The Mexican revolution against Spain began in 1810 and was finally successful in 1821. The Mexican Empire of 1822-23 included Central America, but this area soon became independent. The republican government that succeeded the empire was marked by instability and strife.

The weakened condition of the country cost it Texas (1836) and the large northern area that now comprises the southwestern U.S. (1848). An additional area in the north was sold to the U.S. in 1853.

During 1861-67, Mexico was torn by a civil war between the aristocracy, supported by France, and the lower classes, led by Benito Juarez.

The French were finally expelled from Mexico, and Juarez came to power.

During most of the period between 1877 and 1911, the country was ruled by the dictator Porfirio Diaz, who restored stability and secured foreign investment.

After Diaz's death, Mexico entered a period of civil war, which lasted from 1913-20. During this period, the U.S. intervened in Veracruz (1914) and sent a punitive expedition into northern Mexico (1916-17).

Since 1929, Mexico has been ruled by the Institutional Revolutionary Party. The PRI is a broad-based political confederation, encompassing a wide political spectrum.

Mexico has rich natural resources, including what may be the world's largest petroleum reserves, but its rugged topography and arid climate have been major obstacles to economic development.

Considerable economic and social progress has been made since 1940, but unemployment remains extremely high, and many Mexicans have yet to share in the benefits of the country's development.

## MEXICO-REVOLUTIONARY OVERPRINTS (1914)

With the seizure of power in 1913 by Gen. Huerta following the assassination of President Madero, a group of Madero's former supporters launched a revolution.

This group, led by Carranza and including such leaders as Obregon, Villa, and Zapata, called themselves the "Constitutional Government."

During 1914, a number of Mexican cities and states under Constitutionalist control, provisionally overprinted stocks of regular Mexican stamps — Acambaro (Guanajuato State); Aguascalientes (Aguascalientes); Chihuahua (Chihuahua); Colima (Colima); Culiacan (Sinoloa);

Guaymas (Sonora); Juarez (Chihuahua); Leon (Guanajuato); Lower California; Coahuila; Gonzales (Guanajuato); Matehuala (San Luis Potosi); Monterrey (Nuevo Leon);

Queretaro; Salamanca (Guanajuato); San Juan de Allende (Coahuila); San Luis Potosi (San Luis Potosi); San Pedro; Sinaloa (Sinaloa); Sonora; Torreon (Coahuila); Tuxtla; Viezca; Yucatan; and Zacatecas.

## MIDDLE CONGO (1907-36)

Former French colony on the northern side of the Congo River. Created from existing French territory in 1907, it was confederated with Gabon, Ubangi-Shari and Chad to form French Equatorial Africa.

After 1936, issues of French Equatorial Africa replaced those of the individual colonies.

## MIDDLE EAST FORCES (1942-50)

During World War II, British and New Zealand forces occupied Italian colonies in East Africa, North Africa and the Aegean Sea.

British stamps overprinted "M.E.F." were used in these areas until 1950, after which the remainders were used in Great Britain.

## MILAN (1897)

A city in northern Italy. For a time, local stamps were issued by the municipal authorities.

## MINORCA (1939)

One of the Balearic Islands, in the western Mediterranean Sea.

Locally typeset stamps were used provisionally after the occupation of the island by the Nationalists in February 1939.

## MODENA (1852-60)

Former duchy in northern Italy. In 1859, the duchy was overthrown and in 1860, the area merged with Sardinia, whose issues came into use.

## MOHELI (1906-12)

One of the Comoro Islands in the Mozambique Channel near Madagascar. Moheli was attached to Madagascar in 1911 and was again separated, as one of the Comoro Islands, in 1947.

Comoro stamps have been in use since 1950.

## MOLDAVIA (1858-61)

Former principality in northeastern Romania. Under Turkish suzerainty after the 16th century, Moldavia united with Wallachia in 1861 to form the Kingdom of Romania.

## MOLDAVIA-WALLACHIA (1862-65)

The united principalities forming Romania.

## MONACO (1885-)

A principality on the southern coast of France. Long autonomous under the protection, at various times, of France, Spain and Sardinia, Monaco is independent, except for the right of France to approve the successor to the throne.

By the treaty of 1918, Monaco will be annexed by France, should the ruling Grimaldi family fail to provide an heir.

## MONGOLIA (1924-)

A republic in central Asia, located between China and Soviet Siberia. The homeland of the Mongol Empire that in the 13th-14th centuries stretched from Poland to Korea. By 1689 Mongol power had declined to the point where the region came under Chinese control.

In 1911, Mongolia declared its independence but in 1921 was occupied by Soviet troops. In 1924, a pro-Soviet republic was established and in 1945, after China renounced all claims in the country, the Mongolian People's Republic was established.

In recent years, the Mongolian government has carried out an active program to transform the country's economy from a nomadic to a more modern, settled form.

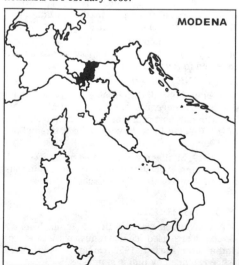

MODENA

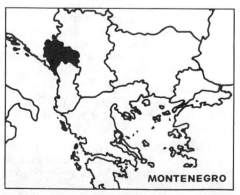

MONTENEGRO

## MONTENEGRO (1874-1918, 1941-45)

A former kingdom in the Balkans, situated north of Albania. Montenegro became independent in 1452 and for centuries successfully resisted the Turks, who held the rest of southeastern Europe.

In January 1916, the Austrians occupied Montenegro, and the government fled to Bordeaux, France, where overprinted French stamps were used for a time.

In November 1918, King Nicholas was deposed in a pro-Serbian coup, and Montenegro was united with Serbia.

During World War II, Montenegro was reestablished as an Italian protectorate. In 1943-44, it was occupied by Germany, which overprinted Yugoslavian stamps and issues of the Italian administration. After the German defeat, Montenegro was again occupied by Yugoslavia, which initially overprinted issues of the Italian Montenegrin regime. Since 1945 regular Yugoslavian stamps have been used.

## MONTSERRAT (1876-)

An island in the Leeward group in the West Indies, southeast of Puerto Rico. Montserrat was under British control after 1632 and attached to the Leeward Island colony until 1956.

## MOROCCO (1956-)

A kingdom in northwestern Africa, bordering on the Atlantic Ocean and the Mediterranean Sea. A powerful state embracing much of Spain and North Africa in the 12th century, Moroccan power declined thereafter.

European encroachment led to the division of the country into French (southern) and Spanish (northern) protectorates in 1912.

In 1956, the two zones were reunited and Morocco again became independent. Morocco has since expanded by absorbing Tangier (1956), Ifni (1969), the northern two-thirds of the Spanish Sahara (1976) and the southern portion of the Spanish Sahara in 1980.

Morocco is closely linked to the U.S. and France by military and economic agreements. In recent years, Moroccan troops have aided against leftist uprisings in Mauritania and Zaire.

Morocco continues to wage a bitter war in the former Spanish Sahara against the Polisario Front, supported by Algeria, which claims independence for the region.

## MORVI (1931-51)

A former feudatory state in western India. Morvi's issues were replaced by Indian stamps in 1950.

## MOSCHOPOLIS (1914)

A town in southern Albania. Stamps were issued by local authorities during the Greek occupation of the area.

## MOUNT ATHOS (1909-13)

The holy mountain of the Orthodox Church, located in northern Greece, near Salonika. In 1909-13, Russian Levant stamps were overprinted "Mount Athos" in French or Russian for use in the Russian consular post office at Daphne, the seaport at the foot of the mountain.

This post office was closed when Greece occupied the area in 1913.

## MOZAMBIQUE (1877-)

A republic on the southeast coast of Africa. Portuguese settlements began in the 16th century, and the colony remained a Portuguese possession until June 25, 1975, when it became independent as the People's Republic of Mozambique.

Closely linked to the U.S.S.R. and Cuba, Mozambique provided bases for rebels fighting the white Rhodesian regime. Since the end of the civil war and the establishment of a majority government, Mozambique has made a number of tentative overtures to the West.

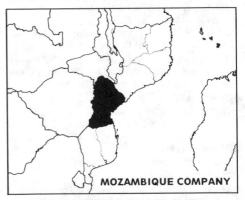

MOZAMBIQUE COMPANY

## MOZAMBIQUE COMPANY (1892-1942)

A private company which, by royal charter, acquired extensive rights in the Mozambique districts of Manica and Sofala.

Most rights, including the direct administration of the territories and the issuing of stamps, reverted to Portugal in 1942.

## MYTILENE (1909-13)

The chief port of the Greek island of Lesbos in the eastern Aegean Sea, off the coast of Turkey. The Russian post office in Mytilene used stamps of the Russian Levant overprinted "Metelin" after 1909.

In 1912, Mytilene was occupied by Greece and overprinted Turkish stamps were used, being superseded by regular Greek issues in 1913.

— N —

## NABHA (1885-1951)

A convention state of British India. Nabha's issues were used concurrently with those of India after April 1, 1950. On Jan. 1, 1951, they were replaced by Indian stamps.

**NANDGAON (1892-95)**

A former feudatory state in central India. Nandgaon's issues were replaced by those of India in July 1895.

**NATAL (1857-1909)**

A former British crown colony on the southeast coast of Africa. A short-lived Boer republic, Natal came under British control in 1843. It was incorporated into the Union of South Africa in 1910.

**NAURU (1916-)**

An island in the west central Pacific Ocean. Nauru was a German possession from 1888-1914 and was occupied by Australian forces during World War I.

From 1920-68, Nauru was a mandate under Australia, New Zealand and Great Britain. It became an independent republic on Jan. 31, 1968.

This 8 square mile island is rich in phosphates, giving the 4,000 plus Naureans one of the highest per capita incomes in the world.

**NAWANAGAR (1875-95)**

A former feudatory state in western India. Nawanagar's issues were replaced by those of India in December 1895.

**NEAPOLITAN PROVINCES (1861-62)**

In October 1860, Garibaldi deposed the ruling Borban dynasty in the Kingdom of the Two Sicilies, and the country was annexed to Sardinia.

Sardinia issued a separate series of stamps for the Neapolitan Provinces in 1861, similar to contemporary Sardinian stamps but inscribed in Neapolitan currency. This set was superseded by regular Italian issues in 1862.

**NEGRI SEMBILAN (1891-)**

Sultanate on the west coast of the Malay Peninsula. Placed under British protection in 1891, the sultanate was occupied by Japan 1942-45.

Negri Sembilan joined the Federation of Malaya in 1948 and is now part of the Malaysian Federation.

**NEJD (1925-26)**

A region in central Arabia united by the puritanical Wahhabi Moslem movement, led by the Saud family, in the 18th century.

During 1914-25, Nejd conquered the Hasa, Asir and Hejaz regions and expanded the kingdom to include most of the Arabian Peninsula.

In 1925, the Kingdom of Hejaz, Nejd and Dependencies was formed, and in 1932, the kingdom was renamed Saudi Arabia.

**NEPAL (1881-)**

Kingdom in the Himalaya Mountains between India and Tibet. United in 1768, Nepal remained independent during the British occupation of India and has since maintained that independence, enjoying good relations with both India and China.

**NETHERLANDS (1852-)**

Constitutional monarchy in northwest Europe, bordering on the North Sea.

Originally under Spanish rule, The Netherlands declared independence in 1581 and during the 17th century became one of the predominant naval and commercial powers, controlling a far-flung empire in the Caribbean, North and South America, Africa, India and the East Indies.

Conflict with England weakened Dutch power until, in 1794, it was overrun by France. The Netherlands again became independent in 1815.

Neutral during World War I, it was occupied by Germany from 1940-45. The last major remnant of The Netherlands' once vast overseas empire was lost in 1950, when Indonesia became independent.

The Netherlands abandoned its policy of neutrality after World War II and aligned itself with the West. It is a member of NATO and of the Common Market.

Although it has undergone substantial industrialization since World War II, the agricultural sector of the country's economy remains strong.

**NETHERLANDS ANTILLES (CURACAO) (1873-)**

Two groups of islands in the West Indies, north of Venezuela. They were originally occupied by Spain, but have been in Dutch possession since 1634.

In 1954, the colony was made an integral part of the Kingdom of The Netherlands.

**NETHERLANDS INDIES (1845-1949)**

A former Dutch colony occupying the greater portion of the East Indies. The area was originally dominated by Hindus, who were supplanted by Moslems after the 14th-15th centuries.

During the 16th century, Portugal dominated the region until forced out by the Dutch and British. After the 17th century, the Dutch ruled most of the area.

The Netherlands Indies were occupied by Japan from 1942-45, during which time a great variety of occupation issues were used.

Two days after Japan's surrender, Indonesian nationalists declared independence, starting the revolution that ended with Dutch withdrawal in 1949.

**NETHERLANDS NEW GUINEA (1950-62)**

The western half of the island of New Guinea, retained by the Dutch after Indonesian independence. An Indonesian invasion in 1962 caused the U.N. to assume temporary executive authority in the area, which was transferred to Indonesia in 1963.

**NEVIS (1861-90)**

A former presidency in the British Leeward Islands, southeast of Puerto Rico.

**NEW BRITAIN (1914-15)**

An island off the northeast coast of New Guinea, in the Pacific Ocean. Formerly part of German New Guinea, New Britain was occupied by Australian forces in 1914.

After World War I, it became part of the mandated territory of New Guinea.

**NEW BRUNSWICK (1851-68)**

Former British colony in eastern Canada. New Brunswick joined the Canadian Confederation in 1867.

**NEW CALEDONIA (1859-)**

An island in the southwest Pacific Ocean. In 1853, New Caledonia became a French Colony, and in 1946 it was designated a French Overseas Territory.

**NEWFOUNDLAND (1857-1949)**

An island off the eastern coast of Canada. With the mainland territory of Labrador, Newfoundland formed a British dominion until its incorporation into Canada in 1949.

**NEW GREECE (1912-13)**

The districts of Turkey occupied by Greece in the First Balkan War. Overprinted Greek issues and one specially printed set were used, until they were replaced by regular Greek stamps.

**NEW GUINEA (1925-42)**

The territory formerly constituting German New Guinea, the northeast portion of the island of New Guinea, in the South Pacific Ocean.

New Guinea was occupied by Australia in 1914 and administered by Australia under a mandate from the League of Nations and after 1947 under a mandate from the United Nations.

New Guinea joined with Papua in 1949 to form the territory of Papua and New Guinea, the name later changed to Papua New Guinea.

**NEW HEBRIDES (1908-)**

A group of islands in the South Pacific Ocean, north of New Caledonia. New Hebrides was declared neutral by Great Britain and France in 1878 and was administered jointly by the two nations from 1906 to 1980. On July 30, 1980, the islands became independent as the Republic of Vanuatu.

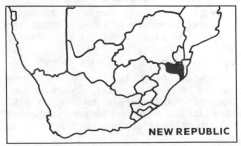

**NEW REPUBLIC (1886-88)**

A short-lived Boer republic in southern Africa. It was absorbed by Transvaal in 1888.

**NEW SOUTH WALES (1850-1913)**

Former British crown colony in southeast Australia. In 1901, New South Wales merged into the Commonwealth of Australia.

**NEW ZEALAND (1855-)**

Two large islands and a number of smaller islands in the South Pacific Ocean. New Zealand was annexed by Great Britain in 1840 and since 1907, has been a self-governing dominion within the British Commonwealth of Nations.

New Zealand has a number of dependencies in the South Pacific, among them the Cook Islands, Niue, the Tokelau Islands, and Ross Dependency in the Antarctic.

**NICARAGUA (1862-)**

A republic in Central America. Independent since 1838, Nicaragua's political history has been turbulent.

The British controlled the eastern coast until 1893, and the U.S. effectively controlled the country from 1912-33.

During 1934-79, the Somoza family ruled Nicaragua. The Somoza regime brought order and considerable economic progress to the country. It also brought widespread corruption and ruthless political repression. In 1974, in response to the activities of the Marxist Sandinista guerrillas, the government imposed martial law. The subsequent excesses of the National Guard alienated virtually all elements of Nicaraguan society, and in August 1978, civil war erupted.

The U.S., which had unsuccessfully attempted to moderate the government's policies, withdrew its support. In May 1979, a Sandinista force invaded Nicaragua, and by July had overthrown the Somozas.

The Sandinista regime has consolidated its position and has suppressed political opposition. It maintains close ties with Cuba and supports Marxist revolutionary movements in neighboring countries.

**NIGER (1921-45, 1959-)**

A republic in northern Africa, directly north of Nigeria.

Under French control after 1890, Niger underwent several administrative incarnations, finally emerging as the Niger Territory in 1920, which became the Niger Colony two years later.

Niger became part of French West Africa in 1904 and used French West African stamps during 1944-59.

In 1958 Niger became an autonomous republic and became fully independent in 1960. It has since maintained close ties with France.

**NIGER COAST PROTECTORATE (1892-1900)**

Former British holdings in southern Nigeria. The area was absorbed into the Southern Nigeria Protectorate in 1900.

## NIGERIA (1914-)

Republic in West Africa, on the Gulf of Guinea. Nigeria was formed from the union of the British protectorates of Northern Nigeria and Southern Nigeria in 1914.

Nigeria became an independent federation in 1960 and a republic in 1963.

Intertribal tensions have been strong since independence. A period of political strife during 1966-67 brought the secession of Biafra, which comprised the mineral-rich southeastern portion of the country. In the ensuing civil war, one million people died, most of them Biafran Ibos. In January 1970, Biafra surrendered and was reabsorbed into Nigeria.

Nigeria has rich petroleum deposits and is a member of OPEC. The massive oil price increases of the 1970s has enabled Nigeria to launch an ambitious campaign of economic development. Drastic cutbacks in oil exports during 1981-82, however, have made it increasingly difficult to maintain these programs.

## NIKLASDORF (1938)

A city in the Sudetenland (Czechoslovakia). In 1938 the municipal authorities overprinted a large number of Czechoslovak stamps to commemorate the union with Germany.

## NISIROS (1912-32)

One of the Dodecanese Islands in the eastern Aegean Sea. Nisiros was obtained from Turkey by Italy in 1912, at which time Italian stamps overprinted "Nisiros" were issued.

These were superseded by the general Aegean Islands' issues in 1929, although two sets overprinted "Nisiro" were released in 1930 and 1932.

## NIUE (1902-)

Island in the South Pacific Ocean, northeast of New Zealand. The area was annexed to New Zealand in 1901. In 1974, Niue became self-governing, although New Zealand retains responsibility for defense and foreign affairs.

## NORFOLK ISLAND (1947-)

Island in the South Pacific Ocean, east of Australia, under Australian administration.

The inhabitants of Norfolk Island are largely descendants of the Bounty mutineers, whose ancestors immigrated to Norfolk from Pitcairns in 1856.

## NORTH BORNEO (1883-1964)

Former British colony, occupying the northeast portion of the island of Borneo in the Malay Archipelago.

Renamed Sabah, British North Borneo joined with Malaya, Sarawak and Singapore to form the Malaysian Federation in 1963.

## NORTH CHINA (1937-49)

The North China Liberation Area comprised Chahar, Hopeh, Shansi and Suiyan. Seven postal districts issued stamps during this period.

## NORTH EAST CHINA (1946-51)

Communist administrative area comprising the provinces of Liaoning, Kirin, Jehol and Heilungkiang, and after 1948, all of Manchuria.

In 1951, the issues of the regional postal administration were replaced by the general issues of the People's Republic of China.

## NORTH GERMAN CONFEDERATION (1868)

A confederation of German states, formed under the leadership of Prussia in 1868, after Austria's defeat in the Austro-Prussian War.

On Jan. 1, 1868, the stamps of all member nations were replaced by those of the confederation, with the area forming the North German Postal District.

## NORTH INGERMANLAND (1920)

A district in Russia lying between the Neva River and Finland. In 1920, the area revolted, established a provisional government and sought union with Finland.

Soviet troops quickly suppressed the revolt.

## NORTHERN EPIRUS (1914-16, 1940-41)

That portion of southern Albania occupied by Greece in 1914-16 and 1940-41. During 1914-16, issues of Epirus and Greek stamps overprinted "Northern Epirus" were used, and in 1940-41 overprinted Greek stamps were used.

## NORTHERN NIGERIA (1900-13)

Former British protectorate comprising holdings in northern Nigeria. Northern Nigeria merged with the Southern Nigeria Protectorate in 1914.

## NORTHERN RHODESIA (1925-64)

Former British protectorate in southern Africa. Northern Rhodesia became the independent republic of Zambia in 1964.

## NORTHWEST CHINA (1946-49)

The northwestern area of China proper, which after the "Long March to Yenan" was the center of the Communist revolution in China. It included the provinces of Kansu, Ninghsia, Tsinghai and, after 1949, Sinkiang. General Chinese issues replaced those of the region in 1949.

## NORTHWEST CHINA (SHENSI-KANSU-NINGHSIA) (1935-49)

The center of the Communist revolution in China after the "long march to Yenan."

In 1949, Sinkiang was added to the region. The regional issues were replaced by the general issues of the People's Republic of China in 1949.

## NORTH WEST PACIFIC ISLANDS (1914-24)

During World War I, Australian forces occupied the German possessions in New Guinea and the adjacent islands.

Australian stamps overprinted "N.W. Pacific Islands" were used on Nauru from 1915-16 and in former German New Guinea from 1915-24.

## NORWAY (1855-)

A constitutional monarchy occupying the western portion of the Scandinavian Peninsula in northern Europe. A powerful kingdom in the Middle Ages, Norway later came under the domination of Denmark, and after 1814, Sweden.

In 1905, Norway became completely independent. The country was occupied by the Germans from 1940-45.

Following World War II, Norway abandoned its traditional neutrality and joined NATO.

The country's abundant hydroelectric resources have produced an ongoing economic boom that has given Norway one of the highest standards of living in the world.

## NOSSI-BE (1889-98)

An island in the Indian Ocean, lying off the northwestern coast of Madagascar, to which it was attached in 1898.

## NOVA SCOTIA (1851-68)

Former British colony in east Canada. Nova Scotia joined the Canadian Confederation in 1867.

## NUGGEN (NOO) (1941)

A city in Estonia. During July-Aug. 13, 1941, Russian stamps were surcharged for use in the city by the German military commander.

## NYASALAND PROTECTORATE (1907-54, 1963-64)

Former British protectorate in south central Africa. Established as British Central Africa in 1890, the name Nyasaland Protectorate was adopted in 1907.

During 1953-63, it was a member of the Federation of Rhodesia and Nyasaland. Nyasaland became independent in 1964, changing its name to Malawi.

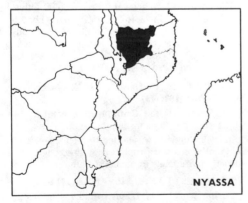

NYASSA

## NYASSA (1897-1929)

A district in northwestern Mozambique. Nyassa was administered by the private Nyassa Co. until 1929 when the company's rights reverted to Portugal.

# — O —

## OAXACA (1914)

A state in central Mexico, which issued its own stamps during the Mexican Civil War.

## OBOCK (1892-94)

A seaport in eastern Africa, on the Gulf of Aden. Acquired by France in 1862 and actively occupied after 1884, it was merged with other French holdings in the area to form the French Somali Coast in 1902.

## ODENPAH (1941)

A city in Estonia. In 1941, the German military commander issued a set of stamps for use in the city.

## ODESSA (1918-20)

A Russian port on the northern coast of the Black Sea. In 1918, Odessa overprinted Russian stamps with the Ukrainian trident for use in its postal district.

During 1919, the Polish Consulate at Odessa overprinted contemporary Polish stamps "ODESA" for use on mail carried from Odessa to Poland through the cooperation of Gen. Denikin. This postal agency was closed Jan. 31, 1920.

## OIL RIVERS PROTECTORATE (1892-93)

Former British protectorate in southern Nigeria. In 1893, the name of the territory was changed to Niger Coast Protectorate.

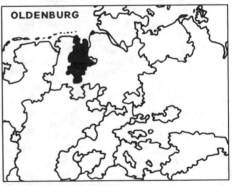

OLDENBURG

## OLDENBURG (1852-67)

A former grand duchy in northern Germany. Oldenburg's issues were replaced by those of the North German Confederation in 1868.

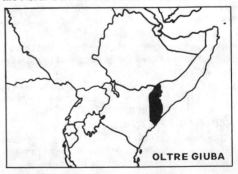

OLTRE GIUBA

**OLTRE GIUBA (1925-26)**

A district in eastern Africa, northeast of Kenya. In 1924, Britain ceded the area to Italy, and in 1926, it was incorporated into Italian Somaliland.

**OMAN-MUSCAT AND OMAN (1944-)**

Independent sultanate on the southeast coast of Arabia. During the first half of the 19th century, Oman ruled an empire stretching from the coast of Persia to Zanzibar, but its power declined until it came under British protection in the late 19th century.

Rebellious tribesmen in the interior fought the central government in the 1950s but were suppressed with British support. Later uprisings were quelled by 1975, with Iranian help.

In 1964 petroleum was discovered and has since become Oman's major export.

In 1979, leftist guerrilla activities resumed in the southwestern portion of the country, supported by the South Yemen People's Republic.

Accords signed with the United States in 1980 give American forces access to bases in Oman, which has become one of the cornerstones of U.S. military policy in the region.

**OPATOW (1918)**

A city in southern Poland. Local stamps were issued by the municipal authorities in 1918. The series was philatelically inspired and very speculative.

ORANGE FREE STATE

**ORANGE FREE STATE (1868-1900)**

A former independent republic in South Africa. The Orange Free State became the British Orange River Colony in 1900 and was incorporated into the Union of South Africa in 1910.

**ORCHHA (1913-50)**

A former feudatory state in the Bundelkhand agency in central India. On May 1, 1950, Orchha's issues were replaced by those of India.

**ORENSE (1936)**

A province of northwestern Spain. In October 1936, two sets of overprinted Spanish stamps were issued under the authority of the National Civil Governor of the province.

**ORLEANS (1953)**

A city in northern France. During a postal strike, in August 1953, the Orleans Chamber of Commerce issued stamps for use in the city.

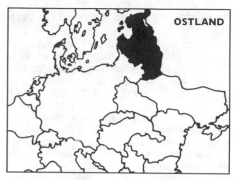

OSTLAND

**OSTLAND (1941-43)**

The German military district comprising Estonia, Latvia, Lithuania and adjacent portions of occupied Russia. German issues overprinted "Ostland" where used in the district.

**OSTROVA (MAHRISCH-OSTRAU) (1939)**

A city in Moravia (Czechoslovakia). In 1939 the municipal authorities overprinted Czechoslovakian stamps to commemorate union with Germany.

— **P** —

**PAHANG (1889-)**

The largest Malay state, under British protection after 1888. Pahang was occupied by Japan from 1942-45 and joined the Federation of Malaya in 1948. It is now a part of Malaysia.

**PAKHOI (1903-22)**

A port in the province of Kwangtung in southern China. France maintained a post office in Pakhoi from 1902 to 1922 using overprinted stamps of French Indo-China after 1903.

**PAKISTAN (1947-)**

Republic in south central Asia. Pakistan was formed in 1947 from the predominantly Moslem areas of India.

In April 1971, Eastern Pakistan seceded and in December 1971, after the Indo-Pakistani War, became independent as the Republic of Bangladesh.

Since 1977, Pakistan has been ruled by a repressive military dictatorship.

Tension with India has remained at a high level since the two countries became independent, and a number of wars have resolved little. Both nations maintain relatively large military forces.

**PALESTINE-BRITISH MILITARY ADMINISTRATION (1918-20)**

In 1918, British and Arab forces occupied the Turkish Asian provinces bordering on the eastern Mediterranean.

Britain's military administration issued stamps inscribed "E.E.F." (Egyptian Expeditionary Forces) that were used in Palestine, Trans-Jordan, Lebanon, Syria and in parts of Cilicia and northeast Egypt.

## PALESTINE-BRITISH ADMINISTRATION (1920-47)

In 1920, British civil administration was established in Palestine, the southernmost of the formerly Turkish provinces bordering on the Mediterranean.

In 1923, the League of Nations formally placed the territory under a British mandate. The Zionist Movement brought increasing Jewish immigration into Palestine, causing an increasingly bitter rivalry between Jewish Palestinians seeking to recreate the ancient Jewish homeland and Arab Palestinians, who wished to create an independent Arab Palestinian state.

In 1948, Britain partitioned the country between the two groups and withdrew her forces, precipitating the first Arab-Israeli War.

## PANAMA (1878-)

A republic occupying the Isthmus of Panama, between North and South America.

The area was a department of the Republic of Colombia until 1903 when U.S. intervention enabled the Panamanians to secure their independence.

The new Panamanian government immediately conceded to the U.S. a 10-mile wide strip of land bisecting the isthmus. Construction of the Panama Canal began the following year and was completed in 1914.

While the Panamanian economy benefited greatly from the Canal, the presence of a foreign sovereignty on their soil was a constant irritant to Panamanians' national pride.

During 1964-77, U.S.-Panamanian relations deteriorated over the status of the Canal, which became an emotionally charged issue throughout Latin America.

In 1978 a revised Canal treaty was ratified by the U.S. Senate. Implemented in 1979, this treaty provides for the gradual transfer of authority, with full Panamanian ownership by the end of the century. Panama assumed political sovereignty in the Canal Zone on Oct. 1, 1979.

## PAPUA NEW GUINEA (1952-)

Independent state occupying the eastern half of the island of New Guinea, in the western Pacific Ocean, north of Australia.

The southern portion of the country, Papua, was united administratively with the northern U.N. mandate of New Guinea in 1949, as Papua and New Guinea.

In 1972, the name of the territory became simply Papua New Guinea. In 1974, it achieved self-government under Australian authority and in 1975 became independent. The country retains close ties with Australia.

Papua New Guinea has numerous tribal divisions, with 750 local languages, and so the maintenance of the country's territorial integrity is a major priority. A secession movement in Bougainville brought violence in 1973 and 1976, and Indonesian incursions from West Irian occurred in 1978.

## PARAGUAY (1870-)

A republic in central South America. Paraguay became independent from Spain in 1811 and from La Plata in 1813.

In 1865, its territorial ambitions precipitated the War of the Triple Alliance (1865-70), in which Argentina, Brazil and Uruguay united to defeat Paraguay, annexing large areas of the country.

In 1935, Paraguay defeated Bolivia in the Chaco War, securing most of the disputed Gran Chaco region.

Paraguay has been ruled by Gen. Alfredo Stroessner since 1954. His regime is one of the most repressive in Latin America.

Since the 1960s, Paraguay has issued a huge number of attractive, philatelically inspired stamps. Most of these issues are omitted by the major catalogs.

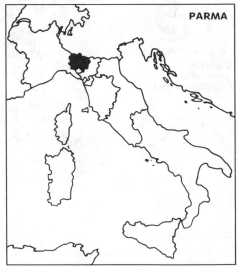

PARMA

## PARMA (1852-60)

Former duchy in northern Italy. Parma was annexed to Sardinia in 1860.

## PARNU (PERNAU) (1941)

A city in Estonia. Overprinted Russian stamps were issued by the German military commander.

## PATIALA (1884-1951)

A former convention state of British India. Patiala's issues were used concurrently with those of India after April 1, 1950. They were replaced by those of India on Jan. 1, 1951.

## PATMOS (1912-32)

One of the Dodecanese Islands in the eastern

Aegean Sea. The area was obtained from Turkey by Italy in 1912, at which time Italian stamps overprinted "Patmos" were issued.

In 1929, Patmos' issues were superseded by the general Aegean Island's issues, although two sets overprinted "Patmo" were released in 1930 and 1932.

## PEKING (1917-22)

The capital of China. Italian post offices in the city used Italian stamps overprinted "Pechino."

## PENANG (1948-)

A former British possession on the west coast of the Malay Peninsula. Penang has been a member of the Federation of Malaya since 1948.

## PENRHYN ISLAND (1902-32, 1973-)

A small island in the South Pacific Ocean, administered by New Zealand as part of the Cook Islands.

Penrhyn was annexed by Britain in 1888 and placed under New Zealand in 1901. Cook Islands stamps were used in Penrhyn prior to 1902 and during 1932-73.

Since 1973, stamps inscribed "Penrhyn Northern Cook Islands" have been in use on the island and on six neighboring islands.

## PERAK (1878-)

A sultanate on the west coast of the Malay Peninsula. Under British influence after 1795, Perak was incorporated into the Federated Malay States in 1895.

Perak joined the Federation of Malaya in 1948.

## PERLIS (1948-)

Former Siamese tributary state in the south Malay Peninsula. Perlis was under British control after 1909, joining the Federation of Malaya in 1948.

## PERU (1857-)

A republic on the west coast of South America. Peru was the center of numerous early Indian cultures. During the 14th-15th centuries, the Inca empire, expanding from its heartland in southeastern Peru, conquered an area stretching from northern Ecuador to central Chile, including Bolivia and northwestern Argentina.

In 1532-33, Spanish adventurers overthrew the Incas, and for three centuries, Peru was the center of Spanish power in South America.

Peru became independent from Spain in 1824, although independence did little to improve the condition of the lower classes of the country. A few wealthy families, along with foreign mining interests, controlled the economic life of Peru until recent years, often ruling through military juntas.

During 1968-80, Peru was ruled by a socialist military regime, which pursued an arduous program of nationalization and social reform. This program slowed after 1976, when popular dissat-

isfaction with the regime's economic policies brought a new military government to power.

In 1980, democratic civilian rule replaced the military dictatorship. The new government is attempting to stimulate Peru's inflation-ravaged economy by luring back private investment.

## PERU-PROVISIONAL ISSUES (1881-85)

During the Chilean-Peruvian War of 1879-84, Lima and Callao, the two chief cities of Peru, were occupied by Chile. Since stamps were supplied from these cities, outlying areas soon ran out of regular stamps and were forced to issue provisional stamps.

The post offices which issued such provisionals were Ancachs, Apurimac, Arequipa, Ayacucho, Chachapoyas, Chala, Chiclayo, Cuzco, Huacho, Moquegua, Paita, Pasco, Pisco, Piura, Puno and Yca.

## PETAH TIQVA (1908-9)

A city in Israel, near Tel-Aviv. Jewish National Fund labels were used for a time by the Austrian post office in the city.

## PETROVSK (1920)

A city in the Caucasus, southern Russia. Russian stamps surcharged with new values were issued by the local authorities.

## PHILIPPINES (1854-)

A large group of islands in the Malay Archipelago, north of Borneo. Occupied by Spain since the 16th century, the Philippines were ceded to the U.S. in 1898.

Nationalist resistance was suppressed by the U.S. by mid-1902, but local self-government was expanded until 1935, when the Philippine Commonwealth was established.

During World War II, the Philippines were occupied by Japan.

Following the defeat of the Japanese in September, 1945, prewar plans for independence were resumed, and on July 4, 1946, the Republic of the Philippines was declared.

Communist Huk guerrillas fought the central government after 1946 but were defeated by 1954.

Increasing leftist terrorism and student riots during 1970-71 led to a declaration of martial law by President Ferdinand Marcos. Marcos has continued to rule by decree, and, although some limited reforms have been made, political opposition has been suppressed, and corruption within the government is rampant.

The Philippines has traditionally been aligned with the United States, but Philippine disillusionment after the U.S. withdrawal from Indo-China in 1975 and U.S. displeasure with the Marcos dictatorship have cooled relations in recent years.

## PISCOPI (1912-32)

One of the Dodecanese Islands in the eastern Aegean Sea. Piscopi was obtained from Turkey by Italy in 1912, at which time Italian stamps overprinted "Piscopi" were issued.

Piscopi's issues were superseded by those of the Aegean Islands in 1929, although two sets overprinted for the island were issued in 1930 and 1932.

## PITCAIRN ISLANDS (1940-)

A group of small islands in the South Pacific Ocean. Originally settled in 1790 by mutineers from HMS "Bounty," Pitcairn, the only inhabited island in the group, has been a British colony since the 19th century.

## POLA (1945)

A city on the Adriatic coast of Yugoslavia. Stamps of Italy and the Italian Social Republic were surcharged for use under the authority of the Yugoslavia military forces.

## POLAND (1860-65, 1918-)

A republic in eastern Europe, between Germany and Russia. During the Middle Ages, Poland was the dominant Christian power in eastern Europe, but after c. 1700, its power declined.

Between 1772 and 1795, it was absorbed by Russia, Prussia and Austria and did not reappear as an independent nation until 1918.

In the aftermath of World War I, Poland fought both Germany and Russia, acquiring large territories from both, as well as from Austria and Lithuania. During this period, many locals were used.

In 1939, Poland was invaded by Germany and the Soviet Union, igniting World War II. The two powers divided Poland between them, Germany occupying all of the country after its invasion of Russia in 1941. During the war, Poland suffered terribly, and some six million Poles, half of them Jews, were killed.

A Polish Government in Exile was established in London and was recognized by the Western Allies, but after Soviet forces occupied Poland during 1944-45, a more malleable government was established by the Russians.

The U.S.S.R.'s 1939 acquisitions were recognized by the new Polish regime. In return for this loss of about 70,000 square miles in the east, Poland was awarded about 40,000 square miles of German territory in the west.

In 1947, the Communist regime was finally established and began a thorough program of socialization. Declining farm production and harsh working conditions sparked riots in 1956, which brought a moderation of government policy. In 1970, a new series of riots brought a change of government and increased emphasis on the production of consumer goods.

Although more moderate than many other Communist states, Poland is closely linked with the U.S.S.R. It joined in the 1968 invasion of Czechoslovakia.

In the summer of 1980, the Polish labor movement Solidarity launched a series of strikes that brought major concessions from the government. Increasing democratization brought intense Soviet pressure to bear on the Polish leadership, resulting in a government crackdown in late 1981.

## POLISH CORPS IN ITALY (1945)

Several issues were made by the Polish Corps in Italy, under Gen. W. Anders, for use by the troops and by civilians in areas occupied by Polish forces.

## POLISH CORPS IN RUSSIA (1918)

In 1917, Polish prisoners of war, captured by the Germans, were formed into the Polish Corps to fight, under German Command, against the Russians.

A number of Russian stamps were overprinted for use by this unit.

## POLISH GOVERNMENT IN EXILE (1941-45)

After the German-Soviet invasion of 1939, the Polish Government in Exile operated from London. During 1941-45, stamps were issued for use on letters posted from Free Polish merchant vessels and warships fighting against the Axis powers.

## POLISH MILITARY POST IN RUSSIA (1917-18)

After the Russian Revolution of 1917, the Polish forces fighting with the Russian Army regrouped into a separate army corps.

Contemporary Russian stamps were overprinted for their use.

## POLISH OFFICES ABROAD (1919-21, 1925-39)

Poland maintained post offices in Constantinople from 1919-21 and Danzig from 1925-39.

## PONCE (1898)

A town in Puerto Rico. U.S. forces issued a provisional stamp for use after the occupation of the city from Spain in August 1898.

## PONEWESCH (PANEVEZYS) (1941)

A city in central Lithuania. Overprinted Russian stamps were issued by the German military commander.

## PONTA DELGADA (1892-31)

An administrative district of the Azores. Stamps of Ponta Delgada were replaced by issues of the Azores in 1905, which in turn were replaced by regular Portuguese issues in 1931.

## PONTEVEDRA (1937)

A province of northwestern Spain, bordering the Atlantic Ocean and Portugal.

The Nationalist authorities overprinted contemporary Spanish stamps for use in the province in 1937.

## POONCH (1876-94)

A former tributary state of Jammu and Kashmir in northern India. Poonch's issues were replaced by those of India in 1894.

## PORT ARTHUR AND DAIREN (1946-51)

Port and peninsula in southern Manchuria, bordering on the Strait of Pohai. Under Japanese rule from 1895-1945, the area was occupied by the Soviets after World War II and turned over to the Chinese Communists in 1946.

In 1951, the regional issues were overprinted by the general issues of the People's Republic of China in 1951.

## PORT LAGOS (1893-98)

A port in northern Greece. Unoverprinted French stamps were used by the French post office in the city after 1870 and during 1893-98, stamps of France, overprinted "Port-Lagos" and new values in Turkish currency were used.

## PORT SAID (1899-1931)

A major Egyptian port on the Mediterranean Sea. The French post office in the city operated from 1867 through March 31, 1931.

## PORTUGAL (1853- )

A republic on the western coast of the Iberian Peninsula in southwest Europe. Independence was established in 1095 and during the 15th and 16th centuries, Portugal built a far-flung overseas empire.

Portuguese power declined rapidly after 1580, although Portugal maintained much of her colonial empire until 1975. Portugal was a kingdom from 1139 until 1910 when the republic was established.

From 1932 to 1968, Portugal was ruled by Premier Antonio de Oliveira Salazar, an authoritarian dictator. After 1968, Salazar's policies were continued by his successors, and the regime became increasingly unpopular, largely because of the country's debilitating wars against nationalist movements in the African colonies.

In 1974, a military coup overthrew the government, and the new liberal regime quickly granted independence to Angola, the Cape Verde Islands, Guinea-Bissau, Mozambique and St. Thome-Principe. Autonomy was granted to Macao, Madeira and the Azores, while the collapse of authority in Portuguese Timor brought that territory's occupation by Indonesia in 1976.

The government moved increasingly to the left during 1975, and the Communists, despite set-backs at the polls, increased their influence. In November, a counter-coup halted this trend, and free elections in 1976 gave Portugal a Socialist government.

Portugal's swift change from a rigidly controlled rightist dictatorship, through a flirtation with communism, to a socialist democracy has brought enormous economic strains. Despite considerable Western aid, Portugal's economic and political life remains in disarray.

## PORTUGUESE AFRICA (1898, 1919, 1945)

Three general issues were released by Portugal for use in its African colonies (Angola, Cape Verde, Portuguese Guinea, St. Thomas and Prince Islands, and Mozambique).

These were used concurrently with the issues of the separate colonies.

## PORTUGUESE CONGO (CABINDA) (1893-1920)

A district of Angola lying north of the Congo River, separated from Angola by Zaire. It was administered as the Portuguese Congo until its incorporation with the colony of Angola.

## PORTUGUESE GUINEA (1881-1974)

Former Portuguese colony in West Africa. The area was explored by the Portuguese in the 15th century but was not colonized until the 19th century. In the 1960s an independence movement in the interior of the colony began a guerrilla war that culminated in the country's independence in 1974.

## PORTUGUESE INDIA (1871-1962)

A number of Portuguese holdings on the west coast of India. Occupied by Portugal since the 16th century, these territories were seized by India in 1961 and absorbed into the Indian republic.

Existing stocks of Portuguese Indian stamps were sold for about 10 days following the invasion and were valid until Jan. 7, 1962.

Two sets for the colony were issued in early 1962 by Portugal, who did not recognize India's action. The stamps were never used in the territories.

## PRAGUE (1918)

Capital city of Czechoslovakia. During November 1918, the Czech Revolutionary Committee operated a local postal service in Prague, staffed by Boy Scouts.

## PRIAMUR AND MARITIME PROVINCES (1921-22)

A region in southeastern Siberia, west of Manchuria. In May 1921, a monarchist, anti-Bolshevik regime was established, with Japanese support. This government was never secure, and with the Japanese withdrawal from Siberia in October 1922, it collapsed.

## PRINCE EDWARD ISLAND (1861-73)

An island in the Gulf of St. Lawrence, in northeastern North America. Prince Edward Island was a British colony until 1873 when it joined the Canadian Confederation.

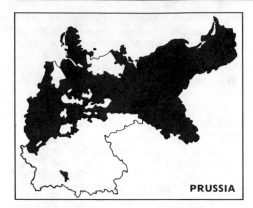

**PRUSSIA**

### PRUSSIA (1850-67)

Former kingdom in northern Germany. By the early 18th century, Prussia was a major European power, and by 1870, she occupied most of northern Germany and ruled two-thirds of the German population.

Prussia dominated the German Empire established in 1870.

Stamps of Prussia were issued from 1850-67 and were replaced on Jan. 1, 1868, by issues of the North German Postal District.

### PRZEDBORZ (1917-18)

A city in south-central Poland. Several series of stamps were issued during World War I by the municipal authorities, under the authority of the Austrian military commander.

### PSKOW (PLESKAU) (1941-42)

A city in northwestern Russia. During World War II, stamps were issued for the district by the German military commander.

### PUERTO RICO (1855-1900)

A large island east of Hispaniola in the West Indies, Puerto Rico was discovered by Columbus on his second voyage in 1493.

Puerto Rico remained a Spanish colony until 1898 when it was occupied by the U.S. during the Spanish-American War. The island was subsequently ceded to the U.S. and since 1952, has been a commonwealth in association with the U.S.

Puerto Rican issues of 1855-73 were issued in Cuba as well as Puerto Rico. Separate issues appeared after 1873. In 1898, two provisional stamps were issued by the U.S. military forces in Puerto Rico, followed by overprinted U.S. stamps during 1899-1900. Since 1900, regular U.S. issues have been in use.

### PUKA (1941)

A city in Estonia. Russian stamps were overprinted for use in the city during July and August 1941 by the German military commander.

## — Q —

### QATAR (1957-)

An Arab sheikdom on the Persian Gulf.

Long under Persian rule, Qatar became independent in the 19th century. It was occupied by the Ottoman Turks from 1871 to 1913 and came under British protection in 1916.

In 1971, Qatar declared its independence, after considering and rejecting a plan to join in a federation with the United Arab Emirates.

Qatar is oil-rich, and its sole economic weakness is a lack of skilled labor. Its oil earnings give it one of the highest per capita incomes in the world.

### QU'AITI STATE (1942-67)

Former British protectorate in south Arabia. The Qu'aiti sultan was recognized as ruler of the entire Hadhramaut, although the Kathiri State of Seiyun maintained a measure of autonomy.

The region was absorbed by the People's Republic of Southern Yemen in 1967.

### QUEENSLAND (1860-1913)

A state in northeast Australia. A British crown colony from 1859-1901, Queensland joined with five other British colonies to form the Commonwealth of Australia in 1901.

### QUELIMANE (1914-22)

A province of Mozambique. Quelimane issues were superseded by those of Mozambique in 1922.

## — R —

### RAJASTHAN (1948-50)

A state in northern India created by the merger of 18 Rajput states, several of which had hitherto issued their own stamps.

### RAJPEEPLA (1880-86)

A former feudatory state in western India.

### RAKWERE (WESENBERG) (1941)

A city in Estonia. During July-August 1941, the German military commander overprinted Russian stamps for use in the district.

### RAS AL KHAIMA (1964-72)

A sheikdom in the Trucial States, in eastern Arabia, bordering on the Persian Gulf. Under British protection from 1892-1971, Ras al Khaima joined the United Arab Emirates in 1972.

### RASEINIAI (ROSSINGEN) (1919, 1941)

A city in central Lithuania. A local stamp was issued by the municipal authorities in January 1919. For a period after the city's occupation by Germany in June 1941, overprinted Russian stamps were used.

### REDONDA (1979-)

A tiny, uninhabited island dependency of Antigua. On Jan. 10, 1979, Antigua began to issue stamps for Redonda, on the premise that planned economic development of the island would create a need for them. In the meantime, they are postally valid on Antigua.

### REICHENBERG-MAFFERSDORF (1938)

Two cities in the Sudetenland (Czechoslovakia). In 1938 they overprinted a number of Czechoslovakian stamps to commemorate union with Germany.

### REUNION (1852, 1885-1974)

An island in the Indian Ocean. Reunion was a French colony from the 17th century until 1947, when it became an integral part of France.

On Jan. 1, 1975, Reunion's stamps were replaced by those of France.

### RHINE PALATINATE (1947-49)

A district of western Germany occupied by France after World War II.

### RHINELAND (1923)

The area of Germany lying west of the Rhine River. After World War I, France attempted to establish a satellite state in the region, which contained rich mineral deposits and much of Germany's heavy industry. An abortive Rhineland Republic (October 1923-January 1924) produced a number of overprints on contemporary German issues.

### RHODES (1912-45)

The largest of the Dodecanese Islands in the eastern Aegean Sea. The center of a prehistoric civilization from c. 3500 B.C., Rhodes' strategic position in the eastern Mediterranean area brought many foreign masters including the Greeks, Romans, Arabs, Crusaders and after 1522, the Turks.

In 1912, Rhodes was obtained from Turkey by Italy, and Italian stamps overprinted "Rodi" were issued. Rhodes continued to issue its own stamps which were used throughout the Dodecanese Islands, concurrently with the general issues of the Aegean Islands.

During 1943-45, Rhodes was occupied by the Germans. Occupied by British forces in 1945, Rhodes, along with the rest of the island group, was annexed to Greece in 1947.

### RHODESIA (1890-1924, 1965-)

A former British administrative unit in southeastern Africa. The area was under the British South Africa Co. until 1924, when Rhodesia was divided into Northern Rhodesia and Southern Rhodesia, under direct British rule.

During 1953-63, these two colonies were united with the Nyasaland Protectorate to form the Federation of Rhodesia and Nyasaland.

With the dissolution of the federation, the three colonies were again separated. Northern Rhodesia became independent as Zambia in 1964, and in 1965, Southern Rhodesia assumed the name Rhodesia and declared its independence from Great Britain.

### RHODESIA AND NYASALAND (1954-63)

A former federation comprising the British territories of Northern Rhodesia, Southern Rhodesia and Nyasaland in southeast Africa.

### RIO DE ORO (1905-24)

A former Spanish colony on the northwest coast of Africa. Rio de Oro was incorporated into the Spanish Sahara in 1924.

### RIO MUNI (1960)

Former Spanish colony on the Gulf of Guinea, bordering on Cameroon and Gabon.

Rio Muni was claimed by Spain in 1885 and formed part of Spanish Guinea 1909-59. In 1959 it became an overseas province of Spain. In 1968 it merged with Fernando Po to form the independent Republic of Equatorial Guinea.

### RIOUW ARCHIPELAGO (1954-60)

A group of islands in Indonesia, located south of Singapore. Because of differing rates of exchange between the currency used in the islands with that used in the rest of Indonesia, several series of Dutch Indies and Indonesian stamps were overprinted for use in the area.

### RIZEH (1909-14)

A Turkish port (now Rize) on the Black Sea. After 1909, stamps of the Russian Levant overprinted "Rizeh" were used by the Russian postal service in the city.

### ROKISKIS (RAKISCHKI) (1941)

A city in Lithuania. Overprinted Russian stamps were issued by the Germany military authorities after Rokiskis' occupation in June 1941.

### ROMAGNA (1859-60)

A territory in north-central Italy, under Papal rule after 1503. In 1859 a provisional government replaced the Papal authorities, and in 1860 Romagna was annexed to the Kingdom of Sardinia.

ROMAN STATES

## ROMAN STATES (1852-70)

The greater part of central Italy, over which the Pope acted as temporal, as well as religious, ruler.

During 1859-61, most of the area joined Sardinia. The districts around Rome remained under Papal control, which was maintained by French troops. In 1870, the French withdrew, and Italy absorbed the remaining Papal territory, except for the enclave of Vatican City.

## ROMANIA (1865-)

A republic in southeastern Europe, bordering on the Danube River and the Black Sea.

Under Turkish rule since the 15th century, Romania was formed from the union of the principalities of Wallachia and Moldavia in 1861, under Ottoman suzerainty. In 1878, as a result of the Russo-Turkish war, Romania became independent.

Although ruled by a Hohenzollern dynasty, related to the ruling family of Germany, Romania did not enter World War I until August 1916, and then joined the Allies. After initial successes, Romanian forces were routed, and by January 1917, almost all of the country had been overrun by Germany, Austria and Bulgaria.

Romania enjoyed considerably greater military success after the armistice, overrunning a large part of Hungary and occupying territories from Austria, Russia and Bulgaria. By the final peace (1920), Romania doubled in size.

During the 1930s, the Iron Guard, a Romanian fascist movement, gained control of the government, and in 1941, Romania entered World War II as an ally of Germany. In 1944, the regime was overthrown by King Michael, with Soviet support, and Romania joined the Allies.

Soviet troops occupied the country after World War II, forcing Michael to abdicate and establishing the people's republic on Dec. 30, 1947.

From the 1950s, Romania has pursued an increasingly independent foreign policy. In 1959, Soviet troops were refused entry into the country, and during the 1960s political ties were strengthened with China, Israel and the West.

## ROMANIAN OFFICES IN TURKEY (1896-1914, 1919)

During 1896-1919, Romania maintained a post office in Constantinople, overprinting regular issues for use there.

## ROSS DEPENDENCY (1957-)

The sector of Antarctica under New Zealand administration.

## ROUAD, ILE (1916-20)

An island in the Mediterranean, off the coast of Latakia. Ile Rouad was occupied by the French from Turkey in 1916, after which stamps of the French offices in Levant were overprint- ed "Ile Rouad." The area was attached to Syria in 1920.

## RUANDA-URUNDI (1924-62)

Two areas of central Africa, between Zaire and Tanzania. Formerly part of German East Africa, they were occupied by Belgian Congo forces during World War I and subsequently were administered by Belgium under a League of Nations (later U.N.) mandate.

They became independent in 1962 as the Republic of Rwanda and the Kingdom of Burundi.

## RUMBERG (1938)

A city in the Sudetenland (Czechoslovakia). Municipal authorities overprinted Czechoslovakian stamps to commemorate the union with Germany.

## RUSSIA (1857-)

A country comprising the greater portion of eastern Europe and northern Asia. European Russia was ruled by Norse dynasties until the Mongol conquest in the 13th century.

After the 16th century, Muscovy (Moscow) became the center of a resurgent Russian state, which for several hundred years steadily expanded its borders.

A major European power after 1700, Russian strength deteriorated in the late 19th and early 20th centuries. Mounting frustrations with the autocratic rule of the tsars and military defeats in World War I brought the fall of the monarchy in March 1917.

In November, the liberal Kerensky regime was overthrown by the Bolsheviks (Communists) who made peace with Germany and began consolidation of their power.

Anti-Bolshevik forces (the "White Russians") quickly formed throughout the country. White Russian regimes were established in western and southern Russia and throughout Siberia, and Bolshevik control was limited to northern and central Europe and Russia. Britain, France, Japan and the U.S. became involved in the civil war, but the inability of the various White Russian governments to cooperate with each other, or to meet the legitimate needs of the people, made it possible for the Bolshevik Red Army to have generally established Soviet authority by the end of 1920.

During 1920-23 the government consolidated its position. Although a number of border provinces (Poland, Finland, the Baltic States and Bessarabia) were lost, the newly formed Union of Soviet Socialist Republics included almost all of the territory of the old empire.

Lenin's death in 1924 precipitated a power struggle within the Communist leadership, with Josef Stalin ultimately emerging as the absolute ruler of the country. During the 1920s and early 1930s, Stalin exiled his opponents within the party. From the mid-1930s through 1953, he purged any suspected opposition through show trials and executions. Millions of Russians died.

Following World War I, when both Germany and Russia were ostracized by the powers, the two countries worked closely and secretly, the Russians supplying Germany with armaments forbidden by the Treaty of Versailles, while German officers trained the Red Army. Alarmed by the German threat after Hitler's rise to power, the U.S.S.R. at first attempted to take a strong stand against German expansionism in the 1930s.

By 1938, however, Russia was convinced that the Allies would not fight and in 1939 the Soviet-German Non-Aggression Pact was signed. A few months later, Germany invaded Poland, while the Soviets occupied southern Poland, the Baltic States and Bessarabia.

In 1941, Germany attacked Russia, and the U.S.S.R. joined the Allies. At first successful, the Germans were pushed back after the end of 1942, and during 1944-45, Soviet forces occupied most of Eastern Europe.

With the peace, the Soviets retained their 1939-40 acquisitions, and Soviet troops forced the establishment of satellite regimes in the rest of the area during 1945-48.

Since World War II, the U.S.S.R. has concentrated on economic and military development. It has exercised an aggressive foreign policy and has not hesitated to use military force as an accepted instrument of policy.

After 1956, the brutal policies of Stalin were officially denounced, and under his successor, Nikita Khrushchev, the government was less harsh. Krushchev was himself deposed in 1964, and his successors have become increasingly rigid and totalitarian.

## RUSSIA-ARMY OF THE NORTHWEST (1919)

Overprinted Russian stamps were used briefly in 1919 by Gen. Nicolai N. Yudenich's White Russian Army operating in the Baltic area, southwest of Leningrad.

## RUSSIAN COMPANY FOR STEAM SHIPPING AND TRADE (ROPIT) (1865-68)

The offices of this private company were used as postal branches under agreement with the Russian government. The company issued several stamps for this service, which were supplanted by official issues for the Russian Levant in May 1868.

In 1918, a number of the company's agencies in the Turkish Empire were reopened. Anticipating the revival of business following World War I, ROPIT overprinted its stocks of Russian Levant stamps with its initials and new values. The collapse of General Denikin's South Russian government, however, brought the closing of the agencies, and the overprinted stamps were never placed in use.

## RUSSIAN OFFICES IN CHINA (1899-1920)

During 1899-1920, Russia maintained post offices in a number of Chinese cities. Russian stamps overprinted "China" in Russian or surcharged in cents and dollars were used for these post offices.

## RUSSIAN OFFICES IN THE TURKISH EMPIRE (1863-1923)

Russia, along with many other European nations, maintained post offices in the Ottoman Empire until the Treaty of Lausanne (1923) abolished their extraterritorial postal privileges.

## RWANDA (1962-)

A republic in East Africa. Until 1916, it was part of German East Africa. The territory, along with Burundi, was administered by Belgium under a League of Nations (later U.N.) mandate as the Trust Territory of Ruanda-Urundi.

On July 1, 1962, Rwanda became an independent republic.

Rwanda is one of the most densely populated countries in Africa and is very poor. The government is attempting to implement ambitious economic and social improvement programs.

## RYUKYU ISLANDS (1947-72)

A chain of islands located between Japan and Taiwan, the Ryukyus were under Japanese rule until 1945, when they were occupied by the U.S. after one of the bloodiest campaigns in the Pacific Theater of World War II.

They remained under U.S. administration until May 15, 1972, when they reverted to Japan.

Japanese stamps, overprinted by local postmasters, and one crude printed provisional were used until 1948, when the occupation authorities began issuing stamps for general use.

Since the return of the islands to Japan, regular Japanese stamps have been in use.

## — S —

## SAAR (1920-35, 1947-59)

A coal-rich district of Germany, southeast of Luxembourg. The Saar was occupied by France after World War I and was placed under League of Nations administration, with France controlling the mines as part of the German war reparations.

In 1935, a plebiscite resulted in the reunion of the area with Germany. The Saar was reoccupied by France in 1945, returning to the German Federal Republic in 1957.

Saar stamps continued to be used until their final replacement by German issues in 1959.

## SABAH (1964-)

A state in northeastern Borneo. Formerly British North Borneo, the territory assumed the name Sabah in 1963 when it joined with Malaya, Sarawak and Singapore to form the Federation of Malaysia.

## ST. CHRISTOPHER (ST. KITTS) (1870-90)

An island in the West Indies, southeast of Puerto Rico. Formerly a presidency of the Leeward Islands, St. Kitts was united with Nevis in 1903 to form the presidency of St. Kitts-Nevis.

In 1952, this designation was changed to St. Christopher-Nevis-Anguilla.

## ST. HELENA (1856-)

An island in the southern Atlantic Ocean. Under British rule since 1673, the colony includes the dependencies of Ascension and Tristan da Cunha.

## ST. KITTS-NEVIS (1903-)

A group of islands in the West Indies, southeast of Puerto Rico. Formed in 1903 as a presidency of the British Leeward Islands colony, the designation of St. Christopher-Nevis-Anguilla was adopted in 1952.

In 1956, this became a separate British colony, securing independence in 1967 as St. Kitts-Nevis-Anguilla. Soon after independence, Anguilla seceded from the union, declaring its independence from both St. Kitts-Nevis and Great Britain.

## ST. LUCIA (1860-)

An island in the West Indies. The island was disputed between France and Britain from 1627-1803, with Britain acquiring control after 1803.

On March 1, 1967, St. Lucia became an independent associated state in the British Commonwealth. It became fully independent on Feb. 22, 1979.

Funded by foreign aid, St. Lucia is pursuing an ambitious economic development program.

## ST. MARIE DE MADAGASCAR (1894-98)

An island off the east coast of Madagascar. Occupied by the French in the 17th century, it was a French colony until 1898, when it was attached to Madagascar.

## ST. NAZAIRE (1945)

A city in northern France, at the mouth of the Loire River. In 1945, Allied advances cut St. Nazaire off from the rest of German-occupied France.

During this period, the local Chamber of Commerce issued provisional stamps for local use.

## ST. PIERRE AND MIQUELON (1885-)

Two small islands off the southern coast of Newfoundland. Originally occupied by the French in 1604, they are the only remnants of a once-vast French North American empire.

## ST. THOMAS AND PRINCE ISLAND (1869-1975)

Two small islands in the Gulf of Guinea. Portuguese possessions since 1490, St. Thomas and Prince became the independent Democratic Republic of Sao Tome and Principe on July 12, 1975.

## ST. VINCENT (1861-)

An island in the West Indies. St. Vincent was a British colony from 1763-1969. On Oct. 27, 1969, St. Vincent became an independent associated state in the British Commonwealth. It became fully independent on Oct. 27, 1979.

## ST. VINCENT-GRENADINES (1973-)

A small group of islands administered by St. Vincent.

## SALONICA (1909-13, 1944)

A major port in northern Greece, on the Aegean Sea. The Russian post office in Salonica used overprinted Russian Levant stamps after 1909, along with the general issues of the Russian offices in Turkey.

The Russian set was quickly followed by a similar series issued by Italy for its post office in Salonica.

During 1916, British issues, overprinted "Levant" were used by the British forces in Salonica.

During the last stages of World War II, Italian stamps were overprinted by the German military commander for use in Salonica.

## SALVADOR, EL (1867-)

A republic in Central America, bordering on the Pacific Ocean.

El Salvador was conquered by the Spanish in the 1520s and was ruled as part of the captaincy-general of Guatemala until 1821. It came under Mexican rule briefly, then formed part of the Central American Confederation until 1839.

Since independence, El Salvador's history has been marked by political instability. Coups, countercoups, inequitable land ownership and a long-running civil war between Marxist guerrillas and right-wing elements of the military make the country's future extremely uncertain.

## SAMOA (1877-)

A group of islands in the South Pacific Ocean, east of Fiji. The native kingdom of Samoa was under the influence of the U.S., Britain and Germany until 1899 when the islands were partitioned between the U.S. and Germany with Great Britain withdrawing her claims.

The eastern portion of the islands were ceded to the U.S. by the local chiefs from 1900-04. American Samoa has since been administered by the U.S., using regular U.S. stamps.

Western Samoa was seized from Germany by New Zealand forces in 1914, and New Zealand subsequently administered the western islands under a mandate from the League of Nations (later the U.N.).

Western Samoa became independent on Jan. 1, 1962. In 1977 the country's name was changed to Samoa. Ties to New Zealand remain strong.

## SAMOS (1878-1915)

An island in the Aegean Sea. Under Turkish

rule since the 15th century, Samos became an autonomous principality in 1832, under British, French and Russian protection.

In September 1912, a provisional government was established, and Turkish troops withdrew. In 1913, Samos was united with Greece.

### SAN MARINO (1877-)

A tiny independent republic in central Italy. Surrounded on all sides by Italy, San Marino has maintained its independence since the 4th century A.D. It is the world's smallest republic and claims to be Europe's oldest state.

Postage stamps and tourism are the country's major industries.

### SAN SEBASTIAN (1936-37)

The capital of the province of Guipuzcoa in northern Spain.

Nationalist authorities overprinted a number of Spanish stamps for use in the city during the Spanish Civil War.

### SANTA CRUZ DE TENERIFE (1937)

A province of Spain in the Canary Islands.

A set of overprinted Spanish stamps was issued in 1937 by the Nationalist authorities.

### SANTA MARIA DE ALBARRACIA (1937)

A city in the province of Teruel in northern Spain.

Two overprinted Spanish stamps were issued in 1937 under the authority of the Nationalist Inspector-General of Posts.

### SAO TOME AND PRINCIPE (1975-)

The Portuguese colony of St. Thomas and Prince became the independent Democratic Republic of Sao Tome and Principe on July 12, 1975.

### SARAWAK (1869-)

A state on the northwestern coast of Borneo. In 1893, the area was ceded to Sir James Brooke

SARDINIA

by the sultan of Brunei, and Sarawak remained an independent state until 1888 when it accepted British control of its foreign affairs.

The Brooke dynasty ruled until 1946, when the last rajah ceded Sarawak to Britain. In 1963, the colony joined with Malaya, Singapore and Sabah (North Borneo) to form the Federation of Malaysia.

### SARDINIA (1851-62)

A former kingdom in northwestern Italy. The Sardinian House of Savoy led the Italian nationalist movement, absorbing most of the many Italian states during 1859-61.

In 1861, the Sardinian kingdom became the Kingdom of Italy, which began to issue stamps in 1862.

### SARNY (1941)

A city in the western Ukraine. After the German occupation of the city in 1941, stamps were issued by the German military commander.

### SASENO (1923)

A small island off the coast of Albania. Occupied by Italy in 1914, it was formally returned to Albania in 1947.

### SAUDI ARABIA (1932-)

Nejd, in northern Arabia, was long the center of the fundamentalist Wahabbi Moslem sect. Under Turkish control until 1913, Nejd was freed by Ibn Saud, a warrior king who immediately set about the enlargement of his domain. He conquered the Turkish province of Hasa in 1913, the Kingdom of the Hejaz in 1925, and most of Asir in 1926. In 1932 the kingdom adopted the name Saudi Arabia.

Oil was discovered in 1936, and petroleum soon became the country's major export and economic mainstay. Saudi Arabia has played a leading role in OPEC.

Saudi Arabia is an absolute monarchy, ruled by the Saud family. Mecca and Medina, the holy cities of Islam, are within the country, and the Koran is the law of the land.

Saudi Arabia has been an active force in the Arab movement for a Palestinian state. Since the 1967 Arab-Israeli War, it has given annual subsidies to the Arab frontline states, as well as to the various Palestinian political groups. The Saudis were among the leaders in the 1973-74 oil boycott of the West.

### SAURASHTRA (1864-1949)

A former feudatory state, actually named Junagadh, in western India. Its stamps were replaced by those of the United State of Saurashtra in 1949.

### SAURASHTRA, UNITED STATE OF (1949-50)

A state formed in 1948 with the merger of over 400 states and territories in western India. Indian stamps have been used in the state since April 1, 1950.

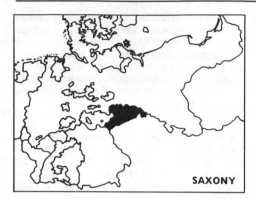

SAXONY

## SAXONY (1850-67)

Former kingdom in central Germany. Saxon issues were replaced by those of the North German Confederation in 1868.

## SCARPANTO (1912-32)

The Greek island of Karpathos in the Dodecanese Islands in the eastern Aegean Sea.

Obtained from Turkey by Italy in 1912, at which time Italian stamps overprinted "Scarpanto," the Italian name for the island, were issued.

Scarpanto's issues were superseded by those of the Aegean Islands in 1929, although two sets were overprinted for the island in 1930 and 1932.

## SCHLESWIG (1920)

An area of the central Jutland Peninsula, in Germany and Denmark. Under German rule from 1864-1918, the province was divided into two districts after World War I.

A plebiscite in 1920, resulted in the northern portion voting to join Denmark and the southern district voting for reunion with Germany.

## SCHLESWIG-HOLSTEIN (1850-67)

Former duchies in northern Germany, forming the southern portion of the Jutland Peninsula. Under Danish control until 1864, the duchies were seized by Austria and Prussia, who subsequently fought the Austro-Prussian War (1866), after which they were absorbed by Prussia.

A plebiscite in 1920 resulted in northern Schleswig being returned to Denmark.

## SCINDE (1852-54)

A district on the lower Indus River, bordering on the Arabian Sea. Scinde is now part of Pakistan.

The Scinde was occupied by Great Britain in 1850 and separate stamps were used until their replacement by the first Indian issue in 1854.

## SCUTARI (1909-11, 1915-20)

A seaport in northern Albania. The Italian post office in Scutari used overprinted Italian stamps from 1909-11 and during the World War I Italian occupation.

In December 1918, the Italians withdrew and Scutari was placed under an international commission to protect it from Serbia.

Until March 1920, various stamps were issued specifically for use in Scutari, after which time the city was replaced under Albanian administration.

## SEGOVIA (1937)

A province of north central Spain.

Contemporary Spanish stamps were overprinted by the National Civil Governor in October and November 1937.

## SEIYUN, KATHIRI STATE OF (1942-67)

A former British protectorate in south Arabia. The area was autonomous until its incorporation into the People's Republic of Southern Yemen.

## SELANGOR (1881-)

Sultanate in the south Malay Peninsula. Selangor was under British protection after 1874 and joined the Federation of Malaya in 1948.

## SENEGAL (1887-)

A republic on the west coast of Africa. The first French settlement began in 1626, and the area remained under either French or (temporarily) British rule.

After 1854, France used Senegal as its base for expansion in West Africa. In 1904 French West Africa was established, with its capital at Dakar, Senegal's capital. French West African stamps were used 1944-59.

In 1958, Senegal became an autonomous state within the French Union, and in 1959 it joined with the French Sudan to form the Federation of Mali. Senegal withdrew from the union in 1960, and on June 26, 1960, became independent. It retains close ties with France.

## SENEGAMBIA AND NIGER (1903-06)

A French African administrative unit (1902-04) comprising French holdings in the Senegal and Niger area.

In 1904, the area was renamed Upper Senegal and Niger, and in 1906, stamps of this new entity were released.

SERBIA

**SERBIA (1866-1918, 1941-44)**

A former state in the Balkans, now part of Yugoslavia. Serbia was a powerful kingdom until its conquest by the Turks in 1389.

Serbia gained autonomy in 1829 and independence in 1878. Serbia assumed leadership of the movement to unite the southern Slavs in the early 20th century, especially after the military defeat of Turkey during the Balkan Wars (1912-13).

The assassination of the heir to the Austro-Hungarian crown by a Serbian nationalist in 1914 led to an Austro-Hungarian declaration of war on Serbia, which rapidly expanded into World War I.

By the end of 1915, Serbia was occupied by German, Austrian and Bulgarian forces, while the Serbian government and army retired to Corfu.

With the collapse of Austria-Hungary in the autumn of 1918, Serbia became the nucleus of the Yugoslav state. The Kingdom of the Serbs, Croats and Slovenes was established on Dec. 1, 1918, under the Serbian monarchy. In 1929 the state was renamed Yugoslavia. During 1941-44, Serbia was recreated as a German puppet state.

**SEVILLE (1936-38)**

A province in southern Spain.

During the Civil War, a large number of contemporary Spanish Republican stamps were overprinted under the authority of the local Nationalist military commander.

**SEYCHELLES (1890-)**

A group of 86 islands in the western Indian Ocean. Formerly occupied by France, the Seychelles have been under British rule since 1810.

The Seychelles were ruled as part of Mauritius until 1903. During 1903-76, the islands were administered as a separate colony. Although the ruling party preferred to continue the Seychelles' association with Britain, continuing pressure from the OAU and United Nations forced it to declare independence on June 29, 1976.

In 1977, the government was overthrown in a coup, and a socialist regime came to power. In 1979, opposition political parties were abolished. The U.S.S.R. has actively attempted to establish its influence in the country.

**SHAN STATES (1943)**

During 1942-43, the Shan States of eastern Burma were separated from the puppet Burmese government established by the Japanese.

In December 1943, the Shan States were reincorporated into Burma, and their stamps were overprinted for use throughout the country.

**SHANGHAI (1865-98)**

One of the major cities and ports of China. Shanghai was opened to European settlement in 1843. In 1864, dissatisfied with the high charges of the Chinese private postal agencies, a postal system was organized under the Municipal Council.

Agencies of the Shanghai Local Post eventually operated in 16 cities within China. In 1898 the service was integrated with those of the Chinese government.

**SHANSI (1941-42)**

A province in northern China, west of Peking. Regular Chinese stamps were overprinted by occupying Japanese forces during World War II.

After 1945, the area was in Communist hands, using the stamps of North China (1946-50) and then of the Peking regime.

**SHANTUNG (1941-42)**

A province of northern China, for which overprinted Chinese stamps were issued under the Japanese occupation.

**SHARJAH (1963-72)**

A sheikdom in eastern Arabia, on the Persian Gulf. One of the Trucial States under British protection from 1892-1971, Sharjah joined in the United Arab Emirates in 1971.

**SIBENIK (SEBENICO) (1944)**

A city on the Adriatic coast of Yugoslavia. After Italy joined the Allies, the area was occupied by Croatian partisans, who overprinted Italian stamps for use in the region.

**SIBERIA (1919-20)**

In November 1918, anti-Bolshevik forces in Siberia formed a moderate socialist government under Adm. Kolchak. The armies of this regime soon occupied most of Siberia and invaded European Russia. At one point, they threatened Moscow, but they were eventually routed by the Red Army in late 1919. The Red counteroffensive overthrew Kolchak in January 1920, and the Siberian state rapidly disintegrated.

**SIERRA LEONE (1859-)**

A republic in west Africa. The coastal area was occupied by Great Britain after 1791, the hinterland coming under British protection in 1896.

In 1961, Sierra Leone became independent. Long one of the most progressive of Britain's west African colonies, Sierra Leone's early political stability and economic growth have given way to coups, countercoups, rampant corruption, and an economy heavily dependent on foreign aid.

**SIMI (1912-32)**

One of the Dodecanese Islands in the eastern Aegean Sea. The area was obtained from Turkey by Italy in 1912, at which time Italian stamps overprinted "Simi" were issued.

These issues were superseded by the general issues for the Aegean Islands in 1919, although two sets, overprinted with the name of the island, were released in 1930 and 1932.

### SINALOA (1923)

A state of northern Mexico bordering on the Pacific Ocean. Stamps were used briefly during 1923, when a revolution against the central government was centered in the state.

### SINGAPORE (1948-)

An island off the southern tip of the Malay Peninsula. Singapore was a British territory administered as part of the Straits Settlements from 1826-1942 and under Japanese occupation from 1942-45.

In 1946, Singapore became a separate crown colony, joining with Malaya, Sarawak and Sabah in 1963 to form the Federation of Malaysia.

In 1965, Singapore withdrew from the federation and proclaimed itself an independent republic. Singapore has a dynamic economy and enjoys the second highest per capita income in the Far East.

### SINKIANG (1915-49)

The westernmost province of China. Because the currency used in Sinkiang differed in value from that used in the rest of China, the province used overprinted Chinese issues until 1949, when the Communists assumed control.

### SIRMOOR (1879-1902)

A former feudatory state in northern India.

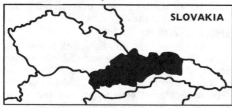

### SLOVAKIA (1939-45)

A province in eastern Czechoslovakia. In March 1939, it declared its independence under German protection. In 1945, Slovakia was reincorporated into Czechoslovakia.

### SLOVENIA (1919-21, 1941- 45)

A province of northwestern Yugoslavia. Slovenia was a part of Hungary until 1918, when it became part of the independent Kingdom of the Serbs, Croats and Slovenes. Slovenia issued stamps until 1921, when the first national issues were released.

During World War II, Slovenia was divided between Germany and Italy, both of which issued separate stamps for their zones. After the war, the province was reoccupied by Yugoslavia, and overprinted stamps of the German occupation (Ljubljana), Germany proper, and Hungary were used, until replaced by regular Yugoslav issues.

### SMILTEN (1919)

A city in Latvia. Russian stamps were surcharged by the municipal authorities for local use in 1919.

### SMOLENSK (1922)

A city in western Russia. Surcharged Russian stamps were issued for local use by the city authorities in 1922.

### SMYRNA (1909-14, 1919)

The major port of western Turkey. The Italian and Russian post offices in the city used stamps of Italy and the Russian Levant, respectively, overprinted with the name of the city.

During the Greek occupation of 1919-22, overprinted Greek stamps were issued for the area.

In 1922, a similar overprint was applied to contemporary Italian stamps for use by the Italian forces occupying the port, but this set was never released.

### SOLOMON ISLANDS (1907-)

A group of islands in the western South Pacific. The islands were a British protectorate designated as the British Solomon Islands until 1975, when, as the group approached independence, the "British" was dropped. The Solomons became self-governing in 1976 and fully independent in 1978.

### SOMALIA (1903-)

An area on the eastern coast of Africa. The colony was established as Italian Somaliland in 1905.

In 1936, it was merged with Eritrea and Ethiopia to form Italian East Africa. In 1941, the area was occupied by Great Britain who held it until 1950, using overprinted British stamps.

In 1950, the area was returned to Italy, under a U.N. trusteeship. In 1960, the area became independent, merging with the former British Somaliland Protectorate to form the Republic of Somalia.

In 1970, the nation's name was changed to the Somali Democratic Republic.

In 1969, a military coup brought an increasingly socialistic regime to power. Relations with the U.S.S.R. were strengthened, and a major Soviet naval base was established at Berbera.

Soviet-Somali relations cooled, however, when Moscow switched its support to Ethiopia in the two nations' dispute over the Ogaden, a large eastern region of Ethiopia populated primarily by Somalis. In 1977 Soviet advisors were expelled from Somalia.

In 1978, Somali forces were expelled from the Ogaden by Ethiopian and Cuban troops. Over one million Somali refugees from the region have fled to Somalia.

### SOMALI COAST (1894-1967)

A former French African colony on the Gulf of Aden. In 1967, the colony's name was changed to the French Territory of the Afars and Issas. In 1977, the name was changed to Djibouti.

**SOMALILAND PROTECTORATE (1903-60)**

A former British protectorate in eastern Africa, bordering on the Gulf of Aden. The area was occupied by Italy from 1940-41.

On June 26, 1960, the territory became independent as part of the Somali Republic.

**SOPRON (1956-57)**

A town in western Hungary. During the 1956 anti-Communist uprising, contemporary Hungarian stamps were overprinted for use in the area held by the rebels.

**SOSNOWICE (1916)**

A city in southern Poland. Local stamps were issued by the municipal authorities during the World War I Austrian occupation.

**SOUTH AFRICA (1910-)**

Republic occupying the southernmost portion of Africa. In 1910, the British colonies of Cape of Good Hope, Natal, Transvaal and Orange River Colony united to form the Union of South Africa, a self-governing dominion within the British Commonwealth.

In 1961, the republic was established.

Since 1948 South African internal policy has been based on apartheid, a program of separate development of the races. This policy has reserved for the white minority (17.5 per cent of the population) the best jobs, political control of the government, and much higher wages than those of other ethnic groups. The plan aims at the eventual creation of a large number of independent ethnic states.

Four of the black states (Bantustans) have been created to date: Transkei (1976); Bophuthatswana (1977); Venda (1979); and Ciskei (1981). None have received international recognition. All issue stamps which are routinely used within their borders, although some catalog editors have not included them in their listings, for political reasons.

South Africa has been ostracized by most of the nations of the world because of apartheid. Its economic strength, however, and the economic dependence of its black African neighbors has enabled the country to prosper.

The surprisingly peaceful transition to majority rule in Zimbabwe (Rhodesia) in early 1980 has strengthened the position of those elements in South Africa who oppose apartheid.

**SOUTH ARABIA (1959-67)**

A former federation of British territories in southwestern Arabia. South Arabia became independent in 1967 as the People's Republic of Southern Yemen.

**SOUTH AUSTRALIA (1855-1913)**

A state of Australia, occupying the south central part of the continent. South Australia was a British colony from 1836-1901 when it joined with five other colonies to form the Commonwealth of Australia.

**SOUTH BULGARIA (1885-86)**

The former province of Eastern Rumelia in the southeast Balkans. In September 1885, a coup overthrew the nominally Turkish administration and established South Bulgaria, uniting with Bulgaria.

Bulgarian stamps replaced those of South Bulgaria in 1886.

**SOUTH CHINA (1949-50)**

The Communist South China Liberation Area included the provinces of Kwangtung and Kwangsi. Regional issues were used after the occupation of Canton.

**SOUTH GEORGIA (1963-)**

An island in the South Atlantic Ocean. In 1962, when neighboring areas were detached from the Falkland Islands to become the British Antarctic Territory, South Georgia remained a Falklands' dependency.

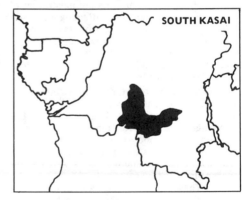

**SOUTH KASAI (1961)**

A district of Zaire which declared itself autonomous after the Congo became independent from Belgium. This revolt was subsequently suppressed by the central government.

**SOUTH MOLUCCAS (1950)**

A group of islands in the Indonesian archipelago, west of New Guinea.

During 1950, the South Moluccas revolted against the Indonesian central government and overprinted 17 Dutch Indies and Indonesian stamps "Republik Maluku Selatan." These stamps were apparently placed into local use.

The main island, Amboina, was occupied by Indonesian troops in November 1950, although Moluccan resistance continued in the outer islands until 1955.

During 1951-54, a long series of South Moluccan issues were marketed in the U.S., but there is no evidence that these were ever actually used in the areas under Moluccan control.

Some 35,000 South Moluccans emigrated to The Netherlands, and among this group nationalist sentiments still run high.

## SOUTH RUSSIA (1919-21)

In October 1918, the Volunteer Army, composed primarily of veterans of the Russian Imperial Army, was formed under the command of General Denikin. Denikin soon assumed leadership of almost all of the anti-Bolshevik elements in southern Russia and in the summer of 1919 directed a major offensive against the Reds. By October, South Russian forces had occupied much of European Russia and threatened Moscow.

A vigorous Red Army counteroffensive, the withdrawal of British and French support, and generally poor leadership brought the rapid collapse of Denikin's command in late 1919. In April 1920, having overseen the loss of all the region except the Crimea, Denikin resigned.

Command was then assumed by Baron Peter Wrangel, probably the most effective of the White Russian leaders. Wrangel was an excellent military leader, and his administration of the areas was enlightened, reflecting an understanding of the economic goals of the revolution. Unfortunately, his superiors kept him from assuming a leadership position that equalled his talents, until the White Russian cause had been lost by less able leaders.

Wrangel consolidated the Volunteer Army and held the Crimea until November 1920, when the army and its dependents were evacuated. The remnants of the South Russian forces temporarily settled in a number of refugee camps in Turkey and the Balkans, and a large number of Russian, Ukrainian and South Russian stamps were overprinted and surcharged for use in the camps. These issues were used until the camps were shut down in June 1921.

## SOUTHERN NIGERIA (1901-14)

A former administrative unit comprised of British holdings in southern Nigeria. In 1914, it was merged with Northern Nigeria to form the Colony and Protectorate of Nigeria.

## SOUTHERN RHODESIA (1924-53, 1964-65)

A former British colony in southeastern Africa. Administered as part of Rhodesia until 1923, Southern Rhodesia was ruled as a separate colony from 1923-53.

The territory was part of the Federation of Rhodesia and Nyasaland from 1953-64, and again became a separate colony from 1964-65.

In 1965, the controlling white minority declared Southern Rhodesia independent of Great Britain.

## SOUTH-WEST AFRICA (NAMIBIA) (1923-)

A territory in southwestern Africa. South-West Africa was a German colony until 1915, when it was occupied by the Union of South Africa.

It has since been administered by South Africa, originally under a mandate from the League of Nations.

In 1968, the U.N. General Assembly, in response to demands by 36 African states, created a council to administer the region, which was renamed Namibia. South Africa refused to transfer control, and in 1970 it was condemned by the U.N. Security Council.

A 1977 pre-independence referendum (in which only whites could vote) was rejected by black nationalist groups, and the Marxist group, SWAPO, began a guerrilla war against South Africa.

## SOUTHWEST CHINA (1949-50)

The Communist Southwest China Liberation Area included the provinces of Kweichow, Szechwan, Yunnan, Sikang and Tibet.

## SPAIN (1850-)

A kingdom in southwestern Europe, occupying the greater part of the Iberian Peninsula. Part of the Roman Empire from c. 200 B.C. until 412 A.D., Spain was subsequently overrun by Germanic tribes, which formed the Kingdom of the Visigoths (West Goths) until 711.

The Arabs invaded Spain in that year, soon occupying all of the peninsula except a few Christian enclaves in the north.

During the Middle Ages, Spain was reconquered by the Christians, who gradually pushed the Arabs south in a series of wars lasting from the 9th century until 1492, when the Arab stronghold of Granada fell.

During this period, the states of Aragon and Castile came to include most of modern Spain, and the marriage of Ferdinand of Aragon and Isabella of Castile brought the union of the two states and the beginning of modern Spain.

Their conquest of Granada and the discovery by Columbus, in the same year, of America, brought Spain rapidly into the position of a great power.

During the 16th century, Spain built a vast American empire and dominated western European affairs. Spanish power peaked c. 1580, when the Spanish king became king of Portugal as well, bringing that nation's empire under Spanish rule.

The rise of The Netherlands, which overthrew Spanish rule in the late 16th century, along with the growing power of Britain on the seas and France on the Continent, marked the beginning of a long decline for Spain. Although she continued to rule a huge American empire, by 1700 Spain had become a second-class power.

During the Napoleonic Wars, Spain was conquered by France, and Napoleon's brother, Joseph, was placed on the Spanish throne. Spain's colonies refused to accept this and proclaimed their allegiance to the legitimate monarch, Ferdinand VII. Because of this, Spain's American colonies were, in effect, self-governing for most of two decades.

With Ferdinand's restoration in 1815, Spain attempted to restore the strict controls that had characterized her pre-war administration. Unwilling to return to their subservient status, the colonies revolted, and by the mid-1820s, Spanish rule had been overthrown on the American mainland. Lacking the wealth of her empire, Spain was thereafter a cipher in European affairs.

In 1898-99, Spain was defeated by the U.S. in the Spanish American War, losing her last American (Cuba and Puerto Rico) and Pacific (the Philippines and Guam) colonies.

In 1931, the monarchy was ousted by a leftist republican movement, which instituted many liberal reforms but was unable to restore order in the country.

On July 18, 1936, a conservative army officer, Francisco Franco Bahamonde, led a mutiny against the regime in Morocco, beginning the Spanish Civil War (1936-39).

Franco was supported by Germany and Italy, while the Republicans were supported by the U.S.S.R.

The Spanish Civil War was in effect a dress rehearsal for World War II. The efficacy of modern weapons, the emphasis upon aircraft as a primary combat tool, and the principal of total war (against civilian as well as military personnel) were tested here.

After a bloody war in which one million died, the Nationalists finally defeated the Republicans, and Franco assumed complete control of the country.

During World War II, Spain remained neutral, much to the disgust and frustration of Franco's German and Italian allies. Despite this, in 1946, because of the regime's close fascist associations, Spain was expelled from the United Nations. It was readmitted in 1955.

In 1947 Franco declared that Spain was a monarchy and provided for his succession by an heir to the Bourbon dynasty overthrown by the Republicans in 1931. Upon his death in November 1975, Prince Juan Carlos assumed the crown.

Juan Carlos immediately dissolved the harsher institutions of the Franco regime, and in June 1976, free elections brought moderates and democratic socialists to power.

A right-wing coup in February 1981 failed, when the army remained loyal to the government.

## SPAIN-CARLIST GOVERNMENT (1873-75)

In 1833 King Ferdinand VII abrogated the Salic Law (which required that succession be through the male line), so that his daughter, Isabella, could succeed him on the Spanish throne. His brother, Don Carlos, who would otherwise have assumed the throne, refused to accept this, and upon Ferdinand's death in 1834 pressed his claim. This brought the First Carlist War of 1834-39.

In 1872, Don Carlos' grandson, also named Don Carlos, reasserted his family's claim and soon controlled large areas in northern Spain. The establishment of a republican regime in Madrid in 1873 brought many Spanish monarchists into his camp.

In December 1875, the Spanish monarchy was restored, and the Carlists rapidly lost ground. By February 1876, the Carlist movement had collapsed completely.

## SPAIN-CIVIL WAR MUNICIPAL ISSUES (1936-37)

During the Spanish Civil War, many cities and districts on both sides issued provisional overprints on Spanish postage and fiscal issues.

These were used as propaganda, as controls to distinguish regular stocks of stamps from looted stocks, and as philatelic productions.

Among those overprints legitimately used are those of Burgos, Cadiz, the Canary Islands, Malaga, San Sebastian, Santa Cruz de Tenerife and Seville.

## SPANISH GUINEA (1902-60)

Former Spanish colony in western Africa, bordering on the Gulf of Guinea. The territory is comprised of Rio Muni, Fernando Po (after 1909) and Elobey, Annobon and Corisco (after 1909).

Fernando Po and Rio Muni were separated in 1960, reuniting in 1968 to form the independent Republic of Equatorial Guinea.

## SPANISH MOROCCO (1903-56)

The northern portion of Morocco, administered by Spain until 1956, when it was merged into the independent Kingdom of Morocco.

## SPANISH SAHARA (SPANISH WESTERN SAHARA) (1924-76)

A former Spanish possession in northwestern Africa, comprising Cape Juby, La Aguera and Rio de Oro. A large (100,000 square mile), sparsely populated (12,793 in 1960) area, the Spanish Sahara is mostly desert and was of little interest to outsiders until the discovery of rich phosphate deposits.

From the 1960s, Morocco, Mauritania and Algeria all pressed claims to the area. In November 1975, thousands of unarmed Moroccans crossed into the territory (the "Green March"), and in February 1976, Spain withdrew from the colony. The Spanish Sahara was divided between Morocco and Mauritania, although a nationalist group, Polisario, declared the area independent and, with Algerian support, continues to wage a guerrilla war against Morocco and Mauritania.

In 1980, Mauritania made peace with Polisario and gave up its portion of the area to Morocco. Fighting between Polisario and Morocco continues.

## SPANISH WEST AFRICA (1949-51)

The former administrative unit comprising the Spanish colonies of Ifni, Spanish Sahara and southern Morocco.

## SPASSK (1920-22)

A city in central Russia. Russian stamps were overprinted with new values by the local authorities.

## SRI LANKA (1972-)

The name of Ceylon was officially changed to Sri Lanki on May 22, 1972.

## STAMPALIA (1912-32)

The westernmost of the Dodecanese Islands in the eastern Aegean Sea. Now the Greek island of Astipalaia.

Stampalia was obtained from Turkey by Italy in 1912, at which time Italian stamps overprinted "Stampalia" were issued.

The island's stamps were superseded by those of the Aegean Islands in 1929, although two sets were overprinted for use in Stampalia in 1930 and 1932.

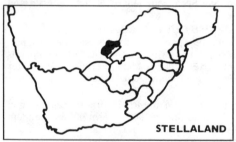

STELLALAND

## STELLALAND (1884-85)

A short-lived Boer republic in southern Africa. The republic was suppressed by Great Britain in 1885 and was incorporated into British Bechuanaland.

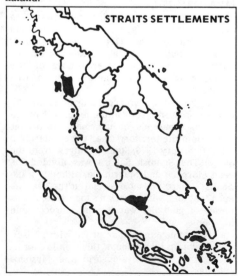

STRAITS SETTLEMENTS

## STRAITS SETTLEMENTS (1867-1946)

Former British colony in Malaya, comprising Singapore, Penang, Province Wellesley and Malacca, along with the dependencies of the Cocos (Keeling) Islands, Christmas Island and Labuan.

Prior to 1867, unoverprinted British Indian stamps were in use. The colony was occupied by Japan in 1942-45 and dissolved in 1946.

## SUDAN (1897-)

A republic in northeastern Africa, south of Egypt. Under Egyptian control from 1820-85, the Sudan was united under native control after the Mahdi led a religious war against foreigners from 1881-85.

In 1898, the area was reconquered by the British, and an Anglo-Egyptian condominium was established. In 1954, the Sudan became self-governing and on Jan. 1, 1956, became an independent republic.

Since independence, Sudan has fought a prolonged civil war in the southern third of the country, where the predominantly black, pagan population seeks independence from the Arab, Moslem north.

In 1969, a military coup brought a socialist regime to power, and in 1970 the government nationalized a number of businesses. In 1971, an abortive Communist coup brought a temporary break in relations between the Sudan and the U.S.S.R. Relations later improved, but since 1975 the Sudan has moved away from the Soviet Union and has strengthened ties with the U.S.

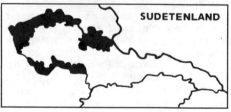

SUDETENLAND

## SUDETENLAND (1938)

The western border area of Czechoslovakia in which the majority of the population is German-speaking. After the Munich Agreement of Sept. 21, 1938, transferring the region to Germany, local Nazis seized control, pending formal German annexation on Oct. 1.

Czechoslovakia stamps overprinted "Wir sind frei" (We are free) were used during this brief period in Asch, Karlsbad, Konstantinsbad, Niklasdorf, Reichenberg-Maffersdorf, Mahrisch-Ostran and Ramburg.

## SUEZ CANAL (1868)

During 1859-69, the Campagnie Universelle du Canal Maritime de Suez constructed the Suez Canal in Egypt, linking the Mediterranean and Red seas.

Until 1867, the company transported mail between Port Said and Suez for free. The company then decided charges for this service, and in July 1868, special stamps were issued.

The stamps were not popular and were withdrawn from sale Aug. 16, 1868. They were demonetized Aug. 31, and the service was taken over by the Egyptian government.

## SUNGEI UJONG (1878-95)

Former Federated Malay State under British protection. The territory was incorporated into Negri Sembilan in 1895.

## SUPEH (1941-42)

A province of central China, for which overprinted Chinese stamps were issued during the Japanese occupation.

## SURINAM (1873-)

A state in northern South America. Disputed by Great Britain, France and The Netherlands during the 17th-18th centuries, Surinam became a Dutch possession after 1815.

In 1954, Surinam, along with The Netherlands Antilles, became an integral part of the Kingdom of The Netherlands.

In 1975, it became fully independent at the initiative of The Netherlands. Some 40 per cent of Surinam's population (mostly East Indians) emigrated to The Netherlands in the period immediately prior to independence.

## SWAHILILAND (1889)

Until the late 19th century, the Sultan of Zanzibar controlled much of the coast of East Africa. Germany secured concessions from the sultan in the area around Lamu, Kenya, which in 1890 were ceded to Britain as part of the settlement for the British transfer of Heligoland to Germany. Prior to this (July-August 1889) the German postal agent at Lamu printed and issued some 100 stamps for use in the region.

## SWAZILAND (1889-)

An inland kingdom in southern Africa, surrounded by the Republic of South Africa and Mozambique. The kingdom was formed by the Bantu tribes in the area in the 19th century, partly in defense against the warlike Zulu Kingdom.

In 1881, Great Britain and the South African Republic (Transvaal) guaranteed Swaziland's independence. During 1894-99, the state was under the protection of the Transvaal, and after 1902, came under British administration.

In 1963, it was recognized as a British protectorate and on Sept. 6, 1968, became independent.

Swaziland is an absolute monarchy. Its fertile lands and abundant mineral resources have made significant economic growth possible. It is closely linked with South Africa, and a handful of South African whites dominate the economy.

## SWEDEN (1855-)

Constitutional monarchy in northern Europe, occupying the eastern portion of the Scandinavian Peninsula. Militaristic expansion in the 17th century made the Baltic Sea a Swedish lake, but after 1709, a series of defeats stripped Sweden of most of her empire.

In 1813, Sweden joined in the war against Napoleon, receiving Norway (independent 1905) as compensation.

Sweden has since maintained a policy of armed neutrality and has devoted her energies to social and industrial development.

Although long under a socialist government, some 91 per cent of the economy is privately owned. Swedish social programs are extensive, although in recent years the high cost of maintaining them has encouraged the growth of a black market of goods and services unreported to the tax collector.

## SWITZERLAND (1850-)

A land-locked federation in central Europe, situated between France, Germany, Austria and Italy. The country has three official languages: German, French and Italian.

The nucleus of modern Switzerland appeared in the late 13th century, and in 1648 the Confederation became independent. Switzerland has not been involved in a foreign war since 1515, and, learning the lesson of Napoleon's seizure of the country, has since 1815 maintained an armed neutrality.

Switzerland has no military alliances and does not belong to the United Nations, although it participates in a number of U.N. programs and has U.N offices in Geneva. In recent years, there has been some pressure within the Swiss government to join the organization officially.

The stability of Switzerland and of the Swiss franc has made the country one of the world's banking centers.

## SYRIA (1919-)

A republic in western Asia, bordering on the Mediterranean Sea.

Under Turkish control after 1516, Syria was occupied by the Allies late in World War II. British and French forces occupied the coastal areas, while the interior was taken by an Arab Army, led by T.E. Lawrence ("Lawrence of Arabia") and Faisal, son of King Hussein of the Hejaz.

Lawrence and Faisal established an independent government, which claimed authority over Lebanon, Jordan, Palestine and Iraq, as well as Syria. This regime was recognized by a Syrian congress, but France soon overthrew the government and occupied the country.

Faisal was compensated by being made king of Iraq, which his family ruled until 1958.

In 1922, France assumed formal control of Syria under a League of Nations mandate. In 1941, a republic government was established, and the country became independent, although French troops remained until 1946.

Syria was united with Egypt during 1958-61.

Since 1963 it has been ruled by the Baathist party, a socialist, pan-Arab group.

Syria is one of the "front-line" Arab states opposing Israel, which has held the Syrian Golan Heights since the 1967 Arab-Israeli War. It has received massive military aid from the Soviet Union, as well as annual subsidies from the oil-rich Arab states. It has consistently taken a hard line against Israel, although in recent years there has been some rapprochement with the West.

### SZECHWAN (1933-36)

A province in southern China. For a time, surcharged Chinese issues were used in the province, because of the devaluation of the local currency.

### SZEGED (1919)

A city in southern Hungary. Between May and November 1919, Szeged was the seat of the anti-Bolshevik Hungarian National Government, under Admiral Horthy. The occupying French forces prevented Horthy from attacking the Bolsheviks, but after the fall of the regime, the Nationalists occupied Budapest and established the National Republic.

In June 1919, the Horthy government overprinted Hungarian issues for use in the area under its authority.

## — T —

### TAHITI (1882-93, 1903, 1915)

An island in the South Pacific. A former French colony, Tahiti merged into French Polynesia in 1893. Except for the issues of 1903 and 1915, stamps of French Polynesia have been in use since 1893.

### TAIWAN (FORMOSA) (1886-95, 1945-50)

Island off the coast of China, in the west Pacific Ocean. Formosa was a Chinese province until 1895, when it was ceded to Japan.

Local Chinese inhabitants objected and proclaimed an independent republic, which was soon suppressed by Japanese forces.

In 1945, it was reoccupied by China, and in 1949, became the last stronghold of Nationalist resistance to the Communists.

The Republic of China on Taiwan has continued to operate since that time.

### TAMMERFORS (1866-81)

A city in west-central Finland. Several issues were made by the local postmaster for use within his district.

### TANGANYIKA (1921-35, 1961-64)

The major portion of the former German East Africa colony, placed under British administration after World War I.

A part of Kenya, Uganda and Tanganyika after 1935, it became independent on Dec. 9, 1961. In 1964, it merged with Zanzibar to become the United Republic of Tanganyika and Zanzibar, renamed Tanzania in 1965.

### TANGIER (1927-57)

In 1923, Great Britain, France and Spain declared Tangier, in northern Morocco, an international zone.

Stamps of French Morocco and Spanish Morocco, as well as special British, French and Spanish issues for Tangier, were used.

In 1957, the city was annexed by Morocco.

### TANZANIA (1965-)

A republic in southeastern Africa, bordering on the Indian Ocean. The territory formed with the union of Tanganyika and Zanzibar in 1964 as the United Republic of Tanganyika and Zanzibar.

In October 1965, the name was changed to the United Republic of Tanzania.

Tanzania has maintained socialist policies at home and a neutral policy in its foreign affairs. Its relations with its two northern neighbors, Kenya and Uganda, have been strained. During 1978-79, clashes occurred with Uganda, culminating in a successful Tanzanian invasion, which overthrew Ugandan dictator Idi Amin.

TANNU TUVA

### TANNU TUVA (1926-34)

An area in northern Asia between Mongolia and Siberia. Long disputed between Russia and China, the district was established in 1926 as an independent republic under Soviet protection.

In 1946, it was absorbed into the Soviet Union.

### TASMANIA (VAN DIEMEN'S LAND) (1853-1913)

Island off the southeastern coast of Australia. A dependency of the British colony of New South Wales from 1803-25, the island became the colony of Van Diemen's Land in 1825.

In 1856, the name of the colony was changed to Tasmania. In 1901, Tasmania joined in the Commonwealth of Australia.

### TELSIAI (TELSCHEN) (1941)

A city in northwestern Lithuania. Overprinted Russian stamps were issued by the German military commander of the area during July and August 1941.

### TEMESVAR (1919)

A district of the Banat, occupied by Serbia after World War I. After the Serbian evacuation, Romanian forces occupied the area, and Temesvar was subsequently annexed by Serbia.

Both Serbian and Romanian forces overprinted Hungarian stamps for use in the area.

## TERUEL (1937)

A province in northeastern Spain. Overprinted Spanish stamps were issued in 1937 by the local Nationalist authorities.

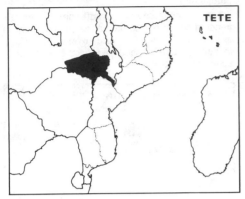

## TETE (1913-14)

A district in western Mozambique.

## TETUAN (1908-09)

A city in northern Morocco, formerly part of Spanish Morocco.

## THAILAND (SIAM) (1883-)

A kingdom in southeast Asia. After 1350, Thailand was the dominant power in the Malaya-Indo-China region.

European encroachments in the 19th century reduced this power, although Thailand, alone among the native states of the region, was able to maintain its independence.

An ally of Japan during World War II, Thailand was able to reoccupy some of its lost territory. These were given up when, in 1945, the Thai government repudiated its declaration of war against Great Britain and the U.S.

After World War II, Thailand aligned itself with the West. During the Vietnamese War, Thai troops were active in South Vietnam (until 1972)

THESSALY

and in Laos (until 1974). Since that time, it has been under increasing pressure from Laos and Cambodia, which support Communist guerrillas within Thailand.

## THESSALY (1898)

During the Turko-Greek War of 1898, a set of five octagonal stamps was issued for use by the Turkish forces in Thessaly.

## THRACE (1913-20)

A district in the southeastern Balkans, bordering on the Aegean and Black Seas.

Under Turkish rule from the 14th century, the western portion of Thrace was occupied by Bulgaria in 1912. In 1913 an autonomous Moslem regime briefly ousted the Bulgarians. During its ephemeral existence, this regime issued lithographed stamps, as well as overprints on Turkish, Greek and Bulgarian issues.

In 1913 western Thrace was incorporated into Bulgaria, using regular Bulgarian issues. In October 1918, this area was taken from Bulgaria by the Allies, who overprinted Bulgarian stamps for use in the zone. In May 1920, western Thrace was mandated to Greece, and in August, Greece annexed the territory.

Eastern Thrace remained in Turkish hands until 1918, when it, too, was occupied by the Allies. Like the western portion of the province, it was turned over to Greece in 1920. After the Greek defeat in the Graeco-Turkish War (1922), it was returned to Turkey.

## THURN AND TAXIS (1852-67)

A princely house which maintained a postal monopoly in central Europe from the 16th century until 1806.

After 1815, it operated postal services in parts of western Germany. In 1867, its rights were purchased by Prussia.

## TIBET (1912-65)

Former theocracy in the Himalaya region of central Asia. An independent kingdom from the 7th century, Tibet was under Mongol influence after its conquest in 1270.

In the 17th century, the grand lama of the Red Hat Lamaistic order secured both spiritual and temporal power, and Tibet remained a more or less independent state under the grand lamas until 1904, after which British influence was strong.

During 1910-12, a pro-Chinese regime was in power, but Chinese troops were withdrawn following the 1912 Revolution, and Tibet again became independent.

In 1950, eastern Tibet was seized by China, and in 1953, a communist government was installed in Tibet itself, supplanting the theocratic regime of the Dalai Lama.

In 1956, a Tibetan revolt within China spread to Tibet, resulting in the dissolution of the Tibetan government in 1959. Although the uprising was crushed ruthlessly (charges of genocide were made against the Chinese in 1961), periodic uprisings have broken out as recently as 1976.

## TIENTSIN (1917-22)

City in northern China. The Italian post offices in Tientsin used Italian stamps overprinted with the name of the city.

## TIFLIS (1857)

The capital city of Georgia (U.S.S.R.). In 1857, the Russian viceroy of the area issued a stamp for local use.

## TIMOR (1885-1975)

An island in the Malay Archipelago. Divided between the Dutch and Portuguese since the 17th century, the island was formally partitioned in 1919.

After the liberal Portuguese revolution in 1974, the Portuguese portion of Timor declared itself independent of Portugal, but was soon disputed by internal factions.

Indonesia restored order in Timor, which remains under de facto Indonesian control.

## TLACOTALPAN (1856)

A village in the state of Veracruz in eastern Mexico.

## TOBAGO (1879-96)

An island in the West Indies, north of Trinidad. In 1889, Tobago was united with Trinidad to form the colony of Trinidad and Tobago.

## TOGO (1897-)

A republic in West Africa, bordering on the Gulf of Guinea. Togo was a German protectorate until 1914, when it was occupied by Anglo-French forces.

After World War I, the territory was divided between Britain and France, under League of Nations mandate. The British portion subsequently became part of Ghana, while the French zone became the present republic (1958).

Togo became fully independent in 1960.

Togo has been ruled as a military dictatorship since 1967. Although the government is repressive, the political stability that it provides has made possible steady economic progress.

## TOKELAU ISLANDS (1948-)

A group of islands in the Pacific Ocean, north of Samoa. Attached to the Gilbert and Ellice Islands, Tokelau Islands were placed under Western Samoan administration in 1926.

On Jan. 1, 1949, they became a dependency of New Zealand.

## TOMSK (1920)

A city in western Siberia. During the Russian Civil War, the local authorities issued a surcharged Russian stamp for use in the area.

## TONGA (1886-)

A group of islands in the South Pacific Ocean, south of Samoa. United during the mid-19th century, Tonga came under British protection in 1900.

On June 4, 1970, Tonga again became fully independent.

Tonga's economy has traditionally been dependent on copra and bananas. The discovery of offshore oil in the 1970s and government efforts to develop tourism bode well for the country's economic future.

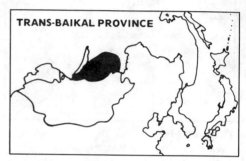

## TRANSBAIKAL PROVINCE (1920)

Shortly after the fall of the Kolchak regime in January 1920, a local warlord in eastern Siberia, the Ataman Semenov, proclaimed himself ruler of Siberia. He maintained control of the area around Chita and Lake Baikal until October, when his government was overthrown by partisans of the Far Eastern Republic. Semenov fled to Mongolia, and all vestiges of his regime vanished.

## TRANSCAUCASIAN FEDERATED REPUBLICS (1923-24)

A former Soviet administrative district in the Caucasus, comprising Armenia, Azerbaijan and Georgia.

In 1917, a short-lived independent Transcaucasian Republic was proclaimed, but this state soon fell to invading German, Turkish and British forces.

After considerable turmoil, the area was occupied by Soviet forces in 1922, and in that year, the Transcaucasian Soviet Federated Socialist Republic was proclaimed. In the following year, it joined the U.S.S.R.

In 1936, this unit was dissolved, and its three component states were separated.

## TRANSKEI (1976-)

A South African state which became independent Oct. 26, 1976. Located between Lesotho and the Indian Ocean, largely surrounded by the Republic of South Africa, of which it had been a part.

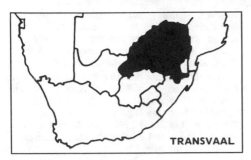

TRANSVAAL

## TRANSVAAL (1870-1910)

Former Boer republic (South African Republic) and British colony in southern Africa; now a province of the Republic of South Africa.

Boer settlements north of the Cape Colony were recognized as the independent South African Republic in 1852, but during 1877-82, British forces occupied the area.

In 1881, the Transvaal again became independent, but increasing tension with the British led to the Boer War of 1899-1902, after which the country became a British colony.

In 1910, the Transvaal joined with Natal, Cape Colony and the Orange River Colony to form the Union of South Africa.

## TRANSYLVANIA (1919)

A principality annexed from the Turks by Hungary in the 18th century, Transylvania was occupied and absorbed by Romania after World War I.

During 1940-44, it was reoccupied by Hungary, finally being returned to Romania after World War II.

## TRAVANCORE (1888-1949)

A former feudatory state in southern India. In 1949, it merged with Cochin to form Travancore-Cochin, which issued stamps for use in the new territory.

## TRAVANCORE-COCHIN (1949-51)

The United State of Travancore-Cochin was formed on July 1, 1949, by the merger of Travancore and Cochin, along with the formerly British-held towns of Tangasseri and Anjengo. Indian stamps have been used since April 1, 1951.

## TREBIZONDE (1909-14)

A Turkish port on the Black Sea. The Russian post office in the city used stamps of the Russian Levant overprinted "Trebizonde" after 1909.

## TRENGGANU (1910-)

Former nonfederated Malay state under Siamese influence until a British protectorate was established in 1909. Trengganu joined the Federation of Malaya in 1948.

## TRIESTE (1947-54)

A formerly Italian territory at the northern end of the Adriatic Sea. After World War II, it was occupied by Allied forces and in 1954, was partitioned between Italy (the northern portion of the seaport of Trieste) and Yugoslavia (the southern section).

These two zones, A and B respectively, issued stamps during 1947-54, while Trieste was a free territory — zone A being under Allied administration, while zone B was administered by Yugoslavia.

## TRINIDAD (1851-1913)

An island in the Caribbean, off the coast of Venezuela. Taken from Spain by Great Britain in 1797, Trinidad was united with Tobago in 1889 to form the colony of Trinidad and Tobago.

## TRINIDAD AND TOBAGO (1913-)

Two islands in the Caribbean, off the coast of Venezuela. The two British colonies were united in 1889, Tobago becoming a ward of the united colony in 1899.

From 1958-1962, the colony was a member of the West Indies Federation, becoming independent in August 1962.

Trinidad has long been an oil refining center and has begun exploiting recently discovered oil reserves of its own. It is one of the most prosperous of the Caribbean states.

## TRIPOLITANIA (1923-35, 1948-50)

Former Italian colony in North Africa. Tripolitania was occupied from Turkey in 1912 and merged with Cyrenaica in 1934 to form the colony of Libya.

During World War II, Libya was occupied by Anglo-French forces, and Tripolitania was occupied by the British until 1950, when it was incorporated into the independent Kingdom of Libya.

## TRISTAN DA CUNHA (1952-)

A group of islands in the mid-South Atlantic Ocean. A British possession since 1816, Tristan da Cunha became a dependency of the colony of St. Helena in 1936.

## TRUCIAL STATES (1961-63)

A group of Arab sheikdoms — Abu Dhabi, Ajman, Dubai, Fujeira, Manama, Ras al Khaima, Sharjah and Kalba, and Umm al Qiwain — in eastern Arabia, bordering on the Persian Gulf.

These states were under British protection from 1892-1971, joining to form the United Arab Emirates in 1971. In June 1963, Trucial States issues were replaced by those of the individual states, which, in turn, were superseded by those of the U.A.E. in 1972.

## TUNISIA (1888-)

Republic in North Africa. Tunisia was under Turkish rule from 1574 until 1881, when it became a French protectorate.

After World War II, nationalist feeling increased, and in 1955, France granted Tunisia internal autonomy. In March 1956, Tunisia became independent.

Tunisia has maintained a moderate, generally pro-Western policy since it became independent. Since the 1960s, it has urged a policy of negotiation with Israel.

In 1974, Tunisia and Libya tentatively agreed to merge, but Tunisia soon withdrew from the agreement, and relations between the two countries have been strained. In 1979, a Libyan-backed invasion of Tunisia from Algeria was thwarted.

TURKEY

Turkey Today

Ottoman Turkish Empire 1863

## TURKEY (1863-)

A republic in southeastern Europe and western Asia.

The area now occupied by Turkey was the center of a number of ancient civilizations, and it remained the center of the Eastern Roman Empire for nearly a thousand years after the fall of Rome itself. During most of this period, the empire was the dominant power of the region.

The empire, weakened by the inroads of Crusaders who found it easier to ransack Christian lands than to fight infields, rapidly lost ground in the 13th and 14th centuries. The Ottoman Turks conquered the outlying provinces, and in 1453 they occupied Constantinople, which became their capital and the center of their own empire.

During the next century, the Turks conquered southeastern Europe, North Africa and much of the Middle East. At its apex (1550-1683), the Turkish Empire stretched from the borders of Poland and the Russian steppes to the Sahara, and from Algeria to Arabia.

From the late 17th century on, the Turkish Empire became increasingly weak and poorly administered, and its military power declined rapidly. During the 19th century, the territorial integrity of the state was maintained only because the European powers could not agree upon the division of the spoils.

In a series of generally unsuccessful wars during 1878-1913, most of Turkey's outlying provinces became independent or were lost to its more powerful neighbors.

In 1914, the Turks joined the Central Powers. Their defeat cost Turkey most of its remaining territory, and by 1919 only Asia Minor re-mained. At that point, it became apparent that the Allies intended to dismember Turkey altogether. In reaction to this threat, a nationalist Turkish government was formed in Ankara in 1920, with Mustafa Kemal as president.

The Nationalists defeated the Greeks, whom they expelled from Western Asia Minor and Eastern Thrace and compelled the Allies to withdraw from the Dardanelles and Cilicia. The Treaty of Lausanne (1923) confirmed Turkish independence and established its borders along roughly ethnic lines.

Kemel established the republic and launched an ambitious program of social reform and industrialization.

Turkey remained neutral during most of World War II, declaring war on the Axis in February 1945. Since that time, it has been aligned with the West, although tension with Greece, a fellow NATO member, over the status of Cyprus, has at times threatened to estrange Turkey from its Western allies.

In 1974, Turkey invaded Cyprus, following a pro-Greek coup which threatened to unite the island with Greece. The Turkish sector (roughly the eastern third of the island) has since been administered as the Turkish Federated State of Cyprus.

## TURKS ISLANDS (1867-1900)

A group of islands in the West Indies, south of the Bahamas. In 1848, along with the Caicos Islands, they were transferred from Bahamian to Jamaican administration, first as a separate colony (1848-73) and later as a dependency of Jamaica (1873-1959).

Stamps inscribed "Turks and Caicos Islands" replaced those inscribed "Turks Islands" in 1900.

## TURKS AND CAICOS ISLANDS (1900-)

Two groups of islands in the West Indies, south of the Bahamas. Ruled by Great Britain from the Bahamas after the early 18th century, the Turks and Caicos were separated as a colony in 1848 and became a dependency of Jamaica in 1873.

In 1959, they again became a separate British colony.

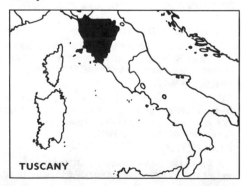

TUSCANY

## TUSCANY (1851-60)

A former grand duchy in west-central Italy. In 1859, the duke was deposed, and in 1860, Tuscany was united with Sardinia.

## TUVALU (1976-)

A group of islands in the Pacific Ocean northeast of Australia. Formerly the Ellice Islands, forming part of the colony of the Gilbert and Ellice Islands, Tuvalu became a separate colony on Jan. 1, 1976 and became independent in 1978.

TWO SICILIES

## TWO SICILIES (1858-62)

Former kingdom comprising southern Italy and Sicily. First created by the Normans in the 11th century, the kingdom passed through various hands until the Bourbon dynasty was overthrown by Garibaldi in 1860.

The area was united with Sardinia in 1860, and Italian stamps have been used since 1862.

## — U —

## UBANGI-SHARI (1915-37)

Former French colony in central Africa. Occupied by France during 1887-98, Ubangi-Shari was established as a colony in 1904. In 1910, it joined Gabon, the Middle Congo and Chad to form French Equatorial Africa. From 1936 to 1960, French Equatorial African stamps were used.

In 1958, Ubangi-Shari became the autonomous Central African Republic. It became fully independent in 1960.

## UDINE (1918)

A city in northeastern Italy, occupied by Austrian forces during World War I. During this period, the municipal authorities issued a stamp for local use.

## UGANDA (1895-1902, 1962-)

An independent state in East Africa. Formerly a British protectorate, Uganda became independent in 1962.

In 1971, General Idi Amin seized control of the government. His administration was erratic and blood-thirsty. Some 45,000 East Indians were expelled in 1972, disrupting the economy, since much of the commerce had been in their hands. In 1973, the U.S. broke relations with Uganda, and most Western nations suspended aid, which was replaced by Soviet and Libyan support.

During the next few years, some 300,000 Ugandans were killed, all opponents or suspected opponents of the regime. This reign of terror, along with generally poor government administration, reduced the Ugandan economy to a shambles.

In March 1979, after a period of increasing tension, Uganda was invaded by a Tanzanian force, supported by Ugandan exiles. In April, Amin was forced to flee the country, and found asylum in Libya, one of the few nations with whom he had remained on friendly terms.

A provisional government was established to administer the country and to normalize Ugandan affairs. The government since has been climactically unstable and the economic and social structures remain in chaos. Anarchy and ruthless government repression are again becoming the norm.

## UKRAINE (1918-23, 1941-43)

A large district in southwestern Russia, now a republic within the Soviet Union.

Under Russian rule since the 18th century, the Ukraine declared its independence in 1917. After several years of warfare, the Bolsheviks finally occupied the Ukraine in 1920, establishing a Soviet Republic, which was absorbed into the Soviet Union in 1923.

During World War II, the Ukraine was occupied by Germany, and overprinted German stamps were used in the area.

## UMM AL QIWAIN (1964-72)

A sheikdom in the Trucial States in eastern Arabia. Under British protection from 1892-1971, Umm al Qiwain joined the independent United Arab Emirates on Dec. 2, 1971.

## UNITED ARAB EMIRATES (1972-)

A union of sheikdoms in eastern Arabia. Formed Dec. 2, 1971, by Abu Dhabi, Ajman, Dubai, Fujeira, Sharjah and Umm al Qiwain.

Ras al Khaima joined the U.A.E. in February 1972. In August 1972, general U.A.E. issues superseded those of the individual states.

This region was long extremely poor, but in recent years the exploitation of large petroleum reserves, with the staggering increase in petroleum prices, has given the UAE one of the highest per capita gross national products in the world.

## UNITED NATIONS (1951-)

The U.N. is an organization for the maintenance of international security and peace. Established in 1945, the U.N. now includes virtually every sovereign nation in the world.

U.N. stamps are used on all mail handled at United Nations post offices in New York, Geneva, and Vienna. Separate issues are released for the use of the Geneva and Vienna offices.

## UNITED STATES OF AMERICA (1847-)

Republic occupying the central portion of North America, along with Alaska, Hawaii and a large number of island possessions in the Caribbean Sea and the Pacific Ocean.

The U.S. was formed from the union of the 13 British mainland North American colonies south of Canada in 1783, after an eight year war against Great Britain.

During 1803-53, the U.S. expanded rapidly westward, increasing its territory through conquest, purchase and negotiation.

Alaska was purchased from Russia in 1867, and in 1898, Hawaii was annexed, at the request of its inhabitants. In the following year, Puerto Rico, Guam and the Philippines were acquired from Spain, following the short Spanish-American War.

The U.S. long avoided involvement in foreign affairs, except in the Western Hemisphere, where U.S. interest was concentrated. In 1917, the U.S. entered World War I and played an instrumental role in the defeat of the Central Powers. Following the war, it reverted to its isolationist policy.

During the first two years of World War II, the U.S. resisted involvement, although its sympathies were strongly with the Allies, to whom it supplied economic aid. The Japanese attack on the major U.S. Pacific naval base at Pearl Harbor forced the country into the war. Again, the U.S. played the decisive part in defeating Germany and its allies.

Following World War II, the U.S. realized that it could not avoid international problems by ignoring them and embarked on a policy of active involvement in the regions where its interests were paramount.

U.S. economic aid sparked the European postwar economic boom, and its administration of Japan saw the rapid expansion of Japanese industry.

U.S. stamps were first issued in 1847, although a number of local postmasters had been issuing local stamps since 1845. U.S. issues have been used in many nations throughout the world, reflecting, in most cases, the presence of American troops. All U.S. possessions, except the Panama Canal Zone, use U.S. stamps.

## UNITED STATES POST OFFICE IN CHINA (1919-22)

From 1867-1922, the U.S. maintained a post office in Shanghai, China. During 1867-1919, unoverprinted U.S. stamps were used, and during 1919-22, surcharged issues were used. This post office was closed on Dec. 31, 1922.

## UNITED STATES-POSTMASTERS' PROVISIONALS (1845-47)

In 1845, the postmaster of New York City began using postage stamps for mail handled by his office. Other postmasters' provisionals appeared during the next two years.

In 1847, the U.S. Post Office, convinced of the desirability of utilizing postage stamps, began to issue national issues, which replaced the provisionals.

Postmasters' provisionals were used by Alexandria, Va.; Annapolis, Md. (envelope); Baltimore, Md. (both stamps and postal stationery); Boscawen, N.H.; Brattleboro, Vt.; Lockport, N.Y.; Millbury, Mass.; New Haven, Conn. (postal stationery); New York, N.Y.; Providence, R.I.; and St. Louis, Mo.

During 1846, the New York provisionals were used experimentally on New York-bound mail from Boston, Albany and Washington.

UPPER SILESIA

## UPPER SILESIA (1920-22)

A former German territory on the Polish border. A plebiscite in 1920 was indecisive, and in 1922, the League of Nations partitioned the district between Germany and Poland.

After World War II, the German portion of the area was annexed by Poland.

## UPPER VOLTA (1920-32, 1959-)

A republic in West Africa, north of Ghana. A French colony from 1919-32, Upper Volta was subsequently divided between the French Sudan, Ivory Coast and Niger.

In 1947, it was reconstituted within French West Africa, and in 1958, was established as a republic within the French community.

In 1960, Upper Volta became independent.

## URUGUAY (1856-)

A republic in South America, on the Atlantic coast between Brazil and Argentina. Under Spanish rule until 1810, associated with La Plata from 1810-16, and conquered by Brazil in 1816, Uruguay finally became independent in 1827.

Uruguay's history during the 19th century was one of anarchy and civil war, with occasional armed intervention by Argentina and Brazil.

After 1900, a stable government enabled the country to make considerable economic and social progress. The rise of radical terrorism by the leftist "Tupamaros" during the 1960s, however, disrupted the country and brought a rightist military takeover in 1973.

## — V —

### VADUZ (1918)

The capital of Liechtenstein. During World War I, the Austrian War Office disrupted the ordinary postal system, necessitating the issuance of a provisional stamp in Vaduz.

This stamp was valid for local use and for transmittal to Sevelen, Switzerland.

### VALENCIENNES (1914)

A city in northern France, near the Belgian border. Soon after the city's occupation by German forces at the beginning of World War I, the Chamber of Commerce issued a stamp for local use.

This stamp was in use from Sept. 3-Oct. 30, 1914.

### VALONA (1909-11, 1914-18)

Albanian seaport. The Italian post office used overprinted Italian stamps from 1909-11.

In October 1914, Moslem revolutionaries issued a series of stamps, used briefly before Valona was occupied by Italian troops.

During the Italian occupation, overprinted Italian stamps were again used in the city.

### VATICAN CITY (1929-)

A tiny (108.7 acres) enclave in Rome, the Vatican City is the sole remnant of the once-extensive Papal state in Italy.

During 1870-1929, the Papacy and Italy disputed sovereignty, but the Lateran Pact of 1929 restored normal relations, with temporal authority of the Pope recognized in the Vatican City, which became an independent state, subject to certain limitations.

### VEGLIA (KRK) (1920)

An island off the northwestern coast of Yugoslavia. During d'Annunzio's occupation of Fiume, regular Fiume issues were overprinted for Veglia.

### VENDA (1979-)

An "independent" nation created out of northern South Africa in 1979. The third of the bantustans to become a separate state under South Africa's program of creating a patchwork of ethnic states from its territory. Venda is not internationally recognized, although its government, albeit a South African satellite, is the sovereign power in the country.

### VENEZIA GIULIA (1918-19, 1945-47)

Former Austrian territory at the northern end of the Adriatic Sea, including the port of Trieste.

The area was occupied by Italy after World War I, during which time overprinted Austrian stamps were used. After World War II, the area was occupied by the Allies, and overprinted Italian stamps were issued from 1945-47 (Trieste zone A).

Yugoslavia occupied part of the territory (zone B), issuing stamps for use there.

### VENEZIA TRIDENTINA (1918-19)

A territory in northern Italy, also known as Trentino. The area was occupied by Italy from Austria after World War I, at which time overprinted Austrian stamps were used.

### VENEZUELA (1859-)

Republic on the northern coast of South America.

Under Spanish rule after 1546, Venezuela expelled the Spanish after a bloody ten-year civil war (1811-21). It at first formed part of Bolivar's Great Colombia, separating from that union in 1830.

Venezuela's history during the 19th century was marked by a succession of military dictatorships and chronic internal disorder.

During 1907-45, Venezuela saw significant economic growth, and in 1945, democratic government was established. Several military coups followed, but since 1959 Venezuela's governments have been progressive and democratically elected.

One of the founding members of OPEC, Venezuela had benefitted enormously from the massive increases in oil prices during the 1970s. Oil revenues are funding major economic expansion and public works projects.

### VICTORIA (1850-1913)

A state in southeastern Australia. Detached from New South Wales in 1851, Victoria joined the Commonwealth of Australia in 1901.

### VICTORIA LAND (1911)

A region of Antarctica. In 1911-12, Robert Falcon Scott organized his ill-fated South Pole Expedition, and two New Zealand stamps were overprinted "Victoria Land" for use by the expedition members.

Scott and four members of his party reached the South Pole on Jan. 18, 1912, but died on the return trip to their base.

## VIETNAM (1945-54)

Country in Southeast Asia, occupying the eastern half of the Indo-Chinese Peninsula.

Vietnam comprises Annam, Tonkin and Cochin China, which have been under Chinese control or influence for most of their history since 111 B.C.

In 1854, France began to extend its control in the area, which was completed by 1884. During World War II, Vietnam was occupied by the Japanese, who supported the regime of the Emperor Bao Dai of Annam.

The Vietminh League, a union of nationalists aiming for an independent Vietnam, grew up in opposition to the Japanese, and in 1945, deposed Bao Dai, declaring Vietnamese independence.

During 1946-54, France fought the Vietminh, hoping to preserve their Indo-Chinese Empire. In July 1949, the State of Vietnam was established under Bao Dai, in association with the French Union.

The defeat of France by the Vietminh forces which had come under complete Communist control brought the partition of the country in 1954.

The northern half became the Communist Democratic Republic of Vietnam, and in the following year, the southern portion became the Republic of Vietnam.

## VIETNAM, DEMOCRATIC REPUBLIC OF (NORTH VIETNAM) (1954-)

A Communist people's republic occupying the northern half of Vietnam.

The Democratic Republic of Vietnam was established in 1954, after the defeat of French forces by the nationalist Vietminh. The North continued to support the Communist Vietcong in the South against the South Vietnamese regime, increasing its aid after 1959.

In 1964, North Vietnamese troops began to fight in the South, bringing the U.S. actively into the war.

During 1965-69, the war was largely a stalemate, with neither side able to achieve any permanent success. Growing domestic opposition to the U.S. involvement in the war brought a cease-fire in January 1973, after which U.S. forces were withdrawn, and U.S. aid to the South was reduced.

In early 1975, a renewed Communist offensive brought about the rapid collapse of the South Vietnamese regime, and a Communist government was installed in the South.

In 1976 the two countries were merged into the Socialist Republic of Vietnam.

Since its 1975 victory, Vietnam has exercised control of Laos and in 1978-79 established a client regime in Kampuchea, where scattered Khmer Rouge resistance continues. A Chinese invasion of Vietnam in February 1979, brought heavy fighting but did not escalate into a full-blown war.

Since the Communist victory, millions of South Vietnamese have been forcibly resettled in the countryside, and hundreds of thousands have fled the South.

## VIETNAM, REPUBLIC OF (SOUTH VIETNAM) (1955-75)

After the loss of the northern half of Vietnam to the Communists in 1954, the southern portion of the country withdrew from the French Union and deposed its ruler, Bao Dai. On Oct. 26, 1955, the Republic of Vietnam was established.

After 1956, fighting with the Communists continued, the southern Communist Vietcong being supported and supplied by North Vietnam. The U.S. supported the South with aid and after June 1965, with troops.

After 1969, because of growing opposition to involvement among Americans, the U.S. began to reduce its involvement and in January 1973, a cease-fire between the U.S., North Vietnam and the Vietcong provided for the withdrawal of U.S. forces.

The U.S. reduced aid to the South, weakening that regime's position, so that in early 1975, a North Vietnamese invasion, in violation of the cease-fire, quickly brought the South Vietnamese collapse.

A Provisional Revolutionary Government, under North Vietnamese direction, assumed control of the South in May 1975.

## VILNIUS (1941)

A city in Lithuania. Vilnius was occupied by German forces from 1941-44. During the early stage of the occupation, overprinted Russian stamps were used.

## VITORIA (1937)

The capital of the province of Alava in northern Spain. The Nationalist authorities overprinted contemporary Spanish stamps for use in the area in April 1937.

## VRYBURG (1899-1900)

A town of British Bechuanaland, occupied by the Boers in November 1899 and reoccupied by the British in May 1900. Both forces overprinted one another's stamps for use in the town.

## — W —

## WADHWAN (1888-c. 1895)

A former feudatory state in western India.

## WALLIS AND FUTUNA ISLANDS (1920-)

Two archipelagos in the South Pacific Ocean, under French protection since 1888.

## WARSAW (1915)

The capital of Poland. During World War I, stamps were issued by the Warsaw Citizens Committee under the authority of the German military commander.

**WARWISZKI (1923)**

A city in northeastern Poland. Formerly part of Lithuania, the city was occupied by Polish forces in 1923, at which time Polish stamps were overprinted for local use.

**WENDEN (LIVONIA) (1862-1902)**

A former district of the Russian province of Livonia, which issued stamps until 1902, when Russian stamps replaced those of Wenden. The area was divided between Latvia and Estonia in 1918.

**WESTERN AUSTRALIA (1854-1913)**

A large state of western Australia. Formerly a separate colony, Western Australia joined in forming the Commonwealth of Australia in January 1901.

**WESTERN HUNGARY (LAJTABANAT) (1921)**

Following World War I, the Allies assigned the formerly Hungarian province of Burgenland to Austria, because of its proximity to Vienna and its predominantly German population. Hungarian irregulars were in occupation of the province, however, and refused to evacuate.

Through Italian mediation, a plebiscite was held in December 1921, with the district around Odenburg (Sopron) being awarded to Hungary and the rest of the province to Austria.

During the Hungarian occupation, overprinted Hungarian stamps and a locally produced set were in use.

**WESTERN UKRAINE (1918-19)**

A briefly independent state in central Europe. Formed in October 1918, from the Austro-Hungarian territories of central and eastern Galicia and Bukovina in an attempt to unite the region with the Ukraine.

In November 1918, Romania occupied Bukovina, and in January 1919, the balance of the Western Ukraine united with the Ukrainian National Republic. In July 1919, the area was occupied by Poland, which, in turn, lost it to the U.S.S.R.

**WEST IRIAN (1962-70)**

Formerly Netherlands New Guinea. Under U.N. administration from 1962-63, West Irian was placed under Indonesian administration on May 1, 1963.

**WILKOMIR (UKMERGE) (1941)**

A city in central Lithuania. During the early months of the German occupation during World War II, overprinted Russian stamps were used in the area.

**WOSNESSENSK (1942)**

A city in the southern Ukraine. During World War II, a provisional issue was made by the German military commander.

**WRANGEL ISSUES (1902-21)**

The last major White Russian (anti-Soviet) commander during the Russian Civil War,

Baron Peter Wrangel was forced to evacuate his forces and followers to refugee camps in Turkey and the Balkans in 1920.

Stamps of Russia, Russian Offices in Turkey, South Russia and Ukraine were overprinted for use in these camps.

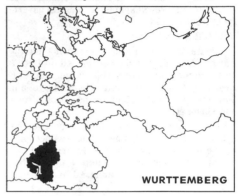

**WURTTEMBERG (1851-1923)**

Former kingdom in southern Germany. Wurttemberg joined the German Empire in 1870. Its regular issues were replaced by those of Germany in 1902, although its official issues continued in use until 1923.

— **Y** —

**YEMEN (1926-)**

An ancient state in southwest Arabia. Under Turkish suzerainty until 1918, Yemen became independent after Turkey's defeat in World War I.

During 1958-61, Yemen was loosely affiliated with Egypt in the United Arab States. In 1962, a military coup ousted the imam and a pro-Egyptian republic was established.

Royalist resistance continued in the interior until 1969, during which time both sides issued a vast number of stamps, most aimed strictly at the philatelic market.

The civil war ended with the victory of the republican regime, and at about the same time, the country's stamp-issuing policy settled back to normal.

**YEMEN (PEOPLE'S DEMOCRATIC REPUBLIC) (1968-)**

A republic in southwest Arabia, south of the Yemen Arab Republic. Established in 1967, when the Federation of South Arabia became independent from Great Britain.

The area was originally named the People's Republic of Southern Yemen; the current name was adopted in 1970.

South Yemen has maintained close ties with the U.S.S.R. It has supported Marxist guerrillas in northern Yemen and in Oman, and a number of Cuban troops are stationed in the country. In 1978, South Yemeni troops aided Ethiopian and Cuban forces against the rebels in Eritrea. In

July 1978, Egypt, the Yemen Arab Republic and Saudi Arabia suspended relations with South Yemen, following a coup that brought the most radical elements of the region to power.

## YUCATAN (1924)

A state in southeastern Mexico. Yucatan was the center of a revolt against the central government from 1923-24.

## YUGOSLAVIA (1918-)

A state in south Europe, bordering on the Adriatic Sea. Yugoslavia was formed on Dec. 1, 1918, from the union of Serbia, Bosnia and Herzegovina, Croatia, Dalmatia, Montenegro and Slovenia, as the Kingdom of the Serbs, Croats and Slovenes.

In 1925, the name Yugoslavia was adopted. During World War II, Yugoslavia was occupied by the Axis, with a number of German and Italian puppet states being created, while the balance of its territory was annexed by its neighbors.

Resistance groups were active during the war, and in late 1944, German forces were driven from the country and a people's republic was proclaimed.

The Communist postwar regime, under the late Josip Broz Tito, broke with Moscow in 1948 and has since maintained its independence from the U.S.S.R.

Many Yugoslavs work in western Europe, and trade with both western and eastern Europe is active.

Separatism remains a major threat to the nation, and since Tito's death in 1980, leadership has been rotated among members of each republic and autonomous province.

## YUGOSLAVIAN OFFICES ABROAD (1943-44)

During World War II, 14 stamps and a souvenir sheet were issued by the Yugoslav government in exile in London. These issues were valid for use aboard Yugoslav vessels fighting against the Axis powers.

## YUNNAN (1926-35)

A province of southwestern China. Regular Chinese stamps were overprinted for use within the province, due to a difference in exchange rates between Yunnan and the rest of the country.

## — Z —

## ZAIRE (1971-)

The Congo Democratic Republic, formerly the Belgian Congo, adopted this name in November 1971.

After the turbulence of the first decade of independence, the relative political stability of the 1970s enabled the government to improve the economic condition of Zaire.

In 1977 and 1978, Cuban-trained Shaban (Katangan) exiles invaded Zaire from Angola.

These invasions were defeated with assistance from Morocco, France, Belgium, Egypt and the U.S.

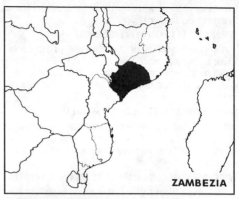

ZAMBEZIA

## ZAMBEZIA (1894-1917)

A former district of Mozambique, in southeast Africa. In 1913, Zambezia was divided into two districts, Quelimane and Tete, which briefly issued their own stamps, until these were replaced by those of Mozambique.

## ZAMBIA (1964-)

A republic in southern Africa. Formerly the British protectorate of Northern Rhodesia, Zambia became independent on Oct. 24, 1964.

## ZANTE (1941, 1943-44)

One of the Ionian Islands, off the western coast of Greece. Zante was occupied by Italy in 1941, and locally overprinted Greek stamps were used for a time. During 1943-44 overprinted issues of the Italian Ionian Islands were used under the German authorities, who occupied the island, following Italy's surrender to the Allies.

## ZANZIBAR (1895-1968)

A group of islands off the coast of Tanganyika in East Africa. An important trading center, Zanzibar was occupied at various times by the Portuguese and Arabs, the latter establishing a powerful state in East Africa when the sultan of Muscat moved his capital to Zanzibar.

In 1885, the sultanate's mainland possessions were divided between Germany, Great Britain and Italy, and in 1890 the islands were placed under a British protectorate.

On Dec. 10, 1963, Zanzibar became independent, and in January 1964, the sultan was deposed. The new regime ousted British and Americans and slaughtered thousands of Arab residents. In April 1964, Zanzibar joined with Tanganyika to form the United Republic of Tanganyika and Zanzibar, renamed Tanzania in 1965.

## ZARA (ZADAR) (1943)

A province on the eastern coast of the Adriatic. Occupied from Austria by Italy after World War I, it was taken from the Italians by Germany in 1943, at which time Italian issues were overprinted by the German authorities.

After World War II, the area became part of Yugoslavia.

### ZARAGOZA (1937)

A province of northern Spain. The Nationalist authorities overprinted contemporary Spanish issues for use in the province in 1937.

Through the late 1940s a number of large, colorful charity stamps were issued in Zaragoza. Although inscribed "Sin Valor Postal" ("Without postal value"), these are often mistaken for postage stamps.

### ZARASAI (ZARGRAD) (1941)

A city in Lithuania. During the early months of the city's occupation during World War II, the German military commander issued overprinted Russian stamps for use in the area.

### ZARKI (1918)

A city in southern Poland. Local issues were made by the municipal authorities, under the auspices of the German military command.

### ZAWIERCIE (1916)

A city in southern Poland. Local issues were made by the municipal authorities, under the auspices of the German military command.

### ZELAYA (1904-12)

A province of Nicaragua on the eastern coast. For a time, the use of silver currency along the coast, while paper currency was used in the rest of the country, necessitated separate stamp issues for the area.

### ZIL ELWAGNE SESEL (1980-)

A British crown colony comprising a number of small islands in the Indian Ocean. Zil Elwagne Sesel was formerly known as the British Indian Ocean Territory.

### ZIMBABWE (1980-)

In May 1979, Rhodesia was offically renamed Zimbabwe Rhodesia, a combination of the African and European names of the country. After six years of bitter civil war, the white regime in Salisbury and the black nationalist factions finally reached a compromise during 1979 negotiations, resulting in the relatively peaceful transition to majority rule in early 1980.

### ZULIA (1891)

A state in northwestern Venezuela, surrounding Lake Maracaibo. In 1891, the state authorities issued two stamps, valid for inland postage, which were in use for three months.

### ZULULAND (1888-98)

An area of southeastern Africa, which was united into a native kingdom under the Zulu tribe in the 19th century.

Conquered by Great Britain in 1887, Zululand was incorporated into Natal in 1898.

### ZURICH (1843-50)

A canton of Switzerland, which issued a number of stamps prior to the release of general Swiss issues in 1850.

# Country Name Cross-Index

Over the years, and especially since the breakup of the European colonial empires since the 1960s, many nations have adopted new names. Below is a short list of some of the changes that most often confuse us as stamp collectors.

| IS | WAS |
|---|---|
| Bangladesh | (East) Pakistan |
| Belize | British Honduras |
| Benin | Dahomey |
| Botswana | Bechuanaland Protectorate |
| Burundi | Urundi |
| Colombia | Grenadine Confederation(1858-61) |
| | United States of New Granada (1861) |
| | United States of Colombia (1861-85) |
| Cambodia | Khmer Republic (1971-75) Democratic Kampuchea (1975-79) |
| Djibouti Republic | Somali Coast (1902-67) |
| | French Territory of the Afars and Issas (1967-77) |
| Equatorial Guinea | Fernando Po + Rio Muni (Spanish Guinea) |
| Ghana | Gold Coast |
| Guinea | French Guinea |
| Guinea-Bissau | Portuguese Guinea |
| Guyana | British Guiana |
| Indonesia | Netherlands Indies |
| Iran | Persia |
| Iraq | Mesopotamia |
| Israel | Palestine |

| IS | WAS |
|---|---|
| Jordan | Trans-Jordan |
| Kenya | British East Africa |
| Kiribati | Gilbert Islands |
| Lesotho | Basutoland |
| Malagasy Republic | Madagascar |
| Malawi | British Central Africa (1891-1907) |
|  | Nyasaland (1907-64) |
| Malaysia | Malaya + Sarawak + Sabah (North Borneo) |
| Mali | French Sudan |
| Rwanda | Ruanda |
| Sabah | North Borneo |
| Somalia | Italian Somalia + British Somaliland Protectorate |
| Sri Lanka | Ceylon |
| Tanzania | Tanganyike + Zanzibar |
| Thailand | Siam |
| Tuvalu | Ellice Islands |
| United Arab Emirates | Trucial States |
| Vanuatu | New Hebrides |
| West Irian | Netherlands New Guinea |
| Yemen People's | Aden (1937-65) |
| Democratic Republic | South Arabia (1965-67) |
|  | People's Republic of Southern Yemen (1967-71) |
| Zaire | Congo Free State (1885-1908) |
|  | Belgian Congo (1908-60) |
|  | Congo Democratic Republic (1960-71) |
| Zambia | Northern Rhodesia |
| Zil Elwagne Sesel | British Indian Ocean Territory |
| Zimbabwe | Southern Rhodesia (1924-65) |
|  | Rhodesia (1965-80) |

# Universal Postal Union

The world postal service forms part of the daily life of people everywhere. Moreover, the proper running of this service is essential to society and even more to the life of the international community. Although one of the oldest intergovernmental organizations in existence, the Universal Postal Union is not widely known to the public at large. Therefore, a brief description of its main bodies may throw some light on an organization playing a leading role in the field of international cooperation.

Without going back to the origin of the post in remote antiquity or dwelling on its embryonic state in the Middle Ages, it should be pointed out that the dispatch of letters then depended on the messenger services of royal households, universities and major religious orders.

Not until the 16th century was an international postal service worthy of the name set up, on the initiative of Franz von Taxis.

The exchange of mail between Austria, Germany, The Netherlands, Italy, France and Spain was, henceforth, to be governed by international agreements.

These, however, were bilateral agreements, adapted to the specific situation of each country. This gave rise to a great many postal rates, calculated in various currencies according to different units of weight and measurement.

Just how complex it was to run the service at both national and international levels can easily be imagined.

Faced with this extreme complexity (there were more than 1,200 different rates before the UPU was founded) and faster means of transport (it was the era of steamships and railways), the postal administrations realized the need to standardize charges and simplify formalities of all kinds.

The introduction of a single rate — the penny postage — hand in hand with the introduction of the postage stamp by Rowland Hill in 1840 opened up new horizons.

In 1863, on the initiative of Montgomery Blair, postmaster general of the United States, a conference was held in Paris.

This conference, which was attended by delegates from 15 European and American countries, established the general principles recommended to administrations as a basis for their mutual agreements.

It had become clear that bilateral agreements were no longer sufficient. In fact, they were an obstacle to the development of international postal communications.

To cope with the situation, a single convention between states concerning postal relations was needed. The honor of bringing this about rests with Heinrich von Stephan, a high-ranking official of the postal administration of the Confederation of Northern Germany.

At his suggestion, the Swiss Government convened at Bern, on Sept. 15, 1874, a conference which was attended by representatives from 22 states. These included:

Austria, Belgium, Denmark, Egypt, France, Germany, Great Britain, Greece, Hungary, Italy, Luxembourg, The Netherlands, Norway, Portugal, Romania, Russia, Serbia, Spain, Sweden, Switzerland, Turkey and the United States.

An agreement was quickly reached, and on Oct. 9, a treaty concerning the establishment of a General Postal Union — commonly known as the Bern Treaty — was signed.

This was the forerunner of the multilateral convention governing the international postal service. Although Montenegro did not take part in the Bern Congress, it signed the treaty on July 1, 1875.

The Bern Treaty came into force on July 1, 1875 (in the case of France on Jan. 1, 1876). In 1878, the name General Postal Union was replaced by Universal Postal Union.

## General Principles

Any member of the United Nations may accede to the UPU, according to current provisions, and also sovereign countries which do not belong to the U.N. may request admission to the UPU. They are admitted if the request is approved by at least two-thirds of the member countries of the Union.

The basic act of the Union is the Constitution, the conditions governing the application of which are specified in "General Regulations."

The constitution sets forth the aims of the Union and lays down precise rules concerning its organic structure. Member countries are considered therein as forming "a single postal territory for the reciprocal exchange of letter-post items."

A derivation of this principle is that of freedom of transit, i.e., the obligation of intermediary administrations also to transport letter-post items delivered to them in transit by another postal administration.

Mention should be made of other fundamental principles essential to the operation of the service — those on fixing charges within specific limits and those relating to standard weight steps.

From 1875 to 1971, the administrations of origin were authorized to retain the entire charges levied by them, and the administrations of destination were not remunerated for the distribution of letter-post items.

This was based on the presumption that a letter elicits a reply and that mail traffic was, therefore, the same in both directions.

However, the 1969 Tokyo Congress, to take account of the growing imbalance of exchanges, decided that an administration which, in its exchanges with another administration, receives more letter-post items than it sends, has the right to collect from the dispatching administration, as compensation, a payment for the costs incurred by the conveyance, sorting and delivery of the excess international mail received (terminal dues).

Certain common rules applicable to the different branches of international postal services and the provisions governing letter-post services are contained in the convention report, supplemented by "Detailed Regulations."

The concept of letter post applies to five categories of items — letters (including aerogrammes), post cards, printed matter, literature in raised relief for the blind, and small packets.

The convention fixes the rates, the maximum and minimum weight and size limits, and the conditions of acceptance.

In addition, the convention prescribes the methods for calculating and collecting transit charges (for letter-post items passing through the territories of one or more countries) and terminal dues.

It also establishes regulations for the registered item service, the air conveyance of mail (increasingly widespread today), as well as that of certain objects, the transport of which requires special precautions (infectious substances and radioactive substances).

The constitution, general regulations, the convention and its detailed regulations are binding on all member countries.

Since some 164 countries now come under these acts, their provisions affect practically the entire population of the world.

Optional agreements moreover govern the operation of postal services as regards the handling of insured values, parcels, postal orders, giro, reimbursement, collection, savings and subscriptions to newspapers and periodicals.

To keep abreast of technical advances and their impact on the postal field, the acts of the Union as a whole are periodically revised by Congress.

## Union Organization

Congress, the Executive Council, the Consultative Council for Postal Studies and the International Bureau are the main bodies of the Union.

Congress, composed of representatives of all member countries, is the supreme authority in the Union. It is convened in principle every five years.

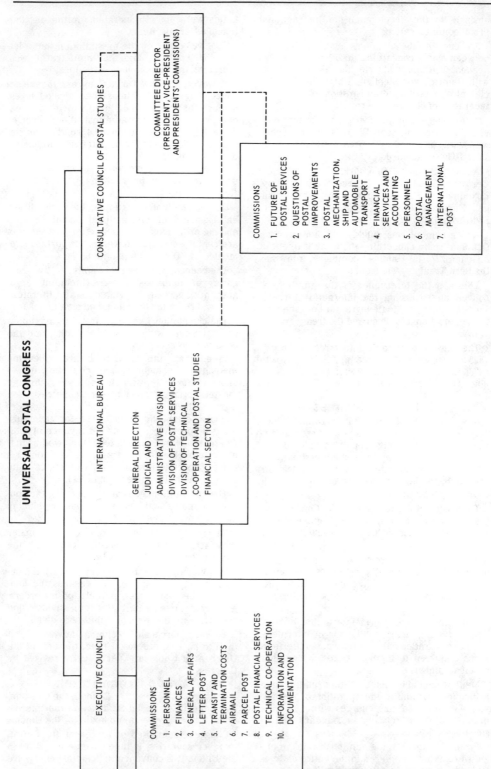

Its main function is to study and revise the acts of the Union, taking as a basis proposals put forward by member countries, the Executive Council or the Consultative Council for Postal Studies.

The Executive Council is composed of 40 members elected by Congress with due regard for equitable geographic distribution, and it meets each year at UPU Headquarters.

It ensures the continuity of the Union's work, coordinating and supervising all Union activities between Congresses, to some extent supervises the activities of the International Bureau, studies administrative, legislative and legal problems of interest to the postal service, draws up proposals, and makes recommendations to Congress.

It is responsible for encouraging, supervising and coordinating international cooperation in the form of postal technical assistance and vocational training.

The Consultative Council for Postal Studies is composed of 35 members elected by Congress for the period between one Congress and the next, that is, normally for 5 years.

In principle, the body meets annually at UPU Headquarters. It is responsible for organizing studies of major problems affecting postal administrations in all UPU member countries, in the technical, operational and economic fields and in the sphere of technical cooperation.

The Council also provides information and opinions on these matters and examines teaching and training problems arising in the new and developing countries.

Since the establishment of the Union, a central office known as the International Bureau has functioned at Bern.

It is responsible for the coordination, publication and dissemination of all manner of information about the international postal service.

At the request of the parties concerned, it gives opinions on disputes. It considers requests for amendments to the acts of the Union, gives notice of changes adopted, and takes part in the preparation of the work of Congress.

It provides secretarial services for UPU bodies and promotes technical cooperation of all types. It can also act as a clearinghouse for the settlement of debts between postal administrations regarding the cost of transit, termination fees, and international reply coupons.

## Technical Cooperation

The principle of technical assistance is contained in Article 1 of the UPU Constitution. It was couched in general terms in order to leave the bodies of the Union the requisite flexibility in the use of all forms of technical cooperation, present and future.

Direct technical assistance between the administrations of UPU member countries (sending officials abroad and exchanging information, documentation and the results of tests) has been a traditional practice.

Technical cooperation activities conducted by the Union itself started in only relatively recent times.

Its participation since 1963 in the U.N. Enlarged Program of Technical Assistance, whose merging with the Special Fund in 1966 produced the U.N. Development Program, was for the UPU one of the outstanding features of recent years.

The UNDP has, in fact, become the main source of finance for UPU assistance to developing countries.

Requests for UPU assistance in technical cooperation matters cover all sectors of the post — planning, organization, management, operations, training and financial services.

The aid provided comes in three forms — recruiting and sending experts, UPU consultants or volunteers; granting vocational training or further training fellowships for individual or group courses (training courses and study cycles); supplying equipment and training or demonstration aids.

Its application is currently based on the following guidelines:

1. Intensifying by the best means available the activities of the UPU in matters of technical assistance in the general context of new order of world economics.

2. Giving priority to the needs of the administrations of the postally least developed countries.

3. Recognizing as priorities the actions aimed at:

— Creation in developing regions of postal works under the standard of the superior framework;

— Improving management of postal services including the utilization of personnel;

— Increasing the number of postal establishments and improving the progress and distribution of mail, particularly in the rural zones, and improving international relations;

— General establishing of postal financial services, including the service of postal authorities and postal savings banks;

4. Concentrating Union efforts on actions aimed at:

— Attribution of UPU aid with priorities going to countries which are most in need and that seem to want to manage the greater part;

— Programs concerning technical assistance;

— Decentralization of technical assistant activities of the UPU thanks to the presence of the UPU on the site;

— Development of the collaboration of the UPU with restricted unions, bearing in mind the political aspects and procedures established by the UPU and the UNDP, as well as the means which arrange the regional organizations;

— The multiplication of the operations of evaluation and the communication of these results to the interested countries in a retroactive manner;

— Systematization of consecutive actions (follow-up) destined to reinforce the results already acquired to facilitate the preparation of recommendations already formulated;

— Active promotion of technical cooperation between developing countries.

## Program of Activities

Within the framework of the UNDP, the UPU executes country and intercountry projects covering all aspects of the postal services and the three components of experts, fellowships and equipment.

Projects common to several countries, which form a very important part of the program, make it possible to solve cheaply and rationally the problems which arise in a certain region (notably, by setting up intercountry postal training schools).

Funds from the UPU budget make it possible to provide additional assistance to that of the UNDP in the form of short consultant missions (three months at most) in specific fields, at the request of the postal administrations concerned.

A noteworthy feature is that, for many missions, the consultants' countries of origin also share the cost of this form of technical cooperation by continuing to pay all or part of the salaries of their officials during the mission.

Since 1981, the UPU has financed, under the title of its "proposed resources," integrated projects comprised of many elements:

Missions of consultants of short duration, formation money, small equipment.

The UPU Special Fund, set up in 1966 and maintained by voluntary contributions from Union member countries, is mainly designed to finance training and further training activities in the form of fellowships, equipment and training courses or study cycles.

Some developed countries provide the International Bureau with funds for the management of associate experts in order to supplement the staff of ongoing projects and give young people with sufficient training the possibility of improving their professional qualifications.

Lastly, under a resolution adopted by the UPU Executive Council in 1967, governments may avail themselves of technical assistance against payment, which they finance themselves from funds in trust.

The International Bureau then undertakes to manage the projects implemented in this way.

The UPU, through the International Bureau, continues to act as an intermediary, wherever expedient, for supplying assistance in kind to developing countries on the basis of offers from developed countries.

It has also made a special effort in the field of vocational training by assessing the needs to be met and listing the facilities available in the various member countries.

In addition, this action is reflected in the establishment or reinforcement of national or multinational schools and the organization of study cycles for the further training of senior staff and of instructor-training courses with the aid of which a large number of postal administrations now have qualified postal instructors.

The UPU also makes sustained efforts to promote technical cooperation among developing countries (TCDC) in order to facilitate mutual assistance between these countries.

## Union's Finances

Each Congress fixes the maximum UPU expenditure for the five succeeding years. At its annual session, the Executive Council examines and approves the Union's annual budget.

The Union's expenses are borne jointly by all member countries which, for this purpose, are divided into eight contribution classes. The contributions vary according to class, in the ratio of 1 to 50.

## Cooperation with U.N.

The UPU maintains excellent relations with the U.N. Under an agreement concluded between the U.N. and the UPU, in 1947, "the United Nations recognizes the Universal Postal Union as the specialized agency responsible for taking such action as may be appropriate under its basic instrument for the accomplishment of the purposes set forth therein . . ."

With this agreement, which came into force on July 1, 1948, the UPU legally became a member of the huge U.N. system of organizations.

Cooperation between the UPU and the U.N. took another major step forward in 1968 when the UNDP gave a favorable reception to large-scale postal projects for setting up or expanding national or multinational training schools in Africa, Asia, Latin America and the Middle East.

The UPU is also in close contact with the International Telecommunication Union and makes great efforts to take part in preparing and implementing joint technical assistance projects with it, especially in the vocational training field.

The UPU also cooperates with other specialized agencies and organizations connected with the U.N. in all matters of common interest, e.g., with the International Civil Aviation Organization on the development of airmail traffic, with the International Atomic Energy Agency on methods relating to the postal conveyance of radioactive substances, and with the World Health Organization on the transport of perishable biological substances.

In addition, the UPU has set up contact committees with other international organizations (International Air Transport Association, Customs Cooperation Council, and International Organization for Standardization).

These committees are mixed bodies with equal representation whose job it is to study general policy questions and find constructive solutions.

## Restricted Postal Unions

The UPU authorizes its members to create restricted postal unions. These are for the purpose of improving reciprocal relations between member countries and resolving specific postal problems of a continent, a region or a subregion.

The restricted unions are juridically independent of the UPU which gives them, nevertheless, a status of observer in that measure or the equal acceptance of the UPU observers at its meetings.

The UPU requires that the restricted unions do not introduce conditions that are less favorable for the public than those laid down in the UPU acts.

The UPU currently maintains relations with eight restricted unions.

## International Postal Traffic

The existence of a worldwide network and of offices scattered even in the most remote localities ensures the operation and flow of international postal traffic everywhere.

There are about 620,000 post offices in the world. These employ some 5 million persons who spare no effort to ensure that the postal services operate in the best interests of users.

More than 280 billion postal items are thus handled yearly in accordance with the time-honored principles of the post which is considered an international public service.

Separate from the postal presentations, the bureaus offer financial services (postal money orders, giro, postal savings, banks) under the national plan and often likewise under the international plan.

## Achievements

The establishment of the UPU has made it possible to standardize the fixing of charges applied to postal items. Thus, the rate of postage paid by users is based on international standards.

Whereas obstacles are still raised in man's path at the boundaries of his territory, there are no frontiers for the post.

A postal item must reach the addressee regardless of his social status, religion or race or the political views of his country. Mailings with impressions in relief are being used for the blind.

To profit from the rapid growth of air transport, the UPU has launched, in the past few years, an action in favor of maximum usage of aircraft for the transport of mail.

The progress realized is encouraging. Hopefully, in the near future, all mail will be sent by air.

Lastly, by allowing free postage for items concerning prisoners of war and civilian internees, as well as for literature for the blind, and by conveying periodicals at a reduced rate, the UPU has transformed its humanitarian aims into reality.

## Conclusion

This touches solely on the salient features of an organization over a century old and gives no more than a brief outline of the UPU's activities.

The Union's role is the development of communications between people by an effective operation of postal services and to contribute to attaining the highest mark of international cooperation in cultural, social and economic domains, as well as offering assistance in postal technology as is demanded by member countries.

Throughout the years, the UPU has been wholly devoted to the task assigned by the founders and has done even more, for it has managed to adjust to new requirements of technology and development.

Even in the critical days of the two world wars, its stability was evident. By constant efforts intensifying international collaboration, the UPU is contributing to bringing people and nations closer together.

## Congresses

Eighteen congresses have been held by the UPU since its organization, with the following providing a thumbnail sketch and principal business of each of these.

1. Berne, Switzerland, Sept. 15 - Oct. 9, 1874. Treaty concerning the creation of a General Postal Union. Number of countries represented, 22; number of participants, 42.

2. Paris, France, May 2 - June 4, 1878. Insured letters and money orders. Number of countries represented, 37; number of participants, 63; number of proposals, 413.

3. Lisbon, Portugal, Feb. 4 - March 21, 1885. Postal cards, collection of bills. Number of countries represented, 48; number of participants, 84; number of proposals, 818.

4. Vienna, Austria, May 20 - July 4, 1891. Insured parcels, subscriptions to newspapers, Cash-on-Delivery. Number of countries represented, 49; number of participants, 99; number of proposals, 553.

5. Washington, D.C., U.S.A., May 5 - June 15, 1897. Number of countries represented, 56; number of participants, 103; number of proposals, 653.

6. Rome, Italy, April 7 - May 26, 1906. Reply coupons. Number of countries represented, 63; number of participants, 133; number of proposals, 798.

7. Madrid, Spain, Oct. 1 - Nov. 30, 1920. Gold franc becomes base currency, provisions concerning postal identity cards included in convention, transfers. Number of countries represented, 69; number of participants, 171; number of proposals, 2,248.

8. Stockholm, Sweden, July 4 - Aug. 28, 1924. Fiftieth anniversary of UPU. Number of countries represented, 78; number of participants, 182; number of proposals, 1,501.

9. London, England, May 10 - June 28, 1929. Small packets, airmail provisions. Number of countries represented, 85; number of participants, 179; number of proposals, 1,895.

10. Cairo, Egypt, Feb. 1 - March 20, 1934. Postal travelers' checks. Number of countries represented, 81; number of participants, 153; number of proposals, 1,666.

11. Buenos Aires, Argentina, April 1 - May 23, 1939. Number of countries represented, 81; number of participants, 174; number of proposals, 1,108.

12. Paris, France, May 7 - July 5, 1947. U.N.-UPU Agreement, Executive and Liaison committee. Number of countries represented, 79; number of participants, 291; number of proposals, 821.

13. Brussels, Belgium, May 14 - July 11, 1952. Extension to literature for the blind of the exception from postal charges granted to prisoners of war. Number of countries represented, 91; number of participants, 283; number of proposals, 1,712.

14. Ottawa, Canada, Aug. 14 - Oct. 3, 1957. Consultative Committee for Postal Studies, savings. Number of countries represented, 96; number of participants, 290; number of proposals, 1,288.

15. Vienna, Austria, May 29 - July 11, 1964. Constitution, technical cooperation. Number of countries represented, 122; number of participants, 520; number of proposals, 1,244.

16. Tokyo, Japan, Oct. 1 - Nov. 14, 1969. Possibility of compensating very high inward handling charges. Number of countries represented, 133; number of participants, 528; number of proposals, 1,156.

17. Lausanne, Switzerland, May 22 - July 4, 1974. UPU Centenary. Number of countries represented, 141; number of participants, 714; number of proposals, 1,035.

18. Rio de Janeiro, Brazil, Sept. 12-Oct. 22, 1979. Revision of Acts of Union; incorporation into Universal Postal Convention of Insured Letters Agreement. Number of countries represented, 143; number of participants, 824; number of proposals, 1,351.

## Director General

Mohamed Ibrahim Sobhi of Egypt, is director-general of the International Bureau and secretary-general of the Union. He was named to that post during the conference at Lausanne, Switzerland, to take office Jan. 1, 1975. His term of office was renewed during the 1979 Congress.

Thomas Scott of Great Britain is deputy director-general.

## Member Countries

As of May 1, 1980, the membership of the UPU had increased to a total of 164.

The following list constitutes the membership of the Universal Postal Union as of January 1977. The date of current membership is shown in brackets.

| | | |
|---|---|---|
| Afghanistan (April 1928) | Botswana (January 1968) | Colombia (July 1881) |
| Albania (March 1922) | Brazil (July 1877) | Comoros (1976) |
| Algeria (1964) | Bulgaria (July 1879) | Congo (July 1961) |
| Angola (1977) | Burma (October 1949) | Costa Rica (January 1883) |
| Argentina (April 1878) | Burundi (May 1969) | Cuba (October 1902) |
| Australia (October 1907) | Byelorussian S.S.R. (May 1947) | Cyprus (November 1961) |
| Austria (1946) | Cameroon (July 1960) | Czechoslovakia (May 1920) |
| Bahamas (1974) | Canada (July 1878) | Denmark (July 1875) |
| Bahrain (1973) | Cape Verde, Republic of (1976) | Djibouti (1979) |
| Bangladesh (February 1973) | Central African Republic (December 1961) | Dominica (1979) |
| Barbados (November 1967) | | Dominican Republic (October 1880) |
| Belgium (July 1875) | Chad (June 1961) | |
| Benin (April 1961) | Chile (April 1881) | Ecuador (July 1880) |
| Bhutan (March 1969) | China, People's Republic of (March 1914) | Egypt (July 1875) |
| Bolivia (April 1886) | | El Salvador (April 1879) |

Equatorial Guinea (July 1970)
Ethiopia (1945)
Fiji (June 1971)
Finland (February 1918)
France (July 1875)
French Overseas
(various dates)
Gabon (July 1961)
Gambia (October 1974)
German Democratic Republic
(1974)
Germany, Federal Republic of
(1955)
Ghana (October 1957)
Great Britain (July 1875)
British Overseas Territories
(various)
Greece (July 1875)
Grenada (1979)
Guatemala (August 1881)
Guinea (May 1959)
Guinea-Bissau (1974)
Guyana (March 1967)
Haiti (July 1881)
Honduras (April 1879)
Hungary (July 1875)
Iceland (November 1919)
India (July 1876)
Indonesia (1951)
Iran (September 1877)
Iraq (April 1929)
Ireland (September 1923)
Israel (December 1949)
Italy (July 1875)
Ivory Coast (March 1961)
Jamaica (August 1963)
Japan (June 1877, dropped
in 1948, restored 1949)
Jordan (May 1947)
Kampuchea (Khmer)
(December 1951)
Kenya (October 1964)
Korea, Republic of (1949)
Kuwait (February 1960)
Laos, People's Democratic
Republic (May 1952)
Lebanon (May 1946)
Lesotho (September 1967)

Liberia (April 1879)
Libyan Arab Yamahiziya
(June 1952)
Liechtenstein (April 1962)
Luxembourg (July 1875)
Madagascar (November 1961)
Malawi (October 1966)
Malaysia (January 1958)
Maldives (August 1967)
Mali (April 1961)
Malta (May 1965)
Mauritania (March 1967)
Mauritius (August 1969)
Mexico (April 1879)
Monaco (October 1955)
Mongolia (August 1963)
Morocco (October 1956)
Mozambique (1979)
Nauru (April 1969)
Nepal (October 1956)
Netherlands (July 1875)
Netherland Antilles
(December 1954)

New Zealand (October 1907)
Nicaragua (May 1882)
Niger (June 1961)
Nigeria (July 1961)
Norway (July 1875)
Oman (August 1971)
Pakistan (November 1947)
Panama (June 1904)
Papua New Guinea (1976)
Paraguay (July 1881)
Peru (April 1879)
Philippines (January 1922)
Poland (May 1919)
Portugal (July 1875)
Portuguese Provinces in Asia
and Oceania (various)
Qatar (January 1969)
Romania (July 1875)
Rwanda (April 1963)
Saint Lucia (1980)
St. Vincent & Grenadines (1981)
St. Thomas & Prince
Islands (date unknown)
San Marino (July 1915)

Saudi Arabia (January 1927)
Senegal (June 1961)
Seychelles (1979)
Sierra Leone (January 1962)
Singapore (January 1966)
Somalia (July 1960)
South Africa, Republic of
(date unknown)
Spain (July 1875)
Sri Lanka (Ceylon) (July 1949)
Sudan (July 1956)
Surinam, Republic of (1976)
Swaziland (November 1969)
Sweden (July 1875)
Switzerland (July 1875)
Syrian Arab Republic
(May 1946)
Tanzania (March 1963)
Thailand (July 1885)
Togo (March 1962)
Tonga (January 1972)
Trinidad and Tobago
(June 1963)
Tunisia (November 1956)
Turkey (July 1875)
Tuvalu (date unknown)
Uganda (February 1964)
Ukrainian S.S.R. (May 1947)
Union of Soviet Socialist
Republic (As Russia July 1875)
United Arab Emirates
(March 1973)
United States of America
(July 1875)
U.S. Territories (October 1907)
Upper Volta (March 1963)
Uruguay (July 1880)
Vatican City (June 1929)
Venezuela (January 1880)
Vietnam (October 1951)
Yemen Arab Republic
(January 1930)
Yemen (People's Democratic
Republic) (June 1968)
Yugoslavia (December 1921)
Zaire (July 1960)
Zambia (March 1967)
Zimbabwe (April 1980)

## Post Codes of the World

On Nov. 3, 1961, the Federal German Post Office became the first administration to introduce post codes for the purpose of speeding the delivery of mail. Since that time postal administrations in many parts of the world have come to recognize the advantages of such a system and have also adopted similar procedures that serve to identify individual postal localities.

As might be expected, these systems vary considerably in structure and information content, according to communications and geographical factors in each country, different postal conveyance systems, traditional habits of postal users, and demands the respective postal administrations make on their own post code systems.

Basically, all systems have the following objectives in common.

— They create the prerequisites for mechanized or automated processing of mail;

— They facilitate and speed up mail sorting and forwarding to the various destinations and in many cases to the delivery or withdrawal office.

The following listing from Union Postale-UPU, summarize principal information regarding post codes, the countries using such a system, type of code and an example:

The information included is:

1. *Coded country name* — In relations between certain member countries the coded name (one, two or three letters) of the country of destination generally followed by a dash precedes the post-code number. The abbreviation consists of the letters used in certain international codes (for example the Road Traffic Convention). It must only be used in relations with member countries which expressly accept it.

2. *Type and position of code* — This column gives the number and variations of the constituents of the code and its position with regard to other parts of the address.

3. *Specimen address* — In the various specimen addresses, the spacing, interval, code, name of place of destination and capital letters are given in the manner requested by administrations. It should be noted that in Article 113 of the Detailed Regulations of the Universal Postal Convention, users are recommended to write the name of the place and country of destination in capital letters. Some constituents of the address are also underlined when this is formally requested by the country of destination.

| Name of country | Name code | Nature and position of code | Specimen address for items addressed to the country |
|---|---|---|---|
| Argentina | | 4 digits on left of place-name | Senor Jose PEREZ<br>Montiel No. 113<br>5501 GODOY CRUZ, MENDOZA<br>ARGENTINA |
| Australia | | 4 digits on right of name of State | Mr. J. B. Brownhall<br>264 High Street<br>FAWKNER VICTORIA<br>3060 AUSTRALIA |
| Austria | A- | 4 digits on left of place-name, 2 spaces between place-name and code number | Herrn Franz Huber<br>Beethovenstrasse 55<br>A-9020 KLAGENFURT<br>AUSTRIA |
| Belgium | B- | 4 digits on left of place-name, 2 spaces between place-name and code number | Monsieur Emile Dubois<br>Rue du Diamant 215<br>B-4800 VERVIERS<br>BELGIUM |
| Bermuda | | 3 digits on right of parish name; dash between first and second digit | Mr. Sydney B. Corbett<br>Tee Street<br>DEVONSHIRE 4-21<br>BERMUDA |

| Name of country | Name code | Nature and position of code | Specimen address for items addressed to the country |
|---|---|---|---|
| Brazil | | 5 digits on left of place-name, dash between place-name and code name | Senor Antonio de Oliveira<br>Cachoeira<br>18430-RIBEIRAO, BRANCO, SP<br>BRAZIL |
| Bulgaria | | 4 digits on left of place-name | Stojan Ivanov<br>Rue V Droumev 58<br>1505 SOFIA<br>BULGARIA |
| Canada | | 6 alphanumeric constituents in the following order ANA NAN (A 1 Alphabetical, N 1 numeric) on the last line of the address, with a space between the 3rd and 4th constituents. (If there is not room: on the right of the name of the country and separated from it by 2 spaces) | Monsieur Jean Durand<br>150, Rue Nepean, Apt. 5<br>OTTAWA, Ont.<br>CANADA<br>K2P 0B6<br>or<br>Monsieur Paul Dupont<br>12, Rue Verte, Apt. 65<br>OTTAWA, Ont.<br>CANADA K2P 0B6 |
| Chad | | 5 figures preceded by the letter E | |
| Czecho-slovakia | | 5 digits on left of place-name, a space between the 3rd and 4th digits, 2 spaces between the place-name and the code. When the name of the delivery office differs from that of the place of destination, the code-number should be put on the left of the delivery office | M. Jan Kemr<br>Olsanska 18<br>276 01 MELNIK<br>CZECHOSLOVAKIA |
| Denmark | DK- | 4 digits on left of place-name, 2 spaces between place-name and code number | Herr Thor Nielsen<br>Tietgensgade 137<br>DK-8800 VIBORG<br>DENMARK |
| Finland | SF- | 5 digits on left of place-name | M. Asko Teirila<br>Case postale 511<br>SF-39140 AKOENMAA<br>FINLAND |
| France | F- | 5 digits on left of name of delivery office<br>The French post offices listed alphabetically in ILPO are followed by the name of the delivery office. There are two possibilities:<br>a. When the office is the *delivery office* (the name of the office and the name written after the country-code are identical)<br>b. When the office is *not the delivery office* (the name of the office is | <br><br><br><br><br>a. Monsieur Jean Page<br>  Impasse s. Georges<br>  F-80100 ABBEVILLE<br>  FRANCE<br><br>b. Monsieur Robert Marin<br>  Rue de l'Eglise<br>  Dunes |

| Name of country | Name code | Nature and position of code | Specimen address for items addressed to the country |
|---|---|---|---|
| France (cont.) | | different from the name written after the country-code). The name of the office of destination should be written on a line above the post-code and delivery office | F-82340 AUVILLAR<br>FRANCE |
| German Dem. Rep. | DDR- | 2, 3 or 4 digits on left of place-name. Three spaces between code-number and place-name, one space between addressee's name and place-name, and between street name (or postal box, etc.) and name of country | a. When address is typed or printed.<br><br>Herrn Alfred Krause<br><br>DDR-402 HALLE<br>Burgstrasse 16<br><br>GERMAN DEM. REP.<br>(or GDR)<br><br>b. When address is handwritten:<br><br>Herrn Richard Wolf<br><br>DDR-402 HALLE<br>Burgstrasse 16<br><br>GERMAN DEM. REP.<br>(or GDR) |
| Germany, Fed. Rep. of | D- | 4 digits on left of place-name. The zeros at the end of the code can no longer be omitted | Herrn Erich Muller<br>Goethestrasse 13<br>D-2000 HAMBURG<br>GERMANY, FED. REP. of<br>(or GFR) |
| Great Britain | | 5, 6 or 7 digits or letters on the right of the name of the country, with a space before the last three components | Mr. Walter C. Brown<br>500, North Park<br>DULVERTON, SOMERSET<br>GREAT BRITAIN TA22 9EX<br>(or: England) |
| Hungary | H- | 4 digits on left of place-name, double-spacing between the latter and the addressee's name and between the name of the street (or post office box) and the name of the country | Nagy Sandor<br><br>H-1022 BUDAPEST<br>Hermann Otto ut 2<br><br>HUNGARY |
| Iceland | IS- | 3 digits on left of place-name | Hr. Jon Jonsson<br>Einimel 80<br>IS-107 REYKJAVIK<br>ICELAND |
| India | | 6 digits on right of place-name, a dash between place-name and code number | Mr. Ali Jerath<br>PO Box 11-56<br>MADRAS - 600027<br>INDIA |
| Israel | | 5 digits on left of place-name, space between 2nd and 3rd digits | Monsieur Dan Tamir<br>2, Rue Ben Yehuda<br>94 622 JERUSALEM<br>ISRAEL |

| Name of country | Name code | Nature and position of code | Specimen address for items addressed to the country |
|---|---|---|---|
| Italy | I- | 5 digits on left of place-name | Sig. Bernardino Masci<br>Via G Garibaldi 27<br>I-47037 RIMINI (FORLI)<br>ITALY |
| Japan | | 5 digits on left of country name, a dash between 3rd and 4th digits. 3 digits for main post offices | Mr. Kaga Imamura<br>PO Box 12-45<br>YOKOHAMA<br>231-91 JAPAN |
| Korea (Rep) | | 5 digits on right of place-name, dash between 3rd and 4th digit. For large towns, the first 3 digits are enough | M. Kim Kang<br>PO Box 1165<br>SEOUL 100<br>KOREA REP. |
| Liechtenstein | FL- | Same code as Switzerland | |
| Malaysia | | 4 digits on right of place-name, a dash between 2nd and 3rd components | M. Ali Bin Mohd<br>112, Jalan Pudu<br>KUALA LUMPUR 05-03<br>SELANGOR<br>MALAYSIA |
| Namibia | | 4 digits on left of place-name | |
| Nepal | | 6 digits | Mr. L. Manandhar<br>15/665 Naxal Nagpokhari<br>Bagmati Zone<br>KATHMANDU<br>NEPAL 711000 |
| Netherlands | | 6 components (4 digits and 2 letters) on left of place-name, a space between 4th and 5th components, 2 spaces between the code and place-name | M. J. Lucassen<br>Morsstr 111<br>2312 BK LEIDEN<br>NETHERLANDS |
| Norway | N- | 4 digits on left of place-name. Exception: Oslo is divided into 12 delivery districts (see example b.) and has no code number | a. Herr Ole Olsen<br>   Bergsmuget 19<br>   N-3700 SKIEN NORWAY<br>b. Herr Nils Nilsen<br>   Hammergase 27<br>OSLO 4, NORWAY |
| Philippines | | 4 digits on right of place-name | Mr. Juan de la Cruz<br>30 M H del Pilar St<br>PASIG RIZAL 3130<br>PHILIPPINES |
| Poland | | 5 digits on left of place-name, a dash between 2nd and 3rd digits | M. Jan Nowak<br>ul Cicha 5 m. 7<br>62-806 KALISZ<br>POLAND |
| Romania | R- | 4 digits on left of place-name (City of Bucharest: 5 digits) | M. Gheorghe Popesti<br>Bd Golescu nr 38<br>R-3581 CHISTAG, BIHOR<br>ROMANIA |
| San Marino | I- | Same code as Italy | |

| Name of country | Name code | Nature and position of code | Specimen address for items addressed to the country |
|---|---|---|---|
| South Africa | | 4 digits on left of, or below place-name | Mr. James Smith<br>PO Box 2211<br>0001 PRETORIA<br>SOUTH AFRICA<br>or<br>Mrs. A. L. Jones<br>Red Park<br>SPRINGS<br>1560 SOUTH AFRICA |
| Sweden | S- | 5 digits on left of place-name, a space between 3rd and 4th digits, 2 spaces between code number and place-name | Fru Inger Lilja<br>Vasavagen 3, 4 tr<br>S-582 20 LINKOPING<br>SWEDEN |
| Switzerland | CH- | 4 digits on left of place-name | Monsieur Andre Perret<br>Pension Mirabeau<br>CH-1874 CHAMPERY<br>SWITZERLAND |
| USSR | | 6 digits on left of place-name. This name must be given on the first line of the address. The symbol accompanying a post-code in ILPO means that the last two or three zeros must be replaced by the digits constituting the number of the urban post office serving the addressee. Where that symbol does not appear, the post-code is that of the head office concerned | 270045 BRESTSKAJA<br>Medyn, oulitsa Gagazin 7<br>Ivanov AP<br>USSR |
| United States of America | | 5 digits on right of, or below place-name, 2 spaces between name of State and code number | Mr. Joe Engle<br>1612 Dexter Street<br>FORT WAYNE, IN 46805<br>USA<br>or<br>Mrs. Betty Johnson<br>1801 Fox Avenue<br>TOWN AND COUNTRY VILLAGE, CA<br>USA 95821 |
| Vatican | I- | Same code as Italy | |
| Vietnam | VN- | 5 digits on right of place-name | M. Nguyen Van Nam<br>Pac Bo<br>Hoa An<br>CAO LAN<br>VIET NAM VN-22494 |
| Yugoslavia | YU- | 5 digits on left of place-name | M. Ante Rankovic<br>Palmoticeva 2<br>YU-11001 BEOGRAD<br>YUGOSLAVIA |

# U.S. Stamp Popularity Polls

**2**

## Reader-Surveys

Starting with the United States stamp issues of 1948, Linn's Stamp News each year has conducted a reader-survey to determine the Most Popular, Worst, and Least Necessary stamp emissions of the previous year. In the earlier polls only two categories were used, Best and Worst. Over the years, many changes have been made until, starting in 1979, readers voted in six different categories.

In the earlier polls participants voted for first place, second place, and sometimes third place in the categories offered. The following tabulation lists the first, second and third (if used) choices in that order. Stamp reproductions follow the survey listing.

### 1948

BEST — Lincoln's Gettysburg Address commemorative; Rough Riders commemorative.

WORST — American Turners Society centennial commemorative; Fort Kearney commemorative.

### 1949

BEST — Universal Postal Union 25¢ airmail commemorative; Annapolis Tercentenary commemorative; Washington and Lee commemorative.

WORST — Edgar Allan Poe Famous American issue; Puerto Rico Gubernatorial Election commemorative.

### 1950

BEST — Freedom stamp which was one of four in National Capital Sesquicentennial series; Legislative stamp from the same series.

WORST — Railroad Engineers of America (Casey Jones) commemorative; California Statehood commemorative.

LEAST NECESSARY — American Bankers Association commemorative; Samuel Gompers Famous American issue.

### 1951

BEST — Nevada commemorative; Landing of Cadillac commemorative.

WORST — Colorado Statehood commemorative; United Confederate Veterans commemorative.

LEAST NECESSARY — Battle of Brooklyn commemorative.

APPROPRIATE DESIGN — American Chemical Society commemorative.

### 1952

BEST — International Red Cross commemorative; Airmail stamp in denomination of 80¢.

WORST — Mount Rushmore National Memorial commemorative; North Atlantic Treaty Organization commemorative.

LEAST NECESSARY — Baltimore and Ohio Railroad Charter commemorative.

APPROPRIATE DESIGN — International Red Cross commemorative.

### 1953

BEST — 300th Anniversary of New York City commemorative; Commodore Matthew Calbraith Perry commemorative.

WORST — Trucking Industry commemorative; Ohio Statehood Sesquicentennial commemorative.

LEAST NECESSARY — Trucking Industry commemorative.

APPROPRIATE DESIGN — Sagamore Hill commemorative.

### 1954

BEST — Lewis and Clark commemorative; Statue of Liberty 8¢ issue.

WORST — Nebraska Territorial commemorative; Kansas Territorial commemorative.

LEAST NECESSARY — Airmail 4¢ issue.

APPROPRIATE DESIGN — Special Delivery issue.

## 1955

BEST — Rotary International commemorative; Atoms for Peace commemorative.

WORST — Fort Ticonderoga commemorative; Land Grant Colleges commemorative.

LEAST NECESSARY — Andrew W. Mellon Famous American issue.

## 1956

BEST — Wildlife Conservation showing Pronghorn Antelope; Wheatland commemorative.

WORST — Pure Food and Drug Laws commemorative; Nassau Hall commemorative.

LEAST NECESSARY — Pure Food and Drug Laws commemorative.

BEST DESIGN (not considering color) — Wheatland commemorative.

## 1957

BEST — American Flag commemorative; Wildlife Conservation issue showing Whooping Crane.

WORST — Polio commemorative; Oklahoma Statehood commemorative.

LEAST NECESSARY — Ship-building commemorative.

BEST DESIGN (not considering color) — Flushing Remonstrance commemorative.

## 1958

BEST — Forest Conservation issue; Mackinac Bridge commemorative.

WORST — Gardening—Horticulture commemorative; Journalism — Freedom of the Press commemorative.

LEAST NECESSARY — Gardening—Horticulture commemorative.

## 1959

BEST — 49-star American Flag commemorative; St. Lawrence Seaway Opening commemorative.

WORST — Dental Health commemorative; Balloon Jupiter commemorative.

LEAST NECESSARY — Dr. Ephraim McDowell commemorative in Famous American issue.

## 1960

BEST — United States—Japan commemorative; Pony Express 4¢ commemorative.

WORST — World Refugee Year commemorative; Boys Clubs of America commemorative.

LEAST NECESSARY — American Woman commemorative.

## 1961

BEST — Frederic Remington commemorative; Range Conservation commemorative.

WORST — Nursing commemorative; Naismith—Basketball commemorative.

LEAST NECESSARY — Naismith—Basketball commemorative.

## 1962

BEST — Winslow Homer commemorative; New Mexico Statehood commemorative.

WORST — Apprenticeship commemorative; Battle of Shiloh commemorative.

LEAST NECESSARY — Apprenticeship commemorative.

## 1963

BEST — John James Audubon commemorative; City Mail Delivery commemorative.

WORST — Emancipation Proclamation commemorative; Science commemorative.

LEAST NECESSARY — Science commemorative.

## 1964

BEST — Homemakers commemorative; Charles M. Russell American Painting commemorative.

WORST — Fine Arts commemorative; Amateur Radio Operators commemorative.

LEAST NECESSARY — Fine Arts commemorative.

## 1965

BEST — Copley American Painting commemorative; Adlai Stevenson Memorial issue.

WORST — Salvation Army commemorative; Traffic Safety commemorative.

LEAST NECESSARY — Dante Alighieri commemorative; Physical Fitness—Sokol commemorative.

## 1966

BEST — Beautification of America commemorative; Christmas issue.

WORST — Great River Road commemorative; Humane Treatment of Animals commemorative.

LEAST NECESSARY — Great River Road commemorative.

## 1967

BEST — Twin Space commemorative pair; Christmas issue.

WORST — Henry David Thoreau commemorative; Canada Centennial commemorative.

LEAST NECESSARY — Urban Planning commemorative.

## 1968

BEST — Waterfowl Conservation commemorative showing ducks in flight; American Indian commemorative showing Chief Joseph.

WORST — Support our Youth commemorative; Leif Erikson commemorative.

LEAST NECESSARY — Arkansas River Navigation commemorative.

## 1969

BEST — First Man on the Moon airmail commemorative; Apollo 8 commemorative.

WORST — W. C. Handy commemorative; Professional Baseball commemorative.

LEAST NECESSARY — W. C. Handy commemorative; Dartmouth College Case—Daniel Webster commemorative.

## 1970

BEST — Maine Statehood commemorative; Natural History issue.

WORST — Wildlife Conservation issue; South Carolina commemorative.

LEAST NECESSARY — Christmas Toys block.

## 1971

MOST POPULAR — Wildlife Conservation issue; Space Achievement Decade issue.

WORST — Blood Donor issue; American Revolution Bicentennial issue.

LEAST NECESSARY — American Wool Industry issue; Christmas Partridge issue.

## 1972

MOST POPULAR — Wildlife Conservation block; Cape Hatteras block.

WORST — Osteopathic Medicine issue; Parent Teachers Association issue.

LEAST NECESSARY — Osteopathic Medicine issue; Family Planning issue.

## 1973

MOST POPULAR — Boston Tea Party block; Love issue.

WORST — Love issue; Postal Service Employees issue.

LEAST NECESSARY — Postal Service Employees issue; Love issue.

## 1974

MOST POPULAR — Mineral Heritage block of four; Skylab issue; Universal Postal Union stamps.

WORST — Preserve the Environment issue; Zip Code issue; Energy Conservation issue.

LEAST NECESSARY — Horse Racing issue; Universal Postal Union stamps; Zip Code issue.

## 1975

MOST POPULAR — Apollo-Soyuz pair; Banking and Commerce issue, two designs; U.S. Military Services (uniforms) four designs.

WORST — Collective Bargaining issue; International Women's Year issue; Contributors to the Cause, four designs.

LEAST NECESSARY — Collective Bargaining issue; International Women's Year issue; D.W. Griffith issue.

## 1976

MOST POPULAR — State Flags issue, 50 different designs; Bicentennial souvenir sheets, four designs; Spirit of '76 triptych.

WORST — A.S. Ochs issue; Telephone Centennial issue; Interphil '76 issue.

LEAST NECESSARY — A.S. Ochs issue; Bicentennial souvenir sheets, four designs; Chemistry issue.

## 1977

MOST POPULAR — Butterflies block; Pueblo Pottery block; Lindbergh Transatlantic Flight.

BEST DESIGN — Pueblo Pottery block; Butterflies block, Colorado Statehood Centennial.

WORST — Energy pair; Talking Pictures; Peace Bridge.

LEAST NECESSARY — Energy pair; Talking Pictures; Butterflies block.

## 1978

MOST POPULAR — American Owls block; CAPEX souvenir sheet; American Trees block.

BEST DESIGN — American Trees block; CAPEX souvenir sheet, American Owls block.

LEAST POPULAR — Harriet Tubman; American Quilts block; Carl Sandburg.

LEAST NECESSARY — CAPEX souvenir sheet; American Quilts blocks; Photography.

## 1979

MOST POPULAR — Endangered Flowers block; Summer 1980 Olympics block; Pennsylvania Toleware block.

BEST DESIGN — American Architecture block; Endangered Flowers block; Pennsylvania Toleware block.

MOST IMPORTANT — Vietnam Veterans (regular); International Year of the Child; Summer 1980 Olympics.

LEAST POPULAR — Dr. Martin Luther King; Robert F. Kennedy; Santa Claus (Christmas).

WORST DESIGN — Dr. Martin Luther King; Santa Claus (Christmas); Robert F. Kennedy.

LEAST NECESSARY — Robert F. Kennedy; Pennsylvania Toleware block; Dr. Martin Luther King.

## 1980

MOST POPULAR — Coral Reefs block; Winter Olympics block; Letter Writing strip of six.

LEAST POPULAR — W.C. Fields; American Education; Edith Wharton.

BEST DESIGN — Coral Reefs block; American Architecture block; Northwest Indian Masks block.

WORST DESIGN — American Education; Veterans Administration; Edith Wharton.

MOST IMPORTANT — Winter Olympics block; Helen Keller/Anne Sullivan; American Architecture block.

LEAST NECESSARY — W.C. Fields; Frances Perkins; Edith Wharton.

## 1981

MOST POPULAR — Space Achievements, block of eight; Desert Plants, block of four; Wildlife Habitats, block of four.

LEAST POPULAR — Professional Management; Savings and Loans; Whitney Moore Young.

BEST DESIGN — Desert Plants block; Space Achievements block; Wildlife Habitats block.

WORST DESIGN — Professional Management; Savings and Loans; Space Achievements.

MOST IMPORTANT — Space Achievements block; International Year of Disabled Persons; Wildlife Habitats block.

LEAST NECESSARY — Professional Management; Savings and Loans; James Hoban 18-cent.

1948

1949

1950

1951

1952

1953

1954

1955

1956

1957

1958

1959

1960

1961

1962

1963

1964

1966

1965

1967

1968

1969              1970

1971

1972

1973

1974

1975

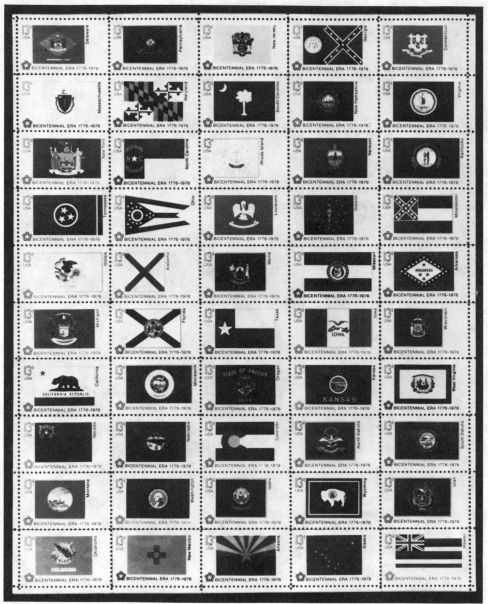

1976

1977

1978

1979

1980

1981

# History of U.S. Postal Communications 3

## Development of the Posts

Americans love to talk about their postal service. Usually it's to tell the sad tale of letters gone astray and mangled packages. What many of us fail to realize is that we are dealing with a tremendous corporation, maintaining tens of thousands of offices, and recording receipts of hundreds of millions of dollars annually in New York City alone.

The story of how our postal service developed from humble beginnings to the present giant parallels the history of the United States itself.

### Early Services

In the early days of European settlement in America, communications with family and friends back on the Continent, or with persons in other colonies, was a very uncertain affair. Letters were entrusted to the crews of sailing vessels, with the expectation that they would take the missives to their destinations or to places where more formal service was available.

As time passed, efforts were made to standardize and safeguard the treatment of mail matter. Collecting points for the dispatch and receipt of overseas correspondence were established, and by the 1650s local laws allowed for the movement of letters inland from plantation to plantation under specific penalties for lack of cooperation.

Later in the 17th century colonial officials, among them New York Governor Francis Lovelace, sought to set up regular communications among the colonies. Lovelace's 1673 effort was short-lived, but it did establish the first precedent for the mutual correspondence that was to prove of such great importance in keeping communications open in the days of the Revolution.

### Neale Patent

The first real project to link the colonies came in 1693, when Andrew Hamilton, governor of New Jersey, opened a service as agent for British Master of the Mint Thomas Neale. The latter official had been granted a monopoly on establishing a colonial post office.

Researcher Alex L. ter Braake notes that Neale and Hamilton had to overcome the many problems of individual economies and currencies, poor roads, previous rights, and other difficulties, but that all the colonies except Virginia eventually cooperated.

Hamilton's system did not pay its expenses, and in 1707 the Crown purchased the rights of the patent holders. The Neale patent was, however, an ambitious, colonies-wide endeavor, one that has brought Andrew Hamilton the title "Father of the American Post."

### Crown Authority

In 1710, the Queen Anne Act established an American postal structure under the administration of a deputy postmaster general in New York. The service was expensive and relatively unreliable, and thus it was not very popular. When Hugh Finlay inspected the American postal system in 1774, he still described a disappointing situation, at least in the south.

The middle of the 18th century did, however, see major improvements under the vigorous administration of Benjamin Franklin, deputy postmaster general and one of the great figures of American postal history.

Franklin inspected post offices personally, introduced stagecoaches, and made other innovations; at times he invested his own funds when revenues ran short. Eventually the service began to show a profit. The Crown removed Franklin from office as a political undesirable in 1774.

## The Independent United States

On July 26, 1775, the new revolutionary government took over the postal services as an essential avenue of communications. Groups of leaders within the colonies had relied upon the mails for the exchange of philosophical letters and plans. As the fighting began, security became an even more important consideration.

Benjamin Franklin was appointed the first postmaster general, although he soon went abroad as a diplomat and was succeeded by his son-in-law Richard Bache.

The Constitution of 1789 made the postal service a federal prerogative, and Samuel Osgood became postmaster general.

## Expansion and Innovation

The 19th century was a time of rapid expansion and development. As the country's boundaries and population moved westward, postal routes and offices moved with them. Transport was improved, with steamboats making their mail debut in 1813, and railroads in 1838. The number of post offices increased dramatically.

The first adhesive postage stamps were the New York City Despatch Post issues of 1842, and various Postmasters' Provisionals in 1845. In 1847 came 5-cent and 10-cent general issues. Soon letters began to have the appearance of today's mail, envelopes with a stamp in the upper right corner, rather than a folded sheet of paper with the address written on the outside and the postage marked in manuscript by the postmaster.

The mid-century period saw important changes in the postal rate structure. The 1840 Penny Post reforms in Great Britain had substantial effects throughout the world, and the U.S. was no exception.

In 1845 rates were reduced and were charged on weight rather than the number of sheets in the letter. Rates were further reduced in 1851. Four years later prepayment of postage was made compulsory. In 1863 came the first standard domestic rate not based on the distance carried.

The 1848 discovery of gold in California put a new emphasis on long-distance routes. The famed Pony Express was inaugurated in 1860, and the transcontinental telegraph completed in 1861. A railroad linked the country together from 1866.

Also during this period, the Civil War had important postal repercussions. Union postage stamps in southern offices were demonetized, and ways had to be found to bring communications lines through troubled areas. A colorful aspect of the period is the patriotic envelope, bearing wording and cartoons designed to have a propaganda impact.

## Introduction of New Services

In the latter part of the 19th century new services were made available. Free city delivery began in earnest in 1863, special delivery in 1885, and rural free delivery in 1896. All of these innovations had a great impact on American society, for they drew closer together a populace long divided by vast distances, and, more recently, by the animosities still remaining from the Civil War.

The growing mail system encouraged the improvement of roads, the circulation of printed materials, and the distribution of a wide variety of goods by mail order. The latter aspect was further improved by the introduction of parcel post in 1913.

The mails were rendered more secure by the introduction of domestic registration in 1855, and of domestic money orders in 1864.

The United States was also coming into greater and greater contact with the outside world. Substantial mails had been exchanged with other nations for some time, and bilateral parcel post conventions were set up long before the same services were available on a domestic basis. In 1874 the creation of the General (Universal) Postal Union had standardized international postal affairs.

U.S. post offices on foreign territory had begun with the short-lived Montreal service during the Revolution, and official American extraterritorial services were established in China in 1867.

At the turn of the 20th century Hawaii was incorporated into the U.S. postal system, and the Spanish-American War brought new territories which had to be given postal service.

A major innovation of the 20th century, one which ranks with the impact of trains in the 19th century, has been the introduction of airmail carriage. In 1911 mail was so carried between two sites on Long Island, and in 1918 a regular route linked New York, Philadelphia, and Washington. The first through transcontinental flight came in 1921, and the now familiar contract routes let to commercial airlines, in 1926.

Over the years there has been a tremendous increase in the volume of mail handled by the postal service, and, in general, in the rates charged for the service. Exceptions to the latter aspect have been the charge for airmail carriage, which decreased once the expensive experimentation and development was over, and decreases in the letter rate in 1883 and 1885. Since 1932, however, the rise for first-class mail has been inexorable.

## Mechanization of Postal Services

At the same time, efforts have been made to match higher rates with better service. One way that mail carriage has been improved is through increasing mechanization.

The cancellation of mail became a machine operation in the late 19th century. At the turn of the 20th century came the meter impression, which testified to the prepayment of postage but did not require a cancellation. Precanceled stamps, and permit markings, have had the same effect in cutting down on the processing necessary for a large commercial mailing.

Because undersized envelopes can jam sorting machinery and destroy mail, and oversized envelopes require special, manual handling, the Postal Service implemented a new envelope standard. As of July 15, 1979, letters and post cards smaller than 3½ inches high by 5 inches long were no longer accepted for mailing; letters and post cards weighing one ounce or less and larger than 6⅛ inches high by 11½ inches long required a 7¢ surcharge.

At the present time, nonstandard pieces mailed without payment of the surcharge are returned to the sender with a special note to the effect that the piece may be remailed with payment of the surcharge and without another charge for the basic postage upon remailing.

Mechanization has now progressed tremendously from the early level of conveyor belts, pneumatic tubes, and similar items. The postal system is today using machines which automatically sort letters when the proper keys are depressed on a console. Sometimes a machine-readable code is impressed on the envelope. There is also apparatus which can actually read the address directly from the envelope. All of this is a natural outgrowth of the ZIP Code system, introduced in 1963.

The Zoning Improvement Plan (ZIP Code) was initiated to speed and improve mail handling. Currently, the ZIP Code is a five-digit system where the first digit represents one of ten geographic areas, the second two numbers indicate a metropolitan area or sectional center, and the last two digits represent a small town or delivery unit within a metropolitan area.

Mandatory presorting by ZIP Code for second and third class bulk mail took effect Jan. 1, 1967.

On Sept. 13, 1978, the USPS announced a plan to assign four add-on digits to the existing ZIP Code group. The additional digits are expected to be in use by 1983.

The first three ZIP Code numbers will continue to designate areas served by a sectional center or major post office, while the last two will identify areas served by associated post offices or stations and branches of the main post office.

The add-on four digits are intended primarily for use by businesses. The new system is expected to hold down future rate increases through faster, more economical, and more accurate mail routing.

Of the four add-on digits (separated from the first five by a hyphen) the first two will denote a "sector" and the last two a "segment" within a sector. The sector could be several blocks or a large building; the segment could be one side of the block or a floor in a large building. Expanded ZIP Code numbers will also denote post of-

fice boxes, business reply mail, and organizations receiving large volumes of mail.

Over 97 per cent of all the mail processed by the Postal Service contains a ZIP Code. By 1983, the USPS hopes that 50 per cent will contain the expanded codes and by 1986, 90 per cent will be add-on coded.

The state of the art is continuing to develop. Western Union now offers a Mailgram service which transmits messages via space satellite to the addressee's post office. This system was introduced in 1974. The International Telephone and Telegraph Corporation is working with glass optical fibers which can carry tremendous amounts of information in a small space through the use of laser beams. The Xerox Corporation has introduced a communicating electronic typing system which sends up to 120 characters per second over ordinary telephone circuits.

The USPS inaugurated Electronic Computer Originated Mail (E-COM) Service on Jan. 4, 1982. E-COM allows volume mailers to electronically transmit computer messages to 25 specially equipped post offices for delivery as First-Class anywhere in the continental U.S.

The Postal Service entered into agreements with five telecommunications carriers. The carriers include: ITT World Communications, Inc.; Dialcom, Inc.; TRT Telecommunications; Netword, Inc.; and Taipan Industries. In addition, Western Union Mail, Inc. has indicated it plans to introduce a "dial-up" phone link with E-COM in 1982.

Among the first firms to have applied to use E-COM service were Shell Oil, Merrill Lynch, Union Oil of California, Temple University, Hallmark Cards, the AFL-CIO, and the Equitable Life Assurance Company of New York.

The cost of an E-COM message is 26-cents for the first page and 5-cents for the second page. E-COM messages are limited to two pages.

In addition to postage fees, a mailer must pay a $50 annual fee and establish an advance deposit account for the payment of E-COM postage and fees. Mailers must also pay the fees charged separately by the telecommunications carriers which must transmit the messages to the 25 E-COM serving post offices.

Once the computer originated message is received by the serving post office, electronic signals are converted into printed message format by the E-COM equipment, which was developed under a $31.8 million contract with RCA Government Systems of Camden, N.J. The messages are automatically printed on quality letter-size paper, trimmed, folded, enveloped, and sealed for delivery.

Message transmission and receiving services are provided 24 hours a day, seven days a week.

E-COM service is available through serving post offices located in Atlanta, Ga.; Boston,

Mass.; Charlotte, N.C.; Chicago, Ill.; Cincinnati, Ohio; Dallas, Tex.; Denver, Colo.; Detroit, Mich.; Kansas City, Mo.; Los Angeles, Calif.; Milwaukee, Wis.; Minneapolis, Minn.; Nashville, Tenn.; New Orleans, La.; New York, N.Y.; Orlando, Fla.; Philadelphia, Pa.; Phoenix, Ariz.; Pittsburgh, Pa.; Richmond, Va.; St. Louis, Mo.; San Antonio, Tex.; San Francisco, Calif.; Seattle, Wash.; and Washington, D.C.

Market research carried out by Opinion Research Corporation indicates that current market potential for E-COM service is approximately 515 million pieces of nongovernmental mail per year. The study further estimates that by 1986 the annual service volume may approach 1.1 billion pieces.

Another electronic transmission system is International Electronic Post (INTELPOST) Service. This service, inaugurated in 1980, is a high-speed computerized digital facsimile system which provides postal customers with a rapid means of transmitting and receiving replicas of original letters, documents, graphics, and other display messages.

With the INTELPOST system, the original document and associated transmittal form are scanned by a facsimile reader operator by postal personnel at an INTELPOST facility and transmitted to the designated post office, where a black-and-white image of the original document is printed by a facsimile printer and prepared for normal mail delivery.

Initially, New York City and Washington, D.C., were linked via land lines to a corresponding site in Canada. Canadian satellite service enabled the USPS to add London to its INTELPOST network in January 1981 and Amsterdam in June of that year.

The postal administrations of Argentina, Australia, Belgium, France, West Germany, and Switzerland plan to join the system, and Brazil, Ireland, Kuwait, Mexico, Venezuela, and Saudi Arabia have expressed an interest in joining.

## Reorganization of the Post Office

The post office is also seeking to improve the situation through the improvement of administration and the removal of the political influences which traditionally dictated decisions. In 1970 legislation created the United States Postal Service, an independent agency designed to operate the mails in a "businesslike" fashion without the long-standing dependencies symbolized by Congressional oversight of policy and appropria-

tions. Inauguration of the new agency came on July 1, 1971.

Rather than the traditional cabinet-level agency headed by a politically appointed postmaster general, the new United States Postal Service is directed by an 11-member Board of Governors. Nine of these persons are appointed by the president, and they then choose the postmaster general. This official and his deputy complete the composition of the board.

Fees are considered by the Postal Rate Commission, an independent body. In the years since the formation of the new organization there has been substantial controversy between the commission and the postmaster general, for the latter has often felt that the former has acted too slowly on rate increases essential to the proper discharge of USPS responsibilities.

In many ways the USPS represents a new departure for the American postal system. Not only is there a new structure of operation, but financially the mail is now to pay its own way as completely as possible, with the income from rates equaling costs.

This theory is directly opposed to that of some observers who see the postal system as a service, designed less to make money than to provide essential communications on commercial and personal levels.

Thus far the financial goals have not been successfully met, and the current policy is to seek ways in which services can be reduced to decrease costs. This has led to further controversy, as local communities protest the loss of small post offices, and the frequency of mail deliveries will probably be reduced. Services rendered have often been roundly criticized.

The continuing difficulties have resulted in a number of suggestions for improvement. One that has gained adherents in recent years is the ending of the government's monopoly over first-class mail carriage, thus encouraging efficiency brought on by competition. Other suggestions include increased subsidies, reduced requirements, all the way to a return of the Postal Service to regular Congressional supervision.

The USPS is thus, like so many post offices throughout the world, strongly embattled in its efforts to provide suitable services within the parameters of available funds and standing regulations. With the increased technological communications alternatives now available, the future may well hold additional major changes for the Postal Service.

## Statistical Background

The following tables, taken from the "Annual Report of the Postmaster General" and "Comprehensive Statement on Postal Operations (January 1982)," demonstrate the development of the U.S. post office since the establishment of the nation's Constitution. While the provision of a vast "sea" of numbers sometimes tends to obscure what was happening on the "grass roots" level, there is a great deal to be learned from such mundane facts as the number of post offices and the number of postal pieces in any given year.

Generally, one can see the growth and expansion of postal communications. For the first two years of service there were only 75 post offices; by 1900 there were more than 76,000. The amount of mail matter carried has reached mind-boggling proportions.

There is also the other side of the story. The number of post offices is now much reduced from the turn of the century, due to such factors as the introduction of the Rural Free Delivery system, and the current drive to reduce postal costs. The number of pieces carried decreased during the Depression, and the last few years also show some examples of slackening off, possibly in response to rising rates and improving alternatives.

Statistical tables can be important sources of useful data, but they must be read with a critical eye and reference to supplementary information.

**Post Office Development and Growth for Fiscal Years 1789-1846 (pre-stamp period)**

| Year | Number of post offices | Income[3] | Expenses[3] | Dead letters received | Amount received from dead letters[21] |
|---|---|---|---|---|---|
| 1789 | 75 | [1] $7,510 | [1] $7,560 | | |
| 1790 | 75 | 37,935 | 32,140 | | |
| 1791 | 89 | 46,294 | 36,697 | | |
| 1792 | 195 | 67,443 | 54,530 | | |
| 1793 | 209 | 104,746 | 72,039 | | |
| 1794 | 450 | 128,947 | 89,972 | | |
| 1795 | 453 | 160,620 | 117,893 | | |
| 1796 | 468 | 195,066 | 131,571 | | |
| 1797 | 554 | 213,998 | 150,114 | | |
| 1798 | 639 | 232,977 | 179,084 | | |
| 1799 | 677 | 264,846 | 188,037 | | |
| 1800 | 903 | 280,804 | 213,994 | | |
| 1801 | 1,025 | 320,442 | 255,151 | | |
| 1802 | 1,114 | 327,044 | 281,916 | | |
| 1803 | 1,258 | 351,822 | 322,364 | | |
| 1804 | 1,405 | 389,449 | 337,502 | | |
| 1805 | 1,558 | 421,373 | 377,367 | | |
| 1806 | 1,710 | 446,105 | 417,233 | | |
| 1807 | 1,848 | 478,762 | 453,885 | | |
| 1808 | 1,944 | 460,564 | 462,828 | | |
| 1809 | 2,012 | 506,633 | 498,012 | | |
| 1810 | 2,300 | 551,684 | 495,969 | | |
| 1811 | 2,403 | 587,246 | 499,098 | | |
| 1812 | 2,610 | 649,208 | 540,165 | | |
| 1813 | 2,708 | 703,154 | 631,011 | | |
| 1814 | 2,670 | 730,270 | 727,126 | | |
| 1815 | 3,000 | 1,043,065 | 748,121 | | |
| 1816 | 3,260 | 961,782 | 804,022 | | |
| 1817 | 3,459 | 1,002,973 | 916,515 | | |
| 1818 | 3,618 | 1,130,235 | 1,035,832 | | |
| 1819 | 4,000 | 1,204,737 | 1,117,861 | | |
| 1820 | 4,500 | 1,111,927 | 1,160,926 | | |
| 1821 | 4,650 | 1,059,087 | 1,165,481 | | |
| 1822 | 4,709 | 1,117,490 | 1,167,572 | | |
| 1823 | 4,043 | 1,130,115 | 1,156,995 | | |
| 1824 | 5,182 | 1,197,758 | 1,188,019 | | |
| 1825 | 5,677 | 1,306,525 | 1,229,043 | | |
| 1826 | 6,150 | 1,447,703 | 1,366,712 | | |
| 1827 | 7,300 | 1,524,633 | 1,469,959 | | |
| 1828 | 7,530 | 1,659,915 | 1,689,945 | | |
| 1829 | 8,004 | 1,707,418 | 1,782,132 | | |
| 1830 | 8,450 | 1,850,583 | 1,932,708 | [12] 380,000 | |
| 1831 | 8,686 | 1,997,811 | 1,936,122 | 500,000 | |
| 1832 | 9,205 | 2,258,570 | 2,266,171 | | |
| 1833 | 10,127 | 2,617,011 | 2,930,414 | | |
| 1834 | 10,693 | 2,823,749 | 2,910,605 | | |
| 1835 | 10,770 | 2,993,556 | 2,757,350 | | |
| 1836 | 11,091 | 3,408,323 | 2,841,766 | | |
| 1837 | 11,767 | 4,101,703 | 3,288,319 | 900,000 | |
| 1838 | 12,519 | 4,238,733 | 4,430,662 | | [13] 12,060 |
| 1839 | 12,780 | 4,484,657 | 4,636,536 | | |
| 1840 | 13,468 | 4,543,522 | 4,718,236 | | |
| 1841 | 13,778 | 4,407,726 | 4,499,687 | | |
| 1842 | 13,733 | 4,546,850 | 4,627,717 | | |
| 1843 | 13,814 | 4,296,225 | 4,374,754 | | 2,668 |
| 1844 | 14,103 | 4,237,288 | 4,298,513 | | 20 |
| 1845 | 14,183 | 4,289,842 | 4,320,732 | | 1,192 |
| 1846 | 14,601 | 3,487,199 | 4,076,037 | | 1,824 |

See footnotes at end of tables.

## Post Office Development and Growth for Fiscal Years 1847-1920

| Year | Number of post offices | Income [3] | Expenses [3] | Postage stamps issued [4] | Stamped envelopes [5] and wrappers issued [6] | Postal cards issued [8] |
|---|---|---|---|---|---|---|
| 1847 | 15,146 | 3,880,309 | 3,979,542 | | | |
| 1848 | 16,159 | 4,555,211 | 4,326,850 | 860,380 | | |
| 1849 | 16,749 | 4,705,176 | 4,479,049 | 955,727 | | |
| 1850 | 18,417 | 5,499,985 | 5,212,953 | 1,540,545 | | |
| 1851 | 19,796 | $6,410,601 | $6,278,402 | 1,246,548 | | |
| 1852 | 20,901 | 5,184,526 | 7,108,459 | 54,136,319 | | |
| 1853 | 22,320 | 5,240,725 | 7,982,757 | 56,344,006 | 5,000,000 | |
| 1854 | 23,548 | 6,255,586 | 8,577,424 | 56,330,000 | 21,384,100 | |
| 1855 | 24,410 | 6,642,136 | 9,968,342 | 72,977,300 | 23,451,725 | |
| 1856 | 25,565 | 6,920,822 | 10,405,286 | 126,045,210 | 33,764,050 | |
| 1857 | 26,586 | 7,353,952 | 11,508,058 | 154,729,465 | 33,033,400 | |
| 1858 | 27,977 | 7,486,793 | 12,722,470 | 176,761,835 | 30,971,375 | |
| 1859 | 28,539 | 7,968,484 | 15,754,093 | 192,201,920 | 30,280,300 | |
| 1860 | 28,498 | 8,518,067 | 14,874,601 | 216,370,660 | 29,280,025 | |
| 1861 | 28,586 | 8,349,296 | 13,606,759 | 211,788,518 | [6] 26,027,300 | |
| 1862 | 28,875 | 8,299,821 | 11,125,364 | 251,307,105 | 27,234,159 | |
| 1863 | 29,047 | 11,163,790 | 11,314,207 | 338,340,385 | 25,548,750 | |
| 1864 | 28,878 | 12,438,254 | 12,644,786 | 334,054,610 | 28,218,800 | |
| 1865 | 28,882 | 14,556,159 | 13,694,728 | 387,419,455 | [7] 26,206,175 | |
| 1866 | 29,389 | 14,386,986 | 15,352,079 | 347,734,325 | 39,094,725 | |
| 1867 | 25,163 | 15,237,027 | 19,235,483 | 371,599,605 | 63,086,650 | |
| 1868 | 26,481 | 16,292,001 | 22,730,793 | 383,470,500 | 73,364,650 | |
| 1869 | 27,106 | 17,314,176 | 23,698,132 | 421,047,460 | 81,675,100 | |
| 1870 | 28,492 | 18,879,537 | 23,998,838 | 468,118,445 | 86,289,500 | |
| 1871 | 30,045 | 20,037,045 | 24,390,104 | 498,126,175 | 104,675,275 | |
| 1872 | 31,863 | 21,915,426 | 26,658,192 | 541,445,070 | 113,925,750 | |
| 1873 | 33,244 | 22,996,742 | 29,084,946 | 601,931,520 | 131,172,600 | 31,094,000 |
| 1874 | 34,294 | 26,471,072 | 32,126,415 | 632,733,420 | 136,418,500 | 91,079,000 |
| 1875 | 35,547 | 26,791,314 | 33,611,309 | 682,342,470 | 149,766,400 | 107,616,000 |
| 1876 | 36,383 | 28,644,198 | 33,263,488 | 698,799,090 | 165,520,250 | 150,815,000 |
| 1877 | 37,345 | 27,531,585 | 33,486,322 | 689,580,670 | 170,651,450 | 170,015,500 |
| 1878 | 38,253 | 29,277,517 | 34,165,084 | 742,461,940 | 183,500,350 | 200,630,000 |
| 1879 | 40,588 | 30,041,983 | 33,449,899 | 774,358,780 | 177,561,950 | 221,797,000 |
| 1880 | 42,989 | 33,315,479 | 36,542,804 | 875,681,970 | 207,137,000 | 272,550,500 |
| 1881 | 44,512 | 36,785,398 | 39,592,566 | 954,128,450 | 227,067,050 | 308,536,500 |
| 1882 | 46,231 | 41,876,410 | 40,482,021 | 1,114,560,330 | 256,565,450 | 351,498,000 |
| 1883 | 46,820 | 45,508,693 | 43,282,944 | 1,202,743,800 | 259,266,450 | 379,516,750 |
| 1884 | 48,434 | 43,325,959 | 47,224,560 | 1,459,768,460 | 322,232,050 | 362,876,750 |
| 1885 | 51,252 | 42,560,844 | 50,046,235 | 1,465,122,935 | 322,751,400 | 339,416,500 |
| 1886 | 53,614 | 43,948,423 | 51,004,744 | 1,620,784,100 | 354,008,100 | 355,648,000 |
| 1887 | 55,157 | 48,837,609 | 53,006,194 | 1,746,985,520 | 381,611,300 | 355,939,250 |
| 1888 | 57,376 | 52,695,177 | 56,458,315 | 1,867,173,140 | 433,635,750 | 381,797,500 |
| 1889 | 58,999 | 56,175,611 | 62,317,119 | 1,961,980,840 | 451,864,300 | 386,808,500 |
| 1890 | 62,401 | 60,882,098 | 66,259,548 | 2,219,737,060 | 513,832,950 | 429,515,350 |
| 1891 | 64,329 | 65,931,786 | 73,059,519 | 2,397,503,340 | 556,226,250 | 424,216,750 |
| 1892 | 67,119 | 70,930,475 | 76,980,846 | 2,543,270,210 | 593,684,700 | 511,433,500 |
| 1893 | 68,403 | 75,896,993 | 81,581,681 | 2,750,293,090 | 656,279,436 | 530,505,600 |
| 1894 | 69,805 | 75,080,479 | 84,994,112 | 2,602,278,355 | 571,475,218 | 468,499,750 |
| 1895 | 70,064 | 76,983,128 | 87,179,551 | 2,795,424,808 | 598,848,900 | 492,305,550 |
| 1896 | 70,360 | 82,499,208 | 90,932,670 | 3,025,481,467 | 616,040,250 | 524,820,140 |
| 1897 | 71,022 | 82,665,462 | 94,077,242 | 3,063,633,885 | 585,032,000 | 523,608,250 |
| 1898 | 73,570 | 89,012,618 | 98,053,523 | 3,418,458,360 | 606,447,000 | 556,380,650 |
| 1899 | 75,000 | 95,021,384 | 101,632,161 | 3,692,775,815 | 628,456,000 | 573,634,150 |
| 1900 | 76,688 | 102,353,579 | 107,740,268 | 3,998,544,564 | 707,555,000 | 587,815,250 |
| 1901 | 76,945 | 111,631,193 | 115,554,921 | 4,239,273,696 | 772,839,000 | 659,614,800 |
| 1902 | 75,924 | 121,848,047 | 124,785,697 | 4,621,285,723 | 853,128,000 | 547,204,090 |
| 1903 | 74,169 | 134,224,443 | 138,784,488 | 5,270,549,115 | 948,654,000 | 770,657,950 |
| 1904 | 71,131 | 143,582,624 | 152,362,117 | 5,330,886,845 | 1,020,255,250 | 702,907,450 |
| 1905 | 68,131 | 152,826,585 | 167,399,169 | 5,751,017,915 | 1,074,918,000 | 728,285,100 |
| 1906 | 65,600 | 167,932,783 | 178,449,779 | 6,284,450,495 | 1,230,287,750 | 798,917,850 |
| 1907 | 62,658 | 183,585,006 | 190,238,288 | 7,061,036,615 | 1,418,840,250 | 805,568,700 |
| 1908 | 60,704 | 191,478,663 | 208,351,886 | 7,651,400,405 | 1,266,002,559 | 809,426,750 |
| 1909 | 60,144 | 203,562,383 | 221,004,103 | 8,731,875,393 | 1,509,626,246 | 926,478,900 |
| 1910 | 59,580 | 224,128,658 | 229,977,225 | 9,067,164,886 | 1,506,861,598 | 726,441,000 |
| 1911 | 59,237 | 237,879,824 | 237,648,927 | 10,046,068,728 | 1,690,775,385 | 975,138,748 |
| 1912 | 58,729 | 246,744,016 | 248,525,450 | 9,929,173,748 | 1,684,624,161 | 909,411,045 |
| 1913 | 58,020 | 266,619,526 | 262,067,541 | 10,812,507,736 | 1,724,730,140 | 946,861,679 |
| 1914 | 56,810 | 287,934,565 | 283,543,769 | 11,112,254,281 | 1,864,713,929 | 962,072,326 |
| 1915 | 56,380 | 287,248,165 | 298,546,026 | 11,226,386,415 | 1,793,764,296 | 975,542,228 |
| 1916 | 55,935 | 312,057,689 | 306,204,033 | 11,671,842,200 | 1,853,791,461 | 1,047,894,800 |
| 1917 | 55,414 | 329,726,116 | 319,838,718 | 12,451,522,117 | 2,161,108,013 | 1,112,337,760 |
| 1918 | 54,347 | [2] 388,975,962 | 324,833,728 | 13,065,784,862 | 1,819,307,148 | 707,111,300 |
| 1919 | 53,084 | [2] 436,239,126 | 362,497,636 | 15,020,470,168 | 1,844,884,905 | 456,924,490 |
| 1920 | 52,641 | 437,150,212 | 454,322,609 | 13,212,790,033 | 2,350,073,359 | 986,156,087 |

See footnotes at end of tables.

### Post Office Development and Growth for Fiscal Years 1847-1920, Continued

| Registered certified, insured, and c.o.d. mail[19] | Dead letters received | Amount received from dead letters[21] | Post offices issuing money orders[14] | Amount of domestic money orders issued | Amount of postal notes issued[15] | Amount of money orders issued[18] | Number of pieces of mail of all kinds handled[20] | Year |
|---|---|---|---|---|---|---|---|---|
| .......... | 1,800,000 | 187. | .......... | .......... | .......... | .......... | 124,173,000 | 1847 |
| .......... | .......... | 1,296. | .......... | .......... | .......... | .......... | .......... | 1848 |
| .......... | 2,100,000 | 99. | .......... | .......... | .......... | .......... | .......... | 1849 |
| .......... | .......... | 1,748. | .......... | .......... | .......... | .......... | .......... | 1850 |
| .......... | 2,750,000 | $1,675. | .......... | .......... | .......... | .......... | .......... | 1851 |
| .......... | .......... | 8,265. | .......... | .......... | .......... | .......... | .......... | 1852 |
| .......... | .......... | 1,384. | .......... | .......... | .......... | .......... | .......... | 1853 |
| .......... | .......... | 4,346. | .......... | .......... | .......... | .......... | .......... | 1854 |
| .......... | .......... | 4,976. | .......... | .......... | .......... | .......... | .......... | 1855 |
| [9] 620,332 | .......... | 8,383. | .......... | .......... | .......... | .......... | .......... | 1856 |
| 717,537 | .......... | 6,756. | .......... | .......... | .......... | .......... | .......... | 1857 |
| 562,903 | .......... | 3,410. | .......... | .......... | .......... | .......... | .......... | 1858 |
| 501,059 | 2,500,000 | 3,134. | .......... | .......... | .......... | .......... | .......... | 1859 |
| 500,774 | 2,000,000 | 3,803. | .......... | .......... | .......... | .......... | .......... | 1860 |
| 386,113 | 2,550,000 | .......... | .......... | .......... | .......... | .......... | .......... | 1861 |
| 302,987 | 2,282,018 | 1,052. | .......... | .......... | .......... | .......... | .......... | 1862 |
| 372,893 | 2,550,416 | .......... | .......... | .......... | .......... | .......... | .......... | 1863 |
| 259,798 | 3,508,825 | .......... | .......... | .......... | .......... | .......... | .......... | 1864 |
| 282,533 | 4,368,087 | 5,222 | 419 | $1,360,122. | .......... | .......... | .......... | 1865 |
| 275,103 | 5,198,605 | 18,393 | 766 | 3,977,259. | .......... | .......... | .......... | 1866 |
| 249,075 | 4,306,508 | 17,485 | 1,224 | 9,229,327. | .......... | .......... | .......... | 1867 |
| .......... | 4,162,144 | 30,502 | 1,468 | 16,197,858. | .......... | .......... | .......... | 1868 |
| .......... | 3,952,862 | 8,818 | 1,466 | 24,848,058. | .......... | .......... | .......... | 1869 |
| .......... | 4,152,460 | 8,023 | 1,694 | 34,054,184. | .......... | $22,189. | .......... | 1870 |
| .......... | 4,194,748 | 10,596 | 2,076 | 42,164,118. | .......... | 38,489. | .......... | 1871 |
| .......... | 4,241,374 | 7,299 | 2,452 | 48,515,532. | .......... | 833,006. | .......... | 1872 |
| .......... | 4,402,348 | 6,208 | 2,775 | 57,516,216. | .......... | 1,863,512. | .......... | 1873 |
| .......... | 4,601,773 | 8,721 | 3,069 | 74,424,854. | .......... | 2,265,242. | .......... | 1874 |
| .......... | 3,628,808 | 9,180 | 3,404 | 77,431,251. | .......... | 1,964,574. | .......... | 1875 |
| 4,007,817 | 3,542,494 | 9,889 | 3,401 | 77,035,972. | .......... | 2,068,668. | .......... | 1876 |
| 4,348,127 | 3,288,290 | 4,945 | 3,697 | 72,820,509. | .......... | 1,844,053. | .......... | 1877 |
| 4,898,804 | 3,186,805 | 8,937 | 4,143 | 81,442,364. | .......... | 2,047,696. | .......... | 1878 |
| 5,429,022 | 2,996,513 | 3,323 | 4,512 | 88,254,641. | .......... | 2,240,454. | .......... | 1879 |
| 6,996,513 | 3,057,141 | 6,506 | 4,829 | 100,352,818. | .......... | 3,463,862. | .......... | 1880 |
| 8,338,918 | 3,233,621 | 6,584 | 5,163 | 105,075,769. | .......... | 4,683,926. | .......... | 1881 |
| 9,627,922 | 4,160,554 | 7,657 | 5,491 | 113,400,118. | .......... | 6,536,514. | .......... | 1882 |
| 10,594,716 | 4,379,398 | 12,279 | 5,927 | 117,329,406. | .......... | 7,717,832. | .......... | 1883 |
| 11,246,545 | 4,564,451 | 9,619 | 6,310 | 122,121,261 | $7,411,992 | 7,688,776. | .......... | 1884 |
| 11,043,256 | 4,710,240 | 12,097 | 7,056 | 117,858,921 | 9,996,274 | 6,840,358. | .......... | 1885 |
| 11,648,227 | 4,791,698 | 8,858 | 7,357 | 113,819,521 | 11,718,010 | 7,178,786 | 3,747,000,000 | 1886 |
| 12,524,421 | 5,335,363 | 10,976 | 7,853 | 117,462,660 | 11,768,825 | 9,035,530 | 3,495,100,000 | 1887 |
| 13,677,169 | 6,217,876 | 10,535 | 8,241 | 119,649,064 | 12,134,459 | 11,293,870 | 3,576,100,000 | 1888 |
| 14,061,866 | 6,206,893 | 12,103 | 8,727 | 115,081,845 | 12,082,191 | 12,280,516 | 3,860,200,000 | 1889 |
| 14,947,081 | 6,517,556 | 12,050 | 9,382 | 114,362,757 | 12,160,490 | 13,230,135 | 4,005,408,000 | 1890 |
| 15,047,602 | 6,829,460 | 13,860 | 10,070 | 119,122,236 | 11,753,849 | 14,443,667 | 4,369,900,000 | 1891 |
| 15,260,094 | 6,780,980 | 15,929 | 12,069 | 120,066,801 | 11,895,766 | 15,120,271 | 4,776,575,000 | 1892 |
| 15,561,410 | 7,131,027 | 13,895 | 18,434 | 127,576,433 | 12,903,077 | 16,341,838 | 5,021,841,000 | 1893 |
| 15,050,554 | 7,101,044 | 14,940 | 19,262 | 138,793,579 | 12,649,095 | 13,792,455 | 4,919,090,000 | 1894 |
| 14,428,081 | 6,319,873 | 12,219 | 19,691 | 156,709,089. | .......... | 12,906,486 | 5,134,281,000 | 1895 |
| 15,106,336 | 6,253,363 | 11,957 | 18,825 | 172,100,649. | .......... | 13,852,615 | 5,693,719,000 | 1896 |
| 14,559,083 | 5,976,960 | 11,454 | 20,031 | 174,482,676. | .......... | 13,588,379 | 5,781,002,000 | 1897 |
| 15,600,220 | 6,295,853 | 10,527 | 22,388 | 191,354,121. | .......... | 13,239,769 | 6,214,447,000 | 1898 |
| 16,086,022 | 6,885,983 | 13,115 | 26,784 | 211,213,592. | .......... | 13,744,770 | 6,576,310,000 | 1899 |
| 18,422,649 | 7,536,158 | 14,465 | 29,649 | 238,921,009. | .......... | 16,749,018 | 7,129,990,000 | 1900 |
| 20,814,501 | 8,507,257 | 15,605 | 30,529 | 274,546,067. | .......... | 20,072,614 | 7,424,390,000 | 1901 |
| 22,831,400 | 9,300,351 | 18,459 | 31,680 | 313,551,279. | .......... | 22,974,473 | 8,085,447,000 | 1902 |
| 25,951,178 | 10,153,528 | 20,961 | 34,547 | 353,627,648. | .......... | 35,237,935 | 8,867,467,000 | 1903 |
| 28,213,870 | 10,923,239 | 22,210 | 35,094 | 378,778,488. | .......... | 42,550,150 | 9,502,460,000 | 1904 |
| 30,200,177 | 10,973,361 | 23,787 | 36,832 | 396,903,433. | .......... | 47,516,027 | 10,187,506,000 | 1905 |
| 34,165,484 | 11,663,377 | 24,090 | 37,444 | 444,515,790. | .......... | 63,047,868 | 11,361,091,000 | 1906 |
| 38,255,649 | 13,005,255 | 26,056 | 37,572 | 479,650,342. | .......... | 84,080,711 | 12,255,666,000 | 1907 |
| 40,151,797 | 13,145,172 | 36,644 | 43,313 | 498,699,637. | .......... | 88,972,388 | 13,364,069,000 | 1908 |
| 40,539,545 | 11,997,325 | 28,913 | 50,043 | 491,074,844. | .......... | 76,754,802 | 14,004,577,000 | 1909 |
| 42,053,574 | 12,545,133 | 30,783 | 51,791 | 547,993,641. | .......... | 99,744,686 | 14,850,103,000 | 1910 |
| 42,766,459 | 13,614,416 | 32,854 | 51,809 | 578,111,005. | .......... | 109,604,639 | 16,900,552,000 | 1911 |
| 42,235,600 | 13,268,199 | 33,122 | 52,815 | 583,337,003. | .......... | 97,660,024 | 17,588,659,000 | 1912 |
| [10] 43,489,172 | 13,214,346 | 31,143 | 54,594 | 624,489,096. | .......... | 102,668,288 | 18,567,445,000 | 1913 |
| [11] 56,397,194 | 12,082,342 | 39,077 | 55,949 | 667,231,064. | .......... | 101,963,428. | .......... | 1914 |
| 60,042,590 | 10,781,927 | 38,514 | 55,670 | 654,139,134. | .......... | 60,772,073. | .......... | 1915 |
| 70,473,197 | 10,839,890 | 45,856 | 56,026 | 719,364,950. | .......... | 46,357,386. | .......... | 1916 |
| 84,117,774 | 13,614,927 | 57,938 | 56,170 | 813,318,927. | .......... | 41,644,878. | .......... | 1917 |
| 109,070,762 | 14,451,953 | 71,709 | 55,668 | 904,649,519. | .......... | 35,864,699. | .......... | 1918 |
| 149,754,951 | 22,982,605 | 199,222 | 54,826 | 1,109,612,859. | .......... | 39,766,077. | .......... | 1919 |
| 192,397,014 | 19,353,413 | 226,962 | 54,395 | 1,332,699,836. | .......... | 32,960,048. | .......... | 1920 |

## Post Office Development and Growth for Fiscal Years 1921-81

| Year | Number of post offices | Income [3] | Expenses [3] | Postage stamps issued [4] | Stamped envelopes [5] and wrappers issued [6] | Postal cards issued [8] |
|---|---|---|---|---|---|---|
| 1921 | 52,168 | $463,491,275 | $620,993,674 | 13,869,934,907 | 2,738,934,489 | 1,081,206,536 |
| 1922 | 51,950 | 484,853,541 | 545,644,209 | 14,261,948,813 | 2,364,372,708 | 1,111,124,439 |
| 1923 | 51,613 | 532,827,925 | 556,850,966 | 15,478,095,130 | 2,721,475,103 | 1,253,195,951 |
| 1924 | 51,266 | 572,948,778 | 587,376,916 | 15,954,475,462 | 2,964,464,261 | 1,293,184,528 |
| 1925 | 50,957 | 599,591,478 | 639,281,648 | 17,386,555,506 | 2,997,177,406 | 1,497,366,700 |
| 1926 | 50,601 | 659,819,801 | 679,704,053 | 16,333,410,317 | 3,001,858,230 | 1,668,240,506 |
| 1927 | 50,266 | 683,121,989 | 714,577,492 | 15,999,701,194 | 3,145,946,376 | 1,834,456,466 |
| 1928 | 49,944 | 693,633,921 | 725,699,766 | 16,676,492,729 | 3,201,458,891 | 1,872,040,126 |
| 1929 | 49,482 | 696,947,578 | 782,343,648 | 16,917,274,874 | 3,228,586,578 | 1,783,897,145 |
| 1930 | 49,063 | 705,484,098 | 803,667,219 | 16,268,856,071 | 3,164,127,424 | 1,643,212,150 |
| 1931 | 48,733 | 656,463,383 | 802,484,840 | 15,559,164,487 | 2,847,439,346 | 1,531,245,650 |
| 1932 | 48,159 | 588,171,923 | 793,684,323 | 14,650,970,133 | 2,384,792,755 | 1,334,753,100 |
| 1933 | 47,641 | 587,631,364 | 699,887,186 | 11,917,442,423 | 1,644,993,351 | 1,389,523,602 |
| 1934 | 46,506 | 586,733,166 | 630,732,934 | 12,525,716,839 | 1,580,819,713 | 1,590,257,450 |
| 1935 | 45,686 | 630,795,302 | 696,503,235 | 13,610,497,410 | 1,617,677,432 | 1,754,030,250 |
| 1936 | 45,230 | 665,343,356 | 753,616,212 | 13,835,399,920 | 1,647,890,978 | 1,917,793,442 |
| 1937 | 44,877 | 726,201,110 | 772,743,145 | 15,108,639,409 | 1,663,818,025 | 2,226,153,250 |
| 1938 | 44,586 | 728,634,051 | 772,307,506 | 14,912,092,916 | 1,643,815,325 | 2,186,720,600 |
| 1939 | 44,327 | 745,955,075 | 784,549,842 | 15,073,795,772 | 1,605,075,706 | 2,170,572,250 |
| 1940 | 44,024 | 766,948,627 | 807,629,180 | 16,381,427,297 | 1,649,548,500 | 2,256,519,650 |
| 1941 | 43,739 | 812,827,735 | 836,858,580 | 16,381,321,410 | 1,645,254,500 | 2,400,188,380 |
| 1942 | 43,358 | 859,817,491 | 873,950,372 | 19,492,121,339 | 1,676,573,172 | 2,370,061,600 |
| 1943 | 42,654 | 966,227,288 | 952,529,098 | 19,123,977,153 | 1,797,400,250 | 2,316,989,950 |
| 1944 | 42,161 | 1,112,877,174 | 1,068,986,872 | 19,106,171,157 | 1,902,312,750 | 1,912,990,100 |
| 1945 | 41,792 | 1,314,240,132 | 1,145,002,246 | 20,239,986,294 | 2,064,773,000 | 2,282,280,350 |
| 1946 | 41,751 | 1,224,572,173 | 1,353,654,000 | 19,180,426,775 | 1,815,915,500 | 2,477,853,770 |
| 1947 | 41,760 | 1,299,141,041 | 1,504,799,000 | 19,542,256,985 | 1,996,449,500 | 2,951,299,600 |
| 1948 | 41,695 | 1,410,971,284 | 1,687,805,000 | 20,432,059,035 | 2,117,572,750 | 3,656,590,675 |
| 1949 | 41,607 | 1,571,851,202 | 2,149,322,000 | 21,047,376,040 | 2,219,743,500 | 3,468,718,950 |
| 1950 | 41,464 | 1,677,486,967 | 2,222,949,000 | 20,647,164,914 | 2,052,155,500 | 3,872,300,900 |
| 1951 | 41,193 | 1,776,816,354 | 2,341,399,000 | 21,521,806,685 | 2,004,568,500 | 4,183,748,200 |
| 1952 | 40,919 | 1,947,316,280 | 2,666,860,000 | 22,067,082,690 | 2,274,659,750 | 2,984,123,500 |
| 1953 | 40,609 | 2,091,714,112 | 2,742,126,000 | 22,960,961,855 | 2,338,622,250 | 2,330,921,050 |
| 1954 | 39,405 | [2]2,268,516,717 | [2]2,667,664,000 | 22,219,068,245 | 2,265,309,250 | 2,360,534,150 |
| 1955 | 38,316 | 2,349,476,528 | 2,712,150,214 | 23,105,454,370 | 2,189,520,750 | 2,515,392,025 |
| 1956 | 37,515 | 2,419,353,664 | 2,883,305,122 | 23,722,488,960 | 2,571,416,250 | 2,911,276,350 |
| 1957 | 37,012 | 2,496,614,310 | 3,044,438,004 | 24,257,859,530 | 1,966,335,500 | 2,046,515,000 |
| 1958 | 36,308 | 2,550,220,791 | 3,440,810,346 | 22,879,828,252 | 2,040,211,000 | 2,375,065,000 |
| 1959 | 35,750 | 3,035,231,808 | 3,640,368,053 | 27,980,885,070 | 2,228,812,720 | 2,969,055,000 |
| 1960 | 35,238 | 3,276,588,433 | 3,873,952,908 | 23,773,570,200 | 2,005,442,000 | 1,773,090,000 |
| 1961 | 34,955 | 3,423,058,716 | 4,249,413,744 | 23,001,808,400 | 2,021,031,500 | 1,653,595,000 |
| 1962 | 34,797 | 3,557,040,595 | 4,331,617,483 | 25,405,928,600 | 1,789,414,500 | 1,463,665,000 |
| 1963 | 34,498 | [3]3,879,127,992 | [3]4,698,527,911 | 31,669,175,000 | 2,344,716,750 | 2,487,038,000 |
| 1964 | 34,040 | 4,276,123,326 | 4,927,824,958 | 24,692,325,800 | 1,928,981,500 | 1,563,165,000 |
| 1965 | 33,624 | 4,483,389,833 | 5,275,839,877 | 22,691,105,600 | 1,670,725,500 | 1,092,380,000 |
| 1966 | 33,121 | 4,784,186,482 | 5,726,522,930 | 23,503,958,800 | 1,627,788,500 | 1,289,000,000 |
| 1967 | 32,626 | 5,101,982,384 | 6,249,026,677 | 26,320,986,420 | 1,512,996,000 | 1,011,675,000 |
| 1968 | 32,260 | 5,660,111,244 | 6,680,971,666 | 34,667,494,050 | 1,853,426,500 | 1,431,310,500 |
| 1969 | 32,064 | 6,255,883,348 | 7,278,849,508 | 27,383,826,600 | 1,374,121,000 | 846,695,000 |
| 1970 | 32,002 | 6,472,737,791 | 7,982,551,936 | 26,182,562,000 | 1,368,097,500 | 830,649,500 |
| 1971 | 31,947 | 8,751,484,000 | 8,955,264,000 . | . . . . . . . . . . | . . . . . . . . . . | . . . . . . . . . . |
| 1972 | 31,686 | 9,245,388,000 | 9,522,378,000 . | . . . . . . . . . . | . . . . . . . . . . | . . . . . . . . . . |
| 1973 | 31,385 | 9,716,405,000 | 9,818,306,000 . | . . . . . . . . . . | . . . . . . . . . . | . . . . . . . . . . |
| 1974 | 31,000 | 10,761,456,000 | 11,298,036,000 . | . . . . . . . . . . | . . . . . . . . . . | . . . . . . . . . . |
| 1975 | 30,754 | 11,552,328,000 | 12,578,429,000 . | . . . . . . . . . . | . . . . . . . . . . | . . . . . . . . . . |
| 1976 | 30,521 | 12,843,714,000 | 13,922,736,000 . | . . . . . . . . . . | . . . . . . . . . . | . . . . . . . . . . |
| 1977 | 30,521 | 14,709,939,000 | 15,310,169,000 . | . . . . . . . . . . | . . . . . . . . . . | . . . . . . . . . . |
| 1978 | 30,518 | 15,854,566,000 | 16,219,619,000 . | . . . . . . . . . . | . . . . . . . . . . | . . . . . . . . . . |
| 1979 | 30,449 | 17,825,629,000 | 17,529,303,000 . | . . . . . . . . . . | . . . . . . . . . . | . . . . . . . . . . |
| 1980 | 30,326 | 19,253,000,000 | 19,559,000,000 . | . . . . . . . . . . | . . . . . . . . . . | . . . . . . . . . . |
| 1981 | 30,242 | 20,898,000,000 | 21,486,000,000 . | . . . . . . . . . . | . . . . . . . . . . | . . . . . . . . . . |

[1] For 3 months only.
[2] Revenues for 1918 and 1919 include $44,500,000 and $71,392,000, respectively, war-tax revenue accruing from increased postage.
[3] Basis of reporting changed. Reporting on accrued cost basis beginning in 1963.
[4] Postage stamps first issued under act of March 3, 1847, and placed on sale at New York, N.Y., July 1, 1847.
[5] Stamped envelopes first issued June 1853 under act of Aug. 31, 1852.
[6] Newspaper wrappers first issued under act of Feb. 27, 1861, not made after Oct. 9, 1934.
[7] Special-request envelopes first issued in 1865.
[8] Postal cards first issued May 1, 1873, under act of June 8, 1872.
[9] Letters first registered July 1, 1855, under act of March 3, 1855.
[10] Insurance service inaugurated Jan. 1, 1913, under act of Congress, Aug. 24, 1912.
[11] C.o.d. service inaugurated July 1, 1913, under act of Congress, Aug. 24, 1912.
[12] Letters returned to writers.

### Post Office Development and Growth for Fiscal Years 1921-81, Continued

| Registered certified, insured, and c.o.d. mail[19] | Dead letters received | Amount received from dead letters[21] | Post offices issuing money orders[14] | Amount of domestic money orders issued | Amount of postal notes issued[15] | Amount of money orders issued[18] | Number of pieces of mail of all kinds handled[20] | Year |
|---|---|---|---|---|---|---|---|---|
| 220,856,945 | 19,683,259 | $223,621 | 54,183 | $1,310,114,354 | .......... | $24,398,542 | ............ | 1921 |
| 238,736,406 | 16,586,419 | 183,965 | 54,201 | 1,205,327,019 | .......... | 20,650,501 | ............ | 1922 |
| 269,840,470 | 19,238,548 | 143,993 | 54,181 | 1,371,454,679 | .......... | 34,118,667 | 23,054,832,000 | 1923 |
| 286,755,587 | 21,618,168 | 176,340 | 54,195 | 1,510,705,439 | .......... | 50,615,153 | ............ | 1924 |
| 294,174,647 | 21,332,232 | 223,197 | 54,269 | 1,532,567,052 | .......... | 52,650,428 | ............ | 1925 |
| 271,871,648 | 24,056,928 | 184,489 | 55,589 | 1,590,485,736 | .......... | 63,171,817 | 25,483,529,000 | 1926 |
| 266,283,318 | 25,854,845 | 149,116 | 54,616 | 1,647,580,285 | .......... | 68,951,620 | 26,686,556,000 | 1927 |
| 265,584,415 | 23,649,044 | 146,322 | 54,803 | 1,630,156,857 | .......... | 71,520,298 | 26,837,005,000 | 1928 |
| 270,577,460 | 23,079,619 | 128,932 | 54,357 | 1,658,442,930 | .......... | 76,112,628 | 27,951,548,000 | 1929 |
| 266,356,558 | 22,685,940 | 147,280 | 54,161 | 1,714,575,751 | .......... | 72,708,105 | 27,887,823,000 | 1930 |
| 233,384,741 | 19,957,684 | 122,992 | 55,040 | 1,559,549,224 | .......... | 62,227,939 | 26,544,352,000 | 1031 |
| 192,580,879 | 17,210,588 | 93,603 | 55,081 | 1,536,889,111 | .......... | 48,848,768 | 24,306,744,000 | 1932 |
| 150,737,943 | 10,708,353 | 89,389 | 56,106 | 1,647,420,645 | .......... | 35,115,947 | 19,868,456,000 | 1933 |
| 149,535,527 | 11,466,622 | 88,391 | 53,803 | 1,776,739,697 | .......... | 30,040,903 | 20,625,827,000 | 1934 |
| 154,950,349 | 12,567,130 | 87,310 | 53,106 | 1,820,597,325 | .......... | 30,429,303 | 22,331,752,000 | 1935 |
| 170,571,613 | 12,328,618 | 118,979 | 51,610 | 1,918,282,806 | .......... | 31,448,914 | 23,571,315,000 | 1936 |
| 176,302,102 | 13,802,638 | 103,722 | 51,304 | 2,170,001,673 | .......... | 33,978,756 | 25,801,279,000 | 1937 |
| 168,216,454 | 13,700,683 | 105,045 | 51,119 | 2,146,752,669 | .......... | 33,515,720 | 26,041,979,000 | 1938 |
| 169,866,593 | 13,226,456 | 96,452 | 50,956 | 2,047,929,528 | .......... | 29,949,091 | 26,444,846,000 | 1939 |
| 168,145,205 | 13,028,111 | 95,696 | 50,705 | 2,094,543,479 | .......... | 21,668,304 | 27,749,467,000 | 1940 |
| 173,827,676 | 13,744,889 | 100,701 | 50,745 | 2,357,012,894 | .......... | 16,862,709 | 29,235,791,000 | 1941 |
| 205,706,286 | 14,990,943 | 133,193 | 51,900 | 3,101,922,936 | .......... | 14,742,898 | 30,117,633,000 | 1942 |
| 297,581,386 | 15,437,258 | 220,705 | 53,694 | 4,435,620,357 | .......... | 17,556,873 | 32,818,262,000 | 1943 |
| 297,455,473 | 15,469,045 | 308,798 | 53,915 | 4,571,573,209 | .......... | 29,981,271 | 34,930,685,000 | 1944 |
| 279,530,763 | 14,144,856 | 351,162 | 53,435 | 4,810,300,270 | [16]$38,756,399 | 38,136,957 | 37,912,067,000 | 1945 |
| 278,800,771 | 18,676,852 | 456,148 | 48,510 | 4,748,066,012 | 132,242,529 | 38,738,035 | 36,318,158,000 | 1946 |
| 310,456,030 | 18,184,742 | 476,690 | 48,344 | 4,199,610,079 | 270,803,722 | 40,928,604 | 37,427,706,000 | 1947 |
| 338,638,938 | 18,100,456 | 507,152 | 48,406 | 4,554,944,265 | 373,829,571 | 51,882,313 | 40,280,374,000 | 1948 |
| 364,807,636 | 18,142,721 | 465,442 | 49,239 | 4,846,917,715 | 470,342,872 | 41,788,188 | 43,555,108,000 | 1949 |
| 347,667,006 | 18,922,309 | 397,107 | 49,269 | 4,598,024,240 | 523,644,668 | 58,744,605 | 45,063,737,000 | 1950 |
| 348,592,983 | 22,935,365 | 443,304 | 48,318 | 5,227,969,853 | [17]415,915,067 | 28,386,090 | 46,908,410,000 | 1951 |
| 342,631,183 | 22,797,455 | 464,397 | 49,599 | 5,933,646,011 | .......... | 38,312,557 | 49,905,875,000 | 1952 |
| 331,151,247 | 23,174,794 | 429,583 | 48,482 | 6,602,585,225 | .......... | 42,090,001 | 50,948,156,000 | 1953 |
| 316,578,914 | 20,043,201 | 379,851 | 47,153 | 6,032,490,082 | .......... | 50,106,005 | 52,213,170,000 | 1954 |
| 310,310,171 | 20,625,463 | 421,573 | 47,789 | 5,851,613,538 | .......... | 44,124,535 | 55,233,564,000 | 1955 |
| 305,244,988 | 21,088,494 | 365,312 | 46,561 | 5,911,182,000 | .......... | 46,525,845 | 56,441,216,000 | 1956 |
| 302,986,760 | 23,808,568 | 439,614 | 45,222 | 5,816,528,746 | .......... | 47,540,375 | 59,077,633,000 | 1957 |
| 262,153,838 | 24,054,103 | 551,372 | 44,804 | 5,441,535,846 | .......... | 49,655,719 | 60,129,911,000 | 1958 |
| 270,403,560 | 21,487,114 | 514,459 | 44,615 | 5,158,274,507 | .......... | 39,970,408 | 61,247,220,000 | 1959 |
| 270,867,819 | 21,969,725 | 560,979 | 44,600 | 5,030,614,549 | .......... | 39,879,890 | 63,674,604,000 | 1960 |
| 267,349,907 | 21,822,853 | 613,307 | 44,764 | 4,957,557,971 | .......... | 35,310,361 | 64,932,859,000 | 1961 |
| 269,707,097 | 22,300,117 | 673,531 | 44,953 | 4,787,351,013 | .......... | 33,677,123 | 66,493,190,000 | 1962 |
| 271,987,671 | 23,547,406 | 680,293 | 44,845 | 4,709,123,431 | .......... | 33,363,651 | 67,852,738,000 | 1963 |
| 274,962,977 | 22,744,417 | 748,784 | 44,684 | 4,719,361,377 | .......... | 32,344,713 | 69,676,477,000 | 1964 |
| 273,352,431 | 24,893,349 | 779,255 | 44,586 | 4,519,693,750 | .......... | 31,752,963 | 71,873,166,000 | 1965 |
| 274,124,608 | 27,332,964 | 770,814 | 44,333 | 4,706,214,335 | .......... | 28,583,079 | 75,607,302,000 | 1966 |
| 280,368,237 | 30,415,977 | 904,571 | 44,150 | 4,697,347,544 | .......... | 26,210,727 | 78,366,572,000 | 1967 |
| 285,009,957 | 32,774,881 | 935,390 | 43,431 | 4,680,686,923 | .......... | 26,001,377 | 79,516,731,000 | 1968 |
| 260,901,000 | 36,363,344 | 1,095,254 | 43,220 | 4,707,947,504 | .......... | 25,340,778 | 82,004,501,000 | 1969 |
| 240,143,000 | 37,422,610 | 1,089,110 | 43,112 | 4,695,138,794 | .......... | 26,576,507 | 84,881,833,000 | 1970 |
| 258,730 | .......... | .......... | 42,287 | .......... | .......... | .......... | 86,983,000,000 | 1971 |
| 259,886 | .......... | .......... | 42,254 | .......... | .......... | .......... | 87,156,084,000 | 1972 |
| 254,023 | .......... | .......... | 41,434 | .......... | .......... | .......... | 89,683,439,000 | 1973 |
| 250,524 | .......... | .......... | 40,914 | .......... | .......... | .......... | 90,098,108,000 | 1974 |
| 252,373 | .......... | .......... | 40,546 | .......... | .......... | .......... | 89,265,979,000 | 1975 |
| 257,721 | .......... | .......... | 40,392 | .......... | .......... | .......... | 89,767,903,000 | 1976 |
| 242,910 | .......... | .......... | 40,322 | .......... | .......... | .......... | 92,223,912,000 | 1977 |
| 226,165 | .......... | .......... | 39,870 | .......... | .......... | .......... | 96,913,154,000 | 1978 |
| 206,910 | .......... | .......... | 39,733 | .......... | .......... | .......... | 99,828,883,000 | 1979 |
| 216,138 | .......... | .......... | 39,486 | .......... | .......... | .......... | 106,311,062,000 | 1980 |
| 218,373 | .......... | .......... | 39,457 | .......... | .......... | .......... | 110,130,400,000 | 1981 |

[13] Aggregate accumulation from 1789 to 1838.
[14] Indicates number of post offices, stations and branches. Money-order system went into operation Nov. 1, 1864, under act of Congress of May 17, 1864.
[15] Postal notes in amounts up to $4.99 first issued Sept. 3, 1883, under act of Congress of March 3, 1883.
[16] From Feb. 1-June 30, 1945. Act of Congress approved June 28, 1944, authorized postal notes in amounts up to $10.
[17] From July 1, 1950, to March 31, 1951, withdrawn from sale March 31, 1951.
[18] Issued for payment in foreign countries. From Sept. 1, 1869, to June 30, 1870. International money orders first issued under Convention, Oct. 12, 1867.
[19] Indicates number of pieces of mail in domestic system given the noted services. Certified mail introduced June 6, 1955.
[20] Beginning 1968 volume based on new probability sample data; not comparable with previous years.
[21] Includes both dead letters and parcels.

# United States Postal Service
# Statement Of Financial Condition

| Statement of Operations | 1979 | 1980 | 1981 |
|---|---|---|---|
| | (in thousands of dollars) | | |
| Operating revenue. | $16,106,000 | $17,143,000 | $19,133,000 |
| Government appropriations. | 1,720,000 | 1,610,000 | 1,275,000 |
| Investment income | 349,000 | 500,000 | 490,000 |
| Total Income. | 18,175,000 | 19,253,000 | 20,898,000 |
| Salaries and related costs. | 15,162,000 | 16,273,098 | 17,479,000 |
| Other expenses. | 2,543,000 | 2,871,489 | 3,351,373 |
| Total Operating Expenses. | 17,705,000 | 19,144,587 | 20,830,759 |
| Income/(-) Loss. | 470,000 | 108,413 | 67,241,000 |

| Balance Sheet | 1979 | 1980 | 1981 |
|---|---|---|---|
| | (in thousands of dollars) | | |
| Assets | | | |
| Current Assets | | | |
| Cash. | $ 144,163 | $ 164,922 | $ 228,512 |
| Investments. | 2,238,716 | 2,476,012 | 1,968,193 |
| Accounts receivable: | | | |
| U.S. Government agencies. | 147,505 | 123,842 | 126,890 |
| Foreign countries | 28,916 | 39,701 | 18,883 |
| Other. | 74,416 | 56,651 | 76,263 |
| Total. | 250,837 | 220,176 | 222,036 |
| Less: Allowance. | -12,915 | -11,935 | -13,070 |
| Accounts receivable, net | 237,922 | 157,437 | 195,643 |
| Inventories. | 55,007 | 76,671 | 82,292 |
| Advances and prepayments | 11,359 | 6,593 | 196,463 |
| Total Current Assets | 2,687,167 | 2,942,439 | 2,691,026 |
| Other Assets. | 955 | 5,402 | 6,362 |
| Property and Equipment—net. | 4,192,986 | 5,673,832 | 5,928,594 |
| Deferred Retirement Costs. | 9,510,743 | 9,925,600 | 10,209,271 |
| Total Assets. | 16,391,851 | 17,204,571 | 17,487,116 |
| Liabilities | | | |
| Current Liabilities: | | | |
| Outstanding money orders | 183,040 | 210,853 | 201,617 |
| Accrued payroll | 100,250 | — | — |
| Payroll Taxes and Civil Service Retirement including amounts withheld | 452,310 | 935,862 | 1,143,317 |
| Workers' Compensation. | 157,082 | 187,225 | 207,455 |
| Accounts payable to other Government agencies | 188,016 | 131,460 | 142,731 |
| Other accounts payable and accrued expenses. | 566,503 | 958,769 | 1,096,381 |
| Notes payable | 67,000 | 232,000 | 67,000 |
| Mortgages payable | 3,600 | 5,000 | 6,000 |
| Prepaid permit mail and box rentals | 269,640 | 279,343 | 329,355 |
| Estimated prepaid postage in hands of the public | 621,000 | 675,000 | 770,000 |
| Total Current Liabilities. | 2,608,441 | 3,428,287 | 3,756,401 |
| Long-term Debt: | | | |
| Notes payable | 1,520,000 | 1,288,000 | 1,221,000 |
| USPS bonds payable. | 250,000 | 250,000 | 250,000 |
| Mortgages payable. | 47,637 | 65,756 | 63,651 |
| Total Long-term Debt | 1,817,637 | 1,603,756 | 1,534,651 |
| Other Liabilities: | | | |
| Employees' accumulated leave | 529,606 | 589,902 | 628,478 |
| Workers' compensation. | 2,190,000 | 2,510,000 | 2,810,000 |
| Other claims. | 300,000 | 20,000 | 25,000 |
| Amounts payable for retirement benefits | 9,389,859 | 9,766,557 | 10,044,286 |
| Total Other Liabilities. | 12,409,465 | 12,891,459 | 13,502,764 |
| Total Liabilities. | 16,835,543 | 17,923,502 | 18,793,816 |

### U.S.P.S. Statement of Financial Condition, Continued

| Balance Sheet Continued | 1979 | 1980 | 1981 |
|---|---|---|---|
| | (in thousands of dollars) | | |
| **Government Equity** | | | |
| Undelivered Orders: | | | |
| Operations .......................................... | 180,399 | 253,236 | 296,954 |
| Capital investment ............................... | 218,833 | 340,236 | 491,224 |
| Total Undelivered Orders ...................... | 399,232 | 593,472 | 788,178 |
| Uncommitted balances: | | | |
| Authority to borrow ............................. | 5,315,549 | — | — |
| Total unexpended balance....................... | 5,714,781 | — | — |
| Undrawn borrowing authorizations .................... | -8,163,000 | -3,574,680 | -4,847,204 |
| Total funded balance .......................... | -2,448,219 | — | — |
| Receivable established for future appropriations........ | 31,000 | 31,000 | — |
| Investment in property, equipment and | | | |
| inventories, net ................................. | 1,973,527 | 2,231,277 | 2,752,326 |
| Total Government Equity/Deficiency (-) ................ | -443,692 | -718,931 | -1,306,700 |
| Total Liabilities and Equity .......................... | 16,391,851 | 17,204,571 | 17,487,116 |
| **Analysis of Changes in Government Equity:** | | | |
| Non interest bearing capital: | | | |
| Start of period ..................................... | -945,222 | -443,692 | -718,931 |
| Transfers and adjustments .......................... | 31,694 | 31,153 | 30,000 |
| Net income or loss (-) for period ..................... | 469,836 | -306,392 | -587,739 |
| Total......................................... | -443,692 | -718,931 | -1,306,700 |

# Operating Statistics

| Classes of Mail | 1981 | 1980 | 1979 | 1978 | 1977 |
|---|---|---|---|---|---|
| | (in thousands) | | | | |
| **1st Class:** | | | | | |
| Pieces, number.............................. | 61,410,172 | 60,276,119 | 57,925,859 | 55,981,255 | 53,654,108 |
| Weight, pounds ............................. | 2,241,731 | 2,135,984 | 2,008,221 | 1,932,251 | 1,840,274 |
| Revenue..................................... | $11,457,145 | $10,145,508 | $ 9,732,720 | $ 8,574,655 | $ 7,831,430 |
| **Priority mail:** | | | | | |
| Pieces, number.............................. | 269,278 | 248,150 | 228,882 | 212,758 | 202,408 |
| Weight, pounds ............................. | 634,688 | 591,258 | 541,323 | 509,526 | 499,314 |
| Revenue..................................... | $ 758,268 | $ 611,635 | $ 560,685 | $ 497,336 | $ 467,602 |
| **Domestic air:**[1] | | | | | |
| Pieces, number.............................. | — | — | — | — | 13,360 |
| Weight, pounds ............................. | — | — | — | — | 1,866 |
| Revenue..................................... | — | — | — | — | $ 5,800 |
| **Express Mail:**[2] | | | | | |
| Pieces, number.............................. | 23,848 | 17,497 | 12,238 | 7,955 | — |
| Weight, pounds ............................. | 93,179 | 77,949 | 64,243 | 30,139 | — |
| Revenue...................................... | $ 269,658 | $ 184,222 | $ 133,582 | $ 88,610 | — |
| **Mailgrams:**[3] | | | | | |
| Pieces, number.............................. | 42,081 | 39,142 | 37,560 | 31,291 | — |
| Revenue..................................... | $ 15,517 | $ 14,552 | $ 14,636 | $ 10,749 | — |
| **2nd Class:** | | | | | |
| Pieces, number.............................. | 9,956,032 | 8,445,625 | 8,399,710 | 8,691,432 | 8,672,530 |
| Weight, pounds ............................. | 3,483,201 | 2,550,121 | 2,984,958 | 2,984,134 | 2,911,543 |
| Revenue..................................... | $ 885,159 | $ 617,584 | $ 643,738 | $ 471,994 | $ 362,783 |
| **Controlled circulation publications:** | | | | | |
| Pieces, number.............................. | — | 1,774,649 | 845,844 | 760,951 | 690,255 |
| Weight, pounds ............................. | — | 927,572 | 357,632 | 299,430 | 266,682 |
| Revenue..................................... | — | $ 245,707 | $ 94,937 | $ 67,165 | $ 52,689 |
| **3rd Class:** | | | | | |
| Pieces, number.............................. | 33,607,405 | 30,380,886 | 27,513,132 | 26,329,813 | 24,049,663 |
| Weight, pounds ............................. | 3,758,295 | 3,240,096 | 2,994,193 | 2,725,160 | 2,473,579 |
| Revenue..................................... | $ 2,643,363 | $ 2,412,326 | $ 2,216,255 | $ 1,986,478 | $ 1,747,519 |

**Operating Statistics, Continued**

## Classes of Mail Continued

| | 1981 | 1980 | 1979 | 1978 | 1977 |
|---|---|---|---|---|---|
| | | (in thousands) | | | |
| **4th Class:** | | | | | |
| Pieces, number............................. | 589,862 | 633,395 | 614,027 | 691,141 | 762,041 |
| Weight, pounds .............................. | 2,479,966 | 2,660,740 | 2,533,889 | 2,778,093 | 3,515,733 |
| Revenue........................ | $ 785,656 | $ 804,644 | $ 747,392 | $ 673,420 | $ 768,671 |
| **International surface:** | | | | | |
| Pieces, number............................. | 412,736 | 450,495 | 447,154 | 426,265 | 386,879 |
| Weight, pounds .............................. | 160,123 | 163,773 | 164,998 | 165,592 | 173,468 |
| Revenue........................ | $ 197,308 | $ 154,380 | $ 146,930 | $ 129,578 | $ 121,932 |
| **International air:** | | | | | |
| Pieces, number............................. | 472,773 | 513,285 | 507,217 | 486,565 | 498,177 |
| Weight, pounds .............................. | 52,055 | 51,868 | 47,764 | 43,274 | 42,102 |
| Revenue[4]........................ | $ 538,093 | $ 441,970 | $ 402,756 | $ 369,151 | $ 370,642 |
| **Penalty:** | | | | | |
| Pieces, number............................. | 2,898,082 | 2,992,110 | 2,895,333 | 2,823,874 | 2,962,047 |
| Weight, pounds .............................. | 568,277 | 503,463 | 503,401 | 497,714 | 564,984 |
| Revenue........................ | $ 706,463 | $ 682,164 | $ 635,064 | $ 579,065 | $ 566,755 |
| **Franked:** | | | | | |
| Pieces, number............................. | 400,647 | 511,869 | 374,099 | 447,925 | 307,030 |
| Weight, pounds .............................. | 14,164 | 15,504 | 16,752 | 14,344 | 12,067 |
| Revenue........................ | $ 53,967 | $ 62,603 | $ 42,532 | $ 47,053 | $ 44,473 |
| **Free for the blind:** | | | | | |
| Pieces, number............................. | 47,484 | 27,840 | 27,828 | 21,929 | 25,414 |
| Weight, pounds .............................. | 56,103 | 39,737 | 36,064 | 32,884 | 42,226 |
| **TOTALS:** | | | | | |
| Pieces, number............................. | 110,130,400 | 106,311,062 | 99,828,883 | 96,913,154 | 92,223,912 |
| Weight, pounds .............................. | 13,514,782 | 12,958,065 | 12,253,438 | 12,012,541 | 12,343,838 |
| Revenue........................ | $18,310,597 | $16,377,295 | $15,371,227 | $13,495,254 | $12,340,296 |

[1] Domestic air mail service discontinued on May 1, 1977.
[2] Express mail established as a class of mail on Oct. 9, 1977.
[3] Mailgram revenue included in other revenue for prior years.
[4] Includes transit special handling and miscellaneous revenue.

## Special Services

| | 1981 | 1980 | 1979 | 1978 | 1977 |
|---|---|---|---|---|---|
| | | (in thousands) | | | |
| **Registry:** | | | | | |
| Number of articles (paid and free).............. | 56,191 | 53,652 | 53,670 | 55,370 | 59,376 |
| Revenue....................................... | $ 168,460 | $ 156,854 | $ 157,160 | $ 123,295 | $ 110,585 |
| **Certified:** | | | | | |
| Number of pieces............................ | 97,185 | 94,305 | 81,385 | 82,060 | 81,439 |
| Revenue....................................... | $ 121,826 | $ 120,168 | $ 98,414 | $ 80,186 | $ 67,648 |
| **Insurance:** | | | | | |
| Number of articles.......................... | 51,993 | 55,445 | 59,642 | 73,330 | 85,599 |
| Revenue....................................... | $ 52,451 | $ 55,355 | $ 56,497 | $ 57,303 | $ 55,877 |
| **Collection-on-delivery:** | | | | | |
| Number of articles.......................... | 13,004 | 12,736 | 12,213 | 15,405 | 16,496 |
| Revenue....................................... | $ 23,480 | $ 20,642 | $ 19,566 | $ 19,519 | $ 19,500 |
| **Special delivery:** | | | | | |
| Number of articles.......................... | 33,160 | 36,394 | 40,971 | 45,326 | 54,243 |
| Revenue....................................... | $ 69,736 | $ 73,037 | $ 84,769 | $ 70,227 | $ 72,427 |
| **Money orders:** | | | | | |
| Number issued .............................. | 117,031 | 119,728 | 108,162 | 123,616 | 136,701 |
| Revenue fees................................. | $ 111,205 | $ 95,331 | $ 91,274 | $ 88,864 | $ 104,757 |
| **Others:** | | | | | |
| Box rents revenue ........................... | $ 168,339 | $ 159,948 | $ 152,930 | $ 123,605 | $ 109,030 |
| Stamped envelope revenue................... | $ 16,398 | $ 15,442 | $ 15,673 | $ 12,976 | $ 13,165 |
| Other revenue, Net........................... | $ 90,549 | $ 68,688 | $ 58,602 | $ 61,827 | $ 104,588 |
| **TOTALS:** | | | | | |
| Special services revenue...................... | $ 822,444 | $ 765,465 | $ 734,858 | $ 637,802 | $ 657,577 |
| Mail revenue.............................. | $18,310,597 | $16,377,295 | $15,371,227 | $13,495,254 | $12,340,296 |
| Operating revenue........................... | $19,133,041 | $17,142,760 | $16,106,085 | $14,133,056 | $12,997,873 |

**Operating Statistics, Continued**

| Employees | 1981 | 1980 | 1979 | 1978 | 1977 |
|---|---|---|---|---|---|
| **Employee Groups** | | | | | |
| Headquarters employees...................... | *3,293 | 2,798 | 2,710 | 2,719 | 2,655 |
| Field regular employees: | | | | | |
| Regional and other field units................... | 6,058 | 6,228 | 5,422 | 5,204 | 5,066 |
| Inspection Service........................... | 5,133 | 5,242 | 5,236 | 5,346 | 5,289 |
| Postmasters................................... | 28,711 | 28,967 | 28,400 | 28,367 | 29,097 |
| Post Office supervisors and technical personnel .... | 37,048 | 36,481 | 36,065 | 36,579 | 36,239 |
| Post Office clerks and mail handlers............. | 232,141 | 229,232 | 230,363 | 226,198 | 227,929 |
| City delivery carriers and vehicle drivers......... | 164,066 | 160,348 | 159,544 | 156,946 | 156,920 |
| Rural delivery carriers........................ | 33,370 | 32,863 | 31,919 | 30,630 | 31,226 |
| Special delivery messengers ................... | 1,929 | 1,987 | 2,094 | 2,235 | 2,372 |
| Building and equipment maintenance personnel.... | 28,070 | 27,586 | 27,366 | 27,243 | 27,050 |
| Vehicle maintenance facility personnel .......... | 4,732 | 4,641 | 4,630 | 4,648 | 4,713 |
| Total full-time employees..................... | 544,557 | 536,373 | 533,749 | 526,115 | 528,556 |
| Total other employees........................ | 125,682 | 130,450 | 129,318 | 129,452 | 126,541 |
| Grand total ............................... | 670,239 | 666,823 | 663,067 | 655,567 | 655,097 |

* Of the 495 people added to Headquarters staff, 240 were temporary employees hired to perform research for a legal action.

| Offices, Stations and Branches | 1981 | 1980 | 1979 | 1978 | 1977 |
|---|---|---|---|---|---|
| Number of post offices.......................... | 30,242 | 30,326 | 30,449 | 30,518 | 30,521 |
| **Number of branches and stations:** | | | | | |
| Classified branches and stations ............... | 4,109 | 4,109 | 4,104 | 4,091 | 4,076 |
| Contract branches and stations ................. | 3,421 | 3,346 | 3,415 | 3,438 | 3,798 |
| Community Post Offices ....................... | 1,685 | 1,705 | 1,765 | 1,823 | 1,927 |
| Total ..................................... | 9,215 | 9,160 | 9,284 | 9,352 | 9,801 |
| Grand Total ............................... | 39,457 | 39,486 | 39,733 | 39,870 | 40,322 |

## Shipments of Accountable Paper

| Fiscal Year | Postage Stamps | Stamped Envelopes | Postal Cards |
|---|---|---|---|
| 1971 ............................. | 33,011,711.5 | 1,517,066.0 | 975,544.75 |
| 1972 ............................. | 26,754,519.9 | 1,320,672.5 | 917,852.75 |
| 1973 ............................. | 26,624,940.3 | 1,172,961.0 | 703,949.25 |
| 1974 ............................. | 29,462,495.6 | 1,266,972.5 | 782,395.75 |
| 1975 ............................. | 24,334,840.1 | 1,016,854.5 | 554,348.25 |
| 1976 ............................. | 30,967,904.9 | 1,118,652.5 | 835,412.25 |
| *Transition Quarter................... | 7,701,885.5 | 292,593.5 | 134,638.25 |
| 1977 ............................. | 26,739,594.8 | 970,319.0 | 502,404.25 |
| 1978 ............................. | 35,889,863.1 | 1,213,335.5 | 664,951.0 |
| 1979 ............................. | 27,362,729.2 | 851,882.5 | 533,012.75 |
| 1980 ............................. | 26,782,003.4 | 898,022.5 | 511,971.75 |
| 1981 ............................. | 38,519,300.0 | 923,317.5 | 751,744.75 |

*Transition Quarter - June 19 thru October 8, 1976. The U.S. Government changed its fiscal year from a July 1 through June 30 basis to an Oct. 1 through Sept. 30 basis effective Oct. 1, 1976.

## U.S. Postmasters General

Following is a listing of Postmasters General of the United States and the authorities under whom they served. Dates of entry into service and home states also are noted.

Benjamin Franklin, Pa.
July 26, 1775
Continental Congress

Richard Bache, Pa.
Nov. 7, 1776
Continental Congress

Ebenezer Hazard, N.Y.
Jan. 28, 1782
Continental Congress

Samuel Osgood, Mass.
Sept. 26, 1789
George Washington

Timothy Pickering, Pa.
Aug. 12, 1791
George Washington

Joseph Habersham, Ga.
Feb. 25, 1795
George Washington

Gideon Granger, Conn.
Nov. 28, 1801
Thomas Jefferson

Return J. Meigs Jr., Ohio
April 11, 1814
James Madison

John McLean, Ohio
July 1, 1823
James Monroe

William T. Barry, Ky.
April 6, 1829
Andrew Jackson

Amos Kendall, Ky.
May 1, 1835
Andrew Jackson

John M. Niles, Conn.
May 26, 1840
Martin Van Buren

Francis Granger, N.Y.
March 8, 1841
William Henry Harrison
and John Tyler

Charles A. Wickliffe, Ky.
Oct. 13, 1841
John Tyler

Cave Johnson, Tenn.
March 7, 1845
James K. Polk

Jacob Collamer, Vt.
March 8, 1849
Zachary Taylor

Nathan K. Hall, N.Y.
July 23, 1850
Millard Fillmore

Samuel D. Hubbard, Conn.
Sept. 14, 1852
Millard Fillmore

James Campbell, Pa.
March 8, 1853
Franklin Pierce

Aaron V. Brown, Tenn.
March 7, 1857
James Buchanan

Joseph Holt, Ky.
March 14, 1859
James Buchanan

Horatio King, Maine
Feb. 12, 1861
Abraham Lincoln

Montgomery Blair, D.C.
March 9, 1861
Abraham Lincoln

William Dennison, Ohio
Oct. 1, 1864
Abraham Lincoln
and Andrew Johnson

Alexander W. Randall, Wis.
July 25, 1866
Andrew Johnson

John A.J. Creswell, Md.
March 6, 1869
Ulysses S. Grant

James W. Marshall, N.J.
July 7, 1874
Ulysses S. Grant

Marshall Jewell, Conn.
Sept. 1, 1874
Ulysses S. Grant

James N. Tyner, Ind.
July 13, 1876
Ulysses S. Grant

David McK. Key, Tenn.
March 13, 1877
Rutherford B. Hayes

Horace Maynard, Tenn.
Aug. 25, 1880
Rutherford B. Hayes

Thomas L. James, N.Y.
March 8, 1881
James A. Garfield
and Chester A. Arthur

Timothy O. Howe, Wis.
Jan. 5, 1882
Chester A. Arthur

Walter Q. Gresham, Ind.
April 11, 1883
Chester A. Arthur

Frank Hatton, Iowa
Oct. 14, 1884
Chester A. Arthur

William F. Vilas, Wis.
March 7, 1885
Grover Cleveland

Don M. Dickinson, Mich.
Jan. 17, 1888
Grover Cleveland

John Wanamaker, Pa.
March 6, 1889
Benjamin Harrison

Wilson S. Bissell, N.Y.
March 7, 1893
Grover Cleveland

William L. Wilson, W.Va.
April 4, 1895
Grover Cleveland

James A. Gary, Md.
March 6, 1897
William McKinley

Charles Emory Smith, Pa.
April 22, 1893
William McKinley
and Theodore Roosevelt

Henry C. Payne, Wis.
Jan. 15, 1902
Theodore Roosevelt

Robert J. Wynne, Pa.
Oct. 10, 1904
Theodore Roosevelt

George B. Cortelyou, N.Y.
March 7, 1905
Theodore Roosevelt

George van L. Meyer, Mass.
March 4, 1907
Theodore Roosevelt

Frank H. Hitchcock, Mass.
March 6, 1909
William Taft

Albert S. Burleson, Tex.
March 5, 1913
Woodrow Wilson

Will H. Hayes, Ind.
March 5, 1921
Warren G. Harding

Hubert Work, Colo.
March 4, 1922
Warren G. Harding

Harry S. New, Ind.
March 4, 1923
Calvin Coolidge

Walter F. Brown, Ohio
March 6, 1929
Herbert Hoover

James A. Farley, N.Y.
March 4, 1933
Franklin D. Roosevelt

Frank C. Walker, Pa.
Sept. 11, 1940
Franklin D. Roosevelt

Robert E. Hannegan, Mo.
  July 1, 1945
  Franklin D. Roosevelt
  and Harry S. Truman

Jesse M. Donaldson, Ill.
  Dec. 16, 1947
  Harry S. Truman

Arthur E. Summerfield, Mich.
  Jan. 21, 1953
  Dwight D. Eisenhower

J. Edward Day, Calif.
  Jan. 21, 1961
  John F. Kennedy

John A. Gronouski, Wis.
  Sept. 30, 1963
  John F. Kennedy
  and Lyndon B. Johnson

Lawrence F. O'Brien, Mass.
  Nov. 3, 1965
  Lyndon B. Johnson

W. Marvin Watson, Tex.
  April 26, 1968
  Lyndon B. Johnson

Winton M. Blount, Ala.
  Jan. 22, 1969
  Richard M. Nixon

E.T. Klassen, Mass.
  Dec. 7, 1971
  Richard M. Nixon
  and Gerald Ford, USPS

Benjamin F. Bailar, Ill.
  Feb. 15, 1975
  Gerald Ford
  and Jimmy Carter

William F. Bolger, Conn.
  March 15, 1978
  Jimmy Carter
  and Ronald Reagan

# Organization of the USPS

Founded in 1971, the United States Postal Service is an independent agency charged with expediting the nation's mails. It is headed by an 11-member Board of Governors, nine of whom are appointed by the president subject to Senate confirmation. The other two members are the postmaster general and deputy postmaster general, who are appointed by the Board.

The presidential appointees serve for terms of from one to nine years. Not more than five may be from the same political party.

The Board generally meets monthly, and the members are compensated with $300 a day for meetings plus $10,000 annually. At these sessions the organization is to direct the exercise of the powers of the Postal Service, direct and control its expenditures, and review its practices and policies."

Day-to-day responsibility for the Postal Service is given to the postmaster general. He is assisted by a number of additional officials, arranged in both subject matter and geographical structure.

The information on incumbents provided here is the latest from the USPS as of May 1982. While there will undoubtedly be changes over time, these data should give a general idea of the individuals who make up the postal management.

## Board of Governors

David E. Babcock (Vice Chairman) .................................... term expires Dec. 8, 1988
  Management consultant, David E. Babcock & Associates
George W. Camp ............................................. term expires Dec. 8, 1985
  Retired postal executive
Robert L. Hardesty (Chairman) ...................................... term expires Dec. 8, 1983
  President, Southwest Texas State University
Paula D. Hughes............................................. term expires Dec. 8, 1987
  First vice president & director, Thomson McKinnon Securities Inc.
Timothy L. Jenkins ............................................. term expires Dec. 8, 1982
  Chairman, MATCH Institution
John R. McKean.............................................. term expires Dec. 8, 1986
  Certified public accountant
William J. Sullivan.......................................... term expires Dec. 8, 1984
  Vice chancellor & treasurer, University of Maine
  Postmaster General William F. Bolger and Deputy Postmaster General C. Neil Benson are also members of the Board.

This leaves two vacancies on the Board of Governors.

## U.S. POSTAL SERVICE OFFICERS
### APMG — Assistant Postmaster General
### SAPMG — Senior Assistant Postmaster General

Postmaster General................................................William F. Bolger
Executive Assistant to the Postmaster General ...............................Gerald F. Merna
APMG, Planning Department ............................................. William R. Cummings
APMG, Public & Employee Communications Department........................ Mary Layton
APMG, Government Relations Department ............................. Edward E. Horgan Jr.
General Counsel, Law Department................................................ Louis A. Cox
Chief Postal Inspector, Inspection Service Department .................... Kenneth H. Fletcher

Senior Assistant Postmaster General . . . . . . . . . . . . . . . . . . . . . . . . . . . . . . . . . . . . . . . . Carl C. Ulsaker
SAPMG, Employee & Labor Relations Group. . . . . . . . . . . . . . . . . . . . . . . . . . . . . . . . .Joseph F. Morris
  APMG, Labor Relations Department . . . . . . . . . . . . . . . . . . . . . . . . . . . . . . . . . . . . . . James C. Gildea
  APMG, Employee Relations Department . . . . . . . . . . . . . . . . . . . . . . . . . . . . . . . . . Nancy L. George
SAPMG, Finance Group . . . . . . . . . . . . . . . . . . . . . . . . . . . . . . . . . . . . . . . . . . . . . . . . . . . . Jim Finch
  APMG, Rates & Classification Department . . . . . . . . . . . . . . . . . . . . . . . . . . Edward J. McCaffrey
  APMG, Finance Department . . . . . . . . . . . . . . . . . . . . . . . . . . . . . . . . . . . . .Anthony P. Cavallo Jr.
    Office of the Treasurer . . . . . . . . . . . . . . . . . . . . . . . . . . . . . . . . . . . . . . . James R. Glassco Jr.
Deputy Postmaster General. . . . . . . . . . . . . . . . . . . . . . . . . . . . . . . . . . . . . . . . . . . . .C. Neil Benson
  Executive Assistant to the Deputy Postmaster General . . . . . . . . . . . . . . . . . . . . . . .John L. Gentile
  Executive Assistant for Information Resources Management . . . . . . . . . . . . . . . . Charles K. Kernan
  APMG, Management Information Systems Department. . . . . . . . . . . . . . . . . . . Ralph M. Feemster
SAPMG, Administration Group . . . . . . . . . . . . . . . . . . . . . . . . . . . . . . . . . . . . . . . . Francis X. Biglin
  Judicial Officer. . . . . . . . . . . . . . . . . . . . . . . . . . . . . . . . . . . . . . . . . . . . . . . . . . James A. Cohen
  APMG, Real Estate & Buildings Department . . . . . . . . . . . . . . . . . . . . . . . . . . . Roger P. Craig
  APMG, Customer Services Department . . . . . . . . . . . . . . . . . . . . . . . . . . . . . . . .Gordon C. Morison
    Consumer Advocate Office . . . . . . . . . . . . . . . . . . . . . . . . . . . . . . . . . . Thomas W. Chadwick
  APMG, Procurement & Supply Department . . . . . . . . . . . . . . . . . . . . . . . . . . . . Jackie A. Strange
  APMG, International Postal Affairs Department . . . . . . . . . . . . . . . . . . . . . . . . . .Walter E. Duka
SAPMG, Operations Group. . . . . . . . . . . . . . . . . . . . . . . . . . . . . . . . . . . . . . . . . . . James V. Jellison
  APMG, Delivery Services Department. . . . . . . . . . . . . . . . . . . . . . . . . . . . . . . Eugene C. Hagburg
  APMG, Mail Processing Department . . . . . . . . . . . . . . . . . . . . . . . . . . . . . . . . Harry C. Penttala
  APMG, Engineering & Technical Support Department. . . . . . . . . . . . . . . . . . . . William V. Chapp
Regional Postmaster General, Central Region. . . . . . . . . . . . . . . . . . . . . . . . . . . . . .Paul N. Carlin
Regional Postmaster General, Eastern Region . . . . . . . . . . . . . . . . . . . . . . . . . . . . . .E. Herbert Daws
Regional Postmaster General, Northeast Region. . . . . . . . . . . . . . . . . . . . . . . . . . . John G. Mulligan
Regional Postmaster General, Southern Region . . . . . . . . . . . . . . . . . . . . . . . . Emmett E. Cooper Jr.
Regional Postmaster General, Western Region . . . . . . . . . . . . . . . . . . . . . . . . . . Michael S. Coughlin

## Postmaster General

William F. Bolger was appointed postmaster general by the Board of Governors of the U.S. Postal Service on March 15, 1978. Previously, he had served as deputy postmaster general and a member of the Board of Governors since Sept. 4, 1975, and postmaster general for the Northeast Region of the Postal Service since July of 1973.

Bolger is only the second career postal employee to hold this position. His first assignment came in 1941 when he went to work for the Post Office Department's Bureau of Finance.

When the USPS was formed, Bolger had been serving as Regional Director of the old Boston Region, responsible for all postal activities in New England. The new administration made him manager of the Boston metropolitan district, and he went on to become acting assistant regional postmaster general in Philadelphia and Eastern Regional postmaster general.

## Consumer Advocate

Thomas W. Chadwick "is responsible for representing consumers within the Postal Service, ensuring their mailing needs are appropriately met." Before taking office in 1972, he was instrumental in setting up The National Postal Forum, "designed to foster an exchange of ideas and views between Postal Service management and mail customers."

Chadwick was a South Carolina newsman and a press secretary. He also has a lengthy service with the USPS, including special assistant to the assistant postmaster general, Finance and Administration; deputy director, Customer Relations Division; director, Complaints Analysis Division.

## Stamps Division

Stamp collectors are strongly affected by the policies of the Stamps Division, Office of Customer Programs, USPS, part of the responsibility of the assistant postmaster general for customer services. It is here that projects involving the production and distribution of philatelic materials, the encouragement of prospective collectors, and the development of USPS philatelic communications are handled.

Other contacts result from USPS participation in various exhibitions, and from Stamps Division publicity releases dealing with newly available stamps and other items. Constructive comments and proposals are always encouraged by mail or through the periodic postal symposia.

For example, the National Postal Forum, created in 1967, is a nonprofit educational corporation chartered for the purpose of improving postal services by developing a close working relationship between postal management and business customers. Operational costs are financed by registration fees and rentals for exhibit booths.

In 1981, five regional forums attracted a total attendance of more than 6,000 mailer and postal officials. A record 260 companies exhibited 460

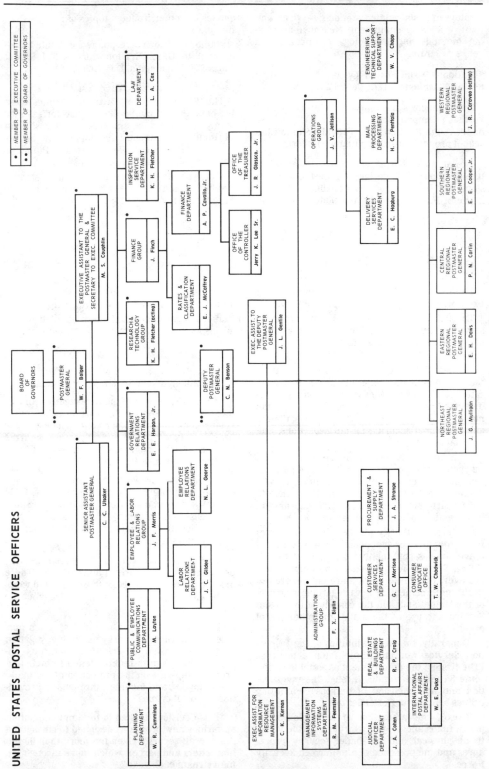

UNITED STATES POSTAL SERVICE OFFICERS

• MEMBER OF EXECUTIVE COMMITTEE
•• MEMBER OF BOARD OF GOVERNORS

BOARD OF GOVERNORS

POSTMASTER GENERAL — W. F. Bolger

SENIOR ASSISTANT POSTMASTER GENERAL — C. C. Ulsaker

EXECUTIVE ASSISTANT TO THE POSTMASTER GENERAL & SECRETARY TO EXEC. COMMITTEE — M. S. Coughlin

DEPUTY POSTMASTER GENERAL — C. N. Benson

EXEC. ASSIST. TO THE DEPUTY POSTMASTER GENERAL — J. L. Gentile

LAW DEPARTMENT — L. A. Cox

INSPECTION SERVICE DEPARTMENT — K. H. Fletcher

FINANCE GROUP — J. Finch

RESEARCH & TECHNOLOGY GROUP — K. H. Fletcher (acting)

FINANCE DEPARTMENT — A. P. Cavallo, Jr.

RATES & CLASSIFICATION DEPARTMENT — E. J. McCaffrey

OFFICE OF THE TREASURER — J. R. Glossco, Jr.

OFFICE OF THE CONTROLLER — Jerry K. Lee Sr.

OPERATIONS GROUP — J. V. Jellison

ENGINEERING & TECHNICAL SUPPORT DEPARTMENT — W. V. Chapp

MAIL PROCESSING DEPARTMENT — H. C. Penfold

DELIVERY SERVICES DEPARTMENT — E. C. Hopburg

WESTERN REGIONAL POSTMASTER GENERAL — J. R. Caraveo (acting)

SOUTHERN REGIONAL POSTMASTER GENERAL — E. E. Cooper, Jr.

CENTRAL REGIONAL POSTMASTER GENERAL — P. N. Carlin

EASTERN REGIONAL POSTMASTER GENERAL — E. H. Dows

NORTHEAST REGIONAL POSTMASTER GENERAL — J. G. Mulligan

GOVERNMENT RELATIONS DEPARTMENT — E. E. Horgan, Jr.

EMPLOYEE & LABOR RELATIONS GROUP — J. F. Morris

EMPLOYEE RELATIONS DEPARTMENT — N. L. George

LABOR RELATIONS DEPARTMENT — J. C. Gildea

PUBLIC & EMPLOYEE COMMUNICATIONS DEPARTMENT — M. Layton

PLANNING DEPARTMENT — W. R. Cummings

ADMINISTRATION GROUP — F. X. Biglin

PROCUREMENT & SUPPLY DEPARTMENT — J. A. Strange

CUSTOMER SERVICES DEPARTMENT — G. C. Morrison

CONSUMER ADVOCATE OFFICE — T. W. Chadwick

REAL ESTATE & BUILDINGS DEPARTMENT — R. P. Craig

INTERNATIONAL POSTAL AFFAIRS DEPARTMENT — W. E. Duka

EXEC. ASSIST. FOR INFORMATION RESOURCE MANAGEMENT — C. K. Kernan

MANAGEMENT INFORMATION SYSTEMS DEPARTMENT — R. M. Feemster

JUDICIAL OFFICER DEPARTMENT — J. A. Cohen

displays of postal-related products, services, and mail processing equipment. New mail-processing methods and technology highlighted this year's program.

National Postal Forum XVI is scheduled to be held in Washington, D.C., Sept. 12-15, 1982.

New collectors are approached through an advertising campaign featuring recent U.S. issues, and through the Benjamin Franklin Stamp Club school program utilizing philatelic materials.

The Stamps Division is involved in the selection of topics and designs for new U.S. emissions, and handles questions dealing with these matters. First day cover and plate number inquiries are other frequent topics of Stamps Division mail.

Stamps Division correspondence should be addressed to USPS Headquarters, 475 L'Enfant Plaza SW, Washington, D.C. 20260.

## Philatelic Sales Division

The Philatelic Sales Division provides over-the-counter and mail-order service for selected stamped paper stock and specialty items. A list of materials currently available may be obtained from the U.S. Postal Service, Philatelic Sales Division, Washington, D.C. 20265.

Total philatelic sales for retained stamps, products, and services were approximately $113.6 million in fiscal 1981.

# Postal Inspection Service

The following information on security and law enforcement relating to the U.S. Postal Service is excerpted from the "Postal Inspection Service Law Enforcement Report," March—April 1976.

The publication is designed to inform interested persons regarding actual cases handled by the service. Further information on the work of the Postal Inspection Service may be obtained from the offices listed in this excerpt.

"Under Public Law 91-375, Aug. 12, 1970, more commonly known as the 'Postal Reorganization Act,' the Postal Inspection Service . . . was delegated responsibility for the protection of the mails, enforcement of postal laws, installation and personnel security, postal inspections, and internal audits.

"The Service is headed by the Chief Postal Inspector, who directs the execution of policies, regulations, and procedures governing all investigations, including presentation of evidence to the Department of Justice and U.S. Attorneys in investigations of a criminal nature.

"Statutory authority has been granted Postal Inspectors to serve subpoenas and warrants, and make arrests, by the provisions of Title 18, U.S.C., Section 3061. It should be emphasized, however, that these powers are only exercised in the enforcement of laws regarding property of the United States in the custody of the Postal Service, the use of the mails, and other postal offenses.

"Generally, the responsibilities of the Inspection Service fall into three main categories. (The first is) the enforcement of postal laws and some 85 federal statutes through the investigation and apprehension of persons committing crimes against the Postal Service.

"(Also), the protection of personnel, mail, postal funds and property through a wide variety of physical and personnel security procedures and the presence of a uniformed Security Force.

"(Finally), the internal audit of all Postal Service financial and non-financial operations.

"About 67 per cent of the investigative time of the Inspection Service is spent on criminal investigations. Nearly 25 per cent of investigative time is devoted to the audit program with the remainder to personnel, physical security and administrative investigations.

"To perform this work, the Inspection Service has approximately 5,600 people of whom 1,700 are Inspectors and 180 are Special Investigators who assist in criminal investigations. These people are located in major cities throughout the United States . . .

"The newest category of Inspection Service personnel is the Security Police Officer. There are presently some 2,600 of these men and women located at postal installations throughout the country . . .

"Historically, the role of the Inspection Service concentrated primarily on the investigation and apprehension of criminals, but this approach (has) had to be broadened to include a greater emphasis on the protection of the mail . . . employees, and facilities, through the prevention of postal crimes.

"This decision resulted in the implementation of various new programs designed to strengthen . . . overall security given the more than 90 billion letters and parcels which move through the mail stream each year."

# ADDRESSES OF POSTAL INSPECTORS

## NORTHEAST REGION

Boston Division
Box 2217
Boston, Mass. 02107
617-223-2223
  Connecticut
  Maine
  Massachusetts
  New Hampshire
  Rhode Island
  Vermont

Newark Division
Box 509
Newark, N.J. 07101
201-596-5400
  Northern New Jersey
  Puerto Rico
  Virgin Islands

New York Division
Box 555
New York, N.Y. 10116
212-971-7641
  Eastern New York

## EASTERN REGION

Philadelphia Division
Box 7500
Philadelphia, Pa. 19101
215-596-5417
  Delaware
  Southern New Jersey
  Eastern Pennsylvania

Pittsburgh Division
1700 Centre City Towers
Pittsburgh, Pa. 15222
412-644-5482
  Western New York
  Western Pennsylvania
  West Virginia

Washington Division
Box 1820
Washington, D.C. 20013
202-523-2551
  District of Columbia
  Maryland
  Virginia

## SOUTHERN REGION

Atlanta Division
Box 16489
Atlanta, Ga. 30321
404-763-7080
  Florida
  Georgia

Chattanooga Division
Box 711
Chattanooga, Tenn. 37401
615-899-9111
  Alabama
  North Carolina
  South Carolina
  Tennessee (All Except
   Shelby County)

Memphis Division
Box 3180
Memphis, Tenn. 38103
901-521-3486
  Arkansas
  Louisiana
  Mississippi
  Oklahoma
  Tennessee (Shelby County)

Fort Worth Division
Box 1230
Fort Worth, Tex. 76101
817-334-2901
  Texas

## CENTRAL REGION

Chicago Division
433 W. Van Buren St.
Chicago, Ill. 60607
312-886-2820
  Northern Illinois
  Northwestern Indiana

Cincinnati Division
Box 2057
Cincinnati, Ohio 45201
513-684-2404
  Kentucky
  Ohio

Detroit Division
Box 119
Detroit, Mich. 48232
313-226-6732
  Indiana
  Michigan

## CENTRAL REGION CONTD.

St. Louis Division
200 S. Hanley Road
St. Louis, Mo. 63199
314-425-3060
  Kansas
  Southern Illinois
  Missouri

St. Paul Division
Box 43558
St. Paul, Minn. 55165
612-725-7318
  Iowa
  Minnesota
  Nebraska
  North Dakota
  South Dakota
  Wisconsin

## WESTERN REGION

Los Angeles Division
Box 30456
Los Angeles, Calif. 90030
213-688-2180
  Arizona
  Southern California
  Southern Nevada
  New Mexico

San Francisco Division
Box 367
San Francisco, Calif. 94101
415-556-2097
  Northern California
  Colorado
  Hawaii
  Eastern Idaho
  Northern Nevada
  Pacific Islands
  Utah
  Wyoming

Seattle Division
Box 400
Seattle, Wash. 98111
206-442-7880
  Alaska
  Western Idaho
  Montana
  Oregon
  Washington

# Postal Rate Commission

The Postal Rate Commission is an independent Federal regulatory agency which was established by Congress to serve as a legal forum for proposed changes in postal rates, fees, mail classifications (which are official definitions of the different services available from the Postal Service); or changes in the nature of available postal service; or appeals from Postal Service decisions to close or consolidate small post offices. The commission also investigates complaints concerning postal rates, fees, mail classifications, or services.

The Commission was created by chapter 36, subchapter I of the Postal Reorganization Act of Aug. 12, 1970 (84 Stat. 759; 39 U.S.C. 3601-3604) and is composed of five commissioners, each appointed to six-year terms by the President, with the advice and consent of the Senate.

The President designates one of the commissioners as chairman, and the chairman's tenure during his term of office is at the pleasure of the President. The commission elects one of its members as vice chairman.

Current Commissioners are:

Simeon M. Bright . . . . . . . . . . . . . . . . . . . . . . . . . . . . . . . . . . . . . . . . . . . . . . . . term expires November 1982
John W. Crutcher . . . . . . . . . . . . . . . . . . . . . . . . . . . . . . . . . . . . . . . . . . . . . . . . term expires October 1986
James H. Duffy . . . . . . . . . . . . . . . . . . . . . . . . . . . . . . . . . . . . . . . . . . . . . . . . . . term expires November 1984
Henry R. Folsom . . . . . . . . . . . . . . . . . . . . . . . . . . . . . . . . . . . . . . . . . . . . . . . . . term expires October 1982
Janet D. Steiger (Chairman) . . . . . . . . . . . . . . . . . . . . . . . . . . . . . . . . . . . . . . . . term expires October 1986

According to the legislation which established the Postal Rate Commission, no more than three commissioners may be members of the same political party.

Organizationally, the chairman of the Postal Rate Commission is responsible for the general administration of the internal affairs of the commission. The staff of the Postal Rate Commission, which includes approximately 80 employees, is organized under three offices: the Office of Technical Analysis and Planning (this office is responsible for technical — as opposed to legal — analyses and the formulation of policy recommendations); the Office of the Commission (which includes both legal and technical staff and represents the interests of the general public in proceedings before the commission); the Office of the General Counsel (which is responsible for legal and advisory services to the commission for all cases before the commission and the courts of the United States, and for all rule making and legislative matters).

The Postal Rate Commission's policies and practices are determined by the commission as a whole, and conform to the guidelines set down in the Postal Reorganization Act of 1970 (the basic charter under which the commission operates), the Administrative Procedure Act, and other applicable laws.

The following charts illustrate how the Postal Rate Commission operates.

## POSTAL RATE COMMISSION PROCEEDINGS CONCERNING CHANGES IN NATIONWIDE SERVICE

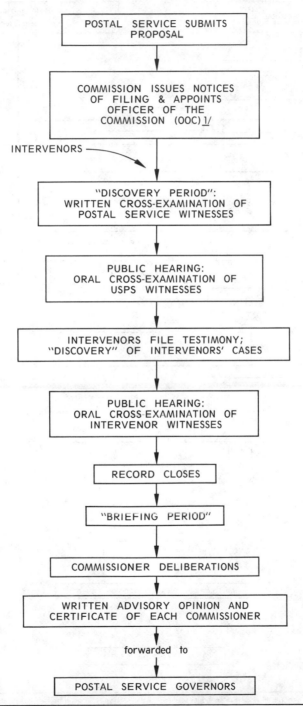

POSTAL SERVICE SUBMITS PROPOSAL

COMMISSION ISSUES NOTICES OF FILING & APPOINTS OFFICER OF THE COMMISSION (OOC) 1/

INTERVENORS —

"DISCOVERY PERIOD": WRITTEN CROSS-EXAMINATION OF POSTAL SERVICE WITNESSES

PUBLIC HEARING: ORAL CROSS-EXAMINATION OF USPS WITNESSES

INTERVENORS FILE TESTIMONY; "DISCOVERY" OF INTERVENORS' CASES

PUBLIC HEARING: ORAL CROSS-EXAMINATION OF INTERVENOR WITNESSES

RECORD CLOSES

"BRIEFING PERIOD"

COMMISSIONER DELIBERATIONS

WRITTEN ADVISORY OPINION AND CERTIFICATE OF EACH COMMISSIONER

forwarded to

POSTAL SERVICE GOVERNORS

1/ This office represents the interests of the general public before the Commission (See 39 USC Sec. 3624 a)

10/79 DW:pic

## POSTAL RATE COMMISSION DECISIONAL PROCEDURE IN MAIL CLASSIFICATION CASE

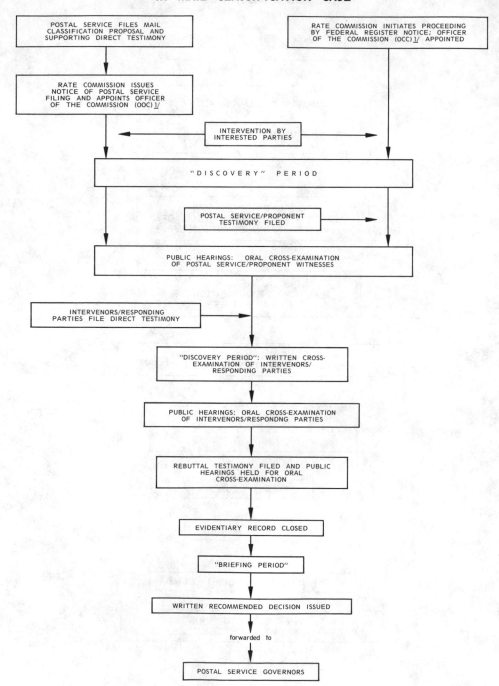

Note: A case may, at any appropriate stage, be disposed of on the basis of a settlement arrived at by the parties. See PRC rules of practice, 529 (39 CFR 53001.29). Disposition of a case on the basis of a stipulation settlement makes some or all of the formal hearing procedures unnecessary.

## MAIL CLASSIFICATION CASE ...

Continued

The Postal Service can respond in
three ways to a decision by the
Postal Rate Commission......

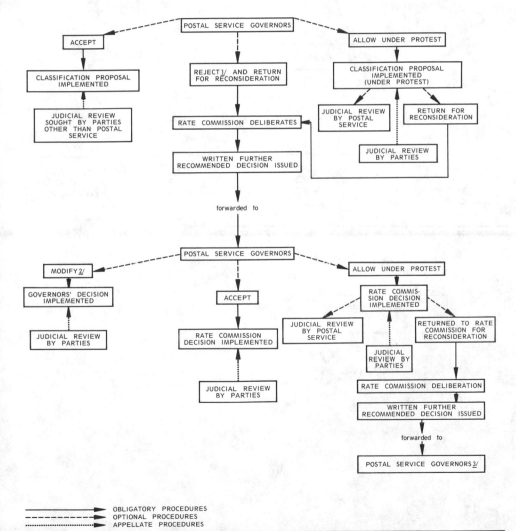

OBLIGATORY  PROCEDURES
OPTIONAL  PROCEDURES
APPELLATE  PROCEDURES

1/  Issue currently unresolved as to whether the Postal Service Governors may reject a Recommended Decision without having the Postal Service file for reconsideration.

2/  Only in very specific circumstances may the Postal Service Governors modify a decision (Sec. 39 USC 53625 d).

3/  At least theoretically; the same process might then be repeated.

10/79 DW:pic

## POSTAL RATE COMMISSION PROCEEDINGS CONCERNING RATE OR SERVICE COMPLAINTS

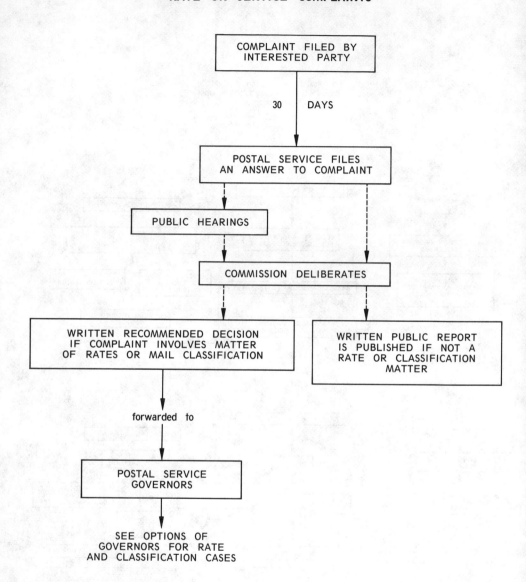

OBLIGATORY PROCEDURES
OPTIONAL PROCEDURES

10/79 DW: pic

## SMALL POST OFFICE CLOSING OR CONSOLIDATION APPEAL PROCEDURE

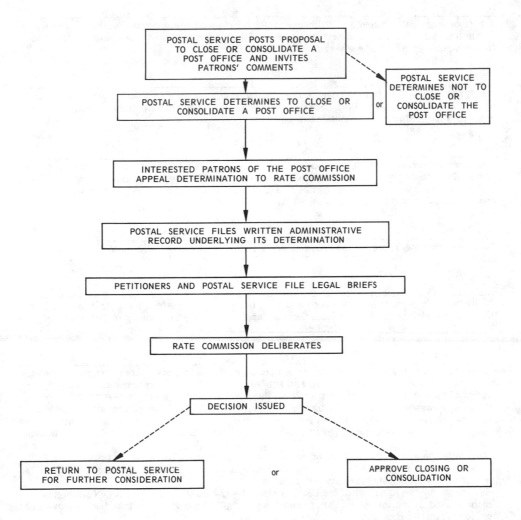

OBLIGATORY PROCEDURE
OPTIONAL PROCEDURES

10/79 DW:pic

## STEPS IN A POSTAL RATE CASE

1. The Postal Service proposes rate changes to the Postal Rate Commission and requests that it issue a recommended decision based upon the proposed changes.

↓

2. Upon due consideration and following public hearings on the proposal, the Rate Commission, within ten months of the Postal Service's original filing of the requested rate changes, must issue a recommended decision to the governors of the Postal Service.

↓

3. If after ten months from the date of the original filing with the Rate Commission it has made no recommended decision, the Postal Service may place the proposed rate changes into effect on a temporary basis, after ten days' notice in the Federal Register.

↓

4. When it receives a recommended decision from the Rate Commission, the governors may approve, allow under protest, reject or modify the decision. (The postmaster general and the deputy postmaster general, who serve as members of the Board of Governors, may not vote on the recommended decisions of the Rate Commission).

↓

5. If the governors approve the recommended decision, they may order the decision placed into effect.

↓

6. If they allow, under protest, a recommended decision to take effect, the governors may return the recommended decision to the Rate Commission for reconsideration and a further recommendation, or seek judicial review of the matter.

↓

7. If the governors reject the recommended decision, the Postal Service may resubmit its request to the commission for reconsideration, and submission of a further recommended decision. Upon receipt of the further recommended decision, the governors may order the new rates placed into effect as recommended or, upon unanimous vote, may modify the further recommended decision, if they find that the commission's reconsidered recommendation would not provide sufficient revenues so that total estimated income and appropriations would equal, as nearly practicable, estimated total costs.

This latter course of action occurred for the first time in 1981. The governors of the U.S. Postal Service took such an unprecedented action when they modified the Postal Rate Commission's recommendation on a postal rate case then under consideration.

In March 1981 the governors of the USPS ordered the 18-cent stamp that the Rate Commission had recommended be put into effect under protest and simultaneously resubmitting the recommended decision for further consideration.

When the Rate Commission again recommended that the USPS stick with an 18¢ stamp in June 1981; the governors rejected this and resubmitted the recommended decision for further consideration. Despite mounting postal deficits, in September 1981 the Rate Commission refused for the third time to modify its recommendation for anything other than an 18¢ stamp.

Rather than rejecting the Rate Commission's position again and filing a new rate case, which would have required approximately 10 more months of review, the Postal Service governors voted unanimously on Sept. 29, 1981 to modify the Rate Commission's recommendation and put the 20¢ rate initially requested into effect.

# Postal Service Publications

The U.S. Postal Service issues a number of documents of interest to philatelists both as hobbyists and as consumers. The titles and prices listed are as of May 1982 and are subject to change.

Subscriptions to periodicals are accepted only for initial periods, but the Superintendent of Documents notes that renewal information will be supplied subscribers in time to maintain continuity of receipt.

Orders should be submitted to the Superintendent of Documents, Government Printing Office, Washington, D.C. 20402. Payment should accompany requests.

The "Postal Operations Manual" (formerly Chapters 3 and 5 of the Postal Service Manual) includes data on retail services, mailing processing, transportation, delivery services, and fleet management. This publication is priced at $37 including domestic postage.

"International Mail" (contains Chapter 2 previously issued in the Postal Service Manual). This information comes in looseleaf form, punched for a 3-ring binder, and is offered by subscription for $34.

"Domestic Mail Manual" (formerly Chapter 1 of the Postal Service Manual) consists of a basic manual and supplementary material for an indeterminate period. The manual includes applicable regulations and information about rates and postage, classes of mail, special services, wrapping and mailing requirements. The subscription price is $28.

The Postal Service also has an "Employee and Labor Relations Manual" (formerly Chapter 4 of the Postal Service Manual) available by subscription. This manual covers personnel policies and regulations governing employment with the Postal Service. The subscription price is $42.

Persons who require advance notice of current orders, instructions, and other information, including philatelic matters, may wish to subscribe to "The Postal Bulletin," issued each Thursday with supplemental issues if needed. The cost is $60 a year with domestic postage.

"Postal Life" is the employees' bimonthly magazine, containing articles on new methods, techniques, and programs. Its cost is $9 per year, with only one year orders accepted.

The "National ZIP Code Directory" makes available the code for every U.S. mailing address. The 1982 edition is priced at $9 (by "trading-in" the front cover of any previous year's ZIP Code Directory, mailers will receive a discount on the single copy price of the 1982 edition).

The "Postal Contracting Manual," dealing with procurement procedures, is $88 including supplements.

"Orientation and Craft Skill Training," designed for Postal Service Craft employees, is available for $4.

"Postage Stamps of the United States" is a detailed and highly illustrated compendium on all U.S. postage stamps. The basic book, continuing through the 1970 Natural History series, is $8. "Transmittal Letter 2" goes through the 1971 Christmas stamps and is priced at $4. "Transmittal Letter 3" is a further continuation priced at $5. Stamps issued during 1974 are covered under "Transmittal Letter 4," which is offered for $4. "Transmittal Letter 5" covers stamps issued in 1975 and is priced at $3.25. Issues released during 1976 and 1977 are covered under "Transmittal Letter 6," which lists for $3.75. Issues released from 1978 through 1980 are featured in "Transmittal Letter 7," which is available for $4. A plastic binder (three-ring looseleaf for small-format book and supplements), when available, is $3.45.

Additional materials, such as leaflets dealing with specific mailing questions, change of address kits, and collectors' aids, are available through local post offices.

## Free publications

The following U.S. Postal Service publications, brochures and pamphlets are available free through many local post offices. The listing is by publication (Pb.) number and title.

1) We Deliver — Story of U.S. Postal Service
2) Packaging for Mailing
4) Importing Animal & Plant Products through Military Post Offices
6) Radioactive Materials
14) Plant Quarantines
15) Parcel Lockers — Regulations and Manufacturing Standards
16) Mail Chute Rules, Regulations and Specifications
17) Apartment House Receptacles, Regulations & Manufacturing Standard
19) Mailers Guide
20) Priority Mail
32) Glossary of Postal Terms
51) International Postage Rates and Fees
61) Information Guide on Presorted First-Class Mail
62) Modern Mailroom Practices
72) Managing Mail Preparation
84) What are the New Letter Mail Dimensional Standards
86) Establishing a Commercial Mail Receiving Agency

# Postal Service Products

### PHILATELIC SALES DIVISION

Stamps and other current U.S. philatelic products can be ordered by mail from the Philatelic Sales Division, U.S. Postal Service, Washington, D.C. 20265. All orders are subject to a $5 minimum order requirement and a handling charge of at least 50¢ per order. Complete details are available in each bimonthly Philatelic Catalog, which is supplied free of charge upon request to the aforementioned address.

The Philatelic Catalog includes all stamps, postal stationery items and retail philatelic products currently available from the Philatelic Sales Division, and is also used as a guide by many of the philatelic centers located throughout the country, which should stock most, if not all, of the items on the current list. The list is revised every two months. Of course, all orders are subject to stock availability, and items may be withdrawn at any time with little or no advance notice.

### PHILATELIC PRODUCTS

The U.S. Postal Service offers a wide variety of retail philatelic products which include, but are not necessarily limited to, the following:

SOUVENIR PAGES: The U.S. Postal Service offers a deposit account service for Souvenir Pages with first day of issue cancellations for all new issues. Information is available from Souvenir Pages, Philatelic Sales Division, Washington, D.C. 20265.

STAMP PANELS: Special American Commemorative Stamp Panels are produced with rare engravings and mint blocks of new commemorative U.S. issues, available individually from the Philatelic Sales Division (at the noted address), or by subscription from U.S. Postal Service, Commemorative Panel Subscription Program, Philatelic Customer Service, Washington, D.C. 20265.

MINT SETS: Each year, the U.S. Postal Service provides single copies of all the commemoratives for the past year, supplied as Souvenir Year Mint Sets. These are often available for one or two years after many of the issues have otherwise gone off sale, and may be obtained by mail from the Philatelic Sales Division at the noted address.

STAMP COLLECTING KITS: The Postal Service produces a variety of stamp collecting kits, with mint and/or used stamps, informational material and supplies for collecting (small album and other accessories). These are also available from the Philatelic Sales Division.

STAMPS AND STORIES: Each year, the Postal Service markets a pocket-sized, concise color catalog of U.S. stamps, available by mail from the Philatelic Sales Division.

Most of these items can be obtained from designated philatelic centers around the country, and some are even available from most post offices. Inquiries directed to the local post office may provide more detailed information on the availability of specific items.

# Significant Dates
# in U.S. Postal History

1639. . . . . General Court of Massachusetts designates Richard Fairbanks' tavern in Boston as collection point for overseas mail.

1692. . . . . British Crown issues a grant to Thomas Neale to set up and maintain a post office in the Colonies for a term of 21 years.

1753. . . . . Benjamin Franklin appointed joint postmaster general for the Colonies under the British.

1775. . . . . Benjamin Franklin named first postmaster general under the Continental Congress.

1789. . . . . Samuel Osgood named first postmaster general under the U.S. Constitution.

1794. . . . . First letter carriers appear on streets of some American cities.

1799. . . . . Government-owned coach service begins. First route between Philadelphia and New York City opened.

1813. . . . . Congress declares all steamship lines to be post routes.

1829. . . . . Postmaster general becomes presidential cabinet post.

1845. . . . . Star route contractor system created.

1847. . . . . Adhesive postage stamps issued by the United States.

1855. . . . . Registered mail introduced.

1855. . . . . Compulsory prepayment of postage takes effect.

1858. . . . . Street letter boxes debut.

1860-61 . . The Pony Express provides east - west postal service.

1863. . . . . Free city mail delivery service starts in 49 cities.

1863. . . . . Uniform letter rates — regardless of distance — enacted by Congress.

1864. . . . . Railway post office introduced.

1874. . . . . Universal Postal Union founded (originally the General Postal Union).

1879. . . . . Domestic mail divided up into four classes.

1885. . . . . Special delivery introduced.

1887. . . . . International parcel post inaugurated.

1893. . . . . Pneumatic tube service starts in Philadelphia.

1896. . . . . Rural free delivery enacted by Congress.

1911 . . . . Postal Savings initiated.

1918 . . . . Airmail service inaugurated between New York City and Washington, D.C.

1920. . . . . First cross-country airmail flight — New York to San Francisco — occurs.

1920. . . . . Metered postage introduced.

1935. . . . . Transpacific airmail service started.

1939. . . . . Transatlantic airmail service introduced.

1941 . . . . Highway post office rolls into operation.

1942. . . . . "V" mail service in use.

1955. . . . . Certified mail service initiated.

1959. . . . . First official Missile Mail dispatched from submarine to mainland, Florida.

1963. . . . . ZIP Code introduced.

1964. . . . . First 24-hour self-service post office in use.

1966. . . . . Postal savings terminated.

1969. . . . . First postage stamp canceled on moon by Apollo 11 mission.

1970. . . . . MAILGRAM (combination letter-telegram) introduced.

1970. . . . . Postal Reorganization Act signed into law.

1970. . . . . Experimental Express Mail Service begun.

**1971** .... U.S. Postal Service begins; postmaster general eliminated from Cabinet.

**1971** .... Star routes become Highway Contract Routes.

**1974.** .... Highway post offices terminated.

**1974.** .... First satellite transmission of MAILGRAMS.

**1976.** .... Post Office class categories eliminated.

**1977.** .... Airmail abolished as a separate rate category.

**1977.** .... Express Mail becomes permanent new class of service.

**1977.** .... Railway post office's final run, June 30.

**1978.** .... U.S. Postal Service begins copyrighting postage stamps and other philatelic products.

**1979.** .... New envelope standards go into effect.

**1980.** .... INTELPOST service introduced.

**1982.** .... E-COM service inaugurated.

# Stamp Production 4

## Bureau of Engraving and Printing

Although the role of the Bureau of Engraving and Printing in supplying this nation's needs for postage stamps may have post-dated the Civil War by some years, the fact is the BEP, which came into existence on Aug. 29, 1862, was an indirect consequence of that conflict.

Primarily the result of the self-confidence, courage, ingenuity, and patriotism of one man — Spencer Morton Clark — it is, as well, the result of the foresight of President Lincoln's first Secretary of the Treasury, Salmon P. Chase; his confidence in Clark's ability and recognition of his accomplishments.

At the time of the firing on Fort Sumter and the president's call for volunteers to quell the rebellion, the nation was already on the fringe of bankruptcy and scarcely in a position to finance a war.

It was this, along with other war matters, that prompted the president to call Congress into special session on July 4, 1861. During this session, Secretary Chase recommended to Congress both a system of taxation and one of floating loans. His scheme for borrowing included the issuance of noninterest-bearing notes which would circulate as money.

Although there was doubt in the minds of many the Government had the constitutional authority to issue paper money, Congress adopted the Chase plan in the act of July 17, 1861 and, as a result, the first Government-issued paper money came into being.

These notes, because of certain provisions of their issuance, became popularly known as "demand notes." These were produced by the "New York bank note companies" — American Bank Note Co. and National Bank Note Co. — under contract with the Government.

One of the provisions of the new law specified that the authorized securities should be "signed by the First or Second Comptroller, or the Register of the Treasury and countersigned by such other officer or officers as the Secretary of the Treasury may designate."

The impracticability of such a procedure soon became evident. If the designated officers were to perform duties other than sign their names to securities, they would have to be relieved of that task.

Corrective action was soon forthcoming and on Aug. 5, just 19 days after enactment of the original legislation, President Lincoln signed a bill that changed the signature requirements to those of the Treasurer of the United States and Register of the Treasury.

The new legislation also provided the secretary might designate other personnel to sign the notes for these officers and ultimately 70 clerks were assigned to the loan branch of the secretary's office for this purpose. These persons signed their own names to the notes.

With such a variety of signatures on notes, security was less than desired. Spencer Clark, the chief clerk of the Bureau of Construction in the department and who was acting engineer in charge of that bureau, suggested to Secretary Chase the notes be imprinted with the facsimile signatures of the required officers.

As additional evidence of lawful issue, he also proposed the notes be imprinted with a copy of the Treasury seal and further suggested this processing be done in the Treasury building.

The secretary approved Clark's proposal and Congress gave its approval with legislation adopted Feb. 25, 1862. Clark was instructed to design a seal for use on the notes and to procure the necessary machinery for the imprinting.

Thus it was that the Treasury began its first actual work in connection with the printing of currency which was eventually to lead to the printing of the nation's postage stamps.

Secretary Chase was so pleased with Clark's machines that he asked him to investigate the possibilities relating to the printing of securities issued by the Government.

Clark's investigation determined the Government was paying substantial prices to the bank note companies for printing notes and he told the secretary he could produce the work in the department for "a comparatively small outlay, at a great saving of cost in the issues."

While the date of the first printing in the department is in question, it is known that in July 1862 Charles Neale, a plate printer, was brought into the department as a clerk in anticipation of authority to print currency at the Treasury.

On Oct. 11, 1862, he was appointed to superintend the plate printing operation and was assigned the task of securing presses, ink and paper, and recruiting workmen.

One of the first products produced by the Bureau, and certainly among the unique, was fractional currency. These were the miniature notes issued by the Government in place of coins during the Civil War and for some years afterwards.

It was the circulation of a variety of items intended as substitute coins which in Secretary Chase's words, "created a manifest necessity for a fractional currency authorized by the National Government."

He proposed alternative remedies: one, reduce the weight of small coins; the other, use revenue or postage stamps in place of coins. Congress preferred the latter and by an act approved July 17, 1862, provided that postage or other U.S. stamps be receivable in payments due to the Government. The same act made the use of any items intended to circulate as money in amounts of less than one dollar unlawful.

Realizing that the glue on stamps would make them inconvenient for the purpose, the secretary requested the postmaster general to supply stocks without adhesive.

The suggestion resulted in an arrangement by the Post Office Department with private bank note companies for printing small notes, comprising in their design reproductions of postage stamps. These were printed in denominations of 5, 10, 25 and 50 cents.

Although the legend appearing on the reverse of these notes implies they were issued under the act of July 17, 1862, that act does not make any mention of postage currency whatsoever.

The same desperate need for Civil War financing, which indirectly led to the creation of the component that eventually grew into the Bureau of Engraving and Printing, resulted in the formation of the U.S. Internal Revenue system.

Until that time, the National Government had relied almost exclusively on tariffs and other customs taxes for its income. An act of July 1, 1862 authorized the president to appoint a commissioner of internal revenue who was given authority to assess, levy, and collect taxes and provide stamps "for expressing and denoting the several stamp duties" imposed by the legislation.

This act became the basis of the present internal revenue system, as far as items taxed and organizations to collect revenues are concerned. Along with other taxing requirements, it provided for stamp taxes on medicines, perfumes, cosmetics, playing cards, and certain commercial papers.

## First Revenue Stamps

Although the bulk of the printing of the first U.S. revenue stamps was assigned to private bank note firms, the Bureau was printing beer and cigar stamps as early as 1867, with the next few years seeing an increase in the number of revenue stamps printed and processed by the Bureau.

The annual report of the chief for fiscal year 1870 indicated deliveries of 31 million stamps embracing distilled spirits, beer, tobacco, custom cigars, and special tax stamps. By 1873, deliveries had arisen to over 244 million stamps and the categories broadly extended.

By 1875, most of the work had reverted to private bank note companies since their bids for producing a variety of stamps were less than those of the Bureau, which continued to print only the custom cigar and special tax stamps.

An act appropriating funds for Government expenses for fiscal year 1877 required that internal revenue stamps should be printed in the Bureau, provided the cost did not exceed that paid under existing contracts to private bank note companies.

However, the secretary of the treasury felt the Bureau would be unable to compete with the private firms and it was not until the following year, under a new secretary, that the Bureau resumed manufacture of almost all the internal revenue items.

Since that time, the Bureau has figured prominently in the production of revenue stamps, although the commissioner has had a prerogative in the placement of stamp orders as these stamps have been needed.

Aside from the staggering amount of revenue stamps manufactured in the Bureau, a further significance of these items derives from the part they played in the introduction of improved machines and processes employed by the Bureau.

The tremendous stamp requirements not only contributed to the introduction of the power plate printing presses in 1878 but spurred the improvements made to this type equipment during the period of its original use by the Bureau.

The need for additional revenue items was also responsible for the extended use of typographic printing made in 1890 and of offset printing made in 1914.

## Early Stamp Production

Although the U.S. postal system dates back to 1782 and first postage stamps were introduced in 1847, it was not until July 1, 1894 that the Bureau took over the production of these stamps.

Prior to that date, there had been only two exceptions to the general procedure followed by the Post Office Department in obtaining its stamps from private bank note companies. The particular reasons why the services of the Bureau were employed in these two instances remains unexplained.

In January 1875, William M. Ireland, acting third assistant postmaster general, advised the Bureau by letter that the Post Office Department was "making preparations to sell to stamp collectors and others, specimens of all postage stamps ever issued under its auspices."

The letter noted that plates existed for all the several issues except those for the first issue of 1847. The Bureau was instructed to reengrave the plates for the 5¢ and 10¢ stamps and from these plates prepare 10,000 of each denomination. There were 11,450 specimens of the 5¢ value and 10,000 of the 10¢ denomination delivered to the Post Office Department.

Strictly speaking, these items produced by the Bureau cannot be regarded as reprints of the original issue. The earlier stamps had been demonetized in 1861, soon after the outbreak of the Civil War. Furthermore, the Bureau prints were specifically declared invalid as postage stamps.

It is interesting to note that in 1947 the Bureau was again called upon to reproduce the original designs in connection with the production of a souvenir sheet commemorating the centenary of U.S. postage stamps.

Another request was received by the Bureau from the Post Office Department on May 20, 1875. It called for the preparation of a die for a new 5¢ ordinary postage stamp. The item was required by the revised foreign letter rate agreed upon by the member countries of the General Postal Union in convention at Berne, Switzerland, in 1874.

This new rate was to become effective July 1, 1875, but the treaty agreement was not ratified until May 3, 1875. This short interval between the time of ratification and the effective date may account for the Bureau being asked to assist in this instance.

The die was prepared from a portrait of Zachary Taylor, already on hand, and engraved with a border of style compatible with that of the ordinary series of postage stamps then current.

The feasibility and propriety of assigning the printing of postage stamps to the Bureau had long been debated. Legislative authority for having the work done at the Bureau on a qualified basis had been included in the appropriation act for the Post Office Department in 1879.

Although the act passed in 1881 repealed the 1879 proviso in full, there was deemed to be no legal impediment to the manufacture of postage stamps by the Bureau.

This fact was borne out by specifications issued by the Post Office Department in 1885, 1889 and 1893 for printing the stamps on a four-year contract basis.

Each expressly stipulated that, should the secretary of the treasury submit bids or estimates found to be more advantageous to the Government than those submitted by private contractors, the postmaster general reserves the right to award the contracts to the Bureau.

There were three private bidders for supplying stamps under the 1893 request, while a proposal to do the work was also submitted by the chief of the Bureau, with approval of the secretary of the treasury. The latter bid was almost $7,000 less than the lowest bid from a private contractor.

When the Bureau's proposal was made public, there was a loud and strong protest voiced by the private contractors. In addition to arguing that the Bureau had no legal authority to perform the service, they contended the agency had not submitted its offer in accordance with terms outlined in the Post Office Department's advertisement for bids.

Submitted to the Department of Justice for review, the latter held there was no legal impediment involved, and the contract was awarded to the Bureau by the Post Office Department on Feb. 21, 1894.

In April, the Department turned over to the Bureau dies, rolls and plates of the then current stamps. No further use was made of the rolls and plates, but the dies, after being slightly altered to distinguish the Bureau printings, were employed in the manufacture of new plates.

Since that date, with but a few exceptions, all postage stamps supplied to the Post Office Department and its successor, the U.S. Postal Service, have come from the Bureau of Engraving and Printing.

## Printing Problems

As might have been expected, the Bureau was not without its trials and tribulations in getting the postage stamp operations under way.

One of the most vexing problems encountered involved the gumming of stamps. While past experience had provided the Bureau the basics for actually printing the stamps, when awarded the contract it had no gumming machines.

Heretofore such stampwork as had been produced in the Bureau had been gummed by hand, but, with the great volume of postage stamps needed, such a procedure would have been totally inadequate.

Since gumming equipment was not manufactured on a commercial basis, it was impossible to purchase the needed machinery. Furthermore, the private bank note firm which previously produced the stamps would not make its equipment available or divulge its mode of operations.

It thus became incumbent upon the Bureau to develop its own machines. Working only upon the recollections of an employe who had previously been in the service of a private contractor and who had operated the equipment, the Bureau was able to accomplish the task.

The first of the work printed by the Bureau was placed on sale by the Post Office Department on July 18, 1894. It was the 6¢ reddish brown regular issue and was followed by the 4¢ denomination which was issued on Sept. 11.

By the end of the first year of operation, the Bureau had printed and delivered more than 21 million sheets of stamps for the Post Office Department, embracing 13 denominations of regular postage as well as miscellaneous values of special delivery, postage due, and newspaper and periodical stamps.

With the termination of the Spanish-American War in 1898, the Bureau found itself involved in still another philatelic operation. Under the terms of the peace treaty, Guam, the Philippine Islands, and Puerto Rico were ceded to the United States, while Cuba was relinquished to the United States in trust for the Cuban people.

Initially, these territories were administered by military governments under the jurisdiction of the U.S. War Department, other than Guam, which was placed under the charge of the Navy Department. The Bureau was called upon to supply the postage stamps used in these territories.

Originally, all four areas were furnished regular U.S. postage stamps overprinted with the name of the respective territory in which the stamps were to be used.

In 1906, the U.S. postage stamps overprinted "Philippines" were replaced by a special issue peculiar to the Islands. The Bureau continued to produce Philippine postage stamps until the Islands took on the status of an independent republic on July 4, 1946. The last stamps so produced were the three denominations of identical design commemorating Philippine independence.

The practice of furnishing regular U.S. postage stamps overprinted "Cuba" was short-lived. In 1899, at the request of the U.S. Post Office Department, the Bureau designed and printed an issue of stamps, comprising 1-, 2-, 3-, 5-, and 10-centavo ordinary values and a 10c special delivery stamp especially for use there.

Although the U.S. military administration of the island ceased in May 1902, the Bureau continued to furnish the stamps for the Republic of Cuba until fiscal year 1905.

With the establishment of regular mail service under the jurisdiction of the U.S. Post Office on Guam and Puerto Rico, overprinted stamps for these islands were not required after 1900. Since that time, regular U.S. postage stamps have been used on the two islands.

## Vending Machines

In this day, when it seems coin-operated vending machines have but recently become standard equipment in factories, office, places of amusement, etc., it may come as a bit of a surprise to learn that a variety of such machines were being marketed in the early 1880s.

With the turn of the 20th century bringing a tremendous increase in the uses to which equipment of this type was being put, it was not long before dispensing machine manufacturers began to look to the sale of stamps as a new use for their products.

At the time, printing of postage stamps was confined to individual sheet form. To obtain stocks for stamp dispensing, it was necessary for either the machine manufacturer or the private user to attach a given number of sheets of stamps, one to another, cut the rows of stamps into strips, and then wind the strips into coils. A tedious task to say the least.

To add to the user's woes, the sheets had already been perforated for separating the stamps by hand and work so perforated often proved too fragile for dispensers. The solution lay in making imperforate sheets available to be produced into coils privately.

Imperforate sheets for this purpose were distributed on an experimental basis in 1906, and by 1908 were available at post offices as a regular stock item.

In the meantime, the Bureau had been experimenting in processing stamps into coil form. The first fruits of this experimental work were issued in February 1908.

These coils were produced from regular sheets of 400 stamps perforated horizontally and cut into strips of 20. The strips were then pasted together to form coils of 500 or 1,000 stamps each. It was not long before the Bureau developed a machine for preparing coils which materially reduced processing costs.

In 1910, an improved model was developed which cut the pasted stream of horizontally perforated sheets of 200 stamps into strips, trimmed the margins, and wound the strips into coils in one operation.

Through the use of this machine, the Bureau was able to produce the stamp coils at a much lower cost and the reduced production rates, in turn, were reflected in the service charges made by the Post Office Department for coiled stamps.

It was fortunate that steps had been taken to develop this type of equipment. Without it, the Bureau would have been hard pressed to meet the unprecedented orders for postage stamps in coil form that were received beginning in mid-1958.

A major factor in this regard was the decision of the Post Office Department to inaugurate an intensive drive to popularize coiled stamps with special emphasis placed on a new 100-stamp roll. Present day coil equipment processes the printed web down to finished products of precisely 100, 500, or 3,000 stamps.

It was the ever increasing demand for stamps in coil form that prompted the third assistant postmaster general in 1909 to recommend that steps be taken looking to a change in the method of printing postage stamps which would enable the Post Office Department to provide improved service and keep abreast of demands.

Inasmuch as up to this time all postage stamps had been printed in sheet form, it was felt the solution lay in the development of a press for printing stamps in a continuous roll form.

Working on this theory, Benjamin F. Stickney, the Bureau's mechanical expert and designer, developed plans for a rotary press which would wet the paper stock, print the stamps, gum and dry them, and perforate the work, while in web form.

With the Bureau lacking in funds to finance construction of such a machine, the Post Office Department was approached on the matter.

## Stickney Press

So promising were Stickney's ideas that in 1910 the postmaster general authorized the expenditure of $5,600 for the construction of an experimental machine in accordance with the plans, from money appropriated to the Post Office Department for expenses incident to investigating and testing mechanical and labor saving devices.

The confidence expressed by the Post Office Department in financing the construction of an experimental press in accordance with Stickney's plans was well placed. Although several years were spent in the development under Bureau supervision, by the spring of 1914, the press was ready to be put into production.

The first stamps produced on the rotary press were the 2¢ ordinary variety of the 1911 series. The initial issue of this work occurred on June 30, 1914. As additional presses were acquired, the production of other denominations of coiled postage and revenue stamps was assigned to the machines.

For a time there were problems to be overcome, but by July 1, 1926, all ordinary postage stamps of 10¢ and under were being produced on the rotary presses. With the gradual increases in the quantities ordered, stamps of the higher denominations, with the exception of the $1, $2, and $5 values, were transferred from the flatbed to the rotary press in 1931. The last of the Stickney presses was decommissioned in March 1962.

## Offset Printing

It was an emergency situation during World War I and the years immediately following that resulted in the printing of U.S. postage stamps by the offset method.

In the early part of 1918, the Bureau received a shipment of barytes (a substance used in the manufacture of printing inks) that was to bring about this temporary innovation in the production of U.S. postage stamps.

While the samples selected from this lot for test purposes passed the basic requirements for the item, it later developed that a large quantity of the total supplied was below standard and the inks manufactured with that portion contained coarse particles which caused the intaglio printing plates to wear rapidly.

Against a normal life expectancy of from six to eight weeks, plates in some cases were wearing out in ten days.

The coarse barytes had been used in the manufacture of the purple ink employed in the printing of the 3¢ regular postage stamp. Requirements for this denomination were running about 25 million stamps per day, largely because of the increase in the domestic letter rate from two to three cents in November 1917.

With stocks becoming rapidly depleted the Bureau director requested and received permission from the Post Office Department to resort to the offset method of printing this item on an interim basis.

Previously, the Bureau had experimented with offset printing of postage stamps in connection with its efforts to manufacture stamps suitable for use in dispensing machines. Based on the findings of these tests, it was known an acceptable stamp could be produced by the offset method.

The necessary offset plates were hastily prepared and printing commenced on March 12, with the first delivery of offset-printed stamps made 10 days later.

About the same time, it was observed that the plates for printing the 1¢ ordinary stamp were also wearing very rapidly and permission was obtained to print stocks of that denomination on offset presses.

The third time in which U.S. postage stamps were printed in their entirety by the offset method occurred in March 1920. Ironically, it was shortly after the first-class domestic postal rate was reduced to its prewar level. At that time it was the printing of 2¢ stamps that necessitated the same treatment, and, as before, it was poor quality barytes that caused the trouble.

## Problems
## of Perforation

From the very beginning of the Bureau's takeover of postage stamp production in 1894, it had been plagued by the excessive amount of spoilage occurring during the perforation operation. The same problem had been experienced by the private bank note companies that produced the stamps prior to that time.

The wetting and drying of the paper, essential to the plate printing method of producing stamps, as well as the gumming of the printed sheets, caused the work to expand and contract. Inasmuch as these physical changes were not uniform throughout a sheet it was difficult to perforate stamps without punching into the printed areas.

So long as postage stamps were produced in single sheet form, the situation could be controlled to some extent by manually adjusting the perforating equipment to allow for variances that occurred.

The printing of stamps in web form on the Stickney presses was another thing. The changing conditions were cumulative and it was not unusual that there would be a variance in size and stamp location between the first and last sheets from the same roll.

There were other contributing factors to the variations that occurred in the work printed in rolls; such as temperature, atmospheric conditions, and water absorption characteristics of the paper.

Experimentation with the perforating of printed rolls of postage stamps by means of electronic controls was begun by the Bureau in 1930. This resulted in development of primary equipment which was designed and built for part manual and part electronic control.

Further improvements were made and a pilot machine constructed that reduced the need for manual corrections to a minimum. First delivery, comprising some nine million stamps perforated on this machine, was shipped in February 1935.

As a result of further extensive experimentation, a production machine was developed by Bureau personnel, incorporating more advanced mechanical and electrical controls. It was put into operation by 1939 and two years later five improved production models were purchased and installed. Over the years, further refinements in the equipment have been made.

## World War II Issues

With World War II approaching a victorious conclusion, the War Department, in mid-1943, placed with the Bureau an order for the production of a special issue of postage stamps to go along as a companion issue for military currency to be used in countries being occupied by U.S. troops.

The initial order for stamps to be used in Italy, was printed at the Bureau by the offset process in 400-subject sheets, each subject being the exact size of the ordinary U.S. postage stamp. The paper used was a pre-gummed, unwatermarked, white sulphite stock.

Orders were subsequently received and processed by the Bureau for additional quantities of Allied Military Italian postage stamps and for furnishing supplemental French, Committee French, Allied Military German, and supplemental Austrian postage stamps.

In 1943, a decision was made by the Post Office Department to issue a series of postage stamps honoring those nations that had fallen victim to the Axis Powers during the second world war. It was proposed these stamps carry a reproduction of the flags of the respective countries in true colors.

With the Bureau lacking suitable equipment for the satisfactory and expeditious production of stamps in multicolor, it became necessary to subcontract the work to a private firm. Thus, for the first time since 1894, an issue of U.S. postage stamps was printed outside the Bureau.

The designing and printing of these stamps was handled by the American Bank Note Co. of New York, with 13 stamps issued, honoring Albania, Austria, Belgium, Czechoslovakia, Denmark, France, Greece, Korea, Luxembourg, The Netherlands, Norway, Poland, and Yugoslavia.

A representative of the Bureau was stationed at the printing plant for the duration of the contract. Borders for the stamps were the same for all of the series and were printed from engraved plates. The central designs for each stamp — a reproduction, in appropriate colors, of the flag of the particular country — was produced by the offset method.

Figures released by the Post Office show slightly less than 20 million stamps issued for each of Poland, Czechoslovakia, Norway, Luxembourg, The Netherlands, Belgium, and France, and slightly less than 15 million stamps issued for Greece, Yugoslavia, Albania, Austria, Denmark, and Korea.

Subsequent years have seen several additional stamps printed outside the Bureau under private contract, in all cases where equipment for gravure printing was available, and before the Bureau's new gravure equipment was installed.

The Eakins "American Painting" commemorative of 1967 was printed by Photogravure and

Color Co. of Moonachie, N.J., the first U.S. stamp to be printed by the gravure method. The following year, the Walt Disney commemorative was printed in the plant of the Achrovure Division of Union Camp Corporation, at Englewood, N.J.

In 1970, the Bureau entered into a contract with Guilford Gravure, Inc., Guilford, Conn., for the lease of their plant and equipment for the printing of the Anti-Pollution commemorative issue and the Christmas stamps on that firm's Andreotti Rotogravure press.

In anticipation of the Bureau's installation of its new Andreotti equipment — then on order — crews from the Bureau of Engraving and Printing manned the equipment, using ungummed rolls of paper for the printing order. These rolls were then returned to the Bureau for gumming on the Cottrell press and perforating.

## Multicolor Problems

The Bureau's role in the production of multicolor postage stamps is a "johnny-come-lately" when the overall picture is viewed. This is not to say there was not an interest along this line, but rather, the ever increasing demands upon existing facilities forestalled and delayed the development of suitable printing equipment.

Although the first bicolor postage stamp was issued by the Post Office Department in 1869, it was to be another 30 years before another set of postage stamps — the first by the Bureau — was to appear.

It was originally planned that the Trans-Mississippi "Omaha" Exposition issue of stamps in 1898 — the first set of commemorative stamps issued by the Bureau — would be produced in bicolor.

However, because of the outbreak of the Spanish-American War in April of that year and the subsequent heavy demands for the Bureau's service in the production of war revenue items, the idea was abandoned.

The commemorative stamps issued in connection with the Pan-American Exposition held in Buffalo, N.Y., in 1901 were the first bicolor stamps produced by the Bureau. The six denominations comprising this series were printed with distinctive borders, each of a different color, with the vignettes, or central subjects, in black.

There were other two-color stamps printed during the intervening years with the 24¢ airmail issue of 1918 probably the most well known. This fame can be attributed to a quirk of fate, but one that could happen with the printing process in use at that time for the producing of the multicolor stamps.

Like stamps in the Pan-American issue, this one had as its central subject a mail plane in flight, printed in blue. Inadvertently, a sheet of these stamps was imprinted with the plane flying upside down.

The error went undetected through a number of examinations and it was only after the sheet of stamps was sold at a post office window that the purchaser realized he had an oddity.

During the post-World War II years, marked by a tremendous advancement in the field of graphic arts, many countries issued varieties of multicolor stamps printed by topographic, lithographic, or gravure methods.

Recognizing this growing interest in multicolor stamps, the Bureau undertook extensive exploration into the potentialities of these processes for the printing of U.S. postage stamps. It was felt, however, that the resultant printed impressions were considerably inferior in quality to intaglio-printed work.

This factor, coupled with the knowledge that the equipment employed in the processes was readily available on the open market and thus could be easily secured by counterfeiters, prompted rejection of the use of the more common printing methods.

It was during the period of evaluation of two intaglio sheet-fed rotary presses in 1955-56 for the dry-printing of currency, that one of the machines showed extensive potentialities for multicolor printing.

In view of the growing demand for more colorful postage stamps, it was decided at the conclusion of the currency tests late in 1956 to acquire this press for further experimentation in connection with the production of stamps.

Initial expectations concerning this machine were soon justified and it was used to produce the 4¢ American Flag stamp issued on July 4, 1957. This was the first time the flag had been reproduced in full color on a U.S. postage stamp, a step that drew wide acclaim.

## Philatelic 'Firsts'

In February 1962, the Bureau teamed up with the Post Office Department in a project that was to mark another "first" in the nation's philatelic history.

Shortly after Astronaut Alan Shepard became America's first space pioneer, Post Office Department officials conceived the idea of a special postage stamp as a suitable tribute to the nation's space exploration efforts.

With officials of the National Aeronautics and Space Administration and the Bureau, the department worked out a proposal for issuing a commemorative stamp simultaneously with the completion of the first orbital flight by an American astronaut.

In light of the fact that the flight might be unsuccessful, it was decided to withhold any advance notice relating to the stamp. The stamp itself was produced under strict security precautions.

Describing the security procedures followed in connection with the production of the stamp, the Bureau in its official "History" notes the "log of the activities relating to the printing and processing of this item would read like a cloak-and-dagger drama."

Instead of the usual formal written orders and receipts between the Post Office Department and the Bureau, in this instance all instructions were given verbally and the proposed designs, models, and die proofs were transmitted by hand-to-hand operations.

Ostensibly, the Bureau's designer of the stamp took annual leave from his job, but actually went into seclusion at his home studio to design the item. The engraver who did the lettering performed his work on weekends when no one else was in the shop.

The picture engraver, supposedly on vacation, came in at night to engrave the central subject for the new stamp. The printing plates were made when the manufacturing division was supposedly closed.

When the plates were ready to go to press, the multicolor pressroom was completely sealed off from the rest of the plant and declared "off limits" except for persons directly concerned.

When production of the stamps was completed, they were removed, over a weekend, to the packaging and shipping area, where they were stored in a newly finished vault.

On weekends, the stamps were dispatched from the Bureau to the registry section of the Washington city post office for shipment throughout the country. In the meantime, postal inspectors at 301 points across the nation were alerted to receive unidentified sealed packages from Washington, to be kept unopened awaiting further instructions.

Two philatelic canceling machines were shipped by the Post Office Department from Detroit to Jacksonville, Fla., with instructions these be held for postal equipment technicians.

While this was going on, the Post Office Department ordered one million unmarked envelopes, ostensibly for headquarters' supplies, but in reality to be processed as "first-day covers" — souvenir day of issue cancellations marking the momentous achievement at Cape Canaveral.

Project Mercury stamps were affixed to the envelopes by employees of the department's philatelic section, working behind locked doors at night and over the weekend.

A large number of the stamped envelopes were transported to Cape Canaveral and the canceling machines were ordered to be delivered to a National Aeronautics and Space Administration official there. Everything was in readiness for release of the new stamp.

At 3:30 p.m., Feb. 20, 1962, the moment that Astronaut John Glenn was retrieved from the ocean and his flight pronounced a success, postal inspectors throughout the country were instructed to open the sealed cartons and release the contents for sale. Immediately, cancellation was begun of the first day covers.

For the first time in American history, a stamp went on sale all over the nation at the exact hour of the event it memorialized, with no advance "leak" that it was forthcoming.

The Bureau and Post Office Department teamed up for another philatelic first on the occasion of the release of the postage stamp saluting the first landing of "man on the moon," on July 20, 1969.

On that occasion, when the first postal astronauts started for the moon they carried with them an engraved master die, reduced in weight, from which the printing plates to produce the stamp were later made.

The master die went to the lunar surface in the module. A die proof on the now famous moon letter was canceled aboard the capsule with the first space postmark, the ring die, containing the words "Moon Landing, U.S.A. — July 20, 1969."

## Production Equipment

We have noted how the development of the Stickney press during the early years of the 20th century virtually revolutionized procedures for the printing of postage stamps, moving production from sheet-fed to rotary web-fed equipment.

Through these years of Bureau service, various improvements were made in the Stickney press and with demand for postage stamps steadily increasing each year, especially in the World War II period, the need for new high-speed equipment became more and more evident.

In 1948 two of the old stalwart Stickney presses were taken out of regular production and installed in the Bureau's engineering facility for study leading to the design of new production equipment.

Through application of the data obtained from that study, specifications were prepared for a high-speed intaglio web press which was delivered in 1950.

This equipment, the forerunner of the Cottrell press, was specially manufactured by the Huck Co. of New York City to Bureau specifications. It became popularly dubbed by Engraving and Printing personnel as "The Huck Press."

Essentially intended for experimental use, with a few additional perfections, it was found suitable for regular production work and the press was used for the printing of the 3¢ International Red Cross commemorative of 1952.

That stamp had the honor of being the first bicolor United States postage stamp produced in web-sheet form.

Further development work conducted with the equipment to achieve maximum operational efficiency and economy culminated in the decision to purchase in 1955 five electronically actuated web-fed presses of similar, but improved design.

These were manufactured to Bureau specifications by the Cottrell Co. of Westerly, R.I., and were first used in the printing of the 3¢ ordinary issue of 1954.

While the basic operation principles of the equipment were the same as those of the Stickney press, the new machines were much larger in size with a speed and production approximately triple that of the old machines.

These presses, equipped with a typographic attachment for precanceling stamps when required, produced about 60 per cent of all U.S. stamps issued in 1981, having been employed in the printing of numerous single-color ordinary and commemorative stamps.

An early morning fire at the Bureau's annex building March 5, 1982 destroyed two of the BEP's five Cottrell presses, and damaged two others.

The 2:45 a.m. blaze was caused by a spontaneous flareup of dust and ink in the pressroom's exhaust ducts.

The two less severely affected presses were put back in service within about 72 hours, while the other pair were declared a total loss. The loss of the two presses actually represented little more than their early retirement. As it was, the Bureau had planned to phase two of its aged Cottrells out of service in May 1982 anyway. The replacement "C" press, a 3-color intaglio press which can print coils and books from roll to roll, is expected to begin operation during mid-1982.

## Giori Equipment

In connection with its responsibility for the production of all United States paper money, the Bureau had long sought means of overcoming the difficulties associated with printing of currency from engraved plates using premoistened paper.

Finally in 1954, investigation developed to the extent that printing by the dry intaglio method was deemed feasible. Two companies which felt they had equipment suitable for the purpose offered their machines to the Bureau for evaluation.

During the ensuing two-year trial period, one of the presses, a product of the Giori organization, showed extensive potentialities for multicolor printing.

As noted earlier, the success of these tests led to the decision to acquire the press for further

experimentation, with the result this machine was used to produce the 4¢ American Flag stamp issued in 1957.

The various stamps produced on this press were so well received that the Bureau purchased another of these machines in 1959. An even larger machine was acquired in 1963.

## Andreotti Press

In 1969, the Post Office Department requested the Bureau to undertake the printing of aerograms. Heretofore, these items were produced by the Government Printing Office, which had to release the job because that agency was not prepared to make equipment changes required by a contemplated design change of the item.

As a consequence, it became incumbent upon the Bureau to acquire the necessary printing equipment for the task. The Bureau's decision to proceed was in part prompted by the fact that the work would be produced by the gravure method, and the availability to the Bureau of such equipment for analysis in the production of postage stamps would be of inestimable help in the Bureau's search to improve its capabilities for the production of multicolor stamp issues.

The gravure process is particularly well suited for printed reproductions of full color art work and designs. It is also especially useful for the high-fidelity reproduction of paintings popularly used for commemorative stamp designs.

Accordingly, the Bureau solicited bids for a rotogravure press and a contract was awarded to the Miehle Company of Chicago, Ill., for a seven-color machine. The design and construction of this press were undertaken for the American firm by Andreotti S.P.A. of Ceprano, Italy.

This machine, which was installed in 1970-71, is approximately 110 feet long and weighs 62 tons. It consists essentially of an unwind rollstand, seven printing units (with provision for an eighth), an extended dryer, and provisions for either sheeting or rewinding.

An additional capability of this unit is that of printing on both sides of the web of paper on the same pass through the press. This feature was used in the production of the Postal Service Employees issue of 1973, and the quartet of stamps honoring the Contributors to the Cause, issued in 1975.

Although the press was not originally equipped for perforating, this feature was added later.

The first postage stamp printed on this press was the 8¢ Missouri Statehood commemorative issue of 1971.

## Web 3-Color Intaglio Press

One of the latest pieces of stamp printing equipment to become operational in the Bureau is the "Web 3-Color Intaglio Press" for the production of coil stamps.

All requirements for coil stamp printing in one operation have been included in this specially designed press, supplied to the Bureau by the Giori organization, and built by Koenig and Bauer of Wurzburg, Germany. These requirements include 3-color intaglio printing, tagging, and precanceling (when required).

This press represents a unique innovation to Bureau press equipment with the introduction of a continuous surface printing form. The printing form is an engraved, concentric, seamless, cylindrical surface containing 936 coil-size stamp engravings (18 across and 52 around).

## Web 8-Color Gravure/Intaglio Press

Another unit of stamp printing equipment recently acquired by the Bureau is an intaglio color press supplied to the Bureau by the Giori organization and built by Koenig and Bauer of Wurzburg, Germany. This press includes five gravure units supplied by Andreotti of Italy.

The press is capable of producing postage stamps in eight colors (three intaglio and five by gravure) and also incorporates additional features required by the Bureau, including perforating and tagging. The gravure and intaglio units have the capability of operating in tandem.

A pregummed paper web is fed into the press from an automatic roll unwind unit. The paper passes through an oven which conditions the paper, then through the five gravure units, the intaglio unit, and a perfecting overprint unit, when applicable.

The paper also passes through a phosphor tagging unit, a perforating unit, and finally to a sheeter.

This press is intended to produce only sheet stamps and does not have the capability to rewind the paper web. After each printing operation, the web is dried in drying units, heated with quartz-tube electric elements.

The gravure printing cylinders are photoengraved copper with a chromium surface. When the press is in the printing mode, the printing cylinder turns in an ink fountain where the image-forming cells are filled with ink. A doctor blade wipes excess ink from the surface of the cylinder prior to its coming into contact with the paper web.

The paper then draws the ink out of the cells; this drawing process is further induced through electrostatic assist equipment. The fifth gravure unit has the capability to print either the obverse or the reverse on the paper web.

The intaglio printing form is an engraved concentric, seamless printing surface.

Printing inks are applied to the engraved form by way of "cut-out" rollers. Raised portions of the cut-out rollers pick ink up from the ink fountain and selectively deposit it on predetermined locations on the printing form.

After each of the three colors has been applied to the form, it moves toward the wiping system. This system consists of a wiper roller and a tank containing a cleaning solution, brushes, and a scraper blade.

The upper portion of the wiper roller is in constant contact with the printing form while the lower portion is partially immersed in the cleaning solution. The wiper roller is cleaned as it rotates in the bath.

The clean wiper roller continues to rotate in a direction opposite to that of the printing form without disturbing the ink in the engraving. The printing operation then takes place by exerting great pressure on the stamp paper as it passes between the printing form and fiber impression roller.

The perfecting overprint unit prints from raised rubber plates and has the capability of printing on both sides of the web in one pass through the press.

This is accomplished by using two plate cylinders which, after being inked, transfer the image to respective blanket cylinders. The paper web is passed between the two blanket cylinders printing the obverse and reverse simultaneously. The two blanket cylinders act as the impression cylinder for each other.

As mentioned earlier, this press is designed to produce sheet stamps. The intaglio form contains an image area to accommodate 460 subjects of regular size commemorative stamps, 10 subjects across and 46 subjects around the form.

The gravure cylinder contains one-half the image area of the intaglio form and can accommodate 230 subjects. Sheet stamps will, however, continue to be printed in 200 subject sizes.

If plate numbers are printed on the sheet, the one to two ratio between the gravure cylinder circumference and the form circumference will require the plate numbers to be printed in different positions on the sheet with each succeeding print.

Initial production from the press came in late 1976 with the printing of part of the 1976 Currier Christmas issue.

Among new pieces of equipment installed in the Bureau of Engraving and Printing for the production of U.S. postage stamps are the booklet-forming machines manufactured by Goebel.

The first unit was installed in the summer of 1976, followed by two others later in the year. A total of six units were operational by the end of 1977.

While the basic unit of this machine is similar to that supplied by Goebel to a number of other countries for the vending of postage stamps by the booklet method, the machines at the Bureau incorporate a number of technical improvements designed by the BEP.

A modern change incorporated in the units for the Bureau is the capability of perforating the stamps as they pass through the machine. This was a separate operation on earlier machines manufactured by Goebel.

At the present time some of the machines are being used for the production of the $1 booklet for distribution from vending machines. The single sheet of eight stamps (seven 13¢ and one 9¢) is bound in a stiff cover that protects the unused stamps until they are removed.

While the machines are presently being used only for assembly of vending machine booklets, they also have the capability of assembling up to 36 stamps and could be used for over-counter booklets.

A roll (12 stamps wide) as it comes from the coil press, feeds the machine. As the stamps progress through, the roll is split and a sheet, eight stamps wide, moves through the perforators and into the binding assembly where it is enclosed in the hard cover.

The other portion of the sheet (four stamps wide) continues on through the machine and is gathered on another roll and will be sent through separately for binding.

It should be noted, this procedure refers specifically to the current operation and can be varied depending on the number of stamps to be bound in an individual booklet.

The machine also has the capability of binding additional sheets, folded sheets, or a combination of the two.

What will eventually become a cover for the booklet starts from a roll of stiff stock which passes through an offset printing unit, capable of printing on both sides and in two colors if desired.

The cover is "scored" and the stamps are attached by moistening the selvage edge. During this operation, a "cohesive" is also applied along the outer edge of the cover. This will serve to keep the booklet closed until all the stamps are removed.

While the average production of the Goebel booklet-forming machine is approximately 15,000 booklets per hour, the production speed will vary, depending on the number of stamps to be enclosed in the booklet.

Because there are no seams in the printing form, "line pairs" have become a thing of the past as related to this equipment. While primarily the Web 3-Color Intaglio press is intended to produce coil stamps, the press has the capability of printing book stamps as well.

A pregummed paper web is fed into the press from an automatic roll unwind unit. It passes through the three-color intaglio unit, then through a precanceling unit (when applicable),

through a phosphor tagging unit, and finally to an automatic rewind unit. After each printing operation, the web passes through a drying oven.

Printing inks are applied to the engraved form by way of "cut-out" rollers. Raised portions of the cut-out rollers pick ink up from the ink fountain and selectively deposit it on predetermined locations on the printing form. After each of the three colors has been applied to the form, it moves toward the wiping system.

This wiping system consists of a wiper roller and a tank containing a cleaning solution, brushes, and a scraper blade. The upper portion of the wiper roller is in constant contact with the printing form, while the lower portion is partially immersed in the cleaning solution. The wiper roller is cleaned as it rotates in the bath.

The clean wiper roller continues to rotate in a direction opposite to that of the printing form without disturbing the ink in the engraving.

The printing operation then takes place by exerting great pressure on the stamp paper as it passes between the printing form and a fiber impression roller. Ink is subsequently dried in drying units, heated with quartz-tube electric elements.

This press became operational in November 1975, producing the 13¢ Flag-Independence Hall stamp. The operational speed of this press is 300 feet per minute, providing a production capacity of 15-20 million stamps per eight-hour shift.

## Intagliocolor '8' Press

The Intagliocolor "8" press is a four-plate, three-color Giori, sheet-fed, high-speed intaglio printing press. It has a production rating of up to 9,000 sheets per hour and is capable of printing in three colors simultaneously from each plate.

The press can feed and deliver individual loads comprising up to 10,000 sheets each. These loads are deposited into one of two delivery elevators at the end of the press. The press continues to print during the removal of a load since the sheets for the following load are switched to the second delivery elevator.

Various sizes and types of paper stock, including pregummed postage stamp paper, can be used on this press in a variety of subject sizes.

Ink rollers are plastic covered and are sectioned on a pantograph capable of routing five areas of these rollers at one time. This routing of each ink roller permits precise placement of the ink into the areas of the engraving designated for the colors applied to the printing plate. A maximum of three ink rollers can apply a like number of colors.

Wiping of the ink from the surface of the plates is accomplished by two wipers. The first wiping utilizes a plastic roller prewiper which simultaneously removes ink from the surface of the plates and compresses ink into the engraved lines. No solvent or water solution is used with this dry wiping unit.

The second wiping utilizes a water-wipe system using a plastic roller which turns in a water-based cleaning solution. This plastic wiper removes all of the remaining ink from the surface of the plates prior to the printing process.

The Interphil postage stamp of 1976 was the first stamp produced on this press.

### First Holiday Closing

For the first time in its history the Bureau was shut down over the 1981 Christmas and New Year's holiday period. The facility was closed in an effort to save an estimated $500,000 in heating, lighting and operating the BEP buildings for the small number of employees which were expected to show up for work during the holiday season.

To make the 10-day shutdown, which extended from December 25 to January 3, a bit easier to swallow, Bureau workers who had vacation time coming to them were allowed to use it during the shutdown and thereby receive full pay. Those who didn't have any leave time left, or didn't want to use up their vacation time over the Christmas and New Year's holiday, were put on leave without pay.

The closing was carried out in phases, with the Bureau's eight different stamp production presses shutting down first, followed within hours by the BEP's 14 currency presses.

The cleanup operation on each press took about two hours to complete.

Following the holiday period, all presses returned to service without incident and neither the Federal Reserve System nor the U.S. Postal Service was affected by the closing with respect to scheduled delivery of currency or postage stamps.

# BEP Organization

Headquarters: Fourteenth and C streets SW, Washington, D.C. 20228. Phone: 202-447-1364.

Director . . . . . . . . . . . . . . . . . . . . . . . . . . . . . . . . . . . . . . . . . . . . . . . . . . Harry R. Clements
Deputy Director . . . . . . . . . . . . . . . . . . . . . . . . . . . . . . . . . . . . . . . . . . . . . . . . . (Vacant)
Assistant Director (Administration) . . . . . . . . . . . . . . . . . . . . . . . . . . . . . . . Robert J. Leuver
Assistant Director (Operations) . . . . . . . . . . . . . . . . . . . . . . . . . . . . . . . . . Larry E. Rolufs
Assistant Director (Research and Engineering) . . . . . . . . . . . . . . . . . . . . . . Milton J. Seidel
Office of Audit and Internal Affairs . . . . . . . . . . . . . . . . . . . . . . . . . . . . . . . Howard J. Katz
Office of Quality Assurance . . . . . . . . . . . . . . . . . . . . . . . . . . . . . . . . . . . Robert E. Clancey
Office of Management and Systems . . . . . . . . . . . . . . . . . . . . . . . . . . . . . . John J. McKenna
Office of Financial Management . . . . . . . . . . . . . . . . . . . . . . . . . . . . . Maurice M. Schneider
Office of Planning and Policy Development . . . . . . . . . . . . . . . . . . . . . . . . . . . . Peter Daly
Office of Currency and Stamp Production . . . . . . . . . . . . . . . . . . . . . . . . . Robert K. Wilcox
Office of Stamp Processing and Surface Printing . . . . . . . . . . . . . . . . . . . Joseph M. DeBose
Office of Engraving . . . . . . . . . . . . . . . . . . . . . . . . . . . . . . . . . . . . . . . . Edward R. Felver
Office of Research and Technical Services . . . . . . . . . . . . . . . . . . . . . . . . . . . David Cohen
Office of Engineering . . . . . . . . . . . . . . . . . . . . . . . . . . . . . . . . . . . . . . Charles H. Thrall
Office of Security . . . . . . . . . . . . . . . . . . . . . . . . . . . . . . . . . . . . . . . . . . . . . . (Vacant)
Office of Industrial Relations . . . . . . . . . . . . . . . . . . . . . . . . . . . . . . . Robert L. Ellenberger
Office of Materials Management . . . . . . . . . . . . . . . . . . . . . . . . . . . . . . . Robert T. Smith

# Directors of the Bureau

Until June of 1896, the head of the Bureau was known as the "Chief." In July of 1896, the title of "Director" came into use. The following list covers all executive officers of the Bureau from the date of its establishment.

| DIRECTOR | TERM | DIRECTOR | TERM |
| --- | --- | --- | --- |
| Spencer Morton Clark | Aug. 22, 1862-Nov. 17, 1868 | Thomas J. Sullivan | July 1, 1906-May 4, 1908 |
| George B. McCartee | Mar. 18, 1869-Feb. 19, 1876 | Joseph E. Ralph | May 11, 1908-Oct. 31, 1917 |
| Henry C. Jewell | Feb. 21, 1876-April 30, 1877 | James L. Wilmeth | Dec. 10, 1917-Mar. 31, 1922 |
| Edward McPherson | May 1, 1877-Sept. 30, 1878 | Louis A. Hill | April 1, 1922-Feb. 14, 1924 |
| O.H. Irish | Oct. 1, 1878-Jan. 27, 1883 | Wallace W. Kirby | June 16, 1924-Dec. 15, 1924 |
| Truman N. Burrill | Mar. 30, 1883-May 31, 1885 | Alvin W. Hall | Dec. 22, 1924-Dec. 15, 1954 |
| Edward O. Graves | June 1, 1885-June 30, 1889 | Henry J. Holtzclaw | Dec. 16, 1954-Oct. 8, 1967 |
| William M. Meredith | July 1, 1889-June 30, 1893 | James A. Conlon | Oct. 9, 1967-July 1, 1977 |
| Claude M. Johnson | July 1, 1893-May 10, 1900 | Seymour Berry | July 2, 1977-April 7, 1979 |
| William M. Meredith | Nov. 23, 1900-June 30, 1906 | Harry R. Clements | July 15,1979 —— |

**BUREAU OF ENGRAVING & PRINTING ORGANIZATION** (effective Jan. 4, 1982)

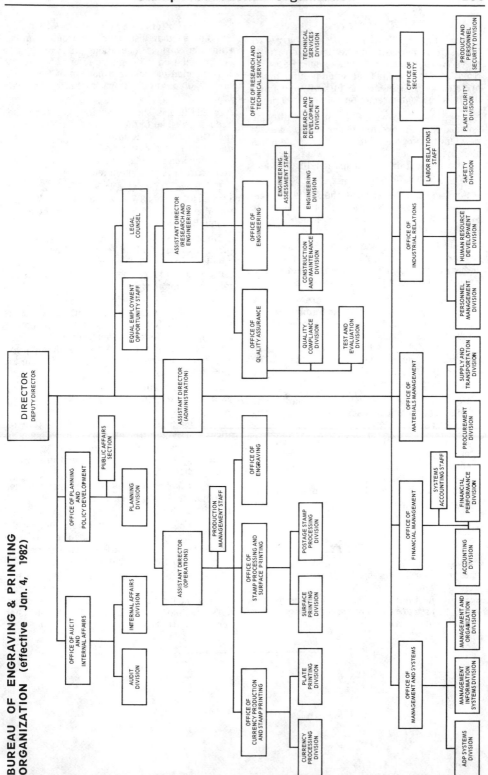

DIRECTOR
DEPUTY DIRECTOR

OFFICE OF AUDIT AND INTERNAL AFFAIRS
- AUDIT DIVISION
- INTERNAL AFFAIRS DIVISION

OFFICE OF PLANNING AND POLICY DEVELOPMENT
- PUBLIC AFFAIRS SECTION
- PLANNING DIVISION

LEGAL COUNSEL

EQUAL EMPLOYMENT OPPORTUNITY STAFF

ASSISTANT DIRECTOR (RESEARCH AND ENGINEERING)

OFFICE OF RESEARCH AND TECHNICAL SERVICES
- TECHNICAL SERVICES DIVISION
- RESEARCH AND DEVELOPMENT DIVISION

OFFICE OF ENGINEERING
- ENGINEERING ASSESSMENT STAFF
- ENGINEERING DIVISION
- CONSTRUCTION AND MAINTENANCE DIVISION

ASSISTANT DIRECTOR (ADMINISTRATION)

OFFICE OF QUALITY ASSURANCE
- QUALITY COMPLIANCE DIVISION
- TEST AND EVALUATION DIVISION

ASSISTANT DIRECTOR (OPERATIONS)

PRODUCTION MANAGEMENT STAFF

OFFICE OF ENGRAVING

OFFICE OF STAMP PROCESSING AND SURFACE PRINTING
- POSTAGE STAMP PROCESSING DIVISION
- SURFACE PRINTING DIVISION

OFFICE OF CURRENCY PRODUCTION AND STAMP PRINTING
- PLATE PRINTING DIVISION
- CURRENCY PROCESSING DIVISION

OFFICE OF SECURITY
- PRODUCT AND PERSONNEL SECURITY DIVISION
- PLANT SECURITY DIVISION

OFFICE OF INDUSTRIAL RELATIONS
- LABOR RELATIONS STAFF
- SAFETY DIVISION
- HUMAN RESOURCE DEVELOPMENT DIVISION
- PERSONNEL MANAGEMENT DIVISION

OFFICE OF MATERIALS MANAGEMENT
- SUPPLY AND TRANSPORTATION DIVISION
- PROCUREMENT DIVISION

OFFICE OF FINANCIAL MANAGEMENT
- SYSTEMS ACCOUNTING STAFF
- FINANCIAL PERFORMANCE DIVISION
- ACCOUNTING DIVISION

OFFICE OF MANAGEMENT AND SYSTEMS
- MANAGEMENT AND ORGANIZATION DIVISION
- MANAGEMENT INFORMATION SYSTEMS DIVISION
- ADP SYSTEMS DIVISION

## Director

The current BEP director — Harry R. Clements — moved from the deputy director's post to acting director when Seymour Berry retired from the Bureau to accept a position in the private sector. Clements was formally appointed the Bureau's 20th director on July 15, 1979.

A native of Blackwell, Okla., the new director entered federal government service as an executive in the program of the President's Commission for Personnel Interchange, where he managed a division of the Occupational Safety and Health Administration.

For two years, he was with the Health, Education and Welfare Department's Rehabilitation Services Administration, serving as deputy commissioner.

From 1975-1978, Clements was chief executive officer of NISH Inc., a private firm providing industrial management services related to government contracting.

Clements' background is in the areas of industrial management and business administration. His bachelor's and master's degrees (from Wichita State University) are in aeronautical engineering, while his additional training in business and government operations comes from the University of California (Los Angeles) and the Federal Executive Institute.

He also has attended additional courses and seminars on technical, management and government operations.

Prior to entering government service, Clements spent 20 years in the aerospace and transportation industry, holding management and executive positions in the fields of engineering, new business development, manufacturing and operations in various major U.S. corporations.

## BEP Tours

The Bureau of Engraving and Printing is charged with the responsibility for the production of major items of a financial character issued by the United States, the two most prominent of which are our Government's paper money and postage stamps.

The BEP offers self-guided tours of its Main Building so that visitors can become familiar with the various operations and production equipment used in the manufacture of currency. It is planned to include a portion of the manufacture of postage stamps in the tour area in 1982.

In addition, a special exhibit/sales area has been established in the foyer of the Main Building. On display is a fully equipped engravers desk and transfer and proof presses. Assorted currency items, postage stamps and Bureau souvenir cards are also exhibited.

The Bureau is located in Washington, D.C., at 14th and C streets SW, just south of the Washington Monument and in the vicinity of the Smithsonian Building.

The tour facility is open each day, Monday through Friday (except legal holidays), from 8 a.m. to 2 p.m. There is no admission charge and the complete tour normally requires approximately 25 minutes. The sales area is open from 9 a.m. to 2 p.m. weekdays.

At times there is a heavier influx of visitors than the tour facility can physically accommodate in the periods available. To assure equity and a pleasant tour for the greatest number possible, admission tickets will be issued when the number of visitors is heavy.

Such tickets will be issued, when necessary, on a first-come, first-served basis. Notices will be posted as soon as all available tickets have been issued to preclude unnecessary waiting for anyone arriving after all tickets have been exhausted. Tickets will be honored on the date of issue only and may not be obtained in advance of the visit.

Current information on the Bureau's tour can be obtained 24 hours each day by dialing 202-447-9709 or 202-447-9916.

Sightseeing buses discharge passengers at the 14th Street entrance and reload at the 15th Street exit point. There are no public parking or restaurant facilities on the premises.

The Bureau is included on the Tourmobile "Washington Mall" Tour. Service operates continually during the day among 11 of Washington's landmarks. There is a Tourmobile stop across the street from the Bureau on 15th Street.

# Varieties, Errors

It may seem a bit odd, but nevertheless true, that while people generally look upon items of defective manufacture to be of less value than the perfect article, for the stamp collector that stamp which shows the results of some mistake arouses greater interest than a correctly printed specimen.

It goes without saying that, with the exercise of proper care, incorrect stamps will be less plentiful than correct ones, and as they are regarded as collectable they quite frequently have a greater value.

When one considers the numerous methods and complicated processes involved in the production of postage stamps, it is small wonder that such things as errors and varieties are not more prevalent.

The term variety, it should be noted, has several different philatelic meanings, which in themselves can lead to considerable confusion.

In relation to stamps generally, the term is used as a synonym for "stamp." In this sense, the term "major variety" is often used to designate every officially approved and issued stamp. To distinguish other variations and distinctions that have been noted by philatelists, the comparative term "minor variety" is often used.

In relation to particular stamps, the term "variety" means a stamp that differs from the norm. In this sense, "variety" includes every error — that is to say, all errors are varieties, but not every variety is an error.

In a special sense in relation to printing, the term "variety" means any stamp that differs from every other stamp because of characteristics imparted by the method and process of printing.

In this sense, varieties are sharply differentiated into "constant varieties" and "inconstant varieties."

A constant variety is one that occurs on every stamp printed from the particular position on the printing base that gives rise to the variety. This would include flaws, etc.

An inconstant variety is one that occurs because some temporary circumstance, affecting only the particular stamp or sheet of stamps on which the inconstant variety appears. This would include all inconstant flaws.

Broadly speaking, for the student of stamp production, constant varieties are important however insignificant their abnormality, while inconstant varieties are of little more than passing interest no matter how striking their appearance.

While the terms "error," "major variety," and "minor variety" are used rather roughly to indicate certain grades of importance, it should also be recognized that these terms are frequently loosely employed.

Except for a few specific references, it is not our intention in these comments to go into detailed explanation of errors, when and how they occur and how they might possibly affect the value of a particular item.

There are a number of excellent treatises on this subject which provide much more comprehensive information of importance to the advanced collector.

One of the most valuable of these tools would be "The Fundamentals of Philately," by L.N. and M. Williams, published under the sponsorship of the American Philatelic Society. There are, however, a number of others.

Rather it will be our intention in these paragraphs to point out some of the more pronounced "mistakes" (for the sake of a more adequate word) that occur in the production of postage stamps and in turn can result in an item of unusual interest or a variety of special concern to the collector of the unusual.

## In the Beginning

The initial opportunity for error arises at the very start of the process of postage stamp production — at the time the artist is preparing his sketch. It may be a misspelled word. He may leave out some essential detail or include something that should not have been included.

In most cases, mistakes of this type are generally discovered before they progress to the finishing stage of the art and are corrected. If, however, the mistake is not discovered and the engraver faithfully follows the artist, these mistakes will be copied and appear on the printing plate and in the designs of the finished stamps.

Mistakes of this type hardly come within the collector's definition of an error, inasmuch as every stamp is alike, while as we have noted earlier, he more often employs the word to designate a variation from the normal run of a particular stamp.

A scratch on an engraved plate or accidental damage to the actual printing plate itself, may result in one particular stamp in the printed sheet having a word misspelled, or result in some slight alteration in the design.

While mistakes of this kind have a certain appeal to the eye and imagination and as such are popular with collectors, attaining considerable value in some cases, they are of no more importance than similar damage which does not alter a letter, or any essential of the pictorial design.

Efforts to repair the actual printing plate through the reentry of an individual stamp cliche can also result in an error of real significance.

One of the more famous of these is the "5-cent red errors" of the United States issue of 1916-17. Actually, there are three such errors involved. They came about through the unintentional mistakes on the part of a technician in the Bureau of Engraving and Printing.

This individual undertook to correct the defects on three positions of plate No. 7942 of the 2¢ stamp by reentering these with the transfer roll. Unfortunately, he selected the wrong roll — the one for the 5¢ stamp.

In the rush of wartime work the sheets printed from the plate were shipped out undetected and used in the normal course of business. These stamps are all accorded major catalog status.

It is when we come to the actual printing of stamps that the possibility for errors and variations are most apt and do occur, largely because of the speed needed to produce stamps in the necessary quantities.

Inasmuch as the printing process is largely mechanical as contrasted with the manual nature of the plate making process, exact control is not always feasible, with the result that a wide assortment of mishaps and combinations of circumstances create a large class of varieties.

As indicated earlier, among those varieties that may occur during the actual process of printing, some will be of considerable interest, while others are of little significance, although they may be very prominent in appearance.

It should be borne in mind that many of the variations discussed in the following paragraphs are to be found in printing by the sheet method.

With the development in recent years of high-speed, multicolor presses, such as those found in the Bureau of Engraving and Printing in Washington, and in many stamp printing firms in other countries, a majority of the early bugaboos have disappeared, only to be replaced with new ones to tantalize the collector.

## Inverted Centers

Inverted centers are among the classic printing errors. Generally speaking these occur when a sheet of stamps to be printed in two colors is placed on the press the wrong way round for receiving the impression of the second color.

More rarely it may happen that one cliche (individual metal unit of the stamp design) in the plate may be inadvertently inverted, so that one stamp in every sheet printed will have an inverted center.

Perhaps the most famous United States stamp falling in this category is the 24¢ airmail of 1918. This stamp, of which a pane of 100 is known to have gone into circulation, is generally recognized as one of the "sacred cows of philately." The other three panes of 100 stamps each were retrieved before they went into circulation.

Stamps with printing on both sides provide a variety of considerable rarity and interest. In the early days, when occasionally a sheet would be poorly printed, a workman might turn the sheet over and print on the other side of it. The result would be a "positive" design printed on both sides of the paper.

It should be clearly understood that both impressions show the design in the correct position and way and one is not reversed as would be the case in an offset. Generally speaking one of the two impressions of a sheet printed on both sides in this manner is faint.

An offset, or what might be more accurately described as set-off, is a comparatively common variety. It is a more or less clear impression of the design of the stamp in reverse on the back of a normally printed stamp. Offset of this type falls into two groupings — machine offset and sheet offset.

Of the two, machine offset is the scarcest variety of offset. If the plate is inked and the machine prints without a sheet of paper on the plate, the impression of the stamps will be transferred to the "tympan" or blanket on the press.

Then, when a sheet of paper is placed on the plate and passes through the press, the back of the sheet will receive the impression which is on the "tympan" or blanket.

Such an offset is usually exceptionally clear, and also usually coincides with the impression on the front. This gives rise to the idea the paper is transparent or that the ink has penetrated through the paper.

Sheet offset occurs in the stacking of the printed sheets as they come off the printing operation and before or after removal from the press. In many cases, to prevent the two printed sheets from touching, a sheet of thin paper is inserted between each damp sheet. This is known as slip-sheeting.

Sometimes the slip sheet is omitted, and the wet impression of one sheet of stamps is transferred or "offset" on the back of the next sheet of stamps placed on the pile. The offset impression will, of course, be in reverse. Generally, sheet offsets rarely coincide with the impression on the front and are usually comparatively faint.

Developments in modern day printing processes and inks have gone a long way toward eliminating this problem in postage stamp production. In some cases a fine spray across the sheet serves to create a barrier to prevent the sheets touching, and in other cases, the printed sheets pass through or over a heating unit that serves to speed up the drying of the ink.

Slurred prints or skid prints result in a variety which is sometimes confused with a double transfer, double strike, reentry or shift, all of which do appear at times. A slurred print, however, is always somewhat blurred and frequently smeary. This result comes from the film of ink between the doubled lines.

The effect is caused by the press not being properly adjusted, loose plates, or the paper not being carefully laid on the plate. When the press roller or scraper passes over the paper a certain amount of "creep" develops, resulting in the paper slipping a little.

Only a portion of the sheet shows the slipping effect, usually at one end of the sheet or the other.

Somewhat spectacular and at times mistakenly called a double impression is the "kiss." It is caused by removing the sheet from the press in a careless manner so that a portion of it comes in contact with the plate a second time. As a rule only a few stamps on a sheet, usually marginal, will show a "kiss."

## Double Impressions

Double impressions and double prints are exceedingly rare. Most of those which have passed into collectors' hands have come from printers' spoils which have been rescued from the wastepaper basket.

A true double impression is the result of putting the sheet of paper through the press twice. Every stamp in the sheet will be double, the displacement of the impression varying considerably. In a double print the two impressions are clearly separated, but are usually of different intensity.

While folded paper varieties may and do occur in most any type of printing process, the fact that wet paper was used for many years in line engravings and lithography, it is a more common occurrence in stamps printed by these processes.

If the paper is not carefully laid on the plate, a small crease or fold may occur. After the sheet has been printed and gummed, it may pass inspection. Eventually the fold opens up and a white band will show across the face of the stamps printed over the fold. This should not be confused with a cracked plate variety.

White areas that appear on stamps are due to a number of causes. If it can be shown that the white spots, scratches, areas, etc., are constant, that is, they occur in the same form again and again, due to a defect in the plate or transfer medium, then they are significant.

However, other examples of white areas may be due to accidents of printing, such as uneven inking, improper adjustment of the press, bubbles of air in the ink, engraved lines becoming clogged with dry ink or chalk and failing to print, and so on.

In line-engraved stamps it sometimes happens that during polishing of the plates some of the ink is pulled from the engraved lines, or where there are solid masses of color the ink may be "scooped" out. Both of these result in white appearing where there should be color.

As was emphasized earlier in these comments, the "errors" and variations noted in the printing process outlined here are by no means all that can and do appear in the production of postage stamps. They do, however, represent the more common items with which the collector is most apt to come into contact.

# Engraved and Lithographed Printings

These Bureau products, unless otherwise indicated, are black-ink engravings produced from intaglio plates in a manner similar to currency and postage stamp reproductions.

Following is a list of portraits, building vignettes, government seals, and miscellaneous printings available from BEP. A price list and ordering form may be obtained by submission of a request to the Office of Public Affairs, Bureau of Engraving and Printing, Washington, D.C. 20228.

## Small Presidential Portraits

Paper six by eight inches, image approximately two by two and a half inches.

| | | |
|---|---|---|
| 1. Washington | 14. Pierce | 27. Wilson |
| 2. J. Adams | 15. Buchanan | 28. Harding |
| 3. Jefferson | 16. Lincoln | 29. Coolidge |
| 4. Madison | 17. A. Johnson | 30. Hoover |
| 5. Monroe | 18. Grant | 31. F.D. Roosevelt |
| 6. J.Q. Adams | 19. Hayes | 32. Truman |
| 7. Jackson | 20. Garfield | 33. Eisenhower |
| 8. Van Buren | 21. Arthur | 34. Kennedy |
| 9. W.H. Harrison | 22. Cleveland | 35. L. Johnson |
| 10. Tyler | 23. B. Harrison | 36. Nixon |
| 11. Polk | 24. McKinley | 37. Ford |
| 12. Taylor | 25. T. Roosevelt | 38. Carter |
| 13. Fillmore | 26. Taft | |

## Portraits of Chief Justices

Paper six by eight inches, image approximately two by two and a half inches.

| | | |
|---|---|---|
| 100. John Jay | 105. Salmon Chase | 110. C.E. Hughes |
| 101. John Rutledge | 106. Morrison Waite | 111. Harlan Stone |
| 102. Oliver Ellsworth | 107. Melville Fuller | 112. Fred Vinson |
| 103. John Marshall | 108. E.D. White | 113. Earl Warren |
| 104. Roger Taney | 109. W.H. Taft | |

## Large Presidential Portraits

Paper nine by twelve inches, image approximately four by five inches.

| | | |
|---|---|---|
| 200. Washington | 207. Wilson | 213. Eisenhower |
| 201. Jefferson | 208. Harding | 214. Kennedy |
| 202. Lincoln | 209. Coolidge | 215. L. Johnson |
| 203. Grant | 210. Hoover | 216. Nixon |
| 204. McKinley | 211. F.D. Roosevelt | 217. Ford |
| 205. T. Roosevelt | 212. Truman | 218. Carter |
| 206. Taft | | |

## Vignettes of Buildings

Paper six by eight inches, image approximately two by four and a quarter inches.

| | |
|---|---|
| 300. Bureau of Engraving and Printing | 308. Wakefield |
| 301. Capitol: East View | 309. Washington City Post Office |
| 302. Capitol: Southeast View | 310. White House: Northeast View |
| 303. Lincoln Memorial | 311. White House: South View |
| 304. Monticello | 312. White House: Southeast View |
| 305. Mount Vernon | 313. Independence Hall |
| 306. Supreme Court | 314. Washington Monument |
| 307. Treasury Department | |

## Government Seals

Lithographed in color, five and three-eights inches in diameter.

400. Obverse of Great Seal of United States
(paper size 7½ by 9 inches)
402. Department of the Treasury Seal
(paper size 8 by 10 inches)

## Miscellaneous Documents

501. Gettysburg Address
(paper size 10 by 13 inches)

# American Bank Note Company

The early history of postage stamp printing in the United States finds a number of firms figuring in the production process covering approximately 50 years before the Bureau of Engraving and Printing took over supplying the requirements of the Post Office Department.

Prior to the year 1845, when uniform rates for postage were set by an act of Congress, postmasters accepted letters for delivery either by receiving payment in advance, in which case they marked "Paid" on the wrapper, or by noting on the wrapper the amount of the established fee which the recipient was to pay.

By the act of 1845, postmasters were authorized to use stamps to indicate prepaid postage and were also authorized to arrange on their own responsibility for the manufacture of stamps until such time as the Post Office Department could do so for the postal system as a whole.

In New York City, Postmaster Robert H. Morris turned to the firm of Rawdon, Wright and Hatch to produce stamps for use by his post office. This same firm in 1842 had manufactured stamps — precursors of postage stamps — for a private message-carrying company in New York.

These first stamps issued for New York City were later to become known as the "New York Postmaster Provisionals." Two years later, in 1847, this same firm was to produce the first U.S. postage stamps.

It is interesting to note that the firm, its identification now increased to Rawdon, Wright, Hatch and Edson, established another milestone in postage stamp history when it executed an order for three denominations for the Canadian Post Office in 1849.

Another predecessor of the present American Bank Note Co., Toppan, Carpenter, Casilear and Co., obtained the contract for the printing of U.S. postage stamps in 1851. Originally scheduled to run through 1856, this contract was later extended four additional years.

In 1861, the National Bank Note Co., a new firm, having been organized only two years earlier, was awarded the contract for the printing of the new series of postage stamps. The change in contractors was apparently made on the basis of designs submitted. With the outbreak of the Civil War, a change in design was felt imperative by government officials.

Still another new company was to enter the postage stamp printing field when the postmaster general awarded the contract in early 1873 to the Continental Bank Note Co.

This firm had entered the bank note and security business in January 1863, at a time when the volume of business, especially in bank notes, increased tremendously as a result of the war.

It is of interest that eventual entrance of the American Bank Note Co. into the field, just as well as its eventual departure as the printer of U.S. postage stamps, came directly as a result of the creation of the Government's Bureau of Engraving and Printing.

As pointed out in another portion of this chapter, the Bureau was organized during the decade following the Civil War and in 1877 an act of Congress provided that all U.S. notes and securities should be printed by the Bureau.

The three companies (American, National and Continental) which had been printing these items had no alternatives other than to face the facts. With the U.S. note business gone, there was enough business left for one major company, but not for three.

In December 1878, the three firms agreed to a "consolidation" with the American Bank Note Co. the surviving unit. The offices of National and Continental were closed.

Lester G. Brookman in his book, "U.S. Postage Stamps of the 19th Century," notes that after the American Bank Note Co. took over the Continental Bank Note Co. on Feb. 4, 1879, the stamp contract held by Continental was apparently assumed by American and fulfilled by that firm.

American was to continue to hold the printing contract for U.S. postage stamps through 1893.

In that year, however, at the time the contract was again up for bids, the chief of the Bureau of Engraving and Printing of the Treasury Department, with the approval of the secretary of the treasury, entered a bid for the work under a clause in the official specifications issued to bidders.

The Bureau's figures were substantially below those submitted by other bidders, and this fact, coupled with the convenience of having the work done in Washington, where nearly all other securities of the Government were then being printed, resulted in the work being awarded to the Bureau.

American Bank Note Co.'s final contribution to this period of U.S. postage stamp production was the famous Columbian issue of 15 stamps produced in 1893 in connection with the Columbian Exposition in Chicago, marking the 400th anniversary of the discovery of America by Christopher Columbus.

This set of stamps, long recognized as the hallmark of U.S. postage, were the last printed for this Government in the 19th century by a private concern. And with but few exceptions, all issues of postage stamps since 1894 have been printed by the Bureau in Washington.

American Bank Note Co. was to figure in one of these exceptions, when it was awarded the contract for the printing in 1943-44 of the Overrun Nations stamps, showing in color the flags of the various countries engaged in World War II which had been overrun by the Axis powers.

There were several factors that apparently played a major role in the awarding of this contract for printing to the American Bank Note Co.

In the first place, the Bureau at the time (again in a war period) was so rushed with other work it did not have the time to devote to such an issue, and secondly, it did not have the equipment to turn out the type of printing planned for this series.

The cooperation of the American Bank Note Co. was solicited in the production of these stamps because its equipment permitted the flags of the various nations to be printed in their actual colors.

As finally released, this wartime series of 13 stamps carried uniform frames printed by the intaglio process, with the centers printed on the company's unique "WLG presses," which could reproduce each flag in its proper colors in perfect register.

Although the philatelic role of the American Bank Note Company has been greatly reduced, the firm currently is responsible for the development and production of the Commemorative Stamp Panels presently offered by the U.S. Postal Service.

These multicolored stamp panels are handsome album pages, containing postal or philatelic information about a current commemorative stamp, illustrated with antique vignettes selected from the files of the bank note company. To each sheet has been attached an encased block of four of the commemorative stamps.

The first of these panels was issued in 1972 in connection with the release of the Wildlife block of four. Since that time some 170 additional panels have been issued through current releases by the Postal Service.

While the supply of a number of these sheets has already been exhausted, the current issues and those still available may be obtained from the Philatelic Sales Unit in Washington and some of the Postal Service Postiques across the country.

In 1978, the U.S. Postal Service awarded a joint contract to the American Bank Note Company and J.W. Fergusson & Sons, Inc., Richmond, Va., for the printing of four commemorative stamp issues.

The bid submitted was $1,260,800 and covers the printing of 160 million stamps for each issue, or a total of 640 million stamps over the course of the two year contract period. The first issues produced under this contract were the John Paul Jones commemorative stamp (released Sept. 23, 1979), and the Benjamin Banneker issue (released Feb. 15, 1980). Later issues included the Veterans Administration Stamp (issued July 21, 1980) and the American Education Issue (released Sept. 12, 1980).

All four issues were printed by J.W. Fergusson & Sons and shipped to the American Bank Note Company for perforating, cutting (from sheets of 200 stamps into post office panes of 50), final processing and distribution.

The Postal Service solicited private sector bids in an attempt to determine if stamp production costs could be lowered through competitive bidding.

Initially, the Postal Service informed 71 firms of its interest in seeking outside sources for the production of stamps. Four companies responded with offers. In addition to the joint venture of American Bank Note and J.W. Fergusson & Sons, bids were submitted by: The Guilford Gravure, Inc., Guilford, Conn.; Imprimerie Courvoisier of La Chaux-de-fonds, Switzerland; and Harrison & Sons of High Wycombe, Buckinghamshire, England.

Similar results occurred when another private printing bid was solicited and awarded in 1982, with the joint venture of the American Bank Note Co. and J.W. Fergusson & Sons taking another order, this time for three commemoratives. The field of competition dwindled slightly, with only Guilford Gravure and Harrison & Sons bidding.

Three other issues of U.S. postage stamps have been printed, in whole or in part, by other private firms.

The first of these was the Walt Disney issue of 1968 which was printed in gravure by Achrovure Division of Union-Camp Corp., Englewood, N.J.

With the Bureau in the process of installing its new Andreotti press for gravure printing, the Anti-Pollution issue of four stamps in 1970 was printed at Guilford Gravure, Inc., Guilford, Conn.

The five stamps of the Christmas-1970 issue were also printed in gravure at Guilford Gravure, Inc. in the Connecticut city. (Reference to these printings will be found elsewhere in this chapter.)

# Law and Philately　　5

# Recent and
# Current Legal Problems

The object of this chapter is to highlight some of the controversial problems which became specific issues during the "Seventies" (1970-79).

## I. Unordered Stamps or Other Philatelic Merchandise

The problem of consumers in the United States constantly receiving merchandise in the mail they did not want and did not request became so annoying a few years back that the Congress of the United States decided to specifically legislate against the mailing of practically all types of unordered goods. The law concerning this matter appeared as Section 3009 of the Postal Reorganization Act, enacted Aug. 12, 1970 (39 USC 3009).

What this law means to the consumer:

There are only two kinds of merchandise that can be sent legally through the mails to a person without his consent or agreement:

1. Free samples which are clearly and plainly marked as such.

2. Merchandise mailed by a charitable organization asking for contributions.

In either of the above cases the consumer can consider the merchandise as a gift if he likes. In all other instances, it is illegal to send merchandise to anyone unless he has previously requested it.

If a person receives unordered merchandise of any kind, he can take it as a gift. He does not have to pay for it, and it is illegal for the individual or firm sending it to him to dun him for it or send him a bill.

If anyone experiences difficulty with unordered merchandise or is tormented with statements demanding payment for such, he should contact the Federal Trade Commission, 6th Street and Pennsylvania Avenue, Washington, D.C. 20580, or the nearest FTC field office. Field offices of the Federal Trade Commission are located in nearly all of the major cities in the United States.

Following the federal government's lead, a number of states have enacted similar legislation forbidding the offer of merchandise to residents of their state which was "not actually ordered or requested by the recipient" (Art.83, Sec.21A, Annotated Code of Maryland).

Conclusion: Anyone receiving unrequested approvals or any other unordered philatelic merchandise may simply keep it as a gift. There is no liability to pay for it nor any responsibility to return it.

## II. Price Control

Under the Economic Stabilization Act of 1970 the president of the United States issued various executive orders with regard to the control of wages, prices and rents, actual authority for regulation thereof being vested in an agency known as the "Cost of Living Council."

In the initial period, up to and including Nov. 13, 1971, the prices of postage stamps were considered to be "frozen" as were practically all other commodities. However, after that date a small number of commodities were excluded from price controls including postage stamps and coins (Federal Register, Vol. 36, No. 220,

Section 101.32 (i)(7)). This was known as "Phase I" of the freeze.

During "Phase II," as economic conditions dictated further changes in the economy, the question of which commodities were included or excluded was completely reexamined, but once again postage stamps were eventually placed on the "excluded list."

At a later date, as inflation appeared to worsen, a temporary 60-day complete freeze, known as "Phase III," was put into effect, and this time all commodities were frozen including stamps and coins.

However, when "Phase IV" regulations (the most sensible of the lot) were finally promulgated as a final step in regulating certain large sectors of the economy, "collectors' stamps and coins" were again unfrozen.

This, of course, was a major victory all along for dealers in these commodities, since any attempt to control prices of these items, particularly early varieties, could have been catastrophic in the industry.

## III. Possession of Counterfeit Postage Stamps

Question: Is it unlawful under the various statutory provisions and court decisions of the United States to retain in one's possession, knowingly or unknowingly, a counterfeit stamp when the owner thereof has no intent whatsoever to dispose of it?

In 1976 a veritable storm of controversy developed in the philatelic press over this question. The legal office of the United States Secret Service, a division of the Treasury Department charged with enforcing violations of any federal statute dealing with securities or obligations, foreign or domestic, has consistently maintained that its agents are entitled to pick up any counterfeit stamps held by private individuals or firms regardless of the intent of the collector or entity as to its usage.

A number of private attorneys, however, collectors themselves, after studying the various provisions of the federal criminal statutes dealing with U.S. and foreign financial obligations and securities (postage and revenue stamps are defined in the statutes as falling within this terminology) have apparently come to the opposite conclusion based on the fact that these statutory provisions indicate there must be "criminal intent," i.e., an intention to victimize or defraud someone in the usage of a counterfeit stamp.

Absent such criminal intent, suggest most of our philatelic attorneys, mere possession of a counterfeit stamp does not violate any provision of law and such stamp may be retained for reference or collection purposes.

The major statutory provisions generally cited are as follows: Title 18, United States Code, Sections 8, 15, 471, 472, 478, 480, 501, 502.

Those sections, especially Section 501, kept philately from being included in the Hobby Protection Act, Public Law 93-167, 93rd Congress, H.R. 5777, Nov. 29, 1973. The Hobby Protection Act is an act to require that reproductions and imitations of coins and political items be marked as copies with the date of manufacture.

The Senate and the House of Representatives felt that the sections mentioned provided ample protection for the hobby of philately.

Those sections are reprinted herewith from the United States Code:

**Sec. 8. Obligation or other security of the United States defined.**

The term "obligation or other security of the United States" includes all bonds, certificates of indebtedness, national bank currency, Federal Reserve notes, Federal Reserve bank notes, coupons, United States notes, Treasury notes, gold certificates, silver certificates, fractional notes, certificates of deposit, bills, checks, or drafts for money, drawn by or upon authorized officers of the United States, stamps and other representatives of value, of whatever denomination, issued under any Act of Congress, and canceled United States stamps. (June 25, 1948, ch. 645, 62 Stat. 685.)

**Sec. 15. Obligation or other security of foreign government defined.**

The term "obligation or other security of any foreign government" includes, but is not limited to, uncanceled stamps, whether or not demonetized. (Added Pub. L. 85-921, Title 3, Sept. 2, 1958, 72 Stat. 1771.)

**Sec. 471. Obligations or securities of United States.**

Whoever, with intent to defraud, falsely makes, forges, counterfeits, or alters any obligation or other security of the United States, shall be fined not more than $5,000 or imprisoned not more than fifteen years, or both. (June 25, 1948, ch. 645, 62 Stat. 705.)

**Sec. 472. Uttering counterfeit obligations or securities.**

Whoever, with intent to defraud, passes, utters, publishes, or sells, or attempts to pass, utter, publish, or sell, or with like intent brings into the United States or keeps in possession or conceals any falsely made, forged, counterfeited, or altered obligation or other security of the United States, shall be fined not more than $5,000 or imprisoned not more than fifteen years, or both. (June 25, 1948, ch. 645, 62 Stat. 705.)

**Sec. 478. Foreign obligations or securities.**

Whoever, within the United States, with intent to defraud, falsely makes, alters, forges, or counterfeits any bond, certificate, obligation, or other security of any foreign government, purporting to be or in imitation of any such security issued under the authority of such foreign government, or any treasury note, bill, or promise to pay, lawfully issued by such foreign government and intended to circulate as money, shall be fined not more than $5,000 or imprisoned not more than five years, or both. (June 25, 1948, ch. 645, 62 Stat. 707.)

**Sec. 480. Possessing counterfeit foreign obligations or securities.**

Whoever, within the United States, knowingly and with intent to defraud, possesses or delivers any false, forged, or counterfeit bond, certificate, obligation, security, treasury note, bill, promise to pay, bank note, or bill issued by a bank or corporation of any foreign country, shall be fined not more than $1,000 or imprisoned not more than one year, or both. (June 25, 1948, ch. 645, 62 Stat. 707.)

**Sec. 501. Postage stamps and postal cards.**

Whoever forges or counterfeits any postage stamp, or any stamp printed upon any stamped envelope, or postal card, or any die, plate, or engraving therefor; or

Whoever makes or prints, or knowingly uses or sells, or possesses with intent to use or sell, any such forged or counterfeited postage stamp, stamped envelope, postal card, die, plate, or engraving; or

Whoever makes, or knowingly uses or sells, or possesses with intent to use or sell, any paper bearing the watermark of any stamped envelope, or postal card, or any fraudulent imitation thereof; or

Whoever makes or prints or authorizes to be made or printed, any postage stamp, stamped envelope, or postal card, of the kind authorized and provided by the Post Office Department, without the special authority and direction of said department; or

Whoever after such postage stamp, stamped envelope, or postal card has been printed, with intent to defraud, delivers the same to any person not authorized by an instrument in writing, duly executed under the hand of the Postmaster General and the seal of the Post Office Department, to receive it —

Shall be fined not more than $500 or imprisoned not more than five years, or both. (June 25, 1948, ch. 645, 62 Stat. 713.)

**Sec. 502. Postage and revenue stamps of foreign governments.**

Whoever forges, or counterfeits, or knowingly utters or uses any forged or counterfeit postage stamp or revenue stamp of any foreign government, shall be fined not more than $500 or imprisoned not more than five years, or both. (June 25, 1948, ch. 645, 62 Stat. 713.)

What few tangential court decisions there have been on this subject, where counterfeit obligations or securities have been seized, such as currency or foreign stamps, would appear to be against the government's position, since without

any showing of criminal intent to defraud, the items seized have generally been ordered returned to the owners.

A contrary decision would, at the very least, seem to be unrealistic and impractical, since most expertizing foundations make considerable use of counterfeit items in determining whether the instant stamp submitted on a comparison basis is genuine or not.

## IV. Reproduction, Duplication, U.S. Postage Stamp Designs

In 1974 a controversy developed between the U.S. Postal Service on the one hand and certain dealers, dealers' organizations and stamp exhibitions on the other, as to whether a private commercial enterprise or stamp exhibition is free to reproduce U.S. postage stamps in souvenir card form or otherwise without the permission of the Postal Service.

A number of dealers and stamp exhibitions have issued souvenir cards in this manner in the past and the Postal Service apparently has no intention to make its position retroactive, nor does its current position have anything to do with the counterfeiting provisions referred to earlier in this chapter.

Purely and simply the Postal Service believes it has the right to license the reproduction of U.S. stamp designs for future commercial use on a paid basis, citing as its authority the legal claim of copyright as set forth in the Act of Jan. 27, 1938, c. 10, 52 Stat. 6. Section 1 of that Act provided:

"That the Postmaster General shall prepare, in such form and at such times as he shall deem advisable, and, upon his request, the Public Printer shall print as a public document to be sold by the Superintendent of Documents, illustrations in black and white of postage stamps of the United States, together with such descriptive, historical, and philatelic information with regard to such stamps as the Postmaster General may deem suitable:

"Provided, that notwithstanding the provisions of Section 52 of the Act of Jan. 12, 1895 (U.S.C., 1934 edition, Title 44, Sec. 58), stereotype or electrotype plates, or duplicates thereof used in the publications authorized to be printed by this section shall not be sold or otherwise disposed of but shall remain the property of the United States:

"And provided further, that notwithstanding the provisions of Section 7 of the Copyright Act of March 4, 1909 (U.S.C., 1934 edition, Title 17, Sec. 7), or any other provision of law, copyright may be secured by the Postmaster General on behalf of the United States in the whole or any part of the publication authorized by this section."

Based on the foregoing statutory provision and the legal history of the Act, the Postal Service is of the opinion it may legally prevent the reproduction or duplication of its stamp designs or license them for such purposes on a fee-paid basis, and apparently would be willing to liberally license such usage with the view to bringing in further revenue to the Postal Service since stamp designs, like delivery of the mail, are, in its opinion, services paid for with the public's funds.

This controversy has not been resolved and will probably take serious negotiation or suit in an appropriate federal court to decide.

N.B. - The Postal Service also claims trademark and service rights in distinctive words and phrases which appear as a part of most postage stamp designs, such as "U.S. Mail," "U.S. Postage," "U.S. Airmail," "Certified Mail," etc.

## V. Importation of Postage Stamps into the United States

Until recently it had generally been assumed that postage and revenue stamps, as well as postal stationery imported into the United States were free of customs duties under the well-known provisions of Sec. 274.40 of the Tariff Schedules of the United States which read as follows:

"Postage and revenue stamps, cancelled or not cancelled, and government stamped envelopes and postal cards bearing no printing other than the official imprint thereon . . . Free"

However, two interesting cases in this connection have recently engaged the attention of the U.S. Customs Service for its interpretation.

A. First Day Covers: The Customs Service has recently ruled that first day covers issued by a foreign government, i.e., "official" first day covers may continue to be imported free of duty, but that first day covers produced by private commercial individuals or firms are subject to duty under the appropriate provisions for certain printed matter.

Apparently the reasoning in this case is twofold — 1) one government does not tax the officially issued documentation of another under the usages of international courtesy; and 2) probably even more important, that the officially issued covers are usually much cheaper than the privately issued ones, costing only a penny or two over the face value of the stamp, whereas the cacheted privately issued cover tends to be considerably more expensive making the entire product into a manufactured paper article.

B. "Local" Stamps: The private owners of islands have for many years been producing adhesives termed in the United States as "local post labels" and in the British Isles as "local labels." So long as the islands were inhabited, even though perhaps only sparsely, so that a claim could legitimately be made that the local labels were needed in addition to the central government's postage stamp in order to deliver

the particular communication to a remote island, there seems to have been little difficulty.

However, cases are now under study where private entrepreneurs own islands which are uninhabited so that the adhesives being issued appear to serve no postal purpose whatever and are apparently produced solely to sell to stamp collectors.

Question: Are such items to be considered "postage stamps" or merely printed labels? The United States Customs Service, after long and exhaustive study, has handed down a landmark decision, the first and only one of its kind, discussing this entire subject in great detail. It is printed here verbatim (with minor style revisions and the deletion of names) with the full permission of the Customs Service.

## Privately Overprinted Stamps

On May 20, 1977 the United States Postal Service issued a 13-cent commemorative postage stamp to mark the 50th anniversary of Col. Charles Lindbergh's historic transatlantic flight from New York to Paris. At the time of the issuance of the stamp, considerable dissatisfaction was expressed by the philatelic public to the effect that not enough descriptive language appears on the stamp to indicate to the present generation the reason for its commemorative issuance; the wording "50th Anniversary Solo Transatlantic Flight," in miniscule type, being considered insufficient to recognize Col. Lindbergh's tremendous historic achievement, and that more explicit wording should have appeared on the stamp.

To remedy this situation an enterprising Florida dealer purchased a larger number of sheets of this stamp and added two lines of larger print — "SPIRIT OF ST. LOUIS" in the upper left corner and "CHARLES A. LINDBERGH" underneath the airplane, making the stamp more attractive and more appealing to the philatelist.

The dealer then sent in his advertisement to the philatelic press offering to sell the "retouched" stamps as mint singles and on cover, but had his advertisement rejected because of the apparent possibility that tampering with an issue of the United States Government might contravene some provisions of Federal law.

Inquiry made by legal counsel on behalf of the dealer in this regard resulted in the following reply from the Postal Service:

This replies to your letter of March 7, 1978, asking on behalf of a client whether it would be unlawful to overprint and sell to collectors the 13¢ U.S. postage stamp commemorating the fiftieth anniversary of the first "Solo Transatlantic (airplane) Flight." The stamp as issued depicts a single propeller airplane flying in the sky over the ocean and the rising (or setting) sun in the background; the only written information on the official stamp design consists of the origin country and postage amount marking ("USA-13¢") required by the Universal Postal Convention, and the brief and relatively inconspicuous legend: "50th Anniversary Solo Transatlantic Flight." The proposed overprinting would consist of the following additional words, in larger print than the original legend: "SPIRIT OF ST. LOUIS" and "CHARLES A. LINDBERGH."

The Postal Service's basic legal authority with respect to postage stamps is to "provide and sell" them, 39 U.S.C. 404(3) (1970), renumbered as 39 U.S.C. 404(a)(3), Pub. L. No. 94-421, September 24, 1976, sec. 9(a), 90 Stat.1310. We have therefore maintained that "postage stamps when purchased by the public become the property of the purchaser." 9 Op. Solic. P.O. Dep't No. 544 at 646 (1944). In the absence of any applicable legal prohibition, therefore, your client may do what he pleases to or with any postage stamps he lawfully purchases.

Since the proposed overprinting would not be in the form of an official postmark, the overprinting would not appear to raise any questions under 18 U.S.C. 503 (1976).

A further letter addressed to the Legal Counsel of the United States Secret Service with regard to the possibility of violating the prohibition in the counterfeiting laws against impressing notices on postage stamps, 18 U.S.C. 8, 475 (1976), or any other provisions resulted in a somewhat similar reply to the effect that "if the overprinting process does not involve the reproduction of any United States stamp, but the overprint is placed on genuine stamps, there would appear to be no legal objection to your client's proposed plan."

In view of the foregoing, the advertisement was placed in the philatelic press and a quantity of mint stamps and covers sold and distributed. The above statement of the Postal Service that the dealer could do what he pleases with the altered stamps included, of course, the obvious fact that they could be validly used as postage even though they might confuse a few sharp-eyed postal clerks.

In this connection, the Postal Service had some later thoughts and decided to issue an amendment to Sec. 142.3 of the Domestic Mail Manual (clause "h"). For the benefit of collectors and dealers, that section of the Manual is set forth in its present entirety as follows:

Amend Sec. 142.3 of the Domestic Mail Manual by revising it to read as follows:

142.3 Validity of Stamps. All postage stamps issued by the United States since 1860 are good for postage from any point in the United States or from any other place where the United States domestic mail service operates, except from the Panama Canal Zone where special Canal Zone stamps are used, and except as provided in this section.

The following are not good for postage:

a. Mutilated or defaced stamps.

b. Stamps cut from stamped envelopes, aerogrammes or postal cards.

c. Stamps covered or coated in such manner that the cancelling or defacing marks cannot be imprinted directly on the stamps.

d. Nonpostage stamps (migratory-bird hunting and conservation stamps, U.S. saving and thrift stamps, etc.)

e. Postage due, special delivery, special handling and certified mail stamps.

f. United Nations stamps, except on mail deposited at United Nations, N.Y.

g. Stamps of other countries.

h. Stamps on which any unauthorized design, message or other marking has been overprinted.

(39 U.S.C. 401(2), 404(a)(2), 404(a)(4), 410(a)).

SUMMARY: This rule amends postal regulations so as to make invalid for use as postage any postage stamps on which any unauthorized design, message or other marking has been overprinted. The need for this regulation was suggested by inquiries by Postal Service customers with regard to the validity as postage of overprinted stamps.

Under present regulations stamps that are mutilated or defaced (i.e., canceled) are considered invalid. The term "unauthorized design, message, or marking" in the final rule is intended to exclude from invalidation authorized markings, such as precanceled stamps and precanceled postmarks under Secs. 143.1 and 143.3 of the Domestic Mail Manual.

EFFECTIVE DATE: August 27, 1979.

SUPPLEMENTARY INFORMATION: On September 8, 1978 the Postal Service published for comment its proposal to revise the regulations as described above. (43 FR39593). The Postal Service received eight letters of comment referring to this proposal, which were divided between those in favor (5), those opposed (1), and those discussing other postal matters (2).

The argument against the proposal was to the effect that stamps individualized through overmarking or overprinting were "in the best American tradition of Freedom of Speech and should not be banned or unduly controlled." The prohibition which was proposed, however, was not an absolute prohibition against the marking or printing of private messages on postage stamps, or against the communication of private messages through the mails.

The rule would leave undisturbed the general rule that "postage stamps when purchased by the public become the property of the purchaser," 9 Op.Solic. P.O. Dep't No. 544 at

646(1944), under which a purchaser of postage stamps may generally mark or overprint his property as he pleases.* Nor would the rule interfere with businesses which overprint stamps with non-commercial messages, and re-sell the overprinted stamp at a profit to collectors of such articles who do not intend to use the stamps as postage.

The prohibition in the regulation is limited only to private markings on stamps to be used for postage, or the attached selvage area beyond the perforations, on which private markings or overprintings may interfere with postal operations in which the prompt and unimpeded recognition of genuine mint postage stamps is necessary. Since the proposal would do just that and nothing more, it would not be an undue restraint of commercial or other speech.

*Footnote — There is a statutory prohibition against impressing commercial messages on postage stamps and other U.S. Government obligations or securities. 18 U.S.C. 8;475(1978). Enforcement responsibility for this prohibition is vested principally in the U.S. Secret Service. 18 U.S.C.3056(1978). This regulation appears to be intended to prevent advertising falsely implying U.S. Government sponsorship of private products or services.

CONCLUSION: Dealers may overprint genuine United States postage stamps and sell them as "philatelic souvenirs," but such stamps will no longer be valid for postage.

# Treasury Department Dictum Regarding Stamp Reproduction

Reprinted here are applicable sections of the law which provide guidance for reproduction of U.S. and foreign postage stamps in souvenir card formats. Briefly, the law does not allow private citizens the right to produce U.S. security items except under restrictions which are spelled out here.

The use of illustrations and motion picture films and slides of postage and revenue stamps is detailed by the Secret Service of the Treasury Department in a facts sheet.

The facts sheet notes that the Treasury Department sponsored legislation to liberalize and clarify laws relating to the use of illustrations and films of paper money, postage and revenue stamps, checks, bonds and other obligations of the United States and foreign governments.

This legislation was passed by Congress and approved by the president on Sept. 2, 1958 (Public Law 85-921, 85th Congress), and was further amended on June 20, 1968, to permit reproductions of postage stamps in color under certain conditions (Public Law 90-353, 90th Congress).

The facts sheet includes the following information:

## United States Postage Stamps

Black and White Illustrations - Canceled and uncanceled United States postage stamps may be illustrated in any size in black and white in articles, books, journals, newspapers, or albums for philatelic educational, historical, and newsworthy purposes.

No individual facsimiles of United States postage stamps are permitted. No individual photographs are permitted, except glossy prints necessary to reproduce the illustrations in publications.

Colored Illustrations - Canceled and uncanceled United States postage stamps may be illustrated in color in articles, books, journals, newspapers or albums for philatelic, educational, historical and newsworthy purposes. Illustrations in color of uncanceled United States postage stamps must be of a size less than three-fourths or more than one and one-half, in linear dimension of each part of the stamps illustrated. Colored illustrations of canceled United States postage stamps may be in any size. The canceled stamps illustrated must bear an official cancellation mark, i.e., the stamps must have been used for postage.

## Foreign Postage Stamps

Black and White Illustrations - Black and white illustrations of uncanceled foreign postage stamps in any size are permitted for philatelic, educational, historical, and newsworthy purposes in articles, books, journals, newspapers, and albums. Black and white illustrations of canceled foreign postage stamps are permissible in any size and for any purpose.

As in the case of United States stamps, no individual facsimiles or photographs of foreign postage stamps are permitted, except glossy prints necessary to reproduce the illustrations in publications.

Colored Illustrations - Uncanceled foreign postage stamps may be illustrated in color in articles, books, journals, newspapers or albums for philatelic, educational, historical and newsworthy purposes, provided such illustrations are of a size less than three-fourths or more than one and one-half in linear dimension of each part of the stamp illustrated. Colored illustrations of canceled foreign postage stamps are permissible in any size and for any purpose. The canceled foreign postage stamps illustrated must bear an official cancellation mark, i.e., the stamps must have been used for postage.

Motion-Picture Films and Slides of United States and Foreign Postage Stamps - Motion picture films and slides of United States and foreign postage stamps in black and white or in color for projection upon a screen or for use in telecasting are permissible, but not for advertising purposes except philatelic advertising.

## Advertising

Printed Illustrations - Black and white illustrations in any size of canceled and uncanceled United States and foreign postage stamps are permitted in philatelic advertising of legitimate dealers in stamps or publishers of or dealers in philatelic articles, books, journals, newspapers, or albums.

Colored illustrations of canceled United States and foreign postage stamps may be used for philatelic advertising in any size. Uncanceled United States and foreign postage stamps may be illustrated in color for philatelic advertising, providing such illustrations are of a size less than three-fourths or more than one and one-half in linear dimension of each part of the stamps illustrated.

Films - The use of reproductions of canceled and uncanceled United States and foreign postage stamps in films for philatelic advertising purposes is permissible.

## U.S. and Foreign Revenue Stamps

Printed Illustrations of United States Revenue Stamps — Printed illustrations of United States revenue stamps are permitted under the same conditions and for the same purposes as illustrations of United States postage stamps, except that colored illustrations of United States revenue stamps are not permitted.

Printed Illustrations of Foreign Revenue Stamps — Printed illustrations of foreign revenue stamps are permitted on the same conditions and for the same purposes as illustrations of foreign postage stamps. Colored illustrations, but only of canceled foreign revenue stamps, are permissible.

Motion-Picture Films and Slides of Revenue Stamps — Films of United States and foreign revenue stamps are permissible in the same manner as films of United States and foreign postage stamps.

## Destruction of Plates and Negatives

The plates and negatives, including glossy prints, of paper money, postage stamps and revenue stamps, bonds, and other obligations and securities of the United States and foreign governments, used in printing the illustrations in publications must be destroyed after their final use for the purpose for which they were made.

No prints or enlargements from motion-picture films or slides of paper money, postage or revenue stamps, bonds, or other obligations are permitted, except prints may be made from such films or slides for the purpose of reproducing illustrations in publications, provided there is compliance with all other restrictions relating to the use of such illustrations.

## Excerpts From Applicable Statutes

. . . Title 18, U.S. Code, Section 474 - whoever prints, photographs, or in any other manner makes or executes, any engraving, photograph, print, or impression in the likeness of any . . . obligation or other security of the United States, or any part thereof, or sells, any such engraving, photograph, print or impression, except to the United States, or brings into the United States, any such engraving, photograph, print, or impression, except by direction of some proper officer of the United States; . . . Shall be fined not more than $5,000 or imprisoned not more than fifteen years, or both.

. . . Title 18, U.S. Code, Section 8 - The term obligation or other security of the United States includes all bonds, certificates of indebtedness, national bank currency, Federal Reserve notes, Federal Reserve bank notes, coupons, United States notes, Treasury notes, gold certificates, silver certificates, fractional notes, certificates of deposit, bills, checks, or drafts for money, drawn by or upon authorized officers of the United States, stamps and other representatives of value, of whatever denomination, issued under any Act of Congress, and canceled United States stamps.

. . . Title 18, U.S. Code, Section 15 - The term obligation or other security of any foreign government includes, but is not limited to, uncanceled stamps, whether or not demonetized.

Title 18, U.S. Code, Section 504 - Notwithstanding any other provision of this chapter, the following are permitted:

(1) the printing, publishing, or importation, or the making or importation of the necessary plates for such printing or publishing, of illustrations of

(A) postage stamps of the United States,

(B) revenue stamps of the United States,

(C) any other obligation or other security of the United States, and

(D) postage stamps, revenue stamps, notes, bonds, and any other obligation or other security of any foreign government, bank, or corporation, for philatelic, numismatic, educational, historical, or newsworthy purposes in articles, books, journals, newspapers, or albums (but not for advertising purposes, except illustrations of stamps, and paper money in philatelic or numismatic articles, books, journals, newspapers, or albums). Illustrations permitted by the foregoing provisions of this section shall be made in accordance with the following conditions —

(i) all illustrations shall be in black and white, except that illustrations of postage stamps issued by the United States or by any foreign government may be color;

(ii) all illustrations (including illustrations of uncanceled postage stamps in color) shall be of a size less than three-fourths or more than one and one-half, in linear dimension, or each part of any matter so illustrated which is covered by sub-paragraph (A), (B), (C), or (D) of this paragraph, except that black and white illustrations of postage stamps issued by the United States may be in the exact linear dimension in which the stamps were issued; and

(iii) the negatives and plates used in making the illustrations shall be destroyed after their final use in accordance with this section.

(2) the making or importation, but not for advertising purposes except philatelic advertising, of motion-picture films, microfilms, or slides, for projection upon a screen or for use in telecasting, of postage and revenue stamps and other obligations and securities of the United States, and postage and revenue stamps, notes, bonds, and other obligations or securities of any foreign government, bank, or corporation. No prints or other reproductions shall be made from such films or slides, except for the purpose of paragraph (1), without the permission of the Secretary of the Treasury.

# Private Express Statutes

## I. United States Code
## Excerpts From Title 18
### CHAPTER 83. POSTAL SERVICE

**Sec. 1693. Carriage of mail generally**

Whoever, being concerned in carrying the mail, collects, receives, or carries any letter or packet, contrary to law, shall be fined not more than $50 or imprisoned more than 30 days, or both.

**Sec. 1694. Carriage of matter out of mail over post routes**

Whoever, having charge or control of any conveyance operating by land, air or water, which regularly performs trips at stated periods on any post route, or from one place to another between which the mail is regularly carried, carries, otherwise than in the mail, any letters or packets, except such as relate to some part of the cargo of such conveyance, or to the current business of the carrier, or to some article carried at the same time by the same conveyance, shall, except as otherwise provided by law, be fined not more than $50.

**Sec. 1695. Carriage of matter out of mail on vessels**

Whoever carries any letter or packet on board any vessel which carries the mail, otherwise than in such mail, shall, except as otherwise provided by law, be fined not more than $50 or imprisoned not more than 30 days, or both.

**Sec. 1696. Private express for letters and packets**

(a) Whoever establishes any private express for the conveyance of letters or packets, or in any manner causes or provides for the conveyance of the same by regular trips or at stated periods over any post route which is or may be established by law, or from any city, town, or place to any other city, town, or place, between which the mail is regularly carried, shall be

fined not more than $500 or imprisoned not more than 6 months, or both.

This section shall not prohibit any person from receiving and delivering to the nearest post office, postal car, or other authorized depository for mail matter any mail matter properly stamped.

(b) Whoever transmits by private express or other unlawful means, or delivers to any agent thereof, or deposits at any appointed place, for the purpose of being so transmitted any letter or packet, shall be fined not more than $50.

(c) This chapter shall not prohibit the conveyance or transmission of letters or packets by private hands without compensation, or by special messenger employed for the particular occasion only. Whenever more than 25 such letters or packets are conveyed or transmitted by such special messenger, the requirements of section 601 of title 39, shall be observed as to each piece.

**Sec. 1697. Transportation of persons acting as private express**

Whoever, having charge or control of any conveyance operating by land, air, or water, knowingly conveys or knowingly permits the conveyance of any person acting or employed as a private express for the conveyance of letters or packets, and actually in possession of the same for the purpose of conveying them contrary to law, shall be fined not more than $150.

**Sec. 1698. Prompt delivery of mail from vessel**

Whoever, having charge or control of any vessel passing between ports or places in the United States, and arriving at any such port or place where there is a post office, fails to deliver to the postmaster or at the post office, within 3 hours after his arrival, if in the daytime, and if at night, within 2 hours after the next sunrise, all letters and packages brought by him or within his power or control and not relating to the cargo, addressed to or destined for such port or place, shall be fined not more than $150.

For each letter or package so delivered he shall receive 2 cents unless the same is carried under contract.

**Sec. 1699. Certification of delivery from vessel**

No vessel arriving within a port or collection district of the United States shall be allowed to make entry or break bulk until all letters on board are delivered to the nearest post office, except where waybilled for discharge at other ports in the United States at which the vessel is scheduled to call and the Postal Service does not determine that unreasonable delay in the mails will occur, and the master or other person having charge or control thereof has signed and sworn to the following declaration before the collector or other proper customs officer:

I, A.B., master — , of the — , arriving from —, and now lying in the port of —, do solemnly swear (or affirm) that I have to the best of my knowledge and belief delivered to the post office at — every letter and every bag, packet, or parcel of letters on board the said vessel during her last voyage, or in my possession or under my power or control, except where waybilled for discharge at other ports in the United States at which the said vessel is scheduled to call and which the Postal Service has not determined will be unreasonably delayed by remaining on board the said vessel for delivery at such ports.

Whoever, being the master or other person having charge or control of such vessel, breaks bulk before he has arranged for such delivery or onward carriage, shall be fined not more than $100.

**Sec. 1725. Postage unpaid on deposited mail matter**

Whoever knowingly and willfully deposits any mailable matter such as statements of accounts, circulars, sale bills, or other like matter, on which no postage has been paid, in any letterbox established, approved, or accepted by the Postal Service for the receipt or delivery of mail matter on any mail route with intent to avoid payment of lawful postage thereon, shall for each such offense be fined not more than $300.

Note: Sec. 1725 is not regarded as a Private Express Statute; however, its provisions may be relevant to Private Express violations.

# Excerpts From Title 39

## CHAPTER 6. PRIVATE CARRIAGE OF LETTERS

**Sec. 601. Letters carried out of the mail**

(a) A letter may be carried out of the mails when —

(1) it is enclosed in an envelope;

(2) the amount of postage which would have been charged on the letter if it had been sent by mail is paid by stamps, or postage meter stamps, on the envelope;

(3) the envelope is properly addressed;

(4) the envelope is so sealed that the letter cannot be taken from it without defacing the envelope;

(5) any stamps on the envelope are canceled in ink by the sender; and

(6) the date of the letter, of its transmission or receipt by the carrier is endorsed on the envelope in ink.

(b) The Postal Service may suspend the operation of any part of this section upon any mail route where the public interest requires the suspension.

**Sec. 602. Foreign letters out of the mails**

(a) Except as provided in section 601 of this title, the master of a vessel departing from the United States for foreign ports may not receive on board or transport any letter which originated in the United States that —

(1) has not been regularly received from a United States post office; or

(2) does not relate to the cargo of the vessel.

(b) The officer of the port empowered to grant clearances shall require from the master of such a vessel, as a condition of clearance, an oath that he does not have under his care or control, and will not receive or transport, any letter contrary to the provisions of this section.

(c) Except as provided in section 1699 of title 18, the master of a vessel arriving at a port of the United States carrying letters not regularly in the mails shall deposit them in the post office at the port of arrival.

**Sec. 603. Searches authorized**

The Postal Service may authorize any officer or employee of the Postal Service to make searches for mail matter transported in violation of law. When the authorized officer has reason to believe that mailable matter transported contrary to law may be found therein, he may open and search any —

(1) vehicle passing, or having lately passed, from a place at which there is a post office of the United States;

(2) article being, or having lately been, in the vehicle; or

(3) store or office, other than a dwelling house, used or occupied by a common carrier or transportation company, in which an article may be contained.

**Sec. 604. Seizing and detaining letters**

An officer or employee of the Postal Service performing duties related to the inspection of postal matters, a customs officer, or United States marshal or his deputy, may seize at any time, letters and bags, packets, or parcels containing letters which are being carried contrary to law on board any vessel or on any post road. The officer or employee who makes the seizure shall convey the articles seized to the nearest post office, or, by direction of the Postal Service or the Secretary of the Treasury, he may detain them until 2 months after the final determination of all suits and proceedings which may be brought within 6 months after the seizure against any person for sending or carrying the letters.

### Sec. 605. Searching vessels for letters

An officer or employee of the Postal Service performing duties related to the inspection of postal matters, when instructed by the Postal Service to make examinations and seizures, and any customs officer without special instructions shall search vessels for letters which may be on board, or which may have been conveyed contrary to law.

### Sec. 606. Disposition of seized mail

Every package or parcel seized by an officer or employee of the Postal Service performing duties related to the inspection of postal matters, a customs officer, or United States marshal or his deputies, in which a letter is unlawfully concealed, shall be forfeited to the United States. The same proceedings may be used to enforce forfeitures as are authorized in respect of goods, wares, and merchandise forfeited for violation of the revenue laws. Laws for the benefit and protection of customs officers making seizures for violating revenue laws apply to officers and employees making seizures for violating the postal laws.

## Questions Answered on Private Express Statutes

Effective Oct. 20, 1974, the Postal Service adopted revised regulations to implement the Private Express Statutes. Adoption of the regulations was preceded by studies of relevant legal and economic factors, and also by the publication of two Notices of Proposed Rulemaking which afforded the public opportunity to provide the Postal Service with views and comments.

The text of the new regulations was published in the Sept. 16, 1974 issue of the Federal Register, 39 F.R. 33211-33213. (An omission of a word was added to section 310.1 (a)(7)(vii) in the October 8, 1974, issue of the Federal Register, 39 F.R. 36114.)

Private carriage of intra-company letters is permitted only if postage is paid or if the carriage is by regular bona fide employees of the company. See Question and Answer IV.

Checks are not letters when traveling from, to, or between financial institutions. See Question and Answer VI. In other cases, checks are considered letters under the new regulations.

The questions and answers which follow are general guidelines but do not constitute an authoritative statement of the governing regulations. The Postal Service's regulations published in the Federal Register provide an authoritative source for guidance in this area. Answers to specific questions may be obtained by writing to the Assistant General Counsel, Opinions Division, Law Department, U.S. Postal Service, Washington, D.C. 20260.

**Q. I. What are the Private Express Statutes?**

A. A group of Federal statutes giving the Postal Service the exclusive right, with certain limited exceptions, to carry letters for others. The statutes are based upon the provision in the U.S. Constitution which empowers Congress "to establish Post Offices and post roads."

**Q. II. What is a "letter" for purposes of the Private Express Statutes?**

A. A "letter," as defined by Postal Service regulations, is a "message" directed to a specific person or address and recorded in or on a tangible object. The word "message" is defined as any information or intelligence that can be recorded by means which include, but are not limited to, written or printed characters, drawings, holes, or magnetic recordings, etc. The phrase "tangible objects" is defined as including, but as not limited to, paper (sheets or cards), recording discs, and magnetic tapes.

**Q. III. What is the basic purpose of the Private Express Statutes?**

A. To protect that portion of the Postal Service's revenues which is derived from the transportation of letters for others. This protection is needed to provide a secure economic foundation so that the Postal Service can render service throughout the country, irrespective of the "loss" or "gain" from its operations in any specific area.

**Q. IV. What, basically, do the Private Express Statutes require?**

A. The Statutes require, in general, that "letters" may be transported for others only by the Postal Service; alternatively, if means other than the Postal Service are used, the applicable postage must, generally, be paid. The basic prohibition is against a person's carrying letters for another person without payment of postage, i.e., operating in competition with the Postal Service. Therefore, an individual may transport his own letters, and a company may transport its own letters (but not those of a parent, subsidiary, or affiliated firm), if it uses its own regular salaried bona fide employees (not contractors or "casual" employees) to do so, even though postage is not paid.

**Q. V. Are intra-company letters covered by the Private Express Statutes?**

A. Yes, but see IV.

**Q. VI. Are any "messages" not treated as letters?**

A. Yes. For example, telegrams, newspapers and periodicals are not letters. In addition, checks, drafts and certain other financial instruments, securities, and title and insurance policies are not letters when shipped to, from or between financial institutions. As to checks and drafts, financial institutions are defined as banks, savings banks, savings and loan institutions, credit unions, and their offices, affiliates, and facilities. As to other instruments, financial institutions are defined as institutions which perform functions involving the bulk generation, clearance, and transfer to such instruments.

A special situation exists with respect to data processing materials. The Postal Service has exercised its authority to suspend the operation of the Private Express Statutes so as to allow any person to carry such materials for others, outside the mails and without payment of postage, if certain conditions are met. The transmission must be completed within 12 hours after leaving the sender, or by noon of the addressee's next business day, and the data processing must commence within 36 hours after receipt at the data processing center.

Persons wishing to transport data processing materials (for others) under the suspension, must file certain information with the Postal Service. The necessary forms may be obtained from the Private Express Liaison Officer, Customer Services Department, U.S. Postal Service, Washington, D.C. 20260.

**Q. VII. Did mailers have a voice in establishing the Postal Service's Private Express regulations?**

A. Yes. The Postal Service informed mailers and the public and its new regulations were published in the Federal Register on July 2, 1973, and again on Jan. 31, 1974. All views and arguments were reviewed and evaluated. The present regulations of the Postal Service were adopted only after this process was completed.

**Q. VIII. Are earlier regulations or issuances of the Postal Service on the Private Express Statutes now obsolete?**

A. To the extent that they are contrary to the regulations published in the Sept. 16 and Oct. 8, 1974 issues of the Federal Register, any opinions, regulations, or publications of the Postal Service (including POD Publication 111, "Restrictions on Transportation of Letters," Fifth Edition, July 1967, republished June, 1973) should no longer be used as the basis for decisions or actions by mailers or others.

**Q. IX. In those situations in which the Private Express Statutes and regulations permit the carriage of letters without the payment of postage, can such letters be placed into, or attached to, or hung from letter boxes or other receptacles for the receipt or deposit of mail?**

A. No.

**Q. X. How can I obtain additional information about the Private Express Statutes?**

A. Write to the Assistant General Counsel, Opinions Division, U.S. Postal Service, Washington, D.C. 20260. If you want information about the applicability of the Private Express Statutes to a specific situation, submit a complete statement of the facts and, if possible, examples of the materials in question. The Assistant General Counsel, Opinions Division, will render advice and will also furnish copies of the Private Express regulations which the Postal Service adopted, effective Oct. 20, 1974.

# Citizens' Stamp Advisory Committee

# 6

# History and Purpose

The purpose of the Citizens' Stamp Advisory Committee is, officially, to "provide the Postal Service with breadth of judgment and depth of experience in various areas which influence subject matter, character and beauty of postage stamps."

The 12 to 16 members, appointed for one-year terms, are selected to reflect a wide range of educational, geographic and professional backgrounds, with the graphic arts, philately, history and education well represented.

## Meetings

They meet at the call of the postmaster general, usually six times a year, for an all-day session, working from an agenda prepared by the Postal Service's Stamp Development Branch.

Actually the committee has two separate but related functions. It is charged with recommending subject matter, and with developing and recommending stamp designs.

In both areas, as its name indicates, the committee is merely advisory. Although most committee recommendations are accepted, the sole responsibility for United States stamps is the postmaster general's and the final decision on both subjects and designs is his.

Some subjects recommended by the committee are not approved; some subjects not recommended by the committee are approved by the postmaster general. Occasionally the committee is notified that the postmaster general has decided to issue a stamp on a subject never before the committee.

Committee recommendations are sent to the postmaster general after each meeting. His decisions, recommendations or statements of policy are reported back to the committee, usually at the start of the next meeting.

There have been two changes of emphasis in the committee's work in recent years. One has been a continuing effort to gain enough lead time to permit the best possible art and printing.

There will always be a few stamps that must be issued on a rush schedule. But this is no longer true of the bulk of the stamp program. In early 1982 programs for 1983 and 1984 were pretty well blocked out with preparation of art well under way, and some subjects were identified as far ahead as 1993.

The other change has been an increasing dependence on the work of subcommittees. Every stamp request that reaches the Postal Service is considered, if only briefly. The committee operates by affirmative action and consensus, though votes are taken when necessary. A new subject is held for further action or referred to a subcommittee if a single member shows an interest in it.

The subcommittees represent a variety of areas — American History, Folk, Literary and Performing Arts, Black Heritage, Sports and Topical subjects — and are headed by committee members with special qualifications or interests in the subjects covered. Reports of the subcommittees provide a better informed basis for full committee discussions.

## Subject Matter

There is no lack of subject matter for the committee to consider. The Postal Service receives about 1,500 different stamp suggestions each year. The committee's job is to select about 15 of them for a coordinated calendar-year program to be recommended to the postmaster general.

The goal is to select the most important, interesting or educational of the available subjects, but decisions are made with all users of the Postal Service, not just stamp collectors, in mind. The mix is important. Topical subjects of the type that repeatedly lead the Linn's popularity poll are not pushed out of the program because something else seems more "important" or because a philatelic organization can be expected to impose a "black blot."

## The Artist

When a subject is approved, usually after considerable discussion, it is turned over to the committee's design coordinators to assign an artist. The artist is selected because he is known for his work in a desired field — wildlife, uniforms or horse racing, for example. A design coordinator briefs him on the special requirements for stamp art and the committee's suggestions for the particular subject. For new artists a visit to the Bureau of Engraving and Printing may be arranged for a thorough briefing on reproduction requirements.

The artist is placed under contract with the Postal Service. Payment is $750 for preliminary art visualizations, rough sketches for the committee's consideration, and an additional $750 for finished art. The maximum $1,500 payment per design is reduced to $1,250 for three to four designs in the same set and $1,000 for five to ten. After that fees are negotiable.

A reproduction subcommittee previews all stamp art to make sure it can be printed effectively by the presses available at the Bureau of Engraving and Printing, and art is not submitted to the full committee until all necessary reproduction revisions have been made.

The full committee makes the decisions on graphic design and the way the subject has been handled by the artist, though naturally the opinions of members with an art or printing background are given special weight, as are the opinions of the design coordinators, who are no longer voting members of the committee. Usually choice of a design is by consensus, but step by step voting is conducted as necessary. Some striking designs are given immediate approval. Others are sent back to the artist three or four times with suggestions for revision, or rejected outright. If necessary, a new artist is commissioned.

## Compensation

Members of the committee who are officials or employees of other government agencies, such as the Bureau of Engraving and Printing, the National Gallery of Art or the Smithsonian Institution, receive no compensation for their work on the committee. Members appointed "from private life" are entitled to a fee of $188 a day, a figure tied to the entry level of the Postal Service's senior executive service. Those from outside the Washington area are provided with travel requests for air transportation and actual travel expenses for food and lodging.

## History and Membership

The idea of an advisory committee to improve United States stamp design developed in the 1930s and 1940s. Foreign countries were beginning to issue colorful stamps in modern graphic designs and both stamp collectors and artists were asking why the United States could not have colorful stamps. Harry L. Lindquist, publisher of "Stamps" magazine and friend of many New York artists, provided a bridge between philatelists and artists.

In 1941 Paul Berdanier, a New York advertising agency art director, formed a Committee of Volunteer Artists in an effort to improve stamp art. Members included W. A. Dwiggins, Clarence Hornung, Gordon Grant, Robert Fawcett, Gustav Jensen, Fred Cooper, Stanley Crane, Warren Chappell, Sam Marsh, Lucien Bernhard, Walter Dorwin Teague and later Paul Manship and Leon Helguera.

In 1942, through Lindquist's contacts with the Post Office Department, the committee was given an opportunity to design a "United Nations for Victory" commemorative. After an informal competition postal officials selected a "United Nations" sketch by Helguera and a plaster cast by Manship on a "Four Freedoms" theme. Characteristically, both designs were modified extensively without consulting the artists.

The next decade has been described as the lowest point in United States stamp design. Stamp art was assembled at the Bureau of Engraving and Printing from bits and pieces provided by stamp sponsors and approved by postal officials with no knowledge and little appreciation of art. But with the inauguration of President Eisenhower in 1953 a new element entered the picture.

The Republicans had promised to get government out of areas that could be better handled by private industry and Postmaster General Arthur E. Summerfield decided to make a start with stamps. As it turned out, the lithographic firm given an opportunity to print a new bicolor 8-cent stamp couldn't do it as well as the Bureau.

Meanwhile, the Fine Arts Commission, which had been actively supervising commemorative coin design, indicated an interest in stamps, much to the consternation of postal officials, who didn't want another agency looking over their shoulders.

The political implications made stamp subjects and designs difficult enough. But in 1955 the commission, the National Academy of Design and the Post Office Department agreed to set up a committee of artists to advise on stamp design.

It was a distinguished group — Norman Kent, Fritz Eichenberg and Anthony de Francisci with Thomas Maitland Cleland, Paul Manship and Edward A. Wilson as alternates. But there was considerable foot-dragging in the Post Office Department. No formal meeting was ever held, and apparently the artists were consulted informally only once or twice.

## Summerfield Committee

The situation changed abruptly in 1957 when L. Rohe Walter, Summerfield's special assistant for public information, suddenly realized the public relations potential of an effective stamp program and arranged to have the Division of Philately, which had been under Finance, placed under his control.

Walter checked the files, asked advice, and killed several birds with one stone by forming his own seven-member Citizens' Stamp Advisory Committee — three philatelists, three artists and an official of the U.S. Information Agency to coordinate stamps with the government's then extensive foreign propaganda activities.

Members of the Summerfield committee were:

**ABBOTT WASHBURN**, Washington, D. C. (March 1957-January 1961). Washburn, deputy director of the U.S. Information Agency, technically was an alternate for the director, Arthur Larson. **ROBERT SIVARD and C. ROBERT PAYNE** at times attended meetings as alternates for Washburn.

**H. L. LINDQUIST**, New York, N.Y. (March 1957-January 1961). Lindquist, named as chairman of the National Federation of Stamp Clubs, had been active in President Eisenhower's People to People program.

**FRANKLIN R. BRUNS JR.**, Takoma Park, Md. (March-November 1957). Bruns was named as curator of the Smithsonian Institution's Division of Philately and Postal History. He resigned from the committee on accepting appointment as director of the Post Office Department's Division of Philately, but served as the committee's ex officio chairman.

**SOL GLASS**, Baltimore, Md. (March 1957-January 1961). Glass, a department store official, was named as president of the Bureau Issues Association.

**ARNOLD COPELAND**, Fairfield, Conn. (March 1957-January 1961). Copeland was named as president of Westport Artists, Inc., Westport, Conn. He was director of visual planning for the Kudner advertising agency in New York.

**ERVINE METZL**, New York, N. Y. (March 1957-January 1961). Metzl, named as president of the Society of Illustrators, was by far the strongest force on the committee for improvement of stamp design.

**WILLIAM H. BUCKLEY**, New York, N. Y. (March 1957-January 1961). Buckley was named as president of the Art Directors Club of New York. He was art director for Benton and Bowles, Inc.

**ROBERT E. FELLERS**, Washington, D.C. (August 1957-January 1961). Fellers was named a member ex officio after his retirement as director of the Post Office Department's Division of Philately.

**BERNARD DAVIS**, Philadelphia, Pa. (December 1957-January 1961). Davis, who succeeded Bruns on the committee, was named as founder and director of the National Philatelic Museum in Philadelphia and chairman of the Stamp Committee of President Eisenhower's People to People program.

**DONALD R. McLEOD**, Chevy Chase, Md. (April 1958-January 1961). McLeod was named ex officio as superintendent of the Engraving Division, Bureau of Engraving and Printing.

The committee, with Metzl leading the way, did succeed in improving stamp designs considerably, but fought without success to increase color flexibility through use of photogravure and lithography as well as recess engraving.

Committee members, ex officio members and alternates were presented the Post Office Department's Benjamin Franklin Service Award by Postmaster General Summerfield at the committee's final meeting on Dec. 15, 1961.

## Day Committee

The inauguration of President Kennedy in 1961 and his selection of J. Edward Day as his postmaster general brought some sharp changes of direction. James F. Kelleher took over the supervision of philatelic policy and Day named a new Citizens' Stamp Advisory Committee conspicuously lacking the U.S. Information Agency representative.

Members of Postmaster General Day's committee were:

**BRUCE CATTON**, Bethesda, Md. (April 1961-February 1963). Catton, a historian noted for his works on the Civil War and editor of American Heritage magazine, was named to provide sound historic judgment within the committee.

**JOHN WALKER**, Washington, D.C. (April 1961-January 1969). One of the world's leading art gallery directors, Walker brought with him not only art judgment but the resources of the National Gallery. **J. CARTER BROWN**, his deputy, served frequently as his alternate.

**NORMAN TODHUNTER**, New York, N.Y. (April 1961-January 1969). Todhunter, an art director with the J. Walter Thompson advertising agency in New York, was the strong art figure on the committee with a coherent stamp design policy. He fought for and eventually won greater flexibility in color printing.

**JOHN MAASS**, Philadelphia, Pa. (April 1961-February 1965). Maass, visual presentation director for the City of Philadelphia, like Todhunter, served as an art director in the development of many stamps.

**DONALD R. McLEOD**, Chevy Chase, Md. (April 1961-February 1965). McLeod, who as superintendent of the Engraving Division at the Bureau had served ex officio on the former committee, was named a regular member of this one.

**GEORGE W. BRETT**, Washington, D.C. (April 1961-August 1963). Brett, a geologist with the U.S. Geological Survey, was vice president (later president) of the Bureau Issues Association and an authority on United States stamp production.

**DAVID LIDMAN**, New York, N.Y. (April 1961-January 1969). Lidman, chief makeup editor and stamp columnist for the New York Times, was president of the American Philatelic Congress and a director of the American Philatelic Society. Lidman was named chairman of the committee in May 1962 after the resignation of Franklin Bruns as director of the Division of Philately, a post in which he had been serving ex officio as chairman.

**DR. JAMES J. MATEJKA JR.**, Chicago, Ill. (April 1961-August 1963, and February 1965-January 1969). Dr. Matejka was an active philatelist and co-founder of Chicago's COMPEX show.

**ROBERT W. BAUGHMAN**, Liberal, Kan. (April 1961-August 1963). A wealthy wheat farmer and stamp collector, vice president (later president) of the Society of Philatelic Americans.

**ROGER KENT**, San Francisco, Calif. (April 1961-January 1969). An attorney, stamp collector, and chairman of the California Democratic Central Committee.

**WILLIAM N. POSNER**, Rochester, N.Y. (April 1961-March 1967). Certified public accountant, topical collector, and chairman of the Democratic County Committee in Monroe County, N.Y.

**STANLEY H. FRYCZYNSKI JR.**, Bayonne, N.J. (April 1962-August 1963). A funeral director active in New Jersey politics and president of the American First Day Cover Society.

**MRS. CATHERINE DRINKER BOWEN**, Philadelphia, Pa. (February 1963-August 1963). A historian named to replace Bruce Catton, who had resigned.

## Gronouski Committee

Postmaster General Day resigned in August 1963 and his Stamp Advisory Committee went out of existence. His successor was John A. Gronouski, who selected as his special assistant for public information and philately a young newspaperman, Ira Kapenstein. A new committee was not named until February 1964 when Lidman, Walker, Todhunter, Maass, McLeod, Kent and Posner were reappointed.

In February 1965 Dr. Matejka was reappointed to the committee and there were three other changes.

**REUBEN K. BARRICK**, Arlington, Va. (February 1965-January 1969). Chief of the Office of Designing, Engraving and Development at the Bureau of Engraving and Printing, replaced Donald McLeod, who had retired.

**WALTER KRAWIEC**, Chicago, Ill. (February 1965-March 1966). An editorial cartoonist for the Polish Daily News in Chicago, replaced John Maass, who had resigned because of ill health.

**ROGER L. STEVENS**, Washington, D.C. (February 1965-January 1969). Special assistant to the president on the arts and chairman of the John F. Kennedy Center for the Performing Arts, was added.

## O'Brien Committee

When Lawrence F. O'Brien replaced John Gronouski as postmaster general in November 1965 he asked members of the committee to continue to serve, and also retained Ira Kapenstein, who quickly became his right-hand man in many areas.

In March of 1966 O'Brien made three new appointments.

**STEVAN DOHANOS**, Westport, Conn. (March 1966-January 1969). An artist, illustrator and designer of a number of stamps, was added in place of Krawiec and immediately began serving as an art director, working with other artists assigned to design stamps. Although his term, like that of the rest of the committee, expired in January 1969, he in fact served continuously until his designation as a nonvoting design coordinator in January 1978.

**ANDREW WYETH**, Chadds Ford, Pa. (March 1966-March 1967). One of the best known and most popular of American painters. He resigned at the end of his one-year appointment.

**KURT WIENER**, Washington, D.C. (March 1966-January 1969). Wiener, owner of H. K. Press in Washington, lithographers of art gallery and museum publications, brought a needed background in modern printing techniques to the committee.

In March 1967, with the departure of Wyeth and Posner, O'Brien named two new members.

**BELMONT FARIES**, Clifton, Va. (March 1967-January 1969). News editor of the Washington Star, stamp columnist and editor.

**DR. ELSIE M. LEWIS**, Washington, D.C. (March 1967-January 1969). Dr. Lewis, acting head of the Department of History at Howard University in Washington, provided a needed professional background in American history.

## Watson Committee

In April 1968 Marvin Watson, President Johnson's special assistant and appointments secretary, was named postmaster general replacing O'Brien, who had resigned to direct Robert Kennedy's campaign for the presidency. Watson named Bill McSweeny his special assistant for public information and philately and asked O'Brien's Stamp Advisory Committee to continue. He did make three additions during a little more than nine months in office.

**DR. JOHN P. ROCHE**, Washington, D.C. (June 1968-January 1969). A special consultant to the president on leave from Brandeis University, where he had been professor of history and politics.

**MRS. ALBERT D. LASKER**, New York, N.Y. (July 1968-January 1969). Philanthropist in many medical fields who had been interested in the Beautification of America program sponsored by Lady Bird Johnson.

**WILBUR J. COHEN**, Silver Spring, Md. (November 1968-January 1969). Secretary of Health, Education and Welfare and a stamp collector.

## Blount Committee

With the inauguration of President Nixon, his postmaster general, Winton M. Blount, asked for the resignations of the Citizens' Stamp Advisory Committee. Four members, Chairman David Lidman, Norman Todhunter, John Walker and Roger Kent, had served continuously since 1961.

Blount named James M. Henderson as his special assistant for public information and philately, and Virginia Brizendine, director of the Division of Philately, was persuaded to remain for a few months to aid in the transition. In July 1969 Blount announced his new Citizens' Stamp Advisory Committee.

**STEVAN DOHANOS**, Westport, Conn. (July 1969-January 1978). Dohanos, the only member of the old committee reappointed, had carried on the stamp art work of the department during the interim. He was named chairman of the new committee.

**J. CARTER BROWN**, Washington, D.C. (July 1969-January 1978). Newly appointed director of the National Gallery of Art. He had served as an alternate for John Walker from 1961-1969. **JOHN BULLARD** and **HOWARD ADAMS** served as his alternates.

**JAMES A. CONLON**, Burke, Va. (July 1969-July 1977). Director of the Bureau of Engraving and Printing. **KENNETH DeHART** and **EDWARD FELVER** served as his alternates.

**BRADBURY THOMPSON**, Riverside, Conn. (July 1969-January 1978). One of the country's most distinguished designers and an authority on typography who had been responsible for several postage stamps. Along with Stevan Dohanos, he was named a nonvoting design coordinator in January 1978.

**JAMES B. WYETH**, Chadds Ford, Pa. (July 1969-January 1978). Son of Andrew Wyeth and an outstanding young artist (he was then 23.)

**MRS. PAUL MELLON**, Upperville, Va. (July 1969-October 1973). Philanthropist and art patroness.

**WALTER G. MacPEEK**, North Brunswick, N.J. (July 1969-died Jan. 21, 1973). Retired Boy Scout official and stamp editor of Boys' Life magazine.

**COL. RANDLE B. TRUETT**, Arlington, Va. (July 1969-September 1975). Historian for the National Park Service, lecturer and philatelist.

**FRED W. SPEERS**, Escondido, Calif. (July 1969-died Aug. 30, 1971). Savings and loan official and philatelist.

**EDWIN A. MORRIS**, Greensboro, N.C. (July 1969-June 1971). Business executive and clothing manufacturer.

**MRS. IKE KAMPMANN JR.** (later Mrs. Holt Atherton), San Antonio, Tex. (October 1969-June 1971).

## New Blount Committee

In October 1971 Postmaster General Blount, shortly before resigning, named a new Citizens' Stamp Advisory Committee for the Postal Service, reappointing all of the old members except Fred Speers, Edwin Morris, and Mrs. Kampmann, and adding five new members.

**WILLIAM DOUGLAS ARANT**, Birmingham, Ala. (October 1971-September 1975). A past president of the Alabama Bar Association.

**FRANKLIN R. BRUNS JR.**, Takoma Park, Md. (October 1971-died March 24, 1979). Bruns, who had served on the first Stamp Advisory Committee in 1957, and then had been ex officio chairman as director of the Division of Philately from 1957 to 1962, returned as curator of the Smithsonian Institution's Division of Postal History.

**EMERSON CLARK**, Burbank, Calif. (October 1971 — ). An aeronautical engineer with Lockheed Aircraft Corp., chairman of the American Philatelic Society's recruiting program and later APS president.

**BELMONT FARIES**, Clifton, Va. (October 1971 — ). Newspaperman, stamp columnist and editor who had previously served from March 1967 through January 1969.

**ROBERT OSTERHOFF**, Rochester, N.Y. (October 1971-September 1975). Founder and executive secretary of the Junior Philatelic Society of America, then 24.

## Bailar Committee

Postmaster General Elmer T. Klassen continued the Blount committee, but his successor, Benjamin F. Bailar, made several changes in

September 1975. Belmont Faries was designated chairman and Stevan Dohanos and Bradbury Thompson design coordinators with responsibility for stamp art. Col. Truett, Douglas Arant and Robert Osterhoff were dropped, and six new members named.

**ERNEST BORGNINE,** Beverly Hills, Calif. (September 1975 — ). Movie and television actor and stamp collector.

**JAMES J. MATEJKA JR.,** Chicago, Ill. (September 1975-January 1978). Dr. Matejka, prominent Midwest philatelist, had served twice on earlier committees, April 1961 to August 1963 and February 1965 to January 1969.

**DR. VIRGINIA NOELKE,** San Angelo, Tex. (September 1975 — ). Professor of history, Angelo State University.

**JOHN SAWYER III,** Chicago, Ill. (September 1975 — ). Educator, superintendent of a Cook County school district.

**JOHN THOMAS,** New York, N.Y. (September 1975-July 1981). Well known stamp collector long active in the American Topical Association. He resigned because of illness in July 1981 and died Jan. 6, 1982.

**DR. DOROTHY WORCESTER,** Somers, Conn. (September 1975-October 1979). Design specialist, director of consumer research for the Milton Bradley Company.

## Bolger Committee

In January 1978 Postmaster General William F. Bolger reappointed Faries, Bruns, Clark, Borgnine, Noelke, Sawyer, Thomas and Worcester. Wyeth, who had been too busy with his art career to attend meetings, and Dr. Matejka, who had a conflicting assignment, were dropped. Carter Brown declined reappointment because of pressures of his duties at the National Gallery of Art. Conlon had not been replaced after his retirement as director of the Bureau of Engraving and Printing, but the Bureau was represented by his successors as director, Seymour Berry and Harry Clements, with technical advice of Edward Felver and Leonard F. Buckley. Dohanos and Thompson continued to serve as design coordinators, but without a committee vote.

The changes left the committee rather short on voting members, and in October, 1979 Postmaster General Bolger reorganized it with six reappointments and ten new members.

Chairman Belmont Faries, Ernest Borgnine, Emerson Clark, Dr. Virginia Noelke, John Sawyer and John Thomas were reappointed. New members were:

**THEODORIC C. (TED) BLAND,** Kansas City Mo.(August 1979 — ). Retired district manager/postmaster at Kansas City, and stamp collector. Joined the committee in August 1979, filling the vacancy left by the death of Franklin Bruns. His appointment was announced with that of the other new members in October.

**HARRY CLEMENTS,** Washington, D.C. (October 1979 — ). Director of the Bureau of Engraving and Printing. He had represented the Bureau at committee meetings since his appointment as director in January 1979.

**WILBUR J. COHEN,** Austin, Tex. (October 1979 — ). Former Secretary of Health, Education and Welfare and a stamp collector. He had been a member of the committee from November 1968 to January 1969.

**RAUL GANDARA,** Santurce, Puerto Rico (October 1979 — ). Retired fire chief of Puerto Rico and stamp collector.

**DR. C. DOUGLAS LEWIS,** Washington, D.C. (October 1979 — ). Curator of sculpture, National Gallery of Art.

**EDWARD MALLEK,** Honolulu, Hawaii (October 1979 — ). Retired businessman and stamp collector.

**JAMES A. MICHENER,** St. Michaels, Md. (October 1979 — ). Novelist, historian and stamp collector. Accepted appointment with the understanding that he would not be able to attend meetings immediately. Became an active member in January 1981.

**MRS. MARY ANN OWENS,** Brooklyn, N.Y. (October 1979 — ). Accredited international stamp show judge, officer of the American Topical Association and topical stamp collector.

**HOWARD E. PAINE,** Washington, D.C. (October, 1979 - May 1981). Art director of National Geographic magazine, expert in graphics, printing and typography and stamp collector. Named design coordinator succeeding Stevan Dohanos, who gave up the assignment to devote full time to his painting.

**MS. CLAIRE WILBUR,** New York, N.Y. (October 1979 — ). Film producer and topical stamp collector. Ms. Wilbur did not serve.

Two new members were named to the committee in 1981:

**DERRY NOYES,** Washington, D.C. (May 1981 — ). Illustrator and designer, head of her own graphics firm, Derry Noyes Graphics. She filled the vacancy left by Howard Paine's acceptance of the design coordinator post.

**DR. JOHN WEAVER,** Rancho Palos Verdes, Calif. (September, 1981 — ). Geographer and educator, president emeritus of the University of Wisconsin System and professor of geography at the University of Southern California. Filled the vacancy left by the resignation of John Thomas.

One new member was announced early in 1982:

**JERRY PINKNEY,** Croton-on-Hudson, N.Y. (March 1982 — ). Well known artist and graphic illustrator, designer of all of the stamps in the

Black Heritage series through the Whitney Young issue of 1981.

## Liaison

Postal Service liaison with the Citizens' Stamp Advisory Committee is through Mary Margaret Grant, manager of the Stamp Development Branch, and Jack Williams, coordinator for the committee.

Because of the administrative burden associated with the large number of stamp subject suggestions each year, the Postal Service does not encourage direct correspondence with members of the committee, but will forward presentations. The address is Citizens' Stamp Advisory Committee, c/o Stamp Development Branch, U.S. Postal Service, Washington, D.C. 20260.

Formal requests for issuance of a stamp should be sent to the Postmaster General, U.S. Postal Service, Washington, D.C. 20260.

# The Butterflies Block of Four

The history of every stamp is different, and the amount of involvement by the Citizens' Stamp Advisory Committee varies considerably. From the committee's point of view the results may be a failure, adequate, or a real success. This is the story of a success.

The Butterflies block of four was by far the most popular stamp issue of 1977, piling up nearly three times as many votes as its closest competitor in the annual Linn's Stamp News Poll.

The result was no surprise to the Stamp Advisory Committee of the Postal Service's Stamps Division. The stamps had been carefully planned in every step of design and production to appeal not only to collectors but to the general public. This time the planning paid off.

The record on the Butterfly stamps begins with a late 1973 letter to Postmaster General

Elmer T. Klassen from Robert M. Pyle, director of the Xerces Society and at that time a graduate student at the Yale University School of Forestry and Environmental Studies. The society, he explained, consisted of more than 200 scientists and lay citizens from 41 states united by a concern for endangered populations of butterflies and moths. It took its name from the Xerces Blue, a butterfly species that became extinct due to environmental changes around San Francisco Bay in the 1940s.

The Xerces Society, Pyle wrote, would host the First World Conference on the Conservation of Lepidoptera, to be held in the Pacific Northwest in 1977, and they would like to have a commemorative stamp, or preferably a block of four, picturing endangered American species from various parts of the country — The Ponceanus Swallowtail, the Karner Blue, the Atala Hairstreak and the Nakomis Fritillary, or if only one, the Ponceanus Swallowtail, an endangered Florida butterfly of great beauty.

It was a model stamp request — a scientific sponsor interested in wildlife conservation, an international meeting, and even specific design suggestions for an obviously popular subject.

The request was placed on the agenda of the Citizens' Stamp Advisory Committee for its next meeting on Feb. 21, 1974. The committee didn't reach the item at that meeting but did at its next on June 5, 1974. To a committee well aware of the popularity of topical collecting, any request for stamps picturing butterflies was a winner. It was placed on hold for 1977, but with the suggestion that the butterflies need not be endangered.

Early in 1976 Donald McDowell, manager of the Stamp Development Branch, asked the Advisory Committee's design coordinator, Stevan Dohanos, to select an artist. There was quick agreement on Stanley Galli, the California wildlife artist who had already designed three stamp issues selected as the most popular of the year — the Wood Ducks of 1968 and the Wildlife Conservation blocks of four of 1971 and 1972, all produced by a combination of offset lithography and recess engraving. Galli was available and was placed under contract.

Although the art should be the major consideration in selecting the method of printing for a stamp, press scheduling and costs also must be considered. Officials at the Bureau of Engraving and Printing, looking at the rest of the 1977 program, suggested gravure on the Andreotti press, which could use six inks, five for the butterflies and the sixth for a background color.

The most flexible form of gravure printing is process color, in which tiny dots of yellow, magenta, cyan and black create a visual illusion of full natural color. But the dot structure makes it an inherently fuzzy process. If the art is suitable, sharper results can be obtained by adding one or two flat or self colors, or by using all self color.

When Galli called McDowell for guidance he was told that though the butterflies should come from different areas of the country, the choice was his, with pattern and color the chief consideration. He should avoid process color if at all possible, selecting four butterflies that could be painted in the same five self colors and a background that would be appropriate to all.

Galli understood what was wanted and quickly came up with sketches, some with background foliage, one with a shadow effect on a neutral background. He was told to work out a block of four using that approach.

The Advisory Committee, at its meeting of April 9, 1976, saw Galli's sketches and a previously unannounced block of four attractive designs by Frank Waslick of the Bureau of Engraving and Printing. Unable to make a fair comparison between Waslick's finished art and Galli's sketches, the committee directed the Stamps Division to procure finished art from Galli and send it and Waslick's art to the postmaster general for a final choice.

When Galli's art, done in yellow, orange, purple, umber, gray and black arrived, Postmaster General Benjamin F. Bailar approved it. It was sent to the Bureau on May 10, 1976, followed on June 9 by carefully checked overlay lettering. The Stamp Advisory Committee saw the already approved art at its meeting of June 18. It was all they had hoped — four different butterflies, colorful wing patterns sharply defined, shadows lifting them from the neutral background. Only one thing more was needed — high quality printing.

The Bureau had provided photographic models on June 16. There was no need to rush, but cylinder proofs were approved on Dec. 22, 1976. Printing began on March 24, 1977.

First day arrangements had been unusually smooth. Back in April 1976, when the Stamps Division began coordinating first days and press utilization for 1977, it became obvious that plans for the First World Conference on the Conservation of Lepidoptera had collapsed. The stamps no longer had a sponsor. But this was not a problem. The stamps had no inscriptions referring to the conference, and the habitats of the four butterflies covered most of the United States. Almost any city would be suitable and any warm weather month would do. May was selected in arranging the year's production schedule.

Processing first day covers is a heavy burden on post offices and the Postal Service likes to spread the work as fairly as possible. Usually it is difficult. With the butterflies it was merely a matter of checking which region had the lightest load assigned for 1977. It was the Midwest Region with two. The butterflies made it three.

Picking a first day city was delegated to the regional office in Chicago, with the criteria that it should not have had a first day recently and should have an active stamp club to help with the first day ceremony. The choice fell in Indianapolis, which had not had a first day since the 30-cent special delivery stamp of 1957 and did have an enthusiastic club.

Indianapolis postal officials found equal enthusiasm everywhere they asked for help. The city's new Children's Museum provided an ideal site. The Indianapolis Stamp Club provided volunteers. Purdue University's Department of Entomology joined in, and enlisted the support of the Entomological Society of America, which had failed to get a stamp for an international conference the year before. The Indiana Department of Resources helped. Two collectors of Butterfly stamps offered exhibits. A Boy Scout honor guard and a high school band were enlisted. Assistant Postmaster General Robert H. McCutcheon came from Washington to speak at the ceremony.

The arbitrarily assigned first day ceremony was one of the most successful of the year. The Butterfly stamps were a success with the public, too. They had proved, if proof was needed, that all you need for a popular stamp is a subject people will like, a colorful and graphically effective design by an experienced artist, and a first class job of reproduction by the printing process best suited to the art.

You can't get that combination with every issue, but it pays off when you do.

# Stamp Selection Who and Why

Contained in the U.S. Postal Service booklet "Stamp Selection Who and Why" are the seven criteria against which all stamp proposals are measured. In order to acquaint the general public — from whom virtually all suggestions for stamp subjects come — these criteria are listed.

## Criteria

1. Living Persons — No living person shall be honored by portrayal on any United States postage stamp.

2. Significant Anniversaries — All postage stamps, including commemoratives, honoring individuals will be issued preferably on significant anniversaries of their births, and not before 10 years after their deaths. The exceptions are memorial stamps and regular issues honoring recently deceased presidents. The 10-year rule was adopted in 1971.

(It should be noted it is not always possible to issue stamps on exact anniversary dates. Stamps are seldom issued on Sundays or national holidays, and occasionally stamps cannot be delivered to post offices in time to be placed on sale on the most appropriate day.

(For instance, Clara Maass was born June 28, 1876, but the stamps honoring her were not issued until Aug. 18, 1976. It is important to note, however, that it was issued during the year marking the centennial of her birth. It should be further noted that the United States does not issue stamps on anniversaries of death, and those who assume the Clara Maass issue marks the 75th anniversary of her death in 1901 are making a mistake).

3. Historical Anniversaries — Commemorative postage stamps of historical significance shall be considered for issuance on even-date anniversaries, preferably starting with the 50th year and continuing at 50-year intervals.

4. Themes and Events — Only themes and events of widespread national appeal and significance will be considered as subjects for postage stamps.

(The Committee acknowledges that "widespread national appeal and significance" is impossible to define, and that decisions made on stamp proposals always have been, and always will be, debated. Most suggestions for stamp issues come from people who do not collect stamps. Committee members for years have been puzzled by the reluctance of the people who know most about stamps to offer suggestions for them).

5. Organizations — Commemorative stamps shall not be issued to honor fraternal, political or sectarian organizations, a commercial enterprise, or a specific product.

6. Charitable Organizations — Commemorative stamps are not considered appropriate for charitable organizations. Posters, labels or seals issued by philanthropic organizations to raise funds, as well as postal slogan cancellations, are more useful in arousing public interest.

7. Cities, Counties, Schools — Commemorative stamps shall not be issued for cities, towns, municipalities, counties, schools or institutions of higher learning, since so many are reaching anniversaries primarily of local or regional significance. Due to the restrictions which must be placed on the stamp program, it would be most difficult to single out one anniversary for commemoration.

Stamp eligibility criteria tend to evolve, and present criteria are subject to change. The committee is receptive to suggested policy changes, and from time to time it adopts additional standards in response to changing situations.

For example, during 1976, the committee developed a policy which allows the issuance of single stamps to commemorate statehood anniversaries at 50-year intervals on the actual anniversary date. Prior to enactment of the statehood policy, the committee realized that of the 50 states, 47 would be observing significant anniversaries of statehood between 1978 and 2001. By disallowing the recognition of the 25th and 75th anniversaries, the committee prevented the stamp program from being inundated with the proposals for statehood issuances.

### REPRODUCTION OF POSTAGE STAMPS

Designs of postage stamps issued after Jan. 1, 1978, are copyrighted and may not be reproduced except under license granted by the U.S. Postal Service. Earlier designs are in the public domain and may be reproduced without permission for philatelic, educational, historical and newsworthy purposes. When reproducing any designs, those protected by copyright or those in the public domain, it is necessary to comply with Title 18, U.S. Code, Section 504 as amended. This statute provides that uncanceled stamps when reproduced in actual colors must be depicted less than 75 per cent or more than 150 per cent of actual size in any linear dimension.

# Fun and Profit 7

## The Investment Scene

### By Dr. Stan Showalter
### (All Rights Reserved)

Dr. Showalter is a psychologist and criminologist at Western Michigan University. In addition, he provides consulting services to law enforcement agencies and is in private practice. He has authored Linn's "Stamp Investment Suggestions" column since 1971 and is presently the philatelic investment editor for Linn's, and is a contributor to Stamp World magazine.

### Warming Up

To make my job easier, let's assume that there are only three reasons why you are reading this chapter. Probably most of you are philatelists who have an interest in seeing a profit out of your hobby for once rather than a long line of check stubs for money spent with little financial return.

A second reason may be that you're a philatelist who has invested in stamps already — sometimes wisely, sometimes foolishly — and you just want to see if you can find anything new here.

The third reason could be that you know nothing at all about stamp collecting but want to put some capital into stamps as an investment vehicle; so you hope that by reading this chapter you can become a well-informed stamp investor.

I hope to be able to reach you to one degree or another, and I hope the information provided will be useful, particularly if it encourages you to be cautious.

My own personal philosophy about philatelic investing can best be characterized as "conservative." I believe stamps are an excellent investment vehicle, but I also believe they should be purchased and held for longer periods of time — three to five years at least. It's important that you understand this because that philosophy will make itself felt throughout this chapter.

Since 1970 or so I have been writing columns and articles for stamp investors; for more than ten years my columns have appeared almost ex-

clusively in Linn's Stamp News. I gave up watching my own track record several years ago, but some of my readers have not, and what they tell me is that the record has been pretty good. So I feel my credentials are in order, and now that you know that we can proceed.

### Wisdom or Folly?

So you think you want to invest in stamps? Seems to make a good deal of sense. After all, practically everyone has heard over the years that money invested in stamps has done as well or even better than other "collectibles." On the other hand, the past two years have seen some pretty severe fluctuations in the stamp market, with some stamps booming and some busted. But, to confuse things, many stamps have continued right on rising in price through all the smoke and furor.

And who hasn't heard of all the "big" money which large corporations are putting into buying up stamp companies, philatelic publishers, and the like? What it all says is that the big guys with the "smart" money are plunking large chunks of their assets down on stamps. If it's good enough for them, it certainly ought to be good enough for you, right?

Well, not necessarily. I've already stated that I am bullish on stamps as investments, but let me spend several paragraphs trying to scare you off if I can. That way we'll get rid of the faint-hearted and perhaps save them both grief and money in the long run.

First, there is no guarantee that the money you put into stamps will grow. Even in inflationary times, there still is no guarantee, and especially is there not a guarantee that your stamps will grow in value faster than the current rate of inflation, whatever it may be.

Just indiscriminately buying up stamps to salt away in a safe deposit box is folly of the worst kind. Don't do it. Stamps are a commodity whose supply and demand both fluctuate considerably from time to time and place to place. No one — repeat — no one can guarantee profit from stamps.

A second argument against investing in stamps is that they are not as easily disposed of as stocks and bonds, or even gold and silver. The people who buy and sell stamps all day long are a comparatively small group when lined up against stock brokers and commodity brokers.

Furthermore, selling a hundred shares of stock is simply a matter of picking up your phone, initiating a sell order to your broker, and that's that. Under normal market conditions, the sale is guaranteed, although perhaps not at the price you had hoped.

With stamps, the picture is different. Perhaps no one wants your stamps at all — that's happened to more "stamp investors" than I would like to think about. There simply is no market for your stamps at the time you wish to get rid of them. No sale.

Or, you may find to your horror that stamps which cost you dearly may be sold at a stamp auction (one of the major methods of disposal) for a fraction of what you paid. Some investment.

Third, many observers feel that a large number of philatelic items are beginning to top off — they've gone as high as the market will take and now are beginning to soften.

Put another way, some advisors would counsel that it's too late for you to get into stamps because the best material has long since been secreted away, and all that is left is inferior material at exhorbitant prices.

While I personally believe that is not true in general, it certainly is the case for large numbers of philatelic properties. The idea, my father used to tell me, is to buy cheap and sell dear. If you enter the stamp market when prices are already higher than the market warrants, obviously the only way to go is down, reversing the advice.

Fourth, some of the properties of the beast itself make fiddling with it difficult. Stamps are small and easily lost, stolen, or damaged. If they are bought with unused gum on the backs, they require special storing and care, for if the gum becomes disturbed, the value of the stamp decreases. (The gum was only for licking and sticking in the first place, but stamp buyers become very emotional about "undisturbed gum.") Along with the problems of storage and theft, it obviously becomes necessary to take out insurance on your stamp properties, an additional expense.

Fifth, stamps tend not to be good vehicles for the short-term investor who is unable to follow closely what the market is doing. This means they make more sense for long-range investment instead, and some investors want a quicker turnover for their money.

In addition, stamps are often the subjects of intense market manipulations by speculators who buy up all they can find of a particular set, allow its "scarcity" to drive up the price, then dump their entire stock on the philatelic marketplace, take their profit, and watch as prices plummet.

Only a handful of people in the know ever really have inside information regarding which stamps are being thus artificially manipulated; the rest of the collecting/investing world trudges on unknowingly until it is too late, and their investment is lost.

There are ways to avoid this problem, and I'll discuss them later. But it is a very real situation which anyone contemplating putting money into stamps should understand. There is no Securities and Exchange Commission to watchdog the philatelic community; all we rely on is the integrity of a large number of dealers, and knowing who they are takes a long time.

For the nonphilatelist, stamp investment can be a total disaster. There are several reasons why, so I want to address that particular person in the section which follows.

But for now, suffice it to say that it will take a good year for an interested — repeat — interested nonphilatelist to develop the basic skills and knowledge necessary for him to avoid losing his shirt in stamps.

The world of philately has its own vocabulary, which is enough to stump a neophyte: "fine, unused, original gum" describes the condition of a stamp. But who is to fathom such jargon at the onset?

Since I have brought up the subject of condition, let me add a seventh caution. The value of a stamp is partly decided by its condition. Stamps are made of paper, are flimsy at best, and are subject to the rigors of kicking about in life for rather long periods. In this case, how well the stamp has fared on its journey determines in part the price to be paid.

A common disadvantage to stamp investment is that stamps are often described by sellers in higher grades than they might be by impartial third parties. Only an experienced philatelist or a very well-read newcomer can determine the true condition of a stamp about to be purchased.

Finally, large numbers of stamps over the years have been altered in various ways or forged completely. Once again, the neophyte has no way of knowing that he is being sold a dead horse unless he has had the horse examined by someone who knows about those things.

There are other drawbacks to investing in stamps, but these are among the major ones, and they are, I feel, things you should consider before you even think about committing your funds to developing a stamp investment portfolio.

In spite of all this, I continue to believe that stamps can be superb investments for the wary and the astute.

## First Things First

The foregoing paragraphs deal with what's wrong with stamps as an investment. Now I want to change the focus from stamps to you. Too many people jump into stamp investment without looking carefully first. It seems to me that a prospective investor has to take a hard look at himself and his total financial picture before he can with justification and confidence sink hard-earned money into a stamp portfolio. Let's examine rather briefly some of those considerations and in so doing, put first things first.

Investing in stamps is a risk; there is no sure-thing, regardless of what various advertisements may tell you. Risk implies that you could lose money as well as make it; risk implies that you could lose practically everything you have invested.

Are you financially prepared to assume that kind of risk potential? If you're retired and on a conservative fixed income, I think not. If you're a kid with a paper route and hope to get your money back out of your stamps by the onset of spring baseball, forget it.

What I am really saying is this; if you are in a tight fix for funds and can't afford to risk your investment, stay out of stamps in lieu of something with a guaranteed return. If there is a good possibility that you may suddenly need to convert your stamps into cash on very little notice, stay out of the stamp market.

First because it is difficult to accomplish, and second because if that is the case you have spread your investments too thinly and have overextended the safety factor. Having to sell investment stamps in a hurry is a horrible experience which almost always bottom-lines in red ink.

Another question which you ought to examine about yourself is whether or not you have the temperament to invest in stamps. As stated earlier, stamp prices tend to move with less volatility than stock and bond prices. There is no daily ticker to ponder, no broker calling breathlessly to tell you it's time to get rid of the stock.

Things move at a more leisurely pace within the philatelic marketplace, and that means you will have to have great patience. That patience requires that you feel comfortable buying stamps thoughtfully and carefully, putting them away in your safe deposit box, and letting them sit there for very long periods of time, usually years.

Not everyone has the personality to handle that kind of investment. Some people want to see the action going down, receive the breathless calls, feel the adrenalin surge as they make a killing. That just doesn't happen in stamps. Prices tend to float up and down, not leap. And that's just too dull for many investors used to more exciting markets.

A final question I believe you should ask yourself is to what degree your investment in stamps will compare with your other investments. I do not believe stamps should be the sole investment vehicle in which you are involved; such a plan is very risky and may result in a financial calamity for you.

A balanced investment picture makes more sense, with assets distributed in a variety of vehicles, including ready cash assets, real estate, automobiles, education, various other financial instruments, and other collectibles. If the only thing you invest in is stamps, you could be in for a stunning awakening.

Jumping into the stamp market without thinking carefully about these things and without balancing other assets is suicidal. If you're inclined to do so, then you'd better get some very solid advice from someone less emotionally involved and more experienced.

## To The Unwashed

If you're not a philatelist, then you are confronted with several problems, among them ignorance, inexperience, and perhaps naivete. All of these or any of them can spell financial disaster for you if you go into stamp investment blindly.

As you will see in the fifth section of this chapter, it takes knowledge of stamps and the stamp market in order to be a successful investor. While some people may disagree as to just how much a prospective investor in stamps really needs to know about his purchases, I don't think anyone would disagree that the uninformed buyer is doomed before he begins.

Some of you simply do not have the time or inclination to spend boning up on philately, yet you want to invest in stamps. I think that is a dangerous proposition, but there is a way around it. In fact, there may be several ways around it. I know of one chap who is sold on stamps for investment but doesn't know a perforation from a commemorative. But he has an advantage. He has a brother who does!

So what he does is to follow a leading investment writer's biweekly investment suggestions. He lists the stamps he wants, copied directly from the newspaper, sends his list to his brother who in turn knows where and with whom to deal in order to find good stamps at decent prices. Brother A sends the stamps to Brother B, who locks them up at the bank.

There is a variation on the same theme, and that is to have a friend who can perform the same favor — perhaps even with a small commission for his trouble.

There is a danger to this plan. It puts you entirely in the hands of some writer's expertise. There are plenty of people writing about stamp investment today, but not all of them pick winners, and not all of them provide sensible advice. Before I would even think about following this plan, I think I'd want to study the fellow's track record for awhile.

For the nonphilatelist without brothers, friends, or time to read investment columns, there is another possibility for investing in stamps, and that is the stamp investment folio service. Since even experienced philatelists often rely on folio services, I will make them the subject of the next section.

Before leaving the neophyte, let me say this: If you haven't the time or interest to invest in learning about stamps, but you are determined to use them as an investment vehicle, perhaps the selection of a reputable, competent stamp investment advisor or folio service is the only realistic avenue open to you.

## Folio Services

Because the investment folio service is of interest to people other than nonphilatelists, I've chosen to make this a separate section. It seems to me that there are several questions which ought to be answered: What is a stamp investment folio service? Who might profit from using one? How do they work? How do I pick a good one? Are there things to look out for? How do I find one?

As noted in the preceding section, I believe that the nonphilatelist who has no interest or time to find out about stamps is suicidal if he thinks he can make a profit from stamps all by himself. He needs the advice and expertise of someone more knowledgeable than himself. For many, that "someone" is a philatelic investment broker, or operator of a folio service, to be more exact.

But I think philatelists, too, might profit from investing a portion of their funds with a specialist in investment. Unless you are exceedingly informed about stamps and their market, and unless you have plenty of good buying and selling contacts, then you may not be much more ahead of the neophyte who knows practically nothing about stamps.

The stamp market is a rapidly changing business arena where millions of dollars are spent annually. Only someone who deals regularly inside that arena really knows what's going on; all others are spectators at best, and that usually includes the collector who has now decided to put some of his funds into investment grade stamps.

So that collector needs advice, and he needs good advice. Some philatelists obtain their investment advice from the many investment writers who abound. Philatelists at least know something about stamps, so they probably take a number of stamp publications, have a few catalogs and books on stamps, and make good conversation frequently with other collectors.

That background of knowledge and information should give them an assist in dealing with their stamp investment folio service, and they ought then to have an edge when it comes to deciding whether or not this fellow knows what he's talking about.

But they still need his expertise, just as the nonphilatelist does, because he is (hopefully) an insider. Incidentally, I think a very good plan for those with adequate funds is to apportion so many dollars per month to be used by the folio service and another, smaller amount to be used by the investor who likes playing his own hunches and wants to be in on the fun of picking some winners himself. Sometimes he discovers that he does as well as or better than the folio service.

So what is a stamp investment folio service? Usually it is an individual working either independently or with a larger philatelic firm. He is supposedly very much involved in the philatelic market, knows what's good and what's a dog, what may be good in the months and years ahead, and what should be avoided like the plague.

To my knowledge, there is presently no philatelic investment folio service representative who is a registered investment broker with the Securities and Exchange Commission, so we're not using the word "broker" in the same sense as if we were talking about stocks.

In the past six or seven years, folio services have proliferated as more stamp people have seen the depth of the attraction which stamps have for a variety of buyers.

In other words, lots of "folio services" have crept out of the woodwork because there's profit to be made (and perhaps investors to be had). I do not mean that simply because a service is new it is disreputable; that just is not the case. I'll point out more about how to spot a good one later on.

How does the service work? In a variety of ways, but usually like this. Each month, you send the service a check for a specified amount.

In return, the service uses its knowledge and information to select what it feels are stamps for your folio which have potential for increased value. They send you the stamps, and you put them away in your safe deposit box. Some services may also buy your stamps back, while others will assist you in selling your stamps when you decide to do so.

One other extra which you might find with some services: they may produce a newsletter or market advisory. I have a personal belief that these things are frills and that you end up paying for them in the long run in the price charged you for your stamps. Some services make a subscription charge for the newsletter, and only a regular perusal of its advice will tell if it is really worth it or not.

How do you find a folio service, and once you do, how do you know if it is a good one? Most services advertise widely in the philatelic press. Others operate, as noted previously, as just one of many philatelic services offered by larger stamp companies. A few letters of inquiry and the examination of several philatelic periodicals should provide you with many possibilities.

I think you should send for their information to see what they offer. If someone responds by phone and starts putting the old "time is of the essence" bit on you, that should be all the warning you need to fend him off.

Don't be overly impressed by glossy, slick brochures; having money enough to pay the printer says nothing at all about the wisdom and safety of the investment program that advertiser is selling. Unfortunately, too many woeful readers have written me that sad tale over the past several years: "I thought they must know what they're doing — their brochure looked so good!"

It seems to me that what you are looking for is someone who already has built a solid reputation as a philatelic investment advisor-broker. This someone should be happy to answer all your questions regarding his qualifications, his basic investment philosophy, and, perhaps most important of all, his track record.

Caution is advised on the last, because anyone can spit out sets of stamps he allegedly sold customers five years ago which have tripled in value since then. What kind of printed information does he have available? Have his selections been made public over time in a newsletter or some other form of publication? That's a proven track record, not a manufactured one.

How well balanced is the total portfolio over a year's time? Too many "experts," in my opinion, limit themselves to a very narrow range of stamps. As you will see later, I think that is foolish; it bespeaks the "all the eggs in one basket" syndrome, and if it were my money, would make me very nervous indeed. So balance is important.

Another factor is price. Your profit will be based almost entirely on two values: what you pay for the stamp and what you sell it for; it's that simple. If you find that you are paying the earth for stamps which sell much (15 per cent or more) cheaper elsewhere, you may want to move on.

Some folio dealers charge a commission for their services; others simply sell you the stamps and take their "commission" out of the profit they made between wholesale and retail.

Both systems are all right, unless you find you are paying double — retail markup and seller's commission. Again, that's time to look for someone else, because the price you are paying is so high that it may be months or years (if ever) before your purchase begins to appreciate over the buying price.

So good reputation, availability to clients, a reasonable investment strategy, a proven track record, a balanced portfolio, and the prices charged are all factors which should interest you before you commit your funds to any investment service.

Finally, there are cautions. Because of the recent proliferation of investment services, many of us who are vitally concerned with stamp investment have been horrified at some of the tales sorrowful investors have brought to us. Unfortunately, every investment "broker" is not honest and competent; some are as dishonest as can be, and they only want to shear the sheep.

If you start getting stamps in your folio from off-beat places, or if you find nothing but very recent new issues from large countries, or if you just start getting the feeling that your "broker" is a collector cleaning out his album, it's time to get out while you can.

This has by no means been a comprehensive discussion of investment folio services, but I hope it has given you something to think about.

There is nothing wrong with investment folio services provided you can find one run by a philatelist who is honest, competent, and on the inside of the market. They are uncommon but well worth the hunt, because they usually will help you make a profit.

## What It Takes

So here you are, money clenched tightly in fist, crouched to leap upon the first good opportunity that comes along, and more than ready to make a profit in stamps. The only question left to be answered, it seems, is how do you do it?

Well, on the surface it looks fairly simple. First, you buy stamps which will increase in value. Next, you hold them for a specified period of time, preferably in a safe place such as a safe deposit box at your local bank. Third, you sell them for more than you paid, thus realizing a profit. Then, you pay your capital gains tax and sit back to enjoy your profits.

You see? There's nothing to it. But wait. If it's that simple, why aren't more people doing it? And how come you don't have to go very far to hear from people who didn't make a profit in stamps?

A good question, because it seems there is no philatelic publication you can read or stamp show you can attend that you won't run into several people who snort in disgust at the idea of making money in stamps. They've tried it and lost their shirts (or to be less melodramatic, didn't make a profit). Some of them are very intelligent people who should have had an edge on the whole business, but they lost money instead. Why?

There could be a number of explanations, but one which seems to hit home more often than not is that they were not properly prepared to invest in stamps in the first place. They never took the time to sit down and effect an investment strategy. They didn't have time to learn how to invest in stamps; they just wanted to make a killing in the stamp market, so in they plunged. And that's where they drowned.

It's important, I believe, to do some thinking and preparing before you invest your money in stamps. In the sections which follow, I want to develop first of all that concept for you; then we will look specifically at the three phases of stamp investing — buying, holding, and selling.

## Before You Buy

Knowledge. Everything else I am about to say in this section points directly back to that word, for the "secret" of successful stamp investing lies in obtaining, sorting, and using knowledge about yourself, about stamps, about the philatelic market, and about economics in general.

If you are not prepared to invest a considerable amount of time in seeking this knowledge, then I suggest you stop reading now and either let an advisor invest your money for you or stay completely out of the stamp market. To do otherwise in such a frame of mind is guaranteed folly. You will not make money in stamps. You will stand an excellent chance of losing what you already have to begin with.

That's a pretty strong statement, but I believe it completely. Too many letters and telephone calls have come my way, too many tales of woe and knowledge come too late, for me to believe otherwise. In the end it is the uninformed and uncaring who get soaked — either by themselves or by the many eager hands waiting in the shadows of the philatelic marketplace.

The first step in successful stamp investing is to spend no money at all. Rather, it is to begin preparing yourself to understand stamps and their market so that when you do invest your money you have improved the chances of seeing it again.

The second step is to read everything you can about stamps and the market and stamp investing. Be sure you read from a wide variety of sources (while I am often flattered by readers who claim to read nothing but my column, I feel guilty and concerned for them, too, because they need to be obtaining other viewpoints at the same time for a balanced picture).

While you are thus educating yourself, marshal your ready cash reserves. Give serious thought to how much of your extra available funds will go into stamps. Set a limit on how much you will spend in any given period: monthly, quarterly, annually, etc. (I always like to keep a small "hot find" fund around so I can take advantage of those occasional, rare opportunities to buy something really good at a savings. That's an event on which you can't always plan, but it often presents an unusual opportunity to acquire something special.)

Remember, you haven't actually spent a nickel yet; you're still in the preparatory stage. As you continue reading publications and studying catalogs, you should expand now to investment-specific writings: regular columns in the philatelic press, special publications devoted exclusively to stamp investors, and other things which begin to provide specific answers to your questions.

By now you should be following the market rather closely so that you cannot only watch what is happening to the prices of specific stamps, but also so you can begin to perceive the broader trends in the market. As with gold or stocks or gems, it makes little sense to buy at the top of the market along with everyone else; that's too late. What you want to do, it seems to me, is to foresee the wave and ride it in.

Now I think you're ready for the next phase, called "let's pretend." You've read everything you could; you've set aside adequate funds; you think that at last you're getting pretty good at picking winners. Now you should put yourself on the spot. Begin selecting a few sets which you would like to buy. Don't buy them. Just select them, perhaps half a dozen a month. Then start charting their progress (you hope).

This is actually easier to do if your "picks" start downward; it means you aren't so hot after all. When it gets tough is when they all start to zoom. That is the point at which you will have to exert greatest self-control to avoid throwing all this preparation to the wind, rushing into a phone booth, and emerging as Supervestor. Be patient. Give it some time and see what happens.

Believe me, there will always be other opportunities to make a profit in stamps; don't talk yourself into believing that this is the last ship for home, because it just isn't. You may find the "zoom" is short-lived and the bottom falls out of your wonderful winners. Thank goodness you only invested time, not money. Now try to find out why things went awry and what you might have done to foresee just such an event.

After several months (yes, months) it is time to check your track record. I know this is inane, because you've probably been sneaking a peek every night under the blanket with your flashlight. But now, officially, formally, the time has come to make out your own report card. How have you done? All losers? Then something is wrong with your input. All winners? Then, my friend, you are ready to do it for real. (Actually, not many of us could pick all winners, so don't expect perfection; being able to pick a majority of winners should satisfy most investors.)

By now you are a different person. You know so much more about the stamp market than you did awhile ago that it amazes you. You know that you can exert the self-control which is mandatory in stamp investing because you have done it. You know that you have developed a calm, rational, unemotional basis for deciding what will go into your investment portfolio and by so doing you have multiplied your chances of success.

In my opinion, it should have taken you about a year to accomplish this goal. I base that estimate on the assumption that you have had to continue working while you learned, that you have had other requirements of your time and attention, and that this self-learning project has had to be accomplished on a spare-time basis.

I want to emphasize again that investing a year in learning about stamps and their market is a very small investment compared to losing what capital you may have. Unfortunately, you can't convince some people of that until they've learned it the hard way.

Now you are ready!

## Buying

In this section I am combining really two aspects of stamp investment: a brief description of the sources of supply for stamp investors as well as some general comments and observations about some of these sources and the strategies for using them.

What follows is based on what I believe to be a fundamental premise, and that is that the price you pay for a set of stamps is extremely important. (There is an exception to that rule, and I'll discuss it later.)

Since you are going into stamp investment precisely with the motive of making a profit, then it seems to me to be important to get the price you pay for your stamps down as advantageously as possible so that when you sell the net profit can be as large as possible.

This is not the old business of "buy stamps cheap and sell them dear," because these days the best investment material is already priced "dear" to begin with. Rather, I am saying that

the stamp business is a competitive one and that very seldom does one dealer and only one dealer have an item which you might like to add to your investment portfolio. Thus it behooves the potential buyer to do some shopping around whether he does so in person (going from shop to shop) or by mail.

There is one major exception and perhaps a minor one, too. The major exception to this rule is when you are after a unique or practically unique philatelic piece, one which just never comes on the market or is so rare that even by paying a premium price you have ensured future profits. In that case — and I believe it is rare — you may decide to buy the stamp at whatever price it takes to get it.

The minor exception has to do with the feeling which some investors have that it pays in the long run to develop an on-going relationship with one or two dealers and to do most of your business through them. While often you may pay a bit more for the material they sell you, you can be assured that it is genuine, that it is in the described condition, that they will stand behind the merchandise, and, perhaps most important, that as the dealer comes to know what you are doing, he can assist you by being on the lookout for special items of value.

Some of the nicest items I have purchased for my own folio have come through dealer-friends who knew they had found something in which I would be interested. So this is something you will have to weigh for yourself. Of course there is a compromise; you can regularize your purchases with a dealer or two but continue to do some shopping around with a percentage of your monthly or quarterly investment money.

But I'm getting ahead of myself. Investors seeking to purchase stamps in person are usually more limited than those who use the mails to buy. Buying in person usually restricts the buyer to the following sources: collectors, retail shops, sellers at stamp shows and bourse.

If you live in New York City, that's not much limitation, but most of you don't; you're up in Vermont or out in Montana or on an Indiana farm, and you just don't have access to the kinds of sources a New Yorker might.

Fortunately, the majority of the stamp business is done by mail. Buyers and sellers send checks and stamps back and forth in a bustling commodity market which the mercantile exchange never sees. Using the mail broadens the buying horizons enormously by expanding your purchasing potential into six areas.

First, if you wish, you can run a "buy ad" in the philatelic press for the stamps you seek: "Private collector seeks early Swiss semipostals in MNH condition. Send description (not stamps) for offer." That sort of thing.

Frankly, I have never found this to be a very effective source of good investment material. It can be a source of some headaches as you begin to deal with some "crawl out of the woodwork" types. Considering the buying rule mentioned, this method greatly increases your purchasing price if you are lucky enough to find some decent material. If you are contemplating large purchases of selected items, you may want to consider the buy ad, but otherwise I don't recommend it.

A second and often overlooked source of investment stamps is the philatelic society sales circuits. Of course, you must be a member (but if you're legitimately interested in stamps you ought to be a member anyway), which entails dues, etc.

The interesting thing about buying investment grade stamps through sales circuits is that, in inflationary times, most of these circuits have been tossing about the country for months, even a year or so. This means that when they were originally priced and put up for sale, the value was probably lower than it is now.

So a careful investor can purchase excellent investment items at a considerable saving over the current retail price. Disadvantage? It's a slow method. Answer? Have your name placed on several countries lists so that you can keep the circuits coming on a rather regular basis.

I'm not personally crazy about new issues for investment, but some people are and have done rather well at it. So, for the investor who likes the challenge of very high risk, buying stamps from the government of issue at the time of issue is a third source of supply which should be mentioned.

Unless there is something funny going on behind the counter, there is no cheaper way to buy stamps than at the time of issue. The trick is knowing which stamps to pick, and I can't help you there, because there simply is no "system" other than the obvious one of buying the new issues of whatever countries are currently "hot." I don't like that kind of buying because I think it interjects too great a risk element into investing.

Probably the greatest single source of supply for investors is the retail dealer. There are all kinds of dealers, ranging from the huge retail company which stocks the entire world's philately to the part-time shoestringer whose complete stock will fit into two shoeboxes in the bedroom closet.

Some dealers are retail only; others are wholesale only; and still others sell at all levels. Some are generalists while others specialize in periods or topics or specific countries. It's a rugged, individualized, dog-eat-dog marketplace out there in spite of what you may have heard. You begin to realize that when you carefully study dealers' advertisements over a long period and see how many come and go as opposed to how many come and remain.

It takes time for most investors to find the right dealers with whom to develop a buying relationship. I recommend taking plenty of time in this process, because five or ten years from now, the quality of your investment folio will directly reflect the quality of your dealer relationships. If you picked competent people to help you, your folio will show that. And it will show it if you didn't, too.

Begin with a smaller order, and don't tell your dealer that you're an investor. Just sit back and see what kind of quality and service you get for your money. Does he send really nice quality stamps? Are his prices reasonable (not necessarily the lowest)? Does he have any special personal touches which indicate to you that if you become a "regular" he will take good care of you? How does he handle your complaints and questions?

All these things are important to the investor who is in search of a good marriage between his money and a dealer. Don't give your money to a dealer who won't give you something in return.

Another reason for a strategy of small beginning orders is to protect you from dishonest dealers. Oh yes, the woods are full of them, as many of you can attest. It's far better to lose a few dollars than a few hundred or several thousand, and I've heard from investors of all three categories when it comes to unscrupulous dealers who have bilked them out of their cash. So go cautiously; you'll be glad you did.

Another suggestion. After you have established yourself as a steady, serious buyer, there's nothing wrong with asking your dealers if they will allow a quantity purchase discount (either if you purchase so many sets or if your purchases run to a specified amount). Many dealers are very happy to do this, but generally they won't make the offer if you don't ask first.

Remember, many dealers are "small guys," and you may have become one of their biggest customers; that ought to be worth something to them and to you, and I suggest it should come out as a discount on your purchases. So ask; you've nothing to lose. If your dealers agree, the price you are paying goes down and allows for a greater profit margin at the other end.

This brings me to another source of supply, the wholesaler. If you frequently make large quantity purchases (either sets or dollars), you could be able to buy at wholesale, not retail. How? Simply by following the wholesalers' advertisements, writing, asking for a price list or quote, and sending a check.

Some wholesalers will refuse your order because you are not a dealer, but there are others who just can't turn down that check, and they'll sell to you at the wholesale price.

This brings a howl of protest from retailers, but wait just a minute. If you remember that most stamp retailers are "little guys" themselves, buying fairly small amounts of stamps from the same wholesalers, the perspective changes a bit. In fact, you may be buying more from the same wholesaler than your former retail dealer did!

Obviously, this suggestion does not fit well for the investor who is putting $30 a month into stamps; but it can work well for the large, regular purchaser, and I suggest it to you as another means of cutting down on the price you pay.

Finally, philatelic auctions provide a fine source of stamps for discriminating investors. Here, perhaps more than anywhere else in the philatelic marketplace, you will pay closest to the actual value of the stamp. (This is not always true because some unscrupulous auction dealers play little games with their unseen customers, but in the main, especially with the public auction, it holds.) Investors can either go to auctions or — and most of them do it this way — simply mail in or telephone in their bids on specific items up for sale. The stamp goes to the highest bidder.

If your controls are poor, stay away from the public auction! Bid by mail and mail only. I've seen too many buyers get the glint of combat in their eyes during a public auction and end up with overpriced stamps, an empty checking account, and a very large lump in their throats.

On the other hand, if you are steelyminded and can control yourself, the public auction can be great fun and often profitable. I suggest getting the catalog well in advance, studying market prices, and setting a very firm limit on what you will bid for each item. Stick with it and don't waver at all, or you're done for.

If you bid by mail, be sure to get the "prices realized" leaflet so you can see why it was you either (a) paid a foolishly high price for stamps, or (b) sent in two hundred bids and got nothing. The prices realized information is a perfect source of market information and feedback to you so you can bid more successfully the next time.

Don't be discouraged if you get nothing the first time or two; as you grow in knowledge and bidding sophistication, the results will begin to show, and you will pick up some really valuable items for your portfolio.

One last comment about these sources of supply. It might be a good idea to try a variety of them; I have not intended to suggest that only one method is ideal, because that simply is not accurate. Successful investors derive their properties from a variety of the sources I have briefly discussed here, and so should you.

A caution or two.

If you are contemplating the purchase of an especially valuable philatelic property, insist on having it expertized prior to purchase. Often this already has been done, and a certificate of authenticity will accompany the stamp. But frequently it has not been done.

Most dealers, provided with adequate surety, will permit the property to be examined by a philatelic expert prior to its purchase. There are simply too many regummed stamps being sold as "original gum, mint, never-hinged," and the potential buyer should be aware of exactly what he is buying.

There are too many forgeries afloat from practically every country to make expertization unnecessary. Of course it costs to have it done.

I've saved this point for last. We have paid particular attention where to buy your investment material and the importance of paying a good price for it, but there is one factor which begs mentioning and emphasis, and that is condition. If I were underlining words, that one would have five or six lines beneath it, because condition is essential in evaluating a stamp.

What I'm saying is this: make sure you find stamps of the very best quality you can afford. Here, as in gems, there is always something even better for a higher price, so of course you must set some limits in this area.

But by all means don't be hoodwinked into buying some scrubby looking reject under the guise of a "superb investment." The condition of the front and the back of the stamp is vital to investors: brightness of color, clarity of design, centering, absence of damage such as missing perforations, bends, folds, tears, "thins," etc. All of these factors and more go into judging the condition of the stamp.

True, a very few stamps are so rare that their condition in unimportant, but this will usually not be the case for the stamps which you are considering for inclusion in your investment folio. Condition is vital, and you should insist on stamps of the finest condition you can afford.

I have no intention of saying anything at length about the gum side of the stamp, or the so-called "never-hinged craze." Personally, I oppose devaluing a perfectly magnificent stamp simply because it has the trace of a hinge mark on its gummed side.

Realistically, however, this is important to investors because so many buyers place the never-hinged qualification on their purchases. This drives up the price, and we are increasingly seeing a widening of the prices between stamps which remain with virgin gum and those which have been violated.

Finally, some stamps simply cannot be found in never-hinged condition; some copies cannot be found with anything except broken gum; some stamps are very old and simply have not survived well, but their value is still great, and they should not be ignored when it comes to their possible folio inclusion.

The hallmark to follow is whether or not the stamp can commonly be found in better condition; if it can, buy it instead of the inferior edition you have before you. If it cannot and the stamp is scarce in any condition, consider it carefully before you reject it for something newer and shinier — and possibly of less real value.

## Care and Feeding

Typically, the person who invests in postage stamps does so in smaller purchases and over a longer period of time. True, there are a few who make one huge buy and then salt the stamps away, but generally it happens the way I first described.

Many investors in stamps seem to think that once they have made a purchase, their work is over. All they need do now is sit back, wait for time to pass, and then collect their rewards for being so smart. They are wrong.

Two extremely vital processes are still ahead, and how the investor handles his purchases in both processes will have a great determination not only as to how much profit he will realize, but also as to whether or not he will even make a profit at all. The first of the processes will be discussed here, the second in the following section.

It just isn't good enough merely to buy stamps and drop them in an old shoe box to wait for them to appreciate in value. Investment stamps require a certain amount of care and feeding, just as any other valuable property would. First, remember that stamps are extremely fragile; they are easily creased, torn, or lost; they can have perforations bent or lost if improperly handled.

So a primary step to be taken is to protect the stamps from those exigencies. This means finding a means of storing them which will enhance their protection, such as card stock with pockets and protective covering. It also means denial of the temptation to handle your stamps excessively.

I recommend in the strongest possible way that you store your stamps in a safety deposit box. That kind of protection will help you avoid overhandling, but there is a much greater reason: it will reduce the chance of loss by theft or robbery.

You may not realize it, but stamp investment is big business and involves a great deal of money. Thieves recognize it, you can be assured, and they work very hard to find out who is investing in stamps and where they keep them. Home invasions, robberies, and thefts of stamps are increasing alarmingly, and partly because investors are so completely thoughtless about how they store their purchases.

Investment stamps (a) should never be kept at home or office, (b) should be well insured, and (c) should be safely locked up at the bank until they are sold. To do less than that, in my opinion, is very foolish. You can't make a profit on stamps you don't have!

Along the same line, use a post office box for your stamp dealings; don't advertise to the world where you live so burglars can locate you any easier than they already do. Maintain a low profile as a stamp investor with the same principle in mind. And when you do cash in your stamps, be careful to whom you brag about how much you made — he may talk to the wrong people, too!

So far, I've said stamps are fragile and need to be kept protectively in a safe deposit box. I've said you ought to keep them insured, and you should keep a low profile as an investor.

Care and feeding of the folio also mandates that you keep careful records of your purchases and sales. This is so you can know for sure if you are making a profit, but it is also because you will need these records in case of loss of the stamps and in case you experience an IRS audit. I won't say more about stamps and taxes because that subject is covered more exhaustively and thoroughly in a separate chapter by the Crumbleys. Keep records; you'll be sorry if you don't.

Assuming that your investment in stamps is made in an on-going fashion as opposed to the single-purchase method, there is something else you should be doing regularly with your portfolio. I call it "emptying the garbage."

At least every six months, I feel you should get out your folio inventory sheet and start looking at the trends in the market. Your purpose should be to evaluate which stamps are doing well and will continue to do so and which ones need to be disposed of quickly.

This is a tough job. No one likes to be confronted with his mistakes, but that is exactly what I am suggesting you need to do in order to maintain a healthy stamp portfolio. It is imperative that you acknowledge when you've made an unwise purchase and then sell it and take your loss. Easy to say; tough to do.

But let me suggest that if you won't do that, then you really ought either to get out of the stamp market or let someone else manage your folio for you. Nobody is perfect. We all may as well face up to the fact and realize that a set of stamps that looks terrific today may be spoiled leftovers in six months, and there's only one place for spoiled leftovers — toss them in the garbage.

If, over a period of time, you find you are throwing out the balance of your portfolio, then you should also face another fact — you just can't pick them, and it's time to find someone who can — if you still have the heart to stay in the stamp market.

The bottom line on this section is simple. If you are going to spend good money on a collectible, then add the care and time it takes to protect your investment. Periodically reexamine your purchases to see how they are doing, and when it is necessary, admit your errors and empty the garbage.

## Selling

"Let me tell you a little secret," said the stamp dealer, leaning across the table. "I buy stamps off people as cheap as I can and sell them as quick as I can for much as I can. That's the secret of my success."

While I know of many dealers who are as embarrassed as I am about that quote, there are plenty of others who live by it and make money with it.

Selling your stamps should be viewed, in my opinion, as an adversary proceeding, since that is exactly what it is. You want to make as much on your investment as possible, while your potential buyer wishes to obtain your property for as little as he honestly can.

I'm not suggesting that the selling atmosphere needs to be charged with anger and hostility, but I think you should understand the fundamentally opposing dynamics which occur in the selling situation.

How and where to sell investment stamps is a very controversial subject. It is further complicated by the fact that there are many different avenues and methods which you can use. Some of them can bring you maximum profit while others will leave you in bitter tears.

While many stamp people will disagree intensely about this next statement, I feel you should know that you either sell your stamps at retail, or you sell them at below (repeat, below) wholesale. Those are your choices; there is very little room in between.

Let's begin with the methods of selling at retail, look at the advantages, and then consider the disadvantages. Later we'll look briefly at selling below wholesale prices.

The highest profit potential when it comes to selling your investment stamps is if you have local collector-investor contacts who will buy the stamps you have to sell. Prices can be at retail or even slightly below in order to give your local buyer a good buy. There is no commission; there are no registration costs; there is little delay; there is simply a quick sale in which you pass on a good investment property and put the profit in the bank, or wherever.

Selling an entire holding this way could be difficult unless it all goes to a single buyer. Obviously the investor living in a large urban area where he has spent years keeping up philatelic contacts and relationships will do better selling through this method than the loner who has a ranch in the west and never met a collector he liked.

For that last fellow there is another retail method of disposing of his investment stamps — the philatelic society sales circuit. I've already described in a previous section how the investor can use sales circuits to buy stamps. He can also use them to sell his stamps.

Stamps are placed in the society's circuit books, photographed by the society, and circulated to many members. Prices should be fixed at slightly less than retail to be competitive. The major advantages are, of course, the ability to get a near-retail price for your stamps, protection by the society, and the knowledge that generally your stamps will be in ethical hands.

The major disadvantage is that it takes a very long time to sell your stamps this way; you should plan on six months to a year before you begin seeing any checks from the society. A second disadvantage is that many books will only be partially sold, and you will have "remainders" to worry about. This can be avoided by pricing the lesser items at really bargain values to ensure their being bought.

One way of avoiding the time problem is to submit several books over a regular period so that when the checks do begin they will tend to come in regularly. Of course, the society deducts a sales charge, and you are responsible for costs of shipping, insuring, etc., but in the end, you could do much worse than selling through the society sales circuits.

A third, more direct method is to take out an advertisement in the philatelic press. I just don't recommend this method unless you have a sizable stock of high-quality material for sale. You can go one of two routes on selling by advertisement.

First, you can simply list what is for sale and price it to sell, then wait hopefully for orders. If your holding is not deep (if you don't have several sets of everything you've advertised), you will have the problem of duplicate orders for material you cannot provide; checks will have to be returned, and that means time and money lost.

Another way to go is to advertise a mail bid sale — a mini-auction, if you will. In the mail bid sale, you list the stamps available and allow would-be buyers to send in their best offers. The items go to the highest bidders, and you've sold your material.

There is the expense of the ad or ads, and there is some time delay because potential buyers have to be given sufficient time to make their bids and get them to you, but many investors have done nicely with this method, and perhaps you could too.

Another near-retail means of disposing of your investment portfolio is the private treaty arrangement. Many larger philatelic companies have a private treaty department. Essentially, private treaty is the putting together through the company of a seller and buyer — a bit like the finder's fee operation.

You send the stamps to the company's private treaty department after having made arrangements by mail or phone in advance; a fair price is agreed upon; the company then finds a buyer at that price and sells your stamps. For their services, the stamp company charges a prearranged commission and sends you the balance.

Advantages? This is a fairly quick method of disposal; it ensures a reasonably fair price for your stamps; it is practically hassle-free; and often the company has so much confidence in your stamps and its ability to sell them that it will even extend an advance on the potential sale.

Disadvantages? Well, there is the commission, but selling stamps almost always entails some expense. Other than that, I come up empty on the negative side. I have used this method myself and recommend it highly.

The key, of course, is in picking the right company to handle your material. In fact, what often works best is to break up your holding among several private treaty departments (British colonies to a B.C. specialist, Germany to a Germany dealer, etc.) since the customers of some dealers buy there because their dealers sell specialist material.

Finally, in the near-retail department, I recommend the auction house. Here again, I feel that a major firm with a strong reputation is mandatory. Material is inventoried and the description sent to the auction firm. They then decide whether or not they would like to add your material to one of their auctions.

Stamps are sent, lotted, described in the auction brochure or catalog, and sold to the highest bidder. The method has the advantage of being a no fuss, no muss system for the seller.

It has a couple of disadvantages, however. First is the delay between the time you send the stamps, the time before they are actually auctioned, and the time before you finally receive your check. Second is that you take a definite chance that your stamps won't bring the price you anticipate and, in fact, that you could even lose money on the arrangement.

If you have selected intelligently, held a reasonably long time, and the market is good, then the chance of something like that happening is rather small; but it does happen. I know from experience! You will pay a seller's commission on your sale, of course, but again, that may be the only pain in the whole process, and that isn't bad at all.

Probably more investors sell to retail dealers than through any other method. In so doing,

they present that dealer — and therefore themselves — with a problem.

While they have evaluated their holding on the basis of current retail market value, the dealer obviously cannot purchase their stamps on that basis, for if he did, there would be no profit. The dealer can only pay a price which allows him to make a profit in turn (it's amazing how huffy investors get about this, but that is the simple logic of the matter).

What I am saying is that the dealer really needs to be able to buy that material at less than wholesale for the purchase to be enticing to him. Why should he pay more for your German semipostals than he can if he continues buying the same material from his regular wholesaler? It doesn't make sense, and that's exactly why his offer to you will seem to be an insult to your intelligence. But remember, he is in business to make money.

So unless the material you have for sale is unique, or unless his own supplies of the same kind of thing have absolutely dried up and he just can't find it anywhere, you will be in the position of having to sell your stamps to that dealer for less than he can ordinarily buy them, and that means "less than wholesale."

One advantage, however, is that if the material is at all decent, the deal can be consummated rather quickly, and you have the money in hand. As one investor put it to me: "I can always make more by going to another guy, but even at the price he has offered me, I am making such a profit, it isn't worth the bother."

I guess there is a lesson in that for us; if we bought wisely and well and our profit is large enough, perhaps we can afford to sell to that retail dealer just to get the quick check.

Finally, and absolutely at the low end of the list, you can sell your investment portfolio to a wholesale stamp dealer. Now remember, this is the guy who sells to the dealer we just mentioned. So what?

Well, he has to sell your stamps to his dealer clients at wholesale, which means that the price he can afford to pay you will be even smaller than if you had sold to the retailer in the first place. Once again, the exceptions are if the kind of material you have is unique or just can't be found at any price.

To the best of my experience and information, these are the major methods in disposing of your investment grade stamps. If I have left a method out, write the editor of this almanac, and the next time we update this chapter, I will expand on methods of selling.

Some final points on selling. Remember to maintain your records for tax purposes. Remember that paper profits mean absolutely nothing; the only thing that really counts is the price you actually obtain on the day you sell your stamps. Sometimes the reality that hits that day is more than many investors can handle.

The value of your holding should never be seen in terms of current retail prices; the value of the holding is ascertained in terms of what you actually can get for the stamps — that's what they're worth. What the Scott catalog says, what Linn's Trends of Stamp Values says, what I say in my column, what you say to yourself in the dark of night — none of these is an accurate value of your investment stamps. The only accurate value is what you can sell them for; when you hold the cash in hand, then you really know what your stamps were worth!

## Remainders

This chapter is not a crash course in philatelic investment. What I have tried to do is make some remarks, observations, and suggestions to investors and would-be investors which I hope will prove helpful.

Some topics have been left out — most intentionally, but a few without doubt by accident. There remain just a few topics which didn't seem to fit, but on which I want to comment briefly.

The question of the balanced folio. Should the investment folio have balance? Well, that depends on what you mean by balance. I recommend that the folio contain a selection of stamps which comprises old classics as well as some newer issues, "dead" countries as well as live ones, foreign sets as much as U.S., and used stamps, lightly-hinged stamps, as well as mint, never-hinged. If that's what balance means, then I am for it. But most important of all, the folio should contain really significant stamps which will appreciate in value.

Another question surrounds the matter of how long stamps should be held. I don't think there is

an intelligent answer to that. It depends on your investment goals to begin with. My own feeling is that most investors put money into stamps on a continuing basis (I recommend that strategy).

That means they will also sell on a continuing basis. I have a quarrel with the "buy 'em and forget 'em" theory. You can't do that and empty the garbage at the same time; in my opinion, the folio must be reviewed periodically and poor material dumped no matter what the cost.

Last, I want to make a special place here in favor of the stamp collection as an investment, because I believe it can be just that. I am not referring to that little kid's album stuck full of unrecognizable bits of used postage. I believe that a truly fine specialized collection can be one of the finest stamp investments to be made.

This plan is tailored for the investor who is also a philatelist; he loves collecting stamps but wants to reap a profit someday. A fine collection of early U.S., of Swiss philately, of first-day air covers — the list is practically endless — these all make great pastimes and good investments simultaneously.

So please, if you love philately but want a profit out of it too, don't overlook the production of a really nice specialized collection as a source of fun and profit!

## Conclusion

I believe that stamps make a good investment in bad economic times as well as good; their history supports the belief. I believe that philatelic investment can be a fascinating hobby as well as a profitable one. I believe that a studious, careful buyer who has the right personality and motivation can make money in the stamp market. If this brief discussion has served to help you achieve that goal, then I am truly pleased.

# Postal Administrations    8

# Printing Establishments
## Foreign

The postage stamps of the world are produced by either individual government-owned establishments or commercial security printing firms.

Brief historical synopses of some of the major stamp-producing organizations and firms follow.

## SOCIEDAD DEL ESTADO CASA DE MONEDA ARGENTINA

**Sociedad del Estado Casa de Moneda, Av. Antartida Argentina 1385, Buenos Aires, Republic of Argentina,** was founded by law in September 1875 and later organized as a commercial society in November 1977.

Stamps, bank notes, coins, bonds, tax labels, checks, passports and all types of securities are printed with modern equipment in a 42,000-square meter building.

Normally, the firm supplies all stamps for the local postal authority and for foreign countries upon request.

Casa de Moneda utilizes, for stamp printing, a four-color rotogravure webfed press and three two-color sheetfed offset presses. Actual production is about two million to four million stamps daily, depending on size.

Casa de Moneda has its own art department, creating or developing designs. It also can offer intaglio-printed stamps, applying all the knowledge of bank note printers.

During 1982, Casa de Moneda was to install a new offset-intaglio webfed press that allows production of four-color offset, three-color intaglio or any combination thereof. This specially designed press starts a new era in stamp printing.

Being a bank note printer, Casa de Moneda developed sophisticated security systems coverings all its products, including stamps, and it is prepared to bring a complete service to the customer.

## LEIGH-MARDON PTY. LTD. AUSTRALIA

**Security Products Division, Leigh-Mardon Pty. Ltd., 15-31 Keys Road, Moorabbin, Victoria 3189, Australia,** incorporates the operations of Asher & Co. which was formed in 1874 and began security printing in the 1940s together with other firms which operated as fine lithographic printers.

Leigh-Mardon Pty. Ltd. is a member of the AMATIL group of companies.

The first postage stamp production at Leigh-Mardon was in 1973 for the Ethiopian Government with an issue depicting tropical fish.

This was followed by a large order for Bangladesh.

In 1975, the company printed the first Australian stamp to be produced by photolithography. All Australian issues are now printed by this process.

The company prints stamps for many countries, including Australia, Malaysia, Cocos (Keeling) Islands, and New Zealand.

Leigh-Mardon Security Products Division has its own graphics department for the creation of designs or refinement of customer-submitted artwork. Two four-color presses are used for stamp production.

Careful control over the process assures quality with respect to both stamps and paper. Supervision for the destruction of waste is carried out by an employee of the Australian Postal Commission.

# AUSTRIA STATE PRINTING OFFICE
# AUSTRIA

**Oesterreichische Staatsdruckerei-Wiener Zeitung, Rennweg 12A und 16, A-1030 Vienna, Austria,** was founded in 1804 in Vienna during the reign of Emperor Franz I as the Government Printing Office and manufactures, in addition to a multitude of printing orders received from the government, postage stamps and securities.

In March/April 1850, the institute started printing postage stamps for all parts of the monarchy. Since 1946, the printing office has printed, apart from Austria, postage stamps for 42 countries and counts many foreign postal administrations among its permanent customers.

The technical equipment available at the Austrian State Printing Office is suitable for printing postage stamps by offset, photogravure, and steel-engraving printing methods, as well as by combinations of such process applications.

The presses used in this production are such units as the Roland for one and two-color offset, Rembrandt and Palatia for single or four-color photogravure, and Intagliacolor for three-color steel engravings.

For manufacturing postage stamps by the combined process of photogravure and steel engraving, a compound postage stamp roller-rotation Goebel press (for four-color photogravure and three-color steel engraving) is used.

The office employs approximately 1,000 persons.

# STATE PRINTING OFFICE
# BELGIUM

**Algemene Werkplaats van het Zegel - Atelier General du Timbre, 60 Stationsstraat, 2800 Mechelen, Belgium,** the State Printing Office of Belgium, was initially housed in the Brussels Northern Railway Station where it functioned from 1848 until 1868. The name of the founder cannot be determined with certainty.

The organization first printed stamps for Belgium in 1848, and used only the rotogravure process for such until 1865. That year the printing office was moved to its present location in Mechelen.

Currently, the office prints stamps for Belgium only using typography, rotogravure or line engraving on its complement of nine presses.

Three presses have capabilities of producing one-color typography work, while one other offers two-color typography. All four are sheetfed. Another press is capable of producing one-color rotogravure plus up to a maximum of three-color engraving.

Additionally, two presses are capable of one-color engraving plus four-color rotogravure work, and another produces stamps by the three-color indirect engraving (similar to offset) plus three-color direct engraving methods. These three presses are webfed.

The ninth press is capable of four-color engraving, sheetfed.

The Belgian postal authorities call on private designers and engravers to carry out the necessary design and plate work.

# ASHTON-POTTER LTD.
# CANADA

**Ashton-Potter Ltd., 110 Sudbury St., Toronto, Ont. M6J 1A7, Canada,** was founded by C.E. Ashton and incorporated in Toronto in 1939. It remains a privately owned firm.

Postage stamp production for Canada began in 1969, with stamps being produced for the United Nations initially in 1972.

The main printing process of Ashton-Potter is sheetfed offset lithography with current capabilities of lithographing five colors at one time.

Ashton-Potter utilizes finished stamp designs submitted by its customers, but has the resources to prepare finished designs itself, if required.

The firm is not strictly a security printer as it is engaged in the printing of trade and school books, plus the production of packaging and labels, direct mail, greeting cards, maps and seed envelopes.

# CHINA COLOR PRINTING CO., INC.
# REPUBLIC OF CHINA

**China Color Printing Co., Inc., 6th Floor, No. 60 Po Ai Road, Taipei, Taiwan 100, Republic of China,** started printing postage stamps for the Republic of China in 1974 on its presses capable of two-color lithographic production utilizing finished designs.

The company, founded in 1961, possesses two laser scanners, five four-color offset presses, as well as related printing and binding equipment, and employs over 400 people in the production of color brochures, catalogs, magazines, posters, calendars, post cards, and books, in addition to postage stamps. It prints aerogrammes for Kuwait.

# CHINA ENGRAVING AND PRINTING WORKS
# REPUBLIC OF CHINA

**China Engraving and Printing Works, 30 Erh-Cheng Road, Hsin Tien, Taipei Hsien, Taiwan, Republic of China,** was founded by the Central Bank of China (ROC) in 1941 at Chung-

King City and started printing stamps for the ROC that year.

The organization was established for the printing of bank notes, stamps, bonds and other securities and is currently performing these functions using the lithography and intaglio methods of printing. It prints stamps for the ROC.

The firm employs its own designers and engravers for the production of orders and also utilizes finished designs submitted by its customers.

# CARVAJAL, S.A.
# COLOMBIA

**Carvajal, S.A. (Division Valores), Apartado 46, Cali, Colombia,** was founded by Manuel Carvajal Valencia in 1904 in Cali as a graphic arts workshop called Imprenta Comercial.

The firm started printing postage stamps for Colombia in April 1975 and is currently producing postal emissions for Costa Rica, El Salvador, Guatemala, Peru, and Honduras as well on its offset and photogravure presses capable of printing up to four colors at a time.

Carvajal, S.A. employs its own designers to meet the requirements of contracting governments or utilizes their finished designs.

In addition to postage stamps, the firm prints such security items as checks, bonds, security notes, lottery tickets, and stock certificates.

Carvajal, S.A. also prints magazines, business forms, textbooks, children's story books (in seven languages), directories, guide books, labels, and boxes.

Statistics of the firm for 1981 include 1,050,000 square feet of industrial working space, an employee staff of 3,720 persons, a paper and paperboard annual consumption of over 45,000 short tons, and $13 million U.S. in exports.

# STAMP PRINTING OFFICE, PTT
# DENMARK

**Post Office Printing House, Stamp Printing Office, Telegrafvej 7, Box 25, DK 2750 Ballerup, Denmark,** was founded by the Danish PTT in 1931 and started printing Danish stamps in 1922.

In February 1982, it moved to a new plant at Ballerup. The office is currently capable of printing up to three colors at one time on the old press by intaglio method and up to six colors in half width.

On the new press, it is possible to print a combination of up to four-color offset and up to three-color intaglio at one time; one-color photogravure and up to three-color intaglio at one time; and in half width up to six colors.

The firm prints the stamps of Greenland, as well as those of Denmark from finished designs and produces stamp booklets.

# THOMAS DE LA RUE
# AND CO., LTD.
# ENGLAND

**Thomas De La Rue and Co., Ltd., P.O. Box 10, De La Rue House, Basingstoke, Hampshire, England,** was founded in 1813 by Thomas de la Rue as a stationery and card-making firm in London, England.

The firm started printing British fiscal stamps in 1853 and postage stamps in 1855 using the typography or surface-printing method.

With the changeover in 1861-62 of the printing of stamps for the Crown Agents from the firm of Perkins Bacon and its recess or line-engraved process to the typography of De La Rue, the majority of British Colonial postage stamps were subsequently produced by De La Rue and Co.

The company introduced the "key plate" system in 1870 enabling an unlimited number of colonies to utilize the same "head" plate with individual overprinted "duty" plates.

It was the firm of De La Rue that produced the only issued United States postage stamps printed abroad (Confederate States of America 5-cent issue of 1862).

The company has its own staff of designers and engravers for the execution of designs for ordering governments, if desired.

The firm is utilizing presses capable of producing from one to four colors at a time in the lithography and intaglio printing processes. Typography is no longer used by the firm to print stamps.

Over the years, De La Rue and Co. has developed and printed adhesive postage and fiscal stamps for about 200 stamp-issuing authorities.

# THE HOUSE OF QUESTA LTD.
# ENGLAND

**The House of Questa Ltd., Parkhouse Street, Camberwell, London SE5 7TP, England,** was founded in London in 1966 by the trio of Wally F. Rodgers, Kenneth M. McAllen and Charles G. Haswell.

The firm started printing postage stamps in 1969 for countries through the British Crown Agents. Utilizing the offset lithography printing process, the firm's presses are capable of printing any number of colors at a time, with some designs requiring press passes running into double figures.

The House of Questa Ltd. has its own staff of designers to add the finishing touches to customer-submitted artwork, as well as initiate designs based on customer wants.

Over 50 per cent of The House of Questa's production is stamps which are shipped to more than 70 countries throughout the world. The firm is currently printing some British Post Office special issues and definitives.

# JOHN WADDINGTON OF KIRKSTALL ENGLAND

**John Waddington of Kirkstall Ltd., Commercial Road, Leeds LS5 3AJ, Yorkshire, England,** is a member company of John Waddington Ltd., producing printing, packaging and publishing.

The security print division specializes in the design and production of postage stamps, having supplied security work for over 70 different countries.

The studio concentrates on the design of security artwork, both rough and finished, and also offers a complete photographic service. The stamp production includes the most up-to-date four-color lithographic equipment.

# WALSALL SECURITY PRINTERS LTD. ENGLAND

**Walsall Security Printers Ltd., Box 26, Midland Road, Walsall, England,** was formed as an independent company in 1966, although the parent company, Walsall Lithographic Co. Ltd., has been in operation since 1894.

WSP, as the firm is known, has the capability of printing on lithographic and letterpress machinery, as well as offering additional facilities such as hot-foil blocking and embossing on stamps.

The firm printed the world's first foil stamp (Tonga) and free-form, self-adhesive stamp (Sierra Leone).

Though famous for its many self-adhesive stamp issues, WSP is now better known for high-quality gummed postage stamps which form the majority of its production.

WSP prints for more than 60 countries and agencies working on direct contract or through agencies such as the British Crown Agents or Inter-Governmental Philatelic Corp.

The firm provides research facilities and original designs for new issues through its own experienced studio or utilizes finished designs submitted by contracting governments.

If required, the company will undertake to provide a complete service, handling all the philatelic requirements of a territory on a contract basis.

The company also prints maps, trading stamps, savings stamps, and discount vouchers for government and commerical organizations.

# FEDERAL PRINTING OFFICE FEDERAL REPUBLIC OF GERMANY

**Bundesdruckerei, Oranienstrasse 91, 1 Berlin 61, Federal Republic of Germany,** evolved from the Printing Office of the German Reich founded in 1879.

In 1877, the Royal Court Printing House of Von Decker, which specialized in typographic arts, was purchased by the German government, and in 1879, the Royal Prussian State Printing House (founded in 1852), which specialized in security paper printing, was likewise taken over by the German government.

The Federal Printing Office functions as a commercial institution under the direct supervision of the Federal Minister for Posts and Telecommunications. The main office is in Berlin with branches in Bonn and Neu-Isenburg.

The facilities, which cover an area of 42,100 square meters in Berlin, employ altogether 3,000 persons, approximately 400 of them in Neu-Isenburg and approximately 180 in Bonn.

It produces not only postage and revenue stamps but also bank notes, all types of securities and bonds, passports and nonmonetary government printing requirements.

The stamp-production processes used include intaglio, photogravure, offset and relief printing or a combination of them.

The Federal Printing Office workshops in Berlin has 42 letterpress presses, 27 single-color or multicolor lithography presses, photogravure press, three diestamping machines, as well as intaglio presses and required related auxiliary machinery.

The office has its own staff of designers and engravers and does postage stamp printing for other countries.

# ASPIOTI ELKA GRAPHIC ARTS GREECE

**Aspioti Elka Graphic Arts, Inc., 276 Vouliagmenis St., Athens 459, Greece,** was founded by Gerasimos Aspiotis on the island of Corfu in 1873, a year which marked the beginning of the printing tradition in Greece.

Later, in 1938, the operations were moved to Athens by his successor, Liakos Iliopoulos.

The first copperplate engraved postage stamps in Greece were printed by Aspioti in 1911 with hand-operated direct-plate printing machines.

Shortly afterwards, the coming issues were printed by the offset method which was to succeed the direct-plate printing used today only in special stamp issues.

Today, Aspioti Elka, apart from the General Printing Section, keeps up the Security Printing Department, fully organized for the execution of all security orders and mainly the postage stamps which are printed for the Greek State by multicolor lithographic process.

In addition to Greek stamps, Aspioti Elka, under tender participation, prints regularly the postage stamps for Cyprus, Ethiopia, and occasionally has printed stamps for Togo, Nigeria and the United Nations.

The firm has established a studio with experienced artists for the correction of customer-submitted designs or the complete artwork according to client's instructions.

The Security Department is supervised by a permanently appointed committee by the Greek Post Office, as well as occasionally appointed supervisors by the Greek State when other state security orders are in process.

Thus, a thorough control is performed with respect to stamps, paper and quality before the official destruction of waste materials.

## JOH. ENSCHEDE EN ZONEN HOLLAND

**Joh. Enschede en Zonen Grafische Inrichting B.V., Klokhuisplein 5, Haarlem, Holland,** was founded by Isaac Enschede in June 1703, making this one of the oldest printing firms in Europe.

Postage stamp production began in 1864, after having printed bank notes for the Netherlands Bank since 1814. The firm was the first to develop a movable type for music, and this was used for the ornamental borders on its first bank notes.

The letterpress operation was augmented by offset equipment in 1914 and by photogravure equipment in 1924, thus affording the production of postage stamps by these individual processes, as well as combinations of the methods.

The firm has its own staff of designers and engravers, plus makes use of designs submitted by the ordering governments.

Enschede en Zonen has printed stamps for 42 countries in addition to those of The Netherlands, Netherlands Antilles, and Surinam. The firm employs 1,100 people in its two Haarlem establishments.

## KULTURA TRADING CO. HUNGARY

**Kultura Hungarian Foreign Trading Co., P.O. Box 149, 1389 Budapest 62, Hungary,** is a state enterprise founded in 1950. It has the exclusive right to export Hungarian printing products and to have foreign products printed.

The firm has also printed stamps for several other countries using the offset, engraving, photogravure and foil-printing processes. Its presses are capable of printing two to four colors at one time.

Kultura Trading Co. utilizes the designs of its own artists for the most part, but uses designs submitted by customers if required. In-house artists prepare all designs for printing.

Strictest security prevails in the Kultura printing houses which are state property. Minute details of plate production, utilization and destruction, quantity of stamps printed including spoiled sheets, and disposition are supplied to the customer.

## INDIA SECURITY PRESS INDIA

**India Security Press, Nasik Road, New Delhi, India,** was established by the British Government at Nasik Road in November 1925 to print postage and fiscal stamps, as well as postal stationery for India.

When India achieved freedom in 1947, the company continued printing stamps, stationery and other security products for the republic.

Photogravure printing was added to the existing processes of letterpress and offset in 1952 with the purchase of two single-color rotary and one two-color rotogravure presses.

In 1972, a sheet-fed, four-color gravure machine was added. In subsequent years, the photogravure process was improved and computerized with the introduction of a scanner, processor, step-and-repeat camera, automatic etching machines, proofing press, etc.

In addition to printing stamps for India, the company produces issues for Nepal, Bangladesh, Bhutan, and Ethiopia. Production of postage stamps on three rotary presses in a single color amounts to 22 million stamps daily for internal use in India.

A studio prepares designs based on ideas suggested by the government. Security and quality control are exercised by separate departments.

## SECURITY PRINTING AND MINTING COMPANY INDONESIA

**Indonesia Government Security Printing and Minting Co. (Perum Peruri), Jln. Palatehan 4, Kebayoran Baru, Jakarta, Selatan, Indonesia,** was founded as a result of the consolidation of two former state-owned enterprises, i.e., the P.N. Percetakan Kebayoran (Banknote and Stamp Printing) and P.N. Arta Yasa (Mint) on Sept. 15, 1971.

All postage and revenue stamps demanded by the Indonesian Directorate General of Posts and Giros and the Directorate General of Taxation are met by Perum Peruri.

Printing is done on uncoated (for normal postage and revenue stamps) or coated (for special/commemorative stamps) paper, which is gummed by Perum Peruri beforehand.

Most printing is done on one five-color and three three-color photogravure rotary presses. The necessary printing cylinders are prepared in-house using a galvanic setup and etching equipment.

All operations, from designing to printing and finishing, including ink making, are done by the company.

# GOVERNMENT POLYGRAPHIC INSTITUTE
## ITALY

**Istituto Poligrafico e Zecca dello Stato, Piazza Verdi 10, Rome, Italy,** currently prints government postage stamps, bank notes for Italy, Vatican City, San Marino, Somalia and other European and extra-European countries.

Furthermore, it mints the Italian Government coins, having at its disposal equipment that can offer production for foreign countries, too.

The production of the art printing department is not of minor importance and concerns the manufacture of valuable editions, art books, and printing.

Founded by the Italian Government by Law No. 2744 on Dec. 6, 1928, the institute has existed since 1866, when it was known as the Government Official Papers Office located in Turin. It moved to Rome in 1928.

The institute has five production plants — two paper mills, two graphic plants, and a Mint Department for the minting of coins. It realizes graphic products in copperplate, lithography, linotyping and rotogravure printing.

For the various production cycles, the institute has, on the whole, more than 600 machines, 20 of which are lithographic, three rotogravure, eight copperplate and several typographic, able to print seven colors.

The institute employs its own designers and engravers, also using finished designs submitted by the ordering governments.

The public corporation produces and supplies pulp, papers, postage stamps, stamped paper, paper money, art printings, publications of the government and the institute. It mints coins and commemorative medals.

The institute employs more than 6,000 people. The minting and security paper productions are effected under the control of the Italian Treasury.

# GOVERNMENT PRINTING AGENCY
## REPUBLIC OF KOREA

**The Government Printing & Mint Agency of the Republic of Korea, Tae Pyeong-dong, Dae Jeon-city, Choong Cheong Nam Do, Republic of Korea,** was founded Oct. 1, 1951, under the direct control of the country's Ministry of Finance.

The organization started printing postage stamps for the home country May 7, 1952, and is currently using both the photogravure and lithography methods of printing for this purpose.

Its photogravure presses are capable of printing four colors at one time.

The organization employs designers of postage stamps appointed by the Ministry of Communications, plus uses its own engravers.

# PRINTEX LTD.
## MALTA

**Printex Ltd., Mill Street, Qormi, Malta,** was established in 1971 in Malta as a subsidiary of Joinwell Ltd. The firm started printing postage stamps for the Malta Government in 1972 and has since printed postage stamps for the Sovereign Military Order of Malta in Rome, Italy.

The firm utilizes the offset printing process with capabilities of running four colors at a time.

Printex Ltd. has facilities for color separation, relettering and retouching as necessary.

The firm's work area covers 50,000 square feet and was built and equipped to meet modern quality color printing and binding exigencies. The firm also prints passports.

# MEXICAN STATE PRINTING OFFICE
## MEXICO

**Talleres de Impresion de Estampillas y Valores, Calzada de Legaria Num. 662, Mexico 10, D.F., Mexico,** was initially called the Oficina de Estampas (Stamp Office) and later the Treasury Printing Office.

The workshops were initiated in 1875 to print revenue stamps which were designed to substitute for stamped paper that was used at that time.

The office was originally established in the area occupied today by the Chief Accounting Office of the Treasury in the former Archbishop's Palace on Moneda Street and later moved to a location on San Cosme Street where two workshops were installed — one for engraving and the other for engraved printing. For security reasons, the workshops were moved to a location inside the National Palace.

The first production equipment with which the first issues were printed consisted of six small hand presses. Later, the machinery was improved in line with the country's needs, and in 1952, the present building was constructed. The building covers 11,541 square meters and has a staff of 337 people.

# STATE PRINTING WORKS OF SECURITIES
## POLAND

**The State Printing Works of Securities, ul. Sanguszki 1, Warsaw, Poland,** is a governmental organization that started printing postage stamps in 1929.

Its complement of printing presses is capable of letterpress, offset, line engraving and rotogravure processes, with the possibility of printing up to six colors at one time.

Currently, the State Printing Works prints postage stamps for Poland and sometimes for other countries, e.g., Morocco, utilizing designs submitted by the ordering country or works of its own designers and engravers.

## FABRICA NACTIONAL DE MONEDA Y TIMBRE SPAIN

**Fabrica Nacional de Moneda y Timbre, Jorge Juan 106, Madrid 9, Spain,** is the official center of Spanish production of stamps, coins, bank notes, lottery tickets and other documents and types of securities requested by the Minister of Treasury and other government departments.

The firm printed all public instruments, writings and other documents for the Spanish government in the 17th century.

It began printing postage stamps in 1850, and in 1893, the union of the stamp printing section and the Spanish Mint was completed.

The company has three rotary offset presses, two of one color and one of five colors, for the production of postage stamps. A combination offset, dry offset and engraving press is also used with the capacity of printing stamps in a total of eight colors.

In 1980, the national printer produced 1,600 million Spanish definitives bearing the king's portrait. An additional 650 million special stamps were printed (400 million on the dry offset multicolor press and 250 million intaglio and combination).

The printer has its own artists and engravers. Security controls are very strict.

In addition to the stamps of Spain, the company produces definitives and special issues of Spanish Andorra and the Republic of Equatorial Guinea and occasionally prints stamps for other countries, including Colombia, Ecuador, and Paraguay.

## HERACLIO FOURNIER, S.A. SPAIN

**Heraclio Fournier, S.A., H. Fournier 19, Vitoria, Spain,** was founded by Heraclio Fournier in Vitoria in 1868 and remains a family company to this day.

The organization uses six two-color and five four-color Roland offset printing presses plus seven one-color Palatia model and one four-color gravure presses. A rotary press WIFAG with 10 printing units is also used.

It first started printing stamps for Spain in 1936, and today produces printed postal paper for several countries throughout the world, including the United Nations.

The Fournier firm has its own staff artists to develop and create the artwork for stamps based on suggestions by customer governments. The firm produces its own paper.

The company is situated in Vitoria, which is the capital of Alava Province in northern Spain. It covers 300,000 square feet and employs approximately 700 people.

The firm also produces various graphic artwork such as art books, pamphlets, calendars, posters, magazines, post cards, and playing cards.

## POST OFFICE STAMP PRINTING WORKS SWEDEN

**The Post Office Stamp Printing Works, S-105 02 Stockholm, Sweden,** started producing Sweden's postage stamps in 1920 using a Benjamin R. Stickney rotary intaglio press which was replaced in 1937 by a machine manufactured by Goebel AG of Darmstadt, Germany.

Prior to 1920, the country's stamps were produced by a private contractor, AB Jacob Bagge's Banknote Printing Works, using two American Hoe copperplate printing machines.

Using the steel-engraving method throughout its stamp-producing years, the Stamp Printing Works is currently utilizing two intaglio presses — one capable of one-color production and the other three-color reproduction (since 1964).

The organization prints only the postage stamps of Sweden using the works of its own designers and engravers.

Sweden was the first country in the world to manufacture stamps in coils and remains as one of the few to use this system.

## COURVOISIER S.A. SWITZERLAND

**Courvoisier S.A., rue Jardiniere 149, CH-2301 La Chaux-de-Fonds, Switzerland,** was founded by Alexander Courvoisier in December 1880. He was a descendant of a family associated with the printing industry since 1806.

Guido Essig-Courvoisier is credited with utilizing the photogravure printing process to produce postage stamps, and the first stamps so printed are the Switzerland 1931 Pro Juventute series produced by the Courvoisier firm.

The firm utilizes three rotary photogravure presses capable of producing five colors at one time. Production on the five-color unit runs between two million and three million stamps per day.

Starting in 1933, Liechtenstein and Luxembourg had some of their stamps produced by the Courvoisier firm. Today, the organization prints postage stamps for 68 nations around the world.

Courvoisier S.A. has its own graphics department for the refinement of customer-submitted designs or the complete artwork based on the customer's preference.

Security is supervised by an appointee of the Swiss Postal Authority. This authority carries out the ultimate controls of quantity with respect to stamps and paper.

## SWISS PTT POSTAGE STAMP PRINTING OFFICE SWITZERLAND

**Swiss PTT Postage Stamp Printing Office, Bern, Switzerland,** was set up in 1930. Previously, the PTT had its postage stamps and other security items printed by government and private establishments.

The office, which has a staff of some 60 persons, specializes in steel-engraved recess printing, producing more than 550 million stamps a year.

Each minute its main unit, a 26-ton, three-color rotary press, turns out 8,000 cut into 160 countersize sheets of 50, which are already numbered, dated and perforated. This corresponds to a daily output of three million stamps.

Recess printing offers protection against forgery which is made even more difficult by expert choice of the paper used.

Careful selection of the designers and engravers, as well as continuous production monitoring and meticulous checking of the finished product, have all contributed to the high reputation Switzerland's stamps enjoy throughout the world.

The office also has an offset press on which it prints Swiss and foreign issues of which only small quantities are required, along with such items as post cards and stamp prospectuses.

In addition, there is a wide range of ancillary work, including the production of stamp booklets, special (pictorial) cancellations, and display material.

# Worldwide Postal Agencies

Most countries of the world maintain an agency or bureau through which they sell their recent and current postal emissions direct to collectors or dealers.

Each agency has its own set of regulations governing ordering instructions, acceptable methods of remittance, deadline for ordering, items offered (stamps, postal stationery, first day covers, postmarks, etc.); therefore, interested collectors should write to the desired agency(ies) initially to ascertain their individual requirements and procedures.

One's name and address should be printed or typed very clearly on all correspondence, especially to foreign-language nations, in order to prevent delays or nonreplies.

Enclosure of an International Reply Coupon aids in facilitating a reply from many countries. IRCs are usually available at any post office in the United States and abroad.

Some countries do not sell their postal paper in small amounts direct to collectors but rather in large quantities to dealers and wholesalers. This listing so indicates where such is known.

When sending inquiries or orders to a foreign country, it is best to utilize airmail, as surface mail can take several weeks to reach its destination(s).

Standard abbreviations used throughout this listing of postal agencies are as follows:

FDC = First Day Covers.

CTO = Canceled to Order.

SODA = Standing Order Deposit Account.

CBC = Certified Bank Check.

BD = Bank Deposit.

PC = Personal Check.

CDA = Certified Deposit Account.

IMO = International Money Order.

IBD = International Bank Draft.

USPSMO or USMO = U.S. Postal Service Money Order.

IRC = International Reply Coupon.

BPO = British Postal Order.

A/M = Airmail.

S/M = Surface Mail.

The remittance of funds by personal check is always subject to collection or negotiation charges, thus reducing the actual payment value of said remittance.

These are mail addresses only; the country's over-the-counter sales agency can well be in a different section of the stipulated city or even in a different city altogether.

Many countries' postal administrations produce philatelic bulletins outlining forthcoming postal emissions and make these announcements available to interested collectors either for a nominal fee or free of charge.

Currency exchange rates are omitted because of continual fluctuation. The latest exchange rates can be ascertained through a local banking establishment.

# AFGHANISTAN

Director of Posts, Philatelic Section, Kabul, Afghanistan. Details of services not provided.

# AITUTAKI

Aitutaki Post Office, Aitutaki, Cook Islands, South Pacific Ocean. Deals with individual orders for mint stamps, FDCs. SODA available with minimum deposit of U.S. $20 required. SODA orders shipped post-free; transient orders are postage extra. CBC accepted.

# ALBANIA

Exportal, Rue 4 Shkurti, Tirana, Albania. Deals with orders for over five sets. Details of services not provided.

# ALGERIA

Receveur Principal des Postes, Alger R.P., Algeria. Deals with individual orders for mint stamps, FDCs (extra charge), special postmarks. SODA available. Orders shipped postpaid. CBC, IMO accepted.

Government Agency: Ancienne Maison Theodore Champion, 13, rue Drouot, 75009 Paris, France.

# ANDORRA (French)

Service Philatelique des Postes et Telecommunications, 61-63 rue de Douai, 75436 Paris, France. Deals with individual orders for mint stamps. SODA available with the first remittance covering at least three-month purchases, plus postage by registered mail. All orders shipped postage extra. CBC, IMO accepted. Printer: Government Printing Office, Perigueux. Also handles postage stamps of UNESCO, Council of Europe, all French issues, and permanent issues of Monaco under same terms.

# ANDORRA (Spanish)

Direccion General de Correos, Servicio Filatelico International, Madrid 14, Spain. Deals with individual orders for mint stamp sets only. No SODA available. Orders sent postage and handling extra. IMO accepted.

# ANGOLA

Centro Filatelico de Angola, Lda., C.P. 2688, Luanda, Angola. Deals with individual orders for mint stamps, FDCs, special postmarks (agency supplies envelopes). SODA available with minimum deposit required. Orders shipped postage extra. CBC, PC, IMO accepted.

# ANGUILLA

The Postmaster, Department of Posts, The Valley, Anguilla, West Indies. Deals with individual orders for mint stamps, FDCs. SODA available with minimum deposit required. Orders shipped postage extra. CBC, IMO, USMO, BPO accepted.

Government Agency: John Lister Ltd., 37 Bury St., St. James's London SW1, England.

# ANTIGUA-BARBUDA

Philatelic Bureau, Barbuda Post Office, Codrington, Barbuda, West Indies (Via Antigua). Deals with individual orders for mint or CTO stamps, FDCs. SODA available with unspecified minimum deposit required. Orders shipped postage extra. CBC, BD accepted.

# ARGENTINA

Seccion Filatelia, Correo Central, Local 55, 1000 Buenos Aires, Argentina. Deals with individual orders for mint stamps. No SODA available. Postage is extra. IMO, CBC accepted. Minimum order for foreign residents is U.S. $25. Also offers postmarks from Argentina's Antarctic bases.

# ASCENSION

Postmaster, Jamestown, St. Helena, South Atlantic. Deals with individual orders for mint stamps, FDCs, special postmarks (bureau or customers supply envelopes). No SODA available. Orders shipped postage extra. CBC on London bank, U.S. bank notes, BPO, IMO accepted.

Government Agencies: Crown Agents Stamp Bureau, St. Nicholas House, Sutton, Surrey SM1 1EL, England; StanGib Ltd., 1325 Franklin Ave., Garden City, N.Y. 11530; British & Overseas Philatelic Agency Ltd., P.O. Box 80, Shibuya, Tokyo 105-91, Japan.

# AUSTRALIA

Philatelic Bureau, GPO Box 9988, Melbourne, Victoria 3001, Australia. Deals with individual orders for mint and CTO stamps, FDCs, special postmarks (bureau supplies pictorial envelopes for $A0.12 each). SODA available with recommended minimum deposit of U.S. $11. Orders shipped post-free by surface, postage extra by air. CBC, IMO, BD accepted.

Also handles postal emissions of Australian Antarctic Territory.

Government Agencies: Australian Stamp Bureau, International Postal Marketing Corp., 128 Passaic Ave., Fairfield, N.J. 07006 (offers SODA services to all North American collectors); British & Overseas Philatelic Agency Ltd., Box 80, Shibuya, Tokyo 150-91, Japan; and Australian Stamp Bureau, St. Nicholas House, Sutton, Surrey SM1 1EL, England.

# AUSTRALIAN ANTARCTIC TERRITORY

Philatelic Bureau, GPO Box 9988, Melbourne, Victoria 3001, Australia. Deals with individual orders for mint and CTO stamps, FDCs, special postmarks (bureau supplies pictorial envelopes for $A0.12 each). SODA available with recommended minimum deposit of U.S. $11. Orders shipped post-free by surface, postage extra by air. CBC, IMO, BD accepted.

**Government Agencies: Australian Stamp Bureau, International Postal Marketing Corp., 128 Passaic Ave., Fairfield, N.J. 07006 (offers SODA services to all North American collectors); British & Overseas Philatelic Agency Ltd., Box 80, Shibuya, Tokyo 150-91, Japan; Australian Stamp Bureau, St. Nicholas House, Sutton, Surrey SM1 1EL, England.**

## AUSTRIA

**Oesterreichische Post, Briefmarkenversandstelle, A-1011 Vienna, Austria.** Deals with standing and individual orders for mint and CTO stamps, FDCs (sales agency supplies envelopes). Orders shipped postage extra plus cost of the FDC and a fee for affixing stamps. CBC, IMO accepted. Printer: Austrian State Printing Office, Vienna.

**Government Agencies: Ancienne Maison Theodore Champion, 13, rue Drouot, 75009 Paris, France (sales in France only); Austrian Philatelic Bureau, 866 Kingston Road, Toronto, Ont. M4E 1S3, Canada (SODA available).**

## AZORES

**Philatelic Office, Av. Casal Ribeiro 28-2°, 1096 Lisbon Codex, Portugal.** Deals with individual orders for mint stamps, FDCs (agency supplies envelopes). SODA available with minimum deposit of $15. Orders shipped postage extra. IMO, CBC, bank notes (except escudos) accepted.

**Government Agencies: J.A. Visser Postzegelgroothandel B.V., Box 184, 3300 AD Dordrecht, The Netherlands; Georg Roll Nachfolger, Holbeinstrasse 2, Postfach 1346, D-2880 Brake, Federal Republic of Germany.**

## BAHAMAS

**Postmaster General, GPO, P.O. Box N8302, Nassau, Bahamas.** Deals with individual orders for mint stamps, gutter pairs, complete sets, FDCs, first day cancellations (customer supplies addressed envelopes) post cards/maximum cards, presentation packs. SODA available with minimum deposit of $10. IMO, BPO, BD, PC in sterling (United Kingdom), U.S. dollars, or Canadian dollars accepted. Printers: Handled by Crown Agents.

**Government Agencies: Crown Agents Stamp Bureau, St. Nicholas House, Sutton, Surrey SM1 1EL, England; StanGib Ltd., 1325 Franklin Ave., Garden City, N.Y. 11530; British & Overseas Philatelic Agency Ltd., Box 80, Shibuya, Tokyo 150-91, Japan.**

## BAHRAIN

**Philatelic Bureau, Postal Directorate, Box 1212, State of Bahrain, Arabian Gulf.** Deals with individual orders for mint stamps, FDCs,

special postmarks (customer supplies envelopes). SODA available with minimum deposit of $20 required. Orders shipped postage extra. PC, BD accepted. Printers: Harrison and Sons Ltd., England; De La Rue & Co., England; Oriental Press, Bahrain.

**Government Agency: James Davis & Sons Ltd., 45 Church St., Rickmansworth WD3 1DG, England.**

## BANGLADESH

**Senior Postmaster, Philatelic Bureau, GPO, Dacca, Bangladesh.** Deals with individual orders for mint stamps and FDCs (extra charge). SODA available with minimum deposit of U.S. $50 required. Orders over U.S. $10 are sent airmail post-free. BD accepted.

**Government Agency: John Lister Ltd., 37 Bury St., St. James's, London SW1, England.**

## BARBADOS

**Philatelic Bureau, GPO, Bridgetown, Barbados, West Indies.** Deals with individual orders for mint stamps, FDCs, special postmarks (bureau supplies envelope at a charge, or customer supplies envelopes). SODA available. Orders shipped postage extra plus service fee. CBC, IMO, USMO accepted. Printer: Various as recommended by British Crown Agents.

**Government Agencies: Crown Agents Stamp Bureau, St. Nicholas House, Sutton, Surrey SM1 1EL, England; StanGib Ltd., 1325 Franklin Ave., Garden City, N.Y. 11530; British & Overseas Philatelic Agency Ltd., Box 80, Shibuya, Tokyo 150-91, Japan.**

## BELGIUM

**Regie des Postes, Service des Collectionneurs, Division 1.3.0.2., 1000 Brussels, Belgium.** Deals with individual orders for mint and CTO stamps. SODA available with minimum deposit of 600 francs. Orders shipped postage free. CBC, IMO accepted. Printer: Malines Stamp Printing Office, Mechelen.

## BELIZE

**Belize Philatelic Bureau, GPO, Belize City, Belize, Central America.** Deals with individual orders for mint and CTO stamps, FDCs, postmarks, stamp booklets and postal stationery. Minimum orders applied. No SODA available. CBC, IMO accepted. Orders shipped postage and handling extra. Printer: Litografia Nacional, Porto, Portugal.

**Government Agencies: Cia. Filatelica Mundial, Box 626, Panama 9A, Republic of Panama, and F.P. Delta SA, Box 1733, Montevideo, Uruguay.**

## BENIN

**Office des Postes et Telecommunications, Direction des Services Postaux et Financiers,**

Cotonou, Republique Populaire du Benin. Deals with individual orders for mint stamps, FDCs. SODA information not provided. Orders sent postage extra. CBC accepted.

Government Agency: Ancienne Maison Theodore Champion, 13, rue Drouot, 75009 Paris, France.

## BERLIN

Versandstelle fur Postwertzeichen, Postfach 12 09 50, 1000 Berlin 12, Federal Republic of Germany. Deals with individual orders for mint and CTO stamps and postal stationery. SODA available with a minimum deposit of 50 Deutsche marks required. Orders shipped postage extra. IMO, BD, CBC accepted. Printer: Federal Printing Works, Berlin.

Government Agencies: J.A. Visser Postzegelgroothandel B.V., Box 184, 3300 AD Dordrecht, The Netherlands; Ancienne Maison Theodore Champion, 13, rue Drouot, 75009 Paris, France (sales in France only).

## BERMUDA

Bermuda Philatelic Bureau, GPO, Hamilton, Bermuda. Deals with individual orders for mint stamps, FDCs. SODA available with minimum deposit of $20 required. Orders shipped postage extra. IBD, CBC accepted.

Government Agencies: Crown Agents Stamp Bureau, St. Nicholas House, Sutton, Surrey SM1 1EL, England; StanGib Ltd., 1325 Franklin Ave., Garden City, N.Y. 11530; British & Overseas Philatelic Agency Ltd., Box 80, Shibuya, Tokyo 150-91, Japan.

## BHUTAN

Philatelic Officer, Philatelic Bureau, GPO, Phuntsholing, Bhutan. Deals with individual/dealer orders for mint and CTO stamps, FDCs, postal stationery. SODA available with minimum deposit of U.S. $15 required. Orders shipped postage extra plus a packing charge. CBC, PC, IMO accepted.

Government Agency: Inter-Governmental Philatelic Corp., 48 W. 48th St., New York, N.Y. 10036.

## BOLIVIA

Direccion Nacional de Correos, Seccion Filatelica, La Paz, Bolivia. Details of services not provided.

## BOPHUTHATSWANA

Philatelic Services and INTERSAPA, GPO, Pretoria 0001, Republic of South Africa. Deals with individual orders for mint stamps, CTOs, FDCs, special postmarks (agency supplies datestamp cards). SODA available with minimum deposit of U.S. $15 required. Orders dispatched post-free with RSA 20¢ per order handling charge. CBC drawn on Pretoria bank made payable to INTERSAPA accepted. Printer: Government Printer, Pretoria.

Government Agencies: Global Philatelic Agency Ltd., P.O. Drawer AC, Katonah, N.Y. 10536; Richard Borek Agenturen, Breite Strasse, 25/26, 3300 Braunschweig, Federal Republic of Germany.

## BOTSWANA

Department of Posts and Telegraphs, Philatelic Bureau, P.O. Box 700, Gaborone, Botswana. Details of services not provided.

Government Agencies: Inter-Governmental Philatelic Corp., 48 W. 48th St., New York, N.Y. 10036; Crown Agents Stamp Bureau, St. Nicholas House, Sutton, Surrey SM1 1EL, England; British & Overseas Philatelic Agency Ltd., Box 80, Shibuya, Tokyo 150-91, Japan.

## BRAZIL

Empresa Brasileira de Correios e Telegrafos, ED. Apolo, SCS, Quadra 13, B1.A, Lote 36, 7° Andar, 70300 Brasilia, DF, Brazil. Deals with individual orders for mint stamps, FDCs, special postmarks (agency supplies envelopes). SODA available with minimum deposit of U.S. $30 required. Orders shipped postage extra plus a handling charge. CBC, IRC accepted. Printer: Brazilian Mint, Rio de Janeiro.

Government Agency: Georg Roll Nachfolger, Holbeinstrasse 2, Postfach 1346, D-2880 Brake, Federal Republic of Germany.

## BRITISH ANTARCTIC TERRITORY

Postmaster for British Antarctic Territory, c/o GPO, Port Stanley, Falkland Islands. Deals with individual orders for mint stamps, FDCs, special postmarks (customer supplies envelopes). SODA available. Orders shipped postage extra plus handling fee. CBC, PC, IMO accepted.

Government Agencies; Crown Agents Stamp Bureau, St. Nicholas House, Sutton, Surrey SM1, 1EL, England; StanGib Ltd., 1325 Franklin Ave., Garden City, N.Y. 11530; British & Overseas Philatelic Agency Ltd., Box 80, Shibuya, Tokyo 150-91, Japan.

## BRITISH VIRGIN ISLANDS

The Postmaster, Philatelic Bureau, Road Town, Tortola, British Virgin Islands. Deals with individual orders for mint and CTO stamps, FDCs, special postmarks (agency supplies envelopes). SODA available with minimum deposit of U.S. $8 required. Orders shipped post-free via surface mail, postage extra via airmail. Extra handling charge of 10¢ per cover only on large quantities of stamps to be affixed to envelopes. CBC, IMO, BPO accepted. Printers: Various through British Crown Agents.

Government Agencies: Inter-Governmental Philatelic Corp., 48 W. 48th St., New York, N.Y. 10036; Crown Agents Stamp Bureau, St. Nicholas House, Sutton, Surrey SM1 1EL, England; StanGib Ltd., 1325 Franklin Ave., Garden City, N.Y. 11530; British & Overseas Philatelic Bureau, Box 80, Shibuya, Tokyo 150-91, Japan.

## BRUNEI

Postal Services Department, GPO, Bandar Seri Begawan, Brunei. Deals with individual orders for mint or CTO stamps, FDCs, postmarks (customer supplies addressed envelopes). SODA available with minimum deposit required. Orders shipped postage extra plus service fee. IMO, CBC, BD accepted. Printers: Various British security printing firms.

Government Agencies: Crown Agents Stamp Bureau, St. Nicholas House, Sutton, Surrey SM1 1EL, England; Inter-Governmental Philatelic Corp., 48 W. 48th St., New York, N.Y. 10036; British & Overseas Philatelic Bureau, Box 80, Shibuya, Tokyo 150-91, Japan.

## BULGARIA

Ministere du Transport et Communications, Service Philatelique Postal, 44 Rue Dencoglou, Sofia, Bulgaria. Details of services not provided.

## BURMA

Myanma Export Import Corp., Export Division, Philatelic Section, Rangoon, Burma. Deals with individual orders for mint stamps. No information on SODA provided. Orders shipped postage extra, plus a packing charge. CBC accepted.

## BURUNDI

Agence Philatelique du Burundi, Boite Postale 45, Bujumbura, Burundi. Deals with individual orders for mint stamps, FDCs. SODA available with minimum deposit of $30 for stamps (blocks of four) or $15 for FDCs required. Orders shipped postage extra. CBC accepted.

## CAICOS ISLANDS

Caicos Philatelic Bureau, South Caicos, Turks & Caicos Islands. Deals with individual orders for mint stamps. Orders shipped postage extra. IMO, PC, cash accepted.

## CAMEROON

Receveur General des PTT, Yaounde, Cameroon. Details of services not provided.

Government Agencies: Inter-Governmental Philatelic Corp., 48 W. 48th St., New York, N.Y. 10036; Ancienne Maison Theodore Champion, 13, rue Drouot, 75009 Paris, France; John Lister Ltd., 37 Bury St., St. James's, London SW1, England (except in U.S.).

## CANADA

Philatelic Mail Order Service, Canada Post Corp., Ottawa, Canada K1A 0B5. Deals with individual orders for mint stamps, official FDCs, postal stationery, annual and thematic stamp collections, customer's own FDCs. SODA available with minimum deposit of Canada or U.S. $20 required. Orders shipped post-free with 50-cent service charge on orders under $5; 50¢ service charge on SODA orders under $2.50; 15¢ service charge on customer's own FDCs. Canadian or U.S. funds only by CBC (if over $250), PC, USPSMO, IMO accepted.

Printers: Various Canadian firms.

Government Agency: James Davis & Sons Ltd., 45 Church St., Rickmansworth WD3 1DG, England.

## CAPE VERDE ISLANDS

Direccao dos Servicos de Correios e Telecomunicacoes, Praia, Republica de Cabo Verde. Deals with individual orders for mint stamps. SODA not available. Orders shipped postage extra. CBC, PC, IMO accepted.

## CAYMAN ISLANDS

Postmaster General, Philatelic Department, Grand Cayman, Cayman Islands, West Indies. Deals with individual orders for stamps, FDCs, special postmarks (customer supplies envelopes). SODA available with minimum deposit of U.S. $25 required. Orders shipped postage extra. IMO, BD, USPSMO, Canada PMO, BPO, sterling bank notes, CBC accepted. Printers: Various through Crown Agents Stamp Bureau.

Government Agencies: Ancienne Maison Theodore Champion, 13, rue Drouot, 75009 Paris, France; StanGib Ltd., 1325 Franklin Ave., Garden City, N.Y. 11530; British & Overseas Philatelic Agency Ltd., Box 80, Shibuya, Tokyo 150-91, Japan; Crown Agents Stamp Bureau, St. Nicholas House, Sutton, Surrey SM1 1EL, England.

## CENTRAL AFRICAN REPUBLIC

Service Philatelique des PTT, Bangui, Central African Republic. Details of services not provided.

Government Agency: Ancienne Maison Theodore Champion, 13, rue Drouot, 75009 Paris France.

## CHAD

Receveur General des PTT, Ndjamena, Chad. Details of services not provided.

## CHILE

Departamento Filatelico, Subdireccion de Correos, Santiago, Chile. Deals with individual orders for mint stamps, FDCs, special post-marks. SODA available with minimum deposit of U.S. $8 required. BD accepted.

## CHINA, PEOPLE'S REPUBLIC OF

China National Stamp Corp., 28 Dong An Men St., Beijing, China. Details of services not provided.

Government Agencies: China Stamp Agency in North America, 1 Unicover Center, Cheyenne, Wyo. 82008-0001 (SODA available); Richard Borek Agenturen, Breite Strasse 25/26, 3300 Braunschweig, Federal Republic of Germany.

## CHINA, REPUBLIC OF (TAIWAN)

Philatelic Department, Directorate General of Posts, Taipei 106, Taiwan, Republic of China. Deals with individual orders for mint stamps, FDCs, special postmarks (bureau supplies envelopes). SODA available with minimum deposit of U.S. $10 required. Orders shipped post-free via registered surface mail, postage extra via airmail. CBC, PC, IMO, U.S. bank notes accepted. Printer: Several local and European firms.

Government Agencies: World Wide Philatelic Agency, Inc., 116 W. 32nd St., New York, N.Y. 10001; Ancienne Maison Theodore Champion, 13, rue Drouot, 75009 Paris, France (sales in France only); John Lister Ltd., 37 Bury St., St. James's, London SW1, England (except in U.S.).

## CHRISTMAS ISLAND

Philatelic Bureau, Christmas Island, Indian Ocean. Deals with individual orders for mint and CTO stamps, FDCs, special postmarks (bureau or customer supplies envelopes). SODA available with minimum deposit of Australia $10 required. All orders dispatched by airmail. Orders exceeding $100 for clients in Australia and $50 for other clients are dispatched by registered mail with clients paying appropriate fee. Orders of lesser value are dispatched by registered mail at client's request and expense. CBC drawn on Australian bank, IMO, Australian postal order accepted.

Government Agencies: Crown Agents Stamp Bureau, St. Nicholas House, Sutton, Surrey SM1 1EL, England; StanGib Ltd., 1325 Franklin Ave., Garden City, N.Y. 11530; British & Overseas Philatelic Agency Ltd., Box 80, Shibuya, Tokyo 150-91, Japan.

## CISKEI

Philatelic Services and INTERSAPA, GPO, Pretoria 0001, Republic of South Africa. Deals with individual orders for mint stamps, CTOs, FDCs, special postmarks (agency supplies date-stamp cards). SODA available with minimum deposit of U.S. $15 required. Orders sent post-free with RSA 20 cents required for handling charge. CBC accepted. Printer: Government Printer, Pretoria.

Government Agencies: Global Philatelic Agency Ltd., P.O. Drawer AC, Katonah, N.Y. 10536; Richard Borek Agenturen, Breite Strasse 25/26, 3300 Braunschweig, Federal Republic of Germany.

## COCOS (KEELING) ISLANDS

Philatelic Bureau, Post Office, Cocos (Keeling) Islands, Indian Ocean. Deals with individual orders for mint and CTO stamps, FDCs, stamp packs. SODA available. Orders shipped airmail post-free. CBC in Australian currency, IMO, IRC accepted.

Government Agency: Cocos (Keeling) Islands Stamp Bureau, International Postal Marketing Corp., 128 Passaic Ave., Fairfield, N.J. 07006 (offers SODA services to all North American collectors).

## COLOMBIA

Oficina Filatelica, Administracion Postal Nacional, Oficina 209, Edificio Murillo Toro, Bogota 1, Colombia. Deals with individual orders for mint stamps, FDCs, special postmarks (agency supplies envelopes). SODA available with minimum deposit of U.S. $10 required. Orders shipped postage extra. CBC, IMO accepted.

## COMORO ISLANDS

Direction Generale des PTT, Service Philatelique, Moroni, Comoro Islands. Details of services not provided.

Government Agency: Ancienne Maison Theodore Champion, 13, rue Drouot, 75009 Paris, France.

## CONGO PEOPLE'S REPUBLIC

Direction Generale des PTT, Service Philatelique, Brazzaville, Congo People's Republic. Details of services not provided.

Government Agency: Ancienne Maison Theodore Champion, 13, rue Drouot, 75009 Paris, France.

## COOK ISLANDS

Philatelic Bureau, P.O. Box 200, Rarotonga, Cook Islands, South Pacific. Deals with individual orders for mint stamps, FDCs. SODA available with minimum deposit required. SODA orders are shipped post-free; transient orders are postage extra. CBC accepted.

## COSTA RICA

Oficina Filatelica de Costa Rica, San Jose, Costa Rica. Deals with individual orders for mint stamps, FDCs. SODA available with minimum deposit of U.S. $50 ($250 for dealers) required. CBC, IMO accepted. Printer: Casa Grafica, San Jose.

## CUBA

COPREFIL (Empresa de Correos, Prensa y Filatelia), Box 100, Havana 1, Cuba, or office in Canada, COPREFIL, 1415 Pine Ave. W, Montreal, Que., Canada H3G 1B2. Details of services not provided.

Government Agency: Ancienne Maison Theodore Champion, 13, rue Drouot, 75009 Paris, France (sales in France only).

## CYPRUS

Philatelic Branch, GPO, Nicosia, Cyprus. Deals with individual orders for mint stamps, FDCs, special postmarks (either agency or customer supplies envelopes). SODA available with minimum deposit required. Orders shipped postage extra. CBC, IMO, BPO accepted. Printers: Aspioti-Elka of Greece, and Harrison & Sons Ltd., England.

Government Agencies: Inter-Governmental Philatelic Corp., 48 W. 48th St., New York, N.Y. 10036; J.A. Visser Postzegelgroothandel B.V., Box 184, 3300 AD Dordrecht, The Netherlands; Crown Agents Stamp Bureau, St. Nicholas House, Sutton SM1 1EL, England; Ancienne Maison Theodore Champion, 13 rue Drouot, 75009 Paris, France (sales in France only); British & Overseas Philatelic Agency Ltd., Box 80, Shibuya, Tokyo 150-91, Japan.

## CZECHOSLOVAKIA

Artia Foreign Trade Corp., P.O. Box 790, Prague 1, Czechoslovakia. Deals only with bulk orders for mint and used stamps, FDCs, postal stationery, kiloware. SODA available with minimum of 100 sets mint or used and minimum deposit of U.S. $200 required. CBC accepted.

## DENMARK

Postens Filateli Raadhuspladsen 59, DK-1550 Copenhagen V, Denmark. Deals with individual orders for mint stamps, FDCs (with service charge), special postmarks (customer supplies envelopes). SODA available with minimum deposit depending on quantity ordered. Orders shipped post-free. CBC, IMO, bank notes accepted. Printer: PTT Stamp Printing Office, Copenhagen.

## DJIBOUTI

Office des Postes et Telecommunications, Djibouti, Republic of Djibouti. Deals with individual orders for mint stamps. Orders shipped postage extra. CBC accepted.

Government Agencies: L'Agence des Timbres-poste d'Outre-Mer, 85, avenue La Bourdonnais, 75007 Paris, France (exclusive agent for first day covers); Maison Theodore Champion, 13, rue Drouot, 75009 Paris, France.

## DOMINICA

Postmaster, Stamp Order Division, GPO, Roseau, Dominica, West Indies. Deals with individual orders for mint stamps, FDCs. No SODA available. Orders shipped postage extra plus handling fee. CBC, IMO, USMO accepted.

Government Agency: Inter-Governmental Philatelic Corp., 48 W. 48th St., New York, N.Y. 10036.

## DOMINICAN REPUBLIC

Oficina Filatelica, Direccion General de Correos, Santo Domingo, Dominican Republic. Deals with individual orders for mint stamps, FDCs, special postmarks (customer supplies envelopes). SODA available with minimum deposit of U.S. $10 required. Orders shipped postage extra with handling charge of 50 cents per order. CBC, IMO, USPSMO accepted. Printers: Litografia Ferrua Hnos of Santo Domingo and Editorial Padilla of Santo Domingo.

## ECUADOR

Departamento Filatelico, Museo Postal del Estado, Direccion General de Correos, Correo Central, Quito, Ecuador. Details of services not provided.

## EGYPT, ARAB REPUBLIC OF

Philatelic Office, Cairo, Arab Republic of Egypt. Deals with individual orders for mint stamps, FDCs, special postmarks (customer supplies envelopes). SODA available with minimum deposit of U.S. $25 required. Orders shipped postage extra. CBC, IMO, PC accepted. Printer: Postal Printing House, Cairo.

## EQUATORIAL GUINEA

Oficina Filatelica de la Direccion General de Correos, Malabo, Republic of Equatorial Guinea. Details of services not provided.

## ETHIOPIA

Ethiopian Postal Service, Philatelic Section, P.O. Box 1112, Addis Ababa, Ethiopia. Deals with individual orders for mint stamps, FDCs. SODA available (no details). Utilizes special National Postal Museum cancellation on FDCs. Details of additional services not provided.

Government Agencies: Les Editions Rodan, Ch. de Waterloo Stwg. 868/870, 1180 Brussels, Belgium; Stamp Values, P.O. Box 4107, Grand Central Post Office, New York, N.Y. 10017.

## FALKLAND ISLANDS

Postmaster, Philatelic Bureau, GPO, Port Stanley, Falkland Islands. Deals with individual orders for mint stamps, FDCs, special postmarks (customer supplies envelopes). SODA available. Orders shipped postage extra plus handling fee. CBC, PC, IMO accepted. Also handles issues of the British Antarctic Territory.

**Government Agencies: Crown Agents Stamp Bureau, St. Nicholas House, Sutton, Surrey SM1 1EL, England; StanGib Ltd., 1325 Franklin Ave., Garden City, N.Y. 11530; British & Overseas Philatelic Agency Ltd., Box 80, Shibuya, Tokyo 150-91, Japan.**

## FALKLAND ISLANDS DEPENDENCIES

**Manager, Philatelic Bureau, GPO, Port Stanley, Falkland Islands.** Deals with individual orders for mint stamps, FDCs, special postmarks (customers supply envelopes). SODA available. Orders shipped postage extra. CBC, PC, IMO accepted.

**Government Agencies: Crown Agents Stamp Bureau, St. Nicholas House, Sutton, Surrey SM1 1EL, England; StanGib Ltd., 1325 Franklin Ave., Garden City, N.Y. 11530; British & Overseas Philatelic Agency Ltd., Box 80, Shibuya, Tokyo 150-91, Japan.**

## FAROE ISLANDS

**Frimerkjadeildin, 3800 Torshavn, Faroe Islands.** Deals with individual orders for mint and CTO stamps, FDCs, special postmarks (customer supplies envelopes). SODA available with no minimum deposit required. Orders shipped post-free. CBC, IMO accepted. Printers: Various European firms.

**Government Agency: StanGib Ltd., 1325 Franklin Ave., Garden City, N.Y. 11530.**

## FIJI

**Philatelic Bureau, GPO Box 40, Suva, Fiji.** Deals with individual orders for mint, CTO stamps, FDCs. SODA available with minimum deposit of F$20 required. Orders dispatched by registered airmail free of postage and registration fee. BD, BPO, IMO accepted.

**Government Agencies: Crown Agents Stamp Bureau, St. Nicholas House, Sutton, Surrey SM1 1EL, England; StanGib Ltd., 1325 Franklin Ave., Garden City, N.Y. 11530; British & Overseas Philatelic Agency Ltd., Box 80, Shibuya, Tokyo 150-91, Japan.**

## FINLAND

**General Direction of Posts and Telecommunications, Philatelic Section, Paasivuorenkatu 3, P.O. Box 654, SF-00101 Helsinki 10, Finland.** Deals with individual orders for mint stamps, FDCs (bureau supplies envelopes), postal stationery. SODA available with 50-markka minimum deposit required. Orders shipped post-free. CBC, IMO, IRC accepted. Printer: Bank of Finland Security Printing House.

## FRANCE

**Service Philatelique, 61-63 rue de Douai, 75436 Paris Cedex 09, France.** Deals with individual orders for mint stamps. SODA available with the first remittance covering at least three-month purchases, plus postage by registered mail. All orders shipped postage extra. CBC, IMO accepted. Printer: Government Printing Office, Perigueux. Also handles postage stamps of UNESCO, Council of Europe, French Andorra, and permanent issues of Monaco under same terms.

## FRENCH COMMUNITY

**Agence Comptable des Timbres Poste d'Outremer, 85 Avenue de la Bourdonnais, Paris 75007, France; Bureau d'Etudes des Postes et Telecommunications d'Outremer, 5 Rue Oswaldo Cruz, 75016 Paris, France.** Agencies supply new issues of most existing and former French colonies. Details of services not provided.

## FRENCH POLYNESIA

**Centre Philatelique, Papeete, Tahiti, French Polynesia.** Deals with individual orders for mint and CTO stamps, FDCs, special postmarks (customer or agency supply envelopes). SODA available with minimum deposit of 5,000 francs. Orders shipped post-free. IRC, CBC, IMO accepted.

## FRENCH SOUTHERN AND ANTARCTIC TERRITORIES

**Agence Comptable des Timbres Poste d'Outremer, 85 Avenue de la Bourdonnais, Paris 75007, France; Bureau d'Etudes des Postes et Telecommunications d'Outremer, 5 Rue Oswaldo Cruz, 75016 Paris, France.** Agencies supply new issues of most existing and former French colonies. Details of services not provided.

## GABON

**Service Philatelique, Direction Generale des PTT, Libreville, Gabon.** Details of services not provided.

**Government Agency: Ancienne Maison Theodore Champion, 13, rue Drouot, 75009 Paris, France.**

## GAMBIA

**Postmaster General, GPO, Banjul, The Gambia.** Details of services not provided.

**Government Agencies: Crown Agents Stamp Bureau, St. Nicholas House, Sutton, Surrey SM1 1EL, England; StanGib Ltd., 1325 Franklin Ave., Garden City, N.Y. 11530; British & Overseas Philatelic Agency Ltd., Box 80, Shibuya, Tokyo 150-91, Japan.**

## GERMANY, DEMOCRATIC REPUBLIC OF

**VEB Philatelie Wermsdorf, Abt. Export/Import, Postfach 266, 7010 Leipzig, German Demo-**

cratic Republic. Deals only with bulk orders for mint stamps, FDCs. SODA available with minimum deposit required. Orders shipped post-free within Europe; postage extra elsewhere. CBC, PC accepted. Printer: VEB Security Printing Works, Leipzig.

# GERMANY, FEDERAL REPUBLIC OF

Versandstelle fur Postwertzeichen, Postfach 20 00, 6000 Frankfurt 1, Federal Republic of Germany. Deals with individual orders for mint and CTO stamps and postal stationery. SODA available with a minimum deposit of 50 Deutsche mark required. Orders shipped postage extra. IMO, BD, CBC accepted. Printer: Federal Printing Works, Berlin.

Government Agencies: World Wide Philatelic Agency, Inc., 116 W. 32nd St., New York, N.Y. 10001; J.A. Visser Postzegelgroothandel B.V., Box 184, 3300 AD Dordrecht, The Netherlands; Ancienne Maison Theodore Champion, 13, rue Drouot, 75009 Paris, France (sales in France only).

# GHANA

Philatelic Bureau, Department of Posts, Accra, Ghana. Details of services not provided.

Government Agency: Inter-Governmental Philatelic Corp., 48 W. 48th St., New York, N.Y. 10036.

# GIBRALTAR

Gibraltar Post Office, Philatelic Bureau, P.O. Box 5662, Gibraltar. Deals with individual orders for mint stamps, FDCs, special cancellations (customer or bureau supply envelopes), postal stationery. SODA available with minimum deposit of £5 required. Orders shipped postage and handling extra. Orders over £5 in value sent by registered post (unless instructions are received to the contrary) and appropriate fee must be included. BD, IMO, CBC, BPO accepted. Printers: Various European firms.

Government Agencies: Richard Borek Agenturen, Breite Strasse 25/26, 3300 Braunschweig, Federal Republic of Germany (Germany and West Berlin); Inter-Governmental Philatelic Corp., 48 W. 48th St., New York, N.Y. 10036 (Western Hemisphere and Japan); Crown Agents Stamp Bureau, St. Nicholas House, Sutton, Surrey SM1 1EL, England (remainder of world).

# GREAT BRITAIN

British Post Office, Philatelic Bureau, 20 Brandon St., Edinburgh EH3 5TT, Scotland. Deals with individual orders for mint stamps, FDCs (extra charge plus value-added tax). SODA available with minimum deposit required. Orders shipped postage extra plus handling fee. CBC, PC, IMO accepted. Printers: Various British firms.

Government Agencies: StanGib Ltd., 1325 Franklin Ave., Garden City, N.Y. 11530; Max Stern & Co., GPO Box 997H, Melbourne 3001, Australia; Ancienne Maison Theodore Champion, 13, rue Drouot, 75009 Paris, France (sales in France only); Georg Roll Nachfolger, Holbeinstrasse 2, Postfach 1346, D-2880 Brake, Federal Republic of Germany; British & Overseas Philatelic Agency Ltd., Box 80, Shibuya, Tokyo 150-91, Japan; Asia Philatelic Co., Pte. Ltd., Suite 811/812, 8th Floor, Straits Trading Building, 9 Battery Road, Singapore 0104 (SODA available).

# GREECE

Greek Post Office, Philatelic Service, 100 Aiolou St., Athens 131, Greece. Deals with individual orders for mint stamps, FDCs. SODA available with minimum deposit of U.S. $10 required. Orders shipped postage extra. CBC, PC, IMO accepted.

# GREENLAND

Gronlands Postvaesen, 100 Strandgade, P.O. Box 100, DK-1004 Copenhagen K, Denmark. Deals with individual orders for mint stamps, FDCs, special postmarks (customers supply addressed envelopes three weeks before issue date). SODA for mint stamps, FDCs, postmarks, etc., available with no minimum deposit required. Orders shipped post-free. IMO, CBC, IRC, PC accepted. Printer: Danish Post Office Stamp Printing Office.

# GRENADA

Postmaster General, GPO, St. George's, Grenada, West Indies. Details of services not provided.

Government Agency: Inter-Governmental Philatelic Corp., 48 W. 48th St., New York, N.Y. 10036.

# GRENADA, GRENADINES OF

Postmaster General, GPO St. George's, Grenada, West Indies. Details of services not provided.

Government Agency: Inter-Governmental Philatelic Corp., 48 W. 48th St., New York, N.Y. 10036.

# GUATEMALA

Direccion General de Correos y Telegrafos, Departamento Filatelico, Guatemala, Central America. Deals with individual orders for mint stamps. SODA available with minimum deposit of U.S. $20. IMO, CBC, BD accepted.

# GUERNSEY

States Philatelic Bureau, Head Post Office, Guernsey, Channel Islands (Great Britain). Deals with individual orders for mint stamps, FDCs, postal stationery, and special postmarks (customer supplies envelopes). SODA and non-SODA available with minimum deposit of $15 required. Orders over $20 shipped post-free. CBC, PC, BPO, cash, Barclaycard, Visa, Access cards accepted. Printers: Various British firms, Courvoisier SA, of Switzerland.

Government Agencies: Inter-Governmental Philatelic Corp., 48 W. 48th St., New York, N.Y. 10036; Stanley Gibbons Ltd., 391 Strand, London WC2R 0LX, England; Richard Borek Agenturen, Breite Strasse 25/26, Braunschweig, Federal Republic of Germany; Goldphila SA, Via Volta 2, 6830 Chiasso, Switzerland; Frimex Ingrid Berkle, Skebokvarnsvagen 370, 12434 Bandhagen, Sweden; J.A. Visser B.V., Box 184, 3300 AD Dordrecht, The Netherlands; Ancienne Maison Theodore Champion, 13, rue Drouot, 75009 Paris, France (sales in France only).

## GUINEA

Agence Philatelique, Boite Postale 814, Conakry, Republic of Guinea. Deals with individual orders for a minimum of U.S. $15.60. SODA information not provided. Orders shipped postage extra. CBC, BD accepted.

## GUINEA-BISSAU

Direccao dos Servicos dos Correios, Telegrafos e Telefones, Bissau, Guinea-Bissau. Details of services not provided.

## GUYANA

Guyana Post Office Corp., Robb Street, Georgetown, Guyana. Deals with individual orders for mint stamps. SODA available. Orders shipped postage extra.

Government Agencies: Crown Agents Stamp Bureau, St. Nicholas House, Sutton, Surrey SM1 1EL, England; StanGib Ltd., 1325 Franklin Ave., Garden City, N.Y. 11530; British & Overseas Philatelic Agency Ltd., Box 80, Shibuya, Tokyo 150-91, Japan.

## HONDURAS

Departamento Filatelico, Direccion General de Correos, Tegucigalpa, D.C., Honduras, Central America. Deals with individual orders for mint stamps. SODA available with minimum deposit of 40 lempiras required. CBC, BD, USPSMO, IMO accepted.

## HONG KONG

Philatelic Bureau, GPO, Hong Kong. Deals with individual orders for mint stamps, FDCs. SODA available with minimum deposit of U.S. $7 required. Orders shipped postage extra plus handling fee. CBC, BPO, IMO accepted. Printer: Harrison & Sons Ltd., England (definitives).

Government Agencies: Crown Agents Stamp Bureau, St. Nicholas House, Sutton, Surrey SM1 1EL, England; StanGib Ltd., 1325 Franklin Ave., Garden City, N.Y. 11530; British & Over-seas Philatelic Agency Ltd., Box 80, Shibuya, Tokyo 150-91, Japan.

## HUNGARY

Philatelia Hungarica, P.O. Box 600, Budapest 1373, Hungary. Deals only with bulk orders (dealers). Details not provided. Also supplies postal emissions of Mongolia.

## ICELAND

Frimerkjasalan, Postboks 1445, Reykjavik, Iceland. Details of services not provided.

## INDIA

Philatelic Bureau, GPO, Bombay 400001, India. Deals with individual orders for mint stamps, FDCs. SODA available with minimum deposit of U.S. $15 required. Orders shipped postage extra plus a handling fee of 1 per cent on all orders. BD in foreign currency payable at any bank in India. Printer: India Security Press.

Government Agencies: James Davis & Sons Ltd., 45 Church St., Rickmansworth WD3 1DG, England; Richard Borek Agenturen, Breite Strasse 25/26, 3300 Braunschweig, Federal Republic of Germany; Inter-Governmental Philatelic Corp., 48 W. 48th St., New York, N.Y. 10036.

## INDONESIA

Philatelic Subdivision, State Enterprise Posts and Giro, 34 Jalan Jakarta, Bandung, Indonesia. Deals with orders for mint stamps, FDCs, and postal stationery. SODA available with minimum deposit of U.S. $6. Orders shipped postage extra. CBC, IMO accepted. Printer: Indonesian Government Security Printing and Minting Co.

Government Agencies: Hugo J. van Reijen, International Philatelic Agencies, Koninginneweg 133, Box 5497, Amsterdam 1007, The Netherlands (Europe and Africa).

## IRAN

Philatelic Bureau, General Directorate of Posts, Tehran, Iran. Deals with individual orders for mint stamps, FDCs (service fee extra). SODA available with minimum deposit of U.S. $10 required. Orders shipped every four months, postage extra. CBC, IMO, bank notes, IRC (for 15 rials). Printer: Government Printing Press Organization, Iran.

## IRAQ

Posts and Savings Administration, Stamp Department, Philatelic Bureau, Baghdad, Republic of Iraq. Deals with individual and bulk orders for mint stamps, FDCs, special postmarks (customer supplies envelopes). SODA available with minimum deposit of U.S. $1 required. Orders shipped post-free, handling fee extra. CBC, IMO, bank notes accepted. Printers: Several European firms.

## IRELAND

The Controller, Philatelic Bureau, GPO, Dublin 1, Ireland. Deals with individual orders for mint stamps, FDCs, special postmarks (customer supplies envelopes), postal stationery, postage due labels, stamp booklets, coils. SODA available with minimum deposit of U.S. $10. Orders shipped postage extra. CBC, BPO, IMO accepted. Printers: Irish Government Printers and Irish Security Stamp Printing.

Government Agency: James Davis & Sons Ltd., 45 Church St., Rickmansworth WD3 1DG, England.

## ISLE OF MAN

Philatelic Bureau, P.O. Box 10M, Douglas, Isle of Man. Deals with individual orders for mint, CTO stamps, booklets and postal stationery. FDCs and presentation packs are also available. SODA and non-SODA available with minimum deposit of U.S. $10. Standing orders and additional orders amounting to more than £10 are supplied without handling charge. Additional orders for less than £10 are subject to handling charge of 15 pence for account holders and 20p for nonaccount holders. PC, BPO, IMO accepted. Printers: Courvoisier, SA, Switzerland, and various British firms.

Government Agencies: Richard Borek Agenturen, Breite Strasse 25/26, 3300 Braunschweig, Federal Republic of Germany; J.A. Visser Postzegelgroothandel B.V., Box 184, 3300 AD Dordrecht, The Netherlands; Crown Agents Stamp Bureau, St. Nicholas House, Sutton, Surrey SM1 1EL, England; Inter-Governmental Philatelic Corp., 48 W. 48th St., New York, N.Y. 10036; Ancienne Maison Theodore Champion, 13, rue Drouot, 75009 Paris, France (sales in France only); Stanley Gibbons Ltd., 391 Strand, London WC2R 0LX, England.

## ISRAEL

Ministry of Communications, Philatelic Services, Tel Aviv-Yafo 61 080, Israel. Deals with individual orders for minimum of three units of mint stamps, FDCs, special postmarks (agency supplies envelopes). SODA available with minimum deposit of U.S. $30 required. Orders shipped postage extra. CBC accepted. Printer: Government Printer, Jerusalem.

Government Agencies: Israel Philatelic Agency in America, Inc., 116 W. 32nd St., New York, N.Y. 10001; Messrs. Harry Allen, Box 5, Rickmansworth, Herts., WD3 1EY, England.

## ITALY

Ufficio Principale Filatelico, Via Mario de' Fiori, 103/A, 00187 Rome, Italy. Deals with individual orders for mint stamps, FDCs, special postmarks (agency supplies envelopes for 200 lire each or customer supplies envelopes). SODA available with minimum deposit of 10,500 lire. Orders shipped postage extra. IMO accepted. Printer: State Polygraphic Institute, Rome.

## IVORY COAST

Office des Postes et Telecommunications, Direction des Services Postaux, Service Philatelique, Abidjan, Ivory Coast. Deals with individual orders for mint stamps, FDCs. SODA available with minimum deposit. Orders sent postage extra. IMO accepted.

Government Agency: Ancienne Maison Theodore Champion, 13, rue Drouot, 75009 Paris, France.

## JAMAICA

Head Postmaster, Philatelic Bureau, GPO, Kingston, Jamaica. Deals with individual orders for mint stamps, FDCs. SODA available with minimum deposit of J$4 required. Orders shipped postage extra. IMO, USPSMO, Canadian MO, BPO, BD, CBC accepted.

Government Agencies: Crown Agents Stamp Bureau, St. Nicholas House, Sutton, Surrey SM1 1EL, England; StanGib Ltd., 1325 Franklin Ave., Garden City, N.Y. 11530; British & Overseas Philatelic Agency Ltd., Box 80, Shibuya, Tokyo 150-91, Japan

## JAPAN

Philatelic Section, CPO Box 888, Tokyo 100-91, Japan. Deals with individual orders for mint stamps only. SODA available with a minimum deposit of $20 required. Orders shipped postage extra. Payment by IMO accepted.

## JERSEY

The Jersey Post Office, Philatelic Bureau, P.O. Box 304, Jersey, Channel Islands, via Great Britain. Deals with individual orders for mint and CTO stamps, FDCs, special postmarks (customer supplies envelopes). SODA available with minimum deposit of U.S. $10 required. Orders shipped post-free plus handling fee (postage extra for airmail). CBC, PC, IMO, USMO accepted. Printer: Courvoisier, SA, Switzerland; The House of Questa Ltd., England; others.

Government Agencies: J.A. Visser Postzegelgroothandel B.V., Box 184, 3300 AD Dordrecht, The Netherlands; Inter-Governmental Philatelic Corp., 48 W. 48th St., New York, N.Y. 10036; Crown Agents Stamp Bureau, St. Nicholas House, Sutton, Surrey SM1 1EL, England; Ancienne Maison Theodore Champion, 13, rue Drouot, 75009 Paris, France (sales in France only); Stanley Gibbons Ltd., 391 Strand, London WC2R 0LX, England; Richard Borek Agenturen, Breite Strasse, 25/26, 3300 Braunschweig, Federal Republic of Germany.

# JORDAN, HASHEMITE KINGDOM OF

Ministry of Communications, Philatelic Section, P.O. Box 71, Amman, Jordan. Deals in complete mint sets only. SODA not available. Orders sent postage extra. CBC accepted.

# KAMPUCHEA (CAMBODIA)

Agence Philatelique, Direction Generale des PTT, Phnom Penh, Kampuchea (Cambodia). No information available.

# KENYA

Philatelic Bureau, P.O. Box 30368, Nairobi, Kenya. Deals with individual orders for mint stamps, FDCs, special postmarks, postal stationery, stamp booklets, coils, and postage due labels. SODA available with no minimum charge. IMO, BD accepted. Orders sent postage extra. Also provides mailing list service for Kenya 15 shillings annually. Printers: Various.

Government Agencies: Crown Agents Stamp Bureau, St. Nicholas House, Sutton, Surrey SM1 1EL, England; Inter-Governmental Philatelic Corp., 48 W. 48th St., New York, N.Y. 10036; British & Overseas Philatelic Agency Ltd., Box 80, Shibuya, Tokyo 150-91, Japan.

# KIRIBATI (Gilbert Islands)

Philatelic Bureau, Box 494, Betio, Tarawa, Kiribati. Deals with individual orders for mint or CTO stamps, FDCs. SODA available. Orders shipped postpaid. CBC, BD, PC, BPO accepted.

# KOREA, DEMOCRATIC PEOPLE'S REPUBLIC OF

Korea Stamp Corp., Pyongyang, Democratic People's Republic of Korea. Details of services not provided.

# KOREA, REPUBLIC OF

Korean Philatelic Center, Division of Bando Sangsa Co. Ltd., CPO Box 1899, Seoul, Republic of Korea. Deals with individual orders for mint stamps, FDCs, special postmarks (agency supplies envelopes for fee). SODA available with minimum deposit of U.S. $10 required. Orders shipped postage extra. CBC, PC, IMO accepted. Printer: Korean Government Printing Agency.

# KUWAIT

Director, Post Office Department, Philatelic Bureau, Safat Post Office, Kuwait. Deals with individual orders for mint stamps, postal stationery, FDCs (customer provides envelopes). SODA information not provided. Orders shipped postage extra. CBC, BD accepted.

# LAOS

Service Philatelique des PTT, Vientiane, Laos. Details of services not provided.

# LEBANON

Receveur Principal des Postes, Service Philatelique, Beirut, Lebanon. Details of services not provided.

# LESOTHO

Philatelic Bureau, P.O. Box 413, Maseru, Lesotho. Deals with individual orders for mint and CTO stamps, FDCs (customer supplies envelopes) serviced for 5¢ each. SODA available with minimum deposit of U.S. $30 required. Orders shipped post-free. CBC, IMO accepted.

Government Agencies: Crown Agents Stamp Bureau, St. Nicholas House, Sutton, Surrey SM1 1EL, England; StanGib Ltd., 1325 Franklin Ave., Garden City, N.Y. 11530; British & Overseas Philatelic Agency Ltd., Box 80, Shibuya, Tokyo 150-91, Japan.

# LIBERIA

Liberia Philatelic Agent, Ministry of Posts and Telecommunications, Monrovia, Liberia. Details of services not provided.

# LIBYA

Service Philatelique, Direction Generale des PTT, Tripoli, Libya. Details of services not provided.

# LIECHTENSTEIN

Official Philatelic Service, FL-9490 Vaduz, Principality of Liechtenstein. Deals with individual orders for minimum of two copies of mint stamps, FDCs, maximum cards, special postmarks (customer supplies envelopes). SODA available by advance payment. SODA orders shipped post-free. CBC accepted. Printers: Austrian Government Printing Office, Austria (line engraving); Courvoisier, SA, Switzerland (photogravure).

# LUXEMBOURG

Direction des Postes, Office des Timbres, L-2020, Luxembourg, Grand Duchy of Luxembourg. Deals with individual orders for mint and canceled stamps and FDCs (bureau supplies envelopes for 8 francs each). SODA available with minimum deposit of U.S. $12 required. CBC, IMO, bank notes accepted. Printers: Courvoisier SA, Switzerland; Joh. Enschede en Zonen, The Netherlands; French Government Printing Office; Austrian Government Printing Office.

# MACAO

CTT, Divisao de Filatelia, Largo do Senado, Macao. Deals with individual orders for mint stamps, FDCs. SODA available with minimum deposit of U.S. $20 required. Orders shipped postage extra. PC, cash accepted.

## MADEIRA

Philatelic Office, Av. Casal Ribeiro 28-2°, 1096 Lisbon Codex, Portugal. Deals with individual orders for mint stamps, FDCs (agency supplies envelopes). SODA available with minimum deposit of $15. Orders shipped postage extra. IMO, CBC, bank notes (except escudos) accepted.

Government Agency: J.A. Visser Postzegelgroothandel B.V., Box 184, 3300 AD Dordrecht, The Netherlands.

## MALAGASY REPUBLIC (Madagascar)

Service Philatelique, Direction Generale des PTT, Tananarive-RP, Malagasy Republic. Details of services not provided.

Government Agency: Ancienne Maison Theodore Champion, 13, rue Drouot, 75009 Paris, France.

## MALAWI

Post Office Philatelic Bureau, P.O. Box 1000, Blantyre, Malawi. Deals with individual orders for mint and CTO stamps, postal stationery, FDCs, special postmarks (bureau supplies envelopes). SODA available with no minimum deposit required. Orders shipped post-free. CBC, IMO accepted.

Government Agencies: Crown Agents Stamp Bureau, St. Nicholas House, Sutton, Surrey SM1 1EL, England; StanGib Ltd., 1325 Franklin Ave., Garden City, N.Y. 11530; British & Overseas Philatelic Agency Ltd., Box 80, Shibuya, Tokyo 150-91, Japan.

## MALAYSIA

Director General of Posts, Post Office Headquarters, Kuala Lumpur, Malaysia. Details of services not provided.

Government Agency: British & Overseas Philatelic Agency Ltd., Box 80, Shibuya, Tokyo 150-91, Japan.

## MALDIVES, REPUBLIC OF

Philatelic Bureau, GPO, Male, Republic of Maldives, Indian Ocean. Deals with individual orders for mint stamps, FDCs. SODA not available. Orders shipped postage extra plus handling fee. Orders restricted to U.S. $20 each. CBC, IMO accepted.

Government Agency: Inter-Governmental Philatelic Corp., 48 W. 48th St., New York, N.Y. 10036.

## MALI

Service Philatelique, Direction Generale des PTT, Bamako, Mali. Details of services not provided.

Government Agency: Ancienne Maison Theodore Champion, 13, rue Drouot, 75009 Paris, France.

## MALTA

Philatelic Bureau, GPO, Auberge d'Italie, Valletta, Malta. Deals with individual orders for mint and CTO stamps, FDCs, special postmarks (customer supplies envelopes). SODA available with minimum deposit of M£2 required. Orders shipped postage extra. BD, IMO (except from U.S.) accepted. Printer: Printex Ltd.

## MAURITANIA

Service Philatelique, Direction Generale des PTT, P.O. Box 99, Nouakchott, Mauritania. Details of services not provided.

Government Agency: Ancienne Maison Theodore Champion, 13, rue Drouot, 75009 Paris, France.

## MAURITIUS

Department of Posts and Telegraphs, GPO, Port Louis, Mauritius. Deals with individual orders for mint stamps, FDCs, special postmarks (agency supplies envelopes). SODA available with minimum deposit of U.S. $10 required. Orders shipped postage extra plus handling charge. CBC, IMO accepted.

Government Agencies: Crown Agents Stamp Bureau, St. Nicholas House, Sutton, Surrey SM1 1EL, England; StanGib Ltd., 1325 Franklin Ave., Garden City, N.Y. 11530; British & Overseas Philatelic Agency Ltd., Box 80, Shibuya, Tokyo 150-91, Japan

## MEXICO

Departamento Filatelico, Edificio de Correos, 2° Piso, Tacuba 1, 06000 Mexico 1, D.F., Mexico. Deals with individual orders for mint stamps. SODA available with minimum deposit of U.S. $10. Orders shipped postage extra. CBC, IMO accepted. Printer: Mexican Government Stamps and Values Printing Office.

## MONACO

Office des Emissions de Timbres-Poste, Departement de Finances, Principality of Monaco. Deals with orders from subscribers only. Subscription fees are U.S. $2 paid once. No standing order is available. Subscribers receive at each issuance an order form to be returned within indicated period. Mint and CTO stamps available at face value, FDCs (plus cost of envelope). Orders shipped post-free. Deposit accounts, PC, IMO accepted. Printer: French Government Printing Office.

## MONGOLIA

Directeur de Bureau des Philatelistes, P.O. Box 175, Ulan Bator, Mongolia. Details of services not provided.

## MONTSERRAT

**Montserrat Philatelic Bureau, GPO, Plymouth, Montserrat, West Indies.** Deals with individual orders for mint stamps, FDCs, postmarks (agency supplies envelopes with charge). SODA available with no minimum deposit. Ordering deadline is six months after issue date. Orders shipped post-free. BPO, CBC, BD, IMO accepted.

## MOROCCO

**Ministere des PTT, Division Postale, Rabat, Morocco.** Deals with individual orders for mint stamps, FDCs, special postmarks (customer supplies envelopes). SODA available with minimum deposit of U.S. $12 required. Orders shipped postage extra. CBC, IMO accepted.

**Government Agency; Ancienne Maison Theodore Champion, 13, rue Drouot, 75009 Paris, France.**

## MOZAMBIQUE

**Philatelic and Numismatic Enterprise, Box 4444, Maputo 1, Mozambique.** Deals with individual orders for mint stamps (complete sets only), FDCs, special postmarks (customer supplies envelopes). SODA available with unspecified minimum deposit required. Orders shipped postage extra. CBC, bank notes accepted. Printer: National Printers (governmental agency) of Maputo.

## NAURU

**Officer-in-Charge, Philatelic Bureau, Republic of Nauru, Central Pacific.** Deals with individual orders for mint and CTO stamps, FDCs (bureau supplies envelopes). SODA available with minimum deposit of A$15 (U.S. $16). PC from Australia; from other areas, BD in Australian dollars or currency notes. Orders shipped post-free via surface, airmail, etc.

## NEPAL

**Officer-in-Charge, Nepal Philatelic Bureau, Sundhara, Kathmandu, Nepal.** Deals with individual orders for mint stamps, postal stationery, FDCs, special postmarks (bureau supplies envelopes). SODA available with U.S. $10 minimum deposit. Orders shipped postage extra. CBC, BD, IMO accepted.

## NETHERLANDS

**Netherlands Post Office Philatelic Service, P.O. Box 30051, 9700-RN Groningen, The Netherlands.** Deals with individual orders for stamps. SODA available. Orders shipped free, handling charge extra on small orders. Payment by IMO, certain bank notes accepted. Payment can be made directly into account through General Bank of The Netherlands, 84 William St., New York, N.Y. 10038 (for U.S. customers), or General Bank of The Netherlands, 61 Threadneedle St., London, England (for U.K. customers).

**Government Agency: World Wide Philatelic Agency, Inc., 116 W. 32nd St., New York, N.Y. 10036.**

## NETHERLANDS ANTILLES

**Philatelic Service Office, Postmaster, Willemstad, Curacao, Netherlands Antilles.** Deals with individual orders for mint stamps, FDCs, special postmarks (agency supplies envelopes). SODA available with minimum deposit of U.S. $5. Orders shipped by airmail registered. Payment by cashier's check or CBC. Printer: Joh. Enschede en Zonen, The Netherlands.

**Government Agencies: World Wide Philatelic Agency, Inc., 116 W. 32nd St., New York, N.Y. 10001; International Philatelic Agencies, P.O. Box 5497, Amsterdam, The Netherlands.**

## NEVIS

**Nevis Philatelic Bureau, GPO, Charlestown, Nevis, West Indies.** Deals with individual orders for mint, CTO stamps, FDCs, PHQ cards, presentation packs. SODA available. Orders shipped post-free. PC, IMO, USPSMO accepted.

## NEW CALEDONIA

**Philatelic Bureau, Recette Principale des Postes, Noumea, New Caledonia.** Deals with individual orders for mint stamps, FDCs, special postmarks (customer supplies envelopes). SODA available with minimum deposit of 2,500 francs. Orders shipped postage extra. IMO accepted. Printer: Government Stamp Printing Office, Perigueux, France.

## NEW ZEALAND

**Post Office, Philatelic Bureau, Private Bag, Wanganui, New Zealand.** Deals with individual orders for mint stamps, FDCs, special postmarks (bureau supplies special post cards on SODA only). SODA available with minimum deposit of U.S. $5.25 required. Orders shipped postage extra. CBC, IMO, BPO accepted.

**Government Agencies: Stanley Gibbons Ltd., 391 Strand, London WC2R 0LX, England; British & Overseas Philatelic Agency Ltd., Box 80, Shibuya, Tokyo 150-91, Japan.**

## NICARAGUA

**Division de Especies Postales y Filatelia, Telcor, Edificio Zacarias Guerra, 7MO. Piso, Apartado 325, Managua, Nicaragua, Central America.** Deals with individual orders for mint stamps, FDCs, special postmarks (agency provides envelopes). SODA available with minimum deposit of U.S. $20 required. Orders shipped postage extra. CBC, PC, IMO accepted.

## NIGER

**Service Philatelique, Direction Generale des PTT, Niamey, Niger.** Details of services not provided.

Government Agency: Ancienne Maison Theodore Champion, 13, rue Drouot, 75009 Paris, France.

## NIGERIA

**Nigerian Philatelic Service, GPO, Tinubu Street, P.M.B. 12647, Lagos, Nigeria.** Deals with individual orders for mint stamps, FDCs, special postmarks (bureau or customer supply envelopes). Orders for CTOs not accepted. SODA available with minimum deposit of U.S. $20. Orders shipped postage extra plus handling charge. BPO, IMO, British and American PC accepted. Printer: Nigerian Security Printing and Minting Co. Ltd., Lagos.

Government Agencies: StanGib Ltd., 1325 Franklin Ave., Garden City, N.Y. 11530; British & Overseas Philatelic Agency Ltd., Box 80, Shibuya, Tokyo 150-91, Japan; Crown Agents Stamp Bureau, St. Nicholas House, Sutton, Surrey SM1 1EL, England.

## NIUE

**Philatelic Bureau, Box 150, Niue Post Office, Government of Niue, Alofi, Niue, South Pacific (via New Zealand).** Deals with individual orders for mint stamps, FDCs, special postmarks (bureau supplies envelopes). SODA available with minimum deposit of U.S. $20 required. Orders shipped postage extra. CBC, IMO, CPO accepted.

## NORFOLK ISLAND

**Senior Philatelic Officer, Norfolk Island 2899, South Pacific.** Deals with individual orders for mint and CTO stamps, FDCs (bureau supplies envelopes). SODA available with unstipulated deposit required. Orders shipped postage extra. CBC, IMO accepted.

Government Agencies: British & Overseas Philatelic Agency Ltd., Box 80, Shibuya, Tokyo 150-91, Japan; Philatelic Bureau, GPO Box 9988, Melbourne, Vic. 3001, Australia; International Postal Marketing Corp., 128 Passaic Ave., Fairfield, N.J. 07006 (offers SODA services to all North American collectors); and Crown Agents Stamp Bureau, St. Nicholas House, Sutton, Surrey SM1 1EL, England.

## NORWAY

**Postens filatelitjeneste, Postboks 1085 Sentrum, Oslo 1, Norway.** Deals with individual orders for mint stamps, FDCs. SODA available. Orders shipped post-free. CBC, IMO accepted.

Government Agencies: StanGib Ltd., 1325 Franklin Ave., Garden City, N.Y. 11530; Stanley Gibbons Ltd., 391 Strand, London WC2R 0LX, England; Richard Borek Agenturen, Breite Strasse 25/26, 3300 Braunschweig, Federal Republic of Germany.

## OMAN, SULTANATE OF

**Philatelic Bureau, Department of Posts, Telegraphs & Telephones, Muscat, Sultanate**
of Oman. Deals with individual orders for mint stamps, FDCs (agency supplies envelopes). SODA available with minimum deposit of U.S. $10 required. Orders shipped postage extra plus service fee. CBC, British and U.S. currencies accepted.

Government Agencies: Crown Agents Stamp Bureau, St. Nicholas House, Sutton, Surrey SM1 1EL, England; StanGib Ltd., 1325 Franklin Ave., Garden City, N.Y. 11530; British & Overseas Philatelic Agency Ltd., Box 80, Shibuya, Tokyo 150-91, Japan.

## PAKISTAN

**Pakistan Philatelic Bureau, GPO, Karachi, Pakistan.** Deals with individual orders for mint and CTO stamps, FDCs, special postmarks (customer supplies envelopes). SODA available with no minimum deposit required. Orders shipped postage extra. CBC, BPO, IMO accepted. Printer: Pakistan Security Printing Corp.

Government Agency: James Davis and Sons Ltd., 45 Church St., Rickmansworth WD3 1DG, England.

## PANAMA

**Direccion General de Correos y Telecomunicaciones, Departamento de Filatelia, Apartado 3421, Panama 1, Panama.** Deals with individual orders for mint stamps, FDCs, special postmarks (customer supplies envelopes). SODA available with minimum deposit of U.S. $15 required. Orders shipped postage extra plus handling charge. CBC, IMO accepted.

## PAPUA NEW GUINEA

**Philatelic Bureau, P.O. Box 160, Port Moresby, Papua New Guinea.** Deals with individual orders for mint stamps, FDCs, issue postmarks (bureau supplies envelopes). SODA available with minimum deposit of U.S. $15.76 required. Orders sent post-free. BPO, CBC, IMO, BD, and bank notes accepted.

Government Agencies: Crown Agents Stamp Bureau, St. Nicholas House, Sutton, Surrey SM1 1EL, England; StanGib Ltd., 1325 Franklin Ave., Garden City, N.Y. 11530; British & Overseas Philatelic Agency Ltd., Box 80, Shibuya, Tokyo 150-91, Japan.

## PARAGUAY

**Oficina Filatelica, Direccion General de Correos, Asuncion, Paraguay.** Details of services not provided.

## PENRHYN ISLAND

**Penrhyn Post Office, Penrhyn Island, Northern Cook Islands, South Pacific Ocean.** Deals with individual orders for mint stamps, FDCs. SODA available with minimum deposit of U.S. $20 required. SODA orders shipped post-free; transient orders postage extra. CBC accepted.

## PERU

Chief, Philatelic Postal Museum, GPO, Lima, Peru. Details of services not provided.

## PHILIPPINES

Stamp and Philatelic Division, Bureau of Posts, Manila, Philippines. Details of services not provided.

## PITCAIRN ISLANDS

Postmaster, Philatelic Bureau, GPO Box 40, Suva, Fiji, South Pacific. Deals with individual orders for mint stamps, CTOs, FDCs. SODA available with minimum deposit of F$20 required. Orders shipped by registered airmail, postage extra. BD, CBC, IMO accepted. CTO stamps available from Postmaster, Pitcairn Islands, South Pacific.

Government Agencies: Crown Agents Stamp Bureau, St. Nicholas House, Sutton, Surrey SM1 1EL, England; StanGib Ltd., 1325 Franklin Ave., Garden City, N.Y. 11530; British & Overseas Philatelic Agency Ltd., Box 80, Shibuya, Tokyo 150-91, Japan.

## POLAND

Ars Polona, P.O. Box 1001, 00-950 Warsaw, Poland. Deals only with bulk quantity orders for mint and CTO stamps, FDCs, special postmarks (wholesale lots only; agency supplies envelopes). SODA available with minimum deposit required. Orders sent postage extra. CBC accepted. Printer: State Printing Works of Securities, Warsaw.

## PORTUGAL

Philatelic Office, Av. Casal Ribeiro 28-2°, 1096 Lisbon Codex, Portugal. Deals with individual orders for mint stamps, FDCs (agency supplies envelopes). SODA available with minimum deposit of $15. Orders shipped postage extra. IMO, CBC, bank notes (except escudos) accepted.

Government Agencies: J.A. Visser Postegelgroothandel B.V., Box 184, 3300 AD Dordrecht, The Netherlands; Ancienne Maison Theodore Champion, 13, rue Drouot, 75009 Paris, France (sales in France only); Georg Roll Nachfolger, Holbeinstrasse 2, Postfach 1346, D-2880 Brake, Federal Republic of Germany.

## QATAR

Philatelic Bureau, Department of Posts, Doha, State of Qatar. Deals with individual orders for mint stamps, postal stationery, FDCs (bureau supplies envelopes). SODA available. No shipping details provided. BD, CBC accepted.

Government Agencies: James Davis & Sons Ltd., 45 Church St., Richmansworth WD3 1DG, England; Inter-Governmental Philatelic Corp., 48 W. 48th St., New York, N.Y. 10036.

## REDONDA

Redonda Philatelic Bureau, Redonda, Antigua. Deals with individual orders for mint stamps. SODA available with minimum deposit required. Orders shipped postage extra. PC, IMO accepted.

## ROMANIA

ILEXIM, 13 Decembrie St. No. 3, P.O. Box 136-137, Bucharest, Romania. Deals with individual orders for mint stamps, kiloware, packet material, FDCs. SODA available. Orders sent by registered airmail postage extra (minimum U.S. $1.50). CBC accepted.

## ROSS DEPENDENCIES

Post Office Philatelic Bureau, Private Bag, Wanganui, New Zealand. Deals with individual orders for mint stamps, FDCs, special postmarks (bureau supplies special post cards on SODA only). SODA available with minimum deposit of U.S. $5.25 required. Orders shipped postage extra.

Government Agencies: Stanley Gibbons Ltd., 391 Strand, London WC2R 0LX, England; British & Overseas Philatelic Agency Ltd., Box 80, Shibuya, Tokyo 150-91, Japan.

## RWANDA

Direction Generale des PTT, Kigale, Rwanda, or Agences Philateliques Gouvernementales, Chaussee de Waterloo 868/870, 1180 Brussels, Belgium. Deals with individual orders for mint stamps, FDCs, special postmarks (agency supplies envelopes for fee). SODA available with no minimum deposit required. Orders shipped postage extra plus handling fee. CBC, PC, IMO accepted.

## ST. HELENA

Postmaster, Jamestown, St. Helena, South Atlantic. Deals with individual orders for mint stamps, FDCs, special postmarks (bureau or customers supply envelopes). No SODA available. Orders shipped postage extra. CBC on London bank, U.S. bank notes, BPO, IMO accepted.

Government Agencies: StanGib Ltd., 1325 Franklin Ave., Garden City, N.Y. 11530; British & Overseas Philatelic Agency Ltd., Box 80, Shibuya, Tokyo 150-91, Japan; Crown Agents Stamp Bureau, St. Nicholas House, Sutton, Surrey SM1 1EL, England.

## ST. KITTS

The Manager, St. Kitts Philatelic Bureau, GPO, Basseterre, St. Kitts, West Indies. Deals with individual orders for mint stamps, FDCs, presentation packs, PHQ cards. SODA available. Orders shipped post-free. PC, CBC, IMO, USPSMO, BPO accepted.

## SAINT LUCIA

Postmaster, GPO, Castries, Saint Lucia, West Indies. Deals with individual orders for mint stamps, FDCs (customer supplies envelopes). No SODA available. Orders shipped postage extra. CBC, IMO, USPSMO, BPO accepted.

Government Agency: Inter-Governmental Philatelic Corp., 48 W. 48th St., New York, N.Y. 10036.

## ST. PIERRE & MIQUELON

Service Philatelique, 61-63 rue de Douai, 75436 Paris Cedex 09, France. Deals with individual orders for mint stamps. SODA available with the first remittance covering at least three-month purchases, plus postage by registered mail. All orders shipped postage extra. CBC, IMO accepted. Printer: Government Printing Office, Perigueux. Also handles postage stamps of UNESCO, Council of Europe, French Andorra, and permanent issues of Monaco under same terms. (French stamps are used on St. Pierre & Miquelon.)

## ST. THOMAS & PRINCE ISLANDS

Direccao dos Correios e Telecomunicacoes, Seccao Filatelica, St. Thomas, Democratic Republic of St. Thomas and Prince Islands. Deals with individual orders for mint stamps and postal stationery. No information on SODA provided. Orders sent postage extra. CBC accepted.

## ST. VINCENT

Bureau Manager, St. Vincent Philatelic Services, GPO, Kingstown, St. Vincent, West Indies. Deals with individual orders for mint and CTO stamps, FDCs. SODA available with minimum deposit of U.S. $15 required. Orders shipped post-free. PC, IMO, BD, BPO accepted.

## ST. VINCENT, GRENADINES OF

Bureau Manager, St. Vincent Philatelic Services, GPO, Kingstown, St. Vincent, West Indies. Deals with individual orders for mint and CTO stamps, FDCs. SODA available with minimum deposit of U.S. $15 required. Orders shipped postfree. PC, IMO, BD, BPO accepted.

## EL SALVADOR

Direccion General de Correos, Departamento de Filatelia, Republic of El Salvador, Central America. Deals with individual orders for mint stamps, FDCs, special postmarks (customer supplies envelopes). SODA not available. Orders shipped postage extra.

## SAN MARINO, REPUBLIC OF

Philatelic Office, 47031 Republic of San Marino. Deals with individual orders for mint stamps, FDCs, special postmarks (customer supplies envelopes). SODA available with minimum deposit of U.S. $20 required. Orders shipped postage extra. CBC, IMO accepted.

## SAUDI ARABIA

Division of Posts and Telegraphs, Philatelic Section, Riyadh, Saudi Arabia. Details of services not provided.

## SENEGAL

Office des Postes et Telecommunications du Senegal, Bureau Philatelique, Dakar, Senegal. Deals with individual orders for mint stamps, FDCs (bureau provides envelopes). SODA information not provided. Orders sent postage extra. CBC accepted.

Government Agency: Ancienne Maison Theodore Champion, 13, rue Drouot, 75009 Paris, France.

## SEYCHELLES

Philatelic Bureau, P.O. Box 60, Victoria, Mahe, Seychelles, Indian Ocean. Deals with individual orders for mint stamps, FDCs (bureau provides envelopes). SODA available. No ordering details provided.

## SIERRA LEONE

Postmaster General, GPO, Freetown, Sierra Leone. Details of services not provided.

Government Agencies: Crown Agents Stamp Bureau, St. Nicholas House, Sutton, Surrey SM1 1EL, England; Inter-Governmental Philatelic Corp., 48 W. 48th St., New York, N.Y. 10036; StanGib Ltd., 1325 Franklin Ave., Garden City, N.Y. 11530; British & Overseas Philatelic Agency Ltd., Box 80, Shibuya, Tokyo 150-91, Japan.

## SINGAPORE

Postal Services Department, 8th Floor, World Trade Centre, Maritime Square, Singapore 0409, Republic of Singapore. Deals with individual orders for mint and CTO stamps, FDCs (bureau supplies envelopes with service charge). SODA available with minimum deposit of S$30 required. Orders shipped postage extra. CBC, IMO, BPO accepted.

Government Agencies: Crown Agents Stamp Bureau, St. Nicholas House, Sutton, Surrey SM1 1EL, England; British & Overseas Philatelic Agency Ltd., Box 80, Shibuya, Tokyo 150-91, Japan; Inter-Governmental Philatelic Corp., 48 W. 48th St., New York, N.Y. 10036.

## SOLOMON ISLANDS

Philatelic Bureau, GPO, Mendana Avenue, Honiara, Solomon Islands, South Pacific. Deals with individual orders for mint and CTO stamps, FDCs, maximum cards, presentation packs. SODA available with minimum deposit of U.S. $20 (adequate for one year supply of stamps) required. BD, PC, IMO accepted. Mint stamps sent airmail postage extra; FDC and CTOs shipped post-free. Printers: Various British firms.

Government Agencies: Crown Agents Stamp Bureau, St. Nicholas House, Sutton, Surrey SM1 1EL, England; StanGib Ltd., 1325 Franklin Ave., Garden City, N.Y. 11530; British & Overseas Philatelic Agency Ltd., Box 80, Shibuya, Tokyo 150-91, Japan.

## SOMALI DEMOCRATIC REPUBLIC

Philatelic Service, Ministry of Posts & Telecommunications, Mogadishu, Somali Democratic Republic. Deals with individual orders for mint stamps, FDCs, special postmarks (either agency or customer supplies envelopes). SODA available with minimum deposit of U.S. $20 required. Orders shipped postage extra. BD, IMO (United Kingdom and Italy only) accepted. Printer: State Polygraphic Institute, Rome.

## SOUTH AFRICA, REPUBLIC OF

Philatelic Services, GPO, Pretoria 0001, Republic of South Africa. Deals with individual orders for mint stamps, CTOs, FDCs, special postmarks (agency supplies datestamp cards). SODA available with minimum deposit of U.S. $15 required. Orders dispatched post-free with RSA 20¢ handling charge. CBC drawn on Pretoria bank accepted. Printer: Government Printer, Pretoria.

Government Agencies: Global Philatelic Agency Ltd., P.O. Drawer AC, Katonah, N.Y. 10536; Richard Borek Agenturen, Breite Strasse 25/26, 3300 Braunschweig, Federal Republic of Germany.

## SOUTH-WEST AFRICA

Philatelic Services and INTERSAPA, GPO, Pretoria 0001, Republic of South Africa. Deals with individual orders for mint stamps, CTOs, FDCs, special postmarks (agency supplies datestamp cards). SODA available with minimum deposit of U.S. $15 required. Orders dispatched post-free with RSA 20¢ per order handling charge. CBC drawn on Pretoria bank made payable to INTERSAPA accepted. Printer: Government Printer, Pretoria.

Government Agencies: Global Philatelic Agency Ltd., P.O. Drawer AC, Katonah, N.Y. 10536; Richard Borek Agenturen, Breite Strasse 25/26, 3300 Braunschweig, Federal Republic of Germany.

## SPAIN

Direccion General de Correos, Servicio Filatelico Internacional, Madrid 14, Spain. Deals with individual orders for mint stamp sets only.

No SODA available. Orders sent postage and handling extra. IMO accepted. Also handles Spanish Andorra.

Government Agency: Cafisa Philatelic International-America, Inc., 1695 N. County Road 18, Minneapolis, Minn. 55441-4298 (SODA available).

## SRI LANKA

Philatelic Bureau, Ceylinco House, Colombo 1, Sri Lanka. Deals with individual orders for stamps, postal stationery, FDCs (covers provided by customer or bureau), postmarks. SODA available with minimum deposit of U.S. $15 required. IMO, BPO, BD drawn on Bank of Ceylon accepted.

Government Agencies: Crown Agents Stamp Bureau, St. Nicholas House, Sutton, Surrey SM1 1EL, England; British & Overseas Philatelic Agency Ltd., Box 80, Shibuya, Tokyo 150-91, Japan; Inter-Governmental Philatelic Corp., 48 W. 48th St., New York, N.Y. 10036.

## SUDAN

Philatelic Office, Posts and Telegraphs, Public Corp., Khartoum, Sudan. Deals with individual and bulk orders of mint stamps, FDCs, special postmarks (customers and bureau supply envelopes). SODA available with minimum deposit of U.S. $2. Orders are dispatched postage extra. CBC, BPO, U.S. and sterling bank notes and BD accepted.

## SURINAM

Postal Administration, Philatelic Department, Paramaribo, Surinam. Details of services not provided.

Government Agency: World Wide Philatelic Agency, Inc., 116 W. 32nd St., New York, N.Y. 10001.

## SWAZILAND

Swaziland Stamp Bureau, Department of Posts & Telecommunications, P.O. Box 555, Mbabane, Swaziland. Deals with individual orders for mint stamps, FDCs (private FDCs canceled for charge of 5 cents each, plus postage), special postmarks (agency supplies envelopes), year packs, postal stationery. SODA available with minimum deposit of U.S. $25 required. Orders shipped post-free. CBC, IMO, U.S. dollars accepted.

Government Agencies: Crown Agents Stamp Bureau, St. Nicholas House, Sutton, Surrey SM1 1EL, England; StanGib Ltd., 1325 Franklin Ave., Garden City, N.Y. 11530; British & Overseas Philatelic Agency Ltd., Box 80, Shibya, Tokyo, 150-91, Japan.

## SWEDEN

PFA Postens Frimarksavdelning, S-105 02 Stockholm, Sweden. Deals with individual orders for mint and used stamps, FDCs. SODA available with no initial deposit required. Orders shipped post-free. CBC, IMO or to PFA Postal Giro account 1049-6 Stockholm.

Government Agency: Ancienne Maison Theodore Champion, 13, rue Drouot, 75009 Paris, France (sales in France only).

## SWITZERLAND

Philatelic Service PTT, Zeughausgasse 19, CH-3030 Bern, Switzerland. Deals with individual orders for mint stamps, FDCs, special postmarks (agency supplies envelopes). SODA available with minimum deposit of U.S. $30 required. SODA orders shipped post-free. CBC, PC, IMO accepted. Printers: Swiss Government Printing Office and Courvoisier, SA of Switzerland.

## SYRIAN ARAB REPUBLIC

Etablissement des Postes et des Telecommunications, Service Philatelique, Damascus, Syrian Arab Republic. Details of services not provided.

## TANZANIA

Tanzania Posts and Telecommunications, Department of Posts, Stamp Bureau, P.O. Box 2988, Dar-es-Salaam, Tanzania. Deals with individual orders for mint stamps, FDCs, special postmarks (customer supplies envelopes). SODA available with minimum deposit of U.S. $1.20 required. Orders shipped postage extra for mint stamps, post-free with handling charge otherwise. CBC on London bank, U.S. bank notes, BPO, IMO accepted.

Government Agencies: British & Overseas Philatelic Agency Ltd., Box 80, Shibuya, Tokyo 150-91, Japan; Crown Agents Stamp Bureau, St. Nicholas House, Sutton, Surrey SM1 1EL, England; Inter-Governmental Philatelic Corp., 48 W. 48th St., New York, N.Y. 10036.

## THAILAND

Philatelic Promotion Centre, Commercial Division, The Communications Authority of Thailand, Bangkok, Thailand. Deals with individual orders for mint stamps. SODA available with minimum deposit of U.S. $10 required. Orders shipped postage extra. CBC, IMO, IRC accepted.

## TIMOR

Postmaster, Cili, Timor, Asia. Details of services not provided.

## TOGO

Direction Generale des Postes et Telecommunications, Direction des Services Postaux et Financiers, Lome, Togo. Deals with individual orders for mint stamps. SODA information not provided. Orders shipped postage extra. CBC, IMO accepted.

Government Agency: Inter-Governmental Philatelic Corp., 48 W. 48th St., New York, N.Y. 10036.

## TOKELAU

Post Office Philatelic Bureau, Private Bag, Wanganui, New Zealand. Deals with individual orders for mint stamps, FDCs. SODA available with minimum deposit of U.S. $5.25 required. Orders shipped postage extra. CBC, IMO, BPO accepted.

Government Agencies: Stanley Gibbons Ltd., 391 Strand, London WC2R 0LX, England; British & Overseas Philatelic Agency Ltd., Box 80, Shibuya, Tokyo 150-91, Japan.

## TONGA

The Stamp Section, Treasury Building, Nuku'alofa, Tonga. Deals only with orders for U.S. $15.20 or more for mint stamps. SODA not available. Orders shipped postage extra (minimum of U.S. $2). CBC, BPO, certain bank notes accepted. Printer: Walsall Security Printers, England.

## TRANSKEI

Philatelic Services and INTERSAPA, GPO, Pretoria 0001, Republic of South Africa. Deals with individual orders for mint stamps, CTOs, FDCs, special postmarks (agency supplies datestamp cards). SODA available with minimum deposit of U.S. $15 required. Orders dispatched post-free with RSA 20¢ per order handling charge. CBC drawn on Pretoria bank made payable to INTERSAPA accepted. Printer: Government Printer, Pretoria.

Government Agencies: Global Philatelic Agency Ltd., P.O. Drawer AC, Katonah, N.Y. 10536; Richard Borek Agenturen, Breite Strasse 25/26, 3300 Braunschweig, Federal Republic of Germany.

## TRINIDAD & TOBAGO

Postmaster General, GPO, Port of Spain, Trinidad. No SODA provided.

Government Agencies: Crown Agents Stamp Bureau, St. Nicholas House, Sutton, Surrey SM1 1EL, England; StanGib Ltd., 1325 Franklin Ave., Garden City, N.Y. 11530; British & Overseas Philatelic Agency Ltd., Box 80, Shibuya, Tokyo 150-91, Japan.

## TRISTAN DA CUNHA

Postmaster, Jamestown, St. Helena, South Atlantic. Deals with individual orders for mint stamps, FDCs, special postmarks (bureau or customers supply envelopes). No SODA available. Orders shipped postage extra. CBC on London bank, U.S. bank notes, BPO, IMO accepted.

Government Agencies: StanGib Ltd., 1325 Franklin Ave., Garden City, N.Y. 11530; British & Overseas Philatelic Agency Ltd., Box 80,

Shibuya, Tokyo 150-91, Japan; Crown Agents Stamp Bureau, St. Nicholas House, Sutton, Surrey SM1 1EL, England.

## TUNISIA

Service Philatelique des PTT, Bureau Directeur de Tunis Recette Principale, Tunis, Tunisia. Deals with individual orders for mint stamps, FDCs. SODA available. CBC, IMO accepted.

Government Agencies: World Wide Philatelic Agency, Inc., 116 W. 32nd St., New York, N.Y. 10001; Ancienne Maison Theodore Champion, 13, rue Drouot, 75009 Paris, France.

## TURKEY

Direction Generale des PTT, Department des Posts, Section de Timbres Poste, Ankara, Turkey. Deals with individual orders for mint stamps. SODA available. Orders shipped postage extra. IMO, BD, CBC accepted.

Government Agency: Richard Borek Agenturen, Breite Strasse 25/26, 3300 Braunschweig, Federal Republic of Germany.

## TURKISH FEDERATED STATE OF CYPRUS

Turkish Federated State of Cyprus, Directorate of Postal Department, Philatelic Branch, Lefkosa, Mersin 10, Turkey. Deals with individual orders for mint and CTO stamps, FDCs. SODA available. Orders sent postage extra. BD, IMO (certain countries) accepted.

## TURKS & CAICOS ISLANDS

Philatelic Bureau, Grand Turk, Turks & Caicos Islands, West Indies. Deals with individual orders for mint and CTO stamps, FDCs (agency supplies multicolored envelopes). SODA available with minimum deposit of U.S. $25 required. Orders shipped post-free. CBC, PC, IMO, USPSMO, BPO, U.S. currency accepted.

Government Agency: Inter-Governmental Philatelic Corp., 48 W. 48th St., New York, N.Y. 10036.

## TUVALU

Tuvalu Philatelic Bureau, Funafuti, Tuvalu, Central Pacific. Deals with individual orders for mint stamps, FDCs, special postmarks (either agency or customer supply envelopes). SODA available with no minimum deposit required. Orders shipped post-free. BD, IMO, BPO accepted.

## UGANDA

Uganda Posts and Telecommunications Corp., Department of Posts, Stamp Bureau, P.O. Box 231, Kampala, Uganda. Deals with individual orders for mint stamps, CTOs, FDCs, souvenir sheets, postmarks (customer supplies envelopes). SODA available with minimum deposit of 1,500 shillings. Only Uganda shillings accepted. Printers: various firms selected on tender basis.

Government Agency: Inter-Governmental Philatelic Corp., 48 W. 48th St., New York, N.Y. 10036.

## UNION OF SOVIET SOCIALIST REPUBLICS

Philatelic Department, V/O Mezhdunarodnaya Kniga, Moscow 121200, U.S.S.R. Deals with individual orders for complete year sets of mint stamps and souvenir sheets for U.S. $59 per year. SODA available for wholesale quantity orders with minimum deposit requirements dependent on quantity ordered. Orders shipped post-free via surface mail, postage extra via airmail. CBC, certain foreign bank notes accepted.

Government Agency: Ancienne Maison Theodore Champion, 13, rue Drouot, 75009 Paris, France (sales in France only).

## UNITED ARAB EMIRATES

Philatelic Bureau, GPO, Dubai, United Arab Emirates, Arabian Gulf. Deals with individual orders for mint stamps, FDCs, special postmarks (customer supplies envelopes). SODA available with minimum deposit of U.S. $10 required. Orders shipped postage extra. CBC, IMO, U.S. and British bank notes accepted. Printers: Harrison and Sons Ltd., England; Thomas de la Rue & Co., England.

## UNITED NATIONS

United Nations Postal Administration, P.O. Box 5900, New York, N.Y. 10017. Deals with individual orders for mint stamps and FDCs (prepared FDCs, Geneva and Vienna). CDA available with minimum deposit of U.S. $35 required. Orders shipped postage extra plus handling charge if under U.S. $2. CBC, PC, USPSMO accepted.

U.N. Postal Administration, Palais des Nations, CH-1211 Geneva 10, Switzerland. Same details with Swiss currency applying.

U.N. Postal Administration, Vienna International Centre, A-1400 Vienna, Austria. Same details with Austrian currency applying.

Government Agencies: J.A. Visser Postzegelgroothandel B.V., Box 184, 3300 AD Dordrecht, The Netherlands; James Davis & Sons Ltd., 45 Church St., Rickmansworth WD3 1DG, England; Ancienne Maison Theodore Champion. 13, rue Drouot, 75009 Paris, France. (sales in France only).

## UNITED STATES OF AMERICA

U.S. Postal Service, Philatelic Sales Division, Washington, D.C. 20265, U.S.A. Deals with individual orders for mint stamps and postal stationery. Stock lists of stamps and stationery may be obtained by a request to Philatelic Sales Division, Washington, D.C. 20265. Orders subject to postage and handling charge and $5 minimum order level. CBC, PC, IMO, USPSMO, BPO accepted. Printers: U.S. Bureau of Engraving and Printing, U.S. Government Printing Office, U.S. Envelope Co., and private contractors.

**Government Agencies: Stanley Gibbons International Ltd., 391 Strand, London WC2R 0LX, England; DeRosa S.n.c., Naples, Italy; J.A. Visser Postzegelgroothandel B.V., Box 184, 3300 AD Dordrecht, The Netherlands (SODA available); Herman E. Sieger SA, Lorch/Wurttemberg, Federal Republic of Germany; Japan Philatelic Co., Tokyo, Japan.**

## UPPER VOLTA

**Service Philatelique, Office des Postes et Telecommunications, Ouagadougou, Upper Volta.** Details of services not provided.

**Government Agency: Ancienne Maison Theodore Champion, 13, rue Drouot, 75009 Paris, France.**

## URUGUAY

**Direccion Nacional de Correos, Departamento de Filatelica, Casilla de Correo 1296, Montevideo, Uruguay.** Deals with individual orders for mint stamps, FDCs, special postmarks (customer supplies envelopes). SODA available with minimum deposit required. IMO, IRC accepted. Printer: Uruguay National Printing Office.

## VANUATU

**Philatelic Section, Post Office, Port-Vila, Vanuatu, South Pacific.** Deals with individual orders for mint and CTO stamps, FDCs, special postmarks (agency supplies envelopes). SODA available with no minimum deposit required. Orders shipped postage extra (mint stamps), post-free (CTOs, FDCs). CBC, BPO, IMO accepted.

**Government Agencies: Crown Agents Stamp Bureau, St. Nicholas House, Sutton, Surrey SM1 1EL, England; StanGib Ltd., 1325 Franklin Ave., Garden City, N.Y. 11530; British & Overseas Philatelic Agency Ltd., Box 80, Shibuya, Tokyo 150-91, Japan.**

## VATICAN CITY

**Ufficio Filatelico, Governatorato, Vatican City.** Deals with individual orders for mint stamps and special postmarks (customer supplies envelopes). No SODA available. Orders shipped post-free. IMO, CBC, bank notes accepted.

## VENDA

**Philatelic Services and INTERSAPA, GPO, Pretoria 0001, Republic of South Africa.** Deals with individual orders for mint stamps, CTOs,

FDCs, special postmarks (agency supplies datestamp cards). SODA available with minimum deposit of U.S. $15 required. Orders dispatched post-free with RSA 20¢ per order handling charge. CBC drawn on Pretoria bank made payable to INTERSAPA accepted. Printer: Government Printer, Pretoria.

**Government Agencies: Richard Borek Agenturen, Breite Strasse, 25/26, 3300 Braunschweig, Federal Republic of Germany; Global Philatelic Agency Ltd., P.O. Drawer, AC, Katonah, N.Y. 10536.**

## VENEZUELA

**Instituto Postal Telegrafico de Venezuela, Oficina Filatelica Nacional, Apartado 4080, Caracas, 1010-A Venezuela.** Deals with individual orders for mint stamps, FDCs, special covers. SODA available with minimum deposit of U.S. $25 required. IMO accepted.

## VIETNAM

**Xunhasaba, Philatelic Department, 32 Hai Ba Trung St., Hanoi Vietnam.** This agency has exclusive distribution rights of all issues of this country. Details of services not provided.

**Government Agency: Ancienne Maison Theodore Champion, 13, rue Drouot, 75009 Paris, France (sales in France only).**

## WALLIS & FUTUNA ISLANDS

**Service Philatelique, Direction Generale des PTT, Futuna, Wallis & Futuna Islands, South Pacific.** Deals with individual orders for mint stamps, FDCs (agency supplies envelopes). No SODA information provided. Orders shipped postage extra. CBC accepted.

## WESTERN SAMOA

**Supervisor, Philatelic Bureau, GPO, Apia, Western Samoa, South Pacific.** Deals with individual orders for mint and used stamps and FDCs. SODA and special order deposit account available. Bureau also maintains mailing list for advance information on new issues. Orders of WS$1 or more are sent registered mail post-free; others by ordinary airmail. BPO, IMO, BD, and U.S. and Australian bank notes (sent by registered mail) accepted.

**Government Agencies: Crown Agents Stamp Bureau, St. Nicholas House, Sutton, Surrey SM1 1EL, England; StanGib Ltd., 1325 Franklin Ave., Garden City, N.Y. 11530; British & Overseas Philatelic Agency Ltd., Box 80, Shibuya, Tokyo 150-91, Japan.**

## YEMEN ARAB REPUBLIC

**Ministry of Communications, Philatelic Bureau, GPO, Yemen Arab Republic.** Deals with individual orders for mint and CTO stamps and souvenir sheets. SODA information not provided. CBC (forwarded by registered mail) accepted.

# YEMEN, PEOPLE'S DEMOCRATIC REPUBLIC

**Director General of Posts & Telegraphs, GPO, Aden, People's Democratic Republic of Yemen.** Deals with individual orders for mint stamps, souvenirs, postal stationery, postmarks (agency supplies envelopes), and FDCs (agency supplies envelope). SODA available. Orders will be shipped postage extra. CBC, IMO accepted.

**Government Agencies: StanGib Ltd., 1325 Franklin Ave., Garden City, N.Y. 11530; British & Overseas Philatelic Agency Ltd., Box 80, Shibuya, Tokyo 150-91, Japan; Crown Agents Stamps Bureau, St. Nicholas House, Sutton, Surrey SM1 1EL, England.**

# YUGOSLAVIA

**Jugomarka, Palmoticeva 2, Belgrade, Yugoslavia.** Deals with individual orders for mint stamps, FDCs. SODA available with minimum deposit of U.S. $10 required. Orders shipped postage extra. CBC, IMO accepted. Printers: various European firms.

# ZAIRE

**Bureau Philatelique, P.O. Box 1981, Kinshasa 1, Republic of Zaire, or Agences Philateliques Gouvernementales, Chaussee de Waterloo 868/870, 1180 Brussels, Belgium.** Details of services not provided.

# ZAMBIA

**Philatelic Bureau, P.O. Box 1857, Ndola, Zambia.** Deals with individual orders for mint stamps, FDCs (service fee extra), special postmarks (customer supplies envelopes). SODA available with minimum deposit of 10 kwacha required. Orders shipped postage extra. BD, IMO, Zambian PO accepted.

**Government Agencies: Inter-Governmental Philatelic Corp., 48 W. 48th St., New York, N.Y. 10036; Crown Agents Stamp Bureau, St. Nicholas House, Sutton, Surrey SM1 1EL, England; StanGib Ltd., 1325 Franklin Ave., Garden City, N.Y. 11530; British & Overseas Philatelic Agency Ltd., Box 80, Shibuya, Tokyo 150-91, Japan.**

# ZIL ELWAGNE SESEL

**Philatelic Bureau, P.O. Box 60, Victoria, Mahe, Seychelles, Indian Ocean.** Deals with individual orders for mint stamps, FDCs (bureau provides envelopes). SODA available. No ordering details provided.

# ZIMBABWE (Rhodesia)

**Posts and Telecommunication Corp., Philatelic Bureau, Box 4220, Salisbury, Zimbabwe.** Deals with individual orders for mint and CTO stamps, FDCs (on or before first day). SODA available with minimum deposit required. Orders shipped postage extra. BPO, IMO, BD and most western currencies accepted. Printer: Mardon Printers (Pvt) Ltd., Salisbury.

# Skills and Approaches    9

## Basic Knowledge

While there are no general rules established for the stamp collector, a little basic knowledge of the hobby is essential. This chapter does not attempt to explain fully every aspect of philately, but rather is intended to present some of the basic fundamentals necessary for the enjoyment of stamp collecting and an understanding of some of its tools, methods and language.

If you are just starting out in stamp collecting, decide first what you want — or are able — to collect. The beginner usually starts with a general collection, but since it is virtually impossible ever to complete such a vast area, he or she usually branches out into some sort of specialization. Choice of a specialty is limited only to one's imagination, and the variety of specialized areas is almost limitless.

For example, a collection can be limited by geographic location (North America, Middle East, Latin America), political groupings (British colonies, Soviet sphere of influence, Third World countries), individual countries (United States, Great Britain, France, Japan), types of stamps (definitives, commemoratives, airmails, revenues), units of stamps (souvenir sheets, miniature sheets, booklets, coils, plate blocks, marginal blocks), postal stationery (envelopes, postal cards, airletter sheets), postal history (first flight covers, first day covers, postmarks) and other related areas (souvenir cards, local posts, meters, proofs, essays). There are also numerous topics and themes that can form the basis for a collection, like animals, Boy Scouts, flags, maps, space and areas as broad as transportation or as narrow as the Model T Ford.

Such a listing is merely representative, but it does show the wonderful diversity of choice within the realm of philately. Joe Brockert, in Linn's general reference handbook "Basic Knowledge for the Stamp Collector," emphasizes a few aspects of the hobby which are worthwhile to emphasize here as well. These are general suggestions, and not absolute facts; each collector must decide how and what to collect, and seek advice and guidance from any available sources.

First, rely on your own common sense. If you really like colorful new stamps, regardless of their postal validity, then collect what you like. If you discover that you can't afford everything available, then limit yourself to what you like best. First and foremost in the hobby of stamp collecting should be enjoyment. A hobby should be fun, not frustrating.

Second, be aware of your financial limitations. Wasting money on worthless labels or less-than-genuine material can be frustrating and disappointing. We hesitate even to mention stamp investment within the context of beginning advice, because there is no generally true or perfect advice in that field. Stamp prices and investment potential are constantly changing, and research in that area is essential for any sort of economic security. In general, beware of unbelievable bargains or outrageously high prices — in the first instance, you will often get exactly what you pay for, and in the second, you may just get taken. If you know your subject and study your material, you will be less likely to make serious and costly mistakes, which leads to the third, and possibly most important, point.

Third, be guided by any and all authoritative sources. Read avidly, seek information and assistance in research, follow the philatelic press, and never be afraid to ask for help from fellow collectors and dealers. The philatelic community is generally willing to help the beginner, but that help often has to be sought. The personal contact of fellow collectors and stamp clubs can be the easiest and most enjoyable learning method available. Advice of more experienced collectors is a valuable aid to the beginner, and the market is full of books and periodicals designed to aid both the beginners and the advanced collectors.

Learn as much as you can about your hobby — its language, methods, techniques and tools. Few reference works are any finer than the basic catalog, and much can be learned from the introduction. Learn how to use a catalog properly, and you will discover a world of magnificent variety in design, printing and production. By all means, do not overlook the techniques of stamp production; though complex, the varieties in printing and production are essential to a basic understanding of stamps. When you realize that a slight difference in perforations can mean the difference between a scrap of paper and a fortune, you may begin to appreciate stamp production techniques.

In learning, one must never impose limitations. If subjects and ideas are avoided simply because of their complexity, the collector will miss a great deal of the enjoyment and appreciation of philately. The same is true in forming a collection. While it is good to specialize, that specialization should not exclude new areas and new interests. It is natural to collect one's native stamps, but that should not be allowed to exclude other countries, topics and interests. Don't collect what everyone else collects, unless of course that is what you really want and enjoy. Philately is not much different from other hobbies and activities, in which the popular course is usually the most expensive (the application of basic economic standards).

Finally, always be willing to share your knowledge and experience with others. Remember, even the greatest philatelist was a beginner at one point, and we can all work to advance philately by sharing our interests and knowledge.

## Care of Stamps

### Handling stamps

One of the first and most important lessons that a collector should learn is the use of stamp tongs, i.e., tweezers especially made for the handling of stamps.

Stamps should seldom (ideally never) be handled by hand, and so it is wise to develop early the habit of always using tongs in working with stamps. Even the cleanest, driest hands may leave traces of skin oil that can stain the stamp or disturb the gum. Obviously, stamps should never be handled with wet or dirty hands.

One should be especially careful in handling modern issues printed with metallic ink, since these inks will tarnish upon contact with the skin, in the same way that a new penny will quickly pick up fingerprints.

Stamp tongs are inexpensive, available in a wide variety of shapes and sizes, and are easy to use with only minimal practice. They are an essential tool if one wants to preserve the freshness of his stamps.

### Removing stamps from paper

Most stamps may safely be soaked from extraneous paper in cold water. Some inks used in stamp printing, however, are fugitive and will run when they come into contact with moisture. Such issues are usually noted in the standard catalogs. Stamps printed in such fugitive inks are best left on paper, since even the most careful handling may cause the ink to run slightly.

In removing stamps from envelope clippings, one should separate colored papers and colored cancellations, especially purple, before soaking. These inks will often run when immersed in water and may discolor any other stamps in the bath.

Normal stamps should be allowed to soak until they float free from the paper. They may then be removed from the water and allowed to dry. To ensure their drying flat, they should be pressed under a light weight, allowing a day or two for thorough drying.

### Storing stamps

Stamps may be stored in any number of ways — in albums, stock books, envelopes, boxes, etc. However stored, stamps should be kept in an area free from excessive heat or humidity. In tropical regions or during the summer months in temperate areas, the use of an air conditioner or dehumidifier is advisable, although, if this is not possible, the danger can be lessened by storing stamps loosely and by not handling mint copies when their gum is soft.

Stamps and albums should be stored away from direct sunlight, since sunlight will fade stamps, while the heat, of course, can cause the gum to soften and become adhesive.

Albums and stock books should be stored upright, rather than flat, since the weight of the pages may cause mint stamps to stick down if their gum softens at all. One should also occasionally leaf through the albums so that the stamps will be aired.

The mass of loose stamps, mostly duplicates, that most collectors eventually accumulate, may be safely relegated to the proverbial cigar box. It is best not to use any sort of container that may have some residue that could affect the stamps, such as grease, wax, etc.

It is generally best to select and use album pages that are intended for use only on one side. When stamps are mounted on both sides of a page in albums, stamps on facing pages can "grab" each other and become damaged when pages are turned. Chances of damage are reduced when only one side of each page is used.

The use of only one side of an album page is also handy when planning to exhibit material, since framed displays can only show one side at a time. Pages for exhibit should be planned with good but minimal graphics; the stamps should tell their own stories as much as possible. The philatelic material can be overwhelmed by excessive write-up, color or ornamentation. Good taste and good graphics are the best guidelines to follow for exhibition pages.

The subject of exhibiting is covered extensively in a book by C.E. Foster, Albuquerque, N.M., a leading authority on the subject. Information on the work, "How to Prepare Stamp Exhibits," is available from the New Mexico Philatelic Association (which produced the book), Box 25706, Albuquerque, N.M. 87125.

### Affixing stamps to album pages

For affixing stamps to display pages, one may generally choose between commercially made stamp hinges or hingeless mounts. Hingeless albums and pages are also available, with the mount incorporated into the page, but these are rather expensive for the beginner.

A variety of good quality stamp hinges exist on the market. A stamp hinge should be peelable, i.e., one should be able to remove it from a stamp without tearing or thinning the stamp and without leaving unsightly hinge remnants.

In using stamp hinges, one should be careful not to apply too much moisture, since the excess may seep out to dampen the gum of the stamp, causing it to stick to the page. Never attempt to remove a hinge until it has completely dried. A hinge may be peeled when dry, but its removal while still wet will almost certainly thin the stamp.

Hingeless mounts are sleeves of acetate which may be trimmed to the size of the individual stamp. The chief advantages of such mounts are the added protection they give fragile stamps and the preservation of the full gum on mint stamps.

One should be careful to use the proper size mount. If a mount is too large, the stamp may slip out, while if it is too small, it will cause the stamp to bend or curl.

Never use tape, gummed paper, general adhesives or glue in mounting stamps. At best they may require soaking to remove the stamp from the album page; at worst they may cause the stamp to be irreparably stained or to be stuck irremovably to the page.

### Awareness

CONDITION: Condition is the all-important factor in the value of a stamp. Flaws such as smudges, creases, tears, pulled perfs, thin spots, etc., will lower a stamp's worth, often substantially. Most experienced collectors will collect damaged stamps only as space-fillers.

AUTHENTICITY: Many reprints and forgeries exist, especially of 19th-century issues. Such items are of interest only to the specialist and, as a rule, are worth very little. Most may be fairly easily recognized by reference to the standard catalogs, which will often give enough information to distinguish at least the most common of the clinkers. Copies of expensive stamps that have been reprinted or forged should be expertized or, at least, purchased from a reputable and knowledgeable source. Reperforated and regummed stamps also present a real danger to the inexperienced collector.

UNUSUAL FEATURES: Many common stamps may be worth substantially more because of some feature that makes them of interest to the specialist, e.g., first day or special event postmarks, "used abroad" cancellations, marginal attachments such as plate numbers or inscriptions, uncommon perforation, etc. Multiples (strips, blocks, etc.) of older issues may also command a substantial premium, and such pieces should not be broken up until this possibility has been checked. For the same reason, some stamps should not be removed from envelopes until it has been determined that the envelope or postmark do not add significantly to the interest of the philatelic item.

## Types of Stamps

DEFINITIVE (REGULAR ISSUE) stamps include the majority of general usage postage stamps. Such issues are all-purpose stamps with a long duration of availability and use. For this reason, they are generally the easiest to find, since they are produced in the greatest quantity by any country.

COMMEMORATIVE stamps, on the other hand, are usually available for only a limited time. These are issued in honor of some person, place or event, and are usually the more colorful issues. While they are not as widely produced as the definitives, their general use and wide circulation makes most stamps of this type relatively easy to acquire.

POSTAL STATIONERY for general use is also widely circulated in many countries. This category includes the widely used and lower rate postal cards, stamped envelopes and printed, stamped lettersheets. These are not as widely produced as regular issue stamps, but they are generally available for an equally long period of time.

AIRMAIL (AIRPOST) stamps came into use with the general delivery of mail by airplane, although a number of airmail stamps represent other means of air transportation, such as balloon or zeppelin. Airmail delivery is so common and widely used in the United States that the domestic airmail classification was terminated May 1, 1977, although international airmail is still in use. Most countries have special stamps for airmail use, including postal stationery (post cards, envelopes and aerogrammes). Some countries even have airpost semipostal stamps and airpost special delivery stamps, which indicate a combination of services or designations.

SEMIPOSTAL (CHARITY) stamps are issued by some countries to provide part of the amount of a postal issue for a charitable cause, relief fund or public welfare project. Many such stamps are inscribed with two values, one representing the post rate, and the other the surtax to be given to the designated fund (sometimes the entire amount will go to the fund). The total of the two values, when so designated, represents the total price of the stamp, although it may be used only for the amount of the postal portion of the cost. Such stamps as Christmas and Easter seals, while related, are not in any way postally valid, and are generally collected only because of their stamp-like quality and common appearance on mailed items. These are issued by the charitable cause strictly as a fund-raising effort.

SPECIAL DELIVERY stamps represent higher fee for the immediate delivery of mail upon arrival at the post office, as opposed to waiting for regular mail shipments.

REGISTRATION (REGISTERED LETTER) stamps indicate a form of monetary guarantee, providing for compensation in case of loss. A receipt is also provided.

INSURED LETTER stamps are also issued by some countries to guarantee delivery and provide compensation in the event of loss. Many parcels and letters are simply marked with postal insurance labels to indicate payment of the insurance fee.

CERTIFIED MAIL stamps, on the other hand, do not guarantee compensation in the event of loss. These only provide a type of documentation for the mailing and delivery of an item.

ACKNOWLEDGEMENT-OF-RECEIPT stamps are issued by some countries to inform the sender of the arrival of an article at its destination.

PERSONAL DELIVERY stamps ensure delivery only to the person designated, much like the telephone equivalent, the person-to-person call. These are useful in confidential or private letters.

AUTHORIZED DELIVERY stamps are sometimes affixed to mail carried by some operation other than the official postal service of a country that delivers mail by the authorization of the official service.

POSTAGE DUE stamps are generally affixed by postal clerks to indicate the amount of postage due on a certain piece of mail (indicating nonpayment or underpayment by the sender, and generally paid by the receiver). Many times, rather than affixing stamps, the amount due will simply be handstamped or written on the article.

PARCEL POST stamps are affixed to some fourth-class mailings, to indicate bulk shipment at the parcel post rate. Special postage due stamps have in the past been issued for parcel post items.

SPECIAL HANDLING stamps are related to parcel post, since they indicate first-class handling of parcels.

METER stamps are affixed by special machines, which not only stamp, but also provide a form of precancellation, speeding up the mail operations of large mailings. These are generally used by large firms or other businesses with large volumes of outgoing mail.

BULK RATE stamps are used to indicate a lower rate for bulk or massive mailings, along with the lower-rate service.

NEWSPAPER (and PERIODICAL) stamps are used for postage on single or bulk newspaper or journal mailings.

OFFICIAL POSTAGE stamps are used for postage on official mail from government offices. Much of this is now done with meter stamps or by officially imprinted envelopes.

OFFICIALLY SEALED (POSTAL SEAL) stamps are placed on mail accidentally opened in the course of processing by the post office. The article is then "officially sealed" at some point, to indicate that it was so opened and duly closed.

MILITARY POSTAGE stamps are used by the armed services in a foreign country, generally during times of war.

OCCUPATION stamps, on the other hand, are issued by a country during its wartime occupation of a foreign country, for use in the occupied territory.

HUNTING PERMIT (DUCK) stamps are so called because of the ducks depicted in the designs. These hunting permit stamps, a type of revenue stamp, have become popular collectors' items.

REVENUE (TAX) stamps have been issued for many items, strictly to represent the payment of taxes in certain types of transactions, not for postal use. Some types of these stamps include stamped paper, documentary, proprietary and private die proprietary, motor vehicle use, boating, wine, playing cards, cigarette and tobacco sales tax, alcohol, firearms, customs fees, consular service fees, narcotic and stock transfer stamps.

OFFICES IN FOREIGN COUNTRIES stamps are issued by one country for postal use in a foreign country.

INTERNATIONAL REPLY COUPONS are produced by the Universal Postal Union for prepayment of return postage on a letter from a foreign country.

HANDSTAMPED COVERS are covers with no postage stamps affixed which are postally validated for delivery by means of some authorizing handstamp.

LATE FEE stamps are affixed to note additional payment for an article to catch up with a regular shipment that has already departed.

LOCAL stamps are issued by private local postal operations competing with, or supplemental to, the regular mail service.

POSTAL NOTE stamps were issued to supplement the regular money order service, generally to make up fractions of a dollar.

SAVINGS stamps were issued for the redemption of some form of savings certificate, either postal savings accounts or bonds (U.S. Savings or War Bonds).

TELEGRAPH stamps were issued by telegraph companies for use on their own telegraphs for payment or collection purposes.

POSTMASTERS' PROVISIONAL stamps were issued by area postmasters in the United States prior to the uniform mail system's establishment in 1847.

CARRIERS' stamps were issued to supplement regular postage in the early days of mail delivery in this country, when postage would only pay for delivery from one post office to another. Carriers' stamps would then pay for delivery by carrier to the destination.

## Postmarks

The following section deals with the postmark (and/or cancellation). Included is a short history and evolution of the postmark, different types, and information on how to obtain current postmarks.

DATESTAMPS are postmarks which indicate the date and/or the time of day when a letter is posted, or at least processed through the initial post office before its delivery. The datestamp is generally attributed to mid-17th century England, when they were applied to discourage unnecessary delays in the delivery of mail. Technically, datestamps have only the date, with no place of origin indicated, while namestamps include the name of the originating office, with no indication of date. The most common type of postmark today is the combination name-datestamp, which supplies both types of information.

POSTMARKS are those parts of the cancellation which indicate date, time and place of posting. Transit postmarks are sometimes applied by some office or station along the complete route of the letter, while receiving marks are sometimes applied by the receiving station. The initial postmark will generally be the only one to include a cancellation.

CANCELLATIONS are those parts of the postal markings which serve to void postage stamps affixed for the prepayment of mail. Before the advent of prepayment and postage stamps, postmarks only served as an information device on the outside of mailed matter. After stamps came into use, however, cancellations became necessary to prevent the reuse of postage stamps. The cancellation portion of the postmark is also known by other various names, such as obliterator, killer or various types of cancellations, such

as flag cancels (flag design), bar cancels (heavy lines or bars), cork cancels (early cancellation devices carved out of cork or wood), slogan cancels (containing some slogan or trademark), gridiron cancels (generally oval shaped) or other designations to indicate the method of transport, such as ship cancels, railroad cancels, mailboat (paquebot) cancels or airmail cancels.

PRECANCELED stamps are those that are canceled before sale to the public, generally in large quantities for large cities. This then eliminates the need to cancel the stamps, and speeds the mail operation in large cities, when dealing with large volumes of mail. They can be precanceled by the Bureau of Engraving and Printing before distribution to various large cities (Bureau precancels), or they can be precanceled by the local postal authorities (local precancels).

SELF-CANCELED stamps refer to metered mail, which automatically stamps and cancels in one operation. This also saves time in the postal operation.

CANCELED TO ORDER stamps are usually made in full sheets, generally as a concession to collectors by the issuing authorities. These are stamps that are never postally used, but still have a cancellation applied, and generally have the original gum and all other characteristics of mint stamps at the same time.

CANCELED BY FAVOR stamps are those that are canceled by the specific request of the purchaser. This can involve regular or special cancellations, and is generally connected with the philatelic requests for first day covers, or other postmarks of significance.

In order to obtain specific postmarks, requests should always be addressed to the postmaster of the specific office from which the postmark is desired. This information, on philatelic events of importance to collectors of significant postmarks, is generally contained in the philatelic press. Less frequent publications will often provide such information after the fact, so a publication from an official source, such as the United States Postal Service, or one with frequent publication to provide sufficient advance notice, would be the best source of information.

Requests should include the specific event or postmark desired, and may include a request for a clear, readable postmark. First day of issue requests are generally self-explanatory, and their philatelic importance will usually assure a clear postmark, so that such a request will be unnecessary, as it is generally assumed. Requests for other types of postmarks, if not widely recognized as a major philatelic event, may require more specific instructions, such as day, time or type of cancel. It is generally safer to include too much detail, rather than not enough.

Envelopes to be specifically postmarked should contain a thin, but stiff, cardboard stock stuffer (about the thickness of an average postal card), which will usually help prevent damage to the envelope and ensure a clearer, firmer postmark. Stamps should be affixed in the upper right corner, at least one-fourth inch away from both the top and the right edges; addresses should be placed in the lower right portion of the envelope.

All envelopes for philatelic servicing are supposed to include a return address (as the address portion), and postal clerks and postmasters are not generally authorized to return unaddressed covers under separate cover (philatelic covers returned unaddressed in a separate, self-addressed, stamped envelope). Some postmasters will perform this service as a favor, but there are no guarantees; some bulk orders for large shipments (such as commercial first day covers) may also be processed unaddressed and returned in bulk under separate cover.

In most cases, however, serviced covers must be addressed for return through the normal mailstream. Peelable return address labels are recommended for this purpose. This is easier than addressing covers in pencil and then attempting to erase it to produce an unaddressed cover. For many types of philatelic covers of recent vintage — especially first day covers — clean, unaddressed covers may command a premium. As always, prices will vary greatly depending on the market.

In recent years, even U.S. first day covers could be prepared in the aforementioned manner, because of a 30-day "grace period" — 30 days during which collectors may purchase new stamp and postal stationery issues at the local post office after the first day of issue, and still prepare and submit their own prepared philatelic covers for first day cancellation. Postal stationery items — postal cards, embossed envelopes, airletter sheets, etc. — were just added to this "grace period" provision in early 1982; at the same time the stamp "grace period" was increased from 15 to 30 days. First day covers may still be prepared in advance, with postal personnel supplying the stamps or stationery items.

U.S. first day cover orders have certain patterns, by which most orders can be prepared with very little information. When submitting first day cancellation requests on covers to which stamps have already been affixed (within the 30-day "grace period"), orders should be submitted to Customer Affixed Envelopes, Postmaster, (Name of City, State and ZIP Code — plus "-9991" for those who care to use the expanded ZIP+4 — for first day site). Since the

stamps are already affixed, no remittance is required for such servicing.

For postal stationery items, the procedure is similar. When submitting postal stationery items for first day servicing within the 30-day "grace period," stationery items should be submitted to Customer Provided Stationery, Postmaster, (Name of City, State and ZIP Code-9991 for the first day site). Again, since the material is provided by the customer, no remittance is required.

For all first day cover requests for which postal personnel are expected to supply the new issue(s), orders and remittance (for the cost of the stamps or stationery items) should be submitted to (Name of Issue), Postmaster, (Name of City, State and ZIP Code-9992 for the first day site). For all U.S. new issues, requests may be submitted and must be postmarked within 30 days of the first day of issue. For all other "special event" or other postmark requests — unless extensions are granted under unusual circumstances — requests must arrive at the necessary post office by the desired date.

When submitting requests for special or first day cancellations — ignoring the "grace period" for the moment — they should be timed to arrive, if possible, just a few days prior to the required date of the postmark. Significantly early requests do not help speed processing, and in most cases, postmasters are not authorized to hold postmark requests for substantial lengths of time. In other words, early requests will not help a collector "get ahead of the crowd," so to speak. They might simply be discarded or ignored. It is best to get requests in ahead of time, but not so far in advance that they have to "sit" for any length of time.

Collectors are also reminded that some new issues may not meet the applicable return postage rate — such as a new issue stamp that is less than the first-class rate, or a special-purpose stationery item (nonprofit, bulk rate, etc.) that is less than the necessary return postage rate. In such cases, collectors must be certain that the full amount of the applicable return postage is included, or remittance is sufficient to cover the full rate of stamps to be affixed. For example, if a new 13¢ stamp is being issued, and the first-class rate is 20¢, the collector must account for at least 7¢ in additional postage — or, as is often done, simply overpay the rate and request a pair of the new 13¢ stamp. Special provisions or restrictions may be imposed by postal authorities in such cases, so again, the philatelic press will be the best source of current information and instructions.

# Multilingual Guide

Often the stamp collector will encounter stamps and catalogs with foreign words that may not be familiar to him. Therefore, the following section is offered to help with some of the basic philatelic terms (150), including colors, processes and directional guides that are often encountered by the average collector.

This glossary is not intended to be complete — indeed, there are too many foreign languages in the world to include even a small portion. This will provide some of the most basic terms for the stamp collector, and help with most translations that should ever arise, in five of the most frequently encountered languages: French, Spanish, Italian, German and Dutch.

Often there may be more than one translation (no more than two are included here), or there may be no exact word that corresponds to the English, so that a term close in meaning must be used instead.

Here, then, are 150 basic philatelic terms and descriptive words in English and five commonly found foreign languages. Typesetting restrictions make it impossible for this listing to include standard foreign accents, which can change the pronunciation of many vowels. Still, the basic translations and spellings are correct. For uniformity, no words are capitalized; nouns in German would typically begin with a capital letter.

| ENGLISH | GERMAN | DUTCH | FRENCH | SPANISH | ITALIAN |
|---|---|---|---|---|---|
| airmail | flugpost, luftpost | luchtpost | poste aerienne | correo aereo | posta aerea |
| auction | versteigerung | veiling | encan, enchere | almoneda, subasta | incanto |
| back | ruckseitig | achterkant | verso | dorso | dorso |
| background | (hinter)grund | achtergrond | fond | fondo | fondo |
| bar | balken | balk | barre | barra | barra |
| bisected stamp | geteilt, halbiert | gehalveerd | timbre coupe | cortado por la mitad | frazionato |
| black | schwarz | zwart | noir | negro | nero |
| block | block | blok | bloc | bloque | blocco |
| blue | blau | blauw | bleu | azul | azzurro |
| booklet (stamps) | markenheftchen | (postzegel) boekje | carnet | cuardernillo | libretto |
| border | rahmen | omlijsting | cadre | marco | cornice |
| bottom | unten | onderkant | bas | abajo | basso |
| bright | lebhaft | helder | vif | vivo | vivo |
| broken | unterbrochen | onderbroken | interrompu | interrumpido | interrotto |
| brown | braun | bruin | brun | castano | bruno |
| canceled | gestempelt | gestempeld | annule | cancclado | annullato |
| cancellation | entwertung | afstempeling | obliteration | matasellado | annullo |
| catalog | katalog | catalogus | catalogue | catalogo | catalogo |
| center | mittelstuck | middenstuk | centre du timbre | centro | centro |
| centering | zentrierung | gecentreerd | centrage | centrado | centratura |
| chalky paper | kreidepapier | krijtachtig papier | papier couche | papel estucado | carta gessata |
| charity stamp | wohltatig-keitsmarke | weldadig-heidszegel | timbre de bienfaisance | sello de beneficenza | francobollo di beneficenza |
| closed | geschlossen | gesloten | ferme | cerrado | chiuso |
| coil | markenrolle | rol | rouleau de timbres | rollo de sellos | rotoli di francobolli |
| color | farbe | kleur | couleur | color | colore |
| commemorative | gedenkausgabe | herdenking-suitgave | commemoratif | conmemorativo | commemorativo |
| corner | ecke | hoek | angle | esquina | angolo |
| counterfeit | falschung | vervalsing | faux | falsificacion | falsificazione |
| cover | brief | brief | lettre | carta | lettera |
| cut square | ausschnitt | briefstuk | coupure | recorte | ritaglio |
| damaged | beschadigt | beschadigd | abime | defectuoso | difettoso |
| dark | dunkel | donker | fonce | oscuro | cupo, oscuro |
| date | datum | datum | date | fecha | data |
| definitive | endgultig | bepaald | definitif | definitivo | definitivo |
| design | entwurf, zeichnung | ontwerp | dessin | dibujo | disegno |
| die | urstempel, type | stempel, originele gravure | matrice | cuno | conio, matrice |
| double impression | doppeldruck | dubbele druk | impression double | impresion doble | impressione doppia |
| dull | trub | dof | terne | turbio | smorto |
| embossed | pragung | in relief | relief | relieve | rilievo |

| ENGLISH | GERMAN | DUTCH | FRENCH | SPANISH | ITALIAN |
|---|---|---|---|---|---|
| engraved | graviert, gestochen | gegraveerd | grave, gravure | grabado, caliografia | incisione, stampato |
| envelope | briefumschlag | envelop | enveloppe | sobre | busta |
| error | fehldruck, fehler | fout (druk) | erreur | error | errore |
| essay | essay, probedruck | proef | essai | ensayo | saggio |
| faulty | mangelhaft | onvolmaakt | defectueux | defectuoso | difettoso |
| figure | ziffer | cijfer | chiffre | cifra | cifra |
| first day | ersttag | eerste dag | premier jour | primer dia | primo giorno |
| foreign | ausland | buitenland | etranger | extranjero | estero |
| forerunner | vorlaufer | voorloper | precurseur | precursor | precursore |
| forgery | falschung | vervalsing | falsification, faux | falsificacion | falsificazione |
| genuine | echt | echt | authentique | autentico | autentico |
| glossy paper | glanzpapier | glanzend papier | papier glace | papel estucado | carta patinata |
| granite paper | faserpapier | papier met zijdevezels | papier melange de fils de soie | papel con filamentos | carta con fili de seta |
| gray | grau | grijs | gris | gris | grigio |
| green | grun | groen | vert | verde | verde |
| gum | gummi | gom | gomme | goma | gomma |
| gutter | zwischensteg | tussenstrook | interpanneau | pasillo | interspazio |
| half | halfte | de helft | moitie | mitad | meta |
| handstamp | handstempel | handstempel | cachet a la main | matasello de mano | timbro a mano |
| hinge | falz | plakker | charniere | fijasello | linguella |
| horizontal | liegend | horisontaal | horizontal | horizontal | coricato |
| imperforate | geschnitten | ongetand | non dentele | sin dentar | non dentellato |
| inscription | inschrift | opschrift | inscription | inscripcion | dicitura |
| inverted | kopfstehend | kopstaand | renverse | invertido | capovolto, invertito |
| issue | ausgabe | uitgave | emission | emision | emissione |
| laid (paper) | gestreiftes | gestreept (papier) | verge | listado | vergato |
| large | gross | groot | grand | grande | grosso |
| left | links | links | gauche | izquierdo | sinistro |
| letter card | kartenbrief | briefkaart | carte-lettre | carta tarjeta | carta-lettera |
| light | hell | licht | clair | claro | chiaro |
| lithography | steindruck | steendruk, lithografie | lithographie | litografia | litografia |
| local issue | lokalausgabe | plaatselijke uitgave | emission locale | emision local | emissione locale |
| margin | rand | rand | marge | borde | margine |
| mint | ungebraucht | ongebruikt | neuf | nuevo | nuovo |
| multicolored | mehrfarbig | meerkleurig | polychrome | multicolores | policromo |
| multiple | mehrfach | meervoudig | multiple | multiple | multiplo |
| narrow | eng | nauw | etroit | estrecho | stretto |
| not issued | unverausgabt | onuitgegeven | non emis | no emitido | non emesso |
| numeral | ziffer | nummer, cijfer | chiffre | cifra | numerale |
| occupation | besetzung | bezetting | occupation | occupacion | occupazione |
| official stamp | dienstmarke | dienstzegel | timbre de service | sello de servicio | francobollo servizio |
| offset printing | offsetdruck | offsetdruk | impression en offset | impresion offset | stampa in offset |
| on back | ruckseite | op de achterkant | au verso | al dorso | a tergo |
| orange | orange | oranje | orange | naranja | arancio |
| original gum | originalgummi | originele gom | gomme originale | goma original | gomma originale |
| overprint | aufdruck, uberdruck | opdruk | surcharge | sobrecarga | soprastampa |
| pair | paar | paar | paire | pareja | coppia |
| pale | blass | licht | pale | palido | pallido |
| pane | gruppe | vel | panneau | grupo | gruppo |
| paper | papier | papier | papier | papel | carta |
| parcel post | paket | pakketpost | colis-postaux | paquetes | pacchi |
| pen canceled | federzug-entwertung | penvernietiging | oblitere a plume | cancelado a pluma | annullato a penna |
| perforated | zahnung, gezahnt | getand | dentele | dentado | dentellato |
| photogravure | aetztiefdruck | rasterdiepdruk | heliogravure | huecograbado | fotocalcografia |
| piece | briefstuck | briefstuk | fragment | fragmento | frammento |
| pink | rosa | rose | rose | rosa | rosa |
| plate | platte | plaat | planche | plancha | lastra |
| postage due | portomarke | portzegel | timbre-taxe | sello de tasa | segnatasse |
| postage stamp | briefmarke | postzegel | timbre-poste | selle de correos | francobollo postale |
| post card | postkarte | briefkaart | carte postale | tarjeta postal | carta postale |

| ENGLISH | GERMAN | DUTCH | FRENCH | SPANISH | ITALIAN |
|---|---|---|---|---|---|
| postmark | poststempel | stempel | obliteration postale | matasello | bollo |
| post office | postamt | postkantoor | bureau de poste | oficina postal | ufficia di posta |
| precancel | vorausenwertung | voorafstempeling | pre-oblitere | preobliteracion | preannullato |
| price | preis | prijs | prix | precio | prezzo, quotazione |
| printing | druck | druk | impression | impresion | stampa |
| proof | probe(druck) | proef | epreuve | prueba | prova |
| provisional | aushilfsausgabe | hulpzegel | provisoire | provisional | provvisorio |
| purple | purpur | purper | pourpre | purpura | porpora |
| rare | selten | zeldzaam | rare | raro | raro |
| recess printing | stichtiefdruck | diepdruk | taille douce | calcografia | calcografia |
| red | rot | rood | rouge | rojo | rosso |
| reengraving | neugravierung | nieuwe gravure | regravure | regrabado | rincisione |
| registration stamp | einschreibemarke | aantekenstrookje | timbre pour lettre chargee | sello de certificado | francobollo per lettere raccomandate |
| repaired | repariert | gerapareerd | repare | reparado | riparato |
| reprint | neudruck | herdruk, nadruk | reimpression | reimpresion | reimpressione |
| revenue stamp | stempelmarke | plakzegel | timbre fiscal | sello fiscal | francobollo fiscale |
| reversed | umgekehrt | omgekeerd | retourne | invertido | rovesciato |
| ribbed | geriffelt | geribbeld | cannele | acanalado | scanalatura |
| right | rechts | rechts | droite | a la derecha | destro |
| rotary printing | walzendruck | rotatiedruk | impression par cylindre | impresion cilindrica | stampa rotativa |
| rouletted | durchstochen | doorstoken | perce | picado | forato |
| se-tenant | zusammendruck | samenhangend | se-tenant | combinacion | combinazione |
| semipostal | wohltatig- keitsmarke | weldadig- heidszegel | bienfaisance | beneficencia | beneficenza |
| set | satz | serie | serie | serie | serie |
| shade | tonung, farbton | tint | nuance | tono | gradazione di colore |
| sheet | bogen | vel | feuille | hoja | foglio |
| side | seite | zijkant | cote | lado | lato |
| small | klein | klein | petit | pequeno | piccolo |
| souvenir sheet | gedenkblock | velletje | bloc commemoratif | hojita-bloque conmemorativa | foglietto commemorativo |
| special delivery | eilmarke | expresse | expres | urgente | espresso |
| specimen | muster | specimen | specimen | muestra | saggio |
| strip | streifen | strook | bande | tira | striscia |
| surcharge | zuschlag | toeslag | surcharge | sobrecarga | soprastampa |
| thick | dick | dik | epais | grueso | spesso |
| thin | dunn | dun | mince | delgado | sottile |
| tinted paper | getontes papier | gekleurd papier | papier teinte | papel coloreado | carta tinto |
| top | oben | bovenkant | haut | arriba | alto |
| trial printing | druckprobe | proefdruk | epreuve essai | prueba | prova di stampa |
| typography | buchdruck | boekdruk | typographie | tipografia | tipografia |
| unused | ungebraucht | ongebruikt | neuf | nuevo | nuovo |
| used | gebraucht | gebruikt | oblitere | usado | usato |
| variety | abart | soort, varieteit | variete | variedad | varieta |
| vertical | senkrecht | vertikaal | vertical | vertical | verticale |
| watermark | wasserzeichen | watermerk | filigrane | filigrana | filigrana |
| white | weiss | wit | blanc | blanco | bianco |
| wide | weit | wijd | espace | ancho | largo |
| with | mit | met | avec | con | con |
| without gum | ohne gummi | zonder gom | sans gomme | sin goma | senza gomma |
| worn | abgenutzt | versleten | use | gastado | usato |
| wove paper | einfaches papier | velijnpapier | papier ordinaire | papel avitelado | carta unita |
| yellow | gelb | geel | jaune | amarillo | giallo |

# Foreign Currency Guide

As an aid to the identification of foreign currency values as found on stamps, this list will give the current names for the currency of stamp-issuing countries. This list is primarily intended to help the collector with unidentified new issue stamps or reports. Older values are not included, since names of currency, value, country and territory are constantly changing. For guidance on older issues or countries, consult the extensively cross-referenced foreign identifier.

Many times, the currency values for a former colony or territory will correspond to the values of the mother country. For complete historical currency information, consult an encyclopedia or international stamp catalog.

To explain the following list, look at the second entry, "AITUTAKI," as an example. The major currency unit of Aitutaki is the New Zealand dollar, which indicates that the currency of that island is tied to that of New Zealand. Unless noted as a specific type or area of currency, each currency unit will be unique to that country — in other words, entries marked simply "dollar" will not be related to other entries marked "dollar." The equivalent figures indicate that one New Zealand dollar is equal to 100 cents.

The most current information on exchange rates should be available from banks or other financial institutions or publications.

AFGHANISTAN: 1 afghani (af) = 100 pouls (p).
AITUTAKI:
   1 New Zealand dollar ($) = 100 cents (¢).
ALBANIA: 1 lek (l) = 100 qindarka (q).
ALGERIA: 1 dinar (d) = 100 centimes (c).
ANDORRA (FRENCH):
   1 French franc (fr) = 100 centimes (c).
ANDORRA (SPANISH):
   1 Spanish peseta (pta) = 100 centimos (c).
ANGOLA: 1 kwanza (kw) = 100 lweys (l).
ANGUILLA:
   1 East Caribbean dollar ($) = 100 cents (¢).
ANTIGUA:
   1 East Caribbean dollar ($) = 100 cents (¢).
ARGENTINA: 1 peso (p) = 100 centavos (c).
ASCENSION:
   1 pound sterling (£) = 100 pence (p).
AUSTRALIA: 1 dollar ($) = 100 cents (¢).
AUSTRIA: 1 schilling (s) = 100 groschen (g).
BAHAMAS: 1 dollar ($) = 100 cents (¢).
BAHRAIN: 1 dinar (d) = 1000 fils (f).
BANGLADESH: 1 taka (t) = 100 poishas (p).
BARBADOS: 1 dollar ($) = 100 cents (¢).
BARBUDA:
   1 East Caribbean dollar ($) = 100 cents (¢).
BELGIUM: 1 franc (fr) = 100 centimes (c).
BELIZE: 1 dollar ($) = 100 cents (¢).
BENIN: 1 CFA franc (fr) = 100 centimes (c).
BERMUDA: 1 dollar ($) = 100 cents (¢).
BHUTAN: 1 ngultrum (nu) = 100 chetrum (ch).
BOLIVIA: 1 peso (p) = 100 centavos (c).
BOPHUTHATSWANA:
   1 South African rand (r) = 100 cents (¢).
BOTSWANA: 1 pula (p) = 100 thebe (t).
BRAZIL: 1 cruzeiro (cr) = 100 centavos (c).
BRITISH ANTARCTIC TERRITORY:
   1 pound sterling (£) = 100 pence (p).
BRITISH VIRGIN ISLANDS:
   1 U.S. dollar ($) = 100 cents (¢).
BRUNEI: 1 dollar ($) = 100 cents (¢).
BULGARIA: 1 lev (l) = 100 stotinki (st).
BURMA: 1 kyat (k) = 100 pyas (p).
BURUNDI: 1 franc (fr) = 100 centimes (c).

CAMEROON:
   1 CFA franc (fr) = 100 centimes (c).
CANADA: 1 dollar ($) = 100 cents (¢).
CAPE VERDE:
   1 escudo (esc) = 100 centavos (c).
CAYMAN ISLANDS: 1 dollar ($) = 100 cents (¢).
CENTRAL AFRICAN REPUBLIC:
   1 CFA franc (fr) = 100 centimes (c).
CHAD: 1 CFA franc (fr) = 100 centimes (c).
CHILE: 1 peso (p) = 100 centavos (c).
CHINA, PEOPLE'S REPUBLIC:
   1 yuan (y) = 100 fen (f).
CHINA, REPUBLIC OF:
   1 New Taiwan dollar (NT$) = 100 cents (¢).
CHRISTMAS ISLAND:
   1 Australian dollar ($) = 100 cents (¢).
CISKEI:
   1 South African rand (r) = 100 cents (¢).
COCOS (KEELING) ISLANDS:
   1 Australian dollar ($) = 100 cents (¢).
COLOMBIA: 1 peso (p) = 100 centavos (c).
COMORO ISLANDS:
   1 CFA franc (fr) = 100 centimes (c).
CONGO PEOPLE'S REPUBLIC:
   1 CFA franc (fr) = 100 centimes (c).
COOK ISLANDS:
   1 New Zealand dollar ($) = 100 cents (¢).
COSTA RICA: 1 colon (col) = 100 centimos (c).
CUBA: 1 peso (p) = 100 centavos (c).
CYPRUS: 1 pound (£) = 1000 milliemes (m).
CYPRUS (Turkish): 1 lira (l) = 100 kurus (k).
CZECHOSLOVAKIA:
   1 koruna (k) = 100 haleru (h).
DENMARK: 1 krone (kr) = 100 ore (o).
DJIBOUTI: 1 franc (fr) = 100 centimes (c).
DOMINICA:
   1 East Caribbean dollar ($) = 100 cents (¢).
DOMINICAN REPUBLIC:
   1 peso (p) = 100 centavos (c).
ECUADOR: 1 sucre (s) = 100 centavos (c).
EGYPT: 1 pound (£) = 1000 milliemes (m).
EL SALVADOR:
   1 colon (col) = 100 centavos (c).

EQUATORIAL GUINEA:
1 ekuele (ek) = 100 centimos (c).
ETHIOPIA: 1 birr (b) = 100 cents (¢).

FALKLAND ISLANDS:
1 pound (£) = 100 pence (p).
FAROE ISLANDS:
1 Danish krone (kr) = 100 ore (o).
FIJI: 1 dollar ($) = 100 cents (¢).
FINLAND: 1 markka (mk) = 100 pennia (p).
FRANCE: 1 franc (fr) = 100 centimes (c).
FRENCH POLYNESIA:
1 franc (fr) = 100 centimes (c).
FRENCH SOUTHERN & ANTARCTIC TERR.:
1 CFA franc (fr) = 100 centimes (c).

GABON: 1 CFA franc (fr) = 100 centimes (c).
GAMBIA: 1 dalasy (dal) = 100 bututs (b).
GERMANY (Democratic Republic):
1 mark (m) = 100 pfennigs (pf).
GERMANY (Federal Republic):
1 Deutschemark (m) = 100 pfennigs (pf).
GHANA: 1 cedi (c) = 100 pesewas (p).
GIBRALTAR: 1 pound (£) = 100 pence (p).
GREAT BRITAIN:
1 pound sterling (£) = 100 pence (p).
GREECE: 1 drachma (dr) = 100 lepta (l).
GREENLAND:
1 Danish krone (kr) = 100 ore (o).
GRENADA:
1 East Caribbean dollar ($) = 100 cents (¢).
GUATEMALA: 1 quetzal (q) = 100 centavos (c).
GUERNSEY:
1 pound sterling (£) = 100 pence (p).
GUINEA: 1 cauries (c) = 100 sylis (s).
GUINEA-BISSAU: 1 peso (p) = 100 centavos (c).
GUYANA: 1 dollar ($) = 100 cents (¢).

HAITI: 1 gourde (g) = 100 centimes (c).
HONDURAS: 1 lempira (l) = 100 centavos (c).
HONG KONG: 1 dollar ($) = 100 cents (¢).
HUNGARY: 1 forint (ft) = 100 filler (f).

ICELAND: 1 krona (kr) = 100 aurar (a).
INDIA: 1 rupee (re) = 100 paise (p).
INDONESIA: 1 rupiah (rp) = 100 sen (s).
IRAN: 1 rial (r) = 100 dinars (d).
IRAQ: 1 dinar (d) = 1000 fils (f).
IRELAND: 1 pound (£) = 100 pence (p).
ISLE OF MAN:
1 pound sterling (£) = 100 pence (p).
ISRAEL: 1 shekel (s) =
10 pounds (£) = 1000 agorot (a).
ITALY: 1 lira (l) = 100 centesimi (c).
IVORY COAST:
1 CFA franc (fr) = 100 centimes (c).

JAMAICA: 1 dollar ($) = 100 cents (¢).
JAPAN: 1 yen (y) = 100 sen (s).
JERSEY: 1 pound sterling (£) = 100 pence (p).
JORDAN: 1 dinar (d) = 1000 fils (f).
JUGOSLAVIA: 1 dinar (d) = 100 paras (p).

KAMPUCHEA: 1 riel (r) = 100 cents (¢).
KENYA: 1 shilling (/-) = 100 cents (¢).
KIRIBATI:
1 Australian dollar ($) = 100 cents (¢).
KOREA, NORTH: 1 won (w) = 100 chon (ch).

KOREA, SOUTH: 1 won (w) = 100 chon (ch).
KUWAIT: 1 dinar (d) = 1000 fils (f).

LAOS: 1 kip (k) = 100 cents (¢).
LEBANON: 1 piaster (pi) = 100 centimes (c).
LESOTHO: 1 loti (m, from plural maloti) =
100 lisente (s from singular sente).
LIBERIA: 1 dollars ($) = 100 cents (¢).
LIBYA: 1 dinar (d) = 1000 dirhams (dh).
LIECHTENSTEIN:
1 Swiss franc (fr) = 100 rappen (rp).
LUXEMBOURG:
1 franc (fr) = 100 centimes (c).

MACAO: 1 pataca (pa) = 100 avos (a).
MALAGASY REPUBLIC:
1 ariary (a) = 5 francs (fr).
MALAWI: 1 kwacha (k) = 100 tambalas (t).
MALAYSIA: 1 rufiyaa (rf) = 100 lari (1).
MALDIVES: 1 rupee (re) = 100 larees (l).
MALI: 1 franc (fr) = 100 centimes (c).
MALTA: 1 pound (£) = 100 cents (¢).
MAURITANIA: 1 franc (fr) = 100 ouguiya (um).
MAURITIUS: 1 rupee (re) = 100 cents (¢).
MEXICO: 1 peso (p) = 100 centavos (c).
MONACO:
1 French franc (fr) = 100 centimes (c).
MONGOLIA: 1 tugrik (t) = 100 mung (mu).
MONTSERRAT:
1 East Caribbean dollar ($) = 100 cents (¢).
MOROCCO: 1 dirham (dh) = 100 francs (fr).
MOZAMBIQUE:
1 metica (mt) = 100 centimos (c).

NAURU: 1 Australian dollar ($) = 100 cents (¢).
NEPAL: 1 rupee (re) = 100 paise (p).
NETHERLANDS:
1 gulden (g) = 100 cents (¢).
NETHERLANDS ANTILLES:
1 gulden (g) = 100 cents (¢).
NEVIS:
1 East Caribbean dollar ($) = 100 cents (¢).
NEW CALEDONIA:
1 Polynesian franc (fr) = 100 centimes (c).
NEW ZEALAND: 1 dollar ($) = 100 cents (¢).
NICARAGUA:
1 cordoba (cor) = 100 centavos (c).
NIGER: 1 CFA franc (fr) = 100 centimes (c).
NIGERIA: 1 naira (n) = 100 kobo (k).
NIUE: 1 New Zealand dollar ($) = 100 cents (¢).
NORFOLK ISLAND:
1 Australian dollar ($) = 100 cents (¢).
NORWAY: 1 krone (kr) = 100 ore (o).

OMAN: 1 rial (ri) = 1000 baizas (b).

PAKISTAN: 1 rupee (re) = 100 paisa (p).
PANAMA: 1 balboa (b) = 100 centesimos (c).
PAPUA NEW GUINEA:
1 kina (k) = 100 toea (t).
PARAGUAY: 1 guarani (g) = 100 centimos (c).
PENRHYN:
1 New Zealand dollar ($) = 100 cents (¢).
PERU: 1 sol (s) = 100 centavos (c).
PHILIPPINES: 1 piso (p) = 100 sentimos (s).
PITCAIRN ISLANDS:
1 New Zealand dollar ($) = 100 cents (¢).

POLAND: 1 zloty (zl) = 100 groszy (gr).
PORTUGAL: 1 escudo (esc) = 100 centavos (c).
QATAR: 1 riyal (ri) = 100 dirhams (d).
REDONDA: 1 dollar ($) = 100 cents (¢)
ROMANIA: 1 leu (l) = 100 bani (b).
ROSS DEPENDENCY:
  1 New Zealand dollar ($) = 100 cents (¢).
RWANDA: 1 franc (fr) = 100 centimes (c).

ST. CHRISTOPHER (ST. KITTS):
  1 East Caribbean dollar ($) = 100 cents (¢).
ST. HELENA:
  1 pound sterling (£) = 100 pence (p).
ST. LUCIA:
  1 East Caribbean dollar ($) = 100 cents (¢).
ST. PIERRE & MIQUELON:
  1 CFA franc (fr) = 100 centimes (c).
ST. THOMAS & PRINCE ISLAND:
  1 dobra (db) = 100 centavos (c).
ST. VINCENT:
  1 East Caribbean dollar ($) = 100 cents (¢).
SAN MARINO:
  1 Italian lira (l) = 100 centesimi (c).
SAUDI ARABIA: 1 riyal (ri) = 100 halalas (h).
SENEGAL: 1 CFA franc (fr) = 100 centimes (c).
SEYCHELLES: 1 rupee (re) = 100 cents (¢).
SIERRE LEONE: 1 leone (l) = 100 cents (¢).
SINGAPORE:
  1 Australian dollar ($) = 100 cents (¢).
SOLOMON ISLANDS:
  1 Australian dollar ($) = 100 cents (¢).
SOMALIA: 1 shilling (sh) = 100 centesimos (c).
SOUTH AFRICA: 1 rand (r) = 100 cents (¢).
SOUTH GEORGIA:
  1 pound sterling (£) = 100 pence (p).
SOUTH WEST AFRICA (NAMIBIA):
  1 South African rand (r) = 100 cents (¢).
SPAIN: 1 peseta (pta) = 100 centimos (c).
SRI LANKA: 1 rupee (re) = 100 cents (¢).
SUDAN: 1 pound (£) = 100 piastres (p).
SURINAM: 1 gulden (g) = 100 cents (¢).
SWAZILAND: 1 emalangeni (e) = 100 cents (¢).
SWEDEN: 1 krona (kr) = 100 ore (o).
SWITZERLAND:
  1 franc (fr) = 100 centimes (c).
SYRIA: 1 pound (£) = 100 piastres (p).

TANZANIA: 1 shilling (/-) = 100 cents (¢).
THAILAND: 1 baht (b) = 100 satang (s).
TOGO: 1 CFA franc (fr) = 100 centimes (c).

TOKELAU ISLANDS:
  1 New Zealand dollar ($) = 100 cents (¢).
TONGA: 1 pa'anga (pa) = 100 seniti (s).
TRANSKEI:
  1 South African rand (r) = 100 cents (¢).
TRINIDAD & TOBAGO:
  1 dollar ($) = 100 cents (¢).
TRISTAN DA CUNHA:
  1 pound sterling (£) = 100 pence (p).
TUNISIA: 1 dinar (d) = 1000 millimes (m).
TURKEY: 1 lira (l) = 100 kurus (k).
TURKS & CAICOS ISLANDS:
  1 U.S. dollar ($) = 100 cents (¢).
TUVALU:
  1 Australian dollar ($) = 100 cents (¢).
UGANDA: 1 shilling (/-) = 100 cents (¢).
UNION OF SOVIET SOCIALIST REPUBLICS:
  1 ruble (rub) = 100 kopecks (kop).
UNITED ARAB EMIRATES:
  1 dirham (d) = 100 fils (f).
UNITED NATIONS: uses U.S. currency
  in New York, Swiss currency in Geneva,
  and Austrian currency in Vienna.
UNITED STATES OF AMERICA:
  1 dollar ($) = 100 cents (¢).
UPPER VOLTA:
  1 CFA franc (fr) = 100 centimes (c).
URUGUAY:
  1 new peso (N$) = 100 centesimos (c).
VANUATU: 1 vatu (v) = 100 francs (fr).
VATICAN CITY:
  1 Italian lira (l) = 100 centesimi (c).
VENDA:
  1 South African rand (r) = 100 cents (¢).
VENEZUELA: 1 bolivar (b) = 100 centimos (c).
VIETNAM: 1 dong (d) = 100 xu.

WALLIS & FUTUNA:
  1 CFA franc (fr) = 100 centimes (c).
WESTERN SAMOA: 1 tala (t) = 100 sene (s).
YEMEN ARAB REPUBLIC:
  1 riyal (ri) = 100 fils (f).
YEMEN, (People's Democratic Republic):
  1 dinar (d) = 1000 fils (f).
ZAIRE: 1 zaire (z) = 100 makuta (k).
ZAMBIA: 1 kwacha (kw) = 100 ngwee (ng).
ZIL ELWAGNE SESAL:
  1 rupee (re) = 100 cents (¢).
ZIMBABWE: 1 dollar ($) = 100 cents (¢).

# Foreign Stamp Prohibitions

For political or diplomatic reasons, the stamps of certain countries are prohibited in this country, as part of a general embargo against the importation of goods from certain countries. This means that the purchase or importation of stamps from these countries is prohibited in the United States, except in cases where goods are returned in the course of personal travel.

The affected countries, along with effective dates of the restrictions, are: North Korea, Dec. 17, 1950; Cuba, July 8, 1963; North Vietnam, May 5, 1964; Kampuchea (Cambodia), April 17, 1975; and South Vietnam, April 30, 1975. The following explanations and clarifications of these restrictions are taken from correspondence with the U.S. Department of Treasury, Foreign Assets Control Division.

In the course of personal travel to any of the affected countries, persons may bring up to $100 worth of goods from these countries back to the United States. This relaxation of the general embargo went into effect in the first part of 1977.

Merchandise returned under these provisions, including stamps, may not be sold or traded commercially under any circumstances. Such commercial use of imported goods from these countries would subject the traveler to criminal penalties.

Such penalties would also be invoked against a traveler returning with more than $100 worth of foreign goods from these countries; imports from these countries valued in excess of $100 would subject the entire amount acquired abroad to confiscation by customs agents and criminal penalties.

Regulations against the mail importation or buying and selling of stamps of prohibited origin affect all stamps, including those issued before the effective date of the regulations.

The prohibitions extend both to unused and used stamps of prohibited origins, and to stamps of such origins purchased or imported from any foreign country.

Licenses for the purchase or importation of such stamps are granted only where satisfactory documentary proof is submitted that the stamps have not been in the prohibited countries on or after the effective date of the applicable regulations, and that there has been no interest of nationals of these countries therein since that date.

Persons desiring to obtain such licenses have found it extremely difficult to obtain proof sufficient to satisfy licensing standards.

Stamps of the affected countries may be purchased and sold within the United States unless there is reason to believe that the stamps were imported in violation of the relevant regulations.

Apart from one exception, unused stamps of any affected country issued after the effective date of the regulations with respect to that particular country should be in the United States only if imported under license, and few, if any, have been licensed for importation.

Accordingly, persons who buy or sell in the United States unused stamps of the affected countries after the applicable effective date may well become involved in violations of the regulations or the relevant customs laws through their acquisition or sale of merchandise which has been imported into the United States contrary to law.

The exception applies to stamps of all prohibited origins, and refers to "packets" as that term is commonly used in the stamp trade.

Packets of predominantly used stamps which are obtained directly or indirectly from North Korea, North Vietnam, South Vietnam, Cambodia or Cuba may be purchased abroad or imported provided the number and value of such stamps does not exceed 10 per cent of the total number or value of the packet.

This exception does not apply if any of the stamps of North Korean, North Vietnamese, South Vietnamese, Cambodian or Cuban origin have in any way been segregated from other stamps in the packet.

Persons who have received from foreign sources unordered stamps that cannot legally be imported are advised that they may not make payment for the stamps or make any disposition of them without a license. Such stamps need not be destroyed; if the supplier can document that shipment was made without knowledge of the relevant prohibitions, their reexportation may be licensed.

Otherwise, and if they are of more than a nominal value, they are subject to seizure and forfeiture under customs regulations affecting importations contrary to law.

# Foreign Stamp Identifier

To aid in the identification of foreign stamps, this section is designed to help identify foreign spellings, words and overprints that might indicate the origin of certain stamps. As a general rule, look for a word, first in the overprint, then in the stamp itself, that looks like a country name. If it's spelled exactly like the country in question, look to the chapter in this almanac which deals with "Stamp-Issuing Entities — Role in History" for some historical background.

If this fails to produce results, then consult this index, which is arranged alphabetically. Foreign characters are not indexed unless close to English characters (due to typesetting restrictions). This should enable you to locate most foreign stamps with identifiable English characters in any catalog. For possible alternate names or country changes, consult the historical background contained in the aforementioned "Stamp-Issuing Entities" chapter. Countries may frequently be listed under a variety of names in different catalogs.

Note that all stamps indexed here are postal stamps, as typically cataloged. Therefore, reference to "tax stamps" means "postal tax stamps," etc. Reference to "locals" is not the usual philatelic sense of the word. As used here, it refers to stamps issued in local areas or internal states within larger stamp-issuing entities, such as the Indian states, Malayan states, and provisional states of some Latin American countries. In some cases, these will be true locals, while in other cases, such stamps may be postally valid within larger areas. In general, then, "local" refers to the issue of an internal state.

Reference dates are not intended to be inclusive. They are merely a guide to the period when various indexed characteristics appeared on certain stamps. In no case will indexed stamps appear before the first indicated date, but use of stamps after a second date (when included) may be common.

# — A —

A.B. on stamps of Russia: Far Eastern Republic (1923).

ABLOSUNG; local official stamps for use in Prussia (1903): Germany.

A CERTO on stamps of Peru; provisionals of Ancachs (1884): Peru.

ACORES: Azores.

AFGAN, AFGHANES: Afghanistan.

AFRICA CORREIOS: Portuguese Africa.

AFRICA OCCIDENTAL ESPANOLA: Spanish West Africa.

AFRICA ORIENTALE ITALIANA: Italian East Africa.

AFRIQUE EQUATORIAL FRANCAISE, A.E.F.: French Equatorial Africa.

AFRIQUE EQUATORIALE GABON: Gabon.

AFRIQUE OCCIDENTALE FRANCAISE: French West Africa.

AITUTAKI on stamps of Cook Islands: Aitutaki.

AITUTAKI on stamps of New Zealand: Aitutaki.

ALAOUITES on stamps of France: Alaouites.

ALAOUITES on stamps of Syria: Alaouites.

ALBANIA on stamps of Italy; offices in Turkey: Italy.

ALEXANDRIE on stamps of France; offices in Egypt: France.

ALEXANDRIE; offices in Alexandria, Egypt: France.

ALGERIE on stamps of France: Algeria.

ALGERIE: Algeria.

ALLEMAGNE DUITSCHLAND on stamps of Belgium: occupation of Germany (1919-21).

A.M.G.: Allied Military Government, appeared on various stamps throughout Europe during Allied occupation.

A.M.G. — F.T.T.: free territory of Trieste (1947-54).

A.M.G. — V.G.; Venezia Giulia: Italy (1945-47).

A.M. POST; Allied occupation: Germany (1945-46).

ANDORRA on stamps of Spain: Andorra.

ANDORRE on stamps of France: Andorra.

ANDORRE: Andorra.

ANTIOQUIA; provisionals of Antioquia (1868-1904): Colombia.

A.O. on stamps of Congo; semipostal stamps under Belgian occupation (1918): German East Africa.

A.O.F. on stamps of France; semipostal stamps (1945): French West Africa.

A.O.I. on stamps of Italy; postage due stamps (1941): Italian East Africa.

A PAYER TE BETALEN; postage due stamps: Belgium.

APURIMAC; provisionals of Apurimac (1885): Peru.

ARABIE SAODITE: Saudi Arabia.

ARCHIPEL DES COMORES: Comoro Islands.

AREQUIPA; provisionals of Arequipa (1881): Peru.

ASCENSION on stamps of St. Helena: Ascension.

A&T on stamps of French Colonies: Annam and Tonkin.

ATT., ATTS.; surcharges (1893-1908): Siam (Thailand).

AUNUS on stamps of Finland; Finnish occupation (1919): Russia.

AUR.; values: Iceland.

AUSTRALIAN ANTARCTIC TERRITORY; territorial issues: Australia.

AVISPORTO; newspaper stamps: Denmark.

AYACUCHO; provisionals of Ayacucho (1881): Peru.

AZERBAIDJAN: Azerbaijan (1919-22).

# — B —

B on stamps of Straits Settlements: Bangkok (1882-85).

B.A. on stamps of Great Britain: offices in Africa.

BADEN; stamps of French occupation (1947-49): Germany.

BAGHDAD on stamps of Turkey; British occupation (1917): Mesopotamia.

BAHAWALPUR; issues of internal state (1945-49): Pakistan.

BAHRAIN on stamps of Great Britain: Bahrain (1948-60).

BAHRAIN on stamps of India: Bahrain (1933-44).

BAHT; value: Siam (Thailand).

BAJAR PORTO; postage due stamps: Indonesia.

BAMRA; locals (1888-94): India.

BANAT BACSKA on stamps of Hungary; Serbian occupation (1919): Hungary.

BANI on stamps of Germany; German occupation (1917-18): Romania.

BANI on stamps of Hungary; Romanian occupation (1919): Hungary.

BARANYA on stamps of Hungary; Serbian occupation (1919): Hungary.

BARBUDA on stamps of Leeward Islands: Barbuda (1922).

BARWANI; locals (1921-48): India.

BASEL; locals (1845): Switzerland.

BASUTOLAND on stamps of South Africa: Basutoland (1945).    ♦

BATAAN AND CORREGIDOR on stamps of the Philippines; Japanese occupation (1942): Philippines.

BATYM on stamps of Russia: Batum.

BAYERN: Bavaria.

B.C.A. on stamps of Rhodesia: British Central Africa (1891-95).

B.C.M.; British Consular Mail (1884-86): Madagascar.

B.C.O.F. JAPAN 1946; military stamps (1946-47): Australia.

BECHUANALAND on stamps of South Africa: Bechuanaland Protectorate (1945).

BECHUANALAND on stamps after 1900: Bechuanaland Protectorate.

BECHUANALAND PROTECTORATE on stamps of a) Cape of Good Hope or b) Great Britain: Bechuanaland Protectorate a) (1899) or b) (1897-1926).

BELGIE: Belgium.

BELGIEN on stamps of Germany; German occupation: Belgium.

BELGIQUE: Belgium.

BELGISCH CONGO: Congo (1910-60).

BELIZE on stamps of British Honduras: Belize (1973).

BENADIR: Italian Somaliland (Somalia) (1903-26).

BENGASI on stamps of Italy; offices in Africa: Italy.

BENIN on stamps of French Colonies: Benin (1892).

BERLIN on stamps of Germany: Berlin (1948).

BESETZTES GEBIET NORDFRANKREICH on stamps of France; German occupation (1940): France.

BEYROUTH on stamps of a) France or b) Russia; offices in Turkey (Levant): a) France (1905) or b) Russia (1910).

BHOPAL; locals (1908-49): India.

BHOR; locals (1901): India.

BIAFRA on stamps of Nigeria; revolutionary forces (1968-69): Nigeria.

BIJAWAR; locals (1935-37): India.

B.I.O.T. on stamps of Seychelles: British Indian Ocean Territory (1968).

B.M.A. on stamps of Great Britain; offices in Africa (1948): Great Britain.

BMA MALAYA on stamps of Straits Settlements: Straits Settlements (1945-48).

BOCTOYHAR; offices in Turkey (1868-84): Russia.

BOFTGEBIET on stamps of Germany; German occupation (1916-17): Lithuania.

BOGACHES, BOGCHAH, BOGSHA(S); values: Yemen.

BOHMEN UND MAHREN: Bohemia and Moravia.

BOHMEN U. MAHREN on stamps of Czechoslovakia: Bohemia and Moravia (1939).

BOLIVAR; locals (1863-1904): Colombia.

BOLLODELLA POSTA DI SICILIA: Two Sicilies (1859).

BOLLO DELLA POSTA NAPOLETANA: Two Sicilies (1958).

BOLLO POSTALE: San Marino.

BOSNA I HERCEGOVINA on stamps of Bosnia and Herzegovina; locals (1918): Yugoslavia.

BOSNIEN HERCEGOVINA: Bosnia and Herzegovina (1912-18).

BOSNIENI HERZEGOWINA: Bosnia and Herzegovina (1906-12).

BOYACA; locals (1902-04): Colombia.

DRASIL: Brazil.

BRAUNSCHWEIG: Brunswick.

BRIEFPOST; French occupation (1945-46): Germany.

BRITISH BECHUANALAND on stamps of Cape of Good Hope or Great Britain: Bechuanaland.

BRITISH BECHUANALAND: Bechuanaland.

BRITISH EAST AFRICA on stamps of British India or Zanzibar: British East Africa (1895-97).

BRITISH NEW GUINEA: Papua New Guinea (1901-05).

BRITISH OCCUPATION on stamps of Russia: Batum (1919-20).

BRITISH PROTECTORATE OIL RIVERS on stamps of Great Britain: Niger Coast Protectorate (1892-93).

BRITISH SOMALILAND on stamps of India: Somaliland Protectorate (1903).

BRITISH SOUTH AFRICA COMPANY: Rhodesia (1890-1920).

BRITISH VICE CONSULATE: Madagascar (1884-86).

BR. VIRGIN ISLANDS: Virgin Islands.

BRUNEI on stamps of Labuan: Brunei (1906).

BRUXELLES BRUSSEL; surcharge precancellation (1929): Belgium.

BUENOS AIRES; locals (1858-62): Argentina.

BUITEN BEZIT on stamps of Netherlands Indies: Netherlands Indies (1908).

BULGARIE: Bulgaria.

BUNDI; locals (1941-47): India.

BUNDI SERVICE; local official stamps (1919): India.

BUREAU INTERNATIONAL D'EDUCATION; International Bureau of Education official stamps (1944-60): Switzerland.

BUREAU INTERNATIONAL DU TRAVAIL; International Labor Bureau official stamps: Switzerland.

BURMA on stamps of India: Burma (1937).

BUSHIRE on stamps of Persia: Bushire (1915).

BUSSAHIR; locals (1895-1901): India.

BUU-CHINH: Vietnam.

# — C —

CABO on stamps of Nicaragua; Cabo Gracias a Dios (1904-09): Nicaragua.

CABO JUBI on stamps of Rio de Oro: Cape Juby (1916).

CABO JUBY on stamps of Spain: Cape Juby (1919-33).

CABO JUBY on stamps of Spanish Morocco: Cape Juby (1934-48).

CABO VERDE: Cape Verde.

CADIZ; revolutionary overprint (1936): Spain.

CALCHI on stamps of Italy; Calchi, Aegean Islands (1930): Italy.

CALIMNO, CALINO on stamps of Italy; Calino, Aegean Islands: Italy.

CAMBODGE: Cambodia.

CAMEROONS U.K.T.T. on stamps of Nigeria: Cameroons (1960-61).

CAMEROUN on stamps of French Congo, Gabon or Middle Congo: Cameroun (1915-25).

CAMPECHE; provisionals (1876): Mexico.

CAMPIONE D'ITALIA; locals (1944): Italy.

CANAL ZONE on stamps of the United States or Panama: Canal Zone.

CANARIAS on stamps of Spain; Canary Islands (1936-37): Spain.

CANTON on stamps of Indo-China; offices in China (1901-23): France.

CARCHI on stamps of Italy; Calchi, Aegean Islands (1932): Italy.

CARNARO on stamps of Fiume: Fiume (1920).

CARUPANO; locals (1902): Venezuela.

CASO on stamps of Italy; Caso, Aegean Islands: Italy.

CASTELLORIZO on stamps of offices of France in Turkey: Castellorizo (1920).

CASTELLORISO on stamps of France: Castellorizo (1920).

CASTELROSSO on stamps of Italy: Castellorizo (1922-32).

CAUCA; locals (1890): Colombia.

CAVALLE; offices in Turkey: France.

CCCP: Russia.

C.CH. on stamps of French Colonies: Cochin China (1886-87).

CECHY A MORAVA; Bohemia and Moravia: Czechoslovakia.

C.E.F. on stamps of Cameroun; Cameroon Expeditionary Force (1915): Cameroons.

C.E.F. on stamps of India; China Expeditionary Force (1900-21): India.

CEFALONIA E ITACA on stamps of Greece; Italian occupation (1941): Ionian Islands.

CENT, CENTS on stamps of a) France or b) Russia; offices in China (1901-22): a) France or b) Russia.

CENTENAIRE ALGERIE: France (1929).

CENTENAIRE DU GABON: French Equatorial Africa (1938).

CENTESIMI on stamps of Austria; Austrian occupation (1918): Italy.

CENTESIMI on stamps of Bosnia and Herzegovina; postage due and special delivery, Austrian occupation (1918): Italy.

CENTESIMI DI CORONA on stamps of Italy; Italian occupation: Austria (1919) or Dalmatia (1921-22).

CENTIMES on stamps of Austria; offices in Crete (1903-07): Austria.

CENTIMES on stamps of Germany; offices in Turkey (1908): Germany.

CENTIMOS on stamps, no country name: Spain (1905).

CENTIMOS on stamps of France: French Morocco (1891-1910).

CERIGO on stamps of Greece; fraudulent overprints: Ionian Islands.

CERVANTES; official stamps (1916): Spain.

CESKOSLOVENSKA, CESKOSLOVENSKO: Czechoslovakia.

CESKO-SLOVENSKO; Slovakia (1939): Czechoslovakia.

CESKO-SLOVENSKO on stamps with Russian characters; Carpatho-Ukraine (1939): Czechoslovakia.

CFA on stamps of France: Reunion (1945— ).

C.G.H.S. on stamps of Germany; official stamps (1920-22): Upper Silesia.

CH preceding oriental characters: Korea.

CHALA; provisionals (1884): Peru.

CHAMBRA on stamps of India; Chambra: India.

CHARKHARI; locals (1894-1945): India.

CHEMINS DE FER SPOORWEGEN; parcel post: Belgium.

CHIHUAHUA; provisionals (1872): Mexico.

CHINA on stamps of a) Germany or b) Hong Kong; offices in China: a) Germany (1898-1913) or b) Great Britain (1917-27).

CHINE on stamps of France; offices in China (1894-1922): France.

CHRISTMAS ISLAND on stamps of Australia: Christmas Island (1958-62).

C.I.H.S. on stamps of Germany; official stamps (1920): Upper Silesia.

CILICIE on stamps of France: Cilicia (1920-21).

CILICIE on stamps of Turkey: Cilicia (1919).

CINQUAN TENAIRE on stamps of French Colonies; postage due (1903): New Caledonia.

CIRENAICA on stamps of Italy: Cyrenaica.

CIRENAICA on stamps of Tripolitania; air post (1932): Cyrenaica.

C.M.T. on stamps of Austria; Romanian occupation (1919): Western Ukraine.

CN; value: Korea.

COAMO; U.S. administration (1898): Puerto Rico.

COCHIN; locals (1892-1949): India.

CO. CI. on stamps of Yugoslavia; Ljubljana (1941): Yugoslavia.

COLIS POSTAUX; parcel post: Belgium.

COLOMBIA on stamps with map of Panama: Panama (1887-97).

COLONIA ERITREA on stamps of Italy: Eritrea (1892-1928).

COLONIALE ITALIANE: Italian Colonies.

COLONIE ITALIANE on stamps of Italy: Italian Colonies (1932).

COLONIES DE L'EMPIRE FRANCAISE. French Colonies (1859-65).

COLONIES POSTES: French Colonies (1881-86).

COMITE FRANCAIS DE LA LIBERATION NATIONALE; semipostals (1943): French Colonies.

COMORES: Comoro Islands.

COMP A DE MOCAMBIQUE on stamps of Mozambique: Mozambique Company (1892).

COMPANHIA DE MOCAMBIQUES: Mozambique Company.

COMPANHIA DO NYASSA: Nyassa (1921-23).

COMPANIA COLOMBIANA; airpost (1920): Colombia.

COMUNE DI CAMPIONE; locals of Italian enclave in Switzerland (1944): Italy.

COMUNICACIONES: Spain (1870-99).

CONFEDERATE STATES; Confederate States (1861-65): United States.

CONFOEDERATIO HELVETICA: Switzerland.

CONGO BELGE: Congo.

CONGO FRANCAIS: French Congo.

CONGO FRANCAIS GABON: Gabon (1910).

CONGRESO DE LOS DIPUTADOS; official stamps (1896-98): Spain.

CONSEIL DE L'EUROPE; Council of Europe official stamps: France.

CONSTANTINOPLE on stamps of Russia; offices in Turkey (1909-10): Russia.

CONSTANTINOPOL on stamps of Romania; offices in Turkey (1919): Romania.

COO on stamps of Italy; Coo, Aegean Islands (1930-32): Italy.

COOK ISLANDS or COOK IS'DS on stamps of New Zealand: Cook Islands (1936-46).

COOK NIUE ISLANDS: Niue (1938-46).

CORDOBA; provincials (1858): Argentina.

COREAN: Korea (1884-94).

COREE: Korea (1902-03).

CORFU on stamps of Greece; Italian occupation (1941): Corfu.

CORFU on stamps of Italy; Italian occupation (1923): Corfu.

CORONA on stamps of Italy; Italian occupation: Austria (1919) or Dalmatia (1919-22).

CORREIO on stamps, no country name: Portugal (1853-65).

CORREO AEREO on stamps, no country name: Spain.

CORREO ESPANOL MARRUECOS on stamps of Spain: Spanish Morocco (1903-10).

CORREO ESPANOL TANGER; Tangier semipostals (1926): Spanish Morocco.

CORREOS ARGENTINOS: Argentina (1888-90).

CORREOS INTERIOR: Philippines (1859-63).

CORREOS MEXICO GOBIERNO REVOLUCIONARIO; Yucatan (1924): Mexico.

CORREOS NACIONALES, CORREOS NALES: Colombia (1859-86).

CORREOS Y TELEGS, CORREOS Y TELEGEOS: Spain (1879).

CORREO or CORRESPONDENCIA URGENTE; special delivery: Spain.

CORRIENTES; provisionals (1856-78): Argentina.

COS on stamps of Italy; Coo, Aegean Islands (1912-22): Italy.

COSTA ATLANTICA B on stamps of Nicaragua; Zelaya (1907): Nicaragua.

COSTA ATLANTICA C on stamps of Nicaragua; Cabo Gracias a Dios (1907): Nicaragua.

COSTANTINOPOLI on stamps of Italy; offices in Turkey (1909-23): Italy.

COTE D'IVOIRE: Ivory Coast.

COTE (FRANCAIS) DES SOMALIS: Somali Coast.

COUR PERMANENTE DE JUSTICE INTERNATIONALE; International Court of Justice official stamps: Netherlands.

CROISSANT ROUGE TURC; tax stamps: Turkey.

CRUZ ROJA DOMINICANA; tax stamps (1932): Dominican Republic.

CRUZ ROJA HONDURENA; tax stamps: Honduras.

CRUZ VERMELHA; Red Cross franchise stamps: Portugal.

CTOT, CTOTHNKA: Bulgaria.

CUAUTLA; provisionals (1867): Mexico.

CUBA on stamps of the United States; U.S. administration (1899): Cuba.

CUCUTA; provisionals (1904-07): Colombia.

CUERNAVACA; provisionals (1867): Mexico.

CUNDINAMARCA; locals (1870-1904): Colombia.

CURACAO: Netherlands Antilles (1873-1948).

CUZCO on stamps of Peru or Arequipa, Peru; provisionals (1882-84): Peru.

C.X.C. on stamps of Bosnia and Herzegovina; Bosnia and Herzegovina (1918): Yugoslavia.

CYPRUS on stamps of Great Britain: Cyprus (1880-81).

# — D —

DAI NIPPON on stamps of Malaya or Malayan States; Japanese occupation (1942): Malaya or Malayan States.

DANMARK: Denmark.

DANSK-VESTINDIEN, DANSK-VESTINDISKE: Danish West Indies.

DANZIG on stamps of Germany: Danzig (1920-23).

DARDANELLES on stamps of Russia; offices in Turkey (1910): Russia.

DATIA; locals (1897): India.

DBL on stamps of Russia: Far Eastern Republic (1920).

DDR; German Democratic Republic: Germany.

DEDEAGH; offices in Turkey (1893-1903): France.

DEFICIT; postage due: Peru.

DEL GOLFO DE GUINEA: Spanish Guinea.

DEN WAISEN SIROTAM on stamps of Italy; German occupation (1944): Ljubljana, Yugoslavia.

DEUTFCHES REICH=DEUTSCHES REICH (old-style printers "S" looks like "f")

DEUTFCHOFTERREICH DEUTSCHOSTERREICH: Austria (1918-21).

DEUTSCH DEMOKRATISCHE REPUBLIK; German Democratic Republic: Germany.

DEUTSCH NEU GUINEA: German New Guinea.

DEUTSCH OSTAFRIKA: German East Africa.

DEUTSCH SUDWEST AFRIKA: German Southwest Africa.

DEUTSCHE followed by BUNDEPOST, FELDPOST, NATIONALVERSAMMLUNG, POFT or POST: Germany.

DEUTSCHE MILITAER-VERWALTUNG MONTENEGRO on stamps of Yugoslavia; German occupation (1943): Montenegro.

DEUTSCHE POST OSTEN on stamps of Germany; German occupation (1939): Poland.

DEUTSCHES REICH(-POST): Germany.

DEUTSCHES REICH GENERALGOUVERNEMENT; German occupation (1941-44): Poland.

DEUTSCHLAND; Allied occupation (1945-46): Germany.

DHAR; locals (1898-1901): India.

DIEGO-SUAREZ on stamps of French Colonies: Diego-Suarez (1892-96).

DIENST on stamps of Netherlands Indies; official stamps (1911): Netherlands Indies.

DIENST SACHE: official stamps of Wurttemberg: German States, Germany.

DILIGENCIA: Uruguay (1856-57).

DINERO on stamps, no country name: Peru (1858-72).

DISTRITO on stamps of Arequipa; provisionals of Cuzco (1881-85): Peru.

DJ or DJIBOUTI on stamps of Obock: Somali Coast (1894-1902).

DJIBOUTI: Somali Coast.

DOLLAR on stamps of Russia; offices in China (1917): Russia.

DOPLATA; postage due: Central Lithuania or Poland.

DOPLATIT or DOPLATNE; postage due: Czechoslovakia.

DPRK: Korea, North (1977—).

DRZAVA on stamps of Bosnia and Herzegovina; Bosnia and Herzegovina (1918): Yugoslavia.

DRZAVA SHS; Slovenia (1919): Yugoslavia.

DRZAVNA; Bosnia and Herzegovina (1919): Yugoslavia.

DUITSCH OOST AFRIKA BELGISCHE BEZETTING on stamps of Congo; Belgian occupation (1916-22): German East Africa.

DURAZZO on stamps of Italy; offices in Turkey (1909-16): Italy.

DUTTIA; locals (1893-1921): India.

# — E —

EAAAC, EAAAE, EAAAS or similar Greek letters: Greece.

E.A.F. on stamps of Great Britain; East Africa Forces (1943-46): Great Britain.

ECUADOR on stamps of Colombia; airpost (1928-29): Ecuador.

E E F; British occupation (1918): Palestine.

EESTI: Estonia.

EE. UU. DE C.; provisionals of Tolima (1870): Colombia.

EGEO on stamps of Italy; Aegean Islands: Italy.

EGYPTE, EGYPTIENNES: Egypt.

EINZUZIEHEN; postage due: Danzig.

EIRE: Ireland.

EJERCITO RENOVADOR; provisionals of Sinaloa (1923): Mexico.

ELFAFS (ELSAS) on stamps of Germany; German occupation (1940): France.

EL PARLAMENTO A CERVANTES; official stamps (1916): Spain.

EL SALVADOR: Salvador.

ELUA KENETA: Hawaii (1861-93).

EMP. OTTOMAN: Turkey (1876-90).

EMPIRE FRANC(AIS): France (1853-71) or French Colonies (1871-72).

ENAPIOMON; postage due: Greece.

EONIKH; tax stamps (1914): Greece.

EPMAKB: South Russia (1919).

EQUATEUR: Ecuador (1887).

E.R. on stamps, no country name: Great Britain (1952-67).

ERITREA on stamps of Great Britain; offices in Eritrea (1948-51): Great Britain.

ESCUELAS: Venezuela (1871-95).

ESPANA: Spain.

ESPANA SAHARA: Spanish Sahara.

ESPANOLA, ESPANS: Spain.

ESTADO DA INDIA: Portuguese India (1946-62).

ESTADOS UNIDOS DE NUEVA GRANADA: Colombia (1861).

EST AFRICAIN ALLEMAND on stamps of Congo; Belgian occupation (1916-22): German East Africa.

ESTERO on stamps of Italy; offices abroad (1874-85): Italy.

ETABLIS(SEMENTS FRANCAIS) DANS L'INDE: French India (1914-54).

ETABLISSEMENTS DE L'INDE: French India (1892-1907).

ETABLISSEMENTS or ETS. (FRANCAIS) DE L'OCEANIE: French Polynesia.

ETAT FRANCAIS: France.

ETHIOPIE, ETHIOPIENNES: Ethiopia.

ETIOPIA; Italian occupation (1936): Ethiopia.

EUPEN on stamps of Germany; Belgian occupation (1920-21): Germany.

EXPED. SCIENT.: China (1932).

EXPOSICION . . . BARCELONA: Spain (1929-30).

EXPOSITION COLONIALE INTERNATIONALE: France (1930-31).

## — F —

FACTAJ on stamps of Romania; parcel post (1928): Romania.

FARIDKOT STATE on stamps of India; locals (1887-1901): India.

FDO. POO: Fernando Po (1897-99).

FEDERATED MALAY STATES: Malaya (1900-35).

FELDPOST on stamps of Germany; military stamps (1944): Germany.

FEN on stamps of Poland; locals (1918): Poland.

FEN, FN; values: Manchukuo.

FERNANDO POO: Fernando Po.

FEZZAN; French occupation (1943-51): Libya.

FIERA CAMPIONARIA TRIPOLI: Libya (1934).

FIERA DI TRIESTE on stamps of Italy: Trieste (1950-53).

FILIPINAS: Philippines.

FILLER, FT; values: Hungary.

FIUME on stamps of Hungary; Fiume (1918-19).

FLUCHTLINGSHILFE MONTENEGRO on stamps of Yugoslavia; German occupation, semipostals (1944): Montenegro.

FORCES FRANCAISES LIBRES LEVANT on stamps of Syria; French military stamps (1942): Syria.

FOROYAR: Faroe Islands.

FR. on stamps of Senegal or Mauritania: French West Africa (1943-44).

FRANC on stamps of Austria; offices in Crete (1903-04): Austria.

FRANCA on stamps of Peru; provisionals (1884): Peru.

FRANCAIS, FRANCAISE: France or French Colonies.

FRANCE D'OUTRE-MER; semipostals (1943): French Colonies.

FRANCO BOLLO: Italy or Italian States.

FRANCO MARKE; Bremen (1856-60): German States.

FRANCO SCRISOREI; Moldavia-Walachia (1862-63): Romania.

FRANQUICIA; franchise stamps (1881): Spain.

FREI DURCH ABLOSUNG; local official stamps (1903-05): Germany.

FREIMARKE: German States.

FREIFTAAT (FREISTAAT) BAYERN on stamps of Germany or Bavaria; Bavaria (1919-20): German States.

FRIMAERKE KGL POST: Denmark (1851).

FUNF GROTE; Bremen (1856-60): German States.

FURSTENTUM, FUERSTENTUM, FVERSTENTUM: Liechtenstein.

## — G —

G on stamps of Cape of Good Hope: Griqualand West (1877-80).

GAB on stamps of French Colonies: Gabon (1886-89).

GABON on stamps of French Colonies: Gabon (1889).

GARCH: Saudi Arabia (1929-30).

GARZON; Tolima provisionals (1894): Colombia.

G.E.A. on stamps of East Africa and Uganda Protectorates; British occupation (1917): German East Africa.

G.E.A. on stamps of Kenya, Uganda & Tanganyika: Tanganyika (1921-22).

G ET D, G & D on stamps of Guadeloupe: Guadeloupe (1903-04).

GENERALGOUVERNEMENT; German occupation (1940-44): Poland.

GENEVE; Geneva locals (cantonals) (1843-49): Switzerland.

GEN.-GOUV. WARFCHAU on stamps of Germany; German occupation (1916-17): Poland.

GEORGIE: Georgia (1919).

GEORGIENNE: Georgia (1920).

GERUSALEMME on stamps of Italy; offices in Turkey (1909-11): Italy.

GHADAMES; French occupation (1949): Libya.

GHANA on stamps of Gold Coast: Ghana (1957-65).

GIBRALTAR on stamps of Bermuda: Gibraltar (1886).

GILBERT & ELLICE PROTECTORATE on stamps of Fiji: Gilbert and Ellice Islands (1911).

GIORNALI STAMPE; newspaper stamps (1861), Sardinia: Italian States.

GOLFO DE GUINEA: Spanish Guinea (1907-49).

GORNY SLASK; unrecognized private issue: Upper Silesia.

GOVERNO MILITARE ALLEATO on stamps of Italy; Allied occupation (1943): Italy.

GOYA: Spain (1930).

G.P.E. on stamps of French Colonies: Guadeloupe (1884-91).

GRAHAM LAND on stamps of Falkland Islands; Graham Land (1944): Falkland Islands.

GRANA; Neapolitan provinces (1861), Two Sicilies: Italian States.

GRANADA: Colombia (1861).

GRANADINA: Colombia (1859-60).

GRANDE COMORE: Grand Comoro (1897-1912).

GRAND LIBAN: Lebanon (1924-27).

G.R.I. on stamps of a) German New Guinea or b) German Samoa; British administration: a) New Britain (1914-15) or b) Samoa (1914).

G.R.I. on stamps of Marshall Islands: New Britain (1914).

GRONLAND: Greenland.

GROSSDEUTSCHES REICH; semipostals (1943-45): Germany.

GROSSDEUTSCHES REICH GENERAL-GOUVERNEMENT; semipostals (1943-44), German occupation: Poland.

GROSZY on stamps of Poland; surcharge (1950): Poland.

GUADALAJARA; provisionals (1867-68): Mexico.

GUADELOUPE on stamps of French Colonies: Guadeloupe (1889-91).

GUAM on stamps of United States: Guam (1899).

GUANACASTE on stamps of Costa Rica; Guanacaste locals (1885-90): Costa Rica.

GUINE: Portuguese Guinea.

GUINEA CONTINENTAL on stamps of Elobey, Annobon and Corisco: Spanish Guinea (1906).

GUINEA CONTIAL ESPANOLA: Spanish Guinea (1903-09).

GUINEA CORREOS on stamps of Spanish Guinea; fraudulent overprints (1914): Spanish Guinea.

GUINEA ECUATORIAL: Equatorial Guinea.

GUINEA ESPANOLA: Spanish Guinea (1902, 1949-60).

GUINEE: French Guinea.

GULTIG 9. ARMEE on stamps of Germany; German occupation (1918): Romania.

GUYANA on stamps of British Guiana: Guyana (1966-68).

GUYANE, GUY. FRANC. on stamps of French Colonies: French Guiana (1886-92).

GUYANE: French Guiana.

G.W. on stamps of Cape of Good Hope: Griqualand West (1877).

GWALIOR on stamps of India or British India; locals: India.

## — H —

HABILITADO on stamps of Cuba; U.S. administration (1898-99): Cuba.

HADHRAMAUT; locals (1955— ): Aden.

HANG-KHONG; airmail: Vietnam.

HANNOVER; Hanover (1850-66): German States.

HASHEMITE KINGDOM: Jordan (1949— ).

HAUTE SILESIE: Upper Silesia.

HAUTE VOLTA: Upper Volta.

HAUT-SENEGAL NIGER: Upper Senegal and Niger (1914-17).

HBA on stamps of Russia: Siberia (1921).

H.E.H. THE NIZAM'S; Hyderabad locals (1927-49): India.

HEJAZ & NEJD, HEDJAZ & NEDJDE: Saudi Arabia (1929-33).

HELLAS: Greece (1966— ).

IIELVETIA: Switzerland.

H.H. NAWAB SHAH (or SULTAN) JAHANBE-GAM; Bhopal locals: India.

H.I.: Hawaii (1851-93).

HIRLAPJEGY: newspaper stamps (1900-22): Hungary.

HOBY: Montenegro (1874-96).

HOI HAO on stamps of Indo-China; offices in China (1901-19): France.

HOLKAR STATE; Indore locals (1886-1908): India.

HOLSTEIN; Schleswig-Holstein (1865-66): German States.

HONDA on stamps of Colombia; Tolima provisionals (1896): Colombia.

H.P. followed by Russian characters: Bulgaria.

HRVATSKA; Croatia or Croatia-Slavonia: Yugoslavia.

HRZGL; Holstein (1864), Schleswig-Holstein: German States.

HT SENEGAL-NIGER: Upper Senegal and Niger (1906-14).

HYDERABAD; locals (1946): India.

## — I —

I.B.: West Irian (1970).

ICC on stamps of India; International Commission in Indo-China (1965-68), Laos and Vietnam: India.

IDAR; locals (1939-44): India.

I.E.F. on stamps of India; India Expeditionary Force military stamps (1914): India.

I.E.F.'D' on stamps of Turkey: Mesopotamia (1919).

IERUSALEM on stamps of Russia; offices in Turkey (1909-10): Russia.

ILE ROUAD on stamps of French offices in Levant: Rouad (1916).

ILES WALLIS ET FUTUNA on stamps of New Caledonia: Wallis and Futuna Islands (1920-40).

IMPERIO COLONIAL PORTUGUES; postage due (1945): Portuguese Africa.

IMPUESTO DE GUERRA; war tax stamps (1874-98): Spain.

INDE: French India.

INDIA PORT(UGUEZA): Portuguese India (1871-86).

INDIA and Portuguese inscriptions: Portuguese India.

INDOCHINE: Indo-China.

INDONESIA with REPUBLIK: Indonesia.

INDONESIA without REPUBLIK; Indonesia (1948-49): Netherlands Indies.

INDORE STATE; locals (1904-47): India.

INDUSTRIELLE KRIEGSWIRTSCHAFT; War Board of Trade official stamps (1918): Switzerland.

INHAMBANE on stamps of Mozambique: Inhambane (1895).

INKERI: North Ingermanland (1920).

INLAND on stamps, no country name: Liberia (1881).

INSELPOST on stamps of Germany; military stamps: Germany.

INSTRUCAO on stamps of Portuguese India; tax stamps (1934-35): Timor.

INSTRUCCION: Venezuela (1893-95).

INSUFFICIENTLY PREPAID; postage due (1931-33): Zanzibar.

IONIKON KPATOE: Ionian Islands (1859).

I.O.V.R.; tax stamps (1948): Romania.

IRAN: Persia (1935— ).

IRANIENNES: Persia (1935-37).

IRAQ on stamps of Turkey: Mesopotamia (1918-22).

IRIAN BARAT: West Irian (1963-68).

I.R. OFFICIAL on stamps of Great Britain; official stamps (1882-1904): Great Britain.

ISLAND: Iceland.

ISOLE ITALIANE DELL'EGEO on stamps of Italy; Aegean Islands (1930-40): Italy.

ISOLE JONIE on stamps of Italy; Italian occupation (1941): Ionian Islands.

ISTRA; locals for Istria and the Slovene Coast (1945-46): Yugoslavia.

ITA-KARJALA; Finnish occupation (1941-43): Karelia.

ITALIA, ITALIANE, ITALIANO: Italy.

IZMIR HIMAYEI ETFAL CEMIYETI; tax stamps (1933): Turkey.

## — J —

J on stamps of Peru; Yca provisionals (1884): Peru.

JAFFA on stamps of Russia; offices in Turkey (1909-10): Russia.

JAIPUR; locals (1904-49): India.

JAMHURI: Zanzibar (1964-68).

JANINA on stamps of Italy; offices in Turkey (1909-11): Italy.

JAPANESE: Japan (1876-96).

JAVA on stamps of Netherlands Indies; locals (1908): Netherlands Indies.

JEEND STATE on stamps of India; Jind locals (1885): India.

JHIND STATE on stamps of India; Jind locals (1885-1913): India.

JIND on stamps of India; locals (1913-43): India.

JOHOR with MALAYSIA; regional issues of Johore (1965— ): Malaysia.

JOHOR, JOHORE on stamps of Straits Settlements; regional issues of Johore (1876-91): Malaya.

JOHORE; Johore (1892-1960): Malaya.

JOURNAUX DAGBLADEN on stamps of Belgium; newspaper stamps: Belgium.

JUAN FERNANDEZ on stamps of Chile: Chile (1910).

JUBILE DE L'UNION POSTALE UNIVERSELLE: Switzerland (1900).

JUGOSLAVIA, JUGOSLAVIJA: Yugoslavia.

— K —

KAIS KON(IGL): Austria (1853-1907).

KALAYAAN NANG PILIPINAS; Japanese occupation (1943): Philippines.

KAMERUN on stamps of Germany: Cameroun (1897).

KAMERUN: Cameroun (1900-18).

KAP; values (1918-22): Latvia.

KARJALA: Karelia (1922).

KARJALA on stamps of Finland; Finnish occupation (1941-43): Karelia.

KARKI on stamps of Italy; Aegean Islands (1912-22): Italy.

KARNTEN UBFTIMMUNG on stamps of Austria; Carinthian plebiscite (1920): Austria.

KAROLINEN: Caroline Islands.

KASAI (SOUTH KASAI) and KATANGA; non-recognized states (1960-61): Congo.

KATHIRI STATE OF SEIYUN; locals (1942 —): Aden.

K.C.-NOUITA: Serbia (1866).

KEDAH; locals: Malaya, Malaysia.

(KEELING): Cocos Islands.

KELANTAN; locals: Malaya, Malaysia.

KENTTA-POSTI FALTPOST on stamps of Finland; military stamps (1943): Finland.

KENTTAPOSTIA; military stamps (1941-63): Finland.

KENYA AND UGANDA: Kenya, Uganda and Tanzania (1922-33).

KENYA UGANDA TANGANYIKA (in any order): Kenya, Uganda and Tanzania (1935-64).

KENYA UGANDA TANZANIA (in any order): Kenya, Uganda and Tanzania (1965— ).

KERASSUNDE on stamps of Russia; offices in Turkey (1909-10): Russia.

K.G.C. 19A20 on stamps of Yugoslavia; Carinthian plebiscite (1920): Yugoslavia.

K.G.L. with cents: Danish West Indies (1855-73).

K.G.L. with skillings: Denmark (1851-68).

KHMERE: Cambodia (1971— ).

KHOR FAKKAN; locals (1964— ): Sharjah and Dependencies.

KIAUTSCHOU: Kiauchau.

KIBRIS: Cyprus (1960— ).

KIBRIS CUMHURIYETI: Cyprus (1960).

KIONGA on stamps of Lourenco Marques: Kionga (1916).

KISHANGARH; locals (1904-47): India.

KISHENGARH; Kishangarh locals (1899-1904): India.

K-number-K on stamps of Russia: Far Eastern Republic (1920).

K 60 K on stamps of Russia: Armenia (1919).

KLAIPEDA; Lithuanian occupation (1923): Memel.

KONGELIGT: Denmark (1851).

KOP KOH: Finland (1856-66).

KORCA, KORCE(S): Albania (1914-18).

KORONA; values (1900-26): Hungary.

KOUANG-TCHEOU on stamps of Indo-China; offices in China (1906-41): France.

KPHTH: Crete (1900-10).

KRALJEVINA, KRALJEVSTVO: Yugoslavia (1921-33).

KRONE, KRONEN; values (1899-1925): Austria.

KSA: Saudi Arabia (1975—).

K-U-K-MILITARPOST: Bosnia and Herzegovina (1912-18).

K.U.K. FELDPOST on stamps of Bosnia and Herzegovina; military stamps (1915): Austria.

K-U-K-FELDPOST; military stamps (1915-18): Austria.

K-U-K-FELDPOST with BANI or LEI; Austrian occupation (1917-18): Romania.

K-UND-K FELDPOST; military semipostals (1918): Austria.

KUPA on stamps of Yugoslavia; Italian occupation (1941-42): Yugoslavia.

KURLAND on stamps of Germany; German occupation (1945): Latvia.

KUWAIT on stamps of a) India or b) Great Britain: Kuwait a)(1923-45) or b)(1948-58).

K. WURTT. POST; Wurttemberg (1875-1900): German States.

— L —

LA AGUERA: Aguera (1920-22).

LABUAN on stamps of North Borneo: Labuan (1905-06).

LA CANEA on stamps of Italy; offices in Crete (1900-12): Italy.

LA GEORGIE: Georgia (1919).

LAIBACH; German occupation (1944-45), Ljubljana: Yugoslavia.

LAND-POST; postage due (1862), Baden: German States.

LANSA; airmail (1950): Colombia.

L.A.R.; Libyan Arab Republic (1969— ): Libya.

LAS BELA; locals (1897-1907): India.

LATTAQUIE on stamps of Syria: Latakia (1931-33).

LATVIJA, LATWIJA: Latvia.

LEI on stamps of Austria; Austrian occupation (1917-18): Romania.

LERO on stamps of Italy; Aegean Islands (1930-32): Italy.

LEROS on stamps of Italy; Aegean Islands (1912-22): Italy.

LESOTHO on stamps of Basutoland: Lesotho (1966).

LEVANT; offices in Turkey (1902-23): France.

LEVANT on stamps of a) Great Britain or b) Poland; offices in Turkey: a) Great Britain (1905-06) or b) Poland (1919-21).

LIBAN, LIBANAISE: Lebanon.

LIBAU on stamps of Germany; German occupation (1919): Latvia.

LIBIA: Libya (1912-51).

LIBYA on stamps of Cyrenaica: Libya (1951).

LIBYE: Libya.

LIETUVA, LIETUVOS: Lithuania.

LIETUVA on stamps of Russia; South District (1919): Lithuania.

LIGNES AERIENNE; military airmail (1942): Syria.

LIMA: Peru (1871-89).

LIMBAGAN on stamps of Philippines; Japanese occupation (1943): Philippines.

LIPSO on stamps of Italy; Aegean Islands (1912-32): Italy.

LIRE on stamps of Austria; Austrian occupation (1918): Italy.

LISBOA; tax stamps (1913) or franchise stamps (1903-38): Portugal.

LISSO on stamps of Italy; Aegean Islands (1930): Italy.

LITAS; values (1922-40): Lithuania.

LITWA, LITWY: Central Lithuania.

LJUBLJANSKA; German occupation (1944-45), Ljubljana: Yugoslavia.

L. MARQUES on stamps of Mozambique: Lourenco Marques (1895-97).

LMcL; Lady McLeod, private internal issue (1847): Trinidad.

LOSEN; postage due: Sweden.

LOTHRINGEN on stamps of Germany; German occupation (1940): France.

L.P. on stamps of Russia; Russian occupation (1919): Latvia.

LTSR on stamps of Lithuania; Russian occupation (1940): Lithuania.

LUBIANA on stamps of Yugoslavia; Italian occupation (1941), Ljubljana: Yugoslavia.

LUEBECK; Lubeck (1863-67): German States.

LUFTFELDPOST; military airmail (1942): Germany.

LUXEMBURG on stamps of Germany; German occupation (1940-41): Luxembourg.

# — M —

MACAU: Macao.

MACAV; tax stamps: Macao.

MADAGASCAR on stamps of France: Madagascar (1895).

MADEIRA on stamps of Portugal: Madeira (1868-98).

MADRID: Spain (1920-30).

MAFEKING on stamps of Bechuanaland Protectorate or Cape of Good Hope: Cape of Good Hope (1900).

MAGYAR, MAGYAR—: Hungary.

MAGYAR NEMZETI KORMANY SZEGED on stamps of Hungary; Serbian occupation (1919), Szeged: Hungary.

MAHRA SULTANATE OF QISHN AND SOCOTRA; locals (1967): South Arabia.

MALACCA; locals: Malaya.

MALAGA on stamps of Spain; revolutionary issues (1937): Spain.

MALAGASY: Madagascar (1961— ).

MALDIVES on stamps of Ceylon: Maldive Islands (1906-09).

MALGACHE: Madagascar (1959-61).

MALMEDY on stamps of Belgium; Belgian occupation (1920-21): Germany.

MALUKU SELATAN; local or private issues (South Moluccas): Indonesia.

MANAMA; locals: Ajman.

MANIZALES; local private post: Colombia.

MARIANAS ESPANOLAS on stamps of the Philippines: Mariana Islands (1899).

MARIANEN: Mariana Islands (1899-1919).

MARIENWERDER on stamps of Germany; plebiscite (1920): Marienwerder.

MARKA; values (1919-28): Estonia.

MARKKA, MARKKAA; values: Finland.

MAROC: French Morocco or Morocco.

MAROCCO on stamps of Germany; offices in Morocco: Germany.

MAROKKO on stamps of Germany; offices in Morocco (1911): Germany.

MARRUECOS on stamps of Spain or with ESPANOL: Spanish Morocco.

MARRUECOS without ESPANOL; Northern Zone (1956-58): Morocco.

MARSHALL-INSELN: Marshall Islands.

MARTINIQUE on stamps of French Colonies: Martinique (1886-92).

MAURITANIE: Mauritania.

M.B.D. on stamps with Indian characters; Nandgaon locals (1893-95): India.

MBLEDHJA KUSHTETUESE on stamps of Albania; Italian dominion (1939): Albania.

MBRETNI(J)A: Albania.

MECKLENB.; Mecklenburg-Schwerin (1856-67): German States.

MEDELLIN; provisionals (1888-89), Antioquia: Colombia.

MEDIA ONZA; official stamps (1854-63): Spain.

MEDIO REAL: Dominican Republic (1865-79).

M.E.F. on stamps of Great Britain; Middle East Forces offices (1942-50): Great Britain.

MEJICO: Mexico (1856-64).

MELAKA; Malacca locals: Malaysia.

MEMEL on stamps of France: Memel (1920-23).

MEMEL with KLAIPEDA; Lithuanian occupation (1923): Memel.

MEMEL-GEBIET on stamps of Germany: Memel (1920).

METELIN on stamps of Russia; offices in Turkey (1910): Russia.

MEXICANO: Mexico.

MILITARPOST: Bosnia and Herzegovina.

MILL., MILLIEME(S) on stamps of France; offices in Egypt (1921-28): France.

M. KIR.: Hungary (1916).

MN; values (1884-95): Korea.

MOCAMBIQUE: Mozambique.

MODONES; Modena (1859): Italian States.

MONASTIR on stamps of Turkey: Turkey (1911).

MONGTSEU, MONGTZE on stamps of Indo-China; offices in China (1903-19): France.

MONT ATHOS on stamps of Russia; offices in Turkey (1909-10): Russia.

MONTE CASSINO on stamps of Poland (exile in Great Britain); Polish government in exile in Great Britain (1944): Poland.

MONTENEGRO on stamps of a) Austria or b) Yugoslavia; a) Austrian (1917-18) or b) Italian (1941-42) occupation: Montenegro.

MONTEVIDEO: Uruguay (1858-67).

MONTSERRAT on stamps of Antigua: Montserrat (1876).

MOQUEA on stamps of Peru; Moquegua provisionals (1885): Peru.

MOQUEGUA on stamps of Arequipa, Peru; provisionals (1881-85): Peru.

MOROCCO AGENCIES on stamps of Gibraltar or Great Britain; offices in Morocco: Great Britain.

MORVI STATE; locals (1931-48): India.

MOYEN CONGO: Middle Congo.

MQE on stamps of French Colonies: Martinique (1886-91).

MUSCAT & OMAN: Oman (1966-70).

M.V.i.R. on stamps of Romania or Germany; German occupation (1917-18): Romania.

— N —

NABHA on stamps of India; locals: India.

NACIONES UNIDAS: United Nations.

NANDGAM; Nandgaon locals (1891-95): India.

NAPA, NAPE: Serbia.

NAPOLETANA; Two Sicilies (1858-60): Italian States.

NA SLASK; semipostals (1921): Central Lithuania.

NATIONALER VERWALTUNGSAUSSCHUSS on stamps of Montenegro; German occupation (1943): Montenegro.

NATIONS UNIES: United Nations.

NATIONS UNIES with HELVETIA; official stamps, United Nations European office: Switzerland.

NAURU on stamps of Great Britain: Nauru (1916-23).

N.C.E. on stamps of French Colonies: New Caledonia (1881-93).

N.D. HRVATSKA: Croatia.

NEDERLAND: Netherlands.

NED(ERLANDSE) ANTILLEN: Netherlands Antilles (1949— ).

NED(ERLANDSCH)-INDIE: Netherlands Indies (1864-1949).

NED(ERLANDS) NIEUW GUINEA: Netherlands New Guinea (1950-62).

NEGERI SEMBILAN; Negri Sembilan locals; Malaysia.

NEGRI SEMBILAN; locals: Malaya.

NEW HEBRIDES CONDOMINIUM on stamps of Fiji: New Hebrides (1908-10).

NEZ(AVISNA) DRZ(AVA) HRVATSKA: Croatia.

N.F. on stamps of Nyasaland Protectorate; British occupation (1916): German East Africa.

NIEUW GUINEA: Netherlands New Guinea (1950-62).

NIEUWE REPUBLIEK: New Republic (1886-88).

NIPPON: Japan (1966— ).

NISIRO on stamps of Italy; Aegean Islands (1930-32): Italy.

NISIROS on stamps of Italy; Aegean Islands (1912-22): Italy.

NIUE on stamps of New Zealand: Niue.

NLLE. CALEDONIE: New Caledonia.

NO HAY ESTAMPILLAS; locals (1894-1912): Colombia.

NOPTO on stamps of Bosnia and Herzegovina; postage due (1919), Bosnia and Herzegovina: Yugoslavia.

NOPTO MAPKA; postage due: Serbia.

NORDDEUTSCHER POSTBEZIRK; North German Confederation (1868-71): German States.

NORD-DEUTSCHE-POST; North German Confederation official stamps (1870-71): German States.

NOREG: Norway.

NORFOLK ISLAND on stamps of Australia: Norfolk Island (1959).

NORGE: Norway.

NOSSI-BE on stamps of French Colonies: Nossi-Be (1891-94).

NOUVELLE CALEDONIE: New Caledonia (1905— ).

NOUVELLES HEBRIDES; French issues: New Hebrides.

NOWANUGGUR; locals (1877): India.

NOYTA: Russia.

NOYT MAPKA with foreign characters: Azerbaijan (1922-24).

NSB on stamps of French Colonies: Nossi-Be (1890-93).

N.S.W.: New South Wales.

N.W. PACIFIC ISLANDS on stamps of Australia: North West Pacific Islands.

NYASALAND: Nyasaland Protectorate.

NYASSA on stamps of Mozambique: Nyassa (1898).

N.Z.: New Zealand.

## — O —

OAHA MAPKA: Finland (1866-74).

OAXACA; civil war issue (1914): Mexico.

OBOCK on stamps of French Colonies: Obock (1892).

OCCUPATION FRANCAISE on stamps of Hungary; French occupation (1919): Hungary.

OCEANIE: French Polynesia (1892-1958).

OESTERR POST with KAIS KOENIGL: Austria (1883-1907).

OESTERR-POST with LIECHTENSTEIN: Liechtenstein (1912-20).

OEUVRES DE SOLIDARITE FRANCAISE; semipostals (1943-44): French Colonies.

OFF(ENTLIG) SAK; official stamps: Norway.

OFFICIAL on stamps of Kenya and Uganda; official stamps (1959-60): Tanganyika.

OFFISIEEL without OFFICIAL; official stamps: South-West Africa.

OFFISIEEL OFFICIAL; official stamps: South Africa.

OFTERREICH (OSTERREICH): Austria.

OIL RIVERS: Niger Coast Protectorate (1892-93).

OKCA; Army of the North (1919): Russia.

OLTRE GIUBA on stamps of Italy: Oltre Giuba.

O.M.F. SYRIE on stamps of France: Syria (1920-22).

ORANGE RIVER COLONY on stamps of Cape of Good Hope: Orange River Colony (1900-02).

ORANJE VRIJ STAAT: Orange River Colony.

ORCHA POSTAGE; Orchha locals (1913-17): India.

ORCHHA STATE; locals (1939-40): India.

ORGANISATION INTERNATIONAL POUR LES REFUGIES on stamps of Switzerland; International Organization for Refugees official stamps (1950): Switzerland.

ORGANISATION METEOROLOGIQUE MONDIALE; World Meteorological Organization official stamps: Switzerland.

ORGANISATION MONDIALE DE LA SANTE; World Health Organization official stamps: Switzerland.

ORTS(-)POST: Switzerland (1850).

O.S.; official stamps (1951-52): Norway.

OSTEN on stamps of Germany; German occupation (1939): Poland.

OSTERREICH: Austria.

OSTERR(EICHISCHE) POST: Austria.

OSTLAND on stamps of Germany; German occupation (1941-43): Russia.

OTVORENIE SLOVENSKENO on stamps of Czechoslovakia; Slovakia (1939): Czechoslovakia.

OUBANGUI-CHARI(-TCHAD) on stamps of Middle Congo: Ubangi (1915-24).

O.W. OFFICIAL on stamps of Great Britain; Office of Works official stamps (1896-1902): Great Britain.

## — P —

P on stamps of Straits Settlements; Perak (1878): Malaya.

P with numeral and queen's cameo, no country name: Great Britain (1971— ).

PACCHI POSTALI; parcel post: Italy, San Marino (diagonal value) or Somalia (star and crescent).

PACKHOI on stamps of Indo-China; offices in China (1903-04): France.

PAHANG; locals: Malaya, Malaysia.

PAISA; values: Nepal.

PAITA on stamps of Peru; provisionals (1884): Peru.

PAK-HOI on stamps of Indo-China; offices in China (1906-19): France.

PAKISTAN on stamps of India: Pakistan (1947-49).

PAKKE-PORTO; parcel post: Greenland.

PALESTINE on stamps of Egypt; occupation of Palestine (1948-67): Egypt.

PAPUA on stamps of British New Guinea: Papua New Guinea (1907).

PAPUA AND NEW GUINEA: Papua New Guinea (1952-71).

PARA on stamps of a) Austria, b) Germany, c) Russia or d) Italy; offices in Turkey: a) Austria, b) Germany, c) Russia or d) Italy.

PARAS on stamps of a) France, b) Great Britain or c) Romania; offices in Turkey: a) France, b) Great Britain or c) Romania.

PARM; Parma (1852-55): Italian States.

PARMENSI; Parma (1853-59): Italian States.

PASCO on stamps of Peru; provisionals (1884): Peru.

PATIALA on stamps of India; locals (1891-1947): India.

PATMO on stamps of Italy; Aegean Islands (1930-32): Italy.

PATMOS on stamps of Italy; Aegean Islands (1912-22): Italy.

PCOCP: Russia (1921-23).

PECHINO on stamps of Italy; offices in China (1917-19): Italy.

PEN, PENNI(A); values: Finland.

PENANG; locals: Malaya.

PENRHYN on stamps of Cook Islands: Penrhyn Island (1973— ).

PENRHYN ISLAND on stamps of New Zealand: Penrhyn Island (1902-20).

PEOPLE'S REPUBLIC OF SOUTHERN YEMEN on stamps of South Arabia: Yemen (1968).

PEOPLE'S DEMOCRATIC REPUBLIC OF YEMEN: Yemen (1971— ).

PERAK; locals: Malaya, Malaysia.

PERLIS; locals: Malaya, Malaysia.

PERSANE(S): Persia (1881-1935).

PERSEKUTUAN TANAH MELAYU: Malaya (1957-63).

PERUANA: Peru.

PERV: Peru.

PESA on stamps of Germany: German East Africa (1893).

PFG. on stamps of Russia; German occupation (1918): Estonia.

PFENNIG; values: German States, Germany.

P.G.S. on stamps of Straits Settlements; official stamps (1890), Perak: Malaya.

PHILIPPINES on stamps of the United States: Philippines (1899-1906).

PIASTER on stamps of a) Austria or b) Germany; offices in Turkey: a) Austria or b) Germany.

PIASTRE(S) on stamps of a) France, b) Great Britain, c) Italy, d) Romania or e) Russia; offices in Turkey: a) France, b) Great Britain, c) Italy, d) Romania or e) Russia.

PIASTRE on stamps of Italy; offices in Turkey: Italy.

PILGRIM TERCENTENARY: United States (1920).

PILIPINAS: Philippines.

PINSIN(E); values: Ireland.

PISCO on stamps of Peru; provisionals (1884): Peru.

PISCOPI on stamps of Italy; Aegean Islands (1912-32): Italy.

PIURA on stamps of Peru; provisionals (1884): Peru.

PLEBISCITE OLSZTYN ALLENSTEIN on stamps of Germany; plebiscite issue (1920): Allenstein.

PLEBISCIT with SLESVIG; plebiscite issue (1920): Schleswig.

P.M. on stamps of Italy; military stamps (1943), regular issue during shortage (1944-45): Italy.

POCZTA (POLSKA): Poland.

POHJOIS INKERI: North Ingermanland.

POLSKA: Poland.

POLYNESIE FRANCAISE: French Polynesia (1956— ).

PONCE: Puerto Rico (1898).

PORTEADO; postage due: Portugal.

PORTE DE CONDUCCION; parcel post: Peru.

PORTE DE MAR; a form of postage due for ship mail (1875): Mexico.

PORTE FRANCO with CORREOS: Peru (1858-72).

PORT GDANSK on stamps of Poland; offices in Danzig (1925-38): Poland.

PORT LAGOS on stamps of France; offices in Turkey (1893): France.

PORTO GAZETEI; Moldavia (1858-59): Romania.

PORTOMARKE; postage due: Bosnia and Herzegovina.

PORTO RICO on stamps of the United States: Puerto Rico (1899).

PORT SAID; offices in Egypt (1899-1928): France.

POSTA CESKOSLOVENSKA on stamps of Austria; semipostals (1919): Czechoslovakia.

POSTAGE with CAMB AUST SIGILLUM NOV: New South Wales (1850-51).

POSTAGE (REVENUE) with portrait of king or queen, no country name: Great Britain (1840-1967).

POSTALI: see PACCHI POSTALI.

POSTA ROMANA CONSTANTINOPOL on stamps of Romania; offices in Turkey (1919): Romania.

POSTAS LE NIOC; postage due: Ireland.

POSTE AERIENNE with plane on stamps of Persia; airmail (1927-29): Persia.

POSTE AERIEO with plane on stamps of Persia; airmail (1928): Persia.

POSTE ESTENSI; Modena (1852): Italian States.

POSTEK NEDEUIERGIZIANE, POSIEXHEDEUIEEGIZIANE: Egypt (1872-79).

POSTE LOCALE: Switzerland (1849-50).

POSTES with red crescent and 1954; tax stamps (1954): Afghanistan.

POSTES OTTOMANES: Turkey (1913-22).

POSTES SERBES on stamps of France: Serbia (1916-18).

POSTGEBIET OB. OST, POFTGEBIET OB. OFT on stamps of Germany; German occupation (1916-17): Lithuania.

POST STAMP, POST & RECEIPT or POSTAGE with ANNA(S); Hyderabad: India.

POST ZEGEL without country name: Netherlands (1852-67).

POULS; semipostals (1952): Afghanistan.

P.P. on stamps of France: French Morocco (1903).

P.P.C. on stamps of Poland; offices in Turkey, consular mail: Poland.

PREUSSEN; Prussia (1861-67): German States.

PRINCE FAROUK: Egypt (1929).

PRISTINA on stamps of Turkey: Turkey (1911).

PRO (PLEBISCITO) TACNA Y ARICA; plebiscite tax stamps (1925-28): Peru.

PROTECTORADO ESPANOL: Spanish Morocco.

PROTECTORATE on stamps of Bechuanaland: Bechuanaland Protectorate (1888-89).

PROTECTORAT FRANCAIS on stamps of France or French Morocco: French Morocco (1914-21).

PRO TUBERCULOSOS POBRES; tax stamps (1937-38): Spain.

PRO UNION IBEROAMERICANA: Spain (1930).

PROVISIONAL 1881-1882 on stamps of Peru; Arequipa provisionals (1881-85): Peru.

PS in intertwined script letters; Cauca locals (1882-83): Colombia.

P.S.N.C. in corners, with ship: Peru (1857).

PTO-RICO: Puerto Rico (1877-98).

PUL; values: Afghanistan.

PULAU PENANG; Penang locals: Malaysia.

PUNO on stamps of Peru or Arequipa, Peru; provisionals (1882-85): Peru.

PUTTIALLA STATE; Patiala locals (1884-90): India.

PYCCKAR NOYTA on stamps of Ukraine; offices in Turkey (1921): Russia.

# — Q —

QATAR on stamps of Great Britain: Qatar (1957-60).

QARKU: Albania (1918).

QEVERRIES SE PERKOHESHME: Albania (1913).

QIND(AR), QINTAR; values: Albania.

QU'AITI STATE OF SHIHR AND MUKALLA; locals (1942-53): Aden.

QU'AITI STATE IN HADHRAMAUT; locals (1955— ): Aden.

QUAN BUU; military stamps: Vietnam.

QUELIMANE on stamps of various Portuguese colonies: Quelimane (1913).

# — R —

R centered on stamps with foreign characters; Jind locals (1874-84): India.

R following numeral on stamps with foreign characters, no other English letters: Persia.

R on stamps of Colombia; registration stamps (1898): Panama.

RABAUL; registration label: German New Guinea.

RABAUL with G.R.I.: New Britain (1914).

RAJASTHAN on stamps of Jaipur or Kishangarh; locals (1949): India.

RAPPEN; values (1854-62): Switzerland.

RAROTONGA: Cook Islands (1919-31).

RAU on stamps of Syria; United Arab Republic (1958): Syria.

RAYON: Switzerland (1850-54).

RECARGO; war tax stamps (1898): Spain.

RECUERDO DEL I'DE FEBRERO: Honduras (1916).

REGATUL ROMANIEI on stamps of Hungary; Romanian occupation (1919): Hungary.

REGENCE DE TUNIS: Tunisia (1888-1908).

REGNO D'ITALIA on stamps of Austria; Italian occupation (1918): Austria.

REGNO D'ITALIA on stamps of Fiume: Fiume (1924).

REICH(SPOST): Germany (1872-1944).

REIS with CORREIO, without country name: Portugal (1853-64).

REP(UBBLICA DI) S(AN) MARINO: San Marino.

REPUB(BLICA) SOCIALE ITALIANA; Italian Social Republic (1944): Italy.

REPUBLICA DOMINICANA: Dominican Republic.

REPUBLICA INHAMBANE on stamps of various Portuguese colonies: Inhambane (1913).

REPUBLICA ORIENTAL: Uruguay (1864-66).

REPUBLICA O(RIENTAL) DEL URUGUAY: Uruguay (1866-1961).

REPUBLICA PORTUGUESA: Portugal.

REPUBLIC OF BOTSWANA on stamps of Bechuanaland Protectorate: Botswana (1966).

REPUBLIEK VAN SUID-AFRIKA: South Africa (1961-71).

REPUBLIK MALUKU SELATAN: see MALUKU SELATAN.

REPUBLIK INDONESIA: Indonesia.

REPUBLICA NG PILIPINAS; Japanese occupation (1944): Philippines.

REPUBLIQUE ARABE UNIE: United Arab Republic (1958): Syria.

REPUBLIQUE CENTRAFRICAINE: Central African Republic.

REPUBLIQUE D'AZERBAIDJAN: Azerbaijan (1919-22).

REPUBLIQUE GABONAISE: Gabon (1959—).

REPUBLIQUE ISLAMIQUE DE MAURITANIE: Mauritania (1960— ).

REPUBLIQUE RWANDAISE: Rwanda.

REPUBLIQUE TOGOLAISE: Togo (1961— ).

REPUBLIQUE TUNISIENNE: Tunisia (1957— ).

RETYMNO: Crete (1899).

REUNION on stamps of French Colonies: Reunion (1891).

R. COMMISSARIATO CIVILE on stamps of Yugoslavia; Italian occupation (1941), Ljubljana: Yugoslavia.

RF (POSTES) without country name: France.

RF intertwined, without country name: France.

R.H.; postage due: Haiti.

RHEINLAND-PFALZ; French occupation (1947-49): Germany.

RHODESIA on stamps of Rhodesia and Nyasaland; postage due (1965-67): Rhodesia.

RIALTAR SEALADAC NA HEIREANN on stamps of Great Britain: Ireland (1922).

RIAU on stamps of Indonesia; Riouw Archipelago (1954-60): Indonesia.

RIGSBANK SKILLING: Denmark (1851-54).

RIN, RN; values: Japan.

RIS on stamps of Netherlands Indies: Indonesia (1950-51).

RIZEH on stamps of Russia; offices in Turkey (1910): Russia.

RO on stamps of Turkey: Eastern Rumelia (1880).

RODI; Rhodes, Aegean Islands: Italy.

ROMAGNE; Romagna (1859-60): Italian States.

ROMANA, ROMINA: Romania.

ROSS DEPENDENCY; Ross Dependency (1957— ): New Zealand.

ROUMELIE ORIENTALE on stamps of Turkey: Eastern Rumelia (1880).

ROYAUME DE L'ARABIE S(A)OUDITE: Saudi Arabia.

ROYAUME DU MAROC: Morocco.

R.P.E. SHQIPERISE: Albania.

RPF with numerals on stamps of Luxembourg; German occupation (1940): Luxembourg.

RSA: South Africa (1967— ).

R.S.M.: San Marino (1949-51).

RUANDA on stamps of Congo; Belgian occupation (1916): German East Africa.

RUANDA(-)URUNDI on stamps of Congo: Ruanda-Urundi.

RUMANIEN on stamps of Germany; German occupation (1918): Romania.

RUSSISCH-POLEN, RUFFIFCH-POLEN on stamps of Germany; German occupation (1915): Poland.

RWANDAISE: Rwanda.

RYUKYUS: Ryukyu Islands (1950-72).

# — S —

S(ELANGOR) on stamps of Straits Settlements; Selangor (1878-91): Malaya.

S.A.: Saudi Arabia.

SAARGEBIET: Saar (1920-34).

SAARLAND: Saar (1957-59).

SAARPOST: Saar (1948).

SABAH on stamps of North Borneo: Sabah (1964).

SACHSEN; Saxony: German States.

SAHARA ESPANOL, SAHARA OCCIDENTAL: Spanish Sahara.

SAINT-PIERRE ET MIQUELON: St. Pierre & Miquelon.

SAINT CHRISTOPHER(-)NEVIS(-)ANGUILLA: St. Kitts-Nevis (1952-57).

SALONICCO on stamps of Italy; offices in Turkey (1909-11): Italy.

SALONIKA on stamps of Turkey: Turkey (1911).

SALONIQUE on stamps of Russia; offices in Turkey (1909-10): Russia.

SAMOA on stamps of Germany: Samoa (1900).

SAMOA without WESTERN on stamps of New Zealand: Samoa (1914-34).

SANDJAK D'ALEXANDRETTE: Alexandretta.

SANTANDER; provisionals (1884-1907): Colombia.

SAORSTAT EIREANN on stamps of Great Britain: Ireland (1922-23).

SAR: Syria (1961— ).

SARKARI on stamps of Soruth; Soruth official stamps: India.

SARRE on stamps of Germany: Saar (1920).

SASENO on stamps of Italy: Saseno (1923).

SAURASHTRA; Soruth locals (1929-49): India.

SCARPANTO on stamps of Italy; Aegean Islands (1912-32): Italy.

SCHLESWIG; Schleswig-Holstein (1864-65): German States.

SCINDE DISTRICT DAWK: India (1852).

SCUDO; values (1852), Roman States: Italian States.

SCUTARI DI ALBANIA on stamps of Italy; offices in Turkey (1909-16): Italy.

SEGNA TASSA or SEGNATASSE without country name; postage due: Italy.

SEIYUN; locals: Aden.

SEJM(-)WILNIE: Central Lithuania (1922).

SELANGOR; locals: Malaya, Malaysia.

S(E)N; values: Ryukyu Islands (1948-50) or Japan.

SENEGAL on stamps of French Colonies: Senegal (1892).

SENEGAMBIE ET NIGER: Senegambia & Niger (1903).

SERBES on stamps of France: Serbia (1916-18).

SERBIEN on stamps of a) Bosnia and Herzegovina or b) Yugoslavia; a) Austrian (1916) or b) German (1941) occupation: Serbia.

SEVILLA(-)BARCELONA: Spain (1929).

S - H in upper corners; Schleswig-Holstein (1850): German States.

SHANGHAI on stamps of United States; offices in China (1919-22): United States.

SHIHR AND MUKALLA; locals (1942-53): Aden.

SHQIP- - -, SHQYP- - -: Albania.

S.H.S.: Yugoslavia (1918-20).

SIEGE (OF) MAFEKING: Cape of Good Hope (1900).

SIMI on stamps of Italy; Aegean Islands (1912-32): Italy.

SINGAPORE MALAYA: Singapore (1948-59).

SIRMOOR; locals (1879-1901): India.

SIVAS on stamps of Turkey: Turkey (1930).

SLESVIG; plebiscite issue (1920): Schleswig.

SLOVENSKA, SLOVENSKENO, SLOVENSKO or SLOVENSKY; Slovakia (1939-44): Czechoslovakia.

SLOVENSKO-PRIMORJE; Istria (1945-46): Yugoslavia.

SLOVENI on stamps of Yugoslavia; Italian occupation (1941): Yugoslavia.

S. MARINO: San Marino.

SMIRNE on stamps of Italy; offices in Turkey (1909-22): Italy.

SMYRNE on stamps of Russia; offices in Turkey (1909-10): Russia.

S.O. 1920 on stamps of Czechoslovakia; plebiscite issue (1920): Eastern Silesia.

SOBRETASA AEREA; airmail (1929): Colombia.

SOCIEDAD-COLOMBO-ALEMANA; airmail (1920-21): Colombia.

SOCIEDADE DE GEOGRAPHIA DE LISBOA; franchise stamps (1903-38): Portugal.

SOCIETE DES NATIONS; official stamps (1922-44), League of Nations: Switzerland.

SOLDI; values (1858-65), Lombardy-Venetia: Austria.

SOLIDARITE FRANCAISE; semipostals (1943-44): French Colonies.

SOMALIA (ITALIANA) on stamps of Italy: Somalia (1922-32).

SOMALI DEMOCRATIC REPUBLIC: Somalia (1970-73).

SOMALIS: Somali Coast (1902-67).

SOMALIYA: Somalia (1973— ).

SONORA; civil war issues (1913-14), Sonora: Mexico.

SORUTH; locals (1877-1914): India.

SOUDAN on stamps of Egypt: Sudan (1897).

SOUDAN on stamps of a) French Colonies or b) Upper Senegal and Niger: French Sudan a)(1894) or b)(1921-30).

SOUDAN: French Sudan.

SOURASHTRA; Soruth locals (1923-29): India.

SOUTHERN RHODESIA on stamps of Great Britain; postage due (1951— ): Southern Rhodesia.

SOUTH GEORGIA on stamps of Falkland Islands; South Georgia (1944— ): Falkland Islands.

SOUTH ORKNEYS or SOUTH SHETLANDS on stamps of Falkland Islands; South Orkneys or South Shetlands (1944-62): Falkland Islands.

SOUTH WEST AFRICA on stamps of South Africa: South-West Africa (1923-27).

SOWJETISCHE BESATZUNGS ZONE on stamps of Germany; Russian occupation (1948), Berlin: Germany.

SPM on stamps of French Colonies: St. Pierre & Miquelon (1885-91).

S.Q. TRSTA-VUJA ZRACNA P; airmail (1949), Yugoslav Zone B: Trieste.

SRI LANKA: Ceylon (1972— ).

SRODKOWA with LITWA: Central Lithuania.

ST. without country name; values (1932-43): Thailand.

STAMPALIA on stamps of Italy; Aegean Islands (1912-32): Italy.

STATI PARM(ENSI); Parma (1852-59): Italian States.

STEMPEL with CENTES.; Lombardy-Venetia (1850): Austria.

STEMPEL with KREUZER: Austria (1850).

ST. CHRISTOPHER(-)NEVIS(-ANGUILLA): St. Kitts-Nevis (1952— ).

S. T(H)OME E PRINCIPE: St. Thomas & Prince Islands.

STOCKHOLM: Sweden (1924).

STOTHNKH; values (1911-24): Bulgaria.

ST-PIERRE M-ON on stamps of French Colonies: St. Pierre & Miquelon (1891-92).

ST. PIERRE ET MIQUELON: St. Pierre & Miquelon.

STRAITS SETTLEMENTS on stamps of Labuan: Straits Settlements (1907).

S.T. TRSTA-VUJA; Zone B (1949-51): Trieste.

S.T.T.-V.U.J.(N.)A.; Zone B: Trieste.

S(UNGEI) U(JONG) on stamps of Straits Settlements; Sungei Ujong (1878-91): Malaya.

SUBMARINO with CORREO; submarine covers (1938): Spain.

SUID(-)AFRIKA: South Africa.

SUIDWES(-)AFRIKA: South-West Africa.

S. UJONG; Sungei Ujong (1891-94): Malaya.

SUL BOLLETTINO, SULLA RICEVUTA; parcel post: Somalia (with star and crescent) or Italy.

SULTANT D'ANJOUAN: Anjouan.

SUOMI: Finland.

SVERIGE: Sweden.

S.W.A.: South-West Africa.

SWAZIELAND: Swaziland (1889-95).

SWAZILAND on stamps of South Africa: Swaziland (1945).

SYRIAN ARAB REPUBLIC: Syria (1961— ).

SYRIE(NNE): Syria (1920-58).

SZEGED 1919 on stamps of Hungary; Szeged issue (1919): Hungary.

## — T —

T on stamps a) in four corners, b) with F, numeral and heraldic lion or c) of various countries; postage due: a) Dominican Republic (1901-42), b) Belgium (1966-70) or c) country of stamp origin.

T in circle on stamps of Peru; Huacho provisionals (1884): Peru.

TACNA Y ARICA; plebiscite issue tax stamps (1925-28): Peru.

TAHITI on stamps of French Colonies or French Polynesia: Tahiti.

TAKCA; postage due (1884-99): Bulgaria.

TAKSE; postage due: Albania.

TALCA; Talca tax stamp (1942): Chile.

TANGANYIKA & ZANZIBAR: Tanzania (1964).

TANGANYIKA with KENYA and UGANDA: Kenya, Uganda and Tanzania (1935-64).

TANGER on stamps of France or French Morocco: French Morocco (1918-24).

TANGER with CORREO(S); Tangier: Spanish Morocco.

TANGIER on stamps of Great Britain; offices in Morocco (1927-57): Great Britain.

TANZANIA with KENYA and UGANDA: Kenya, Uganda and Tanzania (1965— ).

TANZANIA with ZANZIBAR or MUUNGANO; Zanzibar and Tanzania (1965-68): Zanzibar.

TASSE GAZZETTE; newspaper tax stamps (1859), Modena: Italian States.

TAXA DE GUERRA on stamps with a) one or two numerals other than 0, b) two numerals beginning with 0, c) two numerals ending with 0 or d) seven numerals; war tax stamps (1919): a) Macao, b) Portuguese Africa, c) Portuguese Guinea or d) Portuguese India.

TAXE on stamps of Albania; postage due (1919): Albania.

T.C. on stamps of Cochin; Travancore-Cochin locals (1950): India.

T.C.E.K.; tax stamps (1946): Turkey.

TCHAD: Chad.

TCHONGKING on stamps of Indo-China; offices in China (1903-19): France.

T.C. POSTALARI: Turkey (1931).

TE BETALEN with A PAYER; postage due: Belgium.

TE BETALEN with PORT; postage due: Netherlands, Surinam, or Netherlands Indies, Antilles or New Guinea.

TEHERAN on stamps of Persia: Persia (1902).

T.E.O. with CILICIE on stamps of Turkey: Cilicia (1919).

T.E.O. with MILLIEMES on stamps of France or French Offices in Turkey: Syria (1919).

T.E.O. on stamps of French Offices in Turkey: Syria or Cilicia (1919).

TERRES AUSTRALES ET ANTARCTIQUES FRANCAISES: French Southern and Antarctic Territories.

TERRITORIO DE IFNI on stamps of Spain: Ifni (1941-50).

TERRITOIRE DE L'ININI on stamps of French Guiana: Inini (1932-41).

TERRITOIRE DU NIGER on stamps of Upper Senegal and Niger: Niger (1921-26).

TERRITOIRE FRANCAIS DES AFARS ET DES ISSAS: Afars and Issas.

TETUAN on stamps of Spain or Spanish Offices in Morocco; Tetuan (1908): Spanish Morocco.

TETE on stamps of various Portuguese colonies: Tete (1913).

THAI(LAND): Siam (1942— ).

THAILAND with CENT(S); Siamese occupation (1943-45): Malaya.

THRACE on stamps of Bulgaria; Allied occupation (1919-20): Thrace.

TIENTSIN on stamps of Italy; offices in China (1917-21): Italy.

TIMBRE IMPERIAL JOURNAUX; newspaper stamps: France.

TIMBRE POSTE on stamps of France: French Morocco (1893).

TIMBRE TAXE with A PERCEVOIR; postage due (1945): French Colonies.

TIMOR on stamps of Macao: Timor (1885-95).

TIMOR on stamps of Mozambique: Timor (1946).

TJENESTE with FRIMAERKE; official stamps (1871-1924): Denmark.

TJENESTEFRIMERKE; official stamps (1926-32): Norway.

TOGA: Tonga (1897-1949).

TOGO on stamps of Germany: Togo (1897-99).

TOGO on stamps of a) Gold Coast or b) Dahomey: Togo a) (1915-16) or b) (1916-25).

TOGOLAISE: Togo (1961— ).

TOKELAU ISLANDS on stamps of New Zealand: Tokelau Islands (1966-67).

TOLIMA; provisionals (1871-1904): Colombia.

TO PAY; postage due: Great Britain.

TOSCANO; Tuscany: Italian States.

TOU; airmail (1928): Persia.

TOUVA: Tannu Tuva (1927-35).

TRAITE DE VERSAILLES on stamps of Germany; plebiscite issue (1920): Allenstein.

TRANSJORDAN: Jordan (1927-52).

TRANSPORTO PACCHI IN CONCESSIONE; parcel post authorized delivery stamps: Italy.

TRAVANCORE with COCHIN; Travancore-Cochin: India.

TRAVANCORE with ANCHAL or ANCHEL; Travancore or Travancore-Cochin: India.

TREBIZONDE on stamps of Russia; offices in Turkey (1909-10): Russia.

TRENGANNU; locals: Malaya, Malaysia.

TRENTINO on stamps of Austria; Italian occupation (1918): Austria.

TRIESTE on stamps of Italy: Trieste.

TRIDENTINA on stamps of Italy; Italian occupation (1918): Austria.

TRIPOLI DI BARBERIA on stamps of Italy; offices in Africa (1909-15): Italy.

TRIPOLI with CAMPIONARIA: Libya (1927-38).

TRIPOLITANIA on stamps of Italy: Tripolitania.

TRIPOLI MAGGIO on stamps of Libya; airmail (1934): Tripolitania.

TRISTAN DA CUNHA on stamps of St. Helena: Tristan da Cunha (1952-63).

T.TA.C.; airmail tax stamps (1931-33): Turkey.

TUMACO; Cauca provisionals (1901-12): Colombia.

TUNIS(IE): Tunisia.

TURK(IYE): Turkey.

TUVALU on stamps of Gilbert & Ellice Islands: Tuvalu (1976).

TWO PENCE without country name, under enthroned queen: Victoria (1852-54).

# — U —

UAE on stamps of Abu Dhabi: United Arab Emirates (1972).

U.A. EMIRATES: United Arab Emirates.

UAPCTBO: Bulgaria (1937-44).

U.A.R. with values in a) "p" or b) "m"; United Arab Republic: a) Syria (1958-61) or b) Egypt (1958-71).

U.G.: Uganda (1895).

UGANDA on stamps of British East Africa: Uganda (1902).

UGANDA with EAST AFRICA or KENYA: Kenya, Uganda and Tanzania.

UKRAINE on stamps of Germany; German occupation (1941-43): Russia.

U.K.T.T. on stamps of Nigeria; Southern Cameroons (1960-61): Cameroons.

ULTRAMAR with year (1800s): Puerto Rico (1873-76, with script overprints) or Cuba (1867-76).

ULTRAMAR with values of a) one numeral or b) two numerals: a) Macao (1911) or b) Portuguese Guinea (1919 war tax stamps).

UNEF on stamps of India; military stamps (1965): India.

UNESCO; official stamps (1961-71), U.N. Educational, Scientific and Cultural Organization: France.

U.N. FORCE (INDIA) CONGO on stamps of India; military stamps (1962): India.

UNION INTERNATIONALE DES TELECOMMUNICATIONS; official stamps, International Telecommunications Union: Switzerland.

UNION POSTALE UNIVERSELLE with HELVETIA; official stamps (1957-60), U.P.U. International Bureau: Switzerland.

UNTEA on stamps of Netherlands New Guinea: West Irian (1962).

UOPTO CKPNCOPN; Moldavia (1858): Romania.

UPHA TOPA; Italian occupation (1941-43): Montenegro.

URUNDI without RUANDA on stamps of Congo; Belgian occupation (1916): German East Africa.

U.R.I. on stamps of Yugoslavia; semipostals without official postal value (1923): Yugoslavia.

U.S.(A.): United States.

USKUB on stamps of Turkey: Turkey (1911).

— V —

VALLEES D'ANDORRE: Andorra (1932-43).

VALONA on stamps of Italy; offices in Turkey (1909-16): Italy.

VANCOUVER ISLAND: British Columbia and Vancouver Island (1865).

VAN DIEMEN'S LAND: Tasmania (1853-69).

VATHY on stamps of France; offices in Turkey (1894-1900): France.

VATICANE, VATICANA: Vatican City.

VENEZA: Venezuela (1865-76).

VENEZIA with GIULIA or TRIDENTINA on stamps of Italy; Italian occupation (1918): Austria.

VENEZOLANA: Venezuela (1863-65).

VEREINTE NATIONEN: United Nations, Vienna (1979—).

VIET(-)NAM with BUU(-)CHINH, without CONG(-)HOA: Vietnam (1951-56).

VIET(-)NAM CONG(-)HOA with BUU(-)CHINH; South Vietnam (1956-75): Vietnam.

VIET(-)NAM DAN(-)CHU CONG(-)HOA; North Vietnam: Vietnam.

VIVA ESPANA on stamps of Spain: Spain (1936-37).

VOJNA UPRAVA JUGOSLAVENSKE ARMIJE on stamps of Yugoslavia; Istria and Slovene Coast (1947): Yugoslavia.

VOM EMPFANGER EINZUZIEHEN; postage due: Danzig.

V.R. on stamps of Fiji: Fiji (1874-77).

V.R. with TRANSVAAL on stamps of Transvaal: Transvaal (1877-79).

V.R.I. on stamps of Transvaal: Transvaal (1900-02).

V.R. SPECIAL POST on stamps of Transvaal: Cape of Good Hope (1900).

V.U.J.(N.)A. S.T.T. on stamps of Yugoslavia; Zone B: Trieste.

— W —

WADHWAN STATE; locals (1888-89): India.

WALLIS ET FUTUNA on stamps of New Caledonia: Wallis and Futuna Islands (1920-40).

WARSZAWA: Poland (1918).

WEIHNACHTEN on stamps of Rhodes (Aegean Islands, Italy); unofficial German overprint, Aegean Islands (1944): Italy.

WENDEN(SCHEN); Wenden (1862-84): Russia.

W(EST) AUSTRALIA: Western Australia.

WESTERN SAMOA: Samoa (1935-55).

WIR SIND FREI on stamps of Czechoslovakia; German occupation (1938), unofficial: Czechoslovakia.

W(O)N; values: Korea.

WURTTEMBERG with values PF or M; French occupation (1947-49): Germany.

WURTTEMBERG with KREUZER or FREIMARKE; Wurttemberg: German States.

— X —

XAPTOEHMON; tax stamps (1917): Greece.

XEAEPA, XEJEPA: Montenegro (1902-05).

XEIMAPPA with Greek lettering; questionable postal value: Epirus.

XII FIERA CAMPIONARIA TRIPOLI: Libya (1938).

— Y —

YAR: Yemen Arab Republic (1963—).

YCA on stamps of Peru; Yca provisionals (1884): Peru.

Y.C.P.P.; semipostals (1923): Ukraine.

YCTAB: Montenegro (1905).

YEMEN PDR: Yemen People's Democratic Republic.

Y(E)N; values: Japan, Manchukuo, Ryukyu Islands.

Y(KP.) H. P(EN) on stamps of Austria: Western Ukraine.

YKPAIHCbKA: Ukraine (1918-19).

YKSI MARKKA: Finland (1866-74).

YUNNAN(-)FOU on stamps of Indo-China; offices in China (1906-19): France.

YUNNANSEN on stamps of Indo-China; offices in France (1903-05): France.

— Z —

Z(UID) AFR(IKAANSCHE) REP(UBLIEK): Transvaal.

ZAIRE: Congo (1971— ).

ZANZIBAR on stamps of a) France or b) British East Africa or India: a) France (offices in Zanzibar, 1894-1900) or b) Zanzibar (1895-96).

ZANZIBAR with TANZANIA: Zanzibar (1965-68).

Z.A.R. on stamps of Cape of Good Hope: Boer occupation (1899): Cape of Good Hope.

ZEGELREGT: Transvaal (1895).

ZELAYA on stamps of Nicaragua; Zelaya (1904-11): Nicaragua.

ZENTRALER KURIERDIENST; official stamps (1956-57), German Democratic Republic: Germany.

ZONA DE OCUPATIE ROMANA; Romanian occupation (1919): Hungary.

ZONA DE PROTECTORADO ESPANOL EN MARRUECOS on stamps of Spain: Spanish Morocco (1916-25).

ZONE FRANCAISE; French occupation (1945-46): Germany.

ZRACNA POSTA; airmail, Zone B: Trieste.

ZUID(-)WEST AFRIKA on stamps of South Africa: South-West Africa (1923-25).

ZULULAND on stamps of Great Britain or Natal: Zululand (1888-94).

ZURICH: Switzerland (1843-46).

# Difficult Identification

Many foreign stamps, especially those with lettering of Greek, Russian or Oriental origin, are impossible to identify by an index of English type-set characters. The most commonly found of these are listed, by country, in the following section, with an attempt to describe certain distinguishing characteristics. Most stamps after 1900 are readily identifiable, either by name or distinguishing characteristic.

This list is merely a general guide, in an attempt to help collectors find at least general guidance toward the origins of certain difficult-to-identify stamps. All references herein, unless otherwise stated, are to regular postage stamps only, since many official and tax stamps, intended primarily for the use and benefit of persons within the country, often exclude the name of the issuing country. Dates, too, are only general reference points, as use of certain issues after the indicated dates is quite possible.

AFGHANISTAN; 1871-1930: circular designs, "tiger's head," mosque and Eastern characters identify certain issues.

ARMENIA; 1919-23: Socialist emblems and handstamped Russian stamps identify some issues. Issues after 1921 also have many high denominations, with numerals from 3-6 figures.

AUSTRIA; 1867-1908: KR. or KREUZER will identify values for most early issues. Newspaper stamps in this period will have "Mercury," with winged helmet, pictured.

AZERBAIJAN; 1922-24: Russian NOYT MAP-KA appears on most issues, with crescent, star, hammer and sickle. Also many large numerals, with many zeros, overprinted.

BANGLADESH; 1972: crooked tower and "20 P." value identify the one non-English issue.

BATUM; 1919-20: Russian characters, NOYTA or NOYTOBAP. Later issues overprinted "BRITISH OCCUPATION."

BOSNIA AND HERZEGOVINA; 1879-1906: shield and eagle emblem.

BRAZIL; 1843-66: numerals in stylized oval, last digit "0." Values are 10, 20, 30, 60, 90, 180, 280, 300, 430 and 600.

1

2

3

4

5

1) Azerbaijan
2) Bangladesh
3) Batum
4) Bosnia and Herzegovina
5) Brazil

BULGARIA; 1879— : most issues have the Russian NOWA, or the Russian name of Bulgaria, which begins with two characters similar to lower case "b"s (bbATAPNR).

BURMA; Japanese occupation 1942-44: peacock overprint on Burma stamps and stamps similar to Japanese stamps are typical.

CHINA; 1921-66: values in dollars and cents, as well as the sun emblem, identify many issues.

CHINA, PEOPLE'S REPUBLIC; 1949— : numerals followed closely by a single Chinese character identify many issues.

CRETE; 1898-99: Greek letters similar to TAX-YAPOM, METAAAIK, or PEOYMNHE identify most issues.

EGYPT; 1866-1924: values in PARA or PE identify many issues.

EPIRUS; 1914-16: Greek letters similar to HNEIPOE identify most issues.

ETHIOPIA; 1894-1909: lion holding banner or king's bearded profile identify most issues.

FAR EASTERN REPUBLIC; 1920-23: script DBL overprinted on Russian stamps or NOYTO-BAR MAPKA identify most issues.

FINLAND; 1891-1916: values in PEN or MARKKA with the Russian NOYTOBAR MAP-KA distinguish most issues. 1891-96 stamps are generally identical with Russian stamps, except they are more "cluttered," i.e., have more dots, lines, etc. in background. Can only be distinguished by comparison or illustration.

6

7

8

10

11

9

6) Bulgaria
7) Burma, Japanese occupation
8) China, People's Republic

9) China, Republic of
10) Ethiopia
11) Far Eastern Republic

GEORGIA; 1922-23: Russian characters similar to L.L.L.R. and values of 500 or thousands identify most issues.

GREECE; 1861-1966: Greek letters similar to ΕΛΛΑΣ identify most issues.

HUNGARY; 1871-72: regular issue has value KR with bearded profile, while newspaper stamps have no value and posthorn under crown.

INDIA; native states: many native states had plain stamps, generally crowded with Eastern characters. Identification by illustration only.

ISRAEL; 1948: coins and Hebrew writing identify the first Israeli issue.

JAPAN; 1871-1966: most issues through 1947 are identified by the stylized chrysanthemum, including numerous issues for other countries under Japanese occupation. After 1947, the Japanese characters for JAPAN appear, the first of which appears as a squat, angular "8."

JORDAN; 1920-27: nondescript rectangles with Arabic writing, generally subdivided into many smaller rectangles.

KOREA; 1884: a single early issue has a value of 5 Mn., plus a stylized, half-and-half circle in the center.

12

13

14

16

15

17a

17b

12) Georgia
13) Greece
14) Hungary

15) India, Native States
16) Israel
17 a&b) Japan

KOREA, NORTH; 1946-77: later issues include year dates beside the Oriental characters, while most issues have the four-character country name, the last character of which appears as two stacked Roman numeral "II"s, with the preceding character appearing as "O" over "T."

KOREA, SOUTH; 1946-66: similar to North Korea, with addition of CH or stylized circle, appearing as two interlocking apostrophes.

MALAYA; 1935-63, including Japanese occupation: most occupation stamps appear similar to Japanese stamps. Issues of the various Malay states, frequently inscribed MALAYA, are sometimes distinguishable only by the Eastern inscription, including issues of Kelantan, Pahang, Perak, Negri Sembilan, Selangor and Trengganu.

MANCHUKUO; 1932-45: values of FEN or FN., or stylized "snowflake" (five-pronged, star-like object with internal decorations) identifies most issues.

MONGOLIA; 1924-59: Russian characters similar to "bHMAY" appear on most issues after 1950.

MONTENEGRO; 1874-1913: Russian characters similar to NOWTE, NAPA, or HOBY identify most issues.

NEPAL; 1881-1949: sun in upper right corner identifies some issues.

PAKISTAN; 1948: issue with crescent and stars and inscription "15 AUGUST 1947."

PERSIA (IRAN); 1870-1946: lion holding sword over sun identifies many issues, while values of "D" or "R" identify others.

PHILIPPINES; 1943-44, Japanese occupation: Japanese inscription across top beginning with characters similar to two lower-case "t"s identify most issues.

RUSSIA; 1857-1922: Russian characters similar to NOYTA, NOYTOBAP, MAPKA, P.C.O.C.P., POCCIR and PYb identify most issues. Illustrations of slight differences and overprints are generally helpful in distinguishing such similar country issues as ARMENIA, AZERBAIJAN, FAR EASTERN REPUBLIC, BATUM, FINLAND, GEORGIA, SIBERIA, SOUTH RUSSIA, TRANSCAUCASIAN FEDERATED REPUBLICS and UKRAINE.

RYUKYU ISLANDS; 1948-62: year dates and values in dollars and cents in addition to the Oriental characters identify most issues.

18

19

20

21

18) Korea, South
19) Manchukuo
20) Nepal
21) Ryukyu Islands

SAUDI ARABIA; 1916-29: nondescript stamps with Arabic lettering, undistinguishable without illustration.

SERBIA; 1866-1920: Russian characters similar to NOWTA or CPbNJA identify most issues.

SIBERIA; 1919-22: various handstamps on Russian stamps.

TANNU TUVA; 1926: eight-pronged wheel design identifies this issue.

THRACE; 1913: Greek and Arabic inscriptions on stamps of Turkey or Bulgaria, as well as stamps marked "1913," identify most issues.

TRANSCAUCASIAN FEDERATED REPUBLICS; 1923: "3COCP" identifies most issues, many with values of 7-8 digits.

TURKEY; 1863-1913: values in PARAS or crescent with starburst or script identify most issues.

UKRAINE; 1918-19: Russian characters similar to WATIB or УКРAIHCbKA, or stylized facing "R"s on Russian stamps, identify most issues.

22

23

25a

24

25b

22) Siberia
23) Tannu Tuva
24) Thrace
25 a&b) Transcaucasian Federated Republics

# Terms and Abbreviations 10

## Glossary of Philatelic Terms

In the course of stamp collecting and research, numerous terms will be encountered which are either unique to the field, or specialized from more common terminology. This glossary is intended to define and specialize those terms most frequently encountered by collectors.

Unfortunately, no standards exist for the precise definition of philatelic terms. One collector, dealer or society may define a term in one way, and others will see the definition differently. The lines of distinction between and among various terms are often fine, if not nonexistent.

Therefore, this glossary of nearly 300 terms cannot presume to be "the last word" in philatelic discussion, but in terms of stamp condition, at least, it does reflect the policy of Linn's.

### — A —

**Accessories** — Any of the large variety of collecting tools and aids (e.g., hinges, mounts, stamp tongs, perforation gauges, stock books, etc.). Such basic items as stamp albums and catalogs might also be regarded, in a general way, as accessories.

**Adhesive** — In the philatelic sense, an adhesive is a label to be affixed to an article to prepay postal fees, in contrast to designs printed directly on the piece, as with postal stationery.

**Admirals** — A philatelic nickname for three British Commonwealth definitive series, those of Canada, 1912-25 (Scott 104-34), New Zealand, 1926 (182-84) and Rhodesia, 1913-19 (119-38), all of which depict King George V in naval uniform.

**Aerogramme** — The official Universal Postal Union designation for an airletter sheet. These lightweight sheets, with gummed flaps, may be folded into themselves to form their own envelope and are carried at less than the usual airmail rate. No enclosures are permitted.

**Aerophilately** — A specialized area of collecting which concentrates on any form of stamps or postal usage relating to mail carried by air.

**Agency** — **1)** The extraterritorial post offices maintained at various times by governments in the territory of other governments, e.g., the post offices maintained by many European powers in the Turkish Empire until 1923. **2)** An official or private organization which publicizes or sells new issues of stamps on behalf of stamp-issuing entities.

**Air Labels** — Air labels, or "etiquettes," are standard-sized blue labels used by UPU member nations to denote airmail carriage. They are inscribed "Par Avion" (French for "By Air") at the top, with the same message beneath in the language of the native country. Also, adhesives issued by private organizations for specific, unofficial flights.

**Airmail** — The carriage of mail by air. The first regular airmail service was operated in 1870, when mail was carried from Paris, France, then besieged by German forces, over the enemy lines by balloon. The first of many stamps issued specifically for payment of airmail fees was that of Italy in 1917 (Scott C1).

**Albino** — An uninked impression made by a printing plate. Such errors are very scarce on stamps, but are more often found on postal stationery.

**Album** — In philately, albums are books especially prepared for the mounting and display of stamps. Albums come in a great variety of sizes, styles and themes.

**"Album Weeds"** — The title of one of the most extensive and widely used reference works on forged stamps, published at the turn of

1

2

3

4

1) Admirals (margin, selvage)
2) Arrow (plate number, block, definitive)
3) Backstamp
4) Bilingual (commemorative)

the century by the Rev. R. Brisco Earee. The term is rather broadly applied to forgeries and to unusual items that resemble postage stamps but were never intended actually to pay postage, i.e., publicity labels, "stamps" of nonexistent countries, etc.

**Ambulante** — This word ("moving") appearing in the cancellations of various nations indicates that the item was processed by a mobile post office.

**Aniline** — Inks with a coal-tar base. Such inks are used in stamp printing to prevent erasure of cancellations and reuse of the stamps. Aniline inks are very sensitive and may dissolve in water or other liquids or chemicals.

**Approvals** — Priced selections of stamps sent to collectors by mail. The collector purchases whichever items he chooses, returning the balance with payment for those kept.

**Army Post Office (APO)** — An official U.S. post office for use by U.S. military units abroad.

**Arrow** — On many sheets, small arrow-like markings appear in the selvage, generally serving as guides for the cutting of the sheets into predetermined units. Some collectors save pieces displaying these marks, as "arrow blocks."

**Art Paper** — A very fine paper with a highly enameled surface.

**"As Is"** — A term often used in auctions, indicating that the item so designated is sold without guarantee or return privilege. Stamps are usually sold "as is" when they are in poor condition or are very possibly not genuine.

**Authentication Mark** — A marking, such as initials, placed on the reverse of a stamp examined and certified to be genuine by an expert. Such markings do not detract from the value of the stamps, where they represent the endorsement of recognized authorities.

## — B —

**Backprint** — An "overprint" placed on the reverse of a stamp.

**Backstamp** — 1) The postmark applied to the reverse of a mailing piece by the receiving post office. 2) A handstamp applied to the reverse of a stamp, e.g., an expertiser's mark.

**Bank Mixture** — A high quality mixture of stamps. Generally represents clippings from the correspondence of banks and other businesses with extensive overseas business, thus including a relatively high proportion of foreign stamps of high face value.

**Bantams** — The nickname of the South African definitive series of 1942-43 (Scott 90-97), in which wartime economy measures were reflected in the reproduction of the 1941-42 series (81-88) in much-reduced sizes.

**Batonne** — Thin, lined letter paper, which has often been used in stamp printing.

**Bicolored Stamps** — Stamps printed in two colors.

**Bilingual** — Refers to stamps inscribed in two languages, e.g., Canadian (English and French) or South African (English and Afrikaans) issues.

**Bisect** — A stamp cut or perforated into two parts, each half representing half the face value of the original stamp. Officially authorized bisects have often been used during temporary shortages of commonly used denominations. Unauthorized bisects have been even more frequently used, but are generally less desirable. Bisects should be collected on the full cover, or at least on piece, tied by the cancellation as evidence of their genuineness.

**Bishop Mark** — The earliest postmark, introduced by Henry Bishop in England circa 1661. This postmark indicated the month and day that the letter was received by the post office, thus encouraging more rapid delivery by letter carriers.

**Black Jack** — The nickname of the U.S. 2¢ black Andrew Jackson stamp, issued in various forms between 1863-75. This has long been one of the most popular U.S. stamps of this period.

**Blind Perforation** — Perforations that have been only lightly impressed by the perforating pins, leaving the paper intact, but cut. Blind perfs may appear to be imperforate, but some impression is visible on the paper. Blind perfs are minor varieties carrying little, if any, premium over normally perforated copies.

**Block** — A unit of four or more unsevered stamps, including at least two stamps both vertically and horizontally. Most commonly used for "block of four," a block of stamps two high and two wide.

**Bluenose** — The nickname of the Canadian 50-cent issue of 1929, picturing the schooner "Bluenose."

**Bogus** — A completely fictitious "stamp," created solely for sale to collectors. Bogus issues include labels for nonexistent countries, nonexistent values appended to regularly issued sets, issues for nations without postal systems, etc.

**Bond Paper** — A thin, crisp paper of high quality, used to a limited extent in early stamp printing.

**Booklets** — One or more small panes or blocks (known as booklet panes) glued, stitched or stapled together between thin card covers to form a convenient unit for mailers to purchase and carry. The first officially issued booklet was produced by Luxembourg in 1895.

**Bourse** — A meeting of stamp collectors and/or dealers, where philatelic items are sold or exchanged.

**"Bull's-Eyes"** — **1)** The nickname for the first issue of Brazil, 1843 (Scott 1-3). **2)** A "socked-on-the-nose" cancellation, i.e., one that is centered

directly on the stamp, showing location and date of mailing.

**Burelage, Burele** — A fine design of some sort printed on either the face or back of a stamp, either to discourage counterfeiting, or to prevent the cleaning and reuse of the stamp.

— C —

**Cachet** — French, meaning a stamp or seal. Philatelically, a cachet usually refers to some printed design on an envelope denoting some special feature of the cover, e.g., on first day, first flight, or special event covers, etc.

5

6

9

7

8

5) Bisect (on piece)
6) Black Jack
7) Bluenose
8) Bull's-Eye, "socked on the nose" cancellation
9) Bull's-Eye, Brazil

**Canceled To Order (CTO)** — Stamps are "canceled to order," usually in full sheets, by many governments. Such stamps can then be sold to the trade at large discounts from face value. Canceled to order stamps have never seen actual postal use, and are usually less desirable than postally used copies.

**Cancellation** — The marking of a stamp on cover to indicate that it has been used, so that its value is "canceled." Cancellations often include the location of the post office from which the item is mailed, and the date of mailing.

**Cantonal Stamps** — Issues of the Swiss cantons used before the release of national stamps. The cantonal issues of Basel (1845), Geneva (1843-50) and Zurich (1843-50) are among the classics of philately.

**Cape Triangles** — Nickname for the triangular Cape of Good Hope issues of 1853-64, the first stamps printed in this format. Given a distinctive shape to aid illiterate postal clerks, distinguishing letters originating in the colony, the Cape Triangles have long been among the most popular classic issues.

**Catalogs** — Comprehensive compilations of stamp issues, providing descriptions and, usually, values for the items included. Catalogs are an indispensable tool for the collector.

10

11

10) Charity seals (imperf between)
11) Charity stamp (semipostal)

**Catalog Value** — The value of a stamp as listed in any given catalog. Because of changing market conditions, the difficulty in keeping completely up-to-date on pricing and varying conditions of stamps, catalog values should be regarded as a guide rather than as actual retail value. Some stamps are a bargain at double their catalog value, while others may be overpriced at one quarter of their catalog value.

**Censored Mail** — Cover bearing a handstamp or label indicating that the envelope has been opened and read by a censor. Such covers are actually sought by specialists.

**Centering** — The relative position of the design in relation to the margins of a stamp. Assuming that the stamp is undamaged, centering is generally the most important single factor in determining condition.

**Certified Mail** — A U.S. service providing proof of mailing and delivery without indemnity for loss or damage.

**Chalky Paper** — A chalk-surfaced paper introduced in 1902 for stamp printing. Any attempt to remove the cancellation will also remove the design. Immersion of such stamps in water will cause the entire design to lift off. Chalky paper may be easily distinguished by touching it with silver, which will leave a discernible, pencil-like mark.

**Changeling** — A stamp whose color has been changed by contact with some chemical.

**Charity Seals** — Stamp-like labels which are produced by some charity. They have no postal validity, although they are often affixed to envelopes, usually on the reverse.

**Charity Stamps (Semipostals)** — Stamps sold at a surcharge over postal value, the additional charge being earmarked for some special fund.

**Cinderellas** — Stamp-like labels that are not postage stamps. Cinderellas include a wide variety of material, from revenue stamps to bogus issues.

**Classic** — An early issue, with a connotation of rarity, although classic stamps are not necessarily rare. A particularly scarce recent item may be referred to as a "modern classic."

**Cleaning (Stamps)** — Soiled or stained stamps may often be cleaned by a variety of processes, chemical baths, etc. Such cleaning should be done carefully and by someone familiar with the individual stamp and the processes involved. A cleaned stamp can also mean one from which a cancellation has been removed.

**Coils** — Stamps prepared in rolls for sale and use in stamp-vending and affixing machines. Coils are often imperforate on two parallel sides, bear distinctive perforations, or are numbered on the back, distinguishing them from stamps removed from regular sheets.

**Collateral Material** — Any sort of supportive or explanatory material relating to a given philatelic topic. May be either directly postal in nature, as in post office news releases, rate schedules, etc., or nonpostal, as in maps, photos of scenes appearing on stamps, etc.

**Combination Cover** — Cover bearing the stamps of more than one country, which occurs when separate postal charges have been paid for transport of the cover by each country, or when the sender has sought to make a point by adding foreign stamps.

**Commatology** — Specialized collecting of postmarks.

**Commemorative** — A stamp issued to commemorate a special event of some sort. Commemoratives are usually in use for a limited period, while definitive series are usually in use for a number of years.

**Compound Perforations** — Different gauge perforations on different (normally adjacent) sides of a single stamp.

**Condition** — The general state of a stamp, including all factors in relation to the state of the stamp as issued. Condition is one of the prime factors in determining a stamp's value; in only the rarest stamps does condition become unimportant.

**Controlled Mail** — A system whereby the mailer selects philatelically desirable issues for outgoing mail, arranges for light cancellation and secures the stamps' return by the addressee. Such controlled mail operations, once common, ensured a steady stream of collectable stamps into the trade.

**Copyright Block** — U.S. marginal marking block, to which is attached that portion of the marginal selvage bearing the U.S. Postal Service notice of copyright (typically a block of four stamps). The Copyright marking was introduced in 1978, and replaced the "Mail Early" marking.

**Corner Card** — An imprinted return address, generally in the upper left corner of an envelope, from a commercial, institutional or private source, similar to business cards or letterheads.

**Counterfeit** — In philately, any stamp or cancellation created for deception or imitation, intended to be passed as genuine.

**Cover** — Any type of container which "covers" an article sent through the mail; usually, however, used to refer to an envelope that has passed through the mail.

**Crash Cover** — A cover that has been salvaged from the crash of the airplane, train or other vehicle in which it was carried. Such covers often carry a postal marking explaining their damaged condition, making them of interest to collectors.

**Crease** — A noticeable weakening of the paper of a stamp, having been caused by its being folded or bent at some point. Creases substantially lower a stamp's value.

**Cut Cancellation** — A cancellation which cuts the stamp. On most issues, such cancellations indicate nonpostal use, e.g., use of the stamps as fiscals or telegraph stamps. Cut cancellations were used experimentally on early U.S. postage stamps to prevent re-use.

**Cut Square** — The common term for a postal stationery cut-out, whereby the vignette has been clipped from the entire in a square or rectangular piece.

**Cut To Shape** — A nonrectangular stamp or postal stationery imprint cut to the shape of the design, rather than cut square, the manner in which such items are preferred. While this greatly lowers a stamp's value, the unique 1856 British Guiana 1¢ magenta, the world's most valuable stamp, falls in this category.

## — D —

**Dead Country** — A former stamp-issuing entity that has ceased to issue its own stamps or has changed its name, so that the old name will no longer be used.

**Definitives** — Stamps issued for an indefinite period, usually for several years or more, e.g., the U.S. Presidential issue, in use from 1938-54. Designs do not honor a specific time-dated event.

**Deltiology** — Specialized collecting of post cards.

**Denomination** — Printed face value of stamp.

**Die** — The original piece upon which a stamp design is inscribed. Printing plates are made from the original die, producing a constant design in the sheet. Where more than one die is used in the production of an issue, distinctive varieties are usually identifiable.

**Directory Markings** — Postal indication of delivery attempt, stating reason for failure, e.g., "No Such Number," "Address Unknown," etc.

12

13

12) Cut square
13) Cut to shape

14

15

16

17

14) Duck stamps (revenues, plate number)
15) Dummy stamps (coil, pair)
16) Error (block, bilingual)
17) Essay

**Duck Stamps** — Popular name of U.S. Hunting Permit stamps, issued to be used on hunting licenses. Each annual stamp depicts waterfowl.

**Dummy Stamps** — Officially produced stamps used for tests of processing or dispensing equipment, usually blank or carrying special inscriptions, blocks or other distinguishing ornamentation. These are not valid stamps, nor are they intended to reach the market, although some do.

**Duplex Cancel** — Two-part cancellation, both cancellation and postmark, to ensure identification of postmark and proper cancellation.

**Duplicates** — Additional copies of stamps that one already has in his collection. Such copies should be examined closely to prevent overlooking varieties of perforation, watermark or color.

## — E —

**Embossing** — A process whereby the paper is raised to give relief to the design. The use of embossed designs is often found in postal stationery, and has occasionally been used for adhesive postage stamps.

**Encased Postage Stamps** — Stamps inserted into small cases with transparent fronts and circulated as currency. Encased postage stamps have been used during periods of scarcity for small denomination coins as some provisional medium of exchange.

**Entire** — An intact piece of postal stationery, in contrast to a cut-out of the printed design. This term is sometimes used in reference to an intact cover.

**Error** — A major mistake in the production of a stamp. Printing errors may include imperforate or part-perforate varieties, missing or incorrect colors, inversion or doubling of part of the design or overprint, etc. Such errors are usually far scarcer than the normal stamps and thus command considerable premiums.

**Essay** — A proposed design, submitted to, and rejected by, the postal authorities.

**Europa** — The "United Europe" theme, celebrated on stamps of Common Market and affiliated nations since 1956. These are actively collected in Europe, causing a number of nations to issue Europa commemoratives, although they have no local reason for doing so.

**Expertization** — The examination of a philatelic item by an acknowledged expert, to determine whether it is genuine, or something less than completely authentic.

**Exploded** — A stamp booklet is said to be "exploded" when it has been separated into its various components for purposes of display.

## — F —

**Face Value** — The value of a stamp as inscribed on its face. Usually, this represents the value for which the stamp will be honored for postage.

**Facsimile** — Reproduction of a genuine stamp, with no intent to deceive collectors or postal officials. Catalog illustrations are facsimiles.

**Fake** — A genuine stamp that has been altered in some way to make it more attractive to collectors, e.g., repaired, reperfed or regummed alteration to resemble a more valuable variety.

**Farley's Follies** — During 1933-34, Postmaster General James A. Farley supplied a few imperforate sheets of current commemorative issues to President Roosevelt and other government officials. The resulting uproar from U.S. collectors forced the government to release some 20 stamps in imperforate condition for public sale.

**Fast Colors** — Inks resistant to fading.

**Fieldpost** — A military post office operating in the field.

**Find** — A new and/or valuable discovery (e.g., a rare stamp, a startling error, etc.)

**First Day Cover (FDC)** — A cover bearing a stamp tied by a cancellation showing the date of the first day of issue of that stamp. Such cancellations are often distinctive and are usually confined to one, or a limited number of post offices.

**Fiscal** — A stamp-like label denoting the payment of taxes. Fiscals, or revenue stamps, are ordinarily affixed to documents and canceled by pen, canceler, mutilation, etc. Because of their similarity to postage stamps, fiscals have occasionally been used provisionally in that capacity (postal fiscals).

**Flat Plate** — Printing from a flat-bed plate, as opposed to a curved or cylindrical plate.

**Flaw** — A defect in the plate, causing an identifiable variety in the stamp itself.

**Fleet Post Office (FPO)** — An official U.S. post office for use by U.S. military naval units abroad.

**Forerunner** — The philatelic precursor of a stamp-issuing entity, e.g., Turkish stamps before 1918 canceled in Palestine are forerunners of Israeli issues, as are the various European issues for Turkey used in Palestine, and the subsequent issues of the Palestine Mandate.

**Forgery** — A completely fraudulent reproduction of a postage stamp. There are two general types of forgeries: **1)** those intended to defraud the postal authorities; and **2)** those intended to defraud the collectors. The former are avidly collected by specialists and are usually more valuable than the genuine stamps, while the latter are usually worth little and represent a real danger to collectors.

**Frame** — The outer portion of the stamp design.

**Franks** — Some indication on the face of a cover that it is to be carried free of postage.

Franks may be written, handstamped, imprinted or represented by special adhesives. Such free franking is usually limited to official correspondence of various kinds, sometimes including soldiers' mail. Stamps may be referred to as "franks," although this usage is not common, nor is it technically correct.

18

19

20

18) Europa
19) Farley's Follies (imperf)
20) First Day Cover (FDC)

**Freak** — An abnormal variety, created by a set of unique circumstances (e.g., paper fold, overinking, perforation shift, etc.), as opposed to a continually appearing variety or a major error.

**Front** — The obverse of a cover, detached from the reverse. Fronts, while desirable if they bear unusual or uncommon postal markings, are less desirable than the intact cover.

**Fugitive Inks** — To counter attempts at forgery or the removal of cancellations, many governments have used fugitive inks in printing their stamps. Such inks easily fade and will run if placed in contact with water or other liquid chemicals.

## — G —

**"Ghost" Tagging** — The appearance of a light impression apart from the normal inked stamp impression, caused by misregistration of the phosphor "tag" impression in relation to the ink. Sometimes, the plate number impression will have an entirely different number from the ink plate, thus giving the impression of an error: one dark (normal) number and one light (ghost) number.

**Goldbeater's Skin** — A thin, tough, translucent paper. The 1886 issue of Prussia was printed in reverse on Goldbeater's Skin, with the gum applied over the printing. These stamps were virtually impossible to remove from the paper to which they were affixed because of the brittleness of the paper, making subsequent removal and reuse impossible.

**Granite Paper** — A paper with small colored fibers mixed with the pulp; used as a safeguard against forgery.

**Grill** — A pattern of parallel lines (or of dots at the points where the lines would cross) forming a grid. Philatelically, "grill" is usually used in reference to: **1)** the grill embossing used as a security measure on stamps of the United States (1867-71) and Peru (1874-79); or **2)** the grill-like canceling devices used on various 19th century issues.

**Gum** — The mucilage applied to the backs of adhesive postage stamps. Gum represents a problem to stamp collectors, since it may crack (thus harming the paper of the stamp itself), stain, or adhere to other stamps, album pages, etc., under certain climatic conditions. On the other hand, one should not simply remove the gum from unused stamps, because a considerable premium is placed on its presence, particularly if it is completely intact and undisturbed.

**Gutter** — The selvage, usually unprinted, between the panes of a sheet of stamps.

**Gutter Snipe** — Typically used in reference to U.S. items, meaning one or more stamps to which is attached the full gutter from between panes (plus any amount of adjoining stamps), caused by misregistration of the cutting device, paper foldover, etc.

## — H —

**Handstamp** — Cancellation or overprint applied by hand to an adhesive.

**Highway Post Office (HPO)** — Portable mail-handling equipment for sorting mail in transit on highways (normally by truck). The last official U.S. HPO ran June 30, 1974.

**Hinge** — Stamp hinges are small, rectangular-shaped pieces of paper, usually gummed on one side, used in the mounting of stamps. Most modern hinges are peelable, i.e., once dry, they may be removed from the stamp easily, leaving little trace of their having been applied.

## — I —

**Imperforate** — Imperforate stamps are those issued without perforation or rouletting between the individual stamps in the sheet. The earliest stamps were issued imperforate, but after about 1860, most stamps were perforated. Modern imperforates are usually either errors, or have been produced for sale to collectors as philatelic varieties.

**Impression** — Any stamped or embossed printing.

**Imprimatur** — Latin for "let it be printed." Philatelically, the first sheets of stamps from an approved plate, normally checked, or kept for file purposes, prior to final directive that the plate be used for stamp production.

21

22

21) Gutter
22) Imperforate, imperf (block)

**India Paper** — A thin, tough printing paper of high quality, used primarily in the production of proofs.

**Indicia** — Imprints on postal stationery, as opposed to adhesive stamps, indicating prepayment and postal validity.

**Intaglio** — A form of printing in which the inked image is produced by that portion of the plate sunk below the surface, i.e., line engraving and photogravure.

**International Reply Coupon (IRC)** — Coupons issued by members of the Universal Postal Union to provide return postage from recipients in foreign countries.

**Invert** — The term generally used to describe any error where one portion of the design is inverted in relation to the other portion(s).

## — K —

**Keytype** — A basic design utilized for the issues of two or more postal entities, usually differing only in the country name and often inscription of value. Many of the earlier colonial issues of Britain, France, Spain, Germany and Portugal are keytypes.

**Kiloware** — A form of stamp mixture, consisting of miscellaneous stamps on paper, often from various sources. Kiloware derives its name from the fact that it is often sold by the kilogram (about 2.3 pounds).

## — L —

**Label** — The term "label" is philatelically used in reference to any stamp-like adhesive that is not a postage stamp.

**Laid Paper** — One of the two basic types of paper used in stamp printing. Laid paper is distinguished from the other type — wove paper — by the presence of thin, parallel lines when held to the light.

**Letterpress** — A form of printing wherein the design is printed directly from the inked, raised surface of the printing plate.

**Line Engraving** — A form of printing wherein the design is printed from an intaglio plate, produced from a hand-engraved die.

**Line Pair** — A pair of stamps with a guide line or joint die line between. A joint die line indicates a space where ink has collected between two dies. This term usually refers to joint die line pairs, which command a substantial premium over ordinary coil pairs.

**Lithography** — A form of printing wherein the design area of the plate is ink-receptive, while the nonprinting area is ink-repellant.

**Locals** — Stamps that are valid only within a limited area, or within a limited postal system, requiring the addition of nationally or internationally valid stamps for further service. Locals have been produced both privately and officially.

## — M —

**Mail Early (ME) Block** — U.S. marginal marking block, to which is attached that portion of the marginal selvage bearing the inscription "Mail Early (in the Day)," which first appeared on U.S. marginal selvage in 1968, and was subsequently replaced by the Copyright notice. Typically a block of four or six stamps.

**Margin** — Has two philatelic meanings: **1)** the selvage surrounding the stamps in a sheet, often carrying inscriptions of various kinds; and **2)** the unprinted area between the design and the edges of the stamp. The grades for sound stamps are determined by the position of the design in relation to the edge of the stamp as perforated, or, in the case of imperforate stamps, as cut from the sheet.

**Maximum Card** — A pictorial postal card tying together an illustration, a stamp and a cancellation in a common theme, usually relating to the stamp itself.

**Meter** — Government permit of specified face value applied as prepaid postmarks in lieu of stamps.

**Metered Mail** — Mail franked by a postage meter, a device that automatically imprints the

23a     23b

24

25

23 a&b) Keytype
24) Line pair (coil line pair)
25) Locals

proper postal rate, recording this information by means of a distinctive imprint in the upper right-hand area of the envelope. Meters were authorized by the U.P.U. in 1920 and are used today by many businesses and large mailers to simplify the franking of correspondence.

**Miniature Sheet** — A smaller-than-normal sheet of stamps, often bearing marginal inscriptions of some sort.

**Mint** — A stamp in the same state as issued by the post office: unused, undamaged and with full original gum (if so issued).

**Mirror Print** — Negative or reverse impression, like an offset.

**Mission Mixture** — The lowest grade of stamp mixture, containing unsorted but primarily common stamps on paper, as purchased from missions or other institutions.

**Missionaries** — The first stamps of Hawaii, issued in 1851-52. These are extremely rare and are generally ranked among the great classics of philately.

**Mixed Perforation** — Refers to stamps whose perfs are of a different gauge on one or more sides.

**Mixed Postage** — Refers to a cover bearing the stamps of two or more stamp-issuing entities, properly used.

**Mixture** — A lot of stamps, understood to contain duplication.

**Mobile Post Office (MPO)** — Portable mail-handling equipment, generally in trucks or trains.

**Money, Stamps As** — During periods of currency shortage, stamps have often circulated officially in place of small change. Often, stamps used in this way are printed on thin card stock, enclosed in cases of various kinds, affixed to cards, etc.

**Mounts (Stamp)** — A variety of acetate sheaths, clear on the obverse and bearing some sort of adhesive on the back, are offered to collectors who wish to mount their stamps without disturbing the gum. These mounts are then trimmed to the desired size and mounted directly on the album page.

**Multicolor** — More than two colors.

**Multiple** — An unseparated unit of stamps including at least two stamps, but less than the number included in a full sheet.

# — N —

**Native Paper** — Crude, hand-made papers produced locally, as opposed to finer, machine-made paper.

**Never Hinged (n.h.)** — A stamp with original gum and no hinge marks.

**New Issue Service** — A service whereby a dealer automatically supplies all new issues of a given country, area or topic, to service subscribers. Issues provided are determined by previous agreement, in which the quantity, types of issues, etc., are defined.

**Newspaper Stamps** — Stamps issued specifically for prepayment of newspapers and other periodicals and printed matter sent through the mail.

# — O —

**Obliteration** — Has two philatelic meanings: **1)** a form of cancellation intended solely to deface the stamp, i.e., a "killer;" and **2)** an overprint intended to deface a portion of the design of the basic stamp.

**Obsolete** — A stamp no longer available from the post office, although possibly still postally valid.

**Occupation Issue** — An issue released for use in territory occupied by a foreign power.

**Off Center** — A stamp whose design is not centered in relation to the edges of the stamp. An off center stamp is less desirable than a stamp more nearly centered in relation to the edges.

**Offices Abroad** — At various times, many nations have maintained post offices in other countries, usually because of the unreliability of the local postal system. In China and the Turkish Empire, especially, many foreign nations maintained their own postal systems as part of their extraterritorial powers. Usually, special stamps were used for these offices, most often being overprinted regular stamps of the nations maintaining the offices.

**Officials** — Stamps issued solely for the use of government departments and officials. Such stamps may or may not be available to collectors in unused condition from the post office.

26) Occupation issue
27) Offices abroad
28) Omnibus issue

**Offset** — The transfer of part of the design or overprint from one sheet to the back of another, before the ink has dried (also called "set off"). Such impressions are in reverse, and so should not be confused with "printed on both sides" varieties, which are actual errors and command very healthy premiums. Offset may also refer to a printing process of rotary press transference.

**OHMS** — "On His (Her) Majesty's Service." Used in perfins, overprints or franks to indicate official use in the British Commonwealth.

**Omnibus Issue** — Any issue released by several postal entities celebrating a common theme. Omnibus issues may or may not share a keytype design.

**On Paper** — Stamps "on paper" are those which still bear portions of the original envelope or wrapper upon which they were used.

**On Piece** — A stamp on a portion of the original envelope or wrapper, showing enough of the cancellation to ensure authenticity, as in the case of bisects.

**Original Gum (o.g.)** — The original gum on a mint or unused stamp, i.e., not lacking gum or regummed.

**Overprint** — Any printing over the original design of a stamp. An overprint that changes the value of a stamp is more properly termed a "surcharge."

**Oxidation** — Oxidation, or "rust," causes a darkening of certain inks used in printing stamps, especially oranges, which may in time turn brown or black.

## — P —

**Packet** — A pre-sorted unit of all different stamps. One of the most common and economical ways to begin a general collection.

**Packet Letter** — Carried by government-owned ship, or ship authorized by a post office to carry mail.

**Pair** — Two unseparated stamps.

**Pane** — The unit into which a full sheet is divided before sale at the post office. The "sheets" that one normally sees at U.S. post offices are, in fact, panes, full sheets being divided into four panes before shipment to the post offices. A booklet pane is one complete pane (page) as released in the booklet.

**Paquebot** — Cancellation indicating that the article was mailed aboard ship.

**Par Avion** — French for "By Air."

**Parcel Post Stamps** — At various times, many countries have issued stamps especially for payment of parcel post fees.

**Part-Perforate** — A stamp which is not perforated on one or more sides, but with at least one side perforated.

**Paste-Up** — The point where the ends of rolls of coiled stamps are joined by pasting up the

two pieces, often employing unprinted selvage on one coil, over which the other coil is pasted.

**Pelure Paper** — A strong, thin paper occasionally used in stamp printing. Pelure paper is readily distinguishable by its translucence, resembling a slightly dark onion-skin paper.

**Pen Canceled** — Many of the earliest stamps were routinely canceled by pen. In the case of most stamps, however, pen cancellation usually indicates the stamp's use as a fiscal.

29

30

31

29) Overprint
30) Paquebot (cover)
31) Pen canceled

**Penny Black** — The British 1-penny stamp, issued May 6, 1840, bearing the portrait of Queen Victoria, is generally acknowledged as the world's first adhesive postage stamp. The format of this issue influenced stamp design for many years.

**Perfins** — Stamps punched with "perforated initials" or designs. Perfins are normally used as a control to prevent pilferage or misuse of stamps by employes. Perfins may be either privately or officially produced.

**Perforation** — The punching out of holes between stamps in a sheet or coil to facilitate separation. There are three basic forms of perforation used today: **1)** Comb perforation, in which three sides of a stamp are perfed at once, with the process repeated in rows; **2)** Harrow perforation, in which the entire sheet or unit of stamps is perforated in one operation; and **3)** Line perforation, in which holes are punched one row at a time, distinguished by the uneven crossing of perforation lines and irregular cor-

32

33

32) Penny Black
33) Perfins

ners. Comb and harrow perforations show more neatness at the corners, and may be difficult to distinguish, although the rows in harrow perfs are perfectly aligned, while those in comb perforation may be off slightly where the vertical and horizontal rows of perfs cross.

**Perforation Gauge** — Printed scale to facilitate the measurement of the perf numbers, i.e., the number of perf holes or teeth within two centimeters. Perf gauges are available on a variety of materials.

**Permit** — Special postage system of imprinting mailer's assigned permit number on each piece of mail, eliminating the need to affix and cancel stamps on large mailings.

**"Phantasy"** — A bogus stamp.

**Phantom Philately** — The collection of bogus stamps, the name being derived from Fred Melville's "Phantom Philately," one of the pioneer works on bogus issues.

**Philately** — The collection and study of postage stamps.

**Phosphor** — In 1959, Great Britain began to print phosphor lines in the face of some of its stamps to facilitate mail processing by machines that reacted to the phosphor under ultraviolet light. Since then, mail processing has become more and more automated, and many nations now utilize a phosphor "tagging" on their stamps.

**Photogravure** — A modern stamp-printing process that has become increasingly common in recent years. The plate is made from a photograph of the designer's drawing of the stamp. A form of intaglio printing, the ink in this process rests in the design depressions, the actual surface of the plate being wiped clean. The paper then picks up ink from these depressions, in a manner much like the line-engraved process.

**Pictorials** — Stamps bearing a picture of some sort, other than portraits or static designs such as coats of arms.

**Plate** — The basic printing unit which is placed on the press and used to produce stamps. In the U.S., each plate has an identifying number which is imprinted in the selvage of each pane.

**Plate (Number) Block** — A block of stamps to which is attached that portion of the marginal selvage bearing the number(s) of the plate(s) used in printing that particular sheet. The size varies according to the total of plate numbers appearing, and block size is always at least four stamps, and may be equal to twice the total of plate numbers (i.e., an issue with six plate numbers on any given sheet may require a plate block of 12 stamps).

**Plating** — The reconstruction of a sheet by collecting individual stamps representing the various positions. This is possible for many older issues, but most modern issues are too uniform to make the identification of most individual positions possible.

**Plebiscite Issue** — After World War I, a number of disputed areas were placed under temporary League of Nations administration, pending plebiscites to determine which nation the populace wished to join. Special issues were used in several of these areas, among them Allenstein, Carinthia, Eastern Silesia, Marienwerder, Schleswig and Upper Silesia.

**PNC** — Philatelic Numismatic Combination: a cover carrying both a stamp and a coin, medal or token. The two are usually related, as when the cover is canceled on the first day of use of the coin.

**Pneumatic Post** — A form of letter distribution through air tubes. Pneumatic posts are used in some of the larger towns of France and Italy, and Italy has since 1913 issued special stamps for correspondence so serviced.

**Postage Dues** — Stamps indicating that insufficient postage has been affixed to the mailing piece. Postage dues are usually affixed at the office of delivery, and the additional postage is collected from the addressee upon delivery.

**Post Card** — A small card, often carrying a picture on one side and a space for a written message on the other, privately produced and without imprinted stamp.

**Postal Card** — An officially produced post card, bearing an imprint in the upper right corner representing prepayment of postage.

**Postal Fiscal** — Revenue or fiscal stamps used postally.

**Postal History** — Refers to the study of postal markings, rates, routes, etc., that reflect the history and development of postal systems.

**Postal Stationery** — Any type of stationery bearing imprinted stamps, as opposed to adhesive stamps. Postal stationery includes imprinted envelopes, wrappers, postal cards, aerogrammes, etc.

**Postally Used** — Refers to the condition of a stamp that has seen legitimate postal use, as opposed to a copy that has been canceled to order, favor-canceled, etc.

**Postmark** — Any sort of official postal marking. Usually used specifically in reference to cancellations bearing the name of the post office of origin and the mailing date.

**Precancels** — Stamps with special cancellations applied by the post office to facilitate processing of large mailings, since precanceled stamps usually require no further cancellation. Precanceled stamps are sold to mailers who have a permit to use such stamps in the same manner as regular stamps — they may differ from normal stamps only in the precancellation itself. U.S. precancels may be divided into two categories: **1)** "Locals," applied by a town or city

post office; and **2)** "Bureaus," applied by the Bureau of Engraving and Printing.

**Pre-Stamp Covers** — Covers used before the introduction of adhesive postal stamps or of postal stationery.

**Prexies** — The nickname of the U.S. 1938-54 Presidential definitive series.

**Printer's Waste** — Refers to stamps that are badly misprinted and which should have been destroyed at the printing plant. Such items have entered the philatelic market through private channels, rather than slipping past the postal quality controls and being unknowingly sold across the counter.

34 a

34b

35

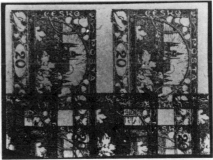

36

34 a&b) Plebiscite issues
35) Precancel (pair)
36) Printer's waste

37a                 37b

38

Guernsey       Isle of Man       Jersey

39

40

37 a&b) Pro Juventute (semipostal)
38) Proofs
39) Regionals
40) Registered mail

**Printing** — The process of imprinting designs on paper from an inked surface.

**Pro Juventute** — Swiss semipostals, the surtax from which is given to child welfare institutions. A Pro Juventute series has appeared nearly every year since 1913.

**Proofs** — Trial impressions from the die or printing plate before actual stamp production. Proofs are made to examine the die or plate for defects and, often, to compare different colored inks, to determine which is to be used for the issue.

**Provisional** — A temporary postage stamp, issued to meet postal demands until new or regular stocks of stamps can be obtained.

## — R —

**Railway Post Office (RPO)** — Portable mail-handling equipment for sorting mail in transit on trains. The last official U.S. RPO ran June 30, 1977.

**Receiving Mark** — A postmark or other postal marking applied by the receiving, rather than the originating, post office.

**Redrawn** — A stamp design that has been slightly altered, maintaining the basic design as originally issued.

**Regionals** — Since 1958, Great Britain has issued short series of definitive sets for the regions of Guernsey (1958-69), Jersey (1958-69), Isle of Man (1958-71), Northern Ireland (1958 —), Scotland (1958 — ) and Wales (1958 — ). These regionals are usually sold only in the appropriate region, but are valid for postage throughout the country.

**Registered Mail** — First class mail with a numbered receipt, including a valuation of the registered item, for compensation if lost. Sometimes, registered mail stamps are specifically used. Registered mail is specially signed for by each postal employee who handles it.

**Registration Labels** — Adhesive labels indicating the registry number and, usually, city of origin, for registered articles sent through the mail.

**Reissue** — An official reprinting of a stamp, valid for postage, from an obsolete or discontinued issue.

**Remainders** — Stocks of stamps remaining unsold at the time that an issue is declared obsolete by the post office. Some countries have sold these remainders to the trade at substantial discounts from face value, often marking them in some way, such as canceling them with a distinctive cancellation. Uncanceled remainders usually cannot be distinguished from stamps sold over the counter before the issue was invalidated.

**Repaired Stamps** — Damaged copies that have been repaired in some way to reinforce them or to make them resemble more valuable undamaged stamps.

**Replicas** — Reproductions of stamps sold as space-fillers during the early days of collecting. Usually printed in one color in a sheet containing a number of different designs. Replicas differ from forgeries in that they were never intended to deceive either the post office or the collector.

**Reprint** — A stamp printed from the original plate, after the issue has ceased to be postally valid. Official reprints are sometimes made for presentation purposes, official collections, etc., and are often distinguished in some way (different colors, perfs, etc.). Private reprints, on the other hand, are usually produced strictly for sale to collectors and often closely resemble the original stamps. Private reprints normally sell for far less than original copies.

**Retouch** — The minor repairing of a damaged plate or die, often producing a minor, but detectable, difference in the design of the printed stamp.

**Revenues** — Labels representing the payment of various taxes, affixed to official documents, merchandise, etc. Some stamps, including many issues of the British Commonwealth, were inscribed "Postage and Revenue," and were available for either use. Such issues are worth far less fiscally canceled. In some cases, revenues have been used provisionally as postage stamps. Such use should be confirmed by collecting the stamp on cover or piece.

**Rocket Mail** — Many experiments have been conducted since 1931, utilizing rockets for the transporting of mail. Special labels have been produced to mark the carrying of mail on such flights.

**'Roos** — The nickname of the first Australian issue (1913), which featured a kangaroo on a map of Australia. This design was used as late as 1945.

**Rotary Plate (Cylinder)** — Printing from curved plates (cylinders) or rotary presses, enabling more continuous stamp production, as opposed to flat plates, which make single impressions.

**Rouletting** — The piercing of the paper between stamps, to make their separation more convenient. No paper is actually removed from the sheet, as is the case in the punching method used in perforating. Instead, rouletting gives the appearance of a series of dashes.

**Rural Free Delivery (RFD)** — System for free home delivery of mail in rural areas of the United States, begun just prior to the turn of the 20th century.

**"Rust"** — A brown mold, resembling the rust in iron, which affects stamps in tropical regions.

# — S —

**SASE** — Self-Addressed, Stamped Envelope. An unused envelope bearing address of sender and return postage. Sent to facilitate reply.

**Secret Marks** — Many stamps have included tiny reference points in their designs to foil attempts at counterfeiting and to differentiate issues.

**Seebeck** — The nickname for various Latin American issues produced by Nicholas Frederick Seebeck, the agent for the Hamilton Bank Note Company of New York, during 1890-99. Seebeck agreed to provide new issues of stamps each year at no charge, in return for the right to sell remainders and reprints to collectors. The resulting furor destroyed Seebeck and blackened the philatelic reputations of the countries involved. "Seebecks" are still common as both mint originals and reprints. Genuinely used copies are often scarce.

**Selvage** — The unprinted marginal paper on a sheet or pane of stamps.

**Semipostal (Charity Stamp)** — Stamp sold at a surcharge over postal value, with the additional charge being earmarked for some special purpose. Usually recognized by the presence of two (often different) values, separated by a "+" sign, on a single stamp.

**Series** — All the variations of design and value of a particular issue.

41

42

41) Replica
42) 'Roos

**Set** — A unit of stamps issued at one time for a common purpose, or over an extended period, embracing a common design or theme.

**Se-Tenant** — French for "joined together." Two or more unseparated stamps of different designs, colors, denominations or types.

**Shade** — The minor variation commonly found in any basic color. Shades are not usually accorded catalog status, unless they are very distinctive.

**Sheet** — The complete unit of stamps as they are printed. Stamps are often printed in large sheets, being separated into two or more panes before shipment to the post offices for sale to the public.

**Ship Letter** — Letter carried by private ship.

**Short Set** — An incomplete set of stamps, usually lacking either the high value(s) or one or more key values.

43

The Declaration of Independence, 4 July 1776 at Philadelphia
From a Painting by John Trumbull

44

45

43) Se-tenant (strip, triptych)
44) Souvenir sheet
45) Specimen

**Sleeper** — Stamps or other collectable items that seem to be unaccountably underpriced, sometimes indicating good investment potential.

**Sleeve** — A cylindrical printing plate of solid construction, eliminating the need to join two or more curved plates for rotary printing.

**Soaking** — The removal of stamps from the paper to which they were affixed when mailed. Most stamps may be safely soaked in water, if handled carefully. Fugitive inks, however, will run in water, and chalky-surfaced papers will lose their designs entirely, so some knowledge of stamps is a necessity.

**Souvenir Card** — A philatelic card, not valid for postage, issued in conjunction with some special event.

**Souvenir Sheet** — A small sheet of stamps, usually including one value or a set surrounded by a wide margin, upon which generally appears a commemorative inscription of some sort.

**Space-Filler** — A stamp used to simply "fill the space" in an album, until a better copy can be found. Space-fillers are normally damaged copies of relatively expensive stamps, but may include reproductions of stamps that the collector cannot afford to purchase.

**Special Delivery** — A U.S. service providing expedited delivery of mail matter.

**Special Handling** — A. U.S. service providing expeditious handling for fourth-class material.

**Special Printing** — Stamps of current or recent design reissued, often with distinctive color, paper, perforations, etc.

**Specialist** — A philatelist who has intensively studied and collected the stamps and postal history of a given country or area, or has otherwise limited his collecting field.

**Specimens** — Stamps distributed to U.P.U. members for identification purposes, to the philatelic press and trade for publicity purposes. Specimens are distinguished by being overprinted or punched with the word "SPECIMEN" or its equivalent, or by being overprinted or punched in a different, but distinctive way. Specimens of scarce stamps tend to be less valuable than normal copies, while those of relatively common issues are more valuable.

**Speculative** — A stamp or issue released primarily for sale to collectors, rather than to meet any legitimate postal need.

**Splice** — The repair of a break in the roll of stamp paper, or the juncture of two rolls in continuous printing. These are normally destined for the wastebasket, but sometimes reach the public.

**Stamp** — Initially used as a verb, meaning to imprint or impress; e.g., to stamp a design. Philatelically, stamp is the common term for a postal adhesive label.

**Stampless Cover** — A cover that has been carried in the mails without a postage stamp. This term is usually confined to those covers predating the requirement that stamps be affixed to all letters (in the United States, 1856).

**Stock Book** — A book containing rows of pockets to hold loose stamps. Stock books are virtually essential for any collector, and may be purchased in a variety of styles and materials, offered at correspondingly varying prices.

**Straight Edge** — Marginal copies from sheets imperforate at the edges will bear one or two (adjacent) imperf sides. Such "straight edges" may or may not have a colored line along the imperf side. Although usually scarcer than normal copies, they are sold at substantial discounts.

**Strip** — Three or more unseparated stamps in a row.

**Surcharge** — An overprint which changes, or restates, the denomination of the stamp.

**Surface-Colored Paper** — Paper colored on the surface only, with a white or uncolored back.

**Sweatbox** — A closed box employing a wet sponge-like material, over which stuck-together unused stamps are placed on a grill. The humidity softens the gum, facilitating separation of the stamps without removal of the gum.

## — T —

**"T"** — Abbreviation for the French "Taxe." Handstamped on a stamp, this letter indicates the stamp's use as a postage due. Handstamped on a cover, it indicates that postage due has been charged. Several countries have used regular stamps perforated with a "T" as postage dues.

**Tagging** — The marking of stamps with a phosphor coating (which may be in lines, bars, letters, overall design area or entire stamp surface), done by many countries for use with automatic mail-handling equipment. When a stamp is issued both with and without this tag, catalogs will often note varieties as "tagged" or "untagged."

**Telegraph Stamps** — Labels used for the prepayment of telegraph fees. Telegraph stamps usually resemble postage stamps, and at one time, the two were collected indiscriminately.

**Tete-Beche** — French for "head to tail." Two or more unsevered stamps, one of which is inverted in relation to the other(s).

**Thematic** — The collection of stamps relating to a specific theme, generally arranged with much research to present a logical story and progression. Generally a type of topical collection.

**Tied** — A stamp is "tied" when the cancellation extends over both the stamp and the adjacent wrapper.

**Tongs** — Tweezers used to handle stamps. Tongs are an essential tool for the collector, since handling stamps with one's hands may soil them, while perspiration can easily affect the gum. Many modern stamps printed in metallic inks will show fingerprints (like a newly minted coin) if handled by hand.

**Topical** — **1)** A stamp that may be categorized under a given topic or theme, such as space, flowers, art, animals, etc.; **2)** The collection of stamps by the topic depicted on them, rather than by date or country of origin.

**Transit Mark** — A postal marking applied by an intermediate post office, between the originating and receiving post offices.

**Triptych** — A se-tenant strip of three related stamps, often forming one overall design.

**Type** — Philatelically, a type is a basic design.

47a

46

47b

48

46) Surcharge
47 a&b) Telegraph stamps
48) Tete-beche (pair)

## — U —

**Underprint** — A fine printing underlying the main design of a stamp. Most often used as a security measure to deter counterfeiting.

**Ungummed** — Stamps without gum. May refer either to stamps issued without gum, as have been released by many tropical countries, or stamps that have been stuck together and subsequently soaked apart, losing their gum in the process. Stamps that have lost their gum in this way are worth less than original gum specimens.

**Unhinged** — A stamp without hinge marks, but not necessarily with original gum.

**Universal Postal Union (UPU)** — Formed in Bern, Switzerland, in 1874, to regulate and standardize postal usage to facilitate the movement of mail between member nations. Today, most nations belong to the UPU.

**Unused** — An uncanceled stamp. An unused stamp has, by definition, not been used, although in the case of uncanceled stamps without gum, one cannot differentiate between a copy that has missed being canceled and one that has somehow lost its gum along the way.

**Used** — A stamp that has been canceled.

## — V —

**Variety** — A variation from the standard form of a stamp. Varieties range from the major (imperfs, missing colors, etc.) to the trivial (slight variations in the plate, minor color shifts, etc.).

**Vignette** — A picture that shades off gradually into the surrounding area. Vignettes are used in printing bicolored stamps to minimize the effect of the normal misregistration in printing. The term is used generally to denote the center illustrative area of a stamp.

49

49) Zeppelin issues (airmail)

## — W —

**Want List** — A list of needed stamps, identified by catalog number, submitted by a collector to a dealer, usually including requirements on condition and price.

**Watermark** — A deliberate thinning of paper during its manufacture, to produce a semitranslucent pattern. Watermarks appear frequently in paper used in stamp printing, and differences in watermarks are considered major varieties.

**Wing Margin** — British sheets printed before 1880 were perforated down the center of the gutter, producing oversized margins on one side of stamps adjacent to the gutter. Such copies are distinctive and scarcer than normal copies.

**Wove Paper** — A paper showing few differences in texture and thickness when held to the light. In producing wove paper, the pulp is pressed against a very fine netting, producing a virtually uniform texture. The most commonly used paper in modern stamp production.

**Wrapper** — A flat sheet folded and sealed around a newspaper or periodical, open at the ends. Wrappers in the past often bore printed indications of value.

## — Z —

**Zemstvos** — Local stamps issued by Russian zemstvos (municipal governments), in accordance with an imperial edict of 1870. A great many such issues appeared, and some are quite scarce.

**Zeppelin Issues** — Includes both stamps issued for, or in honor of, zeppelin flights, and covers carried on such flights, which were franked with either Zeppelin or normal stamps.

**ZIP Block** — U.S. marginal marking block, to which is attached that portion of the marginal selvage bearing the cartoon "Mr. ZIP" character and/or an inscription advising "Use ZIP Code," which first appeared on U.S. marginal selvage in 1964. Typically a block of four stamps.

**ZIP Code** — Zoning Improvement Plan; the U.S. numerical post code used to speed and mechanize mail handling and delivery.

# Uniform Stamp Condition Terms

At the beginning of 1971, Linn's presented a set of Uniform Stamp Condition Terms, which was updated after numerous suggestions and recommendations could be considered and incorporated.

## Stamp Descriptions

When stamps are described, they are usually detailed in a convenient shorthand method of using abbreviations. These abbreviations (or symbols) provide general information regarding a stamps's condition, centering and gum.

For example, M, NH, OG, VF tells a reader that a stamp is mint, never hinged, with original gum and very fine centering. Special features or faults are usually spelled out in greater detail in most descriptions. The specific properties of each term are outlined in the following sections, divided by condition, centering and gum (including hinging).

## General Condition

The general condition of a stamp or set has been broken into four major classifications:

M — MINT — A stamp that has never been postally used or hinged, clean, with original gum (if so issued).

UNUSED — A stamp that has never been postally used, but may have been hinged, lacks gum, or has undergone some other change since it was issued.

U — USED — A stamp that has been postally used.

CTO — CANCELED TO ORDER — A stamp canceled by the issuing government, not including precancels (which would be classified as USED).

## Centering

When viewed from the front or face, the most important consideration is the position of the design from perforation to perforation (if so issued) or from cut edge to cut edge (if imperforate). Centering has been broken down into six major classifications:

S — SUPERB — The design is perfectly centered on the face of the stamp. Opposite margins are equal.

XF — EXTRA FINE — The design is nearly perfectly centered, with all margins not less than three-fourths equal to what they would be on a SUPERB centered copy.

VF — VERY FINE — The design is well centered, but noticeably off center. All margins are not less than one-half equal to what they would be on a SUPERB centered copy.

F — FINE — Perforations are not into the design, but the design is well off center. All margins are not more than one-half equal to what they would be on a SUPERB centered copy, but the perforations do not intrude on the frame or design of the stamp.

AVE — AVERAGE — The perforations cut slightly into the frame and/or design.

FAIR — The perforations are well into the design.

P — POOR — These are usually space fillers, with such poor centering that they should be replaced by better copies whenever possible. However, some rare or valuable items might be nearly impossible to find in better condition, making such copies more acceptable.

## Gum

Gum condition has been broken down into six major classifications:

OG — ORIGINAL GUM — The stamp has the same gum as when issued.

RG — REGUMMED — New gum has been applied to the stamp.

NG — NO GUM — Either the stamp was issued without gum, or the gum has been removed.

NH — NEVER HINGED — The stamp has never been hinged and the gum has never been disturbed in any manner. If the gum has been disturbed, it should be reclassified, even though it may never have been hinged.

LH — LIGHTLY HINGED — The stamp has been hinged with a peelable hinge, and there are only slight traces where the hinge has been removed.

HH — HEAVILY HINGED — The stamp has been hinged and there are hinge remnants and/or missing gum where the hinge has been. If the paper has been thinned, the thin should be listed in accordance with the next section as a fault.

## Faults

Any fault in the stamp should be listed in the description, or the buyer will expect none. These include thins (caused by hinges or any other reason), short perfs, creases, tears, stains, ink marks, pinholes, or unusual wear. Other sources of faults not included here should also be listed.

This listing constitutes the recommendations of Linn's, and may be modified by certain dealers or collectors. These are suggested guidelines, not absolute facts. Some terms are judgment matters, as, for example, the centering. These Uniform Stamp Condition Terms are presented to aid the dealer and collector in the honest and fair appraisal of a stamp's or set's condition.

# Symbols, Abbreviations Guide

As a service designed primarily for the newcomer to philately, following is a guide to symbols and abbreviations most frequently used by Linn's advertisers and editorial staff writers.

★ or * — Mint

⊙ — Used

P — Poor

Av. or Avg. — Average

G — Good

VG — Very Good

F — Fine

VF — Very Fine

XF — Extra Fine

S or Sup. — Superb

MD — Minor Defect(s)

NG — No Gum

OG — Original Gum

HH — Heavily Hinged

LH — Lightly Hinged

VLH — Very Lightly Hinged

NH — Never Hinged

FDC — First Day Cover

FFC — First Flight Cover

⊠ — Cover

☐ — Piece

⊞ — Block

PB — Plate Block

ME — Mail Early (Block)

S/S or SS — Souvenir Sheet

M/S — Miniature Sheet

Opt. or Ovpt. — Overprint

LP — Line Pair

SE — Straight Edge

MI — Marginal Inscription

MS — Matched Set

CMS — Complete Matched Set

Canc. or Ccl. — Canceled or Cancellation

CTO — Canceled To Order

CDS — Circular Date Stamp

PM — Postmark

MPP — Mailer's Postmark Permit

EFOs — Errors, Freaks and Oddities

Imperf — Imperforate

Perf — Perforated or Perforation

w/o — Without

MB — Minimum Bid

Est. — Estimated

APO — Army Post Office

FPO — Fleet Post Office

HPO — Highway Post Office

MPO — Mobile Post Office

RPO — Railway Post Office

SAE — Stamped Addressed Envelope

SASE — Self-Addressed Stamped Envelope

Mi. — Michel

Mk. or Mink. — Minkus

Sc. — Scott

SG — Stanley Gibbons

Yv. — Yvert et Tellier

USPS — U.S. Postal Service

BEP — Bureau of Engraving and Printing

BPO — British Post Office

UNPA — United Nations Postal Administration

UPU — Universal Postal Union

# Souvenir Cards    11

## Official Issues

Souvenir cards have been issued for many years with reproductions of stamps and philatelic engravings, but it is only since 1968 that such cards have been issued on a regular basis from official sources. The three major issuing agencies that now provide souvenir cards are the Bureau of Engraving and Printing, the United States Postal Service and the United Nations Postal Administration.

Souvenir cards are not actual stamps, and as such, have no postal value. In recent years, however, they have become increasingly valuable to the collector. This is due mainly to the limited availability of such cards, especially the older issues. Originally, the cards were either given away to patrons of the philatelic exhibitions at which they were issued, or sold by the issuing agency for about $1.

The Bureau cards are generally issued for U.S. philatelic and numismatic exhibitions, while the U.S. Postal Service cards are issued for foreign, international exhibitions. The United Nations issues are released on the same day as the U.N. commemorative stamps they depict, in honor of some U.N. event or anniversary.

Because these cards are available for only a limited amount of time in most cases, they are mostly in the hands of collectors and potential collectors. Therefore, the value of such souvenir cards, no longer available from the issuing agency, is now determined by the collectors who deal with them.

The following sections list all the souvenir cards that have been issued, divided by the issuing agencies, along with a brief history, descriptions and production information when available.

### Bureau of Engraving and Printing

The Bureau of Engraving and Printing has officially produced souvenir cards in honor of special philatelic (and numismatic) events since 1969. All these cards have been released for exhibitions and events in the United States, and contain engraved reproductions of various U.S. stamp and currency issues.

In December 1975, the BEP changed its policy concerning the sale of souvenir cards. As of the first of that month, the Bureau would supply cards for only 90 days after the issue date. Before December 1975, there had been no time limit. Also on this date, back issues of remaining cards were offered for the last time (up until Jan. 15, 1976), and then all remaining cards were destroyed.

The present policy states: for the first 30 days, quantities of individual purchases are limited to five cards; for the remaining 60 days, unless supplies are depleted sooner, the cards are available in unlimited quantities. Cards remaining after 90 days will be destroyed. The current price of BEP souvenir cards may vary. Before 1975, cards generally sold for $1; as of 1982, prices ran as high as $5. Orders may be mailed to **Office Services Branch, Bureau of Engraving and Printing, 14th and C streets SW, Washington, D.C. 20228.**

Following is a list of all BEP souvenir cards issued, a description of each card and how it was produced, and the number of cards issued and sold. Number sold, based on final figures from the BEP, should represent an accurate number of cards in circulation. Also included are two earlier issues by Bureau union members which served as forerunners to the Bureau cards, though they were not official issues. All cards measure 8½ by 10½ inches, except where noted.

**March 13, 1954, Postage Stamp Design Exhibition, National Philatelic Museum, Philadelphia, Pa.**

Card of four single-color engravings of buildings in Washington, D.C.: the Washington Monument (pale green), National Gallery of Art (lavender), Washington Cathedral (reddish orange) and U.S. Capitol (black). Inscription: "Souvenir sheet designed, engraved and printed by members, Bureau, Engraving and Printing. Reissued by popular request."

The original engravings were created by the Bank Note Engravers Guild in 1946 for the convention catalog of the International Plate Printers, Die-Stampers and Engravers Union of North America. The design was used again for a 1951 convention, using different colors. The originals were in a single color, but were reengraved for multicolor in a 1965 souvenir program. Gallery, designer Robert L. Miller, picture engraver Carl T. Arlt, letter engraver Axel W. Christensen; Capitol, designer Robert L. Miller, picture engraver Charles A. Brooks, letter engravers George L. Huber and John S. Edmondson; Cathedral, designer William K. Schrage, picture engraver Edward R. Grove, letter engraver Charles A. Smith, ornamental borders Richard M. Bower; Monument, designer Victor S. McCloskey Jr., picture engraver Matthew D. Fenton, ornamental engraver Arthur W. Dintaman, letter engraver John S. Edmondson. These scenes would reappear on future souvenir cards.

**May 21-30, 1966, SIPEX, Sixth International Philatelic Exhibition, Washington, D.C.**

Card of three multicolored views of Washington, same as the above card without the Monument. Inscribed: "Designed, Engraved, and Printed by Union Members of Bureau of Engraving and Printing."

Quantity issued: 4,000. Size: 7 by 9 inches.

**July 16-20, 1969, SANDIPEX, 200th anniversary of settlement of California, San Diego, Calif.**

Card of three multicolored views of Washington, same as the above card (Capitol, Art Gallery, Cathedral). This was the first official souvenir card released by the Bureau of Engraving and Printing. Collectors may also recall that a 6-cent postage stamp, Carmel Mission Belfry, designed by Leonard Buckley and Howard C. Mildner, also was issued for the California anniversary.

Quantity sold: 10,706.

**Aug. 12-16, 1969, 78th annual convention of the American Numismatic Association, Philadelphia, Pa.**

The large American Eagle on this card is a reproduction of the die designed and engraved by craftsmen of the Continental Bank Note Company for use on various U.S. securities. This eagle is flanked by smaller eagles from the engravings used on the $10 U.S. notes of series 1869, 1875, 1878 and 1880. According to the legend on the card, the large American Eagle design notes were dubbed "Jackass Notes," the explanation being that "over the years many fanciful explanations have been proffered concerning the engraver's intent in executing the design. None has any real basis in fact. The resemblance of the eagle, in inverted position, to the lowly donkey's head is purely illusionary."

Quantity issued: 12,400. Quantity sold: 12,347. Size: 6 by 9 inches.

**Oct. 2-12, 1969, Fresno Numismatic Society District Fair, Fresno, Calif.**

City of Washington scenes similar to SANDIPEX card (Art Gallery, Capitol, Cathedral). See first three entries in this section.

Card production: Giori multicolor intaglio vignettes, flatbed typographic text.

Quantity issued: 3,804. Quantity sold: 3,798.

**Nov. 21-23, 1969, American Stamp Dealers' Association National Postage Stamp Show, New York, N.Y.**

Block of four from engraved vignette of design of first U.S. special delivery stamp produced by BEP in blue color of this issuance.

Basic design of vignette had been used in production of all issuances of the 10¢ special delivery stamp by the American Bank Note Company (in blue and orange) prior to the printing of postage stamps by the BEP in 1894, which modified the vignette to distinguish it from the American Bank Note issues. The original ABNC designer was Thomas F. Morris Sr.

Card production: die stamped vignettes, flatbed typographic text.

Quantity issued: 14,969. Quantity sold: 14,964.

**March 20-22, 1970, International Stamp Exhibition (INTERPEX), New York, N.Y.**

Vignettes of four U.S. stamps with New York City subjects, printed in original colors: 3¢ ordinary 1954 Statue of Liberty (designer Charles R. Chickering); 3¢ 300th Anniversary of New York City commemorative, 1953 (designer Charles R. Chickering); 15¢ 1947 airmail (designers Victor S. McCloskey Jr. and Leon Helguera); 5¢ 1948 Golden Anniversary of New York City airmail (designer Victor S. McCloskey Jr.).

Card designed by Howard Mildner. Production: die stamped vignette, flatbed typographic text.

Quantity issued: 12,463. Quantity sold: 12,454.

**May 29-31, 1970, Combined Philatelic Exhibition of Chicagoland (COMPEX), Chicago, Ill.**

Vignettes from original engraving used for 50¢ Graf Zeppelin airmail stamp, 1933, in a block of four in green color of original stamp (designer Victor S. McCloskey Jr.).

Production: die stamped vignettes, flatbed typographic text.

Quantity issued: 27,344. Quantity sold: 27,336.

**Aug. 18-22, 1970, 79th annual convention of the American Numismatic Association, St. Louis, Mo.**

Collage in original colors of portions of various securities from original dies used in their production by the BEP to exemplify arts and skills of high-quality engraving and intaglio printed reproductions.

Card designed by Leonard Buckley. Production: die stamped vignette, flatbed typographic text and Treasury Department Seal (with collage).

Quantity issued: 12,017. Quantity sold: 12,013.

**Nov. 5-8, 1970, 84th annual convention, American Philatelic Society (HAPEX), Honolulu, Hawaii.**

Vignettes from engravings used in design of three stamps related to Hawaiian history: 7¢ 1959 Hawaii Statehood commemorative airmail (designer Joseph Feher); 3¢ 1937 Hawaii Territorial series (designer A.R. Meissner); 80¢ 1952 airmail (designer Victor S. McCloskey Jr.).

Card designed by Howard Mildner. Production: die stamped vignettes, flatbed typographic text.

Quantity issued: 30,249. Quantity sold: 30,235.

**March 12-14, 1971, 13th International Stamp Exhibition (INTERPEX), New York, N.Y.**

Block of four of vignette of original engravings of 4¢ 1962 Project Mercury commemorative in colors of original (designer Charles R. Chickering); text superimposed over background beige tint of enlargements of subsequent issues with astronautical themes: 5¢ 1967 Space Twins commemorative, 6¢ 1969 Apollo 8 commemorative, and 10¢ 1969 First Man on the Moon commemorative airmail.

Card data: Giori multicolor intaglio vignettes, offset surface background tints, flatbed typographic text.

Quantity issued: 80,946. Quantity sold: 80,904.

**April 23-25, 1971, 12th annual National Western Philatelic Exposition (WESTPEX), San Francisco, Calif.**

Vignettes from engravings of four commemorative issues related to California history, each in color of original: 3¢ 1950 California Statehood (designer Victor S. McCloskey Jr.); 1¢ 1934 Yosemite National Park (designer Victor S. McCloskey Jr.); 3¢ 1948 Mount Palomar Observatory (designer Victor S. McCloskey Jr.); 3¢ 1939 Golden Gate International Exposition (designer William A. Roach).

Card designed by Howard Mildner. Production: die stamped vignettes, flatbed typographic text.

Quantity issued: 48,228. Quantity sold: 48,199.

**May 21-23, 1971, National Philatelic Exhibition (NAPEX), Washington, D.C.**

Vignettes of stamps representative of the three branches of U.S. Government from 150th anniversary of National Capital series, 1950, in colors of originals: 3¢ Judicial, the U.S. Supreme Court Building (designer Charles R. Chickering); 3¢ Executive, the White House (designer William K. Schrage); 3¢ Legislative, the Capitol (designer Robert L. Miller).

Card designed by Howard C. Mildner. Production: die stamped vignettes, flatbed typographic text.

Quantity issued: 44,478. Quantity sold: 44,429.

**Aug. 10-14, 1971, 80th Anniversary Convention of the American Numismatic Association, Washington, D.C.**

Face of the $1 silver certificate, series 1896, designed by Will H. Low, New York City artist, and printed from a plate prepared from original master die.

Production: rotary sheetfed intaglio vignette, flatbed typographic text.

Quantity issued: 54,721. Quantity sold: 54,694.

**Aug. 26-29, 1971, joint 85th annual convention of the American Philatelic Society and 75th annual Texas Philatelic Association (TEX-ANEX), San Antonio, Tex.**

Vignettes of stamps concerned with Texas history: 9¢ 1956 ordinary, the Alamo (designer Charles R. Chickering); 5¢ 1964 Sam Houston commemorative (designer Tom Lee); 3¢ 1945 Texas Statehood (designer James B. Winn).

Card designed by Howard C. Mildner. Production: die stamped vignettes, flatbed typographic text.

Quantity issued: 68,215. Quantity sold: 68,131.

**Nov. 19-21, 1971, 23rd ASDA National Postage Stamp Show, New York, N.Y.**

Reproduction, in color, of vignettes of original engravings for 1930 Graf Zeppelin airmail, 65¢, $1.30 and $2.60 (designers A.R. Meissner and C.A. Huston).

Production: die stamped vignettes, flatbed typographic text.

Quantity issued: 94,625. Quantity sold: 94,563.

**Nov. 26-Dec. 1, 1971, 75th anniversary of the Collectors Club, New York, N.Y. (ANPHILEX).**

Simulations of basic designs of first U.S. stamps, 1847, reproduced from engravings of basic designs prepared for souvenir sheet issued in 1947 for centennial of U.S. postage stamps, and printed in colors similar to original stamps. Souvenir sheet: designer Robert L. Miller Jr.; portrait of Franklin 5¢ stamp, Charles A.

Brooks; portrait of Washington 10¢ stamp, Carl T. Arlt.

The 1947 sheet design was based on Post Office Department layout, the die proofs of the 1847 stamps having been supplied by Centenary International Philatelic Exhibition Committee.

Card production: die stamped vignettes, flatbed typographic text.

Quantity issued: 80,148. Quantity sold: 80,110.

**March 17-19, 1972, 14th International Stamp Exhibition (INTERPEX), New York, N.Y.**

Block of four reproduction of vignette of 4¢ 1960 Echo I Communications for Peace commemorative (designer Ervine Metzl); text over blue tint background of four other stamps depicting space-related subjects: 1948 Centennial of Fort Bliss, army center for rocket and guided missile research; 1964 Dr. Robert H. Goddard airmail commemorative; 1971 twin 8¢ Space Achievement commemorative.

Card production: die stamped vignette, offset surface printed background tint and text.

Quantity issued: 110,257. Quantity sold: 79,646.

**April 6-9, 1972, New Orleans Philatelic Exposition (NOPEX), New Orleans, La.**

Block of four of vignette of 3¢ 1953 Louisiana Purchase commemorative of sculpture theme of Louisiana Purchase Exposition, St. Louis, 1904 (designer William K. Schrage). Text over blue tint background of enlarged reproductions of the five stamps of the 1904 Louisiana Purchase commemorative series.

Card production: die stamped vignette, offset surface printed background tint and text.

Quantity issued: 65,067. Quantity sold: 60,518.

**Aug. 15-19, 1972, 81st anniversary convention of the American Numismatic Association, New Orleans, La.**

Reproduction of face of $2 silver certificate, series 1896, printed from plate specially produced from original master die. Design, "Science Presenting Steam and Electricity to Commerce and Manufacture," by Edwin H. Blashfield, 19th century allegorical painter.

Card production: rotary sheetfed intaglio vignette, flatbed typographic text.

Quantity issued: 74,172. Quantity sold: 69,078.

**Oct. 20-22, 1972, combined 78th annual convention of the Society of Philatelic Americans and 33rd national exhibition of Associated Stamp Clubs of Southeast Pennsylvania and Delaware (SEPAD), Philadelphia, Pa.**

Reproduction of block of four Independence Hall ordinary 10¢ 1956 (designer Charles R. Chickering).

Card production: die stamped vignette, offset surface printed text.

Quantity issued: 87,285. Quantity sold: 53,722.

**Nov. 17-19, 1972, 24th ASDA National Postage Stamp Show, New York, N.Y.**

Reproduction of four portraits of 10¢ 1940 Famous Americans series: composer Ethelbert Nevin, author Samuel L. Clemens (Mark Twain), poet James Whitcomb Riley, artist Frederic Remington (designer William L. Roach).

Card production: die stamped vignettes, offset surface text.

Quantity issued: 77,153. Quantity sold: 64,161.

**Nov. 24-26, 1972, Stamp Expo, San Francisco, Calif.**

Block of four of vignette of 25¢ 1947 airmail (designer William K. Schrage).

Card production: die stamped vignette, offset surface text.

Quantity issued: 82,838. Quantity sold: 53,220.

**March 9-11, 1973, 15th International Stamp Exhibition (INTERPEX), New York, N.Y.**

Block of four of vignette of 3¢ 1948 Centennial of Fort Bliss (designer Charles R. Chickering).

Card production: die stamped vignette, offset surface text and tint.

Quantity issued: 88,541. Quantity sold: 49,911.

**May 25-27, 1973, Combined Philatelic Exhibition of Chicagoland (COMPEX), Chicago, Ill.**

Block of four of vignette of $5 1893 Columbian Exposition series (designer Alfred Sarony Major), medallion profile of Columbus, copied from 50¢ silver coin of Chicago World's Columbian Exposition. Block, in black of original stamp, framed by border of green, flanked at left by enlargement of vignette entitled "Columbus in his Study," printed in green.

Card designed by Esther Porter. Production: die stamped vignette, offset surface tint and text.

Quantity issued: 50,459. Quantity sold: 49,038.

**Aug. 23-27, 1973, 82nd anniversary convention of the American Numismatic Association, Boston, Mass.**

Reproduction of face of $5 silver certificate, series 1896, printed from a plate specially produced from original master die. Design, "America," executed by Walter Shirlaw, illustrator and bank note engraver.

Card production: rotary sheetfed intaglio vignette, offset surface text.

Quantity issued: 49,544. Quantity sold: 49,530.

**Sept. 14-16, 1973, joint 25th anniversary National Philatelic Exhibition (NAPEX) and 50th anniversary convention of American Air Mail Society, Washington, D.C.**

Reproduction in block of four of engraved frame and vignette on 24¢ 1918 airmail (designer C.A. Huston), denomination and postal data eliminated. Flanked on right by portrayal of airplane "Jenny" used to carry mail on first route, 1918, Washington-Philadelphia-New York.

Card designed by Peter Cocci. Production: die stamped vignette, offset surface tint and text.

Quantity issued: 42,276. Quantity sold: 41,492.

**Nov. 16-18, 1973, 25th ASDA National Postage Stamp Show, New York, N.Y.**

Block of four of vignette of 1¢ 1943 Four Freedoms stamp (designer Paul Manship) in upper right corner flanked at left by reproductions of the 4¢ 1960-1961 American Credo stamps (designer Frank Conley).

Card production: die stamped vignette, offset surface tint and text.

Quantity issued: 52,449. Quantity sold: 42,761.

**Dec. 7-9, 1973, Stamp Expo-North, San Francisco, Calif.**

Block of four of vignette used for 25¢ 1935 Trans-Pacific airmail (designer A.R. Meissner).

Card production: die stamped vignette, offset surface text.

Quantity issued: 70,487. Quantity sold: 35,098.

**March 8-10, 1974, 75th anniversary of Milwaukee Philatelic Society, Milwaukee, Wis.**

Block of four of vignette used on 15¢ 1949 Universal Postal Union airmail commemorative (designer C.R. Chickering), flanked at left by artist's rendition of monument at Bern, Switzerland, symbol of the UPU.

Card production: die stamped vignette, offset surface tint and text.

Quantity issued: 42,992. Quantity sold: 34,742.

**Aug. 13-17, 1974, 83rd anniversary convention of the American Numismatic Association, Bal Harbour, Fla.**

Reproduction of proposed "Agriculture and Forestry" obverse of $10 silver certificate, 1897 "Educational" series, which never appeared on the note (designer Walter Shirlaw).

Card production: rotary sheetfed intaglio vignette, offset surface text.

Quantity issued: 41,591. Quantity sold: 41,591.

**May 9-11, 1975, National Philatelic Exhibition of Washington, D.C. (NAPEX).**

Block of four of vignette from original engraving for 3¢ 1932 Washington Bicentennial commemorative (designer C.A. Huston), from a painting by Charles Willson Peale.

Card production: die stamped vignette, offset surface text and background tint (artist's conception, Washington taking command).

Quantity issued: 67,500. Quantity sold: 26,313.

**Aug. 15, 1975, International Women's Year.**

Brochure with removable souvenir card. Reproduction of series 1886 $1 silver certificate portrait of Martha Washington (painting by Jalabert, designer Thomas F. Morris); 5¢ 1940

Frances E. Willard commemorative (Washington, D.C., Public Library photograph by Perry Pictures); 3¢ 1948 commemorative of 100 years of progress for American women depicting Elizabeth Stanton, Carrie C. Catt and Lucretia Mott (designer Victor S. McCloskey Jr.); 10¢ 1940 Jane Addams commemorative (photograph by Moffett, Chicago, designer William A. Roach).

Card production: rotary sheetfed intaglio vignettes, offset surface text and tint.

Quantity issued: 28,039. Quantity sold: 28,022.

**Aug. 19-24, 1975, 84th anniversary convention of the American Numismatic Association, Los Angeles, Calif.**

Reproduction of engraving on reverse of 1896 $1 silver certificate, designed and executed by Thomas F. Morris, with portraits of Martha (1878) and George Washington (1867).

Card production: rotary sheetfed intaglio vignette, offset surface text.

Quantity issued: 54,981. Quantity sold: 45,593.

**Nov. 21-23, 1975, ASDA National Postage Stamp Show, New York, N.Y.**

Block of four of vignette of 3¢ 1951 Battle of Brooklyn commemorative (designer C.R. Chickering). Flanked on right by engraving of Washington as Army colonel by Lorenzo J. Hatch, from a painting by John Trumbull.

Card production: die stamped vignette, offset surface text and logos.

Quantity issued: 34,370. Quantity sold: 33,411.

**May 29-June 6, 1976, INTERPHIL '76, International Philatelic Exhibition, Philadelphia, Pa.**

Reproduction of block of four of vignette of 1869 24¢ Declaration of Independence stamp; flanked on right by an engraving of Thomas Jefferson, and on the left by an engraving of the reading of the Declaration of Independence from Independence Hall, Philadelphia, Pa.

Card production: engraved vignettes, offset surface text and logo, printed on cream certificate deed paper. Size: 6¼ by 9 inches.

Quantity sold: 44,864.

**May 29-June 6, 1976, INTERPHIL '76 — Special souvenir card prepared by the Bureau of Engraving and Printing for the American Revolution Bicentennial Administration for insertion in the INTERPHIL '76 souvenir catalog.**

The BEP produced a special souvenir "card" on cream-colored paper stock for the ARBA for insertion in the special 6 by 9 inch INTERPHIL '76 catalog. A total of 9,230 six-subject sheets, or 55,380 souvenir cards, were produced, with total catalog production around 50,000. Remaining cards were destroyed, while catalogs were still available for some time afterwards from the American Philatelic Society.

The cards are perforated about ¼ inch from the bound edge of the catalog for removal. Featured is a reproduction of the 10¢ Independence Hall (series 1954-61) definitive (designer C.R. Chickering), as well as an enlarged vignette of the obverse of the $100 currency note (current, Independence Hall).

Final quantity sold is unknown; there are no reports of how many, if any, of the catalogs finally may have been destroyed.

**May 30-Sept. 6, 1976, Bicentennial Exposition on Science and Technology, Kennedy Space Center, Cape Canaveral, Fla.**

Reproduction of two engravings: a 1949 engraving by Charles Brooks, modeled by Charles Chickering, depicting the first flight of the Wright brothers at Kitty Hawk; and a 1967 engraving by Edward Felver depicting man's first walk in space.

Card production: engraved vignettes, offset surface text and logo.

Quantity sold: 27,795.

**June 11-13, 1976, Stamp Expo '76 Bicentennial, Los Angeles, Calif.**

Third in Bicentennial series from BEP (following ASDA '76 and INTERPHIL '76). On the right are four flags from the 1968 6¢ Historic Flag series (designers Robert J. Jones, Leonard C. Buckley and Howard C. Mildner), in this order, vertically: 1775 Bunker Hill, 1776 Grand Union, 1776 Fort Moultrie, 1777 Bennington.

On the left is an engraved vignette of a Continental soldier and long rifle, backed by a replica of the first U.S. "Stars and Stripes."

Card production: engraved vignettes, offset surface text and logo.

Quantity sold: 24,323.

**Aug. 24-29, 1976, 85th anniversary convention of the American Numismatic Association, New York, N.Y.**

Card complementing previous issues on the Educational Series of currency. Reproduction of the back of the 1896 $2 Silver Certificate (the face appeared on the 1972 ANA card), picturing Robert Fulton and Samuel F.B. Morse, with portraits probably engraved by Lorenzo Hatch. Design and execution of the note was by Thomas F. Morris. Also included are the ANA and Bicentennial logos.

Card production: engraved currency reproduction, offset surface text and logos.

Quantity sold: 38,636.

**March 4-6, 1977, MILCOPEX '77, Milwaukee, Wis.**

Reproduction of 1933 3¢ Byrd Antarctic Expedition II issue (designer V. S. McCloskey Jr.); 1959 4¢ Arctic Explorations issue (designer George Samerjar); and working model of dog team and sled from 1959 4¢ Arctic Explorations issue.

Card production: engraved vignettes, offset surface text and logo.

Quantity sold: 24,686.

**May 20-22, ROMPEX '77, Denver, Colo.**

Reproduction of block of four of the 1951 3¢ Colorado issue (designer William K. Schrage), plus a background rendition of Colorado scenery, executed by a BEP artist.

Card production: engraved vignettes, offset surface text and logo.

Quantity sold: 23,287.

**Aug. 23-28, 1977, 86th anniversary convention of the American Numismatic Association, Atlanta, Ga.**

Reproduction of the obverse of the $5 Silver Certificate, series 1899, engraved by G.F.C. Smillie from a model adapted from an 1872 photograph of Running Antelope by Alexander Gardner.

Card production: engraved currency reproduction, offset surface text and logo.

Quantity sold: 56,806.

**Sept. 2-5, 1977, PURIPEX '77, San Juan, Puerto Rico.**

Reproduction of a block of four of the 3¢ 1937 Puerto Rico Territorial issue, showing La Fortaleza (designers William Schrage and William Roach), plus an enlarged background impression of the "San Juan Gate" from the same 1937 3¢ Puerto Rico issue.

Card production: engraved vignettes, offset surface text and logos.

Quantity sold: 23,056

**Nov. 16-20, 1977, ASDA National Postage Stamp Show, New York, N.Y.**

Reproduction of block of four of the vignette of the 1949 6¢ Wright Brothers commemorative airmail issue (modified stamp design by Gary Chaconas); view of Kitty Hawk Memorial modeled by Charles R. Chickering based on illustration from a 1947 "National Geographic" magazine; stock die engraved by Richard Bowery; card modeled by Clarence Holbert.

Card production: engraved vignettes, offset text and illustration.

Quantity sold: 28,272.

**June 2-4, 1978, International Paper Money Show, Memphis, Tenn.**

Reproduction of the vignette of the reverse of the $10 National Bank Note (Act of 1863), vignette used again on the reverse of the $500 Federal Reserve Note, Series 1918. Vignette engraved in 1869 by Frederick Girsch from a painting by W.H. Powell, which hangs in the U.S. Capitol Rotunda, depicting the discovery of the Mississippi.

Card production: engraved vignette, offset text.

Quantity sold: 28,004.

**June 23-25, 1978, CENJEX '78, Freehold, N.J.**

Reproduction of block of four of the vignette of the 1936 1¢ Army issue depicting Gen. Washington, Gen. Greene and Mount Vernon (designer William K. Schrage); also reproduced are enlarged reproductions of other U.S. stamps, including the 1928 2¢ Molly Pitcher, 1930 2¢ Gen. Von Steuben, 1929 2¢ Battle of Fallen Timbers, 1957 3¢ Alexander Hamilton, and 1977 13¢ Lafayette.

Card production: engraved vignettes, offset text and illustrations.

Quantity sold: 23,493.

**July 4, 1979, private card produced by the International Plate Printers, Die Stampers and Engravers Union of North America.**

On this date, with the permission of the BEP, the union members donated their time and effort (using BEP equipment by special permission) to produce a special souvenir card which reproduces "Miss Liberty Rising from the Capitol," an engraving by George F.C. Smillie originally used on the reverse of Liberty Loan bonds, 1927-42 (modified to show clouds rather than the Capitol dome). Sale of this unofficial, privately produced 8 by 11 inch souvenir card was to benefit the widow of Ed Sipe, former president of the BEP plate printers union. The text describes the engraving process.

Card production: fully engraved.

Quantity issued: 2,500. Quantity sold: 2,500.

**Feb. 15-17, 1980, ANA '80, American Numismatic Association midyear convention, Albuquerque, N.M.**

Reproduction of the reverse of the $5 Silver Certificate, Series 1896, designed by Thomas F. Morris, portraits engraved by Lorenzo Hatch, central symbolic design (head and wings) engraved by George F.C. Smillie. Card completes the BEP Education Series of currency reproductions for numismatic events.

Card production: engraved vignette, offset text.

Quantity sold: 24,500 (estimate).

**June 6-8, 1980, International Paper Money Show, Memphis, Tenn.**

Reproduction of the face of the $10 U.S. Note, Series 1901, known as the "Buffalo Bill." Lewis and Clark portraits engraved by G.F.C. Smillie; bison engraved by Marcus W. Baldwin, designed by Ostrander Smith based on a Charles R. Knight wash drawing.

Card production: engraved vignette, offset text.

Quantity issued: 25,000 (estimate).

**July 4-6, 1980, NAPEX, National Philatelic Exhibition of Washington, Bethesda, Md.**

Reproduction of block of four of the U.S. 1923 $5 definitive featuring the head of the Freedom statue on the Capitol dome, designed by C.A. Huston and engraved by J. Eissler, H.I. Earle, E.M. Weeks and E. Hass. Card modeled by Clarence Holbert.

Card production: engraved vignettes, offset text.

Quantitiy issued: 25,000 (estimate).

**Sept. 8, 1980, BEP Visitors Center, Washington, D.C.**

Reproduction of a simulated postage stamp, showing progressive color proofs of multicolor stamp production in various stages. The design shows an eagle in flight, plus the word "Freedom."

Card production: intaglio and offset.

Quantity issued: 50,000 (initial order, estimate).

**Sept. 25-28, 1980, ASDA Stamp Festival, New York, N.Y.**

Reproduction of a block of four of the 1948 U.S. 3¢ Francis Scott Key commemorative (designer Victor S. McCloskey Jr.).

Card production: intaglio and offset.

Quantity issued: 25,000 (estimate).

**March 20-22, 1981, STAMP EXPO '81 (South), Anaheim, Calif.**

Reproduction of a block of four of the 1967 U.S. 13¢ Kennedy definitive (designer Stevan Dohanos, based on a photograph by Jacques Lowe).

Card production: intaglio and offset.

Quantity issued: 25,000 (estimate).

**April 22, 1981, BEP Visitors Center, Washington, D.C.**

Numismatically oriented card to complement 1980 philatelic Visitors Center souvenir card. Includes illustrations of the art of currency engraving. Indefinite period of availability.

Card production: intaglio and offset.

Quantity issued: 50,000 (initial order, estimate).

**June 19-21, 1981, MEMPHIS '81, Memphis, Tenn.**

Reproduction of the face of the $20 Gold Certificate, series 1905. Canceled cards include 18¢ Flag stamp and first day Visitors Center cancel.

Card production: intaglio and offset.

Quantity issued: 25,000 (estimate).

**July 28-Aug. 2, 1981, ANA '81, American Numismatic Association convention, New Orleans, La.**

Reproduction of the "Silver Dollar" back of the $5 Silver Certificate, Series 1886. Canceled cards include 18¢ Flag stamp and first day Visitors Center cancel.

Card production: intaglio and offset.

Quantity issued: 25,000 (estimate).

**March 5-7, 1982, MILCOPEX '82, Milwaukee, Wis.**

Reproduction of a modified block of four of the 1959 Ernst Reuter commemorative, part of the U.S. Champion of Liberty series at the time.

Canceled cards include 20¢ Flag stamp and first day Visitors Center cancel.

Card production: intaglio and offset.

Quantity issued: 25,000 (estimate).

# United States Postal Service

Souvenir cards have been issued by the United States Postal Service, and its predecessor the U.S. Post Office Department, since 1960. They are generally issued for international philatelic exhibitions outside the U.S., or for special purposes of a domestic nature.

The actual forerunner of the U.S. souvenir card was a 1938 issue by the U.S. Post Office Department in conjunction with the Philatelic Truck which toured the U.S. from 1939-1941. It was a 3 by 4½ inch card, showing the White House on blue and white paper. Over 750,000 copies were printed and distributed nationwide, and the last copies were printed on ungummed stock, after the gummed issues began to appear affixed in unwanted places, apparently due to the original recipients throughout the country.

Current records and information provide more figures regarding the quantity of those souvenir cards issued. Officially, 187,000 gummed cards, and 579,500 ungummed cards were issued. These figures are probably more accurate in accounting for actual numbers in public circulation.

All cards after these two pictorial forerunners measure 6 by 8 inches, and the cards issued for foreign exhibitions are generally distributed free to patrons at those foreign, international exhibitions. Until 1976, the mint price for cards in the United States was $1, when the price increased to $1.25 per mint card. As of 1982, the price was about $2 for mint cards. Canceled cards were also offered, starting in 1976, franked with U.S. postage and canceled with the special USPS show cancellation for the event being noted. Canceled cards are generally priced at the cost of mint cards, plus the cost of the stamps used in franking. Mail orders are subject to a $5 minimum order requirement, and a 50-cent handling charge per order. Orders may be mailed to **Philatelic Sales Division, U.S. Postal Service, Washington, D.C. 20265.**

Although there are no specific time limits imposed on USPS souvenir card orders, most cards are removed from sale within approximately one year from the date of issuance. Some may remain on sale longer, and others may be withdrawn sooner, especially if stocks become depleted. USPS policy on future issues may be subject to change.

**March 26-April 5, 1960, First International Philatelic Congress, Barcelona, Spain.**

Reproduction of vignette of 1893 2¢ Columbian issue, Landing of Columbus, printed in black,

from the painting by Vanderlyn in the Rotunda of the U.S. Capitol.

Quantity sold: 10,391.

**Nov. 1-9, 1968, EFIMEX, International Philatelic Exhibition, Mexico City, Mexico.**

Reproduction of $1 1898 Trans-Mississippi (Cattle in Storm) issue (designer R. Ostrander Smith); after a John A. MacWhirter painting, "The Vanguard."

Quantity sold: 50,000 (estimate).

**Sept. 18-26, 1970, PHILYMPIA, London International Stamp Exhibition, London, England.**

Reproductions of Pilgrim Tercentenary issue of 1920: the Mayflower (1¢), the Landing of the Pilgrims (2¢) and the Signing of the Mayflower Compact (5¢); designer C.A. Huston, original sketches (2¢ and 5¢) by Edwin White.

Quantity sold: 75,000 (estimate).

**Nov. 6-14, 1971, EXFILIMA, Third Inter-American Philatelic Exhibition, Lima, Peru.**

Reproduction of three stamps: the 1958 Simon Bolivar and the 1959 Jose de San Martin commemoratives of the Champion of Liberty U.S. issues, modeler William K. Schrage, designers Arnold Copeland, Ervine Metzl and William H. Buckley; and the 1936-37 10-centavo Inca Courier issue of Peru.

Quantity sold: 50,000 (estimate).

**June 24-July 9, 1972, BELGICA, Brussels International Philatelic Exhibition, Brussels, Belgium.**

Reproduction of 1943 5¢ Belgian Flag of Overrun Countries series, designed and engraved by the American Bank Note Company; 1953 3¢ Gen. George S. Patton Jr. commemorative, designer William A. Schrage; and 1958 3¢ Brussels Universal and International Exhibition commemorative, modeler V.S. McCloskey Jr., designer Bradbury Thompson.

Quantity sold: 167,119.

**Aug. 18, 1972, OLYMPIA Philatelie Munchen, Munich, Germany.**

Reproduction of Olympic emblem and 1972 Olympic issue of four stamps: 6¢, bicycling; 8¢, bobsledding; 15¢, running; and 11¢ airmail, skiing; designer Lance Wyman.

Quantity sold: 139,031.

**Aug. 26-Sept. 2, 1972, EXFILBRA, Fourth Inter-American Philatelic Exhibition, Rio de Janeiro, Brazil.**

Reproduction of U.S. 1930 $1.30 Graf Zeppelin issue, designers C.A. Hall and A.R. Meissner; and two 1929 Brazil airmail issues: the 200 rcis Santos-Dumont Airship, and the 300r Augusto Severo Airship "Pax."

Quantity sold: 118,904.

**Aug. 28-30, 1972, National Postal Forum, Washington, D.C.**

Reproduction of block of four of 1971 8¢ USPS emblem regular issue, designer Raymond Loewy-William Smith, Inc., modeler Ronald C. Sharpe.

Quantity sold: 114,000.

**April 30, 1973, Special issue souvenir card to U.S. Postal Service employees for "Postal People Day."**

The USPS issued a special 11 by 14 inch souvenir card to all postal employees; the card was distributed free, and was not available to the general public. Card reproduces the ten 8¢ 1973 Postal People stamps, designed by Edward Vebell, and the inscriptions imprinted on the backs.

**May 11-20, 1973, IBRA, International Philatelic Exhibition, Munich, Germany.**

Reproduction of the official show emblem, and 1930 65¢ U.S. Graf Zeppelin issue, designers C.A. Hall and A.R. Meissner.

Quantity sold: 133,292.

**July 4-7, 1973, APEX, International Airmail Exposition, Manchester, England.**

Reproduction of 1918 24¢ U.S. airmail error, with inverted illustration of the Curtiss Jenny airplane, designer C.A. Huston; the 1927 Newfoundland 60¢ De Pinedo airmail issue; and the 1925 Honduras 25¢ airmail surcharge.

Quantity sold: 115,932.

**Aug. 19-Sept. 2, 1973, POLSKA, World Philatelic Exhibition in Poznan, Poland.**

Reproduction of three stamps honoring Nicolaus Copernicus: 1973 8¢ U.S. commemorative, designed by Alvin Eisenman from an 18th-century engraving; and two 1972 Polish issues, of 1 zloty and 1.50zl values.

Quantity sold: 156,536.

**Feb. 3-6, 1974, National Hobby Industry Trade Show, Chicago, Ill.**

Reproduction of block of four of 1972 Colonial Craftsmen from Bicentennial series, designed by Leonard Everett Fisher, flanked on left by enlarged views of silversmith and glassblower vignettes.

Quantity sold: 93,994.

**June 7-16, 1974, INTERNABA, International Stamp Exhibition, Basel, Switzerland.**

Reproduction of eight 1974 10¢ stamps commemorating the centennial of the Universal Postal Union, above four-language message from Postmaster General E.T. Klassen, honoring UPU centennial and the Swiss Philatelic Societies.

The eight stamps were designed by Bradbury Thompson from the following paintings: Hokusai's "Five Feminine Virtues;" John Fredrick Peto's "Old Scraps;" Jean Etienne Liotard's "The Lovely Reader;" Gerard Terborch's "Lady Writing Letter;" Thomas Gainsborough's portrait of Mrs. John Douglas; Francisco de Goya's portrait of Don Antonio Noriega; Raphael's Michelangelo from "School of Athens;" and Jean-Baptiste Simeon Chardin's inkwell and quill from "Boy with a Top."

Quantity sold: 65,000.

**Sept. 21-29, 1974, STOCKHOLMIA, International Philatelic Exhibition, Stockholm, Sweden.**

Reproduction of 1938 3¢ U.S. Swedish-Finnish Tercentenary issue, designer A.R. Meissner, from painting "Landing of the First Swedish and Finnish Settlers in America," by Stanley M. Arthurs; 1946 10-ore Swedish reengraved regular issue of King Gustaf V, from the 1939 10o regular issue; and the 1967 45o King Gustav VI Adolf issue on his 85th birthday.

Quantity sold: 75,500.

**Oct. 26-Nov. 3, 1974, EXFILMEX, Inter-American Philatelic Exposition, Mexico City, Mexico.**

Reproduction of 1960 commemorative of the 150th anniversary of Mexican independence, one from both countries of the joint U.S.-Mexican issue, designers Leon Helguera and C.R. Chickering; U.S. 4¢ value and English inscriptions, Mexican 30-centavo value and Spanish inscription.

Quantity sold: 75,000.

**April 4-13, 1975, ESPANA, World Stamp Exhibition, Madrid, Spain.**

Reproduction of 4¢ 1893 U.S. Columbian issue of the fleet of Columbus, from a Spanish engraving of the ships Nina, Pinta and Santa Maria; and the 5¢ 1965 Florida Quadricentennial commemorative joint issue with Spain (3-peseta value), designer Brook Temple.

Quantity sold: 106,765.

**June 6-16, 1975, ARPHILA Exhibition, Paris, France.**

Reproduction of three stamps commemorating art: 1965 French issue, Raoul Dufy's "The Red Violin;" U.S. 1961 4¢ issue of Frederic Remington's "The Smoke Signal," designer C.R. Chickering; and 1962 4¢ issue of Winslow Homer's "Breezing Up," designer V.S. McCloskey Jr. Beneath the stamps is a two-language message from Postmaster General Benjamin Franklin Bailar.

Quantity sold: 79,932.

**April 1-4, 1976, WERABA '76, Third International Space Stamp Exhibition, Zurich, Switzerland.**

Reproduction of se-tenant pair, 1971 8¢ U.S. Space Achievement issue, designer Robert McCall. Canceled card franked with 10¢ 1975 Apollo-Soyuz se-tenant pair (20¢ total postage).

Quantity sold: 79,000.

**May 30-Sept. 6, 1976, Bicentennial Exposition on Science and Technology, Kennedy Space Center, Fla.**

Reproduction of 1969 10¢ airmail "Moon Landing" stamp, designer Paul Calle. Canceled card franked with 1975 10¢ Pioneer and 1975 10¢ Mariner stamps (20¢ total postage).

Quantity sold: 108,983.

**July 26, 1976, Colorado Centennial (Aug. 1), U.S. Bicentennial commemorative card.**

Reproduction of 1898 5¢ Trans-Mississippi issue, "Fremont on Rocky Mountains" (designer Raymond Ostrander Smith, from J.W. Orr illustration); 1934 4¢ Mesa Verde National Park issue (designer V.S. McCloskey Jr.); 1976 13¢ Colorado state flag from 50 State Flags issue (designer Walt Reed, modeler Peter Cocci). Canceled card franked with 1976 13¢ Franklin stamp.

Quantity sold: 84,833.

**Aug. 20-29, 1976, HAFNIA '76, Copenhagen, Denmark.**

Marks the 125th anniversary of Denmark's first postage stamp, reproduced on the card, along with the 1851 1¢ Franklin stamp, designer Edward Purcell (questionable designation). Canceled card franked with 1976 13¢ Franklin stamp.

Quantity sold: 85,558.

**Oct. 14-24, 1976, ITALIA '76, Milan, Italy.**

Reproduces 1951 Italian stamp honoring Christopher Columbus and 1952 Italian stamp noting Leonardo da Vinci, plus the 1960 U.S. 4¢ "Champion of Liberty" issue in honor of Guiseppe Garibaldi, designers Arnold Copeland, Ervine Metzl and William H. Buckley. Canceled card franked with 1976 13¢ Franklin stamp.

Quantity sold: 86,854.

**Oct. 30-31, 1976, NORDPOSTA '76, Hamburg, Germany.**

Reproductions of 1959 10 pfennig+5pf German stamp marking the centenary of Hamburg stamps, 50pf+25pf 1966 German stamp honoring Gen. (Baron) Friedrich Wilhelm von Steuben, designer A.R. Meissner. Canceled card franked with 1976 13¢ Clara Maass stamp.

Quantity sold: 82,652.

**May 26-June 5, AMPHILEX '77, Amsterdam, The Netherlands.**

Reproductions of two Netherlands definitives depicting Queen Wilhelmina (1894 5¢ issue and 1947 25¢ issue) and the U.S. 1953 3¢ New York commemorative, designer C.R. Chickering. Canceled card franked with 1977 13¢ Lindbergh flight stamp.

Quantity sold: 87,973.

**Aug. 28-Sept. 4, 1977, SAN MARINO '77, Republic of San Marino.**

Reproduction of the first-issue 1877 San Marino 2-centesimi stamp and the first two U.S. stamps, the 5¢ Franklin and 10¢ Washington of 1847. U.S. stamp reproductions taken from new engravings closely matching the originals (not the official reprints); 5¢ Franklin reproduction vignette engraver Edward P. Archer, lettering engraver Robert G. Culin; 10¢ vignette engraver John S. Wallace Jr., lettering engraver James L. Goodbody. Card designed and modeled by Peter Cocci. Canceled card franked with 1977 13¢ Lafayette stamp.

Quantity issued: 75,000 (estimate).

**March 20-29, 1978, ROCPEX '78, Taipei, Taiwan, Republic of China.**

Reproduction of block of four 1977 13¢ Pueblo Pottery stamps (denominations removed), designed by Ford Ruthling, and two values ($1 and $8) from the second Porcelain Series of the Republic of China, 1973. Canceled cards were not offically prepared; sold mint only.

Quantity issued: 75,000 (estimate).

**May 20-25, 1978, NAPOSTA '78, Frankfurt am Main, Federal Republic of Germany.**

Reproduction of the 70-pfennig German stamp of 1976 honoring Carl Schurz and the U.S. Bicentennial, and the 3¢ Lincoln and 11¢ Hayes issues of the U.S. 1922-25 definitive series. Canceled card franked with 1975 13¢ Eagle and Shield definitive.

Quantity issued: 75,000 (estimate).

**Sept. 15-23, 1979, BRASILIANA '79, Rio de Janeiro, Brazil.**

Reproduction of 1973 20-centavo stamp honoring Alberto Santos-Dumont and the 1978 31¢ U.S. airmail se-tenant pair honoring the Wright Brothers, designed by Ken Dallison. Canceled card franked with 1978 Wright Brothers airmail pair (two 31¢ stamps).

Quantity issued: 75,000 (estimate).

**Nov. 2-4, 1979, JAPEX '79, Tokyo, Japan.**

Reproduction of the 15-yen Japan EXPO '70 stamp (first issue) and the 1960 4¢ U.S. issue honoring ties between the United States and Japan, designed by Gyo Fujikawa. Canceled card franked with 1978 15¢ Fort McHenry Flag definitive.

Quantity issued: 75,000 (estimate).

**May 6-14, 1980, LONDON 1980, London, England.**

Reproduction (enlarged) of the 1907 2¢ U.S. commemorative honoring Jamestown, designed by M.W. Baldwin. Canceled cards not officially prepared; sold mint only.

Quantity issued: 80,000 (estimate).

**June 13-22, 1980, NORWEX '80, Oslo, Norway.**

Reproduction of the 1975 Norwegian 1.25-krone American emigration sesquicentennial issue and the U.S. 2¢ and 5¢ Norse-American stamps, designed by C.A. Huston. Canceled cards franked with 1980 15¢ Winter Olympics commemorative.

Quantity issued: 80,000 (estimate).

**Nov. 15-19, 1980, ESSEN '80, Essen, Federal Republic of Germany.**

Reproduction of a 1954 West German stamp noting the 500th anniversary of printing by movable type, and a U.S. 1952 3¢ stamp with the same theme (designer V.S. McCloskey Jr.). Canceled cards have the 15¢ Albert Einstein commemorative affixed.

Quantity issued: 80,000 (estimate).

**May 22-31, 1981, WIPA '81, Vienna, Austria.**

Reproduction of a 1967 Austrian stamp marking the 125th anniversary of the Vienna Philharmonic Orchestra, and a 1964 U.S. 5¢ commemorative for American Music (designer Bradbury Thompson). Canceled cards have the 18¢ Flag stamp affixed.

Quantity issued: 80,000 (estimate).

**Oct. 1-31, 1981, National Stamp Collecting Month.**

Reproduction of the $5 Columbian commemorative from the United States in 1893, plus the U.S. 18¢ Space Achievements stamp picturing the Space Shuttle "Columbia" from the eight-design se-tenant issue of 1981 (single design showing landing approach only). Canceled cards have the 18¢ Flag coil stamp affixed.

Quantity issued: 100,000 (estimate).

**Oct. 9-18, 1981, PHILATOKYO '81, Tokyo, Japan.**

Reproduction of 1963 Japanese stamp noting letter writing, plus U.S. 1974 Universal Postal Union commemorative depicting letter writing (single Hokusai design only from eight-design set, designed by Bradbury Thompson). Canceled cards have a pair of the 15¢ Letter Writing se-tenant stamps affixed.

Quantity issued: 80,000 (estimate).

**Nov. 7-9, 1981, NORDPOSTA '81, Hamburg, Federal Republic of Germany.**

Reproduction of a German semipostal with a ship theme, plus the 1944 U.S. 3¢ Steamship issue (designer V.S. McCloskey Jr.). Canceled cards have the nondenominated "C" stamp (20¢) affixed.

Quantity issued: 80,000 (estimate).

**May 20-24, 1982, CANADA '82, Toronto, Ontario, Canada.**

Reproductions of the 1859 Canada Beaver issue and the 1869 U.S. Eagle and Shield pictorial issue. Canceled cards franked with 20¢ Flag definitive.

Quantity issued: 80,000 (estimate).

**June 11-21, 1982, PHILEXFRANCE '82, Paris, France.**

Reproductions of the 1976 French American Bicentennial commemorative and the 1978 U.S. French Alliance commemorative. Canceled cards franked with a se-tenant pair of the 18¢ Battles of Yorktown-Virginia Capes commemoratives.

Quantity issued: 80,000 (estimate).

**Oct. 1-31, 1982, National Stamp Collecting Month.**

Details unavailable as this goes to press.

**Oct. 12-17, 1982, ESPAMER '82, San Juan, Puerto Rico.**

Details unavailable as this goes to press.

# United Nations Postal Administration

Souvenir cards have been issued by the United Nations at the rate of two per year since 1972. Each card bears reproductions of the U.N. commemorative stamps issued on the same day in conjunction with the same event as the card.

The cards also include past U.N. issues on similar themes, with foreign denominations (when included) expressed in Swiss and/or Austrian units. The 8 by 6 inch cards also include an English message from the U.N. secretary-general.

Cards are only available for 90 days after issue. For the first 60 days, sales are limited to five cards per order, then unlimited quantities are available for the last 30 days of sale, while supplies last. Since the cards are generally issued in the first half and the second half of the

year, there is never more than one card available at any one time.

The cards generally sell for $1 mint, with additional charge for postage and cancellation determined by the value of the stamps issued. Orders may be mailed to **UNPA, Box 5900, New York, N.Y. 10017.**

Following is a list of all UNPA souvenir cards, with descriptions of the stamps depicted, card printing, and quantities, when available. Quantity sold should be the closest indication of cards now in circulation.

### April 7, 1972, World Health Day.

New 15¢ issue, designed by George Hamori of Australia, with Leonardo da Vinci's "Proportions of Man" over graphic design; 1956 3¢ World Health Organization issue, designed by Olav S. Mathiesen of Denmark, engraved by A.B. Crossett; 1962 4¢ World Against Malaria issue and 1966 WHO headquarters issue, designed by Rashid-ud Din of Pakistan; 1970 6¢ Fight Cancer issue, designed by Leonard Mitchell of New Zealand.

Card designed by Herbert M. Sanborn of the U.S., printed by Arts Graphiques/Imprimeries Populaires of Geneva, Switzerland (in two printings, with two varieties in both printings). Colors: eight, with engraving.

Quantity issued: 160,000. Quantity sold: 158,934 (all sold mint).

### Nov. 17, 1972, Art on U.N. Stamps.

New 8¢ issue with reproduction of Jose Maria Sert's "The Five Continents," four 1967 issues (4¢ Peace, 5¢ Justice, 10¢ Fraternity and 15¢ Truth) from reliefs on General Assembly Hall doors by Ernest Cormier, 1967 6¢ issue depicting Marc Chagall's "The Kiss of Peace" from a Hans Lippmann photograph, 1968 6¢ issue from Henrik Starcke's statue in the Trusteeship Council, 1970 6¢ "Peace Bell" gift to U.N. from the Japanese, and 1971 8¢ issue of Pablo Picasso's "Maia," all designed by Ole Hamann; two 1969 issues, 6¢ and 13¢ stamps from a detail of "The Four Seasons and the Genius of the Year" mosaic in the Delegates' North Lounge at the U.N.

Card designed by Olav S. Mathiesen, Denmark; printed by Bruder Rosenbaum, Austria. Colors: 10.

Quantity issued: 400,000. Quantity sold: 304,476 (146,889 mint, 81,301 first day New York, 76,286 first day Geneva).

### March 9, 1973, Disarmament Decade (1970-1979).

New 8¢ issue, designed by Kurt Plowitz of the U.S. and Ole Hamann of Denmark; 1964 5¢ locked Atomic Blast issue and 1967 6¢ Isaiah Quotation issue, designed by O. Hamann; 1965 15¢ issue of the U.N. Charter's opening words, designed by Olav S. Mathiesen of Denmark; 1972 8¢ Nuclear Nonproliferation issue, designed by Arne Johnson of Norway.

Card designed by Olav S. Mathiesen, Denmark; offset printed by Heraclio Fournier, S.A. of Spain. Colors: 16.

Quantity issued: 400,000. Quantity sold: 299,700 (142,149 mint, 81,020 first day New York, 76,531 first day Geneva).

### Nov. 16, 1973, 25th anniversary of the Universal Declaration of Human Rights.

New 8¢ issue, designed by Alfredo Guerra of the U.S.; annual Human Rights issues from 1952-1958: 1952 3¢ issue, designed by Hubert Woyty-Wimmer, engraved by A.B. Crossett; 1953 5¢ issue, designed by Leon Helguera, engraved by A.B. Crossett and H. Woyty-Wimmer; 1954 3¢ issue, designed by Leonard C. Mitchell, engraved by A.B. Crossett; 1955 3¢ issue, designed by H. Woyty-Wimmer, engraved by E. Dickinson; 1956 3¢ issue, designed by Rashid-ud Din, engraved by A.B. Crossett; 1957 8¢ issue, designed by Olav S. Mathiesen, engraved by A.B. Crossett; 1958 8¢ issue, designed by Leonard C. Mitchell, engraved by W. Hauck; 1963 5¢ 15th anniversary issue, designed by Rashid-ud Din; 1968 6¢ International Human Rights Year issue, designed by Robert Perrot of France.

Card designed by Olav S. Mathiesen, Denmark; offset printed by Ashton-Potter of Canada. Colors: 15.

Quantity issued: 350,000. Quantity sold: 233,364 (102,678 mint, 70,445 first day New York, 60,241 first day Geneva).

### March 22, 1974, Universal Postal Union Centennial.

New 10¢, 30-centime and 60c issues, designed by Arne Johnson of Norway; 1971 20¢ and 75c UPU issues, designed by Olav S. Mathiesen of Denmark; 1953 3¢ and 5¢ UPU issues, designed by Hubert Woyty-Wimmer, engraved by A.B. Crossett.

Card designed by Olav S. Mathiesen, Denmark; offset printed by Ashton-Potter Limited of Canada. Colors: 13.

Quantity issued: 350,000. Quantity sold: 259,696 (132,585 mint, 61,801 first day New York, 65,310 first day Geneva).

### Oct. 18, 1974, World Population Year.

New 10¢, 18¢, 60c and 80c issues, designed by Henry Bencsath of the U.S.; 1965 4¢, 5¢ and 11¢ Population Trend issue, designed by Olav S. Mathiesen of Denmark.

Card designed by David Dewhurst of the United States, offset printed by Heraclio Fournier, S.A. of Spain. Colors: 14.

Quantity issued: 350,000. Quantity sold: 173,039 (75,258 mint, 50,082 first day New York, 47,699 first day Geneva).

### March 14, 1975, Peaceful Uses of Outer Space.

New 10¢, 26¢, 60c and 90c issues, designed by Henry Bencsath; 1962 4¢ (English inscription) and 11¢ (French inscription) Peaceful Uses of Outer Space Committee issue, designed by Kurt Plowitz, engraved by H. Cole.

Card designed by Olav S. Mathiesen, Denmark; offset printed by S. Setelipaino of Finland. Colors: eight.

Quantity issued: 300,000. Quantity sold: 191,594 (91,215 mint, 52,375 first day New York, 48,004 first day Geneva).

**Nov. 21, 1975, United Nations Peace-Keeping Operations.**

New 13¢, 26¢, 60c and 70c issues, designed by Eeva Oivo of Finland; 1957 8¢ U.N. Emergency Force and 1966 15¢ U.N. Observer issues, designed by Ole S. Hamann of Denmark; 1962 11¢ U.N. Congo Operation and 1965 5¢ U.N. Cyprus Force issues, designed by George Hamori of Australia; 1963 25¢ UNTEA issue, designed by Henry Bencsath of the U.S.

Card designed by Olav S. Mathiesen, Denmark; printed by S. Setelipaino of Finland. Colors: 15.

Quantity issued: 300,000. Quantity sold: 185,934 (93,193 mint, 49,607 first day New York, 43,134 first day Geneva).

**March 12, 1976, 30th Anniversary, World Federation of United Nations Associations.**

New 13¢, 26¢ and 90c issue, designed by George Hamori of Australia; 1966 5¢ (English) and 15¢ (French) issues, designed by Olav S. Mathiesen of Denmark.

Card designed by Olav S. Mathiesen, Denmark; printed by Heraclio Fournier, S.A. of Spain. Colors: nine.

Quantity issued: 300,000. Quantity sold: 165,298 (81,607 mint, 43,971 first day New York, 39,720 first day Geneva).

**Nov. 19, 1976, United Nations World Food Council.**

New 13¢ and 70c issues, designed by Eliezer Weishoff of Israel; 1963 5¢ and 11¢ Freedom from Hunger issue designed by Ole S. Hamann of Denmark; 1971 13¢ and 50c World Food Program issue, designed by Olav S. Mathiesen of Denmark.

Card designed by Olav S. Mathiesen, Denmark; printed by Questa Colour Security Printers Ltd. of England. Size was 1/4-inch shorter than normal in both dimensions. Colors: 12.

Quantity issued: 250,000. Quantity sold: 108,325 (45,137 mint, 34,172 first day New York, 29,016 first day Geneva).

**March 11, 1977, United Nations World Intellectual Property Organization.**

New 13¢, 31¢ and 80c issues, designed by Eliezer Weishoff of Israel; 1953 3¢ UPU and 1956 3¢ ITU issues, designed by Hubert Woyty-Wimmer of Austria; 1955 3¢ ICAO and 1960 4¢ IBRD issues, designed by Angel Medina-Medina of Uruguay; 1961 4¢ International Monetary Fund, designed by Roy E. Carlson of the United States and Hordur Karlsson of Iceland; 1964 6¢ IMCO, designed by Henry Bencsath of the United States (emblem by Olav S. Mathiesen of Denmark); 1956 3¢ WHO, designed by Olav Mathiesen; 1954 3¢ FAO, de-

signed by Dirk Van Gelder of The Netherlands, and 3¢ ILO, designed by Jose Renau of Mexico; 1955 3¢ UNESCO, designed by George Hamori of Australia; 1957 3¢ WMO, designed by Alan L. Pollock of Canada; 1958 3¢ IAEA, designed by Robert Perrot of France.

Card designed by Olav S. Mathiesen, Denmark; printed by Heraclio Fournier, S. A. of Spain. Colors: 20.

Quantity issued: 250,000. Quantity sold: 151,227 (65,219 mint, 41,495 first day New York, 44,513 first day Geneva).

**Sept. 19, 1977, Combat Racism.**

New 13¢ and 25¢ issues, designed by B.K. Wiese of Germany, and 40c and 1.10fr issues, designed by M.A. Munnawar of Pakistan; 1971 8¢ and 30¢ stamps designed by Daniel Gonzagup and 13¢ and 50¢ stamp designed by Ole Hamann, noting "Eliminate Racial Discrimination."

Card designed by Olav S. Mathiesen, Denmark; printed by S. Setelipaino of Finland. Colors: 12.

Quantity issued: 250,000. Quantity sold: 151,464 (69,484 mint, 41,335 first day New York, 40,645 first day Geneva).

**May 5, 1978, Namibia.**

New 13¢, 18¢ and 80c issues, designed by Cafiro Tomei, Italy; 1975 10¢, 18¢, 50c and 1.30fr Namibia issues, designed by Henry Bencsath, U.S.; 1973 8¢, 15¢ and 60c Namibia issues, designed by George Hamori, Australia.

Card designed by T. Lee, China; printed by Government Printing Office, Austria. Colors: 16.

Quantity issued: 225,000.

**June 12, 1978, International Civil Aviation Organization.**

New 13¢ and 25¢ issues, designed by Cemalettin Mutver, Turkey, and 70c and 80c issues, designed by Tomas Savrda, U.S.; 1955 3¢ and 8¢ ICAO issues, designed by Angel Medina-Medina, Uruguay, engraved by E. Dickinson.

Card designed by Olav S. Mathiesen, Denmark; printed by Heraclio Fournier, S.A., Spain. Colors: 11.

Quantity issued: 225,000.

**May 4, 1979, International Year of the Child.**

New 15¢ and 31¢ issues, designed by Helena Matuszewska, Poland, and 80c and 1.10fr issues, designed by Arieh Glaser, Israel; 1951 5¢ UNICEF issue, designed and engraved by S.L. Hartz, The Netherlands; 1961 3¢ UNICEF issue, designed by Minoru Hisano, Japan; 1966 4¢, 5¢ and 11¢ UNICEF issues, designed by Kurt Plowitz, U.S.

Card designed by Ole Hamann, Denmark; printed by Heraclio Fournier, S.A., Spain. Colors: 12.

Quantity issued: 225,000.

**Nov. 9, 1979, International Court of Justice.**

New 15¢ and 20¢ issues, designed by Henning Simon, Denmark, and 80c and 1.10fr issues, designed by K. Maeno, Japan; 1961 4¢ and 8¢ ICJ issues, designed by Kurt Plowitz, U.S. (based on Scales of Justice by Raphael, Italy).

Card designed by David Dewhurst, United States; printed by S. Setelipaino, Finland. Colors: 12.

Quantity issued: 200,000.

### March 7, 1980, U.N. Decade for Women.

New 15¢ issue designed by Susanne Rotten-fusser, West Germany, 40c issue designed by M.A. Munnawar, Pakistan, and 4s issue designed by Gunnar Janssen, West Germany; 1975 10¢ International Women's Year issue, designed by Asher Kalderon and Esther Kurti, Israel.

Card designed by David Dewhurst, United States; printed by Questa Colour Security Printers, United Kingdom.

Quantity issued: 200,000.

### Nov. 21, 1980, Economic and Social Council.

New 15¢ and 40c issues designed by Eliezer Weishoff, Israel, 40¢ and 4s issues designed by Dietman Kowall, Federal Republic of Germany, and 70c and 6s issues designed by Angel Medina-Medina, Uruguay; 1958 ECOSOC 4¢ and 8¢ issues designed by Ole Hamann, Denmark.

Card designed by Rocco Callari, United States; printed by Ashton-Potter Ltd., Canada.

Quantity issued: 260,000.

### March 6, 1981, International Year of Disabled Persons.

New 20¢, 1.50fr, 4s and 6s issues designed by Sophia van Heeswijk, West Berlin, and 35¢ and 40c issues designed by G.P. Van der Hyde, Australia.

Card designed by Thomas Lee, China; printed by Heraclio Fournier, S.A., Spain.

Quantity issued: 325,000.

### May 29, 1981, New and Renewable Sources of Energy.

New 20¢ and 1.10fr issues designed by Ulrike Dreyer, Federal Republic of Germany, and 40¢ and 7.50s issues designed by Robert Perrot, France.

Card designed by Rocco Callari, United States; printed by S. Setelipaino, Finland.

Quantity issued: 325,000.

### March 19, 1982, Human Environment.

New 20¢ issue designed by Philine Hartert, Federal Republic of Germany, 40c issue designed by Sybille Brunner, Federal Republic of Germany, and 5s issue designed by Peer-Ulrich Bremer, Federal Republic of Germany; 1972 15¢ and 80c Human Environment issues designed by Robert Perrot, France.

Card designed by Thomas Lee, China; printed by J. Enschede en Zonen, Netherlands.

Quantity issued: 325,000.

### June 11, 1982, Exploration and Peaceful Uses of Outer Space.

New 20¢ and 80c issues designed by Wiktor C. Nerwinski, Poland, and 1fr and 5s issues designed by George Hamori, Australia; 1962 4¢ Peaceful Uses of Outer Space issue designed by Kurt Plowitz, United States; 1975 10¢ and 60c Peaceful Uses of Outer Space issue designed by Henry Bencsath, United States.

Card designed by Rocco Callari, United States; printed by Joh. Enschede en Zonen, Netherlands.

Quantity issued: 325,000.

# Rarities                    12

# Major Rarities of Philately

Ownership of rare stamps has been the quest of all great collectors since the first postage stamps were issued. It is the hope of every collector, regardless of his collecting interests, to discover a major variety, error, or uncataloged issue.

Men have deserted their families, lost their businesses, stolen and even killed to attain ownership of the ultimate, a tiny piece of paper with possibly little or no aesthetic or intrinsic value.

Perhaps the most famous collector, Count Phillippe la Renotiere von Ferrari, made it his lifelong ambition to obtain every stamp of the world. In his pursuit, Ferrari attained many forgeries, but he also comprised one of the most remarkable collections of rarities the world has ever known.

Col. Edward H.R. Green, son of financial wizard Hetty Green, was one of the United States' most renowned collectors. He is especially noted for his purchase of the 1918 24-cent airmail invert sheet.

Other collectors who have successfully obtained several of the world's rarities include Arthur Hind, Maurice Burrus, Alfred Caspary, Philip H. Ward Jr., Alfred F. Lichtenstein, and Theodore Champion.

What determines the value of these stamps is somewhat of a mystery, although the stamp's beauty, history and the popularity of the issuing country are often determining factors.

The following listing is by no means an attempt to include every rarity of the world but is rather a presentation of the history of some of the more famous rarities. Scott catalog numbers are given for easy reference.

## Baden 1851
## 9-Kreuzer Blue Green

Only one sheet was believed to have been printed of the Baden 1851 9kr blue-green (Scott 4b). The color error occurred when the stamp was printed on the blue-green paper of the 6kr rather than the proper rose paper.

One copy of the error exists on a piece bearing the numeral cancellation "1" (Aachen) and is located in the Theodore Champion collection in Paris, France.

Baron von Turckheim possessed two covers addressed to his father, a counselor of legation in Karlsruhe, Germany. One cover is dated July 27, 1851 "Orschweier" while the other is dated Aug. 25, 1851 "Ettenheim."

The 9kr error was evidently used to pay the 6kr rate of postage.

The "Orschweier" specimen is a part of the collection in the German Postal Museum. The "Ettenheim" cover was sold to Herbert Bloch for $20,000 during the H.R. Harmer, Inc. sale of the Caspary collection in April 1956. It later found its way into the John R. Boker Jr. collection.

## Bavaria 1849 1-Kreuzer
## Black Tete-Beche

The 1849 1kr black was the first stamp issued in Bavaria. During the printing process, a cliche was inserted into the printing plate upside down, resulting in a tete-beche issue (1b).

Three tete-beches are known of this issue, each in a different position. The most famous of this variety is the block of 12 from the Ferrari collection. The block was purchased in 1923 by Alfred F. Lichtenstein and was acquired by Lichtenstein's daughter, Louise Boyd Dale, upon his death.

The block is presently owned by the Anne Boyd Lichtenstein Foundation.

1

2

3

4

5

1) Bermuda Perot Provisionals
2) Baden 1851 9 kreuzer
3) Bavaria 1849 tete-beche
4) British Guiana Cottonreels
5) British Guiana 1-cent magenta

## Bermuda
## Perot Provisionals

The postmaster of Hamilton, Bermuda, William B. Perot, produced provisional stamps (X1-3) from 1848-54 by striking his postmarking handstamp on sheets of gummed paper.

The 1-penny provisionals, known as the Perot Provisionals, feature the inscription "HAMILTON+BERMUDA+" in a circle with "One Penny" handwritten above the year date. Perot's signature appears below the year.

The provisionals first appeared in black ink, but this was later changed to red. Only 11 have been found. Two 1853 provisionals on thick white paper were the only recorded unsevered pair, but they were separated in 1934.

Baron S. Leuhusen, a Bermuda shipping magnate, paid £30,000 for a Bermuda Perot of 1849, one of only two known. A 1p red, bluish on cover realized $210,000 during the April 5, 1980, Robert A. Siegel auction held in New York City.

On Feb. 18, 1981, a copy was sold at a Stanley Gibbons auction in New York for $46,200. Another known copy off cover resides in the British Royal Collection.

## British Guiana
## 1851 2-Cent Pale Rose

The British Guiana 1851 2¢ pale rose "cotton-reel" (1) was issued to pay postage on local delivery.

The stamps are called "cottonreels" because they resemble the labels on reels of cotton. They were printed in a local newspaper office and were initialed by a postal clerk as a guard against forgery. Only 10 copies of the 2¢ stamp are known to exist.

Of the surviving issues, six appear in pairs on covers paying the normal delivery postage of 4¢. The most famous cover was sent from Demerara to Plantation of Good Hope on Nov. 25, 1851.

This cover was owned by Ferrari and was purchased by Maurice Burrus in 1921. Raymond H. Weill purchased the cover during the 1963 Robson Lowe auction.

The rare "Miss Rose" entire, bearing a pair of the 2¢ stamp, was sold to a South American collector during Stanley Gibbons auction of the Claude Cartier collection on April 21, 1977. The entire realized £70,000.

## British Guiana
## 1856 1-Cent Magenta

The British Guiana 1¢ black on magenta (13) was a provisional stamp issued in Demerara, British Guiana (now Georgetown, Guyana), when a supply of regulars failed to arrive.

The octagon-shaped stamp is imperforate and bears the rimless postmark of Demerara dated "AP 4 1856." The design is similar to the colony's seal depicting a ship and the Latin motto, "Damus Petimus/Que Vicissim," (We Give and We Seek in Return).

As a precaution against forgeries, the typeset provisionals were initialed by an official. The 1856 1¢ bears the initials of assistant postmaster E.D. Wight (E.D.W.) in the upper left corner of the stamp.

The stamp is the only known copy and was discovered by L. Vernon Vaughan in 1873.

Vaughan soaked the stamp from the original cover and sold it to N.R. McKinnon for $1.50. McKinnon later sold his entire collection to Wylie Hill of Glasgow, Scotland.

The 1¢ black on magenta was purchased by Thomas Ridpath for approximately $600 and again sold to Ferrari in the 1880s for a reputed $750.

After Ferrari's death in 1917, his collection, containing the rarity, was confiscated by France and sold, with proceeds being credited to the German War Reparations Account. The collection had been left to the Berlin Postal Museum in Ferrari's will.

The stamp was purchased on April 6, 1922, by Arthur Hind, Utica, N.Y., for approximately $35,250. It was then sold in 1940 to Frederick T. Small, an Australian living in Fort Lauderdale, Fla., for $42,500.

Small purchased the stamp through an agent and remained anonymous until after the sale of the rarity to Irwin Weinberg, Wilkes-Barre, Pa., on March 24, 1970.

Weinberg acquired the 1¢ black on magenta for a record-breaking bid of $280,000 during a world's rarities auction conducted by Robert A. Siegel Auction Galleries, Inc., at the Waldorf-Astoria Hotel, New York, N.Y.

On April 5, 1980, the famed stamp was again brought to the block by Robert A. Siegel Auction Galleries, Inc., when it was purchased by a private collector for a record $935,000 ($850,000 plus a 10 per cent buyer's premium).

## Canada
## 12-Penny Black

The Canada 12p black (3) was one of the first issues of the Province of Canada. The stamp was issued June 14, 1851, and features the portrait of Queen Victoria, a reproduction of a full-length painting by Alfred E. Chalon.

The 12p stamps were printed by Rawdon, Wright, Hatch and Edson on vertically laid paper. This poor quality paper proved quite unpopular with the public as well as with the postal authorities.

The impression of the queen was weak and the stamps did not adhere well to envelopes. The issue was soon discontinued.

Few sales of the stamps were made (possibly 1,510) because of the high value which was used

mostly for foreign correspondence. It is believed that a proof of the 12p black was erroneously used by the Canada Post Office in foreign mail, thus using a proof as a stamp.

On April 30, 1974, a copy of the 12p black was purchased by Andy Kosztandy, manager of the Postage Department of Charlton Numismatics Ltd., for $17,000.

The purchase was made during J.N. Sisson's auction at the King Edward Hotel, Toronto, Ont., Canada.

In 1975, a mint corner marginal pair was acquired by the Canadian National Postal Museum, Ottawa, Ont., Canada. The pair is valued at approximately $125,000.

A single copy realized $90,000 in a Greg Manning auction in 1978, the price being paid by a New York collector.

A single unused copy was also brought to the block April 5, 1980, by Robert A. Siegel Auction Galleries, commanding $75,000.

A record $126,500 was paid by a Canadian collector for a copy at the Greg Manning International Rarity Auction held May 10, 1980, in London, England.

## Canada 1868
## 2-Cent Green

The Canada 1868 2¢ green (32) on laid paper has been a controversial item for several years. The stamp was issued on April 1, 1868, shortly after the formation of the Dominion of Canada.

Most of the stamps of the "Large Queen" issue were printed on wove paper; however, a small quantity of 1¢, 2¢ and 3¢ stamps were printed on horizontal laid paper.

6

7

6) Canada 12-penny black
7) Canada 2-cent green

Only two copies of the 2¢ stamp have been reported. One of these copies was formerly in the L. Gerald Firth collection until it was purchased by Duane Hillmer, Omaha, Neb., during the J.N. Sissons' Firth collection auction in 1971.

The stamp was later purchased by Robert A. Siegel.

## Canada 1959
## Seaway Invert

The United States and Canada released a joint stamp issue June 26, 1959, to commemorate the opening of the St. Lawrence Seaway. Both stamps depict the Canadian maple leaf and the U.S. eagle side by side against a map of the Great Lakes region.

The Canadian Bank Note Co. of Ottawa was responsible for printing the Canada St. Lawrence Seaway issue in red and blue. The inverted error resulted when several panes of 50 were inadvertently fed into the press upside down for the second color (blue).

The 5-cent issue with center inverted (387a) was not detected by the printing inspectors. No more than four panes of 50 were sold to the public, and Canada Post reportedly retained one pane for its archives.

Of the errors which were printed, 162 were known to have survived, and few have appeared which have circulated through the mails.

A mint left sheet margin block of four brought $70,000 at the John W. Kaufmann, Inc. auction

8

9

8) Canada Seaway invert
9) Canal Zone bridge error

held in November 1979 in Washington, D.C. Myron Kaller, a New York philatelic agent and consultant, registered the bid on behalf of a Texas client.

A single copy, part of the collection of E.P. Peachey, was sold to an unidentified Toronto dealer for $10,500 during a November 1978 auction conducted by J.N. Sissons.

A single copy was knocked down at $19,000 during the Robert A. Siegel Auction Galleries sale of April 5, 1980.

A fine to very fine, never-hinged copy brought $17,500 (including 10 per cent buyer's premium) at Chandler's, Inc., May 21-22, 1980, auction in Evanston, Ill., while an extremely fine stamp commanded $17,000 at a Jan. 21-23, 1981, sale conducted by Richard Wolffers, Inc., in San Francisco.

A block of four was auctioned at the Robert A. Siegel Rarities of the World sale April 25, 1981, realizing $57,500.

## Canal Zone 1962
## Bridge Error

The Canal Zone issued a 4-cent stamp Oct. 12, 1962, to mark the opening of the Thatcher Ferry Bridge spanning the Panama Canal.

The Bureau of Engraving and Printing in Washington, D.C., produced the stamp which depicts a gray and black map of the Americas spanned by the Thatcher Ferry Bridge. A single sheet of 200 stamps received the black and gray imprint but erroneously was not sent through a second press for the bridge imprint. This sheet was later divided into panes of 50 stamps each.

The Canal Zone postal officials immediately confiscated three panes which bore the bridgeless errors (157a), but a fourth had already been purchased by Henry Ellis Harris, owner of the Boston-based philatelic firm bearing his name.

After the error was discovered, the Canal Zone Postal Administration ordered an intentional reprinting of 100,000 stamps without the bridge, explaining that these would be sold to the public at face value.

Harris filed suit against the Canal Zone Postal Administration seeking a preliminary and permanent injunction against the reprinting of the error.

After more than two years, Harris won his case, and the Canal Zone Postal Administration was ordered not to release the intentional misprint.

John W. Douglas, assistant attorney general for the U.S. Department of Justice Civil Division, stipulated the fate of three sheets confiscated by the Canal Zone authorities.

In a letter to Harris, Douglas noted that:

"One sheet of 50 Thatcher Ferry Bridge stamp variants will be laminated and donated to the Smithsonian Institution, Washington, D.C.; a second sheet of 50 . . . will be laminated and donated to the Canal Zone Government; and the remaining sheet of 50 . . . will be destroyed."

A plate block of 10 of the Canal Zone error brought $130,000 in the April 5, 1980 auction of Robert A. Siegel Auction Galleries.

A single realized $13,750 at a Peter Kenedi auction Nov. 10-14, 1980, in California. Another single sold for $16,500 at the Robert A. Siegel Rarities of the World sale on April 29, 1981.

Siegel sold a mint example, position 34, for $13,500 during his April 24, 1982 Rarities auction.

## Cape of Good Hope Triangular Errors

The 1 penny and 4p "Triangular" stamps of the Cape of Good Hope were issued in 1861 to meet a shortage of stamps. These stamps, printed by Messrs. Solomon and Co., are known as "woodblocks" because the dies were engraved on steel and reproduced by stereotyping impressions on wood.

During the printing of these stamps, a cliche of the 1p red was erroneously inserted in the printing frame of the 4p blue, resulting in a 1p blue (7b) and a 4p red (9b).

The most famous philatelic item containing these stamps is a cover bearing a block of four with three 1p red and one 4p red.

The cover was formerly in the Alfred F. Lichtenstein collection. Upon his death, the cover was acquired by his daughter, Louise Boyd Dale. The present owner of this rarity is the Anne Boyd Lichtenstein Foundation.

A 1p blue single realized $8,500 during the March 23, 1977 auction conducted by Robert A. Siegel Auction Galleries.

On Dec. 7, 1978, an unused 4p red was auctioned by Stanley Gibbons International for £47,500. Gibbons auctioned used copies of the 1p blue and 4p red on Nov. 20, 1979, for £7,500 and £7,000, respectively.

## France Tete-Beche Pairs

Tete-beche pairs of the French 10 centimes (1c), 15c (2b), 20c black (3c), 20c blue (4c), 25c (6c), 1 franc vermilion (8b), 1fr carmine (9a), 20c blue, bluish (15e), 80c lake (19a), 80c rose (20a) and 1fr lake, yellowish (21a) were among the first issues of France released in 1849.

The rarest item of this issue is the unused block of four with one tete-beche 1fr vermilion. The tete-beche occurred when an inverted cliche was inserted into the printing plate.

The unused block was discovered behind a desk and was acquired by Theodore Champion in 1931. Robert J. Gill later purchased the block which is currently the property of Duane Hillmer of Omaha, Neb.

The 1fr vermilion was discontinued because the color was too similar to the 40c orange in use at the same time. The 1fr carmine replaced the issue.

An unused block of eight and a used block of fifteen of the 1fr vermilion were owned by Maurice Burrus.

The block of fifteen, formed by a block of ten, two pairs and a single stamp, was sold for $56,000.

## Hawaiian Missionaries

The Hawaiian Missionary stamps were issued in October 1851 in denominations of 2¢, 5¢ and 13¢ (1-4). The stamps are so named because they were frequently used by the American missionaries on correspondence to the United States.

The rarest of the Missionary issue is the 2¢, which paid postage on newspapers and printed material to the U.S. Only 15 copies of this stamp are known to exist.

Two are in the Tapling collection at the British Museum and three are in the Hawaiian Postal Museum. Most others are in private collections.

A 2¢ realized $41,000 in 1963 at the H.R. Harmer, Inc. Burrus auction in New York City.

A 2¢ type II was purchased by Stanley Piller of California for $230,000 during the Nov. 18, 1980 Sotheby Parke Bernet Auction Co. sale.

10

11

10) Cape of Good Hope Triangles
11) France tete-beche

Piller was acting as agent for an anonymous collector.

During the same auction, Joseph Krois, president of National Philatelic Advisors Corp. of New York City, purchased a type I copy for $210,000.

Both items were previously in the Hawaiian collection of Ryohei Ishikawa.

A canceled 5¢ stamp was discovered in old correspondence by C.R. Sturtevant of Oakland, Calif., and was sold to H.J. Crocker of San Francisco, Calif.

A 5¢ blue top marginal copy, cut into slightly on part of one side, brought $42,500 during the Harmers of New York June 4-5, 1980 auction.

In 1903, a cover bearing the 2¢ and 5¢ Missionaries, as well as a pair of U.S. 1851 3¢ stamps, was found among papers in New Bedford, Mass.

The cover was purchased by George H. Worthington and later by Alfred H. Caspary. The Raymond H. Weill Co. acquired the cover in 1957 for $25,000 during the H.R. Harmer, Inc. sale of the Alfred H. Caspary collection.

The cover was later acquired by Alfred J. Ostheimer III and is now in the Hawaiian collection of the "Honolulu Advertiser."

In 1977, a set of four Hawaiian Missionary stamps was confiscated by the U.S. Customs Service after storage in a footlocker for more than 30 years.

12

13

12a

12) Hawaiian Missionaries
12a) Missionaries cover
13) "Black" Honduras

A man, who said the stamps were given to him by a German couple, attempted to sell the stamps which were then confiscated by U.S. Customs.

The stamps had reportedly been stolen from the Reichpostmuseum in Germany.

## Honduras 1925 'Black' Airmail

In 1922, Dr. Thomas C. Pounds, an American living in Honduras, requested that the government issue special stamps to be used with regular stamps on his newly formed airmail flight. Dr. Pounds was to receive the profits from the special issues.

The plans, however, were halted during the revolution in 1923. In 1925, obsolete postage stamps were sent to Dr. Pounds to be overprinted for use on the airmail service.

With the help of Karl Snow, Dr. Pounds overprinted the issues with the wording "Aero Correo." Due to a lack of facilities, the stamps are crudely printed.

The most unusual and rarest of the airmail overprints is the 1925 25 centavos on 10c with a black surcharge (C12). Four copies were to have existed at one time; however, only one can be located at this time.

A pair of the "Black" Honduras was reportedly sent in 1927 to John N. Luff of the Scott Stamp and Coin Co., by Raul Duron Membreno. After examination, the pair was returned to Membreno. The location of this pair is not known.

Another copy, originally given to Julio Ustariz by Dr. Pounds, was also sent to Luff for examination but was reportedly never returned.

The stamp later appeared in the Emil Bruechig collection. Its present whereabouts is unknown.

The only variety known today was purchased by H.A. Robinette of Washington, D.C., in 1930. Robinette sold the copy to Nicholas Sanabria, who in turn sold it to F.W. Kessler. Kessler was acting in behalf of Dr. Philip G. Cole.

On Oct. 27, 1939, the Economist Stamp Co. acquired the stamp for Oscar R. Lichtenstein for $5,300. The stamp was purchased by Thomas A. Matthews for $11,500 during the June 1957 auction conducted by Harmer, Rooke and Co.

Josiah K. Lilly acquired the famous "Black" Honduras for a record $24,500 during the F.W. Kessler sale on Feb. 27, 1961.

In 1968, the impressive Lilly collection was brought to the block by Robert A. Siegel. The Harmer, Rooke firm purchased the rarity for $29,000. It was later sold to Jared L. Johnson of Chandler's, Inc.

On Feb. 6, 1976, the stamp was sold by Andrew Levitt for over $80,000 to Johnson, who was acting on behalf of an unknown buyer.

## India 1854
## 4-Anna Red, Blue

The inverted head of Queen Victoria appearing on the 1854 4a red and blue of India (6c) resulted when the red sheets were placed inverted on the blue printing plates.

The error was discovered and corrected during the printing on one piece.

A copy of the error was exhibited at a meeting of the Royal Philatelic Society of London in 1974. Several were obtained by Stanley Gibbons in 1899, including a cover with two single inverts cut to shape. They were later separated and sold.

Thomas Tapling purchased a cover with two of the errors in 1890, and these are now in the Tapling collection, British Museum.

One was purchased by Henry J. Duveen and later sold to Alfred H. Caspary.

The stamp attained a winning bid of $1,150 during the Caspary sale conducted by H.R. Harmer, Inc., Feb. 24-26, 1958. Current standard catalogs value the stamp at $37,500.

## Mauritius 1847
## 1 Penny and 2p

The Mauritius 1p orange (1) and 2p dark blue (2) were the first stamps issued in the British colonies. Joseph Barnard, a watchmaker and jeweler in Mauritius, evidently forgot the inscription to be placed on the stamps and erroneously printed "Post Office" rather than "Post Paid."

The stamps were printed in time for use by Lady Gomm, the wife of Lt. Gov. W. Maynard Gomm, on invitations to a ball held in September 1847.

A total of 500 of each value were issued, although approximately 30 are known to exist today.

Two covers exist each bearing two stamps of the same denomination. The rarest cover, however, bears one stamp of each denomination.

This cover was sent to M. Lurguie in Bordeaux, France, from Port Louis, via Plymouth, England; Boulogne and Paris, France, on Oct. 4, 1847.

The cover was discovered in a file by a French boy in 1902. Mr. Lemaire purchased it on Jan. 17, 1903. It was later acquired by French collector Brunet de l'Argentiere.

In 1922, Arthur Hind purchased the cover; it was later acquired by Maurice Burrus during the H.R. Harmer auction of the Hind collection in London, England, in 1934.

Raymond H. Weill Co. purchased the cover for $78,400 during the 1963 Robson Lowe Ltd. sale in London. It changed hands once again when it was purchased by Hiroyuki Kanai in 1970 to add to his remarkable Mauritius collection.

Two first day covers exist of the Mauritius "Post Office" issues. One is located in the Tapling collection in the British Museum, while the other is reportedly preserved in the Royal collection at Buckingham Palace.

A cover bearing two copies of the 1p, sent from Mauritius to Bombay, India, on Jan. 4, 1850, was discovered in an Indian marketplace in 1897. It was purchased by George H. Worthington in 1906 and sold to Alfred F. Lichtenstein in 1917. Lichtenstein's daughter, Louise Boyd Dale, obtained the cover at the time of his death.

The price of $380,000 was paid by the Raymond H. Weill Co. during the H.R. Harmer, Inc. sale on Oct. 21, 1968.

14

15

15a

14) India 1854 invert
15) Post Office Mauritius
15a) Mauritius cover

"1"

16

17

18

19

A 1p single was acquired by a collector in India in 1870 and brought to England where it was discovered in 1946 in Folkestone.

The stamp was purchased by Sir Andrew Clark in 1947 who later sold it to an unknown collector.

This rarity was purchased by Rene Berlingin of Liechtenstein for $80,000 during the Nov. 25, 1976, auction conducted by Stanley Gibbons.

## Mexico 1935
## 20 Centavos

On April 16, 1935, Mexico released the 20c lake airmail issues with the legend, "AMELIA EARHART/VUELO/DE BUENA VOLUNTAD/MEXICO/1935," overprinted in violet.

The overprints were released to commemorate the nonstop flight of United States aviatrix Amelia Earhart from Mexico City to Newark, N.J., on May 8, 1935.

A total of 300 of the overprinted issues were released. Forty covers were carried on the flight.

Greg Manning Auctions sold a copy for $3,500 during its Jan. 5, 1981 sale.

## Spain 1851
## 2-Reales Blue

The 1851 2r blue error of Spain (10a) occurred when the cliche of the 2r was inserted in the plate of the 6r. Only three specimens are believed to exist.

A block of 14 or 15 containing the error was reportedly offered to A. Galvez in Madrid in 1899, but he refused to buy it. This block was later purchased by another dealer who separated it.

A pair containing the error was acquired by Ferrari and was later sold to King Carol II of Romania. Rene Berlingin purchased the pair in 1951.

An unused specimen is in the British Museum in London, England.

## Sweden 1855
## 3 Skilling-Banco

The color error of the Sweden 1855 3sk-bc orange occurred when the cliche of the 3sk was accidentally inserted in the plate of the 8sk orange.

This resulted in the orange stamp rather than the normal green stamp.

The only surviving copy is canceled and was discovered by G.W. Backman in 1885 in his grandfather's correspondence.

Backman sold the stamp to H. Lichtenstein, a Stockholm dealer, for 7 kronen. During the early 1890s, Lichtenstein sold the rarity to Sigmund Friedl.

Ferrari purchased the stamp in 1894. It then passed from the Ferrari collection to collections belonging to Count E. Leijonhufvud, C.P. Tamm,

16) Mexico 1935 Earhart
17) Spain 1851 error
18) Sweden 3 skilling-banco
19) Switzerland "Double Geneva"

Johann Ramberg, King Carol of Romania and was later offered by Stanley Gibbons.

The cancel reads, "Nya Kopparberget, July 13, 1857." The stamp was used to pay 8sk postage rather than the supplementary postage of 3sk.

The authenticity of this error was questioned in 1975 when Gilbert Svenson, director of the Swedish Postal Museum, announced that the stamp was a forgery. Svenson also made an offer to purchase the stamp at face value at that time.

Svenson stated that the orange of the stamp did not match the orange of the 8sk and that the paper of the upper half of the stamp differs from that of the lower half.

The error was reportedly sold at an October 1978 auction by Edgar Mohrmann and Co., Hamburg, Germany, for 1 million marks (approximately U.S. $500,000). This sale, however, was contested by two U.S. auctioneers.

## Switzerland 1843
## 10-Centimes Yellow-Green

The "Double Geneva" 10c yellow-green (2L1) was issued Sept. 30, 1843, by the Canton Geneva in Switzerland. The stamp was formed by the joining of two 5c stamps with a rectangle above the two stamps reading "10. PORT CANTONAL. CENT."

Varieties include the reversal of the two shields. The stamps were sold in sheets and the users were to cut the stamps themselves, sometimes cutting between the same stamps rather than dividing two sets of the double stamps. A vertical pair realized £26,250 sterling (about $53,500) during the May 5-6, 1976 auction conducted by Stanley Gibbons. Only six such pairs are known.

The Maurice Burrus block of six sold for $121,000 during the Burrus collection sale.

A mint block of 7½ from the Alfred Lichtenstein collection was purchased by Burrus and is now in the Swiss Postal Museum.

## Switzerland 1845
## 2½-Rappen Black

The 1845 2½rp black, crimson and blue of the Canton Basel in Switzerland (3L1) was issued July 1, 1845. The "Basel Dove" was in use for a short time for prepayment of mail services.

The stamps, designed by Melchior Berry, were the first to be printed in three colors. Postage stamps did not prove popular with the people of Basel and were withdrawn.

A block of 15 "Basel Doves" was discovered in a desk drawer and acquired by Ernst Muller of Basel when he purchased, in 1937, the Lichtenstein collection. Henry J. Duveen purchased the block for $1,745. The block was also owned by Iwan Bally before being placed in the Swiss Postal Museum.

## Switzerland
## 'Rayon' Issues

Switzerland was proclaimed a federal republic by the constitution adopted on Sept. 12, 1848. The federal administration of Switzerland issued 10-rappen black, red and yellow stamps in 1850 with a colored frame around the cross.

The stamps are referred to as "rayon" stamps as the amount of postage due was in accordance with the "rayon" or distance.

The three-color impressions proved expensive and the issue was discontinued. Approximately 10 copies are believed to exist with the yellow background inverted to the black and red colors.

The 1851 5rp light blue and red (9) is also a rare "rayon" issue with the colored frame around the cross. The frame was used to separate the colors but was later removed as it was considered to be against heraldic specifications.

An 1850 10rp with complete frame sold for $4,750 during the H.R. Harmer, Inc. sale of the

20

21

20) Switzerland "Basel Dove"
21) Switzerland "Rayon"

Alfred H. Caspary collection, Nov. 18-21, 1957, while an 1851 5rp with complete frame, tied to part of a cover, brought $7,500 at the same sale.

## Tuscany 1860
## 3-Lire Ochre

The Tuscany 3l ochre (23) was issued by the provisional government in 1860 after Garibaldi's victory. The stamps were printed on the paper of 1851. Two unused and three used specimens were offered for sale during the H.R. Harmer, Inc. sale of the Alfred H. Caspary collection, Jan. 28-30, 1957.

## United States
## Alexandria 'Blue'

Only one copy of the U.S. Alexandria 5¢ blue Postmasters Provisional (1X2) is known to exist on cover. Postmasters' Provisionals were issued to prepay postage before the U.S. government began issuing stamps and also during the Civil War.

The Alexandria provisionals were issued by Postmaster Daniel Bryan in Alexandria, Va., in 1846. The provisionals featured the wording "Alexandria Post Office" in a circle with "Paid 5" in the center.

The Alexandria provisionals were normally printed on buff paper; however, the Alexandria blue was discovered on a cover addressed to Richmond, Va., in 1907.

The cover is canceled by a black "paid" and bears the circular "Alexandria, Va., Nov. 25."

George H. Worthington acquired the cover which was later sold to Alfred H. Caspary. The rare provisional was purchased by Josiah H. Lilly in 1955 during the H.R. Harmer, Inc. sale of

the Caspary collection. Lilly paid $10,000 for the cover.

It was sold during the Robert A. Siegel auction of the Lilly collection for $18,500 and later appeared in the collection of John R. Boker Jr.

The cover was displayed at INTERPHIL '76 in Philadelphia, Pa., by David Feldman on behalf of the present owner. Much to the surprise of visitors to INTERPHIL, a second copy of the stamp was displayed at the event by Raymond and Roger Weill.

Prior to this exhibition, the provisional on cover was believed to be the only stamp to exist. The Weill stamp was reportedly certified to be genuine by the Philatelic Foundation and is owned by a client of Weill.

## United States
## Boscawen Provisional

The Boscawen, N.H., 5¢ dull blue on yellowish paper Postmasters' Provisional (4X1) is believed to have been issued in 1846 by Boscawen's postmaster Worcester Webster.

Only one copy of the provisional is known to exist. The copy appears uncanceled on a cover with a manuscript postmark in the upper left corner reading "Boscawen, N.H., Dec 13" with no year.

The cover was addressed to "Miss Achsah P. French, Care of Theodore French, Esq., Concord, N.H."

A postal official acquired the cover shortly after its discovery in 1865. In 1894, it was purchased by Hiram E. Deats, Flemington, N.H., for $5. It was sold to W.H. Colson in 1912 and later appeared in the Ferrari collection.

Arthur Hind acquired the cover in 1922 for $11,115. At the Hind auction in New York in 1933, Frank Marquis purchased it for $5,000.

The cover again changed hands during the H.C. Barr, Inc. sale in 1937 when Roy G. Fitzgerald of Dayton, Ohio, paid $5,100 for the rarity.

In November 1964, the cover was sold to Raymond H. Weill & Co., acting as agent for an unidentified collector during a Robert A. Siegel auction. It realized $23,000.

## United States
## Millbury, Mass., Provisional

The Millbury, Mass., 5¢ bluish Postmasters' Provisional (7X1) was issued by Postmaster Asa H. Waters in 1846. The stamp was printed from a woodcut on a hand press with the portrait of George Washington facing right in a circular band.

The inscription in the circular band reads "Post Office Paid 5 Cents."

The provisional was discovered by John K. Tiffany of St. Louis, Mo., while visiting in Worcester, Mass., in July 1885.

22

23

22) Tuscany 1860 3 lire
23) Alexandria Blue

Tiffany discovered the rarity on bound letters of Isaac Davis in the Library of American Antiquarian Society in Worcester.

Three specimens are believed to exist. An unused copy with full gum was in the Ferrari collection and was purchased by Josiah Lilly. It realized $34,000 during the Lilly sale in 1967.

A canceled variety was owned by Arthur Hind. The stamp attained $7,000 during the H.R. Harmer sale in 1968 and was again sold during the Robert A. Siegel sale on March 23, 1971.

Siegel also sold a Millbury Provisional on March 23, 1977, for $7,500.

A used copy with small faults realized $10,500 during an auction conducted by John W. Kaufmann, Inc., Washington, D.C., on Nov. 27, 1979.

A used copy with two closed tears, neatly tied, was sold for $22,000 during a June 4-5, 1980 auction conducted by Harmers of New York.

## United States
## 1-Cent Z-Grill

The 1867 1¢ Z-grill (85A) depicting Benjamin Franklin set the world record for an auction realization for any American stamp May 25, 1977, during the inaugural auction of Sotheby Parke Bernet Stamp Auction Co., New York, N.Y., when it was sold to the West Coast dealer, Superior Stamp and Coin Co., for $90,000.

It is the only used copy of the stamp, of which only two copies are known. The stamp was sold in 1975 at public auction for $42,500.

## United States
## 1869 Inverts

The 1869 15¢ (119b, 119c), 24¢ (120b) and 30¢ (121b) inverts are among the rarest issues of the United States. The 1869 issues were very unpopular with the public and were withdrawn from circulation within a year of their release.

The most famous 15¢ brown and blue, dark brown and blue, type II, was a part of the Arthur Hind collection and was purchased by Elliott Perry.

The rarest of the inverted frame issues is the 24¢ green and violet. A block of six 24¢ was discovered in Liverpool, England, on a parcel of an importers firm in the 1880s.

The vertical block of six was sold to a dealer who then sold it to Thomas Ridpath for approximately $25. William Thorne of New York, purchased the block and divided it into a block of four. The remaining pair later appeared in the F.W. Hunter collection.

The block was once owned by the Scott Stamp and Coin Co. and a Boston dealer, A.W. Batchelder. William H. Crocker of San Francisco, Calif., acquired it for $800.

The most famous owner of the 24¢ block was Y. Souren who purchased it in 1938 for $12,500.

According to Herman Herst Jr., Souren had the block mounted between two panes of glass and carried it with him in a special coat pocket.

Souren sold his prized possession to Esmond Bradley Martin for $25,000. Martin later returned it to Souren.

The block was acquired by Leslie White and sold in 1949 to the Raymond H. Weill Co. An unknown collector purchased it from the Weill firm who again attained it in 1968.

In 1974, the firm sold the rarity to an unknown Texas collector for an undisclosed amount.

A used 30¢ invert commanded $70,000 during the April 5, 1980 auction conducted by Robert A. Siegel Auction Galleries.

A 30¢ value realized $125,000 during the Siegel Rarities of the World auction on April 29, 1981.

An unused 15¢ type II was pounded down for a record-breaking $180,000 (not including buyer's premium) during the Siegel Rarities sale on April 24, 1982, with Renee Bowden paying the price, acting as agent for an anonymous buyer. A used 30¢ sold for $42,500 at the same auction.

## United States
## 'Running Chicken'

The "Running Chicken" cancellation was hand carved by John W. Hill, postmaster of Waterbury, Conn., one of hundreds of cork carvings which served as canceling devices for the Waterbury Post Office.

24

25

26

24) Boscawen Provisional
25) Millbury Provisional
26) U.S. inverts

Hill's cancellation and those of his associates became known as the Waterbury fancy cancellations, the "Running Chicken" being the most popular.

It is said the "Running Chicken" may actually be a turkey since the cancellation was created and used in late November for Thanksgiving time.

A realization of $45,000 was obtained for an 1869 Waterbury "Running Chicken" cover at the Jan. 31, 1977 auction conducted by Robert A. Siegel Auction Galleries, Inc.

The cover bears three examples of the U.S. 1869 1-cent issue with three separate and complete strikes of the "Running Chicken" cancellation.

A record $240,000 was realized for this cover at the Oct. 30, 1979 auction of Sotheby Parke Bernet Stamp Auction Co., Inc. This price was paid by a San Francisco dealer, William Crowe, who was acting as an agent for an unidentified buyer.

A superb strike of this cancel on an 1869 3¢ realized $3,400 at the April 1-2, 1982 auction conducted by the Robson Lowe Stamp Department of Christie's.

## United States
## Pan-American Invert

Six denominations of stamps were placed on sale May 1, 1901, in commemoration of the Pan-American Exposition held in Buffalo, N.Y., May 1-Nov. 1, 1901.

During the printing process, it was discovered that the first two denominations contained inverted frames. Less than 1,000 copies of the 1¢ invert (294a) are known and less than 200 of the 2¢ (295a).

A total of 400 4¢ (296a) were intentionally printed for specimen purposes after erroneous reports reached the Post Office Department that 4¢ inverts had been found. Approximately half of the 4¢ inverts were printed with the word "SPECIMEN" (296b). A sheet of 100 without the overprint was placed into the government stamp collection and 194 were destroyed, leaving 106 copies for the public.

Other denominations of the Pan-American series were also said to have been printed with inverted frames. These were also destroyed.

Singles and blocks of four of the 1¢ stamp are relatively common. The rarest of this issue is a block of 20 which was included in a collection comprised by Warren H. Colson for an unknown collector.

After the owner's death in 1951, the block was stored in a bank vault in Boston, Mass., until it was purchased by Raymond H. Weill Co. in 1976.

Only one block of four of the 2¢ invert exists. The block was owned by such prominent collectors as Col. Edward H.R. Green and Philip H. Ward Jr. The Ward collection was purchased by the Raymond H. Weill Co. in 1963 and sold to an anonymous collector.

The block was sold April 29, 1980, at an auction conducted by Sotheby Parke Bernet for $220,000.

Another block of four was broken by the Weill firm at the request of a client. The block has since been reconstructed.

A plate block of four of the 4¢ was discovered several years ago. The block was purchased by the Weill firm for an anonymous collector.

A block of four 4¢ realized $150,000 at the Sotheby Parke Bernet April 29, 1980 auction.

A 1¢ invert brought $12,500 during the Robert A. Siegel Auction Galleries sale of April 4, 1979. The April 5, 1980 Siegel sale included a 1¢ inverted center imprint in a plate number strip of four (two known) which realized $55,000, and a 2¢ invert which brought $40,000.

A 1¢ block of four commanded $80,000 at the Sotheby Parke Bernet April 29, 1980 auction.

A block of four of the 1¢ drew a winning bid of $80,000 at the April 29, 1980 sale conducted by Sotheby Parke Bernet Stamp Auction Co. The price was paid by a Florida dealer.

At the same sale, blocks of four of the 2¢ and 4¢ brought $220,000 and $150,000, respectively. The 4¢ block was sold to National Philatelic Advisory Corp.

27

28

27) U.S. Running Chicken
28) Pan-American invert

The auction also featured a 4¢ plate No. 1145 which commanded $55,000.

Suburban Stamp, Inc., Springfield, Mass., sold a 4¢ for $29,000 at its May 31, 1980 auction.

A 1¢ was hammered down at $6,750 during the May 18, 1981 sale conducted by Greg Manning Auctions. A 1¢ with small faults realized $14,000 at the Robert A. Siegel Rarities of the World sale April 29, 1981.

The April 24, 1982 Siegel Rarities sale featured a block of four of the 4¢ which realized $40,000, a price being paid by Irwin Weinberg, despite small thins or specks on each stamp.

## United States 1918 24-Cent Airmail Invert

The 1918 24¢ airmail with an inverted center (C3a) is believed to be the most popular issue of the U.S. The error occurred when a sheet was turned 180 degrees during the printing of the 1918 airmail stamps.

The stamps, featuring the Curtiss "Jenny" biplane, were issued for prepayment of mail carried on the inaugural airmail service flight on May 15, 1918.

One sheet of 100 was released and purchased by William T. Robey at a Washington, D.C., post office on May 14, 1918.

Unable to withstand the harassment inflicted upon him when the news of the rarity reached the world, Robey sold the sheet to Eugene Klein for $15,000. Klein numbered each stamp by position before selling it to Col. Edward H.R. Green for $20,000.

Green broke up the sheet and sold the single stamps and blocks individually. A block of eight was purchased by Y. Souren of New York and broken into a block of four. This block was later acquired by Raymond H. Weill Co. and sold to an anonymous collector.

On June 8, 1976, during INTERPHIL '76 in Philadelphia, Pa., the rare block was sold at an H.R. Harmer auction to the Weill firm for $170,000. The block was sold on behalf of the Princeton University Library.

The Princeton block was sold for $500,000 to a Florida real estate investor during a private sale arranged by Myron Kaller July 19, 1979.

A single 1918 invert was also sold by H.R. Harmer during INTERPHIL '76 and purchased by the Sandler Brothers for $40,000.

The price for single copies continued to escalate with $62,500 being paid by Irwin Weinberg-Miner Stamp Co. at the Robert A. Siegel Aug. 27-28, 1977 sale, and $70,000 at the November 1977 Andrew Levitt auction.

An East Coast dealer paid $100,000 for a single copy at the November 1978 auction held by Sotheby Parke Bernet.

Another record was established during the Robert A. Siegel April 4, 1979 sale when a single was sold for $130,000.

At the April 5, 1980 Siegel auction, two examples brought $75,000 (reperforated at top) and $125,000 (small light thin).

A copy with natural gum and straight edge at top realized $105,000 at an October 1980 auction conducted by Suburban Stamp, Inc.

A winning bid of $160,000 was obtained for a copy during the April 29, 1981 Robert A. Siegel Rarities of the World sale. It was sold to Columbian Stamp Co.

The Sept. 25-26, 1981 John W. Kaufmann auction featured the McCoy invert, realizing $115,000. This stamp was originally owned by Ethel B. McCoy, but was stolen during the American Philatelic Society convention Sept. 21-25, 1955.

In the early 1970s, Victor Spilotro reportedly claimed ownership of the stamp. In mid-1977, Robert Faiman was offered the stamp by Louis John Castelli Jr. (Ace Stamp and Coin Company), and agreed to the purchase following Philatelic Foundation certification.

Later in 1977, the Philatelic Foundation reportedly found that the stamp was one of the block of four stolen in 1955, and turned it over to the Federal Bureau of Investigation.

Mrs. McCoy donated the stamp to the American Philatelic Research Library, and the courts found in favor of the APRL. The invert was subsequently sold by Kaufmann with proceeds going to the APRL.

A record-breaking $180,000 was paid by Raymond Weill of New Orleans for a copy at the April 24, 1982 Siegel Rarities auction. A second copy, not as well centered, with gum disturbance and small thin spot, realized $75,000 during this sale. It was purchased by a collector from an Asian country.

29

29) Airmail invert

30

31

30) Uruguay tete-beche
31) Uruguay 180 centesimos

### Uruguay Tete-Beche
### 120 Centesimos

Three pairs of the Uruguay 120c tete-beche (4c) of 1858 are known to exist. The 120c stamps were printed in sheets of 78 stamps with 13 rows of 6 stamps.

One pair of the 120c tete-beche is located in the Tapling collection in the British Museum, while another, once owned by Pack, is housed in the Hoffman collection of Uruguay.

The Ferrari pair was purchased by Alfred F. Lichtenstein in Paris, France, on June 23, 1921. His daughter, Louise Boyd Dale, became the owner of the stamps upon his death.

An unknown collector purchased the pair during the H.R. Harmer, Inc. auction on May 7, 1970, for $9,000.

### Uruguay Tete-Beche
### 180 Centesimos

The Uruguay 180c of 1858 (5c) was printed in sheets of 78 stamps with 13 rows of 6 stamps. An inverted design occurred in the sheet resulting in tete-beche pairs.

Two pairs of this variety are known, one of which is located in the Tapling collection of the British Museum.

The Ferrari pair was purchased by Alfred F. Lichtenstein in Paris, France, on June 23, 1921. After Lichtenstein's death, his daughter, Louise Boyd Dale, became the owner of the rarity.

On May 7, 1970, the pair was sold for $11,000 to an unknown buyer at the H.R. Harmer sale.

# Museums and Libraries   13

# National Philatelic Collections

## Smithsonian Institution, Washington, D.C.

The National Philatelic Collections, which includes the United States National Postage Stamp Collection and various other foreign area holdings, is maintained by the Smithsonian Institution, and is housed in the National Museum of American History, Constitution Avenue (between 12th and 14th streets), Washington, D.C.

The National Philatelic Collections includes well over 14 million objects — stamps, covers, and postal history objects — and new material is added each year.

An excellent representation of the material embraced within the National Philatelic Collections is displayed in the Hall of Stamps and the Mails. The exhibit area is located on the third floor of the National Museum of American History building.

The exhibition may be visited seven days a week (except Christmas Day), between 10 a.m. and 5:30 p.m. Admission is free.

### History

The cornerstone for the first Smithsonian Institution building was laid May 1, 1847 — two months before official United States postage stamps appeared.

James Smithson, an English scientist, bequeathed his fortune to the United States of America in 1846 for the "increase and diffusion of knowledge." Congress acted quickly, and on Aug. 10, 1846, President James K. Polk signed the act establishing the Smithsonian Institution.

The first philatelic donation — a sheet of 10-cent Confederate stamps (four had been removed) — was made in 1886. A short time later the Smithsonian received 1,733 stamps bequeathed by Spencer Fullerton Baird, secretary from 1878 to 1887. By 1908, some 2,500 stamps had been received as gifts or bequests.

David W. Cromwell, then a prominent New York collector, gave the Smithsonian's philatelic holdings a substantial boost through a series of donations, which totaled 20,000 stamps by 1915.

Some of Cromwell's stamps were exhibited in the Smithsonian's Arts and Industries Building as early as 1911. This display was not pretentious; open albums were placed in glass-topped cases.

A major addition to the collection came in 1911-12 when the United States Post Office Department closed down a postal museum it had operated for roughly 20 years. The collection — representing about 20,000 stamps, postal stationery items, proofs, post office equipment, and related items — was transferred to the Smithsonian Institution.

To manage the collection, Joseph B. Leavy became the Smithsonian's first philatelic specialist in 1913 and, with the help of Catherine L. Manning, who later succeeded him, completed a display of stamps in specially constructed pullout frames. This exhibit, which was opened to the public in early 1915, was housed in the Arts and Industries Building.

Mrs. Manning became government philatelist (later curator) when Leavy died in 1921, and continued in that capacity for 30 years.

Succeeding Mrs. Manning as curators were Franklin R. Bruns Jr. (1951-57), George T. Turner (1958-62), Francis J. McCall (1962-63), Carl H. Scheele (1963-75), and again Franklin R. Bruns Jr. (1975-79). The current curator is Reidar Norby.

In November 1979, the former Division of

Postal History was renamed the National Philatelic Collections and given direct reporting responsibility to the musuem director.

## Hall of Stamps and the Mails

Since 1908, representative portions of the nation's philatelic collection have been on public display. Although initially housed in cramped quarters in the Arts and Industries Building, the exhibit was moved to the newly completed National Museum of History and Technology in 1964.

On display are a variety of different items and replicas which trace the growth of postal communications from the Sumerian cunieform to modern mail handling processes. This exhibit utilizes prints and photographs, models, actual postal objects, and covers to show advances in mail transportation from foot carriers to airmail service.

Among the postal objects on display are mailbags and sacks, mailboxes, locks, cancels, metering devices, and uniforms of mail carriers.

Also on display is a full-size replica of Ben Franklin's colonial post office/print shop.

One highlight of the Hall of Stamps and the Mails is a representative worldwide collection of postal issues. This collection is housed in 473 double-sided pullout frames and numbers about 85,000 stamps.

Another area of the hall is devoted to the "Language of Philately." This exhibit has proven to be one of the most popular in the hall. The display uses actual specimens and objects to explain terms which are unique to the hobby. Production processes and postal operations are also covered.

Special exhibit cases display material on loan from foreign governments and individuals. Recent displays from other countries have included stamps of Germany, Malta, Israel, the British Crown Agents, the five Scandinavian countries, and Mexico.

In addition, there is an area devoted to United States stamp production. On display here is an engraver's booth, with tools and an actual die. Also represented are a transfer press and small Stickney rotary press (both circa 1912), and early perforating machines (c. 1918-39).

To illustrate the various stages in the production of a postage stamp, color transparencies trace each step from design and die engraving to transfer, printing and perforating.

A separate area is also dedicated to the prodution of postal stationery. On display is a hub die, a master die, and a frame die prepared for governmental embossed envelopes by George F. Nesbitt & Company between 1853 and 1861, and the preliminary and final stages of dies for United States postal cards of 1910 (McKinley) and 1911 (Lincoln).

Another attraction in the hall is a rarity case. Among the items on display are a mint specimen of the 24-cent airmail invert; one of three existing panes of the Canal Zone Thatcher Ferry Bridge error (missing the bridge); panes of the 5-cent in 2-cent sheet error; the only Balloon Jupiter cover (with message); the 1869 and 1901 United States inverts; exceptional United States covers; and postal memorabilia.

## Reference Collections

Only representative samples of the National Philatelic Collections are on public display. Present exhibit facilities, large though they currently are, do not permit the display of every postage stamp issued, nor the many stamp varieties of interest to specialists.

The museum does maintain one of the largest philatelic reference collections. Collectors interested in stamps produced by the Bureau of Engraving and Printing, for example, can examine certified plate proofs of every plate from No. 1 on, as well as essays and die proofs of 19th century United States postage and revenue stamps.

Also available are the U.S. Post Office Department/U.S. Postal Service stamp files for much of this century.

United States postal historians and researchers also have access to full panes of many items, multiple pieces and a strong representation of plate number strips and plate block numbers, precancels, stamps with perforated initials (perfins), meter markings, and Christmas and Easter seals.

Cover and postal stationery collectors can examine corner cards, special markings and backstamps, and die varieties.

Also in this area are first day covers, flight covers, war covers (including censor markings and devices), and what may broadly be referred to as cacheted covers.

Postal stationery of the world is also well represented. The museum's collection of worldwide postal stationery references is probably the largest in the world.

The reference area also contains various collections which cover booklet panes and souvenir sheets of the world; Austrian fiscals, Mexican revenues and Swiss military adhesives, as well as one of the finest collections of Israeli ever put together.

Other notable reference strengths are Afghanistan, Albania, Australia, 20th century Belgium, Chile, Colombia, Ecuador, Egypt, France, and Germany.

Also included are materials on India and the Indian Feudatory States, Indonesia, Ireland, Italian States, Japan, Latvia, Nepal, Panama, Peru, the Philippines, Ryukyus, Saar, Salvador,

Spain, Tibet, Transvaal, Trieste, Ukraine, and Venezuela.

There are also thematic areas of note, including United Nations stamps of the world, Rotary and Red Cross issues, and Lincoln and Kennedy material, to name just a few.

Those wishing to refer to any of the reference materials in the National Philatelic Collections should request permission to use the collection at least four weeks in advance of the projected visit. Such a request should clearly state the area to be researched. Requests should be addressed to Curator, National Philatelic Collections, National Museum of American History, Washington, D.C. 20560.

Use of the reference area is restricted to 10 a.m. to 4:30 p.m. Monday through Friday. Access is subject to the availability of staff for supervision and assistance.

## Reference Library

With the addition of the renowned collection of reference materials amassed by the late George T. Turner, the museum's philatelic library is among the largest in the world.

Subjectwise, the monographs, serials, catalogs, manuscripts and documents cover the stamps and postal history of virtually every country of the world.

A notable strength of the philatelic reference library is the photographic collection which includes over 6,000 prints and slides of philatelic and postal history subjects.

The photographic collection has been categorized and arranged in albums or slide cases. Of the slides, transportation is the largest single category, embracing all methods of moving mail, from the runner to rockets.

All of the material in the library is available. In some instances, utilization is restricted to the library itself, during office hours, but parts of the collection are available on interlibrary loan.

## The Headsville Post Office

To complement the philatelic collection, the museum maintains a country store/post office. The structure, which stood in Headsville, W. Va., from about 1861 to 1914, was carefully taken apart, transported to Washington, D.C., and assembled on the first floor of the museum building.

The Headsville Post Office (now designated as the Smithsonian Station) is operated by the United States Postal Service, and museum visitors may purchase current postal issues and have them postmarked with a special Smithsonian Station pictorial cancellation.

The Headsville Post Office, which looks much as it did about 100 years ago, served as the basis for the 8-cent U.S. postage stamp honoring the 100th anniversary of mail order.

## National Air and Space Museum

The National Air and Space Museum is located on the Independence Avenue side of the Smithsonian's museum complex in Washington, D.C. It contains a variety of airmail vehicles and other items relating to postal history.

However, it is in the process of transferring its philatelic holdings to the National Philatelic Collections of the National Museum of American History.

Library hours are Monday through Friday, 10 a.m. to 5 p.m., by appointment only. The museum itself is open daily on the same schedule as the rest of the Smithsonian complex.

# National Archives and Records Service

The permanently valuable documents and records of the United States are housed in the National Archives Building, Eighth and Pennsylvania Avenue NW, Washington, D.C.

The National Archives comprises almost 800,000 cubic feet of historic and important documents, records, maps, recordings, motion pictures and photographs dating from around 1774 to the present.

Included are displays of such original documents as the Declaration of Independence and the Constitution. Also included are the records of the former U.S. Post Office Department. All archival records are available to philatelists and researchers, subject to the regulations for the public use of materials in the National Archives and Records Service.

The hours for the Central Research Room and Microfilm Research Room are 8:45 a.m. to 10 p.m. Monday through Friday, and 8:45 a.m. to 5 p.m. Saturday. Records to be used on Saturday must be requested by 5 p.m. on Friday; those to be used after 5 p.m. Monday through Friday must be requested by 4 p.m. of the day on which they are to be used.

# Library of Congress

The "nation's library," the Library of Congress consists of three buildings on Capitol Hill in Washington, D.C. The oldest, and the one often considered the main Library of Congress building, is the Thomas Jefferson Building completed in 1897. The other two are the John Adams Building (1939) and the James Madison Memorial Building (1980). The Jefferson building is featured on the 1982 U.S. Library of Congress commemorative stamp; the Madison building includes more space than the Jefferson and Adams buildings combined.

The Library of Congress contains over 80 million items on virtually any subject, and is thus likely to contain the largest general reference collection of philatelic materials available anywhere. Researchers can also make good use of the more than 1,200 newspapers in the permanent collection as reference sources. Official documents relating to many presidents and postmasters general are also contained in the Library of Congress.

Researchers should consult with library officials for information on hours and regulations. Interested persons may contact the Library of Congress, Information Office, Washington, D.C. 20540.

# U.S. Libraries and Museums

Philatelic museums and libraries in the United States, except those in the nation's capital previously listed, are presented here alphabetically by state, and by city within each state listing. This listing is as complete and comprehensive as possible, with information current through May 1982. Some changes to this listing are the result of questionnaires sent to all known and previously listed museums and libraries. Future additions and corrections will be appreciated.

Travelers planning a visit to any of these museums or libraries might be advised to make advance contact to confirm hours, location and availability of material. A visit to a postal museum can be a fascinating aspect of any business or pleasure trip. Researchers may also benefit from the resources of libraries with specialized holdings that may not be available elsewhere. There are endless hours of learning and entertainment encompassed in the pages of this U.S. listing, and countless more in the foreign listing which follows afterwards.

## Arizona

**TUCSON.** Western Postal History Museum, Box 40725, Tucson, Ariz. 85717-0725. Founded in 1960, an affiliate of the Arizona Historical Society. Complete U.S. type collection. Postmarks of 13 Western states; Territorial Arizona and New Mexico covers pertaining to "long-gone" camps, forts and mining towns.

Also, State of Arizona revenue collection, specialized collections from other countries such as Mexico and Canada and a United Nations collection.

Exhibits prepared periodically and for special occasions. Permanent exhibit areas are located in the Arizona Heritage Center, 949 E. Second St., while the museum's offices and library are located only two blocks away at 920 N. First Ave. The permanent exhibits include Western dioramas and paintings, and an old-time Territorial Days Post Office formerly used in Benson and St. David.

Museum open to the public Monday through Saturday 9 a.m. to 5 p.m., Sunday 1 to 5 p.m. Free.

The museum's Philatelic Education Department conducts regular courses in local and outlying public schools, coordinating a study of stamps with history, geography and social studies. The museum has philatelic related publications of its own. The Philatelic Research Library is located along with the museum offices.

The museum offices and library are open to the public on Monday, Wednesday and Friday 8 to 11 a.m. and 12:30 to 2 p.m. Closed on Wednes-days during June, July and August, and on holidays observed by the Arizona Historical Society. Facilities available at the discretion of the director.

## California

**ANAHEIM.** Museum of Postal History, Box 3642. Stamps and covers of the United States, United States bicentennial collection, British Empire, Japan and Europe.

Loan exhibits featured including over 35 topical exhibits. Stated to be first and only museum to exhibit within Disneyland; numerous Southern California exhibits including Anaheim Convention Center.

Limited collection of philatelic literature, manuscripts, letters, envelopes and postmarks.

Growth plans include expansion of number and length of exhibits, new facilities, and development of a museum newspaper.

Free. Stamped self-addressed envelope requested with inquiries.

**FRESNO.** Henry Madden Library, California State University, Shaw Avenue at Cedar.

Collection includes U.S. regular, commemorative, airmail and official adhesive postage stamps, 1847-1956; some Panama-Pacific International Exposition cancels, 1910-15. Collection no longer on display; however, it is available for viewing with one day's notice.

Hours are 9 a.m. to 5 p.m. Monday through Friday. Closed weekends and all official holidays. Free.

**LOS ANGELES.** Scandinavian Collectors' Club. Library list of Scandinavian catalogs and periodicals, and general periodicals available through club personnel.

Library materials available on special request. Direct inquiries to Scandinavian Collector's Club, Box 57397, Los Angeles, Calif. 90057.

— Wells Fargo Bank History Museum, 444 S. Flower St. Museum exhibit covers staging, express, banking, mining, gold and early Southern California. Also on exhibit is an original Concord stagecoach.

Open to the public, Monday through Friday, 10 a.m. to 3 p.m. Closed all bank holidays. Free.

**NEW ALMADEN.** New Almaden Museum, 21570 Almaden Road. Letters and envelopes with historical postal markings pertaining to New Almaden and Almaden.

Materials available to public by appointment; used in exhibits on local post office history.

Museum open Monday, Thursday and Friday, 1 to 4 p.m.; and Saturday and Sunday, 10 a.m. to 4 p.m. Closed Tuesday and Wednesday, and during December and January.

Admission $2; children 12 and under 75 cents; senior citizens $1.75.

**POMONA.** Pomona Public Library, 625 S. Garey St. Over 1,000 volumes, 225 periodical volumes in the Willis Kerr Philatelic Library with emphasis on philatelic history of North America.

Established 1959 with donation of entire personal philatelic library of Dr. Willis E. Kerr, former librarian of Pomona College.

Library also has stamps of the Oak Knoll Local Post, Pasadena; collection of 30,000 post cards, some postally used.

Available to the public for use in library only. Free. Open Monday through Thursday, 10 a.m. to 9 p.m.; Friday, 10 a.m. to 5 p.m.; Saturday, noon to 5 p.m. Closed Sunday and on California and national holidays.

Materials also available on interlibrary loan.

**REDLANDS.** The Lincoln Shrine, 120 Fourth St. Located in Smiley Park at rear of A.K. Smiley Public Library.

Stamps relating to Lincoln and the Civil War period, Lincoln commemoratives, stampless covers and Civil War envelopes. Collection also includes foreign stamps.

Lincoln Log, publication of the Lincoln Society of Philately, available.

All materials noncirculating.

Open 1 to 5 p.m., Tuesday through Saturday. Closed Sunday, Monday and holidays, except Lincoln's birthday. Visitors asked to call or write for special appointments for tour groups during morning hours.

—United Postal Stationery Society Central Office.

Books related to postal stationery. Information available from the United Postal Stationery Society, Box 48, Redlands, Calif. 92373.

**SACRAMENTO.** B.F. Hastings Building, 1006 Second St. Once housed office of the Alta Telegraph Co., agents for the Overland Pony Express operated by Russell, Majors and Waddell, 1860-61.

Information available from the Sacramento Convention and Visitors Bureau and Sacramento State Parks, 111 "I" St., Sacramento, Calif. 95814.

**SAN FRANCISCO.** Wells Fargo Bank History Room, 420 Montgomery St. The Wiltsee Memorial Collection of Western Stamps, Franks and Postmarks, left in trust by Ernest A. Wiltsee for public display, over 1,300 covers giving examples from 235 different express companies.

Pony Express stamps, covers, postal markings from California communities, many now "ghost towns."

Entire exhibit centered around an original Concord stagecoach.

Open to the public Monday through Friday, 10 a.m. to 3 p. m. Closed all bank holidays. Free.

**SUNNYVALE.** Western Philatelic Library, philatelic section of the Sunnyvale Public Library, 665 W. Olive Ave., established in 1969 by the Friends of the South Bay Philatelic Library, Inc. A 1971 merger with the trustees of the Philatelic Research Library resulted in the sponsor's change of name to the Friends of the Western Philatelic Library, Inc.

Materials of the Donald F. Dahlquist philatelic library acquired.

Over 750 linear feet on the mezzanine contain better than 2,500 books and 1,500 bound volumes of periodicals.

More than 800 books now available for library use; circulated to library card holders. Occasional in-library lobby displays of philatelic material.

Open Monday through Thursday, 9 a.m. to 9 p.m.; Friday, 9 a.m. to 6 p.m.; Saturday, 9 a.m. to 5 p.m.; Sunday, 1 to 5 p.m. Closed holidays.

**VALLEJO.** The Vallejo Naval and Historic Museum, 734 Marin St.

Naval and historic displays relating to the Navy on the West Coast and Mare Island Naval Shipyard; also material relating to the Spanish Grant "Soscal" and the North San Francisco Bay Area.

Open Tuesday through Saturday, 10 a.m. to 5 p.m. Admission, 50 cents; children, 25¢.

## Connecticut

**HARTFORD.** Connecticut State Library Museum, 231 Capitol Ave. Philatelic collection includes Daniel Nash Morgan (U.S. Treasurer during 1890s) collection of stamps and covers, 1871-1906.

Also, official stamped envelopes of the War and the Post Office departments, 1875; bicentennial commemoratives; Connecticut Tercentenary, 1935; Moon Flights / Space Program, 1962-69; limited variety of local, national and foreign stamps.

Library and museum open to scholars who may do research with the collections. Public may use library facilities and visit museum; research in the museum not permitted general public.

Open Monday through Friday 9 a.m. to 5 p.m., Saturday 9 a.m. to 1 p.m. (except holiday weekends). Closed Sundays and holidays. Free.

## Florida

**FORT LAUDERDALE.** International Swimming Hall of Fame, Inc., 1 Hall of Fame Drive.

The late Axel Nordquist's sports stamp collection features swimming. All stamps, including other sports, displayed and organized by major events — Olympics, World Championships, Pan American and other Continental Games, etc.

Stamps displayed in leatherbound books by country and subject as permanent part of the hall's Special Exhibits Room.

Open daily 10 a.m. to 5 p.m.; Sunday, 11 a.m. to 4 p.m. Admission, $1.25 for adults; 75 cents for students; 50¢ for children. Group rates for stamp clubs; 300-seat auditorium available for regular meetings or special events.

**PENSACOLA.** T.T. Wentworth Jr. Museum, 8382 Palafox Highway. Stamps, letters and envelopes with historical markings framed and on display. Used for occasional exhibits. The collection also includes 100,000 articles relating to the history of Pensacola, Fla., and the United States.

Open Saturday and Sunday, 2 to 6 p.m. Free.

## Illinois

**BROOKFIELD.** Aerophilatelic Federation of the Americas Library, 3532 Oak Ave.

Extensive aerophilatelically related reference material, also substantial numbers of letters and envelopes with historical postal markings including those of Charles A. Lindbergh, Amelia Earhart, Jack Knight and others.

Materials used in exhibitions of the 58 clubs of the AFA and at the five annual exhibitions held in Brookfield.

Library materials available to members only.

**CHICAGO.** Balzekas Museum of Lithuanian Culture, 4012 Archer Ave. Large collection of stamps on permanent exhibit, letters and envelopes, periodicals and history of Lithuanian stamps, also books on philatelic information.

Museum is center for philatelic activities, also offers lectures and has a traveling philatelic exhibit. Materials available to scholars and the general public.

Open seven days a week 1 to 4 p.m.; closed Christmas and New Year's Day. Admission, $1; children and senior citizens, 50 cents.

## Indiana

**FORT WAYNE.** Louis A. Warren Lincoln Library and Museum, 1300 S. Clinton St. Lincoln stamps and patriotic envelopes.

During November through May, open Monday through Thursday, 8 a.m. to 4:30 p.m.; and Friday, 8 a.m. to 12:30 p.m. From May to November, hours are 8 a.m. to 4:30 p.m., Monday through Friday; and 10 a.m. to 4:30 p.m., Saturday. Guided tours for groups; arrangements must be made well in advance. Free.

## Louisiana

**MANSFIELD.** Mansfield State Commemorative Area, Highway 175. Museum displays include Confederate stamps and letters.

Open Monday through Saturday, 9 a.m. to 5 p.m.; Sunday 1 to 5 p.m. Closed Thanksgiving, Christmas and New Year's Day. Admission, $1 adults; 50 cents students.

## Massachusetts

**WESTON.** Cardinal Spellman Philatelic Museum, 235 Wellesley St. Items include the original Cardinal Spellman collection, President Dwight D. Eisenhower, Gen. Matthew Ridgway, and Jascha Heifitz collections, and extensive worldwide stamps.

Also, 10,000 volumes of philatelic and collateral material, extensive acquisitions of letters and envelopes.

Museum has philatelic publications, teaching facilities, traveling exhibits. Materials available to scholars and general public; museum members have room use and library privileges.

Open to the public Sunday, 2 to 5 p.m.; Tuesday through Thursday, 10 a.m. to 4 p.m. Other times by appointment.

Admission is free by donation.

## Michigan

**ANN ARBOR.** Bentley Historical Library, University of Michigan, North Campus. Collecting themes include Michigan political figures, temperance and prohibition, Americans in China, Americans in the Philippine Islands, and the history of the University of Michigan.

Open to general public; closed stacks. Weekdays, 8:30 a.m. to 5 p.m.; Saturday, 9 a.m. to 12:30 p.m.

— Harlan Hatcher Graduate Library, University of Michigan. General section has an extensive collection of philatelic materials, while the Asia Library has extensive Chinese, Japanese and Korean collections of books with many volumes of information on Oriental post office systems (none in English). The Department of Rare Books and Special Collections no longer has any particular strength in postal history material.

Permission required to use collections; permission to research within library granted at main circulation desk, Room 104 Hatcher North.

Open daily 8 a.m. to 10 p.m.; reduced hours during school holidays.

— William Clements Library, University of Michigan, Main Campus, 909 S. University Ave. American works of early Americana (principally pre-Civil War era).

Rare covers, letters, including important works of Washington, Franklin, other early American leaders.

Closed to public; open to advanced historical scholars who have received advance permission from director. Weekdays, 8 a.m. to 5 p.m.

Infrequent exhibits open to the public to display rare philatelic properties.

**DEARBORN.** Henry Ford Museum, Dearborn. George T. Trumbull U.S. collection. Available by appointment only.

Museum open daily 9 a.m. to 5 p.m. Closed Thanksgiving, Christmas, New Year's Day. Admission, $7.

**DETROIT.** Burton Historical Collection, Detroit Public Library, 5201 Woodward Ave. Selective stamps, envelopes, first day covers, Civil War covers, free franks, very early postmarks. Xerox copies or photographs of certain items permitted.

**PLYMOUTH.** West Suburban Stamp Club, Plymouth. Growing library includes reference books, periodicals, auction and show catalogs, etc. No permanent site at present. Several hundred volumes in library for use by membership. Open on request basis only. Contact Box 643, Plymouth, Mich. 48170.

## Missouri

**FULTON.** Winston Churchill Memorial and Library, Westminster College, Fulton. Collection of Churchill commemorative stamps, first day covers.

Items available to scholars and the general public. Some collections may be seen by appointment. The museum has one traveling exhibit of commemorative stamps.

Open daily 10 a.m. to 5 p.m. April through October; Monday through Friday 10 a.m. to 4 p.m. and Saturday and Sunday noon to 4 p.m. November through March. Closed Christmas, New Year's Day and Thanksgiving.

Admission: $1.50 adults; 75 cents children; group rates available.

**ST. LOUIS.** Missouri Historical Society, Jefferson Memorial.

Charles A. Lindbergh collection, including personal belongings, decorations, trophies and mementos. Among stamps in the collection is the first impression of a special airmail stamp issued by the U.S. Post Office Department in

commemoration of the New York to Paris flight, and over 150 first flight covers, some of which were autographed by the pilot.

Open to the public, 9:30 a.m. to 4:45 p.m., Tuesday through Sunday. Free.

## Montana

**HELENA.** Montana Historical Society, 225 N. Roberts St. Miscellaneous world collections, covers from territorial days, early post offices in Montana, early Montana territorial letters, envelopes.

Application for research purposes required; written permission only.

Open Monday through Friday, 8 a.m. to 5 p.m.; Saturday, 9 a.m. to 5 p.m. Closed Thanksgiving, Christmas and New Year's Day. Free.

## Nebraska

**BOYS TOWN.** The PhilaMatic Center, a Museum of Hobbies, Father Flanagan's Boys' Home. Nearly 650 frames of worldwide stamps, including Confederate, Ripley's "Believe It Or Not" 600-pound solid ball of stamps.

Open to the public year round, Monday through Saturday, 8 a.m. to 4:30 p.m.; Sundays and holidays, 9 a.m. to 4:30 p.m. Closed Thanksgiving, Christmas, New Year's Day and a half-day on Good Friday. Free. Group reservations can be made by calling the center in advance.

**GOTHENBURG.** Original Pony Express Station, Ehmen Park. Authentic Pony Express items in the museum. Open to the public May through September, 9 a.m. to 6 p.m.; June through August, 8 a.m. to 9 p.m. Free.

## New Hampshire

**HINSDALE.** Hinsdale Post Office, established Jan. 24, 1815. According to records, it is the oldest continuously operated post office building in the United States.

No current information available.

## New Jersey

**WILDWOOD.** Chester Davis Memorial Library, 5121 Park Blvd. Precanceled postage stamps from United Stamps, England, France, Canada, United Nations, letters, envelopes, philatelic publications.

Revolving exhibits; otherwise shown at Precanex Stamp Shows.

Open only to paid members of the National Association of Precancel Collectors.

## New York

**HYDE PARK.** The Franklin D. Roosevelt Library / Museum, Hyde Park.

Variety of albums given President Roosevelt by other heads of state. Holdings also include singles, sheets, proofs, post cards, envelopes and covers. Museum items available to the public and scholars on a limited basis.

The library has correspondence and literature relating to Roosevelt's interests in the post office and stamps, and stamp collecting. There is no charge for those doing research in the presidential papers.

Museum hours, 9 a.m. to 5 p.m. every day except Christmas and New Year's. General admission, $1.50 (including fee for Vanderbilt Historic Site and home of Franklin D. Roosevelt).

**NEW YORK.** The Collectors Club, 22 E. 35th St. Stamps including Canada, Brazil, Korea, also envelopes, letters, extensive philatelic library. Club meetings, lectures.

Materials available for exhibit on request; research purposes by appointment only.

Open to the public Monday, Wednesday and Friday 10 a.m. to 3 p.m.; longer hours for members. Closed all legal holidays and during summer season, June 15 to Sept. 15. Free.

— Library/Malloch Rare Book Room, New York Academy of Medicine, 2 E. 103rd St.

Library has approximately 375 medical stamps exclusive of the Denker collection, also envelopes with historical postal markings.

Holdings include 53 philatelic publications on medically related topics covering 28 different subjects. Library materials are used in exhibits and facilities are available for reproduction of materials.

Open to general public Monday through Saturday, 9 a.m. to 5 p.m., except holidays. For Fellows of the Academy and holders of library cards, Monday through Saturday, 9 a.m. to 5 p.m.; holidays 10 a.m. to 5 p.m.

Closed Sundays, New Year's, Memorial Day, Fourth of July, Labor Day, Thanksgiving, Christmas, Saturdays during July and August, and before Memorial and Labor Day. Free.

— The Philatelic Foundation, 270 Madison Ave. An extensive collection of Luff reference material including covers with a variety of postal markings, extensive library, photographic reference files, records of postal services from many countries.

Educational program includes publication of analysis of foundation's expertizing work, periodic counterfeit leaflets, and audio-visual programs.

Materials available to the public Monday through Friday, 10:30 a.m. to 4 p.m. by appointment to facilitate service. Closed evenings, all legal holidays.

**RIVERHEAD, LONG ISLAND.** Suffolk County Historical Society, 300 W. Main St. A selection of regional postal history items including a small collection of post office cancellation imprints, postal history and local postal records, plus postcards and charity seals. Materials available upon request.

Open year round, except holidays, Monday through Saturday, 12:30 to 4:30 p.m. Free.

## Ohio

**BELLEVUE.** Margie Pfund Postmark Museum. Owned by Post Mark Collectors Club.

Extensive and growing collection of postal cancellations, items related to post offices and postal service.

Located in the Historic Lyme Village post office building, part of the restored complex at the intersection of Ohio Routes 4 and 113.

The Village is open Tuesday through Sunday, 1-5 p.m., June through August; open weekends May and September. Village admission: adults, $2.50; senior citizens, $2.25; students, $1.25; children under 12 (accompanied by adult), free.

For further information, contact Bernice Mittower, curator, R.R. 2, Box 136, Republic, Ohio 44867.

**COLUMBUS.** Ohio Village, Ohio Historical Society, I-71 and 17th Avenue. This reconstructed village includes a 19th-century postal facility offering special cancellations. May be visited as part of the normal Ohio Village activities.

**SIDNEY.** George W. Linn Memorial Research Library, Amos Press Inc., 911 Vandemark Road.

Approximately 3,000 volumes, 100 current periodicals covering all phases of philately. Noncirculating.

All issues of Linn's Weekly Stamp News on microfilm; printouts available. Xerox services available.

Open year round Monday through Friday, 8 a.m. to 5 p.m. Closed seasonal holidays.

**WAPAKONETA.** Neil A. Armstrong Air and Space Museum, I-75 and Fisher Road. Some space related philatelic items, major first day cover exhibit in preparation.

Open to the public Wednesday through Saturday, 9:30 a.m. to 5 p.m.; Sundays and holidays, noon to 5 p.m. Closed Thanksgiving, Christmas and New Year's Day.

Admission: adults, $1.50; children, 75¢; age 6 and under, free.

**WILLOWICK.** Society of Israel Philatelists Slide Library, 31715 Vine St.

Library has more than 4,000 philatelic slides encompassing 80 different lectures. A written text accompanies all SIP slide lectures.

These slide lectures are available at no charge to responsible philatelic clubs and organizations, as well as nonphilatelic groups.

Request for use of slides must be made at least three weeks prior to meeting date. State exact meeting date when requesting use of a slide lecture.

All slides must be returned by registered or first-class insured mail or United Parcel Service with a declared value of $1 per slide within two days after meeting date.

Slide lectures may not be held for longer periods without prior permission from the slide library's chairman, Dr. Albert Friedberg.

**WRIGHT-PATTERSON AIR FORCE BASE.** U.S. Air Force Museum, six miles northeast of Dayton. Letters, envelopes from servicemen, correspondence forms used by American POWs of World War II and later period, aircraft and balloon flight covers.

Open every day except Christmas, Monday through Friday, 9 a.m. to 5 p.m.; Saturday and Sunday, 10 a.m. to 6 p.m. Free.

## Pennsylvania

**CAMBRIDGE SPRINGS.** Alliance College Library, Polish Library, Fullerton Avenue. Emphasis on issues of Poland, first day covers and blocks, some U.S., some worldwide.

Over 100 periodicals of Poland; Polish and Polish-American newspapers carrying philatelic columns. Available to scholars as well as general public through interlibrary loan service.

Permanent stamp exhibit in the Polish Library.

**PHILADELPHIA.** American Swedish Historical Museum, 1900 Pattison Ave.

Museum has a semicomplete Swedish collection, 1860-1940.

Materials are used on an occasional basis for exhibits, publications and teaching.

Open Tuesday through Friday, 10 a.m. to 4 p.m.; Saturday, noon to 4 p.m. Closed Sundays and Mondays.

— The Franklin Institute, 20th Street and Benjamin Franklin Parkway. Collections include U.S. classics, rarities, covers, Wells Fargo material. Collectors Gallery open to the public.

Open Monday through Saturday 10 a.m. to 5 p.m.; Sunday noon to 5 p.m. Closed most national holidays.

Admission: adults, $3.50; students, $2.50; children under 12, $2; senior citizens, $1.50; children under 4, free.

— B. Free Franklin Post Office, 311 Market St., in an authentically restored house once owned by Benjamin Franklin.

Postal Museum located on second floor houses 168 postal artifacts on loan from the Smithsonian Institution, Washington, D.C. Museum cachets available. Seasonal and topical display changed periodically.

Winter hours 9 a.m. to 5 p.m. daily; summer hours (Freedom Week through Labor Day), 9 a.m to 6 p.m. Closed Christmas and New Year's Day. Free.

— The Free Library of Philadelphia, Logan Square.

Extensive collection of books, periodicals and catalogs on stamps and stamp collecting with continuous acquisitions.

Holdings based on two major collections — Eugene Klein, strong in European books, and Hiram Deats' philatelic literature of American origin.

Philatelic literature available to general public for in-house reference consultation. Library is charged with statewide resource responsibility for philately.

Open 9 a.m. to 9 p.m., Monday through Wednesday; 9 a.m. to 6 p.m., Thursday and Friday; 9 a.m. to 5 p.m., Saturday; and 1 to 5 p.m., Sunday (except in summer). Free for in-person reference use.

— International Coin Museum, National Bank Plaza, 4th and Market Street.

Collection includes stamps of Israel and the United States, postal covers. Displays change periodically.

Philatelic publications and supplies available in museum gift shop.

Open 10 a.m. to 6 p.m. Closed Thanksgiving, Christmas, and New Year's Day.

Admission adults, $1; children, 50 cents.

**STATE COLLEGE.** American Philatelic Research Library, 100 Oakwood Ave. Incorporated in 1968 as the research and educational arm of the American Philatelic Society.

The collection contains numerous research materials covering every aspect of philately. All kinds of informational handbooks, periodicals, catalogs, bibliographies and indexes.

Patrons interested in knowing what books are available on a specific topic should send information on their collecting interest. Subject cards from the card catalog pertaining to the topic are photocopied so that the patron can decide which books he may wish to borrow.

Members may borrow items directly from the library; nonmembers may utilize facilities through the interlibrary loan program.

Handbooks, catalogs and bound periodicals are available for loan through the mail for a 50 cent fee per volume to cover postage and handling. All library fees must accompany requests for service. Address American Philatelic Research Library, Box 338, State College, Pa. 16801.

Open Monday through Friday, 8 a.m. to 4:30 p.m. Free.

Photocopying service available.

## Texas

**RICHARDSON.** University of Texas at Dallas, Wineburgh Philatelic Research Library (Box 643). Extensive collection of books, periodicals and catalogs on stamps and stamp collecting with emphasis on postal history, counterfeits and forgeries and airmail with continuous acquisition. All material available to public for in-house reference.

On permanent display are panels of U.S. postal history, stampless covers and panels of "The Language of Philately." Other exhibits continually changing.

Members may borrow items directly from the library; nonmembers may utilize the facilities through the interlibrary loan program.

Open year round 9 a.m. to noon, and 1 to 5 p.m., or by appointment.

## Vermont

**GRAND ISLE.** Jedediah Hyde Log Cabin. Built in 1783, used as a post office from 1834 to 1841. Now open as a museum, with a display including some old post office documents.

## Virginia

**NORFOLK.** Gen. Douglas MacArthur Memorial, MacArthur Square. Stamps primarily of the Philippines, others of World War II and later origin; first day covers, letters and envelopes. Materials available to scholars and general public.

Open Monday through Saturday, 10 a.m. to 5 p.m.; Sunday, 11 a.m. to 5 p.m. Closed Thanksgiving, Christmas and New Year's Day.

**WILLIAMSBURG.** Colonial Post Office in reconstructed capital. Located in the Printing Office. May be visited as part of the normal Williamsburg activities, and offers special cancellation.

## Washington

**SEATTLE.** Collectors Club of Seattle, 7212 E. Green Lake Drive NE.

Philatelic library available to members only. Open Tuesday, 2 to 9 p.m.; Friday, 5 to 9 p.m.

**YAKIMA.** Yakima Valley Museum, Tieton Drive at South 21st in Franklin Park. Covers, items relating to postal history of central Washington area (territorial and state). Traveling exhibits to schools.

Open Wednesday through Friday, 10 a.m. to 5 p.m.; Saturday and Sunday, noon to 5 p.m.

Admission $1; family, $1.50; students, 50 cents; senior citizens and children under 10, free.

## Wisconsin

**MADISON.** The State History Society, 816 State St. U.S. postage and revenues; Wisconsin tax stamps; and postmarks. Available for study by appointment only.

Open Monday through Friday, 8 a.m. to 5 p.m. Weekdays and night hours when University of Wisconsin is in session. Free.

## Wyoming

**CHEYENNE.** National First Day Cover Museum, 702 Randall Blvd.

On display are first day covers including Great Britain's Penny Black.

The museum is open to the public Monday through Saturday, 9 a.m. to 5 p.m. Free.

# Foreign Libraries and Museums

Throughout the world, public and private museums maintain and display stamp collections for the delight of visiting philatelists. These holdings range from the massive offerings of national postal museums, to the small postal history displays of local historical societies.

Libraries may also be found worldwide, and some have extensive holdings and unusual or specialized philatelic significance.

The following list includes all foreign libraries and museums known to be of interest to philatelists. This listing has been updated with the cooperation of curators and library directors throughout the world. Future additions and corrections will be appreciated, as will information on any museums and libraries that may not be included here.

One interesting aspect of postal museums outside the United States is the frequent inclusion of the telephone, telegraph and other means of communication in the same historical offering — due mainly to the combination of posts and telegraphs (etc.) under the same departmental jurisdiction in many countries. These aspects of technology are frequently also government monopolies, managed by the postal administration or a general telecommunications department

## Australia

### Tasmania

**HOBART.** Hobart Post Office Museum. Located in an 1838 military ordnance building. No additional information available.

### Victoria

**BALLARAT.** Sovereign Hill Gold Mining Township.

This attraction includes a replica of the 1854

Ballarat post office. The facility may be visited as part of the normal activities at Sovereign Hill, and the township offers a special cancellation.

**MELBOURNE.** Melbourne Post Office Museum, 90 Swan St., Richmond, Victoria. Built in 1905, has old timbered ceilings with ornate wooden support brackets, a unique feature of Victorian post office architecture. Served as Richmond post office until April 1974, when it was converted to an Australia Post museum.

Contains displays of historical items associated with the post office, has special posting box, and pictorial postmarker.

All mail posted in the special posting box located inside the museum building is canceled with the pictorial postmarker which features the "Butterfly" design of the postmarkers used to cancel Victoria's first postage stamps in 1850.

Open to the public Monday, Wednesday and Friday, 10 a.m. to 4 p.m.; Sunday, 1 to 5 p.m. Closed Tuesdays and Saturdays.

Clearance for the letter receiver is 4 p.m. Monday, Wednesday, Thursday and Friday.

# Canada
## British Columbia
**KAMLOOPS.** Kamloops Museum, 207 Seymour St., V2C 2E7. Local history museum with small stamp collection usually on display. Available for researchers to study on premises.

Open to public. Summer hours (July 1 through Labor Day): 11 a.m. to 8 p.m. Tuesday through Friday; 11 a.m. to 5 p.m. Saturday; 1 to 4 p.m. Sunday. Winter hours: 11 a.m. to 5 p.m. Tuesday through Thursday and Saturday; 11 a.m. to 8 p.m. Friday; 1 to 4 p.m. Sunday. Free.

## Manitoba
**BRANDON.** John E. Robbins Library, Brandon University, 18th and Princess Avenue. The Gordon Jory collection of early (19th century) covers and postmarks housed in the library.

Hours, Monday through Thursday 8:30 a.m. to 5 p.m. and 6 to 9:30 p.m.; Friday 8:30 a.m. to 5 p.m.; Saturday 1 to 4:30 p.m.; Sunday (fall/winter term only) 1 to 4:30 p.m.

**WINNIPEG.** The Ross House, Sir William Whyte Park, opposite the Canadian Pacific Railway station. Oldest building in Winnipeg proper and first post office in Western Canada, preserved by the Manitoba Historical Society.

No formal postal collections, but some post office equipment. Picture post cards on sale; post cards or letters mailed from Ross House can bear Ross House special cachet if desired.

Open 12:30 to 4:30 p.m. Wednesday through Sunday June 1 to Sept. 1.

## Nova Scotia
**HALIFAX.** Peggy's Cove Lighthouse Post Office. Stated to be the only known post office in the world to be located in a lighthouse.

Open June until September, inclusive, Monday through Saturday, 9 a.m. to 4:30 p.m.

— Public Archives, Coburg Road.
On display are stamps of Nova Scotia, variety of commemorative stamps and other Canadian postage stamps. Open 9:30 a.m. to 10 p.m.

## Ontario
**KINGSTON.** Queen's University Archives, Kathleen Ryan Hall, University Avenue, K7L 3N6. The Austin stamp collection covering Canada, British West Indies, Cape of Good Hope, Great Britain, Gibraltar and Malta; other holdings.

Open Monday through Friday, 9 a.m. to 5 p.m. Closed between Christmas and New Year's Day and on civic holidays. Free.

**OTTAWA.** Public Archives of Canada, 395 Wellington St., K1A 0N3. Offers a collection of philatelic literature materials which will eventually be consolidated with the National Postal Museum collection. Also offers documents dealing with the Canadian Post Office.

Hours, 8:30 a.m. to 4:30 p.m. daily. Free.

— National Postal Museum, 180 Wellington St. (corner of Bank Street), K1A 1C6.

Extensive collection of Canadian, British North American and foreign stamps. Approximately 50 individual panels depicting many aspects of Canadian and foreign postal history; mailboxes from various eras, postal scales and other artifacts; scale models of mail-carrying ships, aircraft and other vehicles, several full size and minidioramas. Replica of a turn-of-the-century post office and general store sales counter.

Canada Post Office records held at Public Archives of Canada, Ottawa, at Record Group 3; museum staff can provide research assistance.

Material at the National Postal Museum and the Public Archives of Canada available to the public, subject to ordinary limitations applicable to archival and museum holdings. Appointment necessary to study archival material and to use museum's library.

Hours, Tuesday to Saturday, 9 a.m. to 5 p.m.; Sundays, noon to 5 p.m. Closed Mondays and Christmas Day. Free.

## Prince Edward Island
**CAVENDISH.** Green Gables Post Office. Replica of a 19th-century post office connected with the writer Lucy Maud Montgomery. Functioning post office offers special philatelic items.

Open daily except Sunday during the summer months (1974 data).

## Quebec
**SAINT-JEROME.** The Castor Laurentien Philatelic Circle Library, 351 de la rue Labelle.

No current information on hours or admission fees available.

# Europe

## Austria

**VIENNA.** Post und Telegraphenmuseum, Technisches Museum, Mariahilfer Strasse 212, 1140 Wien. Collection considers the development of mail communications in Austria. Also stamps and their production, letters, covers, postal markings and other materials. Founded 1889.

A library covering the history of Austrian communications is also available for use.

The collection is open Tuesday through Friday from 9 a.m. to 4 p.m.; Saturday and Sunday from 9 a.m. to 1 p.m. The library is open Tuesday through Friday from 9 a.m. to noon. Closed Monday with the exception of Easter Monday and Whit Monday, also Jan. 1, Good Friday, May 1, Corpus Christi, Nov. 1 and 2, and Dec. 25.

The Technical Museum building charges 10 schilling for adults; handicapped persons, children and students in groups free. Free admission from Sept. 1 to April 30 on Saturdays, Sundays, and holidays.

Museum guidebook available for 18s.

## Belgium

**BRUSSELS.** Musee Postal, Place du Grand Sablon 40 a B-1000 Brussels. Collection deals with the stamps of Belgium and of other Universal Postal Union members.

Also a large variety of postal markings on covers and cards. A library of philatelic works is also available. Original drawings, cliches, and other printing materials also held.

The collection was founded in 1928, and the first museum opened in 1936.

Included in the collection are three major subdivisions: postal history, philately, and the evolution of the telegraph and telephone.

Hours are Tuesday through Saturday, 10 a.m. to 4 p.m., Sundays and holidays, 10 a.m. to 12:30 p.m. The building is closed Mondays, Christmas Day and New Year's Day. Free.

## Denmark

**COPENHAGEN.** Danish Post and Telegraph Museum, 59, Vesterbrogade, 1550 Kobenhavn V. founded in 1907. Collection includes a wide variety of materials dealing with the Danish posts.

Examples of the displays include a reconstruction of the famed "ball-post" vehicle of the 19th century, and the interior of a post office from about 1845. A display deals with ice-breaking ships.

The collection also includes designs and printing materials for Danish stamps, as well as postal history covers.

Open Nov. 1 to April 30, Thursday and Sundays, 10 a.m. to 3 p.m.; May 1 to Oct. 31, Thursdays and Sundays, 10 a.m. to 4 p.m. Free.

## Finland

**HELSINKI.** Post and Telegraph Museum, Tehtaankatu 21 B, 00150, Helsinki, 15.

Collection represents development of Finnish postal service over the past 350 years. On display are examples of all stamps issued by Finland and Universal Postal Union issues from 1941.

Philatelic library of the museum contains nearly 5,000 works; manuscripts on different subjects.

The museum comprises, in addition to the philatelic department, an historical department of Post and Telegraph and libraries.

Rotating exhibits of the collections. The museum also participates in national and international stamp exhibitions.

Collections open to the public according to general usage of museums. Library manuscripts available to scholars and the public. Very old books not circulated.

Open year round Tuesday to Friday, noon to 3 p.m.; Wednesday, 3 to 6 p.m.

Admission, adults, 2Fmk.; children, 1Fmk.

## France

**AMBOISE.** Musee de la Poste, 6, rue Joyeuse, 37400. Collection dealing with postal communications. Special material on the horse-drawn post, including badges, artwork and examples of vehicles.

Exhibits on the posts offer France's first stamp, Paris siege material, maritime post information and airmail artifacts. Military mails and services in foreign countries. Means of urban communications. Housed in 16th century building.

Open all year, daily except Tuesday. Closed Jan. 1, May 1, the Thursday of Ascension, Nov. 1, and Dec. 25.

Hours from April 1 to Sept. 30 are 9:30 a.m. to noon and 2 to 6:30 p.m. From Oct. 1 to March 31, 10 a.m. to noon and 2 to 5 p.m. Admission, adults, 7 francs; children 3fr.

**CHARLEVILLE-MEZIERES.** Galerie postale. A museum which offers both unusual pieces and the everyday apparatus and artifacts of the post office. Many post office boxes and signs.

Exhibits begin in the 18th century, and emphasize the development of services in the Ardennes. Many documents and works of art are included.

Important events covered include early postal codes and the adoption of a decimal currency, both of which occurred about 1800.

Also on display are post office related games, dating stamps, and a wide variety of other items.

Private museum, available only by appointment.

NANTES. Musee Postal, Direction Regionale des Postes, 10 bd Auguste Pageot, 44038 Nantes. Collection ranging from 1426, with documents, artwork, posters, letters, stamps, etc.

Curator served in Germany after World War II and has also collected substantial holdings relating to the German posts.

NICE. Cosmos-Museum Philatelique, Villa Cima-Rosa, Avenue Michel de Cimiez, a facility of Lollini Timbres-Poste.

Emphasis on conquest of space, collections, first day covers. Philatelic literature.

Publications include catalogs, "Conquest of Space" (stamps, first day covers), 13-volume album, monthly information.

PARIS. Musee de la Poste, Maison de la Poste et de la Philatelie, 34, Boulevard de Vaugirard. An official component of the French postal service.

Exhibits dealing with postal markings, early and modern stamps of France and foreign countries. Items range from classic stamps to material related to the siege of Paris to modern mechanization. A substantial library which may be used by visitors on the premises.

Open to the public daily except Thursdays and holidays, 10 a.m. to 5 p.m. Admission 5 francs, half price for children and students. Half price for all visitors on Sunday.

RIQUEWIHR. Musee d'Histoire des PTT d'Alsace. Collection dealing with the history of posts in the northeast part of France, located in the Chateau de Wurtemberg-Montbeliard. Collection of the Amis de l'Histoire des PTT d'Alsace.

Begins with relics of transportation in Roman times. Includes horse post under Thurn and Taxis and after the transfer of Alsace to France in 1648. Modern postal materials include early postage stamps, the siege of Paris and the First World War in Alsace. Early airmail communications.

Open daily from the end of March to mid-November 10 a.m. to noon and 2 to 6 p.m.; Sunday, 10 a.m. to noon, and 3 to 7 p.m. Closed Wednesdays. During July and August the museum is open Wednesdays, and until 7 p.m. Tuesdays and Fridays. Admission, adults 6 francs; children 4fr.

SAINT-MACAIRE (GIRONDE). Musee postal d'Aquitaine. Located in the Relais de poste Henri IV. Collection of the Association pour l'Histoire des Postes et Telecommunications en Aquitaine, founded 1972.

Begins in Roman times, and shows the development of postal communications. Makes use of recreated scenes. Production of postage stamps. Philatelic souvenirs available. Emphasis on postal services.

No current information on hours or admission fees available.

# German Democratic Republic

BERLIN. Postmuseum der DDR, 1066 Berlin, Leipziger Strasse. Collection encompasses stamps from the German States, Germany 1871-1945, the German Democratic Republic, foreign nations and associated materials.

The library includes 20,000 volumes. First day covers, postal history materials, postal stationery and documentary materials may be seen.

Exhibits show the development of communications through the ages.

Hours are 10 a.m. to 6 p.m., Tuesday through Friday; 10 a.m. to 5 p.m. Saturday. Entry is 30 pfennigs, 20pf for students and soldiers, 10pf in groups of 10 persons, and 1 mark for permission to use a camera.

# Germany, Federal Republic of

BERLIN. Berlin Postal and Telecommunications Museum, D-1000 Berlin 30, Urania-House. Collections of stamps of the world since 1945 on exhibit. Various letters and envelopes, Prussian and Berlin area.

Philatelic literature included in "Postgeschichtliche und Philatelistische Bibliothek," D-1000 Berlin 21.

Open to the general public, Tuesday through Friday, 10 a.m. to 4 p.m.; Saturday and Sunday, 10 a.m. to 1 p.m. Closed holidays. Free.

BONN. Postwertzeichenausstellung im Bundesministerium fur das Post- und Fernmeldewesen, Adenauerallee 81.

Special exhibitions in conjunction with the postal museum in Frankfurt. Open Sunday 9 a.m. to 1 p.m.; Wednesday 10 a.m. to 3 p.m. Free.

FRANKFURT AM MAIN. Bundespostmuseum, Schaumainkai 53, D-6000 Frankfurt 70.

Opened in 1958, and contains some of the collections of the former Reichspostmuseum in Berlin. Frankfurt is stated to have many traditions of early postal service activities.

Museum traces the history of postal and telecommunications with such materials as uniforms, works of art, post house signs, postboxes, models, telegraph devices, telephones, radios and other equipment.

Stamps, covers, and printing items are also displayed. Many special exhibits.

The collection also includes substantial archival and library holdings.

Tuesday through Sunday, 10 a.m. to 4 p.m. Free.

FRIEDRICHSDORF IM TAUNUS. Philipp-Reiss-Sammlung, Hugenottenstrasse 93.

This collection is associated with the postal museum in Frankfurt. It is open to visitors Saturday from 10 a.m to noon.

HAMBURG. Philatelistische Bucherei Hamburg, Hamburg 76, Hohenfelder Strasse 10. A library of philatelic publications, open to public use. Hours are Tuesday 5 to 7 p.m., Thursday 5 to 7 p.m., and Saturday 10 a.m. to 1 p.m.

Books may be used in the building, or in most cases withdrawn for circulation. A moderate charge is made for circulation to persons who are not members of the library.

— Postmuseum, Stephanplatz 1-5. Materials relating to postal history of the region on display. Also, an extensive collection of steamer mail. Library and picture holdings associated with the museum.

There is no current information available on hours and fees.

**KOBLENZ.** Oberpostdirektion Postal Museum, Friedrich-Ebert-Ring 14-20.

Stamps on envelopes, post cards and stampless covers on permanent exhibition.

Open to the public Monday through Friday by appointment. Closed Sundays and holidays.

**MAINZ.** Gutenberg-Museum, Liebfrauenplatz 5. Changing exhibitions of stamp collections, philatelic literature includes "Gutenberg im Markenfeld."

Open to the public Tuesday through Saturday, 10 a.m. to 6 p.m.; Sunday, 10 a.m. to 1 p.m. Closed in January for renovation, also certain holidays. Free.

**MUNICH.** Philatelistische Bibliothek (corner of Blumenstrasse and Pestilozzistrasse), a part of the Stadtbibliothek Munchen, founded by Christoph Otto Muller. Because of planned move to new location, address is uncertain.

Library contains 22,000 volumes with 8,000 titles on philately of all countries. Books on specialized subjects, cancellations, forgeries, topicals, postal history; 320 volumes of philatelic periodicals in all languages.

Stamp catalogs of leading German and international publishers; auction catalogs of most European firms. Card file index of philatelic articles in international magazines, with 80,000 entries on all countries.

Open to the general public Monday, 8 a.m. to noon; Tuesday, noon to 7 p.m.; Thursday and Friday, 8 a.m. to 3:30 p.m. Closed holidays. Free.

**NURNBERG.** Der Postabteilung des Verkehrsmuseums, Lessingstrasse 6.

Development of the Bavarian State Post is demonstrated in the rooms of "Taxissaal, Bayernsaal and Postbetriebssaal" containing artifacts of postal history.

General collection with more than 100,000 stamps, special Bavarian collection, alternating special stamp exhibitions.

Open Monday through Saturday, April through September, 10 a.m. to 5 p.m.; October through March, 10 a.m. to 4 p.m. Open Sunday year round, 10 a.m. to 1 p.m. Closed major holidays, and Sunday hours on certain other holidays.

**REGENSBURG.** Furst Thurn und Taxis Zentralarchiv und Hofbibliothek, Emmeramsplatz 5; mailing address Postfach 11 02 46, D-8400 Regensburg 11.

The collection deals with the famed Thurn and Taxis postal system, including the prestamp period and markings on the stamps of Prussia, the North German Confederation, and the German State.

Among the items to be found are documents and artifacts dealing with the communications of the period. Small library is available for use, with a card catalog that also permits access through the Bavarian State Library in Munich.

Hours are Monday through Thursday, 7:30 a.m. to noon and 1 to 4:45 p.m., closing at 3:30 on Friday. It is possible to obtain Xerox and microfilm copies of material in the archives. This is primarily a research facility.

**STUTTGART.** Postgeschichtliche Sammlung der OPD, Kronenstrasse 3. No current information on availability or fees.

## Gibraltar

**GIBRALTAR.** Gibraltar Museum, 18-20 Bomb House Lane. Gibraltar stamps, early local postmarks, "A26" and "G" obliterators. Most of material is on exhibit, occasionally used for publications.

Open Monday through Friday, 10 a.m. to 1 p.m. and 3 to 6 p.m.; closed bank holidays.

Admission, adults 25 pence; children 10p.

## Hungary

**BUDAPEST.** Philatelic Museum of the Hungarian Post Office, H-1400, Budapest, Box 86.

Four exhibits encompass the museum's 220,000 Hungarian and foreign stamps — permanent world exhibition, airmail and zeppelin, Universal Postal Union Centenary, Hungarian fine arts and folk art.

Museum participates on regular basis in national and international exhibitions.

Museum library contains 4,000 volumes on Hungarian and foreign philately, 21 local and foreign periodicals received regularly, more than 30,000 copies of archivalia of the stamps issued by the Hungarian Post Office.

Library also holds extensive collection of letters pertaining to postal history.

Open Wednesday, 10 a.m. to 6 p.m.; Saturday, 10 a.m. to 3 p.m.; Sunday, 10 a.m. to 2 p.m. Admission, 2 forint.

## Ireland

**DUBLIN.** National Museum of Ireland, Kildare Street.

Collection includes British stamps dating from the introduction of the Penny Post of 1840, European and Colonial stamps from the latter half of the 19th century, and recent stamps acquired through the Universal Postal Union.

Letters and envelopes with historical postal markings, primarily of Irish interest.

Available to the public on request and to scholars by prior arrangement.

Open to the public Tuesday through Saturday, 10 a.m. to 5 p.m.; Sundays, 2 to 5 p.m. Closed Christmas Day and Good Friday. Free.

## Italy

**ROME.** Museo Storico delle Poste e Telecomunicazioni, Ministry of Posts and Telecommunications, Viale Cristoforo Colombo.

Postal history of Italian states, canceling devices, stamp designs, relics, documents, seals, bibliographic material and stamps of Italy and the world compose the museum's collection.

Open 9 a.m. to 1 p.m. weekdays. Admission, 500 lire.

## Liechtenstein

**VADUZ.** Postmuseum des Furstentums Liechtenstein, in the same building as the prince's art collection.

The collection, founded in 1930, includes all the stamps of Liechtenstein, with printing and other specialty items, as well as periodical special exhibitions.

Letters, pre-stamp materials and entires are also on display as space permits.

Open daily 10 a.m. to noon and 2 to 6 p.m. Free.

## Luxembourg

**LUXEMBOURG.** Musee des Postes et Telecommunications, 19 Rue de Reims. The museum is located on the first floor of the main post office. It traces the history of postal communications with postal collection boxes, uniforms, devices and other equipment. Stamps, covers and printing items are also displayed, along with documents relating to the establishment of the Luxembourg postal system. Many special exhibits.

Open Tuesday, Thursday and Saturday, 10 a.m. to noon and 2 to 5 p.m. Free.

## Malta

**VALLETA.** General Post Office, Merchants Street.

Stamps and philatelic material, including colorproofs, progressive sheets and original designs, reportedly may be available in the near future for viewing at the post office.

## Monaco

**MONACO-VILLE.** Musee du Palais Princier, MC Monaco. Opened to the public in 1970.

Permanent exhibits include all stamps issued in the Principality of Monaco, the Prince Rainier III collection, letters and envelopes relating to postal history of the principality.

Open July through September, 9:30 a.m. to noon, and 2 to 6 p.m.; other months, 10 to 11:30

a.m. and 2 to 5:30 p.m. Closed Jan. 1 through Feb. 10. Admission, 8 francs.

## Netherlands

**THE HAGUE.** Het Nederlandse Postmuseum, Zeestraat 82 2518 AD. Founded 1929.

General, documentary and specialized collections of The Netherlands, also world collection, on permanent display.

Extensive collection of letters, some bearing what are reported to be oldest known postal markings of the world.

Museum also has collection of designs, engraving materials of Dutch stamps, catalogs, periodicals, books on Dutch philately.

The museum participates in approximately 20 major philatelic exhibitions each year in The Netherlands and abroad.

Open to general public; scholars have access to research material by appointment. Special guided tours on Sundays and during school vacations.

Weekdays 10 a.m. to 5 p.m.; Sundays and public holidays, 1 to 5 p.m. Closed Jan. 1. Admission, adults 50 cents; children 25¢.

A three-year closing for renovation may occur in the near future.

## Norway

**OSLO.** The Post Office Museum of Oslo, Dronningens gate 15 IV, Oslo 1.

Collection on permanent exhibition comprises stamps of Universal Postal Union member countries, cancellations, Norwegian philatelic literature including six booklets published for the museum.

Open to the public Monday through Friday, 10 a.m. to 3 p.m.; Sunday, noon to 3 p.m. Closed New Year's Eve, seasons of Christmas, Easter and Pentecost, May 1 and May 17. Free.

## Poland

**WARSAW.** Musee des Postes et Telecommunications Pologne, ul. Krasinskiego 1, 50-954 Warsaw. Deals with Polish stamps, and with foreign emissions as received through the Universal Postal Union. Library of works in Polish and foreign languages.

Collection includes approximately 5,000 letters and covers, and also proofs and other printing process materials.

The museum takes part in numerous philatelic expositions and also organizes thematic exhibitions of its own. Special programs cater to students, teachers and tour guides.

Founded after World War I and opened to the public in 1928, the collection suffered serious losses during the World War II occupation of Poland. The museum was opened in Warsaw in 1956.

Hours are 10 a.m. to 3 p.m., Sundays 11 a.m. to 2:30 p.m., closed Tuesdays. Entry is 4 zloty, 2zl for students, 1zl for tours. Free on Mondays.

## Portugal

**LISBON.** Museum of the CTT, Rua de D. Estefania. Includes materials relating to the posts, telephone, telegraph and radio.

The collection includes a wide variety of postal and telecommunications devices, including vehicles, mailboxes, canceling devices, and so forth. Also on display are stamps of Portugal and colonies.

Open Tuesday through Saturday, 10 a.m. to noon, and 3 to 6 p.m. Closed Sunday, Monday and holidays. Free.

## San Marino

**SAN MARINO.** Museo Postale e Filatelico di Borgo Maggiore. Early San Marino issues exhibited including sketches, proofs and essays.

A topical display features Olympic Games, airmail history and the like. Museum also has complete collection of Universal Postal Union issues since 1920.

Highly modern design of display area.

No current information on availability and fees.

## Spain

**BARCELONA.** Museo Postal y Filatelico, Palacio de la Virreina, Ramblas 99.

Open Tuesday through Saturday, 9:30 a.m. to 2 p.m. and 6 to 9 p.m.

## Sweden

**STOCKHOLM.** Postmuseum, Lilla Nygatan 6, Old Town, Stockholm (PO Box 2002, S-10311, Stockholm).

Permanent exhibition of Swedish and foreign stamps; temporary exhibitions on special subjects; stampless and stamped letters.

Philatelic library for circulation within Sweden.

Open Monday through Saturday, noon to 3 p.m.; Thursday 9 a.m. to 9 p.m.; Sunday, noon to 4 p.m. Closed major holidays. Free.

## Switzerland

**BERNE.** General Directorate PTT, Library and Documentation, Viktoriastrasse 21, CH-3000 Berne 33.

The facility is open to the public weekdays during office hours. It features books, catalogs, price lists, about 400 titles of philatelic reviews, and a file of postal markings since 1849.

The PTT-Library also serves as the Central Library of the Association of Swiss Philatelic Societies. Most works circulate. Research facilities.

A photocopying service is available.

— Swiss PTT-Museum, Helvetiaplatz 4, CH-3005. Founded in 1907.

Museum collection arranged in three parts, stamps of Switzerland, the world and special collections. Updated yearly. Housed in specially equipped room in the museum basement. A worldwide selection of postage stamps on display in 20 steel cases, each consisting of 50 sliding panels.

Philatelic highlights are provided by special collections such as Old Switzerland, Swiss airmails, international airmails, zeppelin mails, old U.S.A. Also, letters and envelopes with Swiss markings.

Post card sets, individual post cards, copper plate print, variety of books can be bought.

Open to the public weekdays, 9 a.m. to noon and 2 to 5 p.m.; Sundays, 10 a.m. to noon and 2 to 5 p.m. Closed every Monday morning and on the principal religious holidays. Free.

The museum is to be transferred to a new building by 1986.

**GENEVA.** United Nations Philatelic Museum, Palais des Nations, CH-1211 Geneva 10.

Featured are the 11,000-item Prof. Charles Misteli collection — stamps, first day covers and postal documents, strong in League of Nations, early International Labor Office and other material from United Nations agencies.

Also, all U.N. postage stamps issued in Swiss franc, dollar and Austrian schilling values, first day covers and related material, thematic collections.

An audio-visual program is available on request. Library containing international philatelic magazines, handbooks and catalogs open to visitors.

Open to the public Monday through Friday 10 a.m. to noon and 2 to 4 p.m. Free.

## United Kingdom

**BATH.** Bath Postal Museum, 51 Great Pulteney St., BA2 4DP.

On display are covers carried by postboy, mailcoach, pigeon, balloon, cyclist, helicopter, hovercraft, postbus, submarine, plane and rocket. Old and diverse writing artifacts and letters, plus a comprehensive display of British stamps, are also included. Special philatelic exhibitions are featured regularly, augmented by continuous film and audio-visual presentations.

Open 11 a.m. to 5 p.m. daily except Wednesday; 2 to 5 p.m. Sunday. Admission, 50 pence for adults; 25p children; group rates available.

**COLNE (LANCASHIRE).** British in India Museum, Sun Street. Cancellations and stamps issued during British rule; the first air flight between India and the United Kingdom.

Open to the public Saturday and Sunday, May 1 to Sept. 30, 2 to 5 p.m. Parties of more than 20 persons welcome during the "closed season," by appointment. Details upon application.

Admission, adults 50 pence; children 30p.

**GUERNSEY (CHANNEL ISLANDS).** Museum of the States Philatelic Bureau, Guernsey Post Office. Exhibits current stamp issues.

Also displays various items of artwork, proof stamps, progressive sheets and the like. Postal history items, complete sheets of stamps produced during the German occupation of Guernsey from 1940-45.

Publication, "Guernsey Philatelic News," produced two months prior to each new stamp issue.

Renovations had the museum closed temporarily as of early 1982.

**JERSEY (CHANNEL ISLANDS).** Jersey Postal Museum, St. Helier. Opened May 27, 1976 as a section of the Fort Regent Leisure Center.

All philatelic items are related to or issued in Jersey and illustrate postal history of Jersey from 1794 with letters, postmarks, photographs, documents, models and stamps.

Open to general public seven days a week. Admission fee incorporated in entry charge to the Fort Regent complex.

**LONDON.** The British Library, Philatelic Collection, Great Russell Street.

Among famed collections in the museum are the Thomas Keay Tapling holdings, the Dr. E. Mosely collection of Africa, the Mrs. A. Fitzgerald collection of Airmails and Curiosities, the Board of Inland Revenue collection of Great Britain, and the M. A. Bojanowicz collection of the postal history of Poland.

Items on display include Hawaiian Missionary stamps, U.S. Confederate locals, and early Postmasters' Provisionals.

Open Monday through Saturday, 10 a.m. to 5 p.m.; Saturday, 2:30 to 6 p.m. Free.

— British National Postal Museum, King Edward Building, King Edward Street. Established with Reginald M. Phillips collection tracing history of stamps and postal services of Great Britain from 1837-1900.

Also, the post office collection, all postage stamps issued in Great Britain and worldwide offices under control of the British GPO, the Universal Postal Union Collection, and the De La Rue Philatelic Archives.

Exhibitions held; booklet publications including "350 Years of Anglo-American Post Links."

Open Monday through Friday, 10 a.m. to 4:30 p.m.; closed weekends and all bank holidays.

— Bruce Castle Museum, Bruce Castle Park, Lordship Lane, N17 8NU. Collections on local and postal history, material on history of the British Post Office extending from the 16th century to the present day with emphasis on the period 1700-1840.

Postal history collection divided into ten sections: miscellanea; general history; organization of the postal service; staff; finance; collection; distribution and delivery of mails; communications; telegraphs; wireless services and telephones; other services as savings banks, money orders and pensions; and foreign post offices.

Material ranges from 16th century letters, 17th century newspapers, 18th century official notices, 19th century post horns and coaching prints, to books, pamphlets and periodicals on postal history.

Major portion of postal history, the Morten collection, on permanent loan from the Union of Communication Workers.

Stamps, bulk of postal history collection is not on display; specific items for study can be seen by appointment.

Hours, Monday through Friday 10 a.m. to 5 p.m.; Saturday, 10 a.m. to 12:30 p.m. and 1:30 to 5 p.m. Closed Wednesdays and Sundays. Free.

— Imperial War Museum, Lambeth Road, SE1 6HZ.

Extensive holdings of material relating to 20th century warfare, collections of postage stamps, paper money, censorship marks, coins and medallions, most from World War I era.

Some on display but main collection can be viewed on application to the Department of Art.

Open Monday through Saturday, 10 a.m. to 5:50 p.m.; and Sunday, 2 to 5:50 p.m. Closed on most national holidays. Free.

— Gibbons Gallery, 399 Strand, London WC2. This gallery is part of the establishment of international stamp dealer Stanley Gibbons. Each month it presents an exhibition of materials arranged by a well-known collector or group.

Further information is available from the firm. Hours are 9:30 a.m. to 4:30 p.m., except weekends and holidays.

— The Royal Philatelic Society, 41 Devonshire Place, London W1N 1PE.

A membership organization which offers philatelic lectures and displays, expertization, and a library which circulates among United Kingdom members. Founded 1869.

**PRESTON (LANCASHIRE).** Harris Museum and Art Gallery, Market Square.

Stamps of the Victorian era and present day, mainly British; letters and envelopes of World War I and World War II; several hundred Christmas and Valentine cards from the 18th century to the present day. No philatelic items are currently on public display.

Hours, Monday through Saturday, 10 a.m. to 5 p.m.; closed Sunday and all bank holidays.

**YORK.** York Castle Museum, considered an outstanding folk museum, including reconstructed Victorian streets. Exterior of a subpost office can be seen and the Victorian wall-mounted postbox can be used for posting letters. A Victorian pillar-box can be seen outside the William

IV Hotel in Half Moon Court, an Edwardian street.

Open all year except Christmas Day, Boxing Day and New Year's Day. Further details from the curator, The Castle Museum, York YO1 1RY, England.

## Yugoslavia

**BELGRADE.** National Postal Museum, Majke Jevrosime Street 13. Operated by the Yugoslav Postal Administration, displays feature postal history of the country.

Current information on hours or fees not available.

# Other Countries

## Argentina

**BUENOS AIRES.** Posts and Telegraphs. Museum, second floor General Post Office; library on sixth floor, Room 631; 851 Avenida de los Italianos. Philatelic booklets, letters, stamps and envelopes with historical postal markings.

Open to the general public throughout the year. Hours: library, 11:30 a.m. to 7 p.m; museum, 10 a.m. to 6 p.m. Free.

## Colombia

**MEDELLIN.** Philatelic Museum of the Bank of the Republic of Colombia, on 19th floor of bank building.

Collection of stamps, documents and first day covers depicting the development of Colombian culture, plus displays of Colombian and world-wide stamps.

Museum also houses a projection room, exhibition room, special library, and archives of documents on postal and philatelic history of Colombia.

Rotating exhibits of postal material to be scheduled.

Open Monday through Friday, 9:30 a.m. to noon, and 2:15 to 6 p.m.

## Egypt

**CAIRO.** Postal Museum, Aaba Square. Historical postal events of the Middle East and Egypt featured. Also, uniforms of postal carriers and workers, models of buildings that have housed post offices or postal facilities displayed. Handling and transport of the mails also depicted.

Open Saturday through Thursday. Free.

## Ethiopia

**ADDIS ABABA.** Ethiopian National Postal Museum, Post Office Building, Churchill Road.

Complete Ethiopian stamp collection since 1894, Universal Postal Union stamps since 1940. Local and foreign philatelic literature; some envelopes, historical picture post cards.

Stamps preserved and documented in aluminum cases with English-speaking trained personnel available. Exhibits available on request.

Material available to scholars and the general public. Hours are Monday to Friday, 9 a.m. to 1 p.m. and 3 to 6 p.m.; Saturdays, 9 a.m. to 3 p.m. Closed holidays. Admission, Eth. 25 cents for adults; children free.

## India

**NEW DELHI.** National Philatelic Museum, Posts and Telegraphs Directorate (Dak Tar Bhavan), Parliament Street.

Extensive collection of early Indian stamps, essays, trial proofs, postmarks and postal stationery, also foreign issues.

Holdings also include the "Scinde Dawks" of the Province of Sind (now in Pakistan) issued in 1852, the first stamps of Asia, and rare material such as essays, proofs, and other items relating to the first (1854) issues of India.

Also exhibited are general issues of India since independence and pioneer airmail events involving India.

No current information on availability or fees.

## Japan

**TOKYO.** The Communications Museum (Teishin Sogo Hakubutsu Kan), 1-3 Otemachi 2-chome, Chiyoda-ku. Established June 20, 1902, for mutual understanding of postal-communication culture.

Universal Postal Union and general collections on exhibit. Museum also has 1904 official and military use postal cards, philatelic literature. Postal Corner of museum contains philatelic artifacts relating to postal history.

Open Jan. 4-Dec. 28, 9 a.m. to 4:30 p.m. Closed Mondays and holiday season, Dec. 29-Jan. 3.

Admission, adults, 50 yen; juniors under college age (nonstudents considered as adults), 20y; group of adults over 20 persons, 25y; group of junior students, 10y.

## Mexico

**MEXICO CITY.** Postal Museum of Mexico, Postal Palace, Tacuba Street, No. 1, first floor.

Emphasis on stamps and postal history of Mexico, some postally related items of other countries. Museum also has a collection of mailboxes from the United States, France and the Austro-Hungarian Empire.

No current information on availability or fees.

## New Zealand

**CHRISTCHURCH.** The Rhodes Collection of New Zealand is reported to contain many unusual rarities and items. Details unavailable.

## Peru

**LIMA.** Museo Postal y Filatelico, Hall del Correo Central de Lima, Jr. Conde de Superunda No. 170.

Official collections of the Peruvian posts, exhibited chronologically. Philatelic souvenirs are available.

Hours are 7:45 a.m. to 4 p.m. Monday through Saturday, April to December. Sundays and holidays, 10 a.m. to noon. January to March 7:45 a.m. to 1:30 p.m., 10 a.m. to noon on Sundays and holidays.

English-speaking personnel available.

## South Africa

**JOHANNESBURG.** Public Library, Market Square.

Comprehensive collection of books, journals, periodicals and catalogs on philately, both general and specialist in nature.

Books loaned to members of the philatelic societies of Johannesburg and Germiston on presentation of a membership card.

Open Monday through Thursday, 9 a.m. to 7:30 p.m.; Friday 9 a.m. to 5:30 p.m.; Saturday 9 a.m. to 5 p.m.

The library also houses an Africana Museum, with a general collection of South African postage stamps and some adjacent territories; also the Curle collection of Transvaal stamps; a collection of postal covers, post and censor marks illustrates the postal history of World War II as it affected South Africa; also, Johannesburg postmarks, Boer War letters, and postal stationery.

Museum hours are Monday through Friday, 9 a.m. to 5:30 p.m.; Saturday 9 a.m. to 5 p.m.; Sunday 1 to 5:30 p.m. Closed Good Friday and Christmas. Professional staff not available on Saturday or Sunday. Free.

## Turks and Caicos Islands

**GRAND TURK.** Postal Museum of the Turks and Caicos Islands. Open Monday through Thursday, 8:30 a.m. to 1 p.m. Free.

## Zimbabwe

**SALISBURY.** The National Archives, Private Bag 7729, Causeway. Founded 1935. Gun Hill location.

Holdings include every issue from 1913 and single specimens of all earlier issues after the occupation in 1890. Some cancellations.

Open to the public Monday through Friday, 9 a.m. to 5:30 p.m.; Saturday, 9 a.m. to 5 p.m.; and Sunday, 2 to 5 p.m. Closed Good Friday and Christmas Day.

# Organizations

# 14

## American Philatelic Society

Starting with but few enthusiasts in the 1850s, the number of collectors of postage stamps steadily increased through the succeeding decades, and by the 1880s must have totaled 25,000 or more. Naturally, with this comparatively limited number of collectors, the avenues for purchasing and exchanging stamps and securing information about stamps were restricted to the few dealers and the diminutive philatelic journals, practically all of which were published only for brief periods.

Responding to the demand of numerous collectors and local societies to form a national stamp society, 400 interested collectors indicated their willingness to assist in founding such an organization. A total of 219 sent in their proxies and each paid 25 cents for the privilege of voting by proxy.

A committee held a meeting in New York City on Sept. 13, 1886. The name, the American Philatelic Association, was adopted for the newly formed organization. The following day, John K. Tiffany, a distinguished businessman and ardent philatelist, was elected president, a position he was to hold for 10 years.

The first five issues of the "American Philatelist" were published in Altoona, Pa., commencing Jan. 10, 1887. A mail vote in June 1887, resulted in the "Western Philatelist" being chosen as the society's official publication.

Because of the dissension caused by this action, the membership at the second annual convention, held in Chicago, Ill., in August 1887, voted to resume publishing the "American Philatelist" as the society's official journal.

The association was first incorporated in the state of West Virginia under date of Nov. 2, 1891; certificate of this incorporation appears in Volume X, November 1896, issue of the "American Philatelist."

On Aug. 24, 1897, at the Boston convention, authority was given the Northwestern Adjustment Co. of Minneapolis to act as agents for the reincorporation of the association in the state of Minnesota.

In 1897, the name of the organization was changed to the American Philatelic Society, then a few months later was changed back to the original name. Since September 1908, the name has remained unchanged as the American Philatelic Society.

The society grew steadily, and when the golden jubilee convention was held in 1936, membership stood at 4,526.

Because of the startling increase in membership and the society's expanding activities, it was considered necessary to consolidate activities in a central office and to hire full-time employees to staff it.

H. Clay Musser was appointed the first full-time secretary. He established the central office at State College, Pa., on April 1, 1945.

In 1947, the APS was elected to membership in the Federation Internationale de Philatelie (FIP) as the United States representative.

In 1958, the Sales Division, previously operated by J.E. Guest in Dallas, Tex., for 37 years, became one of the responsibilities of the executive secretary, who assumed the additional title of sales director. The Sales Division operations were moved to State College, Pa.

In 1962, the Stamp Education Program, using the now famous "Black Blot" and "Big Q" designations to alert the stamp collecting world to stamp issuing policies believed to be undesirable and injurious to the hobby, was inaugurated and has since won worldwide acclaim and acceptance.

Col. James T. DeVoss, U.S. Army, Retired, succeeded H. Clay Musser as executive secretary and sales director upon Musser's retirement on Nov. 15, 1963.

The society was instrumental in the formation of the Federacion Interamericana de Filatelia (FIAF) in 1966.

Daniel W. Vooys, a bank president from Canajoharie, N.Y., assumed office as president in October 1969. Under his able and imaginative leadership, the society improved its services and sought new areas in which to be of service to philatelists everywhere.

Outstanding among his accomplishments was his whole-hearted support of the effort initiated by Edward L. Willard, APS past president, to establish the American Philatelic Research Library and to have it recognized as a top-ranking library available to all stamp collectors regardless of the philatelic affiliation.

Upon the death in 1976 of James M. Chemi — who had edited "The American Philatelist" in Arizona since 1960 — the editorial offices were consolidated with the headquarters. Since then, the monthly journal has been edited by Richard L. Sine.

In the fall of 1978, Pennsylvania State University began work on a comprehensive series of correspondence courses in stamp collecting. A grant from the APS provided initial funding for the project, which is being directed by an advisory committee composed of both Penn State and APS personnel.

A new national headquarters building was dedicated in April 1982. The building stands on a 5-acre plot at the entrance to a planned community on the outskirts of State College.

With more than 20,000 square feet of floor space, the building is asymetric and will permit expansion in whatever direction necessary.

James T. DeVoss, after 20 years with the society, was succeeded in 1981 by Keith A. Wagner as executive director.

On Jan. 1, 1982, the APS boasted 53,415 current members. Membership has more than doubled since 1977.

From its beginning in 1886, the society has constantly striven to establish and improve high standards for American philately. The steady growth of its membership attests to the nationwide acceptance of its role in this field.

Keeping pace with its ever-expanding membership have been the services offered by the society.

These include close rapport with and support of its numerous chapters and units, a large number of slide-lecture programs, an Expertization Service, an Estate Advisory Service, a Sales Division, and the publication of a philatelic journal as well as numerous handbooks.

# American Philatelic Research Library

The American Philatelic Research Library, located in the American Philatelic Building, is the largest public library specializing in philately in the United States. Incorported in 1968 as the research and educational arm of the American Philatelic Society, the APRL processes requests for information and the loan of books.

The library also offers researchers and browsers a wealth of philatelic materials, display racks filled with current periodicals and auction catalogs, and exhibit frames displaying members' collections.

The APRL is the result of the long-expressed wish of thousands of collectors since the emergence of stamp collecting as a major hobby. It has been recognized for decades that a national philatelic library to serve the needs of serious philatelists, regardless of their place of residence, would be a boon to all stamp collectors and a tremendous boost to the hobby.

The need for easy access to books and articles containing information not readily available to the average collector and researcher has been apparent to many prominent philatelists, some of whom have expounded upon the theme in lectures and in articles published both in the 19th and 20th centuries.

John K. Tiffany, a prominent philatelist of the late 19th century, an ardent advocate of the establishment of a national philatelic library, and first president of the American Philatelic Association (as the APS was then called), was instrumental in developing the lasting interest in philatelic literature which now exists.

Edward L. Willard, first president of the APRL, worked diligently for the establishment of a national philatelic library during his term as president of the APS and finally, in 1968, saw the APRL become a reality. The John K. Tiffany Library Fund and the Edward L. Willard Memorial Fund have been established to honor the contribution these two distinguished philatelists made to the philatelic world. Tax deductible donations in any amount may be made to either of these funds.

Now, with the APRL firmly established as a viable philatelic research center, utilization of its resources is steadily increasing. Several ardent researchers who have utilized the resources of the library have published important articles which have appeared in major philatelic publications.

### Library Resources

The present library collection contains numerous research materials covering every aspect of philately. For beginning collectors, there are all kinds of informational handbooks, guides, dictionaries and encyclopedias. For specialist collectors, there are numerous handbooks, periodicals, and catalogs. For those beginning research in new fields of philately, there are many bibliographies and indexes.

A system has been devised to enable members unable to come to the library to request information and borrow materials. Books, catalogs and bound periodicals can be borrowed through the mail for a small fee per book to cover the cost of postage and handling.

The materials borrowed may be kept for two weeks from the day received, and they may be renewed once for the same period. A fine is charged for each day a book is not returned according to the aforementioned rule. As many as five books may be borrowed at one time. Requests, however, can be made for more than five books with the understanding that additional books will be sent upon return of the books loaned originally.

All patrons are asked to fill out a borrower's application form before borrowing books. A borrower's application form will be sent when books are requested, but members may request the appropriate forms in advance of borrowing, so books can be sent without delay.

The appropriate fee must be sent with all book requests; books cannot be loaned on credit. Members who prefer to request books by telephone may deposit funds for future borrowing.

Members of the APS and APRL may borrow books directly from the library, while members of chapters, units, or affiliates of the APS may obtain material from the library through their chapter or affiliate representative.

All others may utilize the facilities of the library by having their local library request material for them through the interlibrary loan program.

For those patrons who are uncertain as to what may be available on a specific topic, the APRL staff can suggest books. Subject cards from the card catalog pertaining to the topic will be photocopied and sent on request so the patron can decide which books he may wish to borrow.

This is done for two reasons. First, it enables the patron to disregard those publications which he may already have in his possession or which he may already have read. Second, a subject card provides a complete bibliographic description of each book so the patron can determine if it is of interest.

A wide variety of reference sources are available to help in answering specific questions. Reference materials, rare books, and unbound periodicals cannot be loaned; however, photocopies can be made of the appropriate pages of items which may be of interest. A cost per page is charged for photocopies.

### APRL Membership

Any person can become a member of the APRL. The annual dues of $8 include a subscription to the library quarterly, "Philatelic Literature Review." Membership in the APS automatically confers use of the library, but does not include a subscription to the "Philatelic Literature Review."

The "Philatelic Literature Review" for many years has been an authoritative and valuable source of information concerning philatelic literature. Formerly published by the Philatelic Literature Association, before its merger in 1969 with the APRL, the "Review" publishes bibliographies on special philatelic subjects and indexes for other specialized periodicals.

One of its features is the "Literature Clearinghouse," where members may advertise their literature for sale or publish their want lists for needed literature. (Sample copies are available for a nominal charge.)

In September 1969, the U.S. Internal Revenue Service recognized the library as a tax-exempt institution, thus making all donations to it tax deductible. To enable philatelists and friends to provide tax-deductible financial support, sustaining ($15) and contributing ($30) memberships have been established.

With these memberships, the amounts in excess of $5 are tax deductible. The names of sustaining and contributing members are published annually in the "Philatelic Literature Review."

Additionally, life memberships ($160) are available and do not require payment of annual dues. Such contributions also qualify under the Internal Revenue Service regulations.

The fiscal and membership year commences Jan. 1. Dues are payable in advance and are prorated the first year of membership.

Donations of all types of philatelic literature are appreciated. Donations are acknowledged in both "American Philatelist" and the "Philatelic Literature Review." All literature donations also are tax deductible, which is particularly helpful in the settlement of an estate.

Many large private libraries, as well as countless individual works, already have been donated to the APRL. All such donations may be mailed to the APRL via library rate.

An active acquisitions program has been established, and both new and important out-of-print publications are being purchased to expand the holdings of the library. However, the active assistance of concerned philatelists in all fields is needed to ensure the continued growth of the library.

Further information is available from the APRL, Box 8338, State College, Pa. 16801.

## APRL Founder Members

Ray C. Ameen
J. Oliver Amos
William T. Amos
Gordon F. Anderson
Earl P.L. Apfelbaum
Leo August
Samuel August
William H. Bauer
George Boiko
Billings E. Burlingame
Richard W. Canman
Anna M. Chemi
James M. Chemi
Sarah Mensinger
  Chemi Memorial
Emerson A. Clark
Joseph M. Clary
Sylvester Colby
Donald F. Dahlquist
George R. Daley
James N. Dalton
Leslie A. Davenport
Robert L.D. Davidson
Kenneth R. de Lisle
James T. DeVoss
Dr. Harold E. Donnell
Peter G. DuPuy
George C. Dyer
Melvin T. Edmonds
Sidney Epstein
Lois M. Evans
William L. Evans
John E. Foxworth Jr.
Joe F. Frye
Marian Frye
Louis Grunin
Bernard D. Harmer
Henry E. Harris

Elizabeth H. Harrison
Horace W. Harrison
Creighton C. Hart
John T. Hastings Jr.
Bernard A. Hennig
Dolores E. Hennig
Herman Herst Jr.
Duane Hillmer
J. King Horner
Henry W. Houser
Georgia B. Hunt
Lucius Jackson
Gayle C. Jones
Lewis M. Kaufman
Arthur M. Kennedy Jr.
A. Murl Kimmel
Joseph L. Kurtzman
Maryette B. Lane
Andrew Levitt
David Lidman
Harry L. Lindquist
Lyons F. Livingston
Harold H. Longfellow
Catherine S. Lowder
Elizabeth S. Martin
George M. Martin
Robert A. Mason
Edward L. Miller
Doris H. Moran
Kendall A. Moran
James A. Morton Jr.
Edward M. Passano
Charles J. Peterson
Samuel Ray
Edward A. Richardson
Jared H. Richter
Arthur E. Ross Jr.
Arthur Salm

Harry C. Sayre III
Robert A. Scheuermann
William E. Shelton
Kelly Shryoc
J.N. Sissons
Hubert C. Skinner
Kent J. Snyder
Lauson H. Stone
Charles H. Sweeting
Alex L. ter Braake
Neil D. Thompson
Ronald J. Tomaszewski
George Trefonas
V.R. Trimmer
Daniel F. Vooys
Daniel W. Vooys
Grace E. Vooys
Lt. Col. Daniel C. Warren
Raymond H. Weill
William L. Welch
Edward L. Willard
Benjamin Wishnietsky
Marian Carne Zinsmeister
APS Writers Unit
Baltimore Philatelic Society, Inc.
Chicago Philatelic Society
Crescent City Stamp Club
The Franklin Mint Corp.
Hollywood Stamp Club
Memphis Stamp Collectors Society
Mt. Nittany Philatelic Society
New Haven Philatelic Society
Scott Publishing Co.
SONEX '72
Vidiforms Co., Inc.
WESTPEX

## APS Accredited Judges

The following collectors and dealers (latter indicated by an asterisk) have been accredited as philatelic judges. The highest level of philatelic exhibition each individual has actually served as judge is indicated in parentheses following each name — (I) International (N) National (R) Regional (L) Local. The principal area of philatelic interest is given for each accredited judge.

Many stamp exhibitions now utilize apprentice judges in order that those interested might gain experience by serving with an accredited judge and thereby become sufficiently compe-

tent to meet the accreditation requirements of the APS.

Members desiring to make application for accreditation as a philatelic judge may obtain the necessary forms by writing to the chairman, Accreditation of Judges, Box 8000, State College, Pa. 16801.

Allen, William C., Michigan (R) U.S.; postal history; Canada; precancels; Great Britain; Germany

Alton, Jacquelyn S., Illinois (N) Germany

*Ameen, Ray C., Texas (N) Western and Central Europe; Germany and Colonies; Scandinavia; postal history

Arnold, Shirley T., Oregon (N) Germany; Great Britain; Switzerland; Iceland; Vatican; U.S.; Surinam; topicals

Arons, Mark L., Louisiana (N) general; postal stationery; Canada; Switzerland; Guatemala

*Baete, John, Belgium (I) classic Europe; postal history

Ball, Charles I., Ohio (N) general; postal history; postal stationery; literature

Balough, Joseph J., Texas (N) Germany; France; U.S.; perfins; topicals; literature

Barovick, Fred, New Jersey (I) general

Bartlett, William R., Tennessee (N) U.S.; British North America; Greece; Czechoslovakia; Philippines; postal history

Bates, Jack B., Florida (N) U.S.; northwest postal history; precancels; meters; revenues; topicals; British North America; Latin America

Bauer, William H., Illinois (I) U.S. postal history; postal stationery; Great Britain; Germany; Japan; Middle East; literature

Beal, James H., Ohio (I) Mexico; Latin American; classical Europe; general; postal history

Beecher, Stanley H., California (N) U.S.; U.N.; Latin America; British North America

Bennink, Richard J., Michigan (N) U.S.; Great Britain; Netherlands and Colonies; Israel; U.N.; postal history; topicals

*Birkinbine, John II, Arizona (N) 19th-century France; U.S.; Confederates; Canada; Sweden; Great Britain; general

Bize, David N. Jr., Nebraska (R) U.S.; Canada; Scandinavia; airmails; perfins; FDCs

Black, I. Lawrence, New York (N) Germany; France; Saar; Zeppelins; topicals

Blau, Fred F., Illinois (N) Palestine; Israel; Austria; Germany; U.S.; airmails

Blecher, F.W., West Germany (I) North German Confederation; Germany; U.S.; airmails

Blizil, George A., Florida (I) Czechoslovakia; Germany; British Colonies; stationery; Straits Settlements; U.S. 1869s; literature

*Bloch, Herbert J., New York (I) general

Bobbitt, Ottis C., Texas (N) U.S.; topicals

Boehret, Jesse D., Pennsylvania (N) Germany and related U.S. maritime mail

Boerma, Albert, Netherlands (I) Central Europe; literature; thematics

Bohne, Werner M., Florida (I) Germany and States; occupation issues; Memel; Danzig; Saar; Trieste; Allied Military Government; locals

Boker, John R. Jr., New York (I) 19th-century general; U.S.

Bonilla-Lara, Alvaro, Chile (I) Latin America

Bowman, James W., Texas (N) U.S.; Confederates; Hawaii

Brandeberry, R.B., Delaware (N) British Empire; Scandinavia; Netherlands and Colonies; Switzerland; Germany

Brasch, Frank O., California (N) Tibet; China; Manchukuo; Shanghai; Siam; Hong Kong

Brock, Charles W., Texas (N) Mexico; U.S.; postal history; Germany; France and Colonies; China; Great Britain; Canada

Brock, Fred C., California (N) Europe; Great Britain and Colonies; war covers; airmails; postal stationery; postal history

Brown, Kenneth L. Sr., Michigan (R) U.S.; Japan; Europe; topicals; Canada; Scandinavia

Buckner, John M., Florida (N) British Empire; U.S.; Confederates; postal stationery; postal history; topicals; revenues

Burton, Leo R.T., Oregon (N) general except literature and U.S. classics

Canman, Richard W., Illinois (N) Asia except India

Cary, Bruce R., Colorado (N) Austria; Germany; U.S.; highway post offices; topicals

Christian, Calvin W., California (N) U.S.

Clark, Emerson A., California (I) U.S.; British North America; Mexico; Latin America

Clary, Joseph M., California (I) general; 20th-century U.S.; western covers; airmails; topicals; literature; Poland

*Clatterbuck, W.C., Ohio (N) Canada; Hawaii; general

Cohn, Ernst M., Alabama (I) Scandinavia; France; Germany; Europe; postal history; airmails; literature

*Cole, Ezra D., New York (N) U.S.; British North America

Conway, Herbert E., New York (R) U.N.

Corless, Robert D., Arizona (N) U.S.; British North America; British Colonies; general; Australasia; postal stationery

Coyne, Sidney J., California (R) Bavaria; Wurttemberg; Austria; Poland; Yugoslavia; South Africa

Craig, Wallace A., California (N) Latin America; Scandinavia; postal stationery

Crain, Warren H., Texas (R) U.S. and Possessions; British Colonies; Zeppelins; Liechtenstein; Ryukyus

Cratsenberg, C.C., Arizona (N) Canada; U.S.; Latin America; general; literature; Newfoundland; Philippines

Cunliffe, Robert H., Pennsylvania (N) U.S.; revenues; general

Davenport, Carl D., California (N) Scandinavia; U.S.; Switzerland

Debo, Arno, West Germany (I) classical Europe; U.S.; South America

de Bodisco, Wadim, New York (R) Europe; general

de Lisle, Kenneth R., New York (N) U.S. postal history; literature

Demuth, Rene, Luxembourg (I) Luxembourg; Belgium; France; Netherlands

DeVoss, James T., Pennsylvania (I) U.S. Possessions; Central America; general; literature

Diena, Enzo, Italy (I) Italy; Italian States; European classics

Dike, Sheldon H., New Mexico (N) U.S.; postal history; general

Dorfman, David, Florida (N) U.S.; Cyprus; India; Israel; Palestine; Holy Land postal history

Dormer, Edward J., Florida (N) Mexico; U.S.; British Colonies; South America; airmails

Dougan, Charles W., Canada (N) China; Tibet; Chinese Treaty Ports; Shanghai

Doyle, Alan F., Texas (N) postal history; maritime mail; polar; space; postal stationery

Dretzke, Donald A., California (N) U.S.; British North America; France; Switzerland; Australia; Bermuda; Jamaica

Dulin, Austin H., New York (N) Germany; Japan; topicals; U.N.; general

*Edelman, Milton, Pennsylvania (N) 19th-century U.S.; 1851/57 issue; postal history; Egypt; mixed franking; general

*Effinger, R.C. Jr., Alabama (N) Germany; France; Iceland; Austria; Spain; Great Britain; Switzerland; Ryukyus

Eisendrath, Joseph L., Illinois (N) airmails; U.S. revenues; U.S. postal stationery; pioneer flight covers

Elnen, Thomas E., Illinois (N) Scandinavia; British Asia and Africa; U.S.

Emery, Charles O., Canada (N) Canada and revenues; British Commonwealth; topicals; literature

Engstrom, Victor E., Florida (N) general; Scandinavian postal stationery; local posts

Erle, Everett C., California (N) U.S.; British Colonies; 19th-century transatlantic and stampless covers; paquebot and seapost

Evans, Lois M., Massachusetts (N) Japan; U.S. used in Japan and China; U.N.; literature

Fink, Ernesto, Mexico (N) Europe; Sweden; Scandinavia

Flack, Wylie H., Pennsylvania (R) U.S.; postal history; stampless; Shanghai; postal stationery; patriotics; Ryukyus; China

Foley, Joseph E., Colorado (N) Ireland; British North America; British; U.S.

Foster, Clarence E., New Mexico (N) general; topicals; airmails; postal history; literature

Foxworth, John E. Jr., Michigan (I) U.S.; Confederates; British North America; Germany; topicals; postal stationery

Freer, Phillips B., California (N) Mexico; Latin America; topicals

Frenkle, Henry H., Louisiana (N) Great Britain; British Empire (less British North America); 19th-century Europe; literature; topicals

Fricke, Charles A., Pennsylvania (N) U.S.; postal stationery

Fricks, Ernest E., New Jersey (N) postal history

Fritzsche, Wolfgang, New York (N) Czechoslovakia; Germany; postal history; postal stationery; Zeppelins; catapult and Navy covers

Frye, Joe F., Tennessee (N) literature

Ganz, P. Felix, Illinois (N) Andorra; Liechtenstein; Switzerland; U.N.; postal stationery; postal history; Arctic; Antarctic

Garabrant, L.V., New Jersey (N) topical; general; Switzerland; Ireland

Garabrant, Melvin, New Jersey (N) France; Netherlands; topicals; general

Garrett, Gordon B., California (N) Egypt; Sudan; Canada; Scandinavia; airmails; literature; general

Gartner, John, Australia (I) British; general; literature

Gaston, Howard J., Connecticut (N) U.S.; British Colonies; British West Indies; topicals; Cuba; Dominican Republic; Haiti; U.S. cancels; postal history

Gilbert, Alex, Oregon (R) British Colonies; general; Scandinavia

Gobie, Henry M., Florida (N) U.S.; British Colonies; literature.

Goldsmith, Edward, Georgia (N) general; topicals; postal history; Spanish Antilles

Gonda, Thomas A., California (N) U.S.; Austria; Hungary; Liberia; Russia; topicals; perfins

Graue, James W., Washington (N) Germany; Zeppelins; catapult mail; Gambia; literature; U.S.

Green, Nonie, Texas (N) Europe; Latin America; U.S. postal history; Canada; Thailand; airmails; postal stationery

Greene, Inslee B., Washington (N) Australia and States; New Zealand; British America and Oceania; French Oceania; U.S.

Gruenebaum, Werner, Illinois (N) Germany; Austria; Hungarian navy

Guzzio, George T., New York (N) general; topical; France; Germany; German States; U.S.

Hahn, Henry, Virginia (N) Czechoslovakia; Austria; postal history; literature

*Halle, Herman L., Maryland (N) Germany and related

Haller, Austin P., California (N) postal stationery

Halm, Herbert S., Uruguay (I) Latin America; topicals; literature

Harris, James P., North Carolina (N) U.S.; U.N.; Confederates; British North America; literature; UPU; Great Britain

Harrison, Horace W., Maryland (N) U.S. stampless; British America; British North America; postal history; postal stationery; literature

Harrison, John B., Canada (N) Canada; Great Britain; Australia; New Zealand; U.S.; topicals

Hatfield, Jack, Ohio (R) France and Colonies; British Colonies; general

Haverbeck, H.D.S., Virginia (I) U.S.; Confederates; airmails; British; Far East; Middle East; Russia; general

Hennig, Bernard A., Illinois (I) Germany and related; France and Colonies; Great Britain and Colonies; Russia; China; Guatemala

*Herst, Herman Jr., Florida (N) general; literature

Hogensen, Marvin C., Utah (R) 20th-century U.S.; general; topicals

Holly, Frank M., California (N) U.S.; France; topicals; British Columbia; Ryukyus; Japan

Hornung, Otto, England (I) Turkey; Holy Land; East and Central Europe; German field post in Turkey; literature

Hyzen, Leon, California (N) 19th-century U.S.; locals; carriers; topicals

Ichida, Soichi, Japan (I) Japan; U.S.; British and general classics

Illyefalvi, Kalman V., Maryland (N) British Africa; Eastern Europe; U.N.; Austria

Ireland, Philip W., Washington, D.C. (N) China; Japan; Great Britain; British North America; Ottoman Empire and successor states

Isaacs, Mark R., Illinois (N); Indochina; Vietnam; French Colonies; U.S. classics; military mail; independent Asia

Ishikawa, Ryohei, Japan (N) U.S. classics; Hawaii; Japan; Hong Kong; China; India; Korea; Straits Settlements; Asia

Jaeger, Dr. Heinz, West Germany (I) Baden; Germany, States and Colonies; Central Europe

Jefferson, James E., California (N) U.S.; Brazil; general; literature

Jennings, Clyde, Florida (N) U.S.; topicals

Kantor, Mrs. Alvin, Illinois (N) U.S.

Kaposta, Julius, Illinois (N) Hungary; U.N.; Austria; Switzerland; airmails; Zeppelins

Keally, James J., Pennsylvania (N) U.S.; Haiti; Canada; Europe; topicals

Kedrierski, Jerry B., Florida (N) Central Europe; Benelux; 19th-century general; U.S.; Confederates

Kehr, Ernest A., New York (I) general

Kessler, Melvin M., Florida (R) U.S.; Russia and states, offices abroad; military covers; Confederates; postal history

Kline, Roger W., New York (N) U.S.; Canada; U.N.; postal history; postal stationery

Kraemer, James E., Canada (N) Canada; Germany; Brazil; Roman States; Vatican; Arctic; Antarctic; British Colonies

Kunzmann, George J., Illinois (N) Germany and related

Larsen, Paul A., Illinois (N) Germany and Colonies; Denmark; British Colonies; French Africa

Lidman, David, Connecticut (I) U.S.; 20th-century France; literature

Lieberman, Eugene, Illinois (N) U.S.; Confederates; Vatican; Italy and States; China; U.N.; Germany and States; Afghanistan

Light, Theodore, Florida (N) Asia; U.S. airmail covers

Lindberg, George B., Sweden (I) Europe

Lloyd, Carroll L., Maryland (N) U.S.; Latin America; Greece

Lurch, E. Norman, New York (N) postal stationery

*Lutz, Abbot, New York (N) Great Britain; Greenland; Denmark; Italy; postal history; Balkans; literature

Maisel, William H., Maryland (I) U.S.; Belgium; Luxembourg; Switzerland; Netherlands; postal stationery

Martin, Bill A., Kansas (R) U.S.

Martin, George M., Washington (N) general; U.S.; Canada; Germany; China; postal stationery; postal history; literature

Matz, Billy, Tennessee (N) U.S.; Confederates

Mayrisch, Lenard Jr., California (N) Europe; postal history; Levant; Philippines; Barbados; Austria; topicals

McClellan, Robert G., Illinois (N) U.S.; postal history

McPherson, Donald M., California (R) airmails; naval and war covers; topicals; U.S.

Meier, Harry C., New Jersey (N) postal history; Germany; U.N.; literature

Menuz, Wayne, California (N) postal stationery; Italy and Colonies; Great Britain and Colonies

Meroni, Charles F., Florida (I) postal history; U.S.; Confederates

Mewes, Emil W., Germany (I) Europe and Colonies; postal history; literature

Mitchell, Milton, Maryland (I) U.S.; British North America; Israel; China; Siam; Central Europe; general

Moen, Georgia M., Washington (N) U.S.; U.N.; topicals; British Colonies

Moll, Herbert H., Peru (I) Latin America

*Nagel, Lawson, Arizona (N) U.S. and Possessions; general

Norton, Walter E., Pennsylvania (N) Lithuania; Latvia; Estonia; Klaipeda; Memel; Balkans

*Nortum, Mrs. John H., Washington (N) Siam; British Colonies; Europe; U.S.

Nunnelley, S.W., Kentucky (N) Confederates; balloon posts; Israel; general

Odenweller, Robert P., New Jersey (I) U.S.; British Empire; classics

Oesch, Robert S., California (I) topicals; polar postal history

Oliver, William J., California (N) Philippines; Korea; Japan; Ryukyus

Orton, Walter J., New York (N) U.S.; Great Britain; Newfoundland; Canada; Australia; New Zealand

Osborn, Wilmont V., Michigan (L) U.S.; Bolivia; Germany; topicals

O'Shea, Mary Margaret, Oregon (N) U.S.; British Empire; Vatican

Ott, Russell E., Texas (N) topicals; polar; postal history; postal stationery

Owens, Mary Ann, New York (I) topicals

Ozment, James L., Utah (N) U.S. and Possessions; U.S. postal history; Canada; Great Britain

Paliafito, Robert A., Arizona (N) U.S.; U.S. postal history; Italian States

Patterson, Curtis, Delaware (N) FDCs

Pearce, Basil C., California (I) U.S.; Confederates; postal history; postal stationery; essays; proofs; airmails; western covers

Peter, Harold E., Illinois (N) Germany and related areas; postal history; postal stationery

Peterson, Charles J., West Germany (I) literature

Phillips, David G., Florida (N) U.S.; Confederates; China; Japan; Manchukuo; Korea; postal stationery

Pidun, Joachim, West Germany (I) Germany and Colonies; Central Europe

Pla, Steven A., Pennsylvania (N) philatelic literature; China

Plyler, Earle F., Oklahoma (N) U.S.; France; Switzerland; British Colonies

Pomeroy, Thomas D., Oregon (R) U.S.; Canada; topicals

Putz, Leon, Luxembourg (I) Luxembourg; Belgium; Netherlands; German States

Rapp, William F. Jr., Nebraska (N) U.S.; Canada; Hungary; El Salvador; Portuguese Colonies; postal history

*Ray, Samuel, Illinois (I) general; literature

Raymond, Gale J., Texas (R) British West Indies; French Colonies; Pacific Islands; Tibet; Bhutan; war covers; polar

Reide, Walter E., California (N) U.S.; Zeppelins; airmails; topicals

Rendon, Alex, New York (I) Central and South America; Europe

Resnick, Lorence, Florida (N) general

Retter, Wilda K., Oregon (N) topicals; Israel; Spain; U.N.; covers

*Rice, Kenneth L., Florida (N) postal history; U.S.

Rogers, Sherman E., California (N) Greece; Great Britain; British postal history; U.S.; Siam; classics; France; Bosnia

Rosen, Herbert, New York (N) postal history; Arctic and Antarctic; western covers

Rosenberg, Howard L., Illinois (N) U.S.; Canada; Holy Land

Rosende, Dr. Roberto M., New York (I) Cuba; Spain and Colonies; Portugal and Colonies; Latin America; postal history

Rowell, Milo D., California (N) Asia; British Colonies; postal history; China; Ryukyus; Japan and occupations

Rubio-Lotvin, Boris, Mexico (I) Mexico

Salm, Arthur, Illinois (N) Germany and related

Sanford, Oliver R., California (N) Great Britain and Colonies; Germany and related; Nepal; Guatemala

Schaffling, Otto G., Connecticut (N) Germany and States; Austria; Netherlands; Hungary; Switzerland

Schwartz, Joseph D., California (N) Israel and related; Turkey and offices in Turkey; U.N.; Palestine; Holy Land

Seifert, Fred F., New Mexico (N) general; British Colonies; literature; postal stationery; postal history

Sellers, F. Burton, New York (I) Latin America; U.S. and Possessions; Canada; British North America; postal history; literature

Selzer, Howard J., Illinois (R) Central Europe; Great Britain and Colonies; postal history; Far East

Shaug, Frank E., Rhode Island (R) general; British Empire; Europe; U.S.; Scandinavia

Shek, Peter, New York (N) China; Hong Kong; Japan; Southeast Asia; postal history; topicals; U.S.; British

Shryoc, Kelly, Texas (N) Mexico; U.S.; Latin America; topicals

Silver, Philip, New Jersey (I) airmails; Confederates; topicals; Uruguay; U.S.

Sine, Richard L., Pennsylvania (N) literature

Siverts, John S., Delaware (N) 19th-century British; British North America; Greece; Chile; Brazil; Hawaii; Scandinavia

Skinner, Hubert C., Louisiana (N) U.S.; postal history; Latin America; Canada; Mexico; Venezuela; Great Britain and Colonies

Smith, Donald W., Pennsylvania (N) topicals

Smith, Gerald B., Oregon (N) U.S.; British North America

Sorensen, James H., Nebraska (N) U.S. postal history; topicals

Stark, John S., Ohio (R) U.S.; luminescent issues

Steinhardt, Hans R., North Carolina (R) British Empire; Switzerland; Germany; Western Europe

Stets, Robert J. Sr., Pennsylvania (N) U.S.; postal history; German Empire

Stevens, Clark H., Florida (N) postal stationery of U.S. and Possessions and Canada

Stieber, Conrad H., California (N) Central and Western Europe; Japan; Germany and related areas

*Stone, Daniel A., Colorado (N) general; Colorado postal history; topicals

Stulberg, Fred G., Canada (I) Canada; topicals; Israel; Great Britain; literature; postal history

Sutherland, Harry, Canada (I) Europe; North America; China

Thomas, Arthur, California (N) U.S.; postal stationery; British; perfins; general

Thomas, John, New York (N) U.N.; topicals; Saar

Thompson, Cyrus R., California (N) general; literature; topicals

Thompson, Mrs. V.N., Arizona (N) U.S.; general; topicals

Tinsley, W. Eugene, California (N) U.S.; British; France; postal history; Netherlands; topicals; Canada; New Zealand; Mexico

Tobias, A.L., California (N) Confederates; 19th-century U.S.; Ryukyus; Bhutan; art; Europa; flight covers

Torrey, Gordon H., Washington, D.C. (N) Europe; Russia and offices; Middle East; China; Ethiopia; Liberia; postal history

*Van Dam, Theodore, New York (N) Spain; Germany; war covers; postal history

van Ingen, Klaas, California (N) Europe; Great Britain and Colonies; literature; postal stationery

van Ingen, Louise, California (R) Western Europe; South Africa; topicals; literature; British Colonies; postal stationery

Vignola, Frank J., California (N) Asia; postal history; topicals; postal stationery

Vogel, Hal, New Jersey (N) U.S.; Ryukyus; postal history; polar; topicals; aerophilately; literature

*von Stein, Donna M., Florida (N) U.S.; postal stationery; topicals; general

Vooys, Maj. Daniel F., Massachusetts (N) topicals; U.S.; Germany; Netherlands; U.S. postal history; literature

*Warren, Daniel C., Maryland (N) U.S.; Germany; postal history; Confederates; British Africa; British West Indies

Wellman, Earl H., Illinois (N) Ryukyus; Mexico; Latin America; U.S.; British North America; airmails; locals; booklets; literature

Wilkinson, S.A. III, Texas (N) U.S.; Central and Western Europe; British Empire; topicals

Willard, John H., Colorado (N) British Empire; western postal history; Switzerland

Winick, Lester E., Illinois (N) literature; thematic; astrophilately; aerophilately

Wishnietsky, Benjamin, Florida (N) U.S. and Possessions; Confederates; Greece; France; postal history

Wood, Kenneth A., Oregon (N) topicals; literature; general

Wunsch, Dr. Charles L., Illinois (N) U.S.; postal stationery

Wunsch, Margaret L., Illinois (N) U.S.; postal stationery; topicals

Zahm, Anton H., New York (N) U.S. postal history; Australia; Bermuda; Northwest Pacific Islands; Canada; Germany; British

Zankel, Nathan, New Jersey (N) U.S.; Israel; Palestine and related

## Judging Seminar

The APS supports a traveling team of accredited judges to conduct judging seminars upon request of organizing committees of stamp exhibitions throughout the U.S.

The judging seminars explain exhibition award levels, the difference between "class" shows vs. "open" shows, fundamental guides for exhibiting and basic qualities judges look for in an award-winning exhibit.

The chairman of the Judges Accreditation Committee will consider all requests to determine whether conducting a particular seminar is within the scope of the planning society.

Accredited judges qualified to conduct seminars who reside closest to the exhibition will be used as team members.

Interested exhibition organizing committees should direct requests to chairman of the Judges Accreditation Committee, 5944 W. Montrose Ave., Chicago, Ill. 60634.

## Estate Advisory Service

When the executive director is advised of the death of a member of the APS, he will notify the family, or the personal representative of the deceased member, that the society is prepared to aid in the disposal of the deceased member's philatelic estate.

Upon the request of the heirs, or personal representative of the deceased member, the board of vice presidents will appoint a member to evaluate the philatelic estate and assist and advise in its disposal.

There are members, both dealers and collectors, of proven integrity and competence throughout the country who serve on a voluntary basis.

No charge is made for this service. An evaluation is usually sufficient for estate purposes, but it is recommended that a lawyer be consulted for confirmation.

However, it is not expected that the member should render service that will require lengthy travel or excessive time in the evaluation of the holdings or assistance to the estate without compensation. Financial arrangements should be determined before service is rendered.

It should be pointed out there is a difference between an evaluation and an appraisal of philatelic holdings.

Members will provide evaluations at no charge. The evaluation usually consists of a perusal of the holdings with an estimate of value based on the evaluator's knowledge of the material and the current market.

On the other hand, an appraisal consists of a detailed analysis of the value of each item and entails considerable study and time.

If an appraisal is required, it is recommended that an agreement for reasonable compensation be reached before the appraisal is made.

Assistance to heirs of deceased members through the Estate Advisory Service is extended for a period of one year or until the estate is officially settled if earlier than one year.

This service does not extend to any non-APS member once the legal ownership of the deceased member's collection has been transferred.

All correspondence about the Estate Advisory Service should be addressed to the recorder of the APS board of vice presidents.

Self-adhesive stamp album identification labels (two-tone blue, 2 by 4 inches) for APS members who may wish their heirs to utilize the Estate Advisory Service may be obtained without charge upon request to the APS executive director, Box 8000, State College, Pa. 16801.

A stamped-addressed envelope must be furnished — first-class postage for one ounce affixed for requests of 1 to 15 labels; first-class postage for two ounces for 16 to the maximum of 30 labels.

## APS Expertizing Service

The APS Expertizing Service is operated in conjunction with the American Stamp Dealers' Association. More than 165 philatelic experts serve on this committee. Items for examination must be submitted on special expertizing service forms. Forms dated 12-78 or later are valid. Expertizing forms and answers to questions concerning the operation of this service may be obtained from the APS National Headquarters, Box 8000, State College, Pa. 16801.

**Rules and Requirements**

1. Each stamp or cover submitted for examination must be mounted or affixed to a separate form. A coil pair or block shall be considered a single item. Sets of stamps will not be accepted unless individually mounted on separate forms.

2. Each item must be the bona fide property of the individual submitting it for examination. The owner may assign an identification number to each item submitted.

3. The fee for a certificate of opinion, in accordance with the following schedule, must accompany each item submitted (current Scott catalog value, APS/ASDA members, non-members): $200 or less, $10, $15; over $200 to $1,000 and all unpriced items, $13, $20; over $1,000, $17, $25.

The fee for an uncataloged item will be the same as for an unpriced item. Stamps will not be accepted. Foreign checks, including Canadian, will not be accepted unless drawn upon a U.S. bank and payable in U.S. dollars at par.

4. One stamped, self-addressed No. 10 (large $9\frac{1}{2}$-inch) envelope must accompany each item submitted plus one small stamped, self-addressed envelope for each item or group of items submitted at one time. The small envelope will be used to acknowledge receipt by returning Owner's Receipt of Expertizing Service form after a number has been assigned to each item. The second envelope (No. 10) will be used to return the item submitted with the report of the opinion rendered.

No insurance against loss in the mails will be provided by the APS Expertizing Service. The owner must affix sufficient postage to the large envelope so the item can be returned by registered mail at full valuation. This requirement is optional only for those items valued at $200 or less.

5. The APS Expertizing Service reserves the right at all times to decline to examine or give an opinion on any item. Single stamps will not be accepted for authentication as coil or imperforate varieties.

Such items must be submitted in pairs or larger pieces. Requests for plate position of a stamp or overprint will not be accepted. Stamps without gum and used varieties must be thoroughly cleaned of all hinges.

6. Requests for the market or net value of an item will not be accepted, nor will an opinion as to the mint, never-hinged condition be given.

7. The decisions rendered by the APS Expertizing Service are not guaranteed and are only opinions. No refunds unless no opinion is given.

8. Since the meanings of the terms superb, very fine, etc., are debatable, no opinion as to general condition will be given. Defects and alterations not readily apparent will be noted.

9. All reasonable care will be taken of items submitted for examination, but all items are accepted with full understanding on the part of the owner that neither the APS, the American Stamp Dealers' Association, nor members of their Expertizing Committees are liable for any loss or damage resulting from any cause whatever except for gross negligence.

Since the APS Expertizing Service is unable to obtain insurance coverage of any kind, an owner desiring coverage must carry his own insurance.

10. The APS and ASDA reserve the right to make such changes without notice to the rules and requirements as they deem necessary, but such changes will be announced as soon as possible.

11. The request for an examination constitutes an acceptance by the owner of all rules and requirements of the APS Expertizing Service.

12. No item will be accepted if the owner insists upon a deadline date for its return. Owners should allow at least 90 days before expecting a reply.

Since items are submitted to expert committee members for their opinion, unavoidable delays are often experienced.

## APS Insurance

Designed, administered, and operated by experienced collectors, APS All Risk Stamp Insurance now covers more than 7,500 APS members. Tailored to the needs of an active stamp collector, it is available to collector-members residing in the United States and Canada. (Dealer-members in the United States and Canada can be covered by a separate dealer plan available to them. Write directly to the insurance plan manager for details.)

Although savings in premiums exceed 30 per cent or more of the cost most other companies charge for the coverage which they offer, more important than the savings are the other exclusive features found only in the APS-sponsored policy:

1. There is no loss-sharing (co-insurance) clause in the APS-sponsored policy;

2. An automatic 1⅔ per cent per month increase in the amount of insurance provides coverage for the average collector's new acquisitions and/or increases in values;

3. Newly acquired high-valued items are automatically covered up to 35 per cent of the total amount of insurance of $15,000, whichever is less;

4. Individual items need not be listed unless their value exceeds $2,000 rather than the $250 required in other policies; and

5. Shipments by UPS or air express, or by first-class mail, priority mail, or special han-

dling parcel post, all insured for $21 or more, are covered, as are shipments by registered mail, the only method of shipping covered by most other policies.

Claims paid in the past 10½ years exceed $1 million. No payment is made for a claim of less than $50, but payment is made in full for claims which exceed $50.

Additionally, loss by burglary at the residence premises is subject to a $200 deductible to encourage a healthy interest in adequate locks on doors and windows at the collector's home.

Replacement value of your collection may be estimated and coverage obtained based upon that estimate, subject to adjustment within five months. Within this five-month period, a list of all albums or other convenient units (such as shoe box, cigar box, file drawer, etc.) and a brief description of the contents of each unit, together with its valuation, must be submitted.

The insurance plan manager does not want you to send him a detailed inventory, if you have one, because he does not have sufficient file space. You keep the detailed inventory in a safe place where it will not be lost with the collection in the event of a fire, burglary, tornado, etc.

A simplified application has been developed for values up to $20,000 where neither a qualified safe nor bank protection is used. This and a more detailed application is available from the Insurance Plan Manager, 10405A Stevenson Road, Stevenson, Md. 21153. (Please enclose a large stamped envelope for a speedy response.)

Coverage under the APS policy provides insurance against all risks of loss or damage to philatelic property, with certain named exceptions. Briefly, the types of losses which are not covered are those caused by: a) careless handling, including damage by insects, vermin, fading, etc.; b) mysterious disappearance of individual stamps unless specifically scheduled in the policy at values greater than $2,000; c) checked baggage and while in the custody of transportation companies (unless shipped by UPS, air express, registered mail, first-class mail, priority mail, or special handling parcel post, all insured for $21 or more); d) theft from an unattended automobile; e) atomic fission or nuclear reaction; and f) war, revolution, or government confiscation.

Further, loss or damage to coins or any numismatic property except postal currency or PNCs is not covered.

Coverage is written for a one-year term, and about a month before expiration, you will receive a renewal premium notice continuing the coverage in force for a further year, provided you pay the premium within the specified time.

Quadrennially, renewal applications are required. The value of all philatelic property must be disclosed on the application, including that kept in bank storage.

If you wish, you can insure for less than the full replacement value. However, experience indicates that most collectors who have suffered losses did not have sufficient insurance at the time of the loss.

If you have any questions, please write to APS Insurance Plan Manager, 10405A Stevenson Road, Stevenson, Md. 21153.

### Loss Notice Procedure

The policy provides that "Notice of Claim" be given to Leizure Associates, Inc., 508 St. Paul Place, Baltimore, Md. 21202.

An independent adjuster will be assigned to investigate the claim and take the proof of loss required by the policy terms. Telephone number is 301-752-3036.

It is also recommended that losses be reported to the APS Insurance Plan Manager, as well as to the chairman of the APS Stamp Theft Committee (216-856-5895), for burglary and holdup losses.

### Changes Procedure

Write to the APS insurance plan manager and set forth the changes required. They will be accomplished, if possible, and you will be billed for the additional premium, if any. Do not send any remittance with a change request.

## APS Sales Division

Many thousands of members of the APS have found the Sales Division to be the ideal system to dispose of their duplicates and to acquire stamps at reasonable prices.

The fact that the Sales Division has functioned since 1886 speaks for itself. Years of experience have resulted in an efficient service designed to produce the ultimate in satisfaction for the buyer and seller.

Multiple circuits are the most popular. They are designed to offer a group of collectors (not more than 10) a selection of 10 sales books containing stamps of the same country or category.

No minimum purchase is required. Multiple circuits are usually sent to members living in relatively close proximity to each other. This speeds transmission of the circuit and reduces parcel post costs.

Each member may retain the circuit up to seven days. Requests for circuits are processed in the order in which received.

Some multiple circuits of extremely popular material in short supply have long waiting lists. A member is placed on the circuit list according to his geographical location. Thereafter his name moves upward on the list each time the same circuit (composed entirely of a new selection) is remailed from the Sales Division.

Eventually, every member has the opportunity to receive the circuit first. Once this happens, his name reverts to the bottom of the list and the process begins anew. There is no relationship between the order of the names on different circuits. Each circuit operates entirely independent of others.

Direct circuits are sent to Hawaii, Alaska, U.S. Possessions and foreign countries. They may contain books of more than one country or category, depending upon the availability of the material requested. They may be retained by the member for a maximum of 20 days.

If the member purchases less than $20 of material from a circuit, he must pay postage to and from State College, Pa. Additionally, if he requests airmail service, he must pay the cost of such service. A member residing abroad receiving a direct circuit must pay an extra insurance charge which varies according to his place of residence.

Chapter circuits are available to APS chapters upon request. These circuits must be mailed to the APS representative or an APS member specially designated by the chapter.

Chapter circuits consist of approximately 20 sales books of countries or categories requested by the chapter and are mailed automatically on a schedule furnished by the chapter. These circuits may be retained for a maximum of 30 days.

There are three types of sales books. One contains 192 spaces designed for single stamps or sets, while another consists of 14 pages, with a pocket on each page designed to hold a maximum of two covers per pocket. The third consists of 96 spaces for blocks of four and plate blocks.

Stamps may be mounted in the sales books as singles or sets, mint or used. Each sales book contains detailed regulations for purchasers and rules for owners, as well as many helpful hints. Low cost acetate envelopes in three sizes are available to members who wish to mount never-hinged material.

Every page of every sales book is photographed on microfilm before the book is dispatched. This is done for the protection of the sales book's owner and to resolve disputes.

The Sales Division accepts no responsibility for items that overlap or are mounted in glassine or other cloudy coverings, since stamps so mounted cannot be properly photographed for identification purposes.

All sales books entered in the Sales Division are checked by competent philatelists. Sales books containing stamps of exceptional value or stamps known to have been counterfeited are sent to qualified examiners. The examiners are recognized specialists and authorities in their particular fields of philately.

Members questioning the authenticity of any stamp may submit it for examination to the Philatelic Foundation or the APS Expertization Service providing the Sales Division is notified of this action within 10 days of purchase of the stamp.

If the item is found to be fraudulent and not as described, the purchase price of the stamp will be refunded to the purchaser. The society will not, however, pay the cost of the examination.

A set of rules has been developed as a result of many decades' experience in handling sales circuits. These have been refined many times. Those not needed have been discarded. For each rule now published within the sales books there exists a definite need or reason.

Included here are some of the more important rules.

### Regulations for Purchasers

1. On receipt of circuit, the member must check to be sure that all books listed on the invoice are present. He should note missing stamps showing no purchaser's mark. If circuit has missing books or stamps, he should notify the individual from whom he received the circuit and send a copy of the letter to the Sales Division.

The member should attach the note to the sales book indicating to the next member that the discrepancy has been reported.

The member must not hold up the circuit, but should retain the postal receipt or signed receipt, if hand carried, for at least four months. The Sales Division will request a copy should it be necessary to file an insurance claim.

2. Members are not permitted to write in the sales book. Only the Sales Division and the sales examiners are permitted to correct or change the owner's original entries.

Any change by a member will make that member responsible for the net value of the item corrected.

If an obvious mistake was overlooked by the Sales Division or sales examiner, the member should attach a separate note to the sales book and give page and space number of the discrepancy over his signature.

Revisions will be made when the circuit is finally returned to the Sales Division and the sales book has been checked against the microfilm.

3. A purchaser may not make any handwritten additions to any sales book nor is it permissible to sign a name or initials in the space from which an item is removed.

Instead, a rubber-stamp symbol showing the chapter's name or member's name or initials and APS membership number will be handstamped in the appropriate space to identify the purchaser. The rubber stamp must not be over one inch in length, and may be purchased locally or from one of the advertisers in the "American Philatelist."

When an item occupying more than one space is removed from a sales book, the symbol must be placed only in one space — the space where the net value is given.

4. Members are fully responsible for the entire value of the circuit from the time of receipt until (a) the circuit, properly packed and addressed to next authorized recipient, is placed in the United States mails, insured or registered for not less than $50, and a receipt obtained therefor;

Or (b) is placed in the foreign mails, registered in accordance with instructions on the invoice, and a receipt obtained therefor;

Or (c) the circuit is hand delivered to the next recipient and a written receipt obtained therefor. Member shall remain liable if the circuit is hand delivered to anyone other than the authorized recipient.

5. Remittance for purchases must be made in full directly to the Sales Division at the same time the circuit is forwarded. Credit and partial payments are not permitted. The circuit invoice or report sheet must be sent to the Sales Division at that time, and the insurance fee paid regardless of method of delivery even though no stamps are purchased.

6. Members must forward circuits promptly. A fine of 50 cents per day per circuit will be imposed against members who retain a circuit beyond the period authorized.

7. Circuit must be wrapped securely before being placed in the mails. Member must follow mailing instructions which accompany every circuit. He must treat every book with the utmost care.

The member must keep the circuit away from heat and moisture. It must be kept in a safe place where it will not be lost, damaged or stolen. Any losses which result from obvious neglect or carelessness in failing to protect a circuit properly will be the responsibility of the sender, and he shall be completely liable for that portion of the value above whatever reimbursement may be obtained from postal insurance.

8. Failure to comply with any of the aforementioned regulations will be sufficient reason to discontinue the privilege of receiving sales circuits. Violations of a serious nature will be reported to the APS board of vice presidents for necessary action.

### Rules for Owners
#### Mounting

1. Arrange stamps by country and in catalog numerical order.

2. Ink must be used for all net prices. For the protection of the owner, books with net prices changed will be rejected except where the item has been completely removed and space left blank.

3. If a stamp has an imperfection of any sort (i.e., thin, crease, tear, clipped perforation, pin hole, unused but gum missing, etc.), it must be so labeled in the space occupied by that stamp.

4. Write legibly. Prices must be entered in the space provided only. It is best if net values are visible with the stamp in place but under no condition will a book be accepted in which a stamp or block covers the net value of another item.

5. Mount stamps securely.

6. Special mounts are permitted.

7. The Sales Division accepts no responsibility for items that overlap or are mounted in glassine or other cloudy coverings since stamps so mounted cannot be properly photographed for identification purposes.

8. Do not use rubber cement or any adhesives which leave a residue that will adhere to other stamps or pages once the item is removed.

9. Blank spaces not used in the sales book need not be marked out. Leave them completely blank.

### Pricing

10. Prices must be competitive if the member desires good results.

11. Do not waste time mounting material that belongs in penny approvals.

12. Sets may be offered as a unit.

13. Do not submit books with a total net value of less than $30 or more than $300 (maximum limit of insurance coverage).

### Charges

14. An insurance charge of 2 per cent of the total net value (minimum 50¢) provides complete coverage against loss or damage while sales book is in the hands of the Sales Division.

15. Commission on sales is 20 per cent with a minimum of $2 per book.

16. Charges cannot be paid in advance. Together with any fines and cost of return postage and insurance, they will be deducted when settlement is made at time sales book is retired and returned to its owner.

### Fines

17. Any stamp adjudged to be reperforated, regummed, repaired, cleaned, fiscally used, or otherwise altered, unless clearly identified as such by marking in ink in the space wherein the stamp is mounted, shall subject the owner to a fine of $2 per stamp if the stamp is priced over $10 and a fine of $1 if priced $10 or less. Counterfeit stamps, even if identified as such, or material offered "as is," will not be accepted.

18. Fines at the same rate may be levied where items are not labeled as required in Rule No. 3 providing the owner has been previously warned in writing by the Sales Division.

### Liability

19. The APS accepts no responsbility for sales books until they are initially received from the owner for entry in the Sales Division. The society liability ceases when the book is retired and delivered to the last known address of the owner.

20. The APS accepts no liability for any loss or damage to sales book caused by climatic conditions unless there is conclusive proof of human negligence and accepts no liability for decrease in value of multiple stamps due to perforation separation.

### Rejection

21. The Sales Division reserves the right to reject any book for any reason it deems appropriate. Reasons most frequently the cause for rejection are stamps overpriced, not properly or securely mounted, or oversupply of material.

### Classification Guide

Experience has revealed that over 90 per cent of the buyers submitting requests for sales books are for specific individual countries or categories.

General or worldwide collectors are becoming scarce. Books containing an unrelated hodgepodge are poor sellers. Likewise, their circulation is limited since buyers do not ask for material mounted in this manner.

To increase sales, U.S. material should be subdivided so that only one of the following categories is contained in a single book.

19th-century postage, regular and/or commemoratives

20th-century postage, regular and/or commemoratives

Mint singles

Used singles

Booklet panes

Coil Pairs

Airmail, singles and/or blocks

Blocks of four, mint and/or used

Plate blocks

Plate number singles

Cancellations

19th-century covers

First day covers

First flight covers

Stationery or cut squares

Revenues

Departments

Postage dues and special delivery

Precancels

U.S. Possessions (individual Possession preferred)

If books cannot be limited to an individual country or colony, the following categories or combinations of countries may be accepted.

The supply of sales books of certain countries sometimes exceeds the demand and for temporary periods are not accepted by the Sales Division. Those countries urgently needed and those in oversupply are published at frequent intervals in the column "Sales Talk" appearing in the "American Philatelist."

British North America

British West Indies

British America

British Africa

British Asia

British Oceania

British Europe

British Middle East (including sheikdoms)

Central America

Latin West Indies

South America

French Colonies

Benelux (Belgium, Netherlands, Luxembourg)

Scandinavia (including Finland, Greenland, Iceland)

Central Europe (Germany, Saar, Austria, Switzerland, Liechtenstein)

Southern Europe (including Greece, Italy, Spain, Portugal)

Eastern Europe (U.S.S.R.-dominated countries)

Baltic States

Balkans

Europe

Middle East (including Iraq, Iran, Turkey, Jordan)

Far East (including Japan, China, Korea)

Southeast Asia (Laos, Cambodia, Vietnam, Thailand)

Asia

Africa (Independent)

Colonies and offices abroad of any country may be included with the mother country if necessary. Europe, Asia and Africa (Independent) categories should be used only if an earlier listed category will not suffice.

Books of an individual country are definitely preferred to any of the aforementioned categories. Further limiting each book to 19th or 20th-century is also desirable but not required.

Better results can be obtained if mint and used are mounted in separate books. Special books are now available for covers. Low-cost mounts for never-hinged material are also available in three sizes.

Sellers should clearly identify the country, countries or category contained in each sales book. The Sales Division cannot ensure that your books will be included in the right classification unless the appropriate information is filled in on the front cover of each sales book.

## APS Stamp Theft Committee

The services of the APS Stamp Theft Committee are not limited to APS members, but are available to all victims of stamp theft.

Members should advise victims of stamp theft in their areas to contact the APS Stamp Theft Committee, and to do so promptly.

Information concerning stamp theft preventive measures may be obtained by writing the chairman of the committee and enclosing a self-addressed, stamped envelope.

Clippings from local newspapers concerning stamp thefts and stamp thieves are urgently solicited from all parts of the country and should be mailed to the committee. Collectors should be sure that the name of the newspaper and the date the article appeared are indicated.

All stamp collections are subject to theft. Large and valuable ones attract professional thieves. None is too small to be taken by thieves in search of money or items which can be converted into money.

It, therefore, behooves the collector to give thought to the matter, and provide appropriate protection for his philatelic holdings, large or small.

If your stamps should be stolen, you are advised to proceed as follows:

1 — Touch nothing.

2 — Call the police. Not all police officers are familiar with the hobby of stamp collecting, and at the outset may not realize the significance of a stamp theft, especially if it is a large one.

It may be helpful to mention to the investigating officers that major stamp thefts have been occurring all across the country, and that professional thieves are known to be engaged in stealing stamps just as they steal coins, jewelry, furs, objects of art, etc. Experience has shown that such stamp thefts are well planned and expertly executed.

3 — Notify the chairman of the APS Stamp Theft Committee, preferably by telephone. The chairman, James H. Beal, may be reached by telephone day or night (216) 856-5895. The address of the committee is Box 2457, Vienna, Ohio 44473.

## Translation Service

The APS offers to members a translation service in practically all major languages. Almost anything philatelic can be translated — letters, cancellations, inscriptions on stamps, FDC cachets, etc. Translations of one page or less are provided at no charge.

All requests for translations should be sent directly to the chairman of the APS Translation Committee, Dmytro Bykovetz Jr., 902 Stratford Ave., Melrose Park, Philadelphia, Pa. 19126.

More than one, but not more than five pages, will be translated for a charge of $1 per page after the first page. Requests for translation of more than five pages will be negotiated by the chairman with the translation committee members, and the requesting member will be advised of the price before the translation is undertaken.

Postage charges on all translations must be paid by the requesting member. As a general rule, three times the postage necessary to send the translation should be enclosed to cover all forwarding and return postage requirements.

Any APS member able to translate from or to a foreign language, who is willing to serve as a member of the Translation Committee, is urged to offer his or her services to the committee chairman.

The translation service has proved to be reliable, and has established and cemented friendships between APS members and citizens of countries throughout the world.

## APS Speakers Bureau

This list is arranged geographically, as most groups will be interested in obtaining a speaker in their own general vicinity. Addresses for the speakers listed may be found in the current membership listing. Telephone numbers may be obtained from the normal telephone company directory assistance or by inquiry to the speakers bureau chairman. The three entries under the "Requirements" heading are:

First column: One way distance in miles beyond which the speaker expects to be reimbursed for his travel expenses. Letter "A" indicates the speaker desires reimbursement for all travel expenses.

Second column: Whether speaker is willing to stay overnight if distance or meeting time requires. Letter "Y" indicates yes; "N" no.

Third column: Amount of honorarium in U.S. dollars expected by the speaker.

Many of the speakers have subjects in addition to those listed and will speak at banquets or act as masters of ceremony, as well as address stamp clubs. Although many will make shorter trips at their own expense, common courtesy indicates that they be luncheon or dinner guests when this is timely. Most speakers who have indicated a willingness to stay overnight will accept accommodations in a private home as well as in a motel or hotel.

In arranging for speakers, please observe the following:

1) All arrangements should be made directly with the speaker by the host group, not through the speakers bureau.

2) Be certain that all arrangements with respect to accommodations, expenses and honorarium are clearly understood by both parties.

3) Give speakers plenty of notice in extending speaking invitations.

4) Advise the speakers bureau of any problems that arise or suggestions for improving the listing.

All members of the American Philatelic Society willing to speak on philatelic subjects to APS chapters or other groups should request an application form from the chairman, APS Speakers Bureau, or from the APS Executive Director, Box 8000, State College, Pa. 16801.

| Location | Name | Requirements | | | Subjects |
|----------|------|----|----|----|----------|
| **ARIZONA** | | | | | |
| Phoenix | Corless, Robert D. | 100 | Y | 0 | Australia-Canada-New Zealand-Postal Stationery |
| Sun City | Cratsenberg, C.C. | 50 | Y | 0 | Stamp Thefts-Club Programs |
| Tempe | Jackson, Thomas J. | 100 | N | 0 | Tonga Tin Can Mail |
| Tucson | Birkinbine, John II | 50 | Y | 0 | 19th-Century U.S.-Mounting for Exhibitions-Promoting Stamp Clubs |
| **CALIFORNIA** | | | | | |
| Burbank | Clark, Emerson A. | 50 | Y | 0 | Canada-Canadian Cancels & Postal Stationery |
| Campbell | Gary, Douglas L. | 25 | Y | 0 | Covers-Philatelic Basics-Book Reports-U.S. General |
| Corma | Parker, William L. | 100 | Y | 0 | 19th-Century U.S. Kansas/Nebraska Overprints-1908-21 Washingtons |
| Hollywood | Tobias, A.L. | 25 | Y | 0 | Ryukyus, Navy Transoceanics-CSA-Bhutan |
| Los Angeles | Freer, Phillips B. | 100 | Y | 0 | Mexican Philately |
| Pasadena | Gilmore, Jack A. | 50 | Y | 0 | Canada-Newfoundland-U.S. Airmails |
| Redwood City | Jefferson, James E. | 100 | Y | 0 | Brazil-Baltic States-General |
| Salinas | Eidson, Earl L. | 50 | Y | 0 | Americana-Germany-Stamp Stories |
| San Carlos | Thompson, Cyrus R. | 50 | Y | 0 | U.S. Stampless-U.S. Cancels-U.S. General |
| San Clemente | Hyzen, Leon | 100 | Y | 0 | Locals & Carriers-19th-Century Classics-Early Printing Methods |
| San Diego | Frank, Dr. Samuel B. | 25 | N | 25 | 1765 Stamp Act-Revenue Stamps of Great Britain & Ireland |
| San Jose | Stieber, Conrad H. | 50 | Y | 0 | Printing Stamps-Booklets-Tete Beche |
| San Mateo | Adler, Sig | — | N | 0 | No. 1's to 1860-General 1840/50-Germany & Italian States |

| Location | Name | Requirements | | | Subjects |
|---|---|---|---|---|---|
| **CALIFORNIA** | | | | | |
| Stockton | Henderson, Stanley G. | 100 | Y | 0 | FDC Collecting-Early FDC Cachets |
| Sunnyvale | Burma, Benjamin H. | 25 | Y | 0 | Philatelic Nudes |
| | Magyar, Steve | 25 | N | 0 | U.S. Issues of 1907/1920 |
| West Covina | Carriker, Clyde | 25 | Y | 0 | French & British Oceania-Northwest Pacific Islands-Fiji |
| West Sacramento | Oliver, William J. | 100 | Y | 0 | Philippines-California Fishing License Stamps-Exhibiting |
| **COLORADO** | | | | | |
| Englewood | Crosby, Joe H. | 200 | Y | 0 | 19th-Century Flag Cancels-U.S. Postal History-1883 2¢-Philatelic Literature |
| Lakewood | Foley, Joseph E. | 50 | Y | 0 | Ireland |
| **CONNECTICUT** | | | | | |
| Cromwell | Tribken, Bennett | 50 | Y | 0 | Greenland-Faroe Is.-Danish West Indies |
| Granby | Chase, Abbott | 50 | Y | 0 | Christ on Stamps-Great Britain-20 Questions |
| New Britain | Brown, H. Haines | 50 | Y | 10 | Communist China-Stamps & Chinese Cultural Revolution |
| West Granby | Gaston, Howard J. | 25 | N | 0 | Jamaica & Postal History-Lifetime of Experience-Errors-Judging |
| **DELAWARE** | | | | | |
| Hockessin | Patterson, Curtis | A | Y | 0 | U.S. First Day Covers |
| Wilmington | Brandeberry, Robert B. | 25 | Y | 0 | Australia-Counterfeits-Norway |
| | Fahs, James R. | 50 | N | 0 | Art on French Stamps-U.S. Cl-Zeppelin Flights |
| | Wooden, Allen C. | 50 | Y | 0 | Medical History/Personalities on Stamps-Space |
| **DISTRICT OF COLUMBIA** | | | | | |
| Washington | Kaufmann, Patricia A. | 25 | Y | 0 | Confederate Postal History |
| | Swit, David A. | 25 | Y | 0 | Flag Cancels-Philatelic Journalism |
| | Torrey, Gordon H. | 50 | Y | 0 | Turkey-Russia-Persia |
| | Werner, Dr. Bert L. | A | Y | 0 | Exhibition Reforms-Catalogs-Superfluous Stamps-Postalics |
| **FLORIDA** | | | | | |
| Boca Raton | Herst, Herman Jr. | 100 | Y | 0 | General-Teabag Philately |
| Hallandale | Shay, Arnold | 25 | Y | 25 | Concentration Camp Mail-Third Reich-Jewish History-Psychological Warfare |
| Hialeah | Rodriguez, Pedro M. | 100 | Y | 0 | Spain & Colonies-Cuba-Puerto Rico-Philatelic Literature |
| Hollywood | Blizil, George A. | 100 | Y | 0 | British Colonies War Tax Stamps-20th-century Postal History |
| Jacksonville | Jennings, Clyde | 100 | Y | 0 | U.S. Freaks & Oddities-"A Man"-U.S. Rarities-Cancellations-Forgeries |
| Longwood | Bohne, Werner M. | 100 | Y | 0 | Forgeries |
| Miami Beach | Smith, Samuel S. | 100 | N | 0 | U.S. Revenue Stamped Paper |
| Palm Harbor | Colby, Sylvester | 100 | Y | 0 | Stamp Auctions-Philatelic Literature-Fakers & Forgeries |
| Point Manalapan | Cody, Dr. H. Graley | 25 | Y | 25 | U.S. Airmails-Philippines-Ecology-World War II |
| Port Charlotte | Schirmer, Joseph E. | A | Y | 25 | Mounting & Write-up-Olympics-Security & Inventory |
| St. Petersburg | Lane, Mrs. Arthur G. | 200 | Y | 0 | U.S. Black Jacks-U.S. First 4¢-Theft Prevention |
| Sarasota | Hudson, Robert E. | A | Y | 15 | Palestine-Lebanon-Middle East |
| **GEORGIA** | | | | | |
| Atlanta | Cole, Clifford C. Jr. | 100 | Y | 0 | U.S.-British Colonies-Airmails-Counterfeits |
| | Moorefield, Robert | 50 | Y | 35 | Laos-Southeast-Asia |
| | White, John W. | 25 | Y | 0 | Japanese Forerunners-Asian Forgeries-Hong Kong-U.S. Administration Forgeries |
| Decatur | Kimball, Alleen B. | 25 | Y | 0 | Nurses on Stamps-FDC Preparation-Postmark Collecting |
| Smyrna | Templeton, J.C. | 25 | Y | 0 | Exhibiting & Mounting-Ryukyus-Specialization |
| **ILLINOIS** | | | | | |
| Bloomington | Edwards, Philip P. | 100 | Y | 0 | Japan |
| Chicago | Algmin, Victor A. | 100 | Y | 0 | Flowers-Colombian World's Fair-Greece-Japan |
| | Blau, Fred F. | A | Y | 0 | Palestine/Israel-Airmail-Graf Zepp over Palestine |
| | Hennig, Bernard A. | 100 | Y | 0 | Danzig-Germany-German East Africa |
| | Lieberman, Eugene | 100 | Y | 0 | Afghanistan-Papal States |
| Glenview | Bachenheimer, Frank | 25 | — | — | Ruhleben POW Camp Post |
| Wheaton | Bauer, William H. | 100 | Y | 0 | Colorado Postal History-Petroleum & Geology |
| **KANSAS** | | | | | |
| Lenexa | Wagner, Richard L. | 50 | Y | 0 | Germany Semipostals-U.S. Washington 2¢ Reds-Legal Protection |
| Quinter | Martin, Bill | 100 | — | 0 | How to Exhibit-U.S. Airmails-Judging Condition-Beginners |

| Location | Name | Requirements | | | Subjects |
|---|---|---|---|---|---|
| **MAINE** | | | | | |
| Bangor | Arata, Bill | A | Y | 100 | U.S. Stamps as Investment |
| South Harpswell | McLin, William H. | 100 | Y | 0 | U.S. Match & Medicine-Precancels-Covers & Cancels-Juniors |
| **MARYLAND** | | | | | |
| Aberdeen | Warren, Lt. Col. Daniel C. | 100 | Y | 0 | Civil War-Postal History of Richmond-Postal History of Tobago |
| Baltimore | Harrison, Horace W. | 200 | Y | 0 | Canada-Philatelic Fables-Stamp Insurance |
| Hagerstown | Kendall, D. Homer | 25 | Y | 0 | Stampless Covers |
| Pikesville | Illyefalvi, Kalman V. | 25 | N | 0 | Hungary-Union of South Africa-Stamp Shows |
| Takoma Park | Denison, Ellery | 50 | Y | 0 | China |
| | Hecht, Arthur | 25 | Y | 0 | Lady PMs-Carrier Service-Philately in National Archives-Stamp Swindles |
| **MASSACHUSETTS** | | | | | |
| North Adams | Waite, Robert K. Sr. | 50 | Y | 0 | No. 1s of the World-Covers-Things That Interest Me |
| Quincy | Evans, Lois M. | 50 | Y | 0 | Japan |
| West Newton | Champagne, Richard A. | 50 | Y | 0 | Postal Stationery-Envelope Rarities |
| Weston | Dillaway, Dr. Guy R. | A | Y | 0 | Great Britain |
| **MICHIGAN** | | | | | |
| East Lansing | Allen, William C. | 100 | Y | 0 | Michigan Postal History-Precancels |
| Holland | Wierenga, Theron J. | 50 | Y | 0 | U.S.-19th-Century-Mounting & Exhibiting 3¢ 1851 |
| West Bloomfield | Foxworth, John E. Jr. | 100 | Y | 0 | Philatelic Publicity-APS Story-Autos on Stamps |
| **MINNESOTA** | | | | | |
| Minneapolis | Clark, Lawrence S. | 25 | Y | 0 | Stamp Collecting as a Hobby-Tin Can Mail-Newfoundland Wayzata |
| **MISSISSIPPI** | | | | | |
| Greenville | Goldstein, Nathan H. II | 100 | Y | 0 | U.S. Plate Blocks-Printing U.S. Stamps |
| **MISSOURI** | | | | | |
| Webster Groves | Pope, Mrs. John D. III | 100 | Y | 0 | Valentines-Spain |
| **NEBRASKA** | | | | | |
| Crete | Rapp, William F. Jr. | 100 | Y | 0 | Cancels-Nebraska-Postal History-Rural Post Office Routes-Transfer Offices |
| **NEW HAMPSHIRE** | | | | | |
| Portsmouth | Gardner, John E. Jr. | 50 | Y | 0 | U.S. Postal Cards |
| **NEW JERSEY** | | | | | |
| Jersey City | Meier, Harry C. | 100 | Y | 0 | Postwar Germany |
| Livingston | Green, Richard | 100 | Y | 0 | Austria |
| Montclair | van Reyen, Paul | A | Y | 0 | Netherlands & Colonies |
| Moorestown | Eggen, Dale R. | 25 | Y | 0 | Swiss Philately |
| Ridgefield Park | Schiff, Jacques C. Jr. | 100 | Y | 0 | U.S. Freaks & Errors-Participating in Stamp Auctions |
| Summit | Stone, Harlan F. | 25 | N | 0 | Switzerland Postal History |
| Verona | Garabrant, Melvin | 50 | Y | 0 | Topical Collecting-Europa-France-Competitive Exhibiting |
| **NEW YORK** | | | | | |
| Albany | de Lisle, Kenneth R. | 100 | Y | 0 | Hudson River Mail-Postal History of Albany & New York State |
| | McGrath, Thomas F. | 100 | Y | 0 | Philippines-Spanish American War Patriotic Covers |
| Ballston Spa | Lange, John A. Jr. | 100 | Y | 0 | U.S. 3¢ 1851-1857 |
| Brooklyn | Owens, Mary Ann | 50 | Y | 0 | Wisconsin Postal History-Topicals-Exhibiting Judging |
| Chappaqua | Mayer, E. Herbert | 75 | Y | 0 | War Covers-French Army Cancellations-Napoleonic Wars |
| East Northport | Spear, Arthur H. | 25 | Y | 0 | Jamaica |
| Forest Hills | Stollnitz, Henry | 25 | Y | 0 | Postal History-USPO Shanghai-New York Supplementary Mail-U.S. Used Abroad |
| Long Beach | Zollman, Joseph | 50 | Y | 0 | History Through Stamps-Stamps in Publicity Work-Why I Collect |
| Middletown | Markovits, Robert L. | 50 | Y | 0 | U.S. Special Delivery-U.S. Registry-Literature-Investing in Stamps |
| New Hyde Park | Conway, Herbert E. | 25 | Y | 20 | U.N. Philately |
| New York | Jarrett, David L. | A | Y | 0 | U.S. Territorial Covers-U.S. Stampless-U.S. Fort Covers |
| Patchogue | Wright, Donald H. | 100 | Y | 0 | Egypt-General-International Hobby Exchange-Inventorying |
| Poughkeepsie | Mahoney, John Tom | 25 | Y | 0 | FDR-French Balloon Posts-U.S. Commemoratives |
| Staten Island | Kocheisen, Joseph | 100 | Y | 0 | Zeppelin Post-Germany Airmails |
| | Shek, Peter | 100 | Y | 0 | Hong Kong-China |
| Troy | Andrews, James C. | 25 | Y | 0 | Guatemala |
| Wyantskill | Harris, Robert Dalton | 50 | Y | 0 | Postal Stationery-Albany Letter Express-Steamboat Names-"Oregon" |

| Location | Name | Requirements | | | Subjects |
|---|---|---|---|---|---|
| **NORTH CAROLINA** | | | | | |
| Asheville | Stroupe, Vernon S. Jr. | 25 | Y | 0 | U.S. Perfins-Stamp Photography |
| Wilmington | Harris, James P. | 100 | Y | 0 | Franklin Carrier Stamp-U.S. Perfins-<br>Why I Collect |
| **OHIO** | | | | | |
| Akron | Koller, Ken M. | 100 | Y | 0 | U.S. Overprints-Postal Cards-<br>Revenue Stamps-U.S. Values |
| Fairview Park | Ball, Charles L. | 25 | Y | 0 | Bishop Mark-Charity Stamps-<br>Fakes & Forgeries-other subjects |
| Wellston | Levine, Dr. Earl J. | 100 | Y | 0 | Medical Covers-Personal Experience-<br>Stamp Missionary |
| Youngstown | Clatterbuck, W.C. | 50 | Y | 0 | Canada-Hawaii-Portugal-U.S. |
| **OREGON** | | | | | |
| Portland | Fisher, John W. | A | Y | 0 | Starting School Clubs-Ship Cancels-<br>Polar Philately |
| **PENNSYLVANIA** | | | | | |
| Boalsburg | Sente Frank L. | 100 | Y | 0 | Philatelic Literature-1898 U.S. Revenues-APS |
| | Sente, Marjory J. | 100 | Y | 0 | Washington Bicentennial Covers-FDC |
| Carlisle | Gratz, J. Roger | 50 | Y | 0 | Buying at Auction-Doctored Stamps |
| Johnstown | Smith, Donald W. | 100 | Y | 0 | Europa-Exhibiting-Topicals |
| Lemont | Sine, Richard L. | 100 | Y | 0 | Philatelic Writing-APS-Philately Today |
| Meadville | Friedberg, Richard | 100 | Y | 0 | U.S.-Auction Bidding-Grading |
| Rosemont | Keally, James M. Jr. | 50 | Y | 0 | U.S. Bank Note Issues-U.S. Freaks & Oddities |
| State College | DeVoss, Col. James T. | 100 | Y | 0 | APS Operations-Canal Zone-Via Panama-<br>de Thuin Affair-Philatelic Photography |
| | Hahn, Joseph D. | 100 | Y | 0 | History of Post-El Salvador-U.S. Classics |
| **SOUTH CAROLINA** | | | | | |
| Rock Hill | Markett, Robert | 50 | Y | 0 | Postal History Basics-Exhibiting-<br>Club Organization-General vs. Speciality |
| **TENNESSEE** | | | | | |
| Memphis | Frye, Joe F. | 150 | Y | 0 | Scandinavia-Stamp Shows-Auctions-<br>Philatelic Slides |
| Nashville | Hersey, Herman L. | A | Y | 0 | Topical-Life of Christ-Postal History-<br>History of Communications |
| **TEXAS** | | | | | |
| Austin | Kerr, Allen D. | 100 | Y | 0 | China-Laos |
| El Paso | Balough, Maj. Joseph J. | 50 | Y | 0 | Perfins-Preparing Exhibits-<br>Organizing School Clubs |
| Jacksboro | Poore, Rev. Elwood S. | 100 | Y | 0 | Oddities-Music & Religion on Stamps-<br>Great Britain Revenues |
| League City | Richardson, Edward A. | 100 | Y | 0 | Canada-Specializing-Fun in Collecting |
| Quanah | Elliott, Leo A. | 100 | Y | 0 | Australia |
| San Antonio | Lande, Lester M. | 25 | Y | 0 | Philatelic Frivolity-Stamps & Artists-<br>Forgeries-Philately in Business |
| Spring | Koutroulis, Nicholas G. | 100 | Y | 0 | Exhibitions & Judging-Greece-Masonry |
| **VIRGINIA** | | | | | |
| Fairfax | Bowyer, Mathew J. | A | N | 20 | Postal History-Postal Jokes-Postal Operations |
| Falls Church | Olcheski, William J. | 25 | — | — | Family Hobby-Beginning-<br>Rediscover Collecting-Philatelic Writing |
| Richmond | Green, Brian M. | 25 | Y | 0 | Confederate Postal History |
| **WASHINGTON** | | | | | |
| Yakima | Greene, Inslee B. | 100 | Y | 0 | Fiji-French Polynesia |
| | Martin, George M. | A | Y | 0 | Postal History-Postal Stationery-U.S. Writing |
| **WEST VIRGINIA** | | | | | |
| Morgantown | Singer, Armand E. | 25 | Y | 0 | Nepal-Tibet |
| South Charleston | MacPeek, Donald L. | 100 | Y | 0 | Venezuela-Ivory Coast-Mexico-Guatemala |
| **WISCONSIN** | | | | | |
| Janesville | Eickemeyer, T.E. | 50 | Y | 0 | Civil War Patriotics-Sanitary Fairs-<br>Duck Stamps |
| Superior | Unterberger, Thomas P. | A | Y | 0 | Juniors & Your Club |
| **CANADA** | | | | | |
| Delta, B.C. | Dougan, Charles W. | 50 | Y | 0 | Shanghai-Chinese Treaty Ports-Tibet-<br>19th-Century China |
| Ottawa, Ontario | Kraemer, James E. | — | Y | 0 | Canada's National Postal Museum |
| Toronto, Ontario | Rowe, Kenneth | 50 | Y | 0 | Canadian Telegraphs-Forwarding Agents-<br>Knowledge for Postal Historians |
| | Woolley, Robert J. | 100 | Y | 0 | Canadian Sidelines-Canadian Perfins |
| **ENGLAND** | | | | | |
| Weston-Super-Mare | Spafford, Maj. Ronald N. | — | Y | 0 | Falkland Is.-Philatelic Research |
| **KOREA** | | | | | |
| Osan | Piver, Lt. Col. Charles | 50 | N | 0 | Palestine Mandate-Israel Forerunners |

# APS Chapters

## Alabama
Birmingham Philatelic Society
Gadsden Stamp Club
Huntsville Philatelic Club
Calhoun County Stamp Club
Mobile Stamp Society
Montgomery Area Stamp Club

## Alaska
Anchorage Philatelic Society
Gastineau Philatelic Society
Ptarmigan Stamp and Coin
  Society

## Arizona
Flagstaff Stamp Club
Mesa Stamp Club
Arizona Society of Topical
  Philatelists
Kachina Chapter 25
  Germany Philatelic Society
Phoenix Philatelic Association
Prescott Stamp Club
Huachuca Stamp Club
Honeywell Employees
  Philatelic Society
Sun City Stamp Club
Sun City West Stamp
  and Coin Club
Arizona Federation of Stamp
  Collectors
Arizona Philatelic Rangers
Tucson Stamp Club

## Arkansas
Westark Stamp Club
Mountain Home Area
  Stamp Club
Razorback Stamp Club
Arkansas Philatelic Association

## California
Council of Northern
  California Philatelic Societies
Federated Philatelic Clubs
  of Southern California
Society of Southern California
  Philatelists
Orange County Philatelic
  Society
San Gabriel Valley Stamp Club
Bakersfield Stamp Club
Bonita Stamp and Coin Club
LERC Stamp Club
Peninsula Stamp Club
Monterey Peninsula
  Stamp Club
Diablo Valley Stamp Club
German American Stamp Club
San Pablo Pines Stamp Club
Humboldt Collectors Club
Aeronutronic Stamp Club
Fremont Stamp Club
Fresno Philatelic Society
Beckman Philatelic Society
Hemet Stamp Club
South Bay Philatelic Society
Collectors Club of Hollywood

McDonnell Douglas Philatelic
  Club
Inglewood Philatelic Club
Laguna Beach Stamp Club
LaMirada Stamp Club
Long Beach Stamp Club
Hughes Culver City Employees
  Association Stamp Club
Philatelic Society of
  Los Angeles
Scandinavian Collectors Club
Southern California Chapter
  Mexico-Elmhurst Philatelic
  Society International
San Joaquin Philatelic Society
Valley Stamp Club
Saddleback Stamp Club
Stanislaus Stamp Club
Hitco Stamp Club
East Bay Collectors Club
Tri City Stamp Club
Pacific Palisades Stamp Club
Palmdale Stamp Club
Palm Springs Philatelic Society
J P L Stamp Club
Pasadena Stamp Clubs
Petaluma Philatelic Society
Poway Stamp Club
Redding Stamp Club
Redlands Stamp Club
TRW Stamp Club
Sequoia Stamp Club
Riverside Stamp Club
Sacramento Philatelic Society
Monterey County Stamp Club
Arrowhead Stamp Club
Philatelic "25"
San Diego County
  Philatelic Council
San Diego Stamp Club
BankAmerica Philatelic
  Society
California Collectors Club
Collectors Club of
  San Francisco
San Francisco Pacific
  Philatelic Society
Japanese American Philatelic
  Society
San Jose Stamp Club
Philatelic Society of San Leandro
San Luis Obispo Philatelic
  Society
Santa Barbara Stamp Club
Santa Cruz County Stamp Club
Central Coast Stamp Club
Santa Monica Stamp Club
Oakmont Philatelic Society
Sonoma County Philatelic
  Society
Leisure World Stamp Club
Tuolumne County Stamp Club
Stockton Stamp Club
Sun City Stamp Club
Friends of the Western
  Philatelic Library

LERA Stamp Club
Sunnyvale Stamp Society
Conejo Valley Philatelic
  Society
Torrance Stamp Club
Redwood Empire Stamp
  Society
Greater Valley Philatelic
  Society
Ventura County
  Philatelic Society
Glendale Stamp Club
Visalia Philatelic Society
Yuba-Sutter Philatelic Society

## Colorado
Aurora Stamp Club
Boulder Collectors' Club
Canon City Stamp Club
Colorado Springs Stamp Club
Collectors' Club of Denver
Denver Masonic Stamp Club
Denver Stamp Club
Rocky Mountain Philatelic
  Exhibitions
Rocky Mountain Stamp Club
Cherrelyn Stamp Club
Stamp Club of Grand Junction
West Side Stamp Club
Arapahoe Stamp Club
Pueblo Stamp Club

## Connecticut
Branford Philatelic Society
Brookfield Philatelic Society
Connecticut Philatelic Society
Cheshire Philatelic Society
Clinton Stamp Club
Ye Old King's Highway
  Stamp Club
Fairfield Philatelic Society
Manchester Philatelic Society
Middletown Stamp Club
Hardware City Stamp Club
New Haven Philatelic Society
Thames Stamp Club
Norden Employees Stamp Club
Norwalk Stamp Club
Plainville Stamp CLub
Farmington Valley Stamp Club
Heritage Village Stamp Club
Nutmeg Stamp Club
Waterbury Stamp Club

## Delaware
Dover Stamp Club
Milford Stamp and Coin Club
Du Pont Stamp Club
Wilmington Stamp Club

## District of Columbia
Capitol View Stamp Club
Library of Congress Philatelic
  Club
PentAF Stamp Club
Washington Philatelic Society

## Florida

Florida Federation
  of Stamp Clubs
Cape Coral Stamp Club
Clearwater Stamp Club
Halifax Area Philatelic Society
Century Village East Stamp and
  Coin Club
Delray Beach Stamp Club
Fort Lauderdale Stamp Club
Germany Philatelic Society
  Chapter 7
Fort Myers Stamp Club
University City Stamp Club
Hialeah Stamp and Coin Club
Hollywood Stamp Club
Jacksonville Stamp Collectors
  Club
Upper Keys Collector's Club
Gold Coast Stamp Club
Club Cubano Da Coleccionistas
Cuban Philatelic Club of Miami
Miami Stamp Club
Collier County Stamp Club
New Port Richey Stamp Club
Collectors Club of North Miami
Oakland Park Stamp Club
Silver Springs Shores Stamp
  Club
Central Florida Stamp Club
Bay County Stamp Club
Golden Bee Stamp Club
Pensacola Philatelic Society
Port Charlotte Stamp Club
Port St. Lucie Stamp Club
St. Augustine YMCA Stamp Club
St. Petersburg Stamp Club
Sarasota Philatelic Club
Highlands County Stamp Club
South Miami Stamp Club
Sunrise Stamp Club
Tallahassee Stamp Club
Tampa Collectors Club
Titusville-Moonport
  Stamp Club
Venice Stamp Club
Indian River Stamp Club
Century Village Stamp Club
Cresthaven Stamp and Coin
  Club
Zephyrhills Stamp Club

## Georgia

Athens Philatelic Society
Atlanta Stamp Collectors Club
Georgia-Carolina Stamp Club
Greater Augusta
  Philatelic Society
DeKalb Stamp Club
South Metro Stamp Collectors
  Club
Macon Philatelic Society
Roswell Stamp Club
Cobb County Stamp Club
Gwinnett Stamp Club
Stone Mountain Philatelic
  Society
Valdosta Stamp Club

## Hawaii

Hawaiian Philatelic Society

## Idaho

Boise Stamp Club
Snake River Stamp Club
Palouse Empire Stamp Club
Pocatello Stamp Club

## Illinois

Northwest Philatelic Club
Fox Valley Stamp Club
Belleville Stamp Club
Corn Belt Philatelic Society
Suburban Collectors' Club
Jackson County Stamp Society
Champaign-Urbana
  Stamp Club
Austin Philatelic Society
Beverly Hills Philatelic
  Society
Chicago Philatelic Society
Germany Philatelic Society
  Chapter 5
Hellenic Philatelic Society
  of America
North Shore Philatelic Society
The Philaterians
Polonus Philatelic Society
Ravenswood Stamp Club
Roosevelt Philatelic Society
Scandinavian Collectors Club
  Chapter 4
Tower Stamp Club
Decatur Stamp Club
Elgin Stamp Club
Evanston-New Trier
  Philatelic Society
Glen Ellyn Philatelic Club
North Suburban Stamp Club
Lincoln Trail Stamp Club
Quad City Stamp Club
LaSalle County Stamp Club
Park Forest Stamp Club
Caterpillar Stamp Club
Peoria Philatelic Society
Tri-County Stamp Club
Quinsippi Stamp Club
Rockford Stamp Club
Scott AFB Stamp Club
Springfield Philatelic Society
Lake County Philatelic Society

## Indiana

Madison County Bicentennial
  Society
Bartholomew County Stamp
  Club
Elkhart Stamp Club
Peachtree Stamp and
  Study Society
Evansville Stamp Club
Anthony Wayne Stamp Society
Calumet Stamp Club
Indiana Stamp Club
Northeastern Indiana Stamp
  Club
Northern Indiana Stamp Club
Wabash Valley Stamp Club

## Iowa

Allison Stamp Club
Hawkeye Stamp Club
Cedar Valley Stamp Club
Cedar Rapids Stamp Club
Mississippi Valley Stamp Club
Des Moines Philatelic Society
Iowa Women's Philatelic
  Society
North Central Iowa Philatelic
  Society

## Kansas

Northwest Kansas Stamp Club
Lawrence Stamp Club
Lindsborg Stamp Club
Flint Hills Stamp Club
Wichita Stamp Club

## Kentucky

Pennyrile Philatelic Society
Louisville Stamp Society
Philatelic Club of Louisville
Pleasure Ridge Park Philatelic
  Society

## Louisiana

Central Louisiana Stamp
  Collectors Club
Baton Rouge Stamp Club
Acadiana Stamp Club
Bayou Stamp Club
Twin City Stamp Club
Crescent City Stamp Club
Red River Stamp Society

## Maine

Penobscot Valley Stamp Club
Pine Tree Stamp Club
Portland Stamp Club
York County Stamp Club

## Maryland

Annapolis Stamp Club
Baltimore Philatelic Society
Chesapeake Philatelic Society
Bowie Stamp Club
Howard County Stamp Club
Harford County Stamp Club
Rockville-Gaithersburg
  Stamp Club
Goddard Space Center
  Stamp Club
Hagerstown Stamp Club
Potomac Philatelic Society
Silver Spring Philatelic Society

## Massachusetts

Amherst Stamp Club
Boston Philatelic Society
Chelmsford Stamp Club
Fall River Philatelic Society
Wachusett Philatelic Society
Lincoln Stamp Club
Samuel Osgood Stamp Club
Lynn Philatelic Society
Malden Stamp Club
New Bedford Stamp
  Collectors Club
Nippon Stamp Club of
  New England

Scandinavian Collectors Club,
  Chapter 5
Angle Tree Stamp Club
Berkshire Museum Stamp Club
Granite City Stamp Club
Cape Ann Stamp Club
Whaling City Stamp Club
Pioneer Valley Stamp Club
William C. Stone Chapter
Old Colony Philatelists
Waltham Stamp Club
Webster Dudley Stamp Club
Westfield Stamp Club
Cardinal Spellman Philatelic
  Museum
Northeastern Federation of
  Stamp Clubs
Dolphin Stamp Club

### Michigan

Peninsular State
  Philatelic Society
Ann Arbor Stamp Club
Birmingham Stamp Club
Dearborn Stamp Club
Collectors Club of Michigan
Detroit Philatelic Society
Michigan Stamp Club
Motor City Stamp and Cover
  Club
Ferndale Stamp Club
Flint Philatelic Circle
Kent Philatelic Society
Central Michigan Philatelic
  Society
Floral City Stamp Club
Oak Park Stamp Club
  of Michigan
West Suburban Stamp Club
  (Plymouth)
Pontiac Stamp Club
Saginaw Valley Stamp Society
Tri County Stamp Society
Grand Traverse Stamp Club
Wayne Stamp Society

### Minnesota

Maplewood Stamp Club
Minnehaha Stamp Club
Twin City Philatelic Society
Rochester Stamp Club
3M Stamp Club

### Mississippi

Gulf Coast Stamp Club
Hattiesburg Stamp Club
Northeast Mississippi Stamp
  Club
Jackson Philatelic Society

### Missouri

Columbia Philatelic Society
Kingdom Philatelic
  Association
Joplin Stamp Club
Collectors Club of Kansas City
Midwest Philatelic Society
Nevada Stamp and Coin Club
Rolla Philatelic Society

St. Joseph Stamp
  Collectors Club
Greater St. Louis Stamp Club
Mound City Stamp Club
Ozark Mountain Stamp Club
St. Louis Branch No. 4

### Montana

Garden City Stamp Club

### Nebraska

Central Nebraska Stamp Club
Lincoln Stamp Club
Buffalo Bill Stamp Club
Omaha Philatelic Society

### Nevada

Nevada Stamp Study Society
Southern Nevada Stamp Club

### New Hampshire

Collectors Club of
  New Hampshire
White Mountain Stamp Club
Monadnock Stamp Club
Manchester Stamp Club
Nashua Philatelic Society

### New Jersey

Association of South Jersey
  Stamp Clubs
Federated Stamp Clubs
  of Central New Jersey
North Jersey Federated
  Stamp Clubs
Bi-State Stamp Club
Elizabeth Stamp Club
American Helvetia Philatelic
  Society Chapter 1
Fair Lawn Stamp Club
Molly Pitcher Stamp Club
Hamilton Township Philatelic
  Society
Hazlet Stamp Club
North Jersey Stamp Club
Morris Hills Stamp Club
Coreyell's Ferry Stamp Club
Merchantville Stamp Club
West Essex Philatelic Society
Southern New Jersey Chapter
Jockey Hollow Stamp Club
Sussex County Stamp Club
Bergen County Stamp Club
Merck Stamp Club
Middle Forge Philatelic
  Society
Association of Bergen County
  Philatelists
Pascack Stamp Club
Teaneck Stamp Club
Ocean County Stamp Club
Trenton Philatelic Society
Cuban Philatelic Society
  New Jersey Chapter
North Jersey Scandinavian
  Collectors Club
Seashore Stamp Collectors Club
Queen City-Warren Stamp Club
Westfield Stamp Club

### New Mexico

New Mexico Philatelic
  Association
Alamogordo Philatelic Society
Albuquerque Philatelic Society
Los Alamos Stamp
  Collectors Association
Santa Fe Stamp Club

### New York

Federation of Central New
  York Philatelic Societies
Niagara Frontier
  Federated Stamp Club
Fort Orange Stamp Club
Auburn Stamp Club
Batavia-Genesee County
  Stamp and Coin Club
Southern Tier Philatelic Society
Buffalo Stamp Club
Plewacki Post Stamp Society
Polish Cadets Stamp Club
Trinity Stamp Club
Cobleskill Stamp Club
Corning Area Stamp Club
Dansville Area Stamp
  and Coin Club
East Aurora Philatelic Society
Elmira Stamp Club
Bethpage-Farmingdale Stamp
  Club (Farmingdale)
Long Island Stamp Club
Northern Chautauqua Philatelic
  Society
Fulton Stamp Club
Finger Lakes Stamp Club
North Shore Philatelic Society
Chenango Valley Stamp Club
Southern Tier Stamp Club
Allegheny Stamp Club
Huntington Stamp Club
Ithaca Philatelic Society
Reuben E. Fenton Philatelic
  Society
Johnson City Stamp Club
Stamp Society of Kingston
Leroy Stamp Club
Nassau Council Stamp Club
St. Lawrence International
  Stamp Club
Mesilla Valley Stamp Club
Sullivan County Philatelic
  Society
Cortland Stamp Club
Newburgh Stamp Club
Atoz Stamp Club
Manufacturers Hanover Trust
  Stamp Club
Texaco Stamp Club
Turtle Bay Philatelic Society
Niagara Frontier Stamp Club
Olean Area Stamp Club
Community Stamp Club
Oswego Stamp Club
Wayne Stamp Club
Patchogue Stamp and Coin Club
Xerox Employees Stamp Club

Dutchess Philatelic Society
Putnam Stamp Club
Kodak Stamp Club
Rochester Philatelic
 Association
Schenectady Stamp Club
Tri-County Stamp Club
Sodus Stamp Club
Western Monroe Philatelic
 Society
Staten Island Philatelic Society
Syracuse Stamp Club
Troy Stamp Club
Utica Stamp Club
Jefferson County Stamp Club

### North Carolina
Asheville Stamp Club
Charlotte Philatelic Society
Fortnightly Collectors Club
Triangle Stamp Club
Cape Fear Philatelic Society
Greensboro Stamp Club
Hendersonville Stamp Club
Hubert Ben Franklin
 Stamp Club
Princeton Philatelic Society
Raleigh Stamp Club
Rocky Mount Stamp Club
Winston-Salem Stamp Club
Franklin Stamp Club

### North Dakota
Lewis & Clark Stamp Club
Fargo-Moorhead
 Philatelic Society

### Ohio
Collectors Club of Akron
Rubber City Stamp Club
Athens Stamp Club
Belmont County Stamp Club
McKinley Stamp Club
Stark County Stamp Club
Chillicothe Stamp Club
Cincinnati Philatelic Society
Philatelic Society of Cincinnati
American Hungarian Stamp
 Club
Garfield-Perry Stamp Club
Columbus Philatelic Club
Nationwide Stamp Club
Cuyahoga Falls Stamp Club
City of Dayton Philatelic
 Society
Dayton Stamp Club
Black River Stamp Club
Euclid Stamp Club
Fort Findlay Stamp Club
Lakewood Exchange Club
 Stamp Lickers
Mansfield Stamp and Coin Club
Medina County Stamp Club
Miami Valley Stamp Club
Tuscora Stamp Club
Southwestern Stamp Club
Shaker Heights
 Philatelic Society
Springfield Stamp Society

Fort Steuben Stamp Club
Tiffin Stamp Club
Stamp Collectors Club of Toledo
Warren Area Stamp Club
Cuy-Lor Stamp Club
Worthington Stamp Club
Mahoning Valley Stamp Club
Zanes Trace Philatelic Society

### Oklahoma
Washington City Philatelic Soci-
 ety
Muskogee Stamp Club
Oklahoma City Stamp Club
Tulsa Stamp Club

### Oregon
Bandon Stamp Club
Corvallis Stamp Club
Greater Eugene Stamp Society
Rogue Valley Stamp Club
Southern Oregon Philatelic
 Society
Beaver Stamp Club
Oregon Stamp Society
Salem Stamp Society

### Pennsylvania
Associated Stamp Clubs of
 Southeastern Pennsylvania
 and Delaware
Allentown Philatelic Society
Ambler Stamp Club
Beaver County Philatelic
 Society
Bethlehem Philatelic Society
Brookhaven Stamp Club
Butler County Philatelic Society
Carlisle Stamp Club
Cumberland Valley Philatelic
 Society
Clearfield Philatelic Society
Susquehanna Valley Stamp and
 Study Club
Presque-Isle Philatelic Society
Westmoreland County
 Philatelic Society
Grove City Stamp Club
Capital City Philatelic Society
Havertown Stamp Club
Hazelton Stamp Club
Bux-Mont Stamp Club
Indiana Stamp Club
Johnstown Stamp Club
Armstrong Activities
 Association Stamp Club
Philatelic Society of Lancaster
 County
Lansdowne Stamp Club
Lebanon Stamp
 Collectors Club
Mount Joy Stamp Club
Newfoundland Philatelic
 Society
Educators Philatelic Society
 of Philadelphia
Frankford Arsenal Stamp
 Club
Germantown Stamp Club

Oxford Philatelic Society
Philadelphia Chapter No. 18
Philatelic Society
 of Pittsburgh
Scandinavian Collectors Club
 Chapter No. 20
North Penn Stamp Club
Reading Stamp Collectors Club
Spring-Ford Philatelic Society
Northeastern Pennsylvania
 Philatelic Society
Sharon Stamp Club
Springfield Delco Stamp Club
Mount Nittany Philatelic
 Society
Pocono Mountain Philatelic
 Society
Penn-Laurel Stamp Club
Warren County Stamp Club
Wyoming Valley Stamp Club
Williamsport Stamp Club
Bux-Mont Stamp Club
White Rose Philatelic Society

### Rhode Island
Newport Philatelic Society
Rhode Island Philatelic
 Society

### South Carolina
Charleston Stamp Club
Columbia Philatelic Society
Greenville Stamp Club
Spartanburg Stamp Club
Thermal Belt Stamp Club

### South Dakota
Ringneck Stamp Club
South Dakota Stamp and Coin
 Association
Vermillion Stamp Club

### Tennessee
Chattanooga Stamp Club
Cumberland Stamp Club
West Tennessee Stamp Club
Holston Stamp Club
Expo City Stamp Club
Memphis Stamp
 Collectors Society
Southern Philatelic
 Federation
Navy Memphis Stamp Club
Nashville Philatelic Society
Atomic City Stamp Club
Kentucky Lake Stamp Club

### Texas
Texas Philatelic Association
Golden Spread Stamp Club
Mid-Cities Stamp Club
Austin Stamp Club
Texas A&M University
 Stamp Club
Sea Gull Stamp Club
Collectors Club of Dallas
Dallas Philatelic Society
Park Cities Philatelic Society
El Paso Philatelic Society
Panther City Philatelic
 Society

Houston Philatelic Society
JSC Stamp Club
South Plains Stamp Club
Marshall Stamp Club
Nacogdoches Stamp Club
Port Lavaca Philatelic Society
Concho Valley Stamp Club
Collectors Club of San Antonio
San Antonio Philatelic
  Association
Waco Stamp Club
Wichita Falls Stamp & Coin
  Club

### Utah

Golden Spike Stamp Club
Timpanogos Philatelic Society
Utah Philatelic Society

### Vermont

Brattleboro Stamp Club
Chittenden County Stamp Club
Washington County Stamp Club
Rutland County Stamp Club

### Virginia

Arlington County Recreational
  Stamp Club
Northern Virginia Stamp Club
Charlottesville Stamp Club
Dan River Philatelic Society
Eastern Prince William
  Stamp Club
Nathan Hale Stamp Club
Fredericksburg Stamp Club
Virginia Philatelic Federation
Rockingham Stamp Club
Northern Neck Stamp Club
Dolley Madison Stamp Club
Shenandoah Valley Stamp
  Club
Peninsula Stamp Club
Tidewater Stamp Club
Norfolk Philatelic Society
Richmond Stamp Club
Big Lick Stamp Club
Springfield Stamp Club
Ayrhill Stamp Club
Virginia Beach Stamp Club
Northern Neck Stamp Club
Williamsburg Stamp Society

### Washington

Greater East Side Stamp
  Society
Olympic Philatelic Society
Sno-King Stamp Club

Tri City Stamp Club
Whidbey Island Stamp Club
Olympia Philatelic Society
Pullman Stamp Club
Boeing Employees Stamp Club
Collectors Club of Seattle
Seattle Timbremania Society
Washington State Philatelic
  Society
Inland Empire Philatelic
  Society
Tacoma Stamp Club
Walla Walla Valley
  Philatelic Society
Wenatchee Valley
  Stamp Association
Yakima Valley Stamp Club

### West Virginia

Mountain State Stamp Club
Kanawha Stamp Club
Huntington Stamp Collectors
  Club
Blennerhassett Stamp Society
Carbide Stamp Club
Ohio Valley Stamp Club

### Wisconsin

Wisconsin Federation
  of Stamp Clubs
Outagamie Philatelic Society
Walworth County Stamp Club
Kenosha Stamp and Cover Club
Madison Stamp Club
Manitowoc Philatelic Society
Milwaukee North Shore
  Philatelic Society
Milwaukee Philatelic Society
Poland Philatelic Society
University of Wisconsin-
  Milwaukee Philatelic Society
Ripon Philatelic Society
Sheboygan Stamp Club
Central Wisconsin Stamp Club
Arrowhead Stamp Club
Waukesha County
  Philatelic Society
Wisconsin Valley Philatelic
  Society

### Wyoming

Casper Stamp Club
Cheyenne Philatelic Society
Central Wyoming Philatelic
  Society

### Puerto Rico

Puerto Rico Philatelic
  Society
San Juan Philatelic Circle

### Belgium

SHAPE International
  Philatelic Club

### Bermuda

BERMUPEX Group

### Canada

Bathurst & Chaleur District
  Stamp Club
Edmonton Stamp Club
Hamilton Philatelic Society
Union Philatelique de Montreal
Oakville Stamp Club
Ottawa Philatelic Society
Lakeshore Stamp Club
Alberni Valley Stamp Club
Regina Philatelic Club
St. John's Philatelic Society
Vancouver Island Philatelic
  Society
Winnipeg Philatelic Society

### Colombia

Club Filatelico de Barranquilla
Club Filatelico de Bogota

### Dominican Republic

Sociedad Filatelica Dominicana

### Ecuador

Club Filatelico Guayaquil

### England

American Stamp Club
  of Great Britain

### Germany

ARGE USA
Heidelberg Stamp & Coin Club

### Mexico

Sociedad Filatelico de Mexico

### Netherlands Antilles

Curacaose Postzegel
  Vereniging

### Norway

Oslo Filatelist Klubb

### Panama

Isthmian Collectors Club

### Saudi Arabia

Arabian Philatelic Association

### Spain

ROTA Stamp and Coin Club

## APS Affiliates and Units

The APS affiliate or unit number appears in parentheses.

Americana Unit (40)
American Air Mail Society (77)
American First Day Cover Society (33)
American Helvetia Philatelic Society (52)
APS Writers Unit (30)
American Revenue Association (51)
American Society for Netherlands Philately (60)

American Society of Polar Philatelists (31)
Associated Collectors of El Salvador (89)
Austria Philatelic Society of New York (59)
Brazil Philatelic Association (32)
British Caribbean Philatelic Study Group (27)
Bullseye Cancel Collectors Club (108)
Canal Zone Study Group (42)
China Stamp Society (10)
Christmas Philatelic Club (74)

Christmas Seal & Charity Stamp Society (101)
Cinderella Stamp Club (91)
Civil Censorship Study Group (86)
Club of Channel Islands Collectors (63)
Commonwealth International Philatelic Society (113)
Confederate Stamp Alliance (73)
Croatian Philatelic Society (53)
Eire Philatelic Association (21)
Empire State Postal History Society (28)
Errors, Freaks and Oddities Collector's Club (103)
Europa Study Unit (17)
Falkland Islands Philatelic Study Group (83)
Fire Service in Philately (80)
Flag Cancel Society (24)
France and Colonies Philatelic Society (45)
Franklin D. Roosevelt Philatelic Society (69)
Germany Philatelic Society (48)
Great Britain Overprints Society (72)
Haitian Philatelic Society (81)
Illinois Postal History Society (112)
India Study Circle (111)
International Churchill Society (49)
International Philippine Philatelic Society (54)
International Society for Japanese Philately (58)
International Society for Portuguese Philately (35)
International Society of Guatemala Collectors (36)
JAPOS Study Group (68)
Junior Philatelists of America (26)
Korea Stamp Society (113)
Latin American Philatelic Society (104)
Mailer's Postmark Permit Club (100)
Malaria Philatelists International (115)
Maritime Postmark Society (37)
Masonic Study Unit (94)
Massachusetts Postal Research League (93)
Maximum Card Study Unit (106)
Meso-American Archeology Study Unit (82)
Mexico-Elmhurst Philatelic Society International (43)
Mobile Post Office Society (64)
New Jersey Postal History Society (95)
Ohio Postal History Society (66)

Old World Archaeological Study Unit (92)
Pennsylvania Postal History Society (50)
Perfins Club (57)
Performing Arts Study Unit (102)
Pictorial Eleven (56)
Pitcairn Islands Study Group (46)
Polonus Philatelic Society (119)
Post Mark Collectors Club (62)
Postal History Society (44)
Postal History Society of Canada (67)
Postal History Society of Minnesota (84)
Precancel Stamp Society (65)
Rhodesia Study Circle (107)
Romanian Philatelic Club (88)
Rotary-on-Stamps (117)
Ryukyu Philatelic Specialist Society (47)
St.Helena &Dependencies Philatelic Society (85)
Sarawak Specialists' Society (110)
Scandinavian Collectors Club (79)
Society for Czechoslovak Philately (18)
Society for Hungarian Philately (34)
Society for Thai Philately (78)
Society of Australasian Specialists/Oceania(22)
Society of Costa Rica Collectors (96)
Society of Indo-China Philatelists (38)
Society of Israel Philatelists (105)
Society of Philatelists and Numismatists (116)
Space Topics Study Group (29)
Sports Philatelists International (39)
Texas Postal History Society (76)
Turkey and Ottoman Philatelic Society (108)
Tuvalu Philatelic Society (90)
United Nations Philatelists (71)
United Postal Stationery Society (20)
United States Cancellation Club (75)
U.S. 1869 Pictorial Research Association (87)
United States Philatelic Classics Society (11)
United States Possessions Philatelic Society (99)
Universal Postal Union Collectors (70)
Universal Ship Cancellation Society (98)
Virginia Postal History Society (41)
War Cover Club (19)
Western Cover Society (14)
Wisconsin Postal History Society (61)
Women on Stamps Study Unit (118)
Zippy Collectors Club (97)

## APS Convention Sites

The 91st annual APS convention, STaMpsHOW '77, held Aug. 25-28 in San Francsisco, Calif., was the first convention to be conducted by the society, rather than being a guest of a host club.

| | | |
|---|---|---|
| 1886: New York, N.Y. | 1902: Springfield, Mass. | 1918: Cleveland, Ohio |
| 1887: Chicago, Ill. | 1903: Clayton, N.Y. | 1919: St. Louis, Mo. |
| 1888: Boston, Mass. | 1904: Pittsburgh, Pa. | 1920: Providence, R.I. |
| 1889: St. Louis, Mo. | 1905: Minneapolis, Minn. | 1921: Milwaukee, Wis. |
| 1890: New York, N.Y. | 1906: Boston, Mass. | 1922: Springfield, Mass. |
| 1891: New York, N.Y. | 1907: Denver, Colo. | 1923: Washington, D.C. |
| 1892: Niagara Falls, N.Y. | 1908: Columbus, Ohio | 1924: Detroit, Mich. |
| 1893: Chicago, Ill. | 1909: Atlantic City, N.J. | 1925: Los Angeles, Calif. |
| 1894: Niagara Falls, N.Y. | 1910: Detroit, Mich. | 1926: New York, N.Y. |
| 1895: Clayton, N.Y. | 1911: Chicago, Ill. | 1927: St. Louis, Mo. |
| 1896: Lake Minnetonka, Minn. | 1912: Springfield, Mass. | 1928: Toronto, Canada |
| 1897: Boston, Mass. | 1913: Put-In-Bay, Ohio | 1929: Minneapolis, Minn. |
| 1898: New York, N.Y. | 1914: Niagara Falls, N.Y. | 1930: Boston, Mass. |
| 1899: Detroit, Mich. | 1915: San Francisco, Calif. | 1931: Memphis, Tenn. |
| 1900: Milwaukee, Wis. | 1916: Boston, Mass. | 1932: Los Angeles, Calif. |
| 1901: Buffalo, N.Y. | 1917: Alexander Bay, N.Y. | 1933: Chicago, Ill. |

1934: Atlantic City, N.J.
1935: Washington, D.C.
1936: Omaha, Neb.
1937: Detroit, Mich.
1938: New Orleans, La.
1939: San Francisco, Calif.
1940: Buffalo, N.Y.
1941: Baltimore, Md.
1942: Cleveland, Ohio
1944: Milwaukee, Wis.
1945: Newark, N.J.
1946: Chicago, Ill
1947: Pittsburgh, Pa.
1948: Denver, Colo.
1949: Boston, Mass.
1950: Washington, D.C.
1951: Toronto, Canada
1952: Philadelphia, Pa.

1953: Houston, Tex.
1954: San Francisco, Calif.
1955: Norfolk, Va.
1956: St. Louis, Mo.
1957: Tampa, Fla.
1958: Cleveland, Ohio
1959: Los Angeles, Calif.
1960: Portland, Ore.
1961: Chicago, Ill.
1962: State College, Pa.
1963: Mexico City, Mexico
1964: Washington, D.C.
1965: Denver, Colo.
1966: Cincinnati, Ohio
1967: Newark, N.J.
1968: Rochester, N.Y.
1969: Baltimore, Md.
1970: Honolulu, Hawaii

1971: San Antonio, Tex.
1972: New Haven, Conn.
1973: Los Angeles, Calif.
1974: Chicago, Ill.
1975: Columbus, Ohio
1976: Memphis, Tenn.
1977: San Francisco, Calif.
1978: Indianapolis, Ind.
1979: Boston, Mass.
1980: Spokane, Wash.
1981: Atlanta, Ga.
1982: Milwaukee, Wis.

**Future Conventions**

1983: Pittsburgh, Pa.
1984: Dallas, Tex.
1985: San Diego, Calif.

## APS Spring Meeting Sites

1958: Cleveland, Ohio
1959: Detroit, Mich.
1960: Richmond, Va.
1961: Phoenix, Ariz.
1962: New York, N.Y.
1963: San Francisco, Calif.
1964: Salt Lake City, Utah
1965: Cleveland, Ohio
1966: Portland, Ore.
1967: New Orleans, La.

1968: San Diego, Calif.
1969: Tucson, Ariz.
1970: Memphis, Tenn.
1971: Atlantic City, N.J.
1972: New Orleans, La.
1973: Williamsburg, Va.
1974: Miami, Fla.
1975: Phoenix, Ariz.
1976: Philadelphia, Pa.
1977: New Orleans, La.

1978: Toronto, Canada
1979: Denver, Colo.
1980: London, England
1981: State College, Pa.
1982: Tuscon, Ariz.

**Future Spring Meetings**

1983: Portland, Ore.
1984: Open
1985: Providence, R.I.
1986: Chicago, Ill.

# Presidents, Vice Presidents and Conventions

| Term of Office | President | Vice President | Convention | Year |
|---|---|---|---|---|
| 1886-88 | *John K. Tiffany Missouri | R.R. Bogert New York | 1st New York, N.Y. 2nd Chicago, Ill. 3rd Boston, Mass. | 1886 1887 1888 |
| 1888-90 | *John K. Tiffany Missouri | Willard C. Van Derlip Massachusetts | 4th St. Louis, Mo. 5th New York, N.Y. | 1889 1890 |
| 1890-92 | *John K. Tiffany Missouri | Charles B. Corwin New York | 6th New York, N.Y. 7th Niagara Falls, N.Y. | 1891 1892 |
| 1892-93 | *John K. Tiffany Missouri | Willard C. Van Derlip[1] Massachusetts | 8th Chicago, Ill. | 1893 |
| 1893-94 | *John K. Tiffany Missouri | Hiram E. Deats New Jersey | 9th Niagara Falls, N.Y. | 1894 |
| 1894-96 | *John K. Tiffany Missouri | Alvah Davison New York | 10th Clayton, N.Y. 11th Lake Minnetonka, Minn. | 1895 1896 |
| 1896-98 | *Col. Frank F. Olney Rhode Island | **Board of Vice Presidents** Boston, Mass. Willard C. Van Derlip John L. Kilbon George L. Toppan | 12th Boston, Mass. 13th New York, N.Y. | 1897 1898 |
| 1898-99 | *Col. Frank F. Olney Rhode Island | Boston, Mass. Willard C. Van Derlip George L. Toppan Ernest M. Carpenter | 14th Detroit, Mich. | 1899 |

| Term of Office | President | Vice President | Convention | Year |
|---|---|---|---|---|
| 1899-00 | *George L. Toppan Wisconsin | New York, N.Y. J.W. George P.F. Bruner Alexander Holland Albert Perrin[2] | 15th Milwaukee, Wis. | 1900 |
| 1900-02 | *George L. Toppan Wisconsin | Chicago, Ill. Samuel Leland C.E. Severn P. M. Wolsieffer | 16th Buffalo, N.Y. 17th Springfield, Mass. | 1901 1902 |
| 1902-03 | *Alexander Holland New York | Boston, Mass. Frank H. Burt Gordon Ireland J. F. Johnson Edwin F. Sawyer[3] | 18th Clayton, N.Y. | 1903 |
| 1903-04 | *Alexander Holland New York | Boston, Mass. Frank H. Burt Willard O. Wylie Gordon Ireland | 19th Pittsburgh, Pa. | 1904 |
| 1904-05 | *Hiram E. Deats New Jersey | Boston, Mass. Frank H. Burt Willard O. Wylie Gordon Ireland | 20th Minneapolis, Minn. | 1905 |
| 1905-06 | *William C. Stone Massachusetts | Chicago, Ill. Henry N. Mudge Alexander Holland Henry A. Fowler | 21st Boston, Mass. | 1906 |
| 1906-07 | *William C. Stone Massachusetts | Chicago, Ill. Henry N. Mudge Fred Michaels Henry A. Fowler | 22nd Denver, Colo. | 1907 |
| 1907-09 | *John N. Luff New York | Boston, Mass. Clifton A. Howes Lorenzo L. Green Edward deZ. Kelley | 23rd Columbus, Ohio 24th Atlantic City, N.J. | 1908 1909 |
| 1909-11 | *Henry N. Mudge Illinois | St. Louis, Mo. Frederick R. Cornwall Adelbert Strauss Chester Myers | 25th Detroit, Mich. 26th Chicago, Ill. | 1910 1911 |
| 1911-13 | *Fredk. R. Cornwall Missouri | Detroit, Mich. Gen. Chas. A. Coolidge Herbert Bowen C. Frederic Heyerman | 27th Springfield, Mass. 28th Put-in-Bay, Ohio | 1912 1913 |
| 1913-15 | *Gen. C.A. Coolidge Michigan | Cleveland, Ohio Henry C. Crowell John F. Rust Alvin Good | 29th Niagara Falls, N.Y. 30th San Francisco, Calif. | 1914 1915 |
| 1915-17 | *Clifton A. Howes Massachusetts | Brooklyn, N.Y. Henry H. Wilson Dr. Carroll Chase Wm. B. Sprague | 31st Boston, Mass. 32nd Alexandria Bay, N.Y. | 1916 1917 |
| 1917-19 | *John W. Scott New York | Omaha, Neb. F.S. Parmelee[4] Dr. W.P. Wherry H.A. Whipple | 33rd Cleveland, Ohio 34th St. Louis, Mo. | 1918 1919 |
| 1919-20 | *Henry H. Wilson New York | Omaha, Neb. F.S. Parmelee Dr. W.P. Wherry H.A. Whipple | 35th Providence, R.I. | 1920 |

| Term of Office | President | Vice President | Convention | Year |
|---|---|---|---|---|
| 1920-22 | *Dr. Carroll Chase<br>New York | Springfield, Mass.<br>Robert C. Munroe<br>John W. Prevost<br>H.P. Atherton | 36th Milwaukee, Wis.<br>37th Springfield, Mass. | 1921<br>1922 |
| 1922-23 | *C. Fred. Heyerman<br>Michigan | Cleveland, Ohio<br>W.W. MacLaren<br>James A. Harris Jr.<br>Otto F. Moses | 38th Washington, D.C. | 1923 |
| 1923-24 | *C. Fred. Heyerman<br>Michigan | Cleveland, Ohio<br>W.W. MacLaren<br>W.H. Barnum<br>Otto F. Moses | 39th Detroit, Mich. | 1924 |
| 1924-25 | *P.M. Wolsieffer<br>Illinois | Kansas City, Mo.<br>Wm. C. Michaels<br>Wilson D. Wood<br>Wm. Jerrems Jr. | 40th Los Angeles, Calif. | 1925 |
| 1925-27 | *August H. Wilhelm<br>California | Milwaukee, Wis.<br>Dr. Frederick A. Kraft<br>W.O. Staab<br>Dr. Samuel G. Keller | 41st New York, N.Y.<br>42nd St. Louis, Mo. | 1926<br>1927 |
| 1927-29 | *August H. Wilhelm<br>California | Cincinnati, Ohio<br>Wm. C. Kennett Jr.<br>Dr. L.G. Tedesche<br>Gustave M. Mosler | 43rd Toronto, Ont.<br>44th Minneapolis, Minn. | 1928<br>1929 |
| 1929-31 | *Gustave M. Mosler<br>Ohio | Chicago, Ill.<br>Chas. F. Mann<br>Adolph F. Boehm<br>Dr. C.W. Hennan | 45th Boston, Mass.<br>46th Memphis, Tenn. | 1930<br>1931 |
| 1931-33 | *Dr. C.W. Hennan<br>Illinois | Cleveland, Ohio<br>Frank W. Grant<br>William D. Preston<br>Michael J. Lloyd | 47th Los Angeles, Calif.<br>48th Chicago, Ill. | 1932<br>1933 |
| 1933-35 | Roscoe B. Martin<br>New York | Lynchburg, Va.<br>Milton Moses<br>Edward F. Haley<br>Don. P. Peters[5]<br>Carter Glass Jr. | 49th Atlantic City, N.J.<br>50th Washington, D.C. | 1934<br>1935 |
| 1935-37 | *Eugene Klein<br>Pennsylvania | Washington, D.C.<br>Hugh M. Southgate<br>Philip Simms Warren<br>Mrs. C.L. Manning | 51st Omaha, Neb.<br>52nd Detroit, Mich. | 1936<br>1937 |
| 1937-39 | *Carter Glass Jr.<br>Virginia | Buffalo, N.Y.<br>Adolph Steeg<br>Frederick L. Koepf<br>Rollin E. Flower | 53rd New Orleans, La.<br>54th San Francisco,<br>   Calif. | 1938<br><br>1939 |
| 1939-43 | *Rollin E. Flower<br>New York | Cleveland, Ohio<br>Donald W. Martin<br>Judge D.F. Lybarger<br>Ralph E. Johnson | 55th Buffalo, N.Y.<br>56th Baltimore, Md.<br>57th Cleveland, Ohio<br>   (no convention) | 1940<br>1941<br>1942<br>1943 |
| 1943-47 | *Donald F. Lybarger<br>Ohio | Baltimore, Md.<br>Sol Glass<br>Judge D.D. Caldwell<br>Mrs. D.B. McEntee | 58th Milwaukee, Wis.<br>59th Newark, N.J.<br>60th Chicago, Ill.<br>61st Pittsburgh, Pa. | 1944<br>1945<br>1946<br>1947 |
| 1947-49 | *Donald F. Lybarger<br>Ohio | New Orleans, La.<br>Fred N. Billingsley<br>Douglas Watson<br>Leonard V. Huber | 62nd Denver, Colo.<br>63rd Boston, Mass. | 1948<br>1949 |

| Term of Office | President | Vice President | Convention | Year |
|---|---|---|---|---|
| 1949-51 | Wilbur F. Cannon<br>Iowa | Milwaukee, Wis.<br>Clarence J. Gruhl<br>Burleigh E. Jacobs<br>Claude W. Degler | 64th Washington, D.C.<br>65th Toronto, Ont. | 1950<br>1951 |
| 1951-53 | Wilbur F. Cannon<br>Iowa | Philadelphia, Pa.<br>Earl P.L. Apfelbaum<br>P. Harbot Sanville Sr.<br>Donald M. Steele | 65th Philadelphia, Pa.<br>67th Houston, Tex. | 1952<br>1953 |
| 1953-55 | Burleigh E. Jacobs<br>Wisconsin | Moline, Ill.<br>Chas. C. Cratsenberg<br>Frank J. Patterson<br>Allen Seiffert[6]<br>Col. Guy W. Ade | 68th San Francisco,<br>Calif.<br>69th Norfolk, Va. | 1954<br>1955 |
| 1955-57 | *L.D. Shoemaker<br>Florida | Moline, Ill.<br>Chas. C. Cratsenberg<br>Allen Seiffert[6]<br>Col. Guy W. Ade | 70th St. Louis, Mo.<br>71st Tampa, Fla. | 1956<br>1957 |
| 1957-61 | C.C. Cratsenberg<br>Illinois | San Francisco, Calif.<br>Joseph M. Clary<br>Charles A. McKeown<br>Fred B. Thomas | 72nd Atlantic City, N.J.<br>73rd Los Angeles, Calif.<br>74th Portland, Ore.<br>75th Chicago, Ill. | 1958<br>1959<br>1960<br>1961 |
| 1961-65 | Fred B. Thomas<br>California | Washington, D.C.<br>George T. Turner<br>Edward S. Conger<br>Paul J. Plant | 76th State College, Pa.<br>77th Mexico City, Mexico<br>78th Washington, D.C.<br>79th Denver, Colo. | 1962<br>1963<br>1964<br>1965 |
| 1965-69 | *Edward L. Willard<br>Pennsylvania | Los Angeles, Calif.<br>Emerson A. Clark<br>Stanley H. Beecher<br>W. Eugene Tinsley | 80th Cincinnati, Ohio<br>81st Newark, N.J.<br>82nd Rochester, N.Y.<br>83rd Baltimore, Md. | 1966<br>1967<br>1968<br>1969 |
| 1969-73 | *Daniel W. Vooys<br>New York | Phoenix, Ariz.<br>Grant Bulkley<br>Dr. Wm. C. Parker<br>Robert D. Corless | 84th Honolulu, Hawaii<br>85th San Antonio, Tex.<br>86th New Haven, Conn.<br>87th Los Angeles, Calif. | 1970<br>1971<br>1972<br>1973 |
| 1973-77 | Emerson A. Clark<br>California | New Orleans, La.<br>Henry H. Frenkle<br>Hubert C. Skinner<br>William H. Bauer<br>John M. Kinabrew Jr.[7] | 88th Chicago, Ill.<br>89th Columbus, Ohio<br>90th Memphis, Tenn.<br>91st San Francisco, Calif. | 1974<br>1975<br>1976<br>1977 |
| 1977-81 | John E. Foxworth Jr.<br>Michigan | New York Area<br>F. Burton Sellers<br>David L. Lidman<br>E.E. Fricks | 92nd Indianapolis, Ind.<br>93rd Boston, Mass.<br>94th Spokane, Wash.<br>95th Atlanta, Ga. | 1978<br>1979<br>1980<br>1981 |
| 1981- | William H. Bauer<br>Texas | Boston Area<br>Lois M. Evans<br>George S. Norton<br>Guy R. Dillaway | 96th Milwaukee, Wis. | 1982 |

NOTE: In 1896 the society bylaws were changed to increase the number of vice presidents from one to three. They are now required to reside within a radius of 200 miles. The chairman of the Board of Vice Presidents is listed first and the secretary, clerk or recorder (title has changed through the years) is listed last.

*—President deceased.
1—Elected in January 1892 to complete the term of Chas. B. Corwin.
2—Succeeded Alexander Holland who resigned as vice president in early 1900.
3—Succeeded J.F. Johnson who died Feb. 8, 1903.
4—Acting president for balance of term following death of John W. Scott on Jan. 4, 1919.
5—Succeeded Edward F. Haley who resigned as vice president in early 1935.
6—Succeeded Frank J. Patterson who resigned as vice president in March 1954.
7—Succeeded William H. Bauer who resigned as vice president in November 1976.

# Current APS Officers

### Board of Directors

President: William H. Bauer

Board of Vice Presidents: Lois M. Evans, George S. Norton, Guy R. Dillaway

Secretary: Patricia S. Siskin

Treasurer: Joseph E. Foley

Directors at Large: James H. Beal, Henry Gobie, Robert Odenweller, Lester E. Winick

Immediate Past President: John E. Foxworth Jr.

### Appointive Officers

Executive Director: Keith Wagner

Editor of American Philatelist: Richard L. Sine

Attorney: George M. Martin

Deputy Attorney: David A. Flood

Resident Agent: W.H. Schilling Jr.

Historian: Robert L.D. Davidson

Assistant Historian: Allan M. Koplar

Representative to the International Federation of Philately: Bernard A. Hennig

Representative to the Federacion Interamericana de Filatelia: Dr. Roberto M. Rosende

Representative to the International Association of Philatelic Journalists: Charles J. Peterson

Representative to FIP Aero Philatelic Commission: Philip Silver

Representative to FIP Astrophilately Subcommission: Lester E. Winick

Representative to FIP Philatelic Literature Commission: Charles J. Peterson

Representative to FIP Postal History Commission: Ernst M. Cohn

Representative to FIP Postal Stationery Commission: John G. Fluck

Representative to FIP Thematic Commission: Vacant

Representative to FIP Traditional Philately Commission: Robert P. Odenweller

Representative to FIP Youth Philately Commission: Ernest A. Kehr

### National Headquarters Staff

Director of Administration: Frank L. Sente

Staff: Deborah H. Fetzer, Krystal R. McVicker, Connie I. Swartz, Judy A. Weaver

Director of Accounting: Jean M. Varner

Accounting Staff: Patricia A. Fryer, Anetta S. Wertz

Director of Conventions/Education: Robert N. DeVoss

Conventions Assistant: Kathleen A. Ross

Executive Director Staff: A. Mercer Bristow, Helen Bruno, Donna S. Ray

Director of Expertizing: James T. DeVoss

Expertizing Assistant: Rita I. Corl

Mailroom Staff: Barbara J. Fink, Barbara J. Meyers

### Sales Division Staff

Director of Sales: Gordon P. Wrenn

Sales Staff: Carol L. Emel, Carol A. Hoffman, Nancy J. Kraus, Ruth Ann Leidy, Lisa M. Park, Cathy L. Rossman, Lisa A. Schreffler, Susan C. Smith, Carol A. Woodring

### Philatelic Staff

William J. Dixon, Thomas W. Horn, Jack C. Standen

### Editorial Staff:

Barbara L. Albert, Barbara A. Staub, Kathleen Wolsiffer

### Committee Chairmen

Accreditation of Judges: Bernard A. Hennig

Affiliate Coordination: Robert de Violini

Awards and Honors: Mary Ann Owens

Bylaws: George M. Martin

Chapter Activities: John M. Hotchner

Chapter Speakers Bureau: Harry C. Meier

Education Advisory: Hubert C. Skinner

Ethics: Emerson A. Clark

Finance: Joseph E. Foley

Hall of Fame: Herbert J. Bloch

Insurance: Horace W. Harrison

International Relations: Bernard A. Hennig

Literature: Robert L.D. Davidson

Luff Awards: Philip Silver

New Issues: Richard L. Sine

Paper Preservation: Charles E. Nolan, chairman

Philatelic Color Designation: Donald L. MacPeek

Postal History: Ernst M. Cohn

Recruiting: Frank L. Sente

Slide Editor: Kalman Illyefalvi

Stamp Theft: James H. Beal

Translation: Dmytro Bykovetz Jr.

Youth Activities: Alfred E. Rosinski

### APRL Staff

Librarian: Steven A. Pla

Assistant Librarians: Joanne Mast, Martha M. Micuda

Library Staff: Mary A. Borden, Kathy C. Brooks, Gladys C. Hoffman, James C. Knudsen, Sally R. Nevins, Mary Jane Sharpe

Janitorial Staff: Edward W. Bistline

## APS Hall of Fame

The APS Hall of Fame for outstanding contributors to philately was established in 1941 when 15 persons from years past were recognized. Except in 1943, 1965 and 1970, one to three individuals have been added annually. The date preceding the name of the individual indicates the year of nomination.

1941: Ralph A. Barry, Sir Rowland Hill, Beverly S. King, Edward S. Knapp, James L. Lindsay, John N. Luff, Frederick J. Melville, Charles Lathrop Pack, Charles J. Phillips, John W. Scott, Charles E. Severn, Hugh M. Southgate, Thomas K. Tapling, John K. Tiffany, Philip M. Wolsieffer

1942: W. Hamilton Barnum, Walter J. Conrath, Evelyn Severn

1944: Eugene Klein

1945: C.R. Richards, Franklin Delano Roosevelt, Willard O. Wylie

1946: J. Murray Bartels, Percy G. Doane

1947: William C. Stone

1948: Alfred F. Lichtenstein

1949: Edward H. Mason, James Starr

1950: Frederick R. Harris, Saul Newbury, Walter S. Scott

1951: Nicolas Sanabria, J.B. Seymour, Rev. William H. Tower

1952: Donald W. Martin, Walter R. McCoy

1953: David Caldwell, E.F. Hurt

1954: Theresa M. Clark, Dr. James Goodwin, Al Van Dahl

1955: Jere. Hess Barr, D.D. Berolzheimer

1956: Clarence W. Brazer, Dr. H.A. Davis, Dr. Clarence W. Hennan

1957: Hugh M. Clark, Max G. Johl, John W. Stowell

1958: Sidney F. Barrett, Theodore E. Steinway

1959: Stanley B. Ashbrook, Stephen G. Rich

1960: Dr. Carroll Chase, Adolph Steeg

1961: Rollin E. Flower, Morris Fortgang, Harry M. Konwiser

1962: F. Van Dyk MacBride, George B. Sloane

1963: L.H. Barkhausen, Hugh Barr, Hiram E. Deats

1964: Henry Chaloner, August Dietz, Howard H. Elliott

1966: Carl E. Pelander, Philip H. Ward

1967: William W. Hicks, George W. Linn, Harry Weiss

1968: Louise Boyd Dale, Vincent Domanski Jr., Francis Cardinal Spellman

1969: Charles S. Hamilton, Henry A. Meyer, Dr. Gregory B. Salisbury

1971: Richard McP. Cabeen, L.B. Gatchell, Donald F. Lybarger

1972: Edward Denny Bacon, Lester G. Brookman, C.H. Mekeel

1973: Edith M. Faulstich, Peter G. Keller, Elliott Perry

1974: Winthrop Boggs, Sol Glass, Edwin Mueller

1975: Henry M. Goodkind, Delf Norona

1976: Manuel M. Risueno, Sir John Wilson

1977: Alfred H. Caspary, James M. Chemi

1978: Alberto Diena, Irwin Heiman

1979: H.E. Harris, Harry L. Lindquist, Lowell Ragatz

1980: J.R.W. Purves, George T. Turner, Daniel W. Vooys

1981: William E. Gerrish, Dr. James J. Matejka Jr., Ethel B. McCoy

## World Series of Philately

The World Series of Philately was introduced at the 82nd annual APS convention held in Rochester, N.Y., in September 1968. It has proved to be a success and has achieved increasing popularity.

The decision to have a competition which would enable grand-award winners at major national stamp exhibitions to compete against each other to determine a "Champion of Champions" was the result of a demand by serious collectors voiced over many years.

From the first announcement, the novel idea earned wide and immediate acceptance. The quality of exhibits entered in competition at Rochester in 1968 and subsequent competitions has been outstanding.

Prior to the institution of the World Series of Philately, the assembling of a number of truly great award-winning exhibits in one place for viewing by the general public rarely occurred. Usually such exhibits were staged at huge international exhibitions.

To the average stamp collector unable to travel to the site of an international exhibition, the "Champion of Champions" competition offers an opportunity to see some of the most outstanding collections ever formed.

Because the APS holds the conventions in various sections of the U.S., all stamp collectors may take advantage of an unparalleled philatelic experience by attending a World Series of Philately exhibition.

The opportunity to see such a wealth of superbly mounted, painstakingly prepared, and hard-to-obtain material has attracted an ever-increasing number of collectors and noncollectors to each successive World Series exhibition.

The inevitable, long-range results of this high-level competition will be the upgrading of exhibits entered in regional or national shows and the opportunity, previously lacking, for large numbers of people in various parts of the country to see philately at its best.

Because of the obvious popularity of the program, the APS board of directors has adopted a set of rules designed to establish nationally recognized and accepted standards for entries in the World Series of Philately. It was decided that grand-award winners of major national stamp exhibitions would be invited to exhibit their award-winning entries in competition with other winners of similar awards.

The following rules were adopted to determine what exhibition will be considered as qualifying and to establish the criteria for the display to be entered in competition:

1. The exhibition must be an established and recognized major show; the show must be held on a regular basis.

2. There must be no restrictions as to who may exhibit either based on membership or residence. To demonstrate the national character of such exhibitions, not less than 40 per cent of the exhibitors and frames must be by exhibitors residing outside the metropolitan area where the show is being held.

3. The size of the exhibition must be at least 250 eight-page frames or the equivalent (i.e., 125 16-page frames) in the open competition section.

4. APS accredited judges must be utilized as members of the jury (minimum of three), and at least 50 per cent of them must reside outside the metropolitan area where the exhibition is being held; the names of the judges shall be submitted to the chairman of the Accreditation Committee for verification and confirmation not less than 90 days prior to the exhibition.

5. Qualification must be established prior to the eligible exhibition by complying with all requirements for two consecutive exhibitions; the third such exhibition complying with all such rules shall be the participating show.

6. Requests for the initial qualifications and reports for each succeeding show must be forwarded to the APS convention manager, Box 8000, State College, Pa. 16801. Attached to the request must be two copies of the last previous prospectus, exhibition program, and award winners.

7. Once qualified, major national exhibitions will continue to be qualified without submitting a request providing they meet all requirements listed, except as to the number of frames. All exhibitions may drop below the 250-frame requirement to the extent of not more than 20 per cent for one year without being disqualified. They must send two copies of their prospectus,

exhibition program, and award winners to the APS convention manager.

8. Qualified shows shall be judged on the basis of five levels — gold, vermeil, silver, silver-bronze, and bronze.

9. The organizing committee shall make available and publicize in the show catalog a convenient time and place to enable the jury to conduct a public critique and discussion of the exhibits at the show.

10. Remunerations to all judges at eligible exhibitions shall be as follows: a season pass to the exhibition and an awards banquet ticket, a minimum of $75 for expenses to each judge required to travel more than 75 miles.

11. Apprentices may number two or fifty per cent of the accredited members of the jury, whichever is greater.

12. All eligible exhibitors at Champion-of-Champions exhibitions must show the winning exhibit up to a maximum of 160 pages, irrespective of the number of pages shown at the time of the winning of the grand award making that exhibit eligible for World Series competition.

13. Exhibits which have won a grand prix national, international, or class of honor in an FIP-sponsored international exhibition shall be ineligible to compete in the APS World Series of Philately competition.

An exhibition must first meet all of the aforementioned requirements and be certified by the APS, and then the grand-award winners of all subsequent exhibitions will be eligible to participate in the World Series of Philately as long as the exhibition continues to meet the minimum requirements.

If a certified exhibition falls below the minimum requirement, it must reapply and requalify.

The following exhibitions have qualified and received certification for their grand-award winners to compete in the World Series competition.

APS Spring Meeting, American Philatelic Society

ARIPEX, Arizona Federation of Stamp Clubs

BALPEX, Baltimore Philatelic Society

BECKPEX, Beckman Employees Philatelic Society

BERMUPEX, Bermupex Group

CENJEX, Federated Stamp Clubs of Central New Jersey

CPS, Chicago Philatelic Society

FILATELIC FIESTA, San Jose Stamp Club

FLOREX, Florida Federation of Stamp Clubs

FRESPEX, Fresno Philatelic Society

GARFIELD PERRY, Garfield Perry Stamp Club

INDYPEX, Indiana Stamp Club

MIDAPHIL, Collectors' Club of Kansas City

MILCOPEX, Milwaukee Philatelic Society

NAPEX, National Philatelic Exhibitions of Washington, D.C.

NOJEX, North Jersey Federated Stamp Clubs

NOPEX, Crescent City Stamp Club

PHILATELIC SHOW, Northeast Federation of Stamp Clubs

PIPEX, Northwest Federation of Stamp Clubs

ROCKFORD, Rockford Stamp Club

ROMPEX, Rocky Mountain Philatelic Exhibition

ROPEX, Rochester Philatelic Association

SARAPEX, Sarasota Philatelic Club

SEPAD, Associated Stamp Clubs of Southeast Pennsylvania and Delaware

SESCAL, Federated Philatelic Clubs of Southern California

SOJEX, Association of South Jersey Stamp Clubs

STaMpsHOW, American Philatelic Society

SUNPEX, Sunnyvale Stamp Society

VAPEX, Virginia Federation of Stamp Clubs

WESTPEX, Association for Western Philatelic Exhibitions

The following exhibitions are in the process of qualifying as Champion of Champions exhibitions and will be certified when qualifications are completed.

AIRPEX, Dayton Stamp Club

JAXPEX, Jacksonville Stamp Collectors Club

OKPEX, Oklahoma City Stamp Club

West Suburban Stamp Club Annual Exhibition and Bourse, West Suburban Stamp Club

Previous winners of the "Champion of Champions" crown are ineligible for further competition except in international competition. They may, however, exhibit noncompetitively or in a Court of Honor.

### Champion of Champions

Winners of the "Champion of Champions" follow with the year of competition, the exhibition they represent, the name of the exhibitor and residence, and the name of the exhibit.

1968, CPS, Robert H. Cunliffe, Pittsburgh, Pa., 19th-Century U.S. Revenues

1969, SOJEX, Col. James T. DeVoss, State College, Pa., Via Panama Mail before 1881

1970, SESCAL, Margaret L. Wunsch, Aurora, Ill., U.S. 1869 Issue

1971, SOJEX, Wilber H. Schilling, Minneapolis, Minn., 19th-Century U.S.

1972, NOPEX, Louis Grunin, Spring Valley, N.Y., U.S. 1847-1857

1973, SESCAL, Robert P. Odenweller, Great Neck, N.Y., New Zealand 1855-1874

1974, APS-STAMPEDE, Dr. Ludwig L. Simon, East Orange, N.J., The Aristocrats of Confederate Philately

1975, NOJEX, Victor E. Engstrom, Upper Montclair, N.J., Postal History of the Danish West Indies

1976, CPS, Robert C. Magnesen, Elmhurst, Ill., Peru

1977, FLOREX, Edward J. Dormer, Miami, Fla., Mexico

1978, WESTPEX, Ryohei Ishikawa, Tokyo, Japan, U.S. 1¢ 1851-61

1979, CPS, George P. Trefonas, Park Ridge, Ill., Large Hermes Heads of Greece

1980, FRESPEX, Lynne S. Warm, Oceanside, Calif., United States First Bureau Issue 1894-1903

1981, GARFIELD PERRY, Blake Myers, Canton, Ohio, Civil War Patriotic Covers

## John N. Luff Awards

The APS Luff awards are presented for meritorious contributions to philately by living philatelists.

1940: Stanley B. Ashbrook, August Dietz

1944: Dr. Carroll Chase, Elliott Perry, Col. Ralph A. Kimble

1946: Clarence W. Brazer, Lester G. Brookman, David Lidman

1948: Lester G. Brookman, Chester Smeltzer, Harry L. Lindquist

1950: Max G. Johl, Donald F. Lybarger, Laurence D. Shoemaker

1952: Winthrop S. Boggs, Van Dyk MacBride, James T. DeVoss

1954: Sol Glass, Dr. Holland A. Davis

1956: Barbara R. Mueller, Daniel W. Vooys

1958: James T. DeVoss, Henry Abt, Bernard Davis

1961: Herman Herst Jr., Frank J. Kovarik, Charles C. Cratsenberg

1962: Mortimer L. Neinken, Earl P.L. Apfelbaum, George A. Blizil

1964: Judge Edward I.P. Tatelman, James M. Chemi, Joseph M. Clary

1966: Richard McP. Cabeen, Henry E. Harris, H. Clay Musser

1968: Arnold H. Warren, Herbert J. Bloch, Anna D. Plant, Paul J. Plant

1970: Creighton C. Hart, Ezra Cole, Mrs. Arthur G. Lane

1972: Alex L. ter Braake, Edward N. Sampson, Frederick B. Thomas

1974: Horace W. Harrison, Eugene Costales, George M. Martin

1976: Denwood N. Kelly, Ernest A. Kehr, George T. Turner

1978: George W. Brett, John R. Boker Jr., Daniel W. Vooys

1979: Philip Silver, William W. Wylie

1980: Emerson A. Clark, George E. Hargest, Robson Lowe

1981: Charles A. Fricke, Enzo Diena, Cyrus R. Thompson

1982: Bernard A. Hennig, Richard H. Thompson, Carl H. Werenskiold

## APS Slide Programs

**1:** U.S. Postal History, from the collection of the late Adolph Steeg.

**2:** Selected Album Pages from the John M. Gardner Collection of U.S. 19th-Century Cancellations and Postal Markings.

**6:** Fancy U.S. Cancellations, from the collection of Burleigh E. Jacobs.

**7:** Alaska and the Mails, by Joseph J. Cavagnol.

**8:** Why Topical Collecting, by James H. McMeen.

**9:** Graf Zeppelin Flights of the World, Part 1, by Wolfgang Fritzsche.

**10:** Graf Zeppelin Flights of the World, Part 2, by Wolfgang Fritzsche.

**11:** Development of Postal History of East Germany, by Wolfgang Fritzsche.

**12:** Development of Postal History of West Germany, French Zone and Saar, by Wolfgang Fritzsche.

**13:** Development of Postal History of West Germany, U.S. and British Occupation, by Wolfgang Fritzsche.

**14:** Maximum Post Cards, by George A. Blizil.

**15:** Hungary up to 1945, by Wolfgang Fritzsche.

**17:** Rocket Stamps of the World, from the collection of George Ritter.

**20:** The Frank C. Atherton Collection of Hawaiian Stamps, by E.M. Pickop.

**21:** Yugoslavia, Part 1, by Wolfgang Fritzsche.

**22:** Yugoslavia, Part 2, by Wolfgang Fritzsche.

**23:** Collecting Postal Stationery, Part 1, by Wolfgang Fritzsche.

**24:** Collecting Postal Stationery, Part 2, by Wolfgang Fritzsche.

**25:** Newfoundland Aerophilately, Part 1, by Dr. James J. Matejka Jr.

**26:** Newfoundland Aerophilately, Part 2, by Dr. James J. Matejka Jr.

**27:** Philatelic Hiways and Byways, by James H. McMeen.

**28:** The Stamps of Panama, by H.T. Van Dyke.

**29:** Selected Covers and Stamps of the Pan-American Exposition, created by Pitt Petri and the Buffalo Historical Society from the collection of Adolph Steeg.

**31:** The Dominion of Canada, Part 1 (Queen Victoria, King Edward and George V issues), by Wolfgang Fritzsche.

**32:** The Dominion of Canada, Part 2 (King George VI and Queen Elizabeth issues), by Wolfgang Fritzsche.

**33:** How to Collect Airmail Covers, by Dr. Perham C. Nahl.

**34:** August Dietz Collection of Confederate Stamps.

**The following programs of the new series are available with cassette tape recording:**

**35:** Canal Zone Gems From the DeVoss Collection, by Col. James T. DeVoss.

**36:** Norway, The Cancellations and Usages of the Skilling Issues, 1855-1875, by Svend Yort.

**37:** The APS Story, revised 1973 by Col. James T. DeVoss and Lois M. Evans with narration by Jack Lazare.

**38:** Errors, Varieties, Freaks and Oddities on U.S. Stamps, by Clyde Jennings Jr.

**39:** Postally Used Valentines of the 19th-Century, by Van Dyk MacBride.

**40:** Number Ones of the World, by Svend Yort.

**41:** Stamp Printing Methods, Identified and Illustrated, by O.L. Harvey.

**42:** The 1851-57 Issues, by the U.S. Philatelic Classics Society with J. David Baker as narrator.

**43:** Postmaster's Provisionals, by J. David Baker.

**45:** The Tale of the Kicking Mule, by Lee H. Cornell.

**46:** Cats on Stamps, by Betty Stevens.

**47:** Ships on Stamps, by Audrey Pandratz.

**48:** Guatemala, by Warren Stevens.

**49:** The U.S. 1847s, by Jacob J. Legeer.

**50:** Canada's Registry System (1827-1893), by Horace W. Harrison.

**51:** 1861 — A Year of Change, by J. David Baker.

**52:** The Universal Postal Union, by Alex L. ter Braake.

**53:** Stamps of the Trans-Mississippi or Omaha Issue of 1898, by Paul J. Wolf.

**54:** Story of the Penny Black, by Albert A. LeShane Jr.

**55:** Canada, Maple Leaf Issues of 1897-1898, by W.J. Banks.

**56:** Denmark, Wavy Lines, Typographed Issues, by W.J. Banks.

**57:** France, First Issue 1849-1850, by the France and Colonies Philatelic Society, Affiliate 45.

**58:** The Black Jack, by Paul J. Wolff.

**59:** The Postal History of the Commune Revolution in Paris, 1871, by the France and Colonies Philatelic Society.

**60:** Stamps of the Steamship Companies, by Denwood N. Kelly.

**61:** The Postage Stamps of Prince Edward Island, by Robert V.C. Carr.

**62:** A History of Hawaii as Told Through Stamps, by Albert J. Schwalm.

**63:** Black Jack in the Foreign Mails, by Paul J. Wolf and John Hendrickson.

**64:** Swedish Postal History, by Swedish Postal Museum.

**65:** The Division of the Union, by Robert L.D. Davidson.

**66:** A Glimpse of the Confederate States of America, from the Harris S. Mueller collection.

**67:** The Postal History of the Civil War, Part 2, Federal Patriotics, by Robert L.D. Davidson.

**68:** The Cape Triangles, by Paul J. Wolff

**69:** Costa Rica, by the Society of Costa Rica Collectors.

**70:** Postal History of Switzerland, by Harlan F. Stone.

**71:** Canadian Postal Stationery as Used by the Canadian Pacific Railway, by Horace Harrison.

**72:** U.S. Private Die Proprietary Stamp Issues, by Richard Riley and Richard Willing.

**73:** The Ten-Cent Frameline of the Confederate States of America — Gems from the Wiseman Collection, by R.P. Gravely Jr.

**74:** French Balloon Posts, by Herman Herst Jr.

**75:** The Doctoring of Postage Stamps — Philatelists Beware, by G.S. Joseph.

**76:** The Mails of the Graf Zeppelin to and from Palestine, by Fred Blau.

**77:** The Wide-Wide World of Postal Stationery, Part 1, by Charles A. Fricke.

**78:** The Wide-Wide World of Postal Stationery, Part 2, by Charles A. Fricke.

**79:** The Wide-Wide World of Postal Stationery, Part 3, by Charles A. Fricke.

**81:** The World's Columbian Exposition, by James Doolin and Gordon Bleuler.

**Film No. 1:** The Early Days (New Zealand Travelogue).

**Film No. 2:** Timbromania.

# The Society of Philatelic Americans

As the 19th century drew to a close, several major national philatelic societies were emerging from the welter of numerous local short-lived organizations. The first of these, the American Philatelic Association (now the American Philatelic Society), was believed by Southern philatelists to have a very distinct "Yankee" flavor, discriminating against Southern devotees as an aftermath of the Civil War.

With this in mind, a group of very young collectors, mostly in their late teens, organized the Southern Philatelic Association in February 1894.

The SPA's first president, J.M. Chappell Jr. of Macon, Miss., was 20 years old, and was an ardent philatelist boasting a U.S. collection of 1,100 varieties, a well-respected young farmer and a gentleman determined to see a second major philatelic organization succeed. His success is now the Society of Philatelic Americans, and he continued in his philatelic and organizational pursuits until his untimely death in 1918, as a victim of the worldwide influenza epidemic.

The new society consisted of 15 charter members, all from states in the deep South (Mississippi, Alabama, Georgia, Louisiana and Texas), and the original constitution of the organization limited membership to philatelists living in the former Confederate States of America. In March 1894, Vol. 1, No. 1 of the "Dixie Philatelist" appeared as the first issue of the official journal of the Southern Philatelic Association.

However, the sectionalism which was felt in 1894 soon disappeared, and as the memory of the Civil War dimmed, and more members and funds were needed to keep the society going, members north of the Mason-Dixon line were permitted to join. In 1902, the SPA elected its first national officer from the North, W.P. Kelley of Kansas City, Mo., who served as the society's new secretary-treasurer.

The society's serious expansion into a national body commenced around 1910, and reached a point in 1916-1917 where it was the largest philatelic organization in North America. A proposal to change the name of the organization from the Southern Philatelic Association to the Society of Philatelic Americans, retaining the same well-known initials, came under serious consideration in 1914, was approved at the 1918 convention, and was officially adopted in 1922 at the time the society was incorporated as a nonprofit membership corporation under the laws of the state of Minnesota.

At this time, the SPA restated its purposes as being: the promotion of stamp collecting; the spreading of philatelic knowledge; the cultivation of friendship and social intercourse among members; assisting its members to acquire and dispose of philatelic properties without profit to the society; to work for the suppression of forgeries and other material of a questionable nature; and to do whatever else might be necessary and convenient to carry out these objectives according to law.

During its lifetime, the SPA has utilized 10 different philatelic publications as its official organ as follows:

March 1894: Dixie Philatelist

September 1896: Lone Star State Philatelist

November 1898: Virginia Philatelist

January 1903: Philatelic West and Camera News

January 1918: The Stamp Herald

November 1921: The Pacific Philatelist

September 1922: The Stamp Herald

September 1924: The Stamp Collectors Magazine

December 1932: Hobbies Magazine

March 1939: S.P.A. Journal

The current monthly publication, now an integral part of the society itself, actually had a trial run in January 1939 which, appearing successful, was put in full operation two months later. The editors of the S.P.A. Journal to date have been:

J. Edw. Vining: March-August 1939

Don Housewarth: September 1939-June 1943

J. Elmer Zinsmeister: July 1943-November 1962

Belmont Faries: December 1962 to the present

The administrative center of the society is the office of the executive secretary. He keeps the day-to-day records and is responsible for collecting and recording dues payments. All requests, complaints and inquiries are handled by his office, as well as the yearly budget and financial matters.

Requests for membership information should also be directed to the executive secretary, Grant Ricksecker, Box 30286, Cleveland, Ohio 44130. The SPA accepts members from all over the world.

# SPA Expertization Service

### Rules

1. Upon request by a member, accompanied by a stamped self-addressed envelope, forms for the SPA identification/expertization service may be obtained from the chairman of the Expert Committee.

2. The Expert Committee will provide opinions as to the identity or genuineness of philatelic items according to the following schedule: up to $500 catalog value, $5. For $500 and up, the basic fee of $5 plus an additional 1 per cent of catalog value over $500, to a maximum fee of $20, is charged. For example, for $1,000 the fee is $5 plus 1 per cent ($5), for a total of $10. Photo certificates will be issued for an additional $3 fee.

3. Each item should be sent to the chairman of the committee and accompanied by a properly completed application form, the appropriate fee, and a return stamped envelope, prepaid for the postal service desired. An item is any single stamp, piece, block or cover. Each stamp in a set is a separate item.

4. The fee is for each item submitted unless more than one certificate is desired in which case the fee is $4 for each additional certificate. The committee will not break up or separate any piece, however, and will only handle items as submitted.

5. The fee will be retained in all cases where an opinion is supplied. The fee will be refunded

only in those instances where the committee declines opinion. The committee generally will not express opinions on single coils or single imperforates as varieties. The committee does not furnish valuations.

6. The committee shall exercise due caution and care with stamps and other materials entrusted to it, but neither the SPA, its officers or members, nor the Expert Committee, its chairman, members or consulted experts, assume any responsibility whatever for loss or damage of any nature.

7. The opinions expressed by the committee are based on the best information available, but no guarantees of any nature are implied. The SPA, its officers or members, the Expert Committee, its chairman, members or consulted experts shall not be held liable in any way for errors of opinion of whatever kind.

8. The committee will make every effort at expending items sent to it for consideration, but time is necessary to consult experts at some distance. Thirty to 60 days should be allowed for each request.

9. The SPA and the Expert Committee reserve the right to make changes in the fees, rules, and regulations without notice, but such changes will be announced as soon as possible in the "S.P.A. Journal."

10. Submittal of an application for examination constitutes an acceptance by the owner of all rules and regulations.

Manager of the Expertization Service is Gordon H. Torrey, 5118 Duvall Drive, Washington, D.C. 20016.

## SPA Insurance Service

The SPA's program is available to members after a full year of membership. Those who have belonged to a major stamp society for one year prior to joining the SPA can usually waive the waiting period.

Virtually all material that forms part of a member's collection is covered, including stamps, albums, covers, envelopes, post cards, philatelic cards and philatelic literature.

Maximum limits are set on the value that can be recovered on a single item. The limits are $2,500 for dealers' coverage and $1,000 for private collectors' coverage. A maximum is also set on the amount covered when carried outside one's premises or sent by post in any one package. The limit is $10,000 for private collectors, while dealers can be insured up to $50,000 for goods carried in their possession.

Larger limits can be arranged through prior agreement with the insurance service.

Sophisticated and costly security equipment is not required of private collectors. Any private collector whose stamps are valued at less than $50,000 is not required to take any precaution other than a normal homeowner would.

If the collection is of greater value than $50,000, the member is required to keep it locked in a safe or a locked fire-proof cabinet protected by a central alarm system.

Since dealers are supposed to present likelier targets for crime, the security provisions apply when total value exceeds $10,000. Where dealers' stock exceeds $25,000 insurers require that it is contained in a locked safe that is wired to a central alarm system.

Full value of a collection is covered while it is out of a safe provided it is under the personal supervision of the owner. If items outside the safe pass out of the control of the owner, the owner is only covered for 25 per cent of the normal amount.

A detailed inventory of all material including values should be included with an application for insurance coverage. The inventory will be used as a basis for settlement of any loss. In all other cases, 100 per cent of Scott or Stanley Gibbons catalog value (whichever is greater) will apply. Proof of loss is required, and purchase receipts are helpful.

Manager of the Insurance Service is William T. Cartwright, 5480 Wisconsin Ave., Suite 216, Chevy Chase, Md. 20015.

## SPA Sales Division

The Sales Division provides members with the opportunity to buy or sell stamps. Only SPA members may participate as buyers.

A maximum of seven persons, all in the same USPS distributing area, are listed on each regular sales circuit. Each circuit contains between 8 to 14 sales books within the collecting interest of the subscribers. Each time a circuit is mailed from the Sales Division, the person who received it first on the previous mailing will drop to the bottom of the mailing list. The previous second person will be the first to receive the new circuit, with each person below moving up one spot.

Members may hold a circuit for seven days following receipt, after which time it must be mailed to the next member on the list. All remittances for stamps purchased must be sent directly to the Sales Division. Circuits when mailed must be insured for $50.

Individual circuits have the same format as the regular sales circuits, except that they are geared to the person who would purchase more than $25 from each circuit received. If this minimum purchasing figure is not met, the subscriber is expected to pay postage and insurance in both directions. Individual circuits may be held 14 days from receipt. This service was initiated to provide circuits for the person who could not participate within the regular rules.

A $1 insurance fee is required when each circuit is received. This allows for payment of insurance losses over and above the amount paid by the USPS insurance. The insurance fee is maintained in a separate account and used only to pay for claims on lost material. Purchases of $25 or more from sales circuits and handbooks may be charged to MasterCard or VISA.

The SPA's Gold Seal Service is available to those more advanced than the average collector. Stamps in this service retail over $5.

Sales books are made up of a varying number of pages. Some 6 to 8 books will be sent in a circuit. Selections may be held for a period of 14 days. The usual insurance fee of $1 is required and when returned to the Sales Division, $50 insurance coverage is needed.

Frequency of these circuits is not guaranteed. Since the Sales Division does not go into the market and purchase stamps for resale, it is entirely dependent on material received from members.

Branch chapters who desire to have circuits available for their meetings can do so by following certain guidelines. A club member, also a member of the SPA, is designated as the person in charge of the circuit.

The circuit is mailed to that person's attention. The circuit manager takes it to the club meeting, and purchases are made by members under the direction of the manager.

Immediately upon return of a circuit the Sales Division sends out a new one. For the convenience of the branch chapter, a form is enclosed with each circuit to order what countries are desired in the next one.

The Sales Division publishes a periodic listing of handbooks and philatelic supplies. The list is available upon written request to the Sales Division.

Information on the Sales Division is available from Raymond W. Ruthrauff Sr., Box SPA, Darby, Pa. 19023.

## Other SPA Services

### Exchange Department

SPA members can become active in the society's Exchange Department. Members submit the duplicate stamps to the Exchange Department and receive credit equal to current catalog prices. With this credit, stamps from other members can be secured. All transactions are by mail.

Information on the Exchange Department is available from Otto L. Steding, Box 1197, Cincinnati, Ohio 45202.

### Translation Service

Translations from a foreign language into English or from English into a foreign language are available to SPA members without cost. Volunteers can handle any language problem related to philately.

Information on the service is available from Dmytro Bykovetz Jr., 902 Stratford Ave., Melrose Park, Philadelphia, Pa. 19126.

### Book Binding Service

The SPA has been operating a service since 1966 to take care of the job of binding philatelic journals. It has been supervised by Ray West of Chicago, Ill., since its inception. Volumes of journals with a maximum thickness of two inches are given a Class A Library binding with the title stamped on the spine in 22-carat gold. The cost is $7.50 a volume, payable in advance.

Information is available from Ray West, 4137 N. Pulaski Road, Chicago, Ill. 60641.

## SPA Branch Chapters

### National

Brazil Philatelic Association
Bullseye Cancel Collectors Club
Canal Zone Study Group
Central Atlantic Stamp Dealers Association
Central Florida Stamp Clubs
Confederate Stamp Alliance
Cuban Philatelic Club
EFO Collectors Club
Federation of Central New York
   Philatelic Societies
FLOREX
Franklin D. Roosevelt Philatelic Society
International Churchill Society
Junior Philatelists of America
Mailer's Postmark Permit Club
Malaria Philatelists International
NEPPEX
New Mexico Philatelic Association

Niagara Federation of Stamp Clubs
   (Northern New York)
NOJEX
Pennsylvania Postal History Society
ROMPEX
ROPEX
Scandinavian Collectors Club
SEPAD
SESCAL
Society of Australasian Specialists/Oceania
Society of Indo-China Philatelists
Society of Philaticians
SOJEX
United Postal Stationery Society
U.S. Philatelic Classics Society
Universal Philatelic Cover Society
VAPEX
Virginia Postal History Society

Zippy Collectors Club

**Local**

Alexandria (Va.)-Mt. Vernon Stamp Club
Allentown (Pa.) Philatelic Society
American Stamp Club of Great Britain
Anchorage (Alaska) Stamp Club
Asheville (N.C.) Stamp Club
Association of Bergen County (N.J.) Philatelists
Aurora (Colo.) Stamp Club
Austin Philatelic Society, Chicago, Ill.
Baltimore (Md.) Philatelic Society
Bandon (Okla.) Stamp Club
Bay County (Fla.) Stamp Club
Beckman Employees Philatelic Society, Fullerton, Calif.
Birmingham (Ala.) Philatelic Society
Boston (Mass.) Philatelic Society
Brookhaven Stamp Club, Chester, Pa.
Calhoun County (Fla.) Stamp Club
Central Florida Stamp Club, Winter Park, Fla.
Charlotte (N.C.) Philatelic Society
Chattanooga (Tenn.) Stamp Club
Chicago ATA Chapter 18
Chicago (Ill.) Philatelic Society
Chicagoland Czechoslovak Philatelic Society
Chicagoland Germany Philatelic Society
Clearwater (Fla.) Stamp Club
Collectors Club of Denver (Colo.)
Collectors Club of Washington (D.C.)
Collier County Stamp Club, Naples, Fla.
Columbia (S.C.) Philatelic Society
Columbus (Ohio) Philatelic Club
Conejo Valley Philatelic Society, Thousand Oaks, Calif.
Corn Belt Philatelic Society, Bloomington, Ill.
Crescent City Stamp Club, New Orleans, La.
Cuy-Lor Stamp Club, Cleveland, Ohio
DeKalb Stamp Club, Tucker, Ga.
DuPont Stamp Club, Wilmington, Del.
Eastern Prince William Stamp Club, Woodbridge, Va.
El Paso (Tex.) Philatelic Society
First Czechoslovak Philatelic Club of America, Cicero, Ill.
Fond du Lac (Wis.) Stamp Club
Fort Findlay (Ohio) Stamp Club
Fredericksburg (Va.) Stamp Club
Fresno (Calif.) Philatelic Society
Germany Philatelic Society, Chapter 7, Lauderhill, Fla.
Germantown Stamp Club, Philadelphia, Pa.
Greater Valley Philatelic Society, Van Nuys, Calif.

Greenville (S.C.) Stamp Club
Harford County (Md.) Stamp Club
Havertown (Pa.) Stamp Club
Hawthorne Stamp Club, Chicago, Ill.
Hollywood (Fla.) Stamp Club
Humboldt Collectors Club, Eureka, Calif.
Huntsville (Ala.) Philatelic Club
Independence Stamp Club, Philadelphia, Pa.
Indiana Stamp Club, Indianapolis, Ind.
Inland Empire Philatelic Society, Spokane, Wash.
Jacksonville (Fla.) Stamp Collectors Club
Jockey Hollow Stamp Club, Morristown, N.J.
Kansas Precancel Society, Wichita, Kan.
Kent Philatelic Society, Grand Rapids, Mich.
Kodak Stamp Club, Rochester, N.Y.
Lebanon (Pa.) Stamp Collectors Club
LERC Stamp Club, Burbank, Calif.
McDonnell-Douglas Stamp Club, St. Louis, Mo.
McKinley Stamp Club, Canton, Ohio
Memphis (Tenn.) Stamp Collectors Society
Merchantville (N.J.) Stamp Club
Michigan Stamp Club, Detroit, Mich.
Mid Cities Stamp Club, Arlington, Tex.
Middletown (N.Y.) Stamp Collectors Club
Midwest Philatelic Society, Kansas City, Mo.
Milwaukee (Wis.) Philatelic Society
Motor City Stamp and Cover Club, Romulus, Mich.
Mound City Stamp Club, St. Louis, Mo.
Mt. Nittany Philatelic Society, State College, Pa.
Nashville (Tenn.) Philatelic Society
Nathan Hale Stamp Club, Falls Church, Va.
North Shore Philatelic Society, Chicago, Ill.
North Suburban Stamp Club, Libertyville, Ill.
Northern Colorado Philatelic Society, Ft. Collins, Colo.
Northern Indiana Stamp Club, Mishawaka, Ind.
Northwest Stamp Society, Detroit, Mich.
Ohio Postal History Society
Oklahoma City (Okla.) Stamp Club
Oregon Stamp Society, Portland, Ore.
Oxford Philatelic Society, Philadelphia, Pa.
Park Cities Philatelic Society, Dallas, Tex.
Pennsylvania Postal History Society
PENTAF Stamp Club, Washington, D.C.
Philadelphia (Pa.) Stamp Club
Philatelic Society of Cincinnati (Ohio)
Philatelic Society of Los Angeles (Calif.)
Philatelic Society of Pittsburgh (Pa.)
Phoenix (Ariz.) Philatelic Association
Pioneer Valley Stamp Club, Longmeadow, Mass.

Pocono Mountain Philatelic Society, East Stroudsburg, Pa.

Polonus Philatelic Society, Chicago, Ill.

Port Charlotte (Fla.) Stamp Club

Quad-City Stamp Club, Moline, Ill.

Rhode Island Philatelic Society, Providence, R.I.

Richmond (Va.) Stamp Club

Rochester (N.Y.) Philatelic Association

Rockville-Gaithersburg (Md.) Stamp Club

Roosevelt Philatelic Society, Chicago, Ill.

Rubber City Stamp Club, Akron, Ohio

Sarasota (Fla.) Philatelic Club

Seashore Stamp Collectors Club, Margate City, N.J.

Silver Springs Shores Stamp Club, Ocala, Fla.

Sociedad Filatelica Puerto Rico, Santuree, P.R.

South Metro Collectors Club, Woodstock, Calif.

South Miami (Fla.) Stamp Club

Southern Oregon Philatelic Society, Medford, Ore.

Southwestern Stamp Club, Parma Heights, Ohio

Spartanburg (S.C.) Stamp Club

Springfield (Pa.)-Delco Stamp Club

Springfield (Va.) Stamp Club

Stark County (Ohio) Stamp Club

Sunnyvale (Calif.) Stamp Club

Susquehanna Valley Stamp & Coin Club, Enola, Pa.

University City Stamp Club, Gaithersburg, Fla.

Utica (N.Y.) Stamp Club

Virginia Beach (Va.) Stamp Club

Wachusett Philatelic Society, Fitchburg, Mass.

Wayne Stamp Club, Detroit, Mich.

Webster Groves (Mo.) Stamp Club

West Essex Philatelic Society, Upper Montclair, N.J.

West Side Stamp Club, Lakewood, Colo.

West Suburban Stamp Club, Plymouth, Mich.

Western Postal History Museum, Tucson, Ariz.

Wichita (Kan.) Stamp Club

Wilmington (Del.) Stamp Club

Wilmington (N.C.) Philatelic Society

Wisconsin Valley Philatelic Society, Wausaw, Wis.

Worthington (Ohio) Coin and Stamp Club

Wyoming Valley Stamp Club, Wilkes-Barre, Pa.

Ye Olde King's Highway Stamp Club, Darien, Conn.

Zane's Trace Philatelic Society, Zanesville, Ohio

## Annual Fall SPA Convention Sites

| | | |
|---|---|---|
| 1924: New York, N.Y. | 1945: Newark, N.J. | 1966: Kansas City, Mo. |
| 1925: Baltimore, Md. | 1946: Cleveland, Ohio | 1967: Boston, Mass. |
| 1926: Cincinnati, Ohio | 1947: Wichita, Kan. | 1968: Detroit, Mich. |
| 1927: Philadelphia, Pa. | 1948: Detroit, Mich. | 1969: Los Angeles, Calif. |
| 1928: Washington, D.C. | 1949: San Francisco, Calif. | 1970: Baltimore, Md. |
| 1929: Cleveland, Ohio | 1950: Philadelphia, Pa. | 1971: Cincinnati, Ohio |
| 1930: Worcester, Mass. | 1951: Cincinnati, Ohio | 1972: Philadelphia, Pa. |
| 1931: Columbus, Ohio | 1952: New York, N.Y. | 1973: Rochester, N.Y. |
| 1932: Washington, D.C. | 1953: Tampa, Fla. | 1974: Norfolk, Va. |
| 1933: Fond du Lac, Wis. | 1954: Chicago, Ill. | 1975: Cleveland, Ohio |
| 1934: Philadelphia, Pa. | 1955: Louisville, Ky. | 1976: Oklahoma City, Okla. |
| 1935: St. Louis, Mo. | 1956: Grand Rapids, Mich. | 1977: San Juan, P.R. |
| 1936: Cincinnati, Ohio | 1957: Long Beach, Calif. | 1978: Elizabeth, N.J. |
| 1937: Asheville, N.C. | 1958: Montreal, Canada | 1979: Chicago, Ill. |
| 1938: Chicago, Ill. | 1959: Cincinnati, Ohio | 1980: New Orleans, La. |
| 1939: Baltimore, Md. | 1960: St. Louis, Mo. | 1981: Baltimore, Md. |
| 1940: Cleveland, Ohio | 1961: Topeka, Kan. | 1982: San Juan, P.R. |
| 1941: Philadelphia, Pa. | 1962: Portland, Ore. | |
| 1942: Detroit, Mich. | 1963: Cleveland, Ohio | **Future Conventions** |
| 1943: St. Louis, Mo. | 1964: Washington, D.C. | 1983: Virginia Beach, Va. |
| 1944: Chicago, Ill. | 1965: Memphis, Tenn. | |

# SPA Presidents

Past SPA presidents are listed by the year in which they were elected or succeeded to the presidency. The year of the following entry indicates the year their presidency ended, and their successors began their terms (thus, those who served for a short time may be followed by another entry with the same year).

1894: J.M. Chappell Jr. (February-September)
1894: A.M. Rareshide
1896: Benjamin Russell (April-October)
1896: E.W. Heusinger
1897: H. Fenton
1899: R.D. Bradley
1901: Oscar Jannusch
1902: J.H. Dubose
1903: F.W. Coning
1904: Charles Roemer
1907: F.G. Fuessel
1909: Dr. H.A. Davis
1910: H.S. Powell
1911: L. Harold Kjellstedt
1912: August Mack
1913: C.W. Kissinger
1923: V.W. Rotnem
1925: William L. Doepke
1927: Guy W.A. Camp
1929: Dr. Norman P. McGay
1931: Albert E. Gorman (August-October)
1931: Dr. Norman P. McGay (October-July)
1932: W.N. McKelvey (July '32-June '33)
1933: Dr. F.M. Coppock
1938: Russell J. Broderick
1940: J. Edward Vining
1944: Vincent Domanski Jr.

1948: Hil F. Best
1952: Ignatz Reiner (August-November)
1952: Ben Reeves
1956: Fred Barovick
1958: Larry Edmunds
1960: Robert W. Yant
1962: Robert Baughman
1967: Dr. James Matejka Jr.
1970-74: Milton Mitchell
1975-78: Clyde Jennings

# Current SPA Officers

President: James P. Harris
Past president: Clyde Jennings
Vice president: Dr. John M. Buckner
Executive secretary: Grant Ricksecker
Board secretary: Grant Ricksecker
Treasurer: Richard B. Jordan
Directors: Jesse Boehret, Richard A. Corwin, Victor E. Engstrom, Erwin Herschkowitz, Ward D. Morton and Michael E. Ruggiero
Chairman, board of regents: Joseph H. Crosby
Society attorney: Joseph H. Crosby
Director of recruiting: Michael E. Ruggiero
Publicity chairman: Raymond W. Ruthrauff Sr.

**Department Managers**
Sales Division: Raymond W. Ruthrauff Sr.
Exchange Department: Otto L. Steding
Insurance: William Cartwright
Expertizing Service: Gordon H. Torrey
Slide Program Service: Mary Stone
Translation Service: Dmytro Bykovetz Jr.
Book Binding Service: Ray J. West

# Lagerloef Award Winners

The SPA gold award for outstanding service to the society was awarded annually from 1944 to 1975 when it was discontinued.

| | | |
|---|---|---|
| 1944: J. Edward Vining | 1955: Helen Longinotti | 1966: Vincent Domanski Jr. |
| 1945: J. Elmer Zinsmeister | 1956: Louis Sloan | 1967: Larry Edmunds |
| 1946: Alfred Diamond | 1957: Henry O. Nouss | 1968: Bernard Hennig |
| 1947: Hil F. Best | 1958: Emily Moorefield | 1969: Belmont Faries |
| 1948: Stephen Rich | 1959: Gerald A. Jacobson | 1970: Dr. James Matejka Jr. |
| 1949: Ben Reeves | 1960: Robert W. Yant | 1971: Inez Papa |
| 1950: Henry A. Meyer | 1961: Fred Barovick | 1972: Franklin R. Bruns Jr. |
| 1951: Arthur Bledsoe | 1962: Ward Alkema | 1973: Howard Selzer |
| 1952: Marian C. Zinsmeister | 1963: Charles E. Meyer | 1974: Milton Mitchell |
| 1953: Ignatz Reiner | 1964: Hilda P. Yant | 1975: Marie Ricksecker |
| 1954: Walter J. Vrendenburgh | 1965: Stewart T. Bailey | |

## SPA Exhibition Awards

The SPA provides a Research Medal at all major national exhibitions, on an open basis, for the exhibit showing the best original research.

The William Cartwright SPA President's Award is presented annually at the fall convention to the SPA member with the best exhibit.

The George Wilson Award is given at the SPA convention for the best exhibit of Confederate material.

The J. King Horner Award is presented at the SPA convention to the best exhibit in the field of Great Britain and British Colonial material.

The Robert Yant SPA Presidents Award is given at the annual spring meeting for the best exhibit by an SPA member.

The SPA Willard Thomas Award is presented at the spring meeting for the best postal history exhibit.

## SPA Slide Films

This list of slide presentations currently available from the SPA is compiled by set number, and followed by the number of slides in the presentation.

1: Mexican Airmails (47)
2: Famous Americans (49)
3: Mariana Islands (24)
4: Alaskan Mails (72)
5: Postal Conference, 1863 (59)
6: Religion (50)
7: Europa (60)
8: Hermes Heads of Greece (52)
9: Flag Cancellations (80)
10: Stop Thief (42)
11: Centenary Issues (52)

12: Booklet Panes (40)
13: Mountains on Stamps (36)
14: Stamp Day (37)
15: Austrian Semipostals (55)
16: Newfoundland (78)
17: Czechoslovakia Scouts (25)
18: Coaches on Stamps (100)
19: Philatelic Quiz (49)
20: Kentucky Postal History
21: Northwest Territory (68)
22: Napoleon (70)
23: Basketball (82)

24: Sailing Vessels (64)
25: One Frame Exhibits (62)
26: Composers on Stamps (76)
27: Roses on Stamps (60)
28: BANPAKU 70 (70)
29: Fairy Tales (57)
30: Explorers (68)
31: British Monarchy (68)
32: Physics (61)
33: Doctoring of Postage Stamps (61)
34: Postal History of Transvaal (34)

## SPA Handbooks

Amsterdam Postal History — DaCosta and Giphart

Centenary Issues (two volumes) — Zinsmeister

Characteristics of Genuine Japanese Stamps — Tyler

Jefferson Davis Postage Stamp Issues of the Confederacy, The — Malpass

Liechtenstein Stamps and Their Background — Zinsmeister

Philately of the Brussels International Exhibition — Zinsmeister

Slovensky Stat 1939 — Kaufmann

Souvenir Sheets of the World (two volumes) — Zinsmeister

Switzerland 1850-1958 — Zinsmeister

Types and Varieties of the U.S. 10-cent Issues of 1855-1859 — Hesly and Diamond

Types of the 2-cent and 3-cent Washington Series of 1912-1921 — Kenworthy and Diamond

United States One Cent Issues of 1850-1857, The — Kenworthy and Diamond

Western Mails, The — Milgram

For additional information on membership and privileges in the Society of Philatelic Americans, contact the society, Box 30286, Cleveland, Ohio 44130.

# American Topical Association

The American Topical Association was founded Sept. 12, 1949, to promote the hobby of topical philately. Its current address is 3306 N. 50th St., Milwaukee, Wis. 53216.

The collecting of stamps for the subject portrayed on the stamp rather than for the country that issued it or its postal use is not new. At the beginning of the 20th-century, there were philatelists in the United States and in Europe who put together collections of stamps depicting animals, ships, mountains, architecture, and famous people.

But topical philately made little headway for decades because there was only a comparatively small number of pictorial stamps available to collect on particular themes. This was remedied with the revolution in lithography and color printing methods.

In 1944, Phebe B. Boothe authored an 86-page handbook listing more than 1,250 different topical subjects. With this stimuli, Jerome Husak, a 12-year-old youngster from Milwaukee, Wis., attended his first philatelic exhibition in search of topical stamps. A faint germ of an idea of expanding topical collecting and exchanging information with others grew over the next five years.

Then at the age of 17, he founded the American Topical Association using a bedroom of his parents' home as an office. Within the first two months, ATA had recruited 203 members; incorporated as a nonprofit organization; and published the first issue of "Topical Time." At the end of ATA's first year, "Topical Time" had become a bimonthly journal, and in another six months the membership had risen to 1,000.

ATA now has more than 10,000 members in more than 90 countries around the world, and whole number 195 of "Topical Time" features 92 pages of topical articles, checklists, topical new issues, publication reviews, philatelic current events, study unit reports, news of members, and a question-and-answer column entitled "Clearing House of Knowledge" which has answered more than 4,000 questions from topicalists worldwide.

"Topical Time" whole number issues 1 through 124 have been reprinted, excluding all advertising matter, and are now available in 10 handbooks, while entire issues from 125 to date are still available from ATA. Commencing with a 10-year cumulative index (1949-59), five year cumulative indexes through 1979 have been published as a reference source of all topical information published in the ATA bimonthly journal. The computer printout of topical new issues appearing in each issue of "Topical Time" is compiled annually by topical categories and published in separate handbooks. The latest in this series provides a listing of more than 150,000 stamps in 20 volumes (1962-81).

Another series of ATA handbooks consists of the "cream of the crop" of thousands of topical articles appearing in hundreds of philatelic and nonphilatelic journals. There are now eight "Topical Digests" — some in their second edition, but all available.

The majority of ATA handbooks are definitive studies with comprehensive checklists for specific topics. These illustrated handbooks include such topics as aircraft; American flag; Americana; animals; astronomy; birds; cooking; education; Europa; fairy tales; fish; flowers; Holy Family; insects; Lions International; Masons; medicine; music; nudes; plants; railways; religion; Roosevelt; science; shells; ships; space; stamps on stamps; theater; United Nations; and women.

On April 29, 1950, the Casey Jones Railroad Unit was founded as the first American Topical Association Study Unit. Today, ATA has more than 40 active study units, each of which publishes its own bulletin.

The scope of the topics covered in this abundance of philatelic literature includes Americana; archaeology; astronomy; automobiles; aviation; bicycles; biology; birds; chemistry; chess; Christmas; Churchill; coins; computers; cooking; dogs; Durer; Europa; fairy tales; fire service; geography; graphics; journalists; lighthouses; Lions International; malaria; maps; Masons; mathematics; medical subjects; meteorology; minerology; performing arts; railroads; Roosevelt; Rotary; ships; space; stamps; telecommunications; textiles; United Nations; UPU; windmills; women; and World's Fairs.

The first ATA chapter chartered was the Thematic Stamp Club of South Africa making ATA truly international in scope. Today, chapters are scattered throughout the United States and in various other countries.

The first ATA cosponsored all topical philatelic exhibit was held in January 1950, at the National Philatelic Museum in Philadelphia, while the first all-ATA meeting was held in September 1950, in Chicago. The first combined ATA annual convention and ATA topical exhibit (TOPEX) was held in Johnstown, Pa., June 20-22, 1952. TOPEX remains as the largest all-topical philatelic exhibit held in the United States

The ATA Membership Directory provides in alphabetical order the names and addresses of members, and lists collectors by topics. Overseas members are listed by country so that ATA members can contact topicalists with similar interests in various parts of the world. Language-translation service is staffed by 42 members, translating 31 languages for ATA members. Other ATA services described in the Directory include:

An Information Board where some 650 members offer specific information on 350 different topics; a Biography Service which offers thumbnail bio-sketches of some 13,000 persons pictured on postage stamps; a slide-lecture library offering over 55 programs to members as well as stamp clubs; Heirs and Estates Service with members in various sections of the country to assist heirs in disposing of collections and labels available for members' collections explaining the service;

Claims Service to arbitrate claims of $25 or more of members against other members, dealers or vice versa; Judges Accreditation Service with procedures for accrediting topical judges and suggesting judges for various philatelic shows; best in topical awards available to any philatelic exhibition which includes a topical classification; Sales Service to assist members in disposing of duplicates and in locating needed stamps.

## ATA Accredited Judges

Barberis, Nino, Milano, Italy
Baum, Werner J., Rochester, N.Y.
Black, Irving L., Little Neck, N.Y.
Garabrant, Lauretta, Verona, N.J.
Garabrant, Melvin, Verona, N.J.
Green, Jack H., Madison, Wis.
Griffenhagen, George, Vienna, Va.
Guzzio, George T., Brooklyn, N.Y.
Hackett, Margaret, R., Whiting, N.J.
Hellard, Ruth E., Lake Kathrine, N.Y.
Koutroulis, Nicolas, Spring, Tex.
Mueller, Barbara, Jefferson, Wis.
Oesch, Robert, San Diego, Calif.
Owens, Mary Ann, Brooklyn, N.Y.
Peterson, Henry, Minneapolis, Minn.
Smith, Donald W., Johnstown, Pa.
Smith, Dorothy F., Savannah, Ga.
Weinberg, Irving, Philadelphia, Pa.
Wetmore, Ruth, Laurinburg, N.C.
Winick, Lester, Homewood, Ill.

For information on judges for your topical show, contact the ATA.

## ATA Chapters

Arizona Society of Topical Philatelists, Phoenix, Ariz.
Aurora Stamp Club
Cedar Rapids (Iowa) Stamp Club
Chelmsford (Mass.) Stamp Club
Chicagoland Chapter, Chicago, Ill.

China Topical Club, Taipei, China
Collectors Club of Seattle (Wash.)
Collectors Club of Washington (D.C.)
Corn Belt Philatelic Society, Inc., Bloomington, Ill.
Cuy-Lor Stamp Club, Westlake, Ohio
DeKalb Stamp Club, Atlanta, Ga.
Greater Detroit (Mich.) Chapter
Greater Los Angeles (Calif.) Chapter
Johnstown (Pa.) Chapter
Junior Topicalists of Johnstown (Pa.)
Kent (Mich.) Chapter
Lincoln (Neb.) Stamp Club
Mexico City Chapter
Minneapolis (Minn.) Chapter
New York Area Chapter
North Texas Chapter, Dallas, Tex.
Northeastern Pennsylvania Chapter, Scranton, Pa.
Northern Indiana Philatelic Society, Mishawaka, Ind.
Oxford Chapter, Woodstock, Ont., Canada
Philadelphia (Pa.) Chapter
Port Huron-Sarnia Stamp Club, Sarnia, Ont., Canada
Seashore Stamp Collector's Club, Atlantic City, N.J.
Thematic Society of Australia, Sydney, Australia
Thematic Stamp Club, Cape Town, South Africa
Union Philatelique de Montreal (Canada), Inc.
Virginia Philatelic Federation Chapter, Williamsburg, Va.
West Suburban Stamp Club, Detroit, Mich.
Western Monroe Philatelic Society, Rochester, N.Y.
Wisconsin Chapter

## ATA Study Units

Americana Unit
Astronomy Study Unit
Automotive Study Unit
Avian Philately Unit (Birds)
Aviation Study Unit
Bicycles on Stamps Study Unit
Biology Unit
Capt. Cook Study Unit
Carto-Philatelists (Maps)
Casey Jones Railroad Unit
Chemistry Study Unit
Chess on Stamps Study Unit
Christmas Study Unit
International Churchill Society
Coins on Stamps Study Unit
Computer Study Unit

Dogs on Stamps Study Unit
Albrecht Durer Study Unit
Earth's Physical Features Study Unit
Embroidery-Stitchery-Textile Unit
Europa Unit
Fire Service in Philately
Folklore-Fairy Tales Study Unit
Gems, Minerals & Jewelry Study Unit
Graphics Philately Association
International Religious Studies
JAPOS Unit (Journalists, Authors and Poets)
Lighthouse Study Unit
Lions Philatelic Unit
Malaria Philatelists International
Masonic Study Unit
Mathematical Study Unit

Medical Subjects Unit
Meso-American Archeology Study Unit
Meteorology on Stamps Unit
Old World Archaeological Study Unit
Performing Arts Study Unit
Franklin D. Roosevelt Philatelic Society
Rotary on Stamps Unit
Ships on Stamps Unit
Space Unit
Stamps on Stamps - Centenary Unit
Telecommunications Study Unit
United Nations Philatelists
Universal Postal Union Collectors
Windmill Study Unit
Women on Stamps Study Unit
World's Fair Collectors Society

## Annual TOPEX Convention Sites

1952: Johnstown, Pa.
1953: Philadelphia, Pa.
1954: Dayton, Ohio
1955: Decatur, Ill.
1956: Detroit, Mich.
1957: Chicago, Ill.
1958: Little Rock, Ark.
1959: New York, N.Y.
1960: Minneapolis, Minn.
1961: Johnstown, Pa.
1962: Colorado Springs, Colo.
1963: Phoenix, Ariz.
1964: Camden, N.J.

1965: Aurora, Ill.
1966: Boston, Mass.
1967: Rochester, N.Y.
1968: Milwaukee, Wis.
1969: Chicago, Ill.
1970: Montreal, Canada
1971: Syracuse, N.Y.
1972: Portland, Maine
1973: Denver, Colo.
1974: Rochester, N.Y.
1975: Lincoln, Neb.
1976: Philadelphia, Pa.
1977: Dallas, Tex.

1978: Atlantic City, N.J.
1979: Spokane, Wash.
1980: Portland, Maine
1981: Chicago, Ill.
1982: Baltimore, Md.*

*TOPEX was not held in 1982, but an ATA convention was held at BALPEX.

**Future Conventions**
1983: San Antonio, Tex.
1984: Atlanta, Ga.
1985: Allentown, Pa.
1986: Chicago, Ill.

## ATA Presidents

Past ATA presidents are listed by the year in which they succeeded to the presidency.

1950: Charles J. Keenan
1954: Homer L. Jones
1956: Allyn H. Wright
1958: Harvey E. Johnson
1962: John H. Groet
1964: Margaret R. Hackett
1968: Fred Korotkin
1972: Henry Peterson
1976: George B. Griffenhagen
1980: Donald W. Smith

## Current ATA Officers

President: Donald W. Smith
First vice president: Donald B. Brenke
Second vice president: Sam Wilkinson III

Secretary: Judith E. Barna
Treasurer: June A. Hellman
Executive director: Jerome Husak
Directors: Melvin Garabrant and George B. Griffenhagen
Advisory committee: Charles J. Keenan, Homer L. Jones, Allyn H. Wright, Margaret R. Hackett, Fred Korotkin, Henry Peterson, and George B. Griffenhagen

**Special Activity Directors**
Chapters director: Alan J. Hanks
Units director: Donald B. Brenke
Topical awards director: Arlene Crosby
Claims director: A. Michael Knapp
Distinguished Topical Philatelist Award director: Margaret R. Hackett
Heirs and estates director: Judith E. Barna
ATA historian: Homer L. Jones

Information director: Edna B. Cummins

Biography service director: Paul G. Partington

Judges accreditation director: George T. Guzzio

Membership recorder: Dona Jaquet

Public relations director: George B. Griffenhagen

Slide-lecture director: Sam Wilkinson III

Translation director: Dmytro Bykovetz Jr.

Sales service operator: William J. Thomas

Topical Time editor: Fred Foldvary

Topical Time executive editor: Jerome Husak

Publications director: Jerome Husak

ATA librarian: Linda Brothen

Editorial board: Edna B. Cummins, John Henry Richter, Ruth Y. Wetmore, Robert S. Oesch, George B. Griffenhagen, Glen Crago, Donald B. Brenke, Walter L. Tasker, Marshall Whitehead, Janet Foldvary, R. Hal Holden, Mrs. W.R. Jaquet and Ann Shoemake

## Distinguished Topical Philatelist Award Winners

The Distinguished Topical Philatelist award has been presented to ATA members since 1952 for service to topical philately and the ATA.

1952: Jerome Husak, Homer L. Jones, Charles J. Keenan, Allyn H. Wright

1953: Rev. S.C. Becker, George Bourgraf, Catherine D. Caspary Fechner

1954: John H. Groet, Ernest A. Kehr

1955: Willard F. Stanley, Dr. Wilson A. Swanker

1956: Margaret R. Hackett, Walter W. Sievers

1957: Clare McAlister, Sidney R. Esten

1958: Jal Cooper, Edward J. Flath

1959: M.P. Polson, Louis K. Sievert

1960: Ennis C. Cleveland, Harvey E. Johnson

1961: Dr. Shirley C. Tucker, Edgar W. Spurgeon

1962: O. Frank Freedner, Fred Korotkin

1963: John Henry Richter, Capt. M.F. Stern

1964: Lt. Col. Fred H. Campbell, Mr. and Mrs. A.H. Pritzlaff Jr.

1965: Robert S. Oesch, H.F. Rayl

1966: Dr. Melvin J. Andrews, Henry Peterson

1967: Brother Camillus Casey, Dr. E. Willis Hainlen

1968: Clarence Beltmann, John Thomas

1969: Mary Ann Owens, Cyril C. Ranschaert

1970: Dorothy F. Smith, George Griffenhagen

1971: K.D. Dinshah, Sophia Webb

1972: Charles S. Diamant (posthumously), Lester E. Kufahl

1973: Edna Cummins, Melvin Garabrant, Lauretta Garabrant

1974: George T. Guzzio, Margaret M. Wurtz

1975: Myrtle I. Watt, Ruth Y. Wetmore

1976: Franklin R. Bruns Jr., Donald W. Smith

1977: Sam Wilkinson III, Jack H. Green

1978: Lester E. Winick, Robert F. Kante

1979: Donald B. Brenke, Kenneth A. Wood

1980: Paul G. Partington, Walter L. Tasker

1981: Ann Shoemake, Henry J. Rajewski

## ATA Exhibiton Award

The ATA will present either a Best In Topicals gold medal or certificate to any annual philatelic show. This award will be given to the exhibitor of the best topical exhibit. Criteria for the award are:

1. The show must provide a separate classification for topicals.

2. The following ATA definition for topicals must be used: "Topical collecting is defined as forming a collection of philatelic material selected and arranged by subject, design or theme rather than by country or issuance of type of postal service rendered."

3. Brochures on ATA and topical collecting must be distributed at the show.

4. The exhibition chairman must supply the name and address of the winner as well as the title of the winning exhibit to the ATA director of awards.

5. The basis of topical judging shall be: Presentation, 20 points; topical/thematic knowledge — Originality, 5 points; development of theme, 25 points; topical research, 15 points; philatelic elements — condition, 5 points; philatelic items, 15 points; scarcity, 5 points; philatelic information, 10 points. Total, 100 points.

For the medal, the show must have more than 500 pages on exhibit. In addition, the ATA medal winner must earn a bronze or better in the competition.

For the certificate, any annual show meeting the five aforementioned criteria and not qualifying for an ATA gold medal will qualify for a Best in Topicals certificate.

Silver and bronze ATA medals are also available for purchase.

All inquiries should be directed to Arlene Crosby, ATA Director of Awards, 1348 Union, NE, Grand Rapids, Mich. 49505.

## ATA Topical Publications

Publications of the ATA will be found listed in Chapter 18 under Literature

## ATA Slide and Film Loan Service

ATA full-color stamp film showings include more than 55 titles and over 5,000 slides. Each show consists of 30 to 100 slides and can run from half to quarter hour programs. All are complete with script and/or captions. Some of the newer programs have cassette tape sound tracks. This service is open to members and nonmembers alike.

For information on any of the following programs, contact the ATA Slide Librarian Sam Wilkinson III, Box 140810, Dallas, Tex. 75214.

Shows are listed in alphabetical order. All are 35mm slides except the four starred titles (*), which are 35mm filmstrips requiring different equipment or attachments than for slides. Titles marked with two stars (**) have cassette tape and sound tracks.

50: ABC's of Topical Collecting
 1: Americana on Foreign
61: American Revolution
 2: Animals
64: Architechture
46: Astronomy
29: Bible Stories*
54: Bicycles on Stamps
 6: Birds, Series A
30: Christian Faith*
62: Columbian Exposition
53: Dogs on Stamps
48: Drugs and Pharmacy
44: Easter, The Story of
38: Elephants
32: English Religion*
55: Europa
57: Fairy Tales
 7: Fine Arts
 8: Fish and Fishing
 9: Flags
11: Flowers, Series B
12: Flowers, Series C
39: Geology
31: Helpers of Mankind*
56: Hive and Honeybee**
40: Horses
13: Insects and Butterflies
42: Lincoln's Life and Monuments
43: Lions International
14: Maps
33: Masonic
37: Medical History
15: Medical Subjects
18: Music
41: National Parks and Monuments
36: Nurses
16: Nutrition
45: Old Glory Around the World
25: Olympic Games
63: Owls
19: Plants and Fruits

60: Prehistory
20: Religion
49: Rotary International
52: Royalty on Stamps
21: St. Benedict
22: Scouts
23: Ships
35: Space
24: Sports
58: Sputnik to Eagle**
26: Stamps on Stamps
27: Trains
17: Tuberculosis
28: United Nations (World)
59: Jules Verne**

# ATA Information Service

The ATA's free Information Service consists of nearly 700 advanced collectors who have volunteered to answer ATA members' questions on more than 300 different topical subjects on stamps. First organized in 1951 for only 45 subjects and constantly expanded by new volunteers, the ATA Information Service aids members in obtaining information needed to write up their collections.

The complete list of service volunteers is available to ATA members.

# ATA Translation Service

Translation Service is available to ATA members for philatelic correspondence and short articles in 31 different languages. This valuable service to ATA members is free of charge except for return postage.

The 42 linguists who serve as translators are proficient in Afrikaans, Arabic, Bengali, Czech, Danish, Esperanto, Farsi, Finnish, French, German, Greek, Gurmukhi, Hebrew, Hindi, Hungarian, Italian, Japanese, Latin, Latvian, Norwegian, Oriya, Polish, Portuguese, Russian, Serbo-Croatian, Slovak, Spanish, Swedish, Tagalog and Ukranian.

# Heirs and Estates Service

The vital Heirs and Estates Service has a worldwide committee willing to help evaluate philatelic holdings of deceased ATA members and make recommendations on the disposal of such collections. ATA urges collectors to keep records of the purchase prices and/or current estimated value of their collections, and to record instructions for disposition upon death to be placed with the person's will so that the wishes of the deceased may be followed.

A specific method of liquidation cannot be recommended until the collection has been evaluated. Once this is completed, an ATA Heirs and Estates Committee member will recommend methods of disposition best suited to the particular collection. These may include sale at auction, private sale to a dealer, private sale of various individual parts of a collection to differ-

ent dealers, ATA sales service, or private negotiation to interested collectors.

Gummed labels for insertion in stamp albums to make heirs aware of this service are available at cost from the ATA. Additional information is available from the ATA.

# Council of Philatelic Organizations

The Council of Philatelic Organizations is composed of nearly 200 national, regional and local stamp clubs, philatelic societies and dealers united to promote stamp collecting. COPO is the largest umbrella group ever assembled within the hobby.

The council was formed for the sole purpose of promoting stamp collecting by providing a means for cooperation, information exchange, and interaction among member organizations and the public.

Membership is open only to organizations; individuals are not eligible to join. Commercial firms and businesses may hold associate memberships with the same rights and privileges as noncommercial groups.

There is no membership fee or required annual membership dues; however, all COPO activities are funded by voluntary contributions from its members.

Every philatelic organization is eligible to become a member of COPO, with equal voting privileges. Each member organization, regardless of size, has one vote and one official delegate, who is eligible to help elect COPO's governing body, the board of directors.

The annual election meeting is held in November in New York City, at the ASDA National Postage Stamp Show.

COPO has received tax-exempt status under Section 501 (c) (3) of the Internal Revenue Code, which means all donations of money or philatelic property are completely deductible on individual Federal Income Tax returns.

The council does not compete for membership with any philatelic group already established and devotes its full efforts and resources to bringing people into stamp collecting.

The council plans a variety of efforts — publicity campaigns, educational programs and special stamp exhibitions — to draw the attention of the noncollector and interest him or her in collecting stamps.

COPO is a united front, representing diverse elements of philately, and it cooperates with the United States Postal Service to promote the hobby. COPO and the USPS jointly sponsored the first National Stamp Collecting Month in October 1981.

The theme of the first National Stamp Collecting Month was "Discover Stamp Collecting — The Hobby of a Lifetime." COPO considered its

1981 effort to be the largest, most concentrated promotional venture on behalf of philately ever attempted in the United States up to that time.

The USPS, in addition to providing post office lobby displays, banners and posters, distributed more than 750,000 copies of "Introduction to Stamp Collecting," a 32-page basic informational booklet.

COPO issued a cacheted cover for National Stamp Collecting Month, and the Postal Service provided a special cancellation.

A direct mail advertising campaign, featuring a special reply coupon, was used for the first time in 15 test cities and about 75,000 requests for further information on the hobby resulted.

Preliminary studies showed that the promotional activities of that month resulted in a significant increase in demand for philatelic products during that period.

Another National Stamp Collecting Month was scheduled by COPO and the USPS for October 1982.

## Formation

The need for an effective organization to represent philately as a whole became apparent in the past ten years, when significant changes in the hobby had been observed.

In spite of many individual promotional efforts, there was no unified effort being made until the late 1970s to advocate the hobby and its educational benefits or to guide its development.

The need for cohesive action was discussed by a group of prominent philatelists at the National Postage Stamp Show in November 1978. There, the seeds of COPO were sown.

Nine major national philatelic organizations were again invited to a discussion in March 1979 in New York, during INTERPEX. As a result, a nonprofit "stamps council" was proposed.

Preliminary organizational work continued and on Oct. 6, 1979, a draft copy of the articles of incorporation was signed by representatives of the nine organizations at the Sheraton Hotel in Philadelphia during SEPAD.

The nine organizations and their representatives were:

American Academy of Philately: Milton Mitchell

American Philatelic Congress: Sidney Schneider

American Philatelic Society: John E. Foxworth Jr.

American Stamp Dealers' Association: Lewis F. Shull

American Topical Association: George B. Griffenhagen

Bureau Issues Association: E. Ray Shank

Collectors Club of New York: F. Burton Sellers

The Philatelic Foundation: John C. Chapin

Society of Philatelic Americans: Milton Mitchell

It was decided that these nine organizations would constitute the acting board of directors for COPO, and the first meeting was set for the following month in New York. The nine representatives elected Foxworth acting president and Shank acting secretary.

COPO was officially voted into existence in New York Nov. 10, 1979, as the articles of incorporation had been signed by the presidents of eight of the nine organizers, and the last signature was imminent.

The first meeting of COPO was held Nov. 22, 1980, in New York. By that time, bylaws had been adopted, an application for federal tax exemption had been filed, and COPO membership had grown to 124 organizations.

The bylaws called for increasing the board of directors to at least 15 organizations. As a result of an election and a drawing of lots, six members were added to the board of directors and the 15 were divided into groups of five, receiving three-year, two-year and one-year terms.

All subsequent elections are for three-year terms, ensuring that one-third of the board membership can change each year.

The organizations receiving one-year terms were all reelected to three-year terms in 1980.

Information on membership or activities of COPO can be obtained from George Grabon, Box 3492, North New Hyde Park Branch, New Hyde Park, N.Y. 11040.

## Leadership

Organizations, not individuals are elected to the COPO board of directors. Each organization appoints a representative to act on its behalf.

Officers are elected from the membership of the board of directors for two-year terms. The next election is scheduled for fall 1984.

Representatives are listed in parentheses.

President: American Philatelic Society (John E. Foxworth Jr.)

Vice President: The Philatelic Foundation (William H. Miller Jr.)

Secretary: Club of Channel Islands Collectors (George Grabon)

Treasurer: American Topical Association (Donald W. Smith)

### Board of Directors
### Term expires 1984

American Philatelic Society (John E. Foxworth Jr.)

Bureau Issues Association (James H. Bruns)

China Stamp Society (Ellery Denison)

Collectors Club of New York (Ira Zweifach)

Nippon Stamp Club of New England (Lois M. Evans)

### Term expires 1983

American Philatelic Congress (Robert B. Brandeberry)

American Stamp Dealers' Association (Lewis F. Shull)

Club of Channel Islands Collectors (George Grabon)

The Philatelic Foundation (William H. Miller Jr.)

Society of Philatelic Americans (James P. Harris)

### Term expires 1982

American Air Mail Society (Dan R. Barber)

American First Day Cover Society (Edward J. Siskin)

American Topical Association (Donald W. Smith)

Potomac Philatelic Society (David U. Groves)

Universal Ship Cancellation Society (David A. Kent)

## COPO Membership

Acadiana Stamp Club, Lafayette, La.
Aeronutronic Stamp Club, Irvine, Calif.
Aerophilatelic Federation of the Americas
Albuquerque (N.M.) Philatelic Society
Allentown (Pa.) Philatelic Society
Allison (Iowa) Stamp Club
Ambler (Pa.) Stamp Club
American Air Mail Society
American First Day Cover Society
American Philatelic Congress

American Philatelic Research Library
American Philatelic Society
American Stamp Dealers' Association
American Topical Association
Americana Unit (ATA/APS)
Arapaho Stamp Club, McKinney, Tex.
Arizona Society of Topical Philatelists, Tempe, Ariz.
Armstrong Activities Association

Associated Stamp Clubs of Southeastern
    Pennsylvania and Delaware
Austin Philatelic Club, Chicago, Ill.
Baltimore (Md.) Philatelic Society
Bick International, Van Nuys, Calif.
Birmingham (Ala.) Philatelic Society
Black River Stamp Club, Elyria, Ohio
Boeing Employees Stamp Club, Kent, Wash.
Bowie (Md.) Stamp Club
Brazil Philatelic Association
Brookhaven (Pa.) Stamp Club
Bureau Issues Association
Bux-Mont Stamp Club, Warminster, Pa.
Carfisa Philatelic International-America Inc.
Central Coast Stamp Club, Lompoc, Calif.
Central Florida Stamp Club, Orlando, Fla.
Central Michigan Philatelic Society,
    Lansing, Mich.
Charleston (S.C.) Stamp Club
Chelmsford Stamp Club, Tewksbury, Md.
Chicago (Ill.) Philatelic Society
China Stamp Society
Cincinnati (Ohio) Philatelic Society
Clearfield (Pa.) Philatelic Society
Club of Channel Islands Collectors
Club Filatelico of Barranguilla (Colombia)
Collectors Club of Dallas (Tex.)
Collectors Club of New York
Collier County (Fla.) Stamp Club
Commonwealth International Philatelic Society
Confederate Stamp Alliance
Connecticut Philatelic Society
Corn Belt Philatelic Society, Bloomington, Ill.
Coryell's Ferry Stamp Club, Yardley, Pa.
Croatian Philatelic Society
Dallas (Tex.) Philatelic Society
Dearborn (Mich.) Stamp Club
Edmonton (Alberta, Canada) Stamp Club
Eire Philatelic Association
Ellyson Collectors Club, Pensacola, Fla.
Empire State Postal History Society
Errors, Freaks and Oddities Collectors Club
Europa Study Unit
Fairfield (Conn.) Philatelic Society
Fall River (Mass.) Philatelic Society
Fire Service in Philately
Fort Findlay (Ohio) Stamp Club
Fort Lauderdale (Fla.) Stamp Club
Fort Steuben Stamp Club, Steubenville, Ohio
Fox Valley Stamp Club, Aurora, Ill.
Franklin D. Roosevelt Philatelic Society
Fulton Stamp Club
Garden City Stamp Club, Missoula, Mont.
Germany Philatelic Society
Greater Hazleton (Pa.) Area Stamp Club
Haiti Philatelic Society
Hardware City Stamp Club, New Britain, Conn.
Harrison Stamp and Coin Club,
    White Plains, N.Y.
Heart of Texas Stamp Club, Waco, Tex.
Hollywood (Fla.) Stamp Club
Home Chapter, Cardinal Spellman
    Philatelic Museum, Wellesley, Mass.

Huachuca Stamp Club, Sierra Vista, Ariz.
Humboldt Collectors Club, Eureka, Calif.
Huntington Stamp Club, East Northport, N.Y.
Illinois Postal History Society
Indiana Stamp Club
International Guild of Vatican Philatelists
Iowa Women's Philatelic Society,
    Des Moines, Iowa
Japanese-American Society for Philately
JAPOS Study Group
Johnstown (Pa.) Stamp Club
Johnson City Stamp Club, Binghampton, N.Y.
Junior Ambassadors
Junior Philatelists of America
K-T Stamps Inc., Kansas City, Mo.
Kachina Chapter, Germany Philatelic Society
Kiribati Philatelic Society
Lake County (Ill.) Philatelic Society
Latin American Philatelic Society
Lewis and Clark Stamp Club, Bismark, N.D.
Long Beach (Calif.) Stamp Club
M.S. Roe, Morganville, N.J.
Mailer's Postmark Permit Club
Malaria Philatelists International
Manchester Philatelic Society, Rockville, Conn.
Medina County (Ohio) Stamp Club
Memphis (Tenn.) Stamp Collectors Society
Mesoamerican Archeology Study Unit
Mexico-Elmhurst Philatelic Society International
Milwaukee (Wis.) Philatelic Society
Mobile Post Office Society
Monadnock Stamp Club, Keene, N.H.
Montgomery (Ala.) Area Stamp Club
Mount Joy (Pa.) Stamp Club
Mulready Research Foundation,
    Laguna Hills, Calif.
National Organization for Women/New York
    (Women's History Series of FDCs)
Nevada (Mo.) Stamp and Coin Club
Newburgh (N.Y.) Stamp Club
Niagara Frontier Stamp Club, Lewiston, N.Y.
Nippon Stamp Club of New England
North Jersey Federated Stamp Clubs
Oak Park Stamp Club of Michigan
Ohio Postal History Society
Old Colony Philatelists, South Easton, Mass.
Olean (N.Y.) Area Stamp Club
Orange County (Calif.) Philatelic Society
Oxford Philatelic Society, Philadelphia, Pa.
Palmdale Stamp Club, Leona Valley, Calif.
Patchogue (N.Y.) Stamp Club
Peachtree Stamp and Study Club, Elkhart, Ind.
Pennsylvania Postal History Society
Pennyrile Philatelic Society, Hopkinsville, Ky.
Pensacola (Fla.) Philatelic Society
Perfins Club
Permit Imprint Collectors Society
Philatelic Emporium, Rumford, Maine
Philatelic Foundation, The
Philatelic Society of Atascadero (Calif.)
Philatelic Society of Cincinnati (Ohio)
Philatelic Society of Pittsburgh (Pa.)
Philatelic "25" Chapter 822, San Diego, Calif.

Pine Tree Stamp Club, Caribou, Maine
Pleasure Ridge Park Philatelic Society,
  Louisville, Ky.
Polonus Philatelic Society
Port St. Louis Stamp Club, Stuart, Fla.
Potomac (Md.) Philatelic Society
Puerto Rico Philatelic Society
Putnam Stamp Club, Patterson, N.Y.
Quail Creek Stamp Club, Grays Lake, Ill.
Rhode Island Philatelic Society
Roadrunner Stamp Club
Rochester (N.Y.) Philatelic Association
Routing Labels Society
Rubber City Stamp Club, Akron, Ohio
Rumex Stamp Club, Rumford, Maine
Sacramento (Calif.) Philatelic Society
Saginaw Valley (Mich.) Stamp Society
San Pablo Pines Stamp Club, Berkeley, Calif.
St. Helena and Dependencies Philatelic Society
Samuel Osgood Stamp Club, Methuen, Mass.
San Francisco Pacific (Calif.) Philatelic Society
San Joaquin Philatelic Society, Manteca, Calif.
Scandinavian Collectors Club
Scott Collectibles, New York, N.Y.
Sharon Stamp Club, Hermitage, Pa.
Silver Spring Shores Stamp Club, Ocala, Fla.
Society of Australian Specialists/Oceania
Society of Costa Rica Collectors
Society of Philatelic Americans
Society of Philaticians

Southern New Jersey Chapter 154, APS
Space Topics Study Group
Sports Philatelists International
Stamp Expo, Van Nuys, Calif.
Stamptrotters Society of Kingston (N.Y.)
Stanislaus Stamp Society, Modesto, Calif.
Staten Island (N.Y.) Philatelic Society
Thames Stamp Club, New London, Conn.
Tower Stamp Club, Chicago, Ill.
TRW Stamp Club, Redondo Beach, Calif.
Tucson (Ariz.) Stamp Club
U.S. Cancellation Club
United States 1869 Pictorial Research Associates
USS Arizona Chapter 78, USCS
Universal Ship Cancellation Society
University City Stamp Club, Gainesville, Fla.
Upper Keys Collectors Club, Key Largo, Fla.
Valdosta (Ga.) Stamp Club
Vancouver Island Philatelic Society
  Saanichton, B.C., Canada
Visalia (Calif.) Philatelic Society
Walla Walla Valley (Wash.) Philatelic Society
Waltham Stamp Club, Newton Centre, Mass.
WaMarVa Philippine Philatelic Study Group
War Cover Club
Westfield Stamp Club, Granby, Conn.
Wisconsin Postal History Society
Ye Olde King's Highway Stamp Club,
  Darien, Conn.
Zippy Collectors Club

# Collectors Club, Inc.

In 1896, a group of New York residents, all stamp collectors, discussed the possibility of forming an association of men interested in stamps, incorporating it, and establishing a headquarters where collectors and dealers could meet at any time and "where the privileges of a club could be enjoyed by city and country members."

These discussions resulted in the formation of a committee, which, on June 24, 1896, sent a circular letter to a selected list of 100 men, 50 of whom resided in the city and 50 of whom resided in the country, outlining their tentative plan and canvassing their favorable response.

In addition to J.M. Andreini, William Herrick, and Charles Gregory, this founding committee included two philatelic patriarchs, John N. Luff and John W. Scott.

Sixty-two of the men became shareholders (sic) and leased quarters for the Collectors Club at 351 4th Ave., New York, N.Y., on Sept. 26, 1896.

The first meeting was held in the club rooms on Oct. 5, and the first exhibition followed on Oct. 19 when John N. Luff showed his collection of United States stamps, essays and proofs.

The number of members increased steadily, and at the sixth meeting of the board of governors, it was announced that the Collectors Club had incorporated on Dec, 14, 1896.

In addition to the founding committee, the first board included H.L. Calman, F.E.P. Lynde, H.E. Deats and F.A. Nast.

Present membership numbers about 1,100 worldwide.

Although founded primarily as an association whose members shared the privileges of a club and the clublike atmosphere generated from their common interest, the Collectors Club did not neglect the more serious aspects of the hobby.

The letters of incorporation state that one of the particular objectives of the club "is to encourage the best interests of philately by all proper means." The constitution reaffirms this objective.

The club has been faithful to this objective through the establishment and maintenance of a library and reading rooms, the publication of the "Collectors Club Philatelist," publication of studies by authorities in their field, lectures at regular meetings, and participation in the extracurricular activities devoted to developing greater appreciation of philately.

Since 1936, the Collectors Club has occupied 22 E. 35th St., in the Murray Hill section of New York City. The club's five-story brownstone rowhouse, faced with red and gray block laid up in Flemish bond with contrasting stone and metal detail, has been designated a National Historical Landmark.

The facilities are made available to other stamp associations and societies, as well as to Scouts and similar organizations who wish to hold exhibitions (public or private) or other gatherings of a philatelic nature.

The John N. Luff reference collection, the property of the Philatelic Foundation, is housed in the John N. Luff Room of the Collectors Club building.

## Meetings

Regular meetings of the Collectors Club are held the first and third Wednesday of the month at 8 p.m. in the Stephen G. Rich Memorial Room. No meetings are held during the summer months.

With the exception of the annual meeting on the second Wednesday in January, which is devoted to the business of operating the club, the meetings are devoted to the scheduled subject.

## J. Brace Chittenden Memorial Library

The Collectors Club library has more than 140,000 manuscripts, maps, pictures, slides, microforms, tear sheets, books, reports, dissertations, pamphlets and journals. With the exception of certain unique periodicals, rare limited editions and presentation copies, all are available for loan to members in accordance with the rules of the library. Conditions for the use of the rarer material by members are also outlined in the rules.

The names of early benefactors, several of whom served as librarian of the J. Brace Chittenden Memorial Library, include Hiram Deats, Joseph S. Rich, John W. Scott Sr., William R. Ricketts, Abraham Hatfield, Alfred F. Lichtenstein, Charles J. Phillips, Theodore E. Steinway, and Dr. Chittenden.

Dr. Chittenden did much to elevate the library to its present state from its earlier status of "a mere collection of books." The board of governors designated the library as the J. Brace Chittenden Memorial on June 6, 1928.

Among the collections in the library are the Victor Suppantschitsch collection of all printed matter on stamp collecting up to 1900 including some 28,000 items;

Pablo Busch collection containing all philatelic publications issued in Argentina and near completion for many other South American countries;

Joseph S. Rich collection of postal guides, postmasters' reports, etc., of the United States.

The library catalog is cross-indexed so that an author, country or subject can be located. The library contains two major divisions of material — periodicals and handbooks, catalogs and subdivisions. Great emphasis is placed on the completion of periodicals.

The reference material is open to the general public Monday, Wednesday and Friday 10 a.m. to 5 p.m. by appointment.

The major portion of the catalog collection is housed in the Joseph S. Rich Room, including auction catalogs.

## Steinway Memorial Publications Fund

Theodore E. Steinway was a dedicated member of the Collectors Club who shook the club loose from the doldrums of World War I, revitalizing its organization and its purpose.

Steinway gave numerous gifts to the library's collection, including the Suppantschitsch collection which embraced any literature printed on stamps and stamp collecting during the 19th century.

The literature of the hobby was to Steinway the keystone to successful research in philately. The Collectors Club established the Steinway Memorial Publications Fund for the publication of philatelic handbooks. This fund has been in operation since June 1957.

## 'Collectors Club Philatelist'

The "Collectors Club Philatelist" is the bimonthly periodical published for members of the Collectors Club. The periodical was established as a quarterly in January 1922 and became a bimonthly in 1950.

The "Collectors Club Philatelist" contains selected articles from members of the club and details of regular meetings and business matters.

Translations from the "Kohl Handbook," to which the Collectors Club has English-language rights, appear as space and interest permit.

## Awards

The Collectors Club program committees have, on occasion, scheduled a competitive display limited to the members present at meetings with appropriate certificates for first, second and third awards.

In recent years, this event has been scheduled as an annual affair. Silver awards are given to the top exhibits.

Collectors Club medals have been awarded to members since 1925 for outstanding achievements. Collectors Club medals are also awarded annually to the author of the best article published in the "Collectors Club Philatelist" during the previous year.

Certificates of Merit are awarded to the articles ranking second.

The program, which, in the opinion of the Awards Committee, has been the best of the season's scheduled meetings, is also awarded a Collectors Club medal.

## Lichtenstein Medal

The Alfred F. Lichtenstein Memorial award was established in 1952 to honor one of America's great collectors. The Lichtenstein medal is given in recognition of distinguished philatelic service.

## Study Groups

The Collectors Club has maintained a program supporting any valid study group. It is not required that all members of these groups be members of the club, but it is requested that a member of the club, who is also a member of the individual group, act for the Collectors Club in matters pertaining to the club and its home.

The chief contribution of the club to study groups is providing a meeting place. It has also been arranged for individual or collective displays by members of the study group at regularly scheduled meetings of the Collectors Club

The pages of the "Collectors Club Philatelist" have been made available for publication of such groups' studies as is consistent with members' wishes and editorial policy.

## Activities

The Collectors Club supplies stamps and philatelic supplies to schools, hospitals, and other institutions, and offers advice and cooperation to qualified institutions.

Lectures are provided on request both nationally and internationally.

The club has actively supported national as well as international exhibitions devoted to philately.

## Membership

No person under 21 years of age is eligible for membership. A resident member is such person who resides, has a business address, or is employed within a radius of 50 miles from the club house.

A nonresident member is such person who resides and is employed entirely outside the areas previously mentioned, which includes Canada and Mexico.

Annual dues are $50 for resident members; $15 for nonresident members; and $15 for overseas members.

Applications should not be accompanied by remittance; dues are payable upon notification of election. Applications may be obtained from Collectors Club, 22 E. 35th St., New York, N.Y. 10016.

## Board of Governors

Governors are men and women who are elected by voting members to administer the services, functions, activities and maintenance of the Collectors Club. The officers of the club are elected from among the board of governors.

Each governor has an assigned responsibility, such as membership, maintenance of the physical plant, club's publications, library, study groups, etc., and is required to account for the charge at each scheduled meeting of the board.

### Governors
**1981**
Sidney M. Schwartz
William H. Miller Jr.
Robert P. Odenweller
John D. Dowd
Ernest E. Fricks
**1982**
Louis K. Robbins
Elliott Coulter
Louis Grunin
Bernard D. Harmer
Ernest Wilkens
**1983**
Ernest A. Kehr
Abbot Lutz
Alex Rendon
Philip Silver
Ira Zweifach

### Trustees
Alex Rendon
Philip Silver
William H. Miller Jr.

### Officers
President: Alex Rendon
Vice president: Louis Grunin
Secretary: Robert P. Odenweller
Treasurer: Ernest Wilkens

# Philatelic Foundation

The Philatelic Foundation was chartered by the University of the State of New York for philatelic study and research in 1945. Since that time, it has been serving the public in a variety of educational activities.

One of the best known of the Foundation's activities has been its expertization service. Since 1945, over 80,000 philatelic items have been examined.

The other areas of activity have been in the educational field. In 1946, a course on stamp collecting was started at the Collectors Club of New York. This course has been attended by hundreds over the years and served as a foundation in the many avenues of philately.

Recently, the Philatelic Foundation began a series of seminars at the Harvard Club of New York. The scope of the seminars is to concentrate on special subjects such as expertizing, judging, investment, restoration and protection of stamps.

The Foundation's origin was the result of the efforts of some of the most prominent collectors of the time who saw a need for an organization that could serve the public in an educational capacity. Until that time, there was no central expertizing service, and collectors were plagued by counterfeits and altered stamps.

Through donations of reference materials and collections, the Foundation was able to embark on a most ambitious program of offering an expertizing service to the public. Today, a Foundation certificate is universally recognized.

## Expert Committee

The function of the Expert Committee is to render opinions on philatelic items submitted for examination. A full-time staff and a number of volunteers study all the items submitted. After an opinion has been reached, a certificate is issued which describes the items and the opinion.

Each certificate from the Foundation has a photo of the item affixed with the seal of the Expert Committee. A copy of each Foundation certificate is kept as a permanent record, and a photo of each item is maintained in a permanent reference library to enable the curatorial staff to study opinions of the past.

Official application forms for the submission of philatelic items and the list of fees for this service are available upon request.

## Education and Publications

Over the years, the Foundation has published a number of important works, such as Bogg's "Foundations of Philately" and most recently, R.H. White's "Color In Philately." The Foundation also publishes counterfeit leaflets and analysis leaflets which go into some detail on the types of counterfeits of certain issues such as the Beaver issue of Canada 1851 and the United Nations 1½¢ precancel.

Analysis leaflets cover facts regarding certain issues and give breakdowns of the number of items submitted for opinions and the findings. The scope of these leaflets range from U.S. coils to the Vatican provisionals overprints of 1934.

The Foundation also prints a quarterly "Foundation Bulletin" which brings supporters of the Foundation recent facts about certain issues and news of Foundation activities.

Another educational function of the Foundation are the audio-visual programs available free to schools, clubs and organizations. These slide and cassette programs were produced by the U.S. Philatelic Classics Society, Junior Ambassadors, Inc., and the Foundation.

The subjects range from the "Pony Express 1860-61," "U.S. Postmaster Provisionals," "The Postal History of the Confederacy" to programs designed for beginners and young people such as "The Romance of Stamp Collecting," "The Drama of Postage Stamp Creation" and "One Giant Step to Stamp Collecting." A directory of these programs is free upon request.

## Information

Information on all activities of the Foundation is available from the Philatelic Foundation, 270 Madison Ave., New York, N.Y. 10016. All contributions to the Foundation are deductible from federal and state taxes.

# World Federation of United Nations Associations

The World Federation of United Nations Associations produces first day covers to accompany each issue of United Nations stamps, from the United Nations Headquarters in New York, the Palais des Nations in Geneva, Switzerland, and the Vienna International Centre in Vienna, Austria.

The designs for the WFUNA covers are also reproduced in numbered limited-edition art prints, which are usually individually signed by the artist.

This philatelic program offers stamp collectors and art lovers alike the opportunity to ac-

quire original designs by some of the greatest of our time.

The program commenced with the presentation of an original watercolor by Salvador Dali to commemorate the federation's 20th anniversary in 1966. The original still hangs in the public area of the United Nations Building.

Since then many noted artists have contributed designs, among them Marc Chagall, Alexander Calder, Norman Rockwell, Chaim Gross, William Gropper, Ole Hamann and Andy Warhol.

Jacques Cousteau contributed a design to WFUNA for the Law of the Sea; Jessie Oonark, a 70-year-old Inuit artist from the Northwest Territory of Canada did the design for Habitat; and Anne Morrow Lindbergh presented the federation with a quotation to be used with the Ole Hamann design honoring ICAO: Safety in the Air.

Garry Trudeau, the Pulitzer Prize-winning cartoonist of "Doonesbury," contributed his design for the 1974 WFUNA definitive cover; Muhammad Ali donated the use of his painting and poem entitled "Freedom" to WFUNA to accompany the 1979 Namibia stamp issue.

Gloria Swanson, the noted film actress, designed the federation's cover and art print to accompany the U.N. stamp issue honoring the United Nations Decade for Women; and Joan Miro contributed a design to accompany the U.N. stamp issue of May 1980 honoring the United Nations Peacekeeping Operations.

Princess Grace of Monaco presented one of her pressed flower collages to WFUNA to accompany the United Nations Conference on New and Renewable Sources of Energy issue.

In November 1980, Friedensreich Hundertwasser contributed the use of his painting "Escape of the Indoor Sky" for the federation's FDC and limited-edition art print to accompany the issue commemorating the economic and social council, and for the 1982 Human Environment issue he has again granted the use of another of his paintings.

Sophia Loren designed the Federation's FDC for the 1982 Flag Series, and 1983 plans include designs by Hans Erni, the renowned Swiss artist, and by Edna Hibel of the United States.

It is truly an international program with artists from Austria, Brazil, Canada, Denmark, Ethiopia, Federal Republic of Germany, France, Honduras, India, Iran, Ireland, Israel, Japan, Monaco, Spain, Sudan, the Soviet Union, the United Kingdom and the United States.

WFUNA covers and art prints have the distinction of being the only semiofficial items to be included in the United Nations permanent exhibit in New York, and also in the United Nations Philatelic Museum at the Palais des Nations in Geneva.

The work of selling and servicing these FDCs and art prints is carried on by a volunteer staff.

The federation's FDCs are a means of bringing a knowledge of the program and activities of the United Nations to an ever increasing and important section of the world's population, the philatelists. Through their FDCs and art prints, WFUNA is stimulating an interest in the United Nations and promoting a continued and more extensive awareness of its programs.

The funds derived from the sale of these items are used to help finance the federation's work in promoting public understanding of the United Nation. Like the United Nations which it serves, WFUNA is a federation of U.N. associations from some 80 countries.

In addition to organizing seminars and other information programs, WFUNA, as an accredited consultant to the United Nations Economic and Social Council and to UNESCO, attends the meetings of both those organizations and presents the views of federation's members.

Address of the WFUNA director is Mrs. Annabelle Wiener, Director at United Nations Headquarters, Room DC-360, United Nations, New York, N.Y. 10017.

# Junior Philatelists of America

The Junior Philatelists of America was formed Jan. 1, 1976, with the merging of the Junior Philatelic Society of America and the Junior Division of the American Philatelic Society Writer's Unit No. 30.

The JPSA was founded July 10, 1963, by Robert J. Osterhoff, the organization's first president. The society fought an uphill battle for recognition and was refused APS affiliation in 1964.

The JPSA participated in its first national or international exhibition at SIPEX held in Washington, D.C., in 1966. The society was established as an APS unit in 1967.

The Junior Division of the APS Writer's Unit was formed in 1971, the year the JPSA was granted national branch status by the Society of Philatelic Americans. The two groups coexisted until Jan. 1, 1976, when the merger was completed.

Since 1976, the JPA has participated to a great extent at INTERPHIL '76 held in Philadelphia, Pa., and CAPEX '78 held in Toronto, Ont., Canada. The society was also the only junior society which held meetings at STaMpsHOW '79 held in Boston, Mass.

The JPA features an auction department, an exchange department, a first day cover service, library service, pen pal service, tape and slide service, stamp identification service, translation service and study groups.

The society's bimonthly, illustrated publication is the "Philatelic Observer."

## Current JPA Officers

President: Dane S. Claussen

First vice president: Eric Stager

Second vice president: Mark Loest

Interim secretary: Alfred Rosinski

Editor, "Philatelic Observer": Vic Pawlak

Public relations director: Dane S. Claussen

Library coordinator: Mark H. Winnegrad

Tape/Slide Service director: Mary Stone

Translation/Pen Pal Service director: Morton A. Potter Jr.

Stamp Identification Service director: Dane S. Claussen

Chapter coordinator: Open

Exhibitions chairman: Bill Scheuermann

Recruiting director: Chris Bogart

Exchange Department director: Keith Souders

First Day Cover Service director: Stuart Litel

## JPA Awards

JPA exhibition awards include the JPA ribbon and accompanying certificate, which are given to the best youth exhibit at any local, regional or national show.

The JPA H.E. Harris medal, made available through a grant from H.E. Harris Co. stamp firm, is awarded at all regional and national, as well as international shows.

The only requisite for receiving this award is a minimum of four youth entries in a show. Award recipients need not be JPA members.

These awards are presented free of charge by the JPA.

Further information concerning JPA membership and/or awards is available from Bill Scheuermann, Box 195, Minetto, N.Y. 13115.

The mailing address for the JPA central office is Box 383, Boonville, N.Y. 13309.

# Trans-Mississippi Philatelic Society, Inc.

The Trans-Mississippi Philatelic Society, since its inception in 1934, has done a great deal to cement the members and clubs it embraces into a strong philatelic organization. While principally a midwestern society, its membership roll lists members from almost every state in the Union and many foreign countries.

The TMPS was incorporated Jan. 2, 1938, in Nebraska and has grown to be recognized as a national society covering the midwestern portion of the United States.

According to its Articles of Incorporation, the purpose of the TMPS is "to assist its members in acquiring knowledge as to philately, to cultivate a feeling of friendship among philatelists, and in furtherance of these objects to assist its members in the acquisition or disposal of stamps of various kinds through its several departments. To permit research, study, investigation, and the dissemination of philatelic knowledge."

Members derive many direct and indirect benefits. They have full access to all departments of the society.

The TMPS Sales Department is one of the society's most popular departments. All members are entitled to its services to both purchase stamps and dispose of duplicates. Members may request books which will meet their own particular requirements. The only obligation is to pay for the stamps retained and to forward the books to the person next on the list.

As the books are sent through the mail, members may carefully examine the books at their leisure and in their home. Specially printed books are furnished at actual cost for the mounting and pricing of duplicates so they can be entered in this department. Chapters are also urged to participate.

The services of an Expertizing Committee of well-qualified, specialist collectors are available to members to obtain opinions on the genuineness of any issued stamp. This service gives members valuable information on questionable stamps in their collections.

An Estate Advisory Committee furnishes aid and advice on the disposal of the philatelic estate of deceased members. Through the advice given by this committee, members are certain their heirs will obtain a fair price for their holdings, by preventing unscrupulous people from taking advantage of survivors.

The highlight of the year is the annual TMPS convention and exhibition which is held in a different city in the midwest each year. Members are welcome to attend and take part in the actual business matters of the society, as well as meet new friends and renew old acquaintances.

The TMPS has visited Omaha, Council Bluffs, Cedar Rapids, Denver, Wichita, Kansas City, Lincoln, Dubuque, Des Moines, Sioux City, Moline, St. Louis, Waterloo, and Davenport. At these conventions, members see exhibits of stamp collections and allied material, meet stamp dealers of national fame, and mingle with collectors who are nationally known in their fields.

Many TMPS chapters and neighboring clubs hold annual or special meetings. These events are really small conventions, complete with exhibition, bourse, auction and banquet. Every effort is made by the TMPS to aid and promote these meetings.

To become a chapter, five or more TMPS members residing near each other may associate themselves together for the purpose of forming a chapter of the society. This applies to either an existing club or a newly formed club. Becoming a TMPS chapter does not change the name of the local club nor interfere in any way with its local administration. It is rather a matter of privileges, prestige and an indication that such a club is a medium of radiating TMPS benefits.

A chapter pays dues of $1 per year, all of which is turned over to and entirely used by the Chapter Program Department for additional program material. The TMPS has a supply of program material for use by its chapters. New programs are constantly being added to this department, and it plays an important part in entertainment of chapter meetings.

Any person of good character interested in philately may become a member of the TMPS. Application blanks may be obtained from any chapter, member, or executive secretary Ruth D. Miller, Box 24, Allison, Iowa 50602.

A bimonthly publication, "Trans-Mississippian," began in 1980.

## TMPS Chapters

Omaha (Neb.) Philatelic Society, Inc. (1)

Council Bluffs (Iowa) Stamp Club (2)

Cedar Rapids (Iowa) Stamp Club (9)

Des Moines (Iowa) Philatelic Society, Inc. (15)

Cedar Valley Stamp Club (20), Waterloo, Iowa

Midwest Philatelic Society, Inc. (24), Kansas City, Mo.

Mound City Stamp Club (26), St. Louis, Mo.

Quad-City Stamp Club (30), Davenport, Iowa

University Place Stamp Club (32), Lincoln, Neb.

Iowa Women's Philatelic Society (34), Des Moines, Iowa

Corn Belt Philatelic Society, Inc. (35), Bloomington-Normal, Ill.

Decatur (Ill.) Stamp Club, Inc. (45)

Fox Valley Stamp Club (49), Aurora, Ill.

Galesburg (Ill.) Philatelic Society (50)

Sioux City (Iowa) Stamp Club, Inc. (56)

Twin City Philatelic Society (59), St. Paul, Minn.

Madison (Wis.) Stamp Club (63)

Boulder (Colo.) Collectors Club (64)

Denver (Colo.) Stamp Club (65)

Sioux Falls (S.D.) Stamp Club (70)

Allison (Iowa) Stamp Club (71)

Collector's Club of Denver (73)

Chicago (Ill.) Philatelic Society (75)

Central Nebraska Stamp Club (76), Grand Island, Neb.

Mankato Area (Minn.) Stamp Club (77)

Rochester (Minn.) Stamp Club (82)

Janesville (Wis.) Stamp Club (83)

Minnehaha Stamp Club (85), Minneapolis, Minn.

Lincoln (Neb.) Stamp Club (86)

Maplewood (Minn.) Stamp Club (87)

North Central Iowa Philatelic Society (88), Mason City, Iowa

Buffalo Bill Stamp Club (89), North Platte, Neb.

3M Stamp Club (90), St. Paul, Minn.

Collectors Club of Kansas City, Mo. (91)

Rockford (Ill.) Stamp Club (92)

Timpanagoes Philatelic Society (93), Orem, Utah

Cushing (Okla.) Stamp Club (96)

Mobile Philatelic Society (97)

Iowa Lakes Stamp Club (98)

Iowa Postal History Society (99)

## TMPS Officers

President: Herbert Roeser

First vice president: Arthur J. Rogers

Second vice president: Dorothy Green

Third vice president: Kenneth Trettin

Secretary: Gladys Henslin

Treasurer: Robert Lambert

Board of directors: Margaret Harrison, Robert Loeck, Robert Barkhurst, Steven Bahnsen, Jack Jenkins

Immediate past president: Ray Hamernick

## TMPS Awards

In 1952, the TMPS board of directors, following the tradition of the Philatelic Congress of Great Britain founded in 1909 and the American Philatelic Congress founded in Philadelphia in 1935, inaugurated a similar program for the TMPS.

Any TMPS member is eligible to submit his or her manuscript. The TMPS Philatelic Congress chairman, assisted by a committee of two, determines the three best papers and advises the winners that they will compete in an oral presentation at the TMPS convention. Three judges determine the final winner. Presentation of the award is made at the annual banquet during the convention.

A silver TMPS medallion is awarded the winner. In addition, his or her name is engraved on the traveling John B. Brain Memorial plaque, which remains in the winner's possession until the succeeding year's winner is announced.

Bronze medallions are awarded by the society to the other two participants.

The John B. Brain Memorial plaque was presented to the TMPS by Mrs. Brain as a memorial to her husband, who was a charter member of the society and served as its second president. He was also one of the three incorporators. He was an outstanding student of U.S. stamps, a member of many philatelic organizations and prominent in civic work in his home city of Omaha, Neb.

# Philatelic Writers' Organizations

Philatelic writers' organizations are established to promote journalism in the field of philately as well as to give recognition to worthy philatelic writers.

## American Philatelic Society
## Writers Unit No. 30

Sixteen interested, nationally known philatelic writers held a breakfast meeting on Sept. 24, 1967, at the Hotel Robert Treat, during the 81st annual convention of the American Philatelic Society at Newark, N.J. At this meeting, the Writers Unit was formed.

An immediate application was made to the American Philatelic Society for "unit" status, which was obtained, and Unit No. 30 was born.

It was the consensus of those present that a national organization be formed that would bring this nation's philatelic writers into one group for the mutual exchange of knowledge, as well as mutual assistance at a very low annual cost.

By unanimous approval of those present, the following were named as the new organization's officers:

Chairman (later changed to president), David Lidman;

Vice chairman (vice president), James M. Chemi;

Secretary-treasurer, C.C. Cratsenberg.

The new officers were also to act as an executive committee to formulate a constitution and bylaws, and establish a meeting, or seminar, on philatelic writing at all future APS spring meetings and annual conventions.

At the Writers Unit meeting during the 1968 APS spring meeting, positive steps were taken to establish a National Philatelic Literature Exhibition as part of the APS annual convention. The first National Literature Exhibition was held in Rochester, N.Y., in September 1968.

A committee composed of Daniel Vooys, James Chemi and George T. Turner agreed to set up the rules of the classification and the entry of exhibits. The committee's work was completed in time to allow 75 entries, which was far beyond the expectation of all concerned.

Since the first literature exhibition, this section of the convention has continually grown in both the number of entries and the quality of the material entered. It is now fully recognized as the National Philatelic Literature Exhibition of the United States.

Entry requirements and classifications have been clarified each year to the satisfaction of the majority of interested exhibitors. The scope of the exhibition has been broadened to allow the entry of exhibits of Canadian and Mexican members, but membership in the Writers Unit, while encouraged, is not a requirement for entry.

David Lidman was the unit's first president, followed by George M. Martin and James M. Chemi. Upon Chemi's death in 1976, vice president John E. Foxworth Jr. became president and served as such until his election as APS president in 1977. William Bauer was elected president to succeed Foxworth.

Previous vice presidents of the unit have been James Chemi, George Martin, John Foxworth, Barbara W. de Violini, and Charles O. Emery. C.C. Cratsenberg was the sole occupant of the office of secretary-treasurer from the inception of the unit until 1979 when the office was separated into its two components. The position of secretary was filled by Barbara W. de Violini and that of treasurer by Ray Crow.

Current officers are Charles J. Peterson, president; Joe F. Frye, vice president; Mary Ann Owens, secretary; and George Griffenhagen, treasurer.

During 1970, the three unit officers found that added, experienced help was required to properly carry out the increasing number of new projects and expand those already introduced. The membership, by individual ballots, overwhelmingly approved the addition of an advisory council with a minimum of four members, up to a maximum of nine, with the immediate past president serving as the council chairman. The work of the council is most evident in the progress of many of the new unit programs and services.

The present council members are George Martin, John Foxworth Jr., C.C. Cratsenberg, Richard Sine, John Willard, William H. Bauer, Lester E. Winick and Kenneth A. Wood.

A new feature of the Writers Unit agenda was a Writer's Breakfast introduced at Rochester. The breakfast was initiated to serve as an enjoyable session for making friends and relaxing.

In 1970, at Honolulu, Hawaii, as a spur-of-the-moment gag award, a hastily made plaque was made from the end of a corrugated packing box for canned pineapple juice. Properly inscribed with a felt tip pen, it became the first of the now-traditional Broken Pen Awards, given each year at the fall APS convention Writer's Breakfast.

Edward L. Willard, then APS president, was the first recipient. Until his death, his Broken Pen Award was hung in a prominent place in his office, treasured as a tongue-in-cheek award that represented a special honor. Each recipient since the original presentation receives a much more attractive plaque. Subsequent winners of the Broken Pen Award, by year and site of the award, have been:

1971 — Herman Herst Jr., San Antonio, Tex.

1972 — C.C. Cratsenberg, New Haven, Conn.

1973 — C.W. Christian, Los Angeles, Calif.

1974 — Dr. Charles W. Wunsch, Chicago, Ill.

1975 — William T. Amos, Columbus, Ohio

1976 — Maryette B. Lane, Memphis, Tenn.

1977 — Fred S. Wolfe, San Francisco, Calif.

1978 — Barbara W. de Violini, Indianapolis, Ind.

1979 — Irwin Weinberg, Boston, Mass.

1980 — Ernest Cohn, Spokane, Wash.

To keep the members informed of Writers Unit events, news of members' articles and worthy tips concerning philatelic writing, James Chemi edited the first issue of the Unit's "News Bulletin," containing only four pages.

Following the first issue, Klass van Ingen was appointed editor and David C. Stump publisher. After 18 months, Stump became both editor and publisher until 1973, when Joe F. Frye became editor-publisher. The "News Bulletin" is now edited by Barbara R. Mueller.

Steps were taken to enlarge the bulletin and produce it from photoengraved plates by offset printing. From the first four-page production, the "News Bulletin" has reached a high of 40 pages, and excellent photographic reproduction has come to be expected.

The Writers Unit is proud of the fact that it was the early donor of a $1,000 pledge for the new American Philatelic Research Library building at State College, Pa., and continues to support this project.

In 1974, the National Philatelic Writers Hall of Fame was established. A large plaque was obtained with 100 individual nameplates, and the initial list of honorees was unveiled at the Writer's Breakfast in Chicago. Each honoree's name, principal writing field, and the year of selection for the Hall of Fame is engraved on the individual plates. Deceased honorees are further noted by dates of birth and death.

The plaque is hung permanently in the new American Philatelic Building Central Office in State College, Pa. It is kept up to date yearly with the addition of new honorees, announced at the APS spring meeting Writer's Breakfast. A list of honorees follows, divided by date named to the Hall of Fame. Deceased members are noted by birth and death dates.

### 1974, Chicago, Ill.

Stanley Ashbrook (1882-1958)

Winthrop S. Boggs (1902-1973)

Lester G. Brookman (1903-1971)

Richard McP. Cabeen (1887-1969)

Dr. Caroll Chase (1872-1960)

August A. Dietz Sr. (1862-1963)

Edith M. Faulstich (1906-1972)

Max G. Johl (1901-1957)

George W. Linn (1884-1966)

John N. Luff (1869-1938)

Delf Norona (1895-1974)

Elliot Perry (1884-1972)

John W. Scott (1845-1919)

Al Van Dahl (1884-1954)

Prescot H. Thorp (1897-1981)

William W. Wylie (1905-1982)

Harry L. Lindquist (1884-1978)

James B. Hatcher

Herman Herst Jr.

George F. Stilpen

### 1975, Columbus, Ohio

Henry M. Goodkind (1904-1970)

Ralph A. Kimble (1893-1973)

Harry Weiss (1888-1966)

Daniel W. Vooys (1914-1978)

Belmont Faries

Dr. Robert M. Spaulding Jr.

### 1976, Philadelphia, Pa.

Ralph A. Barry (1883-1939)

Kent B. Stiles (1887-1961)

Stephen G. Rich (1890-1958)

James M. Chemi (1912-1976)

Everett C. Erle

Douglas A. Patrick

Alex ter Braake

**1977, New Orleans, La.**

Thomas D. Perry (1877-1958)

Bertram W. Poole (1880-1957)

Willard O. Wylie (1862-1944)

Ernest A. Kehr

Fred Jarrett

Mortimer Neinken

**1978, Toronto, Canada**

Dr. L. Seale Holmes (1884-1961)

William R. Stewart (1898-1970)

Lyons F. Livingston (1922-1972)

Edith R. Doane

Barbara R. Mueller

Dr. Felix D. Bertalanffy

**1979, Denver, Colo.**

Franklin R. Bruns Jr. (1912-1979)

Henry W. Holcombe (? - 1973)

Melvin H. Schoberlin (1912-1977)

Lucius Jackson (1915-1978)

George W. Brett

Earl P.L. Apfelbaum

Charles E. Foster

**1980, London, England**

George Turner (1906-1979)

Frederick J. Melville (1882-1940)

Maurice Williams (1905-1976)

Robson Lowe

L. Norman Williams

**1981, State College, Pa.**

Lowell J. Ragatz (1898-1962)

David Lidman

**1982, Tucson, Ariz.**

Edwin Mueller (1898-1962)

Dr. William Reiner-Deutsch (1898-1981)

Maryette B. Lane

From its start with 16 members in 1967, the Writers Unit has grown to more than 800 members, most of whom reside in the United States, Canada and Mexico, although many are from Western Europe, South and Central America, Africa, Asia and the Pacific Islands.

The annual membership dues are $5 for members in the United States, $7.50 for those in Canada and Mexico, and $12 for all others. An applicant must be an author, editor, writer or columnist, but anyone interested in philatelic writing will be accepted and assisted. However, each unit member must be a member in good standing of the American Philatelic Society.

Further information and an application may be obtained from Mary Ann Owens, Box 1164, Brooklyn, N.Y. 11202.

## Association Internationale des Journalistes Philateliques

Association Internationale des Journalistes Philateliques (AIJP) was established in 1962 in Prague, Czechoslovakia, for the advancement of philatelic journalism.

The association conducts annual congresses and publishes a bulletin at intervals.

President of the AIJP is Dr. Anton van der Flier of The Netherlands; vice president (east), Jan Witkowski of Poland; vice president (west), Dr. Werner Bohne of the United States; secretary general, Fritz E. Baeker of West Germany; treasurer, Jean Frising of Luxembourg; and press secretary, Adolf Hujer of Czechoslovakia.

Recognized philatelic writers should contact Dr. Werner Bohne, Box 1005, Longwood, Fla. 32750.

## Philatelic Press Club, Inc.

The Philatelic Press Club, Inc., was organized in 1964 as a guild dedicated to raising the standards of professional philatelic writing and to cooperate with postal administration members of the Universal Postal Union in exercising integrity in policies related to or affecting philately.

By 1975, so many distinguished overseas writers had been invited and admitted that "International" was added to the corporate name.

Membership is by invitation only and is offered to recognized writers who contribute regular columns to stamp periodicals, metropolitan newspapers and other mass media including radio and television.

Eight foreign philatelic press federations are affiliated as associates. The guild publishes and distributes a monthly "Report to Members," which relays worldwide news information and leads received from correspondents on the six continents.

Annual meetings are held in New York in conjunction with the ASDA National Show, but when high-ranking postal officials arrive in the United States the IPPC arranges for exclusive press conference in New York or other cities at mutually convenient times.

For several years, the IPPC has presented annual awards to those postal administrations which provide members with "outstanding news services."

Further membership information is available from Ernest A. Kehr, Box 1, Richmond Hill, N.Y. 11419.

## Society of Philaticians

The Society of Philaticians is an international association of professional and amateur philatelic journalists and publicists. It was organized on Nov. 17, 1972, to advance philatelic journalism, to unite philatelic writers and to gain greater recognition for philatelic literature and the philatelic journalist.

The society promotes philately and the use of philatelic literature and supports any publicity efforts in that respect.

It also seeks additional publicity for stamp collecting in the nonphilatelic press in order to increase interest in this avocation. The society also provides awards for outstanding philatelic writing and publicity.

The society is a national branch of the Society of Philatelic Americans and a member of The Council of Philatelic Organizations.

Membership applicants should be engaged in philatelic writing or philatelic publicity work. Benefits of membership include a membership certificate, subscription to "The Philatelic Journalist," with free advertising privileges of philatelic literature, a philatelic handbook published by the society, as well as inclusion in a membership list which is distributed to worldwide postal administrations, philatelic publications, philatelic exhibitions and the philatelic trade for their press release lists.

The society has prominent members in the field of philatelic journalism throughout the U.S. and Canada, as well as 20 foreign countries. Membership information is available from the secretary, Gustav Detjen Jr., 154 Laguna Court, St. Augustine Shores, Fla. 32084.

# Local Stamp Clubs

Following is a listing of stamp clubs that are registered with Linn's Club Center, including meeting day, location and time and current (as of mid-1982) contact person's name and address, presented as a service to those who might be interestsed in visiting a local club if in the vicinity. Linn's urges local groups inadvertently omitted to contact the Club Center.

## ALABAMA

**BIRMINGHAM:** Birmingham Philatelic Society, second and fourth Tuesday, except December, Jewish Community Center, 3960 Montclair Road, 7 p.m. Alan R. Barasch, Box 3403-A, Birmingham, Ala. 35255-0503.

**MOBILE:** Mobile Stamp Club, first Thursday and third Monday, City Recreation Department, 2300 Government St., 7:30 p.m. Terry Loyce, 4 Sarah Drive, Semmes, Ala. 36575.

**MONTGOMERY:** Montgomery Area Stamp Club, second and fourth Thursday, Plaza Post Office, Conference Room 11, 7:30 p.m. Jim Floyd, Box 11217, Montgomery, Ala. 36111.

**TUSCALOOSA:** Bama Stamp and Coin Club, first and third Thursday, University of Alabama Campus, Room 25, 7 p.m. Constance Sulentic, Box 7403, University, Ala. 35486.

## ALASKA

**ANCHORAGE:** Anchorage Philatelic Society, second and fourth Wednesday, Employment and Training Center of Alaska Building, 2330 Nichols, 7:30 p.m. Sheila Erwin, Box 2214, Anchorage, Alaska 95510.

— Ptarmigan Stamp and Coin Society, second and fourth Monday, Third and Eagle, 7 p.m. Marsha Pody, Box 4-1090, Anchorage, Alaska 99509.

**JUNEAU:** Gastineau Philatelic Society, first and third Thursday, undercroft Episcopal Church, 405 Gold St., 7:30 p.m. Don Garcia, Box 1425, Juneau, Alaska 99802.

## ARIZONA

**CASA GRANDE:** Arizona Federation of Stamp Clubs, third Thursday, Sambo's Restaurant, 8 p.m. Sheila E. Giambruno, 6235 W. Clarendon Ave., Phoenix, Ariz. 85033.

**MESA:** Copper State Stamp Club (aka Mesa Stamp Club), every other Monday, Saint Mark's Episcopal Church, 322 N. Horne, 7 p.m. Mary E. Thompson, 519 E. Wesleyan Drive, Tempe, Ariz. 85282.

**PHOENIX:** Arizona Precancel Club, fourth Monday, except December, Yucca Branch Library, 5648 N. 15th Ave., 7 p.m. Alvin Gerstenberger, Box 839, Glendale, Ariz. 85302.

— Germany Philatelic Society, Kachina Chapter 25, second Tuesday, Recreation Building, 7200 N. 43rd Ave., 7 p.m. L.E. Thumann, Box 1601, Sun City, Ariz. 85372.

— Phoenix Philatelic Association, second Monday and fourth Wednesday, Woman's Club of Phoenix, 3rd Avenue and Earill, 7 p.m. No meetings in November and December. Mary Anne Lewis, 3224 E. Hazelwood, Phoenix, Ariz. 85018.

**SUN CITY:** Sun City Stamp Club, first Monday and second Tuesday, Marinette Recreation Center, 7:30 p.m. Elizabeth Reynolds, 12411 Amethyst Court, Sun City, Ariz. 85351.

### MISCELLANEOUS

Universal Ship Cancellation Society, USS Arizona Chapter 78, third Saturday, members' homes, 2 p.m. Alex L. Lutgendorf, 5260 W. Sweetwater Drive, Tucson, Ariz. 85705.

# ARKANSAS

**JONESBORO:** Northeast Arkansas Stamp Collectors Society, second Tuesday, Jonesboro-Craighead Public Library, 7 p.m. Udell Smith, Box 1456, Jonesboro, Ark. 72401.

**LITTLE ROCK:** Pinnacle Stamp Club, second Thursday, Bonanza Sirloin Pit, 10901 Rodney Parham Road, 7 p.m. Nita Carter, 5 Leswood Circle, Little Rock, Ark. 72205.

**MOUNTAIN HOME:** Mountain Home Area Stamp Club, second Saturday, Chamber of Commerce Building, 1 p.m. Everett Wheeler, Box 203, Mountain Home, Ark. 72653.

**NORTH LITTLE ROCK:** Arkansas Philatelic Association, first Tuesday, Shoney's Restaurant, 7:30 p.m. Earlene Butterworth, 2115 W. Long 17th, North Little Rock, Ark. 72114.

**ROGERS:** Razorback Stamp Club, second and fourth Thursday, Peace Lutheran Church, 805 W. Olrich St., 7 p.m. Christine V. Kumbera, 1003 Longview Drive, No. 37, Rogers, Ark. 72756.

# CALIFORNIA

**ARCADIA:** San Gabriel Valley Stamp Club, second and fourth Tuesday, 7 p.m. Arcadia County Park, Senior Citizen's Building, 405 S. Santa Anita Ave., Arcadia, Calif. 91006.

**ATASCADERO:** Philatelic Society of Atascadero, every Tuesday, Atascadero State Hospital, 7 p.m. C. Sheridan, Drawer A, Atascadero, Calif. 93422.

**BERKELEY:** East Bay Collectors Club, Inc., every Wednesday, 2288 Fulton, 8 p.m. Tom Brougham, Box 19053, Oakland, Calif. 94619.

**BEVERLY HILLS:** Society of Israel Philatelists, Los Angeles Chapter, fourth Sunday, Union Federal Savings and Loan Association, 8485 Wilshire Blvd., 1 p.m. Fred Gerson, 4207 Parva Ave., Los Angeles, Calif. 90027.

**BREA:** Universal Ship Cancellation Society, USS California Chapter 51, third Sunday, Republic Federal Savings and Loan, 2400 E. 17th St., 2 p.m. Alfred J. Moses, Box 752, Brea, Calif. 92621.

**CAMARILLO:** Camarillo Stamp Club, second Thursday, Santa Barbara Savings and Loan, 425 Arneill Road; fourth Thursday, Mercury Savings, 1656 Arneill Road, 7:30 p.m. Ruth G. Cox, 1708 Burnley St., Camarillo, Calif. 93010.

**CARMEL:** Monterey Peninsula Stamp Club, first and third Monday, Carmel High School Library, Ocean and Highway 1, 7:30 p.m. Jack Frimodig, 29 Country Club Gate, Pacific Grove, Calif. 93950.

**CATHEDRAL CITY:** Palm Springs Philatelic Society, first and third Wednesday, Pomona First Federal Savings and Loan, 39-950 Date Palm Drive, 7 p.m. Charles C. Kirshbaum, 845 Calle De Flora Vista, Palm Springs, Calif. 92262.

**CLOVIS:** Fresno Philatelic Society, first Sunday 2 p.m.; third Thursday 7 p.m. Fresno Production Center, 5755 E. Fountain Way. Jay Avila, 4769 N. Polk, Fresno, Calif. 93711.

**CULVER CITY:** Nippon Philatelic Society, fourth Sunday, except December, Culver City Library, 4975 Overland Ave., 2 p.m. Sune Johnson, 1446 Mildino Drive, Glendale, Calif. 91208.

**EL CAJON:** German-American Stamp Club, first and third Sunday, German American Club, 1017 S. Mollison, 11 a.m. R.E. Prall, Box 236, Spring Valley, Calif. 92077.

**EL CERRITO:** San Pablo Pines Stamp Club, first and third Monday, Kidd Manor, 100 Austin Court, San Pablo; second and fourth Monday, El Cerrito Co-op, 1751 Eastshore Blvd., 8 p.m. Leon G. Rahe, 969 Marlesta Road, Pinole, Calif. 94564.

**ENCINO:** Greater Valley Philatelic Society, first Friday and third Thursday, Union Federal Savings and Loan Association, 15962 Ventura Blvd., 7:30 p.m. Edward J. Damits, Box 8191, Van Nuys, Calif. 91409.

**FULLERTON:** Society of Southern California Philatelists, second Sunday, St. Andrews Church, Chapman Avenue, 2 p.m. Louise Van Ingen, Box 369, Placentia, Calif. 92670.

**HUNTINGTON BEACH:** McDonnell Douglas Philatelic Club, first Tuesday, Mercury Savings and Loan, Edinger and Beach; third Tuesday, Security Federal, Brookhurst and Chapman, Garden Grove, 7:30 p.m. William Messecar, Box 2324, Huntington Beach, Calif. 92647.

**LAGUNA HILLS:** Laguna Hills Stamp Club, second and fourth Tuesday, Clubhouse 3, Dining Room 2, 1:30 p.m. Peggy Forsander, 2282 D Mariposa W, Laguna Hills, Calif. 92653.

**LA HABRA:** La Mirada Stamp Club, second and fourth Tuesday, Western Savings and Loan, 10 Fashion Square, 7:30 p.m. George Leete, Box 1891, La Mirada, Calif. 90637.

— Orange County Philatelic Society, first and third Friday, Mercury Savings Building, 1001 E. Imperial Highway, 7 p.m. Gail E. Dolbee, Box 26, La Habra, Calif. 90631.

**LA MESA:** La Mesa Philatelic Society, second and fourth Thursday, Porter Hall, University Avenue and Memorial Drive, 8 p.m. Larry Elliott, 10670 Snyder Road, La Mesa, Calif. 92041.

**LARKSPUR:** Tamalpais Stamp Club, second and fourth Friday, except last Friday in December, Bank of Marin, 1177 Magnolia Ave., 8 p.m. Gail M. Trimble, 731 Montecillo Road, San Rafael, Calif. 94903.

**LONG BEACH:** Long Beach Stamp Club, first and third Tuesday, Millikan High School Cafeteria, 2800 Snowden Ave., 7:30 p.m. S.T. Conrad, Box 15234, Long Beach, Calif. 90815.

**LOS ANGELES:** Mexico-Elmhurst Philatelic Society International, Southern California Chapter, fourth Wednesday, California Federal Savings and Loan, 1900 Sunset Blvd. Phillips B. Freer, Box 43433, Los Angeles, Calif. 90043.

— Scandinavian Collectors Club, Southern California Chapter 17, first Wednesday, Department of Water and Power General Office Building, Conference Room 1273, 111 N. Hope St., 7 p.m. H.J. Schlueter, Box 75281, Los Angeles, Calif. 90075.

**MANTECA:** San Joaquin Philatelic Society, first Thursday, First Federal Savings and Loan Association, 150 W. Yosemite Ave., 7:30 p.m. R.N. Phillips, 834 Nevada St., Manteca, Calif. 95336.

**MODESTO:** Stanislaus Stamp Club, second Tuesday, Homewood Village Mobile Home Park, 2000 Mable Ave., 7:30 p.m. Helen M. Duroy, Box 2614, Modesto, Calif. 95351.

**MOFFETT FIELD:** ARC Stamp Club, first Wednesday, 11:30 a.m.; third Wednesday 7:30 p.m., NASA Ames Research Center. Joan Nelson, NASA Ames Research Center 241-15, Moffett Field, Calif. 94035.

**OAKLAND:** Japanese American Society for Philately, third Sunday, Sumitomo Bank Building, 400 20th St., 1:30 p.m. Margaret B. Munda, 100 Bay Place, Apt. 1103, Oakland, Calif. 94610.

— Scandinavian Collector's Club, Golden Gate Chapter 21, second Thursday, Federal Savings and Loan, 2200 MacArthur Blvd. Dennis E. Dietz, Box 433, Benicia, Calif. 94510.

— Society of Israel Philatelists, NorCal Chapter, fourth Sunday, Beth Jacob Congregation, 3778 Park Blvd., 1:30 p.m. Lenore Dickstein, 1027 Clarendon Crescent, Oakland, Calif. 94610.

**PASADENA:** Jet Propulsion Lab Stamp Club, second Wednesday at noon; fourth Tuesday at 4:30 p.m., Jet Propulsion Lab, 4800 Oak Grove Drive. T.C. Lear, 435 S. El Molino Ave., Pasadena, Calif. 91101.

**PETALUMA:** Petaluma Philatelic Society, first and third Saturday, Bank of Marin, Conference Room, Washington Square, 7:30 p.m. Paul H. Stowring, 725 Pepper Road, Petaluma, Calif. 94952.

**POWAY:** Poway Stamp Club, second and fourth Wednesday, Meadowbrook School Auditorium, 7:30 p.m. Ron Kunavich, Box 673, Poway, Calif. 92064.

**REDONDO BEACH:** Torrance Stamp Club, first and third Monday, Progressive Savings, Community Room, 1670 S. Pacific Coast Highway, 7 p.m. Donald Greaton, 15808 Dalton Ave., Gardena, Calif. 90247.

— TRW Stamp Club, second and fourth Tuesday, TRW Building, noon. W. Kwok S/1435, 1 Space Park, Redondo Beach, Calif. 90278.

**REDWOOD CITY:** Sequoia Stamp Club, second and fourth Tuesday, Community Activities Building, 1400 Roosevelt Ave., 8:15 p.m. Barbara LeBlanc, 997 Alameda, Redwood City, Calif. 94061.

**SACRAMENTO:** Sacramento Philatelic Society, every Wednesday except the fifth, 36th and J streets, 7 p.m. Fran Roberts, Box 13284, Sacramento, Calif. 95813.

— Scouts On Stamps Society International, Pony Express Chapter 25, every Monday, Boy Scout Service Center, Fair Oaks and El Camino, 7 p.m. Betty Bertolli, 2930 23rd St., Sacramento, Calif. 95818.

**SALINAS:** Monterey County Stamp Club, fourth Tuesday, Northern Savings and Loan, 425 S. Main, 7:30 p.m. Jim Dirksen, 1253-31 Los Olivos Drive, Salinas, Calif. 93901.

**SAN FRANCISCO:** California Collectors Club, every Friday, California Hall, 625 Polk St., 7 p.m. Yvonne C. Jarkowski, 2400 17th Ave. No. 4, San Francisco, Calif. 94116.

— Golden Gate Postcard Club, fourth Sunday, Fort Mason Building C, Room 215, 1:30 p.m. Karl Heuer, 3315 Sweet Drive, Lafayette, Calif. 94549.

**SAN JOSE:** San Jose Stamp Club, first Thursday and third Monday, American Legion Post, 1504 Minnesota Ave., 7:30 p.m. Peggy Nash, Box 21429, San Jose, Calif. 95151.

**SAN LEANDRO:** Philatelic Society of San Leandro, Inc., third Tuesday, San Leandro City Library, Harrison Street and Estudillo Boulevard, 8 p.m. Bill Hattwick, 17249 Via Corona, San Lorenzo, Calif. 94580.

**SANTA BARBARA:** Santa Barbara Stamp Club, first and third Tuesday, Community Room, 1035 State St., 7:30 p.m. Ogden Monks, 3929 Harrold Ave., Santa Barbara, Calif. 93110.

**SANTA MARIA:** Central Coast Stamp Club, second and fourth Thursday, Recreation Building, Simas Park, 520 S. McClellend, 7:30 p.m. Albert C. Hardy Jr., Box 814, Lompoc, Calif. 93438.

**SANTA ROSA:** Sonoma County Philatelic Society, second and fourth Thursday, Bank of Sonoma, Guerneville and Fulton roads, 8 p.m. Arthur A. Reynor Sr., Box 81, Guernewood Park, Calif. 95446.

**SEAL BEACH:** Leisure World Stamp Club, first and third Thursday, Clubhouse 3, 1:30 p.m. No meetings in July and August. Ruth E. Stanick, 13240 Fairfield Lane, No. 172-F, Seal Beach, Calif. 90740.

**SONORA:** Tuolumne County Stamp Club, first and third Wednesday, El Capitan Community Room, 172 W. Stockton Road, 7 p.m. Valerie Anderson, Box 42, Columbia, Calif. 95310.

**SUN CITY:** Sun City Stamp Club, second and fourth Tuesday, Coast Federal Savings, Sun City Boulevard, 1:45 p.m. George Halstenson, 26281 McCall Blvd., Sun City, Calif. 92381.

**SUNNYVALE:** LERA Stamp Club, every Monday, Sunnyvale Public Library, Philatelic Section, 665 W. Olive Ave., 7 p.m. N. Papson, 104 Amber Oak Court, Los Gatos, Calif. 95030.

**THOUSAND OAKS:** Conejo Valley Philatelic Society, second and fourth Monday, Conejo Community Center, Dover and Hendricks avenues, 7:30 p.m. Willard Peck, 31 Isabel, Camarillo, Calif. 93010.

**VALLEJO:** Universal Ship Cancellation Society, USS Saginaw Chapter 58, second Sunday, Vallejo Naval Museum, 734 Marin St., 1:30 p.m. R. Rawlins, Box 4634, Vallejo, Calif. 94590.

— Vallejo Stamp Club, first and third Tuesday, Vallejo Community Center, 225 Amador, 8 p.m. Mrs. Kayde England, 155 Kit Carson Way, Vallejo, Calif. 94589.

**VENTURA:** Ventura County Philatelic Society, first and third Monday, E.P. Foster Library, 651 E. Main St., 7:30 p.m. Robert W. Thompson, Box 42148 Point Mugu, Calif. 93042.

**WALNUT CREEK:** Diablo Valley Stamp Club, second and fourth Thursday, Leisure Services Building, Multi-Purpose Room, 1650 N. Broadway, 7:30 p.m. Second Thursday in November and December. Cyril M. Kimpton, 825 Oak Grove Road, No. 17, Concord, Calif. 94518.

**YUBA CITY:** Yuba Sutter Philatelic Society, fourth Monday, Sutter County Library, Clark Avenue and Forbes, 7 p.m. Tony Pollizzi, 916 E. 21st St., Marysville, Calif. 95901.

## MISCELLANEOUS

American Society of Polar Philatelists, Los Angeles Chapter 7, various places. Robert de Violini, Box 5025, Oxnard, Calif. 93031.

Beckman Employees Philatelic Society, third Monday, various homes, 7:30 p.m. Klaas van Ingen, Box 369, Placentia, Calif. 92670.

China Stamp Society, Chiu Chin Shan Chapter, first Sunday, members' homes, 2:30 p.m. Ernest N. Hirschfeld, Box 248, Mill Valley, Calif. 94942.

FAVE Collectors, members' homes. S.W. Fields, Box 82863, San Diego, Calif. 92138.

San Diego Philatelic "25," third Wednesday, various homes, 7:30 p.m. No meetings July and August. Lt. Col. R.A. Kennedy, 9255 Magnolia Ave., Santee, Calif. 92071.

Southern California Precancel Club, third Saturday, noon. Charles Lewis, Box 41, Banning, Calif. 92220.

United States Philatelic Classics Society, Southern California Chapter, various shows, 1 p.m. Louise Van Ingen, Box 369, Placentia, Calif. 92670.

## COLORADO

**AURORA:** Aurora Stamp Club, Inc., first Wednesday and third Monday, Aurora Public School, 875 Peoria St., 7:30 p.m. Grover C. Bock, 11607 E. Kentucky Ave., Aurora, Colo. 80012.

**CANON CITY:** Canon City Stamp Club, first and third Tuesday, American Federal Savings Building, 630 Main St., 7:30 p.m. John H. Simonson Jr., Box 211, Canon City, Colo. 81212-0211.

**ENGLEWOOD:** Cherrelyn Stamp Club, second Monday, Grace Lutheran Church, 4750 S. Clarkson St., 7:30 p.m. Gideon H. Diamon, Box 1621, Englewood, Colo. 80150.

**GRAND JUNCTION:** Stamp Club of Grand Junction, second Wednesday, Mesa County Public Library, 530 Grand Ave., 7 p.m. Charles Teed, 510 W. Mesa Ave., Grand Junction, Colo. 81501.

## CONNECTICUT

**BRANFORD:** Branford Philatelic Society, first and third Monday, Branford Community House, 7:30 p.m. Fred E. Roganson, Box 2304, Short Beach, Conn. 06405.

**BROOKFIELD:** Brookfield Philatelic Society, third Tuesday, Brookfield Public Library, Route 25, 7:30 p.m. Victor Lambert, Box 213, Brookfield, Conn. 06804.

— Brookfield Philatelic Society Junior Club, second Saturday, Brookfield Public Library, Route 25, 2 p.m. Victor Lambert, Box 213, Brookfield, Conn. 06804.

**CHESHIRE:** Cheshire Philatelic Society, first and third Friday, Connecticut Savings Bank, 8 p.m. No meetings in July and August. William F. Neff Jr., M.D., 93 Main St., Cheshire, Conn. 06410.

**DARIEN:** Ye Olde King's Highway Stamp Club, second and fourth Wednesday, First Presbyterian Church, corner Post Road and Noroton Avenue, 8 p.m. James S. Dugan, Box 1101, Darien, Conn. 06820.

**FAIRFIELD:** Fairfield Philatelic Society, second Sunday, American Legion Hall, Reef Road, 2 p.m. Gene C. Trinks, Box 25, Fairfield, Conn. 06430.

**GREENWICH:** Greenwich Stamp Club, second Thursday, Collyer House, Lafayette Place, 8 p.m. Walter I. Teitz, 68 Halsey Drive, Old Greenwich, Conn. 06870.

**MANCHESTER:** Manchester Philatelic Society, second and fourth Tuesday, Mott's Community Hall, 387 Middle Turnpike E, 6:30 p.m. Richard Steele, Box 448, Manchester, Conn. 06040.

**MIDDLETOWN:** Middletown Stamp Club, first and third Tuesday, Main Street Firehouse, Main Street, 7:30 p.m. Walter C. Bielefield, 80 Newtown St., Middletown, Conn. 06457.

**NEW BRITAIN:** Hardware City Stamp Club, first and third Tuesday, New Britain Memorial Hospital, 2150 Corbin Ave., 7:30 p.m. Anthony Simcik, Box 13, New Britain, Conn. 06050.

**NORWALK:** Norwalk Stamp Club, first and third Monday, Nathan Hale School, Strawberry Hill Road, 7:30 p.m. Achilles Cerbini, 38 Richmond Hill Road, South Norwalk, Conn. 06854.

**ORANGE:** Society of Israel Philatelists, New Haven Chapter, first Thursday, Orange Synagogue Center, Old Grassy Hill Road, 8 p.m. Howard Novitch, 1014 Rainbow Trail, Orange, Conn. 06477.

**STRATFORD:** Nutmeg Stamp Club, second and fourth Wednesday, Baldwin Center, 8 p.m. Mary B. Hartnett, 501 Bridgeview Place, Stratford, Conn. 06497.

**UNIONVILLE:** Farmington Valley Stamp Club, second and fourth Monday, Farmington High School, 8 p.m. No meetings in summer and December. W.R. Peterson, 23 Saddle Ridge Drive, West Hartford, Conn. 06117.

**WATERBURY:** Waterbury Stamp Club, first and third Monday, Waterbury YWCA, 85 Prospect St., 7:30 p.m. No meetings in July and August. Vic Russ, Box 1998, Waterbury, Conn. 06721.

**WATERFORD:** Thames Stamp Club, second and fourth Wednesday, Clark Lane Junior High School, Clark Lane, 7:30 p.m. George G. Ryan, Box 244, Waterford, Conn. 06385.

## MISCELLANEOUS

Connecticut Philatelic Society, meets when requested. David A. Kent, Box 13, New Britain, Conn. 06050-0013.

Dynamic Philatelic Society, special meetings as needed. John F. Tierney, Box 849, Groton, Conn. 06340.

Universal Ship Cancellation Society, USS Nathan Hale Chapter 68, first Sunday, members' homes, 2 p.m. David A. Kent, Box 13, New Britain, Conn. 06050-0013.

## DELAWARE

**CAMDEN:** Dover Stamp Club, fourth Tuesday, Caesar Rodney Junior High School, 7 p.m. No meetings in July and August. Carl Hill, Route 2, Box 38, Harrington, Del. 19952.

**MILFORD:** Milford Stamp and Coin Club, second Wednesday, Milford Carlisle Fair Hall, North West Front Street, Florence Gillespie, 2 Nailor St., Milford, Del. 19963.

**WILMINGTON:** DuPont Stamp Club, first Wednesday, DuPont Country Club, except May and June, 8 p.m. No meetings in July and August. Arthur E. Church Jr., 103 Ridgeland Road, Wilmington, Del. 19803.

— Wilmington Stamp Club, second Wednesday, Salesianum High School Library, 8 p.m. No meetings in July and August. Walton T. Connelly, TRL Building, Chestnut Run, Wilmington, Del. 19898.

## DISTRICT OF COLUMBIA

— Capitol View Stamp Club, every Tuesday, except holidays, VOA Conference Room, 330 Independence Ave. SW, 12:30 p.m. Irving Lind, 6722 Bostwick Drive, Springfield, Va. 22151.

— Collector's Club of Washington, D.C., first and third Wednesday, Odd Fellow's Building, 419 7th St. NW, 7:30 p.m. Dr. John N. Hoffman, 2501 Q St. NW, Washington, D.C. 20007.

— Mr. Beasley Stamp Club of Chevy Chase, first Thursday, Blessed Sacrament Church Library, Western Avenue and Quesada Street NW, 7:30 p.m. David S. Orem, 7 Leland Court, Chevy Chase, Md. 20815.

## MISCELLANEOUS

Samuel Gompers Stamp Club, irregular, 815 16th St. NW, Washington, D.C. Edwin M. Schmidt, Box 1233, Springfield, Va. 22151.

Germany Philatelic Society, Chapter 21, second Sunday, members' homes, 1:30 p.m. Robert Dunn, 9413 Ferry Land Court, Alexandria, Va. 22304.

International Society For Japanese Philately, Washington, D.C., Chapter, first Tuesday, to be announced, 7:30 p.m. Lee R. Wilson, 4216 Jenifer St. NW, Washington, D.C. 20015.

Philippine Study Group of Washington, varies meetings once monthly. Dan Peterson, 7408 Alaska Ave. NW, Washington, D.C. 20012.

## FLORIDA

**BOYNTON BEACH:** Tropical Post Card Club, first Sunday, Royal Palm Clubhouse, N.E. 22nd Avenue and North Federal Highway, noon. Thomas Diddle, 802 North Road, Boynton Beach, Fla. 33435.

**BRADENTON:** Manatee Stamp Club, second Tuesday, Central Library, 1301 Barcarrota Blvd., 7 p.m. Ruth Bauder, 3419 Dunbar Drive, Sarasota, Fla. 33582.

**CAPE CORAL:** Cape Coral Stamp Club, second Wednesday, 4732 Del Prado Blvd., 7:30 p.m. Wilma Marik, Box 42, Cape Coral, Fla. 33904.

**CLEARWATER:** Clearwater Stamp Club, first and third Monday, Bank of Clearwater, 600 Cleveland St., 8 p.m. J. Edward Evans, Box 5442, Clearwater, Fla. 33518.

**DEERFIELD BEACH:** Century Village East Stamp and Coin Club, every Thursday, clubhouse, 11 p.m. Harrison Ressler, 2028 Oakridge Drive, Deerfield Beach, Fla. 33441.

**DELRAY BEACH:** Delray Beach Stamp Club, first and third Wednesday, Atlantic High School, 2501 Seacrest Blvd., 7 p.m. Max E. Zhiss, 241F Capri Park, Delray Beach, Fla. 33445.

**EUSTIS:** Mount Dora Stamp Club, third Friday, First Federal Savings and Loan, 2 p.m. Herbert Miller, 1909 Sunset Road, Mount Dora, Fla. 32757.

**FORT LAUDERDALE:** Fort Lauderdale Stamp Club Inc., first and third Wednesday, Broward County Courthouse, 201 S.E. 6th St. and 3rd Avenue, 7:30 p.m. Adolph Lell, 4541 N.W. 23rd St., Fort Lauderdale, Fla. 33313.

— Germany Philatelic Society, Chapter 7, first and third Saturday, 4800 N.E. 20th Terrace, 10 a.m. Ken Simon, 513 6th Ave. S, Lake Worth, Fla. 33460.

**FORT WALTON:** West Florida Stamp Club, second Sunday, Brooks-Beal Center, 3 p.m. Armand B. Coutu, 316 17th St., Niceville, Fla. 32578.

**HALLANDALE:** Society of Israel Philatelists, South Florida Chapter, second Thursday, Ingall's Park Recreation Room, 735 S.W. First St., 7 p.m. Dan Piver, 8851 Carlyle Ave., Surfside, Fla. 33154.

**HOLLYWOOD:** Hollywood Stamp Club, every Tuesday, 2030 Polk St., 6 p.m. Dr. Francis Haas, Box 2171, Miami Beach, Fla. 33140.

**INVERNESS:** Citrus Area Stamp Association, first and third Thursday, New Adult Education Building, Cardinia Street, 7:15 p.m. Dorothy M. Woodington, Star Route 1, Box 137 H-1, Inverness, Fla. 32650.

**JACKSONVILLE:** Jacksonville Stamp Collector's Club, first and third Tuesday, First Presbyterian Church (basement), 118 E. Monroe St., 7:30 p.m. Peter Dearing, Box 4106, Jacksonville, Fla. 32202.

**LAKELAND:** Ridge Stamp Club, first and third Tuesday, Magnolia Building, Lake Mirror Center, 7 p.m. Rita Pritchett, 3160 Tanager E, Mulberry, Fla. 33860.

**LARGO:** Suncoast Philatelic Society, first and third Tuesday, Largo Community Center, 65 4th St. NW, 7:30 p.m. Rudolph Sup, 14130 Rosemary Lane, Apt. 3217, Largo, Fla. 33540.

**LEESBURG:** Lake County Philatelic Society, fourth Monday, First Federal Savings and Loan, Main and Highway 27, 7:30 p.m. Caroline Robertson, 180 Osceola St., Clermont, Fla. 32711.

**MARGATE:** Margate Stamp Club, second and fourth Wednesday, Teen Pavilion, Park Drive, 7:15 p.m. Nelson D. Wagener, 6940 N.W. 14th Court, Margate, Fla. 33063.

**MELBOURNE:** Missile Stamp Club, first Wednesday, United Church of Christ, U.S. 1 and Strawbridge Avenue, 7:30 p.m. Leonard J. Blanzy, 1264 Wilson St., Melbourne, Fla. 32935.

**MIAMI BEACH:** Miami Beach Stamp Club, second and fourth Monday, Miami Beach Public Library, Collins Avenue and 22nd Street, 5:30 p.m. Stanley T. Brownstein, 1140 8th St., Apt. 4, Miami Beach, Fla. 33139.

**NAPLES:** Collier County Stamp Club, Inc., second and fourth Thursday, Federal Fort Myers Building, 3201 Tamiami Trail N, 7 p.m. Ruth Fenton, Route 2, Box 1666, Naples, Fla. 33940.

**NEW PORT RICHEY:** New Port Richey Stamp Club, first and third Sunday, Clearwater Federal Savings and Loan, 1 p.m. Sylvia Kober, Box 684, New Port Richey, Fla. 33552.

**NORTH FORT MYERS:** Fort Myers Stamp Club, third Friday, First Federal Savings and Loan, 121 Pondella Road, 7:30 p.m. Beulah E. Clark, 81-D Blossom Court, North Fort Myers, Fla. 33903.

**NORTH MIAMI BEACH:** Stamp Collectors Club of North Miami, second, fourth and fifth Monday, Southeastern Medical Center, 1750 N.E. 167th St., 7 p.m. David Collins, 1750 N.E. 168th St., North Miami Beach, Fla. 33162.

**OAKLAND PARK:** Oakland Park Stamp Club, second and fourth Thursday, 3900 N.E. 3rd Ave., 7 p.m. Morris Merkur, 406 N.W. 68th Ave., Apt. 519, Plantation, Fla. 33317.

**OCALA:** Silver Spring Shores Stamp Club, fourth Thursday, Silver Spring Shores Presbyterian Church, Box 7003, 7 p.m. Florence Kleinert, 12 Silver Way, Ocala, Fla. 32672.

**ORANGE CITY:** West Volusia Stamp Club, every Wednesday, 201 W. University, 2 p.m. Robert R. Wilson, 160 Dogwood Ave., Orange City, Fla. 32763.

**ORLANDO:** Central Florida Stamp Club Inc., first and third Thursday, John Young Science Center, 810 E. Rollins St., 8 p.m. Howard Leavitt, 810 E. Rollins St., Orlando, Fla. 32803.

— Scandinavian Collectors Club, Central Florida Chapter 19, first Tuesday on even months (February, April, etc.), office of Dr. O.E. Olsen, 2108 N. Orange Ave., 7:30 p.m. Wade Beery, Box 3781, Orlando, Fla. 32802.

**PENNEY FARMS:** Penney Farms Retirement Community Stamp Club, third Thursday, Diebold Arts and Craft Building, 9:30 a.m. William Sacks, Box 157, Penney Farms, Fla. 32079.

**PENSACOLA:** Ellyson Collectors Club, first Tuesday, Saufley Field, NETPDC Conference Room 1, 11:30 a.m. Frank J. Novak, 4251 Morelia Place, Pensacola, Fla. 32504.

**PORT CHARLOTTE:** Port Charlotte Stamp Club, second Thursday 2 p.m.; fourth Thursday 7 p.m., First Federal Savings and Loan, Tamiami Trail. Josephine B. Barrow, Box 3645, Punta Gorda, Fla. 33951-3645.

**PORT SAINT LUCIE:** Port Saint Lucie Stamp Club, second Thursday, Community Center, 200 S.W. Prima Vista Blvd., 7 p.m. Lois M. Gross, 274 N.E. Saleda Drive, Port Saint Lucie, Fla. 33452.

**ST. AUGUSTINE:** St. Augustine YMCA Stamp Club, first Tuesday, St. Augustine YMCA, 7:30 p.m. Charles Colee, 44 Bay View Drive, St. Augustine, Fla. 32084.

**ST. PETERSBURG:** St. Petersburg Stamp Club, every Wednesday, Trinity Lutheran

Church, 401 5th St. N, 7:30 p.m. James Wehle, Box 546, St. Petersburg, Fla. 33731.

**SARASOTA:** Sarasota Philatelic Club, third Thursday, Ellis Bank, corner of Main and Orange streets, 7:30 p.m. Harvey Barnard, 529 Blue Jay Place, Sarasota, Fla. 33577.

**SOUTH MIAMI:** South Miami Stamp Club, every Wednesday, Sylva G. Martin Senior Citizens Center, 6130 Sunset Drive, 7 p.m. Edgar C. Kaplan, 2005 S.W. 83rd Court, Miami, Fla. 33155.

**SUNRISE:** Sunrise Stamp Club, second and fourth Sunday, Roarke Recreation Center, 1720 N.W. 60th Ave., 1 p.m. Sid Mintz, Box 130092, Sunrise, Fla. 33313.

**TAVERNIER:** Upper Keys Collector's Club, third Thursday, Immanuel Lutheran Church, Mile 90, Plantation Key, 7:30 p.m. Audrey Devlin, 153 Navajo St., Tavernier, Fla. 33070.

**TITUSVILLE:** Titusville-Moonport Stamp Club, first Wednesday, Chamber of Commerce, 2000 S. Washington, 7 p.m. Susie Marie Sigg, Box 6071, Titusville, Fla. 32780.

**VENICE:** Venice Stamp Club, third Tuesday, United First Federal Savings and Loan, Community Room, 7:30 p.m. George T. Hayes, 922 Gibbs Road, Venice, Fla. 33595.

**VERO BEACH:** Indian River Stamp Club, second and fourth Monday, Doctors Clinic-Nurses Lounge, Fifth Avenue, 7:30 p.m. M.C. Bradbury, 2800 Indian River Blvd., N-5, Vero Beach, Fla. 32960.

**WEST PALM BEACH:** Century Stamp Club of West Palm Beach, second and fourth Wednesday, Delray Savings and Loan Bank, 1 p.m. Harry Rubin, 150 Cambridge G, West Palm Beach, Fla. 33409.

# GEORGIA

**ATHENS:** Athens Philatelic Society, first Thursday, First Lutheran Church, Fellowship Hall, Dougherty Street, 7:30 p.m. F.E. Barton, 41 Providence Village, Winterville, Ga. 30683.

**ATLANTA:** Atlanta Stamp Collectors Club, second and fourth Wednesday, All Saints Episcopal Church, West Peachtree Street and North Avenue, 7 p.m. Robert J. Maifeld, 522 Drexel Ave., Decatur, Ga. 30030.

**AUGUSTA:** Greater Augusta Stamp Club, first and third Thursday, V.A. Hospital (downtown), C-wing, Conference Room, 7:30 p.m. Richard Stoddard, Box 444, Grovetown, Ga. 30813.

**DECATUR:** Dekalb Stamp Club, third Sunday, Dekalb Federal Savings and Loan Building, 116 Clairmont, Ave., 2 p.m. Alvin E. Dvorshak, Box 784, Stone Mountain, Ga. 30086.

**MACON:** Macon Philatelic Society, first Thursday, Robert Train Recreation Center, Oglethorpe and First streets, 7:30 p.m. Edgar E. Maxwell, 1903 Upper River Road, Macon, Ga. 31211.

**SNELLVILLE:** Gwinnett Stamp Club, first Tuesday, Walton Electric Building, Highway 78, 7:30 p.m. John Hembree, 1845 Oak Ridge Way, Lawrenceville, Ga. 30245.

**STONE MOUNTAIN:** Stone Mountain Philatelic Society, second and fourth Thursday, Peachtree Bank, Memorial Drive at Hambrick Road, 7:30 p.m. J.H. Camp, 1766 Austin Drive, Decatur, Ga. 30032.

**VALDOSTA:** Valdosta Stamp Club, second Monday, South Georgia Regional Library, 7:30 p.m. M.O. Lawrence, 605 Mack Drive, Valdosta, Ga. 31601.

# HAWAII

**HONOLULU:** Hawaiian Philatelic Society, second Monday, Ala Moana Shopping Center, Ala Moana Banquet Hall, 7:30 p.m. Mr. Kay H. Hoke, Box 10115, Honolulu, Hawaii 96816.

— Hawaii-Ryukyu Philatelic Specialist Society, meets monthly, Kaimuki Library, 1041 Koko Head Ave., 7:30 p.m. Walter Chang, 2550 Manoa Road, Honolulu, Hawaii 96816.

# IDAHO

**BOISE:** Boise Stamp Club, second Tuesday, Post Office, 770 S. 13th, 7 p.m. Irene Field, 2055 Wilmington Drive, Boise, Idaho 83704.

**MOSCOW:** Palouse Empire Stamp Club, third Tuesday, Latah County Courthouse, Room 2B, 7:30 p.m. Mac Kittner, Box 8664, Moscow, Idaho 83843.

# ILLINOIS

**ARLINGTON HEIGHTS:** Northwest Stamp Club, first Monday and third Thursday, Arlington Heights Memorial Library, 500 Dunton Ave., 7:30 p.m. Frank F. Fischer, 135 Essex Road, Elk Grove Village, Ill. 60007.

**AURORA:** Fox Valley Stamp Club, second and fourth Tuesday, McCullough Activities Center, North Lake and Illinois avenues, 7:30 p.m. No meetings in July, August and December. Donald R. Clark, 2485 Cambridge, Aurora, Ill. 60506.

**BLOOMINGTON:** Corn Belt Philatelic Society, third Tuesday, Stamp Division; fourth Wednesday, Postcard Division, Bloomington Federal Savings and Loan Association, Community Room, 7:30 p.m. Jack L. Jenkins, Box 625, Bloomington, Ill. 61701.

**BROOKFIELD:** Suburban Collector's Club, second and fourth Wednesday, Sokol Hall, 3907 Prairie, 8 p.m. Gene Palys, Box 207, Brookfield, Ill. 60513.

**CARBONDALE:** Jackson County Stamp Society, second and fourth Thursday, St.Francis Xavier Church, Poplar and Walnut, 8 p.m. Dave Eakin, 823 S. Illinois, Carbondale, Ill. 62901.

**CHARLESTON:** Lincoln Trails Stamp Club, second and fourth Wednesday, Carlyle Realty Building, 7:30 p.m. Jim Mikeworth, 24 Beech Lane, Villa Grove, Ill. 61956.

**CHICAGO:** American Topical Association, Chicagoland Chapter 15, third Friday, Independence Park, 3945 N. Springfield Ave., 7:45 p.m. Henry Rajewski, 5255 S. Newcastle, Chicago, Ill. 60638.

— Chicago Philatelic Society, first and third Thursday, Oxford House, 225 N. Wabash, 7:30 p.m. Aubrey Berman, Box A3953, Chicago, Ill. 60690.

— Hellenic Philatelic Society of Chicago, third Sunday every other month, 2700 N. Austin Blvd., 2 p.m. John Georges, 5955 W. Newport Ave., Chicago, Ill. 60634.

— North Shore Philatelic Society, second and fourth Monday, Loyola Field House (Chicago Park District), 7100 Sheridan Road, 8 p.m. Philip D. Tully, Box 11580, Chicago, Ill. 60611.

— Roosevelt Philatelic Society of Chicago, first and third Tuesday, Hayes Park Fieldhouse, 2936 W. 85th St., 7:30 p.m. Donald J. Van Winter, 7653 S. Roberts Road, Bridgeview, Ill. 60455.

— Scandinavian Collectors Club, Chicago Chapter 4, third Thursday, no meetings in July and August. November and December meetings first Thursday, Swedish Club of Chicago, 1258 N. LaSalle St., 7:30 p.m. Ronald Collin, Box 63, River Grove, Ill. 60174.

— Tower Stamp Club, first and third Tuesday, Brooks Building, 223 W. Jackson Blvd., noon. Frank Bachenheimer, Box 248, Glenview, Ill. 60025.

— United Nations Collectors of Chicagoland, first Tuesday, September thru June, Swedish Club of Chicago, 1258 N. LaSalle St., 7:30 p.m. Charles Berg, Box 1674, Chicago, Ill. 60690.

**DE KALB:** Kishwaukee Valley Stamp Club, second Wednesday, De Kalb Bank, 3rd and Lincoln Highway, 7 p.m. Clifford Elliott, Box 97, Sycamore, Ill. 60178.

**EAST PEORIA:** Caterpillar Stamp Club, first and third Tuesday, Fondulac Administrative Center, 201 Bloomington Road, 7 p.m. Jeanne Jones, 5200 N. Main St., East Peoria, Ill. 61611.

**GLEN ELLYN:** Glen Ellyn Philatelic Club, first and third Monday, Glen Ellyn Civic Center, 535 Duane St., 7:30 p.m. Ron Baumgardner, Box 217, Glen Ellyn, Ill. 60137.

**HERRIN:** Herrin Junior High Stamp Club, first and third Tuesday, Library, 12:30 p.m. John H. Bauernfeind, 700 S. 14th St., Herrin, Ill. 62948.

**HOMEWOOD:** Homewood-Flossmoor Postcard Club, second and fourth Tuesday, Dolphin Lake Clubhouse, 183rd Street and Governors Highway, 7:30 p.m. Les Lawitz, 18820 Highland Ave., Homewood, Ill. 60430.

**KANKAKEE:** Kankakee Valley Stamp and Coin Club, second Tuesday, Governor Small Park, Centennial Room, 7:30 p.m. Donald Merrill, Box 150, Bradley, Ill. 60915.

**LA GRANGE:** La Grange Philatelic Society, fourth Friday, La Grange Library, 10 W. Cossitt, 7:30 p.m. Ruth Keller, 515 S. Spring Ave., La Grange, Ill. 60525.

**LIBERTYVILLE:** North Suburban Stamp Club, first Monday, Cook Memorial Library, 413 N. Milwaukee Ave., 8 p.m. Robert S. Smith, Box 353, Libertyville, Ill. 60048.

**MOLINE:** Quad-City Stamp Club, second Thursday, Moline Township Hall, 620 18th St., 7:30 p.m. Steven J. Bahnsen, 1712 7th Ave., Moline, Ill. 61265.

**PARK FOREST:** Park Forest Stamp Club, first and third Tuesday, Freedom Hall, Lakewood Drive and Orchard Boulevard, 7:30 p.m. Les Lawitz, 18820 Highland Ave., Homewood, Ill. 60430.

**PARK RIDGE:** Park Ridge Stamp Club, first Monday, Drake Funeral Home, 625 Bussee Highway, 7:30 p.m. Bernard Baer, 800 Devon, Park Ridge, Ill. 60068.

**PEORIA:** Wabco Stamp Club, first Thursday, Wabco Personnel Conference Room, 2300 N.E. Adams, 4:15 p.m. Holmes Dille, 2300 N.E. Adams St., Peoria, Ill. 61639.

**ROCKFORD:** Rockford Stamp Club, first Wednesday, Home Federal Savings and Loan, 1107 E. State St., 7:30 p.m. Perry Arnquist, 604 Hollister Ave., Rockford, Ill. 61108.

**ROXANA:** Community Stamp Club, second and fourth Monday, Rox-Arena, Roxana Park, 7 p.m. Loyd Grafford, Box 153, Wood River, Ill. 62095.

**SKOKIE:** Israel-Palestine Philatelic Society of America, Society of Israel Philatelists, Chicago Chapter, second Thursday, Skokie Library, 5215 W. Oakton, 7:30 p.m. C.A. Tuteur, 1438 W. Pratt Blvd., Chicago, Ill. 60626.

— Lincoln Stampers, every other Tuesday, Lincoln Junior High School, Room 116, 3:15 p.m. Shirley Jacobson, 7839 Lincoln, Skokie, Ill. 60077.

**SPRINGFIELD:** Springfield Philatelic Society, fourth Tuesday, Security Federal Savings and Loan, 510 E. Monroe St., 7:30 p.m. Patricia Holmes, 428 Lexington Drive, Rochester, Ill. 62563.

## MISCELLANEOUS

Illini Precancel Stamp Club, spring and fall, Holiday Inn, I-80, 9 a.m. Robert H. Meeske, Route 5, Princeton, Ill. 61356.

Scouts on Stamps Society International, Baden-Powell Chapter 1, March of each year, various locations. Carl R. Hallmann, 253 Sheldon, Downers Grove, Ill. 60515.

Universal Ship Cancellation Society, Moffett Chapter 6, various Sundays, members' homes, 2 p.m. Lawrence R. Groh, 9648 S. Major Ave., Oak Lawn, Ill. 60456.

Vatican Philatelic Society, Chicagoland Chapter, fourth Monday, varies, 7:30 p.m. James Doheny, 3625 McCormick Ave., Brookfield, Ill. 60513.

# INDIANA

**ANDERSON:** Madison County Bicentennial Stamp Club, third Thursday, Madison Heights High School, 7 p.m. Bonnie Lyons, Box 1863, Anderson, Ind. 46011.

**ANGOLA:** Northeastern Indiana Stamp Club, second Tuesday, Kendallville Public Library-Angola United Methodist church basement, 7:30 p.m. Harold Murzyn, 212 First St., Albion, Ind. 46701.

**COLUMBUS:** Bartholomew County Stamp Club, third Thursday, Bartholomew County Library, 7:15 p.m. Frank Ebert, 3109 N. National Road, Columbus, Ind. 47201.

**ELKHART:** Maple City Post Card Club, first Thursday, First National Bank, Eastside Branch, 1320 Middlebury St., 7:30 p.m. David H. Long, Box 644, Elkhart, Ind. 46515-0644.

**EVANSVILLE:** Evansville Stamp Club, Inc., first and third Tuesday, IOS Building, 2900 Lincoln Ave., 7:30 p.m. Tom Ryder, Box 161, Evansville, Ind. 47702.

**FORT WAYNE:** Anthony Wayne Stamp Society, second Monday, Northwood Middle School, 7:30 p.m. Gwen Converse, Box 10504, Fort Wayne, Ind. 46852.

**HAMMOND:** Calumet Stamp Club, every Thursday except second, Calumet Federal Savings and Loan, 7007 Calumet Ave., 7 p.m. P.A. Demkovich, 7520 Magoun Ave., Hammond, Ind. 46324.

**INDIANAPOLIS:** Indiana Stamp Club, Inc., first Monday, Childrens' Museum, 30th and Meridian streets, 7:30 p.m. Jeanette Adams, Box 40792, Indianapolis, Ind. 46240.

**KOKOMO:** Kokomo Stamp Club, second Wednesday, Kokomo Public Library, 7 p.m. Ned P. Booher, 421 S. Phillips St., Kokomo, Ind. 46901.

**LOGANSPORT:** Logansport Stamp Club, third Thursday, Mental Health Building, 125 9th St., 7:30 p.m. Helen L. Wagner, Route 4, Box 26, Logansport, Ind. 46947.

**RICHMOND:** Centerville Stamp Club, third Friday, Richmond National Guard Armory, West Main Street, 7:30 p.m. Ted Parker, 1318 Boyer St., Richmond, Ind. 47374.

**SOUTH BEND:** Northern Indiana Philatelic Society, second and fourth Thursday, St. Joseph Bank, Roseland Branch, U.S. 31 and 33 at Darden Road, 8 p.m. E.A. Bella, Box 393, Mishawaka, Ind. 46544.

— Northern Indiana Philatelic Society Juniors, first Saturday during April, May and June, South Bend Public Library, Main Branch, 9:30 a.m. Box 393, Mishawaka, Ind. 46544.

— Wabash Valley Stamp Club, last Thursday, Vigo County Public Library, 6:30 p.m. Carl M. Tausig, RR 14, Box 239, Brazil, Ind. 47834.

**TERRE HAUTE:** Wabash Philatelic Society, first Thursday, 1509 Wabash Ave., 6:30 p.m. P.N. Martin, Box 4026, Terre Haute, Ind. 47808.

**WEST LAFAYETTE:** Lafayette Stamp Club, third Wednesday, Senior Citizens Center, 300 North St., 7 p.m. Clair C. Conn, 1903 N. 18th, Lafayette, Ind. 47904.

## MISCELLANEOUS

Central States Federation of Stamp Clubs, spring and fall, location varies. Bonnie Lyons, Route 4, Box 37, Anderson, Ind. 46011.

# IOWA

**ALLISON:** Allison Stamp Club, second Saturday, R.E.C. meeting room, North Main Street, 7:30 p.m. Ruth Miller, Box 24, Allison, Iowa 50602.

**DES MOINES:** Des Moines Philatelic Society, second Friday, Staves Memorial United Methodist Church, Madison Avenue and E. 281st Street, 7 p.m. No meetings in July and August. Edwin H. Allen Jr., 2307 49th St., Des Moines, Iowa 50310.

**CEDAR RAPIDS:** Cedar Rapids Postcard Club, third Thursday, Peoples Bank, 3rd Avenue SE, 7:30 p.m. Vivian Rinaberger, 4548 Fairlane Drive NE, Cedar Rapids, Iowa 52402.

— Cedar Rapids Stamp Club, first Monday, Peoples Bank and Trust Company, 7:30 p.m. Betty Rutherford, Route 2, Marion, Iowa 52302.

**GRINNELL:** Grinnell Philatelic Society, fourth Tuesday, Grinnell College Science Building Library, 8 p.m. Dr. K.L. Hoefert, 1426 Spring St., Grinnell, Iowa 50112.

## MISCELLANEOUS

Germany Philatelic Society, Sioux City Chapter 14, monthly in members' homes, 7:30 p.m. Daniel A. Fling, 3226 Grandview Blvd., Sioux City, Iowa 51104.

# KANSAS

**COFFEYVILLE:** Coffeyville Stamp Club, first Tuesday, Statesman Club, 8th and Maple, 7:30 p.m. Lucille McGovney, 912 W. 2nd, Coffeyville, Kan. 67337.

**HAYS:** Fort Hays Stamp Club, third Sunday, Midwest Energy, 111 E. 11th St., 2 p.m. James E. Thorns, Coronado Estates, 500 W. 36th St., Hays, Kan. 67601.

**HUTCHINSON:** Sunflower Stamp Club, third Monday, Hutchinson Public Library Auditorium, 9th and Main, 6:30 p.m. Debra Biery, 1806 Lyman, Hutchinson, Kan. 67501.

**TOPEKA:** Topeka Stamp Club, third Thursday, Topeka Savings Association, 8th and Quincy streets, 7:30 p.m. Walter A. Tuchscherer, 2021 Pembroke Lane, Topeka, Kan. 66604.

**WICHITA:** Cessna Stamp Club, second Thursday, Cessna Activity Center, 2744 George Washington Blvd., 7:30 p.m. No meetings in June, July and August. Bonnie Cheever, 2542 Victoria, Wichita, Kan. 67216.

— Kansas Precancel Society, fourth Friday, except December, GMF, USPS, 7117 W. Harry, 7:30 p.m. Dilmond D. Postlewait, Box 1335, Wichita, Kan. 67201.

# KENTUCKY

**HOPKINSVILLE:** Pennyrile Philatelic Society, third Tuesday, Hopkinsville-Christian County Library, 7 p.m. David Riley, 2527 Cox Mill Road, Hopkinsville, Ky. 42240.

**LEXINGTON:** Henry Clay Philatelic Society, third Monday, Bell House, Sayre Avenue, 7 p.m. A.C. Stagg, 622 Orchard Ave., Lexington, Ky. 40502.

**LOUISVILLE:** Louisville Stamp Society, first and third Friday, Crescent Hill Presbyterian Church, 142 Crescent Ave., 8 p.m. John R. Glick, 3107 Sunny Lane, Louisville, Ky. 40205.

— Shelby Street Stamp Society, first and third Friday, 1404 S. Shelby St., 3 p.m. R. Paul Baker, 1310 Tycoon Way, Louisville, Ky. 40213.

**OWENSBORO:** Owensboro Area Stamp Club, first Friday, Owensboro Area Museum, 2829 S. Griffith Ave., 7:30 p.m. No meetings in June, July and August. Richard Weiss, 2311 S. York St., Owensboro, Ky. 42301.

# LOUISIANA

**BATON ROUGE:** Baton Rouge Stamp Club, first and third Wednesday, East Baton Rouge Parish Library, 7711 Goodwood Blvd., 7 p.m. Estelle H. Vest, 3228 Ontario St., Baton Rouge, La. 70805.

**LAFAYETTE:** Acadiana Stamp Club, second Thursday, Majestic Pools' Office, West Gloria Switch Road, 7 p.m. Ken Johnstone, Box 3939, Lafayette, La. 70502-3939.

**MONROE:** Twin City Stamp Club, first Monday, Monroe Post Office, Sterlington Road, 7 p.m. Pauline Hendrixson, 4106 Roger St., Monroe, La. 71201.

**NEW ORLEANS:** Crescent City Stamp Club, second and fourth Tuesday, 874 Harrison Ave., 7:30 p.m. Box 7096, Metairie, La. 70010.

— The Dixiana Stampers, first Friday, 874 Harrison Ave., 6:30 p.m. 4323 Elba St., New Orleans, La. 70125.

# MAINE

**AUBURN:** Twin Rivers Stamp Club, second and fourth Wednesday, Auburn YMCA, 7 p.m. Ray Gagnon, 23 Sylvan Ave., Lewiston, Maine 04240.

**AUGUSTA:** Maine Philatelic Society, first Saturday, Holiday Inn, 11 a.m. Alvin Sweet, Box 4, Rockport, Maine 04856.

**BANGOR:** Penobscot Valley Stamp Club, second Monday, YMCA, Hammond Street, 7 p.m. Gilbert M. Roderick, 52 Fern St., Bangor, Maine 04401.

**CARIBOU:** Pine Tree Stamp Club, second and fourth Thursday, Loring Federal Credit Union, Downtown Mall, 7 p.m. Donald McDougal, Powers Road, Caribou, Maine 04736.

**PORTLAND:** Pine Tree Postcard Club, second Monday, Public Safety Building, 109 Middle St., 6:30 p.m. Jon Stokes, 30 Sanborn St., Portland, Maine 04103.

— Portland Stamp Club, fourth Tuesday, Portland Public Safety Building, 109 Middle St., 7:30 p.m. No meetings in July and August. Rupert E. MacLean, 30 Providence Ave., South Portland, Maine 04106.

**SKOWHEGAN:** Somerset County Stamp Club, third Sunday, Depositor's Trust Company, Madison Avenue, 1:30 p.m. Rick Lancaster, Box 383, Skowhegan, Maine 04976.

**WATERVILLE:** Waterville Stamp Club, Waterville Public Library, Elm Street, 7 p.m. No meetings in June, July, August and September. Glenice S. Merrill, 19 Union St., Waterville, Maine 04901.

# MARYLAND

**ANNAPOLIS:** Annapolis Stamp Club, second and fourth Tuesday, Annapolis Public Library, West Street, 7 p.m. No meetings in July and August. LCDR L.P. Cavanaugh, USN Ret., 95 Conduit St., Annapolis, Md. 21401.

**BALTIMORE:** Baltimore Philatelic Society, first Friday, second Thursday, third Wednesday and fourth Tuesday, 1224 N. Calvert St., 7:30 p.m. Kalman V. Illyefalvi, 8207 Daren Court, Pikesville, Md. 21208.

— Chesapeake Philatelic Society, every Friday, Zion Church, Harford Road and Iona Terrace, 8 p.m. Connie Plasterer, 1504 Barkley Ave., Baltimore, Md. 21221.

— Germany Philatelic, Chapter 16, third Sunday, Baltimore Philatelic Society Clubhouse, 1224 N. Calvert St., 1:30 p.m. No meetings in July and August. Christopher Deterding, RFD 10, 741 Holly Drive N, Annapolis, Md. 21401.

— The Monumental Post Card Club, fourth Sunday, except December, Star Community Hall, 7405 Windsor Mill Road, 1 p.m. Peggy Bower, 2902 Ontario Ave., Baltimore, Md. 21234.

— Waxter Center Stamp Club, first and third Friday, Waxter Center for Senior Citizens, 861 Park Ave., 12:30 p.m. Mrs. Ruperta S. Waters, 3350 Dolfield Ave., Baltimore, Md. 21215.

**BETHESDA:** American First Day Cover Society, Robert G. Graebner Chapter 17, second Saturday, St. John's Episcopal Church, Wisconsin Avenue and Bradley Boulevard, 10 a.m. Larry Carney, 5565 Columbia Pike, Arlington, Va. 22204.

**BOWIE:** Bowie Stamp Club, second and fourth Monday, Bowie City Hall, 7:30 p.m. James Bono, 12431 Milling Lane, Bowie, Md. 20715.

**COLUMBIA:** Howard County Stamp Club, second and fourth Thursday, Thunderhill Neighborhood Center, 7:30 p.m. Frank E. Kos, 5465 Delphinium Court, Columbia, Md. 21045.

**CUMBERLAND:** Tri-State Stamp Club, second Wednesday, First People's Credit Union Building, 153 Baltimore St., 7:30 p.m. Madeline H. Fazenbaker, 811 Gephart Drive, Cumberland, Md. 21502.

**GREENBELT:** Goddard Space Flight Center Stamp Club, second Tuesday, various buildings on center, 11:30 a.m. John Chovan, Box 261, Greenbelt, Md. 20770.

**LINTHICUM:** North Arundel Philatelic Society, every Tuesday, Linthicum Library, Hammonds and Shipley roads, 6 p.m. Victor N. Hutchinson, Box 725, Glen Burnie, Md. 21061-0725.

**OXON HILL:** Oxon Hill Philatelic Society, first and third Monday, Oxon Hill Library, 6200 Oxon Hill Road, 7:30 p.m. Pat Fowler, 9915 Williamsburg Drive, Upper Marlboro, Md. 20772.

**PIKESVILLE:** Society of Israel Philatelists, Baltimore Chapter, third Thursday, Loyola Federal Savings and Loan Association, 1300 Reisterstown Road, 7:30 p.m. No meetings in July and August. Stanley H. Raffel, 3408 Ripple Road, Baltimore, Md. 21207.

**SILVER SPRING:** Beltway Stamp Club, first and third Tuesday, Good Shepherd United Methodist Church, 9701 New Hampshire Ave., 7:30 p.m. John Murchake, Box 1728, Hyattsville, Md. 20788.

## MISCELLANEOUS

Associated Stamp Clubs of Chesapeake Area, various shows, LCDR L.P. Cavanaugh, USN, Ret., 95 Conduit St., Annapolis, Md. 21401.

Lions Stamp Club No. 2, on call, 13412 Grenoble Drive. Stanley E. Kenison, 13412 Grenoble Drive, Rockville, Md. 20853.

Universal Ship Cancellation Society, Admiral Byrd Chapter 11, first Friday, various locations, 8:30 p.m. Bill Luckett, Box 3, Washington Grove, Md. 20880.

# MASSACHUSETTS

**ADAMS:** Northern Berkshire Stamp Club, first and third Wednesday, Miller Annex-Adams Library, 7 p.m. No meetings in June, July and August. Joseph Dahrouge Jr., 31 Crandall St., Adams, Mass. 01220.

**BOSTON:** Boston Philatelic Society, first and third Thursday, George Sherman Union, Boston University, 775 Commonwealth Ave., 7:30 p.m. Thomas Barrett Jr., 52 Humphrey St., Marblehead, Mass. 01945.

**CENTERVILLE:** Cape Cod Stamp Club, second and fourth Friday, Hyannis Co-Op Bank, West Main Street and Route 28, 8 p.m. Leon G. Smith, Box 615, W. Yarmouth, Mass. 02673.

**CHELMSFORD:** Chelmsford Stamp Club, second and fourth Tuesday, Central Congregational Church, 1 Worthen St., 8 p.m. Emile Vandenbulcke, Box 163, Chelmsford, Mass. 01824.

**DUDLEY:** Webster-Dudley Stamp Club, first Tuesday, Dudley Town Hall, 7:15 p.m. No meetings in July and August. Jennie Kozlowski, 32 E. Main St., Webster, Mass. 01570.

**FALL RIVER:** Fall River Philatelic Society, first Tuesday; third Wednesday, Fall River Public Library, 104 N. Main St., 7 p.m. Alice Kent, 62 Kennedy St., Fall River, Mass. 02721.

**FORT DEVENS:** Fort Devens Stamp and Coin Collectors, first and third Monday, Crossroads Recreation Center, 7 p.m. Russell Robertson, Box 503, Ayer, Mass. 01432.

**FRAMINGHAM:** Lincoln Stamp Club, fourth Monday, Park Street Baptist Church, Franklin and Park streets, 7:30 p.m. David P. Borghi, 30 Wilde Ave., Framingham, Mass. 01701.

**LAWRENCE:** Samuel Osgood Stamp Club, first and third Wednesday, St. Augustine Church, 7:30 p.m. Dr. Jacob J. Apsel, Box 1335, Lawrence, Mass. 01842.

**LEOMINSTER:** Wachusett Philatelic Society, third Tuesday, except second Tuesday in December and June, All Saints Chapel, 7:30 p.m. No meetings July and August. G.R. Vitagliano, 60 Acushnet Ave., Worcester, Mass. 01606.

**MALDEN:** Malden Stamp Club, second and fourth Wednesday, Mystic Side Congregational Church, 8 p.m. Box 214, Malden, Mass. 02148.

**PITTSFIELD:** Berkshire Museum Stamp Club, second and fourth Tuesday, Berkshire Museum, 39 South St., 7:30 p.m. Edward J. Ptak, 16 Alba Ave., Pittsfield, Mass. 01201.

**QUINCY:** Granite City Stamp Club, second and fourth Wednesday, Lincoln Hancock School, 7:30 p.m. No meetings in July and August. Ernest B. Remondini, Box 52, Weymouth, Mass. 02189.

**STOUGHTON:** Old Colony Philatelists, first and third Monday, Congregational Church Hall, Pierce Street, 7 p.m. Alice I. Magee, 126 Britton Ave., Apt. B, Stoughton, Mass. 02072.

**WALPOLE:** Walpole Stamp Club, first and third Thursday, Walpole Public Library, 7 p.m. Robert S. MacDonald, 9 Park Lane, East Walpole, Mass. 02032.

**WESTON:** Philatelic Numismatic Combination Society of Massachusetts, last Sunday of January, March, May, September and November, Cardinal Spellman Philatelic Museum, 2:15 p.m. Eunice Alter, Box 903, Marblehead, Mass. 01945.

## MISCELLANEOUS

Amherst Stamp Club, second Wednesday, members' homes, 7:30 p.m. Phyllis Lehrer, 197 Pondview Drive, Amherst, Mass. 01002.

Northeastern Federation of Stamp Clubs, annual meeting at show. Dr. Guy R. Dillaway, Box 181, Weston, Mass. 02193.

Universal Ship Cancellation Society, Old Ironsides Chapter 1, one Sunday per month, members' homes, 2 p.m. Norman Doucette Jr., 9 Governor's Ave., Winchester, Mass. 01890.

# MICHIGAN

**ALBION:** Albion Stamp Club, first and third Monday, September to May; first Monday, June, July and August, Albion Public Library, 501 S. Superior St., 7 p.m. Mrs. M. Helena Davis, 933 W. Erie St., Albion, Mich. 49224.

**ANN ARBOR:** Ann Arbor Stamp Club, third Monday, 310 S. Ashley St., 7:30 p.m. Harry C. Winter, Box 2012, Ann Arbor, Mich. 48106.

**BIRMINGHAM:** Birmingham Stamp Club, second and fourth Thursday, Pembroke School, 955 N. Eton, 7:30 p.m. No meetings in June, July and August. Charles A. Wood, 244 W. Breckenridge, Ferndale, Mich. 48220.

**DEARBORN:** Michigan Stamp Club, second and fourth Monday, Prince of Peace Lutheran Church, 19104 Ford Road, 7 p.m. Richard Chellevold, Box 2376, Ann Arbor, Mich. 48106.

**DETROIT:** Northwest Stamp Society, first and fourth Tuesday, Advent Lutheran Church, Southfield Service Drive, 7 p.m. Kenneth A. Brock, 9959 Riverdale, Redford, Mich. 48239.

— Scandinavian Collectors Club of Detroit, Chapter 3, first Tuesday, Advent Lutheran Church, 20201 Southfield Road, 7:30 p.m. Petter A. Poppe, 1028 Montrose, Royal Oak, Mich. 48073.

**EAST LANSING:** Central Michigan Philatelic Society, second and fourth Thursday, Recreation Center, 7:30 p.m. Joseph Adams, 4100 Seaway Drive, Lansing, Mich. 48910.

**FERNDALE:** Ferndale Stamp Club, first and third Tuesday, Ferndale Community Center, 400 E. Nine Mile Road, 7 p.m. Bob Jacobs, Box 2, Royal Oak, Mich. 48067-0002.

**HARPER WOODS:** Wayne Stamp Society, second and fourth Wednesday, Surety Federal Savings and Loan Building, 8 Mile and Kelly, 8 p.m. Dr. George V. Holland, 32164 St. Anne's Drive, Warren, Mich. 48092.

**KALAMAZOO:** Southwestern Michigan Post Card Club, first Monday, Kalamazoo Public Library-Museum, 315 S. Rose, 7:30 p.m. Louise B. Northam, 1833 Waite Ave., Kalamazoo, Mich. 49008.

**MONROE:** Floral City Stamp Club, second Monday, First National Bank, Community Room, Monroe and Willow streets, 7:30 p.m. Brother Walter Foken CSC, 108 W. Elm Ave., Monroe, Mich. 48161.

**MUSKEGON:** Muskegon Stamp Club, first and third Wednesday, McGraft Congregational Church, 1617 Palmer, 7:30 p.m. Maxine Veeder, 1087 W. Grand, Muskegon, Mich. 49441.

**OAK PARK:** Detroit-Oak Park Stamp Club, second Tuesday, Oak Park Community Center, 7:30 p.m. Henry C. Lenhoff, 27451 Fairfax, Southfield, Mich. 48076.

**PETOSKEY:** Northwestern Michigan Stamp and Coin Club, fourth Tuesday, Little Traverse Regional Historical Museum, 7:15 p.m. Harold R. Heintz, Box 33, Harbor Springs, Mich. 49740.

**PLYMOUTH:** West Suburban Stamp Club, first and third Friday, Culture Center, 515 Farmer, 7:30 p.m. Hal Williams, Box 643, Plymouth, Mich. 48170.

**PORT HURON:** Port Huron-Sarnia Stamp Club, third Wednesday, St. Clair County Community College, 7:30 p.m. M.E. Wright, 1533 Griswold St., Port Huron, Mich. 48060.

**SAGINAW:** Saginaw Valley Stamp Society, first and third Wednesday, Chemical Bank and Trust, Community Room, M47 and Weiss Road, 7:30 p.m. Patrick A. Walters, Box 413, Freeland, Mich. 48622.

**TRAVERSE CITY:** Grand Traverse Stamp Club, fourth Thursday, TBA Credit Union, 7:30 p.m. Richard E. Bond, Box 224, Traverse City, Mich. 49684.

## MISCELLANEOUS

Blue Water Cover Collectors, when available, members' homes. Box 193, Port Huron, Mich. 48060.

Lindquist Stamp Club, members' homes. Frank N. Kangas, 804 Hamilton Ave., Kingsford, Mich. 49801.

Scouts on Stamps Society International, Great Lakes Chapter 8, spring and fall, members' homes, 8 p.m. Dr. George V. Holland, 32164 St. Anne's Drive, Warren, Mich. 48092.

Universal Ship Cancellation Society, USS Michigan Chapter 80, various dates, 16500 W. 12 Mile Road, Suite 107, 7:30 p.m. Robert Quintero, 22608 Poplar Court, Hazel Park, Mich. 48030.

Wolverine Stamp Club, second Friday, members' homes, 7 p.m. L.A. Pulinski, 7310 Emanon, Dearborn, Mich. 48126.

# MINNESOTA

**MARSHALL:** Lyon County Philatelic Society, third Monday, Municipal Building, 7 p.m. Steve Klein, 301 Robert, Marshall, Minn. 56258.

**MINNEAPOLIS:** Minnehaha Stamp Club, second Thursday, Pearl Park, Portland Avenue and Diamond Lake Road, 7 p.m. George Breiner, 6844 Upton Ave. S, Minneapolis, Minn. 55423.

— Postal History Society of Minnesota, fourth Tuesday, YWCA, 12th and Nicollet, 8 p.m. James Inverarity, 401 9th St. SE, Minneapolis, Minn. 55414.

**NORTHFIELD:** Northfield Stamp Club, third Tuesday, Community Action Center, 7 p.m. Paul W. Tollefson, Route 1, Northfield, Minn. 55057.

**OWATONNA:** Owatonna Stamp and Coin Club, third Thursday, Park and Recreation Building, West Hills, 7:30 p.m. Gary G. Ascher, Box 668, Owatonna, Minn. 55060.

**ST. LOUIS PARK:** Minnesota Israel Philatelic Society, third Sunday, Jewish Community Center, 2:30 p.m. No meetings in February, July and August. Ray Getsug, 4330 S. Cedar Lake Road, St. Louis Park, Minn. 55416.

**ST. PAUL:** Twin City Philatelic Society, first Thursday, YWCA 12th and Nicollet, Minneapolis; third Thursday, Lutheran Church, Park and University, St. Paul, 7 p.m. Ray Hamernick, 522 Rice St., St. Paul, Minn. 55103.

## MISCELLANEOUS

Albert Lea Stamp and Coin Club, third Wednesday, members' homes, 7:30 p.m. Warren W. Rosenau, Box 747, Albert Lea, Minn. 56007-0747.

Germany Philatelic Society, Chapter 10, second Friday, members' homes, 8 p.m. Walter J. Kurth, 2111 Dundee Place, Stillwater, Minn. 55082.

# MISSISSIPPI

**BILOXI:** Gulf Coast Stamp Club, first Saturday, Knights of Columbus Hall, 122 E. Water St., 7:30 p.m. Jim Currie, Box 402, Gulfport, Miss. 39501.

**JACKSON:** Jackson Philatelic Society, second Friday, Electric Building, South Lamar and East Pascagoula streets, 7:30 p.m. M.D. Myers, Box 10553, Jackson, Miss. 39209.

# MISSOURI

**FORT LEONARD WOOD:** Pulaski Stamp and Coin Club, first and second Wednesday, Building 1704, 7 p.m. SFC Philip Bohduc, 57 Young St., Fort Leonard Wood, Mo. 65473.

**KANSAS CITY:** Collectors Club of Kansas City, second Wednesday, Loose Park Library Building, 52nd and Wornall Road, 7:30 p.m. Paul Oesterly, 400 W. 61st Terrace, Kansas City, Mo. 64113.

— Midwest Philatelic Society, first Saturday, First National Drive-In Bank, 13th and Washington, 2 p.m. Adolph Pearson, 802 E. 53rd, Kansas City, Mo. 64110.

**KIRKWOOD:** Gateway Post Card Club, first Monday, except September, Kirkwood Community Center, Room 201, 7:30 p.m. Adele Kempf, 13048 W. Watson Road, St. Louis, Mo. 63127.

**ROLLA:** Rolla Philatelic Society, third Friday, University Center, Meramec Room, 7 p.m. J.W. Jensen, Box 1213, Rolla, Mo. 65401.

**ST. JOSEPH:** St. Joseph Stamp Collectors Club, second Saturday, Senior Citizens Center, 10th and Felix, 1:30 p.m. Merlin Huber, 1307 Sylvanie, St. Joseph, Mo. 64501.

**ST. LOUIS:** Baden Stamp Club, every other Monday, Halls Ferry and McLaran streets, 1 p.m. Vincent J. Lutz, 1546 Sells Ave., St. Louis, Mo. 63147.

— Greater St. Louis Stamp Club, fourth Monday, 2735 Woodson Road, 8 p.m. Vincent J. Lutz, 1546 Sells Ave., St. Louis, Mo. 63147.

— Mound City Stamp Club, first and third Monday, Prudential Savings and Loan, 8020 Forsyth Blvd., 7 p.m. James Adler, 6452 Nashville Ave., St. Louis, Mo. 63139.

— Society of Israel Philatelists, St. Louis Chapter, third Thursday, St. Louis County Library, Mid County Branch, 7821 Maryland, 7:30 p.m. Allan M. Koplar, Box 16072, St. Louis, Mo. 63105.

**SPRINGFIELD:** Ozark Mountain Stamp Club, first and third Thursday, 1730 E. Portland, 7 p.m. Jobelle Burk, 613 S. Main, Springfield, Mo. 65801.

**WEBSTER GROVES:** Webster Groves Stamp Club, first and second Friday, 34 N. Gore, 8 p.m. Hans Stoltz, 34 N. Gore, Webster Groves, Mo. 63119.

## MISCELLANEOUS

Missouri Precancel Club, date varies. Edwin Swafford, 714 Delchester Lane, Kirkwood, Mo. 63122.

# NEBRASKA

**NORTH PLATTE:** Buffalo Bill Stamp Club, first Sunday, Blue Flame Room, 215 E. 5th, 2 p.m. Avis Thomas, 309 S. Walnut, North Platte, Neb. 69101.

**OMAHA:** Omaha Philatelic Society, second Friday, W. Dale Clark Library, 215 S. 15th St.; fourth Friday, Commercial Federal Savings and Loan, 20th and Harney, 7:30 p.m. Richard L. McConnell, 2235 St. Mary's Ave., Apt. 421, Omaha, Neb. 68102.

# NEVADA

**RENO:** Nevada Stamp Study Society, second and fourth Saturday, University of Nevada, Physics Building, 2:30 p.m. Douglas Willick, Box AD, Sparks, Nev. 89431.

# NEW HAMPSHIRE

**CONWAY:** White Mountain Stamp Club, first Tuesday, Conway Recreation Center, Room 1, Main Street, 7:30 p.m. Barbara M. Savary, Box 393, Conway, N.H. 03818.

**MANCHESTER:** Manchester Stamp Club, fourth Tuesday, 210 Mooresville Road, 7:30 p.m. Robert Dion, 210 Mooresville Road, Manchester, N.H. 03103.

**NASHUA:** Nashua Philatelic Society, first Monday; first Tuesday if holiday, Chandler Library, Main Street, 7 p.m. Ralph Bauer, Box 1412, Nashua, N.H. 03061.

# NEW JERSEY

**CALDWELL:** West Essex Philatelic Society, second and fourth Monday, North Jersey Savings and Loan, 268 Bloomfield Ave., 8 p.m. Raymond Laplace, Box 443, Elmwood Park, N.J. 07407.

**CLIFTON:** Clifton Stamp Society, first and third Monday, Clifton Recreation Building, Main and Washington avenues, 7:30 p.m. Gerard J. Neufeld, 33 Comfort Place, Clifton, N.J. 07011.

**GLOUCESTER CITY:** Gloucester City Stamp Club, every Monday, Gloucester City Public Library, Monmouth Street and Railroad Avenue, 7:30 p.m. No meetings on holidays. Carl R. Herr, 109 Oak Ave., Bellmawr, N.J. 08031.

**HAZLET:** Hazlet Stamp Club, second and fourth Tuesday, Hazlet Township Recreation Commission Building, Union Avenue, 8 p.m. No meetings in July and August. Esther Dunn, Box 12, Hazlet, N.J. 07730.

**HIGHLAND PARK:** Society of Israel Philatelists, Central Jersey Chapter, second Tuesday, YMHA and YWHA, 2 S. Adelaide Ave., 7:30 p.m. Ann Rosenzweig, Box 267, New Brunswick, N.J. 08903.

**LAKEHURST:** Leisure Village West Stamp and Coin Club, first and third Wednesday, Leisure Village West, Willow Hall, 10 a.m. Edmond Beldowski, 481C Winfield Court, Lakehurst, N.J. 08733.

**LAMBERTVILLE:** Coryell's Ferry Stamp Club, first and third Monday; third Monday in July, August and September, Lambertville Baptist Church, Bridge Street, 8 p.m. Bertha S. Davis, Box 5, Wrightstown, Pa. 18940-0800.

**MERCHANTVILLE:** Merchantville Stamp Club, first Thursday, third Wednesday, Temple Lutheran Church, 7:30 p.m. Nancy B. Kiser, Box 523, Folcroft, Pa. 19032.

**MIDDLESEX:** Middlesex Stamp Club, third Wednesday, Middlesex High School, Room 115, 2:45 p.m. Paul T. Jackson, Box 231, Raritan, N.J. 08869.

**MOORESTOWN:** American Philatelic Society, Southern New Jersey Chapter 154, second Tuesday, Recreation Center, New Albany Road, 8 p.m. No meetings in July and August. John P. Werst, 285 W. Second St., Moorestown, N.J. 08057.

**MORRISTOWN:** Jockey Hollow Stamp Club, first and third Monday, Frelinghuysen School, West Hanover Avenue, 8 p.m. H.M. Tweedy, Box 2411-R, Morristown, N.J. 07960.

**NEW PROVIDENCE:** Hillview Stampers, every Friday, Hillview School, Room A3, 2:10 p.m. Juanita S. Goldman, 340 Central Ave., New Providence, N.J. 07974.

**NORTH HALEDON:** North Haledon Stamp and Coin Club, second Thursday, 950 High Mountain Road, 7:30 p.m. Janet Post, 351 Belmont Ave., Haledon, N.J. 07508.

**OLD BRIDGE:** Old Bridge Stamp and Coin Club, first and third Tuesday, Hill Lanes Bowling Alley, Route 9, 8 p.m. A.E. Washor, Route 9, Old Bridge, N.J. 08857.

**PHILLIPSBURG:** Bi-State Stamp Club, fourth Tuesday, City Federal Bank, Roseberry Street, 7:30 p.m. Howard Arnold, Box 97, Bloomsbury, N.J. 08804.

**RIDGEWOOD:** North Jersey Stamp Club, second and fourth Wednesday, St. Elizabeth's Church, California Street, 8 p.m. No meetings in July and August. Marguerite J. Doney, 65 New St., Allendale, N.J. 07401.

**SUMMIT:** Garden State Post Card Collector's Club, first Sunday, Jewish Community Center, Kent Place Boulevard and Morris Avenue, 1 p.m. Dolores L. Kirchgessner, Box 1005, Secaucus, N.J. 07094.

**TEANECK:** Teaneck Stamp Club, first and third Thursday, Town Hall, Teaneck Road, 8 p.m. No meetings in July and August. Tom R. Bleeker, Box 331, Allendale, N.J. 07401.

**TRENTON:** Trenton Philatelic Society, second and fourth Friday, Mercer County Administration Building, South Broad Street, 7:30 p.m. No meetings in July and August. F.D. Davis, 11 Morningside Drive, Yardley, Pa. 19607.

**VINELAND:** Association of South Jersey Stamp Clubs, second Sunday, No. 1 Vineland

Fire Hall, 4th and Wood streets, 2 p.m. Helen Rocco, 405 N. 8th St., Vineland, N.J. 08360.

**WARREN:** Queen City-Warren Stamp and Cover Club, first and third Monday, 1st National Bank of Central Jersey, 59 Mountain Blvd., 7:30 p.m. Frank F. Raciti, 273 King George Road, Warren, N.J. 07060.

**WEST ORANGE:** Society of Israel Philatelists, North Jersey Chapter, third Monday, Jewish Center, 300 Pleasant Valley Way, 8 p.m. Chester S. Callen, 27 Marmon Terrace, West Orange, N.J. 07052.

## MISCELLANEOUS

Englewood Stamp Club, contact secretary, David Popkin, Box 528, Englewood, N.J. 07631-0528.

Historic Batsto Philatelic Society, irregular intervals. C.F. Kier Jr., 109 Oak Ave., Elm Towne, N.J. 08037.

Scouts on Stamps Society International, George Washington Chapter, bimonthly, various locations, 2 p.m. Carl F. Schaum, 177 Mohawk Drive, Cranford, N.J. 07016.

# NEW MEXICO

**ALAMOGORDO:** Chaparral Stamp and Coin Club, every Tuesday, Chaparral Junior High School, Room 1, 3:05 p.m. Elise Smith, 2413 Princeton, Alamogordo, N.M. 88310.

**ALBUQUERQUE:** Palo Duro Stamp Club, every Monday, Palo Duro Senior Citizens Center, 5221 Palo Duro NE, 1 p.m. John E. Backman, 3201 Britt NE, Albuquerque, N.M. 87111.

**CLOVIS:** Clovis-Portales Stamp Club, first and third Sunday, First Federal Savings and Loan Association, 2501 Prince St., 2 p.m. Douglas C. Williams, 32 Paseo Village, Clovis, N.M. 88101.

**LAS CRUCES:** Mesilla Valley Stamp Club, first and third Thursday, Mutual Building and Loan, Telshor and Missouri, 7:30 p.m. Lorraine Barbour, Box 546, Mesilla, N.M. 88046.

**LOS ALAMOS:** Los Alamos Stamp Collectors' Association, second and fourth Tuesday, Fuller Lodge, 2132 Central Ave., 7:30 p.m. Eva Lee M. Wentworth, 2161-B 36th St., Los Alamos, N.M. 87544.

## MISCELLANEOUS

Alamogordo Philatelic Society, first and third Sunday, members' homes, 2 p.m. Elise Smith, 2413 Princeton, Alamogordo, N.M. 88310.

Roadrunner Stamp Club, different places, Helen C. Wilcox, 1300 N. Guadalupe, Carlsbad, N.M. 88220.

# NEW YORK

**ALBANY:** Fort Orange Stamp Club, every Tuesday, Albany Institute of History and Art, 125 Washington Ave., 8 p.m. No meetings in June, July and August. Maris Tirums, 125 Washington Ave., Albany, N.Y. 12210.

**AMSTERDAM:** Upstate New York Post Card Club, second Friday, Second Presbyterian Church, Church Street (Routes 5 and 30), 7:30 p.m. No meetings in July, August and September. Dorothy J. Baron, 1832 Fiero Ave., Schenectady, N.Y. 12303.

**BAYSHORE:** Great Southbay Postcard Collectors Club, first Thursday, Bayshore Memorial Building, East Main Street, 6 p.m. Carlton Coulter, Box 251, Brightwaters, N.Y. 11718.

**BETHPAGE:** Germany Philatelic Society, Chapter 30, fourth Monday, Bethpage High School, Faculty Dining Room, 7:30 p.m. Herb M. Hartfield, 197 N. Delaware Ave., North Massapequa, N.Y. 11758.

**BINGHAMTON:** Johnson City Stamp Club, first and third Monday, New York S.E.&G. Building, Old Vestal Road, 8 p.m. Robert Shelanskey, 300 June St., Endicott, N.Y. 13760.

**BROOKLYN:** Benjamin Franklin Stamp Club, Public School No. 16, each Tuesday and Friday, Clubroom 207, 157 Wilson St., 2 p.m. Steven J. Braunstein, 157 Wilson St., Brooklyn, N.Y. 11211.

— St. Matthew-Emanuel Stamp Club, first, third and fifth Wednesday, 421 7th St., 7:30 p.m. Albert J. Bruckner, 1143 E. 42nd St., Brooklyn, N.Y. 11210.

**BUFFALO:** Buffalo Stamp Club, every Friday, Holiday Inn, 1881 Niagara Falls Blvd., 8 p.m. Walter J. Orton III, 2265 Long Road, Grand Island, N.Y. 14072.

— Plewacki Post Stamp Society, every Tuesday, Adam Plewacki American Legion Post 799, 385 Paderewski Drive, 8 p.m. No meetings on holidays. Stanley A. Keane, 385 Paderewski Drive, Buffalo, N.Y. 14212.

— Polish Philatelic Society, fourth Friday, 612 Fillmore Ave., 8 p.m. Jerome Mazurek, 1390 Broadway, Buffalo, N.Y. 14212.

**CARMEL:** Putnam Philatelic Society, first and third Friday, Guidepost Associates, Conference Room, 7:30 p.m. Harry Bryant, Box 196, Patterson, N.Y. 12563.

**COBLESKILL:** Cobleskill Stamp Club, second Thursday, B.P.O. Elks Lodge, Legion Drive, 8 p.m. Muriel K. Jester, Route 20 and RD 1, Sharon Springs, N.Y. 13439.

**COOPERSTOWN:** Leatherstocking Stamp Club, third Tuesday, 28 Pioneer St., 8 p.m. Mary Pangborn, 61 Pioneer St., Cooperstown, N.Y. 13326.

**DANSVILLE:** Dansville Area Stamp and Coin Club, third Sunday, Dansville Town Hall, Clara

Barton Street, 2 p.m. Robert L. Stickney, 45 Van Campen St., Dansville, N.Y. 14437.

**EAST AURORA:** East Aurora Philatelic Society, every other Wednesday, East Aurora Middle School, 7:30 p.m. David L. Smith, 744 Warren Drive, East Aurora, N.Y. 14052.

**EAST ROCKAWAY:** East Rockaway Stamp Club, first and third Monday, 6 James St., 8 p.m. Vernon L. Brenner, 70 Cameron Ave., Hempstead, N.Y. 11550.

**ELMIRA:** Elmira Stamp Club, third Tuesday, Chemung Valley Savings and Loan Association, North Main and First streets, 8 p.m. Kathryn Knapp, Hillcrest Road, RD 1, No. 494, Elmira, N.Y. 14903.

**FREDONIA:** Northern Chautauqua Philatelic Society, first and third Monday, American Legion Post 59, 7:30 p.m. Dolores Dieteman, 208 Pike St., Dunkirk, N.Y. 14048.

**FULTON:** Fulton Stamp Club, second and fourth Wednesday, Fulton Municipal Building, South First Street, 8 p.m. Ronald Traino, Box 44, Fulton, N.Y. 13069.

**GENEVA:** Finger Lakes Stamp Club, second and fourth Wednesday, Jordan Hall, North Street, 7 p.m. Gil Lewis, RD 3, Box 293, Route 88 S, Newark, N.Y. 14513.

**GREENLAWN:** Huntington Stamp Club, first and third Tuesday, Greenlawn Plaza, Travel Office, Palaski Road, 7:30 p.m. Arthur H. Spear, 617 9th Ave., East Northport, N.Y. 11731.

**HAMILTON:** Chenango Valley Stamp Club, second Friday, Colgate University, Huntington Gymnasium, Lyon Lounge, 7:45 p.m. No meetings in July and August. Cliff Glaviano, 404 Franklin St., Oneida, N.Y. 13421.

**JACKSON HEIGHTS:** Philatelic Club of Jackson Heights, second and fourth Tuesday, Queensborough Public Library, 35-51 81st St., 5 p.m. James Brinkman, 34-39 82nd St., Jackson Heights, N.Y. 11372.

**KINGSTON:** Stamptrotters Society of Kingston, second Thursday, Chambers School, Ulster Avenue Mall, 7:30 p.m. Bruce Burgher, 22 Lawrenceville St., Kingston, N.Y. 12401.

**LAKEWOOD:** Reuben E. Fenton Philatelic Society, last Tuesday, Chautauqua Mall Community Center, 7:30 p.m. Mary Lawson, 35 Charles St., Lakewood, N.Y. 14750.

**LONG BEACH:** Long Beach Stamp and Coin Club, second Tuesday, Long Beach Library, 111 W. Park Ave., 8 p.m. A.H. Alexander, 330 W. Pine St., Long Beach, N.Y. 11561.

**MASSAPEQUA PARK:** Bar Harbor Stamp Club, first and third Monday, Bowery Savings Bank, Sunrise Highway, 7:30 p.m. Arthur B. Silverman, 1 Larch Lane, Massapequa Park, N.Y. 11762.

**MILLBROOK:** China Philatelic Study Group, first Monday, North Avenue, 7 p.m. Gene Klein, Box 630, Millbrook, N.Y. 12545.

**MONTICELLO:** Sullivan County Philatelic Society, first Sunday, Temple Sholom, Port Jervis Road, 7:30 p.m. Art Rosenzweig, Box 230, Monticello, N.Y. 12201.

**MONTROSE:** Cortlandt Stamp Club, first and third Friday, Springvale Inn, Route 9A, 8 p.m. Duncan Finlayson, Box 115, Montrose, N.Y. 10548.

**NEWBURGH:** Newburgh Stamp Club, fourth Monday, Newburgh Savings Bank, Vails Gate Branch, Route 32 and Temple Hill Road, 7:45 p.m. Lorna Miller, 310 Nina St., New Windsor, N.Y. 12550.

**NEW YORK:** Atoz Stamp Club, last Saturday, 144 E. 24th St., 7:30 p.m. Melvin Garabrant, 63 Park Ave., Verona, N.J. 07044.

— Austria Philatelic Society of New York, fourth Monday, March, April, May, October and November, Collectors Club, 22 E. 35th St., 8 p.m. Meetings at members' homes during June and September. Jo-Anne W. Theimer, 150 Rumson Road, Rumson, N.J. 07760.

— City Hall Stamp Club, every Saturday, 932 Broadway, third floor, 8 a.m. Jacob Habib, 150 Nassau St., New York, N.Y. 10038.

— Essay-Proof Society, second Wednesday, Collectors Club, 22 E. 35th St., 8 p.m. No meetings in July and August. David E. McGuire, RD 4, Colonial Drive, Katonah, N.Y. 10536.

— Estonian Philatelic Society, second Sunday, Estonia House, 243 E. 34th St., 11 a.m. Rudolf Hamar, 31 Addison Terrace, Old Tappan, N.J. 07675.

— Fine Arts Philatelists, New York Chapter, third Friday, Collectors Club, 22 E. 35th St., 7:30 p.m. No meetings in July and August. Olga Priester, 757 60th St., Brooklyn, N.Y. 11220.

— International Society for Japanese Philately, New York Chapter, first Monday, Collectors Club, 22 E. 35th St., 7:30 p.m. Frank A. Howard, 115 John St., North Massapequa, N.Y. 11758.

— Italy and Colonies Study Circle (USA), last Friday, studio of Domenico Facci, 248 W. 14th St., 8 p.m. Michael Pane, 307 N. Main St., Hightstown, N.J. 08520.

— Masonic Stamp Club of New York, second Wednesday, Collectors Club, 22 E. 35th St., 1:30 p.m. No meetings in July and August. Dr. Irwin M. Yarry, Masonic Hall, Box 10 or 71 W. 23rd St., New York, N.Y. 10010.

— Metropolitan First Day Cover Society, Chapter 19, first Thursday, Collectors Club, 22 E. 35th St., 7:45 p.m. No meetings in July and August. Ben Green, 66-15 Thornton Place, Rego Park, N.Y. 11374.

— Scandinavian Collectors Club, second Wednesday, Swedish Salvation Army, 225 E. 52nd St., 8 p.m. Paul W. Helgesen, 85 Willowbrook Ave., Stamford, Conn. 06902.

**NORTH BABYLON:** Babylon Stamp Club, first and third Wednesday, Deer Park Avenue Elementary School, 7:30 p.m. J.J. Lambert, 18 Leeds Lane, North Babylon, N.Y. 11703.

**OSWEGO:** Oswego Stamp Club, second and fourth Tuesday, Roy C. McCrobic Building, Lake Street, 8 p.m. Jim Oldenburg, RD 1, Box 41, Oswego, N.Y. 13126.

**PATCHOGUE:** Patchogue Stamp Club, second and fourth Monday, Four Sisters Community Center, 96 S. Ocean Ave., 7:30 p.m. Ray A. Boldt, 51 Highland Ave., Patchogue, N.Y. 11772.

**PLATTSBURGH:** Plattsburgh Stamp Club, second and fourth Monday, October-April; fourth Monday, May-September, State Bank of Albany Building, Margaret Street, 7:30 p.m. Glenn Estus, Box 451, Westport, N.Y. 12993.

**POUGHKEEPSIE:** Dutchess Philatelic Society, first and third Tuesday, Friends Meeting House, Hooker Avenue and Whittier Boulevard, 7:30 p.m. No meetings in July and August. Roy Ahlquist, Quaker Lane, Staatsburg, N.Y. 12580.

**REGO PARK:** Long Island Stamp Club, second, fourth and fifth Tuesday, Lost Battalion Hall, 93-29 Queens Blvd., 7:30 p.m. Marcus Julis, 144-04 Gravett Road, Flushing, N.Y. 11367.

**ROCHESTER:** Rochester Philatelic Association, second and fourth Thursday, St. Paul's Episcopal Church, East Avenue and Vick B, 8 p.m. No meetings in July and August. John Kellas, Box 3806, Brighton Station, Rochester, N.Y. 14610.

— Society of Israel Philatelists, Rochester Chapter, third Monday, Jewish Community Center, Edgewood Avenue, 7:30 p.m. Dr. Morris Sherwin, 1840 Monroe Ave., Rochester, N.Y. 14618.

**ROME:** Copper City Stamp Club, second and fourth Thursday, American Legion Home, 325 Erie Blvd. W, 7:30 p.m. No meetings in June, July and August. Franklyn Rudd, 614 N. James St., Rome, N.Y. 13440.

**ROSLYN:** North Shore Philatelic Society, first and third Wednesday, Roslyn Library, 8 p.m. Adolph Stephani, 4 Ann St., Glen Cove, N.Y. 11542.

— Society of Israel Philatelists, Chai Long Island Chapter, fourth Wednesday, Temple Beth Sholom, Roslyn Road, 8 p.m. Richard Cowitt, Box 85, Glen Oaks, N.Y. 11004.

**SHERRILL:** Community Stamp Club (Oneida-Sherrill), third Thursday, CAC Clubhouse, 139 E. Hamilton Ave., 7:30 p.m. No meetings in June, July and August. Don Connelly, 68 Glenwood Ave. RD 1, Oneida, N.Y. 13421.

**SIDNEY:** Tri-County Stamp Club, third Sunday, Sidney Civic Center, 7 p.m. No meetings in July and August. Robert Finnegan, 27 Pearl St. E, Sidney, N.Y. 13838.

**STATEN ISLAND:** Public School No. 8 Great Kills School Stamp Club, every Thursday, School Library, Lindenwood Road, 3 p.m. Fred Sprague, Lindenwood Road, Staten Island, N.Y. 10308.

**UTICA:** Utica Stamp Club, first and third Tuesday, Plymouth-Bethesda Church, State and Plant streets, 7:30 p.m. Herbert F. Sears, Box 394, Utica, N.Y. 13503.

**VAILS GATE:** Half Moon Postcard Club, fourth Friday, Albany Savings Bank, Vails Gate Branch, Route 32, 8 p.m. Karl P. Baisley, Box 21, Lake Peekskill, N.Y. 10537.

**WEBSTER:** Xerox Employees Stamp Club, second Tuesday, Building 337, 800 Phillips Road, 7:30 p.m. R. Altmann, 107 Linden Tree Lane, Apt. 12, Webster, N.Y. 14580.

**WHITE PLAINS:** Texaco Stamp Club, first Wednesday, 2000 Westchester Avenue, noon. H.E. Hagan, 2000 Westchester Ave., White Plains, N.Y. 10605.

## MISCELLANEOUS

Bell Park Gardens Stamp Club, second and fourth Friday, members' homes, 7:30 p.m. No meetings in July and August. Charles Amira, 218-06 68th Ave., Bayside, N.Y. 11364.

The Graf Zeppelin Stamp Club, first and third Thursday, Recreation Center No. 1, Baumholder Post, 7:30 p.m. MSG (Ret) Leon H. Stalker, Box R, General Delivery, APO New York 09034.

Long Island Postal History Society, no regular date. Arthur Fitzpatrick, Box 1178, Southold, N.Y. 11971.

Society of Israel Philatelists, Hudson-Mohawk Chapter 1, third Wednesday, members' homes, 8 p.m. Leonard Rockmore, 71 Paxwood Road, Delmar, N.Y. 12054.

# NORTH CAROLINA

**ASHEVILLE:** Asheville Stamp Club, third Monday, First Congregational Church, 308 Merrimon Ave., 7:30 p.m. Charles W. Siddaway, 119 Spooks Branch Road, Asheville, N.C. 28804.

**CHARLOTTE:** Charlotte Philatelic Society, first and third Sunday, Metrolina Association for the Blind, 704 Louise Ave., 2 p.m. Pradeep N. Jalundhwala, Box 30101, Charlotte, N.C. 28230.

**GREENSBORO:** Greensboro Stamp Club, second and fourth Thursday, Lindley Recreation Center, Springwood Street, 7:30 p.m. F. Dudley Chaffee, 3810 Parkwood Drive, Greensboro, N.C. 27403.

— Tarheel Postcard Club, Saturdays, 1614 Helmwood Drive, 2 p.m. Roberta S. Greiner, 1614 Helmwood Drive, Greensboro, N.C. 27410.

**HENDERSONVILLE:** Hendersonville Stamp Club, last Friday, Meadows Community Center, 3rd Avenue and Justice Street, 7:30 p.m. Hans R. Steinhardt, 202 Waddell Drive, Hendersonville, N.C. 28739.

**HUBERT:** Benjamin Franklin Stamp Club, second Monday, Queens Creek United Methodist Church, 7:30 p.m. Le Vance Myers, 105 Sandy Ridge Road, Hubert, N.C. 28584.

**RALEIGH:** Raleigh Stamp Club, first Monday, Jaycee Center, Wade Avenue, 7:30 p.m. Richard Cramp, Box 26863, Raleigh, N.C. 27611.

**TRYON:** Thermal Belt Stamp Club, first and third Monday, North Carolina National Bank Building, 7:30 p.m. Albert F.W. Jaeger, Drawer A, Tryon, N.C. 28782.

## MISCELLANEOUS

Fortnightly Collectors Club, third Thursday, members' homes, 7:30 p.m. William Heidinger, 4204 Cantey Place, Charlotte, N.C. 28211.

Scouts On Stamps Society International, Tarheel Chapter, meets as announced. W.C. Cowen, Box 31242, Raleigh, N.C. 27622.

# NORTH DAKOTA

**BISMARCK:** Lewis and Clark Stamp Club, second Sunday, basement Gate City Savings and Loan, 4th and Rosser streets, 2 p.m. Dean Conrad, Box 217, Bismarck, N.D. 58502.

**FARGO:** Fargo-Moorhead Stamp Club (F-M Stamp Club), second and fourth Friday, North Dakota State University, Minard Hall, Room 201, 6:30 p.m. Martin Carlson, 1028 3rd Ave. S, Moorhead, Minn. 56560.

# OHIO

**AKRON:** Rubber City Stamp Club, first and third Friday, Montrose Zion United Methodist Church, 565 N. Cleveland Massillon Road, 8 p.m. Thomas Huchko, Box 508, Barberton, Ohio 44203.

**ALLIANCE:** Carnation City Stamp Club, fourth Wednesday, Christ United Methodist Church, 470 E. Broadway, 7:30 p.m. Dave Keirn, 23440 Hartley Road, Alliance, Ohio 44601.

**ASHLAND:** Ashland Stamp and Coin Club, first and third Tuesday, First Federal Savings and Loan, 7:30 p.m. Dwight Morr, Box 124, Ashland, Ohio 44805.

**ASHTABULA:** Ashtabula County Stamp Club, third Wednesday, alternate Cardinal Savings and Loan and Ashtabula Hotel, 7:30 p.m. Mike Clarke, Box 452, North Kingsville, Ohio 44068.

**ATHENS:** Athens Stamp Club, second Wednesday, Electric Company, 200 S. May, 7:30 p.m. No meetings in July and August. Marvin Fletcher, 45 Avon Place, Athens, Ohio 45701.

**AVON LAKE:** Trojan Stamp Club, every Friday, Troy Junior High School, Belmar Boulevard, 3 p.m. Ronald L. Rummel, 149 Avon Belden Road, Avon Lake, Ohio 44012.

**CANTON:** McKinley Stamp Club, fourth Wednesday, Malone College, Campus Barn, 515 25th St. NW, 7:30 p.m. Loretta Hart, 1730 Coventry Road NE, Massillon, Ohio 44646.

**CINCINNATI:** Philatelic Society of Cincinnati, first and third Wednesday, Cincinnati Club, 8th and Race streets, 8 p.m. Clifford W. Shafer, Box 1794, Cincinnati, Ohio 45201.

**CLEVELAND:** American Hungarian Stamp Club, first Saturday, 5 p.m.; third Friday, 7 p.m. West Side Hungarian Reformed Church, 15300 Puritas Road. Andrew Dona, Box 07105, Lakewood, Ohio 44107.

— Garfield-Perry Stamp Club, every Friday, Holiday Inn-Downtown, 2160 Euclid Ave., 8 p.m. Thomas F. Allen, 2160 Euclid Ave., Cleveland, Ohio 44115.

**COLUMBUS:** China Stamp Society, Ko Lun Pu Chapter, fourth Sunday in January, April, July and October, Upper Arlington Public Library, 2 p.m. Paul H. Gault, 140 W. 18th Ave., Columbus, Ohio 43210.

— Germany Philatelic Society, Edward E. Kuehn Chapter 20, third Sunday, Upper Arlington Public Library, 2 p.m. Paul H. Gault, 140 W. 18th Ave., Columbus, Ohio 43210.

**CUYAHOGA FALLS:** Cuyahoga Falls Stamp Club, first and third Monday, Jack Richard's Art Studio, 2nd floor Gallery, 7:30 p.m. No meeting in July. A.R. Lunsford, Box 203, Cuyahoga Falls, Ohio 44222.

**DAYTON:** City of Dayton Philatelic Society, second and fourth Wednesday, Patterson Homestead, 1815 Brown St., 7:30 p.m. Emerson H. Marcum, 155 Antwerp Ave., Brookville, Ohio 45309.

**ELYRIA:** Black River Stamp Club, first Friday, Elyria Savings and Trust Co., Lowell Street, 8 p.m. Robert H. Frederick, 276 Dowd Road, Elyria, Ohio 44035.

**EUCLID:** Euclid Stamp Club, second and fourth Monday, Euclid Lutheran Church, 431 E. 260th St., 8 p.m. Denise Stotts, Box 32211, Euclid, Ohio 44132.

**FINDLAY:** Fort Findlay Stamp Club, second and fourth Wednesday, Tri-County Bank, 7:30 p.m. Donald M. Yeager, Box 426, Findlay, Ohio 45840.

**HAMILTON:** Fort Hamilton Philatelic Society, third Wednesday, Firehouse No. 5, Erie Highway, 7:30 p.m. Len Mueller, 6 Donna Ave., Hamilton, Ohio 45013.

**HAYESVILLE:** Johnny Appleseed Postcard Club, second Thursday, Hayesville Elementary School, 6:30 p.m. Ruth Garrett, Box 2297, Mansfield, Ohio 44905.

**MARION:** Marion Hobby Club, second Wednesday, Redman Hall, 581 Bellefontaine Ave., 7:30 p.m. Berneice White, 3487 Firstenberger Road, Marion, Ohio 43302.

**MARTINS FERRY:** Belmont County Stamp Club, first Friday, 7:30 p.m.; third Sunday, 2 p.m. Municipal Building, Council Room. Vi Marple, 4232 Franklin St., Bellaire, Ohio 43906.

**NEWARK:** Central Ohio Stamp and Coin Club, third Tuesday, State Savings Building, 1235 N. 21st St., 7:30 p.m. Leland Crotinger, Box 696, Newark, Ohio 43055.

**NEW PHILADELPHIA:** Tuscora Stamp Club, first and third Wednesday, Diamond Savings and Loan Company, 7:30 p.m. No meetings in December. Ralph W. Otto, Box 61, New Philadelphia, Ohio 44663.

**NORTH CANTON:** Stark County Stamp Club, second Wednesday, Ameritrust Bank Building, 1200 N. Main St., 7:30 p.m. Brian Mumford, 1210 31st St. NW, Canton, Ohio 44709.

**NORTH OLMSTED:** Cuy-Lor Stamp Club, second and fourth Friday, Ohio Savings, Great Northern Boulevard, 8 p.m. Eric E. Johnson, Box 45042, Westlake, Ohio 44145.

**PIQUA:** Upper Miami Valley Stamp Club, third Tuesday, Piqua National Bank, Community Room, 7:45 p.m. Lowell Storer, Box 206, West Milton, Ohio 45383.

**SANDUSKY:** Sandusky Stamp Club, second and fourth Tuesday, Briar School, South Avenue, 8 p.m. No meetings in June, July and August. Donald Crosby, 331 Brunswick Drive, Huron, Ohio 44839.

**TIFFIN:** Tiffin Stamp Club, third Thursday, Westgate Tri-County Bank, 7:30 p.m. No meeting in August. John Kern, 84 N. Sandusky St., Tiffin, Ohio 44883.

**TOLEDO:** Stamp Collectors Club of Toledo, second and fourth Thursday, Medical College of Ohio, Mulford Library Cafeteria, 3000 Arlington Ave., 8 p.m. Allan M. Cunningham, 706 Spring Grove Ave., Toledo, Ohio 43605.

**UNIVERSITY HEIGHTS:** Society of Israel Philatelists, Cleveland Chapter, first Tuesday, Temple Emanu El, 2200 S. Green Road, 8 p.m. No meetings in July and August. Dr. Albert Friedberg, 31715 Vine St., Willowick, Ohio 44094.

**WARREN:** Warren Area Stamp Club, fourth Friday; third Friday during November and December, Morgandale No. 3 Fire Station, Wilson Drive and Overland Avenue NE, 7:30 p.m. A.H. Aho, 1658 Oak St. SW, Warren, Ohio 44485.

**WORTHINGTON:** Worthington Stamp Club, first and third Monday, Ohio State Bank, Founder's Room, 688 High St., 8 p.m. Wendell L. Thompson, Box 323, Worthington, Ohio 43085.

**YOUNGSTOWN:** Mahoning Valley Stamp Club, second and fourth Thursday, Martin Luther Lutheran Church, 420 Clearmount Drive, 7:30 p.m. Anthony C. Blanch, 15 Lee Drive, Poland, Ohio 44514.

**ZANESVILLE:** Zane Trace Philatelic Society, first and third Tuesday, MAJV School, Richards Road, 8 p.m. Roy Gillespie, 2990 Lookout Drive, Zanesville, Ohio 43701.

## MISCELLANEOUS

Ohio Precancel Club, scheduled shows. Charles Pearson, 1004 Pinehollow Lane, Cincinnati, Ohio 45231.

# OKLAHOMA

**BARTLESVILLE:** Washington County Philatelic Society, fourth Thursday, January through October; third Thursday in November, Disciples Christian Church, 5800 Douglas Lane, 7:30 p.m. No meetings in July, August and December. Joe F. Copeland, Box 741, Bartlesville, Okla. 74005.

**LAWTON:** Lawton-Fort Sill Stamp Club, first and third Tuesday, Town Hall, 7:30 p.m. Lloyd C. Brown, 804 N. 13th St., Lawton, Okla. 73501.

**MUSKOGEE:** Muskogee Stamp Club, first Tuesday, Commercial Bank Building, Louis Duncan Room, 3rd and Broadway, 7:30 p.m. Mrs. J.D. Cole, 1321 W. Broadway, Muskogee, Okla. 74401.

**OKLAHOMA CITY:** Oklahoma City Stamp Club, first and third Tuesday, St. David's Episcopal Church, 3333 N. Meridian, 7:30 p.m. Don Beitsch, Box 26944, Oklahoma City, Okla. 73126.

**TULSA:** Tulsa Stamp Club, first and third Thursday, Tulsa Central Library, 7 p.m. Calvin E. Rohmiller, 10972 E. 3rd, Tulsa, Okla. 74128.

## MISCELLANEOUS

Ponca City Stamp Club, second Friday, indefinite location, 7:30 p.m. Dorothy S. Jones, 1914 N. 6th, Ponca City, Okla. 74601.

# OREGON

**ALBANY:** Linn County Philatelic Society, second Wednesday, State Savings and Loan Association, basement, 3rd and Ellsworth, 7:30 p.m. Carmen Suplee, 39178 Highway 226, Scio, Ore. 97374.

**BANDON:** Bandon Stamp Club, third Friday, Bandon City Hall Council Chambers, 8 p.m. Charlotte Casey, 2678 Stanton St., North Bend, Ore. 97459.

**EUGENE:** Greater Eugene Stamp Society, second and fourth Wednesday, Benjamin Franklin Savings and Loan Building, 11th and Pearl (do not send mail to the above address), 7:30 p.m. A.R. Martin, 768 Ascot Drive, Eugene, Ore. 97401.

**MEDFORD:** Southern Oregon Philatelic Society, first Thursday, Girls Community Club, 229 N. Bartlett, 7 p.m. Barbara Cranston, 229 N. Bartlett, Medord, Ore. 97501.

**PORTLAND:** Oregon Stamp Society, second and fourth Tuesday, society's clubhouse, 4828 N.E. 33rd Ave., 8 p.m. Harold D. Peterson, Box 02121, Portland, Ore. 97202.

**SALEM:** Junior Stamp Collectors of Salem, third Tuesday, Grant School, Market and Winter, 7 p.m. Thomas D. Pomeroy, 1909 Nut Tree Drive NW, Salem, Ore. 97304.

— Salem Stamp Society, third Tuesday, Grant Elementary School, 7:30 p.m. Rae Hanna, 637 Browning Ave., South Salem, Ore. 97302.

— Willamette Valley Stamp Club, first Monday, Ben Franklin Building, 101 High St., 7:30 p.m. Thomas Pomeroy, 1909 Nut Tree Drive NW, Salem, Ore. 97304.

## MISCELLANEOUS

Benton County Philatelic Society, second Wednesday, members' homes, 7 p.m. Thomas Pomeroy, 1909 Nut Tree Drive NW, Salem, Ore. 97304.

Corvallis Stamp Club, first Wednesday, members' homes, 7:30 p.m. Thomas Pomeroy, 1909 Nut Tree Drive NW, Salem, Ore. 97304.

# PENNSYLVANIA

**AMBLER:** Ambler Stamp Club, first Wednesday, third Tuesday, Trinity Memorial Episcopal Church, Parish Hall, Bethlehem Pike and Highland Avenue, 7:30 p.m. James H. O'Mara, 1230 Lois Road, Ambler, Pa. 19002.

**BETHEL PARK:** Bethel Park Junior Stamp Club, every Monday, Neil Armstrong Middle School, 3:30 p.m. Richard Gaetano, Neil Armstrong Middle School, Bethel Park, Pa. 15102.

**CLEARFIELD:** Clearfield Philatelic Society, second Tuesday, Old County Home, Route 322, 7:30 p.m. Philip Thompson, Temple Heights, Curwensville, Pa. 16833.

**GREENSBURG:** Westmoreland County Philatelic Society, second Sunday, Greengate Mall, Community Hall, 2:15 p.m. Grace E. Prinkey, Box 501, RD 1, Hunker, Pa. 15639.

**HAZLETON:** Greater Hazleton Area Stamp Club, first and third Wednesday, Diamond United Methodist Church, Parish House, Diamond Avenue and Locust Street, 7:30 p.m. Kathryn B. Kapuschinsky, 226 Hillcrest Drive, West Hazleton, Pa. 18201.

**JOHNSTOWN:** Johnstown Junior Stamp Club, first Thursday, David A. Glosser Memorial Library, 7 p.m. Donald W. Smith, 1633 Florida Ave., Johnstown, Pa. 15902.

— Johnstown Stamp Club, fourth Monday, Cambria Savings and Loan Association, Franklin Street, 8 p.m. Mary Katherine Roberts, 327 Haverford St., Johnstown, Pa. 15905.

**LEBANON:** Lebanon Stamp Collectors Club, second Thursday, Quality Inn-Lebanon, Route

72 S, 7:30 p.m. Jerry Laconis, Box 114, Palmyra, Pa. 17078.

**LOWER BURRELL:** Tri-County Stamp Club, third Monday, Grace Community United Presbyterian Church, 2751 Grant St., 7:30 p.m. D.L. Robinson, 416 Wedgewood Drive, Lower Burrell, Pa. 15068.

**LYNDORA:** Butler County Philatelic Society, first and third Wednesday, Dunbar Community Center, 7:30 p.m. Harold C. Bartlett, 220 Grandview Blvd., Butler, Pa. 16001.

**MONTOURSVILLE:** Williamsport Stamp Club, fourth Wednesday, American Legion Post, 104-1312 E. Broad St., 8 p.m. Harold E. Gottshall, 1009 Weldon St., Montoursville, Pa. 17754.

**NEW CASTLE:** New Castle Stamp Club, second and fourth Tuesday, Hoyt Institute of Fine Arts, 124 E. Leasure Ave., 7:30 p.m. Clara E. McCandless, 607 S. Market St., New Wilmington, Pa. 16142.

**PHILADELPHIA:** Baltic States Philatelic Study Group, third Thursday, East Girard Savings and Loan Building, Castor and Princeton streets, 8 p.m. W.E. Norton, 2647 Eddington St., Philadelphia, Pa. 19137.

— Educators Philatelic Society, third Thursday, Saul High School, 7100 Henry Ave., 7 p.m. Dr. Ralph Bartholomew, 7100 Henry Ave., Philadelphia, Pa. 19128.

— Frankford Arsenal Stamp Club, second Thursday, Philadelphia Gas Works-Community, 4410 Frankford Ave., 8 p.m. No meetings in July and August. Edward G. Kroupa, 3347 St. Vincent St., Philadelphia, Pa. 19149.

— Germantown-Chestnut Hill Stamp Club, first Tuesday, third Wednesday, Watertown Recreation Center, Hartwell Lane, 7:30 p.m. No meetings in July and August. Dorothy L. Moore, Box 128, Flourtown, Pa. 19031.

— Oxford Philatelic Society, second and fourth Wednesday, 4410 Frankford Ave., 8 p.m. Samuel Brothkoff, 3177 Kensington Ave., Philadelphia, Pa. 19134.

— Scandinavian Collectors Club, Philadelphia Chapter 2, first Tuesday beginning with February and every other month, St. James United Methodist Church, Tabor Road and Water Street, 7:30 p.m. Alpheus P. McCloskey, 91 W. Fern St., Philadelphia, Pa. 19120.

**PITTSBURGH:** Philatelic Society of Pittsburgh, first and third Monday, First Lutheran Church, 615 Grant St., 7 p.m. Third Monday only in July, August and September. G.M. Carr, 995 Greentree Road, Pittsburgh, Pa. 15220.

— Society of Israel Philatelists, Pittsburgh Chapter, second Thursday, Hebrew Institute, 6401 Forbes Ave., 7:30 p.m. C. Daniel Askin, 5702 Beacon St., Pittsburgh, Pa. 15217.

**READING:** Scouts on Stamps Society, Daniel Boone Chapter 29, first Sunday of every other month beginning in January, Hawk Mountain Council Service Center, 4903 Pottsville Pike, 2 p.m. Jean E. Creitz, 830 Berkshire Drive, Reading, Pa. 19601.

**SHARON:** Sharon Stamp Club, third Tuesday, First Presbyterian Church, 600 E. State St., 7:30 p.m. C.N. Zook, 4400 Clifford Drive, Hermitage, Pa. 16148.

**SPRINGFIELD:** Springfield-Delco Stamp Club, second and fourth Thursday, Springfield Township Municipal Building, Springfield and Powell Road, 8 p.m. No meetings in July and August. Chet Draper, 802 Church Lane, Yeadon, Pa. 19050.

**STATE COLLEGE:** Mount Nittany Philatelic Society, first Thursday and third Wednesday, American Philatelic Research Library Building, 7:30 p.m. Mrs. Ardeth L. Frisbey, Box 902, State College, Pa. 16801.

**UPPER DARBY:** Lansdowne Upper Darby Stamp Club, second and fourth Tuesday, Multi-Purpose Building, 69th and Walnut, 8 p.m. Chet Draper, 802 Church Lane, Yeadon, Pa. 19050.

**WARREN:** Warren County Stamp Club, third Tuesday, Northwest Savings, Hospitality Room, 7:30 p.m. David Church, Route 1, Box 1539, Clarendon, Pa. 16313.

**WILKES-BARRE:** Wyoming Valley Stamp Club, first and third Tuesday, YMCA, second floor, East Northampton Street, 7:30 p.m. William F. McMurray, 6 Park Lane N, Mountaintop, Pa. 18707.

**WILKINSBURG:** Wilkinsburg Stamp Club, second and fourth Sunday, Borrough Building, 1 p.m. Joseph M. Bayuk, 4908 Plaport St., Pittsburgh, Pa. 15207.

**WORMLEYSBURG:** Susquehanna Valley Stamp and Study Club, second Tuesday, West Shore Stamps, 5 Market St.; fourth Tuesday, Larry Lee Stamps, 322 S. Front St., 7:30 p.m. Sandra L. Hurst, 2145 Lambs Gap Road, Enola, Pa. 17025.

**WYOMISSING:** Reading Stamp Collectors Club, second and fourth Tuesday, A.A.A. Building, 7:30 p.m. No meetings in July and August. Samuel Charles, 615 Byran St., Pennside, Pa. 19606.

**YORK:** White Rose Philatelic Society, first Tuesday, York Mall Community Room, East Market Street; third Wednesday, State Capital Savings Association, 2701 Eastern Blvd., 7:30 p.m. Clair A. Holtzapple, 313 Pinehurst Road, York, Pa. 17402.

## MISCELLANEOUS

China Stamp Society, Philadelphia Chapter, third Monday, members' homes, 7:30 p.m. Bernard E. Stoloff, 7 Bennington Road, Havertown, Pa. 19083.

Lithuanian Philatelic Society of New York, last Sunday, members' homes, 2 p.m. W.E. Norton, 2647 Eddington St., Philadelphia, Pa. 19137.

Mount Joy Stamp Club, first Wednesday, members' homes, 7:30 p.m. Mrs. Joseph Shaeffer, 127 Park Ave., Mount Joy, Pa. 17552.

Universal Ship Cancellation Society, Decatur Chapter 4, monthly, members' homes, 7:30 p.m. Richard F. Hoffner, 18 Ryers Ave., Cheltenham, Pa. 19012.

Western Pennsylvania Precancel Society, third Sunday may vary, members' homes, 10 a.m. Steve Pavlina, 208 Allegheny Ave., Cheswick, Pa. 15024.

# RHODE ISLAND

**NEWPORT:** Newport Philatelic Society, second and fourth Sunday, Jewish Community Center, Touro and Division streets, 1:30 p.m. Charles W. Birdy Sr., Box 388, Middletown, R.I. 02840.

**PAWTUCKET:** Slater Stamp Club, first and third Wednesday, Centennial Towers, Goff Avenue, 7:30 p.m. Linda R. Collette, Box 1774, Pawtucket, R.I. 02862.

**PROVIDENCE:** Rhode Island Philatelic Society, first and third Tuesday, All Saints Memorial Church, Parish Hall, 674 Westminster St., 8 p.m. John J. Perrino Jr., 34 Wildwood Drive, Cranston, R.I. 02920.

## MISCELLANEOUS

Rhode Island Postal History Society, on demand, members' homes. Brenton P. Thurston, 73 Northampton St., Warwick, R.I. 02888.

# SOUTH CAROLINA

**COLUMBIA:** Columbia Philatelic Society, second Tuesday and fourth Thursday, South Carolina Education Television Center, 2712 Millwood Ave., 8 p.m. Buddy Broome, Box 50328, Columbia, S.C. 29250.

**GREENVILLE:** Greenville Stamp Club, fourth Thursday, St. Francis Community Hospital, 6:30 p.m. Sam Whitehead, Box 1871, Greenville, S.C. 29602.

**NORTH CHARLESTON:** Charleston Stamp Club, first and third Thursday, North Charleston City Hall, 7:30 p.m. George Clark, Box 2164, Station A, Charleston, S.C. 29403.

# SOUTH DAKOTA

**ABERDEEN:** Ringneck Stamp and Coin Club, second Monday, First Bank-Aberdeen Fountain Room, 320 S. 1st St., 8 p.m. Elaine M. Roth, 118 Elizabeth Drive, Aberdeen, S.D. 57401.

**MOBRIDGE:** Bridge City Stamp and Coin Club, first Thursday, Montana-Dakota Utility Company, Social Room, 7:30 p.m. Stan Mack, Box 91, Mobridge, S.D. 57601.

# TENNESSEE

**CHATTANOOGA:** Chattanooga Stamp Club, first and third Thursday, U.S. Postal Facilities, Shallowford Road, 7:30 p.m. Ernest Seagle, 215 Buena Vista Drive, Chattanooga, Tenn. 37404.

**MEMPHIS:** Memphis Stamp Collectors Society, first and third Tuesday, Pink Palace Museum, 232 Tilton Road, 7:30 p.m. W.R. Bartlett, 5559 Ackerman Cove, Bartlett, Tenn. 38134.

**NASHVILLE:** Nashville Philatelic Society, second and fourth Thursday, Inglewood Branch Public Library, Gallatin Road, 6 p.m. Jack Watts, 2633 Western Hills Drive, Nashville, Tenn. 37214.

## MISCELLANEOUS

Mid-South Postcard Club of Memphis, fourth Tuesday, various places, 7:30 p.m. Ben Cox, 4061 Patte Ann Drive, Memphis, Tenn. 38116.

# TEXAS

**ARLINGTON:** Mid-Cities Stamp Club, first Wednesday, Arlington Community Center, South Center Street, Vandergriff Park, 7:30 p.m. Albert Little, Box 1483, Arlington, Tex. 76010.

**AUSTIN:** Austin Stamp Club, first Thursday, third Tuesday, Public Library, Howson Branch, 2500 Exposition, 7:30 p.m. Allen Kerr, 1424 Westmoor, Austin, Tex. 78723.

**BORGER:** Borger Stamp Club, first and third Tuesday, Opportunities Center, 7:30 p.m. Dale R. Smith, Box 334, Fritch, Tex. 79036.

— Hutchinson County Stamp and Coin Club, fourth Thursday, Hutchinson County Library Auditorium, 625 Weatherly St., 7 p.m. No meetings in June, July and August. Eck Spahich, 1512 Lancelot Road, Borger, Tex. 79007.

**EL PASO:** El Paso Philatelic Society, first Wednesday, El Paso Electric Co., Rush Fair Center, Rushing and Fairbanks; fourth Friday, Mutual Savings, Yarbrough and Montwood, 7:30 p.m. John J. Terranova, 10716 Captain Valtr, El Paso, Tex. 79924.

— Germany Philatelic Society, Southwest Chapter 32, second Wednesday, Mutual Savings Association, Trans Mountain Road, 7:30 p.m. Chris Probasco, Box 4286, El Paso, Tex. 79914.

**FORT WORTH:** Panther City Philatelic Society, second and fourth Tuesday, Panther Boys Club, 1519 Lipscomb St., 7:40 p.m. Charles W. Brock, 4633 El Campo Ave., Fort Worth, Tex. 76107.

**HOUSTON:** Houston Philatelic Society, first and third Monday, Central Presbyterian Church, 3788 Richmond Ave., 7:30 p.m. J.W. Paisley, 5 Cape Cod Lane, Houston, Tex. 77024.

— Lyndon B. Johnson Space Center Stamp Club, second and fourth Monday, Gilruth Center, JSC, NASA Road 1, 7:30 p.m. T. Nicodemus, Box 58328, Houston, Tex. 77258.

**KERRVILLE:** Bluebonnet Philatelic Society, first and third Thursday, Dietert Senior Citizens Claim, 617 Jefferson, 7:30 p.m. E. Tom Miller, 1117 Hancock Drive, Kerrville, Tex. 78028.

**LONGVIEW:** Longview Stamp Club, first Tuesday, Longview Community Center, 2nd and Whaley streets, 7:30 p.m. Louise McIntyre, 406 S. White Oak Road, White Oak, Tex. 75693.

**MARSHALL:** Marshall Stamp Club, second Tuesday, SWEPCO Building, 7:30 p.m. Hal Griswold, 4406 John Reagan, Marshall, Tex. 75670.

**NACOGDOCHES:** Nacogdoches Stamp Club, first Thursday, Unitarian Fellowship Building, 1502 Douglass Road, 7:30 p.m. Mrs. Victor Hoff, 90 Carrizo Creek Estates, Nacogdoches, Tex. 75961.

**SAN ANTONIO:** Mexico-Elmhurst Philatelic Society, South Texas Chapter, second Tuesday, 5164 Broadway, 7:30 p.m. Gloria J. Gosdin, 14330 Modesto Place, San Antonio, Tex. 78247.

— San Antonio Philatelic Association, every Friday, St. Luke's Lutheran Church, 514 Santa Monica, 8 p.m. Jack Virta, 2907 Sir Phillip Drive, San Antonio, Tex. 78209.

**WACO:** Heart of Texas Stamp Club, third Thursday, Texas Power and Light Service Center, 3600 Franklin Ave., 7:30 p.m. Mrs. Charles Fritsch, 4111 N. 24th, Waco, Tex. 76708.

## MISCELLANEOUS

Cowtown Postcard Club, third Sunday, members' homes, 2 p.m. Millie Poledna, 7504 Madeira, Fort Worth, Tex. 76112.

Permian Basin Stamp Club, second Tuesday, alternate post offices in Midland and Odessa, 7:30 p.m. Mrs. John W. Walker, 1304 Lawson Ave., Midland, Tex. 79701.

Texas Postal History Society, semiannually, various places. Dr. William H.P. Emery, 1421 Schulle Drive, San Marcos, Tex. 78666.

Texas Precancel Club, various places. David Hanschen, Box 823, Addison, Tex. 75001.

# VERMONT

**BENNINGTON:** Green Mountain Stamp Society, second and fourth Wednesday, Crescent Manor Nursing Home, 7 p.m. John Breen, Box 571, Bennington, Vt. 05201.

**BRATTLEBORO:** Brattleboro Stamp Club, third Monday, Brooks Memorial Library, Main Street, 7 p.m. Irene Kirchheimer, RD 2, Box 20-E, West Brattleboro, Vt. 05301.

**MONTPELIER:** Washington County Stamp Club, third Tuesday, 1st Baptist Church, School and St. Paul streets, 7:30 p.m. Herbert H. Storm, Box 269, Randolph, Vt. 05060.

## MISCELLANEOUS

Vermont Philatelic Society, once or twice a year, various places. Dr. Paul G. Abajian, 93 Saratoga Ave., Burlington, Vt. 05401.

# VIRGINIA

**ARLINGTON:** Fairlington Stamp Club, first and third Monday, South Fairlington Community Center, 7:30 p.m. Ernie F. Philipp, 4200 S. 34th St., Arlington, Va. 22206.

**DANVILLE:** Dan River Philatelic Society, first and third Tuesday, First and Merchant National Bank, Danville Room, Main Street, 7:30 p.m. W.A. Ware, Box 366, Danville, Va. 24543.

**McLEAN:** Dolley Madison Stamp Club, first and third Friday, McLean Community Center, 7:30 p.m. G. Margaret Babb, 6608 Ivy Hill Drive, McLean, Va. 22101.

**NORFOLK:** Society of Israel Philatelists, Tidewater Chapter, second Thursday, 2301-E Colley Ave., 7:30 p.m. Kurt Hirsch, M.D., 943-E Armfield Circle, Apt. 201, Norfolk, Va. 23505.

**RICHMOND:** Carriage House Stamp Club, third Thursday, First Baptist Church, Monument Avenue and Boulevard, 7:30 p.m. Mrs. H. Linwood Snowa, 4634 Hanover Ave., Richmond, Va. 23226.

— Richmond Stamp Club, second and fourth Tuesday, C&P Building, Floyd and Nansemond streets, 8 p.m. Robert C. Moore, 1619 Westbury Drive, Richmond, Va. 23229.

**ROANOKE:** Big Lick Stamp Club, second Sunday, Main Post Office, Room 182, 416 Rutherford Ave. NE, 2:30 p.m. Ranes C. Chakravorty, M.D., 5049 Cherokee Hills Drive, Salem, Va. 24153.

**SPRINGFIELD:** Springfield Stamp Club, second and fourth Wednesday, Lynbrook Elementary School, 5801 Backlick Road, 7:30 p.m. Douglas K. Lehmann, Box 544, Springfield, Va. 22150.

**VIENNA:** Ayrhill Stamp Club, first and third Thursday, Fairfax County Public Library, Vienna Branch, 7:30 p.m. David Lee, 11706 Blue Smoke Trail, Reston, Va. 22091.

**WARRENTON:** Fauquier Stamp Club, first Saturday, Shadow Lawn Center, 70 Culpeper St., 10:30 a.m. Donn R. Kuse, Parks and Recreation, 14 Main St., Warrenton, Va. 22186.

**WOODBRIDGE:** Eastern Prince William Stamp Club, first Monday, Potomac Library, Opitz Boulevard, 7:30 p.m. Francis X. Alexander, Box 1052, Woodbridge, Va. 22193.

## MISCELLANEOUS

Holston Stamp Club, first Thursday, various places, 7 p.m. D.W. Ashley, 709 Navajo Trail, Bristol, Va. 24201.

Universal Ship Cancellation Society, Admiral Richard Byrd Chapter 11, first Friday, members' homes, 8:30 p.m. Kenneth P. Hanson, 6307 Pioneer Drive, Springfield, Va. 22150.

Virginia Philatelic Federation, quarterly, various places. Ranes C. Chakravorty, M.D., 5049 Cherokee Hills Drive, Salem, Va. 24153.

Virginia Postal History Society, last Sunday, 515 Wimgrow Road, 2 p.m. James Thayer, Box 29771, Richmond, Va. 23229.

# WASHINGTON

**SEATTLE:** Collectors Club of Seattle, Tuesdays, noon; Fridays, 7 p.m., 4731 15th Ave. NE, Ed Tupper, Box 15205, Seattle, Wash. 98115.

**SEQUIM:** Strait Stamp Society, second Monday, Sunnyside Village Recreation Room, 7 p.m. Lucille Springer, 234 Dungeness Meadows, Sequim, Wash. 98382.

**SPOKANE:** Inland Empire Philatelic Society, fourth Tuesday, West Central Community Center, North 1603 Belt, 7:30 p.m. J. Graue, Valleyford, Wash. 99036.

## MISCELLANEOUS

Universal Ship Cancellation Society, USS Puget Sound Chapter 74, eight times a year, contact president. Robert C. Clark Jr., 2424 Boyer Ave. E, Seattle, Wash. 98112.

# WEST VIRGINIA

**BUCKHANNON:** Upshur County Stamp and Coin Club, third Wednesday, Mountain Cap Building, 26 N. Kanawha St., 7:30 p.m. Mrs. Edward Sienkiewicz, 26 Meade St., Buckhannon, W.Va. 26201.

**CHARLESTON:** Kanawha Stamp Club, first Sunday, Main Post Office Building, second floor, 2:30 p.m. Sam N. Poolos, 604 S. Park Road, Charleston, W.Va. 25304.

**CLARKSBURG:** Harrison County Stamp Club, third Monday, Harrison County Senior Citizens Center, 7:30 p.m. Michael Ravis, Box 68, Philippi, W.Va. 26416.

— Stamp Club of Harrison County, third Monday, Senior Citizens Center, 6th and Main Street, 7:30 p.m. T.K. Reeves, 445 W. Main St., Clarksburg, W.Va. 26301.

**ELKINS:** Mountain State Stamp Club, second Thursday, Elkins Senior Center, 7:30 p.m. Michael Ravis, Box 68, Philippi, W.Va. 26416.

**PARKERSBURG:** Blennerhassett Stamp Society, first Thursday, third Monday, Trinity Episcopal Church, 5th and Juliana streets, 7 p.m. Evert L. Whitlatch, 1327 42nd St., Parkersburg, W.Va. 26101.

**SISTERSVILLE:** Middle Island Stamp Club, third Thursday, Library, 8 p.m. Donald D. Slider, 115 Rural St., Paden City, W.Va. 26159.

**WHEELING:** Ohio Valley Stamp Club, second and fourth Thursday, St. Matthew's Episcopal Church, Tatum Lounge, 15th and Chapline streets, 7:30 p.m. Hugh T. Harrington, Georgetown Apartments H-31, Wheeling, W.Va. 26003.

# WISCONSIN

**FOND DU LAC:** Fond du Lac Stamp Club, first Tuesday and second Thursday, Care Center East, 115 E. Arndt St., 7:30 p.m. Ray Schmitz, 21 N. Boardman St., Fond du Lac, Wis. 54935.

**LA CROSSE:** La Crosse Stamp Club, first Monday and third Tuesday. Meetings for June, July and August held on third Tuesday, Southside Senior Citizen's Center, 7 p.m. Jan Marie Duckett, 321 Coulee Park Estates, Onalaska, Wis. 54650.

**MANITOWOC:** Manitowoc Philatelic Society, second Tuesday, Jim Lukes Stamp Store, 931 S. 8th, 7:30 p.m. Mary Lou Wagner, 15 South County Trk S, Cato, Wis. 54206.

**MILWAUKEE:** Germany Philatelic Society, Milwaukee Chapter 18 Heinrich von Stephan, fourth Sunday, Ashland Travel Service, 8400 W. Capitol Drive, 7 p.m. Roger J. Szymanski, Box 1690, Milwaukee, Wis. 53201.

— Milwaukee Philatelic Society, third Saturday, Howard Johnson's Motor Inn, 1716 W. Layton Ave., 7:30 p.m. Karl L. Keldenich, Box 1062, Milwaukee, Wis. 53201.

— Poland Philatelic Club of Milwaukee, third Sunday, Polish Army Veteran's Home Post 3, 1629 S. 10th St., 7 p.m. Edith Malson, 320 E. Montana St., Milwaukee, Wis. 53207.

**WAUSAU:** Wisconsin Valley Philatelic Society, first Wednesday, University of Wisconsin Marathon Center, 6:30 p.m. Betty Brown, Box 71, Wausau, Wis. 54401.

**OSHKOSH:** Oshkosh Philatelic Society, first Tuesday and third Monday, Evergreen Manor, 1130 N. Westfield St., 7:30 p.m. Herbert E. Burgett, 615 Amherst Ave., Oshkosh, Wis. 54901.

**WAUKESHA:** Waukesha County Philatelic Society, second and fourth Thursday, First Savings Building, 100 E. Sunset Drive, 7 p.m. M.G. Denney, 2138 Rambling Rose Road, Waukesha, Wis. 53186.

**WAUWATOSA:** Wauwatosa Philatelic Society, first Thursday; third Wednesday, Wauwatosa Civic Center, 76th and North Avenue, 7:30 p.m. Ruth Bock, Box 13102, Wauwatosa, Wis. 53213.

**WEST BEND:** Kettle Moraine Stamp and Coin Club, second Thursday, Recreation Center, 724 Elm St., 7 p.m. David Hunsicker, 319 S. 9th Ave., West Bend, Wis. 53095.

**WISCONSIN RAPIDS:** Central Wisconsin Stamp Club, first Thursday, YMCA, Stevens Point; third Thursday, Chula Vista Manor, 7 p.m. Dave Carney, 3021 Lincoln St., Wisconsin Rapids, Wis. 54494.

## MISCELLANEOUS

Bay View Stamp and Coin Club, irregular schedule. F. Dombrowski Jr., Box 07507, Milwaukee, Wis. 53207.

Sheboygan Stamp Club, irregular schedule, Citizens Bank Forum Room, 821 N. 8th St., 7:30 p.m. Ruth Hoppe, 1654 S. 24th St., Sheboygan, Wis. 53081.

Wisconsin Christmas Seal and Charity Stamp Society, Chapter IV, meets once a year. Herbert E. Burgett, 615 Amherst Ave., Oshkosh, Wis. 54901.

Wisconsin Postal History Society, meets once a year. Frank Moertl, N95 W 32259 County Line Road, Hartland, Wis. 53029.

# WYOMING

**CHEYENNE:** Cheyenne Philatelic Society, third Wednesday, Laramie County Library, 7 p.m. Kenneth W. Schneider, Box 5, Cheyenne, Wyo. 82003-0005.

# PANAMA

**BALLOU:** Isthmian Collectors Club, second and fourth Tuesday, Pancanal Training Center, Building 600, 7 p.m. R.J. Karrer Jr., Box 1807, APO Miami, Fla. 34003.

# PUERTO RICO

**HATO REY:** Puerto Rico Philatelic Society, every Sunday, Andalweia Avenue, Box 1500, 9 a.m. Raul Gandara, 26 Washington St., Santurce, P.R. 00907.

# National Stamp Clubs

Following is a list of National Stamp Clubs that are registered with Linn's Club Center and their contact addresses. Societies affiliated with other organizations are indicated in parentheses.

To determine which organization is best suited to assist you in your collecting speciality, turn to the Specialized Index to National Stamp Clubs, immediately following this national club listing.

**(1)**
**Albrecht Durer Study Unit**
**(ATA)**
Mrs. Ursel E. Kissinger
Beckers Road, Box 399
Temple, Pa. 19560

**(2)**
**Americana Study Unit**
**(ATA, APS)**
June Bancroft
Box 179
Washington, D.C. 20044

**(3)**
**American Air Mail Society**
John J. Smith
102 Arbor Road
Cinnaminson, N.J. 08077-3859

**(4)**
**American First Day**
**Cover Society**
**(APS)**
Marge Finger
Box 23
Elberon, N.J. 07740

**(5)**
**American Philatelic**
**Congress**
Diane D. Boehret
Box 937
Brookhaven, Pa. 19015

**(6)**
**American Plate Number**
**Single Society**
Martin L. Wilson
10926 Annette Ave.
Tampa, Fla. 33612

**(7)**
**American Revenue**
**Association**
**(APS)**
Bruce Miller
1010 S. Fifth Ave.
Arcadia, Calif. 91006

**(8)**
**American Society**
**for Netherlands Philately**
Marinus Quist
124 Country Club Drive
Covington, La. 70433

**(9)**
**American Society**
**of Polar Philatelists**
**(APS)**
S.H. Jacobson
4300 W. Dempster
Skokie, Ill. 60076

**(10)**
**American Topical**
**Association**
Jerome Husak
3306 N. 50th St.
Milwaukee, Wis. 53216

**(11)**
**Armed Forces Stamp**
**Exchange Club**
Karl Bielenberg
8861 Blue Sea Drive
Columbia, Md. 21046

**(12)**
**Associated Collectors**
**of El Salvador**
Michael D. Moore
4621 Meaford St.
Lansing, Mich. 48917

**(13)**
**Atomic/Nuclear**
**Study Group**
Nancy Morrow, Lt. Col.(Ret)
600 Sharon Park Drive, A-208
Menlo Park, Calif. 94025

**(14)**
**Automotive Study Unit**
**(ATA)**
A. Michael Knapp
37 W. Broad St.
Columbus, Ohio 43215

**(15)**
**Avian Philately**
**Study Unit**
**(ATA)**
Susan L. Stoddard
5324 W. Avenue L
Quartz Hill, Calif. 93534

**(16)**
**Belgian Congo**
**Study Circle**
Ralph E. Jacquemin
4132 E. Minnezona
Phoenix, Ariz. 85018

**(17)**
**Biology Unit**
**(ATA)**
Betty Rutherford
Route 2
Marion, Iowa 52302

**(18)**
**Bosnia-Herzgovina**
**Study Group**
William R. Clements
2820 Lambert Trail
Chesapeake, Va. 23323

**(19)**
**British Caribbean**
**Philatelic Study Group**
**(APS)**
Howard C. Austin
4230 N. Woodburn St.
Shorewood, Ill. 53211

**(20)**
**British North America**
**Philatelic Society**
Edward J. Whiting
25 Kings Circle
Malvern, Pa. 19355

**(21)**
**Buildings Series**
**Study Group**
**(GPS)**
Calvin V. Whitsel
65 W. Jackson, Box 10
Chicago, Ill. 60604

**(22)**
**Bullseye Cancel**
**Collectors Club**
Nick Michaluk
5935 S. Kolmar
Chicago, Ill. 60629

**(23)**
**Bureau Issues Association**
Catherine S. Bruns
7215 13th Ave.
Takoma Park, Md. 20912

**(24)**
**Canal Zone Study Group**
**(APS)**
Alfred R. Bew
29 S. South Carolina Ave.
Atlantic City, N.J. 08401

**(25)**
**Captain Cook Study Unit**
**(ATA)**
David Seymour
38 Sherwood Road
Meols, Wirral, Merseyside
L47 9RT, England

**(26)**
**Carto-Philatelists**
**(ATA)**
Thomas H. Sutter
714 E. Maple St.
Appleton, Wis. 54911

**(27)**
**Casey Jones Railroad Unit**
**(ATA)**
Charles A. Korleski
1108 Somonauk St.
Sycamore, Ill. 60178

**(28)**
**Chemistry-on-Stamps**
**Study Unit**
**(ATA)**
Foil A. Miller
960 Lakemont Drive
Pittsburgh, Pa. 15243

**(29)**
**Chess on Stamps**
**Study Unit**
**(ATA)**
Peter W. Thayer
11226 Marlette Drive
Cincinnati, Ohio 45242

**(30)**
**Cheswick Historical**
**Society**
Steve Pavlina
208 Allegheny Ave.
Cheswick, Pa. 15024

**(31)**
**China Stamp Society**
F.C.J. Deridder
100 Font Blvd.
San Francisco, Calif. 94132

**(32)**
**Christmas Philatelic Club**
Vaughn H. Augustin
Box 77
Scottsbluff, Neb. 69361

**(33)**
**Christmas Study Unit**
**(ATA)**
D.L. Dombrowsky
1411 N. Powhatan
Arlington, Va. 22205

**(34)**
**Chrome Card**
**Collectors Club**
Mike Boyar
Box 508
Bound Brook, N.J. 08805

**(35)**
**Civil Censorship**
**Study Group**
Dann Mayo
5443 Paseo
Kansas City, Mo. 64110

**(36)**
**Club of Channel Islands**
**Collectors**
**(APS)**
Matthew Trachinsky
Box 579
New York, N.Y. 10028

**(37)**
**Coin on Stamps**
**Study Unit**
**(ATA)**
Mrs. C.E. Humphrey
304 S. Stewart Ave.
Lombard, Ill. 60148

**(38)**
**Collectors Club**
22 E. 35th St.
New York, N.Y. 10016

**(39)**
**Collectors**
**of Religion on Stamps**
Viola Esau
600 W. Orange Grove Road
Tucson, Ariz. 85704

**(40)**
**Costume Study Unit**
**(ATA)**
Dorothy L. Truhon
4000 N.W. 20th Drive
Gainesville, Fla. 32605

**(41)**
**Cover Collectors Club**
Mrs. Frederic White
237A Rossway Road
Pleasant Valley, N.Y. 12569

**(42)**
**Cover Collector's**
**Circuit Club**
Edward J. Wieme
Box 416
Gladstone, Ore. 97027

**(43)**
**Croatian Philatelic Society**
**(APS)**
Eck Spahich
1512 Lancelot Road
Borger, Tex. 79007

**(44)**
**Deltiologists of America**
Dr. James L. Lowe
10 Felton Ave.
Ridley Park, Pa. 19078

**(45)**
**Dogs on Stamps**
**Study Unit**
**(ATA)**
Morris Raskin
75 Maple Ave.
Newark, N.J. 07112

**(46)**
**Dominican Republic**
**Study Group**
James Smith
431 George Cross Drive
Norman, Okla. 73069

**(47)**
**Dwight D. Eisenhower**
**Philatelic and**
**Historical Society**
**(AFDCS)**
David Pritchard
927 S. Fort Thomas Ave.
Fort Thomas, Ky. 41075

**(48)**
**Earth's Physical**
**Features Study Unit**
**(ATA)**
Bryan Elliott
3919C Richmond Road
Nepean, Ont. Canada

**(49)**
**Eire Philatelic**
**Association**
Joe Foley
Box 2352
Denver, Colo. 80201

**(50)**
**Embroidery-Stitchery Unit**
**(ATA)**
Helen N. Cushman
1001 Genter St., Apt. 9H
La Jolla, Calif. 92037

**(51)**
**Errors, Freaks and Oddities**
**Collectors' Club**
**(APS, SPA)**
John M. Hotchner
Box 1125
Falls Church, Va. 22041

**(52)**
**Europa Study Unit**
**(APS, ATA)**
Donald W. Smith
1633 Florida Ave.
Johnstown, Pa. 15902

**(53)**
**Expo Collectors and**
**Historians Organization**
Edward J. Orth
1436 Killarney Ave.
Los Angeles, Calif. 90065

**(54)**
**Fairy Tales-Folklore**
**Study Unit**
**(ATA)**
Karen Cartier
2500 Buffalo Drive
Arlington, Tex. 76013

**(55)**
**Fine Arts Philatelists**
Ursel Kissinger
Beckers Road, Box 399, RD 1
Temple, Pa. 19560

**(56)**
**Fire Service in Philately**
**(ATA)**
Gustave Knoeckel
Box 3011
Rotonda West, Fla. 33947

**(57)**
**Flag Cancel Society**
**(APS)**
David W. Prosser
7664 State Street Road
Watertown, N.Y. 13601

**(58)**
**France and Colonies**
**Philatelic Society**
**(APS)**
Walter E. Parshall
103 Spruce St.
Bloomfield, N.J. 07003

**(59)**
**Franklin D. Roosevelt**
**Philatelic Society**
**(AFDCS, APS,**
**ATA, SPA)**
Gustav Detjen Jr.
154 Laguna Court
St. Augustine Shores, Fla.
32084

**(60)**
**Gems, Minerals and Jewelry**
**Study Unit**
**(ATA)**
George G. Young
254 Summit St.
Plantsville, Conn. 06479

**(61)**
**Germany Colonies**
**Collectors Group**
**(GPS)**
Col. Wilbur E. Davis
3313 Heritage Drive
Wilmington, Del. 19808

**(62)**
**Germany Philatelic Society**
**(APS)**
Frederick Behrendt
Box 2034
Westminster, Md. 21157

**(63)**
**Graphics Philately**
**Association**
**(ATA)**
Mrs. Dulcie M. Apgar
776 Silver Cloud St.
Thousand Oaks, Calif. 91360

**(64)**
**Hellenic Philatelic**
**Society of America**
Basil Stephenson
1 Wall St. 2-B
Fort Lee, N.J. 07024

**(65)**
**Holocaust Study Group**
Dr. Justin Gordon
Box 322
Skokie, Ill. 60076

**(66)**
**India Study Circle**
**for Philately**
D.B. Griffin
16 The Downs
Tuscaloosa, Ala. 35401

**(67)**
**International Association**
**of Space Philatelists**
**(AFA)**
William P. York
Box 302
Yonkers, N.Y. 10710

**(68)**
**International**
**Churchill Society**
**(ATA)**
R.M. Langworth
Box 385
Contoocook, N.H. 03229

**(69)**
**International Guild of**
**Vatican Philatelists**
Joseph Lo Preiato
Box 11096
Hartford, Conn. 06111

**(70)**
**International Philatelic**
**Press Club**
Ernest A. Kehr
Box 114
Richmond Hill, N.Y.
11419-0114

**(71)**
**International Philippine**
**Philatelic Society**
Eugene A. Garrett
446 Startford Ave.
Elmhurst, Ill. 60126

**(72)**
**International Society**
**for Japanese Philately**
Lois M. Evans
Box 752
Quincy, Mass. 02269

**(73)**
**International Society**
**of Guatemala Collectors**
Julian Graff
17099 W. Bernardo Drive,
Apt. 207
San Diego, Calif. 92127

**(74)**
**International Society**
**of Reply Coupon Collectors**
Dr. Allan Hauck
Box 165
Somers, Wis. 53171

**(75)**
**Iraq Philatelic Study Group**
Norman A. Cohen
Box 29543
Dallas, Tex. 75229

**(76)**
**Israel Plate Block Society**
David Lebson
5902 Winner Ave.
Baltimore, Md. 21215

**(77)**
**Jack Knight Air Mail Society**
Fred L. Wellman
5112 S. Pointe Drive
Inverness, Fla. 32650

**(78)**
**Jamaica Study Group**
**(APC, APS, AIJP, SPA)**
Howard J. Gaston
267 W. Granby Road
West Granby, Conn. 06090

**(79)**
**JAPOS Study Group**
**(ATA, APS)**
Gustav Detjen Jr.
154 Laguna Court
St. Augustine Shores, Fla.
32084

**(80)**
**Judaica Historical**
**Philatelic Society**
Sam Simon
80 Bruce Ave.
Yonkers, N.Y. 10705

**(81)**
**Jugoslavia Study Group**
**(CPS)**
Michael Lenard
1514 N. 3rd Ave.
Wausau, Wis. 54401

**(82)**
**Korea Stamp Society**
Forrest W. Calkins
Box 1057
Grand Junction, Colo. 81502

**(83)**
**Lighthouse Study Unit**
**(ATA)**
P.H. Cole
3900 Dudley St.
Lincoln, Neb. 68503

**(84)**
**Lions International**
**Stamp Club**
F.S. Taft
1430 Holston Drive
Bristol, Tenn. 37620

**(85)**
**Lions International**
**Stamp Club, Chapter 2**
Steve Tripp
6504 Wiscassett Road
Bethesda, Md. 20016

**(86)**
**Lions Philatelic Unit**
**(ATA)**
Stan Galloway
Box 6082
Colorado Springs, Colo. 80934

**(87)**
**Luminescent Stamp Club**
Dale C. Dwyer
3728 Merrimac Lane E
Hanover Park, Ill. 60103

**(88)**
**Mailer's Postmark**
**Permit Club**
John M. Howell
Box 669
Littlerock, Calif. 93543-0669

**(89)**
**Malaria Philatelists**
**International**
**(ATA)**
James Dellinger
426 W. Fremont
Elmhurst, Ill. 60126

**(90)**
**Maritime Postmark Society**
John B. Swenson
Box 1244
La Jolla, Calif. 92038

**(91)**
**Masonic Study Unit**
**(APS, ATA)**
Richard M. Needham
708 N. Mt. Pleasant Ave.
Lancaster, Ohio 43130-2697

**(92)**
**Mathematical Study Unit**
**(ATA)**
Estelle A. Buccino
5615 Glenwood Road
Bethesda, Md. 20817

**(93)**
**Medical Subject Unit**
**(ATA)**
Robert R. Patterson
Box 680
Snyder, Tex. 79549

**(94)**
**Mesoamerican Archeology**
**Study Unit**
**(ATA)**
Chris L. Moser
Box 1442
Riverside, Calif. 92502

**(95)**
**Mexico-Elmhurst Philatelic**
**Society International**
**(APS)**
MEPSI
Box 42165
Tucson, Ariz. 85733

**(96)**
**Mobile Post Office Society**
**(APS)**
Edwin B. Bergman
5030 Aspen Drive
Omaha, Neb. 68157

**(97)**
**National Association**
**of Precancel Collectors**
G.W. Dye
Box 121
Wildwood, N.J. 08260

**(98)**
**New Mexico**
**Philatelic Association**
**(APS, SPA)**
Winifred Amsden
Box 130
Los Alamos, N.M. 87544

**(99)**
**Ohio Postal**
**History Society**
George J. Ball Jr.
2848 Seaman Road
Oregon, Ohio 43616

**(100)**
**Old World Archaeological**
**Study Unit**
**(ATA)**
Heinz Schwinge
913 Grey Ave.
Evanston, Ill. 60202

**(101)**
**The Perfins Club**
**(APS)**
Dorothy L. Savage
10550 Western Ave., Sp. 94
Stanton, Calif. 90680

**(102)**
**Performing Arts**
**Study Unit**
**(APS, ATA)**
Rev. Marshall J. Whitehead
Box 1505
Indianapolis, Ind. 46206

**(103)**
**Permit Imprint Collectors**
**Society**
Lois Brennan
1011 S. 43rd St.
Tacoma, Wash. 98408

**(104)**
**Petroleum Philatelic Society**
**International**
Tom D. McElroy
13815 Kimberley
Houston, Tex. 77079

**(105)**
**Philatelic Music Circle**
**(BPF)**
C.J. Sabados
528 Rimini Road
Delmar, Calif. 92014

**(106)**
**Pictorial Cancellation**
**Society**
**(APS)**
Robert M. Hedges
Box 306
Hancock, Md. 21750

**(107)**
**Pitcairn Islands**
**Study Group**
**(APS)**
Anne A. Hughes
2013 20th Place
Kenosha, Wis. 53140

**(108)**
**Plate Block Collectors Club**
Bill Roberts
Box 4133
Princeton, Fla. 33032

**(109)**
**Polish POW and DP**
**Camp Study Group**
**(RPSC)**
Chris Kulpinski
Box 464
Feasterville, Pa. 19047

**(110)**
**Polonus Philatelic Society**
**(SPA)**
James Mazepa
Box 1217
Oak Park, Ill. 60304

**(111)**
**Postal Stationery**
**Study Group**
**(GPS)**
John F. Matschinegg
5118 N. Drake Ave.
Chicago, Ill. 60625

**(112)**
**Postcard History Society**
**(APS)**
Roy Cox
Box 3610
Baltimore, Md. 21214

**(113)**
**Postcard Club**
**(APS)**
Marie A. Lord
4613 Eugene Drive
Bristol, Pa. 19007

**(114)**
**Post Mark Collectors Club**
**(APS)**
Wilma Hinrichs
4200 S.E. Indianola Road
Des Moines, Iowa 50320

**(115)**
**Post-WWII Study Group**
**(GPS)**
Donald E. Slawson
463 Ridge Road
Winchester, Va. 22601

**(116)**
**Precancel Stamp Society**
**(APS)**
David A. Coates
Carillon House, Apt. 829
2500 Wisconsin Ave. NW
Washington, D.C. 20007

**(117)**
**Romanian Philatelic Club**
George Pataki
84-47 Kendrick Place
Jamaica Estates, N.Y. 11432

**(118)**
**Rossica Society of**
**Russian Philately**
Dr. Kennedy L. Wilson
7415 Venice St.
Falls Church, Va. 22043

**(119)**
**Rossica Society of**
**Russian Philately**
**Northern California Chapter**
Alex Sadovnikov
Box 612
San Carlos, Calif. 94070

**(120)**
**Rotary-on-Stamps**
**Fellowship Unit**
**(ATA)**
Dr. Eugene Atkinson
Box 2006
Tarleton University Station
Tex. 76402

**(121)**
**Ryukyu Philatelic Specialist**
**Society**
**(APS)**
Arthur L. Askins
Box 4092
Berkeley, Calif. 94704-0092

**(122)**
**St. Helena and Dependencies**
**Philatelic Society**
**(APS)**
Vivian W. Finne
Box 366
Calpella, Calif. 95418

**(123)**
**Scouts on Stamps Society**
**International**
Carl R. Hallmann
253 Sheldon
Downers Grove, Ill. 60515

**(124)**
**Society for Czechoslovak**
**Philately**
**(APS)**
Edward J. Sabol
Box 676
Woodbury, N.J. 08096

**(125)**
**Society for Hungarian**
**Philately**
**(APS)**
Thomas Phillips
Box 1162, Samp Mortar Sta.
Fairfield, Conn. 06430

**(126)**
**Society for Thai Philately**
**(APS)**
Gary A. Van Cott
Box 1118
Aiea, Hawaii 96701

**(127)**
**Society of Australasian**
**Specialists**
**(APS, SPA)**
David Proctor
Box 82643
San Diego, Calif. 92138

**(128)**
**Society of Costa Rica**
**Collectors**
Henry P. McGhee
1696 Georgetowne Blvd.
Sarasota, Fla. 33582

**(129)**
**Society of Indochina**
**Philatelists**
**(APS, SPA)**
Mark Isaacs
Box 531
Chicago, Ill. 60690

**(130)**
**Society of Philatelic**
**Americans**
Grant Ricksecker
Box 30286
Cleveland, Ohio 44130

**(131)**
**Society of Philatelists**
**and Numismatists**
**(ANA)**
Joe R. Ramos
1929 Millis St.
Montebello, Calif. 90640

**(132)**
**Society of Philaticians**
**(SPA)**
Gustav Detjen Jr.
154 Laguna Court
St. Augustine Shores
Fla. 32084

**(133)**
**Southern Philatelic**
**Federation**
Donald F. Garrett
1010 Metairie Road
Jackson, Miss. 39209

**(134)**
**Souvenir Card**
**Collectors Society**
Dr. Curtis D. Radford
Box 7116
Rochester, Minn. 55903

**(135)**
**Space Philatelists**
**International Society**
Martin J. Michaelson
Box 171
West Nyack, N.Y. 10994

**(136)**
**Space Topics Study Group**
**(APS, ATA)**
Lester E. Winick
2121 Maple Road
Homewood, Ill. 60430

**(137)**
**Space Unit**
**(APS, ATA)**
Bernice Scholl
Box 2579
Marathon Shores, Fla. 33052

**(138)**
**Sports Philatelists**
**International Society**
**(APS)**
C.A. Reiss
55 Public Square, Suit 1410
Cleveland, Ohio 44113

**(139)**
**Stamps on Stamps**
**Centenary Unit**
**(ATA)**
Eloise B. Kane
Box 56
Palm Springs, Calif. 92263

**(140)**
**State Revenue Society**
**(ARA)**
Harold A. Effner Jr.
425 Sylvania Ave.
Avon-by-the-Sea, N.J. 07717

**(141)**
**Telecommunications**
**Study Unit**
**(ATA)**
F. Dombrowski Jr.
Box 07507
Milwaukee, Wis. 53207

**(142)**
**Texas Centennial Society**
Norman Alan Cohen
Box 29543
Dallas, Tex. 75229

**(143)**
**Third Reich Study Group**
**(GPS)**
R.J. Houston
11 Yorktown Drive
Clark, N.J. 07066

**(144)**
**Tin Can Mail**
**Study Circle**
Janet Klug
Route 1, Box 370B
Pleasant Plain, Ohio 45162

**(145)**
**Turkey and Ottoman**
**Philatelic Society**
Gary F. Paiste
4249 Berritt St.
Fairfax, Va. 22030

**(146)**
**Tuvalu Philatelic Society**
**(APS)**
Ted Castro
Box 2760
Chicago, Ill. 60690

**(147)**
**Ukrainian Philatelic**
**and Numismatic Society**
George I. Pawliczko
Box C
Southfields, N.Y. 10975

**(148)**
**United Nations Philatelists**
**(ATA)**
Ronald Hollinger
2017 Broadway
Blue Island, Ill. 60406

**(149)**
**United Postal**
**Stationery Society**
**(APS, SPA)**
Joann Thomas
Box 48
Redlands, Calif. 92373

**(150)**
**Universal Philatelic**
**Cover Society**
**(SPA)**
T.D. Pomeroy
1909 Nut Tree Drive NW
Salem, Ore. 97304

**(151)**
**Universal Postal**
**Union Collectors**
**(ATA)**
Ray Reaber
740 Wiggins Circle
Pascagoola, Miss. 39567

**(152)**
**Universal Ship**
**Cancellation Society**
Frank Hoak III
Box 668
New Canaan, Conn. 06840

**(153)**
**U.S. Philatelic**
**Classics Society**
**(APS, SPA)**
Robert R. Hegland
Box 1011
Falls Church, Va. 22041

**(154)**
**War Cover Club**
**(APS)**
Lincoln E. Kieffer
Box 173
Jamesburg, N.J. 08831

**(155)**
**Windmill Study Unit**
**(ATA)**
Jim Lunney
301 Thornridge Drive
Midland, Tex. 79703

**(156)**
**Women on Stamps**
**Study Unit**
**(ATA)**
Ms. Ronnelle Genser
2857 Elliott Circle NE
Atlanta, Ga. 30305

**(157)**
**World's Fair**
**Collectors Society**
**(ATA)**
Michael R. Pender
148 Poplar St.
Garden City, N.Y. 11530

**(158)**
**Zippy Collectors Club**
**(APS)**
Helen R. Rocco
405 N. 8th St.
Vineland, N.J. 08360

# Specialized Index
# National Stamp Clubs

Find your particular collecting speciality in the following listing, then turn back to the preceding pages covering National Stamp Clubs to determine which national group is best suited to serve your needs. Example: Persons interested in Archaeology on stamps will find that subject listed below, with the listing followed by numbers 94 and 100. Now turn back to the national club list and find clubs numbered 94 and 100 for the names and addresses of contact persons.

# Foreign Stamp Clubs

### AFRICA
**Mashonaland
Philatelic Society**
Mrs. Cecilie Coventry
Box 2735
Salisbury, Zimbabwe

### AUSTRALIA
**Australian Airmail Society**
Nelson Eustis
GPO Box 954
Adelaide, S.A. 5001

**Ballarat Philatelic Society**
Diana R. Vernon
Box 493
Ballarat, Vic. 3350

**Dalby Philatelic Society**
Mrs. Win Jackman
64 Patrick St.
Dalby, Qld. 4405

**Eastern Districts
Philatelic Society**
Allen Downes
Box 240
Magill, S.A. 5072

**Gumeracha and Districts
Philatelic Society**
Mrs. R.C. Welsh
Box 164
Woodside, S.A. 5244

**Junction Park Stamp Club**
Dell Luxton
Box 177, Annerley
Brisbane, Qld. 4103

**Manning District Stamp
and Coin Club**
Werner Hoch
83 Isabella St.
Wingham 2429 N.S.W.

**Queensland
Philatelic Society**
John E. Crowsley
Box 346
Nundah, Qld. 4012

**Royal Philatelic Society**
Miss Myra Farley
GPO Box 2071
Melbourne, Vic. 3001

**Tasmanian Philatelic Society**
Madeliene E. Percey
GPO Box 594
Hobart, Tas. 7005

**Woomera Stamp Club**
Joan Forster
Box 4
Woomera, S.A. 5720

### AUSTRIA
**Arge-Christkindl e.v.
International Stamp Club**
Otto Taurer
Postfach 34, Ludwiggasse 14
A-4403 Steyr

### CANADA
**Association of Philatelists
and Numismatists**
E. St-Onge
C.P. 111
Boucherville, Que. J4B 5E6

**Brantford Stamp Club**
John Fairgrieve
Box 1
Brantford, Ont. N3T 5M3

**Centre Philatelique Salaberry
De Valleyfield**
Fernand Foucher
408 Giroux St.
Valleyfield, Que. J6T 3M2

**Credit Valley
Philatelic Society**
R. Laker
2118 Dickson Road
Mississauga, Ont. L5B 1Y6

**Crireq Stamp Club**
Raymond Rajotte
Box 1000
Varennes, Que. J0L 2P0

**East Toronto Stamp Club**
Raymond Reakes
188 Woodmount Ave.
Toronto, Ont. M4C 3Z4

**Electrohome Stamp Club**
Ron Heimpel
86 River Road E
Kitchener, Ont. N2B 2G2

**Essex County Stamp Club**
Box 1503, Station A
Windsor, Ont. N9A 6R5

**Fraser Valley Philatelic Club**
G. Horner
Box 3
Abbotsford, B.C. V2S 4N7

**Germany Philatelic Society
Windsor-Detroit Chapter 11**
M.P. Bratzel Jr.
1233 Virginia Ave.
Windsor, Ont. N8S 2Z1

**Granby Philatelic Club**
H.E. Hooper
No. 15-135th St. Michel St.
Granby, Que. J2G 8X8

**Greater Victoria Philatelic
Society**
Don Dundee
928 Claremont Ave.
Victoria, B.C. V8Y 1K3

**Gzowski Polish Philatelic
Society of Toronto**
Mike Lubinski
6 Attercliff Court
Rexdale, Ont. M9V 1H7

**Hamilton Philatelic Society**
J.W. Savage
Box 205, Station A
Hamilton, Ont.

**Lakehead Stamp Club**
Louise Cifarelli
2824 Begin Bay
Thunder Bay, Ont. P7E 5M1

**Lakeshore Stamp Club**
P.R. Keen
Box 1
Pointe Claire-Dorval, Que.
H9R 4N5

**La Societe Philatelique
de Quebec, Chapter 40**
Jean Pierre Forest
Box 2222, Postal Terminal
Quebec, Que. G1K 7N8

**Latvian Philatelic Society**
Rudolfs Zalamans
60 Wakelin Terrace
St. Catharines, Ont. L2M 4K9

**London Philatelic Society**
A. Benjaminsen
298 Neville Drive
London, Ont. N6G 1C3

**Muskoka Philatelic Society**
T.E. Lyon
Box 187
Gravenhurst, Ont. P0C 1G0

**North Toronto Stamp Club**
J.M. Shelton
219 Beechy Drive
Richmond Hill, Ont. L4C 2X6

**North York Philatelic
Society, Chapter 21**
Boris Margau
Box 62
Willowdale, Ont. M2N 5S7

**Nova Scotia Stamp Club**
Dave Harvey
7 Birchdale Ave.
Dartmouth, N.S. B2X 1E6

**Okanagan-Mainline
Philatelic Association**
Fred R. Arnot
111 Hyslop Drive, RR 3
Penticton, B.C. V2A 7K8

**Oxford Philatelic Society**
W.S. Koleszar
11 E. Park Drive
Woodstock, Ont. N4S 3M9

**Philatelic Club of Montreal**
Sheila Usher
Box 264
Westmount, Que. H3Z 2T2

**Postal History Society
of Canada**
Andy M. Palachik
Box 3461, Station C
Ottawa, Ont. K1Y 4J6

**R.A. Stamp Club**
Gerald E. Lepine
2451 Riverside Drive
Ottawa, Ont. K1Y 7X7

**Red Deer Stamp Club**
Ed Tompson
10 Otterbury Ave.
Red Deer, Alta. T4N 4Z9

**Royal Philatelic Society
of Canada**
Ms. Roddie Gould
Box 1054, Station A
Toronto, Ont. M5W 1G5

**St. Francis Collectors Club**
Ted Harris
36 Beattie St., RR 1
Lennoxville, Que. J1M 2A2

**St. Lawrence International
Stamp Club**
Robert Kitchener
114 15th St. W
Cornwall, Ont. K6J 3J8

**Society of Israel Philatelists,
Edmonton Chapter**
Dr. Joel Weiner
11348 57th Ave.
Edmonton, Alta. T6H 1B2

**Stoney Creek Stamp Club**
Vernon G. March
200 Charlotte St.
Hamilton, Ont. L8K 4V6

**Swiatowid Polish Philatelic
and Numismatic Society**
M. Lubinski
8 Attercliff Court
Rexdale, Ont. M9V 1H7

**Toronto Estonian
Philatelic Club**
H. Maeste
91 Old Mill Drive
Toronto, Ont. M6S 4K2

**Union Philatelique
de Montreal**
Michel Gagne
B.P. 398, Station A
Montreal, Que. H3C 2T1

**Winnipeg Philatelic Society**
Florence Hookey
Box 1425
Winnipeg, Man. R3C 2Z1

**World Stamp Exchange
Circuit Club**
Elvin Person
Esther, Alta. T0J 1H0

**Yemen Philatelic Society**
Blair D. Stannard
2001 Greenway Park
Gloucester, Ont. K1B 5B1

## CYPRUS
**Cyprus Philatelic Society**
Dr. John G. Kaimis
Box 1151
Nicosia

## DOMINICAN REPUBLIC
**Sociedad Filatelica Dominicana**
Dr. Antonio Coiscou W.
Apartado Postal No. 1930
Santo Domingo

## FINLAND
**Finnish Topical Association**
Ahti Haapaniemi
Box 53
SF-00131 Helsinki

## FRANCE
**Societe Philatelique
Franco-Britannique**
Langlois Pierre
98, Cours de Vincennes
75012 Paris

## GERMANY
**Rheinland Pfalz Stamp Club**
Robert L. Witkosky
PSC Box 644
APO New York 09021

**Spanish Philatelic Club**
Nicolas A. Moeller
Box 1244
2056 Glinde

## GREAT BRITAIN
**American Stamp Club
of Great Britain**
M. Wallace
148 Bramhall Lane S
Bramhall, Stockport
Cheshire SK7 2ED

**Andorran Philatelic
Study Circle**
Mrs. E. Jacques Ashville
York Road, Cliffe, Selby
North Yorks YO8 7NY

**Anglo-Boer War
Philatelic Society**
J.R. Stroud
28 Oxford St.
Burnham-on-Sea, Somerset

**Austrian Stamp Club
of Great Britain**
H.G. White
1 Chesterton Park
Cirencester, Glos. GL7 1XU

**Belgian Study Circle**
A.G. Wood
5 Sutherland Grove
London, S.W. 18 5PS

**British Aerophilatelic
Federation**
Alexander S. Newall
338 City Road
London EC1V 2PX

**British Decimal Stamps
Study Circle**
Carol Morrison
"Rozel", Bepton Road
Bepton, Sussex SU29 9RB

**British Postmark Society**
Alan J. Howard
9 Gainsborough Ave.
Stockport, Cheshire SK6 5BW

**British Royal Portraits
Study Group**
L.E. Copeland
20 Chapel Hay Lane
Churchdown, Glos. GL3 2ET

**British Society of
Australian Philately**
A.G.W. Scott
5 Breakspeare
College Road
Dulwich, London SE21 7NB

**British Society of Russian
Philately**
R.F. Young
"Highfield" 27
Coxhill Gardens River
Dover, Kent CT17 0PX

**British West Africa
Study Circle**
J.R. Merchant
10 Bushmead Ave.
Bedford, Beds.

**British West Indies
Study Circle**
I.P. Chard
48 The Shrublands
Potters Bar, Herts.
EN6 2BW

**Canadian Philatelic Society
of Great Britain**
David F. Sessions
3 Langfield Close, Henbury
Bristol BS10 7ND

**Channel Islands
Specialists' Society**
Brian Cropp
17 Westlands Ave.
Huntercombe, Slouch
SL1 6AG

**Churchill Collectors Club**
Brian Bugge
8 Clyde Road, Stanwell
Staines, Middx. TW19 7RH

**Cinderella Stamp Club**
Gordon Phillips
35 Ham Farm Road
Ham, Surrey TW10 5NA

**Cyprus Study Circle**
Robert Wheeler
47 Drayton Ave.
London W13 0LE

**East Africa Study Circle**
Roy Dunstan
Chantry Court
1 The Close, Warminster
BA12 9AL

**Egypt Study Circle**
E.M. Hall
6 Bedford Ave.
Little Chalfont, Bucks.

**Ethiopia Collectors' Club**
Rev. F.G. Payne
83 Penn Lea Road
Bath BA1 3RQ

**Falkland Islands Philatelic
Study Group**
M.D. Barton
Sandle Manor, Fordingbridge
Hants SP6 1NS

**Football Study Group**
S.H. Renshaw
27 Ashfield Road, Davenport
Stockport SK3 8UD

**Forces Postal History Society**
M. Dobbs
80 Addison Gardens
London W14 0DR

**France and Colonies Philatelic
Society of Great Britain**
A. Swain
1 Elizabeth Court
70 Sudbury Ave.
Wembley, Middx. HA0 3BD

**Great Britain Decimal Stamp
Book Study Circle**
G.T. Fisk
Oakfield, Shrewley Common
Warwick CV35 7AN

**Great Britain Overprints
Society**
B.H. Pratt
60 Church Lane
Eaton, Norwich NR4 6NY

**Great Britain Philatelic
Society**
Robin R. Tapper
16 Trinity Close
Bromley, Kent BR2 8ND

**Hellenic Philatelic Society
of Great Britain**
R.J. Scott
17 Riddlesdown Ave.
Purley, Surrey CR2 1JH

**Helvetia Philatelic Society
of Great Britain**
G.W. Hubbard
43 Webheath Netherwood St.
London NW6 2HD

**Hovermail Collector's Club**
D.W. Powell
15 The Twitten, Southwick
Brighton BN4 4DB

**Indian Ocean
Study Circle**
Mrs. S. Hopson
The Vineyard
Garden Close Lane
Newbury, Berks. RG14 6PR

**International Society for
Japanese Philately, U.K. Chapter**
D.T. Smith
23 Britannia Road
Norwich NR1 4NP

**Iran Philatelic Study Circle**
B. Lucas
99 Moseley Wood Drive
Leeds LS16 7HD

**Italy and Colonies
Study Circle**
Richard Harlow
6 Marston Road
Teddington, Middx.

**Liechtenstein
Study Circle**
E.J. Dymond
97 Downlands Ave.
Worthing, West Sussex
BN14 9HF

**Masonic Philatelic Club**
T.J. Fray
76 Merrivale Road
Beacon Park
Plymouth PL2 2RP

**Nepal and Tibet Philatelic
Study Circle**
C. Hepper
4 Osric Court, Dames Close
Peterborough, Cambs.

**Netherlands Philatelic Circle**
John C. Milner
202a Old Bath Road
Cheltenham GL53 9EQ

**Nigerian Study Circle**
M. Nicholson
20 Estuary Park, Combwich
Bridgwater, Somerset

**Pacific Islands Study
Circle of Great Britain**
Mrs. R. Tyler
62 Moat Drive
Harrow, Middx. HA1 4RX

**Papuan Philatelic Society**
F.J. Prophet
5 Morcom Close, Menear Road
Boscoppa, St. Austell
Cornwall PL25 3UF

**Philatelic Music Circle**
Irene Lawford
22 Bouverie Gardens
Kenton, Middx. HA3 0RQ

**Polar Postal History
Society of Great Britain**
H.E.J. Evans
12 Longlands Spinney
Charmandean, Worthing
Sussex BN14 9NU

**Portuguese Philatelic
Society**
L. Thompson
73 Grasmere Gardens
Harrow, Middx. HA3 7PS

**Postal History Society**
J.G.S. Scott
Lower Street Farmhouse
Hildenborough, Tonbridge
Kent TN11 8PT

**Postal History Society
of Lancashire and Cheshire**
Eric Hebdon
410 Rossendale Road
Burnley, Lancs. BB11 5HN

**Postmark Club**
Miss E. Granville-Edge
Box 100, Great Ouseburn
York YO5 9SZ

**Postal Mechanisation
Study Circle**
H.J. Lush
9 Leighton Ave.
Pinner, Middx. HA5 3BW

**Precancel Stamp Society
of Great Britain**
D. Philcox
42 Westville Road
Thames Ditton, Surrey
KT7 0UJ

**Railway Philatelic Group**
A. Brookhouse
15 Mount Pleasant Lane
Bricket Wood, St. Albans
Herts. AL2 3UX

**Rhodesian Study Circle**
Margaret Harris
30 Wykeham Road
Netley Abbey
Southampton SO3 5ET

**Scandinavia Philatelic Society**
Miss Susan Worsley
71 Castelnau, Barnes
London SW13 9RT

**Security Endorsement and
Perfin Society of Great Britain**
J.M. Rucklidge
13 Moncrieffe Road
Sheffield S7 1HQ

**South African Collector's
Society of Great Britain**
W.A. Page
138 Chastilian Road
Dartford, Kent DA1 3LG

**Southern Pictorial Envelope
and Caricature Society**
D.J. Nethercleft
1 Chestnut Close
Maidenhead, Berks. SL6 8sy

**Spanish Main**
Bernard Davies
16 Lynwood Close
Gordon Road
South Woodford E18 1DP

**Spanish Study Circle**
Mrs. J.F. Richardson
16 Fairford Ave.
Luton, Beds. LU2 7ER

**Sudan Study Group**
H.L. Bowyer
27 Maidstone Drive
Marton, Middlesbrough
Cleveland TS7 8QW

**United Nations Study Group**
J.S. Peddie
13 Hynmoor Road, Old Brumby
Scunthorpe, Humberside
DN17 1EZ

**Waterlow Study Circle**
Colin Hoffman
9 Oaker Ave.
West Didsbury, Manchester
M20 8XH

### GUATEMALA
**Asociacion Filatelica
De Guatemala**
Col. Romeo J. Routhier
Apartado Postal 39

### INDIA
**Indo-American Society**
N. Krishnan
5 Raveline St.
Kit AB Mahal, Fort Bombay
400 001

**Philatelic Society of India**
K.D. Dinshah
Dharwar Building
Zorastrian Estate
Tardeo Road
Fort Bombay 400 007

**Philatelic Society
of Malawi**
Uttar Pradesh
B.J. Kumar
3-A/149 Azad Nagar
Kanpur 208 002

**Rourkela Philatelic Club**
Ms. Sumitra Sahoo
B/156/20
Rourkela 769005

**United Philatelists**
B.J. Kumar
3-A/149 Azad Nagar
Kanpur 208 002

### MALAWI
**Philatelic Society
of Malawi**
B.J. Bowden
Box 1443
Blantyre

### MALAYSIA
**Philatelic Society
of Malaysia**
C. Nagarajah
Box 588
Kuala Lumpur 01-02

### NATAL
**Philatelic Society of Natal**
D. Reinecke
Box 588
Durban 4000

### NEPAL
**Nepal Philatelic Society**
Bidya Eatna Tuladhar
GPO Box 342
Kathmandu

### NEW ZEALAND
**Federation of New Zealand
Philatelic Society**
Suzanne F. Dick
Box 40-504
Upper Hutt

**Manly Warringah
Philatelic Society**
O.M. Smith
Box 80
Manly, N.S.W. 2095

**New Zealand Junior
Stamp Club**
A. Frank Watters
Box 812
New Plymouth 4600

**New Zealand Stamp
Collectors' Club**
Mrs. R. Porter
Box 1805
Christchurch

**Postal History Society
of New Zealand**
R.G. Armstrong
Box 38.503
Howick, Auckland

**Royal Philatelic Society
of New Zealand**
B.G. Vincent
Box 1269
Wellington

### PAKISTAN
**Rawalpindi Islamabad
Stamp Collectors Society**
G. Salam Hussain
House 1-D Street 56
Sector Ramna 6/4, Islamabad

**Pakistan Stamps
Exchange Club**
Munir Hussain
Box 686
GPO Lahore

### PORTUGAL
**Tap-Air Portugal
Philatelic Club**
Capt. F. Lemos da Silveira
Rua Pedro Ivo, 3-3° EF
P-1700 Lisbon

### SAUDI ARABIA
**Arabian Philatelic Association**
John M. Wilson
Aramco, Box 1929
Dhahran

### SCOTLAND
**Glasgow Thematic Society**
Miss A.C. Mackenzie
23 Albert Road
Glasgow G42 8DL

**Letter Box Study Group**
W.L. Morton
11 Morvem Road, Bearsden
Glasgow G61 3BU

**Scottish Postal
History Society**
W.L. Morton
11 Morvem Road, Bearsden
Glasgow G61 3BU

### SOUTH AFRICA
(Republic of)
**Philatelic Society
of Johannesburg**
I.A. Miller
Box 4967
Johannesburg 2000

### SPAIN
**Sociedad Aerofilatelica
Espanola**
Antonio Ripoll Sabe
Apartado Correos
25028 Barcelona

# Exhibitions

# 15

## The International Federation of Philately

The Federation Internationale de Philatelie (International Federation of Philately) was founded in 1926 as a nonprofit association to promote philately on the international level, to promote peace and friendship through philately worldwide, to establish and maintain close contacts with postal administrations and national and international organizations interested in philatelic matters and to support philatelic events organized by FIP members. The statutes of the FIP were completely revised in Vienna at the WIPA '81 FIP congress.

The registered office of FIP is in Zurich, Switzerland, and administrative headquarters are at the secretariat. FIP membership is comprised of national federations with one representative for each country. Where no national federation exists, FIP membership is granted to the most representative philatelic organization in the country on a temporary basis until a national federation should be formed. The American Philatelic Society is the member for the United States.

Besides giving patronage to international exhibitions held by FIP members, FIP is empowered to organize on its own initiative international philatelic exhibitions with the agreement of the national federation concerned and to bring out publications of philatelic interest.

### Membership

FIP consists of national federations to which the majority of philatelic societies in the country concerned are full members. Only one full member can be admitted to FIP for each country. Where no national federation exists, FIP membership is granted to the most representative philatelic organization in that country. Such full membership shall be on a temporary basis. As soon as a national federation has been formed in that country, it will replace the temporary member. Only full members as in these two cases shall have a vote in congress.

#### Associate Membership — Continental Federations

Regular members of FIP may join into a continental federation with philatelic organizations of countries who are not members of FIP.

These federations shall operate in accordance with the statutes and regulations of FIP.

Proposals for such federations are to be submitted to the board of directors of FIP for approval by the congress.

#### Conditions for Admission

In order to be considered at the next following congress, applications for membership must be submitted to the secretariat of FIP at least three months before the congress convenes.

Applications for membership must be accompanied by the bylaws of the applicant, as well as by a statement of the number of affiliated societies, their total membership and a written undertaking to accept and implement without qualification all FIP rules and regulations.

#### Resignation

The resignation of a member shall be accepted only if all outstanding dues have been paid. The resignation has to be addressed to the secretariat of FIP in writing and sent by registered mail before Oct. 31 of the year in course.

#### Subscriptions

All members are obliged to pay an annual subscription to FIP.

The amount of the subscription shall be determined annually in compliance with the annual budget approved by the congress. The subscription of the amount approved by the congress will become due in the financial year following approval and must be paid not later than June 30 of that year. Failure by a member to pay for the current year or for the previous year will entail forfeiture of that member's right of vote in congress.

Should a member fail to pay his subscription for a period of two years, without justification acceptable to the congress, the board of directors will terminate the membership immediately.

**Disciplinary Action**

Any member who is in breach of the statutes or regulations of FIP, or takes any action which injures the material or moral well-being of FIP, or of a member of FIP, may be called upon for an explanation of his action at the request of either the FIP board of directors or the injured member.

The case shall be examined by the board of directors, and will be submitted to congress for a decision.

# Honorary Membership of FIP

On proposal of the board of directors, the congress may confer honorary membership on persons who have given exceptional service to FIP. These honorary members shall have the right to attend congress.

# Administration

The administrative bodies of FIP are:

1. The Congress
2. The Board of Directors

Congress: The congress is the supreme body of FIP.

Each regular member is represented at congress by a delegation consisting of not more than two persons, of whom only one has a vote.

At the request of a regular member, the board of directors may allow the attendance of two observers for each member.

The names and addresses of the members of each delegation and of any observers accompanying them must be forwarded to the secretariat in writing within three weeks of the receipt of the notice convening the congress.

Regular members can be represented at congress by a proxy.

Every proxy must be authorized in writing and filed with the board of directors before the opening session of congress.

No delegate may represent more than two federations.

Only regular members may vote at the congress.

The following may attend congress in a consultative capacity only:

— members of the board of directors,
— associate members,
— honorary members,
— the presidents of FIP commissions,
— special representatives,
— admitted observers.

Congress shall meet annually at a time and place determined by the congress. Normally two years in advance.

Notice of convocation of congress shall be sent to FIP members and office holders not less than two months before the opening date, and shall include the agenda, reports of primary offices and functions and justified motions.

A motion proposed by a member can be included in the agenda, only if it is submitted to the secretariat not later than three months before the opening of the congress.

Special motions with exception of modifications of the statues or the dissolution of FIP, may be presented after approval of the board of directors without previous announcement.

**Elections**

The congress shall elect by secret ballots:

1. the president
2. three vice presidents
3. other members of the board of directors (five)
4. the auditors

Nominations must be submitted in writing by a regular member to the secretariat of FIP not later than three months before the opening date of congress.

Meetings of the congress can transact business only if a simple majority of the voting members are represented in person or by proxy.

Decisions of the congress require a simple majority except for:

Amendments to the statutes, expulsion of a member other than automatic expulsions for nonpayment of dues, and the dissolution of FIP.

Except for elections, the president shall have the deciding vote in case of a tie. In an election the vote will be repeated until one receives a majority.

All changes of the statutes require a quorum of not less than two-thirds of the regular members of FIP and a simple majority of affirmative votes of the regular members present in person or proxy.

The expulsion of a member on any grounds other than nonpayment of dues or the readmission of a member previously expelled, shall require the affirmative vote of three quarters of the regular members present in person or by proxy.

A member must be represented in person or by proxy to be able to vote.

The proceedings of the congress may be conducted in French, German, English, Spanish or Russian.

The reports of the congress, other reports, audits, as well as motions shall be recorded in the languages as set forth above. The organizers of the congress will provide the necessary facilities.

In case of differing interpretation, the original text shall prevail.

For the report of the congress sessions, the organizers may select one of the languages mentioned above.

### The Board of Directors

The board of directors is the directing body of FIP.

It comprises a president, three vice presidents and five directors-at-large.

All members of the FIP board of directors shall be elected for a four-year term. The president may not serve more than two terms.

No member of the board of directors may at the same time hold office as president of any philatelic commission of FIP.

All members of the board of directors shall be entitled to attend the meetings of any FIP commission.

The president shall represent FIP at all times and shall be its legal representative.

The president shall preside at all meetings of the congress and the board of directors.

In the absence or incapacity of the president, one of the vice presidents nominated by the board of directors shall take his place.

In the event of a vacancy in the office of president, the board of directors will elect one of the vice presidents to act as president until the next congress is convened. A new president will be elected at the next congress for the remaining period of the four-year term.

In the event of a vacancy in the office of any member of the board of directors, an election will be held at the next congress to complete the remaining period of the four-year term.

In carrying out the duties of his office, the president shall have the services of a permanent secretariat, the cost of which shall be paid by FIP. The secretariat will be permanently located at a place decided upon by congress without regards to the domicile of the elected president.

### Auditors

The auditors shall examine and certify all of the accounts and balance sheet of FIP not later than March 15 following the end of the fiscal year in question.

They shall submit their audit report to the congress in writing.

### Recognized Observers of FIP

Recognized observers of FIP are persons who, in their professional capacity, agree to assist FIP in accomplishing its objectives.

Congress may appoint observers from international trade organizations, large catalog publishers, international expert organizations, etc.

They will be admitted to congress as consultants for questions concerning their professional field.

### Philatelic Commissions of FIP

The commissions are technical organs of FIP.

They work under the general guidance of the board of directors and according with the long term program of FIP.

Every regular member of FIP may appoint a delegate to every FIP commission.

Each commission shall elect a bureau from among its own members comprising not more than seven members.

Each commission shall nominate for the approval of the board of directors a member of the Bureau of the Commission to act as its president.

If the board of directors accept the nomination, it shall be submitted to congress for approval.

The congress elects presidents of commissions for a term of four years.

No person may, at one and the same time, hold offices as president of more than one FIP commission.

Commissions must submit all rules governing their own proceedings and all draft regulations to the board of directors for approval by congress.

No commission shall be empowered to enter into obligations on behalf of the FIP except and only to the extent that it shall have been authorized by congress and confirmed in writing by the board of directors.

Each commission shall report to congress:
a) its work during the preceding year
b) motions and proposals
c) programs of work for the coming two years.

These reports shall be submitted to the board of directors by January 31.

No report may be published until it has been approved by the board of directors.

The board of directors submits to congress its recommendations for all allocation of funds to commissions.

The expenditures of the commissions must be submitted with receipt together with the annual report.

### Special Representatives

Congress may appoint recognized specialists for a specified period to undertake special assignments with the consent of the regular member concerned.

## International Exhibitions

In compliance with the general regulations of FIP, international philatelic exhibitions may be organized under FIP patronage or auspices.

Requests for FIP patronage or auspices must be submitted to congress at least two years in advance. They must be sent to the FIP secretariat in writing.

Only exhibitors affiliated with a federation which is a member of FIP may participate in international exhibitions organized under the patronage or auspices of FIP.

The organizing body of any exhibition granted the patronage or auspices of FIP agrees as follows:

a) to pay to FIP the appropriate financial contribution as laid down by congress.

b) to abide by the general regulations for FIP exhibitions.

## Dissolution of FIP

At the request of the board of directors or upon request of more than two-thirds of the active members, the FIP can be dissolved by a congress.

The dissolution of FIP requires the presence of a two-thirds majority of active members and a three-quarters majority of members with a right to vote who are attending or who are represented by proxy.

Upon the dissolution of the FIP, the assets of FIP shall be transferred to the Federation of Swiss Philatelic Societies in trust. This federation shall retain said assets until the organizing of a new federation of international philately.

## Occurrences Not Covered

In cases where the statutes do not cover the matter, the same shall be determined by the board of directors to be confirmed by the congress.

## Interpretation of the Statutes

In the event there are disagreements in the text of the statues by reason of translation, the German text shall be valid.

# Past Congress

Since the founding of FIP in 1926 there have been 46 congress sessions held, with most of those taking place in Europe. During the war years of 1939 through 1942 and 1944 and 1945, there were no congress sessions.

A number of the FIP congress sessions have been held in connection with an international exhibition, at which the leading philatelists from all parts of the world were in attendance for the event being held under FIP patronage.

The only congress session held in the United States was during the INTERPHIL exhibition held in Philadelphia, Pa., in 1976.

The following constitutes a listing of the year and location for FIP congresses of the past:

1926 — Paris, France
1927 — Strasbourg, France
1928 — Vienna, Austria
1929 — Berne, Switzerland
1930 — Brussels, Belgium
1931 — Paris, France
1932 — Heidelberg, Germany
1933 — Vienna, Austria
1934 — Lugano, Switzerland
1935 — Brussels, Belgium
1936 — Luxembourg City, Luxembourg
1937 — Paris, France
1938 — Prague, Czechoslovakia
1939 — World War II, no session
1940 — World War II, no session
1941 — World War II, no session
1942 — World War II, no session
1943 — Geneva, Switzerland
1944 — World War II, no session
1945 — World War II, no session
1946 — Brussels, Belgium
1947 — Prague, Czechoslovakia
1948 — Basel, Switzerland
1949 — Paris, France
1950 — Vienna, Austria
1951 — Copenhagen, Denmark
1952 — Utrecht, The Netherlands
1953 — Lisbon, Portugal
1954 — Geneva, Switzerland
1955 — Stockholm, Sweden
1956 — Helsinki, Finland
1957 — Tel Aviv, Israel
1958 — Brussels, Belgium
1959 — Hamburg, Germany
1960 — Warsaw, Poland
1961 — Budapest, Hungary
1962 — Prague, Czechoslovakia
1963 — Istanbul, Turkey
1964 — Paris, France
1965 — Vienna, Austria
1966 — Munich, Germany
1967 — Amsterdam, The Netherlands
1968 — Prague, Czechoslovakia
1969 — Sofia, Bulgaria
1970 — London, England
1971 — Budapest, Hungary
1972 — Brussels, Belgium
1973 — Munich, Germany
1974 — Stockholm, Sweden
1975 — Madrid, Spain
1976 — Philadelphia, U.S.A.
1977 — Amsterdam, The Netherlands

1978 — Prague, Czechoslovakia
1979 — Sofia, Bulgaria
1980 — Essen (West Germany)
1981 — Vienna, Austria
1982 — Paris, France
1983 — Rio de Janeiro, Brazil

Future congresses (applied for but not necessarily firm)

1985 — Hungary
1986 — Prague, Czechoslovakia
1987 — Amsterdam, The Netherlands
1989 — Bulgaria

# General Regulations

With the change in the FIP statutes it became necessary to change the general regulations for exhibitions. After a great deal of work in close cooperation with many concerned organizations, a final draft appeared in March 1982 for ratification at the Paris congress in June.

Basic changes and features of the proposed draft include:

1. A delineation of categories of shows — World (general or specialized) which would receive full patronage, International (general or specialized) which would be granted auspices, and others which would receive support. The three categories, patronage, auspices, and support, represent decreasing levels of FIP involvement and adherence to the FIP rules.

2. Frame space would be calculated in square meters rather than frames as a unit, with a minimum and maximum specified both for individuals and for the total to be available at a given show.

Normal competitive exhibits would receive from 5 to 10 square meters and honor class exhibits would receive 10 square meters of space.

General World shows would be from 2,500 to 4,500 square meters and specialized exhibitions would be from 1,000 to 2,000.

3. A participation in each show of 20 per cent of the total as first time exhibits will be encouraged.

4. Evaluation sheets for literature exhibits are planned.

5. Honor class rules will be brought into line with those approved at the Essen Congress, i.e., FIP will determine the list of qualified exhibits which will be determined annually. The period of qualification will extend over a 10 year span. All other provisions are essentially unchanged.

6. Medals are proposed to be changed from the silver to the gold level by the following substitution:

silver
large silver
vermeil (gold plated silver)
large vermeil
gold

7. Minimum gold content for gold and large gold medals is specified.

8. Only large vermeil and higher awards will be eligible for special prizes.

9. Exhibitors will receive two admission cards instead of the one presently provided, and will have the opportunity to purchase special issues of the exhibition at a special counter set aside for that purpose for exhibitors only.

10. A major revision has been made to the section regarding national commissioners, including:

— Expanded services for security to be provided both to and from the exhibition for commissioners.

— The right to mount and dismount the exhibits personally.

— A special lounge for commissioners to give them the opportunity to meet and discuss any problems they may have on an informal basis.

— If they bring at least two exhibits; it is proposed that commissioners receive a hotel room for two, a suitable daily allowance, two passes, an exhibition catalog, the awards list, and two tickets to the awards banquet.

Until modified, the general regulations of 1975 remain in effect, and these earlier regulations will continue to be in effect for any show given patronage prior to the approval of the new draft. The current regulations are as follows:

(The organizer may choose between the designations "International Philatelic Exhibition" and "Philatelic World Exhibition.")

### General Provisions

**Art. 1**

1. The following "General Regulations for International Philatelic Exhibitions under the Patronage of the FIP" were accepted on Sept. 30, 1974 by the congress in Stockholm and confirmed on April 14, 1975 by the congress in Madrid. The regulations of June 1, 1967 are thereby superseded.

2. The provisions of these general regulations apply solely for adult exhibitors.

3. The "Special Regulations for International Philatelic Exhibitions of Young Philatelists under the Patronage of the FIP" apply for exhibitions of young philatelists.

**Art. 2**

The exhibitions under the patronage of the FIP are categorized as:

1. General International Exhibitions.

The organizers of such exhibitions must provide for all of the classes listed in Article 3, below.

2. Specialized Exhibitions, which are limited to the following:

2/1. traditional philately,

2/2. postal history,

2/3. thematic philately,

2/4. aerophilately.

**Art. 3**

1. General exhibitions must include all the following philatelic categories and classes:

A. - First Category: **Noncompetitive Participation**

**1.** Court of Honor,

**2.** Official Class,

**3.** "Hors Concours" Class for all other noncompetitive exhibits.

B. - Second Category: **Competitive Participation**

**1.** FIP Class of Honor,

**2.** Class for Traditional Philately,

**3.** Class for Postal History,

**4.** Class for Thematic Philately,

**5.** Class for Aerophilately,

**6.** Literature Class.

2. The subdivision of exhibits within the classes provided in 2 through 5 of the second category is provided for in the various special regulations.

3. The FIP Class of Honor will not be provided for in specialized exhibitions (Art. 2/2).

4. In specialized exhibitions (Art. 2/2), the providing for a related literature class is at the discretion of the Organizing Committee.

5/1. In those years when there is a special international exhibition of young philatelists, the Organizing Committees of the other international exhibitions (see Art. 2), should provide a section for the participation of young philatelists, but are not required to do so.

5/2. In those years when there is no special international exhibition of young philatelists, such a section must be provided for in at least one of the general international philatelic exhibitions, and it will be submitted to the rules of the special regulations for International Philatelic Youth Exhibitions.

6. Exhibits which cannot be placed in one of the foregoing competitive classes (second category, 2 through 6) may be grouped in a special class by the Organizing Committee. The evaluation of these exhibits is left to the discretion of the jury.

**Art. 4**

First Category: **Noncompetitive Participation**

1. The Court of Honor is restricted to collections of philatelists who have been specially invited by the Organizing Committee, and consists of:

a) Collections of notable personages,

b) Collections of particular philatelic interest.

2. The Official Class comprises the participation of postal administrations, postal museums, and postage stamp printers, as well as of artists and engravers.

3. The "Hors Concours" Class comprises the exhibits of those collectors who either are not allowed to participate in the Competitive Participation or do not want to do so.

**Art. 5**

Second Category: **Competitive Participation**

1. FIP Class of Honor:

a) Only those collections will be admitted in the FIP Class of Honor which have previously won three large gold medals in exhibitions under FIP patronage. (A "Grand Prix" is equivalent to a large gold medal.) Only one medal for a given year will be taken into consideration.

b) A collection can only be admitted to compete for the FIP Grand Prize of Honor during the five successive years following its admission to the FIP Class of Honor. After this period, it can again be exhibited in one of the classes listed in Art. 3, second category, 2 - 5.

2. Competitive Classes for traditional philately, for postal history, thematic philately and aerophilately. Only those collections can be admitted to these classes which meet the respective special regulations, and whose owners meet the conditions of Art. 9 of these general regulations.

3. Literature class.

Participation in this class is reserved for those philatelic publications which meet the special regulations of the FIP for literature.

**Art. 6 - Exhibition Frames**

1. The minimum number of frames to be made available for those classes listed in Art. 3, second category, 1 - 5, is set as follows:

a) in general exhibitions 3,000,

b) in specialized exhibitions:

traditional philately 1,500,

postal history 1,000,

thematic philately 1,500,

aerophilately 1,000.

The usable frame area must be at least one square meter, otherwise the number of frames must be proportionately increased.

2. The Organizing Committee of a general exhibition determines the distribution of available frames among the various classes.

3. The number of frames to be made available to each exhibit in the FIP Class of Honor may not be more than 15 and, in principle, not less than 10.

4. In the other competitive classes, with exception of the Literature Class, the Organizing Committee in accepting an exhibit must provide for it a minimum of 5 frames, unless the exhibitor requests a lesser number, which however must be at least 3 frames.

## Art. 7 - Awards

1. FIP Class of Honor.

The sole award in this class is the "FIP Grand Prize of Honor." It consists of a precious work of art. The Organizing Committee will present the other participants in the FIP Class of Honor with a prize of honor or a medal, which however must be distinctively different from those medals awarded by the jury for the competitive classes (Art. 3, second category). The same collection may only once receive the "FIP Grand Prize of Honor."

2. Competitive Classes.

2/1. In international exhibitions under the patronage of the FIP the jury will make the following awards:

a) in general exhibitions:

a "Grand International Prize,"

a "Grand National Prize,"

b) in specialized exhibitions:

a "Grand Exhibition Prize."

These "Grand Prizes" consist of precious art objects which the Organizing Committee will place at the disposal of the jury.

These prizes will be awarded to the most deserving exhibits in the international and the national class, respectively, which the jury has already selected for a large gold medal, and will be awarded in place of such a medal.

The same collection may in no way be awarded the same "Grand Prize" at more than one international exhibition.

2/2. In addition to the above-mentioned "Grand Prizes," the Organizing Committee is free to place special prizes of honor at the disposal of the jury. These special prizes will be awarded to exceptionally deserving collections, which have already been selected by the jury for a large gold medal.

2/3. Further, the following medals exclusively reserved for the competitive classes will be placed at the disposal of the jury with no limitation on number:

    large gold medals (18 carat),

    gold medals (18 carat),

    vermeil medals (silver gilt),

    silver medals,

    silver-bronze medals,

    bronze medals.

2/4. Special prizes may be placed at the disposal of the jury to be awarded to exhibits which have received as a minimum a silver medal, but could not be awarded a higher ranking medal.

These special prizes will be placed at the disposal of the jury with no stipulations.

As appropriate, however, the desires of the donor will be considered in the case of special prizes donated by leading officials of the exhibition host country.

These special prizes may be works of art, plaques or medals. In the latter case they must of necessity be distinctively different from the medals provided for the competitive classes.

3. Awards for nonexhibitors.

All medals which may be offered to nonexhibitors must be distinctively different from those provided for the competitive category.

## Art. 8

1. On the basis of a justified recommendation from the competent national federation (member of the FIP) to the president of the FIP, the "FIP Medal" may be awarded to a personal study collection of exceptional philatelic value, and which presents new knowledge of the philately of a country.

2. This recognition will be presented by the FIP in addition to the competitive medal awarded by the jury.

3. The FIP Medal may only be awarded once to the same study.

4. The medal, engraved with the recipient's name, will be accompanied by a diploma carrying the reason for the award.

## Provisions concerning the participation in International Philatelic exhibitions under the Patronage of the FIP

## Art. 9

1. Only those collectors are allowed to participate in international philatelic exhibitions under the patronage of the FIP who: belong to an FIP member organization according to Art. 8 and 9 of the statutes, and who already have been awarded at least a silver medal for their collection at a national or equivalently ranked exhibition, or else have certification from the competent national federation that the collection is of equivalent quality.

2. Collections belonging to stamp dealers may be accepted in the competitive class under the condition that the competent national federation formally certifies to the Executive Committee that the exhibit is a private collection which has been formed by the dealer over a period longer than the last five years.

## Art. 10

Provisional application for participation must go through the national commissioner. The following is to be listed:

The exact description of the exhibit,

The awards received for the exhibit at exhibitions under the patronage of FIP as well as at national or equivalent exhibitions,

The desired number of frames, the class in which the exhibit is to be entered, as well as the FIP member organization to which the exhibitor belongs.

### Art. 11

1. The Organizing Committee acknowledges the acceptance of the exhibit for participation in the exhibition by sending a definitive entry form through the national commissioner. The Organizing Committee is not required to justify its decision should it reject an exhibit.

2. The Organizing Committee is not required to provide the total number of frames desired, should this exceed the minimum number provided for in Art. 6, par. 3 and 4.

### Art. 12

In the definitive entry form, the exhibitor agrees to accept and abide by:

The general regulations on Exhibitions organized under the patronage of the FIP,

The special regulations mentioned in Art. 3/2,

The special regulations of the exhibition.

He further agrees to meet the instructions of the national commissioner.

Failure to abide by the above regulations and instructions can lead to exclusion from participation.

### Art. 13

1. Collections may only be exhibited in the FIP Class of Honor under the name of the owner, unless the name is provided to the jury.

2. In the regular competitive classes, collections may be exhibited under a pseudonym. However, the owner must advise the Organizing Committee of his true identity, and authorize it to so inform the jury.

### Art. 14

1. The entry must without exception be the property of the exhibitor.

2. The exhibitor will avoid the display of stamps and vignettes whose exhibition does not conform to the directives of the FIP concerning unwanted issues.

3. He is free to mention, very discreetly, the rarity of an item.

Should there be reference to the expertizing of an item, the certificate of expertization must be kept available for the jury.

4. No indication of monetary value is allowed.

### Art. 15

Decisions of the international jury are final. No appeal is allowed.

### Art. 16

Each exhibitor has the right without further charge to:

A permanent entry card,

An exhibition catalog,

A copy of the list of awards made by the jury (Palmares).

### Art. 17

Exhibitors must be advised of the following in the first announcement brochure:

The cost per frame,

Insurance considerations which are not covered by the Organizing Committee,

Customs and currency exchange provisions,

Entry and exit provisions,

The special regulations valid for the exhibition, which however may not be in conflict with these general regulations or with the special regulations for the various competitive classes.

### Provisions for the Organizers

### Art. 18

1. The FIP extends its patronage only to those international philatelic exhibitions which are organized by its members (Art. 7-9 of the statues).

2. Only the congress is empowered to extend the patronage of the FIP.

### Art. 19

1. According to Art. 5 of the statutes, the congress can also extend the technical and moral support of the FIP to international philatelic exhibitions which take place in nonmember countries, with the purpose of encouraging the development of philately there and the formation of a national federation.

2. This support may only be granted once for a given country.

### Art. 20

1. The request for FIP patronage must be presented in writing to the Secretariat of the Executive Committee, no later than Dec. 31 of the third year preceding the exhibition.

2. In the written application for extension of patronage, the following must be formally agreed to:

2/1. to respect all provisions of these general regulations for exhibitions,

2/2. neither to solicit nor accept any other philatelic patronage in addition to that of the FIP,

2/3. within the frame of the FIP patronized exhibition, neither to allow any activities of other philatelic organizations nor to include them in the publicity brochures or the exhibition program without the formal approval of the Executive Committee of the FIP,

2/4. to name commissioners only from countries which are FIP members. The Executive Committee can authorize exceptions,

2/5. to select the members of the jury in strict accordance with Art. 32 of these regulations,

2/6. only to accept entries from collectors who belong to an FIP member federation (Art. 7 through 9 of the statutes). Applications for participation have to be forwarded through the national commissioner, who is competent for the residence of the exhibitor. Applications through another national commissioner are subject to the previous, written authorization by the FIP member, on whose territory the applicant's residence lies. Applications for participation from collectors, who are affiliated to an FIP member, but who reside in a country, which is not a member of FIP, may be forwarded by the national commissioner of this FIP member. In special cases, the decision is for the Executive Committee,

2/7. to prepare the special regulations for the exhibition in strict accord with these general regulations, and, after their approval by the Executive Committee, to publish them on a timely basis,

2/8. to send the FIP the sum determined by the congress at the time it confirms patronage.

**Art. 21**

1. The Executive Committee will present the timely submitted request for patronage to the following congress for the purpose of securing provisional acceptance. Definitive acceptance patronage will be made by decision of the congress two years prior to the exhibition.

2. Should an Organizing Committee fail to respect the obligations provided for in accordance with Art. 20, subsequent to definitive granting of patronage, the Executive Committee has the right at any time to withdraw such patronage. In such a case, all FIP members will immediately be advised of the withdrawal and requested to withdraw their commissioners and jurors, and to advise their members against participation in the exhibition.

**Provisions Concerning Foreign Commissioners**

**Art. 22**

The foreign commissioners will be selected by the Organizing Committee on the basis of recommendations from the respective FIP members.

**Art. 23**

Only the foreign commissioners are responsible for coordination between the Organizing Committee and the participants in the competitive categories from the individual countries.

**Art. 24**

1. The Organizing Committee is authorized only to name commissioners from those countries represented in the FIP.

2. Conversely, for such countries which are under Art. 19, the Organizing Committee may designate commissioners with prior written approval of the Executive Committee for each specific case.

**Art. 25**

The Organizing Committee, by registered letter, will request FIP members to submit recommendations for their designation of foreign commissioners. In the event this request is not answered within three months, the Organizing Committee has the right to turn to the Executive Committee in such a case for clarification of the situation.

**Art. 26**

The list of foreign commissioners will be published in the exhibition brochures.

**Art. 27**

National organizations who do not wish to nominate a commissioner for a particular exhibition must so inform the Organizing Committee and the Executive Committee in writing immediately after the first request for nomination of a commissioner.

**Art. 28**

The commissioner obligates himself:

To publicize the exhibition among the philatelists of his country;

To examine the provisional applications prior to sending them to the Organizing Committee, to assure himself of their philatelic merit, and to check the correctness of the statement of previous awards.

**Art. 29**

Any lapse in the voluntarily undertaken obligations of a commissioner can lead to his being excluded from this function in future exhibitions.

**Art. 30**

1. The commissioner has the right to a permanent entry card, an exhibition catalog and a list of the awards made by the jury (Palmares).

2. The Organizing Committee is at liberty to provide honorariums for special services which a commissioner may render on behalf of the exhibition.

# FIP Rules For Traditional Philately

### Article 1

Traditional philately is based on the collecting of all philatelic and postal items, in a manner which may include, but is not limited to, all

forms of stamps, unused, used, and on cover, as well as philatelic materials such as original essays and proofs, relating to the production of stamps in as specialized or as generalized a nature as the collector desires.

Essentially, traditional philately comprises all philatelic activities except those which are specifically intended to be considered in the specialized fields of postal history, aerophilately, and thematics. Exhibits which do not follow the special rules of those areas may be considered and judged as traditional philately exhibits, particularly if the area concerned does not wish to accept the exhibit for lack of conformity to its rules.

Exhibits in the traditional philately or open competition section of international exhibitions under FIP rules should contain material which may be reasonably related and described as a unit. The coverage should be clearly stated in the exhibition catalog description and the exhibit should present a display which is meaningful to the viewer.

### Article 2

Exhibitors should aim at showing material which is comparable with the best condition obtainable, but where a rare item is unobtainable in good condition, the exhibitor is encouraged to include it, provided its appearance is not so poor as to disfigure the display. The inclusion of forged, faked or repaired material, not described as such, may lead to downgrading, or even disqualification, depending on the severity of the violation, as per FIP rules.

Pre-stamp postal markings may be included in such an exhibit if they add to the scope of the coverage, and are not excessive in proportion to the philatelic element. Exhibits shall not include unwanted issues, as per FIP rules.

### Article 3

Traditional philately exhibits at international exhibitions may be arranged by the Organizing Committee into classes which may be expected to attract significant levels of participation in relation to the location and stated aim of the exhibition. Regardless of the number and scope of classes thus established, the only Grands Prix which are authorized are those provided by FIP general regulations, specifically those for the honor class, the international class, and the national class.

### Article 4

Judging of traditional philately exhibits shall be on the basis of each exhibit's total significance philatelically and how the exhibit in particular compares with a theoretical perfection in its area. In doing so, judges will consider each exhibit on the following bases:

1. Condition
2. Completion
3. Philatelic importance and rarity
4. Philatelic knowledge and research
5. Presentation and balance.

(Adopted by FIP Congress at Sofia, Bulgaria on May 17, 1979)

# Thematic Rules

International rules for thematic collections and subject collections.

### Introduction

The thematic class is composed of two categories of collections: the thematic collection as such and the subject collection.

### Thematic Collections

### Article 1

The thematic collection develops a theme or illustrates an idea following a logical plan, using the motifs offered by the stamps, as well as the information supplied by the philatelic or postal documents. Therefore, the stamps and documents selected shall be in strict relation to the theme or idea selected.

### Article 2

The plan of the collection, presented as a preface, must be logical and correct and will supply the necessary information, including all the divisions, to estimate the size of the collection. A concise and accurate text must clearly indicate the development of the theme.

### Article 3

The originality of the theme will be treated meticulously. The collection will be enhanced by

careful research made by the collector, allowing his personality to be brought forth.

### Article 4

The size of the collection will allow a clear and complete development of the proposed theme.

### Article 5

The philatelic elements; postage stamps and postal documents represent the essential elements of any thematic collection.

### Subject Collections

### Article 6

The subject collection includes all the postage stamps and philatelic documents related to a subject or purpose of issue. The presentation of the philatelic material can be in a systematic, thematic order and/or by country or chronological order.

### Article 7

The subject collection must be preceded by a plan which introduces the material displayed, illustrates the criteria followed in its realization and gives an idea of the extent of the collection and the development of the different parts.

### Article 8

The subject collection must be accompanied by a clear and concise descriptive text. Its only function is to comment on the systematic development and the features of the collection.

### Article 9

The development of a subject collection requires deep philatelic research of the chosen subject or purpose of the issue.

### Article 10

The postage stamps and philatelic documents are the essential elements of the collection.

### Common Directives

### Article 11

The presence and variety of various philatelic elements (stamps, covers, cancellations, handstamps, postal stationery, etc.) will allow the assessment of the collector's philatelic knowledge. These items must be authentic and in good condition. The cancellations should be neat and cover the stamps as little as possible. The FIP decisions concerning harmful or undesirable issues will be applied. Nonphilatelic items cannot — in principle — be admitted.

### Article 12

The presentation of the collections must be clean and neat, and will present a harmonious entity.

### Article 13

In evaluating the collections, the jury will observe the following criteria:

#### Thematic Collections

| | | |
|---|---|---|
| 1. Presentation and general impression | 10 | 10 |
| 2. Theme | —— | 50 |
| 2/1. Plan of the collection and development of the theme | 20 | —— |
| 2/2. Originality and setting up of the theme | 25 | —— |
| 2/3. Size of the condition | 5 | —— |
| 3. Philatelic elements | —— | 40 |
| 3/1. Philatelic knowledge | 15 | —— |
| 3/2. Condition and rarity of stamps and documents | 25 | —— |
| Total | 100 | 100 |

#### Subject Collections

| | | |
|---|---|---|
| 1. Presentation and general impression | 10 | 10 |
| 2. Subject | —— | 40 |
| 2/1. Systematic study and size of the collection | 25 | —— |
| 2/2. Setting up of the subject | 15 | —— |
| 3. Philatelic elements | —— | 50 |
| 3/1. Philatelic knowledge | 20 | —— |
| 3/2. Condition and rarity of stamps and documents | 30 | —— |
| Total | 100 | 100 |

### Article 14

The prizes may be awarded as follows:

Lowest points obtained at an exhibition

| Medals | International | National |
|---|---|---|
| Gold, large | 95 | —— |
| Gold | 90 | 85 |
| Vermeil | 85 | 80 |
| Silver | 75 | 70 |
| Silver (plated) bronze | 70 | 65 |
| Bronze | 60 | 55 |
| A diploma may be delivered to the collectors with | 50 | 45 |

### Regulations of the General Rules of FIP

### Article 15

In an international exhibition, five frames at least shall be at the disposal of each collector allowing him to show the development of the collection plan and present the interesting philatelic items.

### Article 16

The thematic class is evaluated by a jury exclusively formed by specialists of these collections. Their number will be proportionate to the number of frames reserved to the class.

### Article 17

The prizes of the thematic class will be identical to the ones of other classes. They can show, in whole or shortened letters, the inscription "Thematic Class."

### Article 18

The only thematic collections and the subject collections which have been awarded a silver medal at national exhibitions supported by the concerning national federation will be accepted in the competition class of the international exhibitions supported by FIP.

# Regulation For Youth

Special regulations for Youth International Philatelic Exhibitions under the patronage of the FIP.

### CHAPTER I
### General Conditions
### Article 1

1. The present "Special Regulations for Youth International Philatelic Exhibitions under the patronage of the FIP" was approved by the Stock-

holm congress under date of Sept. 30, 1974 and confirmed by the Madrid congress under date April 14, 1975.

It replaces the October 1966 one.

2. It applies both to special exhibitions of young philatelists and special sections provided at special or general exhibitions appearing in Article 2 of the general regulation although the number of frames (1,000) for these sections, laid down in Article 5 is not compulsory.

## Article 2

1. The Youth International Philatelic Exhibitions under the patronage of the FIP or the corresponding sections of other exhibitions are reserved for young philatelists aged from 12 to 25.

2. The age attained on Jan. 1 of the year in which the exhibition takes place determines for the whole year the age group as shown in Article 4.

## Article 3

1. The following competition classes are planned for the participation of young philatelists.

1/1. Traditional philately and aerophilately class.

1/2. Thematic philately class.

1/3. Literature class (literature intended for young philatelists as well as literature written by young philatelists).

2. Apart from these competition classes the organizing committee of the exhibition may plan:

2/1. an official class.

2/2. a "noncompetitive" class such as is defined in Article 4/3 of the general regulation.

## Article 4

1. The collections for competition classes provided in Article 3/1 sub 1 and 2 are open to the following age groups.

— Age Group A    12 and 13
— Age Group B    14 and 15
— Age Group C    16 to 18
— Age Group D    19 to 21
— Age Group E    22 to 25.

2. Collective collections are shown in the age group D.

## Article 5

1. For special youth exhibitions, the exhibition organizing committee will have to put at the disposal of the competitive classes (age groups A to E) a minimum of 1,000 frames planned for 12 normal sized album sheets.

2. For all exhibitions the participation of young philatelists are exonerated of the frame fee except, however, for general exhibitions in which the organizing committee has the option of imposing on the participants of Group E a fee equivalent to 50 per cent of the general fee.

3. In the different age groups the exhibitors will have to fill a minimum number of frames per collection, these being put at the disposal of the exhibition committee according to the following key:

— Age Group A    2 Frames
— Age Group B    2 Frames
— Age Group C    3 Frames
— Age Group D    4 Frames
— Age Group E    5 Frames.

For specialized collections of a single issue a minimum of 3 frames will be accepted.

4. The minimum number of sheets to be assigned to a frame is 12. In case of frames of different dimensions consult the following table.

| Number of sheets per frame | Minimum of frames per age group | | | | |
|---|---|---|---|---|---|
| | A | B | C | D | E |
| 8 | 3 | 3 | 4 | 6 | 7 |
| 9 | 3 | 3 | 4 | 5 | 6 |
| 12 | 2 | 2 | 3 | 4 | 5 |
| 15 | 2 | 2 | 2 | 3 | 4 |
| 16 | 2 | 2 | 2 | 3 | 4 |

## Article 6

1. The number of frames to be assigned to the different members of the FIP (see Articles 8 and 9 of the statutes) is resolved by the exhibition organizing committee in agreement with the "FIP Commission for Youth Philately."

2. At the same time the exhibition organizing committee will forward to the chairmen of the members concerned of the FIP the necessary entry forms.

3. It behooves the concerned members of the FIP to designate the participations to be presented. Should a member of the FIP surrender this right to his section of the youth philately, the secretary's office of the chairman of the FIP will have to be informed in order to transmit the information in writing to the FIP committee for youth philately and to the exhibition organizing committee.

## Article 7

1. The appreciation of the participation by the jury will have to be carried out according to the guidelines enclosed with the present regulations.

2. The jury will establish for each participation a short critical appreciation. Appraisal sheets supplied must be used to this end.

3. Each exhibitor is entitled to receive the appraisal sheet or a copy of the latter.

## Article 8

1. At every Youth International Philatelic Exhibition a sufficient number of the following medals are to be provided for the jury:

— Vermeil medals
— Silver medals

— Silver-bronze medals

— Bronze medals

— Diplomas

— Diploma of participation.

2. Special prizes will also have to be provided for the jury to award without qualification.

3. For particularly deserving collections the jury may add its congratulations to the medal either for the presentation, for the design or for the philatelic study.

## CHAPTER II

Stipulations concerning the participation in Youth International Philatelic Exhibitions under the patronage of the FIP.

### Article 9

1. Will only be eligible to Youth International Philatelic Exhibitions, according to Article 3/1 figures 1 and 2, collections which:

1/1. are the property of a collector affiliated to a member of the FIP, according to Articles 8 and 9 of the statutes;

1/2. have obtained at least a silver-bronze medal in a national exhibition or of equal importance, unless the national federation in question certifies the required qualification.

2. During the same year a collection will only be able to participate once, in a competition class, in a Youth International Philatelic Exhibition or in the section "Youth" of a general International Philatelic Exhibition organized under the patronage of the FIP.

3. A collection having gained a vermeil medal twice in the age group C to E will not be able to compete in the same group.

4. A collection of a young philatelist having participated in an adult class in a general or special exhibition and having gained at least a bronze medal in this exhibition will not be entitled to participate in a competition class in a Youth International Philatelic Exhibition or in a corresponding section in a general exhibition.

### Article 10

Application for a competition class according to Article 3, figures 1 and 2, will be through the national representative.

To be enclosed:

— A short precise description of the participation.

— Distinctions gained in FIP exhibitions and others.

— A statement certified by the national representative affirming that the collection is the personal work of the collector.

### Article 11

Applications for the literature class will be according to the stipulations of the special regulation for the literature class.

### Article 12

On the application form the participant agrees to accept:

— The special regulation of Youth International Philatelic Exhibitions under the patronage of the FIP

— The special regulations of the Exhibition.

— Moreover, he agrees to respect the instructions of the national representative.

Noncompliance with the preceding terms may lead to exclusion of the participation.

### Article 13

Collections may only be displayed under the name of the owner.

### Article 14

1. Collections must be the exhibitor's own property.

2. The exhibitor is asked to respect the arrangements of the FIP relative to undesirable issues.

3. He has the option of mentioning very discreetly the rarity of the items. In case of appraisal the appraisal report should be held at the disposal of the jury.

4. Any indication of value is forbidden.

### Article 15

The decision of the international jury of the exhibition will be binding and final.

### Article 16

Each exhibitor is entitled to:

— a permanent entry card

— an official catalog

— a copy of the exhibition honors list.

### Article 17

The exhibitors should be informed by the initial propaganda pamphlet about:

— insurance not covered by the director of the exhibition;

— customs and monetary regulations;

— entry and exit conditions for travelers;

— the special regulation valid for the exhibition which, however, should neither be contrary to the present special regulation nor to special regulations concerning the different classes.

Any future alteration to these terms should be brought to the notice of the representatives and exhibitors as soon as possible.

## CHAPTER III
### Provisions Concerning the Organizers
### Article 18

1. The FIP will only grant its patronage to international philatelic exhibitions organized by its members (Articles 7 to 9 of the statues).

2. Only the congress is qualified to grant the patronage of the FIP.

## Article 19

1. According to Article 5 of the statutes, the congress can grant the moral and technical backing of the FIP to international philatelic exhibitions organized in non-member countries in order to foster the development of philately and the creation of a national federation.

2. This backing can only be consented once to the same country.

## Article 20

1. The demand for patronage for an exhibition must be presented in writing to the Executive Committee, at the latest, Dec. 31, three years prior to the exhibition.

# Rules For Aerophilately
## Article 1

The present special regulations complete the "General Rules and Regulations for FIP Philatelic Exhibitions;" approved by the Madrid congress, held April 14, 1975, it concerns all questions regarding aerophilatelic collections.

## Article 2

In conformity with Art. 3/2 of the above-mentioned "General Regulations," such regulations are valid for both specialized international aerophilatelic exhibitors and collections displayed in the aerophilatelic class in general exhibitions.

## Article 3

Exhibitions and classes to be grouped as follows:

1. Forerunners collections (balloon mail, pioneer flights, etc.).

2. Collectors of flown covers which involve the study and classification of stamps, hand stamps and other marks used by the post office to distinguish airmail postage.

3. (To be decided upon by the commission) Commemorative collections concerning air demonstrations.

## Article 4

All displayed items should be authentic both where stamps and hand stamps are concerned as well as airmail cancellations and labels.

## Article 5

When judging aerophilatelic collections the jury will take the following into consideration awarding points as follows:

| | |
|---|---|
| a. Presentation, general impression of the collection | 10 points |
| b. Philatelic knowledge and research | 25 points |
| c. Development and size of the collection | 25 points |
| d. Historical, postal and aerophilatelic knowledge | 15 points |
| e. Rarity of items | 20 points |
| f. Special characteristics | 5 points |
| | Total: 100 points |

## Article 6

Collectors will be awarded the following medals according to the number of points awarded by the jury:

| | |
|---|---|
| Large gold | from 95 points |
| Gold | from 91 to 94 points |
| Vermeil | from 86 to 90 points |
| Silver | from 76 to 85 points |
| Silver (plated) bronze | from 71 to 75 points |
| Bronze | from 60 to 70 points |

## Article 7

In the case of any dispute arising from the interpretation of a translation the French version of such regulations will be binding.

## Article 8

These special regulations were approved at the Philadelphia congress.

# Rules For Postal History
## Article 1

A postal history collection is based on the study and classification of postal and philatelic items which are directly relevant to the methods, routing and conditions of dispatch of postal communications of all periods, or to the organization to this end of postal services, whether governmental, local or private.

## Article 2

All items included in the exhibit should be in good condition of preservation, with the exception for example of wreck covers or disinfected mail. The inclusion of forged, faked or repaired material, not described as such, may lead to downgrading or even disqualification.

## Article 3

The postal history class in philatelic exhibitions shall be judged by specialist judges who will be members of the jury.

## Article 4

In judging a postal history class the jury shall be guided in making its awards by the following criteria:

a. Treatment of the subject: knowledge of postal history and research work.

b. Importance of the collection and rarities.

c. Condition of preservation of the collection.

d. Presentation of the collection.

## Article 5

Medals awarded in this class shall be the same as for other classes except they should be inscribed "Postal History" or "P.H."

## Article 6

These rules have been approved by the FIP congress in Madrid, on April 15th, 1975, and came into effect on Jan. 1, 1976.

### Explanatory Note to Article 1

a. A postal history collection consists primarily of used covers and adhesive postage stamps, and postal documents, arranged so as to illustrate a postal historical theme according to Article 1.

b. Such postal history collection themes are, for example:

1. Pre-adhesive postal services.

2. General studies of the development of postal services, national or international.

3. Military mail; field post, siege mail, POW and concentration camp mail.

4. Maritime mail.

5. Wreck covers.

6. Disinfected mail.

7. Railway mail.

8. Censorship of mail.

9. Postage due mail.

And the collections may contain, where strictly necessary, also stamps and their forerunners, maps, prints, sketches, decrees, and the like.

## Rules For Literature

1. The philatelic literature class includes all printed communications related to postage stamps, postal history, their collecting, or to any of the specialized fields connected with the foregoing.

2. The literature class shall consist of the following major sections:

A. **Handbooks and Special Studies:** handbooks, monographs, specialized catalogs, specialized articles (single articles as well as serialized studies) when published as separates, bibliographic works, exhibition catalogs, auction compilations, and similar special works, etc.

B. **General Catalogs:** worldwide, regional and single area catalogs whose depth of coverage does not qualify them as specialized catalogs.

C. **Periodicals:** philatelic journals, philatelic newspapers, society organs, house organs, yearbooks and similar publications.

D. **Articles:** including newspaper columns, periodical articles which have not been separately published, transcripts of philatelic lectures presented to the public (including radio, television and film scripts).

3. Dates of publication may be no earlier than five years prior to year of exhibition for entries in the Handbook and Special Studies division, and no earlier than two years prior to year of exhibition for all other entries. Periodicals shall be exhibited by complete volume or year: at least 10 selections are required for newspaper columns. Revised editions will be considered as new publication. For multivolume works, the date of publication of each volume shall govern.

4. It is the responsibility of the appropriate country federation to verify that prospective exhibits in the literature class have previously received at least a silver medal in a national exhibition, or are of equivalent quality. (General regulations, Art. 9, paragraph 1.)

5. In amplification of Article 14 of the general regulations, literature may be exhibited by the author, compiler, editor, publisher, sponsoring organization or society, or any other individual holding proprietary rights.

6. The highest award provided for the literature class at international exhibitions shall be a (small) gold medal. The awards will be identical to those available to other classes, but will bear in abbreviation or in full the inscription "Literature." Literature exhibits are eligible for special prizes in accordance with Art. 7 of the general regulations.

7. In accordance with Art. 32 and 39 of the general regulations, there will be at least three judges for literature for each international exhibition which includes a literature class, to include one member of the FIP Literature Commission as designated by the FIP Executive Committee. These judges must be recognized as literature specialists by their national FIP member organization, and certified for the international level by the FIP. A major factor in such international certification is the requirement for a reading ability in two or more languages, one of which must be French, English, German, Spanish or Russian.

8. Judges shall in general be guided by the following scale, as adopted from Art. 40 of the general regulations:

a. Originality, significance and
   depth of research.                    40 points

b Presentation of contents: style,
   clarity, skill in communication.      40 points

c. Technical matters: title page
   and imprint, pagination, credits,
   bibliography, index, use of illustrations, etc. (Judges shall not
   consider "appearance" binding, or
   other matters of strictly commercial
   significance)                         20 points

9. The fee for entry of a literature exhibit shall be no higher than the price for hire of one frame of postage stamps material.

10. Two copies of each literature exhibit shall be provided: one copy for judging, and the other for a reading room which shall be made available by the exhibition organizers. Unless the exhibitor formally requests the return of these copies, one copy shall be forwarded by the Exhibition Committee to the FIP library, and the other copy to the local philatelic library or similar institution.

11. The organizing committee shall furnish the judges a list of the literature entries at least 3 months prior to the exhibition. This list may be in the form of the printed exhibition catalog.

# Guidelines For Traditional Philately Exhibitors And Jury

An explanation and expansion of the general rules explains the philosophy of exhibiting to give potential exhibitors and judges more explicit examples of what to do.

### Article 1

The basic intent of this rule is that all philatelic pursuits were once considered "traditional," but it is now recognized that some specialized disciplines have developed. Advocates of these disciplines (aerophilately, postal history, topicals/thematics) desired judges acquainted with the special considerations of their areas.

Although special rules have evolved, not all collectors have changed from the traditional style of exhibiting and have either suffered a low score for not having followed the new rules or have been disqualified.

In principle, then, it may be understood that all collections are considered traditional, but they may also choose to consider themselves under one of the more restricted categories. On this basis, any collection which fails to satisfy the specialized rules may always be evaluated as a "traditional" collection, even though it may receive a different award from that which it would receive in the more restricted category. Judges in the traditional area should be prepared to accept and evaluate any exhibit rejected by the other disciplines.

"Philatelic and postal items" and "philatelic materials" are meant to include virtually all items which are in any way connected with transmission of information by or outside of the post. If any item is in doubt, it may be included, but it should be indicated as such. At the same time it must be remembered and stressed that many of these are not considered significant enough to be shown internationally.

Also, there are national objections to certain items (unaddressed first day covers, for example) which are perfectly accepted and even encouraged in other countries. The FIP does not undertake to pass judgment on such differences in taste, and accepts, within the definition, all items.

### Article 2

The condition of material is essential to a good exhibit. Provision is made, however, for the unique or nearly unique material that does not occur in fine condition. The statement of the article is intended to discourage the inclusion of too many items of a condition which may disfigure an exhibit, particularly if its omission would be unnoticed.

Forged, faked and repaired material should not knowingly be shown as genuine items. Some material may, however, be of such a nature that even experts disagree on the genuineness of the item. Indeed, new research may shed an entirely different light on such a subject. It is left to the judges to decide the individual case and the circumstances which may or may not be involved.

In severe violations of this principle, it is recommended that the jury's observations leading to the application of this rule be communicated to the exhibitor by the organizing committee.

Pre-stamp material or other covers not bearing stamps should in general not occupy more than 10 per cent of a collection's exhibit space unless it may be shown that such material is an essential part of the area being shown.

### Article 3

Each exhibition is a unique situation due to location, changes in collecting and exhibiting habits over the years, personalities of the key members of the organizing committee and other variables which occur in the 10 years or more usual time between shows in a given country. Emphasis may shift in such a way that significant participation in an area at one show may be followed by a very poor turnout in the same area at the next.

The organizing committee is in the best position to evaluate the levels of participation that may occur and to assign separate categories accordingly. The FIP has decided to prevent proliferation of Grands Prix in order to retain the significance of these major awards. Any attempt to augment these three without a change in FIP general regulations is expressly prohibited.

### Article 4

The considerations which are used to judge the relative merits of philatelic exhibits were established before 1900 and are essentially valid today. The vast experience of FIP international judges is the essential element that permits a rapid and accurate evaluation of an international exhibit.

## Bases For Appreciation Of Philatelic Exhibits

Exhibits in the traditional or "open" class at

FIP international or world exhibitions are awarded medals based upon two sets of considerations. The first of these, the philatelic significance of the area shown, is a key initial factor in determining the maximum possible level a perfect exhibit could attain. A fairly easily collected area would obviously be capable of only a much lower level of prize than a more difficult one.

The judges, by their experience in the broader area of disciplines, will be aware of these relative importances as will, usually to a somewhat lesser degree, the exhibitor. It should be stressed, however, that such importances are not absolute, but may change in time as interest, study and acceptance as well as tastes in collecting change. Such importances are also variable within a country and even down to the different approaches to collecting a limited area of the country.

For example, a collection of "used only" examples of "low value" classic issues of a country in its finest state would have lesser capability of a high award than a complete collection of the same issues including the other values, unused and on cover as well, and finely represented in those forms.

It is this element that prevents a collection of very modern issues from receiving a high award in international competition, while at the same time allowing any reasonable collection of the so called "classics" a much better opportunity.

There are many possible approaches to the idea of philatelic significance and perhaps the easiest of these might be the answer to the question "If this were the most perfect possible exhibit in its area, what would be the maximum level it should attain?"

For a collection of the Ajman issues of 1968, the answer would be quite different from that for a collection of Great Britain issues of 1840. Each would be equally capable at the lowest level (no prize) but perfection in one might still be extremely low, if indeed it were accepted as an international exhibit, while the other could win and has won each of the possible Grands Prix.

These relative rankings are, however, transitory things. While the Great Britain will remain capable of maximum levels, the Ajman, in future times, could conceivably advance to much more respectable levels, particularly if the study included true commercial usages and the like.

Collecting tastes would and should become the determinant of capability. Such limits may even change yearly as "respectability" improves or remains constant. It is a demand upon the judges to have an appreciation for these changes although a full current feel for these is very difficult to realize in practice. In the final analysis, it is the "smell" of an exhibit, similar to that indefinable sense that gives an expert a feeling that a particular item is good or bad, that should permit him to make the correct allocation and analysis.

The system of judging in groups will provide the check, while members of the other groups verifying the decision will provide the balance. Although this is the least easily defined, let alone agreed upon, concept of judging, it may be fairly assumed that these considerations are well understood and automatically applied by experienced judges.

Any attempt to quantify such judgments (to assign points for the various areas) would usually fail for two basic reasons — change in the level according to greater acceptance, and the almost infinite number of possible variants that may be chosen by the exhibitor.

Couple this with the inability of individuals to agree on such determinations and the lack of manpower to accomplish it and you have the beginning of a mammoth problem. The application of such a scale of possible points (the multiplier) may be difficult and time consuming to find and allocate, but then, one must consider the second half of the problem.

Each exhibit must then be considered on five bases, each here covered individually.

**Condition.** An obvious criterion, with finest condition, margins, color, lightness or distinctness of postmark, condition of the cover and similar considerations being worthy of highest attainment. Obvious display of items of lesser condition, particularly when better condition is known and available, should be considered as a defect in an exhibition. On rarer stamps, finest condition constitutes a distinct plus in an exhibit.

**Completion.** On an exhibit which is capable of attaining a Grand Prix in the significance determination, completion may be used in making two separate determinations. What is present in a collection will determine whether or not it is worthy of a gold medal. After that point has been reached, it may be more easily considered a matter of what is not present that permits or prevents it from reaching the highest levels. This element also bears on the condition and the rarity factors.

**Philatelic Importance and Rarity.** Although analyzed to some degree in the first analysis of philatelic significance, philatelic importance and rarity completes the triad of necessary attributes in any major philatelic exhibit. Without the rare stamps from an area, many similar collections could be created and therefore none of these can normally expect to win a top award.

On the other hand, a collection which includes the acknowledged rarities of an area may, if these are in fine condition and reasonably complete, expect to attain the highest levels allowed by its significance.

Rarity in general is based on two factors; established value caused by demand for a particular item, and difficulty in obtaining another similar item. The latter could be a relatively inexpensive stamp, but still rare. Each has its place within the definition of this criterion.

**Philatelic Knowledge and Research.** Considered by some to be a very important element of philately, this is nevertheless a difficult area to show or consider. Although important philatelically, perhaps it should remain predominantly the province of published study rather than in a show entry where it may be doomed to bog down an otherwise excellent exhibit. As a rule, though, these elements should be present in an exhibit. The manifestation of them may be to indicate rare cancellations on loose stamps and to offer brief explanations of rates and routes of covers.

Sufficient information should be given to show the exhibitor's knowledge of the area, yet not turn it into a book, illustrated by stamps and covers. Original study should be given extra attention, but the lack of such should not penalize an otherwise excellent exhibit. In some areas, great studies by past experts may have left very little new information to be found by today's collector.

In these cases, philatelic knowledge would mainly be a manifestation of the application of this past information to assemble a balanced collection. New study in such areas should, however, gain special attention from the judges due to the great difficulty of conducting such research with positive results. Felicitations of the jury are normally reserved for those exhibits that show an impressive level of original research.

**Presentation and Balance.** Normally the least important of considerations, presentation and balance reflect the personal taste of the exhibitor in choosing how and what to show. Display on colored pages, unnecessary and repetitive art work, nonuniform combination of written information and other objectionable elements which distract from the philatelic material should be avoided.

Neatness and comprehensiveness of presentation which permit a rapid assessment of what is and is not present in an exhibit are to be encouraged at the international level. Balance is a variable which the exhibitor must exercise to present the best material in the limited space available.

If a particular portion of the area chosen for the exhibit comprises material which is common or remaindered unused, but rare used, and particularly so on cover, the exhibitor may choose to omit the unused if space and other considerations dictate.

This should not affect the consideration of completion if it is obvious that the material could be obtained by the exhibitor but has been omitted to keep a higher level of significant material. Too much of a preponderance of a certain type of material in one area with a correspondingly lower amount in another might constitute a lesser balanced collection.

Although a classic approach to balance would be an equal quantity of unused, used, and covers throughout the area being shown, a slightly heavier concentration on the more difficult issues should normally result in the higher award.

This is a very subjective evaluation, highly variable with each different collectible area, and specific considerations which are valid for one are not necessarily so for another. Experience of the judges will normally reflect the success or failure of meeting this criterion.

## Objective Evaluation Of Philatelic Exhibits

Since occasion might arise for a wide difference between judges on the level that an exhibit should attain, a more objective approach may be used as a guide for further discussion. This approach, often called a "point system," may also be used to train new judges and for the information and guidance of exhibitors.

Since international judges gain their experience at lower levels and move to international status only after first being an observer, it is unlikely that any will choose to use a point system on a regular basis, and due to time considerations could not expect to be asked to do so for the entire show in any case.

Most judges are quite able to reach a swift determination of the final level that an exhibit will attain, even if working individually, and on comparison these determinations will usually differ only slightly between judges. Although given as a medal type (gold, vermeil, silver, etc.), a total number of points could just as easily be assigned, yet would mean the same thing.

As may be seen from the earlier discussion of the criteria which are used to evaluate an exhibit, each area is a subjective determination. Any attempt to reduce each area to numbers, however sophisticated, is sure to be unjust to a significant number of collecting interests in a given show.

For this reason, the point system must remain only a guide. (If this were not so, each page could be scanned by a computer and judges would become unnecessary. At the same time, stamp shows would become very boring in the precise sameness that would result from the likely end need for "uniform" display.)

To avoid the need for a two level system which would first evaluate the total philatelic significance possible and then the level the exhibit achieved within that framework, the significance element may be combined with rarity as "philatelic importance" as in Article 4, item 3 of the basic rules.

There always remains, in either case, the difference of opinion over what is significant in a particular area. In most cases, however, the final results will often be inside a one level spread, and more rarely a two level spread. Another consideration in formulating a point system to be borne in mind is that of individual preferences in the maximum number of points to be allocated to an area.

Someone who cannot afford classics and who chooses to collect more modern issues will usually call for a lower number of points possible for (monetary) rarity. The classicist will usually prefer the opposite. Another who is artistically inclined will favor presentation, and so on.

No firm allocation will please all collectors, and yet, any system adopted by the FIP is likely to cause adoption by national federations for both the authoritative nature of FIP in general as well as the need to use the same system when proceeding with an evaluation from the national to the international level.

National federations who think that their system is more appropriate may decline to change, but the few who proceed to international competition will normally not be judged by a point system in any case, unless the need to establish a basis for that collection and the decision is made to use the point system as a guide.

The following allocation of points is made available for the exhibitor as a guide to the areas of concentration of effort in developing the exhibit, to the judge who feels that his experience is not sufficient to make a proper evaluation of a philatelic exhibit, and for use in case of disputes on the level that an exhibit should attain, in the sense of guidance of the judges for further discussion.

Points allocated to the above criteria shall be awarded according to the maximum levels indicated on the following scale. The five basic criteria have been reordered here in accordance with importance, with the criterion deserving the highest number of points coming first and the remainder in decreasing order of importance.

| | | |
|---|---|---|
| 1. Philatelic Knowledge and Research | —— | 35 |
| a. Philatelic Knowledge | 25 | —— |
| b. Research | 10 | —— |
| 2. Philatelic Importance and Rarity | —— | 35 |
| a. Philatelic Importance | 15 | —— |
| b. Rarity | 20 | —— |
| 3. Condition | 15 | 15 |
| 4. Completion | 10 | 10 |
| 5. Presentation and Balance | 5 | 5 |
| | —— | —— |
| | | 100 |

The total of points obtained will indicate the medal equivalent based on the following scale:

| | |
|---|---|
| Large Gold | 95 |
| Gold | 90 |
| Vermeil | 85 |
| Silver | 80 |
| Silver-Bronze | 70 |
| Bronze | 60 |
| Certificate of Participation | less than 60 |

Application of these may be used as a guide for exhibitors, trainee judges and to help obtain a basis for resolving differences of opinion on unusual exhibits. Experience in making the subjective evaluation necessary for the proper application of these criteria is essential.

(Adopted by the Traditional Philately Commission of the FIP on May 26, 1979, at Sofia, Bulgaria, by unanimous vote.)

# Exhibitions Important To Stamp Collecting

The philatelic exhibition has become an important and interesting adjunct to the hobby of stamp collecting. It is worldwide in its impact, yet at the same time reaching down into even the smallest of clubs, where members share their interests and their philatelic treasures.

## Purpose

Essentially, a philatelic exhibition is a contest. Basically speaking, its primary purpose is to bring together in one place the best of collections, pitting them against each other.

By so doing, other collectors are given the opportunity to enjoy the results of the efforts of others, learning from them, while the owners of those adjudged winners are given tangible evidence of superiority.

The conventional exhibit, it should be noted, is not exactly designed to teach the average layman or the novice in stamp collecting. In fact, such exhibitions frequently become bewildering to them.

Recognizing this fact, more and more experienced philatelists are coming to look with favor on those efforts directed toward displays illustrating fundamentals, on a noncompetitive basis, in conjunction with regular shows.

Exhibitions are staged annually by local clubs, regional groups, national societies and even associations incorporated for the specific purpose of planning and presenting the huge international shows.

These are held in a variety of places — hotels and motels, libraries, YMCAs, clubhouses of fraternal organizations, and great exposition halls. In recent years, shopping centers have become a major locale for local shows.

## When Held

The majority of the shows are held in the spring and early fall, thus climaxing or opening the winter stamp season. It should be emphasized, however, that local shows take place whenever the committees are ready for them.

In many cases, the site for the show is the same year after year, although the changing habits of the American people are being reflected in the selection of new show locations.

## Financing Shows

Local shows, generally, do not have an admission charge, financial support for the effort coming from bourse rental. On the other hand, larger shows charge an admission fee and in some cases there are exhibit entry fees.

In many cases, exhibitions involve more than just the exhibit of postage stamps and other philatelic material. In addition to the bourse, where stamps and philatelic material are for sale by dealers, other features include lectures and slide presentations on various phases of philately, and provisions are made for meetings of societies and clubs.

Additional financing for local and federation shows is frequently secured through the sale of cacheted covers and in recent years the sale of souvenir cards, both with philatelic themes tied to the show's locale.

Many of the larger shows also will feature an auction, which frequently proves an additional drawing card for the more seasoned collectors.

## New Issues

National and regional shows are occasionally used as the locale for the release of new issues of stamps by the United States Postal Service, the United Nations Postal Administration, and foreign governments, creating a demand for first day covers.

## International Exhibitions

The show of shows, of course, is the big international exhibition. In the past, there was one international show each year, generally with Federation of International Philately (FIP) sanction, but recent years have seen two and sometimes three international exhibitions held in various parts of the world.

In the United States, the international exhibitions occur at intervals of approximately 10 years. The first INPEX show in New York City in 1912 was followed by the second INPEX in 1926; TIPEX in 1936; the Centenary Exhibition of 1947; FIPEX in 1956; SIPEX in 1966, and INTERPHIL in 1976.

## Commercial Shows

Commercial shows have played a major role in the exhibition area since the formation of the annual event sponsored by the American Stamp Dealers' Association (ASDA) which held its first show in New York City in 1949.

Although purely commercial initially, more recent shows by ASDA have incorporated competitive exhibits along with special exhibits by governments.

The role of the latter was emphasized by Herbert Rosen, New York City, with the advent of the annual INTERPEX shows in 1958 and held in the spring of each year under his sponsorship until acquisition by the ASDA in 1972.

For its part the ASDA has expanded its activities with area exhibitions, such as LISDA, sponsored by the Long Island chapter of ASDA; INPEX, sponsored by the International Northwest chapter; and ASDA International Philatelic Fairs in the Chicago, Ill., area.

## Early Exhibitions

The first stamp exhibition, as such, apparently took place in Dresden, Germany, as long ago as 1870.

The first public stamp exhibition in the United States was arranged by John Walter Scott, who succeeded in having a collection accepted for display at the Centennial in Philadelphia in 1876. In 1888, another modest exhibition was held in Boston at the convention of the American Philatelic Association.

The first organized exhibition on a comparatively ambitious scale was staged in New York City at the old Eden Musee on West 23rd Street, a popular museum where royalty and the leading figures of the world could be seen in costumed statuary.

This exhibition opened March 11, 1889, the result of efforts of a committee of members of the Brooklyn and Staten Island Philatelic Societies, joined by the National Philatelic Society.

Stamps were mounted on cards and shown in glass frames. The committee had been promised exhibits from 150 collectors, but at curtain call most of these had defaulted and only 31 exhibited. However, 272 sheets were shown, comprising a substantial number of the countries then issuing postage stamps.

John Scott came to the rescue of the troubled committee and volunteered to write a catalog — "official guide" — to the exhibits. The exhibition ran approximately three weeks.

What is believed to have been the first public exhibition of stamps by a stamp dealer on his own initiative was that of a D. Field of London, England. It was held in 1900 in the Albermarle Galleries, Albermarle Street.

Reportedly, during the approximately two weeks it was open, the exhibition was visited by many thousands of people, including a number of famous collectors from England and the continent.

# International Exhibitions

The following list includes a number of the outstanding international philatelic exhibitions held around the world during the past century. Although hardly complete, it does represent a compilation of information available from research at the American Philatelic Research Library, State College, Pa., and Linn's Philatelic Library.

1881 — First World Philatelic Exhibition, held in Vienna, Austria, Nov. 13-20. Largely national in character.

1890 — International Postage Stamp Exhibition, held in Vienna, Austria, under auspices of Austrian Philatelic Club. Marked 50th anniversary of introduction of postage stamps and 40th anniversary of first Austrian postage stamps.

1897 — London Philatelic Exhibition, held in London, England, July 22-Aug. 5.

1905 — Exhibition of British Colonial Fiscal and Telegraph stamps, held in London, England, April 7-8.

1906 — International Philatelic Exhibition, held in London, England, May 23-June 1.

1910 — International Postage Stamp Exhibition (Internationale Postwertzeichen Ausstellung), held in Berne, Switzerland, Sept. 3-12.

1911 — International Exhibition of Stamps, held in Sydney, Australia, October 1911, under auspices of the First Philatelic Congress of Australia.

1913 — International Philatelic Exhibition, held in New York City, Oct. 27 - Nov. 1, under auspices of the Association for Stamp Exhibitions, Inc.

1923 — International Postage Stamp Exhibition (Internationale Postwertzeichen Ausstellung) held in Vienna, Austria. Held at a time of great emergency following World War I.

1925 — International Postage Stamp Exhibition (Exposition Internationale de Timbres-Poste) held in Paris, France, May 2-12.

1926 — International Philatelic Exhibition (second in the United States), held in New York City, Oct. 16-23, under auspices of Association for Stamp Exhibitions, Inc.

1929 — International Philatelic Exhibition held at LeHavre, France, May 18-26, under patronage of the president of the French Republic.

1932 — International LuPosta — International Air Mail Exhibition held in the City of Danzig, July 23-31.

1933 — WIPA 1933 — Vienna International Postage Stamp Exhibition held in Vienna, Austria, in June 1933, sponsored by the Union of Austrian Philatelic Clubs.

1934 — National Stamp Exhibition held in New York City, Feb. 10-18, sponsored by the New York American, and endorsed by Association for Stamp Exhibitions, American Philatelic Society and Collectors Club of New York.

1936 — TIPEX — Third International Exhibition in the United States held in New York City, May 9-17. Sponsored by the Association for Stamp Exhibitions. Occasion for release of the TIPEX sheet.

1937 — PEXIP 1937 — International Postage Stamp Exhibition held in Paris, France, in June. Occasion for release of the special sheet of four stamps (Ceres type) on June 18.

1938 — International Philatelic Exposition held in Rio de Janeiro, Brazil, Oct. 22-30.

1940 — Stamp Centenary Exhibition held in London, England, May 6-11 under the auspices of the Royal Philatelic Society.

— International Centennial Stamp Exhibition held at the British Pavilion, World's Fair in New York City, in cooperation with the New York World's Fair Corporation and British Commission to the World's Fair.

1943 — GEPH — Exposition Philatelique Nationale held in Geneva, Switzerland, Aug. 17-26.

1947 — Centenary International Stamp Exhibition held in New York City, May 17-25, under auspices of the Association for Stamp Exhibitions, Inc. Recognized the 100th anniversary of the first U.S. postage stamps.

1948 — IMABA — International Postage Stamp Exhibition held Aug. 21-29 in Basel, Switzerland.

1949 — CITEX 1949 — Centenary International Exhibition held in June in Paris, France.

1950 — London International Stamp Exhibition held in London, England, May 6-13.

— EFIRA 1950 — Exposicion Filetelica International held Oct. 6-12 in Buenos Aires, Argentina.

— ESCE — Centenary Exhibition of the first Spanish postage stamp held in Madrid, Spain, Oct. 12-22.

1951 — Canadian International Philatelic Exhibition held in Toronto, Sept. 21-25, under auspices of Canadian Association for Philatelic Exhibitions.

1952 — REINTAX — International Philatelic Exhibition held in Monaco, April 26-May 4. FIP patronage.

— CENTILUX 1952 — International Centenary Stamp Exhibition held in Luxembourg City, Luxembourg, May 24-June 4.

—ITEP — International Centenary Stamp Exhibition held in Utrecht, The Netherlands, June 28 to July 5.

1953 — International Stamp Exhibition honoring Centenary of postage stamps in Portugal held in Lisbon, Portugal, Sept. 26-Oct. 5. Recognized by the FIP.

1954 — INDIPEX — International Stamp Exhibition observing the India postage stamp centenary held in New Delhi, India, Oct. 1-15.

1955 — NORWEX — International Stamp Exhibition honoring Centenary of Norwegian postage stamps held in Oslo, Norway, June 4-12. Recognized by FIP.

— STOCKHOLMIA '55 — International Stamp Exhibition held in Stockholm, Sweden, July 1-10, observing Centenary of Swedish postage stamps.

— International Postage Stamp Exhibition held in Prague, Czechoslovakia, Sept. 10-25. FIP patronage.

— International Philatelic Exposition held in Havana, Cuba, Nov. 12-19.

1956 — PHICIPEX — Philippine Centenary International Philatelic Exhibition in Manila, Philippines, April 25-May 9.

1956 — JUFIZ — Jugoslavia International Philatelic Exhibition held in Zagreb, Jugoslavia, May 20-27.

1956 — FIPEX — Fifth International Philatelic Exhibition in the United States held in New York City, April 28-May 6, under auspices of the Association of Stamp Exhibitions, Inc.

— FINLANDIA 1956 — International Stamp Exhibition held in Helsinki, Finland, July 8-16, honoring the Centenary of Finnish postage stamps.

— EXMEX 1956 — International Philatelic Exhibition held in Mexico City, Mexico, Aug. 1-15.

1957 — TABIL — International Postage Stamp Exhibition held in Tel Aviv, Israel, Sept. 17-23. FIP patronage.

1958 — EFICON — Exposicion Filatelica InterAmericana Confederacion held in Parana, Argentina, April 19-27.

— TEMATICA 1958 — International Postage Stamp Exhibition in Buenos Aires, Argentina, Aug. 16-23.

— International Aero Philatelist Exhibition held in Philadelphia, Pa., Oct. 10-12 in connection with the Aero Philatelists convention.

1959 — INTERPOSTA 1959 — International Postage Stamp exhibition held in Hamburg, Germany, May 22-31, recognizing the centenary of the stamps of Hamburg and Lubeck. FIP sanctioned.

— SICILIA 1959 — International Philatelic Exhibition held in Palermo, Sicily, Oct. 10-26, celebrating the centenary of the stamps of Sicily. FIP sanctioned.

1960 — First International Philatelic Congress in Spain, held in Barcelona, March 26-April 5.

— UNIPEX 1960 — International Philatelic Exhibition held in Johannesburg, South Africa, May 30-June 4, observing Golden Jubilee of Union of South Africa.

— London International Stamp Exhibition, held in London England, July 9-16. Sponsored by Royal Philatelic Society and British Philatelic Association.

— POLSKA '60 — International Philatelic Exhibition held in Warsaw, Poland, Aug. 27-Sept. 9, honoring the 100th anniversary of first Polish postage stamp. FIP patronage.

— International Exhibition of Postage Stamps held in Bratislava, Czechoslovakia, Sept. 24-Oct. 9. Sponsored by Federation of Czechoslovak Philatelists.

1961 — BUDAPEST 1961 — International Postage Stamp Exhibition held in Budapest, Hungary, Sept. 23-Oct. 3.

— TEMEX '61 — Exposicion Internationale de Filatelia Tematica held in Buenos Aires, Argentina, Oct. 14-24.

1962 — Canadian National Philatelic Exhibition held in Windsor, Ont., Canada, May 3-5, sponsored by the Royal Philatelic Society of Canada.

— PRAGA 1962 — World exhibition held in Prague, Czechoslovakia, Aug. 18-Sept. 2. Sponsored by Federation of Czechoslovak Philatelists and the Ministry of Transport and Communications. FIP recognized.

— LUPOSTA 1962. International Air Post Exhibition held in Berlin, Germany, Sept. 12-16.

1963 — MELUSINA '63 — International Exhibition in Luxembourg, organized by the Federation of Philatelic Societies of Luxembourg. Held April 13-21. FIP sponsored.

— AEROPHILA '63 — International Airmail Exhibition held in Brussels, Belgium, Sept. 1-8. Third congress of the FISA.

— ISTANBUL '63 — International Stamp Exhibition held in Istanbul, Turkey, Sept. 7-15, sponsored by the Federation of Philatelic Clubs of Turkey, honoring the first Turkish stamps. FIP patronage.

1964 — PHILATEC 1964 — International Philatelic and Postal Techniques Exhibition held in Paris, France, June 5-12.

1965 — WIPA 1965 — The Vienna International Postage Stamp Exhibition held in Vienna, Austria, June 4-13. FIP patronage.

— NABRA '65 — International Postage Stamp Exhibition held in Berne, Switzerland, Aug. 27-Sept. 5.

1966 — SIPEX — Sixth International Philatelic Exhibition in the United States, held in Washington, D.C., May 21-30. FIP patronage.

— AEROPEX — International Airmail and Aerospace Exhibition held in New York City, June 10-12. Sixth FISA congress.

1967 — AMPHILEX '67 — International Philatelic Exhibition held in Amsterdam, The Netherlands, May 11-21, sponsored by The Netherlands Federation of Philatelic Societies.

— FILEX '67 — International Exhibition held in Reykjavik, Iceland, Sept. 2-10.

— International Aerophilatelic Exhibition held in Budapest, Hungary, Sept. 7-8. National Association of Hungarian Philatelists in association with FISA.

1968 — EUROPA '68 — International Philatelic Show held in Naples, Italy, April 26-May 5.

— Red Crescent Thematic Exhibition held in Istanbul, Turkey, June 11-30.

— IFA WIEN 1968 — International Airmail Exhibition held in Vienna, Austria, May 30-June 4. Held under FISA sponsorship and marked by the Eighth FISA congress.

— PRAGA 1968 — World Stamp Exhibition held in Prague, Czechoslovakia, June 22-July 7. Marked by the 37th congress of the FIP.

— TEMATICA-POZNAN '68 — International Philatelic Exhibition held in Poznan, Poland, July 28-Aug. 11. Organized by the Polish Philatelic Federation. FIP patronage.

— EFIMEX '68 — Exposicion Filatelica International held in Mexico City, Mexico, Nov. 1-9. Under FIP patronage.

1969 — Centenary Exhibition, Royal Philatelic Society, London, England, held April 11-20.

— JUVENTUS 1969 — First International Philatelic Exhibition for FIP juniors, held in Luxembourg City, April 3-8. FIP patronage.

— SOFIA '69 — World Philatelic Exhibition held in Sofia, Bulgaria, May 31-June 8.

— LUPO '69 — First Airmail Exhibition in Switzerland, held in Lucerne, Switzerland, April 26-28, sponsored by the International Federation of Aerophilatelic Societies.

— TORINO '69 — International Postage Stamp Exhibition held in Turin, Italy, June 26-29.

— JOEPEX '69 — International Stamp Exhibition held in Colombo, Ceylon, July 3-6.

— EXFILBO '69 — International Postage Stamp Exhibition held in Bogota, Colombia, Nov. 28-Dec. 7. First exposition of Filatelica InterAmericana.

1970 — ANPEX 1970 — Australian National Philatelic Exhibition held in Sydney, New South Wales, April 27-May 1.

— PHILYMPIA — London International Stamp Exhibition held in London, Sept. 18-26. Sponsored by Royal Philatelic Society, British Philatelic Association, and Philatelic Traders' Society.

— XII Philatelic Exhibition held in Barcelona, Spain, Oct. 25-31.

— EXFILCA '70 — Second Exposicion Filatelica InterAmericana held in Caracas, Venezuela, Nov. 27 to Dec. 6. Under FIAF sponsorship.

— Malta Philatelic Exhibition, organized by the General Post Office of Malta, held Dec. 28 to Jan. 9, 1971.

1971 — PHILATOKYO '71 — International Philatelic Exhibition held in Tokyo, Japan, April 20-30, commemorating a century of Japanese Posts. Under FIP patronage.

— International Stamp Exhibition held in Capetown, South Africa, May 22-31, under auspices of the Philatelic Federation of South Africa.

— International Luposta — International Airmail Exhibition held in West Berlin, Germany, June 10-13. 11th FISA congress.

— BUDAPEST '71 — International Philatelic Exhibition held in Budapest, Hungary, Sept. 4-12.

— EXFILIMA '71. International Philatelic Show held in Lima, Peru, Nov. 6-14. Held under FIAF patronage.

— ANPHILEX — Commemorating the 75th year of the Collectors Club of New York City. Held Nov. 26-Dec. 1 at the Waldorf-Astoria Hotel in New York City.

1972 — COPEX '72 — International Philatelic Exhibition held in Kerala, India, Feb. 24-27.

— EFIME '72 — International Philatelic Exhibition held in Medellin, Colombia, April 20-27.

— BELGICA '72 — International Philatelic Exhibition held in Brussels, Belgium, June 24-July 9, sponsored by the Royal Federation of Belgian Philatelic Societies. FIP patronage.

— LIBA — International Show held in Vaduz, Liechtenstein, Aug. 18-27.

— INTERJUNEX 1972 — Second international philatelic exhibition for juniors. FIP sponsorship. Held in Kristiansand, Norway, Aug. 25-Sept. 3.

— EXFILBRA '72 — Fourth Exhibition under FIAF sponsorship, held in Rio de Janeiro, Brazil, Aug. 26-Sept. 2.

— ROCPEX '72 — Republic of China Philatelic Exhibition, held in Taipei, Oct. 24-Nov. 2. Organized by the Directorate General of Posts.

1973 — IBRA-MUNCHEN '73 — International Postage Stamp Exhibition held in Munich, West Germany, May 11-20, under sponsorship of the FIP with the Federation of German Philatelists.

— POLSKA '73 — World Postage Stamp Exhibition held in Poznan, Poland, Aug. 19-Sept. 3, marking the 500th anniversary of the birth of Nicolaus Copernicus. Held with FIP patronage.

— INDIPEX '73 — India International Philatelic Exhibition held in New Delhi, India, Nov. 11-14.

— JERUSALEM '73 — International Stamp Exhibition, originally scheduled for the December holiday season in Jerusalem, postponed to March 25-April 2, 1974. Under FIP patronage, celebrating the 25th anniversary of Israel stamps.

1974 — INTERNABA 1974 — International Postage Stamp Exhibition held in Basel, Switzerland, June 6-17. Under FIP patronage. Marked the centenary of the Universal Postal Union.

— INJUNPEX '74 — First International All-Junior Stamp and Literature Exhibition, July 5-7. Held in New York City.

— STOCKHOLMIA '74 — International Postage Stamp Exhibition held in Stockholm, Sweden, Sept. 21-29. Sponsored by the Philatelic Society of Sweden and the Royal Swedish Post, with FIP patronage.

— EXFILMEX '74-UPU — Fifth Exposicion Filatelica InterAmericana held in Mexico City, Mexico, Oct. 26-Nov. 3. FIAF sponsorship.

— LUBRAPEX '74 — Fifth Lubrapex Exposicion Filatelica Luso Brazileira held in Sao Paulo, Brazil, Nov. 26-Dec. 4.

1975 — ESPANA '75 — International Philatelic Exhibition held in Madrid, Spain, April 4-13, in cooperation with Spanish Philatelic Societies. FIP sponsorship. Forty-fourth congress of FIP.

— NORDIA '75 — Nordic Stamp Exhibition held in Helsinki, Finland, April 26-May 1. Held with cooperation of the Philatelic Society of Finland and Administration of Posts and Telegraph.

— ARPHILA '75 — International Philatelic Exhibition held in Paris, France, June 6-16. Sponsored by Federation of French Philatelic Societies, marking the 50th anniversary of the first stamp exhibition in Paris in 1925.

— INJUNPEX '75 — Second International All-Junior Stamp and Literature Exhibition, July 6-12. Held in Guadalajara, Mexico.

— EXFILMO '75 — Inter American Philatelic Exhibition held in Montevideo, Uruguay, Oct. 10-19. Organized by Club Filatelico del Uruguay and Circulo Filatelico de Montevideo.

— EXFIVIA '75 — First Exhibition of Filatelica Boliviana held in La Paz, Bolivia, Nov. 15-22.

— THEMABELGA — World Exhibition of Thematic Philately held in Brussels, Belgium, Dec. 13-21. First world exhibition of thematic philately held under FIP patronage.

1976 — INTERPHIL '76 — International Philatelic Exhibition held in Philadelphia, Pa., May 29-June 6. Forty-fifth congress of the FIP.

— HAFNIA '76 — First International Postage Stamp Show in Denmark. Held in Copenhagen, Aug. 20-29, marking 125th anniversary of first Danish stamp. FIP patronage.

— ITALIA '76 — World Stamp Exhibition held in Milan, Italy, Oct. 14-24. Organized by the Federation of Italian Philatelic Societies and held as part of the Milan Fair, FIP patronage.

1977 — JUPHILEX '77 — International Exhibition for Juniors held in Bern, Switzerland, April 7-11.

— International Philatelic Youth Exhibition held in Antwerp, Belgium, Aug. 6-16. Sponsored by the Royal Federation of Belgium Philatelic Societies and Pro-Post, under the auspices of the FIP Youth Commission.

— LUPOSTA '77 — International Air Post Exhibition held in West Berlin, West Germany, Aug. 19-21.

— SAN MARINO — International Philatelic Exhibition held Aug. 28-Sept. 4 in honor of the centenary of the first San Marinese stamps.

— PORTUCALE '77 — Second International Thematic Stamp Exhibition held Nov. 19-28 in Portugal. FIP patronage.

1978 — CAPEX '78 — International Philatelic Exhibition held June 9-18 in Toronto, Ont., Canada. FIP patronage.

— PRAGA 1978 — World Postage Stamp Exhibition held Sept. 8-17 in Prague, Czechoslovakia. FIP patronage.

1979 — PHILASERDICA '79 — International Philatelic Exhibition held in Sofia, Bulgaria, May 8-27, noting the 100th anniversary of the first Bulgarian postage stamps. FIP patronage.

— BRASILIANA '79 — First Inter-American Exhibition of Classic Philately and Third World Exhibition of Thematic Philately, held Sept. 15-23 in Rio de Janeiro, Brazil. FIP patronage.

1980 — INDIA '80 — International Philatelic Exhibition held in New Delhi, India, Jan. 25-Feb. 3. FIP patronage.

— LONDON 1980 — International Philatelic Exhibition held in London, England, May 6-14. FIP patronage.

— NORWEX '80 — International Philatelic Exhibition held June 13-22 in Oslo, Norway. FIP patronage.

— JUPOSTEX — Youth Exhibition held in Eindhoven, The Netherlands, May 23-27. Sponsored by Netherlands Federation of Philatelic Societies and Foundation of Philatelic Youth-work, FIP patronage.

— BUENOS AIRES '80 — International Philatelic Exhibition held Oct. 24-Nov. 2 in Buenos Aires, Argentina, under FIP patronage in conjunction with annual meeting of Inter-American Philatelic Federation.

1981 — LURABA 1981 — Organized by Managing Board of Federation of Swiss Philatelic Societies. Held March 20-29 in Lucerne, Switzerland. Sponsored by Foundation Pro Aero and the Funds for Promotion of Philately. FIP patronage.

— WIPA '81 — International Philatelic Exhibition held in Vienna, Austria, May 22-31. FIP patronage.

— PHILATOKYO '81 — First International Stamp Exhibition, held Oct. 9-18 in Tokyo, Japan. FIP patronage.

1982 — CANADA 82 — International Philatelic Youth Exhibition held May 20-24 in Toronto, Canada. Sponsored by Royal Philatelic Society of Canada and Canada Post. FIP patronage.

— PHILEXFRANCE '82 — held June 11-21 in Paris, France.

## FIP International Exhibitions (Patronage By FIP Confirmed)

### 1982

MILANO 82 (Literature), Milan, Italy, Oct. 22-25

BELGICA '82 (Postal history, postal stationery, aerophilately), Brussels, Belgium, Dec. 11-19

### 1983

TEMBAL (Thematic), Basel, Switzerland, May 21-29

BRASILIANA 83, Rio de Janeiro, Brazil, July 29-Aug. 7

BANGKOK 1983 (under auspices), Bangkok, Thailand, Aug. 4-13

FIP International Exhibitions (patronage by FIP requested)

1984 — ATHINA 1984, Athens, Greece, May 20-30
 — AUSIPEX 84, Melbourne, Australia, Sept. 21-30
 — (Youth) Sofia, Bulgaria, unknown
1985 — Argentina, unknown
 — BUDAPEST 85, Budapest, Hungary, September
 — (Youth) Portugal, unknown
1986 — AMERIPEX, Chicago, Ill., May 22-June 1
 — STOCKHOLMIA, Stockholm, fall
 — Israel, unknown
1987 — Toronto, May or June
 — Copenhagen, fall
1988 — Portugal, unknown
 — Prague, Czechoslovakia, unknown
1989 — Sofia, Bulgaria, unknown
1990 — London, May
1992 — Uruguay, unknown
1996 — New York, unknown
2000 — London, May
 — WIPA 2000, Vienna, Austria, June

# First Days

# 16

## United States Stamps
## Day by Day

With the launching of a new regular postage series late in 1922 the United States Post Office Department established a policy of issuing new stamps on specific dates and at places appropriate to their subjects. This policy, which has been continued by the U.S. Postal Service, brought the first day cover into the philatelic picture, adding a new facet to the avocation of stamp collecting.

Since this policy was implemented Oct. 4, 1922 with an 11¢ stamp (Scott 563) featuring the portrait of Rutherford B. Hayes, released at Fremont, Ohio, to mark the birth centenary of this former president, more than 1,000 varieties of U.S. postal adhesives have made their debut on 326 different days of the year. The only dates since late 1922 when one or more varieties of U.S. stamps haven't had first days are:

January 7, 21, 22, 28, 31

February 4, 6, 9, 17, 19, 21, 29

March 9, 17, 27

April 15, 21

May 12

July 6, 8

August 8

September 13

October 3, 25

November 8, 27, 28

December 4, 13, 14, 16, 18, 19, 22, 23, 24, 25, 26

Because holiday mailings tax the facilities of the postal service during December, it avoids release of new stamps in that month as far as possible. Consequently, December has more "stampless" days than any of the other months of the year.

The following "day-by-day" listing of first days covers only adhesive postage stamps issued since Oct. 4, 1922. While a good many earlier U.S. stamps are known to have made their first appearances on specific dates (a fact usually established by postmarks) it seems discreet to limit this listing to those adhesives for which an "official" date of issue exists as a result of a postal service policy.

The listing, by months and Scott catalog numbers, through 1981, follows:

### January

1. Washington Bicentennial series (704-15) 1932
   13¢ (three) Spirit of 1776 (1629-31) 1976

2. 3¢ Betsy Ross (1004) 1952
   26¢ Mount Rushmore airpost (C88) 1974
   25¢, 31¢ International airpost (C89-C90) 1976

3. 3¢ American Banker's Association (987) 1950
   7¢ Alaska Statehood (C53) 1959
   13¢ Washington at Princeton (1704) 1977

4. 3¢ Columbia University (1029) 1954
   10¢ ZIP Code (1511) 1974
   15¢ Everett M. Dirksen (1874) 1981

5. 3¢ George Washington Carver (953) 1948
   10¢ Star Runway airpost, sheet and coil (C72-C73) 1968

6. 4¢ New Mexico Statehood (1191) 1962
   13¢ Carl Sandburg (1731) 1978

7. Not a first day to date

8. 5¢ Battle of New Orleans (1261) 1965

9. 5¢ American Flag (1208) 1963

10. 7¢ Woodrow Wilson (1040) 1956
    5¢ Sam Houston (1242) 1964

11. 13¢ Benjamin Harrison (622) 1926
    4¢ Patrick Henry Credo (1144) 1961
    3¢ Alexander Hamilton (1086) 1967
    18¢ Statue of Liberty airpost (C87) 1974
    13¢ Indian Head Cent (1734) 1978

12. 1¢ Thomas Jefferson (1278) 1968
    15¢ Robert F. Kennedy (1770) 1979

13. 15¢ Statue of Liberty airpost (C63) 1961
    15¢ Martin Luther King Jr. (1771) 1979

14. 2¢ Allied Nations (907) 1943

15. 2¢ George Washington (554) 1923
    4¢ Martha Washington (556) 1923
    9¢ Thomas Jefferson (561) 1923
    10¢ James Monroe (562) 1923
    2¢ Army (786), 2¢ Navy (791) 1937
    5¢ DC-4 Skymaster airpost (C37) 1948
    3¢ 4-H Clubs (1005) 1952
    3¢ Pennsylvania Academy (1064) 1955
    3¢ Polio (1087) 1957

16. 1¢ Benjamin Franklin (552) 1923
    2¢ General Pulaski (690) 1931
    6¢ Beautification (1365-68) 1969

17. 2¢ Washington coil, sidewise (599) 1923
    3¢ Benjamin Franklin (1073) 1956
    13¢ INTERPHIL '76 (1632) 1976

18. 6¢ DC-4 Skymaster airpost (C39) 1949

19. 6¢ America's Wool (1423) 1971

20. Presidential coils, sidewise (839-47) 1939
    4¢ George Washington Credo (1139) 1960
    13¢ (two) Capt. Cook (1732, 1732a, 1733)
    1978

21. Not a first day to date

22. Not a first day to date

23. 18¢ Dr. Elizabeth Blackwell (1399) 1974

24. 3¢ California Gold Discovery (954) 1948

25. 20¢ Map and Planes airpost (C9) 1927
    2¢ Lake Placid Olympics (716) 1932

26. 4¢, 8¢ Mahatma Gandhi, Champion of
    Liberty (1174-75) 1961
    6¢ Douglas MacArthur (1424) 1971
    8¢ Love (1475) 1973

27. Presidential coils, endwise (848-51) 1939
    3¢ Samuel Gompers (988) 1950

28. Not a first day to date

29. 1¢ Washington Irving (859) 1940
    2¢ James Fenimore Cooper (860) 1940
    6¢ Franklin D. Roosevelt (1284) 1966
    40¢ General George Marshall (1292) 1968
    15¢ W. C. Fields (1803) 1980

30. 5¢ Franklin D. Roosevelt (933) 1946
    1¼¢ Albert Gallatin (1279) 1967
    15¢ Whitney Moore Young (1875) 1981

31. Not a first day to date

## February

1. 13¢ Harriet Tubman (1744) 1978
   15¢ (four) Winter Olympics (1795-98) 1980

2. 4¢ Range Conservation (1176) 1961

3. 3¢ Lincoln, rotary (635) 1927
   10¢ James Monroe, rotary (642) 1927
   4¢ Horace Greeley (1177) 1961
   8¢ Sidney Lanier (1446) 1972

4. Not a first day to date

5. 3¢ Ralph Waldo Emerson (861) 1940
   5¢ Louisa M. Alcott (862) 1940

6. Not a first day to date

7. 15¢ (five) Windmills (1738-42) 1980

8. 4¢ Boy Scout Jubilee (1145) 1960

9. Not a first day to date

10. 5¢ Winged Globe airpost (C12) 1930
    National Stamp Exhibition souvenir
    sheet of six 3¢ Byrd (735) 1934
    16¢ Airmail Special Delivery bicolor (CE2)
    1936
    8¢ Pamphleteer (1476) 1973
    10¢ Benjamin West (1553) 1975

11. 3¢ Thomas Edison (945) 1947
    3¢ Coast & Geodetic Survey (1088) 1957
    8¢ Peace Corps (1447) 1972

12. 3¢ Abraham Lincoln (555) 1923
    $1 Lincoln Memorial (571) 1923
    3¢ Gen. Oglethorpe (726) 1933
    1¢ Four Freedoms (908) 1943
    3¢ Land Grant Colleges (1065) 1955
    1¢ Lincoln Centennial (1113) 1959
    6¢ Illinois Statehood (1339) 1968

13. 10¢ Map and Planes airpost (C7) 1926
    10¢ Samuel Clemens (863) 1940

14. 4¢ Oregon Statehood Centennial (1124) 1959
    4¢ Arizona Statehood (1192) 1962
    25¢ Frederick Douglass (1290) 1967

15. 20¢, 50¢ China Clipper airpost (C21-C22) 1937
    5¢ Physical Fitness (1262) 1965
    15¢ International Year of the Child (1772)
    1979
    15¢ Benjamin Banneker (1804) 1980

16. 1¢ James Wadsworth Longfellow (864) 1940
    2¢ John Greenleaf Whittier (865) 1940

17. Not a first day to date

18. 3¢ Army (787), 3¢ Navy (792) 1937
    3¢ San Francisco Exposition (852) 1939
    4¢ Winter Olympics (1146) 1960

19. Not a first day to date

20. 3¢ James Russell Lowell (866) 1940
    5¢ Walt Whitman (867) 1940
    4¢ Project Mercury (1193) 1962

21. Not a first day to date

22. 1½¢ Mount Vernon (1032) 1956
    5¢ George Washington (1283) 1966

23. 3¢ National Guard (1017) 1953
    8¢ Rotary International (1066) 1955
    3¢ Architects (1089) 1957
    13¢ (50) State Flags (1633-82) 1976

24. 10¢ James Whitcomb Riley (868) 1940

25. 2¢ George Rogers Clark (651) 1929
    4¢, 8¢ San Martin Champion of Liberty
    (1125-26) 1959
    15¢ (six) National Letter Writing (1805-10)
    1980

26. 3¢ Merchant Marine (939) 1946

27. 3¢ Lincoln Sesquicentennial (1114) 1959
    15¢ John Steinbeck (1773) 1979

28. 3¢ B.&O. Railroad (1006) 1952

8¢ George Gershwin (1484) 1973
10¢ Pioneer Jupiter (1556) 1975

29. Not a first day to date

## March

1. 8¢ Yellowstone Park Centenary (1453) 1972
2. 3¢ Texas Centennial (776) 1936
   3¢ Ohio Sesquicentennial (1018) 1953
   3¢ Washington Territory (1019) 1953
3. 3¢ Florida Statehood (927) 1945
   3¢ Minnesota Territory (981) 1949
4. 5¢ Roosevelt coil, sidewise (602) 1924
   3¢ Vermont Sesquicentennial (903) 1941
   3¢ American Automobile Association (1007) 1952
   15¢ Albert Einstein (1774) 1979
5. 5¢ Theodore Roosevelt (602) 1924
   9¢ Americana coil (1616) 1976
6. 1¢ Americana coil (1811) 1980
7. 4¢, 8¢ Masaryk Champion of Liberty (1147-48) 1960
8. 15¢ Justice Oliver Wendell Holmes (1288) 1968
   13¢ (four) American Quilts (1745-48) 1978
9. Not a first day to date
10. 13¢ Telephone Centenary (1683) 1976
11. 10¢ Veterans of Foreign Wars (1525) 1974
    13¢ (seven), 9¢ (one) booklet pane (1590(9¢), 1623, 1623a) 1977
12. 6¢ Blood Donors (1425) 1971
13. 10¢ Collective Bargaining (1558) 1975
14. 1¢ Horace Mann, 2¢ Mark Hopkins (869-70) 1940
    8¢ Albert Einstein (1285) 1966
15. Farley Special Printings (752-71) 1935
    3¢ Gardening/Horticulture (1100) 1958
    10¢ Andrew Jackson (1286) 1967
    6¢ American Legion (1369) 1969
    "B" (18¢) sheet, coil, booklet (1818-20) 1981
16. 4½¢ The Hermitage (1037) 1959
    5¢ Migratory Bird Treaty (1306) 1966
17. Not a first day to date
18. 8¢ Family Planning (1455) 1972
19. 1½¢ Harding, profile (553) 1925
    1½¢ Harding, perf 10 rotary (582) 1925
    1½¢ Harding coil, sidewise (598) 1925
    5¢ Charles M. Russell (1243) 1964
    13¢ Commercial Aviation (1684) 1976
20. 12¢ Grover Cleveland (564) 1923
    30¢ Buffalo (569) 1923
    $2 U.S. Capitol (572) 1923
    $5 Head of Freedom Statue (573) 1923
    1¢ Franklin, imperf (575) 1923
21. 8¢ Tri-motored Plane airpost (C26) 1944
22. 8¢ Statue of Liberty (1042) 1958
    1¢ Andrew Jackson (1209) 1963
23. 3¢ Maryland Tercentenary (736) 1934
    4¢ Army (788), 4¢ Navy (793) 1937
    13¢ Sound Recording (1705) 1977
24. 5¢ Roosevelt, perf 11 by 10½ (637) 1927
    7¢ McKinley, perf 11 by 10½ (639) 1927

25. 8¢, 10¢, 10¢, 18¢ Contributors to the Cause series (1559-62) 1975
26. 5¢ DC-4 Skymaster airpost (C33) 1947
    80¢ Diamond Head airpost (C46) 1952
    10¢ Robert Frost (1526) 1974
27. Not a first day to date
28. 3¢ Charles Eliot (871) 1940
    5¢ Frances E. Willard (872) 1940
29. 25¢ (two) Octave Chanute (C93-C94) 1979
30. 4¢ Malaria Eradication (1194) 1962
    8¢ Alaska Statehood (C70) 1967
    6¢ Hemisfair (1340) 1968
31. 4¢ Benjamin Franklin Credo (1140) 1960
    16¢ Americana (Liberty) regular and coil (1599, 1619) 1978

## April

1. 3¢ New York World's Fair (853) 1939
   4¢ North Atlantic Treaty (1127) 1959
   5¢ Crusade Against Cancer (1263) 1965
2. 13¢ booklet pane, "Stamp Collecting" label (1595d) 1976
3. 3¢ Pony Express (894) 1940
4. ½¢ Nathan Hale, flat plate (551) 1925
   1½¢ Harding, imperf (576) 1925
   4¢ Martha Washington, perf 10 rotary (585) 1925
   5¢ Roosevelt, perf 10 rotary (586) 1925
   6¢ Garfield, perf 10 rotary (587) 1925
   1¢, 2¢, 5¢ Lexington-Concord series (617-19) (1925)
   3¢ North Atlantic Treaty Organization (1008) 1952
   $1 Airlift (1341) 1968
   10¢ Mariner 10 (1557) 1975
5. 3¢ Booker T. Washington (1074) 1956
   2¢ Cape Hatteras block (1448-51) 1972
6. 4¢ Arctic Exploration (1128) 1959
   5¢ Carolina Charter (1230) 1963
   13¢ Chemistry (1685) 1976
7. 10¢ Booker T. Washington (873) 1940
   3¢ Mississippi Territory (955) 1948
   4¢ World Refugee Year (1149) 1960
   4¢ Shiloh (1179) 1962
8. 2¢ Massachusetts Bay Colony (682) 1930
   1¢ John James Audubon (874) 1940
   2¢ Dr. Crawford W. Long (875) 1940
   12¢ Americana sheet (1594), coil (1816) 1981
9. 8¢ Statue of Liberty, flat plate (1041) 1954
   5¢ Appomattox (1182) 1965
   5¢ Humane Treatment of Animals (1307) 1966
10. 2¢ Carolina-Charleston (683) 1930
    3¢ Joseph Pulitzer (946) 1947
    15¢ Frances Perkins (1821) 1980
11. 15¢ Special Delivery (E13) 1925
    4¢ Charles Evans Hughes (1195) 1962
12. 3¢ Washington & Lee University (982) 1949
    4¢ Fort Sumter (1178) 1961
13. 20¢ Monticello (1047) 1956
    8¢ Posting a Broadside (1477) 1973

13¢ (four) Pueblo Indian Pottery (1706-09) 1977

14. 3¢ Pan American Union (895) 1940
     29¢ Americana (Lighthouse) (1605) 1978

15. Not a first day to date

16. 5¢ Indiana Statehood (1308) 1966

17. 3¢ Luther Burbank (876) 1940
     5¢ Dr. Walter Reed (877) 1940
     3¢ Brussels Fair (1104) 1958
     5¢ National Grange (1323) 1967

18. 25¢ Paul Revere (1048) 1958
     4¢ Water Conservation (1150) 1960
     10¢ EXPO '74 (1527) 1974

19. 65¢, $1.30, $2.60 Graf Zeppelin airpost (C13-C15) 1930
     3¢ Newburgh Peace (727) 1933
     10¢ Lexington-Concord (1563) 1975
     15¢ (four) Pennsylvania Toleware (1775-78) 1979

20. 3¢ Statue of Freedom (989) 1950
     8¢ World Trade (1129) 1959

21. Not a first day to date

22. 2¢ Arbor Day (717) 1932
     25¢ Abraham Lincoln airpost (C59) 1960
     5¢ New York World's Fair (1244) 1964

23. 8¢ Copernicus (1488) 1973
     7.9¢ bulk rate coil (1615) 1976
     18¢ (four) Flowers (1876-79) 1981

24. 14¢ Fiorello LaGuardia (1397) 1972
     18¢ Flag sheet, coil booklet (1890-93) 1981

25. 1¢ Presidential (Washington) (804) 1938
     5¢ United Nations Conference (928) 1945
     4¢ Seattle World's Fair (1196) 1962

26. 3¢ Charter Oak (772) 1935
     10¢ Jane Addams (878) 1940
     20¢ Columbia Jays airpost (C71) 1967
     13¢ (four) American Dance (1749-52) 1978

27. 3¢ Puerto Rico Election (983) 1949

28. FIPEX souvenir sheet (1075) 1956
     3¢ James Monroe (1105) 1958

29. 3¢ Railroad Engineers (993) 1950
     5¢ John Muir (1245) 1964

30. 3¢ Washington Inauguration (854) 1939
     3¢ Louisiana Purchase (1020) 1953
     3¢ FIPEX commemorative (1076) 1956
     4¢ Louisiana Statehood (1197) 1962
     8¢ Postal People (1489-98) 1973

## May

1. 7¢ William McKinley (559) 1923
     8¢ Ulysses S. Grant (560) 1923
     14¢ American Indian (565) 1923
     20¢ Golden Gate (567) 1923
     1¢, 2¢, 5¢ Huguenot-Walloon series (614-16) 1924
     State overprints (658-79) 1929
     6¢ Support Our Youth (1342) 1968
     6¢ Grandma Moses (1370) 1969
     10¢ Paul Laurence Dunbar (1554) 1975
     18¢ Red Cross (1910) 1981

2. 3¢ Mother's Day (737-38) 1934
     5¢ American Circus (1309) 1966

3. 1¢ Stephen Foster (879) 1940
     2¢ John Philip Sousa (880) 1940
     15¢ Montgomery Blair (C66) 1963
     11¢ City of Refuge (C84) 1972

4. 3¢ Rhode Island Tercentenary (777) 1936
     10¢ Horse Racing (1528) 1974
     13¢ French Alliance (1753) 1978

5. 1½¢ Martha Washington (805) 1938
     3¢ Wild Turkey (1077) 1956
     5¢ Battle of the Wilderness (1181) 1964
     6¢ Apollo 8 (1371) 1969

6. 6¢ (four) Natural History (1387-90) 1970

7. 3¢ Nebraska Territory (1060) 1954
     16¢ Ernie Pyle (1398) 1971
     11¢ Jetliner sheet and coil (C78, C82) 1971
     18¢ George Mason (1850) 1981

8. 8¢ Missouri Statehood (1426) 1971
     8¢ Harry Truman Memorial (1499) 1973
     18¢ Savings and Loans (1911) 1981

9. 1½¢ Harding coil, endwise (605) 1925
     3¢ (four) TIPEX souvenir sheet (778) 1936
     3¢ Honorable Discharge Emblem (940) 1946

10. 3¢ Lincoln coil, sidewise (600) 1924
     2¢ Sesquicentennial Exposition (627) 1926
     3¢ Transcontinental Railroad (922) 1944
     4¢ Kansas Statehood (1183) 1961
     60¢ Special Delivery (E23) 1971

11. 6¢ Alexandria Bicentennial (C40) 1949
     3¢ Minnesota Statehood (1106) 1958

12. Not a first day to date

13. 3¢ Victor Herbert (881) 1940
     5¢ Edward McDowell (882) 1940
     5¢ Winston Churchill (1264) 1965
     13¢ Dr. Papanicolau (1754) 1978

14. 6¢ Eagle airpost (C23) 1938
     10¢ Skylab (1529) 1974
     18¢ (ten) Wildlife booklet (1880-89) 1981

15. 3¢ Grand Coulee Dam (1009) 1952
     10¢ Airmail 50th Anniversary (C74) 1968
     9¢ Delta Wing Plane airpost (C77) 1971

16. 30¢ Transatlantic airpost (C24) 1939

17. 1½¢ Harding, rotary (633) 1927
     4¢ Martha Washington (636) 1927
     9¢ Thomas Jefferson (641) 1927
     3¢ Stamp Centenary (947) 1947
     6¢ Law and Order (1343) 1968
     6¢ W.C. Handy (1372) 1969

18. 2¢, 5¢, Norse-American series (620-21) 1925
     4¢ Thomas Jefferson Credo (1141) 1960
     18¢ Surrey coil (1906) 1981

19. ½¢ Presidential (Franklin) (803) 1938
     5¢, 10¢ CIPEX souvenir sheet (948) 1947

20. 4¢ Homestead Act Centennial (1198) 1962
     13¢ Solo Transatlantic Flight (1710) 1977
     15¢ Dolley Madison (1822) 1980

21. 2¢ Red Cross (702) 1931
     3¢ Air Force Reserve (1067) 1955
     5¢ SIPEX (1310) 1966
     21¢ Airpost (C81) 1971
     13¢ Colorado Statehood (1711) 1977
     18¢ (eight) Space Achievements (1912-19) 1981

22. 3¢ Steamship (923) 1944
    3¢ Steel Industry (1090) 1957
    "A" (15¢) regular and coil (1735-42) 1978
23. 3¢ Annapolis Tercentenary (984) 1949
    5¢ SIPEX souvenir sheet (1311) 1966
24. 3¢ Telegraph Centenary (924) 1944
    13¢ Jimmie Rodgers (1755) 1978
25. ½¢ Nathan Hale, rotary (653) 1929
    1¢, 3¢ Century of Progress (728-29) 1933
    5¢ Canada Centenary (1324) 1967
26. 2¢ Valley Forge (645) 1928
    10¢ Lindbergh airpost, booklet (C10a) 1928
    5¢ Army (789), 5¢ Navy (794) 1937
27. 10¢ David Wark Griffith (1555) 1975
28. 3¢ Four Chaplains (956) 1948
    17¢ Rachel Carson (1849) 1981
29. 7¢ McKinley, perf 10 rotary (588) 1926
    8¢ Grant, perf 10 rotary (589) 1926
    9¢ Thomas Jefferson (590) 1926
    5¢ John Ericsson (628) 1926
    3¢ San Diego Exposition (773) 1935
    3¢ Wisconsin Centennial (957) 1948
    6¢ Powered Flight 50th Anniversary (C47) 1953
    5¢ John F. Kennedy Memorial (1246) 1964
    13¢ John F. Kennedy (1287) 1967
    13¢, 18¢, 24¢, 31¢ INTERPHIL '76 souvenir sheets (1686-89) 1976
30. 3¢ Confederate Veterans (998) 1951
    4¢ Lincoln Sesquicentennial (1116) 1959
31. 3¢ Kansas Territory (1061) 1954
    3¢ Geophysical Year (1107) 1958
    4¢ SEATO (1151) 1960
    15¢ Emily Bissell (1823) 1980

## June

1. 3¢ Kentucky Statehood (904) 1942
   3¢ Tennessee Statehood (941) 1946
   13¢ Benjamin Franklin (1690) 1976
2. 4¢ American Woman (1152) 1960
3. 2¢ Presidential (Adams) (806) 1938
   3¢ Kansas City Centennial (994) 1950
   35¢ Charles Drew (1859) 1981
4. 4¢ William Howard Taft (685) 1930
   5¢ Swedish Pioneers (958) 1948
   5¢ Food for Peace (1231) 1963
   15¢ (four) American Architecture (1779-82) 1979
5. 2¢ Edison's First Light (654) 1929
   15¢ Certified Mail (FA1) 1955
6. 12¢ Benjamin Harrison (1045) 1959
   10¢ (eight) Universal Postal Union Centenary (1530-37) 1974
   13¢ (four) Butterflies (1712-15) 1977
7. 15¢ (four) Endangered Flowers (1783-86) 1979
8. 10¢ James Monroe, perf 10 rotary (591) 1925
   4¢ Silver Centennial (1130) 1959
   2¢ Frank Lloyd Wright (1280) 1966
9. 3¢ Doctors (949) 1947
10. 1¢ Benjamin Franklin, rotary (632) 1927
    8¢ U.S. Grant, rotary (640) 1927

11. 2¢ Edison's Light, rotary (655) 1929
    2¢ Edison's Light, coil (656) 1929
12. 3¢ Baseball (855) 1939
    3¢ Executive Mansion (990) 1950
    3¢ Gunston Hall (1108) 1958
    8¢ Wildlife Conservation (1427-30) 1971
13. 3¢ Marquis de Lafayette (1010) 1952
    10¢ Mineral Heritage (1538-41) 1974
    13¢ Lafayette (1716) 1977
14. 9¢ The Alamo (1043) 1956
    3¢ Oklahoma Statehood (1092) 1957
15. 3¢, 5¢ Olympic Games (718-19) 1932
    3¢ Arkansas Centennial (782) 1936
    11¢ Statue of Liberty, Giori (1044A) 1961
    5¢ New Jersey Tercentenary (1247) 1964
    5¢ Magna Carta (1265) 1965
    10¢ Kentucky Settlement (1542) 1974
    15¢ Seeing Eye Dogs (1787) 1979
16. 3¢ Washington, portrait by Stuart (720) 1932
    3¢ Presidential (Jefferson) (807) 1938
17. 2¢ Sullivan Expedition (657) 1929
    2½¢ Bunker Hill Monument (1034) 1959
    1¼¢ Palace of Governors (1031A) 1960
    10¢ Battle of Bunker Hill (1564) 1975
18. 10¢ Charles Lindbergh's Flight (C10) 1927
    18¢ Professional Management (1920) 1981
19. Bicolored Postage Due series (J88-J101) 1959
20. 5¢ West Virginia Statehood (1232) 1963
21. 3¢ Constitution Ratification (835) 1938
    3¢ New Hampshire (1068) 1955
22. 5¢ Poland Flag (909) 1943
    3¢ Antelope (1078) 1956
    8¢ Post Rider (1478) 1973
23. 8¢ Antarctic Treaty (1431) 1971
24. 3¢ Washington, vertical coil (721) 1932
    3¢ Statue of Liberty (1035) 1954
25. 6¢ Transport Plane (C25) 1941
    3¢ Mackinac Bridge (1109) 1958
    17¢ Electric Auto (1905) 1981
26. 4¢ St. Lawrence Seaway (1131) 1959
    5¢ International Cooperation Year (1266) 1965
    6¢ Wolf Trap Farm (1452) 1972
    15¢ Photography (1758) 1978
    18¢ (four) Wildlife Habitats (1921-24) 1981
27. 3¢ Swedish-Finnish Tercentenary (836) 1938
    3¢ Franklin Roosevelt Memorial (932) 1945
    3¢ Dr. Harvey Wiley (1080) 1956
    6¢ Register and Vote (1344) 1968
    21¢ Amadeo Giannini (1400) 1973
    15¢ Helen Keller and Anne Sullivan (1824) 1980
28. 3¢ Soo Locks (1069) 1955
    15¢ Statue of Liberty airpost (C62) 1961
29. 18¢ Disabled Persons (1925) 1981
30. 3¢ Boy Scout Jamboree (995) 1950
    15¢ Americana (Flag) regular (two) and coil (1597, 1598, 1618C) 1978

## July

1. 6¢ Winged Globe (C19) 1934
   4¢ Presidential (Madison) (808) 1938
   3¢ Teachers of America (1093) 1957
   5¢ Gettysburg (1180) 1963
   5¢ Bill of Rights (1312) 1966
   8¢ U.S. Postal Service Emblem (1396) 1971
2. 5¢ Salvation Army (1267) 1965
   $1 Americana (Rush Lamp) (1610) 1979
3. 3¢ Idaho Statehood (896) 1940
   15¢ George M. Cohan (1756) 1978
4. 3¢ Win the War (905) 1942
   3¢ Indiana Territory (996) 1950
   10¢ Independence Hall (1044) 1956
   4¢ 48-star Flag (1094) 1957
   4¢ 49-star Flag (1132) 1959
   4¢ 50-star Flag (1153) 1960
   5¢ Erie Canal (1325) 1967
   6¢ Historic Flags (1345-54) 1968
   8¢ Bicentennial Commission Emblem (1432) 1971
   8¢ Colonial Craftsmen (1456-59) 1972
   8¢ Boston Tea Party (1480-83) 1973
   10¢ Continental Congress (1543-46) 1974
   10¢ Revolutionary Uniforms (1565-68) 1975
   13¢ (four) Declaration of Independence (1691-94) 1976
   13¢ (four) Skilled Hands for Independence (1717-20) 1977
5. 5¢ Search for Peace (1326) 1967
6. Not a first day to date
7. 3¢ Wisconsin Tercentenary (739) 1934
   5¢ Chinese Resistance (906) 1942
8. Not a first day to date
9. 2¢ Braddock's Field (688) 1930
   6¢ Maine Statehood (1391) 1970
10. 3¢ Wyoming Statehood (897) 1940
    6¢, 8¢, 15¢, 11¢ Progress in Electronics (1500-02, C86) 1973
    18¢ Edna St. Vincent Millay (1926) 1981
11. 4½¢ Presidential (White House) (809) 1938
    3¢ Marine Corps (929) 1945
    4¢ Senator George Norris (1184) 1961
    15¢ Roses (booklet) (1738) 1978
12. 10¢ Special Delivery (E12) 1922
    5¢ Czechoslovakia Flag (910) 1943
    3¢ George Eastman (1062) 1954
    6¢ Bald Eagle airpost (C67) 1963
    5¢ Henry Thoreau (1327) 1967
13. 3¢ Northwest Ordinance Sesquicentennial (795) 1937
    17¢ Statue of Liberty airpost (C80) 1971
    8.4¢ coil (1615C) 1978
14. 3¢ Oregon Territory (783) 1936
    3¢ Nevada Settlement (999) 1951
    5¢ Opening of Japan (1021) 1953
15. 3¢ Northwest Territory (837) 1938
    10¢ Apollo-Soyuz (1569-70) 1975
16. 1¢ Yosemite National Park (740) 1934
    6¢ California Settlement (1373) 1969
    13¢ (four) Olympic Games block (1695-98) 1976
17. 5¢ Dante Alighieri (1268) 1965
18. 1¢ Franklin, coil sidewise (597) 1923
19. 1¢ Franklin coil, endwise (604) 1924
    3¢ Progress of Women (959) 1948
    4¢ Pony Express Centennial (1154) 1960
20. 6¢ Wildlife Conservation (1392) 1970
    15¢ Viking Mission to Mars (1759) 1978
21. 5¢ Presidential (Monroe) (810) 1938
    15¢ Veterans Administration (1825) 1980
22. 5¢ Nevada Statehood (1248) 1964
23. 15¢ Gen. Bernardo de Galvez (1826) 1980
24. 2¢ Grand Canyon (741) 1934
    3¢ Utah Settlement (950) 1947
    3¢ Cadillac's Landing (1000) 1951
    4¢, 8¢, Simon Bolivar, Champion of Liberty (1110-11) 1958
    4¢ Girl Scouts (1199) 1962
    8¢ Amelia Earhart (C68) 1963
25. 5¢ Beacon airpost (C11) 1928
    17¢ Woodrow Wilson, rotary (697) 1931
    25¢ Niagara Falls, rotary (699) 1931
26. 1¢ Franklin Roosevelt Memorial (930) 1945
27. 6¢ James Garfield, rotary (638) 1927
    5¢ Norway Flag (911) 1943
28. 6¢ Presidential (John Q. Adams) (811) 1938
    3¢ Lewis and Clark (1063) 1954
    3¢ Atoms for Peace (1070) 1955
    4¢ Brian McMahon (1200) 1962
    15¢ Mount McKinley (1454) 1972
29. 5¢ Nebraska Statehood (1328) 1967
30. 5¢ Yellowstone National Park (744) 1934
    25¢ Bay Bridge airpost (C36) 1947
    5¢ Poland Millennium (1313) 1966
31. 3¢ William Allen White (960) 1948
    5¢ New York City 50th anniversary (C38) 1948
    5¢ Eagle in Flight airpost (C50) 1958
    7¢ Jet Airliner sheet and coil (C51-C52) 1958

## August

1. 3¢ Lincoln, perf 10 rotary (584) 1925
   3¢ Colorado Statehood (1001) 1951
   6¢ Air Force (C49) 1957
   8¢ "Tagged" airpost (C64a) 1963
   5¢ Register and Vote (1249) 1964
   5¢ Voice of America (1329) 1967
   6¢ John Wesley Powell (1374) 1969
2. 3¢ U.S.-Canada Friendship (961) 1948
   3¢ Supreme Court Building (991) 1950
   6¢ Alabama Statehood (1375) 1969
   8¢ John Sloan (1433) 1971
   8¢ Space Achievement Decade (1434-35) 1971
3. 2¢ Vermont Sesquicentennial (643) 1927
   2¢ Burgoyne Campaign (644) 1927
   3¢ Mount Rainier (742) 1934
   3¢ Iowa Statehood (942) 1946
4. 7¢ Presidential (Jackson) (812) 1938
   13¢ Peace Bridge (1721) 1977
5. 4¢ Martha Washington coil, sidewise (601) 1923
   3¢ Wheatland (1081) 1956
6. 6¢ Dwight D. Eisenhower (1393) 1970

10¢ Chautauqua (1505) 1974
13¢ Herkimer at Oriskany (1722) 1977
7. 6¢ Flag Over White House, Huck press
   (1338D) 1970
8. Not a first day to date
9. 3¢ Francis Scott Key (962) 1948
   15¢ Special Olympics (1788) 1979
10. 5¢ Luxembourg Flag (912) 1943
   3¢ Smithsonian Institution (943) 1946
   5¢ Herbert Hoover (1269) 1965
11. 8¢ Presidential (Van Buren) (813) 1938
   3¢ Youth Month (963) 1948
   3¢ Mount Rushmore (1011) 1952
   28¢ Americana (Fort Nisqually) (1604) 1978
12. 7¢ Airpost, red (C60) 1960
13. 2¢, 5¢ Hawaii Sesquicentennial (647-48) 1928
   15¢ Special Delivery (E16) 1931
   50¢ Lucy Stone (1293) 1968
   8¢ Robinson Jeffers (1485) 1973
14. 3¢ Oregon Statehood (964) 1948
   5¢ Shakespeare (1250) 1964
15. 8¢ Airpost (C4) 1923
   3¢ NRA (732) 1933
   3¢ Panama Canal (856) 1939
   10¢ Airpost (C27) 1941
   3¢ Shipbuilding (1095) 1957
   4¢ Atlantic Cable (1112) 1958
16. 5¢ Emancipation Proclamation (1233) 1963
   10¢ Kansas Winter Wheat (1506) 1974
17. 16¢ Airpost (C5) 1923
   7¢ Balloon Jupiter (C54) 1959
   5¢ Alliance for Progress (1234) 1963
   5¢ Davy Crockett (1330) 1967
   6¢, 8¢, 15¢ Olympic Games (1460-62), 11¢
   (C85) 1972
18. 6¢ James Garfield (723) 1932
   5¢ Virginia Dare (796) 1937
   9¢ Presidential (W.H. Harrison) (814) 1938
   13¢ Clara Maass (1699) 1976
19. 5¢ Winged Globe airpost (C16) 1931
   15¢ Airpost (C28) 1941
   5¢ Robert Fulton (1270) 1965
   18¢ Alcoholism (1927) 1981
20. 15¢ New York Skyline airpost (C35) 1947
   4¢ Naval Aviation (1185) 1961
21. 24¢ Biplane airpost (C6) 1923
   7¢ Hawaii Statehood (C55) 1959
22. 6¢ Edgar Lee Masters (1405) 1970
23. 6¢ Botanical Congress (1376-79) 1969
   $5 Americana (Railroad conductor's
   lantern) (1612) 1979
24. 3¢ Iowa Territory (838) 1938
   5¢ Netherlands Flag (913) 1943
   2¢ Franklin Roosevelt Memorial (931) 1945
   3¢ American Bar Association (1022) 1953
25. 12¢ Cleveland, rotary (693) 1931
   1¢, 3¢ APS souvenir sheets (730-31) 1933
   3¢ Justice Harlan F. Stone (965) 1948
   6¢ DC-4 Skymaster, coil, airpost (C41) 1949
   50¢ Patrick Henry (1051) 1955
   5¢ National Park Service Emblem (1314)
   1966

26. 3¢ Susan B. Anthony (784) 1936
   10¢ SPA souvenir sheet (797) 1937
   1¢ Washington (1031) 1954
   4¢ Soil Conservation (1133) 1959
   6¢ Woman Suffrage (1406) 1970
   10¢ International Women's Year (1571) 1975
   15¢ (four) American Owls (1760-63) 1978
   15¢ (four) Coral Reefs (1827-30) 1980
27. 1½¢ Harding, imperf, rotary (631) 1926
   15¢ Statue of Liberty, rotary (696) 1931
   9¢ Zion National Park (748) 1934
   20¢ Airpost (C29) 1941
   4¢ Lincoln-Douglas Debates (1115) 1958
   4¢ Petroleum Industry (1134) 1959
   10¢ Pan American Games (C56) 1959
   8¢ Lyndon B. Johnson Memorial (1503) 1973
28. 3¢ APS souvenir sheet (750) 1934
   4¢ Hire the Handicapped (1155) 1960
   5¢ Florida Settlement (1271) 1965
   8¢ Emily Dickinson (1436) 1971
   18¢ (four) Architecture (1928-31) 1981
29. 3¢ Grand Army of the Republic (985) 1949
   4¢ World Forestry Congress (1156) 1960
   5¢ Marine Corps Reserve (1315) 1966
30. 16¢ Airmail Special Delivery (CE1) 1934
   10¢ Pan American Union Building airpost
   (C34) 1947
   3¢ Mount Palomar Observatory (966) 1948
31. $1 Wilson, dry printing (832c) 1954
   8¢ Magsaysay, Champion of Liberty (1096)
   1957
   4¢ Apprenticeship (1201) 1962

## September

1. 2¢ Warren G. Harding Memorial (610) 1923
   15¢ Organized Labor (1831) 1980
2. 10¢ Presidential (Tyler) (815) 1938
3. 4¢ Eagle In Flight airpost (C48) 1954
   3¢ Labor Day (1082) 1956
   30¢ Special Delivery (E21) 1957
   5¢ Traffic Safety (1272) 1965
   10¢ (four) Postal Service Bicentennial
   (1572-75) 1975
4. 11¢ Hays, rotary (692) 1931
   13¢ Benjamin Harrison, rotary (694) 1931
   50¢ Arlington Amphitheater, rotary (701)
   1931
   3¢ American Chemical Society (1002) 1951
   4¢ Workmen's Compensation (1186) 1961
5. 6¢ Crater Lake (745) 1934
   1¢ Gilbert Stuart (884) 1940
   2¢ James Whistler (885) 1940
   10¢ Summer Olympics (1790) 1979
   15¢ Edith Wharton (1832) 1980
6. 3¢ Engineering Centennial (1012) 1952
   3¢ Lafayette Bicentenary (1097) 1957
7. 3¢ Coronado Expedition (898) 1940
   3¢ Clara Barton (967) 1948
8. 14¢ American Indian, rotary (695) 1931
   20¢ Golden Gate, rotary (698) 1931
   30¢ Buffalo, rotary (700) 1931
9. 3¢ Poultry Industry (968) 1948
   3¢ California Statehood (997) 1950
   10¢ Moon Landing (C76) 1969

10. 8¢ Henry O. Tanner (1486) 1973
11. 3¢ Service Women (1013) 1952
    5¢ Doctors Mayo (1251) 1964
    6¢ Walt Disney (1355) 1968
    50¢ Americana (Iron "Betty" lamp) (1608) 1979
12. 2¢ Harding, rotary (612) 1923
    5¢ Women's Clubs (1316) 1966
    6¢ South Carolina (1407) 1970
    8¢ San Juan, Puerto Rico (1437) 1971
    15¢ American Education (1833) 1980
13. Not a first day to date
14. 2¢ Battle of Fallen Timbers (680) 1929
    12¢ Presidential (Taylor) (817) 1938
    5¢ Belgium Flag (914) 1943
    3¢ Sagamore Hill (1023) 1953
    4¢ Dental Health (1135) 1959
    4¢ Francis Scott Key Credo (1142) 1960
15. 2¢ Thomas Jefferson (1033) 1954
    8¢ Parent-Teacher Associations (1463) 1972
16. 3¢ Augustus Saint-Gaudens (886) 1940
    5¢ Daniel Chester French (887) 1940
    4¢ Mexican Independence (1157) 1960
    4¢ Sam Rayburn (1202) 1962
    3¢ Francis Parkman (1281) 1967
17. 2¢ General Von Steuben (689) 1930
    3¢ Constitution Sesquicentennial (798) 1937
    5¢ John Singleton Copley (1273) 1965
18. 15¢ Map airpost (C8) 1926
    8¢ Zion National Park (747) 1934
    3¢ Fort Ticonderoga (1071) 1955
    13¢ Adolf Ochs (1700) 1976
19. 4¢, 8¢ Kossuth Champion of Liberty (1117-18) 1958
    6¢ Stone Mountain Memorial (1408) 1970
20. 6¢ Father Marquette (1356) 1968
    8¢ (four) Wildlife Conservation (1464-67) 1972
    8¢ Willa Cather (1487) 1973
21. 3¢ Gold Star Mothers (969) 1948
    30¢ Robert E. Lee (1049) 1955
22. 13¢ Presidential (Fillmore) (818) 1938
    3¢ Fort Kearny (970) 1948
    3¢ Nassau Hall (1083) 1956
    4¢ Freedom of the Press (1119) 1958
    6¢ Dartmouth College Case (1380) 1969
    18¢ Babe Didrikson Zaharias (1932) 1981
    18¢ Bobby Jones (1933) 1981
23. 10¢ Energy Conservation (1547) 1974
    31¢ (two) Wright Brothers (C91-C92) 1978
    15¢ John Paul Jones (1789) 1979
24. 40¢ John Marshall (1050) 1955
    3¢ Devil's Tower (1084) 1956
    5¢ Johnny Appleseed (1317) 1966
    6¢ Professional Baseball (1381) 1969
25. 4¢ Mesa Verde National Park (743) 1934
    3¢ Printing Tercentenary (857) 1939
    30¢ Twin Motor Transport airpost (C30) 1941
    5¢ DC-4 Skymaster airpost (C32) 1946
    15¢ (four) Northwest Indian Masks (1834-37) 1980
26. 8¢ Winged Globe airpost (C17) 1932

6¢ Daniel Boone (1357) 1968
6¢ Intercollegiate Football (1382) 1969
27. 3¢ Corregidor (925) 1944
    8¢ Mail Order Business (1468) 1972
28. 5¢ French Flag (915) 1943
    3¢ U.S. Army (934) 1945
    4¢ U.S.-Japan Treaty (1158) 1960
    8¢ Drummer (1479) 1973
    15¢ (four) Summer Olympics (1791-94) 1979
29. $2 Presidential (Harding) (833) 1938
    4¢, 8¢ Reuter, Champion of Liberty (1136-37) 1959
    5¢ (two) Space Walk (1331-32) 1967
    10¢ Peace Through Law (1576) 1975
30. 3¢ Boulder Dam (774) 1935
    10¢ Frederic Remington (888) 1940
    3¢ Gutenberg Bible (1014) 1952

## October

1. 6¢ Arkansas River Navigation (1358) 1968
   6.3¢ Bulk rate coil (1518) 1974
2. 50¢ Graf Zeppelin airpost (C18) 1933
   7¢ Acadia National Park (746) 1934
   5¢ Urban Planning (1333) 1967
3. Not a first day to date
4. 11¢ Rutherford B. Hayes (563) 1922
   3¢ Volunteer Firemen (971) 1948
   3¢ Newspaper Boys (1015) 1952
   4¢ Frederic Remington (1187) 1961
   8¢ Drug Abuse (1438) 1971
5. 5¢ Cordell Hull (1235) 1963
   8¢ Dr. Robert Goddard (C69) 1964
   5¢ Beautification of America (1318) 1966
   8¢ Angus Cattle (1504) 1973
6. 14¢ Presidential (Pierce) (819) 1938
   11¢ International Telecommunication Union (1274) 1965
   5¢ Finland Independence (1334) 1967
   10¢ (two) Banking and Commerce (1577-78) 1975
7. 1¢ Eli Whitney (889) 1940
   2¢ Samuel F. B. Morse (890) 1940
   3¢ Edgar Allen Poe (986) 1949
   15¢ UPU 75th anniversary (C43) 1949
   $1 Patrick Henry (1052) 1955
8. 10¢ Great Smoky Mountains (749) 1934
   4¢, 8¢ Paderewski Champion of Liberty (1159-60) 1960
9. 3¢ Byrd Antarctic Expedition (733) 1933
   6¢ Leif Erickson (1359) 1968
   8¢ Osteopathic Medicine (1469) 1972
   15¢ (four) American Trees (1764-67) 1978
   15¢ (four) Architecture (1838-41) 1980
   18¢ Coming Through the Rye (1934) 1981
10. 1¢ Trans-Mississippi Exhibition souvenir sheet (751) 1934
    4¢ Overland Mail (1120) 1958
    4¢ Senator Robert Taft (1161) 1960
    4¢ Republic of China (1188) 1961
    10¢ Legend of Sleepy Hollow (1548) 1974
11. 5¢ Eleanor Roosevelt (1236) 1963
    "C" (20¢) sheet, coil, booklet (1946-48) 1981
12. 3¢ Washington, horizontal coil (722) 1932

5¢ Greek Flag (916) 1943
10¢ Retarded Children (1549) 1974
13. 5¢ Kosciuszko (734) 1933
15¢ Presidential (Buchanan) (820) 1938
3¢ Future Farmers (1024) 1953
8¢ Tom Sawyer (1470) 1972
40¢ airmail Philip Mazzei (C98) 1980
18¢, 20¢ James Hoban (1935-36) 1981
14. 3¢ Cyrus McCormick (891) 1940
5¢ Elias Howe (892) 1940
5¢ Science (1237) 1963
6¢ Dwight Eisenhower Memorial (1383) 1969
10¢ (two) Christmas (1579-80) 1975
15. 5¢ American Music (1252) 1944
3¢ Indian Centennial (972) 1948
4¢ Wheels of Freedom (1162) 1960
6¢ Cherokee Strip (1360) 1968
16. 1¢, 2¢, 3¢ National Defense (899-901) 1940
3¢ Kearney Expedition (944) 1946
4¢ Noah Webster (1121) 1958
$1 Eugene O'Neill (1294) 1967
18¢ (two) Yorktown/Virginia Capes (1937-38) 1981
17. 1¢ Franklin, perf 10 rotary (581) 1923
6¢ Fort Snelling (1409) 1970
18. 2¢ Battle of White Plains (629) 1926
2¢ White Plains Souvenir Sheet (630) 1926
3¢ Hawaii Territorial (799) 1937
4¢ Boys' Clubs of America (1163) 1960
6¢ John Trumbull (1361) 1968
15¢ (two) Christmas (1768-69) 1978
15¢ (two) Christmas (1799-1800) 1979
19. 2¢ Ohio River Canalization (681) 1929
2¢ Yorktown Sesquicentennial (703) 1931
20. 2¢ Molly Pitcher (646) 1928
16¢ Presidential (Lincoln) (821) 1938
3¢ 13th Amendment (902) 1940
½¢ Benjamin Franklin (1030) 1955
4¢ Automated Post Office (1164) 1960
21. 3¢ Old Ironsides (951) 1947
5¢ Great River Road (1319) 1966
30¢ John Dewey (1291) 1968
22. 7¢ Airpost coil, red (C61) 1960
23. 4¢ Dag Hammarskjold Memorial (1203) 1962
5¢ Adlai Stevenson Memorial (1275) 1965
10¢ Christmas (1550-51) 1974
24. 3¢ William Penn (724) 1932
3¢ Daniel Webster (725) 1932
20¢ George C. Marshall (1289) 1967
6¢ Wildlife Conservation (1362) 1968
25. Not a first day to date
26. 5¢ Yugoslavia Flag (917) 1943
4¢, 8¢ Mannerheim, Champion of Liberty (1165-66) 1960
5¢ City Mail Delivery (1238) 1963
5¢ Homemakers (1253) 1964
5¢ Savings Bonds/Servicemen (1320) 1966
27. 5¢ Theodore Roosevelt (557) 1922
17¢ Presidential (A. Johnson) (822) 1938
3¢ U.S. Navy (935) 1945
3¢ Rough Riders (973) 1948
3¢ Trucking Industry (1025) 1953

4¢ Forest Conservation (1122) 1958
8¢ CARE Anniversary (1439) 1971
13¢ (two) Christmas (1701-02) 1976
28. 10¢ Alexander Graham Bell (893) 1940
6¢ Anti-Pollution (1410-13) 1970
20¢ (two) Christmas (1939-40) 1981
29. 50¢ Airport (C31) 1941
3¢ Juliette Lowe (974) 1948
5¢ Red Cross Centennial (1239) 1963
8¢ Historic Preservation (1440-43) 1971
30. 13¢, 17¢ Special Delivery (E17-E18) 1944
31. 3¢ Motion Pictures (926) 1944
13¢ Liberty Bell (1595) 1975
15¢ (two) Christmas (1842-43) 1980

## November

1. 3¢ Michigan Centenary (775) 1935
4¢ Camp Fire Girls (1167) 1960
4¢ Christmas (1205) 1962
5¢ Christmas (1240) 1963
5¢ Christmas (1321) 1966
6¢ Christmas (1363) 1968
31¢ Summer Olympics (airmail) (C97) 1979
2. 3¢ Four States (858) 1939
5¢ Korea Flag (921) 1944
4¢, 8¢ Garibaldi, Champion of Liberty (1168-69) 1960
5¢ Christmas (1276) 1965
5¢ Thomas Eakins (1335) 1967
3. 6¢ Christmas (1384) 1969
4. 3¢ Will Rogers (975) 1948
6¢ Chief Joseph (1364) 1968
3¢ Parkman, coil (1297) 1975
15¢ Will Rogers (1801) 1979
5. 3¢ Fort Bliss (976) 1948
4¢ Walter George Memorial (1170) 1960
6¢ Christmas (1414-18) 1970
20¢ John Hanson (1941) 1981
6. 4¢ Basketball (1189) 1961
5¢ Christmas (1336) 1967
7. 8¢ Christmas (1507-08) 1973
8. Not a first day to date
9. 5¢ Albania Flag (918) 1943
3¢ Moina Michael (977) 1948
3¢ King Salmon (1079) 1956
5¢ Christmas (1254-57) 1964
8¢ Christmas (1471-72) 1972
10. 19¢ Presidential (Hayes) (824) 1938
20¢ Presidential (Garfield) (825) 1938
3¢ Coast Guard (936) 1945
8¢ Christmas (1444-45) 1971
8¢ Pharmacy (1473) 1972
11. 15¢ Statue of Liberty (566) 1922
25¢ Niagara Falls (568) 1922
50¢ Lincoln Memorial (570) 1922
3¢ General George S. Patton (1026) 1953
15¢ Vietnam Veterans (1802) 1979
12. 3¢ Alaska Territory (800) 1937
13. 11¢ Freedom of the Press (1593) 1975
14. 4¢ Higher Education (1206) 1962
24¢ Old North Church (1603) 1975
15. 2¢ Harding, imperf (611) 1923
10¢ Christmas, self-stick (1552) 1974

13¢ Flag and Independence Hall (1622) 1975
13¢ Flag, coil (1625) 1975

16. 4¢ Hammarskjold, special printing (1204) 1962

17. $5 Presidential (Coolidge) (834) 1938
8¢ John J. Pershing (1042A) 1961
5¢ Mary Cassatt (1322) 1966
5¢ Washington, redrawn (1283B) 1967
8¢ Stamp Collecting (1474) 1972

18. 10¢ UPU 75th Anniversary (C42) 1949
6¢ Theodore Roosevelt (1039) 1955

19. 3¢ Gettysburg Address (978) 1948
4¢ Abraham Lincoln (1036) 1954
4¢ Lincoln Credo (1143) 1960

20. 6¢ James Garfield (558) 1922
3¢ American Turners (979) 1948
3¢ New York City (1027) 1953
15¢ Statue of Liberty airpost (C58) 1959
6¢ Hope for Crippled (1385) 1969
6¢ United Nations Anniversary (1419) 1970
7.7¢ coil, (1614) 1976
25¢ (two) Wiley Post (airmail) (C95-C96) 1979

21. 3¢ International Red Cross (1016) 1952
5¢ Verrazano Narrows Bridge (1258) 1964
6¢ Landing of Pilgrims (1420) 1970

22. 25¢ China Clipper airpost (C20) 1935
3¢ U.S. Capitol (992) 1950
3¢ Wildlife Conservation (1098) 1957
20¢ USA and Jet airpost (C75) 1968

23. 5¢ Austria Flag (919) 1943
5¢ Washington (1213) 1962

24. 6¢ Disabled American Veterans (1421) 1970
6¢ Honoring U.S. Servicemen (1422) 1970
9¢ Freedom to Assemble (1591) 1975

25. 3¢ Puerto Rico Territory (801) 1937
4¢ Fort Duquesne (1123) 1958
4¢ Andrew Carnegie (1171) 1960
13¢ Liberty Bell, coil (1618) 1975

26. 3¢ Alfred E. Smith (937) 1945

27. Not a first day to date

28. Not a first day to date

29. 10¢ Special Delivery (E15) 1927

30. 25¢ UPU 75th Anniversary (C44) 1949

## December

1. 10¢ Monroe coil, sidewise (603) 1924
1½¢ Harding, full-face (684) 1930
1½¢ Harding coil, full-face (686) 1930
13¢ American Eagle and Shield (1596) 1975

2. 24¢ Presidential (B. Harrison) (828) 1938
25¢ Presidential (McKinley) (829) 1938
5¢ James Monroe (1038) 1954
5¢ Fine Arts (1259) 1964

3. 4¢ Dr. Ephraim McDowell (1138) 1959
$5 John Bassett Moore (1295) 1966
6¢ William Harnett (1386) 1969

4. Not a first day to date

5. 3¢ Everglades National Park (952) 1947
8¢ Airpost, sheet and coil (C64-C65) 1962

6. 4¢ John Foster Dulles (1172) 1960

7. 5¢ Denmark Flag (920) 1943
5¢ John James Audubon (1241) 1963

8. 30¢ Presidential (T. Roosevelt) (830) 1938
50¢ Presidential (W. H. Taft) (831) 1938

9. 3¢ Joel Chandler Harris (980) 1948

10. 2¢ Washington, rotary (634) 1926
3¢ Battle of Brooklyn (1003) 1951
20¢ Fire Pumper (1907) 1981

11. 5¢ Mississippi Statehood (1337) 1967
20¢ (four) Desert Plants (1942-45) 1981

12. 2¢, 5¢ Aeronautics Conference (649-50) 1928

13. Not a first day to date

14. Not a first day to date

15. 1¢ Army (785), 1¢ Navy (790) 1936
3¢ Virgin Islands (802) 1937
3¢ Children's Issue (1085) 1956
4¢ Echo I (1173) 1960
4¢ Winslow Homer (1207) 1962
5¢ Amateur Radio (1260) 1964
9.3¢ Mail Wagon (1900) 1981

16. Not a first day to date

17. 6¢ Wright Brothers (C45) 1949
20¢ Flag Over Supreme Court, sheet, coil, booklet (1894-96) 1981

18. Not a first day to date

19. Not a first day to date

20. 3¢ George Eastman (1072) 1955

21. 1¢, 2¢, 5¢ Pilgrim Tercentenary series (548-50) 1920

22. Not a first day to date

23. Not a first day to date

24. Not a first day to date

25. Not a first day to date

26. Not a first day to date

27. 3¢ Religious Freedom (1099) 1957
13¢ airpost, coil (C83) 1973
19¢ Sequoia (1851) 1980

28. 17¢ Woodrow Wilson (623) 1925
4¢ Nurses of America (1190) 1961

29. 3¢ Texas Statehood (938) 1945

30. 3¢ Gadsden Purchase (1028) 1953
28¢ Airmail Blanche Stuart Scott (C99) 1980
35¢ Airmail Glenn Curtiss (C100) 1980

31. 2¢ Washington coil, endwise (606) 1923

# Periodicals

# 17

# Philatelic Publications

This list contains all periodicals of national, international or topical interest to the philatelist. Bulletins of local clubs have not been included, unless they represent a national or international scope, or some area of specialized research.

This list is compiled alphabetically by countries, with the United States and Great Britain falling ahead of the rest, since these two countries have the largest number of periodicals, and most are in English.

Within each country, the periodicals are indexed alphabetically, using the original name of the journal (translations follow the less-obvious titles). Titles are followed by the frequency of publication (if known), expressed as the minimum number of times per year the publication is issued. When the publication is issued by an organization or firm, that name will follow, generally translated. The general rule for the language of the periodical is: the publication is in English if the title is in English; foreign titles indicate the native language of the source country for the publication or language of the title. Multilingual journals are so noted.

Following the first set of information in each entry will be a contact address. Society or publication addresses are generally used in preference to private addresses. Inquiries should be directed to the society or source firm, or the publication itself (a note, "Attention: Editor," may be added). The editor's name is the fastest changing item listed, and as such, may not be current.

Prices are not included because of constantly changing costs, postal rates and foreign exchange rates. Many publications will provide sample copies for return postage, or a nominal fee. Initial inquiries should request such information, rather than including payment. It is generally appreciated, when requesting information or response, if a self-addressed, stamped envelope or International Reply Coupon is included.

Please address all corrections, updates or deletions from this list to Linn's Almanac Periodicals List, Box 29, Sidney, Ohio 45367.

## United States

**AERO PHILATELIST ANNALS** (2); American Air Mail Society. 102 Arbor Road, Cinnaminson, N.J. 08077. Philip Silver, ed.

**AFA NEWS & JACK KNIGHT AIR LOG** (4); Aerophilatelic Federation of the Americas. Box 269, Brookfield, Ill. 60513. Fred L. Wellman, ed.

**AIRPOST JOURNAL** (12); American Air Mail Society. 102 Arbor Road, Cinnaminson, N.J. 08077. Frank H. Blumenthal, ed.

**AMERICAN PHILATELIC SERVICES REPORT** (6). Box 56, Lewiston, N.Y. 14092. Lee Simonson, ed.

**AMERICAN PHILATELIST, The** (12); American Philatelic Society. Box 8000, State College, Pa. 16801. Richard L. Sine, ed.

**AMERICAN REVENUER, The** (10); American Revenue Association. 1010 S. Fifth Ave., Arcadia, Calif. 91006. Kenneth Trettin, ed.

**AMERICANA PHILATELIC NEWS** (6); Americana Unit. Box 179, Washington, D.C. 20044. August Mark Vaz, ed.

**ARAB WORLD PHILATELIST** (At random). 1325 W. Moss Ave., Peoria, Ill. 61606. R. Howard Courtney, ed.

**ARIZONA PHILATELIST** (6); Arizona Federation of Stamp Clubs. 6235 W. Clarendon Ave., Phoenix, Ariz. 85033. Donn Lueck, ed.

**ASDA NEWSLETTER** (12); American Stamp Dealers' Association. 5 Dakota Drive, Lake Success, N.Y. 11042.

**ASTROFAX** (4); Astronomy Unit. 254 Summit St., Plantsville, Conn. 06479. Ann Shoemake, ed.

**ASTROPHILE** (6); Space Topics Study Unit. 91 Eastern Parkway, Hillside, N.J. 07205. Jim Cattani, ed.

**AUSTRIA BULLETIN** (3); Austria Philatelic Society of New York. 150 Rumson Road, Rumson, N.J. 07760. Richard Green, Ernest Theimer, eds.

**AUTOGRAPHED COVERS FORUM** (6); Autograph Chapter of the AFDCS. Box 433N, Elmwood Park, N.J. 07407. Jan Brennan, ed.

**AVIAN PHILATELY, Journal of** (4); Avian Philately Study Unit. 5324 W. Ave. L., Quartz Hill, Calif. 93534. William W. Cole Jr., ed.

**BADGER POSTAL HISTORY** (4); Wisconsin Postal History Society. N95 W32259 County Line Road, Hartland, Wis. 53029. James B. Hale, ed.

**BERMUDA HIGH** (6); Geosix West. 127 Solar St., Syracuse, N.Y. 13204. Robert W. Dickgiesser, ed.

**BIO-PHILATELY** (4); Biology Unit. B. Rutherford, R.R. 2, Marion, Iowa 52302. Gustavs E. Eglajs, ed.

**B.N.A. TOPICS** (6); British North American Philatelic Society. 25 Kings Circle, Malvern, Pa. 19355. H. Michael Sheet, ed.

**BOLETIN, El** (3); Cuban Philatelic Society of America. Box 450207, Miami, Fla. 33145. Silvia Garcia Frutos, ed.

**BRITISH CARIBBEAN PHILATELIC JOURNAL** (5); British Caribbean Philatelic Study Group. 4230 N. Woodburn, Shorewood, Wis. 53211. George Bowman, ed.

**BULL'S EYE** (4); Brazil Philatelic Association. 3433 Kenneth Drive, Palo Alto, Calif. 94303. William V. Krieble, ed.

**BULLSEYE BULLETIN** (4); Bullseye Cancel Collectors Club. 5935 S. Kolmar, Chicago, Ill. 60629. Nick Michaluk, ed.

**BWI BULLETIN, The** (4); Jamaica (BWI) Study Group. 267 W. Granby Road, West Granby, Conn. 06090. Howard J. Gaston, ed.

**CANAL ZONE PHILATELIST** (4); Canal Zone Study Group. Box 9973, College Station, Tex. 77840. Gilbert N. Plass, ed.

**CARTO-PHILATELIST** (4); Carto-Philatelists. 714 E. Maple St., Appleton, Wis. 54911. Mark D. Larkin, ed.

**CAT MEWS** (4). 607 S. Hamline Ave., St. Paul, Minn. 55116. Virginia A. Haywood, ed.

**CHANNEL ISLANDS REPORTER** (4); Club of Channel Islands Collectors. Box 579, New York, N.Y. 10028. Robert Ausubel, ed.

**CHANTILLY STAMP COLLECTOR** (12). Box 281, Chantilly, Va. 22021. John S. March, ed.

**CHESSTAMP REVIEW** (6); Chess on Stamps Study Unit. 11226 Marlette Drive, Cincinnati, Ohio 45242. Sam Wilkinson III, ed.

**CHINA** (4); China Philatelic Study Group. Box 630, Milbrook, N.Y. 12545. Gene Klein, ed.

**CHINA CLIPPER, The** (6); China Stamp Society. 100 Font Blvd., San Francisco, Calif. 94132. Norman W. Vachowiak, ed.

**CHRISTMAS NOTES** (6); Christmas Study Unit. 1411 N. Powhatan, Arlington, Va. 22205. Robert Haney, ed.

**CHRONICLE OF THE U.S. CLASSIC POSTAL ISSUES** (4); U.S. Philatelic Classics Society. 2030 Glenmount Drive NW, Canton, Ohio 44708. Susan M. McDonald, ed.

**CIVIL CENSORSHIP STUDY GROUP BULLETIN** (6). 274 Harvey Ave., Lincroft, N.J. 07738. John Warren, U.S. ed.; Tony Torrance, U.K. ed.

**CODEX FILATELICA** (6); Mesoamerican Archaeology Study Unit. Box 1442, Riverside, Calif. 92502. Larry Crain, ed.

**COINS ON STAMPS NEWS** (4); Coins on Stamps Study Unit (ATA). 304 S. Stewart Ave., Lombard, Ill. 60148. Michael Dziewulski, ed.

**COLLECTORS CLUB PHILATELIST** (6); Collectors Club of New York. 22 E. 35th St., New York, N.Y. 10016. E. E. Fricks, ed.

**COMMONWEALTH PHILATELY** (6); Commonwealth International Philatelic Society. Box 195, Minetto, N.Y. 13115. Ryan G. Lorenz, ed.

**COMMUNICATOR, The** (6); Telecommunications Study Unit. Box 07507, Bay View Station, Milwaukee, Wis. 53207. F.S. Dombrowski Jr., ed.

**CONFEDERATE PHILATELIST, The** (6); Confederate Stamp Alliance. 1522 K St. NW, Suite 1000, Washington, D.C. 20005. Patricia A. Kaufmann, ed.

**COROS CHRONICLE** (6); Collectors of Religion on Stamps. 600 W. Orange Grove Road, G-184, Tucson, Ariz. 85704. Eileen E. Freeman, ed.

**COSTUME REVIEW** (4); Costume Study Unit. 4000 N.W. 20th Drive, Gainesville, Fla. 32605. Dorothy L. Truhon, ed.

**CURTAIN CALL** (6); Performing Arts Study Unit. Box 1505, Indianapolis, Ind. 46206. The Rev. Marshall J. Whitehead, Dr. Harrold Shiffler, eds.

**CZECHOSLOVAK SPECIALIST, The** (10); Society for Czechoslovak Philately. 427 King St., Woodbury, N.J. 08096. Henry Hahn, ed.

**DELTIOLOGY** (6); Deltiologists of America. 10 Felton Ave., Ridley Park, Pa. 19078. James J. Lowe, ed.

**DISPATCHER, The** (4); Casey Jones Railroad Unit. 1108 Somonauk St., Sycamore, Ill. 60178. H.E. Rankin, ed.

**DOMINICAN REPUBLIC STUDY GROUP BULLETIN** (4). 431 George Cross Drive, Norman, Okla. 73069. James W. Smith, ed.

**DOSSU JOURNAL** (4); Dogs on Stamps Study Unit (ATA). 75 Maple Ave., Newark, N.J. 07112. Morris Raskin, ed.

**DURER JOURNAL** (4); Albrecht Durer Study Unit. Box 399, R.D. 1, Temple, Pa. 19560. The Rev. Jack A. Denys, ed.

**EFO COLLECTOR** (6); Errors, Freaks and Oddities Collectors Club. Box 1125, Falls Church, Va. 22041. John M. Hotchner, ed.

**1869 TIMES** (4); U.S. 1869 Pictorial Research Associates. c/o Rex Stever, First City Bank Tower, Box 167, Corpus Christi, Tex. 78477. Dr. Michael Rosove, ed.

**EISENHOWER PHILATELIST, The** (6); Dwight D. Eisenhower Philatelic and Historical Society. 927 S. Fort Thomas Ave., Fort Thomas, Ky. 41075. David M. Pritchard Jr., ed.

**ENTIRE TRUTH, The** (3); International Study Group of Aerogrammes. Classic Philatelics, Box 5637, Huntington Beach, Calif. 92646. Pat Feiner, ed.

**ESSAY-PROOF JOURNAL** (4); Essay-Proof Society. R.D. 4, Colonial Drive, Katonah, N.Y. 10536. Barbara R. Mueller, ed.

**ESTONIAN PHILATELIST, The** (1); Estonian Philatelic Society. 243 E. 34th St., New York, N.Y. 10016. Rudolf Hamar, ed.

**EUROPA NEWS** (6); Europa Study Unit. 1633 Florida Ave., Johnstown, Pa. 15902. Ruth E. Hellard, ed.

**EXPLORER** (6); International Association of Space Philatelists. Box 302, Yonkers, N.Y. 10710. William P. York, ed.

**EXPO INFO GUIDE** (4); EXPO Collectors and Historians Organization. 1436 Killarney Ave., Los Angeles, Calif. 90065. Edward J. Orth, ed.

**EX-SPAN-SION** (6); Society of Philatelists and Numismatists (philatelic-numismatic combinations). 1929 Millis St., Montebello, Calif. 90640. Ralph A. Holmes, ed.

**FAIR NEWS** (6); World's Fair Collectors Society. 148 Poplar St., Garden City, N.Y. 11530. Michael R. Pender, ed.

**FAP JOURNAL** (4); Fine Arts Philatelists. c/o Ursel E. Kissinger, Beckers Road, Box 399, Temple R.D. 1, Pa. 19560. David W. Christel, ed.

**FARO, El** (4); Associated Collectors of El Salvador. 4621 Meaford St., Lansing, Mich. 48917. Robert A. Fisher, ed.

**FINEST HOUR** (4); International Churchill Society. 134 N. Woodlawn, Lima, Ohio 45805. Richard M. Langworth, ed.

**FIRESIDE CHATS** (6); Franklin D. Roosevelt Philatelic Society. 154 Laguna Court, St. Augustine Shores, Fla. 32084. Gustav Detjen Jr., ed.

**FIRST DAYS** (8); American First Day Cover Society. Box 23, Elberon, N.J. 07740. Sol Koved, ed.

**FLAG CANCELLATIONS** (6); Flag Cancel Society. 7664 State Street Road, Watertown, N.Y. 13601. Bart Billings, ed.

**FLORIDA PHILATELIST** (6); Florida Federation of Stamp Clubs. 210 S. Woodlynne Ave., Tampa, Fla. 33609. Wade H. Beery, ed.

**FLYER, The** (6); Aviation Study Unit. 109 Matterson Ave., Syracuse, N.Y. 13219. Robert Anderson, ed.

**FRANCE AND COLONIES PHILATELIST** (4); France and Colonies Philatelic Society. 103 Spruce St., Bloomfield, N.J. 07003. Robert G. Stone, ed.

**FROM THE DRAGON'S DEN** (4); Ryukyu Philatelic Specialist Society. Box 15368, Plantation, Fla. 33318. Thomas J. Manning, ed.

**GERMAN POSTAL SPECIALIST** (12); Germany Philatelic Society. Box 2034, Westminster, Md. 21157. George A. Blizil, ed.

**GREAT BRITAIN CORRESPONDENCE CLUB NEWSLETTER** (4). Box 4586, Portland, Ore. 97208. Tom Current, ed.

**HAITI PHILATELY** (4); Haiti Philatelic Society. 119 Foote Road, South Glastonbury, Conn. 06073. Mrs. Henry Van Dyke, ed.

**HAWAII-RYUKYU PHILATELIC SPECIALIST SOCIETY BULLETIN** (1-2). 2550 Manoa Road, Honolulu, Hawaii 96822. Harold S.T. Yea, ed.

**HELLENIC PHILATELIC SOCIETY OF AMERICA BULLETIN** (5). 1 Wall St., 2-B, Fort Lee, N.J. 07024. Basil Stephenson, acting ed.

**HJMR NEWSLIST** (3-6); HJMR Co. Inc. Box 6638, Hollywood, Fla. 33021. Larry Resnick, ed.

**HOBBIES** (12); Lightner Publishing Co. 1006 S. Michigan Ave., Chicago, Ill. 60605. Frances L. Graham, ed.

**HOLOCAUST STUDY GROUP BULLETIN** (4). Box 322, Skokie, Ill. 60076. Dr. Justin Fordon, Michael Zolno, eds.

**HOLYLAND JUDAICA PHILATELIST** (6). Box 727, Redwood City, Calif. 94064. Edward G. Rosen, ed.

**ICE CAP NEWS** (6); American Society of Polar Philatelists. 4300 W. Dempster, Skokie, Ill. 60076. Bernard V. Coyne, ed.

**ILLINOIS POSTAL HISTORIAN** (4); Illinois Postal History Society. Box 60244, Chicago, Ill. 60660. Jack Hilbing, ed.

**INDIA POST** (4); India Study Circle for Philately. 16 The Downs, Tuscaloosa, Ala. 35401. Ron Mockford, ed.

**INDO-CHINA PHILATELIST** (6); Society of Indo-China Philatelists. Box 531, Chicago, Ill. 60690. Robert Moorefield, ed.

**INFORMER, The** (11); Society of Australasian Specialists/Oceania. Box 82643, San Diego, Calif. 92138. Dr. Frank Novak, ed.

**INSIDE COVERAGE** (6) (first day covers). 3602 N.W. 84th Ave., Coral Springs, Fla. 33065. Prof. Earl Planty, ed.

**IRAQ POSTAL HISTORY** (1); Iraq Philatelic Study Group. Box 29543, Dallas, Tex. 75229. N.A. Cohen, ed.

**ISRAEL PHILATELIST, The** (6); Society of Israel Philatelists. 31715 Vine St., Willowick, Ohio 44094. Dr. Oscar Stadtler, ed.

**JAPANESE PHILATELY** (6); International Society of Japanese Philately. Box 752, Quincy, Mass. 02269. Dr. Robert M. Spaulding Jr., ed.

**JAPOS BULLETIN** (4); Journalists, Authors and Poets on Stamps Study Group. 154 Laguna Court, St. Augustine Shores, Fla. 32084. Gustav Detjen Jr., ed.

**JOURNAL, The** (6); United Nations Philatelists Inc. 2017 Broadway, Blue Island, Ill. 60406. Duane Lammers, ed.

**JOURNAL OF FIRE SERVICE IN PHILATELY** (6); Fire Service in Philately. Box 3011, Rotonda West, Fla. 33947. Gustave Knoeckel, ed.

**JOURNAL OF THE ROSSICA SOCIETY OF RUSSIAN PHILATELY** (2). 7415 Venice St., Falls Church, Va. 22043. Dr. Kennedy Wilson, ed.

**JUDAICA PHILATELIC JOURNAL** (4); Judaica Historical Philatelic Society. 80 Bruce Ave., Yonkers, N.Y. 10705. Dr. Murray Frost, ed.

**KALEIDOSCOPE, The** (irregular); Bhutan Philatelic Society. 1425 W. Jessamine, No. 302, St. Paul, Minn. 55108. Brian Kuehl, ed.

**KIRIBATI REPORT, The** (4); Kiribati Philatelic Society. 3 Greenville Drive, Barrington, R.I. 02806. Steve Kyner, ed.

**KOREAN PHILATELY** (4); Korea Stamp Society. Box 1057, Grand Junction, Colo. 81502. John Strout, ed.

**LATIN POST** (4); Latin American Philatelic Society. 11327 Laverne Drive, Riverside, Calif. 92505. Piet Steen, ed.

**LATVIAN COLLECTOR** (3); Latvian Collector. Box 5403, San Mateo, Calif. 94402. M. Tirums, ed.

**LIBERIAN PHILATELIC SOCIETY NEWSLETTER** (6). 9027 S. Oakley Ave., Chicago, Ill. 60620. Henry Chlanda, ed.

**LINN'S STAMP NEWS** (52); Amos Press Inc. Box 29, Sidney, Ohio 45367. Edwin O. Neuce, ed.

**LIONS INTERNATIONAL PHILATELIST** (4); Lions International Stamp Club. 1430 Holston Drive, Bristol, Tenn. 37620. Woody Woodman, ed.

**LPSNY BULLETIN** (4); Lithuanian Philatelic Society of New York. 2647 Eddington St., Philadelphia, Pa. 19137. Walter E. Norton, ed.

**LUMINESCENT BULLETIN** (4); Luminescent Stamp Club. 3728 Merrimac Lane E, Hanover Park, Ill. 60103. Dale C. Dwyer, ed.

**LUNDY PHILATELIC QUARTERLY** (4); Lundy Collector's Club. 2021 Ridge Road, Homewood, Ill. 60430. Roger Cichora, ed.

**LUREN** (12); Southern California Chapter No. 17, Scandinavian Collectors Club. Box 57397, Los Angeles, Calif. 90057. Paul Nelson, ed.

**MACHINE CANCEL FORUM** (12). Box 98, Greenbelt, Md. 20770. John R. McGee, John Koontz, eds.

**MANEAPA** (4); Tuvalu Philatelic Society. Box 2760, Chicago, Ill. 60690. Michel Forand, ed.

**MASONIC PHILATELIST** (4); Masonic Stamp Club of New York. 22 E. 35th St., New York, N.Y. 10016. Dr. Irwin M. Yarry, ed.

**MAXIMAPHILY NEWSLETTER** (4); Maximum Card Study Unit. 9891 Huyck Road, Farmersville Station, N.Y. 14060. Merlin F. Teed, ed.

**MEKEEL'S WEEKLY STAMP NEWS** (52). Box 1660, Portland, Maine 04104. George F. Stilphen, ed.

**METER STAMP SOCIETY BULLETIN** (4). Box 1345, Jackson, N.J. 08527. Werner Simon, ed.

**MEXICANA** (4); Mexico-Elmhurst Philatelic Society International. Box 42165-S, Tucson, Ariz. 85733. Dean Carter, ed.

**MIASMA PHILATELIST** (4); Malaria Philatelists International. 426 W. Fremont, Elmhurst, Ill. 60126. J.W. Dellinger, ed.

**MINKUS STAMP AND COIN JOURNAL** (4). 116 W. 32nd St., New York, N.Y. 10001. Belmont Faries, ed.

**MITCHELL'S HAWAIIAN PHILATELIST** (6). Box 1387, Los Angeles, Calif. 90028. James T. Mitchell, ed.

**MONUMENTAL BULLETIN, The** (4); Monumental Postcard Club. c/o George Miller, Department of English, University of Delaware, Newark, Del. 19711. George Miller, ed.

**MOTOR PHILATELICS** (4); Automotive Study Unit. 37 W. Broad St., Columbus, Ohio 43215. R. Benz, ed.

**NATIONAL STAMP NEWS** (36). Drawer Y, Sullivan's Island, S.C. 29482. Marcia Byars-Warnock, ed.

**NETHERLANDS PHILATELY** (4); American Society for Netherlands Philately. 124 Country Club Drive, Covington, La. 70433. Paul E. van Reyen, ed.

**NEW MEXICO PHILATELIST** (6); New Mexico Philatelic Association. Box 130, Las Alamos, N.M. 87544. R.W. Davis, Joyce Franke, eds.

**NEWS BULLETIN** (4); Writers Unit No. 30 of the American Philatelic Society. Box 1164, Brooklyn, N.Y. 11202. Barbara R. Mueller, ed.

**NEWS OF HUNGARIAN PHILATELY** (6); Society for Hungarian Philately. Box 1162, Samp-Mortar Station, Fairfield, Conn. 06430. Al Bauer, ed.

**NIPPON PHILATELIC SOCIETY NEWSLETTER** (11). 1446 Mildine Drive, Glendale, Calif. 91208. Sune Johnson, ed.

**NUCLEUS, The** (4); Atomic/Nuclear Study Group. 600 Sharon Park Drive A-208, Menlo Park, Calif. 94025. Nancy Morrow, ed.

**OBLITERATOR, The** (4); Pictorial Cancellation Society. Box 306, Hancock, Md. 21750. Wesley Smith, ed.

**OHIO POSTAL HISTORY JOURNAL** (4); Ohio Postal History Society. 7130 Claybeck Drive, Dayton, Ohio 45424. Bart Billings, ed.

**OLCHESKI'S STAMP NEWSLETTER, Bill** (12); Olcheski Enterprises. Box 30, Falls Church, Va. 22046. Bill Olcheski, ed.

**OLD WORLD ARCHAEOLOGIST** (4); Old World Archaeological Study Unit. 913 Grey Ave., Evanston, Ill. 60202. David A. Detrich, ed.

**ONCE UPON A TIME** (6); Fairytale and Folklore Study Unit. 2509 Buffalo Drive, Arlington, Tex. 76013. Karen Cartier, ed.

**ONE HALF FATHOM** (11) (oceanographic philately). 4004 Bay to Bay Boulevard, Tampa, Fla. 33609. Irene Fager, ed.

**OXCART** (4); Society of Costa Rica Collectors. 1696 Georgetown Blvd., Sarasota, Fla. 33582. Dr. Harold T. Edwards, ed.

**PANTOGRAPH OF POSTAL STATIONERY** (6); United Postal Stationery Society. Box 48, Redlands, Calif. 92373. Jack L. Jenkins, ed.

**PERFINS BULLETIN, The** (10); Perfins Club. 10550 Western Ave., Space 94, Stanton, Calif. 90680. F.A. Walker, ed.

**PERMIT PATTER** (6); Mailer's Postmark Permit Club. Box 669, Littlerock, Calif. 93543. Helen McGinley, ed.

**PETRO-PHILATELIST** (4); Petroleum Philatelic Society. 5031 Sears Court, Columbus, Ga. 31907. John C. Slater, ed.

**PHAROS** (12); Lighthouse Study Unit. 3900 Dudley St., Lincoln, Neb. 68503. Philip H. Cole, ed.

**PHILAGEMS** (6); Gems, Minerals and Jewelry Study Unit. 254 Summit St., Plantsville, Conn. 06479. Peter I. Manning, ed.

**PHILAMATH** (4); Mathematical Study Unit. 7010 Nashville Drive, Lubbock, Tex. 79413. Joel and Linda Haack, eds.

**PHILAMATIC CENTER QUARTERLY** (4); Father Flanagan's Boys' Home. PhilaMatic Center, Boys Town, Neb. 68010. Leo J. Eckert, ed.

**PHILATELIA CHIMICA** (4); Chemistry on Stamps Study Unit. 960 Lakemont Drive, Pittsburgh, Pa. 15243. Robert E. Witkowski, ed.

**PHILATELI-GRAPHICS** (4); Graphics Philately Association. 776 Silver Cloud St., Thousand Oaks, Calif. 91360. Dulcie M. Apgar, ed.

**PHILATELIC FREEMASON** (6); Masonic Study Unit. 708 N. Mount Pleasant Ave., Lancaster, Ohio 43130. Walter J. Kirby, ed.

**PHILATELIC JOURNALIST** (6); Society of Philaticians. 154 Laguna Court, St. Augustine Shores, Fla. 32084. Gustav Detjen Jr., ed.

**PHILATELIC LITERATURE REVIEW** (4); American Philatelic Research Library. Box 338, State College, Pa. 16801. Charles J. Peterson, ed.

**PHILATELIC NUNCIO** (6); International Guild of Vatican Philatelists. Box 11096, Hartford, Conn. 06111. Joseph Lo Preiato, ed.

**PHILATELIC OBSERVER, The** (6); Junior Philatelists of America. Box 383, Boonville, N.Y. 13309. Victor Pawlak, ed.

**PHILATELION** (10); Lions Philatelic Unit. 314 Ryder Road, Manhasset, N.Y. 11030. Anton K. Dekom, ed.

**PITCAIRN LOG** (4); Pitcairn Islands Study Group. 2013 20th Place, Kenosha, Wis. 53140. Bernard Reilander, ed.

**PLATE BLOCK COLLECTOR, The** (9-10); Plate Block Collectors' Club. Box 4133, Princeton, Fla. 33032. Bill Roberts, ed.

**PLATE NUMBERS** (6); American Plate Number Single Society. 10926 Annette Ave., Tampa, Fla. 33612. Martin L. Wilson, ed.

**PMCC BULLETIN** (11); Post Mark Collectors Club. 4200 S.E. Indianola Road, Des Moines, Iowa 50320. Patti Blanchette, ed.

**PNC COLLECTORS JOURNAL** (12); 99 Co. 804 S. El Camino Real, San Clemente, Calif. 92672. Doris Walker, ed.

**POLISH POW STUDY GROUP NEWS-LETTER, The** (4-6). Box 464, Feasterville, Pa. 19047. Chris Kulpinski, ed.

**PO'OLEKA O HAWAII** (4); Hawaiian Philatelic Society. Box 10115, Honolulu, Hawaii 96816. Mrs. Virginia May Lewis, ed.

**POLONUS BULLETIN** (6); Polonus Philatelic Society. Box 1217, Oak Park, Ill. 60304. James Mazepa, publications chairman.

**PORTU-INFO** (4); International Society for Portuguese Philately. Box 1916, Philadelphia, Pa. 19105. Steve Washburne, ed.

**POSSESSIONS** (4); United States Possessions Philatelic Society. 217 Tyler Ave., Cuyahoga Falls, Ohio 44221. Gilbert N. Plass, ed.

**POSTAGE PAID** (4); Permit Imprint Collectors Society. 1924 Leslie Drive, Independence, Mo. 64055. Paul Wolfgeher, ed.

**POSTAL BELL, The** (6); Japanese American Society for Philately. Box 1049, El Cerito, Calif. 94530. William H. McConnell, ed.

**POSTAL HISTORY JOURNAL** (3); Postal History Society. Box 397, Brookhaven, Pa. 19015. James H. Baxter and Ernest M. Cohn, eds.

**POSTAL HISTORY U.S.A.** (4); Fourth Class Cancellation Club. 430 Ivy Ave., Crete, Neb. 68333. William F. Rapp, ed.

**POSTAL STATIONERY** (6); United Postal Stationery Society. Box 48, Redlands, Calif. 92373. Jack L. Jenkins, ed.

**POSTAL STATIONERY NOTES** ; Postal Stationery Study Group of the British North American Philatelic Society. Box 549, Pinawa, Man. R0E 1L0, Canada. Earle Covert and Robert Lemire, eds.

**POSTAL STATIONERY STUDY GROUP BULLETIN** (4); Germany Philatelic Society Postal Stationery Study Group. 5118 N. Drake Ave., Chicago, Ill. 60625. V.F. Matschinegg, ed.

**POSTCARD CLUB FEDERATION NEWSLETTER** (3). Box 1765, Manassas, Va. 22110. John H. McClintock, ed.

**POSTCARD HISTORY SOCIETY NEWSLETTER** (4). Box 3610, Baltimore, Md. 21214. Roy Cox. ed.

**POSTHORN, The** (4); Scandinavian Collectors Club. Box 276, Newtonville, Mass. 02160. Joe F. Frye, ed.

**PRECANCEL FORUM, The** (12); Precancel Stamp Society. Carillon House, Apt. 829, 2500 Wisconsin Ave. NW, Washington, D.C. 20007. Dilmond D. Postlewait, ed.

**PRECANCEL STAMP COLLECTOR, The** (12); National Association of Precancel Collectors. Box 121, Wildwood, N.J. 08260. Glenn W. Dye, ed.

**P.S. — A QUARTERLY JOURNAL OF POSTAL HISTORY** (4); aGatherin'. Box 175, Wynantskill, N.Y. 12198. Diane DeBois, ed.

**QUETZAL, El** (4); International Society of Guatemala Collectors. 17099 W. Bernardo Drive, No. 207, San Diego, Calif. 92127. Allan Wichelman, ed.

**RAPID NOTICE NEWS SERVICE** (12); Space Philatelists International Society. Box 171, West Nyack, N.Y. 10994. Martin J. Michaelson, ed.

**REPLY COUPON COLLECTOR** (2); International Society of Reply Coupon Collectors. Box 165, Somers, Wis. 53171. Dr. Allan Hauck, ed.

**REPORT TO MEMBERS** (12); International Philatelic Press Club. Box 114, Richmond Hill, N.Y. 11419. Ernest A. Kehr, ed.

**REVEALER** (4); Eire Philatelic Association. Box 2352, Denver, Colo. 80201. John J. Blessington, ed.

**ROMANIAN PHILATELIC STUDIES** (4); Romanian Philatelic Club. 84-47 Kendrick Place, Jamaica Estates, N.Y. 11432. George Pataki, ed.

**ROTARY ON STAMPS, Bulletin of** (5); Rotary on Stamps Fellowship. Box 2006, Tarleton University Station, Tex. 76402. William Eugene Atkinson, ed.

**ST. HELENA AND DEPENDENCIES PHILATELIC NEWSLETTER** (4); St. Helena and Dependencies Philatelic Society. Box 366, Calpella, Calif. 95418. Dr. Russell Skavaril, ed.

**SCALPEL AND TONGS** (12); Medical Subjects Unit. 15049 Cherokee Hills Drive, Salem, Va. 24153. Dr. Ranes C. Chakravorty, ed.

**SCOTT'S MONTHLY STAMP JOURNAL** (12); Scott Publishing Co. 3 E. 57th St., New York, N.Y. 10022. Ira Zweifach, ed.

**SEAPOSTER** (6); Maritime Postmark Society. Box 1244, La Jolla, Calif. 92038. Alfred J. Moses, ed.

**SIEGEL'S NEWSLETTER** (6); Siegel's Holyland Philatelics Ltd. 3777 Independence Ave., Bronx, N.Y. 10463. Marvin Siegel, ed.

**SIGNAL, The** (4); Stamps on Stamps Centenary Unit. Box 56, Palm Springs, Calif. 92263. Louis Guadagno, ed.

**SOSSI JOURNAL** (11); Scouts on Stamps Society International. 253 Sheldon, Downers Grove, Ill. 60515. William Cowen, ed.

**SOUVENIR CARD JOURNAL** (4); The Souvenir Card Collectors Society. Box 7116, Rochester, Minn. 55903. Curtis D. Radford, ed.

**SPA JOURNAL** (12); Society of Philatelic Americans. Box 9041, Wilmington, Del. 19809. Belmont Faries, ed.

**SPANISH-AMERICAN PHILATELIST** (6) (bilingual). 11 Blue Spruce Drive, Upper Saddle River, N.J. 07458. B.N. and R.J. Marlowe, eds.

**SPEC SHEET** (4-6); Building Series Study Group of the GPS. Box 10, 65 W. Jackson, Chicago, Ill. 60604. Phil Rose, ed.

**SPOKEN' WORD** (8); Bicycle on Stamps Study Unit. 817 Drexel Ave., Drexel Hill, Pa. 19026. Frank Havnoonian, ed.

**SPORTS PHILATELY, Journal of** (6); Sports Philatelists International. 55 Public Square, Suite 1410, Cleveland, Ohio 44113. John La Porta, ed.

**STAMP AUCTION NEWS** (12); Richards Publishing Co. Box 37198, Tucson, Ariz. 85740. Kay Klausmeier, ed.

**STAMP COLLECTOR** (52); Van Dahl Publications Inc. Box 10, Albany, Ore. 97321. Michael Green, ed.

**STAMP DEALER** (12); Hentzell Publications. Box 33467, San Diego, Calif. 92103. George Hentzell, ed.

**STAMP MARKET UPDATE** (4); Scott Publishing Co. 3 E. 57th St., New York, N.Y. 10022. Stephan Datz, ed.

**STAMP RESEARCH REPORT** (12). Box 34478, Bethesda, Md. 20817. David U. Groves, ed.

**STAMP SHOPPER** (12); Hentzell Publications. Box 33467, San Diego, Calif. 92103. George Hentzell, ed.

**STAMP SHOW NEWS AND PHILATELIC REVIEW** (12); West-Rock Show Associates. 1839 Palmer Ave., Larchmont, N.Y. 10538. Ina Grant, ed.

**STAMP TRADE INTERNATIONAL** (52); STI Inc. 1839 Palmer Ave., Larchmont, N.Y. 10538. Ina Grant, ed.

**STAMP WHOLESALER, The** (26); Van Dahl Publications Inc. Box 706, Albany, Ore. 97321. James A. Magruder, ed.

**STAMP WORLD** (12); Amos Press. Box 601, Sidney, Ohio 45367. Fred Boughner, ed.

**STAMPS** (52); H.L. Lindquist Publications. 153 Waverly Place, New York, N.Y. 10014. Jim Morton, ed.

**STAMPS, OLD LETTERS AND HISTORY** (6); Cheswick Historical Society. 208 Allegheny Ave., Cheswick, Pa. 15024. Steve Pavlina, ed.

**STATE REVENUE NEWSLETTER** (6); State Revenue Society. 425 Sylvania Ave., Avon-by-the-Sea, N.J. 07717.

**STRICTLY U S** (4); Voncorp. Dunedin, Fla. 33528. Donna von Stein, ed.

**TELL** (11); American Helvetia Philatelic Society. Box 57, Grafton, Mass. 01519. Keith Schall, ed.

**TEXAS PHILATELIST** (6); Texas Philatelic Association. 1421 Schulle Drive, San Marcos, Tex. 78666. William J. Murphy, ed.

**TEXAS POSTAL HISTORY SOCIETY JOURNAL** (4). Box 12814, Austin, Tex. 78711. Charles Deaton, ed.

**TEXTILE-RAMA** (4); Embroidery-Stitchery Unit. 1001 Genter St., Apt. 9H, La Jolla, Calif. 92037. Helen N. Cushman, ed.

**THAI PHILATELY** (4); Society for Thai Philately. Box 1118, Aiea, Hawaii 96701. Gary A. Van Cott, ed.

**THIRD REICH STUDY GROUP BULLETIN** (4); Third Reich Study Group of the GPS. 11 Yorktown Drive, Clark, N.J. 07066. R.J. Houston, ed.

**TIN CANNER** (6); Tin Can Mail Study Circle. R.R. 1 Box 370B, Pleasant Plain, Ohio 45162. Janet Klug, ed.

**TOPICAL TIME** (6); American Topical Association. 3306 N. 50th St., Milwaukee, Wis. 53216. Fred E. Foldvary, ed.

**TOPICAL WOMAN, The** (6); Women on Stamps. 905 Birch Ave., Peterborough, Ont. K9H 6G7, Canada. Davida Kristy, ed.

**TORCH, The** (4); National Association of Bicentennial $2 Cancellation Collectors, 2 Carvel, Annapolis, Md. 21401. Andrew Vero, ed.

**TRANSIT POSTMARK COLLECTOR** (6); Mobile Post Office Society. 5030 Aspen Drive, Omaha, Neb. 68157. Warren Kimball, ed.

**TRANS-MISSISSIPPIAN, The** (6); Trans-Mississippi Philatelic Society. Box 24, Allison, Iowa 50602. Robert J. Lambert, coordinating ed.

**TRUMPETER, The** (4); Croatian Philatelic Society. 1512 Lancelot Road, Borger, Tex. 79007. Charles D. Glavanic, ed.

**UKRAINIAN PHILATELIST** (2); Ukrainian Philatelic and Numismatic Society. Box C, Southfields, N.Y. 10975. Jerry G. Tkachuk, ed.

**USCS LOG** (12); Universal Ship Cancellation Society. 928 Towne Ave., Los Angeles, Calif. 90021. Stanton Honeyman, ed.

**U.S. CANCELLATION CLUB NEWS** (6). Box 286, Bonsall, Calif. 92003. Alyce Evans, ed.

**UNITED STATES SPECIALIST** (12); Bureau Issues Association. 7215 Thirteenth Ave., Takoma Park, Md. 20912. James H. Bruns, ed.

**UNIVERSAL COVER NEWS** (12); Universal Philatelic Cover Society. 1909 Nut Tree Drive NW, Salem, Ore. 97304. T.D. Pomeroy, ed.

**URUGUAY PHILATELIST, The** (4); Uruguay Collectors Club. Box 1214, Des Plaines, Ill. 60016. Herman Kerst, ed.

**VATICAN NOTES** (6); Vatican Philatelic Society. Box 500, Conway, N.H. 03818. William M. Wickert, ed.

**VORLAUFER** (6); German Colonies Collectors Group. 3313 Heritage Drive, Westminster, Wilmington, Del. 19808. Wilbur E. Davis, ed.

**WAR COVER CLUB BULLETIN** (4). Box 173, Jamesburg, N.J. 08831. Ray Merriam, ed.

**WATERCRAFT PHILATELY** (6); Ships on Stamps Unit. 714 Ridge Road, Moscow, Idaho 83843. William A. Coffey, ed.

**WAY MARKINGS** (4); Virginia Postal History Society. Box 29771, Richmond, Va. 23229. Stephen Jaronski, ed.

**WEATHERVANE, The** (6); Meteorology Study Unit of the ATA. 304 Melrose Drive, Thibodaux, La. 70301. Don Gary, ed.

**WESTERN EXPRESS** (4); Western Cover Society. 9877 Elmar Ave., Oakland, Calif. 94603. Everett Erle, ed.

**WINDMILL WHISPERS** (6); Windmill Study Unit. 3875 Arena Road, Atascadero, Calif. 93422. C. Jean Kilmer, ed.

**YULE LOG** (12); Christmas Philatelic Club. Box 77, Scottsbluff, Neb. 69361. Irene Chidester, ed.

**ZIP ME NEWS** (12); Zippy Collectors Club. 118 W. Sixth Ave., York, Pa. 17404. Sherwood D. Suereth Sr., ed.

## Great Britain

**AIR MAIL NEWS**; British Air Mail Society. 39 Jeymour Drive, Greenford, Middlesex UB6 8NS. A.G. Mathieson, ed.

**ANGLO-BOER WAR PHILATELIST** (4); Anglo-Boer War Philatelic Society. 28 Oxford St., Burnham-on-Sea, Somerset. R. & J. Holdeman, eds.

**APC BULLETIN** (12); Aero Philatelic Club of London. Alandale, Radcliffe Gardens, Carshalton Beeches, Surrey SM5 4PQ. Ewart Sanders, ed.

**AUSTRIA** (4); Austrian Stamp Club of Great Britain. 1 Chesterton Park, Cirencester, Glos. GL7 1XU. John F. Giblin, ed.

**BAPIP BULLETIN** (3); British Association of Palestine-Israel Philatelists. 21 High Meadows, Chigwell, Essex 1G7 5JY. N. Collins, ed.

**BATON, The** (3); Philatelic Music Circle. 22 Bouverie Gardens, Kenton, Middlesex HA3 0RQ. U.S. contact: C.J. Sabados, 528 Rimini Road, Del Mar, Calif. 92014. Mrs. Irene Lawford, ed.

**BELGAPOST** (2-3); Belgian Study Circle. 5 Sutherland Grove, London SW18 5PS. J. B. Horne, ed.

**BELGIAN CONGO STUDY CIRCLE BULLETIN** (4). 5 Ascham Lane, Whittlesford, Cambs. CB2 4NT. R.E. Jacquemin, ed.

**BRITISH DECIMAL STAMPS STUDY CIRCLE BULLETIN.** Rozel, Bepton Road, Midhurst, W. Sussex GU29 9RB. A.W. Walton, ed.

**BRITISH JOURNAL OF RUSSIAN PHILATELY** (2); British Society of Russian Philately. 27 Coxhill Gardens, River, Dover, Kent CT17 0PX. I.L.G. Baillie, ed.

**BRITISH PRIVATE POST STUDY GROUP NEWSLETTER** (4). 35 Smith St., London SW3 4EP. John Holman, ed.

**BRITISH SOCIETY OF AUSTRALIAN PHILATELY BULLETIN** (6). 5 Breakspeare, College Road, Dulwich, London. G.N. Durham, ed.

**BRITISH STAMP VALUES** (2); Link House Magazines. Link House, Dingwall Avenue, Croydon, Surrey CR9 2TA. Richard West, ed.

**BULLETIN** (4); British Postmark Society. 9 Gainsborough Ave., Marple Bridge, Stockport, Cheshire SK6 58W. B.P. Pask, ed.

**BULLETIN, The** (4); British West Indies Study Circle. 48 The Shrublands, Potters Bar, Enfield, Herts. EN6 2BW. M. Sheppard, ed.

**BULLETIN, The** (6); Security Endorsement and Perfin Society of Great Britain. 13 Moncrieffe Road, Sheffield S7 1HQ. Ron Bowman, ed.

**CAMEL POST** (4); Sudan Study Group. 27 Maidstone Drive, Martin, Middlesbrough, Cleveland TS7 8QW. H.L. Bowyer, ed.

**CAMEO** (2); British West Africa Study Circle. 10 Bushmead Ave., Bedford. J.J. Martin, ed.

**CEYLON STUDY CIRCLE BULLETIN.** 42 Lonsdale Road, Cannington, Bridgwater, Somerset. R.W.P. Frost, ed.

**CHINESE PHILATELY, Journal of** (6); China Philatelic Society of London. E. N. Lane, Kingsland, Westwell, Ashford, Kent TN25 4SW. P.I. Padget, ed.

**CINDERELLA PHILATELIST, The** (4); Cinderella Stamp Club. 35 Smith St., London SW3 4EP. L.N. Williams and Gordon Phillips, eds.

**CIVIL CENSORSHIP STUDY GROUP BULLETIN** (6). Rozel Cottage, Back Road, Dollar, Clacks. FK14 7EA. A.R. Torrance, ed.

**CONCORDE STUDY CIRCLE NEWSLETTER** (4); Alandale, Radcliffe Gardens, Carshalton Beeches, Surrey SM5 4PQ. Brian L. Asquith, ed.

**COOK'S LOG** (4); Captain Cook Study Unit of the ATA. D. Seymour, 38 Sherwood Road, Meols, Wirral, Merseyside L47 9RT. Ian Borcham, ed.

**CROWN AGENTS TRADE CIRCULAR** (24); Crown Agents Stamp Bureau. St. Nicholas House, St. Nicholas Road, Sutton, Surrey.

**ESPANA** (4); Spanish Study Circle. 16 Fairford Ave., Luton, Beds. LU2 7ER. A.E. Purver, ed.

**FIL-ITALIA** (4); Italy and Colonies Study Circle. 45 Junction Lane, Burscough, Near Ormskirk, Lancs. L40 55W. U.S. contact: Michael Pane, 307 N. Main St., Hightstown, N.J. 08520. Colin Pilkington, ed.

**FORCES POSTAL HISTORY SOCIETY NEWSLETTER** (4). 17 Wimbledon Park Court, London SW19 6NN. A.J. Brown, ed.

**GB JOURNAL** (6); Great Britain Philatelic Society. Anso Corner Farm, Hempstead, Saffron Walden, Essex CB10 2NU. Alan Huggins, ed.

**GEOSIX** (4); King George VI Collectors Society. Ashenhurst, Rectory Lane, Stevenage, Herts. SG1 4BX. Frank Huxley, ed.

**GERMANIA** (6); Germany and Colonies Philatelic Society. The Oaks, Hook Cross, Rotherwick, Basingstoke, Hants. RG27 9BZ. P.G. Husbands, ed.

**GIBBONS STAMP MONTHLY** (12); Stanley Gibbons Magazines Ltd. Drury House, Russell Street, London WC2B 5HD. Russell Bennett, ed.

**HELVETIA NEWSLETTER** (12); Helvetia Philatelic Society of Great Britain. 3 Cranford Gardens, Victoria Drive, Bognor Regis, W. Sussex PO21 2EL. Mrs. E.J. Rawnsley, ed.

**HONG KONG STUDY CIRCLE BULLETIN** (6). 47 Sandcliffe Road, Grantham, Lincs. NG31 8EW. C.C. Gower, ed.

**HOVER COVER** (2); Hovermail Collector's Club. 15 The Twitten, Southwick, Brighton BN4 4DB. C.J. Richards, ed.

**IO** (4); Indian Ocean Study Circle. The Vineyard, Garden Close Lane, Newbury, Berkshire RG14 6PR. Mrs. S. Hopson, ed.

**IRAN PHILATELIC STUDY CIRCLE BULLETIN** (3). 99 Moseley Wood Drive, Cookridge, Leeds LS16 7HO. Bernard Lucas, ed.

**IRISH PHILATELY** (4); Irish Philatelic Circle. 3 Cleves Way, Hampton, Middlesex TW12 2PL. Michael Richards, ed.

**KIKU SHIMBUN** (4); U.K. Chapter of the International Society for Japanese Philately. 23 Britannia Road, Norwich NR1 4HP. D.N. Kilner, ed.

**KIWI** (6); New Zealand Society of Great Britain. 26 Old Cross, Hertford, Herts. SC14 1RD. Allan P. Berry, ed.

**LES ISLES NORMANDES** (3); Channel Islands Specialists. 17 Westlands Ave., Huntercombe, Slough, Berks. SL1 6AG. O.W. Newport, ed.

**LIECHTENSTEIN STUDY CIRCLE BULLE-TIN.** 97 Downlands Ave., Worthing, W. Sussex. J. Beken, ed.

**LION, The** (4); Ethiopian Collectors' Club. 83 Penn Lea Road, Weston, Bath BA1 3RQ. N. Cape, ed.

**LOG BOOK, The** (12); Ship Stamp Society. 33a Ridgeway Road, Timperley, Altrincham, Cheshire WA15 7HA. R.N. Marriott, ed.

**LONDON PHILATELIST, The** (6); Royal Philatelic Society. 41 Devonshire Place, London W1N 1PE. Stuart Rossiter, ed.

**MAINSHEET** (4); Spanish Main Society (Latin America philately). 16 Lynwood Close, Gordon Road, London E18 1DP. John Fosbery, ed.

**MALTA NEWSLETTER** (3); Malta Study Circle. 69 Stonecross Road, Hatfield, Herts. AL10 0HP. R. E. Martin, ed.

**MAPLE LEAVES** (5); Canadian Philatelic Society of Great Britain. 66 E. Bawtry Road, Rotherham, S. Yorks. L.F. Gillam, ed.

**MASONIC PHILATELIC CLUB NEWS-LETTER** (4). 76 Merrivale Road, Beacon Park, Plymouth PL2 2RP. T.U. Fray, ed.

**MAYFLOWER, The** (4); American Stamp Club of Great Britain. 148 Bramhall Lane S, Bramhall, Stockport, Cheshire SK7 2ED. Ernest Malinow, ed.

**METHODIST PHILATELIC SOCIETY NEWSLETTER** (4). 59 Romway Road, Leicester LE5 5SD. U.S. contact: A.R. Ransom, 1303 Woodshole Road, Towson, Md. 21204. B. Thompson, ed.

**NETHERLANDS PHILATELIST, The** (3); Netherlands Philatelic Circle. 202a Old Bath Road, Cheltenham, Glos. GL53 9EQ. Richard Wheatley, ed.

**NIGER NEWS** (4); Nigerian Study Circle. 20 Estuary Park, Combwich, Bridgwater, Somerset. M.P. Nicholson, ed.

**NOTEBOOK** (5); London Postal History Group. 24 Dovercourt Road, Dulwich, London SE22 8ST. Peter A. Forrestier Smith, ed.

**ORANGE FREE STATE STUDY CIRCLE BULLETIN** (4). 28 Oxford St., Burnham-on-Sea, Somerset. L.H. Lomax, ed.

**OVERPRINTER, The** (4); Great Britain Overprints Society. 60 Church Lane, Eaton, Norwich NR4 6NY. Francis Kiddle, ed.

**PACIFICA** (4); Pacific Islands Study Circle of Great Britain. 62 Moat Drive, Harrow, Middlesex H41 4RX. D.H. Vernon, ed.

**PHILATELIC BULLETIN** (12); Philatelic Bureau. 20 Brandon St., Edinburgh EH3 5TT. John Memmott, ed.

**PHILATELIC EXPORTER, The** (12); Philatelic Exporter Ltd. (trade journal, not for collectors). Box 4, Edgware, Middlesex. Arthur D. Stansfield, ed.

**PHILATELIC MAGAZINE** (12); Stamp Collecting Ltd. 42 Maiden Lane, London WC2E 7LL. Douglas N. Muir, ed.

**PHILATELIST, AND PHILATELIC JOURNAL OF GREAT BRITAIN, The** (6); Robson Lowe Ltd. 39 Poole Hill, Bournemouth BH2 5PX. Peter Collins, ed.

**PHILIPPINE PHILATELIC SOCIETY JOURNAL** (4). 61 Elford Close, Ferrier Estate, Kidbrooke, London SE3 9YW. Peter Harradine, ed.

**POLAR POST** (4); Polar Post Historical Society of Great Britain. 12 Longlands Spinney, Charmandeau, Worthing, Sussex BN14 9NU. R.G. Garbutt, ed.

**POLISH PHILATELIC REVIEW;** Polish Philatelic Association of the United Kingdom. 40 Ansell Road, London SW17 7LS. P. Bol, ed.

**PORTUGUESE PHILATELIC SOCIETY BULLETIN** (4). 73 Grasmere Gardens, Harrow, Middlesex HA3 7PS. George R. Pearson, ed.

**POSTAL HISTORY** (4); Postal History Society. Lower Street Farmhouse, Hildenborough, Tonbridge, Kent TN11 8PT. J.D. Hayhurst, ed.

**POSTSCRIPT** (4); Society of Postal Historians. 25 Sinclair Grove, London NW11 9JH. V. Denis Vandervelde, ed.

**PRATIQUE** (4); Disinfected Mail Study Circle. 25 Sinclair Grove, London NW11 9JH. V. Denis Vandervelde, ed.

**PRECANCELS** (6); Precancel Stamp Society. 42 Westville Road, Thames, Ditton, Surrey KT7 0VJ. John G. Watson, ed.

**PRIVATE POST, The** (1); British Private Post Study Group of the Cinderella Stamp Club. 35 Smith St., London SW3 4EP. P. Thornton, ed.

**PTS JOURNAL** (6); Philatelic Traders Society. 27 John Adam St., London WC2N 6H2. Kenneth W. Anthony, ed.

**RAILWAY PHILATELY** (4); Railway Philatelic Group. 15 Mount Pleasant Lane, Brichet Wood, St. Albans, Herts. AL2 3UX. P. Johnson, ed.

**RHODESIAN STUDY CIRCLE JOURNAL** (4). 30 Wykeham Road, Netley Abbey, Southampton SO3 5ET. C.M. Hoffman, ed.

**SARAWAK JOURNAL** (4); Sarawak Specialists' Society. 11 Cherry Close, Linton, Cambridge CB1 6UE. Brian J. Cave, ed.

**SCANDINAVIAN CONTACT** (4); Scandinavia Philatelic Society. 71 Castelnau, Barnes, London SW13 9RT. P.S.S.F. Marsden, ed.

**SCOTTISH STAMP NEWS** (12); Alba Stamp Group. 27 Gilmour Road, Edinburgh EH16 5NS, Scotland. Stanley K. Hunter, ed.

**SCOUT STAMP COLLECTORS CLUB BULLETIN** (6). 16 Effingham House, Kingsnympton Park, Kingston Hill, Surrey KT2 7RU. P.J. Duck, ed.

**SLIPSTREAM** (12); Hovermail Collectors' Club. 15 The Twitten, Southwick, Brighton BN4 4DB. J.K. Pemberton, ed.

**SPRINGBOK, The** (6); South African Collectors Society. 138 Chastilian Road, Dartford, Kent DA1 3LG. C.P. Ravillidus, ed.

**STAMP AND POSTAL HISTORY NEWS**; Epic Publishing Ltd. and British Philatelic Federation. 1 Whitehall Place, London SW1A 2HE.

**STAMP COLLECTING** (52). 42 Maiden Lane, London WC2E 7LL. George Beal, ed.

**STAMP DIGEST** (12); Urch Harris and Co. Ltd. 7 Richmond Hill Ave., Clifton, Bristol BS8 1BQ. J. Weaver, ed.

**STAMP LOVER** (4); National Philatelic Society. 1 Whitehall Place, Room 4, London SW1A 2HE. Arthur Blair, ed.

**STAMP MAGAZINE** (12); Link House Magazines. Link House, Dingwall Avenue, Croydon CR9 2TA, Surrey. Richard West, ed.

**STAMPS** (12); Stamp Publications. Sovereign House, Brentwood, Essex CM14 4SE. Allan Daniell, ed.

**STAMPS OF HUNGARY** (4); Magyar Philatelic Society of Great Britain. Hill Cottage, Lewknor, Oxford OX9 5TS. R. Dawson, ed.

**SWISS PHILATELIST, The;** Amateur Collector Ltd. Box 242, Highgate, London N6 4LW. R.F. Bulstrode, ed.

**THAI TIMES** (3); Thailand Philatelic Society. 5 The Street, Brettenham, Ipswich 1P7 7QP, Suffolk. Peter Collins, ed.

**TPO** (4); TPO and Seapost Society. 9 Beech Park Ave., Northenden, Manchester M22 4BL. D.A. Bullough, ed.

**TRANSVAAL PHILATELIST** (4); Transvaal Study Circle. 36 Wakefield Gardens, London SE19 2NR. Maj. H.M. Criddle, ed.

**UPLAND GOOSE** (4); Falkland Islands Philatelic Study Group. The Mews, Sandle Manor, Fordingbridge, Hants. SP6 1NT. U.S. contact: D.C. Stanton, 8 Thomas St., Springvale, Maine 04083. Maj. R.N. Spafford, ed.

**VALIRA TORRENT** (2); Andorran Philatelic Study Circle. Ashville, Cliffe, Selby, N. Yorks, W.A. Jacques, ed.

**WATERMARK, The** (6); Clacton-on-Sea Philatelic Society, 337 St. John's Road, Clacton-on-Sea, Essex CO16 8DF. G. Parkes, ed.

## Africa, East

**PHILATELIC BULLETIN** (4); East Africa Posts and Telecommunications Stamp Bureau. Nairobi, Kenya.

## Africa, South

**OFS PHILATELIC MAGAZINE** (12); Orange Free State Philatelic Society. Box 43, Plumstead 7800. John W. Hodgson, ed.

**SOUTH AFRICAN PHILATELIST** (12); Philatelic Federation of Southern Africa. Box 375, Johannesburg 2000. J. Groenewald, ed.

## Argentina

**MUNDO FILATELICO** (6). Casilla de Correo 3241, Buenos Aires. Jose Antonio Brovelli, ed.

**POSTAS ARGENTINAS** (4). Sarmiento 151, 2 Piso Oficina 207/210, Buenos Aires.

**REVISTA DE LA SOCIEDAD FILATELICA ARGENTINA** (4). Box 1103, Buenos Aires. Dr. Ricardo U. Gardney, ed.

## Australia

**AUSTRALIAN STAMP BULLETIN** (6); Australia Post. Manager, Stamps and Philatelic Branch, Marketing Services Department, Australia Post, Box 302, Carlton South, Victoria 3053.

**AUSTRALIAN STAMP MONTHLY, The** (12); Ramsay Ware Stockland Pty. Ltd. Box 178, Carlton South 3053. J. Hawker, ed.

**COVERS** (2); Universal Cover Collectors Club. Box 133, Glenelg 5045. Errol J. Hehir, ed.

**PHILAS NEWS** (4); Philatelic Association of New South Wales. Box A495, Sydney South, NSW 2000. Richard C. Peck, ed.

**PHILATELY FROM AUSTRALIA** (4); Royal Philatelic Society of Victoria. Box 2071S, G.P.O., Melbourne, Victoria 3001. Dr. G. Kellow, ed.

**PPS STAMP NEWS** (4); Papuan Philatelic Society. 77 Parkhill St., Pearce, ACT 2607. U.S. contact: V.A. Rutherford, Box 3067, Buena Vista, Colo. 81211. M.T. Bulley, ed.

**SCOUT AND GUIDE STAMP SOCIETY OF AUSTRALIA, Journal of.** 37 Bogong Ave., Glen Waverley, Victoria 3150. Mrs. L. Westfield, ed.

**STAMP NEWS** (12); Review Publications Pty. Ltd. 1 Sterling St., Dubbo, NSW 2830. Bill Hornadge, ed.

**STAMP TALK** (4); Australian Philatelic Specialists Group. GPO Box 919, Adelaide 5001. B.I. Van Tenac, ed.

## Austria

**AUSTRIA-PHILATELIST** (4); Adolf Kosel KG. Box 55, A-1095 Vienna. Leopold Sander, ed.

**BRIEFMARKE, Die;** Verbandes Osterreichischer Philatelisten-Vereine. Getreidemarkt 1, 1060 Vienna.

**CHRISTKINDL NEWS** (2); Arbeitsgemeinschaft Christkindl. Postfach 34, A-4403 Steyr. Otto Taurer, ed.

**POSTRUNDSCHAU** (12); Austrian Post Office. Box 8, 1011 Vienna.

## Belgium

**BALASSE MAGAZINE** (6). 45-45a Rue du Midi, B-1000 Brussels. Willy Balasse, ed.

**ECHOPHIL** (6); Echo Philatelique ASBL. 223 Rue Royale Sainte-Marie, B-1030 Brussels. J. Lepingle, ed.

**L'ENTIER POSTAL.** 6 Ambiorix Square, B-1040 Brussels. Dr. J. Stibbe, ed.

**HISTOPHILA** (4); Histophila Thematic Group. 2 Promenade d'Orleans, B-4880 Spa. Gaspar Roger, ed.

**POSTZEGAL, De** (11); Vlaamse Bond van Postzegelverzamelaars. Werfenplein 6, B-8000 Brugge. J. Ysenbrandt, ed.

**REVUE DU TIMBRE, La** (12); Salm Phila Club. Les Grands Champs 21, B-6690 Vielsalm. Roland Leveque, ed.

## Bolivia

**POSTALES DE BOLIVIA** (4); Bolivian Philatelic Federation. Apartado Postal 8013, La Paz. Eugenio von Boeck, ed.

## Brazil

**BRASIL FILATELICO, Boletim do** (4); Philatelic Club of Brazil. Caixa Postal 195, 20000 Rio de Janeiro. Aureo G. Santos, ed.

**FILATELIA** (3); Philatelic Agency of United Nations for Brazil. Praca de Republica, 270-sbloja, 01045 Sao Paulo. Adalberto Marcus, ed.

## Bulgaria

**PHILATELEN PREGLED** (12); Union of Bulgarian Philatelists and Ministry of Information and Communication. Box 798, BG-1000 Sofia Z.

## Canada

**BURMA PEACOCK, The** (4); Burma Philatelic Study Circle. 1887 Hollywood Crescent, Victoria, B.C. V8S 1J2. Alan Meech, ed.

**CANADIAN PHILATELIST** (6); Royal Philatelic Society of Canada. Box 1054, Station A, Toronto, Ont. M5W 1G5. Peter Mann, ed.

**CANADIAN STAMP NEWS** (26); McLaren Publications Ltd. Box 11,000, Bracebridge, Ont. P0B IC0. Douglas Black, ed.

**CFPS BULLETIN, The** (4); Canadian Forces Philatelic Society. Box 2595, Ottawa, Ont. K1P 5W6. David Gronbeck-Jones, ed.

**KRAJEJS** (4); Latvian Philatelic Society. 60 Wakelin Terrace, St. Catharines, Ont. L2M 4K9. (Latvian language) J. Ronis, ed.

**NATURE'S WONDERS** (4); Earth's Physical Features Study Unit. 3919C Richmond Road, Nepean, Ont. K2H 8T9. Bryan Elliott, ed.

**PHILATELIC BULLETIN** (4); Canada Post Corporation. Philatelic Mail Order, Canada Post, Ottawa, Ont. K1A 0B5.

**POSTAL HISTORY SOCIETY OF CANADA JOURNAL** (4). Box 3461, Station C, Ottawa, Ont. K1Y 4J6. Dr. Robert C. Smith, ed.

## Chile

**CHILE FILATELICO** (4); Philatelic Society of Chile. Casilla 13245, Santiago. Richardo Boizard, ed.

## China, People's Republic of

**CHINA PHILATELY** (4); China National Stamp Corp. 27 Dong Chang An St., Peking. (English language.) Liang Hongguei, ed.

**JIYOU** (12); China National Stamp Corp. 27 Dong Chang An St., Peking. (Chinese.) Yu Xiaohui, ed.

## China, Republic of

**CHENG'S STAMP JOURNAL** (4). Box 1121, Taipei, Taiwan. Bilingual. Warren M.S. Yang, ed.

**CHINA PHILATELIC MAGAZINE;** China Philatelic Society. Box 33, Taipei, Taiwan. J. Prieto, ed.

**POSTAL SERVICE TODAY** (12); Directorate General of Posts. 71 Chinshan St., Taipei 106, Taiwan. T.Y. Lin, ed.

## Costa Rica

**COSTA RICA FILATELICA** (4); Philatelic Association of Costa Rica. Apartado 3441, San Jose. Ricardo Alvarez and William Reuben, eds.

**FILATELIA COSTARRICENSE;** Philatelic Club of San Jose. Apartado 2866, San Jose.

## Cuba

**CAMAGUEY FILATELICO** (4); Circulo Filatelico Ignacio Agramonte. Republica No. 372, Apartado Postal 204, Camaguey. Jose Ramos Palmier, ed.

## Cyprus

**CYPRUS PHILATELY** (6); Cyprus Philatelic Society. Box 1151, Nicosia. Dr. G.I. Michaelides, ed.

## Czechoslovakia

**FILATELIE** (24); Federation of Czechoslovak Philatelists. Celetna 26, 110 00 Prague. Vitezslav Houska, ed.

## Denmark

**DANSK FILATELISTISK TIDSSKRIFT** (8); Denmark Philatelic Union. Ulfeldtsvej 8, Stensballe, DK-8700 Horsens. Tom Plovst, ed.

**FRIMAERKESAMLEREN** (9); Frederiksberg Frimaerke Forening. 4 Birkemosevej, DK 2750, Ballerup. Andreas Abitz, ed.

**POPULAER FILATELI** (12); Aarhus Frimaerkehandel. Bruunsgade 42, DK-8000 Aarhus C. Inger Andersen, ed.

**POSTHISTORISK TIDSSKRIFT** (4); Posthistorisk Selskab. K.C. Vagnkjaer, Nyelandsvej 2, DK2000 Kobenhaven F. J. Chr. Rich, ed.

## Dominican Republic

**FILOTELICO, El** (6); Dominican Philatelic Society. Apartado 1930, Santo Domingo. Danilo A. Mueses, ed.

**REVISTA POSTAL DOMINICANA;** Director-General of Posts. Santo Domingo. Clemente A. Cruz Lopez, ed.

## Egypt

**ORIENT PHILATELIQUE;** Society Philatelique d'Egypte. 16 Rue abd el Khalek Saroit, B.P. 142 Kairo.

## Fiji

**STAMP GOSSIP** (10); Philatelic Society of Fiji. Box 351, Suva. Peter Rodda, ed.

## Finland

**ABOPHIL** (9). Varnankatu 3-F, SF 20310 Turku 31. Mikko Ossa, ed.

**PHILATELIA FENNICA** (9); Philatelic Federation of Finland. Tehtaankatu 21B43, SF 00150 Helsinki 15. Eino Arohanko, ed.

**POSTIMERKKI** (3-4); Lauri Peltonen. Juuvikinkatu 32, 10900 Hanko. Tom Peltonen, ed.

**SUOMEN POSTIMERKKI LEHTI** (8); Suomen Filatelist/Seura. Box 167, SF-00101 Helsinki 10. Pentti Anttila, ed.

## France

**AMICALE PHILATELIQUE FRANCE-ISRAEL** (10); 17 Avenue Suzanne-Buisson, 93140 Bondy. Dr. Jean Kohn, ed.

**BULLETIN DE LA CHAMBRE DES NEGOCIANTS ET EXPERTS EN PHILATELIE.** 5 Rue Drouot, Paris, 9.

**BULLETIN DE LA CHAMBRE SYNDICALE DES NEGOCIANTS ET EXPERTS EN TIMBRES-POSTE.** 6 Place de la Madeleine, Paris 8e.

**BULLETIN MENSUEL** (11); Yvert et Cie. 13 Rue Drouot, 75009 Paris. Theodore Champion, ed.

**DILIGENCE D'ALSACE** (2); Les Amis de l'Histoire des PTT d'Alsace. B.P. 153/R4, 67004 Strasbourg, Cedex.

**DOCUMENTS PHILATELIQUES** (4); Philatelic Academy. 7 Avenue Beaucour, 75008 Paris. Pierre de Lizeray, ed.

**L'ECHO DE LA TIMBROLOGIE** (11). 37 Rue des Jacobins, F-80036 Amiens, Cedex. Jacques Gervais, ed.

**FEUILLES MARCOPHILES, Les** (4); Union Marcophile. 19 Avenue de Chatelet, 77-330 Lesigny.

**MONDE DES PHILATELISTES, Le** (11). 11 bis, Bd. Haussmann, 75009 Paris. Jean-Toussaint Stofati, ed.

**PHILATELIE FRANCAISE, La** (10); Federation of French Philatelic Societies. 7 Rue Saint-Lazare, F-75009 Paris. Pierre Langlois, ed.

**PHILATELIE POPULAIRE** (10); International Philatelic Union. 33 Rue de la Grange-aux-Belles, 75483 Paris 10e.

**PHILATELISTE UNIVERSEL, Le** (6); Editions Dumenil. B.P. 12, 78103 Saint Germain en Lay Cedex. Thierry Wirth, ed.

**SIHP BULLETIN;** Societe International d'Histoire Postale. 46 Rue Victor Kenard, 59000 Lille N. Garcin, ed.

## Germany, East

**LUFTPOST-NACHRICHTEN.** Wilhelm Pieck Strasse 7/183, DDR-6902 Jena-Neulobeda. Dr. Karlheinz Herdt, ed.

**NEUE LIPSIA-RUNDSCHAU** (6); Philatelistenverband. Schonbachstr. 22b, DDR-7027 Leipzig. Horst Engelhardt, ed.

**SAMMLER EXPRESS** (12); Central Commission for Philately. Franzosische Strasse 13/14, DDR-1086 Berlin. Henri Hamann, ed.

## Germany, West

**ARCHIV FUR DEUTSCHE POSTGESCHICHTE** (2); Gesellschaft fur Deutsche Postgeschichte. Zentrale Geschaftsstelle, Postfach 70 04 20, D-6000 Frankfurt 70.

**BOREK-BERICHTE** (12); Richard Borek. Domplaz 4, 33 Braunschweig.

**BRIEFMARKEN POST** (12); Philapress Publications. Postfach 106, D-3400 Gottingen.

**BRIEFMARKEN SPIEGEL** (12); Philapress Publications. Postfach 206, D-3400 Gottingen.

**DBZ-DEUTSCHE ZEITUNG FUR BRIEFMARKEN KUNDE** (52); Werner Kuhn Publication. Postfach 309/310, D-5427 Bad Ems.

**EISENBAHNER-PHILATELIST, Der** (4);Mitteilungsblatt der BSG im Bundesbahn Sozialwerk. Heinrichstr. 72, D-6100 Darmstadt. Otto Ney, ed.

**GABRIEL** (12);Mitteilungsblatt der Sammlergilde St. Gabriel. Kreuzstrasse 10, D-3490 Bad Driburg. Norbert Thiele, ed.

**GANZSACHE, Die** (4); Berliner Ganzsachen-Sammler Verein. Zavelsteinstr. 54, D 7000 Stuttgart 30. Hanspeter Frech, ed.

**INTER PHILA COURIER** (6). Box 700118, D-7000 Stuttgart 70. Eberhard Colle, ed.

**ISCA STAMP CENTENARIES BULLETIN** (4); International Stamp Centenary Association. Im Muhlenfelde 1, D-1000 Berlin 37. Alfred Gerth, ed.

**JAPAN-BERICHTE** (4); Arbeitsgemeinschaft Japan im Bund Deutscher Philatelisten. c/o Leo Stehr, Goethestr. 36, D-5040 Bruhl. Heinz Warmuth, ed.

**LUFTPOST, Die.** Fuggerstr. 38, D-1000 Berlin 30. Kurt Dahmann, ed.

**LITERATUR-NACHRICHTEN** (1); Bund Deutscher Philatelisten Bundesstelle Literatur. Gronaurer Str. 30, D-5000 Koln 80. Robert Hohn, ed.

**MERCVRIVS** (4); Post and Telecommunications Topical Group. Am Osterberg 19, D-3122 Hankensbuttel 1. Fritz E. Baeker, ed.

**MICHEL-RUNDSCHAU** (12); Schwaneberger Verlag. Muthmannstrasse 4, 8000 Munich 45.

**NACHRICHTENBLATT DES BRIEFMARKENHANDELS** (12); APHV. Geibelstrasse 4, D-5000 Koln 41.

**PHILATELIE** (6); Bund Deutscher Philatelisten. Mainzer Landstrasse 221-223, D-6000 Frankfurt am Main 1. Wolf J. Pelikan, ed.

**POLAR-PHILATELIST, Der** (6). Waldemeinestr. 81, D-4902 Bad Salzufleni. Klaus Pumpenmeier, ed.

**SAMMLERDIENST** (26); Verlag Reimar Hobbing GmbH. Box 683, D-8630 Coburg. Gertrud Raum, ed.

## Greece

**PHILATELIC BULLETIN, The** (12); N. Domninos. 20 Pyrras Str., Athens 405. Greek with few pages in English.

**PHILATELIC ECHO** (6); Philatelic Society of Piraeus. Tsamadou Str. 7, Piraeus. Greek, English and French. Elie G. Chronis, ed.

**PHILOTELIA** (6); Hellenic Philatelic Society. 57 Rue Akadimias, Athens. Greek, English and French.

**PHILOTELIKI LESVOS** (12); Philatelic Society of Lesvos. Sapfus Str. 8, Mytilini, Lesvos.

## Hungary

**FILATELIAI SZEMLE** (12); Mabeosz, National Federation of Hungarian Philatelists. Budapest Pf. 4, H-1387. Mihaly Filyo, ed.

## Iceland

**GRUSK** (4); Felag Frimerkjasafnara. Randalaek 21, 105 Reykjavik.

## India

**HYDERABAD PHILATELIST;** Indo-American Philatelic Society of Hyderabad. O.U. 7/12 Jamai Osmania, Hyderabad 7, AP. Dr. S.M. Hyder Raza Zaidi, ed.

**IND DAK** (12). 190 Defence Colony, Indiranagar, Bangalore 530 038. L.G. Shenoi, ed.

**INDIAN PHILATELIST** (4); Indian Posts and Telegraphs Department. Philatelic Section, Director General, New Delhi 110001.

**INDIA'S STAMP JOURNAL** (12); Empire of India Philatelic Society. Standard Building, Dr. Dadabhoy Naoroji Road, Bombay 400001. P.M. Medhora, ed.

**LANDMARK** (12); Indo-American Society. Kitab Mahal, 5 Raveline St., Bombay 400 001. N. Krishnan, ed.

**STAMP DIGEST** (12); Stamp Digest Publications. P-70, CIT-VIM, Calcutta 700 054. Bibhash Gupta, ed.

**STAMP TIMES** (12); Vithagan Institute of Philately. Ayanavaram, Madras 600023.

**STAMPS AND STAMPS** (4); Rourkela Philatelic Club. B/156/20, Rourkela 769005. Sahadeva Sahoo, ed.

**U-PHIL TIMES** (6); United Philatelists. 3-A/149 Azad Nagar, Kanpur 208 002. B.J. Kumar, ed.

## Indonesia

**MAJALAH PHILATELI INDONESIA.** Jalan Sindanglaya 6, Jakarta-Pusat.

## Ireland

**IRISH STAMP NEWS** (4). 3 Fitzwilliam Place, Dublin 2. Ian Whyte, ed.

## Israel

**EXPRESS INTERNATIONAL** (4). Central Post Office Box 2334, Il-Acre 24 122. M. Silbermann, ed.

**ISRAELI PHILATELIC MONTHLY** (12). Box 21224, Tel Aviv. Arie Lindenbaum, ed.

## Italy

**BOLLETTINO PREFILATELICO.** Via dell Arlo 31, 35100 Padova. Corrier Maggiore, ed.

**COLLEZIONISTA, Il** (12); S.C.O.T. srl. Via Cavour 17 F, 10123 Torino.

**CRONACA FILATELICA** (11); Eder s.n.c. Casella Postale 1065, 80100 Napoli-Vomero. Carlo Alberto de Rosa, ed.

**F & N** (4); United National Association for Philatelists and Numismatists. Corso Vittorio Emanuele 73, I-10128, Torino. Carlo S. Cerutti, ed.

**FILATELIA** (12) Sott Corso Garibaldi, 35100 Padova. Also Avsilio, ed.

**FILATELICO, Il.** Casella Postale 176, 95100 Catania. Cateno Nisi, ed.

**FRANCOBOLLI** (12); Sassone Editrice. Piazza Sturzo 9, 00144 Rome.

**ITALIANA** (12). Piazza Italia 5, I-20093 Cologno Monzese. Rolando Gianni, ed.

**NUOVO CORRIERE FILATELICO, Il** (6); Society for the Study of Philately and Postal History. Via Martelli 8, 50129 Firenze.

**SETACCIO, IL** (4). G.Gamba, Boezio 92, 00192 Roma. Fulvio Roccatano, ed.

**TRIBUNA DEL COLLEZIONISTA, La** (11). Via San Nilo 4, 04024 Gaeta. Tommaso Valente, ed.

**VITA VALORE COLLEZIONISMO.** Via Boiardo 27, 20127 Milano. Cesco Giannetto, ed.

## Japan

**KITTE KENKYU** (6); Institute of Philately. Kitte Kenkyu Kai, Box 35, Omori P.O., Tokyo. Masahisa Makino, ed.

**PHILATELIST, The** (12); Japan Philatelic Society. Box 1 Shinjuku, Tokyo 160-91. Meiso Mizuhara, ed.

**PHILATELY IN JAPAN** (4); Japan Philatelic Society. Box 1, Shinjuku, Tokyo 160-91. English Language. Meiso Mizuhara, ed.

**YUSHU** (12); Japan Philatelic Society. Box 1, Shinjuku, Tokyo 160-91. Meiso Mizuhara, ed.

## Korea

**KOREAN STAMP REVIEW** (English, 4) and **KOREAN STAMPS** (Korean, 12); Korean Philatelic Center. CPO Box 495, Seoul.

## Malawi

**CLEFT-STICK**; Philatelic Society of Malawi. Box 1443, Blantyre. B.J. Bowden, ed.

## Malaysia

**MALAYSIAN PHILATELIST, The** (6); Philatelic Society of Malaysia. Box 588, Kuala Lumpur 01-02, Selangor. C. Nagarajah, ed.

## Malta

**PHILATELIC SOCIETY OF MALTA MAGAZINE** (3); The Philatelic Society. 1 Scots St., Valletta. Nick A. Cutajar, ed.

## Mexico

**HANDBOOK OF MEXICAN PHILATELY** (8); La Gaceta Filatelica. Apartado Postal 620, Naucalpan. Roberto Liera and Isaac Backal, eds.

**REVISTA FMF** (4); Mexican Philatelic Federation. Apartado Postal 12, Mexico 1, D.F. Jose Turu Carol, ed.

## Nepal

**PHILATELY** (2); Nepal Philatelic Society. GPO Box 342, Kathmandu. Surendra Lal Shrestha, Jal Krishna Shrestha and Madan Bahadur Shrestha, editorial board.

## Netherlands

**BALLOONPOST BULLETIN** (3); International Society of Balloonpost Specialists. Statenlaan 2A, The Hague. Dr. Jan Boesman, ed.

**BEELDFILATELIST** (5); Nederlandse Vereniging voor de Thematische Filatelie. Langswater 908, 1069 EH Amsterdam. Drews Veenstra, ed.

**MIJN STOKPAARDJE** (My Hobby, 11); B.V. Uitgeverij de Postiljon. P. Nieuwlandstr. 19, 3514 HB Utrecht.

**NOORDERLICHT, HET** (4); NFV Skandinavie. Weesperzijde 91, Amsterdam. J. Dekker, ed.

**PHILATELIE** (4). Bronsteeweg 86, Heemstede. A. Boerma, ed.

**POSTZAK, DE** (4); Nederlandse Vereniging van Poststukken Postempel Verzamelaars (Netherlands Society for Postal Stationery). Beetslaan 134, Rijswijk ZH. J. Giphart, ed.

**POSTZEGEL REVUE** (12); Omni-Trading b.v. Canadalaan 8a, NL-7316 BX Apeldoorn.Victor Hafkamp, ed.

## New Zealand

**CAPTAIN COQK** (11); Christchurch Philatelic Society. Box 29, Christchurch. W.R. Stagg, ed.

**MAIL COACH, The** (12); Postal History Society of New Zealand. Box 275, Masterton 5900. R.M. Startup, ed.

**NEW ZEALAND STAMP COLLECTOR** (4); Royal Philatelic Society of New Zealand. Box 1269, Wellington. J.W. Brodie, A.R. Burge and B.G. Vincent, eds.

**PHILATELIC BULLETIN** (2); New Zealand Post Office. Marketing Manager, Marketing Branch, Waterloo Quay, Wellington.

## Nicaragua

**REVISTA FILATELICA** (4); Philatelic Society of Nicaragua. 512 Bolivar Ave., Managua. Ernesto Kelley, ed.

## Norway

**NORSK FILATELISTISK TIDSSKRIFT** (10); Federation of Norwegian Philatelists. Box 875, Sentrum, Oslo 1. Erling Sjong, ed.

## Pakistan

**PAKISTAN STAMP JOURNAL** (4); Pakistan Philatelic Association. Box 1182, Lahore. Dr. Ijaz Aslam Qureshi, ed.

## Papua New Guinea

**PNG PHILATELIC NEWS** (4); Papua and New Guinea Philatelic Bureau. Box 160, Port Moresby, Papua.

## Peru

**FILATELIA PERUANA** (2); Philatelic Association of Peru. Paseo de la Republica 6090, Miraflores, Casilla 5644, Lima 100. Pedro Castre Andrade, ed.

## Philippines

**AFF JOURNAL** (4); Philatelic Association of the Philippines. Box 2405, Manila. Fabian Carmona Jr., ed.

**PHILIPPINE PHILATELIC SOCIETY NEWS** (6); International Philippine Philatelic Society. Box 437, Manila. Linda Stanfield, ed.

## Portugal

**BOLETIM DO CLUB FILATELICO DE PORTUGAL** (6). Av. Almirante Reis, 70-5° dto., 1100 Lisboa. Dr. Eurico Lage Cardoso, ed.

FRANQUIA (12); Revista Filatelica Portuguesa. Praca Artur Portela, 2-5° dto., Lisboa. Daniel Cordeiro Costa, ed.

NOTICIAS FILATELICO (12); Publica cao Meusal. Rua da Figueira da Foz 126, 3 Coimbra.

SELOS Y MOEDAS (4); Clube dos Galitos. Box 306, 3806 Aveiro Codex. Vitor Santos Falcao, ed.

## Romania

FILATELIA (12); Association of Romania Philatelists. Ilexim, Box 136-137, Bucharest. Dr. Nicolae Tripcovici, ed.

## Singapore

KRETA AYER JOURNAL; Kreta Ayer. Block 4, 115-B Sags Lane, Singapore 0105. Chia Wee Min, ed.

## Solomon Islands

NEWSLETTER (6); Solomon Islands Philatelic Bureau Ltd. G.P.O., Mendana Avenue, Honiara. Reg Taylor, ed.

## Spain

ECO FILATELICO Y NUMISMATICO, El (24). Arrieta 29, Apartado 108, Pamplona. M. Torrea, ed.

FESOFI REVISTA (6); Federation of Spanish Philatelic Societies. San Vincente 16-2, Valencia 2. Gabriel Izquierdo Gimenez, ed.

MADRID FILATELICO (12). Puerta del Sol 4, Madrid 14. Rafaela Reol de Galvez, ed.

VALENCIA FILATELICA (4); Apartado de Correo 912, Valencia 9. Jose M. Gomis Segul, ed.

## Sri Lanka

PHILATELIC SOCIETY OF SRI LANKA NEWSLETTER (4). 32 Castle Lane, Bambalapitiya, Colombo 4. Frederick Medis, ed.

## Sweden

ATALAYA (2). Local postage stamps and cinderellas, in English. Kungsgatan 23, S-302 45 Halmstad. Christer Brunstrom, ed.

NORDISK FILATELI (10); Nordisk Filateli A.B. Box 5303, 102 46 Stockholm. Sven Olof Forselius, ed.

## Switzerland

BERNER BRIEFMARKEN ZEITUNG (12); Zumstein and Co. Box 2585, CH-3001 Berne. Gaudenz Muller, ed.

BULLETIN DE LA SOCIETE PHILATELIQUE DE NEUCHATEL (12). CH-2054, Chezard. Paul Ducommun, ed.

ISRAEL-PHILATELIST, Der (4); Schweizer Verein der Israel-Philatelisten. Silbergasse 32, CH-2503 Biel. Walter Mani, ed.

PHILATELICA (11); Verlag Groth AG. Box 25, CH-6314 Unteraegeri. Hans Groth, ed.

PTT-Zeitschrift (12); Generaldirektion PTT. Viktoria-strasse 21, 3000 Berne 33.

SCHWEIZER BRIEFMARKENZEITUNG (11); Verband Schweizer Philatelisten Vereine. Buri Druck AG, Eigerstr. 71, 3001 Berne. Dr. Alfred Guggisberg, ed.

UNION POSTALE (6); Universal Postal Union. International Bureau, Case Postale, 3000 Berne 15. In seven languages.

## Trinidad

TRINIDAD PHILATELIC SOCIETY BULLETIN (6). 78 London St., San Fernando. G.B. Thompson, ed.

## Union of Soviet Socialist Republics

PHLATELIYN SSSR (12). Davidovski 6, 107140 Moscow B-140.

## Uruguay

URUGUAY FILATELICO (4); Philatelic and Numismatic Clubs of Uruguay. 11 Correo Central, Montevideo. Enrique Sandleris, ed.

## Venezuela

REVISTA DEL CLUB FILATELICO DE CARACAS (4); Philatelic Club of Caracas. Apartado 61197, Caracas 106. E. Martin Guerra, ed.

## Yugoslavia

FILATELIJA (2); Yugoslavia Stamp Journal, Croatian Philatelic Union. Habdeliceva ul. 2, 41000 Zagreb. Velimer Ercegovic, ed.

FILATELISTA (6); Savez Filatelista Srbide. P. fah 702, Sremska 6, 11000 Beograd. Jovan Reljin, ed.

# Literature 18

## Philatelic Books and Monographs

In any field of philatelic endeavor, knowledge of the work that has gone before is of extreme importance. The thoughts of others can aid in the identification of material, open new avenues of research, and bring distant collections and archives to one's own area.

Obviously, the optimal way to obtain this assistance is by direct, detailed communication with fellow researchers. Unfortunately, barriers of distance and time frequently make this impossible.

This chapter is designed to introduce the vast field of published philatelic literature. For almost every area of philately there is literature putting forth some of the work recorded by researchers.

Our list has been compiled from various sources, including the listings of two firms specializing in philatelic literature: HJMR, Box 6638, Hollywood, Fla. 33021, and Roger Koerber, 605 Northland Towers West, Southfield, Mich. 48075.

In addition, assistance in specific country sections has been given by the following: Dr. Arthur Askins, Ryukyu Philatelic Specialist Society; American Topical Association; Victor Berecz, Society for Hungarian Philately; Norman Epstein, Rossica, Society of Russian Philately; Phillips B. Freer, Mexico-Elmhurst Philatelic Society International;

Maurice Friend, Hellenic Philatelic Society of America; Felix Ganz, American Helvetia Philatelic Society; Mrs. T.R. Hughes, Pitcairn Islands Study Group; F.C.J. Ridder, China Stamp Society; Edward J. Sabol, Society for Czechoslovak Philately; Robert G. Stone, France and Colonies Philatelic Society; Yoram Szekely;

E.A. Williams, Society of Australian Specialists/Oceania; Paul E. van Reyen, American Society for Netherlands Philately; Dr. Robert M. Spaulding, International Society for Japanese Philately; Ben Cohen, United Nations Philatelists; Aerophilatelic Federation of the Americas; St. Helena Study Group;

D.B. Griffin, India Study Circle; Carlos Romo, Andorran Philatelic Study Circle; J.W. Sauber,

Society of Costa Rica Collectors; Gary van Cott, Society for Thai Philately; Preston A. Pope, Eire Philatelic Association; and Francis E. Welch, Vatican Philatelic Society.

In addition to numerous philatelic literature dealers in the United States and overseas, books can be obtained through philatelic literature sections in auctions.

As many of the books listed here are out of print, it is suggested collectors also consider borrowing a desired book from the various philatelic libraries, such as the American Philatelic Research Library, Collectors Club of New York library, Western Philatelic Library, etc. Information on libraries can be found in Chapter 13.

Specialist societies are also good sources of information on how to obtain specific books in their fields of interest. Address information on specialty societies appears in Chapter 14.

Linn's Almanac editors will be glad to learn of additional books and monographs not covered in this listing.

### United States

### — A —

**Adams, Harrington** — Comparative Values of Ghost Towns. Seventh edition checked to June 15, 1967.

**Alexander, Thomas** — Simpson's U.S. Postal Markings, 1851-1861. 1980, 448 pages.

**American Philatelic Society** — The Chatham Square Post Office and Swarts' City Dispatch Post. APS handbook, 1941, 34 pages.

**American Air Mail Catalogue** — American Air Mail Society, Volume one, 474 pages; Volume two, 509 pages; Volume three, 1979, 509 pages.

**Antrim, E.** — Civil War Prisons and Their Covers. Collectors Club, 1961, 215 pages.

**Arkansas Precancel** — Arkansas Precancel Notes 1943-1944. Volume 1, No. 1-12.

**Armstrong, Martin** — Washington-Franklins, 1908-1921. 1979, second edition, 224 pages.

Definitive Series, 1922-38. 1977, 120 pages.

**Armstrong, Max** — United States Coil Issues, 1906-1938. 1977, 120 pages.

**Ashbrook, Stanley B.** — Postal Legislation of the C.S.A. 1861-65. 1946, 54 pages.

Special Service. Postal history data. Two volumes.

The U.S. Issue of 1869 and Notes on "The Premieres Gravures of 1861." 1943, 77 pages.

The U.S. One Cent Stamp of 1851-1857. Two volumes, 1938, 338 and 384 pages.

U.S. Ten Cent Stamp of 1855-1857. 1936, 87 pages.

Types and Plates of U.S. One Cent 1851-1857. 1926, 93 pages.

**Atherton, Frank C.** — Hawaiian Stamp List. 1937, 24 pages.

**Atkins, A.T.** — Postmarked Kentucky (1792-1900). 1975, J-B Publishing Co., 163 pages.

## — B —

**Baker, J.D.** — Postal History of Indiana. Two volumes, 1976. 1,061 pages.

**Balough, Joseph J. and Dorothy** — Catalog of U.S. Perfins. 1979, Perfins Club.

**Barker, E.N.** — Early Colorado Mails. 20 pages.

**Barkhausen, L.H.** — U.S. Postal Stationery Recut 2 Cent U.S. Envelope Dies. 59 pages.

The Recut 2 Cent U.S. Envelope Dies of the Series 1904. 59 pages.

**Barrett, L.G.** — Retouched 2 Cent Envelope Dies of 1903. 1911, 22 pages.

U.S. 3¢ Violet War and Victory. 14 pages.

**Barrett, Oliver R.** — Lincoln Collection. 1952, 264 pages.

**Bartels, J.M.** — Catalogue of U.S. Stamped Envelopes and Wrappers of U.S. and Possessions. Fifth edition. Published by Prescott Holden Thorp, 1943. Two volumes.

Checklist of Canal Zone Stamps. Second edition, 1908, 22 pages.

Envelopes of U.S. Fifth edition, 1936, 38 pages.

Nesbitt Envelopes (1853-1869). First edition, 1929, 29 pages.

Stamped Envelopes 1853-1899. Second complete catalog and reference list. 1899, 40 pages.

**Bartels and Berthold** — Rare United States Envelopes. 1908, 16 pages.

**Bartlett, J.D.** — Handbook and Check List of U.S. State Revenue Stamps. 32 pages.

**Bauer, Osment and Willard** — Colorado Postal History. 1971 J-B Publishing Co., 248 pages.

**Baughman, R.W.** — Kansas Post Offices. 1961, 256 pages; 1977 second printing, 264 pages.

**Beaumont, Howard B.** — Printed Cancellations, 1862-1883. 1972, American Revenue Society, 40 pages.

**Bernstein, H.** — The Ledger of Doctor Benjamin Franklin. Reprint 1976, 126 pages.

**Berthold, V.M.** — Bartels' Catalogue United States Stamped Envelopes. Fourth edition, revised. 1911, 195 pages.

Die Varieties of the Nesbitt Series. 1906, 106 pages.

Wells, Fargo and Company's Handstamps and Franks. 1978 reprint of 1926 work, 85 pages.

**Besom, Dale** — Official Printed Dated Control Precancel Catalog. 1981, fifth edition, 164 pages.

**Bidwell, R.W.** — Series of 1941 Wine Revenue Stamps. 1965, 44 pages.

**Billig, Fritz** — U.S. Naval Postmarks. Handbook. Volume 12, Part 1, 192 pages.

**Birch, J.A.** — Postal History of the U.S. Virgin Islands. 1966, 40 pages.

**Blake, Maurice C., and Davis, Wilbur W.** — Postal Markings of Boston, Massachusetts to 1890. Original edition, 1949, 367 pages; 1973 reprint, 392 pages.

**Blanchard, J.** — Durand Engraving Companies. 1951, 20 pages.

Engravers of Portraits on First U.S. Stamps. 10 pages.

**Bloomgarden, Henry S.** — American History Through Commemorative Stamps. 1969, Arco Publishing Co., 141 pages.

**Bloss, R.S.** — Pony Express, The Great Gamble. 1959, 159 pages.

**Boggs, W.S.** — Early American Perforating Machines and Perforations 1857-67. 1954, 33 pages.

Robert Morris, Postmaster of New York. 1960, 206 pages.

"U.S.P.S." Notes on U.S. Watermarked Postage Stamps. 1958, 13 pages.

Notes on the Bluish Paper Stamps of 1909. 1960, 11 pages.

Ten Decades Ago 1840-1850. American Philatelic Society, 1949, 100 pages.

**Boggs, W.S., and Nathan, M.C.** — The Pony Express. 1962, 112 pages.

**Bounds, Harvey C.** — Postal History of Delaware. 1938, 111 pages.

**Bowyer, Mathew J.** — They Carried the Mail. 1972, Robert B. Luce Inc., 223 pages.

**Bradbury and Hallock** — A Chronology of Florida Post Offices. 1962, 91 pages.

**Bradley, James** — The Confederate Mail Carrier or From Missouri to Arkansas. 1894, 275 pages, Mexico, Mo.

**Brannon, P.A.** — Organization of the Confederate Post Office Department at Montgomery. 1960, 164 pages.

**Brazer, Clarence** — Essays for U.S. Adhesive Postage Stamps. 1977 reprint (1941 edition), Quarterman Publications, 320 pages.

Historical Catalog U.S. Essays and Proofs. Trans-Mississippi issue 1898. 48 pages.

Historical Catalog U.S. Stamp Essays and Proofs. The 1847 issue. 32 pages.

Varieties of U.S. Essays and Proofs. 6 pages.

Price List No. 21 of United States Essays and Proofs. Jan. 2, 1956.

**Brenner, C.D.** — Postmarks of Railway Post Offices and Route Agents in California. 1973, 15 pages.

**Brett, G.W.** — The Giori Press. 1961, 109 pages.

**Broderick and Mayo** — Civil Censorship in the United States During World War II. 1980, Civil Censorship Study Group, 110 pages.

**Brookman, Lester G.** — Bank Note Issues of 1870-93. 1941, 98 pages.

1847 Issue of U.S. Stamps. APS handbook series, 1942, 77 pages.

Notes on the Grilled Issues. 1940, 72 pages.

The U.S. Postage Stamps of the 19th Century. Three volumes, 882 pages, 1967, H.L. Lindquist Publications.

**Brooks, Edward** — American Letter Express Co., Louisville and Nashville 1861. 1946, 61 pages.

**Bruns, Franklin R. and James H.** — Catalog of United States Souvenir Cards. 1980, The Washington Press, 98 pages.

**Bureau of Engraving and Printing** — The First Hundred Years, 1862-1962. 1978, Durst reprint, 200 pages.

**Bureau Issues Association Inc.** — Checklist, Postage Stamp Booklet Covers, United States. Second edition. 1975, loose-leaf, 25 pages plus two covers.

**Burns, Edward J.** — Additions to Hawaiian Postal History. Volume I, 1980 reprint of 1972 work, 66 pages; Volume II, (Hawaii's town cancels), 1980, 36 pages.

**Burroughs, Karl** — Five Cents 1847 Plate Proofs. 14 pages.

## — C —

**Cabeen, Richard McP.** — U.S. Stamps Typewritten Booklets. The Chicago Tribune.

**Cabot, G.D.** — Priced Catalogue of the State and City Revenue and Tax Stamps of the U.S. 1940, 138 pages.

**Cavagnol, J.J.** — Postmarked Alaska. 1957, 105 pages.

**Chapman, A.** — The Pony Express. 319 pages.

**Chappell, C.H.** — Proprietary Revenues of 1898, Precanceled Varieties. 1957, 89 pages.

**Chase, Carroll** — Classic United States Stamps, 1845-1869. 1962 edition, 45 pages.

The 3¢ Stamp of the United States 1851-1857 Issue. Reprint of 1942 edition. Quarterman Publications, 1976, 400 pages.

**Chase and Cabeen** — The First Hundred Years of U.S. Territorial Postmarks 1787-1887. 1980 reprint of 1950 book, 341 pages.

**Clark, Douglas N., and Ruckle, F.E.** — The Street Railway Post Offices of Baltimore. 1979, Mobile Post Office Society, 35 pages.

**Coda, R.J.** — U.S. Bureau Issue Precancels. Fourth edition July 1957.

The Standard Catalogue of Precancels. Maine, New Mexico, New Hampshire, Virginia.

**Cole, Maurice F.** — Postal Markings of Michigan. 1955, 198 pages.

Voices in the Wilderness. Michigan postal history. 1961, 336 pages.

**Collectors Institute Ltd.** — Pictorial Treasury of U.S. Stamps. 1974, 224 pages.

**Collin, H., and Calman, H.L.** — Catalogue of the Stamps, Envelopes and Wrappers of the U.S.A. and the C.S.A. 1900, 206 pages.

**Colman, H.F.** — Checklist of Canal Zone Stamps. 1912, 29 pages.

**Combs, W.V.** — First Federal Issue 1798-1801, U.S. Embossed Revenue Stamped Paper. 1979, American Philatelic Society, 128 pages.

U.S. Departmental Specimen Stamps. 1965, 48 pages.

**Cornell, L.H.** — Tale of the Kicking Mule. 1949, 61 pages.

**Coulson, H.E.** — The 2¢ 1893 Columbian, A Philatelic Research. Available in tear sheets.

**Coy, O.C.** — California County Boundaries. Written in 1923, revised 1973.

**Crocker, H.J.** — Hawaiian Numerals. 1909, 108 pages.

**Crown, F.** — Confederate Postal History. 1976, 313 pages. Anthology from the "Stamp Specialist."

**Cullinan, Gerald** — The Post Office Department. 1968, Frederick Praeger, 272 pages.

## — D —

**Datz, Stephen R.** — Datz Philatelic Index of United States Postage Stamps. Scott Publishing Co., 1981 edition, 99 pages.

**Davis, H.A.** — 1887 3 Cent Vermilion. 1922, 24 pages; 1979 reprint, Triad Publications.

**Davis, H.A., and Wiley, H.L.** — A combined reprint of two earlier works: The U.S. 3¢ Green 1870-1887 by H.L. Wiley, and U.S. 1887 3 Cent Vermilion by Dr. H.A. Davis. Triad Publications.

**Davis, J.H.** — U.S. Guide Lines Catalogue and Checklist. 1949.

**Day, J.M.** — Post Office Papers of the Republic of Texas, 1836-1840. 1966-67, two volumes, 239 pages each.

**Deas, Arthur W.** — An Index Showing the Relationship Between Illustrations and a Description of U.S. Postage Stamps. 1937, Bureau Issues Association, 8 pages.

**Deaton, Charles** — Texas Postal History Handbook. 1980, 245 pages.

**Deitzer, B.F.** — Price List of Indiana Towns and Types. 7 pages.

**de Lisle, Kenneth R.** — Peltz Collection of Albany (N.Y.) Postal History, The Hudson River Mail, 1804-1858. 1969, 59 pages.

**Devol and Graham** — Establishment of the First U.S. Government Post Offices in the Northwest Territory. 1975, 48 pages.

**Diamond and Hesley** — Types and Varieties of U.S. 10¢ Issue 1855-1859. 12 pages.

**Diamond and Kenworthy** — The U.S. One Cent Issues of 1851-57. 24 pages.

Distinguishing Types 2¢ and 3¢ Washington 1912-1921. 1960 revised edition.

**Dietz, A.** — Confederate States Catalog and Handbook. Last edition, 1959, 282 pages.

The Confederate States Post Office Department — Its Stamps and Stationery. 1948, 48 pages.

The Postal Service of the Confederate States of America. 1929, 439 pages.

Specialized Confederates. 1931, first edition, 320 pages.

**Dike, Sheldon** — Arizona Territorial Postmark Catalog. 1972, 72 pages.

The Territorial Post Offices of Colorado. 1957.

The Territorial Post Offices of Florida. 10 pages.

New Mexico Territorial Postmark Catalog. 1981, 145 pages.

**Doane, E.R.** — County System of RFD, Dec. 20, 1899-June 30, 1903. Reprint 1977, 199 pages.

**Doubleday, Elwyn J.** — The Post Offices of Massachusetts. 35 pages.

**Dow, Sterling T.** — Postal History of Maine. Volume 1. Reprinted by Quarterman as Maine Postal History and Postmarks, 1976, 256 pages.

**Drakos, F.** — The 2-Cent Recut Dies. The Hartford Issue of U.S. Stamped Envelopes. 1950; reprint 1977, 159 pages.

**Drickamer, Lee C., and Lincoln, Leo L.** — Postal History of Berkshire County Massachusetts, 1790-1981. 1982.

**Drinkwater, John** — The Stamps of the C.S.A. 1861-65. 1931, 20 pages.

**Durland, C.B.** — Durland Standard Plate Block Catalog 1979. V. Nazar and G. W. Patten, 208 pages.

**Durland** — Standard Plate Number Catalog. Dr. Robert Rabinowitz, 1981 edition, 212 pages.

**Dworak Specialized Catalog of United States Air Mail Covers.** 1930, 288 pages; 1931, 422 pages.

## — E —

**Einstein, Kingsley and DeKay** — A handbook of U.S. Revenue Stamped Paper. 1979, American Revenue Association, 88 pages.

**Ellis, F.L., and Maisel, W.H.** — United States Commemorative Stamped Envelopes 1876-1965. 88 pages.

**Empire State Postal History Society** — Manuscript Post Offices of New York State, 1973, 41 pages; 1974 to 1978 supplements.

New York State Post Offices Extant By County and Year, 1792-1969. 1980, 36 pages.

**Engle, John** — Flag Stamp Varieties Catalogue. U.S. Overrun Nations. 1944, 39 pages.

**Ernst, Carl W.** — Postal Service in Boston 1639-1893. 1975 reprint of 1894 article, 70 pages.

**Evans, W.** — Stamps of the Canal Zone. 1911, 35 pages.

## — F —

**Finkelstein, Daniel** — K & S Postal Strike Letter Dispatch. 1976, Harry Hayes.

**Finlay, Hugh** — Journal: Colonial Postal History 1773-1774. Printed by Frank Norton in 1867; reprinted by U.S. Philatelic Classics Society, 1975, 124 pages.

**Flack, Wylie H.** — Introduction to the Postal History of Philadelphia County. 1979, Associated Stamp Clubs of Southeastern Pennsylvania and Delaware, 20 pages.

**Ford, D.L.** — Oklahoma Precancel Types. 4 pages, Hoover Brothers.

**French, Loran C.** — Encyclopedia of Plate Varieties on U.S. Bureau — Printed Postage Stamps. 1979, Bureau Issues Association, 350 pages.

**Fricke, Charles A.** — A Contemporary Account of the First U.S. Postal Card 1870-75. 1973 edition, 151 pages.

The U.S. International Single Postal Cards of 1879, 1897 and 1898. Volume 1, 60 pages.

Plating of First U.S. Postal Card. 1973, 72 pages.

Transitive Relationship to Family Tree of Proofs.

**Frickstad, W.N.** — A Century of California Post Offices, 1848-1954. Original edition, 1955, 414 pages.

A Century of Nevada Post Offices 1852-1957. 1958, 48 pages.

**Fuller, Wayne E.** — The American Mail, Enlarger of the Common Life. General history. 1972, 378 pages.

## — G —

**Gable, J.H.** — United States Stamps — A Subject Index. 78 pages.

**Gallagher, John S.** — The Post Offices of Rhode Island. 1977, 36 pages.

Post Offices of Utah. 1977, 84 pages.

**Gallagher, John S., and Patera, Alan** — Post Offices of Ohio. 1979, The Depot, 320 pages.

Post Offices of Minnesota. 1979, The Depot, 280 pages.

Wyoming Post Offices, 1850-1980. 1980, 176 pages plus 16-page booklet.

**Geschwindner, Morris and Koontz** — Time Marking Machine Company and B.F. Cummins Co. (machine cancellations). 1982, 200 pages.

**Giffard, Walter M.** — Descriptive Catalogue of the Postage Stamps of Hawaii. Reproduction of a work first published at the end of the Hawaiian Kingdom in 1894. Published by Jane Wilkins Pultz, 20 pages.

**Glass, Sol** — U.S. Postage Stamps, 1945-1952. 1954, 280 pages.

**Gobie, Henry M.** — The Speedy, A History of U.S. Special Delivery. 1976, 296 pages.

U.S. Parcel Post — A Postal History. 1979, 250 pages, Postal Publications.

**Goodkind, Henry M.** — The U.S. 24¢ Air Mail Inverted Center of 1918. 1956, 32 pages.

U.S. The 5¢ Beacon Air Mail Stamp of 1928. 1965, 61 pages.

**Goodwin, F.E.** — The Making of U.S. Stamps. 1913, 53 pages.

The 1847 Issue of U.S. Stamps. 1913, 50 pages.

1851-60 Issue U.S. Stamps. 1913, 78 pages.

The 1861-1868 Issue U.S. Stamps. 1914, 39 pages.

Specialized U.S. to 1919. Second edition, 1920, 64 pages.

U.S. Department Stamps. 1915, 14 pages.

**Govern, Robert W., and Lounsbury, Jay W.** — Discontinued and Renamed Post Offices in the Zip Era, 1963-1978. 1979, Post Mark Collectors Club, 135 pages.

**Grant, R.W.** — Handbook of Civil War Patriotic Envelopes and Postal History. Volume 1, 1977, 250 pages.

**Granville, J.E.** — Price Predictions. (U.S. stamps). Volumes I and II, 1947, 117 pages and 93 pages.

**Green, Brian M.** — The Confederate States Ten-Cent Blue Lithograph. 1979, Philatelic Foundation.

The Typographs of the Confederate States of America. 1981, Philatelic Foundation, 36 pages.

**Griffith, S.E.** — Discontinued Post Offices of New Jersey and Summary of New Jersey Post Office Changes 1930 to 1970. Second list prepared by Ruth Dolezal and Marie Kaminky. Published by the New Jersey Postal History Society.

**Griffith, W.H.** — Story of the American Bank Note Company. 1959, 92 pages.

**Gross, E.T.** — The First Window Envelope. 1942, 31 pages.

**Growther and Merolla** — The Post Offices of Delaware and The District of Columbia. 1978, 50 pages.

**Gruber, Ted** — Postal History of Utah 1849-1976. J-B Publishing Co., 45 pages.

**Gruenzner, Norman** — Postal History of American POWs: World War II, Korea, Vietnam. 1979, American Philatelic Society, 138 pages.

**Gunesch, Adolf** — Bureau Print Price List 1938. Second edition, 58 pages.

Guide and Price List to Precancel Collecting.

Handbook on Precancels, Stamps Suggestions and Information for Collectors. Eighth edition.

## — H —

**Hafen, L.R.** — The Overland Mail 1849-1869. 1977 reprint, Quarterman Publications, 368 pages.

**Hahn, G.H.** — U.S. Famous American Series of 1940. 1950, 193 pages.

**Hahn, M.** — Cancellations of Waterbury. 1940, 31 pages.

Postal Markings of the United States 1847-1851. Published by William R. Stewart, 1938, 42 pages.

**Haller, A.P.** — Catalog of Postal Stationery of U.S. Possessions. 1971, 268 pages.

Thorp Catalog Update to 1974. United Postal Stationery Society.

**Hargest, George E.** — History of Letter Post Communication Between the United States and Europe 1845-1875. Second edition, revised Quarterman Publication, 1971, 256 pages.

**Harlan, George** — Colorado, Postmarks and Places. 1976, 225 pages.

**Harrison, G.** — Nesbitt Stamped Envelopes and Wrappers of the U.S.A. 1895, 44 pages.

**Hart, O.S.** — Some Notes on the New York Postmaster's Provisional. 1911.

**Harvey, Jack V.** — Regular Postage Issue of 1922-35. Published by AFDCS, 70 pages.

**Hatcher, James Brush** — A Forerunner of the 1847s. The New York Postmaster Stamp 1845. 1947, New York Journal American, 8 pages.

**Hatfield, A. Jr.** — The New York Postmaster's Stamp. 1921, 22 pages.

**Haydon** — Haydon's Standard Burolist, Buroprinted Precancels. Fourth edition, 1944.

**Heater, E.F.** — 1904 Re-cuts. 1949, 40 pages.

**Helbock, Richard W.** — Military Postmarks of Territorial Alaska. 1977, 197 pages.

Postmarks of Territorial Alaska. 1976, 136 pages.

Frontier Centennial Western Postal Route Atlas. 1981, La Posta, 30 pages.

The Post Offices of New Mexico. 1980, 70 pages.

**Helbock, R.W., and Dimpsey, D.S.** — Naval Postmarks of Territorial Alaska. 1979, 262 pages.

**Herbert, Antonio** — Herbert's Catalogue of Used Plate Number Singles. 1979, 199 pages, Trans Pacific Stamp Co.

**Herst-Sampson** — Fancy Cancellations on U.S. 19th Century Stamps. Fourth edition, Billig Handbook No. 33, 288 pages.

**Herst-Zareski** — 19th Century U.S. Fancy Cancellations. Second edition, revised, 1951, 258 pages.

**Hertz, A.J.** — A Study of the Western Express. 1952, 13 pages.

**Hesley and Diamond** — Types and Varieties of United States 10-cent Issue, 1855-1859.

**Hill, Henry W.** — The United States Five Cent Stamps of 1856-1861. 1955, 79 pages.

**Hines, Terry** — Revenue Study of U.S. Federal Special Tax Stamps. Unlisted in Scott and beginning with the issues of 1873. American Revenue Association, 140 pages.

**Hobson, Burton, and Reinfeld, Fred** — U.S. Commemorative Coins and Stamps. 1964, 64 pages.

**Hogan, Pat** — A History of the Stamps of Hawaii: 1851-1900. 1980, 22 pages.

**Holcombe, Henry W.** — Patent Medicine Tax Stamps. 1979, 632 pages, Quarterman Publications.

**Hooper, R. Malcolm** — A History Survey of Precancels. 1979, Cardinal Spellman Philatelic Museum.

**Hoover Brothers** — Official Catalogue of U.S. Double Line Electro Precancels. 1938 second edition.

Official Precancel Catalogue 1951-1952. Maine, Montana, Mississippi, North Dakota, South Dakota, Tennessee, Texas, West Virginia, Wisconsin.

The Precancel Town List. November 1953.

Specialists Guide Bureau Print Precancels. 1939, 56 pages.

**Horner, W.E.V.** — Stamped Envelopes of the U.S. Second edition, 1884, 76 pages.

**Horowicz, Kay, and Lowe, Robson** — The Colonial Posts in the United States of America 1606-1783. 1967, 52 pages.

**Howard, G.P.** — The Stamp Machines and Coiled Stamps. 1943, 127 pages.

**Howe, James O.** — Precancel Stamp Catalogue for the State of Illinois. 1947.

**Hubbard, Elbert** — U.S. State Revenue Catalog. 280 pages.

**Hubbel, Raynor** — Confederate Stamps, Old Letters and History. 1959, 89 pages.

**Huber, Leonard V., and Wagner, C.A.** — The Great Mail. 1949, 200 pages.

# — J —

**Jarrett, David L.** — Colorado Territorial and Pre-Territorial Postmarks. 1976, Collectors Club of Chicago, 207 pages.

**Jay, John L., and Smith, Chester M.** — New Jersey History — The Post Offices and First Postmasters, 1776-1976. 200 pages, Quarterman Publications.

**Jersey, Stanley C.** — Postal History of United States Forces in British Solomon Islands Protectorate During World War II. 1968, 96 pages.

**Johl, M.** — U.S. Stamps of the Twentieth Century. 1929-38, four volumes.

United States Postage Stamps 1902-1935. Reprint, 1976, 592 pages, Quarterman Publications.

U.S. Commemorative Stamps of the Twentieth Century. 1947, two volumes, 356 and 382 pages.

**Johnson, David A.** — Town List. Published by Central Ohio Precancel Club 1962, 1963, 1964, 1965, 7 pages.

**Johnson, G.F.** — Notes on the APOs (World War II). 1947, 29 pages.

**Jolley, Max W.** — Notes on Berkshire Vermont Post Office and Early Postal Roads, 12 pages.

**Junior Philatelists of America** — Introduction to United States Philately. 29 pages.

# — K —

**Karlen, H.M.** — Chicago Postal History. 1970, 191 pages.

**Kay, J., and Smith, C.** — New Jersey Postal History. 1977, 199 pages.

Pennsylvania Postal History. 1976, 564 pages.

**Kenyon, B.C.** — History of the Postal Issues of Hawaii. 1895, 26 pages.

**Kimble, Ralph A.** — Commemorative Postage Stamps of the U.S. First edition, 1933, 350 pages; revised 1936, 404 pages.

**King, Beverly S.; Bacharach, Justin L.; and Turner, George** — Revenue Unit columns from the American Philatelist. 1981, reprint by Quarterman, 237 pages.

**Kirkpatrick, Inez E.** — A Postal History of Sioux City. 1977, 208 pages, J-B Publishing Co.

Stagecoach Trails in Iowa. 1975, 232 pages, J-B. Publishing Co.

**Kitchen, R.F.** — First Men on the Moon Handbook of Stamps. 139 pages.

**Klein, E.** — U.S. Waterway Packetmarks, 1832-99. 1940, 208 pages; 1942, two supplements.

**Klein, George** — U.S. Bureau Precancels. 1981, fifth edition.

**Knapp, E.S.** — Pony Express. 1936, 27 pages.

**Koeberg, E.G.** — Collected Postal History Notes of Ontario Co., N.Y. 1978, 97 pages.

**Koeppel, Adolph** — Stamps That Caused the American Revolution, Stamps of the 1765 British Stamp Act for America. 1976, 193 pages.

**Konwiser, H.M.** — Texas Republic Postal System. 1933, 72 pages.

Postal Markings. Quarterman reprint, 762 pages.

The American Stamp Collectors, A Complete Guide to U.S. Stamps and the Colonial and Revolutionary Posts. Published by Minkus, 1947, 208 pages.

**Kriege, Owen H.** — Arizona Territorial Postmark Catalog. 1980, third edition, 103 pages.

— **L** —

**Landis, Dr. Robert L.** — Oregon, Washington and Idaho Post Offices. 1969, 262 pages.

**Lane, M.B.** — The Harry F. Allen Collection of Black Jacks. 1969, 147 pages.

**Langford, F.** — Flag Cancel Encyclopedia. 1955, 72 pages.

**Laurence, Robert** — The George Walcott Collection of Used Civil War Patriotic Covers. 1934, 261 pages; 1975 reprint.

**Lauzon, A.A.** — The United States Columbian Issue 1893. 1942, 69 pages.

**Lehman, Howard** — Confederate States, the Two Cent Green Stamp. Reprint Collectors Club, 23 pages.

**Leutzinger, J.F.** — Handstamps of Wells, Fargo and Co. 1852-95. 1968, 273 pages; 1971 supplement.

**Lidman, David** — Treasury of Stamps. 1976, 304 pages.

**Linn, G.W.** — The Paid Markings on the 3¢ U.S. Stamp of 1861. 1955, 104 pages.

**Lloyd, P.W.** — Stamp Investing for Profit. 1977, 130 pages.

**Loso and de Windt** — Twentieth Century U.S. Fancy Cancellations. 1952, 172 pages.

**Lowe, Robson** — Encyclopedia of Empire Postage Stamps, Volume 5, North America. 1973, 760 pages.

**Luff, John N.** — The Postage Stamps of the United States. 1981 reprint of 1902 edition, Quarterman, 318 pages.

Postage Stamps and Stationery of the Hawaiian Islands. 1914, 21 pages.

Postmasters' Provisional Stamps. Revised by Hugh M. Clark, 1937, Scott Stamp and Coin Co., 79 pages.

**Luff, Moe** — United States Postal Slogan Cancel Catalog. 1968 edition revised 1975, 128 pages.

**Lybarger, D.F.** — The U.S. Issues of 1918-1920. 1937, 46 pages.

— **M** —

**McDaniel, Gayle** — Americana: A Salute to the U.S. Bicentennial. Amos Press Inc., 294 pages.

State Flags on Stamps. 1979, Amos Press, 50 pages.

**McDonald, S.M.** — American Philately Miscellany. Reprint 1976, 592 pages, Quarterman Publications.

**McMath, Kenneth** — Precancel Town List. All states and territories listed and priced to June 1971.

**MacBride, Van Dyk** — Confederate Patriotic Covers. Reprint 1979, Triad Publications, 64 pages.

**Malpass, G.N.** — The Jefferson Davis Postage Stamp Issues of the Confederacy. 1954, 24 pages.

**Markovits, R.L.** — U.S. 10¢ Registry Stamp of 1911. 32 pages, 1973.

**Mason, E.H.** — Essays For U.S. Postage Stamps. 1911, 90 pages.

**Mathewson, Craig C.** — Post Offices and Postmasters of Cape May County, N.J. 1802-1970. 1970, 44 pages.

**Means, C.A.** — New Haven Provisional Envelope. 1932, 51 pages.

**Melville, Fred J.** — Confederate States of America. 1913, 72 pages.

Postage Stamps of the Hawaiian Islands in the Collection of Henry J. Crocker. 1908, 9 pages.

United States Postage Stamps 1847-1869. 1910, 92 pages.

U.S. Postage Stamps 1870-1893. 1910, 71 pages.

U.S. Postage Stamps 1894-1910. 1910, 91 pages.

United States Special Service Stamps. 1915, 67 pages.

**Merolla, Crowther and Jackson** — Rhode Island Postal History - The Post Offices. 1977, 136 pages.

**Merolla and Crowther** — The Post Offices of Massachusetts. 1981, 159 pages.

**Meschter, D.Y.** — Wyoming Territorial and Pre-Territorial Post Offices. 1971, 17 pages.

**Meyer and Harris** — Hawaii, Its Stamps and Postal History. 1948, 424 pages.

**Micarelli, Charles N.** — Manual and Identification Guide to the United States Regular Issues, 1847-1934. 1981, Scott Publications, 116 pages.

**Milgram, James W.** — The Express Mail of 1836-1839. 1977, Collectors Club of Chicago, 214 pages.

The Western Mails. 62 pages.

**Milliken, E.** — New York Foreign Mail Cancellations 1870-76. 1942, 31 pages.

**Mills, Earl T.** — Alphabetical Descriptive Arrangement of U.S. Commemorative Stamps. Special issues by inscriptions 1893-1963. 27 pages.

**Minkus** — American Stamp Catalogue. Priced.

**Mitchel-Hoover** — Catalog of United States Bureau Precancels. Published by Hoover Brothers and Stephen Rich. 36th edition.

**Moroney, Rita L.** — Montgomery Blair — Post Master General. 1963, 44 pages.

**Morris, Reg** — American Machine Bar Cancels, 1884-1898. 43 pages.

**Mosher, Bruce** — Discovering US Rotary Booklet Pane Varieties 1926-1978. 1979, 128 pages, Mosher Philatelics.

**Mueller, Barbara R.** — U.S. Postage Precancel Primer. 46 pages.

**Murphy, R.T.** — Postal History Cancellation Study of the U.S. Pacific Islands. 1974, 182 pages.

**Mynchenberg, G.C.** — Official Precancel Catalog. Maine 1951; Texas 1952; Tennessee 1952; and Wisconsin.

## — N —

**Nast, C.A.** — The Revenues of the U.S. 1905, 20 pages.

**Nathan, M.C.** — Franks of Western Expresses. 1973, 281 pages.

**National Philatelic Museum** — The 1851-1857 Issue. 1951, 176 pages.

The Perforation Centennial (1857-1860). 1957, 232 pages.

Postage Stamp Design. 246 pages.

**Neinken, M.L.** — The 1851-57 12¢ Stamp. 1964, 74 pages.

The U.S. One Cent Stamp of 1851-1861. 1972, 552 pages.

U.S. Ten Cent Stamps of 1855-59. 1960, 252 pages.

**New Jersey Postal History Society** — Discontinued Post Offices of New Jersey and Summary of New Jersey Post Office Changes 1930 to 1970.

**New York Sun** — U.S. Commemorative Notes 1893-1934. 73 pages.

**Nichols, C.M.** — Early Post Office of Chautauqua County. 152 pages.

**Noble, Gilbert W.** — Official Catalogue of U.S. Bureau Precancels. 1981, 63st edition, 232 pages.

Official Precancel Stamp Catalogue for the Mountain States. 1953.

Official Precancel Catalogue 1952-1954. Alabama, Connecticut, Florida, Georgia, Iowa, Kentucky, Louisiana, Texas.

The Integral Precancel Type List and Handbook. First edition 1962.

**Norona, Delf** — Cyclopedia of United States Postmarks and Postal History. Reprint (combined 1933 and 1935 editions), 416 pages, Quarterman Publications.

## — O —

**Oakley, B.C., Jr.** — A Postal History of Mississippi. Stampless period 1799-1860. 1967, 290 pages; Volume II, 1980, 663 pages.

**Olcheshki, Bill** — Beginning Stamp Collecting. 135 pages.

**Olson, K.F. and V.M.** — Rapid Cancelling Machines, Manufacturers and Impressions. 1946, 31 pages.

Postal Historian's Note Book. Part 1, 1974, 60 pages.

**Ormsby, Waterman** — The Butterfield Overland Mail. Reprints of articles written for the New York Herald in 1858. 179 pages.

## — P —

**Paher, S.W.** — Nevada Post Offices, an Illustrated History. 1982.

**Patera, Alan H.** — The Post Offices of Connecticut. 1977, 55 pages.

**Patton, Donald S.** — Boyd's Local Posts. History of four posts which served New York City 1844-1882.

The Local Posts in Brooklyn, 1844-1882.

The Private Local Posts of the United States. Volume one, New York State, 1967, 350 pages.

**Penny, Gilbert and Patricia** — Alabama, A Glimpse at Its Postal History. 1969, 22 pages.

**Perry, E.** — Byways of Philately. 1966, 270 pages.

The Chatham Square Post Office and Swarts' City Despatch Post. 1941, 34 pages.

United States 1857-1860 Issue. 1922, 63 pages.

**Perry, T.D.** — Guide to the Stamped Envelopes of the U.S. 1940, 176 pages.

**Petersham, M. and M.** — America's Stamps. 1947, 144 pages.

**Petri, Pitt** — Postal History of Western New York. 272 pages.

**Phillips, C.J.** — Specialized Catalog of Confederate States. General Issues. 1928, Dietz Press, 31 pages.

**Phillips, David** — American Stampless Cover Catalog. 1978 edition, David G. Phillips Publishing Co. Inc., 250 pages.

**Phillips, G.H.** — Postoffices and Postmarks of Dakota Territory. J-B Publishing Co., 74 pages, 1973.

Postoffices of South Dakota, 1861-1930. 1975, J-B Publishing Co., 76 pages.

Handling the Mail in Benton County, Arkansas, 1836-1976. 1979, Benton County Historical Society, 136 pages.

**Pickett, Rice and Spelman** — Florida Postal History Stampless Period. 1957, Palm Beach Stamp Club, 73 pages.

**Poole and Bartels** — U.S. Virgin Islands. 27 pages.

**Power, E.B.** — General Issues of U.S. Stamps. Includes coils and private perfs. 1909, 118 pages; 1917 supplement, 91 pages.

**Powers, R.T.** — Postal Markings of Maryland, 1766-1855. 1960, 100 pages.

**Pratt, Thomas H.** — The Postmaster's Provisionals of Memphis, Tennessee. 1929, Dietz Press, 43 pages.

**Precancel Stamp Society** — The Precancel Stamp Society's Town and Type Catalog of the U.S. and Territories. Third edition, 1979.

Bureau Precancel Catalog. 1979, PSS, 40 pages.

**Price, Dr. John M.** — Street Car R.P.O. Service in Brooklyn and New York City. 1979, Mobile Post Office Society, 50 pages.

**Priester, Thomas W.** — United States Beer Stamps. 1979, 95 pages.

## — Q —

**Quaife, M.M.** — Absalom Grimes, Confederate Mail Runner. 1926, 215 pages.

## — R —

**Rainey, Thomas** — Ocean Steam Navigation and the Ocean Post. 1977 reprint of 1858 book, 224 pages.

**Ramsey, Grover C.** — Confederate Postmasters in Texas. 1963, 71 pages.

**Ramsey, G.R.** — Postmarked Iowa. 1976, 556 pages, J-B Publishing Co.

Postmarked Washington: Island County & San Juan County. Published 1977 by Lopez Island Historical Society, 62 pages. Lewis and Cowlitz counties, 1978, 250 pages; and Jefferson, Challam and Mason counties, 1978, 192 pages.

**Rapp, W.F.J.** — Discontinued Post Offices of Nebraska. 1967.

**Rapp and Willard** — Catalog of Telegraph Message Covers, 19th Century. 77 pages.

**Reinfeld, F.** — Commemorative Stamps of U.S.A. 1956, 359 pages.

Pony Express. 127 pages.

**REM, Inc.** — A Research Work on the United States Postal Service Issue of July 1, 1971. 200 pages.

**Remele, C.W.** — U.S. Railroad Postmarks 1837 to 1861. 1958, 169 pages.

**Rhode Island Postal History Society** — Rhode Island Postal History, The Post Office. 136 pages.

**Rich, J.S.** — U.S. Telegraph Stamps. 1947, 76 pages.

A Comparative List of the Numbers of U.S. Envelopes. 1893, 18 pages.

**Rich, W.** — History of the U.S. Post Office to 1829. 1077 reprint of 1924 book, Quarterman Publications, 190 pages.

**Richards, C.F.** — The Check List of the Stamps of Hawaii. 1916, 38 pages.

**Richow** — Territorial Post Offices of Wisconsin. 1963, 38 pages.

**Rickerson, Wildey** — United States Revenue Stamps. 84 pages.

**Ricks, M.B.** — Directory of Alaska's Postmasters and Postoffices 1867-1963. 1965, 72 pages.

**Riddell, John D. and Sheila** — U.S.A. Consular Post Offices in Japan. 1972, 12 pages.

**Robey, W.T.** — The Story, Discovery, 24 Cent Invert U.S. Airmail Stamps.

**Robinson, H.** — Carrying British Mail Overseas. 1964, 327 pages.

**Rogan, Kevin R., and McGrath, Thomas F.** — Locations and Assignments U.S. Army Post Offices World War II and Later. Third edition, 1973, 102 pages, War Cover Club.

**Rohloff, Paul C.** — The Waterbury Cancellations. 1979, Collectors Club of Chicago, 264 pages.

**Root and Connelley** — The Overland Stage to California. 1950 reprint, 630 pages.

**Rotnem Stamp Company** — Standard Precancel Stamp Catalog. 1929, 700 pages.

**Rusbason, A.J.** — History of U.S. Commemorative Postage Stamps. 1932, 31 pages.

## — S —

**Salley** — History of California Post Offices 1849-1976. 1977, 311 pages.

**Sampson, E.N.** — American Colonial Postmark Catalog. 1953, 30 pages.

**Sampson, J.W.** — Seven Cent Vermilion U.S. 1871-1873 Issue. 16 pages.

**Sampson, Wishnietsky and Skinner** — American Stampless Cover Catalog. 1978 edition, David G. Phillips Publishing Co., 280 pages.

**Sanford, H.F.** — The Mail of the A.E.F. 1940, 56 pages.

**Sargent, R.W.** — Revenue Stamps of the U.S. 1862-1899. 1942, 136 pages.

**Scalley, Rex M.** — 1971 Puerto Rico Stamp Price Catalog. 32 pages.

**Scarlett, O.** — Complete Cyclopaedia of all Revenue Stamps of the U.S. 1893, 98 pages.

**Schoen, R.H., and DeVoss, J.T.** — Counterfeit Kansas-Nebraska Overprints on 1922-34 Issues. Reprint 1976, 34 pages.

**Schueren, F.P.** — The United States 1869 Issue — An Essay Proof History. 1974, 127 pages.

**Schultz, William R.** — Catalog of Rattlesnake Island Local Post Stamps. Third edition, 1980.

**Schwalm, A.J.** — Plating Hawaii 1894-1899 Two Cent Stamps. 20 pages.

**Scott Publishing Company** — U.S. Stamps in Color. Abridged catalog, 112 pages.

United States Stamp Catalogue Specialized. 1982 edition, 790 pages.

**Segal, Stanley B.** — Errors, Freaks and Oddities on U.S. Stamps — Question Marks in Philately. 1979, H.M. Southgate, 100 pages.

**Sherman, J.E. and B.H.** — Ghost Towns and Mining Camps of New Mexico. 270 pages.

**Sherman, Lawrence** — The First Forty Years: Analysis of the Growth in Value of United States Plate Blocks from 1937 to 1977. Published by Almar Stamps, 16 pages.

**Shirk, G.H.** — First Post Offices Within the Boundaries of Oklahoma. 1948, 61 pages.

**Silberberg, B.** — U.S. Stamp Series of 1901. 1976, 120 pages.

**Simchak, Richard** — Journal of United States Stamped Envelopes.

**Simon and Walsh** — The United States Postage Meter Stamp Catalog. 1976, Indicia Associates.

**Simpson, Tracy W.** — U.S. Postal Markings and Related Mail Services 1851 to 1861. 1959, 177 pages; revised by Thomas J. Alexander, U.S. Philatelic Classics Society, 1980.

**Skine, Walter** — St. Vincent to Florida. 1965, 8 pages.

**Skinner, Hubert, and Eno, Amos** — United States Cancellations, 1845-1869; Unusual and Representative Markings. 1980, American Philatelic Society, 362 pages.

**Slawson, George C.** — Postal Stationery of United States Possessions. 1957, 70 pages.

Vermont Postal History. 1969, 308 pages; 1971 index.

**Sloane, G.B.** — William F. Harnden, The Original Expressman. 1932, 19 pages.

Sloane's Column. A compilation of all his articles in Stamps Magazine, 1980 edition, 467 pages.

**Sloat, Ralph L.** — Farley's Follies. 1979, 108 pages.

The Airmail Special Delivery Stamps of the United States. Bureau Issues Association, 1977, 86 pages.

**Smith, Chester M., and Kay, John L.** — Pennsylvania Postal History. 576 pages, Quarterman Publications.

**Smith, Dr. Chester M.** — Index to the Postal History of Vermont. Published by the Vermont Philatelic Society, up to 1969, 56 pages.

American Philatelic Periodicals. 1979, American Philatelic Research Library, 80 pages.

**Solley, Harold E.** — The History of California Post Offices 1849-1976. Acme Philatelic Services, 300 pages.

**Springer, S.** — Handbook of North American Cinderella Stamps. 1980, ninth edition, 56 pages.

**Staff, F.** — Transatlantic Mail. 1956, 191 pages.

**Stanton** — U.S. Revenue Catalogue. 1885, 22 pages; Clemens Standard Historical Revenue Stamp Catalogue. 1887, 12 pages.

United States Letter Rates to Foreign Destinations, 1847 to GPU-UPU. 1982, 160 pages.

**Stern, E.** — History of the Free Franking of Mail in the U.S. 1936, 236 pages.

**Stets, Robert J.** — Street Car R.P.O. Service in Philadelphia. 1979 monograph, Mobile Post Office Society, 41 pages.

**Stets, Robert J., and Kay, John L.** — Independent Post Offices of Philadelphia County (Pa.), 1800-1867. 1979, 44 pages.

**Stevens, T.A.** — Anecdotes About 101 Distinguished Americans. 1964, 264 pages.

**Stevenson, W.L.** — U.S. Grills. Handbook No. 16, Severn - Wylie - Jewett, 1910, 15 pages.

**Stover, Hugo D.** — Philatelic Catalog of Puerto Rico. Puerto Rico Philatelic Society.

**Stratton, F.B.** — Leavitt Machine Cancellations. 1976, second edition, 48 pages.

**Swan, Walter M.** — Catalog of Meter Slogans. Postal Markings Handbook No. 2, 1939, 53 pages.

The Basic Type Meter Stamp Catalog. Third edition, 1959, 79 pages.

## — T —

**Tasker, Walter L.** — U.S. History as Portrayed by U.S. Stamps. 1966, 38 pages.

**Taylor, M.F.** — First Mail West. 1971, 253 pages.

**ter Braake, Alex** — Posted Letter in Colonial and Revolutionary America. 1975, 653 pages.

Texas: The Drama of Its Postal Past. 1970, 298 pages.

**Theobald, John and Lillian** — Arizona Territory, Post Offices and Postmasters. Published by the Arizona Historical Foundation, 178 pages, 1961.

Wells Fargo in Arizona Territory. 1979, Arizona Historical Foundation, 210 pages.

**Thompson, H.K.** — U.S. County and Postmaster Postmarks. 173 pages.

**Thorp, P.H.** — Twentieth Century U.S. Stamped Envelopes. 1968, 205 pages.

**Tiffany, J.K.** — History of the Postage Stamps of the U.S. 1886, 278 pages.

**Tiffany, Bogert and Richert** — Stamped Envelopes, Wrappers and Sheets of the United States. 1892, 126 pages.

**Toppan, Deats and Holland** — Historical Reference List of the Revenue Stamps of the U.S. The Boston Revenue Book. 1980 reprint of 1899 book, 416 pages.

**Toppan, G.L.** — A Tentative Check List of the Proofs of the Adhesive Postage and Revenue Stamps of the U.S. 1904, 30 pages.

Notes on the U.S. and Confederate Stamps. 1906, 27 pages.

Stamps of the Canal Zone. 1906, 38 pages.

**Towle, Charles L.** — The Centennial Catalog of Arizona Railway Postal Markings. 1979, Western Postal History Museum, 44 pages.

New Mexico Catalog of Railway Postal Markings, 1881-1967. 1980, 80 pages.

**Towle and Meyer** — Railroad Postmarks of the U.S. 1861-1886. 1968, 379 pages.

**Tracy and Ashbrook** — Notes on the U.S. Twelve Cents 1851-57. 1926, 23 pages.

**Trout, Horace Q.** — Specialist's Guide to Bureau Print Precancels (Gilbert B. Noble Catalog). 1980, third edition, 766 pages.

U.S. Bureau Precancels, The Noble Official Catalog. 1981, 63rd edition, 232 pages.

**Turner, George T.** — Essays and Proofs of United States Internal Revenue Stamps. Published by the Bureau Issues Association, 475 pages, 1974.

— U —

**United Postal Stationery Society** — Postal Stationery of the U.S. Possessions. Second edition, 1971, 268 pages.

U.S. Postal Card Catalog. 1980 edition, 250 pages.

Precanceled Envelopes of the United States. 1981.

**U.S. Fish and Wildlife Service** — Duck Stamp Data. 1978, 50 pages.

**United States Government Printing Office** — History of the Postal Inspection Service. 1982, 26 pages.

**United States Post Office Department** — Postage Stamps of the U.S. 1847-1979.

Private Express Statutes. Third edition, Sept. 1940, 19 pages.

**U.S. Postal Service** — Stamps and Stories. Regularly issued.

— V —

**Van Dam, Theo.** — The Postal History of the AEF, 1917-1923. 1980, American Philatelic Society, 242 pages.

**Vanderhoof, E.R.** — A Check List of the Beer Stamps of the United States of America. 1934 APS reprint, 15 pages.

**Van Vlissingen and Waud** — New York Foreign Mail Cancellations. 1968, 105 pages.

**Vero, A.J.** — Those Incredible B$2FDC/-B$2J4Cs! Listing of April 13, 1976, and July 4, 1976, cancellations on the United States $2 bill. Published by Andrew J. Vero, 121 pages.

**Von Stein, P.** — Graphi-Guide for U.S. Stamps.

— W —

**Wagner, C.C.** — Postal Facilities and Postmarks, District of Louisiana, Territory of Louisiana and Territory of Missouri 1804-1821. 1954, 38 pages.

**Walcott, G.** — Civil War Patriotic Covers. 1934.

**Walsh, D., and Simon, W.** — The United States Postage Meter Stamp Catalog. 94 pages.

**Warmsley, Arthur J.** — Connecticut Post Offices and Postmarks. Connecticut Printers Inc., 250 pages.

**Waterhouse, N.E.** — A Comprehensive Catalog of Postage Stamps of U.S.A. Published by Frank Godden, 1916, 114 pages; 1921 supplement, 24 pages.

**Weatherly. A. Earl** — North Carolina, Guilford County. 1972, 207 pages.

**Wells, Stanley** — U.S. Army Post Offices and Navy Numbers in Cook Islands, Tonga and Fiji. Pacific Islands Study Circle of Great Britain.

**West, Christopher** — The Revenue Stamps of the United States. 1979, 102 pages.

Private Die Match Stamps. 1980, Castenholz and Sons, 262 Pages.

Match and Medicine Stamps. 144 pages.

**West, R.D.** — Chillicothe, Ohio, A Postal History. 1959, 81 pages.

**Westerburg, J.F.** — Plating the Hawaiian Numerals. 1968, 85 pages.

**Wheat** — Post Offices and Postmasters of Texas, 1846-1930. 1982, 2,000 pages.

**White, R.H.** — Encyclopedia of the Colors of United States Postage Stamps, 1847-1918. 1981, Philatelic Research Ltd., four volumes.

**Whitebourgh, J.** — Philometer Compendium with Price Indications: A Standard Catalogue and Guide of 2,337 U.S. Philometers. First edition, 1957.

**Wiley, H.L.** — U.S. Parcel Post Stamps, Stamp Booklets, Postal Savings Stamps. 1914, 36 pages.

The U.S. Green 1870-1887. 1915, 26 pages.

**Wilhelm, Carl** — Postal Service in Boston 1639-1893. Published by Trustees of the Boston Public Library, 1975.

**Willard, E.L.** — The 2¢ Red Brown of 1883-1887. Two volumes, 1970, 164 pages each.

**Willard, J.H.** — Colorado Postal History, Early Railway Postal Routes. 1974, 61 pages, J-B Publishing Co.

**Wiltsee and Parker** — The Franks of the Everts Expresses. 1931, 16 pages.

**Wiltsee, E.** — Gold Rush Steamers of the Pacific. 1938, 377 pages; 1976 Quarterman Publications reprint.

Pioneer Miner and the Pack Mule Express. 1931, 112 pages; 1976, Quarterman Publications reprint, 160 pages.

**Wisconsin Postal History Society** — Territorial Post Offices of Wisconsin. 38 pages.

**Wishnietsky, Ben** — Confederate States of America Stampless Cover Catalog. 1980, 100 pages.

**Woodward, P.H.** — The Secret Service of the United States Post Office. 1979 reprint, Sanford J. Durst, 600 pages.

**Woolley, M.E.** — The Early History of the Colonial Post Office. 1969 reprint of 1894 edition, American Philatelic Research Library, 33 pages.

**Wyman, W.D.** — California Emigrant Letters. 177 pages.

## — Y —

**Yeomans, S.** — The Booklet Issues of the U.S. 1900-1923. 48 pages.

## Foreign Countries

### Abyssinia

**Baldwin, N. C.** — Abyssinia, 1929-31. An aerophilatelic guide and priced checklist of Abyssinia and French Somaliland. 16 pages.

### Aden

**Graham, M. A. M.** — Aden Censor Marks 1914-19. 8 pages.

**Hornal, Charles** — Perim Outpost of Aden. Postal Historian supplement to Volume 22, No. 3, 1955, 8 pages.

### Afghanistan

**Collins, Peter** — The Afghan Campaign 1841-43. The letters of Capt. William Riddell on his journey from Indore to the North West Frontier.

**Patterson, F. E., III** — Afghanistan, Its 20th Century Postal Issues. 1965, 208 pages.

### Albania

**Wiener, Lionel** — Notes on the Stamps of Albania. London, 1916.

### Algeria

**Halden and de Beaufond** — Catalogue des Marques Postales et Obliterations d'Algerie 1830-1876. 1949, 196 pages.

### Andorra

**Abad, M.** — Cataleg de Segells, Andorra, 1977-78. 1978, Les Escaldes (Andorra), 64 pages.

**Andorra Philatelic Society** — Valles d'Andorre Catalogue National Specialise. 1978, S.A. Maury, 239 pages (French).

**Bacquer, Jean** — Les Emissions Postales de la Principaute d'Andorra. 1956, Le Monde des Philatelistes, 12 pages.

**Battesti, Paul** — Catalogue/Prix Courant, Emissions Postales des Vallees d'Andorre. 1977, French Bureau and Spanish Agencies, 9 pages.

**Jacques, W. A.** — Andorra-Andorre. The story of its stamps and postal history. 1974, Robson Lowe, 68 pages.

### Antigua

**Lowe, Robson** — The Codrington Correspondence 1743-1851. 1968. Robson Lowe. 124 pages.

**Melville, F. J.** — Antigua. 1929, 57 pages.

### Argentina

**Alfaro, R. E.** — Who's Who on the Postage Stamps of Argentina. 1940, 12 pages.

**Bose, W.B., and Korth, R.** — Estafetas Postales Ambulantes Argentinas 1865-1965. 1974, 38 pages.

**Daireaux** — Argentine et le Timbreposte. 104 pages. Spanish with introduction in German and English.

**Delpont** — Sellos Rivadavia 1864-1872. 1946, 66 pages, Spanish.

**Jewell, C.** — Reconstruction of Four Plates of the 5c of the Rivadavia Series. 1937, 15 pages.

**Kunze, A.F.** — Who's Who on the Postage Stamps of Argentina. Revised edition, Pan American Union, 1950, 41 pages.

**Stich, L.** — Corrientes 1856-80. 1957, 88 pages.

**Zago, Manrique.** — Sellos Postales Argentinos con Historia. 1981, Manrique Zago Publications, 200 pages.

### Ascension

**Attwood, J.H.** — Ascension, The Stamps and Postal History. 1981, Robson Lowe, 71 pages.

**Ford, Eric H.** — History and Postage Stamps of Ascension Island. 1972 reprint, Harry Hayes Publications, 68 pages.

**Urch, Harris** — Queen Elizabeth II Ascension Catalogue. 1982.

### Australia

**Australian Commonwealth Specialists' Catalogue** — 1981, 41st edition, Seven Seas Pty. Ltd., 389 pages.

**Australian Dependencies Stamp Catalogue** — First edition 1964, 32 pages, Review Publications.

**Australian Stamp Bureau** — The Australian Stamp Bureau Philatelic Handbooks contain the story of the stamps covered by title.

1) The Early Federal Period 1901 to 1912-13. 24 pages.

2) The Early Commonwealth Period and the Kangaroo and Map Series. 1968, 16 pages.

3) The 1913-14 Recess Printed Series and the King George V Sideface and Pictorial Definitive Stamps. 32 pages.

4) The Definitive Stamps of the Reign of King George VI. 40 pages.

5) The Definitive Stamps of the Reign Of Queen Elizabeth II, 1952-1965. 59 pages.

6) The Commemorative Stamps of the Reign of Queen Elizabeth II, 1952-1969. 56 pages.

7) Australian Commemorative and Air Mail Stamps, 1927-1951. 44 pages.

8) The Postage Due Stamps of Australia 1890-1961. 25 pages.

9) The Commemorative Stamps of the Reign of Queen Elizabeth II 1960-65. 48 pages.

10) A History of the Post Office in Tasmania. 1973.

**Avery, et al** — Tasmania: The Postal History and Postal Markings. Volume II (see Campbell), Royal Philatelic Society of Victoria, 1975.

**Bare** — A Study of the King George V 1½ pence Red Die II Stamps. ACCC, 1962.

**Bassett Hull** — Stamps of Tasmania. Royal Philatelic Society of London, 1890.

The Postage Stamps of Queensland. RPSL, 1930.

The Postage Stamps of New South Wales. RPSL, 1913.

**Brown, A., and Campbell, H.** — New South Wales Cancellations. 1963, Robson Lowe, with supplements.

**Butler, A. R.** — The Departmental Stamps of South Australia. 1978.

**Campbell, H.** — Queensland Cancellations and other Postal Markings, 1860-1913. Royal Philatelic Society of Victoria, 1977.

Tasmania: The Postal History and Postal Markings. (J.R.W. Purves and L.C. Viney, joint authors.) Part I, 1962.

**Collas, P.** — Queensland Postal Stationery, 1880-1912. Hawthorne Press, 1979, 645 pages.

**Collas, P., and Williams, E. A.** — Northern Territory (Australia) Handbook. 1977, Society of Australasian Specialists, 192 pages.

**Cox** — South Australia: The Squared Circle Cancellation. 1975.

**Craig** — The Revenue and Railway Stamps of Tasmania. 1979, American Revenue Association.

**Darke, J.** — The Postal Stationery Catalogue of the Colonies of Australia. Part IV.

**Davidson and Dix** — King George V 4-pence. 1973.

COFA: The George V 3-pence. BSAP, 1977.

**Davidson, Dix and Rowntree** — The King George V 5-pence. BSAP, 1981.

**Davies and Linfield** — The Cancellations of Melbourne. BSAP, 1980.

**Dix and Rowntree** — The Australian Commonwealth KGV 1/2 pence. London, 1959.

**Eustis, H. N.** — Australian Air Mail Catalogue. Third edition, 195 pages.

The Ross Smith Air Stamps. 1979, Hawthorne Press, 72 pages.

**Frankenstein, V.** — Handstamps of the Travelling Post Offices of New South Wales. 1976, Robson Lowe, 8 pages.

**Ham, Thomas** — Victoria Half Lengths. A guide to the classification of the different printings.

**Hamilton, Margaret** — The Stamps and Postal History of Western Australia. 1979, Western Australia Study Group, 471 pages.

**Houison, A.** — History of the Post Office and the Issue of Postage Stamps. 1890, 110 pages.

**Hull, A.F.B.** — The Perkins Bacon Printings, 1854-1861, and the De La Rue Printings, 1864-1902. 20 pages.

**Hutson, G.** — The Stamps of New South Wales. Royal Philatelic Society of London, 1960.

**Hyeronimus, R.P.** — Commonwealth of Australia: Postage Due Stamps. 1980, Hawthorne Press.

**Inglis, et al** — The Railway (and other) Stamps of Mainland Australia. 1981.

**Johl, Max** — Postal Stationery and Postal History of Western Australia. Volume I, the de la Rue Printings, 1981.

**Legge, H. D.** — The Line Engraved Issues of 1914 and the Essays, Die and Plate Proofs of the Georgian 1d. 128 pages.

The 1913 Penny Kangaroo of Australia. 1980, Stanley Gibbons Publications Ltd., 46 pages.

**Lessing, James** — Commonwealth of Australia Slogan Cancellations: 1918-1960. Society of Australasian Specialists, 1974, 72 pages.

**Logigas, Dace** — Parade of Australian History on Postage Stamps. 16 pages, Seven Seas Stamps Ltd., N.S.W.

**Lowe, Robson** — A record of the engravers T. S. Harrison and Son when employed by Waterlow Bros., and Layton Ltd. of London 1897-1912.

Encyclopaedia of Empire Postage Stamps, Volume 3, Part 3, Australasia. Billig Vol. 43.

Encyclopaedia of Empire Postage Stamps, Volume IV, Australia. Reprint of the original work with supplements, HJMR Co.

**Milner, Roy** — Postal History of the Australian Antarctic 1911-1965. Polar History Society of Great Britain, 56 pages.

**Mortimer, David** — The Color Catalogue of Australian Stamps. 1976, 40 pages.

**Neil, D.M.** — 1d King George V Australian Commonwealth Stamps (1914-1937). 1947, 71 pages.

**Pacific Islands, Australasia Stamp Catalogue.** Stamp Publications, issued yearly.

**Pack** — The Half-Lengths Portraits and the Two Pence Queen enthroned. 1923.

**Parker, Colin** — The Catalogue of Australian Pre-stamped Envelopes. 1981, Philatelic Consulting Services, 64 pages.

**Purves J.R.W.** — Victoria: The Registered and Too Late Stamps, 1854-58. 1966.

Victoria: 1901-12 Issue. 40 pages.

Victoria: The Postage Dues. 1960, 88 pages.

Victoria: The V Over Crown Watermarks, Types, Supplies, Varieties, 1867-1905. 1964, 40 pages.

The Barred Numeral Cancellations, 1856-1912. 1949, 224 pages.

The Butterfly and Barred Oval Cancellations. 1965, 48 pages.

The Emblems of Victoria, 1957-63. 1957, 105 pages.

The Postal History of the Port Phillip District, 1837-51. 1950, 68 pages.

Victoria: The Half-Lengths.

Victoria: The 5/- 1867-1891 and the 1/, 5/-, £1 and £2 1901-12. Hawthorne Press, 1979.

South Australia: The Long Stamps, 1902-12. 1978.

The Traveling Post Offices (to 1912). Hawthorne Press monograph.

**Rosenblum, A.** — Australian Air Mails. 1931, 43 pages.

The Stamps of the Commonwealth of Australia. Sixth edition.

**Stobbs, S.** — Postmarks of the Australian Forces from all Fronts 1939 to 1953. Second edition, 1976, Harry Hayes, 64 pages.

**Tasman Catalog of Australia.** 16 pages.

**Tripp** — Location and Assignments of U.S. Army Post Offices in World War II. 1959, War Cover Club.

**Turley** — Official Handbook of the Post Office Registration Labels.

**Ward, Gordon** — Australia, an Introduction to the Study of the King George V 1½d Die 2. The second printings made by A. J. Mullett from 1926. 56 pages.

The George V 5 Pence, 1915-36.

**Whitmarsh, D.** — The Search for Secrecy: Civilian Censorship in Australia, 1939-45. 1977, Oceania Philatelic Society.

**Williams and Collas** — Northern Territory Handbook, 1824-1975. 1977.

## Austria

**Allanello, Raffaele** — Lombardy-Venetia and Austrian Levant (cancellations). Successor to Mueller handbook, 600 pages.

**ANK Nettokataloge** — 1980 edition, 280 pages.

**Clement, Alfred** — Handbuch der Feld-und-Militarpost in Osterreich Handbook on Austrian Army postal service. 1964, Volume 1 (1443-1914), 320 pages.

**DeFrank, P. F.** — Die Erste Ausgabe von Osterreich und Lombardei - Venetien, 1850-1858. First issue of Austria and Lombardy Venetia. 1978, Giorgio Migliavacca, reprint of 1933 German translation of French original, 97 pages.

**Del Bianco, Umberto** — Il Lloyd Austriaco e gli annuli marittimi dell' Austria - Ungheria. Postal history of Austrian Lloyd shipping line and other Austrian maritime activities 1820-1918. Volume I, 1976, Sorani Editore, Milan, 362 pages; Volume II, 479 pages.

**Engelhardt, Wilhelm** — Etude sur les Preobliters Autrichiens (precancels). 1957, 14 pages.

**Erler, Martin, and Hagn, Helmut** — Katalog der Fiskalmarken von Osterreich. Catalog of the adhesive revenues of Austria. 2 volumes, 1978-1979, ORA Verlag.

**Ferchenbauer, Ulrich** — Osterreich 1850-1918. Specialized catalog. 1976, third edition, 623 pages.

**Gauge, Anton** — Die Zeitungsstempelmarken Osterreichs und Lombardei Venetiens. Catalog of the newspaper tax stamps of Austria and Lombardy - Venetia. 1958, 245 pages; 1962 supplement.

**Gindl, Heinz** — Alles uber die Trachtenserie. Specialized handbook of the definitive issue of 1948-62. 1967, Linz, 104 pages.

**Gordon, T. M.** — Checklist of Italian and Jugoslavian Town Cancels on the Stamps of the Austrian Empire, 1850-1883. 1974, 103 pages.

Checklist of Town Cancellations of Bosnia and Herzegovina, 1879-1918. 1973, 78 pages.

Checklist of Hungarian and Romanian Town Cancels on the Stamps of the Austrian Empire, 1850-70. 1971, 127 pages.

Checklist of Czechoslovakian Town Cancels on the Stamps of the Austrian Empire, 1850-83. 1970, 222 pages.

Checklist of Polish Town Cancels on the Stamps of the Austrian Empire, 1850-83. 1970, 77 pages.

Checklist of Austrian Town Cancels on the Stamps of the Austrian Empire, 1850-83. 1974, 158 pages.

**Huber, Karl** — Dass Wappen - Mittelstuck von Osterreich (und) Lombardei-Venetien. Study of plate varieties and errors of first issue of Austria and Lombardy - Venetia. 1969, 62 pages, Linzer Kreis.

**Huber, Karl, and Wessely, Gerhard** — Grosses Handbuch Osterreich und Lombardei - Venetien. Handbook on first issue. 1976, WEKA - Philatelie, 248 pages.

Spezialkatalog fur die erste Emission 1850. Detailed, priced catalog for the first issue. 1979, WEKA-Philatelie, 136 pages.

**Klein, Wilhelm** — Die postalischen Abstempelungen und andere Entwertungsarten auf den Osterreichischen Postwertzeichen Ausgaben von 1867, 1883 und 1890. Postmarks on issues of 1867, 1883 and 1890. Two volumes, 1967-72, Geitner.

**Kropf, Hans** — Die Postwertzeichen des Kaisertum Osterreich und der Osterreich - ungarischen Monarchie. Study of the 19th century issue. 1908, M. Schultz, 447 pages.

**Majetic, Victor** — Spezial Katalog der Feld - und Etappenpoststempel von Osterreich-Ungarn, 1914-18. Catalog of army postmarks, WWI. 1965, 124 pages.

**Michel Osterreich Spezial Katalog.** 1979/80 edition, 195 pages, Schwanenberger Verlag.

**Mueller, Edwin** — Osterreich Spezialkatalog 1850-1918. Fifth edition, J. Kunz and Mercury Stamp Co., 1952, 155 pages, German and English.

Die Poststempel auf den Freimarken Ausgabe 1867 von Osterreich - Ungarn. Postmarks on definitive issue of 1867. 1930-32, Die Postmarke, 416 pages.

The Prestamp Postmarks of Austria. 1960, Collectors Club, 199 pages; supplement 1, 1965; supplement 2, by Karl Kuhn, Die Briefmarke, 1975, 48 pages.

**Mueller, Edwin, and Fitch, Mark** — Handbook of Austria and Lombardy — Venetia Cancellations on the Postage Stamp Issues of 1850, 1858-59, 1860-61, 1863 and 1863-64. 1961, 468 pages; 1978 reprint, German and English.

**National Philatelic Museum, Philadelphia, Pa.** — Austria, 143 pages.

**Osterreichischer Bundesverlag** — Kleine Kunstegeschichte der Osterreichischen Briefmarke. History of the design and printing of Austrian stamps. 1967-68, two volumes.

**Osterreichischer Staatsdruckerei** — 100 Jahre Osterreichische Briefmarke. Official centennial history of Austrian stamps. 1950, 99 pages.

**Passer, Adolf** — Die Postwertzeichen von Bosnien und Herzegovina. Stamps of Bosnia - Herzegovina. 1930, Prague, 215 pages.

**Pfalz, Helmut, and Richter, Helmut** — Osterreich Spezialkatalog amtliche Zahnungen, 1867-1906. Catalog of perforation varieties for issues of 1867-1906. 1969, 56 pages.

**Schneiderbauer, Franz** — Ganzsachen Osterreich - Spezial - Katalog und Handbuch. Standard catalog of Austrian postal stationery. 1977, Vienna, 220 pages.

**Sieger, Hermann** — Osterreichischer Flugpost Katalog. First flight covers of Austrian Airlines, 1955-70. 1971, Sieger Verlag, 228 pages.

**Tranmer, Keith** — Austrian Post Offices Abroad. Part 8, 112 pages.

Postal History of Austria, 1938-45. 1972, Austria Stamp Club of Great Britain, 99 pages.

Austro-Hungarian Army Post Offices, 1914-18. Second edition, 1973, 115 pages.

**Tschilingarian, Simon D., and Stephen, W.S.E.** — Austrian Post Offices Abroad. 1962-1976, Austria Stamp Club of Great Britain, eight parts to date (Part 8 by K. Tranmer).

**Waschutt, Alois** — Osterreich 1867. Plate varieties of definitive issue of 1867. 1972, 125 pages.

**Wurth, Rudiger** — Sonderpostamter in Osterreich. Catalog of Austrian slogan and commemorative special cancels. 1979, Verlag Margarether Thurner, 315 pages.

**Zanetti, Agostino** — Cancellations of Lombardy-Venetia (1856-66) and Austrian Levant (1863-83). 1979, 347 pages (Italian, French, German and English).

## Bahamas

**Ludington, M.H., and Raymond, G.** — Bahama Islands. History and catalog of the handstamps and cancellations between 1802 and 1967.

**Ludington, M.H.** — Bahamas Locally Overprinted 1916-17 Special Delivery Stamps. 12 pages.

**Ludington, M.H., and Osborn, G.** — Royal Mail Steam Packets to Bermuda and the Bahamas. 24 pages.

**Raymond, G.** — Bahamas Post Office. 9 pages.

Bahamas Temporary Rubber Datestamps and Cancellations. Bahamas Postal History Study Circle, 12 pages.

## Bangladesh

**Kessler** — Air Post Stationery of Bangladesh. Lava, 18 pages.

## Basutoland

**Gilbert, G. N.** — Basutoland, Historical Notes. 1973 reprint, 30 pages.

**Scott, Aubrey H.** — The Cancellations and Postal Markings of Basutoland/Lesotho Post Offices and Their Historical Background. 1980, Collectors Mail Auctions, 294 pages.

## Bechuanaland

**Holmes** — Stamps, Stationery and Postmarks. 1971, 189 pages.

## Belgium

**Barefoot, J.** — Belgium Numeral Cancels 1849-1866. European Philately No. 2, 29 pages.

**Belgium Stamp Dealers' Association** — Catalogue Officiel Belgique. 1979 edition, 338 pages.

**Billig, Fritz** — Forgeries. Volume 40, in German.

**Bertrand, Gustave** — Memorial Philatelique il la Belgique. 1934, 217 pages (French).

**Blumental, G.M.** — Belgium Catalogue National Specialise - 10 per cent. 1979.

**Catalog Prinet** — Editions Dereume, issued yearly.

**D'Hondt, D.** — Les Obliterations Mecaniques Belges in Form de Drapeau, de Flammes ou de Lignes Paralleles Ondulees (machine cancels). 1945, 45 pages (French).

Les Obliterations Mecaniques Belges, 1910-51 (machine cancels). Two booklets, 69 pages (French).

**Duson, Jean** — Catalogue des Carnets de Timbres Poste de Belgique et du Congo Belge. 1978, 64 pages (French).

**Grubben** — Essays Belgium & Congo. 1933, 119 pages, in French.

**Herlant** — La Poste Aux Letters au Pays de Liege Avant 1849, with catalog des Marques Postales. 1957, 34 pages, in French.

**Hubinont, Raoul** — Belgium Les vols de Gand 1913. 1963, Academie de Philatelie de Belgique, 73 pages.

Belgium Catalogue des Estampiles et Obliterations Allemandes relevees sur le courrier civil dans les Etapes du Front Ouest, France and Belgium. Guerre Mondiale 1914-1918, with the collaboration of Rene Goin. Academie de Philatelie de Belgique, 1971, 119 pages.

Belgium Bibliographie de La Philatelie Belge. Academie de Philatelie de Belgique, 1972, 43 pages, in French.

**International Philatelic Editions** — Catalogue National Specialise Belgique & Europa. 50th edition, 364 pages; 1977, eight-page supplement.

**Jacob, R.** — Essai de Classification des Obliterations et Griffes des Cantons de L'est de la Belgium et des Communes Belges Annexees parl'Allemagne en 1940-1945. Postal history. 80 pages.

**Karrick, C.E.** — Catalog Cross Reference U.S. Belgium. Belgium Philatelic Society, based on the 1976 editions of the Catalogue Official and Scott's Standard Postage Stamp Catalogue, 29 pages.

**Lepingle, J.J.E.** — Catalogue Illustre des Obliterations Temporaires de Belgique et du Congo Belge. 1956, 54 pages (French).

Petit Lexique des Marques Postales Belges de 1849 a nos Jour (cancellations). 1957, 23 pages (French).

**Mayenge, G.** — Essai de Classification des Obliterations du Car Postal et de ses Cachets non Obliterants (cancels and cachets of postal cars). 1956, 18 pages (French).

### Belgian Congo

**Balasse, Willy** — Catalog, Belgique, Congo Belge. 1949, French.

**Mallet-Veale, H.** — Stamps of the Belgian Congo and Belgian East Africa. 1928, 39 pages.

### Bermuda

**Dickgeisser, Robert W.** — King George VI High Values. 1980, Triad Publications, 96 pages.

**Ludington, M.H.** — Handstruck Stamps and Cancellations. 1956, 40 pages.

Postal History and Stamps of Bermuda. Reprint, Quarterman Publications.

**Ludington, M.H., and Osborn, Geoffrey** — Royal Mail Steam Packets to Bermuda and Bahamas. 24 pages.

### Bhopal

**Barefoot, J.** — Notes on Plating "The Primitives." 22 pages.

### Bolivia

**Alfaro, R.E.** — Who's Who on the Postage Stamps of Bolivia. 1940, 9 pages.

### Brazil

**Alliance Specialized Catalog of Brazil.** 1965.

**Catalogo de Inteiros do Brazil Ariro.** 1957, 52 pages.

**Catalog de Selos do Brazil** — Rolf Harold Meyer, issued yearly.

**Kunze, A.F.** — The Amazon, Has it Been Truly Discovered. A narrative based on the postage stamps of Brazil, Ecuador, Peru. Pan American Union, 1944, 8 pages.

**Meyer, R.H.** — Catalogo de Selos do Brazil. 1979, 37th edition, 352 pages, in Portuguese.

**Schiffer, F.** — Specialized Catalog of Brazil. 1980, 332 pages (Portuguese).

### British Commonwealth
### General

**Alcock and Meredith** — Postage Stamps, Varieties III, QV-KGVI. 1949, 122 pages.

**Baldwin, N.C.** — Air Mails of British Africa 1925-32. 68 pages.

British Air Mails 1784-1946. 213 pages, 1947.

Fifty Years of British Air Mails, 1911-1960. 47 pages.

**Barefoot and Hall** — British Commonwealth Revenues. 1980.

**Bridger and Kay** — Commonwealth Five Reigns Postage Stamp Catalogue. 1979, 14th edition, 528 pages.

**British Post Office** — Collect British Stamps. British and American editions regularly updated.

**Bruns, Frank** — The Stamps of Elizabeth Regina and the Royal Family. 45 pages.

**Commonwealth Catalogue King George VI Stamps** — Ninth edition 1963, 163 pages.

**Commonwealth Catalogue of Queen Elizabeth Period of Postage Stamps.** Regularly updated.

**Crane, A.O.** — Postage Stamps of King George VI. Sixth edition, 1948, 120 pages.

**Donaldson, Neil** — The Postal Agencies in Eastern Arabia and the Gulf. 1975, 280 pages.

**Easton, John** — De La Rue History of British and Foreign Postage Stamps 1855-1901. 1958, 846 pages.

**Forgo, Steve** — Paintings and Graphic Arts on the Stamps of Great Britain and the Nations of the British Commonwealth. 1979, Phil-Art, 315 pages.

**Gibbons, Stanley** — British Commonwealth Catalog. Regularly updated.

Elizabethan Catalogue. Regularly updated.

**Jackson, Capt. H.T.** — Railway and Airway Letter Stamps of the British Isles, 1891-1971. 1979, 179 pages.

**Johnson, C.A.** — British Colonial Handbook. 1945, 57 pages.

**Johnson, S.C.** — British Postage Stamps. 1944, 47 pages.

**Heins, H.H.** — Numeral Cancellations of the British Empire. Third edition, 1967, 64 pages.

**Kenmore** — Price list of stamps of the British Commonwealth of Nations Catalogue. 1942 edition.

**Lister, John** — Queen Elizabeth II Stamp Catalogue. Regularly updated.

**Lowe, Robson** — British Postage Stamps of the 19th Century. 1979 edition, 272 pages.

British Empire Review 1961-68. 92 pages.

The De La Rue Key Plates. 1979, 32 pages.

Encyclopaedia of British Empire Postage Stamps, Volume I Great Britain and the Empire in Europe. 1948 edition; HJMR reprint of original with supplements, two volumes, 468 pages.

Encyclopaedia of Empire Postage Stamps, Volume II Africa. 468 pages, two volumes, reprint by HJMR.

Encyclopaedia of Empire Postage Stamps, Volume III Asia. 575 pages, three volumes, reprint by HJMR.

Encyclopaedia of British Empire Postage Stamps, Volume IV, Australasia. 1962, three volumes, reprint by HJMR.

**Mayo, Dann** — British Empire Censorship Devices, World War II. 1978, Civil Censorship Study Group.

**Melville, F.J.** — British Central Africa. 28 pages.

British Central Africa and Nyasaland. 76 pages.

**Minkus** — British Commonwealth Stamp Catalog. 575 pages.

**Morley, W.** — Catalog and Price List of the Revenue Stamps of the British Colonies. 1895, 88 pages.

**Nodder** — Postal History and Postmarks of British Central Africa and Nyasaland. 140 pages.

**Potter, David** — British Elizabethan Stamps. 190 pages.

**Rose, Stuart** — Royal Mail Stamps, A Survey of British Stamp Designs. 1980, Phaidon Press Ltd., 128 pages.

**Rosen, Gerald** — British Local Stamps Catalog. 152 pages.

**Samuel, Marcus** — Specimen Stamps of the Crown Colonies. 1976, 224 pages.

**Urch, Harris and Co.** — The Commonwealth Catalogue of Queen Elizabeth II Silver Jubilee Postage Stamps. 1979.

Queen Elizabeth II Commonwealth Catalogue. 1979, 700 pages.

**Vallancey, H.** — British Postmarks. 72 pages, Volume 12.

British Photogravure Stamps. 1934-35, 16 pages.

**Wilson, Sir John** — The Royal Philatelic Collection. 1952.

**de Worms, Percy** — Perkins Bacon Records. Security printing. 1953, 867 pages.

### British Guiana

**Townsend, W.A., and Howe, F.G.** — Stamps and Postal History. 1970, 424 pages.

### British North America

**Heath, J.M.** — British Postal Agencies in Mexico.

**Jarrett, Fred** — Stamps of British North America. 1975 reprint of 1929 book, 624 pages.

**Lowe, Robson** — Encyclopaedia of British Empire Postage Stamps. Volume V, North America, 1973, 760 pages.

**Minuse and Pratt** — Essays and Proofs of British North America. 1970, 198 pages.

**Pugh, Kenneth W.** — Reference Manual of BNA Fakes, Forgeries and Counterfeits. Eleven releases to date.

**Smith, William** — The History of the Post Offices of British North America 1639-1870.

### British Solomon Islands

**Voyce, Reverend** — Postal History of Barakoma Airfield. 1966, 40 pages.

### British West Africa

**McCaig, Colin** — Postal History and Handstamps. 1979, 64 pages.

### Brunei

**Lowe, Robson** — Brunei 1895 Star and Crescent Issue. 1973, 32 pages.

**Melville, Fred J.** — Brunei. 1980 reprint of 1930 booklet, 38 pages.

### Burma

**Davis G., and Martin D.** — Postal History of Burma. 1971, 216 pages.

### Canada

**Bailey, Maj. W.J.** — Canadian Military Postmarks. 1978, 72 pages.

**Bileski, K.** — Canadian Postage Stamps, 1953-1974. Elizabethan period. 100 pages.

**Billig, Fritz** — Volume 7, Canada Catalogue of Constant Plate Varieties by Hans Reiche. 48 pages plus 1954 supplement.

Volume 9, Canada Tax, War Tax Stamps. 1959, War Tax Study Group. 36 pages.

**Boggs, W.S.** — Postage Stamps and Postal History of Canada. 1946, two volumes; 1975, Quarterman reprint. 624 pages.

**Bond, N.** — Postal Stationery of Canada. 1953, 132 pages.

**Brandom, Lee W.** — Catalog of Tobacco Tax Paid Stamps of Canada and Newfoundland. 1976, Canadian Revenue Group of the British North American Philatelic Society, 176 pages; 1980 supplement.

**British North American Philatelic Society** — Canadian Perfins Catalog.

**Campbell, Frank W.** — Canada Post Office, 1755-1895. 1972, 191 pages.

**Charlton Stamp Guide** — 1981, second edition, 231 pages.

**Chung, Andrew** — The 1977-1978 Definitives of Canada. 27 pages.

The 1967-1978 Postage Due Issue of Canada. 1980, 46 pages.

**Day and Smythies** — Canadian Fancy Cancellations of the 19th Century. 1962, 122 pages.

**Deaville, Alfred** — The Colonial Postal Systems and Postage Stamps of Vancouver Island and British Columbia, 1849-71. Quarterman reprint of 1928 edition, 226 pages.

**Department of Trade and Commerce** — Canada 1943, 196 pages; 1944, 205 pages.

**Firth, L. Gerald** — Canada, the 15-Cent of 1868. 1963, 211 pages.

**Gandley, Will** — Canada Cover Catalogue. Regularly updated.

**Gandley, W., and Stanley, D.** — Canada/BNA Postage Stamp Catalogue. Regularly updated.

**Gillam, L.F.** — A History of Canadian RPOs. 1979, 179 pages, American Philatelic Society.

**Gronbeck-Jones, D.** — Centennial Definitives of Canada, 1967-1972 Series. 40 pages.

The Caricatures and Landscapes Definitives of Canada. 1979, 48 pages.

**Halliday, W.E.** — Notes on the Postal History of Canada. 11 pages.

**Hamilton, P.** — Canadian Stamps. (c.1940), 116 pages.

**Hanson, G.** — Guidebook & Catalog of Canadian Stamps. Issued yearly, Regency Publishing Co.

**Harrison, H.W.** — Canada's Registry System 1827-1911. 1971, 84 pages.

**Heyn, K.D.** — Checklist of Canada's Definitives, 1954-1976, 35 pages.

**Hillson, John** — The Small Queens of Canada. 1981, Robson Lowe Ltd., 24-page monograph.

**Holmes, L.S.** — Specialized Philatelic Catalogue of Canada and B.N.A. 1963, 10th edition, 410 pages.

**Howes, C.A.** — Canadian Postage Stamps and Stationery. 1974 reprint of 1911 work. 312 pages.

**Irwin, R.W.** — Canadian Meter Postage Stamp Catalog. Second edition. 68 pages.

**Konwiser, H.M.** — Canada and Newfoundland Stampless Cover Catalog. 1946, 50 pages.

**Laroche, J.J.** — Canada 1967-1973 Centennial Definitives. 1973, 120 pages.

**Leclerc, Pierre A.** — Apercu de Bibliophilatelie. A view of bibliophilately with the emphasis on Canada and BNA. 1974, 25 pages.

Elements d'Interest Philatelique. Short articles of Canadian philately. 1975, 24 pages (French).

Propos d'un Ex-Philateliste. 1974, 38 pages, French.

**Lyman** — Lyman's Standard Catalogue of Canada - BNA Postage Stamps. Regularly updated.

**McAlpin, T., and Gandley, W.** — Canada Matched Plate Block Stamp Catalogue. Sixth edition. 56 pages.

**Mackenzie, Kenneth S.** — The Canadian Ocean Mail Clerk, 1860-87 (ships of the Allan Line). Canadian National Postal Museum, 47 pages.

**Marler, G.C.** — Edward VII Issue of Canada. 1975, National Postal Museum. 224 pages, French or English.

The Admiral Issue, 1911-1925. 1949, APS handbook, 75 pages.

**Mechem, T.O.** — Canadian Philatelic Handbook. 38 pages of postal history.

**Morgan, I.C.** — Specialized Catalog of Canadian Airmails. 1931.

**Morin, Climon** — Canadian Philately Bibliography and Index, 1864-1973. 1979, National Library of Canada, 281 pages.

**Pekonen, W.** — Checklist of Canadian Official Stampless Covers Since 1963, 66 pages.

**Philatelic Supply Co.** — Canada Specialized Postage Stamp Catalog. 1979 edition, 128 pages.

**Proulx, David** — Slogan Postal Cancels of Canada. 1978 edition.

**Pugh, K.W.** — Canada Varieties of the Queen Elizabeth Era. Part 1, 36 pages; part 2, 52 pages.

**Reiche, Hans** — Canada Plate Varieties. 48 pages.

The Admiral Stamps of 1911 to 1925. 20 pages.

Canada Large Queen's Report. 70 pages, Canadian Wholesale Supply Co.

Admiral Cancels. 1981, Unitrade Associates, 17 pages.

Constant Plate Varieties of the Canada Small Queens. 1981, Unitrade, 27 pages.

**Richardson, Ed** — Collect Canadian Covers. 1978, 104 pages, American Philatelic Society.

**de Rooy/Hali Booklet Catalogue of Canada.** Regularly updated.

**Rose, Ken** — Canada Tagged Stamps Handbook. 39 pages, Saskatoon Coin and Stamp Centre.

**Royal Philatelic Society** — The Royal Philatelic Society of Canada 1968 Year Book. 56 pages.

**Satfield, Garret W.** — Canadian Secret Mark Stamps, 1935-1966. 19 pages.

**Sisson** — 1978 Standard Catalogue of Canada Revenues and Semi-Official Airmails. Third edition, 50 pages, J.N. Sissons Ltd.

**Smith, Crouch and Jarrett** — Airmail Catalog Canada and Newfoundland. 1929, 53 pages.

**Smythies, E.A.** — Canadian Roller Cancellations 1894-1930.

Canadian Registered Letter Stamps & Cancellations 1875-1902. 63 pages.

Canadian Duplex Cancellations, 1860-1902. Second edition, 55 pages.

**Tomlinson, Frederick** — The Canadian Map Stamp of 1898. 1972 reprint, 47 pages.

**Vaughn, Gordon D.** — The Queen Elizabeth II Era Stationery of Canada.

**Vilter, E.F.** — Catalog of Liquor Bottle Seals of Canada. 1980, Canadian Revenue Group of the BNAPS, 102 pages.

**Walburn, H.G.** — Official Catalog of Canada Precancels. 13th edition, 1981, 55 pages, Gilbert W. Noble.

**Webb, J.F.** — Canada & Newfoundland Postal Stationery Catalog. 1978 edition, 77 pages.

**Whitehead, A.** — Squared Circle Postmarks. 1959, second edition, 56 pages.

**Whitworth, G.** — First Decimal Issue of Canada 1859-68. 1966, 95 pages.

**Wilcox, George** — History of Rural Mail in Canada. 1975 reprint of 1918 work, 74 pages.

**Wrigley, Roy** — Canadian Postage Stamps Checklist and Catalog. 24 pages.

**Wrigley, Roy, and Moir, Brian** — Canadian Official Stamps. Eighth edition.

**Young, Donald A.** — Canada Through the Looking Glass (major and minor varieties of 20 century stamps). 1958, 24 pages.

### Canada-BNA-Provinces

**Argenti, N.** — Postage Stamps of New Brunswick and Nova Scotia. 1962, 223 pages; 1976 reprint, 223 pages.

**Deaville, A.S.** — Colonial Postage Systems and Postage Stamps of Vancouver Island and British Columbia, 1849-71. 1928, 210 pages.

**Jephcott, C.M.** — Postal History of Nova Scotia and New Brunswick. 300 pages.

**Mitchell, R.B.** — Fakes and Forgeries of New Brunswick and Prince Edward Island. 1979, 43 pages.

Nova Scotia Fakes and Forgeries. 1976, 50 pages.

**Poole, B.W.H.** — Nova Scotia (c.1920), 20 pages. (Mekeel's Handbook 34.)

Stamps of Prince Edward Island. 16 pages. (Mekeel's Handbook 27.)

Postage Stamps of British Columbia and Vancouver Island. 14 pages.

**Woodall, R.G.** — Postal History of Yukon Territory. 1976, 267 pages, second edition.

### Cape of Good Hope

**Stevenson, D.A.** — Triangular Stamps of the Cape. 1950, 142 pages.

### Cayman Islands

**Aguilar, E.P., and Saunders, P.T.** — Postal History, Postage Stamps and Postmarks. 1962, 111 pages.

**Melville, F.J.** — Cayman Islands. 1912, 63 pages.

### Channel Islands

**Barefoot Ltd.** — Channel Islands Revenues. 1979, 24 pages.

**Gibbons, Stanley** — Channel Islands Specialized Catalogue of Stamps and Postal History. 1979.

Collect Channel Islands Stamps. 1982, 10th edition.

**Hayes, R.A.** — Modern Channel Islands Flight Covers. 1974.

**Mohle, Heinz, and Wienecke, Michael** — Kanalinseln. Deutsche Besetzung 1940-45. Handbook of the stamps and postal history of the Channel Islands under German occupation during WWII. 1979, Arbeitsgemeinschaft Neues Handbuch der Briefmarkenkunde. 120 pages.

**Newport, W.** — Channel Islands Stamps and Postal History. 214 pages.

Stamps and Postal History of the Channel Islands. 1972, 224 pages.

The Specialized Priced Catalogue of Channel Island Stamps. Channel Islands Specialists Society, 94 pages.

**Wieneke, Michael** — The German Field Post Office in the Channel Islands. 1982, Channel Island Occupation Society.

### Chile

**Alfano, R.E.** — Who's Who on the Postage Stamps of Chile. 1944, 18 pages.

**Mercado, R.A., and Sigismond, Jean** — Les Timbres du Chile. 1980 reprint, 68 pages.

### China

**Bendig, A.W.** — National Revenue Stamps of China. 16 pages.

Revenue Stamps of the Japanese Occupation of Manchuria and Inner Mongolia. 1956, 9 pages.

Formosa Revenue Stamps. 1958, 4 pages.

Revenue Stamps of Taiwan. 1961, second edition.

Notebook on Chinese Revenue Stamps. Electrostatic reproduction of the original. 185 pages.

**Borek** — Volksrepublik China. 1979, 57 pages.

**Bowker, H.F.** — Foochow. 1903, 1938, 11 pages.

**Cane, L.B.** — Stamps of China. 1938, 64 pages.

**Chan, S.H.** — Catalogue of Unit and Silver Yuan Stamps of China. 1976, 74 pages.

**Chang, K.S.** — Catalogue of Chinese Stamps (1879-1949). 1978, 196 pages.

Overprinted New Taiwan Dollar Stamps with Standard Style of Writing of Lead Types. 1980, 150 pages.

**ChenKee Stamp Service** — Catalog Chinese Postage Stamps. 1951, 269 pages.

**Ch'ien, Tsao** — Chinese Postal History — the Part of Taiwan. 1981, Directorate of Posts.

**Chi Wen Yen** — An Illustration of Revenue Stamps of China. 1976-78, Part 1, 35 pages; Part 2, 35 pages; Part 3, 44 pages; Part 4, 51 pages; and Part 5, 53 pages.

**China National Stamp Corp.** — Postage Stamp Catalogue of the People's Republic of China, 1949-1980. 1981, 144 pages.

**China Philatelic Society** — Postage Stamps of the People's Republic of China. 1972, 88 pages.

**China Stamp Collectors Club of Australia** — The Great Wall. Offset reproduction of complete journal (October 1956 - December 1962) in four volumes and index.

**Denison, Ellery** — Chinese Postage Stamp Booklets. 1981, Denison 41 pages.

**Directorate General of Posts** — Postage Stamps of Modern China, the Cultural Interflow of Nations. 120 pages.

Stamps Tell the Story of the Republic of China. 64 pages.

Postage Stamp Catalog of the Republic of China (1878-1978). Centennial edition, 900 pages.

Illustrated Catalog in Color of Postage Stamps of the Republic of China. Periodic supplements.

A Select Collection of Large Dragon Stamps, Covers and Postmarks. 1978.

Prize Selections from the ROCPEX Taipei '81. 1982, 200 plus pages.

**Dougan, Charles** —The Shanghai Postal System, the Stamps and Postal History. 1981, 214 pages.

**Foreign Language Press (Peking)** — Postage Stamps of the People's Republic of China. 1959, 100 pages.

**Fuerst, Robert E.** — Catalogue of the Money Order Stamps of China (Pagoda Design). 1976, 34 pages.

**Gibbons, Stanley** — China Catalogue. 1979, 190 pages.

**Gray, R.E.** — The Northeastern Provinces Sun Yat-Sen Stamps of 1945-1948. 1976, 89 pages.

Airmail Stamps of China (1921-49). 1978, 61 pages.

Counterfeits of Chinese Postage Stamps. 1979, 10 pages.

**Han, Ho-Yun** — Illustrated Catalogue of Chinese Postal Stationery (1897-1977). 1978, 224 pages.

**Hayes, Harry** — The Postal Stationery of the People's Republic of China, 1949-1965.

**Huang Kuang-Sheng** — A Treatise on the Extant Copies of the Small $1. 1977, 350 pages, in Chinese and English.

**Hubbard, H.W.** — Handbook of Early Chinese Communist Stamps, 1928-38. 1969, 54 pages.

Treaty Port Local Posts of China. 1957, 28 pages.

**Ireland, Philip W.** — China - The Large Dragons, 1878-1885. 1978, Robson Lowe, 130 pages.

**Japan Philatelic Society** — 1980 Chinese Stamp Catalogue (P.R.C.).

**Jones, W.E.** — Gold and Silver Currency Stamps of China and Formosa. 1952, second edition, 38 pages.

National Currency Stamps of China. 1955, 26 pages.

The Silver Currency Stamps and Temporary Labels of China. 1975, third edition, 52 pages.

**Kan, W.** — Rare Stamps of China. 1972, 128 pages.

**Kao, C.L.** — Notes on the Postage Stamps of China 1878-97. 1974, 26 pages.

**Kerr, A.D.** — The Local Overprinted Stamps of Manchuria 1945-47. Volumes 1-4, 1976-77, 186 pages.

**Lankester, R.F.** — China 1927-1949, 80 pages.

**Livingston, L.F.** — Classical China. 1956.

Price List of Formosa Postage Stamps. 1958, 24 pages.

The Shanghai Postal System. 1971, 54 pages.

**Ma, Zung-Sung** — Illustrated Catalog of Stamps of China. Reprint of 1947 edition, 568 pages.

**Marsh and Williams** — The Postal Savings Stamps of China. 1976, 41 pages.

**Melville, F.J.** — Postage Stamps of China. 1908, 44 pages.

**Mencarini, J., and Chow, M.D.** — Descriptive Catalogue of Chinese Postal Stationery with Appendices. 1937, Chinese Philatelic Society; 1981, reproduction by Williams, 76 pages.

**Morgan, T.** — Chats on the Stamps of China. 24 pages.

**Negus, James** — Forgeries of China's Large Dragons. 1978, 14 pages.

**Padget, P.I.** — Postal Stationery of the People's Republic of China, 1949-65. 1975 reprint of 1929 book, 33 pages.

The Postal Markings of China. 1978, 111 pages.

The Revenue Stamps of Communist China, 1929-45. 1981, second edition, 24 pages.

**Romans Net Price Catalog of Chinese Treaty Ports Stamps.** Reprint, 46 pages.

**Ruland, L.S.** — Express Letter Stamps of China. 1941, 30 pages.

**Schumann, A.** — China Specialized Catalog. 1941, second edition, 100 pages.

**Siddall, T.** — Catalog of Stamps of China and Chinese Treaty Ports 1926, 42 pages.

**Sieh, Pingwen, and Blackburn, J. Lewis** — Postage Rates of China, 1867-1980. 1981, English edition, Directorate General of Posts, Taiwan.

**Starr and Mills** — The Chinese Air Post 1920-35. 1937, 112 pages.

**Tilles, Dr. Harvey** — The Perfins of China.

**Universal Stamp Service** — Standard Catalog of People's Posts of China. 1952, 282 pages.

**Wan, Jack** — China — Military Postal History of the World War II. 1980, two volumes, 500 pages (Chinese).

**Warner, W.A.** — Emissions of China, Shanghai, Corea and Japan. 1889, 14 pages.

**Williams, J.M.** — The Gold Yuan Stamps of China. 1977, 90 pages.

The China National Currency Stamps of 1945-48. 1981, 100 pages.

**Yang, N.C.** — Postage Stamp Catalog of the People's Republic of China. 1982, fifth edition.

**Yu, K.C.** — Standard Postage Stamp Catalogue of China. 1982, 252 pages.

### Christmas Island

**Pacific Islands Study Circle** — Christmas Island and Its Postal History. Hawthorn Press.

### Colombia

**A Barriga Especialized Catalogue.** 1981, 10th edition, 245 pages.

**Gebauer, E.** — Air Post of Colombia. 1963, 126 pages.

**Gebauer, E., and Tamayo, Jairo L.** — Los Primeros 50 years of Airmail Service in Colombia. 326 pages.

**Inbarren, J.** — Who's Who on the Postage Stamps of Colombia. 1942, 19 pages.

**Myer, J.N.** — Colombia 1904-1917 Types of the 'Numeral' Issues. 1957, 48 pages.

Studies in the Philately of Colombia. 1940, 86 pages.

**Temprano, Leo** — Catalogo Estampillas Tipo de Colombia. 1979, 14th edition, 229 pages, Filatelia Tematica L.T.

### Cook Islands

**Burge, A.R.** — Cancellations of Cook Islands and Niue. 1971, 61 pages.

The Early Cook Islands Post Office. 112 pages.

**Howard-White, F.B.** — Cook Islands Early Postal History. 1975, Postal History Society of New Zealand Monograph No. 5.

**Pacific Islands Study Circle** — Postmarks to 1919, 55 pages.

The Cook Islands to 1919. 1958, Hawthorne Press, 55 pages.

### Costa Rica

**Fossum, Earl G.** — Index to Costa Rican Philatelic Literature, 1863-1973. 1974, Society of Costa Rica Collectors, 64 pages.

**Kunze, A.F.** — Who's Who on the Postage Stamps of Costa Rica. 1943, 18 pages.

**Mata, Dr. Carlos Saenz** — Catalogo de Sellos Postales de Costa Rica. 1979, second edition, Society of Costa Rica Collectors, 104 pages.

**O'Neill, Fred, et al** — Antologia Filatelica Costarricense. 1971, Comision Nacional del Sesquicentennario de la Independencia de Centro America, 185 pages.

### Crete

**Binos, Charilaos, M.** — The Error in the Control Numerals of 10 - lepta Paris Print 1861. 1958 reprint from Philotelia, pages 350-51.

**Lewis, H.L** — Crete, Its Postal History and Stamps. 198 pages.

**Poole, B.W.H.** — Postage Stamps of Crete. 32 pages.

**Tchilinghirian and Stephen** — Part V, Greece, Crete, Aegean Islands, Macedonia. 1964, Austrian Stamp Club of Great Britain, pages 322-400.

**Thompson, C.S.** — Counterfeits of the First Six Issues of Crete. 11 pages.

**Zervoyannis, Nicholas** — Les Timbres - Postes de la Crete. Part 1, 1971, 130 pages; Part 2, 140 pages. Greek and French.

### Croatia

**Croatian Philatelic Society** — Paperback catalog on stamps, coins, paper money and military decorations of Croatia. 1975. 300 pages.

### Cuba

**Garcia, R.R.** — El Correo Aero En Cuba. First flights, 1937, 40 pages.

**Kunze, A.F.** — Who's Who on the Postage Stamps of Cuba. 1943, 29 pages.

### Curacao

**Julsen, F.W., and Benders, A.M.** — Postal History of Curacao. 1976, American Society for Netherlands Philately, 626 pages.

### Cyprus

**Bols, A.N.D.** — The Postal Surcharge and Revenue Stamps of Cyprus. 1979, Robson Lowe, 12 pages.

**Castle, Wilfrid** — Postal History and Postage Stamps. 1971, second edition, 256 pages.

**Erdin's Catalogue of Cyprus Turkish Federated State of Kibris Postage Stamps and Postal History.** 1981, second edition, Erdin Rifat, 88 pages.

**Field, John** — Airmails Over Cyprus, 1930-1952. 12 pages.

### Czechoslovakia

**Catalogue of Postal Stationery of Czechoslovakia.** Society for Czechoslovak Philately.

**Erler, Martin** — Catalog of Federal and Municipal Revenues of Czechoslovakia. English-German, 220 pages.

**First Czechoslovak Philatelic Club of America** — Handbook on Bohemoslovenika. 1978.

**Kaufmann, H.** — Slovensky Stationery. 1939, English translation from Society for Czechoslovak Philately.

**Padelky** — Forgeries. Translation from Society for Czechoslovak Philately.

**POFIS Catalog Ceskoslovenskych Postovnich Znamek.** Postal Philatelic Service, issued yearly.

**Richet, R.** — Czechoslovak Fieldposts.

The Issues and Cancellations of Carpatho-Ukraine and South Slovakia. Translation from Society for Czechoslovak Philately.

The Issues of the Czechoslovak Legion in Siberia.

The Issues of the Sudetenland. Translation from Society for Czechoslovak Philately.

**Velek, S.** — Billig's Volume 10, Czechoslovakia. 60 pages.

**Viklicky, Vladimir** — Public Health as Reflected on Czechoslovak Philatelic Material. 163 pages.

### Danish West Indies

**Danish West Indies Specialized Catalogue** — 1978, Frost Forlag handbook, 114 pages (Danish).

**Engstrom, Victor E.** — Danish West Indies Postal Stationery.

**Hvidberg Hansen, Eric** — Danish West Indies King Stamps, 1907-1917. Frost Forlag Handbook No. 8, 30 pages (Danish).

Danish West Indies Postal History. Frost Forlag handbook, 51 pages (Danish).

**Mathieson, Henning** — Danish West Indies Cancellations, 1809-1877. Frost Forlag Handbook No. 6, 19 pages (Danish).

### Denmark

**AFA Danmark Frimaerkekatalog.** Aarhus Frimaerkehandel, updated yearly.

**Boom, Rob** — Denmark Stamp Booklets Catalogue. 1980, Boonstamps, 96 pages.

**Christensen, Sten** — Denmark, 2 Rigsbank-Skilling, 1851-1852. 1981, Trelleborg Philatelic Society, 159 pages.

**Christensen and Ringstrom** — Private Local Posts of Denmark. 1974, 199 pages.

**Gotfredsen, Jorgen** — Danske Breve, 1851-1979. 1980, Aarhus Frimaerkehandel, 224 pages.

**Gronlund** — Denmark Plating Rigsbankskill 1851-52, 64 pages.

**Hageman** — Denmark and Danish West Indies Handbook. 1964-1970, four volumes.

**Larsen, Arne K.** — Postal History of Nazi Occupation of Denmark, 1939-45. 1980, Frost Forlag (Danish).

**Schmidt-Anderson and Forlow** — Danske, Essays og Provetryk, 1849-1902 (essays and proofs). 1950, 18 pages (Norwegian).

**Schonning-Paaskesen** — Denmark Fire Rigsbank-Skilling. Plating of Plate I, 80 pages, Plating of Plate II, 80 pages, Aarhus Frimaerkehandel (Danish and English).

### Dominican Republic

**Kunze, A.F.** — Who's Who on the Postage Stamps of Dominican Republic. 1945, 23 pages.

### Dutch Indies

**Arratoon, W.J.A.** — Ned. Indies No. 1, tevens Stempelbock, 1860-80. 1972, 43 pages.

**Beer van Dingster, J.H.** — De Ontiwikkeling van het Postwezen in Ned. Oost-Indie. 1935, 183 pages.

**Geuzendam, A.W.** — Vierkantstempels von Ned. Oost-Indie, 1892-1916. 1976, 54 pages.

**de Haan, D.W.** — Overland Mail, 1840-50. 1973, 52 pages.

**Stapel, C.** — De Postbladenkwestie, 1947-49 (military aerogrammes). 119 pages.

**Wolff de Beer, W.S.** — Poststempels No. 1, 1789-1864. 1971, 203 pages.

### East Africa

**Mackay, J.A.** — Story of East Africa and its Stamps. 192 pages.

### Egypt

**Albani and Zeitoun** — Catalog des Timbres d'Egypte. 1948, 135 pages.

**Beneans, F.W.** — Egypt Postage Prepaid Military Datestamps, 1941-47. National Philatelic Society of London, 150 pages.

**Fiske, Willard** — All About Postal Matters in Egypt. 1978, Harry Hayes pamphlet, 26 pages.

**Kehr, Ernest** — Interpostals of Egypt, 1864-92.

Commemorative Stamps of Egypt.

**Lowe, Robson** — Egyptian Essays 1860-1960.

**Melville, F.J.** — Egypt. 1915, 81 pages.

**Sacher** — Army and Field Post Offices of Egypt and the EEF, 1914-20. 1970, 35 pages.

### Epirus

**Cronin, Andrew** — Greek Postmarks of Northern Epirus, 1912-20. 1978, 27 pages.

Epirus Stamps and Postal History of Moschopolis, 1914. Hellenic Philatelic Society, 18 pages.

### Ethiopia

**Kohl, P.** — Die Postwertzeichen von Aethiopien. 1911, 16 pages.

**Payne, Eric** — The Issues of 1894-1903. 1981, Cockrill Booklet No. 13, 28 pages.

The Issues of 1903-1905. 1981, Cockrill Booklet No. 14, 36 pages.

### Falkland Islands

**Andrews, James** — Cancellations of the Falkland Islands. 56 pages.

**Bagshawe, R.W.** — Postal History of the Falkland Islands Dependencies. 1947, 15 pages.

**Barnes, Robert** — Postal Service of the Falkland Islands. 1980, reprint, 96 pages.

**Glass, C.E.** — The Falkland Islands Printings of the Pictorial Issue, 1938-49. 20 pages.

**Spafford, Maj. R.N.** — Falkland Islands Philatelic Digest No. 2. 1979 companion to 1975 publication, 200 pages.

**Urch, Harris** — Queen Elizabeth II Falkland Island Catalogue. 1982.

### Faroe Islands

**Wowern, Eric** — Specialized Catalog of Postage Stamps and Postmarks. Regularly updated.

1976 Meter Marks and Non-Postal Charity Labels. 57 pages.

Specialized Catalog of Freight Stamps. 1976, 22 pages.

### Fezzan

**Taub, M.** — Fezzan Air Stamps. 1955, 11 pages; 1964, 27 pages.

### Fiji

**Botwright, Roy, and Walker, R.K.** — The Post Offices and Postal Cancellations of Fiji. 1979.

**Campbell, H.M.** — Post Offices and Postal Cancellations. 1957, 56 pages.

**Henney, G.** — The U.S. Army Postal Service in Fiji, 1942-45. 1979, Philatelic Society of Fiji Study No. 5, 31 pages.

**Purves** — Stamps of Fiji 1878-1902. 90 pages.

**Rodda, P., and Welsh, D.** — Registration Labels of Fiji. Philatelic Society of Fiji Study No. 1, six pages.

**Rodger, J.G.** — The Story Behind the 2½-pence Surcharge of 1941. Philatelic Society of Fiji Study No. 2, eight pages.

Fiji's Postage Due Stamps. 1979, Philatelic Society of Fiji Study No. 3, eight pages.

Fiji's Internal Air Services. Philatelic Society of Fiji Study No. 4, 10 pages.

**Rodger, J.G., and Duberal, R.F.** — Stamps and Postal History 1870-75. 160 pages.

**Urch, Harris** — Queen Elizabeth II Fiji Catalogue. 1981.

### Finland

**Ganzsachen Handbook** — 1923, 120 pages.

**Leinonen, Jorma** — Cinderella Postal Stationery. 1980, 80 pages (English and Finish).

**Linder, L.** — Finlands Ovalmarken, 1856-1860. 1956, 160 pages (Finnish).

**Moxter, H.G.** — Die Postzensur in Finnland (Finnish Mail Censorship 1914-46). 100 pages, German with English introduction.

Finnland Feldpost. 1978, German Study Group, 280 pages.

**Ossa, Mikko** — Suomen Postimerkkien Vaarenteita. Forgeries. 1978, 107 pages.

**Pelander, C.E.** — Postal Issues of Finland. 1940, 63 pages.

**Norma Postimerkkiluettelo Finland Stamp Catalogue.** 1977 edition, 200 pages.

**Suomi Postmerkkiluettelo.** Catalog issued yearly, Lauri Peltonen.

**Specialized Catalog of the Stamps of Finland.** Regularly updated.

### Fiume

**Magistris** — Specialist Catalog of the Stamps of Fiume. 38 pages.

**Oliva, G.** — Razionale Catalog dei Francobolli di Fiume. 1956.

### France

**Ab der Halden and de Beaufond** — Marques Postales et Obliterations d'Algerie. 1949, 197 pages.

**Academie de Philatelie** — L'Encyclopedie des Timbres Poste de France, Tome I. Two volumes, 1968.

**Argus Catalogue.** Updated yearly, Society des Editions.

**Association des Collecteurs Entiers Postaux** — Catalogue des Entiers Postaux de France, d'Algerie, des Colonies Francaises, Pays de Protectorat et des Mandats, Monaco, Saare. Seventh edition, 1974; supplements with prices issued every few years.

**Barat, Pierre J.** — Le Nouveau Bleues de France 1849-1876. Based on the original editions by A. Suarnet of 1933-1964. 1976, 355 pages.

**Barrier, L.** — Essai sur les Semeuses. 1951, 231 pages.

**de Beaufond, E.H.** — Catalogue des Obliterations de Timbres de France, 1849-1876. 1947, 113 pages; new edition, 1978 by A. Sinais, 116 pages.

Marques Postales des Departements Conquis 1792-1815. 1957, 147 pages.

Catalogue des Marques Postales Dites Noms Revolutionaires, 1793. 1945, 54 pages.

Catalogue des Obliterations des Timbres de France 1876-1900. 1960, 255 pages; reprint 1977, 255 pages plus 12 pages.

**Bentley, W.** — Postal History and Postmarks of the Franco-Prussian War. 1965, 50 pages.

**Berck Catalogue.** Updated yearly, Berck.

**Bergier, J.** — Les Marques d'Entree Maritime du XVIII et du XIX Siecle. 1982, 131 pages.

**Bertrand, G.** — Memorial Philatelique. Volume I: La France depuis 1880, Monaco, Saare, Andorre, 1932, 371 pages; Volume VI: La France Premieres Emissions de 1849-1900, 1948, 162 pages.

**Blanc, E.** — Bibliographie Francaise des Postes et la Philatelie. 1949, 170 pages.

**Blazy and Gauvin** — Les Timbres de L'Ile de France. 1930, 24 pages.

**Boblique, J.** — Cent Ans de Tubes Pneumatiques. 1968, 36 pages.

**Boner, P.** — Handbuch und Katalog von Frankreich 1849-1900. 1981.

**Bourselet, M.** — Les Paquebots Francais et Leur Cachets 1780-1935. 1936, 218 pages.

**Braun, J.** — Catalogue des Publicititimbres des Carnets de France et des Colonies Francaises. Second edition, 1977.

**Bremard, P.** — Obliterations Mecaniques Francaises, par Departements. 1962-1970, four volumes; annual supplements.

**Broustine, P., Francon, R., Mignon, B., and Storch, J.** — Les Roulettes . . . Coils, stamps for automatic vending machines. 1977, 237 pages.

**Brown, Ruth and Gardner** — The Bordeaux Issue of 1870-71. 1981, France and Colonies Philatelic Society, 128 pages.

**Brun, J.-F.** — Faux et Truques. 1980, 131 pages.

**Catalogue Correlator for the Stamps of France** — 1969, 32 pages; 1974 supplement, 3 pages.

**Ceres Catalogue.** Updated yearly.

**Chaintrier, L.** — Balloon Post of the Siege of Paris 1870-71. 1976, 163 pages.

**Chanaryn, V.** — An Introduction to the Posts of France in the Franco-German War of 1870-71. 1976, 120 pages.

**Chapier, G.** — Etude sur les Tarifs Postaux Francaises des Origines a la Creation du Timbres-Poste. 1974.

**Charbon, P.** — Au Temps des Malles Poste et des Diligences. 1979, 216 pages.

**Chase, C.** — Catalogue des Cachets des Courriers-Convoyeurs Boites Mobiles et Gares. 1954, 126 pages.

Napoleonic Postal Decrees, 1791-1808, 37 pages.

**Chase and de Beaufond** — Catalogue des Cachets Ambulants de France (to 1900). 1951, 57 pages.

**Chase and Lenain** — Les Bureaux Francais a l'Etranger du XVIe Siecle a 1817. 1961, 80 pages.

**Chevalier, J.** — Les Cachets a Date aux Types 11-14, 1829-1862. 1981, second edition.

**Cocatre, A.** — Les Mandats et Bons de Poste. 1958, 20 pages.

**Cohn, Ernest M.** — The Flight of the Ville d'Orleans. Flight from Siege of Paris, 1870. 1978, 175 pages.

Die Papillons von Metz . . . 1976, 77 pages.

**Cornuejols, J.** — Les Cachets Grandes Chiffres Refaits de France 1863-76. 1978, 110 pages.

**Deloste, G.** — Histoire Postale et Militaire de L'Armee d'Orient 1915-20. 1968.

Histoire Postale et Militaire de la Deuxieme Guerre Mondiale. 1980, second edition.

Histoire Postale et Militaire de la Premiere Guerre Mondiale. 1975.

Histoire Postale et Militaire de la XXeme Siecle en Dehore des Deux Guerres Mondilaes. 1970, 160 pages.

**DeVries and Van der Vlist** — Les Bureaux de Poste de Paris. 1978, 72 pages.

**Dubus, L.** — Les Acheminees ou Forwarded Francais. 1944, 48 pages; 1976 supplement, 60 pages.

**Forbin, A.** — Catalogue Prix-Courant des Timbres Fiscaux de France et des Colonies Francaises. 1937, 256 pages.

**Frgnac, E.** — Marques Postales de la Corse 1739-1904. 1947, 42 pages.

**Francois, L.** — Cachets et Obliterations de la Poste Francais aux Armees (1849-70). 1929, 100 pages; reprinted 1978.

**Francon, R., and Storch, J.** — Specialise France-Timbres Poste de 1700 a 1940 et de la 2eme Guerre Mondiale 1940-1945. 1973, 539 pages.

**de Frank, Ph.-F.** — Les Marques Postales de la Grande Armees. 1948; revised edition by Dubus et al, 1977.

**Fromaigeat, J.** — Histoire des Timbres-Poste de l'Empire. Four volumes, 1966-72.

La Poste par Pigeon. 1966.

**Gavault, G.** — Timbres Ferroviares Francaises et Colis Postaux; Nomenclature Tariffaire des Entiers Postaux et des Timbres. 1979, 76 pages.

**Geoffroy, R.** — Obliterations Temporaires-France-Union Francaise-Monaco, 1938-57. 1958, 72 pages; annual supplements since 1958 titled "Obliterations des Bureaux Temporaires et Premiers Jours."

**Germain, P.** — Le 25-centime Ceres de 1871-1872. 1952, 1963, two volumes.

Les Chiffre-Taxe Carres Francais 1859-82. 1956, 120 pages.

**Ginestet, R.** — Les Entiers Expliques par les Tarifs Postaux. Two volumes, 1975, 28 pages.

**Grasset, J.** — Les Timbres Faux pur Tromper la Poste de France. 1976, 134 pages.

**Hayhurst, J.D.** — The Pigeon Post into Paris, 1870-71. 1970, 45 pages.

The Pneumatic Post of Paris, 1974, 27 pages.

**Hoogendijk, D.C.** — Catalogue des Obliterations de Paris sur Timbres au Type Sage, 1876-1900. 1973, 236 pages.

**Joany, R.** — Glossaire Philatelique et Postal. 1977, 24 pages.

Nomenclature des Timbres-Poste de France, 1876-1959. 15 volumes, 1958-78.

Les Timbres-Poste au Type Sage. Two Volumes, 1962-63, 83 pages.

Histoire des Timbres-Poste au Type Sage 1875-1976. 1980, two volumes, 223 pages and 30 pages.

**Kremer, J.B.** — French Philatelic Facts. 1949-51, 202 pages; reprinted as Billig Volume 29.

Catalogue of Revenue Stamps of France. 1962, 32 pages; reprinted in Billig Volume II.

**La Bourse de Timbre Catalogue.** Annual

**Lafon, A.** — Catalogue des Obliterations Mecaniques a Flamme Illustree ou Stylisee. Two volumes, 1970, 670 pages; annual supplements.

**Langlois and Bourselet** — Les Obliterations des Bureaux de Poste de l'Afrique du Nord, Algerie, Tunisie, Maroc, 1830-1930. 1930, 100 pages.

**Langlois and Francois** — Les Obliterations des Bureaux Francais a l'Etranger. 1924, 148 pages.

Catalogue des Estampilles et Marques Postales d'Alsace et Lorraine 1698-1870. 1937, 263 pages.

**Langlois and Veneziani** — Nomenclature Generale des Bureaux de Poste Francais 1849-1876. 1939, second edition.

**Lautier, A.** — Nomenclature des Cachets a Date Manuels Posterieure aux Types 17 bis et 24 bis, 1884-1969. 1969.

**Legendre, J.** — Bureaux Speciaux et Franchises des Origines a 1879. 1970; 1976 supplement.

**Lenain, L.** — La Poste de l'Ancienne France des Origines a 1791. 1967; supplements, 1968, 1974.

La Poste aux Armees et les Relations Postales Internationales des Origines a 1791.

**LePileur, J.** — Les Marques Aeropostales. 1936, 52 pages; 1939, Supplement I, 105 pages.

**Leralle, A.** — Les Armees de la Revolution e Leurs Marques Postales 1791-1803. 1954, 47 pages.

A.B.C. de Marques Postales. 1944, 57 pages.

**Lesgor, R.** — France 19th Century Specialized. 1956, 49 pages.

France 20th Century Specialized 1900-1930. 1955, 99 pages.

**Lesgor and Minnigerode** — Cancellations on French Stamps of the Classic Issues 1849-1876. 1948, 131 pages.

**Lion, J.F.** — Les Timbres de la Liberation. 1965, 324 pages.

**de Lizeray, P.** — Les Anciens Timbres Francais Expliques 1849-1876. 1954, 16 pages.

Les Methodes d'Impression des Timbres-Poste. 1955, 32 pages.

Les Poincons Semeuses du Musee Postal. Volume I & Volume II, 1955-56, 62 and 47 pages.

Timbres de France. Eight volumes, 1955-1965.

Timbres et Types. Thirteen volumes, 1960 to date.

**Luft, Stanley J.** — Regular Issues of France, 1876-1945 According to Their Normal Postal Usage. Volume I, 1974, 88 pages; additions 1979, 2 pages.

The Regular Issues of France According to Their Normal Usage. Volume II, 1944-59, 1979, 76 pages.

**Lux, P.** — Obliterations des Racettes Auxiliares de Paris.

Poste et Marcophile Ferroviares, les Ambulants et le Convoyeurs. 1967.

**Marion, P.** — Dictionnaire de Semeuses a Types Multiples. 1974.

Dictionnaire des Types Typographies et Taille-Douce. 1976, 220 pages.

**Mathieu, A.** — Cachets a Date de France sur Type Sage, 1876-1901. 1976, 294 pages.

Catalogue des Obliterations de France sur Timbres Detaches, 1854-76. 1981, 160 pages.

Catalogue des Obliterations de Paris 1849-76.

**Mathieu, Pothion and deMicoulski** — Nomenclature des Bureaux de Postes Francais 1852-1876. 1966, 170 pages.

**Maury, A.** — Catalogue . . . Marques Postales de la France. 1898, 143 pages.

Histoire des Timbres-Poste Francaise. 1907, 635 pages.

**Maury, A., Renault, B., Devoitine, E., Doe, E., and Strowski, S.** — Catalogue des Estampilles de France. 1929, 634 pages; reprinted 1976.

**Mayer, P.** — Catalogue Liberation, La Guerre 1939-45. Third edition, 1979, 121 pages.

**Mazabrey, J.** — Les Faux de Sperati des Timbres Classiques de France. 1981.

**Mignon, B.** — Les Timbres Francaise a Travers les Decrets 1849-1940. 1955, 16 pages.

**Monteaux Catalogue.** Updated yearly.

**Munier, G.** — La France en Thematique. 1973-present, six volumes.

**Naudet, G., et al** — Les Vignettes Francaise d'Aerostation et de L'Aviation des Origines a 1940. 1973, 148 pages.

**Newport and Whitney** — French Islands: A Priced Catalogue of the Postal History of the Islands of North and West Coast of France. 1981, 96 pages.

**Noel, G.** — Catalogue des Cachets a Date d'Entree: France, Algerie, Levant. 1957, 63 pages; second edition 1976.

Catalogue des Marques d'Entree en France 1800-1838. 1961, 45 pages.

Catalogue des Timbres de Journaux de France. 1975.

Catalogue des Timbres-Taxe Carres. 1974.

Obliterations des Chiffres-Taxe Cerres 1859-1878. 1956, 92 pages.

**Nougaret, P.** — Bibliographie Critique de l'Histoire Postale Francaises. 1969, two volumes

**Olivier, E.** — Les Estampilles a Main avec Flamme Type Daguin. Second edition 1966, 48 pages.

**Pothion, J.** — Catalogue des Bureaux Ambulants 1845-1965 et des Cachets de Gares 1854-1960. 1978.

Catalogue des Cachets Courriers-Convoyeurs Lignes. 1979 edition, 88 pages.

Catalogue des Cachets Courriers-Convoyeurs Stations.

Catalogue des Marques Postales des Bureaux de Distribution de France Cursives, 1819-1858. 1976, 82 pages.

Catalogue des Obliterations Temporaires de France Non-Illustrees. 1972, 624 pages.

France Obliterations 1849-1876. 1969; 1976; 1978, 100 pages.

Nomenclature des Bureaux de Postes des Petits Chiffres et de Gros Chiffres, 1852-1876. 1979, 108 pages.

L'Obliteration Francaise, Initiation. 1963; 1979, 70 pages.

Catalogue de Cachets Grilles 1849-52. 1981.

Dictionnaire des Bureaux de Poste Francaises 1575-1904.

Dictionnaire des Bureaux de Poste Francaises 1904-1914. 1977, 61 pages.

**Pouget R.** — La Fabrication des Timbres-Poste Francaises. 1938.

**Ribault, D.** — Catalogue des Timbres Perfores Francaises. 1977.

**Robinson, A.** — Postal Markings of Bureaux de Passe, 1864-82. 1978, 30 pages.

**Rochette A.** — Catalogue Etoiles avec Chiffres de Paris, 1863-76. 1964, 124 pages.

Paris Bureaux de Quartiers 1849-63 et des Gares 1864-76. 1965, two volumes, 265 pages.

**Rochette, A., and Pothion, J.** — Catalogue des Marques Postales et Oblierations de Paris, 1700-1876. 1958, 349 pages.

**Rouques, L.** — Les Preobliterees de France et Leur Varieties. 1976, 24 pages.

**Rykner, P., and Gobillot** — La Poste Pneumatique de Paris. Two volumes, 1975, 1977.

**Salles, Raymond** — La Poste Maritime Francaise. Historique et Catalogue. Nine volumes, 1961-1975.

**Savelon, P.** — La Poste Pendant la Siege 1870-71. Five volumes, 1955-62.

**Silombra, J.** — Histoire de l'Aerostation et de l'Aviation Francaise de 1783 a 1930. 1981.

**Sinais, B.** — Catalogue des Obliterations Militaires Francaises, 1914-1918. 1975; second edition, 1979, 39 pages.

Catalogue des Obliterations Militaires Francaises, 1939-1945. 1978.

Le Service Postale Militaire Francaise pendant la Guerre de 1914-18. 1975, 200 pages.

**Sinais, B., and Delhommez, D.** — Catalogue des Obliterations Navales Francaises, 1771-1979. Two volumes, 1979, 1980.

**Sinais, B., and Sitorek** — Catalogue des Obliterations de Meetings d'Aviation et d'Agences Postales Air. 1981.

**Sinais, B., and Weingarten, A.** — Catalogue des Cartes Postales de Franchise Militaire. 1980.

**Sperati, J. de** — Philatelie sans Expert. 1946, 124 pages.

**Stone, R.G.** — Key to the Ink Color Numbers on French Proofs. 1979, 12 pages.

**Stone, R.G., and Martin, M.** — Glossary of English Equivalents of Terms Commonly used in French Auctions. 1973, 13 pages.

**Storch, J., and Francon, R.** — Les Entiers Postaux de France et Monaco. 1974; second edition, 1978, 188 pages.

Monographie des Timbres au Type Blanc. Second edition, 1977, 216 pages.

Monographie des Timbres de France de 1903 et 1906 au Type Semeuses. 1974, 200 pages.

Les Timbres-Poste au Type Pasteur. 1977, 183 pages.

**Stroh, P.** — Lexique Francais-Anglais-Francaise. 1971, 20 pages.

Les Timbres-Poste au Type Marianne de Bequet. 1980, 96 pages.

Les Timbres-Poste au Type Semeuse Camee. 1981, two volumes, 221 and 233 pages.

**Strowski, S., and Sinais, B.** — Les Estampilles Postales de la Grande Guerre. 1925, 386 pages; revised edition, 1977, 400 pages.

**Teissier, A.** — Carnets de Timbres-Poste France et Colonies. 1956, 125 pages.

**Thiaude Catalog.** Updated yearly.

**Tournier, G.** — Postes Francaises en Italie sous la Revolution et le Ier Empire (1792-1815). 1929, 89 pages.

**Vaille, E.** — Histoire Generale des Postes Francaises. Eight volumes, 1946-50.

Histoire des Postes Francaise Jusqua la Revolution. 1947.

Histoire des Poste Francais Depuis la Revolution. 1947.

**de Vinck de Winnezeele** — Les Types de Timbres de France 1900-1938. Second edition, 1938, 55 pages.

Colonies Francaises et Bureaux a l'Etranger. 1928, 157 pages.

**de Vinck de Winnezeele and Charvet, M.** — L'Impression des Timbres Francaises par les Rotatives. Third edition, three parts, 1946-55.

**Wanos, L., and de Belleville** — Catalogue des Varietes de France. Fifth edition, 1975, 352 pages.

**Waugh, W.W.** — The French Departments Conquis 1791-1815, Their Chronology, Civil Post Offices Having Postmarks, and Typical Markings. 1980, 29 pages.

**Yvert et Tellier** — Catalogue des Timbres-Poste de la France et des Colonies Francaises. Tome III, Bureaux Francaises a l'Etranger et Territoires Occupes. 1940, 321 pages.

Catalogue Specialise des Timbres de France. Tome I, 1849-1900. 1975, 350 pages.

**Zollman** — Minkus Stamp Catalog: France, Monaco, Andorre. 1981, 140 pages.

### French Colonies
### Overseas Territories

**Association des Collectioneurs des Entiers Postaux** — Catalogues des Entiers Postaux de France, d'Algerie, des Colonies Francaises. Seventh edition, 1974; supplements with prices every few years.

**Bertoni, G.** — Les Obliterations de la Reunion. 1977, 23 pages.

**Bouvet, P.** — Le Vol des Aigles. 1938.

**Brambilla, M. et al** — Timbres de Madagascar, 1859-1972. 1972, 323 pages.

**Braun, J.** — Catalogue des Publicititimbres des Carnets de France et des Colonies Francaises. 1958; second edition, 1977.

**Brun, A.** — Les Timbres de Tunisie. 1933, 84 pages.

**Chapier, G.** — Les Obliterations de Maroc. 1955, 72 pages; supplements, 1958, 1961.

**Corbelli, L.** — Afrique Equatoriale Francaise, les Surcharges Locales, 1940-42. 1944, 35 pages.

**Cotter A.** — Catalogue Cotter des Timbres Poste du Maroc. Various editions, 1940-1970s.

**Desrousseaux** — Les Postes Francaises en Extreme Orient (Indochina). Three volumes, 1972-73.

**Dubus, L., Pannetier, P., and Marchand, A.** La Guadeloupe. 1958, 213 pages.

**Dupraz, G., et al** — T.A.A.F. — Catalogue Specialise. 1981, 216 pages.

**Exelmans, Cte., and de Pomyers, O.** — Maroc Poste Francaises. 1948, 223 pages.

**Forbin A.** — Catalogue Prix-Courant des Timbres Fiscaux de France et des Colonies Francaises. 1937, 256 pages.

**Geoffroy, R.** — Obliterations Temporaires-France-Union Francaise, 1938-57. 1958, 72 pages; annual supplements, 1959 to date, titled "Obliterations des Bureaux Temporaires et Premiers Jours."

**Hals, N., and Collas, P.** — The New Hebrides, Their Postal History and Postage Stamps. 1967, 176 pages.

**Hofstetter, H. et al** — La Poste Local du Maroc. 1945, 35 pages; later editions.

**Houwink, R.H.** — Franzosischen Ozeanie, 1927-1963. 1962, 41 pages.

Stamps and Postal History of Tahiti. 1969, 31 pages; 1980, 32 pages, French and English.

**Jamet, M.** — 150 ans d'Histoire Postale des Anciennes Colonies Francaises des Origines a 1860. 1980, 250 pages.

**Janton, H.** — Postage Stamps of French Territories Officially Used for Non Postal Purposes. 1955, 32 pages.

**Joany, R.** — Les Bateau Avion. 1979, 80 pages.

**Joffre, L.** — Histoire des Obliterations et des Timbres des T.A.A.F. 1978, 55 pages.

**Kling, G.** — La Poste et le Timbre en Nouvelle Caledonie. 1975, 31 pages.

**Langlois, M., and Bourselet, V.** — Les Obliterations des Bureaux de Poste des Colonies Francaises. 1927, 57 pages; revised edition for part of "Afrique Occidentale Francaise," 1937, 61 pages.

Les Obliterations des Bureaux de Poste de L'Afrique du Nord, Tunisie, Maroc, 1830-1930. 1930, 100 pages.

**de Langre, J., and Cotter, A.** — Etude sur les Postes Cherifiennes et les Cachets Maghzen. 1971, 40 pages.

**Pannetier, P., and Kricheldorf, H.** — Madagaskar, 1889-1902. 1961, 55 pages.

**de Pomyers, O.** — Les Premieres Timbres des Colonies Francaises. 1957, 157 pages.

Les Timbres du Gabon et du Congo Francaise. 1958, 197 pages.

Les Timbres de la Reunion. 1939, 104 pages.

Les Timbres de Senegal. 1959, 246 pages.

**Salles, R.** — La Poste Maritime Francaise, Historique et Catalogue. Nine volumes, 1961-75.

**Stone, R.G.** — An Alphabetical List of Post Office Names and Other Words in Postmarks Used on the French Colonies General Issues, 1860-92. 1978, 23 pages.

French Colonies, The General Issues. 1961, 116 pages.

A Key to the Lozenge Obliterators of French Colonies 1860-92. 1977, 11 pages.

Bibliography of the Philatelic Literature on French Colonies, Overseas Territories and Protectorates. 1981, Volume I, 110 pages.

**Taub, M.** — Fezzan-Ghadames. 1964, 27 pages.

**Tournier, G.** — Les Marques Postales Militaires du Maroc, 1907-31. 1931, 205 pages.

**Tristant, H.** — Histoire Postale de la Cote des Somalis. Three volumes, 1969-75.

T.A.A.F., Terre Adelie, Iles Australes, Philatelie, Histoire Postales. 1974, 296 pages.

Les Timbres Pour Colis Postaux de la Cote d'Ivoire. 1964, 12 pages.

**Truc, H.** — Poste Aerienne Francaise, Volume I, Afrique du Nord. 1950, 151 pages.

**Vandelli, G.** — Timbres-Poste de Fezzan, 1943-52. 1964, 52 pages.

**de Vinck de Winnezeele** — Colonies Francaises et Bureaux a l'Etranger, Etude des Timbres Surcharges et les Emissions Locales. 1928, 157 pages.

**Wall, J.** — Les Cachets Dateurs Obliterants de la Martinique. 1965, 9 pages.

**Yvert et Tellier** — Catalogue des Timbres Poste de la France et des Colonies Francaises, Tome II, Colonies Francaises. 1936, 841 pages.

## Gambia

**Melville, F.J.** — Gambia. 1909, 68 pages.

## Germany

**Arbeitsgemeinschaft Bautenserie** — Handbuch Bautenserie 1948. In depth study of German definitive issue of 1948-49 (Building Series). 1961 to date, 20 pages.

**Arbeitsgemeinschaft Schiffspost Katalog.** Maritime postal history. 1955 to date, 31 parts to date.

**Ascher, Dr.** — Grosser Ganzsachen Katalog.

**Bachenheimer, Frank** — A Postal History of the Ruhleben P.O.W. Camp, 1914-1918. 1980, Germany Philatelic Society, 40 pages.

**Berlin Postal Stationery Society** — Neuer Ganzsachen-Katalog.

**Bochmann, Julius** — Katalog Der Deutschen Gelegenheirsstempel. Listing of German slogan, commemorative and other special postmarks. Published regularly since 1952 in parts: Part 1, basic work covering through 1951; supplement 1952-55; supplement 1956-59; supplement 1960-64; supplement 1965-73, parts 1-3.

**Borek, R.** — Deutschland Catalog, Germany and colonies. 1980 edition, 322 pages.

**Buchner, Heinz** — Beitrage zur Postgeschichte Mecklenburg-Vorpommerns 1945-52. Postal History of Mecklenburg Province. 1971, Verlag Neues Handbuch der Briefmarkenkunde, 192 pages.

**Burhop, Dedo** — Postkrieg Spezialkatalog. Postmark catalog regularly updated.

**Burneleit, Albert** — Die Deutschen Uberdruckmarken vom Jahre 1923. 1942, Seifert, 100 pages.

**Die Deutsche Ost Afrika Linie** — Arbeitsgemeinschaft Schiffspost 1976-78.

**Deutsche Reichspost** — Ortsverzeichniss. Post offices in Germany and occupied territories as of 1944. Reprint of 1944 edition, Karl Pfankuch, 1979, 480 pages.

**DNK, Deutschland Nettokatalog.** 1981 edition.

**Durst, Heiner, and Glasewald, Ruprecht** — Katalog der Deutschen Freistempel. Meter markings. 1959, Poststempelgilde Rhein-Donau, 90 pages.

**Dusterbehn, Heinrich** — Katalog der Deutschen Eisenbahnmarken. German Railway stamps. 1950, fourth edition, 136 pages.

**East German Philatelic Association** — Bezirksvorstand Halle, Arbeitskreis Ganzsachen.

**Erler, Martin, and Norton, John A.** — Katalog der Stempelmarken von Deutschland. Catalog of the adhesive revenues of Germany. 1977 to date, four volumes to date.

**Faulhaber, Carl, et. al.** — Die OPD Marken 1923. 1940, Seifert, 124 pages.

**Flaschendrager, Werner** — Handbuch der Bezirksaufdruckmarken. 1948 Soviet Zone overprints. 1967-69, two volumes, VEB Transpress.

**Flatters, Hans** — Franzosische Zone. Abarten und Plattenfehler der Landerausgaben. Plate varieties in issues of the French Occupation zones, 1947-49. 1974, 242 pages.

**Germany Philatelic Society** — Hand Overprints Catalog. Hand Overprints Study Group.

**GPS Reference Manual of Forgeries.** 1975 to date, 18 releases to date.

**German-English Dictionary** of Philatelic Terms. 1980 edition, 175 pages.

**Grabowski, Heinz** — Grabowski Lufthansa Spezial Katalog. Lufthansa German Airlines flight covers and markings. 1963-68, third edition plus supplements 1-5.

**Grobe** — Altdeutschland Special Catalog. 1953, 145 pages.

**Hansen, Hans Jurgen** — Postmarks Alte Briefmarken Eine Kultur Und Stilgeschichte der Fruhen Briefmarken. 111 pages.

**Harper, A.** — Postal Stationery of Germany Third Reich. 1933-45, 47 pages.

**Hille, Horst** — DDR Briefmarken, Stempel, Dokumente. Postal History of East Germany. 1969 Transpress, 181 pages.

**Jahn, W.** — Zentraler Kurierdienst and Behorden-Dienstmarken der DDR. 1967, 69 pages.

**Dienstpost DDR Handbuch.** Official mails of East Germay. 1974 to date, two parts, Verlag Heinrich Wittman.

**Kalckhoff, Franz** — Die Briefumschlage der Deutschen Reichspost. Stamped envelopes of the German Empire. 1936, Verlag Robert Noske, 79 pages.

**Katalog der Deutschen und Verwandten R&V Zettelformen.** German registry labels and markings. 1966 to date, 16 parts to date.

**Kohl Briefmarken Handbuch: Deutsches Reich 1872-1925 Und Deutsche Kriegsmarkens 1914-18** — 1974 reprint, Arbeitsgemeinschaft Neues Handbuch der Briefmarkenkunde, 438 pages.

**Kricheldorf, Hellmuth, and Wolter, Karl Kurt** — Neues Handbuch der Briefmarkenkunde. Issues 1925-35; booket panes 1911-21 and 1935-45. 1952-58, 376 pages.

**Kriegel, Kurt** — Deutsches Reich, Falschstempel der Inflation, 1919-23. Fraudulent postmarks on inflation issues. 1978, Infla Berlin, 55 pages.

**Litschke, I.** — English-German Philatelic Dictionary. 32 pages.

**Meier zu Eissen, Hans** — Borek Ganzsachen Spezialkatalog Deutschland 1850 bis 1932. German stationery 1850-1932, official and private. 1979, Verlag Richard Borek, 690 pages.

Borek Ganzsachen Spezialkatalog Deutschland. Post 1933 period stationery. 1976, Verlag Richard Borek, 320 pages.

Katalog und Handbuch der Deutschen Privat-Postanstalten. Volume 1, 1979, Aachen-Berlin, 220 pages, Verlag Richard Borek.

**Metzner, Alfred** — Handbuch der Bogen und Bogenranddrucke der Briefmarken der Deutschen Reichspost. Margin inscriptions and other selvage markings on issues of 1872-1940. 1941-43, two volumes, Seifert.

**Michel** — Briefe Katalog Deutschland. German stamps on cover catalog. Regularly updated.

Briefmarken Catalog Deutschland. Regularly updated.

Ganzsachen Katalog Deutschland. Catalog of officially issued stationery. Regularly updated.

German Specialized Catalog. Regularly updated.

Privateganzsachen Katalog. Stationery issued to private order. Regularly updated.

**Moser, Georg** — Handbuch Katalog der Deutschen Inflationsmarken. Inflation stamps, 1919-23. 1933, 272 pages.

**Muller, J.** — Germany Specialized Catalog. Ninth edition, 1961.

**Muller-Mark, E.** — Brevier Klassischer Marken. 1956, 6th edition, 96 pages.

**Nawrocki, Johannes** — Gebuhrenstempel der Inflationszeit. Reprint of 1940 edition, Verlag Neues Handbuch der Briefmarkenkunde, 236 pages.

**Paul, C.** — Illustrierte Katalog der Barfreimachungs und Franko Stempel nach dem 8.5.1945. 1948, 40 pages.

**Philatelistenverbad im Kulturbund der DDR** — Bezirksvorstand Halle. Arbeitskreis Ganzsachen. Catalog of post WWII German postal stationery, both official and printed to private order. In progress since 1974, East German Philatelic Association.

**Pofis** — German Democratic Republic, 1945-1955. 28 pages.

**Rawlings, John, and Passmore, Michael** — The Postal History of the Nuremberg Rallies. 1980, M.H. Passmore, 112 pages.

**Reinheimer, A.** — Illustrierter Preiskatalog der Deutschen Postalischen Entwertungsarten. 1894, 52 pages.

**Riemer, Karl Heinz** — Die Postzensur der Aliirten im Besetzten Deutschland nach dem 2 Weltkrieg. Handbook of Allied censorship markings of post WWII period. 1977, Stempelgilde Rhein-Donau, 152 pages.

Die Postuberwachung durch Deutsche Dienststellen Wahrend des 2 Welkrieges. German WWI censorship. 1979, 220 pages.

Zensurpost aus dem III Reich. Third Reich mail censorship markings. 1966, Poststempelgilde Rhein-Donau, 82 pages.

**Rommel, O.** — Postwertzeichen der Deutschen Postbezirke (to 1895). 1896, 121 pages.

**Salm, Arthur** — Michel Handbuch-Katalog "Pfennige." Study of color varieties of 1875 definitive issue. 1977, Schwanenberger Verlag, 60 pages.

**Sautter, Karl** — Geschichte der Deutschen Post, Teil 3: Geschichte der Deutschen Reichpost (1871-1945). 1951, Bundesdruckerei, 603 pages.

**Schmidt, Carl** — Handbuch der Deutschen Privat-Postwertzeichen. Handbook of stamps and stationery issued by many private posts which existed in Germany in the late 19th century. 1939-42, two volumes, Verlag Robert Noske.

**Schmidt, Heinz** — Die Bezirksstempel Aufdrucke der Sowjetischen Besatzungszone. 1948 Soviet Zone overprints. 1961, 136 pages.

**Schmuck, Wolfgang** — Philacolor Deutschland Katalog. Updated yearly.

**Sieger, Hermann** — Katalog der Flugpost der Neuen Deutschen Lufthansa. Lufthansa first flight covers, 1955-75. 1976, 12th edition, 498 pages.

**Simon, Sam** — Handbook of the Mail in the Concentration Camps, 1933-45. 1976, 138 pages.

**Stadtbibliothek Munchen** — Deutschland und Deutsche Gebiete. Biblographic catalog, 1975.

**Stereo Stamps** — Catalog of Displaced Persons, Prisoners of War, Concentration Camps and Ghetto Stamps During and After World War II in Germany. 1979, 32 pages.

**Turk, Heinrich** — Der Eingeschriebene Brief, Handbuch. History of registered mail in Germany. Two volumes: Volume 1, 1973, 176 pages; Volume 2, 1977, 124 pages.

**Whittman, H.** — Briefmarken Als Geldanlage und Spekulationsobjekt. 185 pages.

Bautenserie 1948 Special Catalog. 1978 edition, 76 pages.

**Wolfe, F.S.** — Gemany's Post-War Local Post Issues 1945-48. 1964, 48 pages.

**Wolff, W.** — 600 Falsche Stempel. 27 pages.

**Wrona, R., and Goecks, W.** — Deutschland Catalog, 1947, 64 pages.

**Wulbecke** — Deutsche Notfrankaturen 1945-1946. 36 pages.

### German States
### General

**Arbeitsgemeinschift Nachverwendete Altdeutschland Stempel** — Postmarks of old German States used after 1872. In progress, to date 11 parts published.

**Doberer, Kurt Karl** — Die Briefmarken von Altdeutschland. 1977, Verlag Richard Borek, 196 pages.

**Grobe, Hans** — Altdeutschland Spezialcatalog und Handbuch. Catalog of stamps and stationery. 1975, fifth edition, Grobe, 718 pages.

**Lindenberg, Carl** — Die Briefumschlage der Deutschen Staaten. Stamped envelopes. 1892-95, 15 parts. Reprints exist of parts 1, 5/6 and 13.

**Muller-Mark, Ewald** — Altdeutschland unter der Lupe. Stamps and stationery of all states. 1960, fifth edition, two volumes.

**Schloss, Hermann** — Distinguishing Characteristics of Classic Stamps: Old German States. 1948, H.L. Lindquist, 108 pages.

**Stiedl, Otto, and Billig, Fritz** — Grosses Handbuch der Falschungen. Contains illustrations of originals and forgeries of most German States. 1934, 18 parts, Fritz Billig.

### Baden

**Graf, Ewald** — Handbuck der Badischen Vorphilatelie, 1700-1851. 1971, Verlag Neues Handbuch der Briefmarkenkunde, 379 pages.

**Grossman, A.** — Billig's Volume II. Cancellations-Postmarks.

**Lindenberg, Carl** — Briefmarken von Baden. 1894, Verlag H. Brendicke, 171 pages.

**Melville, F.J.** — Baden. 1928, 59 pages, English.

**Simon, Siegfried.** — Handbuch der Baden Poststempel, Ganzsachen, Postscheine und Marken. Postmarks, pre-stamp and post-1851. 1935-37, Fritz Seifert, two volumes.

### Bavaria

**Beck, C.** — Bayern 1849, 1 Kreuzer Schwarz. 1924, 24 pages.

**Doberer, Kurt Karl** — Rauten und Gekronte Lowen. Classic issues. 1972, Bruckmann, 204 pages.

**Eisenbeiss, Wilhelm** — Bayerische Post und Briefkunde. Postal history. 1962, 175 pages.

**Gundel, Hans** — Bayern 1849-62. Compilation of articles on history and plate varieties of the first issue. 1977, 325 pages.

**Holzschuher, K.** — Die Bayerischen Feldpostempel. 1919, 15 pages.

**Maderholz, Erwin** — Bayerisches Briefmarkenalbum. 1972, Suddeutscher Verlag, 130 pages.

**Stenger, E.** — Die Muhlradstempel von Bayern. 8 pages.

**Winkler, Karl** — Handbuch der Bayerischen Poststempel. 19th century postmarks. 1951, Verlag Karl Ulrich and Co., 384 pages.

### Bergedorf

**Knauer, Karl** — Bergedorfer Postgeschichte. Postal history to 1868. 1961, Karl Knauer, 329 pages.

**Krotzsch, Hugo** — Die Postfreimarken des Beiderstadtischen Postamtes Bergedorf. 1876, Krotzsch, 169 pages.

**Rommel, O.** — Die Postwertzeichen des Bergedorfer Postbezirks. 1892, 56 pages. Plus 15 pages supplement.

### Bremen

**Knauer, Karl, and Salm, Arthur** — Bremen Handbuch. 1967, Georg Amm, 102 pages; 1976 supplement, 64 pages.

**Piefke, Christian** — Die Geschichte der Bremischen Landespost. Postal service history. 1947, Kasten, 200 pages.

### Brunswick

**Bade, Henry** — 333 Jahre Braunschweigische Post 1535-1867. Postal history. 1960, Pfankuch, 199 pages.

**Berger, L.** — Die Postwertzeichen des Herzogthums Braunschweig. 1893, 138 pages.

**Kalotay, P.** — Braunschweig: Der Reihe Klassische Sammelgebiete. 1948, 32 pages.

Der Durchstich Einer Braunschweiger Marke. 1891, 35 pages.

### Hamburg

**Lohden, Klaus** — Freie und Hansestadt Hamburg, 1859-67. Stamps and postal history. 1978, 81 pages.

**Meyer-Margreth, Ernst** — Die Poststempel von Hamburg. Postmarks. 1965, Hamburg-Altonaer Verein fur Briefmarkenkunde, 87 pages.

**Ohrt, Paul** — Die Postfreimarken von Hamburg. 1931, Die Postmarke, 208 pages.

### Hanover

**Von Lenthe, August** — Hannover-Postanstalten und Poststempel. Postmark catalog. 1971, reprint of 1957 edition, Hans Grobe, 220 pages.

### Heligoland

**Lemberger, Helmuth** — Heligoland Philatelie. 1970, Verlag Walter Wulf, 144 pages.

**Wulbern, A.** — Die Postwertzeichen Helgolands. 1892, 32 pages.

### Lubeck

**Herzog** — Die Postmarken. 1947, 40 pages.

**Knauer, Karl, and Niese, Johannes** — Lubeck, Stempelhandbuch von den Anfangen bis 1868. 1977, Harry von Hoffman, 80 pages.

### Mecklenburg-Schwerin

**Albert, Georg, et. al.** — Die Briefmarken von Mecklenburg-Schwerin. 1964, Arbeitsgemeinschaft Neues Handbuch der Briefmarkenkunde, 19 pages.

Die Postbriefstempel von Mecklenburg-Schwerin. Postmarks. 1966, Arbeitsgemeinschaft Neues Handbuch der Briefmarkenkunde, 68 pages.

**Moeller, C.** — Geschichte des Landespostwesens in Merklenburg-Schwerin. History of the postal services. 1897, 359 pages.

### Marienwerder

**Landre and Henkel** — Handbook Heft No. 21, 47 pages.

### North German Postal Union

**Krotzsch, Hugo** — Norddeutscher Postbezirk. 1895, second edition, 160 pages.

**Sautter, Karl** — Geschichte der Deutschen Post. Teil 2: Geschichte der norddeutscher Bundespost, 1868-71. 1935, Berger, 135 pages.

**Spalink, H. Friedrich** — Handbuch uber die Deutschen Hufeisenstempel. Catalog of horseshoe-shaped town cancels. 1979, third edition, 187 pages.

### Occupation Issues

**Catalogue special de Timbres d'Alsace-Lorraine, Leur Obliterations et Certaines Pieces Postales, 1870-71.** German occupation issues in Alsace-Lorraine during Franco-Prussian War. 1937, l'Echangiste Universal, 162 pages.

**Mieczkowski, Arthur** — Elsass-Lothringen, 1870. 1 Teil: Die Marken und ihre Entwertungen. Stamps & postmarks of German occupation in Alsace-Lorraine during Franco-Prussian War. 27 pages.

### Oldenburg

**Ohrt, Paul** — Die Postfreimarken vom Grossherzogtum Oldenburg. 1894, Krotzsch, 120 pages.

Die Poststempel von Oldenburg. Postmarks. 1911, Kohl, 361 pages.

### Prussia

**Butow, G.** — Katalog der Preussen-Nummernstempel mit Bewertung. 1925, 48 pages.

**Herzog** — Die Postempel der Stadt Magdeburg. 16 pages.

**Kalckhoff, Franz** — Die Briefumschlage von Preussen. Stamped envelopes. 1943, Seifert, 106 pages.

**Marbach, Kurt** — Die Preussischen Aufgabe und Nummerstempel. Postmarks. 1936, Post, two volumes; 1978 paperback reprint.

**Munzberg, Werner** — Preussen, Postanstalten und Stempel, 1817-67. Postmarks. 1977, in progress, five volumes to date (1980).

**Ohrt, Paul** — Die Postfreimarken des Konigreichs Preussen. 1896, Krotzsch, 232 pages.

**Rasche, W.** — Bewertung der Preussischen Ringnummern-Stempel. 1949.

**Stephan, Heinrich von** — Geschichte der Preussischen Post. History of Prussian postal service by founder of UPU. Classic. 1928, Decker, 747 pages.

### Saxony

**Dieck, F.W.** — Prak. Handbook der Freimarken des Konigsreichs Sachsen. 1921, 55 pages.

**Gobeler, Heinz** — Sachsen Handbuch. 1955, 298 pages.

**Mackey, John P.** — The Saxon Post. 1978, 99 pages.

**Milde, Horst, and Schmidt, Erich** — Die alte Sachsenpost. 1973, Verlag fur Verkehrswesen, 548 pages.

**Rommel, O.** — Geschichte der Sachsichen Zeitungsmarke 3 Pfennige Rot. 1894, 48 pages.

**Schulze-Dirks, Arno Alexander** — Die Postwertzeichen der Provinz Sachsen-Anhalt. 1945-1946, 54 pages.

### Schleswig-Holstein

**Jager, Peter** — Postgeschichte Schleswig-Holstein. Postal history. 1970, 64 pages.

**Katalog der Poststempel und Entwertungen von Schleswig Holstein bis 1875.** Postmarks. 1973, 126 pages.

**Rosenkranz, A.** — Die Postfreimarken der Herzogtumer Schleswig Holstein. 1897, Krotzsch, 138 pages.

### Thurn and Taxis

**Haferkamp, Hans, and Probst, Erwin** — Thurn and Taxis Stempelhandbuch. Postmarks. 1976-78, three volumes, Verlag Neues Handbuch der Briefmarkenkunde.

**Hurt, E.F., and Hollick** — Handbook. Billig's Volume 8, 124 pages in English. 212 pages.

**Munzberg, Werner** — Stationskatalog der Thurn und Taxis Post. Post offices and postal system. 1967, Lassleben, 319 pages.

**Sebastian, Fritz** — Thurn und Taxis 350 Jahre Post. Postal system history. 1948, Wilkens, 253 pages.

### Wurttemberg

**Bruhl, Carlrichard, and Thoma, Heinz** — Handbuch der Wurttemberg Philatelie, 1851-75. 1975-76, two volumes, Verlag Neues Handbuch der Briefmarkenkunde.

**Kohler, Karl** — Die Briefmarken von Wurttemberg, 1851-81. 1940, Lieger, 136 pages.

**Weidlich, Hans A.** — Handbuch der Wurttemburg Philatelie: Die Postscheine der Kreuzerzeit. Postal receipt forms. 1979, Verlag Neues Handbuch der Briefmarkenkunde.

**Wolffling-Seeling, Fritz** — 500 Jahre Post in Wurttemberg. 1965, Sieger, 269 pages.

### German Colonies

**Andersen, Hans** — Die Briefmarken von Nord-Schleswig. 1962, 56 pages.

**Becker, Ernst** — Memel Katalog. 1937, two volumes, Verlag Robert Noske.

**End, Karl, and Becker, Willibald** — Saar Briefmarken Spezialkatalog. 1950, Saardruckerei, 150 pages.

**Ey, Eduard** — Die Briefmarken der Deutschen Postanstalten im Ausland. German colonies and offices abroad. 1964, third edition, 235 pages.

**Friedemann, Albert** — Die Postwertzeichen und Entwertungen der Deutschen Postanstalten in den Schutzgebieten und im Ausland. Stamps and postmarks of German colonies and post office abroad. 1967-69, three volumes, third edition.

The Postage Stamps and Cancellations of the Post Offices in German South West Africa. 1967; first English edition of German South West Africa section, 1980, Collectors Mail Auctions Ltd., 197 pages.

**Hasselhoff, Gerhard** — Freie Stadt Danzig 1920-39. Bewertung der Poststempel. Postmarks of Danzig during interwar period. 1979, 49 pages.

Freie Stadt Danzig. Polnische Post in Danzig 1793-1955. Danzig postmarks of all periods except interwar period. 1979, 130 pages.

**Heinz, A.** — Postmaster Provisionals of Freudenstadt. 1966, 26 pages.

**Hoffmann-Giesecke, G.** — Deutsch Neu-Guinea. 1959, 151 pages.

Sudwestafrika. 1956, two volumes.

**Horr, Hugo J.** — Die Postwertzeichen des Sudentenlandes. 1963, 480 pages.

**Landesverbad der Briefmarkensammler des Saarlandes** — Handbuch der Postwertzeichen des Saargebietes und des Saarlandes. 1958 to date, nine parts.

**Ludin, Emil** — Die Briefmarken der Provinz Zara. WWII German occupation issues of Zara. 1958, Heinrich Wittmann, 64 pages.

**Mecklenburg Special Catalog.** 1945-1946, 23 pages.

**Michaelis, Curt** — Handbook of Complete Stamps from Danzig and of Polnischen Postamts Danzig. 1973, 36 pages.

**Michaelis, Curt** — Flugpost von und nach Danzig. 1973, 36 pages.

**Ritter, Rolf** — Handbuch vom Abstimmungsgebiet Oberschlesien. Handbook for Upper Silesia. 1969 to date, 10 parts.

**Schmidt, W., and Werner, Hans** — Geschichte der Deutschen Post in den Kolonien und im Ausland. History of postal services. 1942, Rudolph, 479 pages.

**Schuler, Gerhard** — Danzig - Die Schragedrucke und ihre Falschungen. Diagonal overprints issues with emphasis on forgeries. 1960, Infla Berlin, 29 pages.

**Schupp, Wilhelm** — Die Postwertzeichen des Saargebietes. Saar issues through 1934. 1935, Verlag Robert Noske, 208 pages.

**Schwenzfeger, Alfred, et al** — Die Briefmarken von Marienwerder. 1964, Arbeitsgemeinschaft Neues Handbuch der Briefmarkenkunde, 47 pages.

**Staedel, Paul** — Etude des Timbres-Post et Obliterations de la Sarre 1945-55. Post WWII issues and postmarks of Saar. 1956, Graffenstaden, 168 pages.

Special Sarre. Specialized Saar catalog. 1959, 96 pages.

**Steuer, Friedrich F.** — Handbuch and Katalog der Deutschen Kolonial-Vorlaufer. Forerun-

ners, stamps of Germany used and postmarked in colonies and post offices abroad. 1973, Schwanenberger Verlag, 454 pages.

**Tust, Wolfgang, and Pickenpack, Werner** — Deutsche Besetzung in Frankreich 1940-45. German occupation of France during WWII. 1971, Arbeitsgemeinschaft Neues Handbuch der Briefmarkenkunde, 64 pages.

### German Military Post Offices

**Butow, Georg** — Die Abstempelungen der Deutsch-Belgischen Besatzungsmarken. German occupation forces postmarks in Belgium during WWII. 1920, 127 pages.

**Clement, Alfred** — Kleines Handbuch der Deutschen Feldpost 13 Jahrhundert - 1914. History of military postal services in Germany from 13th century to 1914. 1952, 67 pages.

**Clement, A.** — Kleines Handbuch der Deutschen Feldpost 1937-1945. 64 pages.

**Crusemann, Friedrich** — Deutsche Marine Schiffpost. Part 1: Die Zeit bis zum Ausbruch des Weltkrieges 1914. Postmarks of all German naval units up to the outbreak of WWI. 1958-62, 980 pages.

**Crusemann, Friedrich, and Schlimgen, Josef** — Deutsche Marine Schiffspost 1914-19. Continues the Crusemann Handbook for the WWI period. 1978 to date, to be complete in seven parts, Poststempelgilde Rhein-Donau.

**Fuchs, Gunter** — Uber die Lokalisierung der Deutschen Feldpostamter 1939-45. Catalog of the locations of German army post offices during WW II. 1972, Verlag Handbuch der Briefmarkenkunde, 96 pages.

**Gericke, Bodo** — Die Deutsche Feldpost im Zweiten Weltkrieg 1939-45. 1971, 164 pages; supplements 1-4, 1974, 30 pages.

**Heberle, E.** — Die Post im Westlichen Etappengebiet und ihre Abstempelungen. German army postal service on the Western front in WWI. 1929, 40 pages.

**Kannapin, Norbert** — Die Feldpost Nummern der Deutschen Kriegsmarine 1939-45. Postal station numbers of the German navy during WWII. Two volumes: Volume 1, second editon, 1974, sea forces, 127 pages; Volume 2, land forces, 118 pages.

Die Deutsche Feldpost Organisation und Localisation 1939-45. 1979, Biblio Verlag, 184 pages.

**Kesselstatt, Franz E.** — Die Tunispakchenmarke und die Palmestempel des DAK. Stamps, markings and postal history of the German forces in North Africa during WWII. 1978, Arbeitsgemeinschaft Neues Handbuch der Briefmarkenkunde, 56 pages.

**Rungas, Wolf, and Sauer, Erich** — Inselpost 1944-45. German forces on the Aegean Seas in WWII. 1978, 232 pages.

**Schmitt, Bruno, and Gericke, Bodo** — Die Deutsche Feldpost im Osten. German army postal system on the Russian front during WWII. 1969, 71 pages.

**Schracke, Karl** — Geschichte der Deutschen Feldpoststempel 1914-18. Official history of the German army's postal services during WWII. 1921, Reichsdruckerei, 345 pages.

**Schriever, Karl Heinz** — Die Deutschen Feldpoststempel 1914-18. German army post office postmarks of WWI. 1967, Poststempelgilde Rhein-Donau, 217 pages.

**Schultz, Hermann** — Handbuch und Stempelkatalog der Deutschen Dienstpost 1939-45. WWII official mail postmarks. 1953-59, Poststempelgilde Rhein-Donau, 444 pages.

**Stephan, Walter** — Kriegsgefangenenpost Deutscher Soldaten und Internierter, 1939-45. WWII German POW mail. 1969, 104 pages.

**Wimmer, Hans** — Die Deutsche Packchenfeldpost. German army parcel post during WWII. 1969, 86 pages.

**Zirkenbach, Kurt** — Die Deutsch Post in Belgien 1914-18. 1926, Germania Berichte, 70 pages.

### Gibraltar

**Duveen, G.E.** — Postage Stamps of Gibraltar. 1973 reprint, Harry Hayes, 88 pages.

**Higham, F.D.** — Postage Stamps of Gibraltar. 1918, 36 pages.

**Hine-Haycock, W.** — Posted in Gibraltar. Postal history. 1978, Robson Lowe, 122 pages.

### Gilbert and Ellice

**Urch, Harris** — Queen Elizabeth II Gilbert Islands/Kiribati Catalogue. 1982.

**Vernon, D.H.** — Cancellation Study of the Gilbert & Ellice Islands. 1968, Pacific Islands Study Circle.

### Great Britain

**Alcock, R.C., and Holland, F.C.** — The Postmarks of Great Britain and Ireland. 314 pages, plus 15 supplements (originally published 1940 through 1950s, basic work).

The Maltese Cross Cancellations. Second editon, 1970, 134 pages.

**Alcock-Meredith** — British Postage Stamp Varieties Illustrated. 122 pages.

**Allen, David** — The Social and Economic Importance of Postal Reform in 1840. 1976, No. 4, 28 pages.

**Archer, M.S.** — Welsh Post Towns Before 1840. 138 pages.

**Arkell, LTC J.O.A.** — The Parcel Post Labels of Great Britain, Part I: Berkshire. 1976, 32 pages.

**Arnot, James** — The 'Brunswick Star.' Edinburgh duplex obliterator.

**Bachelor and Picton-Phillips** — Pre-Victorian Stamps and Franks. 42 pages.

**Barefoot, J.** — Great Britain Revenues. European Philately Series No. 1, 172 pages.

Great Britain Revenue Compendium. 1981, European Philately Series No. 7, 165 pages.

**Billig** — Volume 44, Guide Lines to the Penny Black. Reprint of 1949 work, 224 pages.

**Blair, Neil** — Postal History of Perth. Woods of Perth Ltd.

**Booth, R.G.** — Catalogue of the Adhesive Revenue Stamps of the U.K., Isle of Man and Channel Islands. 1976, 173 pages.

**Brumwell, G.** — British Post Office Numbers, 1844-1906. 1971, 138 pages.

Local Posts of London, 1680-1840.

**Burgess, H.** — Stamps King Edward VII, 1901-1910. 1950, 31 pages.

**Cade, R. Courtney** — Handbook of British Colonial Stamps in Current Use. 1950, Crown Agents, 104 pages; 1955, Crown Agents, 151 pages.

**Chalmers, J.** — Inventor of the Adhesive Postage Stamp. 1970, 149 pages.

**Chandler, John, and Dagnell, H.** — The Newspaper and Almanac Stamps of Great Britain and Ireland. 1981.

**Concordance of British Stamps.** — Listing of Great Britain and regionals by Gibbons, Scott and Minkus numbers. 1979, 32 pages.

**Crofts, J.** — Packhorse, Waggon and Post. Early posting system. 147 pages.

**Crouch and Hill** — British Army Field Post Offices 1939-1950. 1951, 113 pages.

**Crow, D.** — The Post Office How It Works. 1962, 36 pages.

**Dagnall, H.** — John Dickinson and His Silk-Thread Paper. The story of the silk thread paper used for the Mulready letter sheets and envelopes. 32 pages.

**Doupe** — King Edward VII 1902-1910.

**Durham, John** — Telegraphs in Victorian London. 1959, 31 pages.

**Evans, Maj. E.B.** — The Mulready Envelope.

**Farrugia, Jean, and Gammons, Tony** — Carrying British Mails. 1980, National Postal Museum, London, 84 pages.

**Firebrace, J.A.** — Overprinted M.E.F. on Great Britain Stamps of 1942.

**Frank, Schonfeld and Barber** — The Impressed Duty Stamps of Great Britain. 1981, 388 pages.

The Stamp Duty of Great Britain and Ireland. 1974, 231 pages.

**Gibbons, Stanley** — Collect British Stamps. 1981, 29th British edition; 1981, second American edition.

Great Britain Specialized. Volume I, Victoria, 1980 edition; Volume II, The Kings, 1975; Volume III, Queen Elizabeth II, 1982; Volume IV, Decimal Issues Since 1970, 1980, third edition.

Great Britain Elizabeth II Pre-decimal Issues. 1979.

Great Britain and Commonwealth Catalogue. 1982 edition.

**Gilbert, J.F.** — First Class Markings on Government Official Stationery. 1974 edition, Harry Hayes, 64 pages.

**Gilbert and Koehler** — Catalog illustre des Timbres Fiscaux de Grande Bretagne, Irlande, Ecosse. 1906-07, 148 pages.

**Graveson, S.** — Ocean Penny Post. 12 pages.

**Great Britain First Day Covers.** Bredon Hill Stamps and Benham Ltd., 1980 edition, 128 pages.

**Great Britain Philatelic Society** — Queen Victoria, the Plating of the Penny 1840-1864 Die I Plates. 1980, four volumes, 618 pages.

**Haldane, A.R.B.** — Three Centuries of Scottish Posts (to 1836). 336 pages.

**Harrison, T.S.** — Harrisons of Waterlow. 12 pages.

**Hayes, Harry** — The Parcel Post Labels of Great Britain. 1979, 47 pages.

**Hewlett** — A Provisional Guide to the Valuation of the Numerical Cancels of the British Isles.

**Hewlett and Swallow** — Picton's Priced Postcard Catalogue and Handbook. 136 pages.

**Hill, C.W.** — Scotland in Stamps. 144 pages.

**Hill, Norman** — Postal Markings of the Allied Forces in Great Britain WWII. 56 pages.

The Railway Traveling Post Office of Great Britain and Ireland 1838-1975. 24 pages.

The Royal Tour Trains, Their Postal History and Postal Marks. 1977, Harry Hayes, 24 pages.

**Huggins, A.K.** — British Postal Stationery.

**Hughes, W.E.** — Chronicles of Icarus No. 3, British Air Posts 1850-53.

**Hyde** — Royal Mail. 378 pages.

**Jackson, H.T.** — Railway Letter Posts of Great Britain. 58 pages.

Post Office Telegraph Stamps 1869-1881. 60 pages.

**Jennings, Peter** — Aerogrammes. Airmail from 1870 to 1972.

**Jones, Lionel D.** — United Kingdom Savings Stamps, Labels and Coupons. 1979, 125 pages.

**Kidd, Cyril** — Posted in Advance for Delivery on Christmas Day. Robson Lowe, 16 pages.

**Kirk, A.J.** — Great Britain King Edward VIII. Second edition, 30 pages.

**Kreicker and Burrell** — The Penny Black — Philately's No. 1. 1940, 24 pages.

**Lister, R.** — College Stamps of Oxford and Cambridge. 1974 reprint, Harry Hayes, 64 pages.

**Litchfield, P.C.** — Guide Lines to the Penny Black. 1979, Robson Lowe Publications, 224 pages.

**Lovegrove, J.W.** — Herewith My Frank. "Free" markings. 1976, 101 pages, plus supplements to 1980.

**Lowe, Robson** — The Embossed Queen's Head Essay 1840.

Postage Stamps of Great Britain 1661-1942. January 1943, second edition, 186 pages.

Encyclopaedia of British Empire Postage Stamps Volume 1, Great Britain, etc.; HJMR reprints, 468 pages in two volumes.

The Handpainted Essays, 1884-1892. 1975, 12 pages.

Newspaper Postage Stamps; the De La Rue Dies, 1860-1870. 1981, 12-page monograph.

**Lundy, F.G.C.** — Handbook of the Revenue Stamps of Great Britain and Ireland. 1894, 46 pages.

**Mackay, J.A.** — The Story of Great Britain and Her Stamps. 158 pages.

**McDonald, A.** — Telegraph Stamps of Great Britain. 1959, 42 pages.

**Melville, F.J.** — Embossed Adhesive Stamps. 1910, 39 pages.

King Edward VII Stamps. 1911, 83 pages.

Line Engraved Stamps. 1909, 89 pages.

Embossed Revenue Stamps of Great Britain and Ireland. 1911, 32 pages.

Newspaper Tax Stamps of Great Britain. 1912, 55 pages.

Great Britain Line Engraved Stamps. 82 pages.

The Postage Stamps of Great Britain. 1904, 56 pages.

War Stamps Salonika and Long Island. 48 pages.

**Migliavacca, G.** — Francobolli e Timbri dello Sciopero Postale Inglese. (1971 strike post.) 1975, 35 pages.

**Muggeridge, S.J.** — The Postal History of Maidstone and the Surrounding Villages. 45 pages.

**Narbeth, Colin** — Collecting British Stamps, A Beginner's Guide. 143 pages.

**Narbeth, C., and Lyon, D.** — Successful Investing in Stamp and Banknotes. 140 pages.

**Netto** — Catalog of Postage Stamps of Great Britain. G.F. Rapkin, Ltd., 1980 edition.

**Oxley, G.F** — English Provincial Local Posts 1765-1840. 79 pages.

**Pearson** — Slogan Postmarks of the United Kingdom, 1917-1969. 1974, 98 double pages.

Special Event Postmarks of the U.K., 1851-1973. 1973, second edition, 120 double pages.

**Potter, David** — Catalog of Great Britain Railway Letter Stamps, 1957-1976. Railway Philatelic Group, 36 pages.

The Talyllyn Railway Stamps and Postal History. 1969, Railway Philatelic Group, 24 pages.

**Povey and Whitney** — The Postal History of the Manx Electric Railway. 1980, 28 pages

**Purves, J.R.W.** — The V over Crown Watermarks, Types, Suppliers, Varieties 1867-1905, 1912. 1964, 40 pages.

**Redhill Philatelic Society.** — An Introduction to the Postal History of Reigate, Redhill and District. 32 pages.

**Rigo de Righi, A.G.** — The Story of the Penny Black and its Contemporaries. 1980, National Postal Museum, London, 56 pages.

**Robertson, A.W.** — The Maritime Postal History of London 1766-1960.

Great Britain Post Roads, Post Towns and Postal Rates 1635-1839. 64 pages.

The Ship Letter Stamps of Liverpool.

The Maritime Postal History of the British Isles. 1964, three volumes.

**Robinson, Howard** — The British Post Office, a History. 1948, Princeton University Press, 467 pages.

**Rosen, Gerald** — Catalogue of British Local Stamps. Great Britain and surrounding islands. 152 pages.

**Royal Philatelic Society** — Postage Stamps of Great Britain. Volume 1, Imperforate Line-Engraved Issues by Seymour and Hill, 1967 revised edition, 336 pages; Volume 2, Perforated Line-Engraved Issues by Wiggins, 1962 revised edition.

The Royal Philatelic Society of London 1869-1969 (history). Robert Maclehose and Co. Ltd., 192 pages.

**Samuel, Marcus, and Huggins, Alan** — Specimen Stamps and Stationery of Great Britain. 1980, Great Britain Philatelic Society, 310 pages.

**Seymour, J.B.** — The Penny Black of Great Britain. 1934, 31 pages.

**Staff, F.** — The Penny Post, 1680-1918. 1964, 219 pages.

Transatlantic Mail. 1956, 191 pages.

**Stanton** — Study of the Provisional Issue King George V 1934-1935. 1960, Great Britain Philatelic Society, 32 pages.

King Edward VIII, A Study of the Stamps. 1958, Great Britain Philatelic Society, 13 pages.

**Stitt-Dibden, W.G.** — Squared Circle Postmarks. 29 pages.

**Stone, J.W.M.** — The Repairs of the 1841 One Penny, Plates 1-40. 88 pages.

**Stoneham** — The Stoneham Catalogue of British Stamps. Includes Great Britain, Jersey, Guernsey and Isle of Man. Regularly updated.

**Tilles, Dr. Harvey** — Great Britain Perfins. Presently being published in sections.

**Traill and Holland** — The Sideways Duplex Cancellations of England and Wales. 27 pages.

**Wadham, F.** — Penny Blacks Plated. 1920, 22 pages.

**Ward, G.B.** — Postage Stamps of Great Britain. 25 pages.

**Watson, James** — Stamp Varieties Explained. 1979, Stanley Gibbons Publications.

**Westley, H.C.** — Postal Cancels of London, 1840-1890. 170 pages.

**Whitney, J.T.** — Collect British Postmarks. 1980, second edition, 213 pages.

**Wiggins, W.R.D., and Tonna, G.C.** — The Plating of Alphabet II, III and IV. 1973, G.C. Tonna, five volumes.

**Willcocks, R.M.** — England's Postal History to 1840 with notes of Scotland, Wales and Ireland. 1975, 167 pages.

The Postal History of Great Britain and Ireland. 1972, 80 pages.

**Wilson, H.S.** — History of the Travelling Post Offices of Great Britain Part I, 1971, 74 pages; Part II, 1975, 76 pages. Railway Philatelic Group.

## Greece

**Billig, Fritz** — Greece No. 1 and 2 Forgeries. Two handbooks.

**Constantinides, T.** — Etude sur les Timbres de Greece - Grosse Tete de Mercure. 1933, 514 pages; English reprint, 1979, Hellenic Philatelic Society of America, 312 pages.

**Constantinis, M.** — Postal Rates from Foundation of Greek Posts in 1829 until 1909. 28 pages.

The Post Office During the Hellenic Uprising, 1821-27. 138 pages.

**Coutsis, J.C.** — Greek Post Offices and Their Postmarks from 1861-1900. 1959, 172 pages.

**Hartmann, E.** — Samos und Seine Postverhaltnisse. 1936, 32 pages.

**Macrymichalos, S.** — Numbering of the Greek Rural Cancellation Postmarks. 69 pages.

**Monk, H.** — Greece. Volumes 1-4. Translated by Zervos, H.J.

**Nicolaides, S.** — Greek Postal Bureaus and Their Cachets During the 1919-22 War in Asia Minor.

Historical Details of the Greek Post Offices in Moldavia-Walachia and Soulina. 22 pages.

Histoire Du Timbre Grec. 1923, 117 pages.

**Nicolaides, S., and Xanthopoulos, A.** — Early Contracts by Greek Posts for Transmission of Mail Abroad, 1833-60. 29 pages.

**Papaioannou, A.C.** — The Small Hermes Heads of Greece. 125 pages.

**Photiades, G.M.** — First Athens Issue of Large Hermes Heads of Greece. 1965, 39 pages.

**Raftoupoulis Philatelic Editions** — Stamps of Greece and the Hellenic Nation. Catalog regularly updated.

**Raftoupoulis, S.** — The Classical Period of the Hellenic Postmarks. 104 pages.

Le Sovrastampe a Mano di Cefalonia, Itaca, Zante. 1961, 49 pages.

**Samaras, D.** — Cancellations of the Greek Steamship Companies, 1856-1900. 31 pages.

**de Smeth, P.** — Greece, Premier Type. 1925, 75 pages.

**Spink-Truman** — Classification of Large Hermes Heads. Billig's Volume XI.

**Vlastos Catalog of Stamps.** 1980 edition, 472 pages.

### Greenland

**Wowern, Eric** — Greenland (1907-1938). Pakke Porto Stamps. 1978, 64 pages.

Greenland Mail Before 1938. 1976, 69 pages.

Postage Stamps After 1938. 1980 edition, 56 pages.

Greenland, Expeditions and Flights Before 1938. 1976, 69 pages.

Greenland, Expeditions and Flights After 1938. 1976, 69 pages.

Greenland Specialized Stamp Catalog. Regularly updated.

Greenland Postmark Catalog (1938-1974). 1976, 69 pages.

Greenland Catalog of Meter Marks and Non-postal Charity Stamps. 1976, 55 pages.

### Guatemala

**Andrews, J.C.** — Postal Use of the Fiscal Stamps.

**Goodman, R.A.** — Postal History and Philately of Guatemala. Volume 1 to 1902, 1969, 279 pages; Volume 2 through 1971, 1974, 342 pages.

### Haiti

**Kunze, A.F.** — Who's Who on Postage Stamps. 19 pages.

### Hejaz

**Haworth and Sargent** — The Postage Stamps of the Hejaz. 1922, 63 pages.

### Honduras

**Green, Irving** — The Black Honduras. 1962, 32 pages.

### Hong Kong

**Perrin, K.L.** — Hong Kong "China" Overprints. Hong Kong stamps overprinted for use in British Post Offices in China, 1917-1930. 43 pages.

**Tilles, Dr. Harvey** — A Catalog of the Perfins of Hong Kong, 1870s to present. Published by the author.

**White, Arthur** — Hong Kong and the Treaty Ports. 1981, Cardinal Spellman Philatelic Museum, 160 pages.

**Yang, Nai-Chiang** — Postage Stamp Catalog. 1972, 70 pages.

### Hungary

**Barefoot** — Hungary Revenues. 1979, European Philatelic Study No. 5, 85 pages.

**Berecz, V.G** — The Pioneer Period of Hungarian Airmail. Society for Hungarian Philately Monograph No. 1, 1970.

**Ettre, L.S.** — Hungary Error Prints, Variations, 1900-44. Society for Hungarian Philately Monograph No. 2, 1971.

Issues of Western Hungary (Lajtabansag) in 1921. 1971, Society for Hungarian Philately Monograph No. 3.

**Kropf, H.** — Die Postwertzeichen der Oesterr. - Ungar. Monarchie. Early Hungarian issues and postal stationery, 1902 (German).

**Mabeosz** — A Magyar Belyegek Monofrafiaja. Six volumes, 1965-74.

Magyar Belyegkulonlegessegek Kezikonive. 1956, watermark reference.

**Madarasz, G.** — Belyegkatalogus, 1850-71. 1971, Hungarian and English.

**Mueller, E.** — Prestamp Postmarks of Austria. Includes Hungarian pre-stamp covers and cancels. 1960.

**Oliva, G.** — Fiume. A detailed catalog. 1956.

**Payer, B.** — Die Briefmarken des Konigreichs Ungarn. Information on essays of 1871 and envelopes. 1920.

**Philatelia Hungaria** — Magyar Belyegek Arjegyzeke. Annual catalog.

Hungarian Stamp Centenary. 1971, English language catalog.

**Ryan, G.S.** — The Cancellations of Hungarian Post Offices. 1980, 600 pages.

**Schaffling, W. and O.F.** — Hungarian Precancels. Precancels on Hungarian newspaper stamps. Society for Hungarian Philately Monograph No. 4, 1973.

**Szabo, J.** — Baranya Belyegei. Information and background on stamps of the Baranya issue. 1939.

**Szalay, A.B.** — Hohere Philatelie. Authority on the 1919 Transylvania issues. 1935, two volumes.

**Szekely, S.** — Magyarorszag Belyegei. Catalog useful for post-WWII specialized material. 1947.

**Tranmer, Keith** — Austro-Hungarian APOs 1914-18. 1973.

Postal Markings of the Austro-Hungarian Navy, 1914-18. 1961.

**Williams, L. and M.** — Hotel Posts of Hungary and Roumania. 1962.

**Zinsmeister, M.C.** — Hungarian Stamps and their Background. 1948.

### Iceland

**Adalsteinn, Jon** — One Hundred Years of Icelandic Stamps, 1873-1973. 473 pages.

**Scherer, R.W.** — Regulations on How to Use the Mail, with Amendments. 1925, 35 pages.

Handbook of Icelandic Postal Stationery. 52 pages.

**Thorsteinsson, S.H.** — A Catalogue of Icelandic Stamps. 1979 edition, Scanstamps Ltd., 121 pages.

Iceland. Volume I, 25 pages, Danish period; Volume II, 14 pages, manuscript cancels. Frost Forlag's Handbooks No. 10 and 11 (Danish).

## India

**Barefoot** — Bhopal, Plating the Primitives. 1978, 22 pages.

**Bateman** — Postal History of Bussahir. 1968, 84 pages.

**Cooper, Jal** — India Used Abroad. 1972 edition, 74 pages.

Early Indian Cancellations. 1948, 92 pages.

India Used in Burma. 1950, 64 pages.

Stamps of India. 1968 edition, 177 pages.

**Dastur** — Introduction to India Used Abroad. 1977, 67 pages.

**Dawson** — The One and Two Annas Lithographed Postage Stamps of India, 1854-55. 1948, 85 pages.

**Friedman, H.A.** — Azad Hind and Chalo Delhi Stamps. 1972, 16 pages.

**Giles** — Handstruck Postage Stamps of India. VOlume I, 256 pages; Volume II, 1967, 172 pages.

**Government of India** — White Paper on the Indian States. 1950, 395 pages.

**Gupta, V.K.** — A Handbook on Gwalior Postal History and Stamps, 1837-1950. 1980, 218 pages.

**Harkawat** — The Indore State Handbook. 1973, 71 pages.

**India Study Circle of Great Britain** — A Guide to the Postal Stationery of India, 1856-1977.

**Jain, Manik** — Encyclopedia of Indian Postal Stationery. 1973, 167 pages.

**Jatia, D.N.** — Indian Rocket Mails. Philatelic Congress of India, 64 pages.

**Lang, Derek** — A Guide to the Postal Stationery of India, 1856-1977. Part I, 1978, 74 pages, introduction; Part II, 1979, 122 pages, post cards; Part III, 1980, 94 pages, envelopes; and Part IV, 1981, aerogrammes.

**Lowe, Robson** — Indian Field Post Offices, 1903-1904. 1979, 10 pages.

**Luiz** — Stamps of Cochin. 1972, 98 pages.

**Martin, D.R.** — Early Indian Cancellations 1855-84. 1970, 144 pages.

Indian Traveling Post Offices, 1864-91.

**Martin, D.R., and Blair, N.** — Overseas Letter Postage from India, 1854-1876. 1976, 72 pages.

**Mooss** — Travancore Postal History. 1973, 221 pages.

**Nayeem, M.A.** — History of Postal Administration in Hyderabad. Volume I, 320 pages.

Hyderabad Postal History: Postal Markings. 1967, 152 pages.

Hyderabad Philatelic History. 1980, 264 pages.

**Pai, G.B.** — Cochin Postmarks and Cancellations. 110 pages.

**Samuel, Marcus** — Specimen Stamps of British India. 1978, 40 pages.

**Sidebottom, J.K.** — The Overland Mail. 1948, 174 pages.

**Spence, J.A.** — India 1854 Essays, Proofs and Reprints. 1975, 158 pages.

**Virk, D.S.** — Indian Army Post Offices and Philately. 1980, 224 pages.

## Indonesia

**Bruynesteyn, Dr. W.** — Republiek Indonesie de Boekdruk van 1945 (Java machine overprints). 1968, 15 pages.

**Dai Nippon Society** — Catologus van de Postzegels Uitgegeven in Netherlands in die onder Japanse Bezetting, 1942-45 (catalog of Dutch Indies Japanese Occupation stamps). 1975, 173 pages (Dutch).

Catalogus van de Postzegels Uitgegeven door het Rebellerende Regime van de Republiek Indonesie, 17 Augustus 1945-December 1949 (catalog of the postage stamps issued by the rebellious regime of the Republic of Indonesia). 1981, 217 pages (Dutch).

**Esbensen, V.** — Republik Indonesie, 1945-49 (postal history). 1980, 45 pages.

**Ramkema, H.** — Catalogus Weense en Philadelphia Uitgiften van de Republiek Indonesie (cinderella material). 1977, 147 pages (Dutch).

**Uitgiverij Zonnebloem** — Officielle Postzegelcatalogus Indonesie. Annual stamp catalog.

## Ireland

**Booth. R.G.** — A Catalogue of the Adhesive Revenue Stamps of the United Kingdom (including pre-1922 Ireland and Free State overprints). 1976, 173 pages.

**Brady, J.** — Adhesive Revenue Stamps of Ireland. 20 pages.

**Chandler, John, and Dagnall, H.** — The Newspaper and Almanac Stamps of Great Britain and Ireland. 1981.

**Feldman, David** — Stamps of Ireland. Released annually.

The Revenue Stamps of Ireland.

Handbook of Irish Philately. 180 pages.

**Feldman and Kane** — Handbook of Irish Postal History to 1840. 1975, 131 pages.

**Foley, Joseph** — British Stamps Overprinted by Irish Republican Office. Monograph.

The Taylor-Made Fenian Essays.

**Frank and Schonfeld** — The Stamp Duty of Great Britain and Ireland. 1974.

**Hibernian Specialized Catalogue of the Postage Stamps of Ireland.** Regularly updated.

**Hibernian Catalogue of Simplified Stamps of Ireland.** Regularly updated.

**Hill, J.A.** — The Overprinted Stamps of Ireland. 1976. 36 pages.

**Kane, William** — Catalogue of the Postal Markings of Dublin, 1840-1922. 1981.

**Lowe, Robson** — Ireland 1922-72.

**MacDonnell, David** — Stamps of Ireland. 1979, 92 pages.

**Mackay, J.A.** — The Story of Eire and Her Stamps. 160 pages.

**Meredith, W.G.** — The Postage Stamps of Ireland, 1922-27. 1979, Eire Philatelic Association.

**O'Neill, Charles Patrick** — Newspaper Stamps of Ireland. 1978.

**Warren, Brian** — The Gerl Definitives. 1979, Ian White, 68 pages.

**Wilcocks, R.M.** — The Postal History of Great Britain and Ireland (to 1840). 1972.

**Wilcocks, R.M., and Sedgewick, W.A.** — The Spoon Experiment, 1853-58.

### Isle of Man

**Gibbons, Stanley** — Collect Isle of Man Stamps. 1982, sixth edition.

**Massey, A.J.P.** — Isle of Man Postmarks, Surface and Air. 1979, Harry Hayes, 119 pages.

**Urch Harris** — Commonwealth Catalogue of Queen Elizabeth Stamps: Isle of Man. 1982, first edition, 20 pages.

**Von Uexkull, Jakob** — Isle of Man Local Stamps. 1977, 27 pages.

Post Manninagh — The First Isle of Man Postage Stamp Issues. 1977, 15 pages.

**Whitney, J.T.** — Isle of Man Camp Mail. 13 pages.

Priced Catalog of Isle of Man Postal Markings. 84 pages.

### Israel

**Bale** — Catalog of Israel Postage Stamps. Regularly updated.

Catalog of the Stamps of Palestine Mandate. Regularly updated.

**Blake** — Rishon Le Zion Armoured Car Stamp. 1948, 16 pages.

Doar Ivri Plates (No. 1-9). Nine pages.

**Buzzetti and Sorani** — Italian Detachment in Palestine, 1917-21. In Italian with separate English translation, 55 pages.

**DCIB** — Catalog. 275 pages, lists over 1,000 titles of books and periodicals in English.

**Gershon** — Specialized Catalogue of Israel and The Holy Land. 1978, 352 pages.

**Gladstone, N.** — Postal Censorship in Palestine During World War II, 1939-1945. 111 pages.

Postal Censorship in Israel, 1948-1978. 1979, 110 pages.

**Glassman, Emanuel** — The Postal History of Jerusalem From 1948. 1979, 176 pages.

**Heymann, I., and Pertzelan, M.** — Postage Stamps of Israel. Second edition 1956, 193 pages.

**Hoexter, W., and Fluri, E.** — The stamps of Palestine and the Interim Period. 139 pages.

**Hoffman, Barry D.** — Turkish Post Offices in the Holy Land. 1962, 59 pages.

**House of Zion** — Carmel Israel Catalogue. Regularly updated; 1980 edition, 68 pages.

**Israel-Palestine Society** — Minhelet Ha'am Postage Stamps. JNF seals overprinted Doar. 1950 Monograph, 12 pages.

**Kessler and Vogel** — Postal History of Nahariya. 1948, 10 pages.

**Kolar-OR Catalogue** — Regularly updated, Orient Publishing House Ltd.

**Levison, M.E.** — The Doar Ivri.

**Livnat, R.** — Doar Ivri, Plate and Tabs Types. 1978.

**Ministry of Posts** — Catalog. Regularly updated.

**Mosden** — Catalogue of the Postage Stamps of the Holy Land and Judaica. Two volumes, 1969-71, 696 pages.

**Narros Sellos Catalog of Israel** — Regularly updated.

**OR Holyland Catalog Pre-Israel** — Specialties of Turkish and foreign posts. 94 pages.

**Persoff, Meir** — The Running Stag. Stamps and postal history. 1973, 115 pages.

**Pollack, F.W.** — Turkish Post in the Holy Land. 1977 reprint, 59 pages.

**Richter, John H.** — Judaica on Postage Stamps. 181 pages.

**Sacher, Michael** — Government, Certified Official and Post Office Cachets of the British Mandate of Palestine. 1982, British Association of Palestine-Israel Philatelists, 87 pages.

**Schulman and Weisberger** — Israel Postal System. 18 pages.

**Shalit, Uri** — Catalog of Israel Philatelic Items. 1976, 176 pages.

**Siegel, M.** — Introduction to Stamps of Palestine Mandate. 11 page monograph.

**Simmons, David** — Basic Israel Philately. 1979.

**Simon** — Catalog of Israel Stamps. 1967, 311 pages.

Handbook of the Mail in the Concentration Camps, 1933-45. 136 pages.

**Smith, C.H., and Simon, W.** — Catalog of the Meter Postage Stamps.

**Wallach, Josef** — Israel Definitive Postage Stamps Specialized Catalogue. 1979, 70 pages.

**Wallerstein's Specialized Catalog of Israel and the Holy Land Revenues.** 115 pages.

**Wolinetz, Harvey** — Arab Philatelic Propaganda Against the State of Israel. 74 pages.

### Italy

**Allanello, R.** — Lombardy-Venetia and Austrian Levant Cancellations. 600 pages.

**Baldoni, A.** — Dalla Republica Cisalpina a Roma Capitale d'Italia. 1942, 61 pages.

**Balestra-Cecchi** — Postal Services of the Italian Navy in WWII. Cancels and cachets. 219 pages, in Italian.

**Banci, A.** — Catalogo Prefilatelico, Lombardo-Veneto. 1942, 175 pages.

**Barberis, N.** — Studio Sulla Posta da Campo Polacca in Italia Durante WWII. 1964, 37 pages.

**Bazzi, A.** — La Posta Militare Italiana del 1870. 1955, 23 pages.

**Bianchi, Paolo** — Postal History of Italian Colony Eritrea, 1883-1903. 151 pages.

**Billig, Fritz** — Handbooks on Cancellations-Postmarks, Volume V.

Handbooks on Forgeries. In German.

**Bocchialini, J.** — Annulamenti Postali dell'Ex-Ducato di Parma e del Regno (1860-1863). 1948, 47 pages.

**Bolaffi, G.** — Catalogo Nazionale dei Francobolli Italiani. Regularly updated.

Encyclopedia of Ancient Italian States Specialized. 363 pages.

Italy and Colonies Catalog. 655 pages.

**Brown, W.L.** — Descriptive Catalog of Revenue Stamps of Italy, 1836-1878. 23 pages.

**Buzzetti, L., and Sorani, S.** — The Italian Detachment in Palestine, 1917-1921. 56 pages.

**Carozzi, A.** — Billig's Handbooks on Cancellations-Postmarks Volume 3.

Le Timbrature a Numero del Regno d'Italia (1866-1889). 136 pages.

**Catalogo Filagrano degli Interi Postli Postali.** 1980, 256 pages.

**Centro Filatelico Internazionale** — Tuscany Difetti Constanti Nei Francobolli del Granducato di Toscana. Eight pages.

**Chase, C.** — Manuscript notes and lists relating to Italy in the Napoleonic Period.

**Cherubini-Taragni** — Italian Airmail Catalog. 1974, 299 pages, in English and prices in U.S. dollars.

**Chiavarello, G.** — Catalogo dei Francobolli delle Occupazioni Italiane WWII. 1962, 79 pages.

Catalogo Specializzato dei Francobolli di Napoli, 1858-1861. 1955, 63 pages.

**Ciarrocchi, F.** — Catalogo Specializzato dei Francobolli d'Italia. 1953 edition, 116 pages.

**Consonni, P.** — La Posta Aerea d'Italia. 45 pages.

**Cresto, G.B.** — La Nostra Legislazione sui Francobolli dal 1818 ai Nostri Giorni. 1894, 196 pages.

**Dehn, R.A.** — Italian Stamps. 1973, 288 pages.

**Del Bianco, U.** — Italian Maritime Cancellations Prior to 1891. 158 pages.

**Della, S.R.L.** — Catalogo Italiano Francobolli Degli Antichi Stati Italia, San Marino, Vaticano. 1966 edition, 134 pages.

**Delrieu, H.** — Les Timbres de Sardaigne et Leurs Obliterations. 41 pages.

**Faraone, Ettore** — Catalog of the Cancellations of Sardinian-Italian Lombardy, 1860-63. 88 pages, in Italian.

**Ferrini** — Italy 1851-1877 Iconografia Di Vittorio Emanuelo Attaverso I Franco-Bolli. 49 pages.

**Fiecchi, Alfredo E.** — Creation of the Special Service of the Private Post of Milan, 1920. 46 pages, in Italian.

**Gaggero, G.** — The Revolution of Venice and the Siege of Venice (1848-49). Military and naval markings. 142 pages, in Italian.

The Republic of Venice, 1848-49. Postal markings. 210 pages, in Italian.

**Gallenge, M.** — Italian Postal History. Part I, cancellations and handstamps of the Romagna region, 160 pages; Part 2, cancellations and handstamps of the Marche region, 212 pages.

**Gianetto, C.** — Tuscany Contributo Allo Studion dei Francobolli di Toscana con Tavole Fuori Testo. 15 pages.

**Gordon, T.M.** — Checklist of Italian and Jugoslavian town cancels on the stamps of the Austraian Empire, 1850-83. 1974, 103 pages.

**Harris, L.H.** — World's First Air Stamp, Italy 1917. 15 pages.

**Lajolo, C.** — Stamps of the Military and of the Corps of Italian Volunteers, 1848-70. 15 pages.

**Landmans, G.** — Annulamenti del Lombardo-Veneto. 1952, 67 pages.

Catalogo della Posta Aera Italiana. 1929, 87 pages.

Catalogo dello Cartoline e Vignette Ufficiali e Semiufficiali di Posta Aerea Italiana. 32 pages.

Catalogo dei Francobolli d'Italia. 1953, 255 pages.

**de Magistris, L.** — Italy and Colonies Marche Da Bollo. Catalog of revenues, 1947, 279 pages.

**Melillo, Enrico** — Poste e Telegrafi nel Regno de Sardegna, 1800-60. Migliavacca reprint of 1910 booklet, 35 pages.

**Meyer, S.** — I Francobolli di Transizione di Napoli del 1861. 20 pages.

**Migliavacca, G.** — Invito Alla Storia Postale. 51 pages.

Unicum Filatelico. 1973, 220 pages.

The Post and Courier Service of Early Modern Italy. 1980, 32 pages.

Italian P.O.W. and Internees in Africa. 1980. 42 pages.

**Morrone and Rossi** — Catalogo dei Bolli ed Annulamenti Postali del Ducato di Modena (1852-1859). 1954, 82 pages.

**Oliva, G.** — Francobolli Degli Antichi Stati Italiani. 211 pages.

I Francobolli d'Italia. Volume I, 1950 edition, 204 pages.

**Omodeo, A.** — A Listing of Markings for the Kingdom of Sardinia, Jan. 1, 1838. 18 pages.

**Ostrow, P.** — Italy's Liberation Locals of WWII. October 1953, 12 pages.

**Pastine, O.** — L'Organizzazione Postale della Repubblica di Genova. 1926.

**Patton, D.A.** — The Romagna. Study of postal history.

**Penco, Piero** — Italy Le Buste Lettere Postali I Francobolli Soprastampati B.L.P. 19 pages.

**Peroni, B.** — Fonti per la Storia d'Italia dal 1789-1815. 1936, 330 pages.

I Francobolli della IV Emissione di Sardegna (1855-63). 174 pages.

**Rubini, Giulio** — Postal History of Friuli and its Cancellations. 49 pages, in Italian.

**Sassone** — Two Sicilies Cancellations. 1974, 191 pages, in Italian.

Specialized Catalog. Regularly updated.

**Schenone, G.** — Il Volo Verticale in Italia. 35 pages.

**Tchillinghirian, S.D.** — Stamps of Italy Used Abroad. Six parts.

**Tomasini, M.** — Italia 1863. I Falsi Usati Postalmente del 15 centesimi Litografico. 1961, 49 pages.

**Violino, E.** — Catalogue of Zeppelin Mails of Italy, Italian Colonies, San Marino and Vatican City. 112 pages.

**Vittozzi, E.** — Gli Annulamenti sui Francobolli del Regno di Napoli. 1927, 15 pages.

**Vollemeir, Paolo** — Forged Pre-adhesive Postmarks of the Old Italian States. 1979 reprint, Postal History Society, 56 pages.

I Boli, Postali Toscani de Periodo Prefilatelico fino 1851. 300 pages (Italian); Volume II, after 1851 by Felippo Pettrucci, 294 pages (Italian).

**Von Bertalanffy** — Origins of Posts, Italy 15th Century.

**Weisbecker, Walter, G.** — Camp Mail of Italian P.O.W. and Civilian Internees in East Africa, 1940-47. 1981, 100 pages.

### Jamaica

**Aguilar, E.F.** — Handbook of Jamaica. Two volumes, 238 pages.

**Foster, T.** — Postal History of Jamaica, 1662-1860. 1968, 180 pages.

**Melville, F.J.** — Jamaica. 1910, 89 pages.

**Nicholson, L.C.C.** — Temporary Rubber Date Stamps, 1881-1938.

### Japan

**Arai, Toshimoto** — Showa Kitte Kenkyu (regular issues of 1937-1948). 1974, 143 pages. Japanese, but illustrations easily used.

**Bertalanffy, Felix D.** — A Historical Interpretation of the 72 Commemorative Postcards of Japan, Part I. 1971, 40 pages, Japanese American Philatelic Society Monograph No. 1.

**Bishop, John G.** — The Roman Letter Postmarks of Japan. 1979, 114 pages, International Society for Japanese Philately Monograph No. 7.

**Dai Nippon Society** — Catalogus van de Postzegels Uitgegeven in Nederlands Indie onder Japanse Bezetting 1942-1945 (occupation issues). 1975, 173 pages.

**Ekitei Yushu Kai** — The Specialized Catalogue of Showa Regular Stamps 1937-1946. 1980, 120 pages. Japanese, but illustrations easily used.

**Fisher, George A.** — Early Japanese Postmarks and Post Offices. 1965; 1975, 45 pages. International Society for Japanese Philately Monograph No. 1.

Philatelic Cazetteer of Manchoukuo and Kwantung Leased Territory, South Manchurian Railway Zone. 1981, 73 pages, International Society for Japanese Philately Monograph No. 9.

**Gely, Andre** — Les Faux Timbres Anciens du Japon et Leur Expertise 1871-1875 (forgeries). 1958, 67 pages.

**Halliburton, W.H.; Roger, Conrad; and Spaulding, Robert M.** — Pacific Crossings From Japan. 1969, 31 pages, International Society for Japanese Philately Monograph No. 3.

**Hashimoto, Akira** — Checklist of Japanese Scenic Cancellations 1931-1940. 1976, 160 pages. Japanese, but illustrations easily used.

**Hedeman, N.F., and Boekema, Roelf** — Dai Nippon in South East Asia. 1948, 186 pages. Also reprinted in Billig Handbook Vol. 19.

**Ichida, Soichi** — The Cherry Blossom Issues of Japan 1872-1876. 1965, 337 pages.

The Dragon Stamps of Japan 1871-1872. 1959, 221 pages.

**Insatsu Kyoku Choyo Foundation** — Japanese Postage Stamps in the Manufacture. 1975, 155 pages.

**Ishikawa, Ryohei** — The Forerunner Foreign Post Offices in Japan. 1976, 164 pages. Japanese, but illustrations easily used.

**Ito, Yoshimi** — B.C.O.F. Overprints and British Commonwealth and Indian MIlitary Postal Services in Japan and Korea. 1981, 240 pages.

**Japan Stamp Dealers Association** — Japanese Postage Stamp Catalogue. Annual, 144 pages. Japanese, but illustrations easily used.

**Japan Stamp Publicity Association** — Foreign Mail of Japan in the Days of Her Accession to the UPU. 1978, 80 pages. Japanese, but illustrations easily understood.

**JAPEX Committee** — Centenary of Japanese Post Offices in China. 1976, 228 pages. Japanese, but illustrations easily understood.

International Mail Service Centenary. 1976, 192 pages. Japanese, but illustrations easily understood.

Tazawa Series 1913-1937. 1978, 201 pages. Japanese, but illustrations easily understood.

**Johnson, Sune** — A Concordance: The Stamps of Japan, Ryukyus and Manchoukuo 1871-1979. 1981, 47 pages, International Society for Japanese Philately Monograph No. 10.

**Marcus, Margaret** — Paintings on Japanese Postal Issues. 1972, 50 pages, International Society for Japanese Philately Monograph No. 5.

**Metzelaar, Willem and Tyler** — Forgeries and Imitations of the Dragon Stamps of Japan. 1971, 24 pages, International Society for Japanese Philately Monograph No. 4.

**Mizuhara, Meiso** — Sakura Catalog of Japanese Stamps. Annual, 200 pages. Japanese, but illustrations easily understood.

**Mizuhara, Meiso, et al** — Japanese Stamp Specialized Catalog. Annual, 500 pages. Japanese, but illustrations easily understood.

Encyclopedia Japanese Philately. 1974, second edition, 526 pages.

**Montgomery, Milton T.** — A Guide to the Cherry Blossom Series. 1969, 31 pages, International Society for Japanese PLhilately Monograph No. 2.

**Mosher, John** — Japanese Post Offices in China and Manchuria. 1978, 229 pages.

**Murata, Moriyasu** — Murata Collection (of Japanese stamps). 1977, 466 pages. Japanese, but illustrations easily understood.

**Nishino, Shigeo and Tani Takashi** — Date Stamps for Overseas Mail of Japan. 1981, third edition, 100 pages. Japanese, but illustrations easily understood.

**Onishi, Jiro** — Nihon no Gunji Yubin (military postmarks). 1966, 297 pages. Japanese, but illustrations easily understood.

**Sakairi, Hiroshi, and Yoshikawa Yoichi** — Japanese Commemorative Datestamps (Small) List 1934-1940. 1976, 128 pages. Japanese, but illustrations easily understood.

**Salles, Raymond, and Matsumoto Jun Ichi** — Le Bureau Francais de Yokohama 1865-1880. 1976, 121 pages.

**Sawa, Mamoru** — Koban Kitte (1876-1892 regular series). 1974, 443 pages. Japanese, but illustrations easily understood.

**Shimomura, Masaichi** — Standard Catalogue of the Japanese Revenue Stamps. 1981, 155 pages. Japanese, but illustrations easily understood.

**Spaulding, Robert M.** — Specialized Catalogue of the Postage Stamps of Japan. 1955, 48 pages.

**Tanabe, Takeshi, ed.** — Gallery of Japanese Stamps, 1977-1982, 10 volumes, about 300 pages each. Japanese, but illustrations easily understood.

**Tebori Kitte Kenkyu Kai** — The Specialized Catalogue of Japanese Hand Engraved Stamps. 1981, third edition, 185 pages. Japanese, but illustrations easily understood.

**Tyler, Varro E.** — Characteristics of Genuine Japanese Stamps 1872-1876. 1967; 1981, 38 pages.

**Tyler, Varro E., and Montgomery, M.T.** — The Wada Cherry Blossom Forgeries. 1974, 92 pages, International Society for Japanese Philately Monograph No. 6.

**Wilhelmsen, Kristian** — Japans Klassiske Forfalskninger (forgeries). Includes English translation. 1981, 363 pages.

**Wilhelmsen, Kristian, and Tyler, Varro E.** — The Koban Forgeries of Japan. 1979, 63 pages, International Society for Japanese Philately Monograph No. 8.

**Woodward, A.M. Tracey** — The Postage Stamps of Japan and Dependencies. 1928; reprinted 1976 with additions, 548 plus 243 pages.

**Yamashita, Seiichi** — Postal History of Saghalien. 1978, 126 pages. Japanese, but illustrations easily understood.

**Yoshikawa, Yoichi** — Japanese FDC Catalogue. Periodic editions; 1981, 160 pages. Japanese, but illustrations easily understood.

### Jordan

**Souan, K.C.R.** — Philatelic History of Jordan, 1920-1980 Diamond Jubilee. 1980, 345 pages.

### Jugoslavia

**Billig, Fritz** — Handbooks on Forgeries. Jugoslavia I and II, in German.

**Gordon, T.M** — Checklist of Italian and Jugoslavian Town Cancels on the Stamps of the Austrian Empire, 1850-83. 1974, 103 pages.

**Prirucnik** — Specialist Handbooks: Volume 2 Jugoslavia 1918-19 overprints on Bosnia and SHS, 156 pages; Volume 3 Hrvatska 1918-19, 141 pages; Volume 4 Slovenija 1919-20, 160 pages; Volume 5 Slovenska Izdanja Drugi Dio, 253 pages; Volume 6 Slovenska Izdanja Treci Dio, 221 pages; Volume 7 Slovenska Izdanja Cervrti, 206 pages; Volume 10 Crna Gora Montenegro, 156 pages.

**Uroshevich, M.** — Katalog Postanskih Maraka Jugoslovenshik Zemalja. 1975.

### Korea

**Collectors Club** — Philatelic Handbook for Korea, 1884-1905. 128 pages.

**Korean Philatelic Society** — Korean Postage Stamp Catalog. 143 pages.

Philatelic Handbook for Korea, 1884-1905. 128 pages.

**Ministry of Communications** — Postage Stamps of Korea 1884-1956. 132 pages.

### Latvia

**Stereo Stamps** — The Stamps of Latvia. 1979, 52 pages.

### Levant

**Armstrong, D.B.** — The Stamps of the Levant Post Offices. 1972 reprint, 128 pages.

**Zimmerman, David M.** — Free French Censorship in the Levant. 1980.

## Liberia

**Cockrill, Philip** — Liberia Booklet Series. Nine booklets to date.

**Von Saleski, L.** — Liberia Specialized Stamp Catalog. 500 pages.

## Liechtenstein

**Bergmann, J. Wilhelm, and Paikert, Horst-Dieter** — Die Einschreibezettel im Fuerstentum Liechtenstein. Covers registration labels. Duesseldorfer Philatelistenclub Jan Wellem, eight pages.

Die Ganzsachen des Fuerstentume Liechtenstein. Covers postal stationery.

**Betschinger, Gustav** — Liechtenstein Handbuch. Presently in publication, to date three volumes have been published, Ring der Liechtenstein Sammler, to date 950 pages.

**Bluemel, Gerhard W.** — Die Poststempel Liechtensteins. Cancellations. Liechtenstein Collectors Guild.

**Liechtenstein Handbuch and Katalog.** 1953 edition, Sieger Verlag, 212 pages.

**Marxer, Alfons** — Liechtensteiner Briefmarken Katalog. Phila-Verlag, regularly updated.

**Otto, R.** — Die Ganzsachen des Fuerstentume Liechtenstein. Covers postal stationery. Reprint of Bergmann and Paikert work, 16 pages.

**Sieger, Hermann E.** — Die Post in Liechtenstein, 1770-1920. Reprint from the jubilee issue "50 Jahre Liechtensteinische Postwertzeichen 1912-1962." 105 pages.

**Zinsmeister, M.C.** — Liechtenstein Stamps and Their Background, 1912-1973. 88 pages.

**(Note: all Swiss catalogs published in Switzerland include a listing of Liechtenstein stamps. See Switzerland listing.)**

## Lithuania

**Lithuanian Philatelic Society of New York** — Postage Stamps of Lithuania. 1979, Collectors Club, 237 pages.

## Luxembourg

**Billig, Fritz** — Handbooks on Forgeries. Volume 39.

**Godinas** — Airmail and First Flight Catalog. 1958, 62 pages.

**Luxembourg Posts and Telecommunications** — The origin of the First Luxembourg Stamps. 1979, 47 pages.

**Prifix** — Specialized Catalog. Regularly updated, in French.

## Malaya

**Lowe, Robson** — Malaya-Japanese Occupation (catalog of single-line chops). 1962, 16 pages.

## Malaysia

**Malaysia-Singapore-Brunei Stamp Catalog** — Regularly updated, International Stamp and Coin Agency, Kuala Lumpur.

## Malta

**Bannister, A.B., and Martin, R.E.** — Malta 1965 Definitives. 1976, 31 pages.

**Galea, Joseph** — The Quarantine Service and the Lazzaretto of Malta. 1967; reprinted 1975, 36 pages.

**Mackay, J.A.** — Story of Malta and Her Stamps. 96 pages.

**Malta Study Circle** — The 1885-1902 Victoria Adhesives. Monograph.

1965 Definitive Set, Decimal Overprints of 1972. 31 pages.

Prisoner of War Mail. 15 pages.

Village Postmarks. 41 pages.

The Postal History and Postage Stamps. 1980, 411 pages.

War-Time Airmail. 1977, 25 pages.

**Pogson, L.V.J.** — Malta, the 1885-1902 Victorian Adhesives.

**Said Catalog of Malta Stamps.** Regularly updated.

**Turnbull, Mrs. P.L. (drafted by)** — Postal History, Malta 1530-1806. Mail of the Knights of Malta and Napoleonic Occupation. 1976, 24 pages.

## Manchukuo

**Akagi, R.H.** — Postage Stamps of Manchukuo. 1941, 101 pages.

**Schumann, A.** — Special Catalogue of the Stamps of Manchukuo. 1940-1941 editions, 46 pages and 84 pages.

**Zirkle, H.** — Postage Stamps and Commemorative Cancellations of Manchukuo. 1964, 131 pages.

## Mauritius

**Baker, Ken** — The B53 Obliterators of Mauritius. 32 pages.

**Harrison, M.** — Post Office, 1847 Mauritius. 1947.

**Kanai, Hiroyuki** — Classic Mauritius: The Locally Printed Postage Stamps, 1847-59. 1981, 144 pages.

## Mexico

**Aquirre, E.** — Catalogo Especializado de los Sellos Postales de Mexico. Septima edition 1946, 161 pages.

**Bash, J.K., and Yag, Otto** — The Pre-Stamp Markings of Mexico. 1965; 1973 edition, 170 pages.

**Billings, R.R.** — Postal Issue of 1874-1883.

**Brock, C., Eimbcke, A., and Ingham, F.** — A Guide to Collecting Mexico. 32 pages, three-ring binder.

**Cassio, J.L.** — Mexico los Timbres de Tres Centavos del Imperio de Maximiliano. 1936, 31 pages.

Mexico los Timbres Mexicanos de Ocho Reales de 1861 Negro y Cafe con Sobre-Carga a Pam. 1935, 37 pages.

**Celis, Cano** — Catalogo Especializado de los Sellos Postales de Mexico. 1974, 471 pages.

**Chapman, S.** — The Postage Stamps of Mexico 1856-1868. 1976 Quarterman reprint, 407 pages.

**Heath, J.M.** — British Postal Agencies in Mexico, 1825-76. 1971, 21 pages.

**Herrasti, S.** — Study of Relations of Value and Price of the Stamps of Mexico.

**Ingham, Frederick G.** — A Catalog of the Proofs, Essays, Sample, Specimen and Test Stamps of Mexico. 1979 edition, Mexico-Elmhurst Philatelic Society International, 46 pages.

**Linn, G.W.** — Mexico The White and Green Seal Issues of Sonora. Billig's Volume 20.

**Mexico-Elmhurst Philatelic Society International** — The Genuine Characteristics of the Stamps of Mexico. 1979.

**Monterrubio, F.** — Specialized Catalog of Mexico Air Mail Stamps. 1957, 79 pages.

**Odfjell, A.** — Stamps of the Postal Districts of Mexico.

**Schatzkes, J.** — The Cancellations of Mexico, 1856-1874.

**Schimmer, K.H.** — The Postmarks of Mexico 1874-1900. 1977, 472 pages.

1895-98 Mail Transportation Issue of Mexico. 45 pages.

**Stevens, R.B.** — The Revenue Stamps of Mexico. 360 pages.

**Yag, O.** — The Issue of 1872-74. 44 pages.

### Mongolia
**Catalog of Mongolian Stamps** — 1979 edition, Philatelia Hungarica, 200 pages.

### Natal
**Hart, Kantey and Leon** — The Postal Markings of Natal.

### Nauru
**Pacific Islands Study Circle** — Cancellation Study of Nauru.

### Nepal
**Alevizos, G.** — Priced Guide to the 1881-1918 Native Issues of Nepal. 16 pages.

**Hellrigl, W., and Hepper, C.** — The Native Postmarks of Nepal. 1977, Nepal Philatelic Study Circle, 133 pages.

**Ricketts, M., and Vignola, F.** — A Guide to Specialization in Nepal Philately. 1977, 22 pages, California Collectors Club.

**Smythies and Dawson** — Postage Stamps of Nepal. 1950, 47 pages.

**Vignola, Frank, and Sanford, O.R.** — A Philatelic View of the Anglo-Nepalese War of 1814-1816. 1981, George Alevizos, 24 pages.

### Netherlands
**Avezaat, C., and Okker, H.** — Catalogus Erstedag Brievan Nederland en O.R. 1979, 127 pages.

**Balen** — Handboek Nederland Emissie, 1852.

**Blom, F** — Etude sur les Obliterations Roulette des Pays-Bas (roulette precancels). 1955, 32 pages (French).

Handboek Nederlands Postkantoren, 1850-1906.

**Boesman, J.** — Handboek Postvluchten Nederland en O.R. 1970, 400 pages.

**ter Braake** — Handboek Voorfilatelie Nederland. 151 pages.

**Buitenkamp, H., and Muller, E.** — Catalogus Postzegels op Brief Nederland, 1852-1978. 1980, 60 pages.

**Chase** — Histoire et Catalogue des Marques Postales des Dept. Conquis Sous la Revolution 1792-1815. 62 pages.

**Cockrill, Philip** — K.N.S.M. The Royal Netherlands Steamship Co., 1856-1981. 1981, 56 pages.

**Cockrill, Philip, and Traanberg, J.P.** — Maritime Markings and Ship Cancellations (1793-1939) of the Netherlands and Colonies. 1980, 56 pages.

**van Dieten, J.L.** — Catalogus Proeven Nederland en O.R. 1966, 199 pages.

**Doorn** — Handboek Nederlands Censuer, Kamp, en Dienstpost.

Nederlands Postale Problemen na 1945.

**Goldhoorn, Dr. L.** — Overzicht van Nederlands Postzegels. 1979, 91 pages.

**Guezendam's Postzegelhandel** — Catalogus van de Postwaardestukken van Nederland en Overzeese Rijksdelen. Regularly updated.

**Hoogerdijk** — Catalogus Grootrondstempels Nederland.

Catalogus Halfrond Kleinrondstempels Nederland.

Catalogus Langstempel Nederland.

De Puntstempels van Nederland en Ned. Indies. 1970, 75 pages.

**Horn, E.** — Handboek Postzegelbockjes Nederland, Ned. Indies, Curacao. 1980, 201 pages.

**Houwink. Dr. R.H.** — Neues Handboek No. 14 Niederlandisch New Guinea. 19 pages.

**Kuypers, Rene J.** — Philatelic Service, The Netherlands, A Postal History. 1980, Netherlands Philatelic Society of Chicago.

**van de Loo, P.F.A.** — Forgeries, Netherlands and Colonies. 1979, 148 pages.

**Melville, F.J.** — Holland. 1909, 78 pages.

**National Philatelic Museum** — Netherlands Handbook. Philadelphia, 194 pages.

**Nederlandsche Vereeniging van Postzegelhandelaren** — Speciale Catalog. Regularly updated.

**Portheine** — Catalogus Rolzegels Nederlands. 1978.

**de Rooy/Hali** — Special Katalogus Automaatboekjes Nederland (Slot Machine Booklets). 1980-81, 56 pages.

**Schiller and deKruif** — Manual of the Stamps of Netherlands and Colonies. 1940, 217 pages.

**Schweizer, W.F.** — Matrix voor de Indeling van Postzegels met Textial-Motieven. 40 pages.

**Technipress** — Catalogus Prentbriefkaarten Nederland. 1979.

**Trompet** — Catalogus Maximumkaarten Nederland.

**Vellinga** — Handboek Stempels Nederland, 1667-1915.

**de Vliegende Hollander** — Luchtpostcatalogus Nederland en O.R. 1977, 264 pages.

**Ward, V.D.** — Catalogus Reclame/gelegenheidsstempels Nederland.

**Wilgenburg** — Catalogus Plaatfonten Nederland.

### Nevis

**Melville, F.J.** — Nevis. 1909, 60 pages.

### Newfoundland

**Ayshford, John, and Brachi, Mike** — The Last Stamps of Newfoundland. Robson Lowe, 20 pages.

**Boggs, W.S.** — The Postage Stamps and Postal History of Newfoundland. 1942; 1975 reprint, 256 pages.

**Dalwick and Harmer** — Newfoundland Air Mails 1919-1939. 1953, 180 pages.

**Goodkind, H.M.** — The Hawker Stamp of Newfoundland. 1951, 23 pages.

**Meyerson, D.C.** — Newfoundland Specialized. 56 pages.

### New Guinea

**Croaker, H.** — Postmarks of British New Guinea and Papua to 1942. Hawthorne Press.

**Hare, Dan** — The Airmails of New Guinea, 1922-42. 64 pages.

**Harrison and Rutherford** — The Postal History of New Guinea and Papua, 1945-70. 1971.

**Melville, F.J.** — British New Guinea and Papua. 1909, 63 pages.

**Powell** — Postal History of New Guinea, 1880-1942. 49 pages, Hawthorne Press.

### New Hebrides

**Collins, Peter** — New Hebrides. Listing of postal cancellations.

**Crompton and Hals** — Cancellation Study and History of Registered Cachets and Labels of New Hebrides. 1970, Pacific Islands Study Circle.

U.S. Armed Forces Postal Services in the New Hebrides During World War II. Pacific Islands Study Circle.

**Hals, N., and Collas, P.** — Postal Stamps and Their History. 1968.

**Jersey, S.C.** — U.S. Armed Forces Postal History in the New Hebrides During World War II. Pacific Islands Study Circle.

### New Zealand

**Auckland City Stamps** — ACS Colour Catalogue of New Zealand Stamps. 1979, 30 pages.

**Breen, Campbell and Startup** — New Zealand Registered Mail User Cachets. 1975, 23 pages.

**Campbell, G.** — Handbook New Zealand Registration Labels, 1906-65. 82 pages.

**Collins, R.D.J.** — New Zealand Timral, 100 Years of Postal Services. 31 pages.

Oceanic Dependencies of New Zealand. 52 pages.

**Collins and Watts** — The Postage Stamps of New Zealand. 1961, Royal Philatelic Society of New Zealand, six volumes.

**Franks, L.** — Postal History Catalog of New Zealand. Volume 1, 40 pages; Volume 2, 54 pages.

All the Stamps of New Zealand — Collecting for Profit and Pleasure. 1981 edition, 161 pages.

**Jackson, Alan** — New Zealand Relief Date stamps, 1925-74. 17 pages.

**Jury, Len** — Catalogue of New Zealand Stamps. Regularly updated.

**Kaye, G.** — New Zealand. Study of the Richardson printings on large star paper.

**Kiwi Catalogue of New Zealand** (stamps, revenues, postal stationery). Regularly updated.

**Lowe, Robson** — The Chalon Two Pence. Eight pages.

**Paterson, C.** — Pim's Catalog, The Stamps of New Zealand. 1949, 116 pages.

**Robinson, Howard** — A History of the Post Office in New Zealand. 1964, 280 pages.

Squared Circle Cancellations of New Zealand. Postal History Society of New Zealand.

**Samuel, R.D.** — New Zealand Postal Stationery Catalogue. Three volumes: I, postal cards, 1976; II, letter cards, 1976; III, registered envelopes, 1978.

The Second Type Postage Due Stamps of New Zealand. 1980.

**Scott, K.J.L.** — Notes on the Early Cancellations of New Zealand.

**Stamp Publications Pty. Ltd.** — New Zealand and Pacific Islands Stamp Catalogue. 1979, 176 pages.

**Startup, R.M.** — American Post Offices in New Zealand 1908-1959. 17 pages.

Chatham Isles Mails. 1976, 49 pages.

Korean War, New Zealand Military Postal Services 1950-57.

New Zealand Post Offices. 1979, Postal History Society of New Zealand, 241 pages.

New Zealand Postal Slogans. 160 pages.

New Zealand Wairarapa Postal Services. 29 pages.

Through Gorge and Valley. History of the postal district of Nelson from 1842. 1975 edition with addenda, 96 pages.

Westland Postal Services 1860-1960. 23 pages.

Air Mail Cancellations of New Zealand. 1954.

New Zealand Relief Cancellations. 1960.

Traveling Mails (non-rail). 1960.

**Walker, J.R.** — The Great Barrier Island 1898-99 Pigeon Post Stamps. 1968, 109 pages.

### Nicaragua

**Brenke, D.B.** — Preludes and Causes of the American Revolution. 1973, 32 pages.

### Niue and Tokelau

**Burge, A.R.** — The Decimal Currency Arms Type Stamps of Niue Island and the Tokelau Islands.

### Norfolk Island

**Simpson, Ray** — Norfolk Island Postmarks. Pacific Islands Study Circle, 1970.

### North Borneo

**Shipman, L.H.** — The Fiftieth Anniversary Issue of the British North Borneo Company, January 1, 1931. 1970, 28 pages.

The Stamps and Postal History of North Borneo. Part 1, 1883-93, 1977, 375 pages, Sarawak Specialist Society.

### North/South America

**Richardson, H.T.** — Envelope Stamps of North and South America, 1853-1875. 1965, 54 pages.

### Norway

**Billig, Fritz** — Norway-Plating of the First Issues. Billig's Volume III, 62 pages.

**Eriksen, Postmaster H.** — The Norwegian Field Post Office in Great Britain During World War II.

**Hannevig, E.C.** — Handstamps at Sandosund Post Office, 1852-1870.

**Moldenhauer, F.C.** — Maritime Postal History of Norwegian Steamships. 32 pages.

**Oslo Filatelistclubb** — Norwegian Specialized Catalogue. Regularly updated.

**Rasch-Engh, Rolf** — Arms and Weapons in the Norwegian Post Office.

**Sannes** — Norske Poststempler, 1846-1894. 60 pages.

**Tommelstad, B.E.** — The First Postal Franking Machine in the World.

**Utgave** — Tolvte Utgave Catalog over Norges Frimerker. 81 pages.

**Werenskiold, C.H.** — Norway Posthorn Stamps — 100 years.

### Orange Free State

**Wenn** — Postal Markings 1868-1910. 54 pages.

### Pakistan

**Ahmed** — 25 Years of Philately in Pakistan. 1972, 66 pages.

**Martin, D.R.** — Pakistan Overprints on Indian Stamps, 1948-49. 1974 edition, 156 pages.

**Sidhwa, Rustam S.** — Pakistan Stamps, Errors and Varieties. 1979, 40 pages.

### Persia

**Lewis, H.L.** — The Stamps of Persia. 1970, 136 pages.

### Pitcairn Islands

**Foxwell** — Study of Postal History, Stamps, Cancellations to 1967 Discovery Issue.

**Hawley, F.** — Catalog on Postal History. 1975 edition.

**Hornadge and Kitching** — The Pitcairn Island Stamp Catalog. 1981 edition, 224 pages.

**Simpson** — Pitcairn Islands: The Stamps and Postal History. 1972, 40 pages.

**Urch Harris and Co.** — Pitcairn Catalog.

### Poland

**Berek, Jan** — Field Post of the Polish Legion, 1914-18. 93 pages.

**Bojanowicz, M.A.** — The Kingdom of Poland. Covers No. 1, the 1860 stamp. 1979, Royal Philatelic Society of London, 150 pages.

**Bura, Fabin** — Polish Olympic Chronicle in Philately. 148 pages.

**Gryzewski, Tadeusz** — The Stamps and Postal Service of the First Polish Corps in Russia.

**Komunikacyne, D.** — Poland Lat Poczty Polskiej. 1958, 399 pages.

**Laszkiewicz, A.** — Polskie Znaki Pacztowe. 1935, 419 pages.

**Mazepa, J.** — The Occupation of Russia by the Polish I Corps. 40 pages.

**Myslicki, Andrezel** — Katalog Polskich Stempli Okolicnmociowych Zeszyt 12 Wgkazy Tematyczne. 96 pages (Polish).

**Pofis Catalog** — Katalog Znamek Lidova Republica Poland 1944-53. 1954, 32 pages (Polish).

**Ruch** — Ilustrowany Catalog Znaczkow Polskich. Catalog regularly updated.

**Smith, H.M.** — Polish Post, Seven Years War. Covers 1935-49. 82 pages.

### Portugal

**Eladio de Santos**— Selos de Portugal Continental, Insular e Ultramarino. Catalog regularly updated.

**Magalhaes, A.G., and Andrade e Sousa, M.** — Marcas Postais de Portugal Metropolitano Utilizadas no Periodo Pre-Adesivo. Three volumes, 1978-80, Federacao Portuguesa de Filatelia.

**Melville, F.J.** — The Cameo Stamps. 1911, 90 pages.

Postage Stamps, 1880-1911. 85 pages.

**Mercado Filatelico** — Catalog Portugues Simeos Ferreira. Catalog regularly updated.

**Pernes, R.R.** — Crown Stamps of the Portuguese Colonies. 1976, 35 pages.

## Reunion

**de Pomyers, O.** — Les Timbres de la Reunion. 1939, 105 pages.

## Rhodesia

**Drysdall, A.R.** — The stamps and Postal History of Northern Rhodesia and Zambia 1963-1965. 1976, 38 pages.

**Mitchell, D.A., and Tring, H.T.** — The Surcharging of Rhodesia's Mail, 1965-71. 91 pages.

**Rhodesia Philatelic Society** — The Postage Stamps of Rhodesia. 1925, 28 pages.

**Rhodesia Philatelic Agencies Ltd.** — Rhodesia Stamp Catalog. Regularly updated.

**Simpson, Gerald** — 1913 Admirals, Notes on the Bicolored Stamp. 12 pages.

**Smith, R.C.** — Rhodesia, A Postal History. 1967, 470 pages; 1970 supplement, 147 pages.

## Romania

**Billig, F., and Stiedl, O.** — Romania, Original and Counterfeits. Three volumes, 1938, 90 pages, German.

**Birnbach** — Moldavia-Walachia Postal History. German text, 68 pages.

**Cohen, Edouard** — Contributions to the Study of the Romanian Essays. 1945, 90 pages, French.

The Stamps of Romania, 1872-79 Issues. 1952, 41 pages, French.

**Danescu, Marcel** — Philatelic Dictionary. 1979, 222 pages, Romanian.

**Dengel, Ludovic** — History of the Private Posts and Their Stamps Used in the Territory of Today's Romania. 1947, 54 pages, Romanian.

**Dragomir, Kiriac** — Romanian Classical Postage Stamps Lithographed in Period 1865-72. 1971, 48 pages, Romanian.

**Minescu, C.C.** — The History of the Romanian Posts. 1916, 673 pages, Romanian.

**Murea, Petre** — The History of the Romanian Postage Stamps. 1938, 375 pages, Romanian.

**Nicolaides, Sophocles** — Historical Details of the Greek Post Offices in Moldavia-Walachia and Soulina. 1972, 22 pages, Greek and English.

**Philatelic Association of Romania** — Philatelic Guidebook. Regularly updated, Romanian.

**Racoviceane, G.** — Postal Markings Used in Romania Until 1881. 1963, 115 pages, Romanian.

**Romanian Philatelic Club** — Romanian Postage Stamp Catalogue. 1974, 624 pages, Romanian.

**Rompresfilatelia** — Philatelic Almanac. Regularly updated, Romanian.

**Spineanu, Morgenstern and Florescu** — Philatelic Studies. 1965, 317 pages, Romanian.

**Szalay, A.B.** — High Philately. Two volumes, 1935, 1,046 pages, German.

**Tebeica, Val.** — The First Romanian Postage Stamps. 1962, 213 pages, Romanian, German, Hungarian and French editions.

**Wertheimer-Ghika, J.** — Documents of the Romanian Posts. Two volumes, 1944, 1945, 187 and 162 pages, Romanian and French.

**Williams, L.N. and M.** — Hotel Posts of Hungary and Romania. 12 pages.

## Russia

**Ashford, P.T.** — Imperial Russian Stamps Used in Transcaucasia.

**Balat, John** — Illustrated Postal History of Western Ukraine.

**Billig, F.** — Billig's Handbooks on Forgeries. Russia, Empire and Levant. German text.

Billig's Handbooks on Forgeries. Russia, Soviet. German text.

**Bourdi, A.** — Catalog of the Stamps of the Russian Local Posts. 1978 edition, 249 pages.

**Central Philatelic Agency** — Catalog of Postage Stamps of the U.S.S.R. Regularly updated, Russian.

**Ceresa, R.J.** — The Postage Stamps of Russia. 1979, 52 pages.

**Herrick, William** — Catalogue of the Russian Rural Stamps. 1978 reprint of 1896 book, Migliavacca, 128 pages.

**Ian, Russell** — Russian Stamp Finder. 24 pages.

**Kuthre, W.E., and Ashford, P.T.** — Stamps of the Russian Refugee Post.

**Lukac, I.** — Zeppelin Post and Airship Postage Stamps of Russia. 70 pages, German.

**Minkus** — Russia Catalog. 1981-82 edition, 178 pages.

**Rachmanov, V.** — Russia No. 1.

**Roberts, C.W.** — Trident Issues of the Ukraine.

**Speers, Fred W.** — The Zemstvo Gazeteer. Billig's Handbook, Volume 30, 90 pages.

**Tchilinghirian and Ashford** — Postage Stamps of Armenia.

**Tchilinghirian and Stephen** — Stamps of the Russian Empire Used Abroad.

**Xanthopoulos, A.** — Russian Mail of the Monastic Cell of St. John Chrysostomos in Mount Athos. 19 pages.

## Ryukyu Islands

**Askins, Arthur L.** — Bibliography of Source Material for the Study of the Provisional Postal Items of the Gunto Governments of the Ryukyu Islands, 1945-1951. RPSS, 1977, 28 pages.

A Checklist of the Nansei Shoto Provisional Postage Stamps, 1945-50. RPSS, 1976, 20 pages.

**Faries, Belmont** — The Postal Stationery of the Ryukyu Islands.

**Kenkichi, Tachikawa** — Handbook of Ryukyu Postage Stamps. Japan Philatelic Society, Tokyo, 1973, 174 pages.

**Kenya Kai Kanyo** — The Postal Stationery Catalog of Ryukyu

**Schoberlin, Melvin** — Handbook and Specialized Catalogue of the Postal Issues of the Ryukyu (Liu Ch'iu) Islands (Issued Under United States Administrations). Part I, Postal Stationery of the Gunto Governments, second edition revised and updated by Arthur L. Askins, RPSS, 1978, 88 pages; Part II, Postal Stationery of the Central Governments (1948-72), second edition revised and updated by A.L. Askins, RPSS, 1979, 222 pages; Part III, The Nansei Shoto Provisional Postal Stamps (1945-48). 1973, RPSS, 55 pages.

Standard List of Post Offices. RPSS, 40 pages.

**Sera, M.** — Ryukyus Handbook. 1963, Radiopress, Tokyo, 238 pages.

### Saar

**Die Postwertzeichen des Saargebietes - Saarkatalog.** 1922, 120 pages.

**Bentz, G.** — Catalog of the Prussian Cancels in Saar During the Postage Stamp Period, 1856-67. 22 pages.

**Emin, Th.** — Les Timbres de la Saare. 1924, 103 pages.

**Postwertzeichen des Saargebietes** — Band II. 112 pages, German text.

**Schupp, W.** — Die Postwertzeichen des Saargebietes. Second edition, 208 pages.

**Staedel, P.** — Sarre Etude d'Timbres et Obliterat, 1945-1955. 1958, 168 pages, French.

### St. Helena

**Hibbert, Edward** — St. Helena Postal History and Stamps. 1979, 208 pages.

**Melville, F.J.** — St. Helena. 1912, 82 pages.

**Urch Harris** — Commonwealth Catalogue of Queen Elizabeth II Postage Stamps: St. Helena. 1982, first edition, 24 pages.

**Warden, William** — Letters from St. Helena, 1816. Fifth edition, 215 pages.

### St. Vincent

**Pierce, A.D., Messenger, J.L., and Lowe, R.** — St. Vincent. 1971, 184 pages.

### Samos

**Billig, F.** — Billig's Handbooks on Forgeries, Samos. German text.

**Hartman, Ernst** — Billig's Volume 7. Cancellations-Postmarks. Samos: und seine Postverhaeltnisse mit Beruechsichtigung der Entwertungen. German text, 32 pages.

### San Marino

**Amaral, Sebastiao** — San Marino Zeppelins - The Italian Voyage. 72 pages, Italian.

**Government Philatelic Office** — Catalog di Repubblica di San Marino. Regularly updated.

### Sarawak

**Forrester-Wood** — Sarawak Stamps and Postal History. 1957, 576 pages; Forrester-Wood and Shipman supplement, 235 pages.

**Poole** — Sarawak. 1906, 72 pages.

**Shipman, L.H.** — The De La Rue Issues of 1918 to 1928 and the Associated Printings. 1970, 28 pages.

**Shipman and Walker** — Priced Catalog of the Stamps and Postmarks of Sarawak. 1972, 161 pages.

### Saudi Arabia

**Mayo, M. Max** — Specialized Catalog of Hejaz-Nejd and Saudi Arabia. 1973.

### Scandinavia

**Aarhus Frimaerkchandel** — AFA Skandinavien Frimaerkekatalog. Aarhus, Denmark. Covers Denmark, the Faroe Islands, Greenland, Danish West Indies, Finland, Iceland, Norway, Sweden and the United Nations, both New York and Geneva issues. Regularly updated, Danish text.

**Drechsel, E.** — The Paquebots of Norway, Denmark, Finland, Iceland and Sweden. 24 pages.

**Facit** — Scandinavia Specialized. Catalog regularly updated.

**Liwendahl, Lasse** — Swedish and Norwegian Reply License Stamps and Stationery. 1979, C. Nieuwland, 96 pages.

**Luning, Orjan** — Luftpostens Historia i Norden. History of Airmail in Scandinavia. 1979, Philatelic Society of Sweden, 351 pages, Swedish and English.

**Minkus** — Scandinavia and Baltic Stamp Catalog. 1981-82 edition, 134 pages.

**Pelander** — Pelander's Scandinavian Checklists, 1938-48.

**Wise, E. H.** — Stamps of Denmark, Iceland and Norway; Stamps of Sweden and Finland. Both books discuss stamps and postal history of the Scandinavian group up to the pre-World War I issues. Heinemann Philatelic Series.

### Serbia

**Billig, F.** — Billig's Handbooks on Forgeries - Serbia. Volume 30, German.

**Rasic, Mirko R.** — The Postal History and Postage Stamps of Serbia. 1979, Collectors Club Handbook No. 25, 276 pages.

**de Smeth, P.** — Les Timbres de la Principaute de Serbie (1866-1880). 1927, 54 pages.

**Zydek, H.J.** — The Occupation Issues of Serbia in World War II. German.

### Seychelles

**Farmer, H.V.** — Seychelles Postage Stamps and Postal History. 1955, 123 pages.

### Shanghai

**Dougan, Charles W.** — The Shanghai Postal System: The Stamps and Postal History. 1981, American Philatelic Society, 214 pages.

## Singapore

**International Stamp and Coin Agency** — Singapore Stamp Catalogue. 1982 (first edition), 42 pages.

## Solomon Islands

**Hinchcliffe, Colin** — Postage Paid and Meter Franking Machine Marks of the Solomon Islands. 1980, Pacific Islands Study Circle.

Postal Agency Markings of the Solomon Islands. 1979, Pacific Islands Study Circle.

Registration Markings of the Solomon Islands. 1979, Pacific Islands Study Circle.

**Vernon, D.H.** — Cancellation Study of the British Solomon Islands Protectorate. Pacific Islands Study Circle.

**Voyce, A.H.** — The Postal History of Barakoma Airfield. 34 pages.

## South Africa

**Arcade** — Arcade Catalogue of the Stamps of the Union and Republic of South Africa (1910-77), South West Africa (1923-77) and Transkei. 1978 edition, 134 pages.

**Buckley, G.D., and Marriott, W.B.** — Stamps of the Orange Free State. 1980, Orange Free State Study Circle.

**Collectors Mail Auctions Ltd.** — Handbook of Stamps of South Africa. 1979, 450 pages.

**Lobell, H.E.** — The De La Rue Georgians of South Africa. 1944, 100 pages.

**Pirie, J.H.H.** — World War II Philately of Southern and Eastern Africa. 1953, 60 pages.

**Robemark** — Robemark Stamp Catalogue of Southern Africa. 1979.

**Rosenthal, Eric, and Blum, Eliezer** — Runner and Mailcoach (postal history). 1969, Purnell, 180 pages.

**Simenhoff and Basden** — Standard Catalog of the Postage Stamps of the Union of South Africa. 1946, 117 pages.

**Southern Africa Simplified Stamp Catalogue.** 1981, first edition, Glen Carpendale, 200 pages.

**The Special and Commemorative Postmarks, Cachets and Covers of South Africa.** Second edition, 341 pages.

## South West Africa

**Mallet-Veale, H.** — South West Africa - A Check List. 1928, 43 pages.

**Putzel, R.F.** — Handbook of Postmarks of South West Africa Under South Africa Administration. 1978, Collectors Mail Auctions Ltd., 263 pages.

## Solomon Islands

**Voyce, A.H.** — The Postal History of Barakoma Airfield. 34 pages.

## Spain

**Blair, Neil** — The Postal History of Perth. Two parts: Perth's Postal Services 1689-1900 and Postmarks of Perth to 1900.

**Crew, A.C.** — The Post Office Markings of Madrid 1757 to 1900. 52 pages.

**Edifil** — Spain Catalogo Unificado Especializado Edifil y Dependencias Postales. Regularly updated.

**Gomez-Guillemon, P.** — Republican Local Tax Stamps of the Spanish Civil War. 124 pages.

**Graus, F., and Soro, E.** — The Postal Forgeries of Spain. 601 pages, Spanish and English.

**Heller, Ernst** — Town Censormarks of Spain, 1936-1945. 1982, 350 pages.

**Hevia** — Spanish catalog regularly updated.

**Leze, Carlos** — Spanish Cancels 1850-1860 - Matasello de Pecha en Espana. 1952.

**Monge, Pedro** — Pre-filatelia Espanola Apuntes Sobre Timbres Postal Markings Montaneses, 1793-1849 (pre-stamp markings). 1947, 32 pages (Spanish).

Pre-filatelia Espanola Legeros Apuntes Sobre Timbres Postales de Reus, 1791-1849. 1945, 15 pages.

**Nathan, S.** — Castles in Spain. 1976, 24 pages.

The Local Posts of Cadiz Between 1830 and 1860. 115 pages, Spanish.

The Message Carriers of Cadiz, 1830 to 1860. 68 pages.

Ambulantes and Railway Marks of Spain and Ex-Colonies. 1979, 228 pages.

**Negus, J.** — Ifni, Stamps and Cancellations. 1975, 75 pages.

**Purves, Ronald** — The Lithographed Franco Head Issue, a Study of the Madrid Printings, 1939-53. 1974, Robson Lowe, 55 pages.

**Saeftel, H.** — The Town Cancellations from 1854 and 1857 on the 4-Cuartos Stamps from 1856, 1860, 1862 and 1864. 1976, second edition, 61 pages, English, German and Spanish.

**Shelley, R.** — The British Legion in Spain During First Carlist War 1832-39. 72 pages.

The Postal History of the International Brigades in Spain. 1980, Spanish Philatelic Society, 160 pages.

The Postal History of the Spanish Civil War 1936-39. Reprint, 91 pages.

**Soler, Jose, and Monge, Pedro** — Pre-filatelia Mataronesa. 1948, 21 pages (Spanish).

**Tort, Nicolau** — Guide for the Collector of Stamps of Spain, 1850-1900. Three volumes, reprint, 1,179 pages, Spanish.

**Unificado Specialized Catalogue.** 1979 edition, 455 pages, Spanish.

**Van Dam, T.** — Billig's Handbook on Postmarks, Volume 13. The Postal Markings of Spain. 74 pages

A Postal History of Spain. 1973.

## Straits Settlements

**Lockhart, R.H.D.** — The Postage Stamps of the Straits Settlements. 1925, 40 pages.

## Sudan

**Armstrong, D.B.** — Brights Philatelic Library. 1912, 72 pages.

**Stagg, E.C.W.** — Stamps and Postal Stationery, 1867-1970. 1977, 144 pages.

Sudan: The Postal Markings, 1867-1970. 1974, 196 pages.

### Surinam

**Julsen** — The Censor Markings of Surinam 1940-1945. 38 pages.

**de Rooy/Hali** — Automaatboekjes en Kombinaties Suriname-Ned. Antillen (Slot Machine Booklets). 1980-81, 31 pages.

### Sweden

**Besokande, F.** — Sweden Vagledning. I Post Museum. 1956, 140 pages.

**Frimarkshuset AB** — Facit Postal History. 1982.

**Grape** — Sweden Enhetsportot och Frimarket. 1955, 159 pages.

**Lagerstrom, Lennart** — Swedish Slot-machine Booklets, 1954-77. 1978, Sveriges Filatelist Forbund Handbook No. 9.

**Lister** — A Catalogue of Swedish Local Postage Stamps 1941-1947. 1971, Harry Hayes, 24 pages.

**Liwendahl, Lasse** — Sveriges och Norges Svarslosenmarken samt Helsaker, 1968-1978 (the reply license stamps and stationery of Sweden and Norway). 1979, 96 pages.

**Odfjell, A.** — Sveriges Frimerker 1855-1944. 1946, Norsk Filatelistisk Tidsskrift, 61 pages.

**Royal Swedish Postal Administration** — Catalogue of the Postage Stamps of 1920-1926. 20 pages.

Sweden Katalog. Regularly updated.

**Sveriges Filatelist Forbund** — Priskatalog Over Svenska Post - Och Makulerings Stamplar. Specialized catalog of Swedish postage stamps and postal stationery. Regularly updated.

**Swedish Association of Thematic Stamp Collecting** — Motiv Pa Svenska (cover illustrations of Swedish stamp booklets), 1904-1979. 1980, 64 pages.

**Swedish Postal Museum** — Postman Minns. 1956, 280 pages.

### Switzerland

**Amateur Collector Ltd.** — Switzerland Catalogue. Appears annually.

**Amrein, Rene** — Rollenmarken Katalog. Covers Swiss coil stamps. 1976, third edition, 148 pages, Kusnacht, Zurich.

**Andres, F.X., and Emmenegger, Hans** — Grosses Handbuch der Schweizer Abstemplungen, 1843-1882. Cancellations 1843-1882. Association of Swiss Philatelic Societies, 1931, 1940 and 1954 supplements, total 810 pages.

**Andres, F.X.; Emmenegger, Hans; Muller, Alfred; and Lipp, Anton** — Grosses Handbuch der Abstemplungen auf Schweizer Marken, 1843-1907. The updating of the foregoing handbook through 1907. Association of Swiss Philatelic Societies, eight loose-leaf volumes, 1969-1978.

**Auf der Maur Stamps** — Helvetia Catalog: Switzerland and Liechtenstein. 1982 edition.

**Buhler, Joshua** — Altschweiz — was nicht im Katalog steht (Classic Switzerland — what you don't find in catalogs). Fonds zur Forderung der Philatelie, 1968, Zurich, 47 pages.

**Chalfant, Edwin L.** — Classification Guide of Swiss Soldier Stamps 1939-45. 1973, Riviera Stamps.

**Ganz, Felix; Hurlimann, Robert; and Enschede, E.J.** — Perfins of Switzerland. U.S. Perfins Club, 1972, 31 double pages.

**Gees, Rene** — Die Ausgabe Rayon III 15 Rappen Grosse Wertziffer (The Rayon III Stamp with Large Figure 15). Heerbrugg, 1970, 47 pages, reprint from the Swiss Philatelic Journal. Schweiz UPU 1900. 1976 reprint.

**Gilbert and Koehler** — Catalogue illustre des timbres fiscaux de la Suisse, cantons et municipalites. 1906, 87 pages.

**Greminger, Eduard** — Die Entwicklung des Poststempels in den letzten 100 Jahren (The Development of Postal Cancellations over the last 100 years). Reprint from Postzeitschrift, 1949, 18 pages.

**Guinard, P.; Valko, G.; Doorenbos, J.; Hertsch, M.** — 100 Jahre Stehende Helvetia. 1982, Zumstein & Co., 260 pages (German and French).

**Hertsch, Max** — Schweizer Briefmarken. Two volumes, 104 and 93 pages, Silva-Verlag, Zurich, 1973.

**Koch, P.A.** — Die Internationalen Antwortscheine der Schweiz und der UNO Genf (Swiss reply coupons). 1981, Urefeld-Traar, 47 pages (German).

**Kohl, Roland (collator)** — Schweizerisches Luftposthandbuch (Swiss aerophilately handbook). 1978 edition, Swiss Aerophilatelists Society, Zurich.

**Liniger, Nagel and Vuille** — Les Marques Postales de la Suisse Romande. Monographs on early postmarks through 1850 of the French speaking cantons of Switzerland. Printed in four parts, total 92 pages, 1955, Yverdon.

**Locher, Paul** — Die Schweizerischen Soldatenmarken (Swiss Soldiers Issues, World War I). 74 pages and a supplement.

**Locher and Forestier** — Die Schweizerischen Soldatenmarken, 1939-42 (Soldiers Issues, World War II). 188 pages and several supplements, 1943-64.

**Marken-Muller** — Muller Katalog Schweiz and Liechtenstein. Basel, German text, issued annually.

**Mirabaud, Paul** — The Postage Stamps of Switzerland 1843-1862. Alex de Reuterskiold, joint author. 1975 Quarterman reprint, 304 pages.

**Misteli, C.** — Les Timbres-Poste et Obliterations de la Societe des Nations. 1948, 20 pages.

**Muller, Alfred** — Die Schweizerischen Bahnpostempel (Swiss RPO markings). Zumstein and Co., 1977.

**Muller, Ernst** — Die Rayon II Ausgabe der Schweiz. 1968.

Die Markenheftchen, Kehrdruck and Zwischenstegmarken der Schweiz (booklets, tete-beches, interspaces). 108 pages.

**Negrini, Gino** — Note di Storia Postale e Studi Filatelici del Cantone Ticino e Lago Maggiore. Postal History of Ticino Canton. Bellinzona Circolo Filatelico, 1977, 90 pages, in Italian and German.

**PTT Bern** — Verzeichnis der Maschinenstempel und Ortswerbestempel (catalog of Swiss machine cancellations and publicity postmarks). Third edition, 1967 plus three supplements.

**PEN** — Obliterations Speciales (special and automobile office cancellations, 1850-present). Editions PEN, 1950 and 1978 plus annual supplements.

Timbres des Remplacement (Switzerland and Liechtenstein emergency postmarks, 1889-1977). Editions PEN, 63 pages.

Catalogue de vignettes suisses de propaganda (Swiss publicity labels and stickers). 1981, 150 pages.

**Pfenninger, O.** — Handbuch der Schweizer Post-Werth-Zeichen. 1890, 134 pages.

**Rampacher, P.F.** — Katalog der Ausstellungs und Gelegenheitsmarken der Schweiz (catalog of Swiss labels and vignettes). Covers 1864-1950, 1951 edition, Hans Steiner, Grenchen, Switzerland.

**Reuterskiold, A.** — Forgeries of the "Cantonal" Stamps of Switzerland. 1907, 35 pages.

**Ross, Robert C.** — Swiss Internment Cancels and other Markings. 1974, 14 pages.

**Ruttiman, E.** — Die Ausgabe Stehende Helvetia 1882-1907. 44 pages.

Die Post-Vermerk-Etiketten der Schweiz, 1882-1943 (postal labels of Switzerland). Basel, 1944, 24 pages.

**Sager, Peter** — Der Blaue Ikarus (the 65-cent airmail stamp of 1923). 1978, Zumstein and Co., 17 pages.

**Schild, Georges** — Die Post der Internierten in der Schweiz 1940-46 (internment mail cancels, WWI). Ganzsachensammlerverein, Bern, 1975, 40 pages.

**Schio, Max** — Die Buchdruckausgabe 1882 im Ziffermuster (the Cross and Numeral issue of 1882). Zumstein and Co., Bern, 1968, 20 pages.

**Schlunegger, Ernst** — Die Motive Der Schweizer Werbestempel No. 3 (SMV manuscript series). 101 pages, German.

**Schwarzenbach, H.R.** — Ersttags Katalog, Schweiz and UNO Genf. 1982, 150 pages.

**Society of Swiss Cancellation Collectors** — Handbuch Werbedatumstempel Schweiz (publicity town cancellations of Switzerland). Bern, 1976; 1980 supplement.

**Stocker, Hans** — Stehende Helvetia. Bern, 1967, 88 pages.

**Sulser, H.** — Die Soldatenmarken der Schweiz (Soldiers issues of Switzerland). Three volumes, 197 and 60 pages, 1977; 1979, 136 pages.

**Swiss Cancellation Collectors Society** — Schweiz Postwerbestempel Handbuch. 1976, Bern; supplement, 1979.

**Swiss Stamp Dealers' Association** — Helvetia, Schweiz/Liechtenstein. Appears annually.

**Tanner, Hans** — Spezialkatalog. Appears annually. Two parts, first day covers, Day of the Stamp, PTT collection sheets, stamps with tabs, special post and postal cards, etc.

**Valko, Georges** — Uber den Druck Prozess und die Abarten der Stehenden Helvetia, 1882-1907 (printing and varieties of the Standing Helvetia issue). Zumstein and Co., Bern, 1978.

**Vogel, Georg** — Anzeigenpostkartenkarten der Schweiz (advertising postal cards of Switzerland). Two volumes, 78 and 12 pages, 1977 and 1978, Schwieberdingen, Germany.

**Von Grisewald, F.C.** — The Stamps of Switzerland 1843-1854. 1893, C.H. Mekeel, St. Louis, Mo., translated from the German, 64 pages.

**Vuille, Louis** — Les Postes du Valais, 1616-1850. Lausanne, 1978, 80 pages.

**Winkler, J.J.** — Le Service Postal Au Pays de Vaud 1849. 1955, 44 pages.

Handbuch der Schweizer Vorphilatelie, 1695-1850 (early postmarks of Switzerland). Association of Swiss Philatelic Societies, 554 pages, 1968.

**Zumstein** — Schweiz/Liechtenstein. Appears annually.

Handbuch uber die Briefmarken der Schweizerischen Eidgenossenschaft. Bern, 1924.

Spezialkatalog Schweiz-Liechtenstein. 1982 edition, 900 pages, in German with French and English introduction.

Ganzsachen Schweiz (postal stationery catalog). 1976.

### Tannu Tuva

**Kanak, Richard C.** — Tannu Tuva: Postage Stamps 1926-43. 1979, 17 pages.

### Thailand

**Collins, Peter** — Revenue Stamps of Thailand. 1979, Thailand Philatelic Society, 20 pages.

Thailand, The Waterlow Proof Sheets, 1917-1960. 1981, Robson Lowe, 64 pages.

**Fawdry, Cyril W.** — The Airpost in Thailand. Second edition, revised and extended over the period 1935 to 1972, 1973, second edition, Harry Hayes, 31 pages.

**Frajola, Richard** — The Postage Stamps of Siam to 1940. 1980, Postilion Publications, 104 pages plus eight-page price guide supplement.

**Holland, A.** — Postage Stamps of Siam. 1904, 28 pages.

**Kovadhana, P.** — Thailand Postage Stamp Catalogue 1883-1976. 200 pages.

**Le May, R.S.; Williamson, W.J.F.; and Smith, E. Wayon** — Descriptive Catalogue of the Postage Stamps and Post and Letter Cards of Siam. 1920, Siam Philatelic Society, 129 pages.

**Lindenberg, Paul P.** — The Early History of Thailand.1944, Siam Philatelic Society, 18 pages.

**Linnemann, Henry S.** — The Postal Stationery in Siam, 1855-1925. 1925, Ministry of Communications, Bangkok, 36 pages.

**Melville, F.J.** — Siam: Its Posts and Postage Stamps. 1906, 52 pages.

**Row, R.W. Harold** — The Adhesive Postage Stamps of Siam. 1913, London, 75 pages.

**Siam Philatelic Society** — Siam Postage Stamps, Stationery and Postmarks, 1939-1948. Survey Department, Bangkok, 1949, 47 pages.

### Tibet

**Waterfall, Arnold C.** — The Postal History of Tibet. 1981, second edition, Robert Lowe, 188 pages.

### Tokelau/Union Islands

**Burgess, A.H.** — Tokelau/Union Islands — A Philatelic Study. Two supplements.

### Tonga

**Mann, E.W.** — The 1897 Issue of Tonga. 28 pages.

**Melville, F.J.** — Tonga. 1909, 65 pages.

**Rosenblum, A.A.** — The Stamps of Tonga. 1935.

### Transvaal

**Luff, J.N.** — Otto's Printings of the Transvaal Stamps. 1913, 40 pages.

**Robson Lowe** — Transvaal: Plating the 1878-80 Issue. 24 pages.

### Trieste

**Trieste** — Catalogo dei Francobolli del Territorio Libero di Trieste. 1949, 19 pages, Italian and English.

### Trinidad and Tobago

**Wike, Ron G.** — Trinidad and Tobago Postal Meter Stamps. 1978, Harry Hayes, 48 pages.

### Tristan da Cunha

**Crabb, George** — The History and Postal History of Tristan da Cunha,. 1980, 343 pages.

**Gane, Douglas M.** — Handbook of Tristan. 1924, 50 pages.

**Urch, Harris** — Queen Elizabeth II Tristan da Cunha Catalogue. 1982.

### Trucial States

**Minkus** — Trucial States.

### Turkey

**Armstrong, Douglas B.** — The Stamps of the Levant Post Office.

**Billig, F.** — Billig's Handbooks on Forgeries. Turkey I and II, German.

**Higlett, G.A.** — Turkey, Random Notes. 1926, 14 pages.

**Hoffman, Barry D.** — Turkish Post Offices in the Holy Land. 1962, 59 pages.

**Passer, Adolf** — The Stamps of Turkey. Two volumes, Royal Philatelic Society, London, 1938.

**Pulhan, Ali Nusret** — Turk Pullari Katalogu. 12th edition, 1974, 1,030 pages, Turkish.

### Tuvalu

**Urch, Harris** — Queen Elizabeth II Tuvalu Catalogue 1982.

### Uganda

**Robson Lowe** — The Uganda Missionaries Postal History. Eight pages.

### United Arab Republic

**Mosden** — U.A.R. Catalogue. 1960, 48 pages.

### United Nations

**Barnes. W.J.** — The 1945 Unied Nations Slogan Cancellation. 1979, 84 pages.

**Clement, B.L.** — The U.N. Conference Study. 1981, UNOP/UNP monograph, 105 pages.

**Conway, H.E.** — 101 on the U.N. 101 More on the U.N. Eight supplements to date. Regularly released. 25 Years of Philatelic Highlights. 60 pages.

**Dickert, I.** — The United Nations in Austrian Philately. 1979, UNOP/UNP monograph, 47 pages.

**Emmenegger, J.L.** — Postal Facilities of the U.N. Emergency Forces (UNEF II) 1973-1979. 1980, 44 pages.

**Gaines, Arleigh** — United Nations Philately. Loose-leaf catalog with quarterly supplements. 1980, 700 plus pages.

**Gans, R.L.** — Presentation Folders of the United Nations. 1978, UNP monograph, 20 pages.

**Goodey, R.** — A Study of the First United Nations Regulars and Airmail Postage Stamps, 1951-66. Two parts, 249 pages.

**Hanke, W.** — U.N. First Flight Covers, 1959-76. 1976, UNOP monograph (German); 1978 supplement, 196 pages.

**Haussler, R.** — United Nations Stamps. 1965, 28 pages.

**Kelen, Emery** — Stamps Tell the Story of the United Nations. 96 pages.

**Kvarnes-Goodey** — Handbook on the First Issue of United Nations Postage Stamps, 1951-66.

**Linder** — United Nations Specialized Philatelic and Numismatic Catalog and Handbook. 1976, sixth edition.

**Paikert, H.** — OPU Study. 1979, UNOP monograph (German), 332 pages.

**Patrick, D.** — The Postal Stamps and Postal History of the U.N. 174 pages.

**United Nations** — United Nations Postage Stamps. Updated periodically.

**United Nations Philatelic Society** — U.N. and Related Worldwide Stamps. 1973, fourth edition, 122 pages.

**Witzig, Dr. H.** — OIT Study. 1977, UNOP monograph (German), 256 pages.

**Wolke, Otto** — The 1951 Definitives, Air Mail Issues and Reprints. 1974, 96 pages; 1975 follow-up, 63 pages.

### Uruguay

**Castillo, J.F.** — Catalogo de la Emision de 1860. 1939, 15 pages, Spanish.

**Club Filatelico** — Uruguay Specialized Airmail Catalog. 1948, 60 pages.

**Griebert, H.** — The Stamps of Uruguay. 1910, 90 pages.

**Hoffmann, R.** — Estudio de las Fasificationes de los Sellos Postales Uruguay. 1948, 115 pages.

**Jean, S.** — Stamps and Postmarks of Uruguay. 1909, 79 pages.

**Kobylanski, J.K., and Gari, E.C.** — Catalogo de Estampillas del Uruguay. 1981, Mundus, 190 pages (Spanish).

**Mezzottoni, H.** — Catalogo de los Sellos Aereos del Uruguay. 60 pages, Spanish.

**Sejo, J.R.** — Uruguay: Sellos. 1941-46, 136 pages.

**Uruguay Libro de Oro, 1827-1977.** Stamps and history. 1978, 765 pages, Spanish.

### Vatican City

**Bolaffi** — Bolaffi Specialized Stamp Catalog Roman States and Vatican City. Regularly updated, English and Italian.

**Government Philatelic Office** — Stamps of Vatican City State, 1977-1980. 1982.

**Greenan, L.** — I Francobolli dello Stato della Citta del Vaticano. The postage stamps of the Vatican City State. 1979, 212 pages.

**I.C.E.F.** — Volume III of the Catalogo Enciclopedico Italiana. Annually updated (Italian, with glossary in English, French and German).

**Kehr, E.** — Vatican Stamps. 1956, 48 pages.

Vatican. 220 pages.

**Kittel** — Der Vatikanstaat. 1967, 240 pages (German).

**National Museum** — National Philatelic Museum Vatican Stamps. 216 pages.

### Venezuela

**Hernandez, R.S.** — Origenes de las Dos Primeras Emisiones de las Estampillas de Correo de Venezuela. 1956, 71 pages.

Origenes de los Tres Primeras Emisiones de las Estampillas "Escuelas" de Venezuela. 1961, 97 pages.

**Valera, Prof. Juan Jose** — Catalog Especializado de Estampillas de Venezuela. 1976, 412 pages.

**Wickersham, C.W.** — The Early Stamps of Venezuela. 1958, 156 pages.

### Virgin Islands

**Dalwick, R.E.R.** — Virgin Islands. Mekeel Handbook No. 14.

**Melville, F.J.** — Virgin Islands. 1928, 68 pages.

### Western Samoa

**Startup, R.** — Western Samoa Postal History. 1960.

### Western Ukraine

**Baumgarten, J.** — West-Ukraina: Meine Reiseerlebnisse. 1919, 31 pages.

## General Literature

### Aerophilately

**Aeronautica and Air Label Collectors Club** — Air Transport Catalog. Volume I (Europe); Volume II (Great Britain, Ireland and Australasia); Volume III, Sections 1 (Canada), 2 (Caribbean Area), 3 (Puerto Rico, Hawaii, Alaska) and 4 (United States); Volume IV (Latin America); and Volume V, Section I (Africa) and II (Asia).

**American Air Mail Society** — American Air Mail Catalogue. Four volumes.

American Air Mail Catalogue of Air Letter Sheets.

**Berkshire Exchange** — American Catalog of Air Mail and First Day Covers. 1929 edition, 111 pages.

Standard Airpost Catalogue. 1930 edition, 333 pages.

**Champion, Theodore** — Catalogue Historique et Descriptif des Timbres de la Poste Aerienne. 1930, sixth edition, English and French.

**Cole, Philip L.** — Collection of Airmail Stamps and Covers. F. W. Kessler catalogs. Part I, 1939, 70 pages; Part II, 1940, 60 pages.

**Crampon, L.J.** — Aerophilatelic Flights, Hawaii and Central Pacific, 1913-46. 1980, Hawaiian Philatelic Society, 69 pages.

**Curley, W.** — Amelia Earhart. 1966, Cardinal Spellman Philatelic Museum, 28 pages.

Charles A. Lindbergh, a Biographical and Philatelic Study. 1978, Cardinal Spellman Philatelic Museum, 44 pages.

The Graf Zeppelin's Flights to South America. 1970; 1982 reissue, Cardinal Spellman Philatelic Museum.

**Dahman, K.** — Helicopter Post. 1962, fourth edition, 52 pages.

**Danner, James** — Graf Zeppelin and Hindenburg. Detailed listing of all collectables. 243 pages.

**Eisendrath, Joseph L.** — Crash Covers, an Aerophilatelic Challenge. 1979, American Air Mail Society, 210 pages.

**European Aerophilatelic Club of Germany** — Aerogramme Ubersee Katalog. Volume I, South America, Australia, Malaya and Oceania. 1977, 83 pages (German).

**Falk, A.** — Hindenburg Crash Mail — The Search Goes On. 64 pages.

**Fidelma, Sister M.** — Catalog of the Charles A. Lindbergh Collection of the Cardinal Spellman Philatelic Museum. 1968, 75 pages.

**Field, D.** — Priced Catalogue of Air Mail Stamps and Airposts of the World. 1934, second edition.

**Field, F. J.** — Commercial and Historical Atlas of the World's Airways. 1925, 85 pages.

**Field, J.C.W.** — Aerial Propaganda Leaflets. 1954, 87 pages.

**Godinas, F.** — Catalogue Mondial des Entiers Aeropostaux. 1960-1964, one volume; 1967, two volumes (English and French).

**Greiner Katalog.** Greiner's Catalog of European Aerograms. 1978, 169 pages (German and English).

**Heartwell, J.C.** — Air Stamp Records. 1942, 64 pages.

**Heinmuller, J.P.V.** — Man's Fight to Fly. 1945 revised edition, 370 pages.

**Holmes, Donald B.** — Air Mail: An Illustrated History, 1793-1981. 1982, Clarkson N. Potter Inc., 226 pages.

**Jennings, Peter** — Aerogrammes.

**Kessler, F.W.** — Catalogue of Aerograms. 1961, two volumes.

**Kremer, Brainerd** — Siege of Paris Balloon Post. Information on all flights, pigeon post.

**Kronstein, Max** — Pioneer Airpost Flights of the World, 1830-1935. 1978, 310 pages.

1965 Supplement to Rocket Mail Catalogue. Original catalog by Stephen Smith.

**Lieberg, Owen** — The First Air Race. The international competition at Reims, France, in 1909. 229 pages.

**Lipsner, Capt. B.B.** — Airmail, Jennies to Jets. 1951, 306 pages.

**Lissiuk, K.** — Historical Air Mail Catalogue. 1931, third edition, 333 pages.

**MacKay, James A.** — Airmails, 1870-1970. 216 pages.

**Martin, S.F.** — Air Transport Label Catalog. 1934, 52 pages.

**Mauck, M.T.** — Air Mail and First Day Cover List No. 10. Revised 1929-1930.

**Mueller, F.** — Catalogue des Etiquettes Aeropostales. 1947, second edition, 288 pages.

**Partington, P.G.** — Aviators and Aeronauts of Latin America on Postage Stamps. 21 pages.

**Roessler, A.C.** — Standard Historical Souvenir Airmail Catalog. Reprint, 49 pages, 1976.

**Sanabria** — World Airmail Catalog. Regularly updated. Sanabria Publishing Co., Greenwich, Conn.

**Sieger Verlag** — Zeppelin Post Katalog. 1981, 384 pages.

**Smith, Stephen** — Rocket Mail Catalogue. U.S. and foreign flights.

**Stephen, J.** — Airgraph and V-Mail Catalogue. 1948, 48 pages.

**Violini, E.** — Catalogue of Graf Zeppelin Mail. Italy, Italian Colonies, San Marino and Vatican City. 1971, 110 pages.

**Wiegand, Werner** — Aerogramme Catalog. 1977, several volumes.

Other items relating to this field concerning specific countries can be found under the country listings.

### First Day Covers

**Ansink, Hamilton and Monty** — Mellone's First Cachets. 1980, 80 pages.

**August, Leo, and Strauss, Gerald** — United States Specialized Catalog of First Day Covers. 1980-81 edition, Washington Press.

**Baker, Philip R.** — A Compilation of 200 Designers, Producers and Servicers of Identifiable Cachets, 1933-46. 1978, 22 pages.

**BB Philatelic Publications** — Great Britain First Day Covers. 1981, 144 pages.

**Cusick, Allison** — Linprint FDC Photo Catalog. 1923-41. 64 pages.

**Eiserman, Monte** — Handbook for First Day Cover Collectors. AFDC Foundation, 100 pages.

**Fleetwood** — Standard First Day Cover Catalog. James A. Helzer.

**Gasper, Wayne** — Specialized Catalogue of Henry Grimsland Cacheted FDCs and Covers. 45 pages.

**Langer** — First Day Cancellations. 1980, 64 pages.

**Mellone, M.** — Mellone's Specialized Cachet Catalog of First Day Covers of the 1940s. 1979, FDC Publishing Co., 256 pages.

U.S. Early FDC Cachet Identifier. 1976, 59 pages.

Discovering the Fun in First Day Covers. 1980 edition, 175 pages.

**Mellone and Newton** — The Cachet Identifier of U.S. Cacheted First Day Covers. 1979, second edition, 60 pages.

**Mills, Dean** — The FDC Auction Report. 1980, 1981, six-month reports of auction results.

**Monty, Richard** — Specialized Catalogue of Jacques Minkus FDCs and Patriotic Cachets. 93 pages.

**Newton, Barry** — A.C. Roessler Photo Cachet Catalogue. 1977, 111 pages.

Winfred Grandy FDC Cachet Identifier. 1980, 72 pages.

**Parks, M. Douglas** — Photo Cachet Catalog, Harry Ioor. 1976, 92 pages.

The Cachet Catalogue of Staehle and Knapp. 1980.

**Planty, Earl** — Cram Course in First Day Covers. 1980, 32 pages.

**Planty, E., and Mellone, M.** — Planty's Photo Encyclopedia of Cacheted FDCs, 1923-1935. Eight volumes.

**Yoshikawa, Y.** — Japanese FDC Catalogue. 1981, 191 pages.

## Forgeries

**Aretz, Frank** — Know Your Stamps. 1940, four parts, 100 pages.

**Atlee, Pemberton and Earee** — The Spud Papers. Descriptive catalog of early philatelic forgeries. 168 pages.

**British Philatelic Association** — The Work of Jean de Sperati. 1955, four volumes.

**Chemi, Beal and DeVoss** — The Yucatan Affair, the Work of Raoul Ch. de Thuin, Philatelic Counterfeiter. 1974, American Philatelic Society, 523 pages.

**Dalton, Lewis and Pemberton** — Early Forged Stamps Detector. 1863 and 1865; 1979 reprint in one volume, 80 pages.

**Dorn, J.** — Forged Stamps of all Countries. 1950, 240 pages.

**Durst, Sanford J.** — Early Forged Stamp Detector. 1979, 39 pages.

**Earee, Rev.** — How to Detect Forged Stamps. Album Weeds, 1976 reprint in eight volumes covering Afghanistan to Zululand.

**Fletcher, H.G. Leslie** — Postal Forgeries of the World. 1977, 150 pages.

**Johnson, Alden C.** — Forgeries Old and New. 1941, Marks Stamp Co. Ltd., Toronto, 47 pages; Part II, 1945, 46 pages.

**Lowe, Robson** — The Gee-Ma Forgeries. 1980, 12 pages, Robson Lowe Publications.

The Oswald Schroder Forgeries. 1980, 16-page monograph.

The Work of Jean de Sperati. Two volumes.

**Melville, Fred J.** — Phantom Philately. 1950 reprint of 1923 book.

**Pugh, Kenneth W.** — Reference Manual of BNA Fakes, Forgeries and Counterfeits. Seven parts; others planned.

**Ragatz, Lowell** — Fournier Album of Philatelic Forgeries. 1972, 175 pages.

**Serrane, Fernand** — Vade-Mecum du Specialiste-Expert en Timbres Poste Hors d'Europe. Classic work on forgeries. Two volumes, 1929.

**de Sperati, Jean** — La Philatelie Sans Expert. 1946, 120 pages.

**Spying Eye** — Handbook on Philatelic Forgeries. 1948, The Maplewood Press, 48 pages.

**Toaspern, H.** — Philatelic Frauds, Fakes and Fakers. 1936, 16 pages.

**Tyler, V.F.** — Philatelic Forgers: Their Lives and Works. 1976, Robson Lowe Ltd., 60 pages.

**Williams, L.N. and M.** — Forged Stamps of Two World Wars. 1954, 42 pages.

Other items relating to this field concerning specific countries can be found under the country listings.

## Investment

**Datz Philatelic Index** — Index listing percentage changes in catalog value for U.S. and U.N. stamps. Regularly updated.

**Durst, Sanford** — Collector/Investor Guidebook and Inventory. 1977, 124 pages.

**Ellis, Henry M.** — How to Gain Pleasure and Profit from Stamp Collecting. Second printing, May 1947, Funk and Wagnalls Company, New York, 224 pages.

**Forsher, Brunno J.** — More Precious Than Gold and Philately. Sherman Oaks Stamp and Coin Co., 160 pages.

**Garden, Bruce** — Make Money with Stamps. 77 pages.

**Gilbert, Skeet** — The Fundamentals of Profitable Stamp Investing. 74 pages.

**Gunston, Bill** — The Philatelist's Companion. Stamps as an investment. 1975, 256 pages.

**Harris, H.E.** — Postage Stamp Price Index. Regularly updated; 1979, 192 pages.

**Herst, Herman** — Fun and Profit in Stamp Collecting.

**Hornadge, B.** — Stamp Investment Guidelines. 64 pages.

**Kimble, R.A.** — Stamp Collecting for Profit. 1935, 66 pages.

**Lake, K.R.** — Stamps for Investment. 1971, 192 pages.

**Lloyd, P.W.** — Stamp Investing for Profit. 1977, 66 pages.

**Mackay, James A.** — Money in Stamps. 1967, 240 pages.

**Mac Guffin, R.D.** — Stamps as an Investment. 1935, 192 pages.

**Melville, Fred** — Stamp Collecting for Fun and Profit. 1961, 190 pages.

**Milbury, C. E.** — So You Want to Invest in Stamps. 1946, 130 pages.

What Price Philately. 1946, 110 pages.

**Narbeth, C., and Lyon, D.** — Successful Investing in Stamps and Bank Notes. 145 pages.

**Philatelic Data Systems** — Philatelic Market Review, U.S. and Possessions. Several volumes, 3,000 pages; supplements regularly published.

**Phillips, Charles J.** — Postage Stamps as an Investment. 1923, 39 pages.

**Suffet, Stephen L.** — The $500 Way to Start a U.S. Stamp Investment Program. 1980, Pilot Industries Inc., 48 pages.

**Sutton, R.J.** — Stamps are Money. 1959, 195 pages.

**Wagenheim, K.** — Paper Gold. How to make money and hedge against inflation. 202 pages.

**Williams, L.N. and M.** — Check Your Stamps. How to make money from the post office; for noncollectors who ask if their find is worth anything. 25 pages.

### Maritime

**Arnell, Dr. John C.** — Atlantic Mails, A History of the Mail Service Between Great Britain and Canada to 1889. 1980, 412 pages.

**Cockrill, Philip** — The History, Ships and Postal Cancellations of the Woermann Steamship Line of Hamburg. Also a list of ships and cancellations of the Deutsche Ost Afrika Line. Reference for seamail collectors, German postal specialists, Africa collectors, and ship topicalists. 1980 reprint, 34 pages.

**Davey** — Ship Letters of the South Pacific. Hawthorne Press.

**Drechsel, Edwin** — The Paquebots of Scandinavia. 1977, 24 pages.

The Paquebot Marks of Africa, the Mediterranean Countries and Their Islands. 1981, Robson Lowe Ltd., 72 pages.

**Folkman, David I.** — Nicaragua Route. 1972, 185 pages.

**Hosking, Roger** — Paquebot Cancellations of the World. 1977, 190 pages.

**Joesten** — Paquebot Markings of the World. 1973.

**Kemble, John H.** — Panama Route, 1848-69. History of the companies and ships. 1976 reprint of 1938 book, 496 pages.

**McGuire, C.R.** — The Newfoundland Post Office Mail Assorting Office, North Sydney to Nova Scotia, 1906-1949. 1980, 11 pages.

**Murphy, Robert T.** — Getting Started in Paquebot Cover Collecting. 32 pages.

**Polar History Study Group** — Reference Handbook of Postmarks, Cachets, Official Covers and Ship Letters of the USSR Antarctica. 1978, 44 pages.

**Rainey, Thomas** — Ocean Steam Navigation and the Ocean Posts. Reprinted 1977, 224 pages.

**Ringstrom and Tester** — The Private Ship Letter Stamps of the Caribbean. Volume I, 1977, 166 pages; Volume II, all except Caribbean, Finland and Suez Maritime Canal Co., 1981, 215 pages; Volume III, Finland, 1982-83; and Volume IV, Suez Co., 1982-83.

**Staff, Frank** — The Transatlantic Mail. 1980, Quarterman Publication reprint of 1956 work, 191 pages.

**Other items relating to this field concerning specific countries can be found under the country listings.**

### Post Cards

**Bernhard, Willi** — Automobile Postcard Catalog, 1895-1975. 158 pages.

German Picture Post Card Catalogue, 1870-1945. 128 pages.

Picture Postcards of the Third Reich, 1933-45. 160 pages.

**Bowers, Q. David, and Martin, Mary L.** — The Postcards of Alphonse Mucha. 1980, 120 pages.

**Burdick, J. R.** — Pioneer Postcards - Post Cards to 1898. 200 pages.

**Byatt, Anthony** — Picture Postcards and Their Publishers. Great Britain publishers, 1894-1939. 391 pages.

**Carline, Richard** — Pictures of the Post. 127 pages.

**Carver, Sally S.** — The American Postcard Guide to Tuck. 76 pages.

**Durbin, L.S.** — Standard Catalogue of Postal Cards. 1886, sixth edition, 32 pages.

**Filnkossl, Heinz** — 100 Year Postal Cards and Other Postal Card Jubilees. 118 pages.

**Freeman, L.** — Wish You Were Here — A Centennial Guide to Postcard Collecting. 160 pages.

**Gibbons, Stanley** — Gibbons Postcard Catalogue. 1981, second edition, 287 pages.

**Hill, C.W.** — Discovering Picture Postcards. 64 pages.

**Holt, Toni, and Valmi** — Picture Postcards of the Golden Age. 214 pages.

Till the Boys Come Home. Pictures over 730 post cards, 192 pages.

**Johanson, Erik, and Termonen, Teuvo** — Postikortti Suomessa (Finnish post cards). 1981, Oy Kaj Hellman Ltd., 144 pages (Finnish).

**Kaduck, J.M.** — Transportation Postcards. 92 pages.

Mail Memories - Pictorial Guide to Postcard Collecting.

Patriotic Postcards. 67 pages.

Rare and Expensive Postcards. 88 pages.

**Lawson and Warr** — The Postcards of Tom Browne. 60 pages.

**Lowe-Brennan** — Lincoln Postcard Catalog. 144 pages.

Washington Postcard Catalog. 127 pages.

**Radley, C.** — History of Silk Postcards. 32 pages.

**Stadtmiller, Bernard** — Postcard Collecting, A Fun Investment. 78 pages.

**Staff, Frank** — The Picture Postcard and Its Origin. 1979 printing of 1966 book, 96 pages.

Picture Postcards and Travel. 1979, 96 pages.

Picture Postcards and War. 1982.

**Steinhart, Allan L.** — The Postal History of the Post Card in Canada, 1871-1911. 1979; 1980, second printing, 65 pages.

## Postal History

**aGatherin'** — European Postal History Documents. 1980, aGatherin', Wynantskill, N.Y.

**Angus, Ian** — Stamps, Post and Postmarks. 128 pages.

**Branston, Alfred J.** — Introducing Postal History. 1979, Stanley Gibbons Publications.

**Deutsches Post-Archiv** — Pages dealing with postal history. In German. Available from Deutsches Post-Achiv, c/o Archiv-Verlag, 33 Braunschweig, Breite Str. 25/26, Federal Republic of Germany.

**Disraeli, Robert** — Here Comes the Mail. 1939, Little Brown & Company, 117 pages.

**Forster, R.K.** — Postmark Collecting. 1960, London, 187 pages.

World Postmarks. 180 pages.

**Gibson, H.C.** — Henry C. Gibson Classic Foreign Covers 1840-60. 1944, 44 pages, French and German.

**Hahn, Calvet M.** — Postal History Primer. Postal history, pre-stamp covers and folded letter sheets. H & H Marketing, 1975, 44 pages.

**Hargest, George** — History of Letter Post Communication Between the U.S. and Europe, 1845-75. 234 pages.

**Hopkins, A.E.** — A History of Wreck Covers. Wrecks by land, sea, and air.

**Hurt and Williams** — Private Local Posts Handbook. (Billig's Volume 6), 1951 edition, 166 pages.

**Jewell, Charles** — Combination Covers. 1943, The London Philatelist, 19 pages.

**Kandaouroff, Prince Dimitry** — Collecting Postal History. Volume was translated into English 1973 by William Finley, 188 pages.

**Meroni, Charles F.** — Evolution of World Posts. 1952-53.

**Richardson, H.T.** — Envelopes of North and South America 1853-1875. 54 pages.

**Smith, A.D., Allen, Geo., and London, Unwin** — Development of Rates of Postage. 1917, 431 pages.

**Stimson, A.L.** — History of the Express Companies 1858. 287 pages.

History of the Express Business 1881. 389 pages.

**Van derLinden, James** — Postal Treaty Hand Stamp Catalog, 1815-75. 1977, 64 pages.

**Other items relating to this field concerning specific countries can be found under the country listings.**

## Topical

**American Topical Association** — Adventures in Topical Stamp Collecting. Handbook 96 (by Griffenhagen and Husak). 1981, 72 pages.

Aircraft: World Jets on Stamps. Handbook 57 (by De-Mars), 96 pages.

Americana on Foreign Stamps. Volume I. Checklist and stories behind stamps. Handbook 58 (by Wagner), 112 pages.

Americana on Foreign Stamps. Volume II. Checklist, subtopic lists, and cross-referenced index. Handbook 85 (by Wagner).

Astronomy and Philately. Handbook 90, 80 pages.

Bicentennial of American Independence on Foreign Stamps. Handbook 97, 66 pages.

Birds of the World on Stamps. Handbook 82 (by Stanley, Ridgely, and Eglajs), 104 pages.

Cooking with Stamps. Handbook 56 (by Brooks), 120 pages.

Education on Stamps. Handbook 68 (by Brooks), 60 pages.

Europe, Stamp Collecting Guide. 309 pages.

Europa on Stamps. Covers CEPT, Benelux, Council, Common Market, concept, forerunners, NATO, refugee and recovery issues. Handbook 34 (by Europa Study Unit).

Fairy Tales and Folk Tales on Stamps. Handbook 73 (by Partington).

Fishes, Amphibia and Reptiles. Handbook No. 91, 120 pages.

Holy Family on Stamps. Handbook 92, 120 pages.

Horses on Stamps. Handbook 52 (by Wetmore).

Insects and other Invertebrates on Stamps of the World. Handbook 98.

John F. Kennedy Stamps of the World. Handbook 50 (by Green, Czesany).

Lions International on Stamps. Handbook 59 (by Dekom).

Mammals of the World on Stamps. Handbook 79 (by Wagner, Stanley), 76 pages.

Masonic Stamps of the World. Handbook 43 (by Beltmann), 88 pages.

Medical History in Philately. Volume I (Medical Handbook Series, 5 volumes). Contains 280 physician biographies, medical scientists, world events and medical chronology, etc. Handbook 39 (by Newerla), 144 pages.

Drugs and Pharmacy on Stamps. Volume II (Medical Handbook Series). Pharmaceutical personalities, equipment, symbols, drug dosage forms, drug ads on stamps, and private die proprietary medicine stamps. Handbook 55 (by Griffenhagen), 96 pages.

Medical Stamps. Volume III (Medical Handbook Series). Updates doctors list, drugs and pharmacy lists, checklist of nurses, medical cancellations illustrated, etc. Handbook 63 (by Hainlen), 88 pages.

Private Die Proprietary Medicine Stamps. Volume IV (Medical Handbook Series). History of 132 proprietary medicine firms using private die stamps. Handbook 66 (by Griffenhagen), 80 pages.

Medicine Tax Stamps Worldwide. Volume V (Medical Handbook Series). Checklist of pharmaceutical fiscals and study of patent medicine merchandising around the world. Handbook 76 (by Griffenhagen), 128 pages.

Music World of Stamps. Handbook 84 (by Whitehead)

New Issues. Topical annual summaries, regularly issued.

Philatelic Nudes. Babies, children, adults in art, and sports. Handbook 53 (by Deane).

Old Glory Around the World. Handbook 75 (by Buckley, Dockal).

Plants on Stamps. Handbook 94 (Delfield, Sents and Patterson), 164 pages.

Railway Stamps. Handbook 102 (by Burkhalter, Wales), 104 pages.

A History of Religion on Stamps. Two volumes, Handbook 36 (by Morse), 240 pages.

Eleanor and Franklin D. Roosevelt Stamps of the World. Handbook 48 (by Silver, Bart).

Science Stamps. Scientific, philatelic, biographic and historic data for physics, natural history, invention, chemistry, etc. Lists of scientists by name, country and science. Handbook 87 (by Truman).

Space Covers. Listed by missions: Explorer, Discoverer, and Gemini. Astronaut biographies. Handbook 60 (by Peters).

Space Stamps. Checklist by country and subtopic. Handbook 99 (by Malz).

Sports and Recreation Checklist. Complete listing of competitive sports. Handbook 83 (by Bruce), 48 pages.

Stamps on Stamps - Centenaries. Handbook 45 (by Leland).

Theatre Philatelic. Descriptive checklist includes masks, playwrights, and actors. Handbook 67 (by Shiffler), 104 pages.

United Nations Stamps of the World. History of U.N. from the beginning. Handbook 40 (by Parkin, Magee), 84 pages.

U.S. History as Portrayed by U.S. Stamps. Chronological history of the United States and international events on U.S. stamps from Nordic visits to present day. Handbook 51 (by Tasker).

Watercraft on Stamps. Handbook 80 (by Herd), 84 pages.

Women on Stamps. Volume I, Handbook 71 (by Webb); Volume II, Handbook 93 (by Killingbeck).

**Arakawa, Kohman Y.** — Shells on Stamps of the World. 1979, Biological Society of Nagasaki Prefecture, 234 pages, in Japanese and English.

**Ask-Upmark, Erik** — Medicine Told by Stamps. 1976, 116 pages.

**Astronomy Study Unit** — Worldwide Copernicus Cancellations. 48 pages.

**Barber, C.J.** — Butterflies and Moths on Stamps. 1977, 48 pages.

**Barrett, O. W.** — The Animals on Postage Stamps. 1936, 90 pages.

**Berry, K., and Sager, W.A.** — 75 Years of Christmas Stamps. 1973, Collectors of Religion on Stamps, 80 pages.

**Berry, K.** — Six More Years of Christmas Stamps. 1979, Collectors of Religion on Stamps, 124 pages.

**Brabant, Paula** — Astronomie et Philatelie. 1962, L'Echo Philatelique, 60 pages (French).

**Brunstrom, Christer** — DX-Philately (radio stamps and radio stations). 1980, 24 pages.

**Devalick, G.** — Art and Philatelie. In French, 112 pages.

**Domingue, Robert A.** — Masonic Cacheted Covers. 1981, 260 pages.

**Engahen, Carl-Olaf** — Varldens Sportfrimarken. 1951 sports catalog, Swedish, 272 pages.

**Eriksson, Hans** — Postal Stationery Associated with Railways. Part I, Eastern Europe, 1981, 320 pages (Swedish, English and German).

**Esten, Sidney, R.** — Birds of the World on Stamps. 34 pages.

**Forgo, Steve** — Paintings and Graphic Arts on Stamps of Great Britain and the Nations of the British Commonwealth. 315 pages.

**Glover, W.T.** — A Checklist of Telecommunications on Postage Stamps. 1979, National Philatelic Society, 100 pages.

**Goodbody, A.M., and Hart, C.A.** — Railways on Stamps. Two volumes.

**Gouly, Andre, and Henri, Leroy** — L'Art Religeus Dans La Philatelie. 1951, 200 pages.

**Green, D.** — Catalogue of Tuberculosis Seals of the World. Parts 1-3, revised to 1945-46.

**Grimsey, A. H. R.** — Checklist of Postage Stamps about Music. Philatelic Music Circle, 1980 edition.

**Habbel, Wolfgang, R.** — John F. Kennedy Motive-Katalog. 1975, 32 pages (German).

**Houdemer, F.E.** — Les Poissons et le Timbre-Poste Nature II. The fish and the postage stamp. 1955, 164 pages, French.

**Ingram, D.** — Postage Stamps of the Red Cross, 1914-1918. 88 pages.

**Keep, David** — History Through Stamps. Brief outline of modern history, showing the interest in common stamps as distinct from classics and specialist pieces. 110 pages.

**Ken-ichi Hirano** — Postmarks and Official Cachets of Japanese Antarctic Research Expenditions. 1974 revised edition, 26 pages; supplement.

**Kyle and Shampo** — Medicine and Stamps. 1970, 215 pages.

**Lanspeary, Philip J.** — The World of Birds on Stamps. 1975, 328 pages.

**Lollini** — Lollini Catalogue of Space Material. 14th edition; 1975 supplement, 40 pages. Conquest of Space. 1978, 336 pages.

**McKee, J.D.F.** — Checklist of Scout and Guide Stamps of the World. 1980, 76 pages.

**Martin, M.W.** — Topical Stamp Collecting. 1977, distributed by ATA, 192 pages.

**Mayence, Guy** — L'Année Geophysique aux Poles Terrestres. International Geophysical Year and operations at both poles; cancellations, dates, historical date data — of all countries involved. 1962, L'Echo Philatelique, 83 pages (French).

**Minto, Dorothy** — Archaeology Checklist. 1980, Fine Arts Philatelist, 229 pages.

**Minzoni, Don Giovanni** — Scout Stamp Catalogue. Three volumes, Edizioni Scoutismo (Italian, French, English).

**Miyoshi, Mizoi and Kawashima** — Atoms on Stamps Checklist. 1979, 59 pages (Japanese and English).

**Morris, Gerald A.** — The Holy Family. 1979, ATA Christmas Study Unit, 120 pages.

**Morse, F.H.** — Religion on Postage Stamps. 1963, two parts, 238 pages.

**Mueller, B.** — Postage Stamps and Christianity. 1964, 83 pages.

**Nathan, S.** — The Railway Theme in Spanish Philately. 1979, Spanish Philatelic Society, 100 pages.

**Nowicki, W.Z.J.** — Nicolas Copernicus Stamp Catalogue, 1973-76. 1979, 198 pages, Copernicana Ltd.

**Page, H. D.** — The Equipment Register of the Philatelic Railroad. 22 pages.

**Peat, Sylvester** — Music on Stamps. Two volumes, part I, A-B, part II, C-F, 118 pages.

**Podolsky, Sherwin** — The Postal History and Vignettes of the 1932 Olympic Games. 196 pages.

**Rosen, H.** — Radio Philatelia. 1956.

**Ross, J.F** — History of Telecommunications on Stamps. Five volumes, Harry Hayes.

**Schlunegger, E.** — Introduction to Topical Philately. 1978, Richard Borek, 345 pages.

**Schmitt, Frederick P.** — The Whale's Tale as Told on Postage Stamps. Picton Publishing, London, 69 pages.

**Shawen, Lena** — The Story of F.D.R.'s Stamps. A President's Hobby. H.L. Lindquist, N.Y., 1949, 48 pages.

**Sherwood, William** — Handbook of the Dance on Stamps. 1981, Fine Arts Philatelists, 202 pages.

**Smit, F.G.A.M.** — Insects on Stamps. 1978, 78 pages.

**Smith, Wesley** — U.S. Postal Cancellations/Man's Conquest of Space. 1979, 35 pages; 1981, second edition.

**Sports Philatelists International** — Postal History and Vignettes of the 10th Olympiad and the Third Winter Olympic Games. 200 pages.

**Stengel, Hans** — Plants and Animals on Stamps. 1979, Richard Borek, 156 pages, German.

**Stiles, K. B.** — Geography and Stamps. 1931, 286 pages.

Postal Saints and Sinners. 1964, 294 pages.

**Strom and Lewy** — Animals on Stamps. 1968, Philart Products Ltd., 383 pages.

**Sudbury, R.F.** — The Bicycle and the Postage Stamp. 62 pages.

**Swanker, Wilson A.** — Medical Subjects on Stamps. 1954, 20 pages.

**Tankoos, Harry L.** — Collecting Dog and Cat Stamps. 1979, H. and M. Tankoos Publishers, 96 pages.

**Thorsen, Harry Jr.; Hoffman, William; and Kaplan, Howard** — Scouts on Stamps of the World. 1979, sixth edition, SOSSI.

**Timmermann, Herbert** — The Motif of Birds on Stamps. 1978, 1,116 pages.

**Way and Standen** — Zoology in Postage Stamps. 1951, 113 pages.

**Weber, Robert L.** — Physics on Stamps. 1980, A.S. Barnes and Co.

**Wyslotsky, O.** — Philatelic Handbook of Ice Hockey. 43 pages.

### Worldwide Catalogs

**Bolaffi** — Italy Specialized, Europe, Overseas. Regularly updated, Italian. Edizioni Scot, Box 335, 10100 Turin, Italy.

**Borek Briefmarken-Katalog.** — Most countries treated individually or in groups. Regularly updated, German. Richard Borek, Domplaz 4, 33 Brunswick, West Germany.

**Durbin, L. W.** — Illustrated Price Catalogue of the Postage Stamps of All Nations. 1881, eighth edition, 124 pages.

Standard Catalogue of Postal Cards. 1886, sixth edition, 32 pages.

**Forbin A.** — World Revenue Catalog. Second printing of 1915 edition.

**Higgins and Gage** — Postal Stationery Catalogue. 1965, 19 sections covering the world; supplements currently being issued. Classic Philatelics, Box 5637, Huntington Beach, Calif. 92646.

**Michel** — Germany Specialized, Europe, Overseas. Regularly updated, German. Lighthouse Publications, 317 W. 44th St., New York, N.Y. 10036.

**Minkus** — New World Wide Postage Stamp Catalogue. Two international volumes and U.S. Specialized. Regularly updated. Minkus Publications, 116 W. 32nd St., New York, N.Y. 10001.

Regional Catalogs, 12 volumes to 1982.

**Scott Standard Postage Stamp Catalogue.** Five volumes (U.S. Specialized; U.S. and British; three volumes of foreign). Regularly updated. Scott Publishing Co., 530 Fifth Ave., New York, N.Y. 10036.

**Stanley Gibbons** — 21 volumes covering the world. Regularly updated. Gibbons, 391 Strand, London WC2R OLX, England, or StanGib Ltd., 595 Fifth Ave., New York, N.Y. 10017.

Stamps of the World (simplified). 1982 edition, one volume.

**Whitman-Gibbons** — Whitman-Gibbons Postage Stamp Catalogue. Part 1, U.S. and possessions, Great Britain and British Commonwealth. 1968, 621 pages.

**Yvert et Tellier** — France Specialized, Europe and Overseas. Regularly updated, French. Yvert et Tellier, 37 Rue des Jacobins, 80036 Amiens, France.

## Miscellaneous

**Alden, John** — Printers and Printing in Philately. 1976, Picton Publishing, 76 pages.

**Allen, J.L., and Silverstone, P.H.** — Stamp Collector's Guide to Europe. 224 pages.

**American Nations Series** — 18 booklets. Pan American Union.

**American Philatelic Congress** — Congress Book. Issued annually.

**Association for Stamp Exhibitions** — Stamp Exhibitions. A "how-to" book. 1950, 186 pages.

**Bacon, E.D.** — Reprints of 19th Century Postal Adhesive Stamps and Their Characteristics. 168 pages.

**Barefoot, J.** — European Philately. 1978, J. Barefoot Ltd.

**Beckton, Goodfellow** — A Glossary of Philatelic Terms. 1933, 39 pages.

**Bell, Russell S.** — Guide to Stamp Wholesalers. 20 pages.

**Bennett and Watson** — Philatelic Terms Illustrated. 1972, 192 pages.

**Bierman, Stanley M.** — The World's Greatest Stamp Collectors. 1981, Frederick Fell, 296 pages.

**Billig's Philatelic Handbooks** — A philatelic library in miniature. 44 volumes.

**Blair, Arthur** — The World of Stamps and Stamp Collecting. 1972, Hamlyn, 128 pages.

**Boggs, W. S.** — Foundations of Philately. 1955, 187 pages.

**Booth, Phoebe** — Subject Matter of Philately. 1944 checklist, 86 pages; three supplements.

**British Philatelic Association Ltd.** — BPA Philatelic Societies' Directory. Includes a listing of organizations of the world with meeting sites, founding details, current secretaries, and information on the activities of the British Philatelic Association.

**Brockert, Joe** — Basic Knowledge for the Stamp Collector. 1981 printing, Amos Press, 130 pages.

**Brown, Jerry** — Philatelic Terms Illustrated. 192 pages.

**Browne, Glen** — How To Sell Your Stamp Collection. 1979, 30 pages.

**Bruns, F. R.** — Fells Official Stamp Guide. Guide to collecting, selling and evaluating stamps. Reprinted 1961, 125 pages.

**Brunstrom, Christer** — Collect Cinderella Stamps. 1979, 12 pages.

**Bullinger, E.W.** — Bullinger Monitor Guide. 1976 edition.

**Burgess, G. H.** — Minimum Essentials in Stamp Collecting. 1939, 198 pages.

**Burns, Al** — The Essentials of Stamp Collecting. 1934, 80 pages.

**Bush, Joseph V.** — A.M.G. Catalog Handbook. 1979, third printing, 44 pages.

**Buxton Stamp Co.** — The Buxton Encyclopedia of Watermarks. 1978, 114 pages.

**Chapman and Baker** — All Color Book of Stamps. 1974, 72 pages.

**Chlanda, E.A.** — Insurance Guide for Stamp Collectors. 1981, Verba Co., 14 pages.

**Clifton, Robert Bruce** — Murder By Mail and Other Postal Investigations. 1980, second printing, Dorrance and Co., 225 pages.

**Collin, H., and Calman, H.L.** — A Catalogue for Advanced Collectors of Postage Stamps, Stamped Envelopes and Wrappers. 1901, Scott Stamp and Coin Co., 14 parts.

**Colson, W. H.** — Postage Stamps and Their Collection. 1907, 98 pages.

**Cooper, Jeremy** — Under the Hammer. The Auctions and Auctioneers of London. Robson Lowe, 248 pages.

**De Pree, Mildred** — A Child's World of Stamps. 1976.

**Donaldson, N.** — The Postal Agencies in Eastern Arabia Gulf. 280 pages.

**Egan, C. W.** — The Stamp Collectors Handbook Lexicon of Terms and Practical Hints to Philatelists. 1894, Kissinger, 56 pages.

**Ekker, Charles** — Philatelia-1. How-to-do-it stamp dealing handbook.

**Erskine, G. B.** — Approaches to Philately. 1950, 211 pages.

**Evans, Edward B.** — The Philatelic Catalogue of Postage Stamps, Envelopes, Wrappers and Cards. 1891, 486 pages.

Stamps and Stamp Collecting. A glossary of principal philatelic terms. 1913, fourth edition, 112 pages.

**La Federation des Societes Philateliques du Quebec** — The history of philately, how to collect, what to collect, how to exhibit, and an illustrated glossary. In French, 74 pages.

**Felix, E. J.** — How to Collect Stamps, Coins and Paper Money. 1954, 160 pages.

Identify Your Stamps. 1967, 243 pages.

Watermarks and Perforations. 1966, 249 pages.

Worldwide Watermarks and Perforations. 1840 to date. 256 pages.

**Forbin, A.** — Catalogue de Timbres Fiscaux par A. Forbin. 1915, 797 pages (French).

**Forsher, B. J.** — More Precious Than Gold and Philately. Basic facts, threadbare stories, and trivia regarding stamp collecting. 160 pages.

**Foster, C. E.** — How To Prepare Stamp Exhibits. 1974, 212 pages.

Showcasing Your Stamp Collection. 1979, 120 pages.

**Fry, Ed** — Catalogue for Collectors of Post Cards. 1886, 216 pages.

**Gandley, Will** — Things You Should Know About Stamp Collecting. Canadian Wholesale Supply, 38 pages.

**Graham, H. T.** — Glossary of Philatelic Terms. 1951, 108 pages.

**Grossman, Samuel** — Stamp Collector's Handbook. 1975, 192 pages.

**Hahn, Calvet M.** — For Juniors With Love. 1979, H. & H. Marketing, 80 pages.

**Harlow, A. F.** — Paper Chase. 1940, 353 pages.

**Harris, H.E.** — Stamp Collector's Guide and Companion. Second printing 1976, 160 pages.

Classics, Rarities and other Choice Stamps. 1952-1953, 45 pages.

How to Collect Stamps. 1979, 190 pages.

**Harrison and Armstrong** — A New Approach to Stamp Collecting. 1953, London, 188 pages.

**Harrison, T.S., and Harrison, R.A.** — The Harrisons of Waterlow. Art of stamp engraving, 12 pages.

**Heath, G.A.** — How to Sell Stamps By Mail. 1979, Heath Sales.

**Hentzell, George** — Read Before Dealing. 1980, Hentzell Publications, 101 pages.

**Herst, H.** — Nassau Street. 305 pages.

Fun and Profit in Stamp Collecting. 1962 edition, 168 pages.

Stories to Collect Stamps By. 1968 edition, 281 pages.

A Quarter Century of Stamp Dealing. 1960.

The Compleat Philatelist. 1979, Washington Press, 115 pages.

**Hornadge, Bill** — Stamps — A Collector's Guide. 1968, first edition; 1980 revised edition, Review Publication.

Philatelic Fables. 1980, Review Publications Pty. Ltd., 72 pages.

**Ilma, Viola** — Funk and Wagnalls Guide to the World of Stamp Collecting. 1978, 340 pages.

**Irvin, D., and Seshold, M.** — Errors in Postage Stamp Design. 1979, National Philatelic Society, 192 pages.

**Jaffe, Hans, and Kunz, R.E.** — Coils, A Worldwide Catalog. 1980, 84 pages.

**Kean Publications** — Stamps Direct. 1979, 24 pages.

**Kehr, E. A.** — The Romance of Stamp Collecting. 1947, 342 pages.

My Hobby is Collecting Stamps. 1955, 125 pages.

**Kelley, P.** — The World of Local Postage Stamps. 155 pages.

**Kohl Handbooks** — 43 sections on philately of the world. German.

**Konwiser, H. M.** — American Stamp Collector's Dictionary. 1949, 309 pages.

Postal Markings. 1980, Quarterman Publications reprint, 762 pages.

**Lidman, David and Apfelbaum, John D.** — The World of Stamps and Stamp Collecting. 1981, Charles Scribner and Sons, 243 pages.

**Lindquist, H.L.** — The Blue Book of Philately. 1933, 434 pages.

**Linn's Stamp News** — Linn's World Stamp Almanac. 1982 fourth edition.

**Logigas, Dace** — Have Fun Collect Stamps. 48 pages.

**Lowe, Robson** — The Diseases of Philately and their Treatment. Well-known and little-known ailments to which the postage stamp and its collectors are heirs.

**Lyons, J. H.** — Commemorative Stamps of the World. 1914, 132 pages.

**McP. Cabeen, Richard** — Standard Handbook of Stamp Collecting. 1979 revised edition, Thomas Y. Crowell Co., 630 pages.

**Mackay, James A.** — World of Classic Stamps 1840-1870. Putnam Sons, N.Y., 1972, 344 pages.

The Dictionary of Stamps in Color. 296 pages.

Encyclopedia of World Stamps, 1945-1975. 160 pages.

**Magnus, Dr.** — Le Grands Manuel for Stamp Collectors. 173 pages.

**Melillo, E.** — Pigeons Voyageurs. Pigeon posts. 1898, 43 pages.

**Melville, F. J.** — Phantom Philately. 1950 reprint, 204 pages.

Chats on Postage Stamps. 1911, 362 pages.

Postage Stamps in the Making. 1916, 198 pages.

**Michel, Eugene** — Roving the Stamp World with Eugene Michel.

**Mobile Post Office Society** — Mobile Post Office Selections. Volume I, 1980, 38 pages; Volume II, 1982.

**Mueller, E.** — Catalog of the Imperforate Classic Postal Stamps of Europe. 1958, 151 pages.

**Muhitch, Anthony S.** — Stamps That Teach. 1979, 50 pages.

**New, Anthony** — The Observer's Book of Postage Stamps. Includes chapter on printing of stamps and index of 80 artists. 192 pages.

**Newton, Shaw** — The Standard Guide to Stamp Collecting. 1924, Scott Stamp and Coin Co., 35 pages.

**Nicklin, J. W.** — Fabulous Stamps. 1939, 172 pages.

**Ohrt** — Ohrt Handbook. Five volumes covering world philately. German.

**Partington, Pasul G.** — Who's Who on the Postage Stamps of Eastern Europe. 1979, 506 pages.

**Patrick, D. and M.** — Musson Stamp Dictionary. 1972, 277 pages.

**Perry, Elliott** — Pat Paragraphs (compilation of 58 booklets). Bureau Issues Association, 1981, 648 pages.

**Phillips, Stanley** — Stamp Collecting. 58 pages.

**Phillips, Stanley; and Rang, C.P.** — How to Arrange and Write Up a Stamp Collection. 1979, Stanley Gibbons Publications, 32 pages.

**Pirie, Dr. J.H.** — Antarctic Posts. Reprinted 1976, 72 pages.

**Price, W. J.** — It's About Stamps. 1948, A & S.M. Dixon Ltd., 55 pages.

**Precancel Stamp Society** — The ABCs of Precancel Collecting. 20 pages.

**Ray, L.R.** — Background to Philately. 1953, anthology of papers read to Philatelic Congress of Great Britain, 224 pages.

**Renouf, Henry** — Stamp Collecting. 1934, 87 pages.

**Rothschild, S.I.** — Stamps of Many Lands. 1932, 141 pages.

Stories Postage Stamps Tell. 1930, 158 pages.

**Rostenberg, Leona** — Bibliately. 1979, American Philatelic Society, 61 pages.

**Schenk, Gustav** — The Romance of the Postage Stamp. 1962 English version, 231 pages.

**Schmid, Paul W.** — How to Detect Damaged, Altered and Repaired Stamps. 1979, Palmer Press, 105 pages.

**Sefi, A.J.** — An Introduction to Advanced Philately. 1926, 115 pages.

**Sieger-Verlag** — Europaische Blocks. Catalog of souvenir sheets, miniature sheets and sheetlets by the countries of Europe. 1979, fourth edition, 762 pages.

**Smith, A.D.** — The Development of Rates of Postage: An Historical and Analytical Study. 1979 reprint, Quarterman.

**Springer, Sherwood** — Springer's Handbook of North American Cinderella Stamps. 1980, ninth edition, 56 pages.

**Storer, Doug** — Amazing But True Stories Behind the Stamp. 208 pages.

**Sutton, R.J.** — The Stamp Collector's Encyclopaedia. 1966, New York Philosophical Library, 370 pages.

**Tompkins, T.L.C.** — The Persian Gulf. 100 pages.

**Walthouse, Richard G.** — All Nations Stamp Finder and Dictionary. 1980, second edition, Harold Cohn and Co., 75 pages.

**Warner, Frank** — All About Stamps. 1959, 144 pages.

**Watson, James** — Stamp Varieties Explained. 32 pages.

The Stanley Gibbons Book of Stamps and Stamp Collecting. 1981, 256 pages.

**White Ace** — Postage Stamp Identifier. 1979, seventh edition, 65 pages.

**Williams, L.N. and M.** — Techniques of Philately. 1969, 34 pages.

Cinderella Stamps. 1970, 152 pages.

Famous Stamps. 1946 revised edition, 147 pages.

Stamps Day By Day. 1950, 237 pages.

Fundamentals of Philately. 1979 edition, American Philatelic Society, 672 pages.

Rare Stamps. 1967, G.P. Putnam, 120 pages.

**Wilson, Frank L.** — Philatelic Almanac. 1936, 318 pages.

**Wood, Ken** — Basic Philately. 1979, Van Dahl Publications, 68 pages.

**Yeo, Martyn** — How to Arrange and Write Up a Stamp Collection. Stanley Gibbons Publications.

**Zinsmeister, Marian Carne** — Souvenir Sheets World. 2 volume set.

U.P.U. 75th Anniversary Issues. 48 pages.

# The Taxing Task 19

# Taxes and Philately

### By Larry and Tony Crumbley
### (All Rights Reserved)

Dr. Larry Crumbley, Ph.D., CPA, is Professor of Accounting at Texas A&M University. Experienced in public accounting and consulting, he has published a number of books and articles about tax planning and decision making. Tony Crumbley is a research analyst with the Charlotte Chamber of Commerce and the proprietor of Carolina Coin and Stamps.

An old German proverb says we "work and earn, pay taxes and die." We may do other things, stamp collecting among them, but even in our hobbies, taxes are a constant fact of life.

There has been and will continue to be a steady increase in federal, state and local taxes in the United States. Each year more and more of every taxable dollar goes to satisfy the appetite of various governmental units.

Even without a tax increase or surcharge, our constant inflation pushes us into higher tax brackets. We pay more and more taxes each year because inflation is a "silent" tax increase.

A collector may spend hours working with his stamps, checking the perforation, checking to see how well it is centered, looking for thin spots, and hoping for an unlisted variety. But the present high tax rates require a collector, an investor, or a dealer to give serious consideration to the tax implications of his transactions.

An individual can use various methods to avoid or defer his taxes. Often in making an investment decision, he may choose any one of several avenues and still obtain the same desired investment result.

But the tax consequences may be different depending upon the alternative chosen. We like to emphasize that the best income is "tax saved dollars," since this type of income is not taxable.

We have heard at least one collector state:

"The major reason a person invests in stamps is to be able to obtain tax free income since gains can be hidden from the government."

Such an attitude is unfortunate and dangerous, because the government has stopped many other groups from evading taxes.

Philatelists should not make the mistake of failing to report income from transactions in stamps. Some legal tax avoidance is encouraged, but tax evasion is unlawful.

The Internal Revenue Service has many ingenious ways to collect hidden income, and it does not overlook stamp collectors. The Oct. 2, 1974, issue of "Coin World" carried a report of an individual who was convicted of a $350,000 income tax evasion. He was sentenced to a five-year term in Terminal Island.

Don't try to cheat the government, or there may be an article about you in a philatelic publication.

Investing in philatelic items is a good hedge against inflation, but individuals must recognize the dramatic impact taxes have upon their investment.

What good is an investment if you are going to lose most of it in tax payments? Everyone has an obligation as well as a right to legally minimize his tax burden. One court has ruled that "the legal right of a taxpayer to decrease the amount of what otherwise would be taxes, or altogether avoid them by means which the law permits, cannot be doubted."

What we wish to discuss in this chapter are legitimate tax tips and techniques — not dishonest tax gimmicks or tax fraud schemes. But you must help; tax planning is a year-around job.

A philatelist must carefully consider the various tax alternatives before he makes major investment or business decisions. For example, most individuals work more than one-third of their total work hours to pay various taxes. Your "second job" should be trying to legally reduce your tax payments.

One warning is appropriate. Tax laws change as rapidly as a swift-flowing stream. Some of the information you read here may have already changed. It is impossible to keep tax materials up to date without daily and weekly supplements.

Thus, when any major transaction is anticipated, check with a local CPA or lawyer. Rely on this chapter only as a general outline.

## Hobby or Business?

An individual who collects philatelic items falls generally within one of three major groups — a collector, an investor, or a dealer. Under the tax laws the distinction between these three groups is very important. As the three circles in the chart below depict, a person may fall within one, two, or all three tax categories. But overall, the available facts will place an individual in one category.

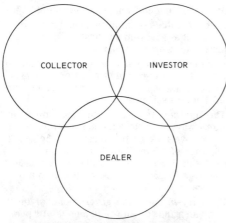

From the point of view of income, a dealer must report income from the sale of rare stamps as ordinary income; whereas an investor or collector may obtain a more favorable capital gain rate.

But a dealer or investor may deduct many more philatelic expenses than a collector. Obviously, the investor is in the most favorable category since he receives favorable capital gain treatment and is allowed to deduct more expenses.

Is a certain expenditure incurred by a collector, investor, or dealer deductible? The answer to the crucial question depends on whether the activity is a hobby or a business. The major criteria which distinguishes between a hobby or business is the profit motive. If the philatelic activity is engaged in for a profit, any associated expenses or losses are deductible if they are considered ordinary and necessary.

However, if the philatelic activity is not engaged in for a profit, then any related expenditures are deductible only as income from the philatelic activity.

A discussion about expenses in general is appropriate at this point. Expenses are deductible under two major areas of tax law. First, all ordinary or necessary expenditures paid or incurred during a tax year in carrying on any trade or business (for example, stamp dealer) are allowable as business deductions.

These allowable business deductions include such items as employee salaries, travel and entertainment expenses, advertising expenditures, depreciation or rent on a stamp shop, supplies, silicone-treated glassine envelopes, insurance, utilities, and so forth.

Second, any ordinary or necessary "nonbusiness" expenditures paid or incurred during a tax year are deductible if they are made (a) for the production or collection of income, or (b) for the management, conservation, or maintenance of property (e.g., rare stamps, stocks, artifacts, etc.) held for the production of income.

A stamp dealer falls within the first category since he is carrying on a trade or business. An investor falls within the second category. But a stamp collector does not fall within any of these categories.

Thus, as a general rule, a stamp collector's philatelic expenses are deductible only as possible hobby income (e.g., gain on sale of stamps), unless the expenses fall into a category which is normally deductible (e.g., interest expense, sales taxes, casualty losses, etc.)

## Profit Motive

Under either of the above dealer or investor categories, stamp activity must still be carried on for a profit in order to create deductible expenses or losses.

But what exactly is a profit motive? Congress tried to clear up this murky area in 1969 by passing a rebuttable presumption by the IRS that an activity is engaged in for a profit if the income from such activity exceeds the deductions from the same activity in two out of five consecutive taxable years. For example, if your philatelic investment activity shows a net income in any two out of five consecutive years, your expenses and losses are presumed to be deductible.

However, if your philatelic activity does not show a net income in two out of five consecutive years, expense and loss deductions are disallowed to the extent that they exceed income from the philatelic activity.

But personal expenses such as taxes and interest, which you may normally deduct, are of course deductible.

This two-out-of-five year rule is, however, a rebuttable presumption. It works more as a blunt instrument rather than as a scalpel.

The IRS may attempt to show that the activity is a hobby rather than a business, and a taxpayer may have difficulty sustaining deductions for business or investing expenses even though there is an indication of a profit motive in addition to a pleasure motive.

In fact, the IRS issued an old Revenue Ruling which indicates that a loss on the sale of a stamp collection accumulated as a hobby is not deductible. Three court cases (two unfavorable and one favorable) can show what criteria may be used to determine the dominant purpose of an activity — a profit motive or a pleasure motive.

In an old case involving a stamp investor, the tax court allowed as a deduction a loss on the sale of a part of his stamp collection. The court wisely reasoned that the taxpayer's primary motive for collecting from the beginning was an investment for the realization of a pecuniary gain.

This taxpayer had shown little interest in stamps and had acquired only a minimum knowledge of stamps. He had not subscribed to any philatelic publications or joined any philatelic organizations.

The investor kept books in which he recorded in chronological order the date of the purchase or sale, the cost or sale price, and the identity of all his investments. He set up a separate bank account and all transactions in stamps were handled through such an account.

The taxpayer worked very closely with a professional philatelist. Unfortunately, during the market crash of 1929, many of his stamps decreased in value, and when he sold part of his stamps, he incurred a sizable loss.

The IRS disallowed the loss, but the tax court agreed with the taxpayer. The court felt that the stamp investor had the "requisite greed" to indicate a profit motive.

In a later court case, an art collector was not so successful, even though he felt collecting works of art was an excellent hedge against inflation and devaluation of currencies.

This taxpayer made every effort to conduct his art collecting in a business-like manner and maintained a record-keeping system that was much better than in the stamp case. Most of the art collector's expenditures were disallowed by the Court of Claims because the IRS was able to establish that personal pleasure or satisfaction was the taxpayer's primary purpose for the art collection.

This court was impressed that the taxpayer had originally started the collection as a hobby, and that the taxpayer and his wife's personal lives revolved around their art collection and related collecting activities.

The pleasure motive was considered primary even though they spent only about a month in their New York apartment where 80 per cent of their art objects were located.

In a case of more recent vintage, a husband and wife started an antique business which they operated out of their home. Although the husband was employed full-time with another company, he assisted his wife (who was the manager of the antique business) with the bookkeeping and in the purchase of antiques.

About 95 per cent of their personal household furnishings were antiques which they were willing to sell, but the furnishings were sometimes held for long periods of time after reasonable offers were made for their purchase.

You guessed it! The taxpayers reported losses from their sale of antiques and deducted these losses from the husband's reportable income.

"No, sir!" said the IRS, and disallowed the losses on the grounds that the taxpayers did not establish that their losses were incurred in a transaction carried on for a profit.

The tax court agreed with the IRS and said the couple established the antique business merely as a mechanism to reduce the cost of living in a home furnished with antiques, rather than for the purpose of making profit (which is an essential element of a trade or business).

The court held that the standard for determining whether the parties had the required intent to obtain a profit from their business operation can be less than a "reasonable expectation" of deriving a profit, but it must be a "bona fide" expectation. Thus, the score is two to one in favor of the IRS.

Although the two-out-of-five years rule was intended to solve the problem of profit versus pleasure, the ultimate determination of many stamp investors' fate may still hinge upon a subjective determination by a court about whether the investor has a profit motive or a pleasure motive.

A stamp investor must take all necessary steps to show that he truly has a profit motive for investing in rare stamps, since the IRS may attempt to classify an investor as a stamp collector in order to disallow his expenses and losses.

The major hurdle that a stamp investor must overcome is showing a profit motive is dominant in his investment program. One tax court case sets forth this criterion clearly:

"The profit or income motive must first be present in and dominate any taxpayer's trade or business before deductions may be taken. While the expectation of the taxpayer need not be reasonable, and immediate profit from the business is not necessary, nevertheless, the basic and dominant intent behind the taxpayer's activities, out of which he claimed expenses or debts were incurred, must be ultimately to make a profit or income from those very same activities.

"Absent that basic and dominant motive, the taxpayer's activities, no matter how intensive, extensive or expensive, have not been construed by the courts as carrying on a trade or business . . . the goal must be to realize a profit on the entire operation, which presupposes not only future net earnings but also sufficient net earnings to recoup the losses which have meanwhile been sustained in the intervening years."

Although this statement refers to a trade or business, this same language also applies to management, conservation, or maintenance of rare stamps held for the production of income.

## IRS Guidelines

The IRS provides some guidelines in published regulations about whether an activity has the dominant objective of making a profit:

1. The manner in which an activity is conducted.

2. Expertise of the taxpayer or his advisors.

3. Amount of time and effort expended.

4. Expectation that assets may appreciate in value.

5. Success of taxpayer in carrying on other activities.

6. History of income or losses with respect to such activity.

7. Financial status of the taxpayer.

8. Elements of personal pleasure or recreation.

Item eight is probably the most worrisome guideline from the point of view of many stamp investors. The IRS is indicating that if there is a degree of personal pleasure or recreation in the activity, this may indicate the activity is a hobby rather than a business or investment activity.

However, the tax court took a different position in a recent decision.

Discussing whether or not expenditures for a yacht were deductible, the court indicated that "a business will not be turned into a hobby merely because the owner finds it pleasurable; suffering has never been made a prerequisite to deductibility."

Certainly, the accumulation of rare stamps is a legitimate and profitable investment enterprise. For example, the set of three Graf Zeppelin (Scott C13-15) was issued in 1930 during the depression for a cost of $5.15.

With only 61,296 sets issued, its value was approximately $350 in 1966 and $7,000 not long ago — a 1900 per cent rise in 14 years, then dropping to $4,000; stamps do decrease in value.

America's rarest stamp, a 24-cent 1918 airmail erroneously printed with the plane flying upside down, sold for $47,000 in 1975, approximately 275 per cent more than the $12,500 price 10 years earlier.

If a stamp investor appreciates or enjoys his investments, the IRS should not use this to convert an investment activity into a hobby.

1. A business-like attitude should be maintained in all of your stamp activities.

2. When you begin investing in stamps, emphasize the investment potential of them, not the hobby aspect.

3. If you collect some stamps as a hobby and other stamps for investment purposes, keep such transactions separate. However, your hobby transactions may "taint" your investment activities.

4. Keep detailed records of all transactions, just as if you were investing in stocks, bonds or real estate.

5. If you attempt to deduct philatelic literature, make sure some of the literature is slanted toward the investment side rather than the hobby side.

6. De-emphasize the hobby side of your collecting with friends, in your records and your transactions with dealers.

7. If a dealer or investment firm suggests that a particular stamp will have investment potential, make a note of such advice.

8. When you purchase a stamp, jot down the reasons why you believe such an investment will be worthwhile (e.g., stamp market at its bottom and must move up, low issuance, etc.).

9. Valuable stamps should be kept in safe deposit boxes and such expenditures deducted as a business expense.

10. The fact that you invest regularly in stamps in a specific program with an investment firm should be a favorable factor.

11. If you have many stamp transactions, a separate bank account can be used to handle all stamp transactions.

## Investor or Dealer?

Just as an investor wishes to have a profit motive in order not to be a collector, an investor does not wish to be classified by the IRS as a dealer.

Thus, once an individual establishes that he is carrying on a business, he must decide whether he is an investor or a dealer.

The distinction between an investor and a dealer is very important for income tax purposes since assets eligible for capital gain treatment are defined in terms of their use and the person holding them.

Generally, if an individual is classified as a dealer, his gains on sale of valuable stamps are taxed as ordinary income irrespective of the length of ownership.

On the other hand, if an individual is an investor, he receives capital gain treatment on the sale of his rare stamps (taxed at a maximum of 20 per cent).

Further, the expenditures of a dealer are deductible as "ordinary and necessary business expenses." In the case of a sole proprietorship, these expenses would be reported on Schedule C of Form 1040 (in effect, they are deductions for adjusted gross income).

Conversely, an investor must claim his deductions as itemized deductions (e.g., deductions from adjusted gross income). Thus if an investor claims the zero bracket amount, he would obtain no benefit from such expenditures.

Although there are major differences in the tax treatment of a dealer and an investor, there is no place in the income tax law that succinctly defines an investor or a dealer (except for securities).

Rather, the definition must be gleaned from the various tax court cases involving this question. The courts have developed some general criteria which may be used to distinguish an investor from a dealer. Let us examine some of these criteria and indicate some factors that might lead to your classification as an investor rather than a dealer.

One important factor is the extent and continuity of buying and selling activities. Continuous weekly sales will likely result in dealer classification; whereas only occasional sales during the year might tend to indicate the activities of an investor.

Certainly, no magic line can be drawn as to the number of sales one could make without being classified as a dealer. The distinction is drawn more in terms of the overall activities and intent of the taxpayer during the periods.

Thus, if an investor purchased a stamp and immediately began advertising it for sale or actively seeking a buyer, there is the distinct possibility that any gain on the sale of the stamp would be taxed as ordinary income irrespective of whether or not it was held over twelve months.

At times the courts have attempted to delineate the distinction between investor and dealer in terms of the taxpayer's motives or expectations. In one leading "intent" case, a dealer was defined as one who buys with the expectation of selling at a profit, not due to a rise in value of the property, but in hopes that he can find buyers to purchase them at a price in excess of their cost. This markup represents payment for their efforts as middle men and for performing the services of retailer or wholesaler.

On the other hand, an investor is characterized as one who buys in expectation of selling at a profit due to a rise in value of the property or an advantageous purchase.

Obviously, this intent approach is difficult. The courts and the IRS have found that it is difficult to "crawl into a taxpayer's mind" and determine his intent for a certain activity.

Under this "intent" approach a dealer could, under certain circumstances, be classified as an investor with respect to certain stamps.

For example, a dealer might purchase certain philatelic items with an expectation of a rise in value over time. If these items were segregated from his ordinary stock in trade, a subsequent sale could result in capital gain treatment. This segregation, however, would require careful establishment and documentation of intent and would likely be questioned by the IRS.

At a certain point the extent of business activities of an investor will turn an investor into a dealer. Some factors to determine if a taxpayer has crossed the border from investor to dealer include:

1. Does the taxpayer rely solely on the sales of stamps for his income?

2. How much time and effort is expended by the taxpayer in buying and selling stamps?

3. Does he have a regular professional business or promotional assistance?

4. What is the nature and extent of his advertising?

5. What is the general business nature of his activity?

Using these guidelines and taking the extreme case, a dealer would be someone who works full-time buying and selling stamps, employs business advisors and employees, advertises extensively and runs a very business-like operation.

To illustrate the other extreme, an investor would clearly be one who occasionally purchases a stamp, holds it hoping for a rise in value, and advertises it a few times in the classified advertising section of a newspaper or magazine.

Closely related to the business activity criteria is the source of the taxpayer's income. If the stamp trader relies solely on sales of rare stamps for his income, it is highly likely that the IRS would classify him as a dealer.

However, if you have invested in rare stamps (rather than stocks) throughout your working life and then retire and begin to sell your valuable stamps in order to live, such a situation (in our opinion) is no different than someone who retires and begins to live on proceeds from the sales of his stocks and bonds.

However, a person who receives the majority of his income from a job or other business unrelated to stamps would be in a better position to maintain his investor status.

On the other hand, it is quite possible under the tax law to be engaged in more than one trade or business. The commissioner could maintain that the trading in stamps constitutes a second trade or business according to the surrounding facts. Again, the source of income is only part of the test for determining dealer or investor classification in conjunction with the other criteria.

There is no clear-cut rule of thumb that can be given to guide the rare stamp investor down the rocky tax road to capital gains. The primary point is that if you do not intend to engage in stamp dealing as a business, conduct your activities by the guidelines given and do not create a situation that would make it appear that you are engaged in a business. By making your actions clearly reflect your intentions, you may avoid future tax problems.

There is a favorable side to the classification of an investor as a dealer. Suppose a dealer takes a long extended trip to several foreign countries and incurs substantial travel expenses on such a purchasing trip for inventory items.

Generally, a dealer or merchant could deduct such travel expenses currently as expenses incurred in purchasing inventory items.

However, an investor might incur similar expenditures in traveling to purchase specific stamps (including incurrence of appraisal fees, etc.). Generally, such costs would be allocable to the cost basis of the stamp investments acquired.

In the former instance (a dealer), the expenditures would be deductible in the year incurred; whereas in the latter situation (an investor) the expenditures would be taken into consideration in the year the stamp investments are sold.

The same situation may be true with regard to selling expenses. A dealer or merchant could deduct selling expenses as an ordinary and necessary business expense in the year incurred.

On the other hand, an investor would take selling expenses into account in determining the gain or loss on the specific stamp investments.

Consider another example. Suppose a dealer investigates a possible purchase of a valuable stamp, but decides against making the acquisition.

For a dealer, these investigative expenses would be deductible. Conversely, if an investor incurs expenses to purchase an investment item but does not purchase the stamp, there is the possibility the IRS will disallow such deductions since the expenditures are not related to an item held for investment.

The chart below summarizes the major tax result of the three categories. In general, the investor is the most favored category.

| Tax Classification | How Gain is Taxed | Deductibility of Expenses | Payment of Sales Tax |
|---|---|---|---|
| Collector | Capital Gain | Only against any income D from AGI | Yes |
| Investor | Capital Gain | D from AGI | Yes |
| Dealer | Ordinary Income | Ordinary deduction | No* |

*But dealer must collect the sales tax from the buyer and remit to the state. A collector or investor might avoid the sales tax on philatelic items by buying them out of state by mail order.

## Capital Gains, Losses

Personal income tax rates are based on a graduated scale, from 14 per cent to 50 per cent. In other words, the higher your income, the higher rate of tax you must pay, basically on a pay-as-you-go basis.

Each individual who has a certain amount of gross income (the amount depending upon a number of variables) must file Form 1040 by April 15 enclosing any taxes he owes or asking for a refund of taxes.

The tax laws provide, however, a tax advantage for persons who hold property for investment purposes. Speaking generally, if such property (e.g., stamps, real estate, stocks) is held for more than twelve months, any gain upon a subsequent sale is classified as a "long-term" capital gain and receives special tax treatment.

The rate at which a long-term capital gain (LTCG) is taxed is 40 per cent of your normal rate bracket, or a maximum of 20 per cent.

For example, if you are in the 30 per cent tax bracket, all capital gains in excess of capital losses will be taxed at 12 per cent (.30 x .40). This special treatment can result in quite a tax savings where your capital gains exceed your capital losses.

The calculation is a little different if your capital losses exceed your capital gains during the year. First, if you have a net short-term capital loss (STCL) position as an individual taxpayer, you may deduct up to $3,000 per year from any other income you may have.

Any STCL in excess of $3,000 may be carried over indefinitely to be used in future years until you use up the loss.

Second, a net long-term capital loss (LTCL) position is penalized by the tax laws. You must have at least a $2,000 LTCL to obtain a $1,000 deduction. That is, each $1 of LTCLs is reduced by 50 cents to obtain your annual $1,000 deduction.

Your period of ownership in a stamp is determined in terms of whole months rather than in days. For example, February counts as one month even though it has less than 30 days. Do not count the day on which you bought the stamp but do count the day on which you sell the stamp.

This special capital gain and loss treatment is not available to anyone whose occupation, either entirely or partially, is buying and selling stamps.

If you are deemed a dealer in stamps, your investment is considered to be your inventory of merchandise and capital gain or loss treatment is not allowed.

This dealer classification, of course, means a tax at your higher ordinary income tax rate. Stamp investors have occasionally been charged with tax deficiencies when investigated by IRS agents only because they conducted their buying and selling of stamps in a manner which made them appear to be dealers.

Too much selling, too often, may indicate to the tax authorities that the person involved is a dealer rather than an investor. For example, if an individual purchased a stamp and immediately began advertising for sale or actively seeking a buyer, there is the distinct possibility that any gain on the sale of the stamp would be taxed as ordinary income irrespective of whether or not it was held over six months.

Several illustrations should make these special rules affecting stamp transactions clearer. Suppose you purchased a plate numbered block of six of the 65¢ U.S. Zeppelin issue (1930) in 1963 for $425 and sell it in 1982 for $2,000.

Also in January you purchased a collection of U.S. plate numbered blocks for $1,000, but four months later you sell the same collection for $965. If you have no other capital transactions during 1982, you would have a net LTCG of $1,540 which receives favorable tax treatment ($2,000 - $425) - ($1,000 - $965) = $1,540.

Consider another example. During 1982, you have the following transactions: LTCG of $600, LTCL of $6,900 and STCG of $200.

Since you have a net LTCL of $6,100, you may deduct the maximum $3,000 ($6,000 x 50¢) from your other income with a $100 LTCL carryover to 1983 ($2,100 - $2,000).

Warning: If in the first illustration you were classified as a dealer in stamps, the $1,540 gain would be treated as ordinary income.

Likewise, if in the second illustration you were a dealer, the $6,100 loss would be an ordinary loss fully deductible against ordinary income (i.e., with no limitations).

Obviously, an ordinary loss is better than a capital loss.

There are several simple suggestions which should help you reduce your income tax liability:

1. Hold, if possible, stamps that you sell at a gain for at least 12 months and one day so they may be classified as "long term."

2. Review your capital gain and loss position near the end of the 12 months holding period of each stamp. If you have a loss position, you may wish to sell and get a short-term capital loss rather than wait and end up with a long-term capital loss.

3. Near the end of your tax year, if you see that you are going to have a net LTCL position, you may wish to sell some stamps for a gain (preferably a STCG). By having some gains to offset against your LTCLs, you avoid throwing half of each $1 of LTCLs away.

4. Unless you are a dealer in stamps, do not make yourself look like a dealer by too frequent transactions.

5. Remember, a short-term capital gain is obviously superior to a long-term capital loss. You must not ignore nontax factors in your philatelic transactions.

## Tax Records

Keeping adequate tax records is very important whether you are a collector, investor or dealer. Many taxpayers fail to appreciate the importance of maintaining and retaining adequate tax records.

# STAMP INCOME GAIN (OR LOSS) RECORD

| Quantity | Country | Catalogue Number | Condition | Purchase Date Amount | Sale Date Amount |
|---|---|---|---|---|---|
|  |  |  |  |  |  |
|  |  |  |  |  |  |

The tax laws require all taxpayers to keep such records the IRS may prescribe and that the willful failure to comply therewith constitutes a misdemeanor. The penalty is a fine of not more than $10,000 or imprisonment for not more than one year, or both, together with the costs of prosecution.

A taxpayer must maintain records enabling him to file a tax return which clearly reflects his taxable income. To clearly reflect income, his income must be recorded with as much accuracy as standard methods of accounting permit. Cases are legion in which a decision went against a taxpayer either at the IRS level or in court because his records were inadequate.

Remember, in most situations the burden of proof is upon the taxpayer to show that any alleged deficiency is incorrect. That is, supporting records may be needed to prove the correctness of items of income or deductions when challenged by an IRS agent.

Suggestion: Set aside a particular drawer which can be used to accumulate applicable tax records such as invoices, etc., during the year.

Following is a suggested chart for recording your stamp gains or losses. The date and description of each purchase can be quite important. The most frequent question asked this author is what to do when a philatelist starts to sell his stamps, not knowing the basis of his stamps because he has no records.

Obviously, the IRS may take the extreme position that the individual's tax basis is the face value of the stamp.

For example, the agent can say that the basis of your line pair of 1938 U.S. 10¢ John Tyler coil stamps is 20¢, even though you may have paid $40 for them. You must be able to prove your basis is $40, and not 20¢.

Let us give an example. A junk peddler collected old auto batteries and resold them for their lead. He reported $4,200 in income, but the IRS claimed $77,870. This figure was based upon a survey of the peddler's sources, nearby service stations and auto-parts stores.

The tax court sided with the IRS because of the taxpayer's utter lack of records. "When the taxpayer has defaulted in his task of supplying adequate records," the tax court said, "he isn't in a position to be hypercritical of the IRS labor."

Keep in mind that under the tax law, a taxpayer is presumed to be guilty until he proves himself innocent (except in fraud cases). You must have records to show the IRS is wrong.

Where the same type of stamp is purchased at different times and you have no way of specific identification, the IRS may use the so-called "First-in, First-out" rule (FIFO). Under this rule the stamps sold are deemed to be the earliest stamps acquired.

Because of differences in holding periods and tax basis, a sale of a stamp may result in either a short-term or long-term gain or loss depending upon which stamps are considered sold first.

By maintaining adequate records, a stamp investor is able to control the type and amount of gain or loss to be recognized when he sells a portion of his position in a type of stamp.

How records should be maintained by a stamp investor is not specified in the law. Such records need not be elaborate or formal. The simplicity of our suggested records should encourage you to make the entries promptly as income items are received and payments for any deductible expenses are made.

Sales slips, bills, invoices, receipts, canceled checks, and other documents are often sufficient evidence to support deductions claimed on your income tax return. Dates of sales and purchases of stamps are very important because of the importance of the long-term and short-term classifications.

How long should records be kept? There is no precise answer to this question since retention period of records vary with the various state and federal statutes and with your future needs.

Copies of old income tax returns should be retained to facilitate the filing of amended returns, the calculation of income averaging and other tax basis problems.

Although copies of old tax returns can be obtained from the IRS for a nominal charge, this procedure can be costly in terms of time and interest charges. Supporting documents should be filed in an orderly manner and stored in a safe place.

The federal government's guide to record retention says, "Records should be retained so long as the contents thereof may become material in the administration of any Internal Revenue Law." Not much help!

At a minimum, the retention period is as long as the statute of limitations for further assessment is open to the particular taxpayer. The normal statute of limitations for federal income tax return expires three years after the tax return is due to be filed or two years from the time the tax was paid, whichever expires later.

That is, after this period expires the IRS can no longer assess additional taxes nor may the taxpayer file an amended return.

This normal three-year period is extended to six years where a taxpayer omits from his tax return an amount of gross income which exceeds 25 per cent of the amount so reported.

Further, in the case of a false return, a willful attempt to evade a tax, or the failure to file a tax return, there is no statute of limitation and the IRS can assess a tax or take a taxpayer to court at any time.

In summary, records should be maintained for at least four years at the minimum after the due date of the tax return or the date the tax is paid, whichever is later.

Due to the importance of the income averaging rule, records should probably be kept from six to ten years. In fact, as long as you keep a stamp, you should keep any applicable information concerning such stamp.

Many expenditures are incurred in maintaining a stamp investment. With proper planning and maintenance of adequate records, these expenses can be turned into valuable tax savings. Tax deductions are valuable. Each extra deduction is worth the same percentage of each dollar as your top tax bracket.

For example, if you fall within the 30 per cent tax bracket, an extra $1,000 of deductions is worth approximately $300 when you file your federal income tax return. You work extra hard to shave a dollar off the price of a stamp which you wish to buy. Yet, many of us forget to keep adequate records in order to claim our maximum legal deductions.

It is important that you keep accurate records of all expenditures relating to the preservation of your stamp investment, such as expenditures for record books, stockbooks, glassine envelopes, sales taxes, advertising expenses, interest expense, safe deposit box rental, postage, stationery, etc.

At the end of the year total these expenses and deduct them under the heading of "Other Deductions" on your income tax return (Form 1040).

Of course, these deductions are allowable only if you are an investor and you elect to "itemize" your deductions rather than claim either of the standard deductions.

That is, a taxpayer is allowed to deduct the larger of (1) itemized deductions, or (2) a standard deduction (zero bracket amount).

A taxpayer should attempt to shift expenses into the year which he itemizes deductions and then use the standard deductions in the year in which his itemized deductions are small in amount.

There are a number of deductions besides the aforementioned obvious ones that may be deductible. For example, accounting or legal advisory services and secretary's salary are deductible. Car fares to visit stamp dealers for consultation or to attend stamp shows are deductible.

Several other expenses may be deductible including home-office expenses, bad debt deductions, casualty losses and advertising expenses.

A caveat is appropriate at this point. Be cautious in claiming deductions which may be attributable to stamp collecting as a hobby rather than as an investment. If a deduction is questioned by an IRS agent, you will be required to prove its relationship to the preservation of your investment.

For example, if you take a vacation to Las Vegas and just happen to purchase several stamps, do not attempt to deduct your vacation expenses.

You may wish to use the following philatelic expense record to keep an accurate record of your deductible expenses. Remember, only deduct expenses that pertain to your stamps as an investment rather than as a hobby.

Most of the aforementioned information about expenses applies equally to dealers. However, a dealer is normally allowed to deduct these expenses as so-called "Deductions for Adjusted Gross Income."

That is, they may be deducted whether or not the dealer itemizes his other personal deductions. However, dealers must generally keep more records than nondealers.

Also, dealers normally have to report on the accrual basis of accounting. If, however, a dealer has no records of his expenses, he will not be allowed a deduction.

## Specialized Stamp Transactions

The stamp market has both "bull" and "bear" markets. But individuals may incur losses on stamp investments. For example, a sheet of a 1958 commemorative stamp from Okinawa, Ryukyu 54, cost 30¢ when issued. In 1971, it was still available for $1, but in 1973 the price shot up to $110, only to plunge to about $15.

There is a way, however, for a stamp investor to obtain losses and still retain similar stamps where he is confident that eventually these stamps will show substantial profits.

The investor may sell the loss stamps near the end of his tax year and obtain any deductible losses. However, keep in mind that an individual may deduct only up to $1,000 of capital losses in any one year.

The investor can take the proceeds from the sale of the stamps and invest in identical stamps. This technique is excellent when an investor has larger than normal taxable income in any tax year, but not large enough so that the income averaging rules apply.

He may immediately invest in similar stamps since the "wash sale" rule which applies to stocks and securities does not apply to stamps.

The "wash sale" rule states that a loss cannot be recognized on the sale of securities where similar securities are purchased within a time period of 30 days before or 30 days after the loss sale.

In this respect, the tax laws favor the sale of stamps rather than the sale of securities. However, keep in mind the major disadvantage of investing in valuable stamps: An investor must often sell his stamps to a dealer at wholesale prices, but may have to pay a higher retail price.

An investor should compute the net advantage or disadvantage: the difference between the value of the losses to him and the transaction cost of selling and buying similar stamps.

The best alternative may be to sell the stamps during the latter part of the year at a stamp auction and buy back similar stamps in the next year at a stamp auction.

In effect, the investor sells somewhere between the retail-wholesale level and buys back near the same price level. But the seller does have auction commissions that may be quite high.

Loss stamps may not be sold to related individuals in order to realize losses and at the same time retain effective control over the stamps.

Tax law prohibits the deduction of losses from the sale or exchange of property between related persons. Related persons include members of a family, brothers, sisters, spouse, ancestors, and lineal descendants. However, any gain recognized on the sale of stamps among related parties will be taxable.

An investor may realize capital gains even during a bear market by selling "short." Here is how this technique works. The investor must find a well-established stamp dealer who retains in his possession stamps for his customers.

The dealer "borrows" these stamps and sells them for the investor to someone else. The dealer may or may not actually deliver the stamps to the buyer (but there is an actual sale).

The investor hopes that the value of the stamps decreases so that he can buy replacement stamps at a lower value, but if the stamps increase in value he loses.

Any difference between the selling price on the short sale and the cost of the stamps later purchased will represent the gain or loss. Naturally, the dealer makes a commission whether the investor wins or loses.

A short sale is much more risky than a long sale (the normal transaction). For example, a stamp selling for $7 today has a tremendous potential gain since the market price can rise 200 per cent, 300 per cent or more, and the stamp cannot fall below about 80 per cent of face value.

Due to this risk, an investor may wish to protect himself against a large rise in the stamps by using a stop-buy order. He should arrange with his dealer to immediately buy him some replacement stamps at a certain price in case the price rises rather than falls.

## Wall Street Techniques

Two Wall Street techniques can be effectively applied to the rare stamp market. One such technique is dollar averaging.

Under dollar averaging, you invest the same amount of money in rare stamps at regular intervals — usually monthly, quarterly, or semiannually.

For example, you may decide to buy $100 worth of stamps per month. Of course, under dollar averaging you buy more stamps for the same number of dollars when their prices are low than when their prices are high.

Thus, you get more stamps when the prices are lower and if the price of the stamps does rise you now have a much larger profit. But dollar averaging does cause you to lose a chance to buy at low prices for big gains.

For example, near the end of 1980 you invested $320 in eight mint 10¢ special delivery E-4, selling for $40 each. In the middle of 1982, when this same stamp was selling for $80, you invest $320 more for four more stamps.

So over the two-year period, you invest $640 and now own 12 specimens. If the special deliveries do go up in the long run, you are better off investing $320 at $40 and $320 at $80 than you would have been by investing $640 at $60 (the middle ground between $40 and $80).

If you purchase $640 of special deliveries at the mid-price of $60, you have only about 10.7 stamps; whereas, by dollar averaging you now own 12.

Of course, you must not ignore all other factors. You and your investment advisor still need to select types of rare stamps that are moving upward. But for dollar averaging you need to select stamps which have some volatility. Also, if the stamps are in a long-term downtrend, do not buy them.

Still another stock market technique can be used where a stamp investor already has a significant sum invested in stamps and would prefer not to commit any further significant capital to this form of investment.

Eric S. Emory in his book "When To Sell Stock" (Dow-Jones-Irwin, Inc., Homewood, Ill. 60430, $7.95) has suggested a "dollar-value" theory for investments in the stock market. This technique can work with philatelic investments.

Assume you have some good, sound philatelic investments — not necessarily the best investments. Select a certain time period each year (or each quarter, etc.) and review your stamp investments and calculate their total value, possibly with the use of the current dealer buy prices.

If the total value of your stamp investments has increased from your last review, sell enough stamps to take out the net gain.

For example, if your total rare stamp investment has increased by $300, sell stamps with a total value of $300 (or as close as possible).

You may wish to dispose of some loss stamps at this time, but the proceeds from the sale should be placed into a reserve for future stamp investments.

On the other hand, if your stamp portfolio has decreased in value, reinvest the reserve to the extent of the decline. You, of course, may wish to invest additional funds.

Emory indicates that this technique has two major advantages. First, you grab any profit and remove funds from further risk when stamp prices are high in relationship to your original investment.

Second, you reinvest from your reserve funds when stamp prices are low relative to your original cost.

Though little research has been done in this field, interest rates obviously play an important role in the success of the stamp investment.

Low interest rates tend to increase the stamp investment activity; likewise high interest rates tend to decrease the investment activity.

This may not be the case in all instances but certain stamps do decrease in value during certain periods of time. Thus, the stamp investor should diversify; he should not put all of his eggs in one basket.

He should diversify both horizontally and vertically. By diversifying horizontally, we are referring to purchasing different stamps (e.g., early commemoratives, airmails, regular issues, etc.). Diversifying vertically refers to investing in different types of investments (e.g., plate blocks, covers and singles from several countries, etc.).

Investment in one or two stamps increases the chance that unforeseen events can reduce your profit (e.g., the collapse of the stamps from Ryukyus).

## Selling Versus Trading

High income tax rates have made it almost a daily occurrence for most real estate brokers to advise their customers to trade their real estate holdings for properties which they wish to acquire, rather than to sell what they have and then buy for cash.

Trading one investment property for another of like kind property involves no gain for income tax purposes.

Trading rather than selling stamps can result in a definite tax advantage. Trading can easily be accomplished by joining an exchange service or exchanging stamps with fellow investors in stamp clubs.

However, eventually the IRS will collect the taxes (unless the investor dies before he sells the stamps in which case the heirs obtain a stepped-up basis).

When he finally decides to sell rather than trade, any gain for income tax purposes depends upon what he paid for the first item traded. The basis in each stamp is transferred to the items for which it is traded.

Trading allows an individual to postpone the tax burden to a later date. This delay may bring important advantages. A trade can forestall the expense of the tax until a time when the individual is in a better position to bear it, or until he is in a lower overall tax bracket.

Remember, any tax liability which he is able to postpone increases his cash flow, and he can earn interest or other investment income on this postponed tax (e.g., invest in more stamps, stock, etc.). Think of a postponement of your tax liability as an interest-free loan from the federal government.

Stamps that have decreased in value below an investor's tax basis should not be traded. If he trades loss stamps, any potential deductible loss is postponed for tax purposes just as any gain would be postponed.

The best tax strategy for loss stamps is to sell the stamps so that the losses are immediately deductible. The investor may use the proceeds from the sale of his loss stamps to purchase the stamps which he wanted to obtain with the trade.

## Investment Clubs

Stamp investment clubs may be one way for a group of investors and collectors to make the most from future rises in the stamp market.

The theory behind a stamp investing club is that a group of individuals agree to make periodic payment to a club to be used to purchase selected philatelic items.

The investment club can buy stamps in volume and should be able to buy closer to wholesale rather than retail. A club can maintain a larger philatelic library and subscribe to investors' newsletters, and could afford a professional administrator or advisor to guide the functioning of the club.

It would be quite beneficial if a dealer is elected the president of the club. A dealer may be able to obtain reduced insurance rates and offer reduced storage costs for the club's stamp investments.

Most important, the dealer may be able to buy stamps at or near wholesale rates. Likewise, there may be a saving on state sales taxes.

In most states, there is no sales tax on sales between two dealers, whereas there is a sales tax on sales between a dealer and a nondealer.

Besides, a dealer is constantly associated with the stamp market, and he will know when to buy and when to sell stamp investments for the maximum profit.

It is imperative that such clubs maintain adequate records of each purchase and each sale with cross-reference to retained sales tickets. These investment clubs are usually treated as partnerships — unless the club elects not to be treated as such.

If no special election is made by the club, any income is allocated among the club members in proportion to their partnership interest (e.g., their holdings).

The investment club files a partnership tax return on Form 1065. The club members then report their fractional share in their individual tax return for the same year, getting the applicable numbers for their Form 1040 from the partnership Form 1065.

Recently, the IRS indicated that a partner may deduct the partnership expense only as deductions from adjusted gross income. In effect, if a partner does not itemize his deductions (i.e., he uses a standard deduction), he is unable to deduct the partnership expenses.

The members must report the income even though they may let it stay in the club. Obviously, when this prior taxed income is finally distributed in a future year, the club member will not be taxed on this income again.

Under this partnership form of organization, any capital gain at the partnership level flows through to the partners as capital gain.

Similarly, any ordinary income at the partnership level will pass through as ordinary income to the partners. Where a club member sells his share of the partnership to another individual, he will recognize a capital gain or loss, depending upon his basis in the club and the amount of the sales price.

Stamp investment clubs may elect not to be treated as a partnership for tax purposes. In order to make this optional election, the investment club must be for investment purposes only, and the club members must be able to compute their individual income without the necessity of computing partnership taxable income.

This optional election is advantageous where the percentage interest of each club member in the purchased stamps does not change (e.g., where there are 20 members and each owns 5 per cent). However, record-keeping problems make this election impracticable where percentages change each month, old members drop out, and new members join the club.

With a large and active investing club, a partnership return will be necessary and an accountant will likely be required to prepare it.

The club must avoid being or acting like a corporation. If the IRS can classify the club as an association, there will be an onerous double tax — one tax at the club level and another tax when distributions are made to the individual members.

Stamp collecting, investing and dealing can be fun, but taxation is serious business. With double-digit inflation we are constantly pushed into higher tax brackets.

Each of us must be conscious of taxation in our day-to-day activities. With the various government levels as our one-third partner (who assumes no risk), we must take all available steps to reduce our overall tax burden.

More information for collectors may be found in *Donate Less To The IRS* ($7.95, Information Services, Box 9027, College Station, Tex. 77840).

## PHILATELIC EXPENSE RECORD

| Date | Expense | Comment |
| --- | --- | --- |
|  |  |  |
|  |  |  |
|  |  |  |
|  |  |  |
|  |  |  |

# United Nations Postal Administration

**20**

# Role in Philately

The idea of establishing a United Nations Postal Administration originally came from Dr. Jose Arce, president of the Argentine Delegation to the U.N. in 1947. It was he who placed before the General Assembly, on Aug. 28, 1947, a draft resolution which eventually led to the signing of an agreement between the United Nations and the United States Post Office Department on March 28, 1951.

The first United Nations postage stamps went on sale later that year, on United Nations Day, Oct. 24, 1951. All were in the definitive and airmail series. There were fifteen denominations of eight different designs. Eleven were definitives of 1¢, 1½¢, 2¢, 3¢, 5¢, 10¢, 15¢, 20¢, 25¢, 50¢, and $1. The other four stamps were airmail issues of 6¢, 10¢, 15¢ and 25¢.

In 1952 the first commemorative issues were released and it has been UNPA's practice ever since to issue an average of five commemorative stamps each year.

By 1968, the success of UNPA, New York, was encouraging enough to make it worthwhile to negotiate an agreement with the Swiss Government for the issue and sale of United Nations stamps in Swiss denominations. After a number of meetings with the Swiss PTT, an agreement was finally signed, making UNPA Geneva a post office in its own right, where the new Swiss-denomination stamps went on sale on Oct. 4, 1969, eight definitives in all. It was not until 1971 that commemoratives were issued in Swiss currency.

In 1979, a treaty was signed between the United Nations and the Government of Austria, permitting the issue and sale of United Nations stamps in Austrian currency. Six definitives were issued on Aug. 24.

The New York, Geneva and Vienna offices offer similar services to United Nations collectors, filling orders for mint stamps and first day covers, providing facilities for bulk mailings and operating Customer Deposit Services whereby accounts may be opened and orders are filled automatically for each new issue. The Customer Deposit Service was instituted in New York in 1961; in Geneva, the first accounts were opened in 1969; in Vienna, the service began in 1980.

The U.N. Postal Administration today sells its stamps, at face value and in local currency, to collectors in more than 100 countries. Originally, U.N. stamps were sold in a small way through a few United Nations offices to U.N. staff members only, in Geneva, Paris and Rome. In July 1961, the UNPA drew up its first agreement to sell stamps overseas, through the Crown Agents in London. In the ensuing years, agreements have been signed in one country after another until today when the stamps are available to collectors in most member nations.

The UNPA was not founded for the purpose of acquiring added revenue. The main function of United Nations stamps is to tell people everywhere about the work, objectives and achievements of the United Nations and its affiliated agencies. The themes of the stamps are international, on subjects such as peace-keeping, food production and agriculture, education, child welfare, human rights, the peaceful uses of outer space and atomic energy, science and technology, various aspects of technical assistance, community development and economic progress.

The stamps are issued in denominations which are necessary for postal needs and the cost is kept within the reach of the smallest collector.

Since 1951, more than a billion stamps and over 25 million pieces of postal stationery have been printed for the United Nations — by firms in Austria, Canada, Czechoslovakia, Finland, Federal Republic of Germany, Japan, The Netherlands, Spain, Switzerland, Turkey, United Kingdom and United States.

The stamps are designed by artists from a panel of nearly 800 professional designers in more than 30 countries, who participate in a world competition for each issue.

Airmail and definitive stamps must be issued when rates change and reprinted whenever stocks run low. Commemorative stamps, issued for special United Nations events, anniversaries or specialized agencies — but never for individual people — are printed only in limited quantities, kept on sale for 12 months unless they sell out beforehand and are never reprinted.

The revenue from philatelic sales is credited to the United Nations annual budget and reduces proportionately the yearly contribution of each member state. The proceeds from stamps sold for postage are another matter altogether.

The United States Postal Service operates the United Nations post office station in New York (the Swiss PTT and the Austrian PTT do likewise in Geneva and Vienna, respectively) and handles all the mail entering and leaving the building, thus receiving the revenue from all stamps used for postage.

Everyone who buys United Nations stamps, either for use on mail or to add to a collection, makes an individual contribution towards the international, humanitarian work of the United Nations.

The stamps tell in miniature the story of the United Nations, promoting a better understanding of the world's problems and of the United Nations' role in helping to cope with them.

The work of the United Nations Postal Administration has been devoted entirely to keeping the world up-to-date about the United Nations and to bringing people of every nationality closer together through a common bond of philately.

Dr. Arce envisaged all of this when he said, more than 20 years ago: "It may be that . . . this simple scheme for making the name and the purposes of the organization known throughout the world may prompt the Nations . . . to unfurl their flags, in a spirit of brotherhood, next to the blue emblem of the United Nations."

## Postal Agreement Between the U.S. and U.N.

"Agreement made this 28th day of March, 1951, between the United States of America and the United Nations.

"Whereas, a certain Agreement between the United States of America and the United Nations, dated the 26th day of June, 1947, regarding the Headquarters of the United Nations (said agreement being hereinafter referred to as the 'Headquarters Agreement') provides that in the event that the United Nations should propose to organize its own postal service, the conditions under which such service shall be set up shall be subject to a Supplemental Agreement; and

"Whereas, the United Nations desires to establish a postal service in conformity with the Headquarters Agreement,

"Now therefore, the parties hereto agree as follows:

"1. Scope of Agreement:

"(i) Subject to the provisions of this Agreement, there shall be established a United Nations Post Office Station in the Headquarters District of the United Nations, as defined in the Headquarters Agreement, which shall be operated by the United States Post Office Department.

"(ii) The United Nations Post Office Station shall provide at the prevailing rates all the services offered by any United States Post Office having comparable operations, except that the United Nations Post Office Station shall use only United Nations postage stamps.

"2. Supply of United Nations postage stamps and stamped paper:

"(i) The United Nations shall at its own expense furnish all United Nations postage stamps required under the terms of this Agreement.

"(ii) In the event that the United Nations shall produce or authorize production of stamped envelopes and post cards, such envelopes or post cards shall conform to the specifications of the United States Post Office Department as to size and as to quality of paper used.

"(iii) No United Nations postage stamps shall be distributed except in accordance with the terms of this Agreement.

"3. Sale of United Nations Postage Stamps:

"(i) The United Nations Post Office Station shall sell only United Nations postage stamps which shall be provided by the United Nations free of charge in such quantities as may be necessary to fulfill all reasonable needs of the United Nations Post Office Station.

"All revenue derived from such sales of United Nations postage stamps and from other services rendered by the United Nations Post Office Station shall be retained by the United States Post Office Department as full and complete compensation for performance of its obligations under the terms of this Agreement, except, however, that the United States Post Office Department shall be reimbursed for performance of any postal services resulting from use of United Nations postage stamps sold for philatelic purposes under the provisions of sub-section (ii) of this section which are used as postage on mail matter posted at the United Nations Post Office Station by being paid an amount equal to the face value of any such stamps so used as postage.

"(ii) The United Nations may maintain a separate agency for the sale of United Nations postage stamps for philatelic purposes in response to orders received by mail. Subject to the provisions of sub-section (i) of this section, all revenue derived from such philatelic sales of United Nations postage stamps shall be retained by the United Nations for its own use.

"4. United Nations postmarks:

"The United Nations shall furnish all postmarking stamps to be applied to mail posted for mailing in the Headquarters District and shall furnish all such postmarking stamps to the United Nations Post Office Station free of charge. All postmarks shall be designated as United Nations postmarks.

"5. United Nations Post Office Station Premises:

"The United Nations shall provide the United States Post Office Department at the expense of the United Nations with quarters, custodial services and utilities necessary to enable the United States Post Office Department to operate the United Nations Post Office Station in the Headquarters District.

"6. Staff and Equipment:

"Except as otherwise provided in this Agreement, the United States Post Office Department will provide at its own expense all staff, equipment and other services and facilities necessary to enable the United States Post Office Department to operate the United Nations Post Office Station under the terms of this Agreement.

"7. Postal Address of the United Nations:

"The postal address of the Headquarters District of the United Nations shall be 'United Nations, New York.'

"8. Duration of the Agreement:

"(i) This Agreement shall take effect on a date to be agreed upon between the United Nations and the United States Post Office Department.

"(ii) This Agreement shall be subject to revision, on the written proposal of either contracting party, after one year from the date of commencement of operations.

"(iii) This Agreement may be terminated by either party giving the other written notice of its intention to terminate such Agreement at least twelve (12) months in advance of the termination date fixed in such notice.

"IN WITNESS WHEREOF the respective representatives have signed this Agreement and have affixed their seals hereto.

"Done in duplicate this 28th day of March, 1951."

The agreement was signed for the Government of the United States of America by the president, and for the United Nations by the secretary-general. In 1968, a similar agreement was signed with the Swiss government. In 1979, a treaty was signed between the United Nations and the Government of Austria.

## U.N. Stamp Designers

Designers of U.N. postage stamps, souvenir cards and postal stationery include the following: The designer's name, country, the stamp's subject, year of issue, denomination and printer, appear in that order. If the designer is responsible for designs of more than one stamp, each additional subject and related information also is given.

**Andrzejewski, Waldemar — Poland** — To Unite Our Strength, 1976, 3 cents, Ashton-Potter Ltd., Canada. Definitive, 1980, 2.50 schilling (adaptation of 1976 3¢ definitive), Bundesdruckerei, Federal Republic of Germany.

**Auchli, Herbert — Switzerland** — Global Eradication of Smallpox, 1978, 13¢, 31¢, H. Courvoisier, S.A., Switzerland.

**Baeten, L. — Belgium** — Postal card, 70 centimes (United States equivalent: 27¢), 1977, S. Setelipaino, Finland.

**Bencsath, Henry — U.S.A.** — U.N. Emblem, 1974, 18¢, H. Fournier, S.A., Spain; United Nations Temporary Executive Authority, 1963, 25¢, H. Courvoisier, S.A., Switzerland; Inter-Governmental Maritime Consultative Organization, 1964, 5¢, 11¢, H. Courvoisier, S.A., Switzerland; International Labour Office Headquarters, Geneva, Switzerland, 1974, 10¢, 21¢, H. Fournier, S.A., Spain; World Population Year, 1974, 10¢, 18¢, H. Fournier, S.A., Spain; Peaceful Uses of Outer Space, 1975, 10¢, 26¢, S. Setelipaino, Finland; Namibia, 1975, 10¢, 18¢, H. Fournier, S.A., Spain; United Nations Conference On Trade And Development, 1976, 13¢, 31¢, H. Courvoisier, S.A., Switzerland; 25th Anniversary of United Nations Postal Administration, 1976, 13¢, 31¢, H. Courvoisier, S.A., Switzerland.

Swiss values: International Labour Office Headquarters, Geneva, Switzerland, 1974, 60 centimes, 80c, H. Fournier, S.A., Spain; World Population Year, 1974, 60c, 80c, H. Fournier, S.A., Spain; Peaceful Uses of Outer Space, 1975, 60c, 90c, S. Setelipaino, Finland; Namibia, 1975, 50c, 1.30 francs, H. Fournier, S.A., Spain; United Nations Conference On Trade and Development, 1976, 1.10fr, H. Courvoisier, S.A., Switzerland. General Assembly, 1978, 70c, 1.10fr, Government Printing Bureau, Japan.

**Bottiau, Claude — France** — Outer Space, 1963, 6¢, H. Courvoisier, S.A., Switzerland; United Nations Day, 1955, 3¢, 4¢, 8¢ and 15¢, also souvenir sheet, Waterlow & Sons, England.

Postal stationery: Outer Space (like 6¢ airmail stamp of 1963), 1963, 6¢, Eureka Specialty Printing Company, Scranton, Pa.

**Calivis, Edmondo — Egypt —** Postal stationery: Air Flight Across the World, 1972, 15¢, J. Enschede en Zonen, Netherlands.

**Callari, Rocco — U.S.A. —** Souvenir cards: Economic and Social Council, 1980, $1, Ashton-Potter Ltd., Canada; New and Renewable Sources of Energy, 1981, $1, S. Setelipaino, Finland.

**Carlson, Roy — U.S.A., with Karlsson, Hordur — Iceland —** International Monetary Fund, 1961, 4¢, 7¢, Government Printing Bureau, Japan.

**Chylinski, Henryk — Poland —** Donaupark, Wien, 1979, 4s, H. Courvoisier, S.A., Switzerland.

**Courvoisier, H., S.A. — Switzerland; Hamann, O. — Denmark, and Mathiesen, O. S. — Denmark —** 25th Anniversary Peace and Progress, also souvenir sheet, 1970, 6¢, 13¢, 25¢ and 44¢, H. Courvoisier, S.A., Switzerland.

**Courvoisier, H., S.A. — Switzerland —** U.N. Volunteers Programme, 1973, 8¢, 21¢, 80c, H. Fournier, S.A., Spain.

**Crombez, V. — Belgium —** Postal card, 40c (United States equivalent: 16¢), 1977, S. Setelipaino, Finland.

**Dewhurst, David — U.S.A. —** International Tourist Year, 1967, 5¢, 15¢, Bundesdruckerei, Berlin. Inalienable Rights of the Palestinian People, 1981, 15¢, 80c, 4s, H. Courvoisier, S.A., Switzerland.

Souvenir cards: World Population Year, 1974, $1, H. Fournier, S.A., Spain; United Nations Decade for Women, 1980, $1, Questa Colour Security Printers Ltd., United Kingdom; International Court of Justice, 1979, $1, S. Setelipaino, Finland.

**Din, Rashid-ud — Pakistan —** U.N. Emblem, 1965, 25¢, Bundesdruckerei, Berlin; Human Rights Day, 1956, 3¢, 8¢, Thomas De La Rue, England; United Nations Day, 1957, 3¢, 8¢, Thomas De La Rue, England; The World United Against Malaria, 1962, 4¢, 11¢, Harrison and Sons Ltd., England; Development through Science and Technology, 1963, 5¢, 11¢, H. Courvoisier, S.A., Switzerland; 15th Anniversary of the Declaration of Human Rights, 1963, 5¢, 11¢, Government Printing Bureau, Japan; United Nations Special Fund, 1965, 5¢, 11¢, Government Printing Bureau, Japan; World Health Organization, 1966, 5¢, 11¢, H. Courvoisier, S.A., Switzerland; Coffee Agreement, 1966, 5¢, 11¢, Government Printing Bureau, Japan; Independence, 1967, 5¢, 11¢, Harrison and Sons Ltd., England; Secretariat, 1968, 5¢, 13¢, H. Courvoisier, S.A., Switzerland; adaptation of 25c reg. (Sept. 20, 1965), 1969, 1fr, Bundesdruckerei, Berlin.

**Doeve, J. F. — Netherlands —** Peace, Justice, Security, 1951, 2¢, J. Enschede en Zonen, Netherlands; Peace, Justice, Security, modification of $1 reg. 1951, 10fr, S. Setelipaino, Finland.

**Dolan, Lyell — Australia —** Symbol of Flight, 1972, 9¢, Government Printing Bureau, Japan.

Postal stationery: Symbol of Flight (like 9¢ airmail stamp of 1972), 1972, 9¢, Government Printing Bureau, Japan.

**Dreyer, Ulrike — Federal Republic of Germany —** New and Renewable Sources of Energy, 1981, 20¢, 1.10fr, S. Setelipaino, Finland.

**El Mekki, Hatim — Tunisia —** Elongated Globe, 1964, 50¢, H. Courvoisier, S.A., Switzerland; Elongated Globe, (modification of 50c reg. 1964), 1970, 2fr, S. Setelipaino, Finland.

Postal stationery: Elongated Globe (like 50¢ definitive stamp of 1964), 1963, 5¢, United States Envelope Company, New York; modification of the 50¢ stamp, 1969, 6¢, S. Setelipaino, Finland.

**Fanais, George — Canada, with Gundersen, George A. — Canada** (of British American Bank Note Co., Ltd., Canada) **—** World Weather Watch, 1968, 6¢, 20¢, Government Printing Bureau, Japan.

**Ferrini, Renato — Italy —** Hands and Globe, 1962, 5¢, Canadian Bank Note Company, Canada; Hands and Globe (modified for reissue), 1967, 5¢, H. Courvoisier, S.A., Switzerland.

**Freudenreich, M. — Poland, with Holdanowicz, L. — Poland —** United Nations, 1969, 13¢, Government Printing Bureau, Japan; United Nations (modification of 13c reg. 1969), 1970, 70c, S. Setelipaino, Finland.

**Fricke, Alrun — Federal Republic of Germany —** Faith in Fundamental Human Rights, 1979, 14¢, H. Fournier S.A., Spain.

**Gardiner, James — United Kingdom —** United Nations Peacekeeping Operations, 1980, 31¢, 6s, Joh. Enschede en Zonen, Netherlands.

**Glaser, Arieh — Israel —** International Year of the Child, 1979, 80c, 1.10fr, H. Fournier, S.A., Spain.

**Gonzague, Daniel — France, with Hamann, Ole — Denmark —** Eliminate Racial Discrimination, 1971, 8¢, 13¢, 30c, 50c, Government Printing Bureau, Japan.

**Guerra, Alfredo — U.S.A. —** 25th Anniversary Declaration of Human Rights, 1973, 8¢, 21¢, 40c, 80c, Government Printing Bureau, Japan.

**Gundersen, George — Canada, with Fanais, G. — Canada** (of British American Bank Note Co., Ltd., Canada) **—** World Weather Watch, 1968, 6¢, 20¢, Government Printing Bureau, Japan.

**Gur, Nejut — Turkey —** Dove, 1974, 2¢, H. Fournier, S.A., Spain; Labour and Development, 1969, 6¢, 10¢, Government Printing Bureau, Japan.

**Hahn, Young Sun — Republic of Korea —** Peace, Justice and Security, 1979, 20¢, H. Fournier, S.A., Spain.

**Hamann, Ole — Denmark —** To Maintain Peace and Security, 1964, 2¢, Thomas De La

Rue, England; U.N. Flag (in breeze), 1962, 3¢, Harrison and Sons Ltd., England; U.N. Flag, 1951, 3¢, 15¢, 25¢, Thomas De La Rue, England; U.N. Emblem, 1966, $1, H. Courvoisier, S.A., Switzerland; Plane and Gull, 1951, 6¢, 10¢, Thomas De La Rue, England; Globe and Wings, 1964, 15¢, Government Printing Office, Austria; Aircraft and U.N. Seal, 1968, 20¢, S. Setelipaino, Finland; United Nations Emergency Force, 1957, 3¢, 8¢, Thomas De La Rue, England; United Nations Day, 1958, 4¢, 8¢, American Bank Note Co., U.S.A.; Economic Commission for Europe, 1959, 4¢, 8¢, Canadian Bank Note Co., Canada; Fifth World Forestry Congress, 1960, 4¢, 8¢, Government Printing Bureau, Japan; Memorial stamp, 1962, 5¢, 15¢, H. Courvoisier, S.A., Switzerland; Freedom from Hunger, 1963, 5¢, 11¢, H. Courvoisier, S.A., Switzerland; Cessation of Nuclear Testing, 1964, 5¢, State Printing Office, Czechoslovakia; Peace-Keeping — United Nations Observers, 1966, 15¢, H. Courvoisier, S.A., Switzerland; Towards Disarmament, 1967, 6¢, 13¢, H. Fournier, S.A., Spain; United Nations Industrial Development Organization, 1968, 6¢, 13¢, Canadian Bank Note Co., Ltd., Canada; Building Series ECLA, 1969, 6¢, 15¢, Bundesdruckerei, Berlin (adapted by photo); Art series — Peace Bell, 1970, 6¢, 25¢, Government Printing Bureau, Japan; Lower Mekong Basin Development, 1970, 6¢, 13¢, H. Fournier, S.A., Spain; Peace, Justice and Progress, 1970, 6¢, 13¢, Government Printing Bureau, Japan; United Nations International School, 1971, 8¢, 21¢, 1.10fr, H. Courvoisier, S. A., Switzerland (adapted for reproduction from work of P. Picasso); adaptation of 3c reg. (May 25, 1962), 1969, 10c, H. Courvoisier, S.A., Switzerland; Palais des Nations, 1969, 30c, H. Courvoisier, S.A., Switzerland; Geneva Headquarters, 1972, 40c, H. Courvoisier, S.A., Switzerland; adaptation of 15c airmail (May 1, 1964), 1969, 75c, Government Printing Office, Austria; Brazilian Peace Mural, 1974, 60c, 1fr, H. Fournier, S.A., Spain, adapted for reproduction from work of C. Portinari; with Courvoisier, H., S.A., Switzerland and Mathiesen, O. S., Denmark — 25th Anniversary Peace and Progress, also souvenir sheet, 1970, 6¢, 13¢, 25¢ and 44¢, H. Courvoisier, S.A., Switzerland; with Gonzague, D. France — Eliminate Racial Discrimination, 1971, 8¢, 13¢, Government Printing Bureau, Japan; Eliminate Racial Discrimination, 1971, 30c, 50c, Government Printing Bureau, Japan. U.N Flag in Breeze, 1979, 1s, H. Courvoisier, S.A., Switzerland. 35th Anniversary of the United Nations, 1980, 46¢, 1.10fr, 10s souvenir sheets, Ashton-Potter Ltd., Canada; Flag series 1980, 16 flags at 15¢ each, H. Courvoisier, S.A., Switzerland; Art Series "Fresco," 1981, 20¢, 31¢, 80c, 6s (adapted for reproduction from work of unknown artist), H. Courvoisier, S.A., Switzerland; Flag series 1981, 16 flags at 20¢ each, H. Courvoisier, S.A., Switzerland.

Souvenir card: International Year of the Child, 1979 $1, H. Fournier, S.A., Spain.

Postal stationery: To maintain Peace and Security (like 2¢ definitive stamp of 1964), 1963, 4¢, Eureka Specialty Printing Company, Scranton, Pa.; Plane and Gull (like 10¢ airmail stamp of 1951), 1961, 11¢, Thomas De La Rue, England.

**Hamori, George — Australia** — Growing Plant, 1964, 7¢, H. Courvoisier, S.A., Switzerland; Unity of the World, 1964, 10¢, H. Courvoisier, S.A., Switzerland; U.N. Flag, 1976, 30¢, Ashton-Potter, Ltd., Canada; Triangular Shapes, 1963, 8¢, H. Courvoisier, S.A., Switzerland; Aircraft with multicolored jet stream, 1974, 13¢, S. Setelipaino, Finland; Aircraft and airmail envelope, 1964, 25¢, Government Printing Office, Austria; United Nations Educational, Scientific and Cultural Organization, 1955, 3¢, 8¢, Waterlow & Sons, England; United Nations Operation in the Congo, 1962, 4¢, 11¢, Bradbury, Wilkinson & Co., England; Peace-Keeping Force in Cyprus, 1965, 5¢, 11¢, H. Courvoisier, S.A., Switzerland; World Health Day, 1972, 15¢, 80c, S. Setelipaino, Finland; Stop Drug Abuse, 1973, 8¢, 15¢, 60c, H. Fournier, S.A., Spain; Namibia, 1973, 8¢, 15¢, 60c, H. Fournier, S.A., Spain; World Federation of United Nations Associations, 1976, 13¢, 26¢, 90c, H. Fournier, S.A., Spain; adaptation of 10c reg. (May 29, 1964), 1969, 20c, H. Courvoisier, S.A., Switzerland; United Nations Security Council, 1977, 80c and 1.10fr, Heraclio Fournier, S.A., Spain. New International Economic Order, 1980, 31¢, 80c, Questa Colour Security Printers Ltd., United Kingdom.

Postal stationery: Triangular Shapes (like 8¢ airmail stamp of 1963), 1963, 8¢, United States Envelope Company, New York; modification of the 8¢ airmail stamp, 1969, 10c, S. Setelipaino, Finland; (like 13¢ airmail stamp of 1974), 1975, 13¢, United States Envelope Company, U.S.A.; 9¢ card, 1977, S. Setelipaino, Finland.

**Hartz, S. L. — Netherlands** — UNICEF, 1951, 5¢, J. Enschede en Zonen, Netherlands.

**Helguera, Leon — Mexico** — Headquarters Building, New York, 1951, 1½¢, 50¢, J. Enschede en Zonen, Netherlands; Human Rights Day, 1953, 3¢, 5¢, Thomas De La Rue, England; United Nations Day, 1959, 4¢, 8¢, Canadian Bank Note Co., Canada.

Postal stationery: Headquarters Building New York (like 1½¢ or 50¢ definitive stamps of 1951), 1952, 2¢, Dennison & Sons, New York; Headquarters Building New York (like 1½¢ or 50¢ definitive stamps of 1951), 1958, 3¢, British American Bank Note Co., Ltd., Canada.

**Hioki, M. — Japan** — Live Together in Peace, 1978, 35c, Questa Colour Security Printers, England. Same design adapted 1979, 50 groschen, H. Courvoisier, S.A., Switzerland.

**Hisano, Minori — Japan** — United Nations Children's Fund, 1961, 3¢, 4¢, 13¢, H. Courvoisier, S.A., Switzerland.

**Holdanowicz, L. — Poland, with Freudenreich, M. — Poland** — United Nations, 1969, 13¢, Government Printing Bureau, Japan; U.N. modification of 13c reg. 1969, 1970, 70c, S. Setelipaino, Finland.

**Janowski, W. and Freudenreich, M. — Poland** — United Nations Security Council, 1977, 13¢, 31¢, Heraclio Fournier, S.A., Spain.

**Janssen, Gunnar — Federal Republic of Germany** — United Nations Decade for Women, 1980, 4s, 6s, Questa Colour Security Printers Ltd., United Kingdom.

**Johnson, Arne — Norway** — Birds in Flight, 1972, 11¢, H. Fournier, S.A., Spain; Non-Proliferation, 1972, 8¢, 40c, H. Fournier, S.A., Spain; Universal Postal Union, 1974, 10¢, 30c, 60c, Ashton-Potter Ltd., Canada; People of all Races, 1976, 4¢, Ashton-Potter, Ltd., Canada; Birds in Flight, 1979, 5s, H. Courvoisier, S.A., Switzerland.

Postal stationery: Birds in Flight (like 11¢ airmail stamp of 1972), 1973, 11¢, Eureka-Carlisle Co., Scranton, Pa.

**Kalderon, Asher — Israel** — Multicolored jet stream, 1972, 21¢, S. Setelipaino, Finland; Law of the Sea, 1974, 10¢, 26¢, 1.30fr, H. Fournier, S.A., Spain; with Esther Kurti, Israel, International Women's Year, 1975, 10¢, 18¢, 60c, 90c, Questa Colour Security Printers, England; with O. S. Mathiesen, Denmark, United Nations 30th Anniversary, also souvenir sheet, 1975, 10¢, 26¢ and 36¢, Ashton-Potter Ltd., Canada; United Nations 30th Anniversary, also souvenir sheet, 1975, 60c, 90c and 1.50fr, Ashton-Potter Ltd., Canada.

Postal stationery: United Nations, 1973, 6¢, Government Printing Office, Japan; (like 6¢ postal card 1973 — new background color), 1975, 8¢, S. Setelipaino, Finland.

**Kanidinc, Salahattin — U.S.A.** — Definitive, 1978, 1¢, Questa Colour Security Printers Ltd., United Kingdom.

**Karlsson, Hordur — Iceland, with Carlson, R. — U.S.A.** — International Monetary Fund, 1961, 4¢, 7¢, Government Printing Bureau, Japan.

**Keter, Simon — Israel, with Pesach, David — Israel** — Technical Co-operation Among Developing Countries, 1978, 13¢, 31¢, 80c, H. Fournier, S.A., Spain.

**Klutmann, Michael — Federal Republic of Germany** — UNDRO Against Disaster, 1979, 80c, 1.50fr, H. Fournier, S.A., Spain.

**Kowall, Dietmar — Federal Republic of Germany** — Economic and Social Council, 1980, 20¢, 4s, Ashton-Potter Ltd., Canada.

**Kurti, Esther — Israel, with Kalderon, A. — Israel** — International Women's Year, 1975, 10¢, 18¢, 60c, 90c, Questa Colour Security Printers, England.

**Kurtz, Lawrence — U.S.A.** — Postal stationery: Contemporary Design, 1969, 8¢, Canadian Bank Note Co., Ltd., Canada; Contemporary Design (like 8¢ airmail postal card 1969), 1972, 15¢, Government Printing Bureau, Japan.

**Lee, Thomas — China** — Souvenir card: Namibia, 1978 $1, Government Printing Office, Austria; International Year of Disabled Persons, 1981, $1, H. Fournier, S.A., Spain.

**Maeno, K. — Japan** — International Court of Justice, 1979, 80c, 1.10 fr, S. Setelipaino, Finland.

**Mason, John — Australia** — Postal stationery: U.N. Seal within a Horn, 1969, 5¢, Canadian Bank Note Co., Ltd., Canada; adaptation of 5c Postal Card (Jan. 8, 1969), 1969, 20¢, H. Courvoisier, S.A., Switzerland.

**Mathiesen, Olav S. — Denmark** — U.N. Headquarters Building, 1968, 6¢, Aspioti Elka-Chrome Mines Ltd., Greece; Headquarters Building, 1971, 8¢, H. Fournier, S. A., Spain; U.N. Headquarters Building, 1974, 10¢, H. Fournier, S.A., Spain; Emblem and Globe, 1962, 11¢, Harrison & Sons Ltd., England; Opening Words, U.N. Charter, 1965, 15¢, Government Printing Office, Austria; Letter Changing Hands, 1972, 95¢, Bundesdruckerei, Berlin; U.N. Stamps in Canadian denomination, 1967, 4¢, 5¢, 8¢, 10¢ and 15¢, British American Bank Note Co., Ltd., Canada (based on the original photo by M. Drummond, Canada); Flag and Plane, 1959, 7¢, Waterlow & Sons, England; Wings and Airmail envelope, 1969, 10¢, S. Setelipaino, Finland; Swallows and Emblem, 1951, 15¢, 25¢, Thomas De La Rue, England; Protection for Refugees, 1953, 3¢, 5¢, Thomas De La Rue, England; United Nations Day, 1953, 3¢, 5¢, Thomas De La Rue, England; World Health Organization, 1956, 3¢, 8¢, Thomas De La Rue, England; Human Rights Day, 1957, 3¢, 8¢, Thomas De La Rue, England; Central Hall, Westminster, London, 1958, 3¢, 8¢, American Bank Note Co., U.S.A.; World Refugee Year, 1959, 4¢, 8¢, Canadian Bank Note Co., Canada; Housing and Community Facilities, 1962, 4¢, 7¢, Harrison and Sons Ltd., England; International Co-operation Year, also souvenir sheet, 1965, 5¢, 15¢ and 20¢, Bradbury, Wilkinson & Co., England; Population Trends and Development, 1965, 4¢, 5¢, 11¢, Government Printing Office, Austria; World Federation of United Nations Associations, 1966, 5¢, 15¢, H. Courvoisier, S.A., Switzerland; United Nations Development Programme, 1967, 5¢, 11¢, H. Courvoisier, S.A., Switzerland; U.N. Institute for Training and Research, 1969, 6¢, 13¢, Government Printing Bureau, Japan; Art Series — Tunisian Mosaic, 1969, 6¢, 13¢, H. Fournier, S.A., Spain; World Food Programme, 1971, 13¢, H. Fournier, S.A., Spain; Universal Postal Union Building, 1971, 20¢, H. Courvoisier, S.A., Switzerland; Bird in

Flight, 1974, 26¢, S. Setelipaino, Finland; adaptation of 15c reg. (Oct. 25, 1965), 1969, 50c, H. Courvoisier, S.A., Switzerland; Emblem and Globe modification of 11c reg. 1962, 1970, 60c, H. Courvoisier, S.A., Switzerland; World Food Programme, 1971, 50c, H. Fournier, S.A., Spain; Universal Postal Union Building, 1971, 75c, H. Courvoisier, S.A., Switzerland; with Courvoisier, H., S.A., Switzerland and Hamann, O., Denmark, 25th Anniversary Peace and Progress, also souvenir sheet, 1970, 6¢, 13¢, 25¢ and 44¢, H. Courvoisier, S.A., Switzerland; with Kalderon, A., Israel, United Nations 30th Anniversary, also souvenir sheet, 1975, 60c, 90c, 1.50fr, Ashton-Potter, Ltd., Canada.

Souvenir cards: Art Series, 1972, $1, Bruder Rosenbaum, Austria; Disarmament Decade, 1973, $1, H. Fournier, S.A., Spain; Human Rights, 1973, $1, Ashton-Potter Ltd., Canada; Universal Postal Union, 1974, $1, Ashton-Potter Ltd., Canada; Peaceful Uses of Outer Space, 1975, $1, S. Setelipaino, Finland; United Nations Peace-Keeping Operations, 1975, $1, S. Setelipaino, Finland; World Federation of United Nations Associations, 1976, $1, H. Fournier, S.A., Spain; World Food Council, 1976, $1, Questa Colour Security Printers, Ltd., England; World Intellectual Property Organization, 1977, $1, H. Fournier, S.A., Spain; International Civil Aviation Organization, 1978, $1, H. Fournier, S.A., Spain.

Postal stationery: Penetration the Universe (abstract form), 1966, 11¢, Eureka-Carlisle Co., Scranton, Pa.; Penetration the Universe (abstract form), 1968, 13¢, Eureka-Carlisle Co., New York; United Nations Flag and Plane (like 7¢ airmail stamp of 1959), 1959, 7¢, International Envelope Corp., New York; United Nations Headquarters, 1973, 8¢, Eureka-Carlisle Co., Scranton, Pa.; Headquarters Building, New York (like 10¢ definitive stamp of 1974), 1975, 10¢, United States Envelope Co., U.S.A.; Swallows and Emblem (like 15¢ and 25¢ airmail stamps of 1951), 1952, 10¢, Dennison & Sons, New York; Swallows and Emblem (like 15¢ and 25¢ airmail stamps of 1951), 1954, 10¢, Dennison & Sons, New York; United Nations Flag and Plane (like 7¢ airmail stamp of 1959), 1960, 10¢, Thomas De La Rue, England; U.N. Headquarters, New York (like 8¢ definitive of 1971), 1975, 18¢, J. Enschede en Zonen, Netherlands; adaptation of 13c airmail Postal Card (May 31, 1968), 1969, 30c, H. Courvoisier, S.A., Switzerland.

**Matuszewska, Helena — Poland, with Tarkowska-Gruszecka, K. — Poland** — International Year of the Child, 1979, 15¢, 31¢, H. Fournier, S.A., Spain.

**Medina-Medina, Angel — Uruguay** — International Civil Aviation Organization, 1955, 3¢, 8¢, Waterlow & Sons, England; International Bank for Reconstruction and Development, 1960, 4¢, 8¢, Government Printing Bureau, Japan; Economic Commission for Europe, 1972,

21¢, 1.10fr, Government Printing Bureau, Japan; Economic and Social Council, 1980, 70c, 6s, Ashton-Potter Ltd., Canada; 10th Anniversary of United Nations Volunteers Program, 1981, 28¢, 5s, Walsall Security Printers Ltd., United Kingdom.

Postal stationery: Superimposed lines in manuscript forming "UN" plus four birds, 1977, 22¢, Joh. Enschede en Zonen, Netherlands.

**Meronti, O. C. — England** — Peoples of the World, 1951, 1¢, 10¢, Thomas De La Rue, England.

**Mirbach, Bernd — Federal Republic of Germany** — 10th Anniversary of United Nations Volunteers Program, 1981, 70c, 7s, Walsall Security Printers Ltd., United Kingdom.

**Mitchell, Leonard — New Zealand** — Human Rights Day, 1954, 3¢, 8¢, Thomas De La Rue, England; Human Rights Day, 1958, 4¢, 8¢, American Bank Note Co., U.S.A.; Fight Cancer, 1970, 6¢, 15¢, Bundesdruckerei, Berlin.

**Muller, Roman — Federal Republic of Germany** — To Practice Tolerance, 1979, 5¢, H. Fournier, S.A. Spain.

**Munnawar, M.A. — Pakistan** — Combat Racism, 1977, 40¢ and 1.10fr, S. Setelipaino, Finland; United Nations Decade for Women, 1980, 40c, 70c, Questa Colour Security Printers Ltd., United Kingdom.

**Mutver, Cemalettin — Turkey** — ICAO: Safety in the Air, 1978, 13¢, 25¢, H. Fournier, S.A., Spain; New International Economic Order, 1980, 15¢, 4s, Questa Colour Security Printers Ltd., United Kingdom; 35th Anniversary of United Nations, 1980, 15¢, 70c, Ashton-Potter Ltd., Canada.

**Nussgen, Gabriele — Federal Republic of Germany** — 10th Anniversary of United Nations Volunteers Program, 1981, 18¢, 40c, Walsall Security Printers Ltd., United Kingdom.

**Oivo, Eeva — Finland** — U.N. Peace-Keeping Operations, 1975, 60c, 70c, S. Setelipaino, Finland.

**Perrot, Robert — France** — Flags, 1971, 60¢, Government Printing Bureau, Japan; International Atomic Energy Agency, 1958, 3¢, 8¢, American Bank Note Co., U.S.A.; Flushing Meadows, New York, 1959, 4¢, 8¢, Canadian Bank Note Co., Canada; United Nations Day 15th Anniversary, also souvenir sheet, 1960, 4¢, 8¢ and 12¢, British American Bank Note Co., Canada; Economic Commission for Latin America, 1961, 4¢, 11¢, Government Printing Bureau, Japan; Economic Commission for Africa, 1961, 4¢, 11¢, H. Courvoisier, S.A., Switzerland; International Year for Human Rights, 1968, 6¢, 13¢, Harrison & Sons Ltd., England; Peace Through International Law, 1969, 6¢, 13¢, H. Courvoisier, S.A., Switzerland; Human Environment, 1972, 8¢, 15¢, 40c, 80c, J. Enschede en Zonen, Netherlands; New and Renewable Sources of Energy, 1981, 40¢, 7.50s, S. Setelpaino, Finland.

Postal stationery: Contemporary design of a jet aircraft, 1968, 13¢, S. Setelipaino, Finland; adaptation of 13c airletter (May 31, 1968), 1969, 65c, S. Setelipaino, Finland.

**Pesach, David — Israel, with Keter, Simon — Israel** — Technical Co-operation Among Developing Countries, 1978, 13¢, 31¢, 80c, H. Fournier, S.A., Spain.

**Pierre-Noel, V. — Haiti** — U.N. Headquarters Building, 1965, 20¢, Government Printing Office, Austria; U.N. Headquarters Building modification of 20c reg. 1965, 1970, 90c, S. Setelipaino, Finland.

**Plowitz, Kurt — U.S.A.** — To Live Together in Peace, 1962, 1¢, Harrison & Sons Ltd., England; To Live Together in Peace, 1965, 1¢, Government Printing Bureau, Japan; Bird formed from Laurel Leaves, 1963, 13¢, H. Courvoisier, S.A., Switzerland; United Nations Day, 1956, 3¢, 8¢, Thomas De La Rue, England; International Court of Justice, 1961, 4¢, 8¢, Government Printing Bureau, Japan; Peaceful Uses of Outer Space, 1962, 4¢, 11¢, Bradbury, Wilkinson & Co., England; General Assembly Building, 1963, 5¢, 11¢, Government Printing Bureau, Japan; Control Narcotics, 1964, 5¢, 11¢, Canadian Bank Note Co., Canada; Education for Progress, 1964, 4¢, 5¢, 11¢, H. Courvoisier, S.A., Switzerland; International Telecommunication Union Centenary, 1965, 5¢, 11¢, H. Courvoisier, S.A., Switzerland; United Nations Children's Fund, 1966, 4¢, 5¢, 11¢, Thomas De La Rue, England; Disarmament Decade, 1973, 8¢, 15¢, 60c, 1.10fr, Ajans-Turk, Turkey.

**Pollock, Alan — Canada** — World Meteorological Organization, 1957, 3¢, 8¢, Thomas De La Rue, England. Stylized jetliner traversing globe, 1977, 31¢, Heraclio Fournier, S.A., Spain.

**Purdy, Earl — U.S.A.** — United Nations Day, 1954, 3¢, 8¢, Thomas De La Rue, England.

**Rahikainen, Pentti — Finland** — Peaceful Uses of the Sea-Bed, 1971, 6¢, 30c, S. Setelipaino, Finland.

**Renau, Jose — Mexico** — International Labour Organization, 1954, 3¢, 8¢, Thomas De La Rue, England.

**Rottenfusser, Susanne — Federal Republic of Germany** — United Nations Decade for Women, 1980, 15¢, 20¢, Questa Colour Security Printers Ltd., United Kingdom.

**Saeed, Mian — Pakistan** — 35th Anniversary of United Nations, 1980, 31¢, 6s, Ashton-Potter Ltd., Canada.

**Sagi, Gidon — Israel** — UNDRO Against Disaster, 1979, 15¢, 20¢, H. Fournier, S.A., Spain; 35th Anniversary of United Nations, 1980, 40c, 4s, Ashton-Potter Ltd., Canada.

**Sanborn, Herbert — U.S.A.** — U.N. Emblem, 1958, 4¢, 8¢, Bradbury, Wilkinson & Co., England; To Unite Our Strength, 1961, 30¢, H. Courvoisier, S.A., Switzerland; with Hamann, Ole, Denmark, Trade and Development, 1964, 5¢, 11¢, Thomas De La Rue, England; To Unite Our Strength, modification of 30c reg. (1961, 1970), 90c, S. Setelipaino, Finland; To Unite Our

Strength, 1979, 10s, H. Courvoisier, S.A., Switzerland.

Souvenir cards: World Health Day, 1972, $1, Arts Graphiques/Imprimeries Populaires, Geneva, Switzerland.

**Savrda, Tomas — USA** — ICAO: Safety in the Air, 70c, 80c, H. Fournier S.A., Spain.

**Schmidt, Paula — Federal Republic of Germany** — General U.N. design, 1978, $1, Questa Colour Security Printers, England.

**Shamir Brothers — Israel** — Colored Pathway from U.N. Emblem, 1974, 18¢, S. Setelipaino, Finland.

Postal stationery: (like 18¢ airmail stamp of 1974), 1975, 18¢, S. Setelipaino, Finland.

**Simon, Henning — Denmark** — International Court of Justice, 1979, 15¢, 20¢, S. Setelipaino, Finland.

**Tarkowska-Gruszecka, K. — Poland, with Matuszewska, Helena — Poland** — International Year of the Child, 1979, 15¢, 31¢, H. Fournier, S.A., Spain.

**Tomei, C. — Italy** — Namibia: Liberation, Justice, Co-operation, 1978, 13¢, 18¢, 80c, Government Printing Office, Austria.

**Tomei, E. — Italy** — United Nations Water Conference, 1977, 13¢, 25¢, Government Printing Bureau of Japan; Live Together in Peace, 1978, 25¢, Questa Colour Security Printers, England.

**Van der Heyde, G. P. — Australia** — International Year of Disabled Persons, 1981, 35¢, 40c, H. Fournier S.A., Spain

**Van Gelder, Dirk — Netherlands** — Food and Agriculture Organizations, 1954, 3¢, 8¢, Thomas De La Rue, England.

**Van Heeswijk, Sophia — Federal Republic of Germany** — International Year of Disabled Persons, 1981, 20¢, 1.50fr, 4s, 6s, H. Fournier, S.A., Spain.

**Van Noten, Jean — Belgium** — United Nations Day, 1952, 5¢, American Bank Note Co., New York.

**Vertel, Jozsef — Hungary** — U.N. Headquarters Building, 1967, 1½¢, H. Courvoisier, S.A., Switzerland; adaptation of 1½¢, reg. (March 17, 1967), 1969, 5c, S. Setelipaino, Finland; General Assembly 1978, 13¢, 18¢, Government Printing Bureau, Japan; Donaupark, Wien, 1979, 6s, H. Courvoisier, S.A., Switzerland.

**Viola, Hector — Argentina** — 25th Anniversary of United Nations Postal Administration, 1976, 80c, 1.10fr, H. Courvoisier, S.A., Switzerland.

**Weishoff, Eliezer — Israel** — United Nations Conference on Human Settlements, 1976, 13¢, 25¢, 40c, 1.50fr, H. Fournier, S.A., Spain; World Food Council, 1976, 13¢, 70c, Questa Colour Security Printers, England; World Intellectual Property Organization (WIPO), 1977, 13¢, 31¢,

80c, Heraclio Fournier, S.A., Spain; United Nations Water Conference, 1977, 80c, 1.10fr, Heraclio Fournier, S.A., Spain; Global Eradication of Smallpox, 1978, 80c, 1.10fr, H. Courvoisier, S.A., Switzerland; Peace Dove and Globe, 1979, 15¢ H. Fournier, S.A., Spain; For a Free and Independent Namibia, 1979, 15¢, 31¢, 1.10fr, Ashton-Potter Ltd., Canada; Economic and Social Council, 1980, 15¢, 40c, Ashton-Potter Ltd., Canada.

Postal stationery: stylized airmail envelope with wings, 1977, 25¢, Heraclio Fournier, S.A., Spain.

**Wiese, B. K. — Federal Republic of Germany** — Combat Racism, 1977, 13¢, 25¢, S. Setelipaino, Finland; United Nations Peace-keeping Operations, 1980, 15¢, 1.10fr, Joh. Enschede en Zonen, Netherlands.

**Wind, Willi Wolf — U.S.A.** — Globe and Wing, 1957, 4¢, Thomas De La Rue, England; Globe and Wing, 1959, 5¢, Waterlow & Sons, England.

Postal stationery: Globe and Wing (like 4¢ airmail stamp of 1957), 1957, 4¢, British American Bank Note Co., Ltd., Canada; Globe and Wing (like 4¢ airmail stamp of 1957) 1¢ in Wreath, 1959, 5¢, revalued 4¢ airmail, United Nations; Globe and Wing (like 5¢ airmail stamp of 1959), 1959, 5¢, Eureka Specialty Printing Company, Scranton, Pa.

**Woyty-Wimmer, Hubert — Austria** — World Unity, 1951, 20¢, Thomas De La Rue, England; Human Rights Day, 1952, 3¢, 5¢, Thomas De La Rue, England; Universal Postal Union, 1953, 3¢, 5¢, Thomas De La Rue, England; Human Rights Day, 1955, 3¢, 8¢, Waterlow & Sons, England; International Telecommunication Union, 1956, 3¢, 8¢, Thomas De La Rue, England; Palais de Chaillot, 1960, 4¢, 8¢, Thomas De La Rue, England; Economic Commission for Asia and the Far East, 1960, 4¢, 8¢, Government Printing Bureau, Japan.

## Never Reprinted

Commemorative U.N. postage stamps remain on sale only for 12 months, unless supplies become exhausted beforehand. They are never reprinted.

Another reason why U.N. stamps are attractive, especially to collectors, is that the printing quantities are low — usually around two million — and this has, in some cases, led to some of the issues being more sought after than others.

The returns from U.N. postage stamp sales are not entirely profit; the United Nations Postal Administration pays the United States and Swiss Postal Services for all stamps used for mailing. On the other hand, the proceeds of sales to collectors are retained by the United Nations and are credited annually to the budget and decrease accordingly the contributions of member states. UNPA provides collectors with information about U.N. activities, thus making it even more worthwhile to collect U.N. stamps.

## Sales Counters

Collectors residing in or visiting New York, Geneva or Vienna, are always welcomed at UNPA sales counters. They are open every day for sales to the public of mint stamps, souvenir cards, postal stationery, stamp sets, souvenir folders and catalogs. Gift sets and posters also are offered.

## Souvenir Folders

Souvenir folders are available of all U.N. stamps issued during the year. The stamps themselves — one mint single of each denomination — are contained in a separate glassine envelope and are not affixed inside the folder, although spaces are provided for this purpose.

Information is included about the United Nations events commemorated by the stamps in the folder. The New York, Geneva, Vienna and Flag stamps are available in separate folders.

## First Day Service

Mail orders for stamps and other postal issues should be addressed to the United Nations Postal Administration, P.O. Box 5900, New York, N.Y. 10017, U.S.A.; to United Nations Postal Administration at Geneva, Palais des Nations, CH-1211 Geneva 10, Switzerland; or to the United Nations Postal Administration at Vienna, P.O. Box 900, A-1400 Vienna, Austria.

Orders should be accompanied by a remittance or money order, personal or certified check, the amount of which should also cover return postage and, when required, registration.

Mail orders under $2 (postage excluded) are subject to a 50¢ handling charge but orders over $2 are filled at face value plus postage.

## Deposit Service

The U.N. maintains a Customer Deposit Service, making it easy to collect U.N. stamps and to receive U.N. publicity material. All the collector has to do is open an account with a minimum deposit of $35, tell the U.N. what his standing requirements are, and the UNPA guarantees to fill his order. The order may be revised at any time or the collector may withdraw from the Customer Deposit Service whenever desired.

For complete information on the UNPA and its many collector services, write to either or all of the addresses listed previously under the heading First Day Service.

## Souvenir Cards

UNPA issues souvenir cards at a rate of two per year. The cards bear reproductions of the U.N. commemorative stamps issued on the same day in conjunction with the same event. Cards also include past U.N. issues relating to the same theme.

For detailed information on UNPA souvenir cards and policy of issuing cards, check the index for proper location in the Almanac.

# Washington Scene

# 21

## Federal Bureau of Investigation

Ninth St. and Pennsylvania Ave. NW, Washington, D.C. 20535 Phone, 202-324-3000.

The Federal Bureau of Investigation (FBI) is a division of the Department of Justice, headed by the Attorney General. The FBI's chief is William H. Webster.

The FBI was established in 1908 by the Attorney General who directed that Department of Justice investigations be handled by a group of special investigators.

The FBI is charged with investigating all violations of federal laws with the exception of those which have been assigned by legislative enactment or otherwise to some other federal agency.

The FBI's jurisdiction includes a wide range of responsibilities in the criminal, civil and security fields. Among these are major philatelic thefts; espionage, sabotage, and other subversive activities; kidnapping; extortion; bank robbery; interstate transportation of stolen property; civil rights matters; interstate gambling violations; fraud against the government; and assault or killing the President or a federal officer. Cooperative services of the FBI for other duly authorized law enforcement agencies include fingerprint identification, laboratory services, police training, and the National Crime Information Center.

### Field Divisions — Federal Bureau of Investigation

| Division | Address | Office Phone |
|---|---|---|
| Albany, N.Y. 12207 | U.S. Post Office and Courthouse | 465-7551 |
| Albuquerque, N.M. 87102 | 301 Grand Ave. NE | 247-1555 |
| Alexandria, Va. 22314 | 300 N. Lee St. | 683-2680 |
| Anchorage, Alaska 99513 | Federal Bldg. | 276-4441 |
| Atlanta, Ga. 30303 | 275 Peachtree St. NE | 521-3900 |
| Baltimore, Md. 21207 | 7142 Ambassador Road | 265-8080 |
| Birmingham, Ala. 35203 | Room 1400, 2121 Bldg. | 252-7705 |
| Boston, Mass. 02203 | John F. Kennedy Federal Office Bldg. | 742-5533 |
| Buffalo, N.Y. 14202 | 111 W. Huron St. | 856-7800 |
| Butte, Mont. 59701 | U.S. Courthouse and Federal Bldg. | 782-2304 |
| Charlotte, N.C. 28202 | 1120 First Union National Bank Bldg. | 372-5485, 372-5484 |
| Chicago, Ill. 60604 | Everett McKinley Dirksen Bldg. | 431-1333 |
| Cincinnati, Ohio 45202 | 415 U.S. Post Office and Courthouse Bldg. | 421-4310 |
| Cleveland, Ohio 44199 | Federal Office Bldg. | 522-1400 |
| Columbia, S.C. 29201 | 1529 Hampton St. | 254-3011 |
| Dallas, Tex. 75202 | 1801 North Lamar, Suite 300 | 741-1851 |
| Denver, Colo. 80202 | Federal Office Bldg. | 629-7171 |
| Detroit, Mich. 48226 | 477 Michigan Ave. | 965-2323 |
| El Paso, Tex. 79901 | 202 U.S. Courthouse Bldg. | 533-7451 |
| Honolulu, Hawaii 96850 | 300 Ala Moana Blvd. | 521-1411 |
| Houston, Tex. 77002 | 6015 Federal Bldg. and U.S. Courthouse | 224-1511 |
| Indianapolis, Ind. 46202 | 575 N. Pennsylvania St. | 639-3301 |
| Jackson, Miss. 39201 | Federal Bldg., 100 W. Capitol | 948-5000 |

| | | |
|---|---|---|
| Jacksonville, Fla. 32239 | 7820 Arlington Expressway | 721-1211 |
| Kansas City, Mo. 64106 | 300 U.S. Courthouse Bldg. | 221-6100 |
| Knoxville, Tenn. 37919 | 1111 Northshore Drive | 588-8571 |
| Las Vegas, Nev. 89101 | Federal Office Bldg. | 385-1281 |
| Little Rock, Ark. 72201 | 215 U.S. Post Office Bldg. | 372-7211 |
| Los Angeles, Calif. 90024 | 11000 Wilshire Blvd. | 272-6161 |
| Louisville, Ky. 40202 | Federal Bldg. | 583-3941 |
| Memphis, Tenn. 38103 | Clifford Davis Federal Bldg. | 525-7373 |
| Miami, Fla. 33137 | 3801 Biscayne Blvd. | 573-3333 |
| Milwaukee, Wis. 53202 | Federal Bldg. and U.S. Courthouse | 276-4684 |
| Minneapolis, Minn. 55401 | 392 Federal Bldg. | 339-7861 |
| Mobile, Ala. 36602 | Federal Bldg. | 438-3674 |
| Newark, N.J. 07102 | Gateway I, Market St. | 622-5613 |
| New Haven, Conn. 06510 | Federal Bldg., 150 Court St. | 777-6311 |
| New Orleans, La. 70113 | 701 Loyola Ave. | 522-4671 |
| New York, N.Y. 10021 | 201 E. 69th St. | 553-2700 |
| Norfolk, Va. 23502 | 870 N. Military Hwy. | 461-2121 |
| Oklahoma City, Okla. 73118 | 50 Pennsylvania Place NW | 842-7471 |
| Omaha, Neb. 68101 | 1010 Federal Office Bldg. | 348-1210 |
| Philadelphia, Pa. 19106 | Federal Office Bldg. | 629-0800 |
| Phoenix, Ariz. 85004 | 2721 N. Central Ave. | 279-5511 |
| Pittsburgh, Pa. 15222 | Federal Office Bldg. | 471-2000 |
| Portland, Ore. 97201 | Crown Plaza Bldg. | 224-4181 |
| Richmond, Va. 23220 | 200 W. Grace St. | 644-2631 |
| Sacramento, Calif. 95825 | Federal Bldg. | 481-9110 |
| St. Louis, Mo. 63103 | 2704 Federal Bldg. | 241-5357 |
| Salt Lake City, Utah 84138 | Federal Bldg. | 355-7521 |
| San Antonio, Tex. 78296 | Federal Bldg. | 225-6741 |
| San Diego, Calif. 92103 | 3211 Fifth Ave. | 231-1122 |
| San Francisco, Calif. 94102 | 450 Golden Gate Ave. | 552-2155 |
| San Juan, P.R. 00917 | Pan Am Bldg. | 765-6000 |
| Savannah, Ga. 31405 | 5401 Paulsen St. | 354-9911 |
| Seattle, Wash. 98104 | 1015 Second Ave. | 622-0460 |
| Springfield, Ill. 62708 | 535 W. Jefferson St. | 522-9675 |
| Tampa, Fla. 33602 | Federal Office Bldg. | 228-7661 |
| Washington, D.C. 20535 | 506 Old Post Office Bldg. | 324-3000 |

**Source: U.S. Government Manual**

# Federal Trade Commission

Pennsylvania Ave. at 6th St. NW, Washington, D.C. 20580 Phone, 202-523-3625

| | |
|---|---|
| Chairman | Michael Pertschuk |
| Commissioner | Paul Rand Dixon |
| Commissioner | (Vacancy) |
| Commissioner | Robert Pitofsky |
| Commissioner | David A. Clanton |
| Secretary | Carol M. Thomas, Acting |
| General Counsel | Michael N. Sohn |
| Deputy General Counsel | Gerald P. Norton |
| Assistant General Counsel, Legal Counsel | Barry R. Rubin |
| Assistant General Counsel, Litigation & Environmental Policy | William D. Cross |
| Assistant General Counsel, Legislation & Congressional Liaison | William J. Baer |
| Director, Office of Public Information | Frank Pollock |
| Executive Director | Christian S. White |
| Deputy Executive Director for Management | Barry J. Kefauver |
| Director, Office of Policy Planning and Evaluation | Robert B. Reich |
| Chief Administrative Law Judge | Daniel H. Hanscom |
| Director, Bureau of Competition | Alfred F. Dougherty Jr. |
| Deputy Director, Bureau of Competition | Daniel C. Schwartz |
| Deputy Director, Bureau of Competition | Alan K. Palmer |

Director, Bureau of Consumer Protection...................... Albert H. Kramer
Deputy Director, Bureau of Consumer Protection............... Tracy A. Westen
Deputy Director, Bureau of Consumer Protection............... Richard C. Foster
Director, Bureau of Economics............................... William S. Comanor
Deputy Director, Bureau of Economics........................ P. David Qualls

The Federal Trade Commission was organized as an independent administrative agency in 1951, pursuant to the Federal Trade Commission Act of 1914.

The basic objective of the Commission is the maintenance of strongly competitive enterprise as the keystone of the American economic system. Although the duties of the Commission are many and varied under law, the foundation of public policy underlying all these duties is essentially the same, to prevent the free enterprise system from being stifled, substantially lessened or fettered by monopoly or restraints on trade, or corrupted by unfair or deceptive trade practices.

In brief, the Commission is charged with keeping competition both free and fair.

This basic purpose finds its primary expression in the Federal Trade Commission Act, cited above, and the Clayton Act, both passed in 1914 and both successively amended in the years that have followed. The Federal Trade Commission Act lays down a general prohibition against the use in commerce of "unfair methods of competition" and "unfair or deceptive acts or practices." The Clayton Act outlaws specific practices recognized as instruments of monopoly. As an administrative agency, acting quasi-judicially and quasi-legislatively, the Commission was established to deal with trade practices on a continuing and corrective basis. It has no authority to punish; its function is to "prevent," through cease-and-desist orders and other means, those practices condemned by the law of federal trade regulation; however, court-ordered civil penalties up to $10,000 may be obtained for each violation of a commission order.

## Sources of Information

CONTRACTS AND PROCUREMENT

Persons seeking to do business with the Federal Trade Commission should contact the Division of Administrative Services, Federal Trade Commission, Washington, D.C. 20580. Phone, 202-962-7606.

PUBLICATIONS

A copy of the "Federal Trade Commission — List of Publications," which lists a number of publications of interest to the general public, is available free upon application to the Division of Legal and Public Records, Federal Trade Commission, Washington, D.C. 20580.

CONSUMER PROTECTION, RESTRAINT
OF TRADE INFORMATION,
AND COMPLAINTS

Persons desiring information on consumer protection, restraint of trade questions, or to register a complaint, should contact the nearest Federal Trade Commission Regional Office.

EMPLOYMENT

Civil Service registers are used in filling positions for economists, accountants, consumer protection specialists, and other professional, administrative, and clerical personnel. The Federal Trade Commission employs a sizable number of attorneys under the excepted appointment procedure. All employment inquiries should be directed to Director of Personnel, Federal Trade Commission, Washington, D.C. 20580.

For further information, contact the Director, Office of Public Information, Federal Trade Commission, Pennsylvania Avenue at Sixth Street NW, Washington, D.C. 20580. Phone, 202-963-1110.

## Activities

The Commission's principal functions are:

To promote free and fair competition in interstate commerce through prevention of general trade restraints such as price-fixing agreements, boycotts, illegal combinations of competitors, and other unfair methods of competition;

To safeguard the consuming public by preventing the dissemination of false or deceptive advertisements of consumer products generally and food, drug, cosmetics, and therapeutic devices, particularly, as well as other unfair or deceptive practices;

To prevent discriminations in price, exclusive-dealing and tying arrangements, and corporate mergers when such practices or arrangements may substantially lessen competition or tend toward monopoly; interlocking directorates under certain circumstances; the payment or receipt of illegal brokerage; and discrimination among competing customers in the furnishing of or payment for advertising or promotional services or facilities;

To enforce truthful labeling of textile and fur products;

To regulate packaging and labeling of certain consumer commodities so as to prevent consumer deception and facilitate value comparisons;

To supervise the registration and operation of associations of American exporters engaged solely in export trade;

To petition for the cancellation of the registration of trademarks which were illegally registered or used for purposes contrary to the intent of the Trade-Mark Act of 1946;

To achieve true credit cost disclosure by consumer creditors (retailers, finance companies, non-federal credit unions, and other creditors not specifically regulated by another government agency); to assure a meaningful basis for informed credit decisions; and to regulate the issuance and liability of credit cards, to prohibit their fraudulent use in interstate or foreign commerce;

To protect consumers against the circulation of inaccurate or obsolete credit reports, and to insure that consumer reporting agencies exercise their responsibilities in a manner that is fair and equitable; and

To gather and make available to the Congress, the President, and the public, factual data concerning economic and business conditions.

ENFORCEMENT

The Commission's law enforcement work falls into two general categories: formal litigation leading to mandatory orders against offenders; and law observance of a voluntary nature.

The formal proceedings are similar to those used in courts. Cases are instituted by issuance of a complaint charging a person, partnership, or corporation with violation of one or more of the statutes administered by the Commission. If the charges are not contested, or if in a contested case the charges are found to be true, an order may be issued requiring discontinuance of the unlawful practices.

Law observance is also obtained through voluntary and cooperative action by way of advisory opinions, trade regulation rules, through issuance of guides delineating legal requirements as to particular business practices, or through informal administrative correction of minor infractions.

LEGAL CASE WORK

Cases before the Commission may originate through complaint by a consumer or a competitor; the Congress; or from federal, state, or municipal agencies. Also, the Commission itself may initiate an investigation to determine possible violation of the laws administered by it. No formality is required in submitting a complaint. A letter giving the facts in detail is sufficient, but it should be accompanied by all evidence in possession of the complaining party in support of the charges made. It is the policy of the Commission not to disclose the identity of any complainant, except as required by law.

FEDERAL TRADE COMMISSION
REGIONAL OFFICES
Telephone and Address Listings

ATLANTA, 1718 Peachtree St. NW; Atlanta, Ga. 30309; Telephone (404) 881-4836; serves Alabama, Florida, Georgia, Kentucky, Mississippi, North Carolina, South Carolina, Tennessee.

BOSTON, 150 Causeway St., Analex Building, Room 1301, Boston, Mass. 02114; Telephone (617) 223-6621; serves Connecticut, Maine, Massachusetts, New Hampshire, Rhode Island, Vermont.

CHICAGO, 55 E. Monroe St., Suite 1437, Chicago, Ill. 60603; Telephone (312) 353-4423; serves Illinois, Indiana, Iowa, Minnesota, Missouri, Wisconsin.

CLEVELAND, 118 St. Clair Ave., Cleveland, Ohio 44199; Telephone (216) 522-4207; serves Michigan, western New York, Ohio, western Pennsylvania.

DALLAS, 2001 Bryan St., Suite 2665, Dallas, Tex. 75201; Telephone (214) 749-3056; serves Arkansas, Louisiana, New Mexico, Oklahoma, Texas.

DENVER, 1405 Curtis St., Suite 2900, Denver, Colo. 80202; Telephone (303) 837-2271; serves Colorado, Kansas, Montana, Nebraska, North Dakota, South Dakota, Utah, Wyoming.

LOS ANGELES, 11000 Wilshire Blvd., Room 13209, Los Angeles, Calif. 90024; Telephone (213) 824-7575; serves Arizona, southern California.

NEW YORK, 6 Federal Plaza, 2243-EB Federal Bldg., New York, N.Y. 10007; Telephone (212) 264-1207; serves New Jersey, New York east of Rochester.

SAN FRANCISCO, 450 Golden Gate Ave., Box 36005, San Francisco, Calif. 94102; Telephone (415) 556-1270; serves northern California, Hawaii, Nevada.

SEATTLE, 915 Second Ave., 28th floor Federal Building, Seattle, Wash. 98174; Telephone (206) 442-4655; serves Alaska, Idaho, Oregon, Washington.

WASHINGTON, D.C., Pennsylvania Avenue at 6th Street NW, Washington, D.C. 20580; Telephone (202) 523-3711 (chairman).

**For further information, contact the Director, Office of Public Information, Federal Trade Commission, 202-523-3830.**

# Dealer Organizations    **22**

## American Stamp Dealers' Association, Inc.

Executive offices of the American Stamp Dealers' Association, Inc., are located at 5 Dakota Drive, Suite 102, Lake Success, N.Y. 11042. ASDA dealers are engaged in every facet of philately and are located throughout the United States and the world. No matter where a collector lives or visits, or what his collecting interests or needs, he is not far from an ASDA dealer who can serve him. The triangle insignia is the symbol of membership in the ASDA.

A membership application to ASDA is approved only after a thorough search has been made regarding the applicant. Before membership is granted, the applicant must agree in writing to abide by the ASDA pledge and code of ethics, which include the assurance of fair dealing to collectors.

To be admitted to regular membership in ASDA, an applicant must have at least four years of professional philatelic experience; for provisional membership at least two years.

Among the functions of ASDA are: sponsoring national and local chapter shows, sponsoring seminars for dealers, maintaining a credit file and information on hundreds of dealers and collectors, publishing a membership directory and encouraging junior collectors to exhibit.

The association also serves as a spokesperson when conflict arises with local, state or federal legislation.

### BYLAWS
#### PREAMBLE

The purpose of this association is to provide an organization for the maintenance and development of high standards of business ethics among those engaged directly and indirectly in the merchandising of stamps and other materials for the hobby of philately, and thereby to promote mutual trust and friendship among its members and public confidence and respect for the trade; to provide a medium for the exchange of trade and credit information of philatelic interest through trade papers, releases, meetings and similar means; to arbitrate disputes, mediate, adjust and settle differences between members and the public.

To assist recognized governmental agencies in the prosecution of violations of law relating to philatelic matters; to do all within its power for the general good of philately and in connection therewith to aid in the establishment of local chapters throughout the United States; to so op-

erate that no part of the income or earnings of the association inure to the benefit of any individual or member; and to insure that no officer, member or employee shall receive or be entitled to receive pecuniary profit from the operations thereof except reasonable compensation for services actually rendered.

# ARTICLE I
## BOARD OF DIRECTORS

**Section 1. Number of Members.** The Board of Directors shall consist of nine members and shall include among its members the president, vice president, secretary and treasurer of the association. The four members elected to fill the respective active offices of the association and five other nominees for directorships receiving the greatest number of votes of the membership shall be deemed elected to the board. The president of the association shall be the chairman of the board. The immediate past president shall be ex-officio to the board and shall not have a vote.

**Section 2. Qualifications.** Only members of the association pursuant to Article VI of these bylaws shall be eligible for nomination and election as a director.

**Section 3. Term of Office.** Directors shall take office on the first day of January in the year following the year of their election and shall serve without compensation for two years and until their successors are elected and qualify. The board, by an affirmative vote of six members may remove any director or officer with cause. A written petition by 200 members of the association in good standing or by 20 per cent of the membership, whichever is greater, shall be sufficient to cause a recall referendum to be conducted for the removal of any officer or officers, director or directors, named therein. The board shall cause such referendum to be conducted within 90 days of receipt of a valid petition by the secretary of the association.

**Section 4. Classes.** Terms of directors shall be divided into two classes so that in the year in which officers are elected by the membership two directors shall also be elected. In the alternate year, the other three directors shall be elected.

**Section 5. Regular and Special Meetings.** Regular meetings of the board shall be held at least four times a year. Special meetings of the board may be called by the president, or upon the written request of five board members. The time and place for all regular meetings shall be fixed by the board and ten days prior notice thereof shall be given by mail or publication in the newsletter. The time and place of all special meetings shall be fixed by the president and shall be given by mail unless less than seven days notice is given in which event notice shall be given by telephone or telegraph not less than three days prior to the meeting date.

Each officer and director of the board must present evidence of ability to be bonded at the time of acceptance of nomination for position and must be bondable throughout the entire term of service.

**Section 6. Quorum.** Five members of the board shall constitute a quorum at regular meetings as the board of directors and five shall constitute a quorum at special meetings. Except as provided in Article III, Section 2 of these bylaws, the act of a majority of the members present at a meeting at which a quorum is present shall be the act of the board.

**Section 7. Action by Mail or Telephone Poll.** If, in the opinion of the president, action upon any matter cannot reasonably be deferred until the next scheduled meeting of the board, he may direct that the members of the board be polled by mail or telephone. The secretary shall notify all board members of the result of each such poll in writing. The results of such poll shall be valid as if adopted at a meeting of the board.

**Section 8. Reimbursement for Expenses.** Members of the board of directors shall, upon appropriate application, be allowed reimbursement of an amount not more than the lowest regularly available economy coach air fare for travel expenses actually incurred by members of the board in connection with attendance at meetings of the board of directors.

# ARTICLE II
## OFFICERS

**Section 1. Officers.** The officers shall consist of a president, vice president, secretary and treasurer, each of whom shall perform the duties incidental to the office. They shall take office on the first day of January in the year following the year of their election and shall serve without compensation for a two-year term and until their successors are elected and qualify. Only members of the association pursuant to Article VI of these bylaws shall be eligible for nomination and election as an officer.

**Section 2. President.** The president shall be chief executive officer of the association. He shall preside over all meetings of the board and of the members pursuant to Article IV. He shall see that all duly adopted orders and resolutions of the association are carried into effect. He shall be ex-officio a member of all committees with the right to vote, except for the nominating committee, and shall have the general powers and duties of supervision, management and responsibilities usually vested in the office of president.

**Section 3. Vice President.** The vice president shall perform the duties and exercise the powers of the president during the absence, death or disability of the president as well as such other duties as may be assigned by the president.

**Section 4. Secretary.** The secretary shall attend all meetings of the members pursuant to Article IV and of the board and shall preserve in books of the association true minutes of the proceedings of all such meetings. He shall keep in his custody the seal of the association and shall have authority to affix the same to all instruments where its use is required. He shall give all notices required by statute, these bylaws or any resolution of the board. He shall perform such other duties as may be delegated to him by the board.

**Section 5. Treasurer.** The treasurer shall have charge of the custody of all corporate funds and securities and the keeping of books belonging to the association including full and accurate accounts of all receipts and disbursements; he shall also have charge of deposit of all monies, securities and other valuable effects in the name of the association in such depositories as may be designated for that purpose by the board. He shall supervise the disbursement of the funds of the association as may be ordered by the board, taking proper vouchers for such disbursements, and shall render to the president and board at regular meetings of the board, and whenever requested by them, an account of all his transactions as treasurer and of the financial condition of the association.

# ARTICLE III
## ELECTIONS AND VACANCIES

**Section I. Election.** Elections for officers and directors shall be held as follows:

A. On or before June 1 of each year the board shall appoint from among members of the association a nominating committee of not less than three (3) members, and designate the chairman thereof. The names of the appointees shall be published in an official publication. Not later than September 15 of each year the president shall appoint such inspectors of election as the president shall deem necessary. Committee members or inspectors of the election may not be members of the board.

B. The nominating committee shall endorse at least one (1) candidate from among the members for each office. The endorsement shall be in writing, signed by the chairman of the nominating committee, and delivered to the secretary not later than September 1.

C. A petition signed by twenty-five (25) members nominating an additional candidate or candidates for a specific office or as a director may be delivered to the secretary not later than September 1.

D. Nominees for office shall immediately and not later than ten (10) days thereafter present to the secretary of the association written evidence of ability to be bonded reasonably acceptable to the secretary and acceptance of the nomination for office.

E. The secretary shall prepare a printed ballot, which shall contain: (1) The name of each person endorsed and the method of endorsement; and (2) Sufficient space for the entry of other candidates by the member voting.

F. Not later than September 30, the secretary shall cause a ballot to be mailed to each member entitled to vote. The ballot shall indicate that it must be returned to the secretary, first class or airmail postage prepaid, by a date specified, which shall not be less than thirty (30) days subsequent to the date of mailing of the ballots. The ballot will be unsigned and transmitted in an unaddressed and sealed envelope marked "Ballot" and be contained in a regular envelope addressed to ASDA Headquarters. The unaddressed ballot envelope will remain sealed until opened by the inspectors of election.

G. Seven days subsequent to the specified date, or as soon thereafter as practicable, the inspectors of election shall tabulate the ballots and certify the results to the secretary, who shall cause a notice of election to be published in an official publication.

H. The board of directors may establish such additional election procedures as it may deem necessary so long as they are consistent with the provisions of these bylaws.

**Section 2. Vacancies.** Vacancies in any office or directorship shall be filled by appointment made by a majority of the remaining members of the board. Each person so appointed shall remain in that position until his successor has been elected by the members and shall qualify.

**Section 3. Appointment and Removal of Employees and Agents.**

A. The board may appoint such employees and agents as it may from time to time consider in the best interest of the association, and fix their powers and compensation. Appointees need not be members of the association.

B. Any officer or agent appointed pursuant to this Section 3 may be removed by the board whenever, in its judgment, the interests of the association will be served thereby.

# ARTICLE IV
## MEETINGS OF MEMBERS

**Section 1. Annual Meetings of Members.** At least once during each calendar year, the board shall direct that an annual meeting of members be held, and fix the time and place thereof.

**Section 2. Special Meetings of Members.** Special meetings of members may be called by the president or any five members of the board acting together in writing.

**Section 3. Notice.** At least thirty (30) days prior to the date fixed, notice of the annual or a special meeting of members shall be published in an official publication of the association to all members.

**Section 4. Attendance by Board.** Unless excused by the president, all members of the board shall attend all annual and special meetings of members.

**Section 5. Order of Business.**

A. If a quorum is not present, meetings of members may adopt resolutions indicating the sense of the meeting, which shall be considered at the next meeting of the board.

B. Whether or not a quorum is present, all members shall be entitled to attend and discuss the affairs of the association with the board.

**Section 6. Quorum.** At any annual or special meeting, a quorum shall consist of the lesser of fifty (50) voting members or five per cent of the voting membership.

## ARTICLE V
### COMMITTEES

**Section 1. Standing Committees.** At the first meeting of the board held after January 1 in each year, the president shall appoint after consultation with the board from among the members of the board to the extent possible:

A. A chairman of the Membership Committee.

B. A chairman of the Expert Committee.

C. A chairman of the Bylaws Committee.

D. A chairman of the Legal Committee.

The committee chairman shall name additional members to the Membership Committee, Expert Committee, Bylaws Committee and Legal Committee who need not be members of the board.

**Section 2. Special Committees.** The board may from time to time create special committees, and designate their function and term of office. Members of special committees shall be named by the chairman of the committee and need not be members of the board or members of the association unless so established by the board. The president shall designate after consultation with the board the chairman of the committee.

**Section 3. Membership Committee.** The Membership Committee shall exercise the functions assigned to it by Article VI of these bylaws.

**Section 4. Expert Committee.** The Expert Committee shall oversee all activities of the association in relation to the American Philatelic Expertization Service, and shall act as the association's liaison with the Philatelic Research Institute and Philatelic Foundation as well as other agencies involved in this service.

**Section 5. Bylaws Committee.** The Bylaws Committee shall keep the bylaws under continuous study for the good and welfare of the association.

**Section 6. Legal Committee.** The Legal Committee shall maintain general supervision over the Code of Ethics disciplinary actions and arbitration procedures under rules adopted by the board.

**Section 7. Vacancies.** Vacancies in the membership of any committee may be filled by appointments made in the same manner as original appointments.

**Section 8. Term.** The chairman and all members of the standing and special committees of the association serve at the discretion of the president of the association after consultation with the board.

**Section 9. Quorum.** Unless otherwise designated in the resolution creating a committee, a majority of the whole committee shall consititute a quorum and the act of a majority of the members present at a meeting at which a quorum is present shall be the act of the committee.

**Section 10. Rules.** Each committee may adopt rules for its own government consistent with these bylaws and the approved policy memorandums on file in the ASDA Policy Manual at ASDA Headquarters. Committee chairs shall review their respective policy memorandums for completeness and consistency with the bylaws welfare of the association.

## ARTICLE VI
### MEMBERSHIP

**Section 1. Regular Member.** Any individual natural person may apply for regular membership in the association if he or she:

A. Has been a dealer in philatelic material, supplies, accessories and publications, or in the opinion of the board of directors is engaged in a trade, business or profession which directly advances and benefits the trade; and

B. Furnishes documentary proof of four years of professional experience in the stamp business; and

C. Subscribes to the Code of Ethics of the association; and

D. Has attained the age of legal majority in the jurisdiction in which he resides.

**Section 1a. Foreign Members.**

A. Foreign applicants must be members of their respective country's IFSDA organization if such exists or an organization of equal status, with board approval.

**Section 2. Other Membership Categories.**

A. Honorary Member. The board may grant honorary memberships to any person or persons who have in their judgment served the trade and hobby of philately with distinction and honor. No dues shall be required of such memberships nor shall such honorary member be entitled to voting rights, and such memberships may be withdrawn by the board at any time for good cause shown. Such membership shall be nontransferable. An honorary member upon payment of regular membership dues will be entitled voting rights.

B. Retired Member. A member having reached 30 years continuous ASDA membership or having become 65 years of age may apply for retired membership status. Retired members will receive all official correspondence, pay reduced dues as set forth in Article VI and may wear the retired membership lapel pin. They may not vote or otherwise represent themselves professionally as members of the association unless specifically authorized by the board.

C. Life Member. Persons who, as of January 1, 1978, were life members pursuant to the bylaws prior to the adoption of this provision shall be life members as are persons granted such membership purusant to Article IX, Section 1 of these bylaws. Life members shall have all of the rights of members and be entitled to such voting rights so long as they may live (unless such membership shall be withdrawn by a vote of three-fourths of all of the board of directors for good cause shown).

No portion of the life member's dues shall be refunded by the association in the event of such withdrawal. Such membership shall be nontransferable.

D. Provisional Membership. Any person that meets the criteria in Section 1 above may apply for provisional membership except such applicant must furnish proof of professional philatelic experience for a period of not less than two years nor more than three and one-half years. Provisional members will be upgraded to regular membership upon fulfilling the four years experience requirement unless in the opinion of the board other action should be taken.

Provisional members dues will be 20 per cent less than regular membership and shall be prorated during any year that upgrade action is taken. A provisional member shall have all the rights and privileges of a regular member except they may not vote nor display the ASDA logo. They may, however, indicate their ASDA provisional member status in advertising and correspondence. ASDA logo, plaque and a lapel pin will be furnished at the time of upgrading to regular status.

**Section 3. Applications.** Applicants for membership shall submit their application on forms prescribed by the membership committee accompanied by the application fee and dues for one (1) year. The application fee shall not be refundable but the dues shall be refunded if the applicant is not accepted.

**Section 4. Publication.** Names of applicants for membership shall be published in an official publication of the association at least once prior to consideration by the membership committee. Such publication shall be mailed at least thirty (30) days prior to consideration of such applicants by the membership committee, it being intended that the membership of the association have time to comment on any applicant.

**Section 5. Approval.** The membership committee shall report to the board as follows: All applicants for membership and its recommendations as to each. If the report is accepted by at least five members of the board, the person recommended for membership by the committee shall become a member of the association as of the date of acceptance of the report.

**Section 6. Nonacceptance.** An applicant whose application for membership is not accepted may reapply no earlier than one (1) year after the date of the applicant's notification of nonacceptance.

**Section 7. Resignation.** No member shall be permitted to resign from the association nor shall a member be dropped for nonpayment of dues, if charges against the member are pending under Article VII. If the board establishes procedures for the determination of complaints against members, no member shall be permitted to resign or be dropped for nonpayment of dues while such complaint is unresolved, unless otherwise specifically ordered by the board.

**Section 8.** Any individual person, upon acceptance to membership, shall register with the association all corporations, partnerships, or other philatelic entities in which he holds a financial or stock interest of substantial nature or in which he holds a position as officer, director, or employee and shall take full responsibility for the obligation of the said entity to meet the same standards of dealing imposed upon him individually by the association and can be disciplined pursuant to the Article VII of the bylaws for the action of such entity.

**Section 9. Reinstatement.** A previous member having been dropped from the rolls for resignation or nonpayment of dues may be automatically reinstated if:

a. Application for reinstatement is made during the same calendar year in which he was dropped from membership; and

b. Forwards with his application dues for the full year plus an administrative fee as may be determined by the board of directors; and

c. Has not had charges filed against him as defined in Article VII which remain unresolved.

**Section 10.** An applicant having been expelled or denied membership for cause may apply for membership or reinstatement in the association if:

A. (1) A period of four (4) years has elapsed since the completion of any sentence or probation period if such person has been convicted of a crime, and

(2) During said four (4) year period the applicant has been active in the stamp business, and

(3) Applicant has, in the opinion of the board of directors, conducted his professional stamp and business activities in a manner consistent with the code of ethics and bylaws; or

B. (1) A period of four (4) years has elapsed since the applicant has been discharged in bankruptcy, and

(2) During said four (4) year period the applicant has been active in the stamp business, and

(3) Applicant has, in the opinion of the board of directors, conducted his professional stamp and business activities in a manner consistent with the code of ethics and bylaws; or

C. (1) A period of four (4) years has elapsed since the applicant has settled and resolved all outstanding debts and claims made against him or her, which have not been discharged in bankruptcy, and

(2) During said four (4) year period the applicant has been active in the stamp business, and

(3) Applicant has, in the opinion of the board of directors, conducted his professional stamp and business activities in a manner consistent with the code of ethics and bylaws.

An individual applying for membership or reinstatement under this provision shall also meet all other criteria provided for regular membership in these bylaws.

## ARTICLE VII
### ETHICS AND DISCIPLINE

**Section 1. Code of Ethics.** The board shall establish a code of ethics for the association, which shall be binding upon all members. The board may amend the code of ethics at any time, provided that no change shall be effective until one (1) month after the amendment has been published in an official publication of the association.

**Section 2. Action by Board of Directors.** If any member is ruled by the board to have committed any of the acts prescribed in Section 3 of this article, the board may censure, suspend, expel or otherwise discipline the member. Notice of such action may be published in an official publication of this association. The board may establish and amend trade practice rules governing the procedure to be followed in such cases, provided, that such rules shall afford the member of a fair hearing and the right to counsel. The board may delegate the conduct of the hearing to a committee of members.

**Section 3. Violation.** Any member may be subject to censure, suspension, expulsion or other action by the board who alone, or through the member's partners, employees, agents or servants:

(1) Violates the code of ethics or the bylaws;

(2) Fails to pay the member's lawful obligations within a reasonable time;

(3) Fails to answer communications addressed to the member by the association or its duly authorized officers or appointees;

(4) Fails to participate in any arbitration proceeding conducted by the association;

(5) Knowingly makes a false statement to the association or its representatives;

(6) So conducts the member's business affairs as to bring disrepute to the trade or to lessen public confidence in stamp dealers; or

(7) Is convicted or pleads nolo contendere (or the equivalent) to a crime involving moral turpitude under the laws of the jurisdiction in which the member is charged or resides;

shall be subject to disciplinary action under Section 2 of this article. So long as charges are pending pursuant to subparagraph (7) of this Section 3 and all appeal rights shall not have been exhausted such member shall be suspended from membership in the association.

**Section 4. Effect of Suspension.** During any period of suspension pursuant to this Article VII, a member shall not be eligible to receive any of the benefits of membership, nor to participate in the affairs of the association.

**Section 5. Suspension.** So long as charges are pending pursuant to subparagraph A (7) of this Section 3 and all appeal rights shall not have been exhausted such member shall be suspended from membership in the association. During any period of suspension, a member shall not be eligible to receive any of the benefits of membership, nor to participate as a member in the affairs of the association.

**Section 6. Costs of Complaints.** Whenever a member shall have filed an outstanding three or more complaints or inquiries in any twenty-four (24) month period involving matters based upon which disciplinary action could be taken by the association, the board of directors may, in its sole but reasonable determination, assess against said member costs of the association related to the handling of these complaints or inquiries, including, but not limited to legal fees, staff time and costs of communication.

## ARTICLE VIII
### LOCAL CHAPTERS

**Section 1. Creation.** Not less than ten (10) voting members may apply to the board for the establishment of a chapter of the association. The application shall contain the proposed name of the chapter and the geographic area which it proposes to encompass. Upon acceptance by the board, the members may proceed to establish the chapter.

**Section 2. Regulation.** Each chapter may establish its own bylaws and rules, not inconsistent with these bylaws and any resolution of the board, which shall include the following.

A. Only members of the association shall be members of the chapter.

B. The chapter shall file with the secretary the names and addresses of its officers as elected from time to time.

C. The chapter shall not hold less than three (3) meetings during each calendar year.

D. Copies of the minutes of all chapter meetings shall be sent to the executive officer at the principal offices of the association; and

E. No chapter shall be or hold itself out to be an agent of the association.

**Section 3. Suspension or Revocation of Authority.** The board may suspend or revoke the authority of any chapter for any cause which would result in like action against an individual member, or if the chapter in the sole discretion of the board of directors of the association becomes inactive.

**Section 4. Chapter Shows.** Chapters are encouraged to sponsor and support philatelic bourses and exhibitions. The board may by resolution agree to advance initial costs as a loan or guarantee a chapter against losses in the operation of a philatelic event, to the extent specified in its resolution.

# ARTICLE IX
## DUES AND FEES

**Section 1. Establishment of Dues.** There shall be four classes of membership in the organization: to wit: regular, life, honorary and retirement. For each dues period the board of directors shall establish the annual rate to be paid by all members. Any regular member in good standing may, by paying 20 times the annual dues in one payment, become a life member, subject to the approval of the board and shall thereafter no longer be required to pay dues.

**Section 2. Notice.** If the annual dues established by the board exceeds the rates for the current period, notice of the new rates shall be published in an official publication not later than November 15.

**Section 3. Payment.** All dues shall be payable on January 1 for the year beginning on that date for all persons who are members on that date. Dues for new members after January 1 shall be prorated on a quarterly basis to the beginning of the quarter preceding their admission to membership.

**Section 4. Failure to Pay.** If the dues of any member remain unpaid on March 1, the treasurer shall notify the member of the member's delinquency and assess the member a ten per cent surcharge on the amount due which shall also become a part of the amount due and payable by the member. If the member's dues remain unpaid on April 1, the member's membership shall then terminate and notice of termination shall be published in an official publication.

**Section 5. Refunds.** No dues shall be refunded to any member whose membership terminates for any reason.

# ARTICLE X
## CONTRACTS, CHECKS, DEPOSITS

**Section 1. Contracts.** The board may authorize any officer or officers, agent or agents, in addition to the officers authorized by these bylaws, to enter into any contract or execute and deliver any instrument in the name of and on behalf of the association, and such authority may be general or confirmed to specific instances.

**Section 2. Checks, Drafts, etc.** All checks, drafts or orders for the payment of money, notes or other evidences of indebtedness issued in the name of the association shall be signed by such officer or officers, agent or agents of the association and in such manner as shall from time to time be determined by resolution of the board. In the absence of such determination, such instruments shall be signed by the treasurer and countersigned by the president, vice president or secretary.

**Section 3. Deposits.** All funds of the association shall be promptly deposited from time to time to the credit of the association in such banks, trust companies or other depositories as the board may elect.

# ARTICLE XI
## AMENDMENTS

**Section 1. Method of Proposal of Amendments.** The board may propose amendments to these bylaws at any time or such amendments may be proposed by petition of 20 per cent of the membership or 200 members thereof, whichever shall be greater, addressed to the board. All such proposed amendments if timely received will be presented by the board to the membership with or without recommendations not later than the next following annual meeting of the association.

**Section 2. Publication.** The proposed amendment shall be published in an official publication, and shall be accompanied by a ballot whereon voting members may vote to approve or disapprove the amendment.

**Section 3. Voting.** The inspectors of election shall establish a date, which shall be at least thirty (30) days after the date of publication, for the return of ballots. A simple majority vote of members voting is sufficient to adopt an amendment.

**Section 4. Certification of Results.** On or after the final date for the return of the ballots, the secretary or the secretary's designee, shall tabulate the results, and certify the same to the president.

**Section 5. Effective Date.** An amendment shall become effective on the date specified in the amendment, if any. If no date is specified, the amendment shall be effective upon the date of certification of adoption which fact shall be included in the publication of the proposed amendment in an official publication.

# ARTICLE XII
## MISCELLANEOUS

**Section 1. Definitions.** As Used in These Bylaws:

A. "Association" means the American Stamp Dealers' Association, Inc.

B. "Board" means the board of directors of the association.

C. "Official Publication" shall mean the ASDA Bulletin, Newsletter, or any other communication addressed to all of the members of the association.

D. "Qualify" when used with respect to election of officers and directors shall mean such time as the officer or director shall become eligible to serve under applicable law and the bylaws of the association.

E. "Member" unless otherwise stated means an individual natural person admitted to membership in the association pursuant to Article VI of these bylaws.

**Section 2. Titles.** The titles of articles and sections are used for reference only, and have no substantive effect.

**Section 3. Fiscal Year.** The fiscal year of the association shall be the calendar year unless otherwise determined by a two-thirds vote of the board.

**Section 4. Notice.** Any notice required to be given under these bylaws is effective upon deposit in the United States mails, postage prepaid.

**Section 5. Audit.** The accounts of the association shall be audited not less than annually by a Certified Public Accountant who shall be appointed by the board. A summary of such audit shall be published as soon as practicable after receipt and acceptance of same by the board in an official publication of the association.

**Section 6. Quarterly Financial Reports.** The treasurer of the association shall cause to be prepared and published in an official publication a summary of financial operations of the association in such form as may be determined by the board of directors, such summaries to be provided on a quarterly basis for all periods other than the year end period for which an audit has been prepared in accordance with Section 5 of this Article XII.

**Section 7. Association Sponsored Shows.** No person who is under suspension or who has previously been expelled or denied membership for causes other than insufficient experience may be allowed to act as a dealer's assistant or otherwise appear behind a dealer's booth at any association or chapter sponsored show.

# ASDA CODE OF ETHICS

Membership in the ASDA is a privilege extended to those persons and organizations deemed worthy, and is not a right. Membership may be continued unless the board of directors determines that the conduct of a member has been such, that in the best interests of the ASDA, the member should be suspended or his or her membership terminated.

As a guide to all members this code of ethics has been duly adopted by the board of directors under the authority vested in by the constitution and bylaws of the ASDA.

1. I will support and be subject to the constitution and bylaws of the ASDA and such amendments, resolutions and policies as may be established.

2. I will abide by all federal, state and local laws related to philatelic matters.

3. I will conduct myself so as to bring no discredit to the ASDA, or to diminish the prestige of the membership therein.

4. I will neither buy nor sell philatelic items of which the ownership is in doubt and will promptly report to the proper law enforcement agencies information on suspected stolen material.

5. I will correct promptly any error I make in any transaction.

6. I will assist in the prosecution of violations of law pertaining to philatelic matters, of which I have knowledge, and will report promptly to the proper law enforcement agencies any violations.

7. I will properly, carefully and honestly grade and describe all merchandise offered for sale by me and indicate any faults, defects or alterations that may exist, to include indication of canceled to order material.

8. I will immediately refund on any item sold by me where the description was not accurate or misleading, within a reasonable period of time after the transaction.

9. I will publish and make available my terms of sale so that all clients have an opportunity to become familiar with them.

10. I will hold intact, pending written acceptance from the seller all merchandise sent to me for offer, and should the offer be unacceptable to promptly and carefully return it to its proper owner.

11. I will honor any buying prices that I have published within a reasonable period after their publication. Price lists will include a statement as to expiration of offer or give an actual expiration date and explain any limitations.

12. I will make prompt cash refund on all "out of stock" or returned merchandise.

13. I will advertise for sale only those items that are available to me at the time the advertisement is placed.

14. I will provide all consignors of merchandise with a contract stating my legal commitments.

15. I will pay for all material I purchase according to the terms of sale at the time of purchase.

16. I will not sell, produce, nor advertise counterfeit material in any form in violation of law.

17. I will never substitute or alter material submitted to me without the consent of the owner.

18. I will abide by the "terms of sale" and will publish prices realized within a reasonable time after a public auction.

19. I will conduct myself according to accepted standards of morality and courtesy in all philatelic activities not specifically cited in this code.

20. Insofar as possible I will use the ASDA logo in my advertising.

21. If I should be found guilty of unethical or unlawful conduct, the record thereof may be disclosed to other philatelic societies of which I am a member.

22. I will submit any dispute concerning philatelic transactions in which I may become involved to arbitrators mutually agreed upon by the parties.

## ASDA PLEDGE

A member shall be required to subscribe to the following pledge upon joining the American Stamp Dealers' Association, Inc.:

"As a member of the American Stamp Dealers' Association, Inc., I recognize my obligation to the public and pledge:

1. To buy and sell at prices commensurate with a reasonable return on my investment and at prevailing market conditions.

2. To give advice to my clientele in philatelic matters to the best of my ability.

3. To refrain from dealing in stolen philatelic and counterfeit material, and to furnish buyers of repaired, regummed, reperforated, reprinted or otherwise altered philatelic material with a complete written statement showing in detail the nature of the changes and alterations in such material.

4. To purchase philatelic material from the public at reasonable prices, with due allowances for my risk and prevailing market conditions; to be truthful in my advertising; to refrain from denigrating my competitors; and to make no false claim to a policy or practice of generally underselling competitors."

## CURRENT OFFICERS

Current officers of the American Stamp Dealers' Association are:

Lewis Shull, Crofton, Md., president.

William E. Shelton, San Antonio, Tex., vice president.

William S. Trevvett Jr., Richmond, Va., treasurer.

John G. Ross, Chicago, Ill., secretary.

Herman Herst, Boca Raton, Fla, director.

Gordon McHenry, Osprey, Fla., director.

John W. Kaufmann, Washington, D.C., director.

S. Robinson Kusinitz, Fall River, Mass., director.

John Peters, San Francisco, Calif., director.

The executive officer is Joseph B. Savarese. Inquiries should be directed to American Stamp Dealers' Association, Inc., 5 Dakota Drive, Suite 102, Lake Success, N.Y. 11042.

## ASDA CHAPTERS

Current contact persons for the chapters are:

### MID-ATLANTIC
Daniel C. Warren
Drawer E
Aberdeen, Md. 21001

### NORTH CALIFORNIA
Stanley Piller
3351 Grand Ave.
Oakland, Calif. 94610

### SOUTH CALIFORNIA
J.H. Crum
2720 E. Gage Ave.
Huntington Park, Calif. 90255

### CHICAGO
Donn Ebert
Box 807
North Chicago, Ill. 60064

### NEW ENGLAND
Robert Gibb
Lord Chesterfield Apts.
Building 14, No. 3
Framingham, Mass. 01701

### FLORIDA
Carl J. Kish
1250 Court St.
Clearwater, Fla. 33516

### SOUTH FLORIDA
Robert Hagler
Box 610425
North Miami, Fla. 33161

### INTERNATIONAL NORTHWEST
Charles Gillespie
Box 13145
Portland, Ore. 97213

**LONG ISLAND**
John Zaso
Box 310
New Hyde Park, N.Y. 11040
**MICHIGAN**
R.E. Lippert
23800 Greater Mack
St. Claire Shores, Mich. 48080

**SOUTHWEST CHAPTER**
Melvin Edmonds
Box 2066
Universal City, Tex. 78148

# Regional, Foreign
# Dealers Associations

## UNITED STATES

**Central Atlantic Stamp Dealers Association.** The CASDA serves dealers in Pennsylvania, New Jersey, Delaware, Maryland, Washington, D.C., Virginia and West Virginia. Contact M. Mitchell, 3166 Adderly Court, Silver Spring, Md. 20906.

**Florida Stamp Dealers Association.** Box 4585, Clearwater, Fla. 33518.

**New Jersey Stamp Dealers Association.** Box 412, East Brunswick, N.J. 08816.

**Professional Coin & Stamp Dealers' Association of Long Island.** The association serves the Long Island, N.Y., area and is open to any legitimate stamp dealer with a tax resale number and the sponsorship of two members. Contact Stan Roe, Box 354, Lynbrook, N.Y. 11563.

**Stamp Dealers Association of Georgia.** 133 Carnegie Way NW, Room 203, Atlanta, Ga. 30303.

**Texas Stamp Dealers Association.** Box 30442, Dallas, Tex. 75230. The TSDA has approximately 70 members in Texas, nearby states and one in Mexico.

## CANADA

The Canadian Stamp Dealers' Association is comprised of regular, and honorary members. The organization is headed by a staff of four officers, including the president, vice president, secretary and treasurer. Membership in the Canadian organization is open to qualified dealers based in other countries. Additional information is available from any of the CSDA officials.

### Officers

President: John H. Talman, 35 Victoria St., Toronto, Ont. M5C 2A1.

Vice president: Harold Beaupre, 44 King St. S, Box 424, Waterloo, Ont. N2J 4A9.

Secretary: Case Bastmeyer, 2740 Danforth Ave., Toronto, Ont. M4C 1L7.

Treasurer: Vance Carmichael, Box 267, Smithville, Ont. L0R 2A0.

## CSDA
## Code Of Ethics:

1. At all times to conduct myself in a business-like and professional manner.

2. To advise my clients in philatelic matters to the very best of my ability and in questions of doubt to consult with other respected members of the association.

3. Not to sell, knowingly, repaired, improved, or in any way altered stamps as sound, or for anything else than what they are.

4. To refrain from misleading advertisements and statements.

5. To refrain from dealing in stolen material.

6. To honor and fulfill my contracts and undertakings.

7. To cooperate in all matters which tend to the betterment of the Canadian Stamp Dealers' Association and philately in general.

## FOREIGN ORGANIZATIONS

A few of the foreign dealer organizations supplied details on their services, others did not. In the latter instance it is suggested that contact be made by mail at the address noted.

**Philatelic Traders Society Ltd.** 27 John Adam St., London WC2N 6HZ England. Over 800 members. For full membership a minimum of two years in the trade with proper references. Provisional membership immediately with proper references, subject to approval by the council.

PTS is able to give members an opinion on their stamps for a small fee, but does not provide expert certificates.

**Suomen Postimerkkikauppiaiden Liitto r.y.** Fredrikinkatu 51-53 SF-00100 Helsinki 10, Finland. Thirteen members. Does not sponsor national exhibition and does not provide expertization service.

**Schweizerischer Briefmarkenhandler-Verband.** Gallusstrasse 22, CH-9000 St. Gallen, Switzerland. 68 members. Open only to Swiss or Liechtenstein stamp dealers. No expertization service.

The following organizations are listed alphabetically by country. No other information available.

**Argentina:** Asociacion de Empresarios Filatelicos de la Republica Argentina, Casilla de Correo 3296, 1000 Buenos Aires, Argentina.

**Australia:** The Australasian Stamp Dealers Association. Box 5378, Melbourne, Australia 3001.

**Austria:** Oesterreichischer Briefmarkenhandler-Verband, Mariahifer Strasse 105, Wien VI, Austria.

**Belgium:** Chambre Syndicale Belge des Negociants en Timbres-Poste-A.S.B.L., 14bd M Lemonnier, Bruxelles, Belgium.

**Brazil:** Associacao Brasileria dos Comerciantes Filatelicos, Caixa Postal 5188, Sao Paulo, Brazil.

**Denmark:** Danmarks Frimaerkenhandlerforening, Fuglebakkevej 9, 2000, Copenhagen, Denmark.

**France:** Chambre Syndicale Francaise des Negociants et Experts en Philatelie (CNEP), 4 Rue Drouot, 75009 Paris, France.

**Germany:** Bundesverband des Deutschen Briefmarkenhandels APHV e.h., Klettenberggurtel 60, 5000 Koln-Klettenberg, Germany.

**Greece:** Greek Stamp Dealers Association "Hermes." Aristidou Str. 12, Athens 122, Greece.

**Italy:** Sindicato Nazionale Commercianti di Francobolli, Via Carlo Alberto 71, Rome, Italy.

**Norway:** Norsk Frimerkenhandler Forening, Box 113, Jessheim, Norway.

**Philippines:** Philippine Stamp Dealers Association, Box 1860, Manila, Philippines.

**Spain:** Gremio Nacional de Comercjantes Filatelicos de Espana, Grupo de Filatelia de Madrid, Carretas 1⁹, 14,5, Madrid 12, Spain. Also, Grupo de Filatelia de Barcelona, Paseo de Gracia 44, Barcelona 7, Spain.

**Sweden:** Sveriges Frimarkshandlarforbund, Slottsvagen 103, Nasbypark, Sweden.

**Turkey:** Pul Tuccariari Cemiyeti, Galipdede Caddesi 51, Beyoglu - Istanbul.

# INTERNATIONAL

**International Federation of Stamp Dealers' Associations.** The ground work for IFSDA was laid in London, England, in 1950 during the first postwar international exhibition. Committee meetings were held on May 8, 1950, Grosvenor House, London; on May 29, 1951, Waldorf Hotel, London; and on April 28, 1952 in the Hotel Metropole, Monte Carlo. The first General Assembly was held in Ultrecht, Holland, on July 2, 1952.

The objects of the federation are:

(a) To promote and maintain a high standard of professional integrity among stamp dealers throughout the world.

(b) To promote the interchange between member organizations of all information and literature likely to be of service to the stamp trade.

(c) To endeavor in all possible ways to reduce the barriers to international trade in stamps.

(d) To promote the interchange of information regarding the marketing of forged, faked, repaired or otherwise unsatisfactory stamps.

(e) To take any action which may be thought fit to prevent or reduce the sales of stamps which in the opinion of the federation have not been issued under satisfactory circumstances.

(f) To take any action which in the opinion of the federation would promote the interests of stamp dealers in any part of the world.

(g) To cooperate with the United Nations or any other national or international organization for the attainment of any of the above objects.

(h) To provide for the use of all member organizations international machinery to carry out the above objects.

(i) To take any action which may be thought fit against novelties issued under speculative titles and without any postal reason.

## Membership

Membership in the IFSDA shall be confined to national trade organizations.

Each member country of the federation may send two delegates to the general assembly. Trade organizations with less than 15 members have one vote in the assembly. Trade organizations with a minimum trade membership of 15 have two votes in the assembly. When such an organization sends only one member, that member is entitled to two votes.

The rules of the federation shall specify the rights, duties and financial obligations of members.

The organs of the federation are the general assembly and the executive committee. The general assembly meets normally once a year, if possible at a city where an international exhibition or other international philatelic function is being held. There may also be extraordinary general meetings held as required.

The general assembly and extraordinary general meetings are the authoritative organs of the federation.

The general assembly may elect a president and vice presidents of honor, and shall elect a chairman and two vice chairmen, honorary president and 12 members of the executive committee and two auditors. If at any election a candidate does not secure an absolute majority of the votes which are cast at the first ballot, a second ballot will be held at which the vacancy(ies) shall fall to the candidate(s) receiving the highest number of votes.

The terms of the chairman and vice chairman shall be for one year but they are eligible for reelection. The executive committee shall consist of delegates representing the following regions: Europe, four members; Africa, one member; Asia, one member; Australia and New Zealand, one member; North America, four members; and Latin America, one member.

In the event of any of these places not being filled the general assembly may elect a delegate(s) from another continent to fill the vacancy(ies.) The general assembly shall determine the manner in which this representation can best be attained, keeping in view the different branches of the trade.

Organizations that attended the 1950 International Conference of National Stamp Dealers' Association, London, were eligible to become founder members. Prospective member organizations shall be proposed and seconded for membership by affiliated organizations, and accepted by the next general assembly upon advice by the executive committee.

On the recommendation of the executive committee, the general assembly is equally entitled to exclude members by a two-thirds majority.

The official languages of the federation are English, French and German.

Contact person is Chairman S. Rietveld, Laan van Meerdervoort 360, 's-Gravenhage, The Netherlands.

Vice President of honor in the United States is Kurt Weishaupt, Box 37, Flushing, N.Y. 11358. The American Stamp Dealers' Association, 5 Dakota Drive, Suite 102, Lake Success, N.Y. 11042, is the American member society of IFSDA.

## JAPAN

The official name of the Japan Stamp Dealers' Association is "Nihon Yubin Kitte-sho Kyodo Kumiai." The direct interpretation in English is "Japan Postage Stamp Dealers Cooperative Trade Union." It is the only organization in the philatelic business field which is registered by and authorized by the Japanese government. The authorization is in accordance with the Law of the Cooperative Trade Union, and its operation and activities are strictly under the supervision of the Ministry of Industry and Trade.

### Membership Qualification

1. A member must be a full-time stamp dealer.

2. A member must own his office, his store or his residence in Japan.

3. The application for the entry must be examined by the board of directors of the association.

4. Nonresidents of Japan are not eligible for membership in the association.

The association consists of 172 dealers in all parts of Japan. Meetings are held two times per month and the association publishes the annual "Japanese Postage Stamp Catalog."

The JSDA is located at Room 612, New-Shinbashi Bldg., 2-16-1, Shinbashi, Minato-ku, Tokyo 105 Japan.

# Postal Regulations

# 23

# Philatelic Guidelines

The United States Postal Service is sometimes restricted as to what it can do in providing special services for stamp collectors. Guidelines to be followed by postal personnel are detailed in the U.S. Postal Service Domestic Mail Manual, sections 160, 170 and 140, as well as other guides, such as the Postal Operations Manual and the Postal Bulletin. Those sections of the manual are reproduced in part as follows, with slight variations being made to eliminate unnecessary repetition and sections dealing with Postal Service internal affairs, accounting, etc. These are the postal regulations that most directly affect philately and the mailing public.

## Section 160: Philately

### 161 POLICY

**161.1** There is a single national policy governing the release, sale and discontinuance of postage stamps and postal stationery. The policy is established by Customer Services Department, USPS Headquarters, Washington, D.C. 20260.

**161.2** The policy governing philatelic products shall be administered by the Philatelic Marketing Division. All other policies are administered by the Stamps Division.

**161.3** Uniform application of policies provides a high degree of integrity to the entire program, and all post offices, postal employees and contractors shall comply with the policies set forth in this subchapter. The Postal Service will avoid the creation of philatelic rarities.

### 162 PURPOSE AND SELECTION OF COMMEMORATIVE STAMPS, AND POSTAL STATIONERY AND PHILATELIC PRODUCTS

**162.1 Purpose.** Commemorative stamps and postal stationery (postal cards, embossed stamped envelopes and aerogrammes) explain the cultural and historical heritage of the United States. They describe our nation's achievements, portray the natural wonders of our country, instill pride in America, and focus attention on worthy causes, issues and interests that are of national concern. The Postal Service encourages the widespread use of these stamps and stationery items to promote our national ideals, progress and heritage. Commemorative stamps are not intended to replace regular stamps of the same class, but are provided upon request when available.

**162.2 Selection.** Subjects for commemorative postage stamps and postal stationery may be proposed by the public through correspondence to the Citizens' Stamp Advisory Committee. The committee, which is composed of individuals from outside the Postal Service appointed by the postmaster general, reviews suggestions and makes recommendations for commemorative stamps and postal stationery to the postmaster general, who makes the final selections. Because the committee works far in advance of actual stamp issuance, all proposals should be submitted at least two years prior to the desired issuance date. All suggestions should be forwarded to the Citizens' Stamp Advisory Committee, U.S. Postal Service, c/o Stamp Development Branch, 475 L'Enfant Plaza SW, Washington, D.C. 20260.

**162.3 Philatelic Products.** Philatelic products are produced and sold to expand interest in the hobby of stamp collecting by demonstrating both the fun and the informative value of stamps.

## 163 DISTRIBUTION AND SALE OF STAMPS, POSTAL STATIONERY AND PHILATELIC PRODUCTS

### 163.1 Distribution

.11 All post offices receive initial supplies of new issue commemorative stamps without requisition. Philatelic products such as Mint Sets, Stamp Collecting Kits, etc., are distributed automatically to Stamp Distribution Post Offices.

.12 Stamp Distribution offices shall:

a. Establish a program for the distribution of new philatelic products and the replenishment of existing philatelic products to associate post offices.

b. Assure that less-than-bulk quantities of stamps are supplied to all post offices so they can be placed on sale in accordance with instructions issued in the Postal Bulletin.

### 163.3 Retail Sales

.31 **General.** Stamps, postal stationery and philatelic products are sold at various types of postal retail facilities which are described in this part. Most of these facilities have regular stamp windows or have been designated as Stamp Collecting Centers. Stamp Collecting Centers sell the current commemorative stamps and philatelic products. Other post offices provide specialized philatelic services and sell the full range of stamps and philatelic products offered by the Postal Service. These facilities, as well as the Philatelic Sales Division, are referred to collectively as philatelic outlets.

.32 **Philatelic Centers.** Philatelic Centers are retail selling areas or self-contained facilities separate from the lobby window positions. Some philatelic outlets are referred to as Postiques. (Postique is a registered trademark of the U.S. Postal Service.) They display and sell all current stamps and related philatelic products. The stamps and postal stationery stock offered for sale include commemorative stamps, definitive and regular issue stamps, coils, postage due stamps, airmail and special delivery stamps, booklets and booklet panes, packets of stamped, embossed envelopes, postal cards, and message reply cards and aerogrammes. The Philatelic Sales Division is a Philatelic Center.

.33 **Dedicated Philatelic Windows.** A Dedicated Philatelic Window is a lobby window designated to sell stamps and related philatelic products only. No other postal services are available at Dedicated Philatelic Windows, which are to be identified so that customers desiring normal postal services are directed to other windows. The same items sold at Philatelic Centers are also sold at Dedicated Philatelic Windows.

.34 **Temporary Philatelic Stations**

.341 **Purpose of Participation.** Post offices establish special temporary stations to provide philatelic services, and to sell commemorative stamps and philatelic products. These stations may include specially constructed counters or mobile retail units. They are most frequently located at stamp shows, philatelic exhibitions, stamp dedications, state fairs, conventions, parades or at other locations or activities of significant public or philatelic interest.

.342 **Requests for Participation.** Requests for Postal Service participation at such events should be made by the sponsors or organizers to the local postmaster for initial action. Only requests for first day of issue or other special support, which must come from the national level, should be directed to the Stamps Division. All first day ceremonies are conducted under the direction of the Stamps Division. The payment of fees for space may not be authorized below the headquarters level. Once a postmaster has agreed to participate in an exhibition, a unilateral withdrawal from such a commitment may not be made without the approval of the regional retail branch based upon a showing of good cause.

.343 **Authorization.** Temporary philatelic stations may be authorized by the postmaster with approval by the regional retail manager. Postmasters are authorized to participate at events where admission fees are charged by the sponsor, but in these cases the same cancellation used at the event must be available on request to those not attending the event.

.344 **Ceremonies.** Postmasters and other local officials are encouraged to participate in opening ceremonies for stamp exhibitions or other stamp ceremonies arranged by philatelic groups whether or not a temporary philatelic station has been authorized.

.345 **Announcement and Publicity**

a. Posters.

(1) An announcement of temporary philatelic station and any show cancellation must be posted on the main post office lobby bulletin board and may be posted in other post offices within a 10-mile radius of the event so that collectors will be advised of the USPS' participation. In case of larger shows the posting may occur throughout the sectional center.

(2) Posters should be placed on display at least 15 days before the event but in no case more than 30 days before the event.

(3) All announcements must emphasize the temporary philatelic station. The announcement should mention the name of the stamp show, pictorial or standard cancellation (if any), the dates and hours open to the public, and the location. Promotional material for the show itself must not be incorporated.

b. Press Releases. The postmaster should also announce through press releases to local newspapers the planned establishment of this station. The post office, however, must not distribute free flyers to homes, sell or distribute tickets, exchange ticket coupons, or authorize the use of post office facilities for direct show promotion.

### .346 Arrangements

a. General. Postmasters should insure that detailed planning begins well in advance of the show so that participation brings credit to the USPS and provides a wide range of stamps and philatelic products to collectors. Particular attention should be taken in selecting sales personnel who are knowledgeable about stamp collecting and who have retail experience. All clerks should be fully trained in philatelic sales and cancellation policies.

b. Stamp Stock.

(1) The postmaster should secure a wide range of philatelic products and current postage, using the Philatelic Sales Division stock list (Form 3300) as a guide. Consideration should be given to prepackaging sets of regular issues or postage dues for sale to collectors. No stamp which has been withdrawn from sale by the Philatelic Sales Division may be sold by any philatelic station. Withdrawals are noted in the Postal Bulletin.

(2) Postmasters should requisition philatelic stock not already available in their post office from the Regional Accountable Paper Depository on Form 17, Stamp Requisition, indicating the quantity required and that it is for a stamp show. For stamp shows, stamps with a denomination higher than $1 may be requisitioned in plate blocks of four as noted in 163.2

(3) At the conclusion of the show, excess philatelic stock, including remainders from commemorative sheets, should be sold at the regular windows for postage purposes.

c. Philatelic Products. Postmasters should display and sell philatelic products such as Souvenir Mint Sets, "Stamps & Stories," and Stamp Collecting Kits.

d. Sales Restrictions. The sales policies regarding plate number blocks, marginal markings and line markings on coil stamps are described in 163.532 and .533.

e. Security and Facilities. Postmasters should insure that sufficient security for the stamp stock is provided at the show site and that all other facilities are adequate.

f. Appearance. Postmasters should insure that the appearance of the temporary philatelic station brings credit to the Postal Service by utilizing attractive signs and having space for satisfactory service. The hours that the station is open should be posted.

g. Prompt Service. At those exhibitions where a large number of collectors are expected, postmasters should consider utilizing a speedy line or customer numbers which can be distributed and announced so that customers will not have to wait to make their purchases.

h. Cancellation Service.

(1) Cancellation service should be provided separately from stamp sales. A sufficient number of clerks should be available to provide speedy service.

(2) Clerks should be trained in advance how to provide handstamped postmarks of philatelic quality. Refer to 164.3 for cancellation regulations.

### 163.4 Mail Order Sales

.41 The Philatelic Sales Division services mail orders for postage stamps of selected quality and other philatelic items. Customers may obtain an order form listing items available by writing to the Philatelic Sales Division, U.S. Postal Service, Washington, D.C. 20265.

.42 Post offices may not fill mail orders for stamps and other philatelic items other than mail orders under the Stamps by Mail program and orders for local precancels.

.43 Customers must furnish a self-addressed, stamped envelope for return of precanceled stamps.

.44 Postmasters may not order precancel devices solely to satisfy collector demands.

.45 Philatelic Centers and Dedicated Philatelic Windows may accept and fill mail orders for special cacheted envelopes with cancellations authorized under 165.1. This section shall not affect procedures outlined in 164.83 for purchase of newly issued stamps by cover services from the first day of issue post office.

### 163.5 Sales Policies

.51 New Issues. Only the post office or offices designated as the official first day of issue office(s) shall sell a new item on the first day of sale. New issues shall be placed on sale at all other offices on the day after the first day of sale.

### .52 Regular Stamp Windows and Stamp Collecting Centers

#### .521 Commemorative Stamps

a. It is the Postal Service's intent that all commemorative stamps be sold and none destroyed.

b. Offices shall place commemorative stamps on regular sale, holding aside only enough for the local philatelic demand. All supplies should be sold within 60 days after being placed on sale. After 60 days, clerks should sell all remaining commemorative stamps to customers in place of other sheet stamps.

c. Commemorative stamps of local interest may remain on sale for a longer period but in no case after the date of withdrawal from sale announced in the Postal Bulletin.

#### .522 Plate Number Blocks/Marginal Markings (All Stamps)

a. Definition. Plate number blocks are the stamps located on one corner of a pane of stamps with a plate number or numbers printed on the margin (selvage). Plate number blocks may include as few as four stamps where a single number appears, or as many as 20 where multiple floating numbers and other marginal markings, such as Mr. ZIP and notice of Copyright appear.

b. Setting Aside Plate Number Blocks. Clerks shall break panes of stamps for regular sale purposes, as follows:

(1) First tear stamps from the edge of the panes farthest from the plate number or marginal markings in order to preserve the plate block for collectors.

(2) Set aside quantities of plate blocks or marginal markings as panes are broken during regular sales transactions, but do not set them aside in advance.

c. Minimum Purchase Requirements and Sales Limitations.

(1) When the clerk has a broken pane of stamps from which the plate block or other marginal marking has been sold, and when no plate block or other marginal marking has been set aside, the following minimum purchases must be made by a customer desiring the plate block or other marginal marking:

| Denomination | Minimum Purchase |
|---|---|
| 1 cent to 50¢ | Full marginal strip of stamps (two rows deep having all marginal markings) |
| 51¢ to 99¢ | Half marginal strip |
| $1 to $7.50 | Block of four stamps |

Exception: There are no minimum purchase requirements when a clerk has: (a) only full panes of the requested stamp in stock, or (b) a broken pane that contains the plate block or other marginal marking.

(2) There are limitations to sales as follows: Each customer for whom a pane has been broken is limited to one marginal strip (1¢-50¢); a half marginal strip (51¢-99¢); or a block of four stamps ($1-$7.50) for each stamp subject, per day. It is necessary to place a limit on individual sales of plate blocks and other marginal markings so that the stamp stock available at post office windows may accommodate as many collectors as possible each day. Customers requesting more than the maximum permissible purchase in denominations of the first-class rate and below, should be asked to inquire on another day. Customers requesting more than the maximum permissible purchase in denominations higher than the first-class rate should be asked to inquire on another day, or should be referred to the Philatelic Sales Division.

d. Return of Unsold Stamp Stock. Broken panes of stamps without marginal strips and which exceed clerk requirements for regular stamp sales or use on parcel post, should be returned to the main stamp stock. To return stock, the clerk shall complete Form 17 in accordance with section 552 of Handbook F-1. The returned stock must be redistributed in the following priority: (1) to fulfill Stamps by Mail requests; (2) to be utilized in locally prepared stamp packages for vending machines; and (3) to be sold at other regular stamp windows. After 30 days, any stock remaining unsold at regular stamp windows is returned (using Form 17) to the main stamp stock.

e. Exceptions to Sales Policies. The Stamps Division may establish exceptions to the sales policies on selected stamp issues. Exceptions are announced in the Postal Bulletin.

**.523 Coiled Stamps.** These offices may not open and break coils of stamps.

Exception: Coils of new issue stamps may be opened and sold in less than full coil quantities, subject to the following limitations:

a. Sales of new issue coiled stamps in less than full coils are restricted to a one-month period beginning with the authorized first day of sale for each particular stamp issue.

b. These sales are further restricted to a single stamp window at each location designated by the postmaster to conduct such sales.

c. Coiled stamps of fractional denomination must be sold in multiples that reach full-cent amounts.

d. Stamps remaining in partial coils after expiration of the sales period will be used for general postage if practical.

**.524 Precanceled Stamps.** There is no limitation on the sale to collectors of sheet stamps or full coils of each of the precanceled denominations available. Purchases may be made in person or by mail by nonpermit holders for collection purposes only. Mail order requests must be accompanied by stamped, self-addressed envelopes for the return of the stamps purchased by the collector. Precanceled stamp policy is described in detail in 143.

**.53 Philatelic Outlets**

**.531 Commemorative Stamps.** These offices may keep an issue on sale until a notice of its removal from sales at the Philatelic Sales Division is published in the Postal Bulletin.

**.532 Plate Number Blocks/Marginal Markings (All Stamps).** The sales and disposition policies described in 163.522 apply except as follows:

a. Clerks may sell each customer one matched-set of four marginal strips for any stamp in stock.

b. There are no limitations on the sale of plate blocks of stamps having denominations from $1 to $7.50.

c. The Philatelic Sales Division mail order section, may, however, sell any quantity of marginal strips of stamps of issues having a face value above the first-class letter rate. For issues having a face value at or below the first-class letter rate, marginal strips will be sold only when full panes are ordered.

**.533 Coiled Stamps.** These offices may open coils of stamps as requested, except that coils having fractional denominations can only be sold in multiples that reach full-cent amounts. To guarantee receipt of "line pairs" or "line markings" on coils, the following minimum purchases are required:

a. Bulk rate denominations (when fractional) — minimum of 30 stamps;

b. $1—minimum of six stamps;

c. All other denominations—minimum of 25 stamps. Note: A "line marking" is the vertical line of color appearing at intervals of 25 stamps made by the joint or seam where printing plates meet on a rotary press. The "line pair" consists of the two coil stamps on either side of the "line marking." Line markings may not be visible on all coils.

**.534 Precanceled Stamps.** The sales policy described in 163.524 applies except that coils of precanceled stamps may be opened for the sale of individual stamps to collectors.

**.535 Stamp Credit (Accountability).** Philatelic outlets should maintain a good working level of stamp stock, postal stationery and philatelic products to encourage philatelic interest and to meet the needs of collectors and encourage philatelic interest. Therefore, postmasters may maintain a postage stock of up to $125,000 for each philatelic outlet at their office. This stock may be in excess of normal authorized stock limits. (This does not apply to the Philatelic Sales Division).

**.536 Inventory of Available Items.** Updated lists (Form 3300) of items available at the Philatelic Sales Division will be furnished periodically to philatelic outlets to guide them in maintaining a current inventory for collectors. All listed stamps shall be maintained by permanent philatelic outlets unless sold out and not available by requisition.

**.537 Stamp Packets.** Stamps withdrawn from sale which are incorporated in philatelic products such as Mint Sets or Collecting Kits may be sold by philatelic windows, postal stores, stamp collecting centers, and the Philatelic Sales Division.

**163.6 Stamp Withdrawals.** Notices concerning stamp withdrawals are published in the Postal Bulletin and give effective dates for removing stamps from sale. On the effective withdrawal date, philatelic outlets must immediately return their supply of the withdrawn stamp to the main stamp stock, using a Form 17. The stock must

then be redistributed to regular stamp windows for sale for a period of 30 days.

## 164 CANCELLATIONS FOR PHILATELIC PURPOSES

### 164.1 Definition and Policy

**.11** A postmark is a postal cancellation which contains the post office name, state, ZIP Code and month, day and year the canceling post office accepted custody of the material except as provided in 164.71 and 164.74. Other postal markings are made by validators, obliterators or special purpose cancelers.

**.12** The Postal Service shall endeavor to make all unusual postmarking services widely known to collectors through advance national publicity so as to avoid such postmarks being available only to small groups of people.

**.13** It is the policy of the Postal Service to prohibit backdating of mail except:

a. When postal operating requirements and public demand necessitate that cancellation commence prior to and continue after date contained in the postmark;

b. When replacements are being made of damaged, defective, or missing cancellations or covers; or

c. When all requirements for cancellations were met by customers and cancellations were not applied because of errors of postal personnel.

### 164.2 Philatelic Postmarking

**.21 General.** Postmarking for philatelic purposes is provided at the request of collectors or cover servicers for postmarking outside ordinary mail processing. This service requires special procedures and arrangements so that other postal operations and services are not interferred with or disrupted. It may involve handstamping requested either on a hand back or mail back basis and may entail the holding of mail for cancellation. Before this specialized service can be provided, all its conditions must be met. As a free service it is limited to transactions with fewer than 50 envelopes or other items. For 50 or more envelopes or other items, advance approval of the Stamps Division is required before service can be provided.

### .22 Cooperation With Collectors

a. Employees should strive to furnish clear and legible postmarks to stamp collectors by insuring that cancellation machines and handstamp devices are properly inked. Postal employees shall give special attention to mail bearing an endorsement that is of philatelic value or to requests for light cancellations and should avoid canceling stamps by pen or illegible smudging; however, stamps must be canceled sufficiently to protect postal revenue.

b. The Postal Service cannot provide special attention to a philatelic cover if it has been routinely entered into the mailstream by the sender.

c. Postmarking devices may be used only under the supervision of authorized postal personnel.

d. All handstamped postmarks shall be made with black ink unless the customer specifically indicates a preference for the color otherwise in use.

e. Employees should exercise care in handling all philatelic covers to assure that they are not damaged in mail handling. These covers are generally identifiable by a design printed on the left side of the envelope.

f. Postal employees should assure that philatelic covers are not overcanceled, backstamped, marked "received this date" or otherwise defaced on front or back, used as a top piece in a bundle for destination package for labeling purposes or bent, folded, mutilated or damaged by rubber bands.

**.23 Hand Back and Mail Back Service.** Postmarks rather than other obliterations should be used to provide the following services whenever they are available:

a. Hand Back Service.

(1) Post offices shall honor requests for hand back cancellation service where a customer personally presents an addressed or unaddressed envelope, postal card or other item described in 164.73 to a postal clerk for cancellation with the current day's postmark and immediate return or hand back to the customer.

(2) The envelope, card or other item does not enter the mailstream. All such materials must bear uncanceled postage at the applicable first class rate.

(3) So that service to other customers is not disrupted, there is a limit of 50 cancellations which can be provided for any single customer.

(4) This service may be provided for special die hub or regular machine cancellations only when the particular cancellation machine is readily accessible to the postal clerk, where the providing of such service will not interfere with other sales or mail processing operations and will not inconvenience other customers.

b. "Mail Back" Service. "Mail Back" service refers to that service authorized by the Stamps Division for stamp dealers and cover servicers which permits envelopes, cards or other items submitted for cancellation to be returned in bulk through the mail. Conditions of service are further described in 164.83. This form of "mail back" service must be approved in writing in advance by the Stamps Division. Mail back service shall not be provided for special die hub or machine cancellations.

**164.3 Permissible Cancellation Devices**

**.31 Handstamped Cancellations for Collectors.** The following postmark devices may be used to provide handstamped cancellations for collectors:

a. Standard cancellation with killer bars (Item 550).

b. Circular cancellation without killer bars.

c. First day of issue cancellation at post office where an item is first issued.

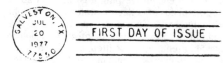

d. Bull's-eye cancellation.

e. Pictorial cancellation subject to conditions set forth in 164.42.

**.32 Obliteraters.** The following devices are obliterators and may be used for philatelic purposes in cases where none of the postmarks or postmarking devices described in 164.31 are available:

a. Validator stamp (also known as a registry stamp or round dater—Item 570).

b. Parcel post canceler (Item 502).

c. Rubber oval stamp (Item 0-681).

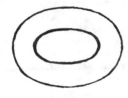

d. Receiving or dating stamp (Item 552).

**164.4 Types of Postmarks or Cancellations**

**.41 First Day of Issue.** These cancellations are provided by the post office when a philatelic issue is first placed on sale and are dated to show that day. They include both machine and handstamp cancellations. The words "First Day of Issue" appear in the killer bars. Requests for first day cancellations must be postmarked no later than the date specified in the Postal Bulletin to qualify for service. Bull's-eye cancellations are used when the conventional first day of issue postmark will not cancel all the unused stamps on an item presented for postmarking.

**.42 Pictorial Cancellations.** The cancellations are authorized to be used only at temporary philatelic stations and at other philatelic outlets. They shall not be used at regular stamp windows for special local celebrations. Cancellations used are generally handstamps except when volume requires the use of a machine cancellation. They may be used only during the operation of the temporary philatelic station. Requests for such cancellations must be at the post office offering the service no later than the date of the cancellation to qualify for service. A station may be authorized only one pictorial cancellation during its operation at an event. Different cancellations for each day of an event are authorized only for international philatelic exhibitions recognized by the Stamps Division and held in the United States.

**.43 Special Die Hub Cancellations.** Special die hub cancellations contain words relating to an event. These cancellations are applied by machine to live mail. Hand back service may be provided only as described in 164.23a. Mail back (return in bulk) service shall not be provided, but cancellation can be provided on addressed envelopes or postal cards which are delivered to the addressee or addressees through mail delivery. Cancellations of philatelic quality are often not possible.

**.44 Standard Cancellations.** Circular handstamped cancellations with or without killer bars may be provided upon request at post offices, stations and branches. They are available every day the office is open for business. No slogan or pictorial material may be included. Mail requests for these cancellations must be at the post office offering the service on the date of the cancellation to qualify for service.

**.45 Flight Cancellations.** Refer to 164.6. These cancellations are made by regular cancellation equipment or by handstamp depending on volume.

**.46 Regular Machine Cancellations.** Post offices may not machine cancel mail with the regular postmark when the envelopes are unaddressed or when the customers requests hand back service except as described in 164.23a. Mail back (return in bulk) service shall not be provided, but cancellations can be provided on addressed envelopes or postal cards which are delivered to the addressee or addressees through mail delivery.

**164.5 First Day of Issue**

**.51 First Day Sale.** A particular post office or postal facility is usually designated to have the exclusive sale of a new issue on the day it is issued. No other postal facility may begin general sale of the new issue until the following day. For purposes of this section, the word issue shall mean postage stamp, stamp booklet, or booklet pane, postal card, stamped envelope or aerogramme.

**.52 Notification.** New stamps and other philatelic issues are announced by notices displayed in post office lobbies, in the Postal Bulletin and through news releases distributed to the press and philatelic periodicals.

**.53 First Day Covers**

a. Definition. A first day cover is an envelope, post card, or other item of reasonable dimension bearing a new stamp or booklet pane or a new postal card, a new stamped envelope or a new aerogramme canceled with a die reading First Day of Issue and showing place and date of first day sale.

b. Procedures. Customers who want first day cancellations of new stamps have two options:

(1) Buy stamps at local post offices and affix them to their own envelopes. Mail the stamped envelopes to the postmaster at the city of issuance for cancellation. Preferential service is accorded covers on which collectors have affixed their own stamps.

(2) Submit envelopes with proper remittance to cover the cost of the stamps desired. The Postal Service will affix and cancel the stamps except as indicated in d. of this section. Remittance should be made by money order or cashier's, certified or personal check made payable to the U.S. Postal Service. Orders containing personal checks will be held until the checks have cleared. Cash will not be accepted, nor will postage stamps or foreign coins and currency; any orders containing such remittance will be returned unserviced. All covers must bear addresses to the right side of the envelope and at least ⅝ of an inch up from the bottom of the envelope. Requests must be postmarked no later than the date specified in the announcement (usually 15 calendar days from the date of issuance) to qualify for cancellation service. Covers must not be returned in outer envelopes even when furnished by collectors because to do so impedes operating efficiency.

c. Requirements. Envelopes submitted by collectors must be of ordinary letter size and must be properly addressed. Collectors should place a filler of postal card thickness in each envelope, and either turn in the flap or seal it. If applicable, collectors should put a pencil notation in the upper right corner of each cover to show the position and number of postage stamps to be placed there.

d. Unacceptable Covers. The issuing post office shall not provide cancellation service on covers submitted through the mail which are unaddressed, or bear stamps issued after the issue date and before the submittal cut-off date,

or bear previously canceled stamps nor may the post office provide hand back service on any items presented after the first day of issuance. These restrictions can be waived only by written authorization of the Stamps Division.

e. Bulk Orders. The post office servicing first day covers shall not accept from any one customer more than 50 envelopes requiring that stamps be affixed. When more than 50 envelopes are submitted, they must be returned unserviced to the customer, with a statement that service will be provided upon resubmittal of stamped envelopes of 50 or fewer envelopes. Care must be taken to prevent customers from avoiding this rule by placing multiple smaller orders. Customers desiring cancellations on more than 50 covers must buy and affix their own stamps to their envelopes.

f. Handstamped Cancellations. Handstamped cancellations will be applied at the first day ceremony location, at the main office windows of the first day post office, and on covers which cannot be fully canceled by postal cancellation machines. In all other cases, machine cancellations will be supplied, except as provided in 164.83.

g. Hand Back Service. Hand back service for first day cancellations is limited to the first day of issue. Material to be canceled must be presented to the main office window of the first day post office.

h. Mail Orders for Mint Stamps. The first day post office may not accept mail order requests for uncanceled stamps from customers outside their service area, except for cover servicers as provided in 164.83a.

**.54 Unofficial First Day Covers.** Stamps acquired at the first day post office may be canceled at any post office. Envelopes containing new stamps canceled on the first day of sale at a post office other than the issuing office are known as "unofficial first day covers."

**164.6 Flight Covers**

**.61 Definition.** The Postal Service authorizes special cachet and cancellation services for mail carried on inaugural flights and other aviation events of national interest. Flight covers generally bear official USPS cachets, the postmark of the city of origin and the backstamped postmark of the city of destination.

**.62 Authorization.** The Stamps Division may authorize cachet and cancellation service for:

a. All stop points on a new airmail route;

b. New stop points on an existing route; and

c. Other aviation events of national interest.

Notices authorizing official cachets and cancellation services are published in the Postal Bulletin. This service will not be authorized for new aircraft used on an existing airmail route. Backstamped postmarks may be authorized where international airmail service is inaugurated to a stop point in the United States when the postal administration of the country of the flight's origin officially requests that the U.S. Postal Service provide philatelic treatment to mail carried on the flight.

**.63 Preparation of Covers.** Collectors must preaddress each cover to the right of the envelope and at least ⅝ of an inch from the bottom of the envelope. Each envelope must bear postage at the applicable airmail rate. Each envelope should include a uniform enclosure of the approximate weight of a postal card to assure a good impression. A clear space, 2½ inches by 2½ inches, on the lower portion of the envelope and to the left of the address must be allowed for the cachet. An additional 1½ inches to the left of the innermost stamp must be provided to permit a clear postmark.

**.64 Submittal of Covers.** Collectors should send the envelopes for inaugural cachets under cover and endorsed "Flight Covers" to the post office or airport mail facility applying the cachet and postmark. A request to hold covers for the inaugural service should be enclosed, indicating the directional service and cachet desired.

**.65 Compliance With Collectors' Requests**

a. Direction Specified. Post offices should comply with requests for dispatch in a particular direction to the greatest extent practicable unless otherwise specified by the Stamps Division. No directional service will be accorded for events of national aviation interest.

b. Direction Not Specified. In the absence of specific requests, post offices should dispatch covers on the actual first flight, regardless of direction.

c. Incomplete Instructions. If the collector's request is not clear, post offices should dispatch covers in accordance with the judgment of the dispatching office.

d. Color of Ink Used for the Cachet. The Stamps Division will determine the color of ink to be used on the cachet at each stop point. Requests from collectors for other ink colors must not be honored.

e. Position of Cachet. Post offices should apply cachets legibly and neatly to the left side of the address side of the cover.

**.66 When Cachets Must Not Be Applied.** Cachets must not be applied to:

a. Covers for immediate return to sender. All covers must be dispatched on the flight.

b. Covers bearing a previous official or unofficial cachet.

c. Covers lacking sufficient clear space for application of cachet without obscuring the address.

d. Aerogrammes and postal cards.

e. Double postal or post cards intended for return reply purposes.

f. Covers received after the flight.

g. Covers on which postage is not fully prepaid.

h. Covers containing previously canceled postage stamps.

i. Anything other than a flight cover.

**.67 Backstamping.** All inaugural covers will be backstamped with machine or hand cancellation devices at the destination post office. Postage stamps are not required for the second cancellation. Requests for additional or special backstamping must not be honored.

**.68 Delay of Flight.** If, after postmarking of covers has begun, the flight is canceled or the scheduled date of departure is delayed to a subsequent date, the postmark dates already stamped on the flight covers will not be changed, replacement covers will not be issued, nor will any liability be accepted.

**164.7 When and Where Philatelic Postmarking May Be Done**

**.71 Date and Place of Postmarking**

a. Postmarking provided for philatelic purposes may commence prior to the actual date of the cancellation requested and may continue after that date when demand, processing capability, or other requirements of the Postal Service dictate it. Under no circumstances may any postmarked materials be released before the date of the cancellation.

b. The regional retail branch may determine that local processing capability requires that philatelic cancellation services be performed at an office other than the post office whose cancellation is used; in these cases, however, all materials to be postmarked must be received at or deposited in the post office whose cancellation is being used, or at an office designated by the regional retail branch or the Stamps Division.

**.72 Preparation Requirements.** Post cards, postal cards and envelopes submitted through the mail must bear postage at the applicable rate and complete addresses, except as provided in 164.83d. Materials submitted for hand back service need not be addressed.

**.73 Special Materials on Which Cancellations Are Requested.** The materials herein described may be canceled as indicated. These provisions do not apply to any arrangements made with cover servicers and dealers by the Stamps Division under 164.8.

a. Plain Cards, Slips of Paper, and Blank Envelopes. Postal employees may not place postmarks for customers on plain slips of paper, plain cards or blank envelopes which do not bear unused postage in an amount equaling or exceeding the first-class rate.

b. Picture Post Cards (Maximum Cards). Picture post cards with the stamp placed on the face of the card rather than on the address side are known as maximum cards. Postmasters may cancel these cards and hand them back to the person presenting them.

c. Posters, Portfolios and Other Memorabilia. These items with the stamps placed thereon may be canceled when presented in person for hand back service. Submittal and return through the mail is not permitted.

d. Already Canceled Stamps/Multiple Cancellations. Items bearing previously canceled stamps and postmarks are acceptable for additional cancellations when presented for hand back service. First day of issue cancellations may not be provided on a hand back basis after the first day of issuance. Mint stamps to cover the first-class rate must be affixed for each cancellation. Materials bearing multiple cancellations may not be submitted or returned through the mail in outer envelopes.

e. Currency. Currency bearing unused postage stamps of first-class value or items bearing currency with stamps affixed or adjacent thereto may be canceled when presented in person for hand back service. Submittal and return through the mail is not permitted. The Postal Service does not accept responsibility for currency in its possession in conjunction with philatelic services.

f. Backs of Envelopes. Post offices may cancel unused stamps when they are affixed to the reverse side of envelopes bearing already canceled stamps. This service is available only for envelopes presented for hand back service. They may not be returned through the mail even when outer envelopes are provided. Such a cancellation denotes only that the item was presented to the post office for postmarking on that date; it does not denote that the envelope was carried by the Postal Service and should be differentiated from flight covers described in 164.6. This type of cover may be presented, for instance, in situations reenacting Pony Express routes, promoting special airline flights, balloon ascents, and the like, on which covers are carried outside the mail service.

g. Foreign Postage Stamps. Unused foreign postage stamps may be canceled with a U.S. Postal Service postmark only when unused U.S. postage of the appropriate rate is canceled with the same stroke.

#### .74 Holding the Mail

a. Post offices may hold mail to comply with customers' requests that the mail be postmarked on a specified date. Post offices may not, however, hold mail for an event where the date of occurrence is not certain or where it is subject to change or for cancellation on a day when the office will be closed, except as authorized by the Stamps Division. In these latter in-

stances, the envelopes submitted should be returned unserviced in an outer envelope to the customer with a short note explaining why the requested service cannot be performed.

b. There will be a limit of 50 covers per customer which can be held for cancellation. Except on first day covers where customers have affixed their own stamps, quantities above this number must receive the prior written authorization of the Stamps Division. The Stamps Division may also authorize the holding of mail for events of nationwide interest.

#### .75 Damaged or Missing Covers

a. Requests for replacement of first day cancellations, pictorial cancellations, and standard cancellations may be accepted at the appropriate post office for a period of 60 days from the date of issuance for first day covers, or 30 days from the date of cancellation for pictorial and standard cancellations.

b. Replacement cancellations will be made for poor quality of cancellation, damage to the envelope, or other similar defects. Replacements will not be made, however, in cases where envelopes were marked on the back by letter sorting machine code numbers as they moved through the mail system.

c. The customer must return the unsatisfactory cover or covers to the appropriate post office for replacement.

d. Replacement covers must be returned to the customer in a penalty envelope so that a stale postmark does not appear in the mail stream.

e. Damaged covers should be disposed of in accordance with section 553 of Handbook F-1.

f. The Postal Service will not replace missing or unsatisfactory standard machine cancellations, special die hub cancellations, or flight cancellations as these cancellations are made in the course of live mail processing.

g. All claims for nonreceipt of other covers submitted for servicing by the Postal Service must be sent to the appropriate post office no later than 60 days from the date of postmark or from the date cancellations were last applied. Claims for replacement cancellations filed after this time will not be honored and will be returned to the customer with a short explanation as to why the request cannot be honored.

h. The Postal Service is not responsible for damage or loss of cacheted covers or of other items of value.

#### .76 Special Requests.
Requests for cancellations at postal facilities that normally do not cancel mail must be made in writing to the regional retail branch at least 60 days in advance to permit regional authorization and appropriate national publicity. These requirements also apply to requests for cancellations at offices which are inaccessible to the public or to re-

quests for cancellations at any offices on dates when mail is not normally canceled (i.e., Sundays and holidays). Cover servicers, as described in 164.8, must submit their requests for cancellations to the Stamps Division.

**.77 Military Post Offices.** Military post offices, including APOs and FPOs, may handstamp covers both on a hand back basis and on mail order requests in conformance with all policies and in accordance with all conditions and procedures herein stated, except that:

a. The postal chief at each such installation may establish the maximum number of covers individual collectors or dealers may submit;

b. Military post offices may not establish temporary philatelic stations or provide pictorial cancellations.

### 164.8 Cover Servicers and Dealers

**.81 Definition.** Cover servicers and dealers include those individuals, groups or commercial enterprises that submit 50 or more envelopes or other items for cancellations, whether presented in one or more packages, and that request return in bulk.

**.82 Mail Back Service**

a. Service subject to a service charge as indicated in 164.83 may be provided by postmasters only when the customer requesting it has received the prior written approval of the Stamps Division.

b. Mail back service, or return under cover in bulk, is available to dealers only when return postage, registration if desired, and all other applicable fees such as special handling and special delivery are remitted to the postmaster at the place of postmarking. Such requests which do not include such payment will be held until the proper amount is received. In the event of overpayment by the cover servicer, the amount in excess of postage and fees required shall be returned separately in mint postage stamps. If the refund is $10 or more, it must be sent under registered mail.

c. Mail back service is generally permitted on first day of issue, pictorial or standard cancellations requested on the following materials: envelopes, postal cards, maximum cards and posters, portfolios or other memorabilia. The Postal Service will not accept covers for first day of issue cancellation which bear a stamp issued after the date of the postmark but before the expiration date for submittal.

d. Unless the cover servicer has received written headquarters' approval for cancellation service, the envelopes will be returned to the cover servicer unserviced with a letter stating that advance approval from the Stamps Division must be obtained before the request can be honored.

**.83 Conditions of Service**

a. First Day of Issue Cancellations. Customers recognized as first day cover servicers will be permitted, though not required, to purchase mint stamps by mail from the first day post office or from the Philatelic Sales Division on the date of issuance. Machine cancellations will be provided to dealers free of charge only when stamp-affixed envelopes are submitted. All stamped envelopes must be returned for servicing within the prescribed time limit. Hand cancellations will be provided subject to a service charge established by the Stamps Division.

b. Pictorial Cancellations. These handstamped cancellations are provided subject to approval by and a service charge established by the Stamps Division, except for exhibition or convention sponsors as indicated in 164.95.

c. Special Die Hub Machine Cancellations. All envelopes must be addressed. They will be canceled free on any quantity of envelopes submitted, but may not be returned in bulk.

d. Standard Cancellations. These handstamped cancellations may be applied on unaddressed covers and returned in bulk only when authorized by the Stamps Division. Orders are subject to a service charge established by the Stamps Division.

e. Flight Cancellations. These covers must be addressed, and service is subject to approval by the Stamps Division. A service fee is charged when handstamped cancellations are requested.

### 164.9 Cancellation Services at Temporary Philatelic Stations

**.91 Approval.** Postmasters may request authority from the regional retail branch to provide cancellation service at temporary philatelic stations. Only the standard circular cancellation shall be provided, unless the sponsors or organizers apply to the postmaster for use of a pictorial cancellation at least 10 weeks prior to the event. The sponsors or organizers must also propose a design and finished artwork for a pictorial cancellation. The cancellation service and design require the approval of the postmaster, the district manager, and the regional retail manager.

**.92 Requirements.** All cancellations must carry the name of the exhibition or event, followed by the word station or sta, the city, state and ZIP Code, and the month, day and year. Pictorial cancellations that endorse the ideals, policies, programs, products, campaigns, or candidates of religious, anti-religious, commercial, political, fraternal, trade, labor, public interest, or special interest organizations will not be approved. However, cancellations may be approved that recognize events such as meetings or conventions sponsored by or involving such organizations, providing their designs do not include words, symbols, or illustrations referring to ideals, policies, programs, products, campaigns, or candidates. If there is doubt as to whether a proposed cancellation meets these requirements, regional retail managers must consult with the general manager, Stamps Division, USPS headquarters, before granting approval. Overall dimensions cannot exceed 4 inches horizontally and 2 inches vertically.

**.93 Publicity.** The regional retail manager must submit a reproducible copy of the pictorial cancellation (actual size) to the Stamps Division so that appropriate national publicity can be arranged. The use of standard cancellations at temporary philatelic stations must also be reported. All reports should include the dates the temporary philatelic stations will be open. Reports and copies of pictorial cancellations shall be submitted the first of each month for those cancellations authorized two months later (e.g., January 1 for March authorization; February 1 for April, etc.).

**.94 Equipment.** Pictorial and standard cancellations shall be applied by rubber handstamps purchased by the region. If more than 100,000 pieces of mail is anticipated, the region may apply to the Stamps Division at least 60 days in advance for purchase of a metal die for machine cancellation. These cancellations may only be provided for the duration of the temporary philatelic station.

**.95 Service Limitations.** Except for the exhibition or convention sponsor, handstamping as a free service will be limited to a maximum of 50 covers for any single individual or group. The sponsor may obtain any reasonable amount of hand backs free of service charge for its members, and special folders or programs prepared by the sponsor may be canceled and made available upon the opening of the show. Individuals or groups requiring more than 50 handstamped cancellations may obtain this service only by paying a special fee. Written application for this service must be made in advance to and authorized by the Stamps Division.

**.96 Use and Return of Equipment.** Philatelic cancellation handstamps, like other canceling devices, may be used only under the supervision of authorized postal personnel and must be returned by the postmaster to the regional retail branch 65 days after close of the exhibition or convention, by which time all replacement requests will have been handled. The regional retail manager shall destroy the cancellation device upon receipt.

**165 SPECIAL PHILATELIC SERVICES, PRODUCTS AND PROGRAMS**

**165.1 Postal Cacheted Envelopes.** Postal Service produced cachets or cacheted envelopes are permitted only for first flights and for major postal or aviation events, such as the opening of a new Philatelic Center or Dedicated Philatelic Window. All such cachets or cacheted envelopes must be approved by the appropriate regional and headquarters organizations, and their approval must be communicated to the Stamps Division at least two months prior to the event so

that national publicity of their availability can be arranged.

**165.2 Presentations.** The postmaster general, the assistant postmaster general, Customer Services, and the Stamps Division general manager are authorized to approve the use of canceled and uncanceled U.S. postage stamps, postal stationery and other philatelic products for information and official postal business purposes and as official presentations of the U.S. Postal Service. All such presentations shall be approved in writing by one of the three authorized officials with a statement indicating the intended use. These presentations shall not be used as postage and will be restricted to those instances when the best interests of the Postal Service will be served.

**165.3 Autographs.** Postal employees have the prerogative to accept or refuse requests for autographs. Employees should exercise fairness in handling such requests. Nothing of value may be accepted or requested in exchange for autographs.

**166 COPYRIGHT OF PHILATELIC DESIGN**

**166.1 Policy.** The designs of postage stamps, stamped envelopes, postal cards, aerogrammes, souvenir cards and other philatelic items issued on or after Jan. 1, 1978, have been copyrighted by the U.S. Postal Service in accordance with Title 17, United States Code.

**166.2 Permission for Use.** The use of illustrations of the designs covered by such copyrights is permitted as follows:

a. In editorial matter in newspapers, magazines, journals, books, philatelic catalogs and philatelic albums.

b. In advertising matter, circulars or price lists for the sale of the postal items illustrated.

c. In advertising matter, circulars or price lists for the sale of newspapers, magazines, journals, books, philatelic catalogs and philatelic albums containing illustrations of philatelic designs.

d. In motion picture films, microfilms, slides or electronic tape for projection upon a screen or for use in telecasting. No print or other reproduction from such films, slides or tapes shall be made except for the uses permitted in 166.2a, b and c.

**166.3 Reproduction of Designs.** Illustrations permitted by 166.2a, b and c may be in color or in black and white and may depict philatelic items as uncanceled or canceled. When depicting uncanceled items in color, illustrations must be less than 75 per cent or more than 150 per cent, in linear dimension, of the size of the design of the philatelic items as issued. Color illustrations of canceled philatelic items and black and white illustrations of uncanceled or canceled philatelic items may be in any size.

**166.4 Requests for Licenses.** The U.S. Postal Service may grant licenses for the use of illustrations of its copyright designs outside the scope of the above permission. Requests for such licenses should be addressed to the chairman, Intellectual Property Rights Board, Office of Contracts, U.S. Postal Service, Washington, D.C. 20260.

## Section 170: Special Cancellations

### 171 AUTHORIZATION

**171.1 Description.** Special cancellations are machine cancellations in which a slogan or message publicizing an event is engraved on a die hub and used to cancel mail. They may be used only in post offices which have 190 or more revenue units and cancel significant volumes of mail. The special cancellations described in this section are not of philatelic quality.

Other types of cancellations are:

a. First day of issue cancellations authorized by the Stamps Division in accordance with 164.5.

b. Handstamped cancellations for collectors described in 164.3.

c. Pictorial cancellations authorized by the Stamps Division in accordance with 164.42.

d. Postal message cancellations are used to convey official postal messages or slogans and are authorized in accordance with 175.

**171.2 Purpose.** Special cancellations are authorized when the scheduled event to be observed is:

a. For a national purpose for which Congress has made an appropriation, or

b. Of general public interest and importance and is to endure for a definite period of time and is not to be conducted for private gain or profit.

**171.3 Prohibitions.** Special cancellations are not authorized for:

a. Events of interest primarily to a particular local group.

b. Fraternal, political, religious, service, commercial.

c. Campaigns or events promoting the sale or use of private products or services.

d. Idea or slogan promotions not directly connected with an event of general public interest and importance.

e. Post office anniversaries.

f. Recruitment programs.

g. Events which occur during a period when all canceling machines in the post office have already been scheduled for the use of other special cancellation die hubs.

**171.4 Periods of Use.** Special cancellations may not be used longer than 6 months. Special cancellations that are approved on an annual basis are limited to one 60-day period annually.

### 172 Revocation

Permission to use any special cancellation may be curtailed or revoked when it is necessary to use special postmarking dies for Postal Service purposes.

### 173 REQUIREMENTS FOR OBTAINING SPECIAL CANCELLATION DIE HUBS

**173.1 Application**

.11 The application, for a purpose described in 171.2, must be submitted in writing to the postmaster at the post office where the special cancellation is to be used.

.12 The application must be submitted by the sponsor at least four months before the date the special cancellation is to be used.

.13 The application must provide the following information:

a. Complete description and schedule of the event to be observed, including evidence that it is not being conducted for private gain or profit.

b. Wording of the proposed cancellation:

(1) Space available for the wording is shown in the illustration below. Wording is limited to 3 lines of not more than 20 letters, numbers, or spaces each. Do not use illustrations or designs, as in most circumstances, such designs are not easily reproduced on a die hub. The wording must directly reflect the event to be commemorated.

| ONANCOCK, VIRGINIA |
| 300TH ANNIVERSARY |
| 1680—1980 |

(2) Wording on a special cancellation must be standardized and approved by the sponsor's national headquarters when the sponsor is an affiliate or local chapter of a national organization. Standardized requests for national events must be forwarded to the general manager, Special Services Division. Rates and Classification Department, Washington, D.C. 20260-5371.

c. Name and telephone number of the post office where the cancellation is to be used.

d. Period of use desired.

e. Number of die hubs required.

f. Name, address and phone number of the sponsor who will be billed for the cost of manufacturing the die hubs.

g. The application described in this section should be in the form of a letter from the sponsor to the postmaster, giving all of the information required.

**.14** A request must be submitted for reuse of recurring annual cancellations three months prior to the date the sponsor desires the cancellation to be used again. In the case of national cancellations, a single request from the national sponsor is sufficient.

**173.2 Referral by Postmaster**

**.21** Forward the application to your designated mail classification center (see subchapter 130) as soon as it is received. Enclose the information described in 173.22 and 173.23.

**.22** Furnish the name of the manufacturer and the model number of the canceling machine on which the special die hub will be used. If the machine is a Model Flier, Model M, or Model G, the correct die hub part number must be stated. The part number for Model Flier and Model M machines is 1535 for a hub that uses a round base ring die, and 1535 G for a hub that uses a square base ring die. The part number for a Model G machine is 218A for a hub that uses a round base ring die, and 218E for a hub that uses a square base ring die. A part number is not required for other machines.

**.23** State the effect the approval would have on the use of special cancellations already approved for that office.

**173.3 Approval and Disapproval.** The sponsor is informed through the postmaster of the approval or denial of the application. If approved, the Mail Classification Center (MCC) arranges for the manufacture of the die hub and instructs the postmaster on its use by memorandum or Form 3617, Order For Special Canceling Machine Die Hubs. If the request is not approved, the postmaster is advised by the MCC manager of the decision and the reason.

**173.4 Cost.** The sponsor must pay the cost of manufacturing the special cancellation die hub and any cost incurred in adapting canceling machines for its use or for installing the hub. The approximate cost of a die hub can be obtained from the mail classification center or the general manager, Special Services Division, Office of Mail Classification, Rates and Classification Department, Washington, D.C. 20260-5371. The organization or person assuming the cost of manufacturing the die hub will be billed by the manufacturer.

**174 DISPOSITION**

**174.1 After Use.** Used die hubs may not be given to sponsors or transferred to another post office.

Used die hubs not retained for future use must be sent for disposal to Mail Equipment Shops, 2135 5th St. NE, Washington, D.C. 20260-6224.

**174.2 Special Request.** A request from the sponsor that a special cancellation die hub be retained for an appropriate purpose, such as placement in a museum, library, historical site, or other suitable use may be approved by the general manager, Special Services Division.

**174.3 Replacement.** When a special cancellation die hub must be replaced, the local sponsor must be notified immediately so that he may, if he desires, apply for a replacement through the local postmaster. The sponsor must pay for replacement die hubs.

**175 POSTAL MESSAGE CANCELLATIONS**

**175.1 Purpose.** Postal message cancellation die hubs are normally used to convey official Postal Service messages or slogans. They may be used as long as the slogan or message remains timely, or as long as the regional director, Mail Processing, considers necessary.

**175.2 Authorization**

**.21 Application.** Heads of postal installations having 190 or more revenue units, who require postal message die hubs, should submit the requests on Form 4636, Requisition for Postmarking Dies and Engraved Station Die Hubs. Send Form 4636 to the regional director, Mail Processing, accompanied by a letter explaining the intended use and duration.

**.22 Approval.** Approved requests for postal message cancellations should be forwarded to the installation's area supply center. Requests for die hubs to be used on Mark II or M-36 Facer Cancellers should be sent to the Western Area Supply Center, Topeka, Kan. 66624.

**176.1 Postage.** Mailers requesting that their mail be canceled with a special cancellation must affix first-class postage to the mail. The mail must bear a complete address. Stamps issued by foreign countries may not be placed on the mail.

**176.2 Prohibitions**

**.21 Holding the Mail.** Mail must not be held to comply with a customer's request that the mail be postmarked with a special cancellation on a particular date.

**.22 Backdating.** Backdating of mail to comply with customer's requests is prohibited.

**.23 Returns.** Mail bearing the special cancellation must not be enclosed in another envelope for return, even if the customer provides a postage paid envelope for return (see 164.43).

**.24 Replacements.** Replacement of damaged envelopes canceled with a special cancellation is prohibited.

## Section 140: Postage

### 141 STAMPED ENVELOPES, POSTAL CARDS, AEROGRAMMES

#### 141. 1 Plain Stamped Envelopes

**.11 Envelopes Available at Post Offices.** Denominations available depend on current postage rates.

**.12 Sales at Post Offices.** Only sizes 6¾ and 10 regular are sold in less than full box lots. Boxes contain 500 envelopes.

**.13 Precanceled Envelopes.** Only nonprofit organizations and political committees (as covered by postal regulations) may purchase precanceled envelopes. Sales are made in full box lots only except at philatelic outlets (see 141.15).

**.14 Window Envelopes.** Window envelopes are sold in full box lots only, except at philatelic outlets (see 141.15). All windows are 1⅛ inches wide and 4¾ inches long and are located ½ inch from the bottom of the envelope. In size 6¾, the window is located ⅞ inch from the left edge; in size 10 it is ¾ inch from the left edge.

**.15 Envelope Sales at Philatelic Outlets.** Window and precanceled stamped envelopes sizes 6¾ and 10 regular may be sold at philatelic outlets in less than full box lots of 500. The selling price of a single window or precanceled stamped envelope will be that price listed for each appropriate size and type on the current issue of Form 3300, Philatelic Catalog. Philatelic outlets will not sell full box lots of window and precanceled stamped envelopes.

**.16 Envelope Dimensions**

a. Size 6¾ — 3⅝ by 6½ inches

b. Size 10 — 4⅛ by 9¼ inches

(Note: Dimensions may vary 1/16 inch.)

**.16 Private Printing of Return Addresses.** Stamped envelopes may be privately printed in any style, provided at least 3½ inches of clear space is left at the right end of the address side of the envelope.

#### 141.2 Printed Stamped Envelopes (Special-Request)

**.21 Printed Stamped Envelopes Available.** Denominations available depend on current postage rates.

**.22 How to Order Printed Stamped Envelopes.** Prepare Form 3203, Order for Printed Stamped Envelopes. Submit the order through the post office named in the return address. However, if undeliverable letters are to be returned to the main office of a firm in another city, envelopes may be ordered at the post office where they will be mailed.

**.23 Style of Printing Return Addresses**

**.231** All lines of the return address will be printed in capitals and lower-case letters with flush left margin, using 8-point Helvetica type. See sample in 141.232.

**.232 Sample Style of Printing:**

Charles Jones
610 Seventh Avenue
New York, NY 00000

**.24 Required Printing**

**.241 Local Address.** The printed address must include the local address. The adequacy of the address, to insure return of undeliverable mail, will be determined by the postmaster. Any one of the following may be used:

a. Street address.

b. Post office box number.

c. Rural route number and box number.

d. Name of building and room number, including street address.

e. A street address and a post office box number may be shown in the return address. When both addresses are shown, mail will be returned to the address indicated in the line immediately preceding the city, state and ZIP Code. The ZIP Code must be that of the delivery unit serving the address shown in the line immediately preceding the city and state.

**.242 Name of Post Office.** The printed return address must include the name of the post office or branch post office, state and ZIP Code.

**.25 Optional Printing**

**.251 Name**

a. The name may be that of an individual, firm, corporation, institution, association or society. It may include the name and title of an officer of the concern (as John Doe, Treasurer, Washington Educational Association) and such titles as M.D., D.D.S., Rev., and LL.D.

b. Descriptive words, such as druggist, attorney at law, esquire, or C.P.A. are not considered titles, but represent business or professional names, which may also be printed. Such descriptive words are printed subject to the conditions set forth in 141.252.

c. The name of a branch or department of a business may be printed only when necessary to insure return of undeliverable mail; i.e., when other branches or departments are located at the same post office address.

**.252 Advertising**

a. A brief statement or descriptive phrase devoted to advertising may be printed either following the name or on one or two separate lines. There may not be more than two such lines devoted to permissible advertising and these two lines should appear between the name (or main line) and the local address.

b. An individual or organization engaged in business, professional, educational, social, cultural, charitable, political or other endeavors may advertise. The advertisement may describe the nature of the business of the individual or organization, or refer to the goods, services or works provided by the individual or organization.

c. Statements or descriptive phrases which describe the nature of a business and contain a reference to the quality of the goods or services produced, such as Best Tires in Town or Complete Insurance, will be permitted.

d. Nothing will be printed which would make the envelope nonmailable under 18 U.S.C. 1463, which prohibits the mailing of indecent matter on wrappers or envelopes.

**.253 Phone Numbers.** The phone number of any individual or group may be printed on the envelope and must appear immediately preceding the local address.

**.254 Postal Instructions.** Only the postal instructions in this section may be included as part of the printed return endorsement. The request to return endorsement in 141.254a shall appear above the name and address. All other postal endorsements shall appear below the line with the city, state and ZIP Code. A combination of endorsements may be used:

a. Request to Return. A request to return undelivered mail after a specified number of days (not less than 3 and not more than 30) may be printed. If a return request is included on envelopes for third-class mail the words Return Postage Guaranteed must also be used. Sample printing:

**After 5 Days, Return to**

b. Address Correction. A request for address correction service may be printed on mail of any class. The new address of addressee or the reason why the piece is undeliverable will be furnished. The charge is 25¢. Sample printing:

**Address Correction Requested**

c. Third-Class Mail. On single piece rate third-class mail which is sealed (see also 621.4), the following must appear:

**Third-Class**

d. Return of Undelivered Third-Class Mail. A request may be made to return undelivered third-class mail. Sample printing:

**Return Postage Guaranteed**

e. Forwarding Third-Class Mail. A request to forward third-class mail to a new address may be made. If addressee refuses to pay forwarding postage, the mail will be returned, and both forwarding and return postage will be collected from the sender. Sample printing:

**Forwarding and Return Postage Guaranteed**

**.26 Other Requirements**

a. No line of either required or optional printing may exceed 47 characters and spaces.

b. The total number of lines of required and optional printing may not exceed seven.

c. The last two lines of printing shall be reserved for the street address or P.O. box number where mail is to be delivered, and the city, state and ZIP Code.

**.27 Prohibited Printing.** No matter may be printed other than that permitted by 141.24 and 141.25.

**.28 Rejection of Envelopes.** Special request envelopes may be rejected because of defective manufacture, or mistakes in printing, denomination, size, etc. If the mistake was made by the purchaser, the value of the postage only will be returned. If the mistake was made by the post office or its contractor, the entire invoiced value of the envelopes will be returned.

**141.3 Postal Cards Available.** Denominations available depend on current postage rates.

Note: All domestic postal cards are precanceled. Postal cards in sheets for use in printing must be cut to regulation size, $3\frac{1}{2}$ by $5\frac{1}{2}$ inches so that the stamp appears in the upper right corner. Cases of sheet postal cards may be broken for sale. Return addresses are not printed on postal cards by the Postal Service.

**141.4 Aerogrammes.** Denomination depends on current aerogramme rate.

**142 ADHESIVE STAMPS**

**142.1 Availability and Use**

**.11 Types.** Denominations range from 1¢ to $5, with some values available in coil or booklet form.

**.12 Use**

**.121** Fix stamps firmly in the upper right corner of the address side of the mail cover.

**.122** Any stamp partly concealed by an overlapping stamp may not be counted as postage.

**.123** Postal employees (other than rural carriers as prescribed in 156.41) are not required to fix stamps to mail.

**.124** Airmail postage stamps may be used to pay regular postage and fees for special services.

**.13 Perforating.** Postage and special delivery stamps may be perforated with an identifying mark if the holes do not exceed 1/32 of an inch in diameter and if the space taken by the mark is not larger than $\frac{1}{2}$ inch square.

**.14 Reuse Prohibited.** Reuse of stamps with intent to cause loss to the government is punishable by fine and imprisonment.

**142.2 Purchase**

**.21 Acceptable Form of Payment.** Foreign or mutilated money is not acceptable. When the post office cannot make change, the exact amount of the purchase must be paid. Checks are acceptable for all postal supplies and services, except money orders, provided they conform to the Postal Service check acceptance policy. A charge of $5 will be levied against a customer whose check is returned by the bank as uncollectable. In such an event, written notice will be given to the customer that the check was returned by the bank as uncollectable and that a $5 charge plus the amount of the returned check must be promptly remitted. The customer must use money order or certified check if he sends the money by mail.

**.22 Purchase Receipts.** If the customer wants a receipt for purchases and has prepared the receipt in advance, the postal employee will stamp it upon payment. If the customer has not prepared but wants a receipt for purchases, Form 1096, Cash Receipt, will be used for postage and other services for which verification of payment is not already provided. The postal employee will fill in the total amount of the purchase and will stamp the form upon payment.

**.23 Postage Due.** Postage due must be paid in cash. Postage due stamps may not be used for paying postage.

**142.3 Validity of Stamps.** All postage stamps issued by the United States since 1860 are good for postage from any point in the United States or from any other place where the United States domestic mail service operates. The following are not good for postage:

a. Mutilated or defaced stamps.

b. Stamps cut from stamped envelopes, aerogrammes, or postal cards.

c. Stamps covered or coated in such manner that the canceling or defacing marks cannot be imprinted directly on the stamps.

d. Nonpostage stamps (migratory bird hunting and conservation stamps, U.S. saving and thrift stamps, etc).

e. Postage due, special delivery, special handling and certified mail stamps.

f. United Nations stamps, except on mail deposited at United Nations, N.Y.

g. Stamps of other countries.

h. Stamps on which any unauthorized design, message, or other marking has been overprinted.

**142.4 Unlawful Use of Stamps**

**.41 By Postal Employees.** It is unlawful for postal employees entrusted with the sale or custody of postage stamps to:

a. Use stamps in payment of debts or purchase of saleable items.

b. Sell stamps except for cash.

c. Sell stamps for more or less than face value.

**.42 Counterfeit Stamps.** Counterfeit stamps will be confiscated and sent to the postal inspector in charge of the division in which the post

office is located. A receipt identifying the stamps will be given to persons from whom counterfeit stamps are confiscated.

**142.5 Reproduction of Stamps**

**.51** Postmasters may not give opinions to the public concerning the reproduction of foreign or domestic postage stamps.

**.52** Persons desiring information concerning reproductions of domestic stamps issued before January 1, 1978, or of any foreign stamps should address their inquiries to the Office of the Director, U.S. Secret Service, Treasury Department, Washington, D.C. 20220.

**.53** Persons desiring information concerning reproductions of domestic postage stamps issued after January 1, 1978, should first review the general reproduction permission provision set out in 166. Any further inquiries should be addressed to the chairman, Intellectual Property Rights Board, Office of Contracts, USPS headquarters, Washington, D.C. 20260.

**142.6 Imitations of Stamps and Official Markings**

**.61 Postage Stamps.** Matter bearing imitations of postage stamps, in adhesive or printed form, or private seals or stickers which are like a postage stamp in form and design, shall not be accepted for mailing.

**.62 Official Markings and Designs.** Matter bearing decorative markings and designs, in adhesive or printed form, which imitate the markings and designs used to identify official postal services shall not be accepted for mailing. The following illustrations are examples of prohibited imitations:

**.63 Permissible Seals and Stickers.** Seals or stickers that do not imitate postage stamps by having such characteristics as words, numerals, or other markings which indicate a value may be attached to other than the address side of mail.

**143 PRECANCELED STAMPS**

**143.1 General**

**.11 Definition.** Precanceling means the cancellation of adhesive postage stamps, stamped envelopes, or postal cards in advance of mailing. Precanceling may be done either by the Postal Service or by the mailer under a postal permit. Since postage due stamps are not accepted as payment of postage in advance of mailing, they are not precanceled. The use of precanceled postage reduces the time and costs of mail handling. If precanceled mail is sorted and tied in packages by the mailer, it requires less processing time and can be dispatched more quickly. Precanceled commemorative stamps are not made available because commemorative stamps are sold for only a limited time.

### .12 Methods of Precanceling

**.121 Precanceling By the Mailer.** Mailers who meet the requirements of 143.3 may precancel adhesive stamps, postal cards and stamped envelopes by using a mailer's precancel postmark. Postal cards are precanceled at the time of printing and do not require a mailer's precancel postmark unless desired by the mailer.

### .122 Precanceling By Postal Service

a. All Post Offices. All post offices are authorized to requisition precanceled stamps and stamped envelopes in quantities as described in Handbook F-1, 522.2.

b. Local Precanceling. Post offices which have precanceling devices, such as an electroplate or handstamps, may continue to use such equipment to precancel limited quantities of stamps upon request by customers. Requests for large quantities of precanceled stamps are to be filled by requisitioning precanceled stamps, rather than by performing a more costly local precanceling service.

**.13 Place of Mailing.** Mail bearing precanceled postage must be presented to authorized postal employees at weight units, window units, or detached mail units of the post office where the permit is held. Deposit of mail bearing precanceled postage in street collection boxes is not permitted.

**.14 Prohibition.** Precanceled postage stamps may not be used on matter mailed in boxes, cases, bags, or other containers designed to be reused for mailing purposes.

### 143.2 Philatelic Sales

#### .21 Nonpermit Holders

**.211** There is no limitation on the sale to collectors of sheet stamps or full coils of stamps of each of the precanceled denominations available at a post office. Purchases may be made in person or by mail by nonpermit holders for collection purposes only. Complete rolls of precanceled coil stamps may not be broken for philatelic sales except at authorized philatelic outlets. Instructions for selling plate blocks are in 163.5.

**.212** Postmasters will comply with requests for imprints of a precanceling device on their own stamp stock, but not for imprints on blank sheets of paper or on stamps submitted by a collector or other individual. Care should be exercised when precanceling stamps for collectors to assure legible impressions. Permanent ink must be used for precanceling.

**.213** Precanceled stamps are available at post offices which have them on hand or have a handstamp (Item No. 762) for precanceling purposes. Post offices may not acquire a precancel handstamp solely to meet philatelic demand. Care should be exercised by postmasters to ensure providing philatelists with legible and well centered cancellations. Handstamps, once acquired, should be retained by post offices to fill requests from philatelists.

**.214** Each mail order must be accompanied with a stamped, self-addressed envelope for use in returning the stamps to the purchaser.

**.22 Permit Holders.** Precanceled stamps may be purchased for the purpose of paying postage or for philatelic purposes. Permit holders may not sell unused precanceled stamps obtained under their permit.

### 143.3 Mailer's Precancel Postmark

#### .31 Application

a. Applications to use a mailer's precancel postmark on adhesive stamps, postal cards, and stamped envelopes must be filed on Form 3620, Application for Permit to Use Precanceled Stamps or Government Precanceled Stamped Envelopes, at the post office where mailings will be made.

b. A specimen mailing piece bearing the proposed mailer's precanceled postmark must accompany the application.

c. The post office will forward the application and specimen mailing piece to the mail classification center (MCC) for final approval.

#### .32 Approval

**.321** The MCC manager will approve or disapprove the application. The application and specimen mailing piece will be returned to the postmaster.

**.322** The post office will date each approved application upon receipt from the MCC, and number the permits consecutively beginning with No. 1 for the first mailer's precancel postmark permit issued at the post office.

**.323** The Permit To Use Precanceled Stamps or Envelopes will be issued on Form 3620 and endorsed to indicate that it is for a "Mailer's Precancel Postmark."

#### .33 Format

**.331** Upon approval by the MCC manager, mailers may use a precancel postmark on adhesive postage stamps, postal cards and stamped envelopes. The precanceling imprint must include:

(1) The city, state, and 5-digit ZIP Code of the post office where the precancel permit is held and the mailings will be deposited.

(2) The date of mailing.

(3) The permit number, preceded by the words "Mailer's Postmark," and sufficient cancellation lines to fully deface the postage.

**.332** The permit number must not be obscured. Black ink must be used for cancellation and must provide adequate indelibility and sufficient contrast to prevent reuse of the stamp.

**.333** Format A is the authorized design of the mailer's precancel postmark. Format A:

**.334** Format B may be used by mailers who presently have the die, however new dies should not be made in this format. Format B:

**.335** No other format of a mailer's precancel postmark may be authorized.

### .34 Revocation of Mailer's Permit

**.341** Permits may be revoked if used in operating any scheme or enterprise of an unlawful character, or for the purpose of purchasing or acquiring stamps or mailer's precancel postmarks for other than mailing purposes, or for any noncompliance with the format requirement or the instructions on the permit (Form 3620.)

**.342** The postmaster at the post office that issued the permit will notify the permit holder by letter, stating that the permit is to be canceled, and giving the reason(s) for cancellation. The permit holder is allowed 10 days within which to file a written statement showing why the permit should not be revoked.

**.343** When no answer is filed, the postmaster will cancel the permit. If an answer is filed, the postmaster will forward the answer, along with a statement of the facts, to the MCC manager who will determine whether the permit shall be continued in effect. Notice of decision will be given the permit holder through the postmaster.

### 143.4 Stamps Precanceled By Postal Service

### .41 Mailing Permit Required

a. Customers who desire to prepay mailings by using stamps and stamped envelopes precanceled by the Postal Service must complete Form 3620, and file the form at the post office where the precanceled mailings will be deposited.

b. The postmaster will approve or disapprove the application. If approved, he will issue the permit on Form 3620, to the applicant. Each permit must be dated and numbered consecutively beginning with No. 1 for the first permit issued at the post office.

### .42 Required Format

### .421 Stamps Precanceled By Bars Only

a. Endorsements. Stamps requisitioned with a precancel imprint will have only two highly visible lines across the face of each stamp. The precancel imprint will not show the post office of mailing or its two-letter state abbreviation. Mailing pieces bearing this precancel imprint must include a return address. If the return address is not within the delivery area of the post office of mailing, the mailer must either place a cancellation endorsement to the left of the postage showing city, two-letter state abbreviation and ZIP Code where mailed, or submit, at the time of mailing, a duplicate of the mailing statement and a sample mailing piece, both in an envelope stamped and addressed to the postmaster at the post office shown in the return address.

b. Illustrations:

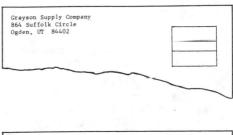

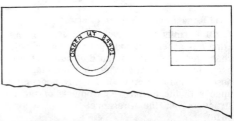

### .422 Stamps Precanceled With City and State

a. Endorsement stamps precanceled by post offices must have two highly visible parallel lines across the face of each stamp. The name of the post office of mailing and its two-letter state abbreviation shall be shown between the two parallel lines. Permanent black ink must be used.

b. Illustration:

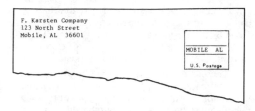

### .423 Overprinting.

If precanceled postage on a single piece is over $1, the precanceled stamps must be overprinted or handstamped in black ink by the mailer with the mailer's initials and the numerical abbreviations of the month and year for use; for example: A. B. Co. 9-78. Precanceled stamps overprinted in this way are acceptable on mail during the month shown, and through the 10th of the following month.

### .424 Stamps precanceled with presorted First-Class Legend

a. Endorsement. Precanceled stamps can be requisitioned with the presorted first-class legend preprinted between the two cancellation lines. These stamps can be used only for the first ounce presort rate with post cards and mail of letter size mailed as part of a qualifying presorted first-class mailing. Mailing pieces bearing the presort imprint must include the return address or cancellation endorsement required by 143.421.

b. Illustration:

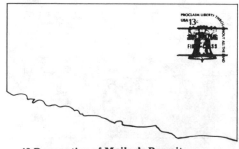

### .43 Revocation of Mailer's Permit

.431 Permits may be revoked if used in operating any scheme or enterprise of an unlawful character, or for the purpose of purchasing or acquiring stamps for other than mailing purposes, including resale, or for any noncompliance with the format requirements or the instructions on the Precancel Permit (Form 3620).

.432 The postmaster at the post office that issued the permit will notify the permit holder by letter, stating that the permit is to be canceled, and giving the reason(s) for cancellation. The permit holder is allowed 10 days to file a written statement showing why the permit should not be revoked.

.433 When no answer is filed, the postmaster will cancel the permit. If an answer is filed, the postmaster will forward the answer, along with a statement of the facts, to the MCC manager who will determine whether the permit shall be continued in effect. Notice of decision will be given the permit holder through the postmaster.

### .44 Requisitioning Stamps

**.441 Small Quantities Precanceled By Handstamp.** Small quantities of stamps may be precanceled by handstamp (Item No. 762) designed to precancel 10 stamps at each impression.

**442. Ordering Precanceled Adhesive Stamps and Stamped Envelopes.** Post offices must requisition precanceled adhesive stamps and stamped envelopes in the same manner as other adhesive stamps and stamped envelopes.

## 144 POSTAGE METERS AND METER STAMPS

### 144.1 Postage Meters

#### .11 Use of Meter Stamps

.111 Postage may be paid by printing meter stamps with a postage meter on any class of mail. Metered mail is entitled to all privileges and subject to all conditions applying to the various classes of mail.

.112 Meter stamps may be used to prepay reply postage on letters and post cards under the following conditions:

a. Meter stamps must be printed directly on the envelope or card that bears the return address of the meter license holder in an amount sufficient to prepay in full the first-class rate.

b. Any photographic, mechanical or electronic process, or any combination of such processes, other than handwriting, typewriting, or handstamping, may be used to prepare the address side of reply mail prepaid by meter stamps. The address side must be prepared both as to style and content in the following form without the addition of any matter other than a return address:

(Meter stamp to be placed here)

NO POSTAGE STAMP NECESSARY
POSTAGE HAS BEEN PREPAID BY

John Doe Company
123 Tremont Street,
New York, N.Y. 10010

c. Reply mail prepaid by meter stamps will be delivered only to the address of the meter license holder. If the address is altered, the mail will be held for postage.

**.113** Postage meter stamps for zero postage shall not be affixed to items delivered by other carriers since this would give the impression of Postal Service delivery. The use of .00 postage meter impressions is not permitted to correct improper dating on any type of matter entered in the mail.

**.12 Description of Meters.** Postage meters are made to print single, several, or all denominations of postage. They contain in one sealed unit the printing die or dies and two recording counters. One adds and keeps a total of all postage printed by the meter. The other subtracts and shows the balance of postage remaining in the meter, after the use of which it will lock. From time to time, mailers take the meter to the post office to have this counter set for additional postage, which is added to the balance remaining. Payment must be made for each additional setting.

**.13 Meter Manufacturers.** Postage meters may be leased from authorized manufacturers who are held responsible by the Postal Service for the control, operation, maintenance and replacement, when necessary, of meters manufactured by them. The following manufacturers are presently authorized to lease meters to mailers:

---

**Manufacturers Authorized to Lease Meters**

POSTALIA, INC., 1423 Centre Circle Drive, Downers Grove, Ill. 60515.

F.M.E. Corporation, 31285 San Clemente St., Hayward, Calif. 94544.

National Cash Register Co., Dayton, Ohio 45409.

Pitney Bowes, Inc., Walter H. Wheeler Jr. Dr., Stamford, Conn. 06926.

Rockaway Corporation, (doing business as International Mailing Systems, a division of Better Packages, Inc.), 8 Brook St., Shelton, Conn. 06484.

---

**144.2 Meter License**

**.21 Application.** A customer may obtain a license to use a postage meter by submitting Form 3601-A, Application for a Postage Meter License (or a form supplied by the manufacturer), to the post office where his metered mail will be deposited. No fee is charged. On approval, the postmaster will issue a license.

**.22 Responsibilities of Licensee**

**.221** After a meter has been delivered to a licensee, he must keep it in his custody until returned to the authorized manufacturer or to the post office. A customer may not have a meter in his possession unless it has been checked into service by the Postal Service. Avoiding the payment of postage through tampering with or misusing a meter is punishable by law.

**.222** Although licensees are not required to maintain a Form 3602-A, Daily Record of Meter Register Readings, they are encouraged to do so, as use of this form will hasten the discovery of meter malfunctions. If at any time the sum of the two figures does not equal the total entered in the Form 3602-A at the last setting, the meter should be taken immediately to the post office, station, or branch where it was set or last examined for examination. If desired, the post office will provide Form 3602-A when the meter is initially checked into service. Additional copies will be provided as the forms are filled.

**.223** The meters in the custody of the licensee and his records relating to meter transactions or latest Form 3603 must be immediately available for examination and audit by the Postal Service or meter manufacturer, upon request (see 144.962).

**.224** If a meter is not reset within a 6-month period, it must be presented together with related Forms 3602-A, or latest Form 3603, for examination at the post office, station, or branch where it is regularly set.

**.225** If the meter's printing or recording mechanism is in any way faulty, it shall be immediately taken to the post office, station or branch where it is regularly set or examined to be checked out of service. Under no circumstances shall the faulty meter be used.

**.226** A licensee must notify the licensing post office whenever the name, address or phone number on Form 3601-A changes.

**.23 Revocation**

**.231** A license will be revoked if a meter is used in operating any scheme or enterprise of an unlawful character, for nonuse during any consecutive 12 months, or for any failure of the licensee to comply with the regulations governing the use of postage meters.

**.232** The meter license holder will be notified by the postmaster if the license is to be revoked and the reasons for revocation. Form 3604, Nonuse of Mailing Permit or Meter License, may be used if revocation for nonuse is being considered. If no written statement of objection is filed by the license holder within 10 days, the postmaster will cancel the license. If a written statement is filed, the appeal will be referred by the postmaster to the Office of Mail Classification for resolution. The Office of Mail Classification will notify the license holder of the decision through the postmaster. If a meter license is revoked, the postmaster will note the date and reason for cancellation of Form 3601-A (see 144.21).

**144.4 Meter Stamps**

**.41 Designs.** The types, sizes, and styles of meter stamps are fixed when meters are approved by the Postal Service for manufacture. Only approved designs may be used.

a. General Examples:

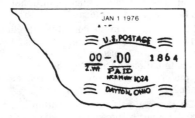

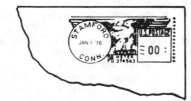

b. Official Mail:

**.42 Legibility.** Meter stamps must be legible and not overlap. Illegible or overlapping meter stamps will not be counted in determining postage paid.

**.43 Fluorescent Ink.** The use of fluorescent ink is mandatory for postage imprints on letter-size metered mail. Failure to use fluorescent ink may result in the revocation of the meter license. Letter-size mail is defined as being from 5 inches to $11\frac{1}{2}$ inches long, $3\frac{1}{2}$ inches to $6\frac{1}{8}$ inches wide, and .007 inches to .25 inches thick.

**.44 Meter Stamps on Tape.** When meter stamps are printed on tape, only tape approved by the Postal Service may be used.

**.45 Position.** Meter stamps must be printed or stuck in the upper right corner of the envelope, address label, or tag.

**.46 Content.** Meter stamps must show the city and state designation of the licensing post office, meter number and amount of postage for all classes of mail. Upon approval of the licensing post office, meter indicia may contain the name and state designation of its local classified branch, which sets the meter. This authorization does not apply to classified stations or contract stations or branches. As an alternative, the ZIP Code designation may be shown in the meter postmark instead of the city/state designation. When this occurs, the words Mailed From ZIP Code must appear in place of the city designation and the mailer's delivery address ZIP Code in place of the state. When it is necessary to print multidenomination meter stamps on more than one tape, the circle showing the post office must appear on each tape.

**.47 Date of Mailing**

**.471** Dates shown in the meter postmark of any type or kind of mail must be the actual date of deposit except when the mailing piece is deposited after the last scheduled collection of the day. When deposit is made after the last scheduled collection of the day, mailers are encouraged but not required to use the date of the next scheduled collection.

**.472** The month, day and year must be shown in the meter postmark on all first-class mail, and on all registered, certified, insured, COD, special delivery and special handling mail, except prepaid reply postage, whether the postmark is printed directly on the mailing piece or on a separate tape.

**.473** The month and year must be shown on meter postmarks printed on a separate tape for second-, third-, and fourth-class pieces. The day may be omitted. Mailing pieces postmarked on a separate tape with only the month and year may be accepted during the month shown and through the third day of the following month when, in the judgment of the postmaster, the mailing was unavoidably delayed prior to its deposit with the Postal Service.

**.474** The date (day, month or year) is not required to be shown on meter postmarks printed directly on a second-, third-, or fourth-class mailing piece.

**.475** The date must not be shown on meter postmarks used to prepay reply postage in accordance with 144.112.

**.48 Hour of Mailing.** The hour of mailing may be shown only on first-class or special delivery mail, and then only when it is mailed in time to be dispatched at the hour shown.

**.49 Ad Plates**

**.491** Advertising matter, slogans, return addresses and the postal markings specified in 144.492 may be printed with the meter stamps within space limitations. Licensees must obtain the plates for the printing of this matter from authorized meter manufacturers to assure suitable quality and content in accordance with the requirements of the Postal Service. Ad plate messages should be clearly distinguished by the inclusion of the name of the mailer or words such as "Mailers Adv." or "Mailers Message." The ad plate must not be obscene, defamatory of any particular person or group, or deceptive, nor shall it advocate unlawful action.

**.492** The following postal markings relating to the class of mail are permissible: FIRST CLASS; PRESORTED FIRST CLASS; THIRD CLASS; BULK RATE.; NONPROFIT ORGANIZATION; FOURTH CLASS; and PRIORITY MAIL. If a postal marking is to appear in the ad plate area, no other matter is to be printed. The marking must fill the entire ad plate area to the extent practicable. All words must be in bold, capital letters which are at least ¼ of an inch in height or 18-point type and legible at two feet. Exceptions for small ad plates that will not accommodate any of the above markings will not be considered.

**145 PERMIT IMPRINTS (MAIL WITHOUT AFFIXED POSTAGE)**

**145.1 Definition.** Mailers may be authorized to mail material without affixing postage if payment of postage is made at the time of mailing from an advance deposit trust account established with the Postal Service for that purpose. Each piece of mail sent by a mailer under this method of payment must bear a permit imprint to indicate that postage has been paid. This method of payment may be used to pay special service fees as well as postage.

**145.2 Permit**

**.21 Application.** A permit to use permit imprints and pay postage in cash at the time of mailing may be obtained by submitting Form 3601, Application to Mail Without Affixing Postage Stamps, with a fee of $40, to the post office where mailings will be made. The postmaster will give the applicant a receipt for the fee on Form 3544. There is no other fee for the use of permit imprints so long as the permit remains active. Note: The applicant must also pay an annual bulk mailing fee if he mails third-class matter at bulk rates. (See 612 and 641).

**.22 Revocation**

**.221** The permit will be revoked if used in operating any unlawful scheme or enterprise, for nonuse during any 12-month period, or for any noncompliance with the regulations governing the use of permit imprints.

**.222** The permit holder will be notified by the postmaster if the permit is to be revoked and the reasons for revocation. Form 3604, Nonuse of Mailing Permit or Meter License, may be used if revocation is for nonuse.

**.223** The permit holder may appeal the revocation to the postmaster. If no written statement of objection is filed by the permit holder within 10 days, the postmaster will cancel the permit.

**.224** If revocation is because of nonuse and the permit holder indicates that he will resume mailings within a 90-day period, the permit will be continued for a period not to exceed 90 days.

**.225** If the postmaster does not grant the appeal, he must notify the customer.

**.226** The permit holder may appeal the postmaster's decision to the general manager, Domestic Mail Classification Division, Office of Mail Classification, USPS headquarters, Washington, D.C. 20260. The appeal must be submitted in writing to the postmaster, who will forward the appeal to the general manager, Domestic Mail Classification Division, who will make the final administrative decision.

**145.3 Preparation of Permit Imprints.** Permit imprints may be made by printing press, handstamp, lithography, mimeograph, multigraph, addressograph, or similar device. They may not be typewritten or hand drawn. The content of the imprint must be in accordance with 145.4, and the format in accordance with 145.5. No other forms of imprints may be used. The imprint must be legible and must be of a color that contrasts sufficiently with the paper to make the imprint readable. The entire imprint must be placed in the upper right corner of the address side of each piece, parallel with the length of the piece. The position of the imprint on fourth-class bound printed matter may be varied so that automatic data processing equipment may be utilized to simultaneously print the address, imprint and other postal information. The permit may be placed on the parcel or on the label for items mailed under the provisions of 664 or 767.6.

**145.4 Content of Permit Imprints**

.41 **First-Class Mail.** Permit imprints must show city and state; First-Class Mail; U.S. Postage Paid; and permit number. They may show the mailing date, amount of postage paid or the number of ounces for which postage is paid. (See 145.5a). The ZIP Code of the permit holder may be shown immediately following the name of the state or in a separate inscription reading ZIP Code 00000 when it is possible to include the ZIP Code without creating uncertainty as to the permit holder's correct address or permit number.

.42 **Second-, Third-, and Fourth-Class Mail.** Permit imprints must show the same information as first class, except the date and the words first-class mail must be omitted. Permit indicia may include the amount of postage paid, weight of piece and markings required by 480, 680 or 780.

.43 **Mail With Special Services.** Permit mail with special services paid by permit must show

first-class mail, if first-class mail; U.S. postage and fees paid; city and state; and permit number. The company's name may be shown in place of the city and permit number in accordance with 145.44.

.44 **Company Permit Imprints for Any Class of Mail.** The city, state, and permit number may be omitted if the permit holder has permits at two or more post offices, provided the exact name of the company or individual holding the permits is shown in the permit imprint. When this style of company permit is used, the mailing piece must bear a complete return address. The permit holder must maintain for a 3-year period and make available for inspection and audit upon request of post office officials, records showing the post office at which any particular mailing was made, date of mailing, total weight of the mailing, weight of a single piece, and the amount of postage paid. A sample piece from the mailing must also be available.

**145.5 Format of Permit Imprints.** Permit imprints must be prepared in one of the following formats. Any of the formats may be used to display the information prescribed by 145.3. The addition of extraneous matter is not permitted.

a. **First-Class Mail**

b. **Second-, Third-, and Fourth-Class Mail (Date and First-Class Mail Omitted)**

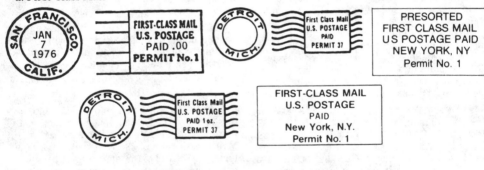

c. **Bulk Third-Class Mail**

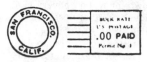 

d. **Special Rates for Authorized Organizations Only**

e. **Official Mail (First-Class)**

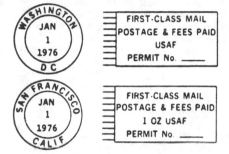

f. **Official Mail (Fourth-Class) (Date and First-Class Mail Omitted)**

 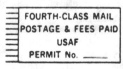

### 145.6 Mailings With Permit Imprints

**.61 Minimum Quantity.** Permit imprint mailings must consist of a minimum of 200 pieces or 50 pounds, except as provided in 145.62. Minimum quantities of mail necessary to mail at the first-class presort rate, the fourth-class zone bulk rate, and the special fourth-class presort rate are higher.

**.62 Exceptions to Minimum Quantities.** A mailing consisting of less than the required minimum will be accepted by the Postal Service if one of the following requirements is met:

a. First-Class Mail. An occasional mailing for a mailer whose total daily mailings are not much more than 200 pieces but who, to cooperate with the post office, presents a portion of his mailings early in the day.

b. All Classes of Mail. A large mailing which extends over two or more consecutive days and the last deposit, made to complete the mailing, is less than the minimum. Note: In order to be

considered an exception, the mailer must include an explanation on the Form 3602, Mailing Statement.

### 145.7 Use of Permit Imprints

**.71 General.** Permit imprints indicate that the postage for matter on which they appear has been paid under the permit imprint system. Therefore, imprints must not ordinarily appear on matter which has not had postage so paid thereon (as, for example, matter which is circulated by means other than mail or which is circulated as an enclosure with other matter either by mail or by means other than mail). Note:

a. See 136.312 for combination mailings containing enclosures which may have postage paid by permit imprint.

b. Permit imprints may appear on address labels, wrappers, envelopes, and other containers, and on complete mailing pieces, which have not had postage paid thereon under the permit imprint system provided it would be impracticable to omit the permit imprint (e.g. when envelopes are shipped from a printer to a permit imprint permit holder).

**.72 Place of Acceptance.** Permit imprint matter will be accepted for mailing only at the post office shown in the permit imprint except: (a) when company permit imprints are used as provided for by 145.44 or (b) when arrangements for acceptance at other post offices are made under the provisions of 145.8.

### 145.9 Alternate Methods of Paying Postage

**.91 Application Procedure**

**.911** All postage must be paid in accordance with the provisions of 146.1 unless an alternate method is approved in writing by the director, Office of Mail Classification, Rates and Classification Department, USPS headquarters.

**.912** Mailers may request authorization to pay postage by an alternate method by submitting a written request to the postmaster at the office of mailing. The request must include a complete description of the type(s) of matter to be mailed, the proposed method of paying postage and a statement of the mailer's reasons for requesting the alternate method.

**.913** The postmaster will forward the request to the Office of Mail Classification through his management sectional center, district, and regional director of finance. Postmasters may not accept mail under any alternate method of paying postage until a written authorization from the director, Office of Mail Classification, is received.

**.92 Conditions of Authorization**

**.921** Authorization to use an alternate method of paying postage may be granted by the director, Office of Mail Classification, when the adoption of such a method would be in the best interests of the Postal Service and when postal revenue can be adequately protected. The authorization will specify the alternate method of postage payment to be used and the terms and conditions of its use, including a time limitation, if applicable.

**.922** As a condition of authorization, the director may require the mailer to agree to pay a surcharge to cover any damages suffered by the Postal Service from the incorrect payment of postage. An authorization to use an alternate method of postage payment may be revoked at any time by the director, Office of Mail Classification, upon the issuance of a written notice to the mailer.

**146 Prepayment and Postage Due**

**146.1 Postage Payment**

**.11 Prepayment Required.** Postage on all mail must be fully prepaid at the time of mailing, with the following exceptions:

a. Business reply mail, or metered reply mail handled as business reply mail, (see 917)

b. Federal Government and free mail, (see 137)

c. Certain mail for the blind, (see 135)

d. Mail sent by members of the Armed Forces, (134)

e. Keys and identification devices returned to owners, (see 610)

**.12 Unpaid Matter Not Bearing Postage Found in the Mail**

**.121** Matter of any class, including that for which special services are indicated, received at either the office of mailing or office of address without any postage (see 146.4), will be endorsed returned for postage and returned to the sender without an attempt at delivery. If no return address is shown, or if the delivery and return address are identical, the piece will be disposed of in accordance with 159.52.

**.122** Metered reply mail, which is prepared in accordance with 144.112, for the mailer's inadvertent failure to imprint a meter stamp on the envelope, will be treated as business reply mail (see 917), and will be delivered upon payment of postage and the corresponding business reply fee.

**.123** Except as provided in 146.123a or b, mailable matter not bearing postage (including but not limited to parcels, newspapers and magazines, books, and records) intended for delivery by a private delivery company but found in collection boxes or other receptacles designated for the deposit of mail by the public or in any facilities or mail processing operations of the Postal Service, will be returned as promptly as possible to the sender postage due, and not delivered to the addressee or returned to the private delivery company. Address correction service or forwarding service will not be provided. Postage due, rated according to 146.221c. will be determined by computing postage due from the point at which the unpaid mailable matter entered the mail to the sender's location. However, when the entry point of the unpaid mailable matter is unknown, postage due will be computed from the point where it was first found in the mail to the sender's location.

a. If the sender cannot be identified or if mailable matter is refused by sender, the procedures in 159.5 will be followed.

b. If it appears that mailable matter was inadvertently delivered to a post office, the private delivery company will be notified as promptly as possible to pick up the matter by the close of the company's next working day. If the company fails to do so, the matter will be returned to sender postage due.

**.13 Insufficient Prepayment**

**.131** Mail of any class, including that for which special services are indicated (except registered mail see 911), received at either the office of mailing or office of address without sufficient postage will be:

a. Marked to show the total deficiency of postage and fees.

b. Dispatched promptly to the addressee by means of the regular or special service indicated.

c. Delivered to addressee on payment of the charges marked on the mail. Note: When quantity mailings of 10 or more pieces are received at the office of mailing without sufficient postage, the mailer will be notified, without charge, preferably by telephone, in order that the postage charges may be adjusted before the mail is dispatched.

.132 When the addressee refuses to pay the deficient postage, or when the mail is undeliverable for any other reason, it will be handled as follows:

a. First-class mail bearing a return address will be returned to the sender and delivered on payment by him of the deficient postage.

b. Mail other than first-class bearing a return address will be returned to the sender and delivered on payment by him of the total of the deficient postage, the forwarding postage, if any, and the return postage.

c. All mail that does not bear a return address will be disposed of in accordance with 159.52

**.14 Postage on Mail Insufficiently Prepaid.** Postage stamps affixed to mail are canceled when the mail is first received in the post office. Postage stamps or meter stamps originally affixed to insufficiently prepaid mail will, when the mail is again presented for mailing, be accepted in payment of postage to the amount of their face value.

**.15 Parcels Containing Written Matter.** At the office of address, parcels subject to postage due will be handled as follows:

a. Postage due at the first-class rate will be charged on parcels consisting mainly of first-class matter.

b. Postage due will be charged for parcels containing nonpermissible written matter which is merely incidental to the entire contents at the following rates:

| Difference between First-Class rate and rate paid | Postage-Due Charge |
|---|---|
| $0.01-$0.25 | Full amount |
| 0.26-1.00 | $0.25 |
| 1.01 or more | 1.00 |

**146.2 Mailable Matter Not Bearing Postage Found In or On Private Mail Receptacles**

**.21 Penalty.** Whoever knowingly and willfully deposits any mailable matter such as statements of account, circulars, sale bills, or other like matter, on which no postage has been paid, in any letterbox established, approved or accepted by the postmaster general for the receipt or delivery of mail matter on any route with intent to avoid payment of lawful postage thereon, shall for each such offense be fined not more than $300.

**.22 Collection of Postage**

**.221 General.** Except as permitted in 156.58, any mailable matter not bearing postage found in, upon, attached to, supported by, or hung from, the private mail receptacles described in 151.11, is subject to the payment of the same postage as would be paid if carried by mail. For mailable matter not bearing postage found in the mail, see 146.12.

**.222 Distribution to less than complete route.**

When there is a distribution of pieces to some, but not all, addresses on a route, they will be handled as follows:

a. Each piece will be taken to the delivery unit.

b. The date and approximate time of finding will be recorded on the piece. if the address where the piece is found is different from the address, if any, on the label, the address where found will be recorded, as well as the approximate time and date.

c. Postage on each piece found will be computed as follows:

(1) First-Class Matter. First-class rates will be applied to matter which would require first-class postage if mailed.

(2) Second-Class Publications. The transient rate in 411.42 will be applied.

(3) Controlled Circulation Publications. The applicable single piece third-class or fourth-class rate in 611.11 or 711 will be applied.

(4) Books, Records, Circulars, Catalogs, and Merchandise. If the piece weighs less than 16 ounces, either the single piece third-class rate, or the applicable fourth-class rate, whichever is lower, will be applied. See 611.12 if the piece weighs 16 ounces or more, the applicable fourth-class rate will be applied.

**.223 Distribution to all or substantially all addresses on a route**

If there is a distribution of identical pieces to all or substantially all addresses on a route, only two copies, each dated, initialed and marked with the address where found, will be taken to the office along with a written notation of the total number of identical pieces observed on the route. The postmaster must prepare a memorandum showing the details to support the claim of postage, which will be computed in accordance with 146.222c.

**.224 Request for payment**

a. If there is reason to believe that a private delivery firm or an individual within the delivery area of the post office is responsible for the delivery, the local postmaster will notify the firm or individual as promptly as possible concerning the number of pieces and the amount of postage due. The applicable provisions of this manual will be explained. If the firm or individual receiving a request for postage offers objection that these regulations have not been applied properly in the particular case, the facts will be investigated before any action is taken. If, within five days after receiving a request for the postage, or within five days after receiving a renewed request following investigation of an objection, the firm or individual agrees to pay the postage due, payment will be accepted and the articles will be delivered to the addresses. The firm or individual paying the postage may choose to redeliver the pieces rather than have the Postal Service deliver them. Receipt for payment will be handled in accordance with 146.224c. If the pieces are found to have been removed improperly, they will be delivered without postage charge.

b. If the firm or individual responsible for delivery is not known or if the firm presented with a request fails to pay the postage, the pieces will be returned as promptly as possible to the publisher or manufacturer, postage due, with each piece endorsed to show that the articles were found in or on the addressee's mailbox without postage. If a publisher or manufacturer provides the name and telephone number of a person to contact about pieces found in mailboxes and orally or in writing guarantees payment of postage, the pieces will not be returned but will be redelivered promptly to the addressees. If the pieces are refused by the publisher or manufacturer or if the publisher or manufacturer is unknown, the procedures in 159.5 will be followed.

c. An equivalent amount of postage due stamps affixed to a sheet of paper and properly canceled as a receipt for money collected will be given the person or firm paying postage. If payment is in the form of uncanceled stamps or meter stamps, they will be affixed to a sheet, canceled and returned as a receipt for payment. No other receipt will be issued.

**.23 Report to Other Office.** If the person or firm or distributor responsible for the impermissible use of the private mail receptacles is located within the area served by another post office, a sample piece will be sent with a report of the facts to the postmaster at that location with request that he take action in accordance with 146.22.

**.24 Repeated Violations.** If the person or firm or distributor responsible for the impermissible use of the private mail receptacles continues the impermissible use after having been notified that the use is impermissible, the postmaster will submit a sample piece and report of the facts (see 146.22) to the postal inspector in charge.

**146.3 Collection of Postage Due**

**.31 Collected On Delivery.** Customers must pay for postage due mail in cash only, prior to delivery to them. However, postage on quantity mailings found in private mail boxes will be collected as provided in 146.22.

**.32 Use of Postage Due Stamps.** Postage due stamps are only used to collect postage due on mail. They may not be used for any other payment of postage or fees.

**.33 Use of Postage Stamps, Permit Imprints, or Customer Meter Strips.** Postage stamps, permit imprints, and customer meter strips may not be used for payment of postage due.

**.34 Advance Deposit.** If postage due collections amount to approximately $10 or more every 60 days, payment may be made by advance deposits of money.

**146.4 When Not Collected**

**.41 Stamps Lost Off Mail.** When it is apparent from the impression of a cancellation that a postage stamp has been wholly or partially lost, the piece must be handled, in the absence of contrary evidence, as if correct postage had been paid for the class and weight of the piece.

**.42 Registered Mail.** Registered mail, except that endorsed to show that it was registered in transit, must be delivered without collection of postage due. Postage due must be collected on matter registered at other than the mailing office.

**147 EXCHANGES AND REFUNDS**

**147.1 Exchanges of Stamps**

**.11 Post Office Mistake.** Mistakes in selling damaged, defective, or otherwise unserviceable stamps may be corrected by the post office by exchanging stamps at full value.

**.12 Purchaser's Mistake.** Mistakes made by purchaser in buying adhesive stamps of the wrong denomination or stamped envelopes or postal cards of the wrong kind, size, or denomination may be corrected by exchanging stamps at full value. Only full panes of stamps, coils of stamps in the original sealed wrappers, full boxes of stamped envelopes, or original sealed packs of postal cards may be exchanged.

Any customer exchanging $250 or more of such stock must furnish proof of identity (driver's license, military I.D., or other valid identification) and must present the stock in exchange to the postal unit at which his or her mail is delivered. This will allow the clerk exchanging the stock to validate the customer's address. A record of each transaction of $250 or more will be made, showing name of customer, type of I.D., business firm, address, amount, and denominations exchanged. Any suspicious circumstances should be reported immediately to the local inspector or inspector-in-charge.

**.13 Unserviceable Postal Stationery and Unused Precanceled Stamps.** Unserviceable and spoiled stamped envelopes or postal cards, if uncanceled, and unused precanceled stamps and postal cards, will be exchanged for other postage-stamped paper as follows:

a. Stamped envelopes (mutilated no more than is necessary to remove contents), for postage value plus value of postage added as a result of rate increase or for additional service.

b. Unmutilated aerogrammes (airletter sheets), for postage value less 1 cent for each aerogramme redeemed.

c. Unmutilated single and double postal cards, for 85 per cent of postage value plus full value of postage added as a result of rate increase or for additional service.

(1) Either half of a double postal card may be redeemed if the double card has been printed and cut for use as single cards.

(2) Unused double postal cards printed for reply purposes should not be separated; however, if they have been separated in error, and the purchaser presents both halves, the cards may be redeemed.

(3) Reply halves of double postal cards that have been returned to sender outside of the mails are not redeemable by the original purchaser even though the reply half received no postal service.

d. Sheet postal cards spoiled in the process of cutting to size, for 85 per cent of postage value plus full value of postage added as a result of rate increase or for additional service, if all cut sections are submitted.

e. Stamps affixed to commercial envelopes and post cards, for 90 per cent of postage value. Envelopes and post cards must be in a substantially whole condition and in lots of at least 50 of the same denomination and value.

f. Unused precanceled stamps in full coils or in full sheets redeemed from precanceled permit holders, for 90 per cent of postage value.

Note: Stamped envelopes or aerogrammes (airletter sheets) with a printed return address and postal cards with any printed matter of the purchaser, may be exchanged only by the purchaser. If there is no purchaser's printing, they may be exchanged by any responsible person. When redemption cannot be made at time of presentation, the postmaster will furnish a receipt on Form 3210 for uncanceled, unserviceable, or spoiled envelopes or postal cards, or for unused, precanceled stamps left in his custody.

### .14 Conversion of Postage Stamps to Other Forms of Postage

**.141 General.** Mailers may submit postage stamps for conversion to a meter setting or advance deposit for permit imprint mailings under the conditions set forth in 147.142 through 147.146. A conversion charge of 10 per cent of the face value of the stamps or $250, whichever is greater, will be deducted when the stamps are converted. No part of any amount applied to a meter setting or trust account from the conversion of postage stamps will be later refundable in cash, or by other means.

**.142 Where to Apply.** All requests to convert postage stamps to meter or permit imprint postage must be sent to the general manager, Stamps Division, U.S. Postal Service, Washington, D.C. 20260. The general manager, Stamps Division, will forward a copy of the request to the inspector-in-charge of the division in which the requestor's post office is located.

**.143 What May be Converted.** Only full panes of stamps, or coils of stamps in the original sealed wrappers, will be accepted for conversion. Commemorative stamps issued no earlier than one year prior to the date of the request for conversion or issues of regular stamps which have not been officially withdrawn from sale at the Philatelic Sales Branch will be accepted under these conditions.

**.144 Conversion Rate.** The amount of postage applied to a meter setting or permit imprint trust account through conversion will be the lesser of the full face value of the stamps submitted minus 10 per cent, or full face value minus $250.

**.145 Submittal of Request.** The customer must submit a letter to the general manager, Stamps Division, requesting conversion of the stamps to meter or permit imprint postage. The letter must include the name, denomination, quantity and value of postage stamps for which conversion is requested, and name of the post office where the stamps were purchased. Evidence of purchase for the stamps must also be included with the request.

**.146 Approval.** The general manager, Stamps Division, will review the request and may ask the mailer to submit additional records to support the information in the request. The general manager, Stamps Division, will approve or deny the request. If the conversion is authorized, the postmaster will be advised of the proper procedures for accepting the postage stamps and making the required accounting entries. The general manager, Stamps Division, will determine the post office which has the capabilities to destroy the postage stamps. The credit will be applied to the post office where the mailer has his meter set or deposits his permit imprint mail.

**.15 Nonexchangeable.** The following are nonexchangeable:

a. Adhesive stamps, unless mistakes were made in purchasing, stamps were defective, or stamps were affixed to commercial envelopes and post cards.

b. Stamps cut from postal cards, stamped envelopes, or aerogrammes (airletter sheets).

c. Parts and pieces of postal cards.

d. Postal cards, stamped envelopes and aerogrammes received for reply purposes.

e. Mutilated and defaced stamps.

### 147.2 Refunds

### .21 Justification

**.211** When postage and special or retail service fees have been paid and no service is rendered, or when the amount collected was in excess of the lawful rate, a refund may be made:

a. Refunds for postage and fees paid by stamps, permit imprints, or meter impressions, unused meter impressions, and unused units set in meters are handled according to 147.24.

b. Refunds for retail services and fees not paid by means of stamps, permit imprint, or meter impressions are handled according to 147.26.

**.212** The Postal Service is assumed to be at fault and no service is rendered in cases involving returned articles improperly accepted in both domestic and international services because of excess size or weight.

**.213** Mailers who customarily weigh and rate their mail are expected to be familiar with basic requirements and the Postal Service is not considered to be at fault when these mailers are required to withdraw articles from the mail prior to dispatch.

**.214** See 147.222 and 147.25 for special provisions for refunding the postage value of unused meter stamps.

**.215** A postage refund may be provided the sender for first-class, third-class single piece, and fourth-class mail torn or defaced during processing by the Postal Service to such extent that identification of addressee or intended delivery point cannot be made. This applies only when the failure to process and/or deliver is the fault of the Postal Service. Where possible, the damaged item will be returned with the postage refund.

**.216** Requests for refunds which are questionable, or which cannot be processed in accordance with the provisions of 147.2 will be forwarded to the mail classification center serving the office where the request originated. The MCC manager will return the request along with his ruling to the office which submitted the request.

**.22 Amount Allowable**

**.221 Refund of 100 Per Cent Will Be Made:**

a. When the Postal Service is at fault.

b. For the excess when postage or fees have been paid in excess of the lawful rate.

c. When service to the country of destination has been suspended.

d. When postage is fire-scarred while in the custody of the Postal Service, including fire in letterbox, and the mail is returned to sender without service.

e. When special delivery stamps are erroneously used in payment of postage, and the mail is returned to the sender without service.

f. When fees are paid for special delivery, special handling and certified mail, and the article fails to receive the special service for which the fee has been paid.

g. When surcharges are erroneously collected on domestic registered mail, or collected in excess of the proper amount, or represented by stamps affixed to matter not actually accepted for registration.

h. For fees paid for return receipts or for restricted delivery when the failure to furnish the return receipt or its equivalent, or erroneous delivery, or nondelivery, is due to the fault or negligence of the Postal Service.

i. For annual bulk mailing fee when no bulk mailings of third-class matter are made during the year for which the annual fee has been paid.

j. When customs clearance and delivery fees are erroneously collected.

k. When fees are paid for registry or insurance service on mail addressed to a country to which such services are not available, unless claim for indemnity is made.

l. When express mail is not delivered according to the terms of the service standards as delineated in Handbook M-68, Express Mail Service.

**.222** A partial refund shall be made:

a. When complete and legible unused meter stamps are submitted within one year from the dates appearing in the stamps. See 147.25.

b. When the face value of the stamps does not exceed $250, refunds of 90 per cent will be made.

c. When the face value of the stamps exceeds $250, refunds will be made for the face value of the stamps less $10 per hour for the actual manhours required to process the refund, with a minimum charge of $25 deducted from the amount of the refund.

d. The employee processing the refund will enter the following endorsement on the reverse of Form 3533:

(1) I certify that (number) hours were required to process this refund.

(2) The certifying and witnessing employees will both sign this certification.

**.223** When mail is returned at the request of the sender or for a reason not the fault of the Postal Service, any difference between the amount paid and the appropriate surface rate chargeable from mailing office to interception point and return will be refunded.

**.23 Unallowable Refunds.** No refund will be made:

a. For an application fee to use permit imprints.

b. For registered, insured and COD fees after the mail has been accepted by the post office even though it is later withdrawn from the mailing post office.

c. For unused adhesive stamps (see 147.11 and 147.12).

d. For adhesive stamps affixed to unmailed matter.

**.24 Application for Postage Refund**

**.241** Customers who wish to request a refund must submit an application on Form 3533, Application and Voucher for Refund of Postage and Fees, to the postmaster together with the envelope or wrapper, or the portion thereof having names and addresses of sender and addressee, canceled postage and postal markings, or other evidence of payment of the amount of postage and fees for which refund is desired.

### .25 Meters and Meter Stamps

**.251 Postage Adjustments.** The postage value of unused units set in a meter surrendered to the post office to be checked out of service may be transferred to another meter used by the same license holder. If the meter is withdrawn from service because of faulty mechanical operation, a final postage adjustment or refund may be withheld pending report of the meter manufacturer of the cause of faulty operation. If the meter is damaged by fire, a refund or transfer of postage will be made only if the registers are legible, or can be reconstructed by the meter manufacturer.

### 148 REVENUE DEFICIENCY

**148.1 General.** The term revenue deficiency refers to insufficient payment by a mailer or other postal customer of postage, fees, or box rent. For example, a deficiency may result from an incorrect setting of a postage meter by a post office employee; from an impermissible enclosure included in a second-class publication; or from sending mail matter at a rate lower than the specified rate. Revenue deficiencies are usually disclosed during the course of a postal inspector's audit or local financial examination. In addition, a revenue deficiency may be assessed initially by the director, Office of Mail Classification, Rates and Classification Department, USPS, Washington, D.C. 20260

**148.2 Appeal of Ruling.** A mailer may appeal any ruling assessing a revenue deficiency, by filing an appeal within 15 days of receipt of the revenue deficiency ruling to the director, Office of Mail Classification, Rates and Classification Department, or to the assistant postmaster general, Rates and Classification Department, USPS headquarters, Washington, D.C. 20260, if the deficiency was assessed initially by the director, Office of Mail Classification.

### 149 INDEMNITY CLAIMS

**149.1 Special Services With Indemnity Provisions**

Indemnity claims may be filed for insured, COD, registered, or express mail. (See the International Mail Manual for international insured and registered mail indemnity claims. See 149.5 for express mail provisions.)

**149.2 General Instructions for Filing Claims on Insured, COD, and Registered Mail**

**.21 Who May File.** A claim for complete loss (wrapper and contents) of an insured article may be filed by the mailer or addressee. A claim for complete loss (wrapper and contents) of a COD or registered article may only be filed by the mailer. All claims for complete loss of contents, partial loss, or damage may be filed by the mailer or addressee.

**.22 When to File**

**.221 General.** Indemnity claims must be filed within one year from the date the article was mailed. Follow-up claims (duplicates, inquiries, etc.) must be filed no sooner than 45 days, nor later than six months from the date the original claim was filed. All appeals concerning Postal Service claim decisions must be filed within three months of the original decision on the claim.

**.222 Loss Claims**

a. Insured and COD. The mailer may not file a claim until 30 days after the date of mailing for insured articles and 45 days after the date of mailing for COD articles. Exceptions: Claims for loss must not be submited until 45 days after the date of mailing for parcels sent by first-class (including priority), SAM or PAL mail, and until 75 days after the date of mailing for parcels sent by surface ocean transportation between:

(1) The contiguous 48 states and any state, territory or possession of the United States located outside the contiguous 48 states (including any location or unit having an APO or FPO designation as part of the address).

(2) Any state, territory or possession of the United States located outside the contiguous 48 states and any other state, territory or possession of the United States located outside the contiguous 48 states (including any location or unit having an APO or FPO designation as part of the address).

b. Registered. The customer may not file a claim involving loss until 15 days after the date of mailing in the case of domestic mail, or articles addressed to or mailed from an APO or FPO.

**.223 Complete or Partial Loss of Contents. Damage or Rifling Claims.** Claims for complete or partial loss of contents, damage, or alleged rifling must be filed immediately.

**.23 Copies of Delivery Records.** Customers may obtain copies of delivery records on numbered insured, COD, registered, and express mail shipments by sending a request to the post office of address. The request must include all mailing information such as article number, date mailed, names and addresses of mailer and addressee, and type of mailing (insured, COD, etc.). The fee is $3.75 for each copy of the delivery record requested and must be sent with the request.

**.24 Required Information**

**.241 Evidence of Insurance, COD, or Registration**

The customer must submit evidence that the article was an insured, COD or registered mailing. Acceptable evidence includes either:

a. The original mailing receipt issued at the time of mailing (reproduced copies are not acceptable); or

b. The wrapper, which must have the names and addresses of both the mailer and addressee and the appropriate mail endorsement indicating Postal Service handling as insured, COD, or registered mail. Note: Indemnity may be limited to $50 for insured; $10 for COD mail and $100 for registered mail if only the wrapper is submitted as evidence.

**.242 Evidence of Value.** The customer must submit evidence of value for all claims. All statements must be dated and signed by the maker. Acceptable evidence includes:

a. Sales receipt.

b. Invoice.

c. Statement of value from a reputable dealer.

d. Catalog value of a similar article.

e. Statement describing the article lost or damaged, including where purchased, date, amount and whether the article was new or used. If handmade, the price of material used and labor must be stated. The items must be described in sufficient detail for the Postal Data Center (PDC) to determine that the value claimed is accurate.

f. Paid repair bills, estimates of repair costs, or appraisals may be used instead of estimates of value in the case of claims for partial damage. When there is a possibility that the cost of repair exceeds actual value, other evidence of value may be required.

g. Statement of costs for duplication and premium for surety bond when the claim is for loss of securities or certificates of stock.

**.25 Payable and Nonpayable Claims**

**.251 Payable Claims.** Subject to 149.252, insurance for loss or damage to registered, insured, or COD mail within the amount covered by the fee paid is payable for:

a. Actual value of lost articles. Depreciation is deducted for used items.

b. Cost of repairing a damaged article or replacing a totally damaged article, not exceeding actual value of the article.

c. Remittance due on a COD parcel for which no remittance has been received by the mailer.

d. Death of bees or baby poultry due to physical damage to the package or delay for which the Postal Service is responsible. In the absence of definite evidence showing responsibility for death of bees or baby poultry, the Postal Service will be presumed to be at fault if 10 per cent or more are dead on delivery, and indemnity will be paid for all dead bees or poultry; otherwise

the Postal Service will not be presumed to be at fault (see 149.252k and l and 124.63).

e. Costs incurred in duplicating or obtaining documents, or their original cost if they cannot be duplicated. These costs include:

(1) Cost of duplicating service.

(2) Notary fees.

(3) Bonding fees for replacement of stock or bond certificates.

(4) Reasonable attorney's fees, if actually required to replace the lost or damaged documents.

(5) Other direct and necessary expenses or costs, as determined by the Postal Service.

f. The extra cost of gift wrapping if the gift wrapped article was enclosed in another container for handling in the mail.

g. Cost of outer container if specially designed and constructed for goods sent.

h. The established fair market value of stamps and coins having philatelic or numismatic value, as determined by a recognized dealer of stamps or coins.

i. Federal, state or city sales tax paid on articles which are lost or totally damaged.

j. Postage (not fee) paid for sending damaged articles for repair. The Postal Service must be used for this purpose. Other reasonable transportation charges may be included if postal service is not available.

k. Photographic film and negatives will be compensated for only at the cost of the film stock. No indemnity will be paid for the content of the film, nor for the photographer's time and expenses in taking the photographs.

**.252 Nonpayable Claims.** Payment will not be made in excess of the actual value of the article, or in excess of the maximum amount covered by the fee paid. Indemnity will not be paid in the following situations:

a. The article was not rightfully in the mail. This includes parcels and COD articles sent to addressees without their consent for purposes of sale or on approval.

b. The claim is filed more than one year from the date the article was mailed; the duplicate claim or inquiry is not initiated within six months of the original claim filing date; or the appeal of the Postal Service decision is not filed within three months of the date of the original decision.

c. Evidence of insurance coverage has not been presented.

d. Loss, rifling, or damage occurred after delivery by the Postal Service.

e. The claim is based on sentimental loss rather than actual value.

f. The loss resulted from delay of the mail.

g. The claim is for consequential loss rather than for the article itself.

h. The contents froze, melted, spoiled or deteriorated.

i. The damage consisted of abrasion, scarring, or scraping of suitcases, handbags and similar articles which were not properly wrapped for protection.

j. The death of baby poultry was due to shipment to points where delivery could not be made within 72 hours from the time of hatch.

k. The death of honeybees and harmless live animals was not the fault of the Postal Service.

l. A failure on the part of the second party (the addressee if the claim is filed by the mailer, or the mailer if the claim is filed by the addressee) to fully cooperate in the completion of the claim.

m. The article is so fragile as to prevent its safe carriage in the mails, regardless of packaging.

n. Personal compensation for time required to replace lost documents.

o. Damaged articles, mailing container and packaging were not submitted to the Postal Service for inspection.

p. The claim was submitted after the article had been transported outside of the mails by other carriers or by private conveyance.

q. The damage was caused by shock, transportation environment, or x-ray and no evidence of damage to the mailing container exists.

r. The container and packaging were not submitted to the Postal Service for inspection on a partial or complete loss of contents claim.

**.26 Replacement Shipments.** If a replacement shipment has been sent to a customer to replace the original article(s) lost, Replacement shipment must be indicated on the claim and a copy of the invoice evidencing the replacement must be attached to the claim form.

**.27 Estimates, Appraisals and Depreciation**

**.271** If necessary, the article may be returned to the customer by the Postal Service so he may obtain an appraisal or estimate. Postal Service personnel must give and take receipts for damaged articles on Form 3831, Receipt for Articles Damaged in Mails. Important: The condition of the article must be noted on the receipt.

**.272** The Postal Service depreciates a used article either lost or damaged based on the life expectancy of the article.

**.28 Processing Claims**

**.281 Post Offices, Classified Stations and Branches**

Post offices, classified stations and branches will:

a. Accept and process registered, insured and COD claims upon the presentation of the required information.

b. Assist customers in preparation of claim form.

c. Complete post office portion of the claim.

d. Route completed forms in accordance with the type of claim being processed.

**.282 St. Louis PDC/Office of Mail Classification.** The St. Louis PDC (or the office of mail classification, USPS headquarters, at its discretion, will adjudicate and pay or disallow all claims.

**.283 Appeals.** Appeals are filed with the director of the St. Louis PDC. If the director of the PDC sustains the denial, the appeal may be forwarded to the director, Office of Mail Classification, USPS headquarters, for a final review and adjudication (see 149.81).

**Insured and COD Claims**

**.31 How to File**

**.311 Required Forms.** A customer may file a claim at any post office, classified branch, or station. Form 3812, Request for Payment of Domestic Postal Insurance, dated August 1977 or later, must be used to request payment for the loss or damage of insured mail. A claim has not been filed until a completed Form 3812 has been accepted by the Postal Service. The form is a four-part snap out set which includes two copies of Form 1510-A, Inquiry for the Loss or Rifling of Mail Matter, and one copy of Form 3841, Post Office Record of Claim. Do not complete a separate Form 1510 or Form 3841 for insured or COD claims.

**.312 Evidence of Loss or Damage**

a. Complete Loss Claims Filed by the Mailer. All mailers filing claims for complete loss of insured mail must provide proof that a loss has actually occurred before post offices will accept a claim for indemnity. This proof may be supplied by any one of the following methods:

(1) The mailer may obtain a claim form, Form 3812, Request For Payment of Domestic Postal Insurance, from any post office. The mailer must then complete the claim form and mail it to the addressee. Postal Service personnel will not mail the claim form for the mailer, but assistance in completing the form will be provided upon request. The addressee must complete Items 15 and 19 on the claim form and return it to the mailer. If the addressee has signed the claim form and indicated the article was not received 30 days or more after the date of mailing, the mailer may then take the claim form, along with the original mailing receipt, to a post office and file the claim.

(2) If the mailer is unable to obtain the cooperation of the addressee in signing Form 3812 for numbered insured articles or, if he prefers,

the mailer may send a check or money order for $3.75 to the post office of address and request a copy of the delivery record, provided 30 days or more have elapsed since the date of mailing. Such requests for delivery records must contain the date the article was mailed, the insurance number and the complete name and address of the mailer and addressee (see 149.23).

(3) If the mailer receives a notice from the post office of address that a delivery record is not on file, the mailer may take this notice and original mailing receipt to any post office and file a claim for loss. Post offices accepting such claims must attach a copy of the notice from the addressee post office to the Form 3812 claim set and send them to the St. Louis PDC for adjudication.

(4) If the mailer has written and signed documentation (such as a letter dated at least 30 days after the date of mailing) from the addressee stating the addressee did not receive the article, the mailer may take this documentation to a post office, along with the original mailing receipt, and file a claim. The Postal Service employee must attach this documentation, or a copy of it, to the claim form.

b. Complete Loss Claims Filed By The Addressee. An addressee may file a claim for the loss of an insured article if the addressee presents the following to the post office accepting the claim:

(1) The original mailing receipt. Copies of original mailing receipts are not acceptable.

(2) A Form 3812 that has been signed by the mailer and on which the mailer has designated the payee.

(3) Evidence of value.

Note: If the addressee does not have all of the above information, only the mailer will be allowed to file a claim for loss of an insured article.

c. Complete or Partial Loss of Contents. For complete or partial loss of contents claims, the container and packaging must be presented to the Postal Service for inspection when the claim is filed. Exception: The claimant may submit a Form 673, Report of Rifled Article, or a Form 3760, Wrapper Found Without Contents (which was received from the Postal Service), to file a claim.

d. Damage Claims. For damage claims, the article with the mailing container and packaging must be presented to the Postal Service for inspection at the time the claim is filed.

**.32 Disposition of Damaged Article.** (See 149.6.)

**149.4 Registered Mail Claims**

**.41 How to File**

**.411 Required Forms.** A customer may file a claim at any post office, classified station or branch. Form 565, Registered Mail Application For Indemnity, dated June 1980 or later, must be used to file a claim for loss or damage of registered mail that was insured by the Postal Service. Do not complete a separate Form 1510-A or 3841 for registered claims. A claim has not been filed until a completed Form 565 has been received by the Postal Service.

**.42 Disposition of Damaged Article.** (See 149.6.)

**149.5 Express Mail Claims**

**.51 How to File**

**.511 Who May File.** Claims for complete loss may be filed only by the mailer. Claims for damage or partial loss may be filed by either the mailer or the addressee. (See 294 and 295.)

**.512 Required Forms.** Claims for loss or damage filed by the mailer must be filed on Form 5690, Express Mail Application For Indemnity. A claim has not been filed until a completed Form 5690 has been accepted by the Postal Service.

**.513 When to File**

a. Loss Claims. All claims for loss may be filed no earlier than seven days following the date of mailing, and all claims must be filed not later than 60 days from the date of mailing.

b. Damage Claims. Claims for damage or partial loss should be filed immediately, but must be filed no later than 60 days from the date of mailing. Claims filed by the addressee must be returned to the post office of mailing for signature by the mailer, designation of the payee by the mailer, and inclusion of the customer receipt copy of the mailing label.

**.514 Required Information**

a. General. The mailer or addressee must present the damaged article and packaging at the post office when the claim is filed. The mailer must also provide the customer receipt copy of the mailing label at the time the claim is filed, or when the claim is returned from the post office of address for signature by the mailer. The customer receipt copy of the mailing label must be attached to the claim form at the time the claim is filed (see 295).

b. Merchandise and Document Reconstruction. In the event claims are required for both merchandise insurance and document reconstruction insurance on the same shipment, two Forms 5690 must be completed and processed. Complete documentation must be attached to each claim form, supporting the type of loss or damage claimed. The two claims must be submitted together.

**.52 Disposition of Damaged Article.** (See 149.6.)

**.53 Adjudication.** The St. Louis PDC (or the office of mail classification, USPS headquarters, at its discretion) will adjudicate and pay or disallow all express mail claims.

**149.6 Disposition of Damaged Articles**

For a completely damaged article that will have little or no salvage value (such as smashed glassware), allow the customer to retain the article if he or she so desired; otherwise destroy it. If the completely damaged insured, COD or express mail article will have salvage value, retain it for 90 days, then forward it to your dead parcel branch (see 159.561b) on the next weekly dispatch. Use Form 3831, Receipt For Article(s) Damaged in Mails. If the customer's claim is denied, the article must be returned upon request. For registered mail damage claims, the article and the packaging must be retained and protected at the post office until released by notification from the St. Louis PDC.

**149.7 Payment Conditions, Recovery of Articles, and Reimbursement**

**.71 Payment Conditions**

**.711 Insufficient Fee.** If, through established error by the Postal Service, a fee was charged which was less than that required to cover the amount of insurance coverage requested at the time of mailing, the mailer may be permitted to pay the deficiency in fee. Indemnity may be paid within the limit fixed for the higher fee. This only applies to the insurance fee when the article is insured. An additional fee may not be paid to register an article previously insured or to increase the indemnity on the registered article.

**.712 Loss or Total Damage.** If the insured, registered or COD article was lost or the entire contents totally damaged, the payment will include an additional amount for the postage (not fee) paid by the mailer.

**.713 Mailer and Addressee Claim Insurance.** If both mailer and addressee claim insurance, they should decide between themselves who should receive payment. If no agreement is reached, payment will be made to the mailer, if a payment is due.

**.714 Incompetent or Deceased Payee.** If the payee is incompetent or deceased, payment will be made to the legal representative. If there is no legal representative, payment will be made to such relative or representative of the payee as is entitled to receive the amount due, in accordance with applicable state laws.

**.72 Disposition of Recovered Article.** When a lost registered, insured, COD or express mail article is recovered, the payee may accept the article and reimburse the Postal Service for the full amount paid if the article is undamaged, or for such other amount as may be determined by the director, office of mail classification, USPS headquarters, if the article is damaged, has depreciated in value, or the contents are not intact.

**.73 Reimbursements**

**.731 Reimbursement Tendered.** If reimbursement is tendered representing an overpayment, erroneous or improper indemnity claim payment, or a voluntary indemnity refund, postal personnel will accept it and issue a receipt. Send all reimbursements to the St. Louis PDC, with all claim identifying information. Personnel checks, money orders, or other negotiable instruments should be made payable to the Postal Service. If the instrument is made payable to the postmaster, he must sign his name and restrictively endorse it pay to postal service and remit as above. Do not mark any entry in the cashbook.

**.732 Reimbursement Not Tendered.** When an overpayment, erroneous or improper indemnity claim payment is disclosed and repayment is not tendered, report it to the director, St. Louis PDC, by memorandum, so it may be placed under accounts receivable control by the PDC.

**149.8 Appeals and Postal Service Authority**

**.81 Appeals.** All appeals of Postal Service claim decisions must be filed within three months of the date of the original decision. Appeals must be sent to: Postal Data Center, P.O. Box 14677, St. Louis, Mo. 63180.

**.82 Postal Service Authority.** The requirements established in 149 may be waived in favor of the customer when the director, Office of Mail Classification, USPS headquarters, determines it is in the best interest of the Postal Service.

# Mail Classification and Rates

The Domestic Mail Manual provides detailed instructions for the proper classification of mail matter, and the computation of postage rates. Familiarity with the regulations can often avoid repacking and needless expense.

The information given here is current through May 1, 1982. Additional changes in some rates may occur, and postal patrons should watch for further announcements.

## First Class

First-class mail consists of mailable postal cards, post cards, most matter wholly or partially in writing or typewriting (except authorized additons to second-, third-, and fourth-class mail and acceptable written or typewritten matter listed in the manual), matter closed against inspection, bills and statements of account, and matter having the character of actual and personal correspondence.

**Postal Cards:** A postal card is a card supplied by the Postal Service with a postage stamp printed or impressed on it, for the transmission of messages. A double postal card consists of two attached cards, one of which may be detached by the receiver and returned by mail as a reply. Each card has a printed impressed postage stamp of the first-class card rate.

**Post Cards:** Post cards are privately printed mailing cards for the transmission of messages. A double post card consists of two attached post cards, one of which may be detached by the receiver and returned by mail as a reply. Each card is subject to the first-class card rate. However, postage need not be paid on the reply portion until it is detached and mailed as a reply. The paper or card stock used for single and double post cards may be of any light color that does not prevent legible addresses and postmarks from being placed thereon. Brilliant colors must not be used. Single post cards and each part of double post cards must conform to the following specifications to qualify for mailing at the card rate:

a. Post cards may not be smaller than $3\frac{1}{2}$ by 5 inches or larger than the size fixed by the Convention of the Universal Postal Union in effect (currently $4\frac{1}{4}$ by 6 inches).

b. They must be rectangular in shape, and of approximately the same form, quality and weight as postal cards.

c. A post card must be made of an unfolded and uncreased piece of paper or card stock of approximately the quality and weight of a postal card. The thickness must be uniform and not less than 0.007 of an inch thick.

**Standards:** The following minimum size standards apply to first-class mail:

a. All mailing pieces must be at least 0.007 of an inch thick.

b. All mailing pieces which are $\frac{1}{4}$ of an inch thick or less must be: rectangular in shape; at least $3\frac{1}{2}$ inches high; and at least 5 inches long.

NOTE: First-class mailing pieces which do not meet the minimum size standards are prohibited from the mails.

To insure prompt and efficient processing of first-class mail, it is recommended that all envelopes, cards and self-mailers have an aspect ratio of width (height) to length between 1 to 1.3 and 1 to 2.5 inclusive, and be sealed or secured on all four edges so that they can be handled by machines.

**Size Limits:** First-class mail weighing one ounce or less is nonstandard if it exceeds any the following size limits:

a. Its length exceeds $11\frac{1}{2}$ inches, or

b. Its height exceed $6\frac{1}{8}$ inches, or

c. Its thickness exceeds $\frac{1}{4}$ of an inch, or

d. Its aspect ratio (length divided by height) does not fall between 1 to 1.3 and 1 to 2.5 inclusive.

Nonstandard mail often results in delays or damage to mail because it does not lend itself to machine processing. For this reason, mailers are encouraged to avoid mailing nonstandard first-class mail. A surcharge of 9 cents is assessed on each piece of nonstandard first-class mail.

## Second Class

Second-class mail matter includes printed publications issued at least four times annually, at regular intervals. The purpose must be the dissemination of information, and there must be a legitimate subscribers' list. The publication must be issued from a "known office of publication," and second-class original entry authorization must be obtained at the post office serving the known office of publication.

Publications not entitled to second-class rates include those primarily for advertising purposes, and those circulated free or at a nominal charge. Some exceptions are made for special groups.

A special classification, with finite qualifications and requirements, exists for "controlled circulation" publications, restricted to use by qualified mailers, and subject to its own schedule of rates and fees.

Special application must be made for permission to use second-class rates.

## Third Class

The Domestic Mail Manual defines third-class matter as material which is "not mailed or required to be mailed as first-class mail; not entered as second-class mail; and less than 16 ounces in weight."

This includes circulars sent in identical terms to several persons, and printed matter weighing less than 16 ounces.

There is a rate for single pieces, and also a bulk rate covering mailings of identical pieces weighing not less than 50 pounds, or encompassing at least 200 pieces; only the size and weight must be the same to qualify as "identical."

The same size standards and restrictions apply to third-class mail as those previously outlined for first-class mail, with the exception of keys and identification devices sent through the mail.

Special rates are authorized for certain types of organizations.

## Fourth Class

"Fourth-class mail consists of mailable matter not mailed or required to be mailed as first-class mail; weighing 16 ounces or more (except special or library rate fourth-class); and not entered as second-class mail (except as specifically provided for transient rate matter)."

A zone system based upon the distance between the point of mailing and the destination is used in computing rates. Special rates are provided for catalogs and similar advertising matter, books and similar educational materials, and materials mailed by libraries.

There are specific size and weight limits for fourth-class matter. Parcels mailed between first-class offices are limited to 40 pounds or a total of 84 inches in length and girth combined; parcels mailed under other circumstances are limited to 70 pounds or a combined measurement of 100 inches.

The larger limits are enforced for rural and star routes; military post offices and those in Alaska, Hawaii, Puerto Rico, and the Trust Territory of the Pacific Islands; official mail; and specified materials including educational items and library mailings.

The regulations specify what may be enclosed with fourth-class mailings.

## Express Mail

This is a type of "guaranteed" rapid delivery system between major U.S. cities, with a widely varied rate schedule. At least one form of express mail guarantees articles received by 5 p.m. (or other deadline time as established by any individual office) at a postal facility offering express mail service will be delivered by 3 p.m. the next day or the shipment can be picked up as early as 10 a.m. the next business day. Rates include insurance, shipment receipt, and record of delivery at the destination post office. Express mail service is available for any mailable articles up to 70 lbs. The Postal Service will refund, upon application to originating office, the postage for any express mail shipments not meeting the service standard except for those delayed by strike or work stoppage.

The program now includes a 100 per cent refund of postage and fees if shipment is not delivered within 25 hours; use of official mail indicia for government agencies; and liability insurance.

There are four major types of express mail services: (1) Customer designed Service — a courier-type service custom tailored to the users' requirements for specific pick-up and delivery times; (2) International service — offers overnight and second-day delivery to eight countries with which reciprocal express has been arranged; (3) Next day service — is an overnight system for delivery of shipments mailed at selected post offices; and (4) Same day airport service — offers dispatch on the next available flight between designated airport mail facilities. The Postal Service maintains the full rate and weight limitation tables. For further information, contact your local post office.

# Domestic Postal Rates

## First Class

The single piece rates are applied to each letter or piece of first-class mail according to its weight.

All first-class mail weighing 12 ounces or less, except postal and post cards: 20 cents for the first ounce or fraction of an ounce; 17¢ for each additional ounce or fraction of an ounce.

Single postal cards sold by the post office: 13¢ each. Double postal cards sold by the post office: 26¢ (13¢ each half). Single post cards: 13¢ each. Double post cards (reply portion of double post card does not have to bear postage when originally mailed): 26¢ (13¢ each half.)

Presort rate: Annual fee of $30, then presort rate is applicable first-class rate, less 3¢ per piece for letters and less 1¢ per piece for cards.

Business reply — rates vary to requirement, consult post office.

## Second Class

Second-class mail includes newspapers and periodical publications with second-class mail privileges.

Copies mailed by public: 19 cents for the first ounce; 35¢ up to two ounces; 10¢ for each additional ounce or fraction of an ounce up to eight ounces; 10¢ for each additional two ounces (or fraction thereof) over eight ounces; or the fourth-class rate, whichever is lower.

## Third Class

Third-class mail includes circulars, books, catalogs and other printed matter, merchandise, seeds, cuttings, bulbs, roots, scions and plants, weighing less than 16 ounces.

| Single piece rate, weight not exceeding: | | | |
|---|---|---|---|
| 1 oz. | $0.20 | 10 oz. | $1.05 |
| 2 oz. | $0.37 | 12 oz. | $1.15 |
| 4 oz. | $0.71 | 14 oz. | $1.25 |
| 6 oz. | $0.85 | 15.99 oz. | $1.35 |
| 8 oz. | $0.95 | | |

For keys and identification devices: first two ounces, 32¢; each additional two ounces or fraction thereof, 18¢.

## Discount Rates

A widely varied schedule of discount rates exist for certain classes of U.S. mail. Most notable are the special bulk rate discounts for large or multiple-piece mailings, and the different presort rates, which provide for varying discounts from applicable postage rates. The most recent innovation, carrier-route presort, allows for the biggest presort discount rate. With the different requirements and rate schedules involved for all these classifications, consultation with the local post office is recommended for any mailers who might qualify for these discounts. Most of these discounts require certain minimum mailing requirements, and qualified nonprofit organizations are often given discounts beyond even the regular discounted rates.

## Priority Mail (Heavy Pieces)

Priority mail provides first-class service for heavy items (over 12 ounces), those that would otherwise go parcel post. It is primarily for heavy items that must go at the first-class rate, or for parcels needing expedited service.

Local zone is within the delivery limits of the local post office; Zone 1 is within the same sectional center, Zone 2 is up to 150 miles; Zone 3, to 300 miles; Zone 4, to 600 miles; Zone 5, to 1,000 miles; Zone 6, to 1,400 miles; Zone 7, to 1,800 miles; and Zone 8, beyond 1,800 miles. The zone mileage figures are approximate. The official zone chart furnished by a post office shows the complete zone structure from that office.

### Priority Mail Rates

| Weight—over 12 oz. but not exceeding (pounds) | Local 1, 2 & 3 | Zone 4 | Zone 5 | Zone 6 | Zone 7 | Zone 8 |
|---|---|---|---|---|---|---|
| 1 | $2.24 | $2.24 | $2.24 | $2.34 | $2.45 | $2.58 |
| 1.5 | 2.30 | 2.42 | 2.56 | 2.72 | 2.87 | 3.07 |
| 2 | 2.54 | 2.70 | 2.88 | 3.09 | 3.30 | 3.57 |
| 2.5 | 2.78 | 2.98 | 3.21 | 3.47 | 3.73 | 4.06 |
| 3 | 3.01 | 3.25 | 3.53 | 3.85 | 4.16 | 4.56 |
| 3.5 | 3.25 | 3.53 | 3.85 | 4.22 | 4.59 | 5.05 |
| 4 | 3.49 | 3.81 | 4.18 | 4.60 | 5.02 | 5.55 |
| 4.5 | 3.73 | 4.09 | 4.50 | 4.97 | 5.45 | 6.05 |
| 5 | 3.97 | 4.37 | 4.83 | 5.35 | 5.88 | 6.54 |
| 6 | 4.44 | 4.92 | 5.47 | 6.10 | 6.74 | 7.53 |
| 7 | 4.92 | 5.48 | 6.12 | 6.86 | 7.60 | 8.52 |
| 8 | 5.39 | 6.03 | 6.77 | 7.61 | 8.46 | 9.51 |
| 9 | 5.87 | 6.59 | 7.42 | 8.36 | 9.32 | 10.51 |
| 10 | 6.35 | 7.15 | 8.07 | 9.12 | 10.18 | 11.50 |
| 11 | 6.82 | 7.70 | 8.71 | 9.87 | 11.04 | 12.49 |
| 12 | 7.30 | 8.26 | 9.36 | 10.62 | 11.89 | 13.48 |
| 13 | 7.77 | 8.81 | 10.01 | 11.38 | 12.75 | 14.47 |
| 14 | 8.25 | 9.37 | 10.66 | 12.13 | 13.61 | 15.46 |
| 15 | 8.73 | 9.93 | 11.31 | 12.88 | 14.47 | 16.45 |
| 16 | 9.20 | 10.48 | 11.95 | 13.63 | 15.33 | 17.44 |
| 17 | 9.68 | 11.04 | 12.60 | 14.39 | 16.19 | 18.43 |
| 18 | 10.15 | 11.59 | 13.25 | 15.14 | 17.05 | 19.42 |
| 19 | 10.63 | 12.15 | 13.90 | 15.89 | 17.91 | 20.42 |
| 20 | 11.11 | 12.71 | 14.55 | 16.65 | 18.77 | 21.41 |
| 21 | 11.58 | 13.26 | 15.19 | 17.40 | 19.63 | 22.40 |
| 22 | 12.06 | 13.82 | 15.84 | 18.15 | 20.48 | 23.39 |
| 23 | 12.53 | 14.37 | 16.49 | 18.91 | 21.34 | 24.38 |
| 24 | 13.01 | 14.93 | 17.14 | 19.66 | 22.20 | 25.37 |
| 25 | 13.49 | 15.49 | 17.79 | 20.41 | 23.06 | 26.36 |

Exception: Parcels weighing less than 15 pounds, measuring over 84 inches but not exceeding 100 inches in length and girth combined, are chargeable with a minimum rate equal to that for a 15 pound parcel for the zone to which addressed.

## Fourth-Class (Parcel Post) Rates
### (See Priority Mail for zone boundaries.)

| Weight 1 pound and not exceeding (pounds) | Local | Zones 1 & 2 | Zone 3 | Zone 4 | Zone 5 | Zone 6 | Zone 7 | Zone 8 |
|---|---|---|---|---|---|---|---|---|
| 2 | $1.52 | $1.55 | $1.61 | $1.70 | $1.83 | $1.99 | $2.15 | $2.48 |
| 3 | 1.58 | 1.63 | 1.73 | 1.86 | 2.06 | 2.30 | 2.55 | 3.05 |
| 4 | 1.65 | 1.71 | 1.84 | 2.02 | 2.29 | 2.61 | 2.94 | 3.60 |
| 5 | 1.71 | 1.79 | 1.96 | 2.18 | 2.52 | 2.92 | 3.32 | 4.07 |
| 6 | 1.78 | 1.87 | 2.07 | 2.33 | 2.74 | 3.14 | 3.64 | 4.54 |
| 7 | 1.84 | 1.95 | 2.18 | 2.49 | 2.89 | 3.38 | 3.95 | 5.02 |
| 8 | 1.91 | 2.03 | 2.30 | 2.64 | 3.06 | 3.63 | 4.27 | 5.55 |
| 9 | 1.97 | 2.11 | 2.41 | 2.75 | 3.25 | 3.93 | 4.63 | 6.08 |
| 10 | 2.04 | 2.19 | 2.52 | 2.87 | 3.46 | 4.22 | 5.00 | 6.62 |
| 11 | 2.10 | 2.28 | 2.60 | 3.00 | 3.68 | 4.51 | 5.38 | 7.15 |
| 12 | 2.17 | 2.36 | 2.66 | 3.10 | 3.89 | 4.80 | 5.75 | 7.69 |
| 13 | 2.21 | 2.41 | 2.72 | 3.19 | 4.02 | 4.96 | 5.95 | 7.97 |
| 14 | 2.26 | 2.46 | 2.78 | 3.28 | 4.13 | 5.12 | 6.14 | 8.24 |
| 15 | 2.31 | 2.51 | 2.83 | 3.36 | 4.25 | 5.26 | 6.32 | 8.48 |
| 16 | 2.35 | 2.56 | 2.89 | 3.44 | 4.35 | 5.40 | 6.49 | 8.72 |
| 17 | 2.40 | 2.59 | 2.94 | 3.51 | 4.45 | 5.53 | 6.65 | 8.94 |
| 18 | 2.44 | 2.64 | 2.99 | 3.59 | 4.55 | 5.65 | 6.80 | 9.15 |
| 19 | 2.48 | 2.68 | 3.04 | 3.66 | 4.64 | 5.77 | 6.94 | 9.35 |
| 20 | 2.52 | 2.72 | 3.10 | 3.73 | 4.73 | 5.89 | 7.09 | 9.55 |
| 21 | 2.56 | 2.76 | 3.14 | 3.79 | 4.82 | 6.00 | 7.22 | 9.73 |
| 22 | 2.60 | 2.81 | 3.20 | 3.86 | 4.90 | 6.10 | 7.35 | 9.91 |
| 23 | 2.64 | 2.84 | 3.26 | 3.92 | 4.99 | 6.21 | 7.48 | 10.08 |
| 24 | 2.68 | 2.93 | 3.36 | 4.02 | 5.07 | 6.31 | 7.60 | 10.24 |
| 25 | 2.72 | 3.00 | 3.47 | 4.15 | 5.14 | 6.40 | 7.75 | 10.40 |

Exception: Parcels weighing less than 15 pounds, measuring over 84 inches but not exceeding 100 inches in length and girth combined, are chargeable with a minimum rate equal to that for a 15 pound parcel for the zone to which addressed.

Special lower rates exist for items such as books, bound printed matter, manuscripts, library items, items mailed in bulk or presorted, and other materials. The local post office should be consulted for such rates and requirements.

## Special Handling

For preferential handling in dispatch and transportation of third- and fourth-class mail, the special handling service is provided. This service does not provide special delivery. The fee for pieces up to and including 10 pounds in weight is 75 cents; and for more than 10 pounds, $1.30. The fees are in addition to the postage fees incurred.

## Special Delivery

Special Delivery means an item of mail is delivered as soon as practicable after it arrives at the addressee's post office. It virtually assures delivery on the day received at the post office but generally does not speed up the transportation time to that point from the origin. The special delivery fee (schedule) is in addition to the regular postage.

| | 2 lbs. or less | Over 2 to 10 lbs. | Over 10 lbs. |
|---|---|---|---|
| First-class | $2.10 | $2.35 | $3.00 |
| All other classes | $2.35 | $3.00 | $3.40 |

## Money Orders

Postal money orders provide for sending money through the mail safely with money notes rather than cash. Fees are 75 cents for domestic money orders up to $25; $1.10 for money orders over $25 to $50; and $1.55 for money orders over $50 to $500. They may be purchased and redeemed at any post office. Domestic U.S. money orders are authorized for payment in U.S. and Canadian post offices and banks.

International money orders can be purchased in amounts up to $500 at all larger first-class post offices. Maximum limit may be lower to some countries. Such money orders are available to countries which accept such orders by mutual or intermediary agreements.

## Insurance Fees

Third-class and fourth-class mail may be insured for protection against loss or damage. Also, first-class mail which contains third- or fourth-class matter may be insured, and should be endorsed "Third-" or "Fourth-Class Mail Enclosed," along with the first-class or priority mail endorsement. Liability for insured mail is limited to $400, and the fee schedule is as follows:

| Liability | Fee |
| --- | --- |
| $0.01 to $20 | $0.45 |
| $20.01 to $50 | $0.85 |
| $50.01 to $100 | $1.25 |
| $100.01 to $150 | $1.70 |
| $150.01 to $200 | $2.05 |
| $200.01 to $300 | $3.45 |
| $300.01 to $400 | $4.70 |

## Certified Mail

Certified Mail service provides for a record of delivery to be maintained by the post office from which delivered. The carrier delivering the item obtains a signature from the addressee on a receipt form which is kept for two years. The charge for Certified Mail is 75 cents. It is primarily for first-class items which have no money value; there is no insurance feature.

Certified Mail may be deposited in a collection box if the mailer has attached a "certified mail" sticker and appropriate postage and fees.

## Registered Mail

Domestic first-class or priority mail may be registered with indemnity limit of $25,000. It is offered for the protection of valuable papers, stamps, jewelry and other items of value. Registered mail provides for a receipt to the customer at the time of mailing and a post office record of the mailing.

Registered mail is accounted for by number from time of mailing to delivery and is transported separately from other mail under lock. The registry fees, in addition to first-class postage, are scaled according to declared value of mail. Minimum fee is $3.25; the full fee schedule may be obtained at any post office. Registered mail may not be deposited in collection boxes because a receipt must be issued at point of mailing.

## Additional Services

**COD Mail** — First-class, third-class and fourth-class mail may be sent COD, which provides the post office to Collect On Delivery the price of the item delivered and return payment to sender by money order. The fee schedule for this service varies according to the value to be collected, as well as the value for which an item is insured. Liability does not exceed $400. Payment and fee schedules are available from the local post office. A combination of registration and COD is also available, with various combined fees.

**Return Receipt** — Return receipts furnish the mailer with evidence of delivery, and are obtainable for mail which is send COD, is insured for more than $15, or which is registered or certified. If requested at the time of mailing, the fee is 60¢ for a receipt showing signature and date of delivery, or 70¢ for a receipt showing signature, date and place of delivery. If requested after mailing, the return receipt fee is $3.75, showing to whom and date delivered.

**Restricted Delivery** — Restricted delivery is a service by which a mailer may direct that delivery be made only to the addressee or to an agent for the addressee when specifically authorized in writing by the addressee to receive his or her mail, and may be obtained for COD mail, mail insured for more than $15, registered or certified mail. In addition to postage and other fees, the restricted delivery fee is $1.

# International Mail

International mail includes letters, letter packages, printed matter, small packages of merchandise and samples, and parcel post destined for foreign countries. APO (Army Post Office) and FPO (Fleet Post Office) mail is not considered international mail.

Below is a listing of international postal rates, including surface and air rates. NOTE: Letter class mail to Canada and Mexico receives first-class service in the United States and airmail service in Canada and Mexico at rates equal to domestic U.S. rates.

## Surface Rates

Canada and Mexico (see note in introduction): 20 cents first ounce; 17¢ each additional ounce or fraction through 12 ounces; eight-zone priority rates for heavier weights. Weight limit is 4 pounds to all countries.

Countries other than Canada and Mexico, 1 ounce, 30¢; 17¢ per ounce for each additional ounce up to 8 ounces; over 8 ounces to 1 pound, $2.76; over 1 to 1½ pounds, $3.78; over 1½ to 2 pounds, $4.80; and 75¢ for each additional ½ up to 4 pound limit.

## Air Rates

Central America, Colombia, Venezuela, the Caribbean Islands, Bahamas, Bermuda and St. Pierre and Miquelon, also from American Samoa to Western Samoa and from Guam to the Philippines: 35 cents per half ounce up to and including two ounces; 30¢ each additional half ounce or fraction.

All other countries, 40¢ per half ounce up to and including two ounces, 35¢ each additional half ounce or fraction.

Post card rates to Canada and Mexico are the same as U.S. domestic rates. To other countries, the surface rate is 19¢, while the air rate is 28¢ per card. Size limits are: 6 by 4½ inches maximum; 5½ by 3½ inches minimum. Double reply cards are not useable outside domestic application.

Aerogrammes, or self-contained airmail letter sheets (in which enclosures arc not permitted), are 30¢.

Following is a more complete country listing, with parcel post data as well.

| Country | Letters and Letter Packages Per ½ Oz. | Max. Wt. for Parcel Post (Air Or Surface) | Parcel Post Insurance Available |
|---|---|---|---|
| Afghanistan | *40 | 22 | No |
| Albania | *40 | 22 | No |
| Algeria | 40 | 44 | No |
| Andorra | 40 | 44 | $420 |
| Angola | 40 | 22 | $21 |
| Anguilla (Leeward Is.) | 35 | 22 | $100 |
| Antigua (Leeward Is.) | 35 | 22 | $100 |
| Argentina | 35 | 44 | $210 |
| Aruba (Neth. Antilles) | 35 | 44 | $200 |
| Ascension | 35 | 22 | No |
| Australia | 40 | 44 | $426 |
| Austria | 40 | 44 | $420 |
| Azores | 40 | 22 | $420 |
| Bahamas | 35 | 22 | $126 |
| Bahrain | 40 | 22 | $100 |
| Bangladesh | 40 | 22 | $200 |
| Balearic Is. (Spain) | 40 | †44 | $210 |
| Barbados | 35 | 22 | $100 |
| Barbuda (Leeward Is.) | 35 | 22 | $100 |
| Belgium | 40 | 44 | $210 |
| Belize | 35 | 22 | No |
| Benin (Dahomey) | 40 | 44 | No |
| Bermuda | 35 | 33 | No |
| Bhutan | *40 | 0 | —— |
| Bolivia | *35 | 44 | No |
| Bonaire (Neth. Antilles) | 35 | 44 | $210 |
| Botswana | 40 | 22 | No |
| Brazil | *35 | 44 | No |
| British Virgin Is. | 35 | 22 | $100 |
| Brunei | 40 | 22 | No |
| Bulgaria | *40 | 22 | No |
| Burma | 40 | 22 | No |
| Burundi | 40 | 22 | No |
| Cambodia (see Kampuchea) | | | |
| Cameroon | 40 | 22 | No |
| Canada (rate is per oz.) | 20 | 35 | $400 |
| Canary Is. (Spain) | 40 | †44 | $210 |
| Cape Verde | 40 | 22 | $21 |
| Cayman (Leeward Islands) | 35 | 22 | No |
| Central African Rep. | *40 | 44 | No |
| Chad | †40 | 44 | No |
| Chile | *35 | 22 | No |
| China, People's Rep. of | *40 | 44 | $420 |
| China, Rep. of (see Taiwan) | | | |
| Colombia | *35 | 44 | $210 |
| Comoros | 40 | 44 | No |
| Congo (People's Rep.) | 40 | 44 | No |
| Corsica | 40 | 44 | $420 |
| Costa Rica | 35 | 44 | No |
| Crete (Greece) | 40 | 44 | $210 |
| Cuba | 35 | 0 | —— |

| Country | Letters and Letter Packages Per ½ Oz. | Max. Wt. for Parcel Post (Air Or Surface) | Parcel Post Insurance Available |
|---|---|---|---|
| Curacao (see Neth. Antilles) | | | |
| Cyprus | 40 | 44 | $213 |
| Czechoslovakia | 40 | 44 | $200 |
| Denmark | 40 | 44 | $420 |
| Djibouti | 40 | 44 | $420 |
| Dodecanese Islands (see Greece) | | | |
| Dominica | 35 | 22 | $100 |
| Dominican | *35 | 44 | No |
| East Timor | 40 | 0 | —— |
| Ecuador | 35 | 44 | $50 |
| Egypt | 40 | 44 | $210 |
| El Salvador | *35 | 44 | No |
| Equatorial Guinea | *40 | 44 | No |
| Eritrea (Ethiopia) | 40 | 44 | $210 |
| Estonia (U.S.S.R.) | *40 | 22 | $210 |
| Ethiopia | *40 | 44 | $210 |
| Faeroe Islands | 40 | 44 | $210 |
| Falkland Islands | 35 | 22 | No |
| Fiji | 40 | 22 | $126 |
| Finland | 40 | 44 | $420 |
| France | 40 | 44 | $420 |
| French Guiana | 35 | 44 | No |
| French Polynesia | 40 | 44 | $420 |
| Gabon | 40 | 44 | No |
| Gambia | 40 | 22 | No |
| German Democratic Rep. | *40 | †44 | $210 |
| Germany, Federal Rep. | 40 | 44 | $420 |
| Ghana | 40 | 22 | $80 |
| Gibraltar | 40 | 22 | $50 |
| Gilbert Is. (See Kiribati) | | | |
| Great Britain | 40 | 44 | $1200 |
| Greece | 40 | 44 | $210 |
| Greenland | 40 | 44 | $420 |
| Grenada and Grenadines | 35 | 22 | $100 |
| Guadeloupe | 35 | 44 | No |
| Guatemala | 35 | 44 | $100 |
| Guernsey (Channel Islands, see Great Britain) | | | |
| Guinea | 40 | 44 | No |
| Guinea Bissau | 40 | 22 | $21 |
| Guyana | 35 | 22 | $210 |
| Haiti | 35 | 44 | No |
| Honduras | 35 | †44 | No |
| Hong Kong | 40 | 22 | $420 |
| Hungary | 40 | 44 | $420 |
| Iceland | 40 | 44 | $210 |
| Ifni (see Morocco) | | | |
| India | 40 | †44 | $210 |
| Indonesia | 40 | 22 | No |
| Iran | 40 | 44 | $210 |
| Iraq | 40 | 44 | No |
| Ireland (Eire) | 40 | 22 | $1000 |
| Ireland, Northern (see Great Britain) | | | |
| Isle of Man (see Great Britain) | | | |
| Israel | 40 | 33 | No |
| Italy | *40 | 44 | $126 |
| Ivory Coast | 40 | 44 | No |
| Jamaica | 35 | 22 | No |
| Japan | 40 | 44 | $420 |
| Jersey (Channel Islands, see Great Britain) | | | |
| Jordan | 40 | 22 | No |
| Kampuchea | *40 | 0 | —— |
| Kenya | 40 | 22 | No |
| Kiribati | 40 | 44 | No |
| Korea, Rep. of | †40 | 22 | $210 |
| Korea, Dem. People's Rep. | *†40 | 0 | —— |
| Kuwait | 40 | 44 | $210 |

| Country | Letters and Letter Packages Per ½ Oz. | Max. Wt. for Parcel Post (Air Or Surface) | Parcel Post Insurance Available |
|---|---|---|---|
| Laos | †40 | 22 | No |
| Latvia (U.S.S.R.) | *40 | 22 | $210 |
| Lebanon | 40 | 44 | No |
| Leeward Islands | 35 | 22 | $100 |
| Lesotho | 40 | 22 | No |
| Liberia | 40 | 22 | $105 |
| Libya | 40 | 44 | No |
| Liechtenstein | 40 | 44 | $420 |
| Lithuania (U.S.S.R.) | *40 | 22 | $200 |
| Luxembourg | 40 | 44 | $210 |
| Macao | 40 | 22 | $126 |
| Madagascar (see Malagasy) | | | |
| Madeira Islands | 40 | 22 | $420 |
| Malagasy Republic | 40 | 44 | No |
| Malawi | 40 | 22 | No |
| Malaysia | 40 | 22 | $105 |
| Maldives, Rep. of | *40 | 22 | No |
| Mali | 40 | 44 | No |
| Malta | 40 | 22 | No |
| Martinique | 35 | 44 | No |
| Mauritania | 40 | 44 | No |
| Mauritius | 40 | 22 | No |
| Mexico (rate is per oz.) | 20 | 44 | No |
| Monaco (France) | 40 | 44 | $420 |
| Mongolia People's Rep. | *40 | 0 | —— |
| Montserrat | 35 | 44 | $100 |
| Morocco | 40 | 44 | No |
| Mozambique | 40 | 22 | $100 |
| Namibia (S.W. Africa) | 40 | 22 | No |
| Nauru | 40 | 22 | $210 |
| Nepal | *40 | 22 | No |
| Netherlands | 40 | 44 | $420 |
| Netherlands Antilles | 35 | 44 | $210 |
| Nevis | 35 | 22 | $100 |
| New Caledonia | 40 | 44 | $420 |
| New Hebrides (see Vanuatu) | | | |
| New Zealand | 40 | 22 | $210 |
| Nicaragua | 35 | 44 | $210 |
| Niger | 40 | 44 | No |
| Nigeria | 40 | 22 | No |
| Norway | 40 | 44 | $420 |
| Oman | 40 | 22 | $100 |
| Pakistan | 40 | 22 | $210 |
| Panama | *35 | 70 | No |
| Papua New Guinea | 40 | 22 | $105 |
| Paraguay | 35 | 44 | No |
| Peru | *35 | 44 | No |
| Philippines | 40 | †44 | $210 |
| Pitcairn Islands | 40 | 22 | No |
| Poland | 40 | 44 | No |
| Portugal | 40 | 22 | $420 |
| Qatar | 40 | 22 | $100 |
| Redonda | 35 | 22 | $100 |
| Reunion | 40 | 44 | No |
| Rhodesia (see Zimbabwe) | | | |
| Romania | *40 | 22 | No |
| Rwanda | 40 | 22 | No |
| Ryukyus (see Japan) | | | |
| Saba (see Netherlands Antilles) | | | |
| St. Christopher (St. Kitts) | 35 | 22 | $100 |
| St. Eustatius (see Netherlands Antilles) | | | |
| St. Helena | 40 | 22 | No |
| St. Lucia | 35 | 22 | $100 |
| St. Pierre and Miquelon | 35 | 44 | No |
| St. Thomas & Prince Is. | 40 | 22 | $21 |
| St. Vincent and Grenadines | 35 | 22 | $100 |
| San Marino (Italy) | *40 | 44 | $120 |
| Santa Cruz Islands | 40 | 22 | No |
| Saudi Arabia | *40 | 22 | No |
| Scotland (see Great Britain) | | | |
| Seychelles | 40 | 22 | No |
| Sierra Leone | 40 | 22 | No |
| Singapore | 40 | 22 | $100 |
| Solomon Islands | 40 | 22 | No |
| Somalia | 40 | †22 | No |
| South Africa (Rep.) | 40 | 22 | No |
| Spain | 40 | †44 | $210 |
| Spitzbergen (see Norway) | | | |
| Sri Lanka | 35 | 22 | $210 |
| Sudan | 40 | 22 | No |
| Surinam(e) | 35 | 44 | $100 |
| Swaziland | 40 | 22 | No |
| Sweden | 40 | 44 | $420 |
| Switzerland | 40 | 44 | $420 |
| Syria | 40 | †44 | $210 |
| Taiwan | †40 | 44 | $210 |
| Tanzania | 40 | 22 | No |
| Thailand | 40 | 22 | $126 |
| Togo | 40 | 44 | No |
| Tonga | 40 | 22 | No |
| Trinidad and Tobago | 35 | 22 | $153 |
| Tristan da Cunha | 40 | 22 | No |
| Tunisia | 40 | 44 | No |
| Turkey | 40 | 44 | $210 |
| Turks & Caicos Is. | 35 | 22 | No |
| Tuvalu (Ellice Is.) | 40 | 22 | No |
| Uganda | 40 | 22 | No |
| U.S.S.R. | *40 | 22 | $210 |
| United Arab Emirates | 40 | 22 | $100 |
| Upper Volta | †40 | 44 | No |
| Uruguay | 35 | 44 | No |
| Vanuatu | 40 | 44 | No |
| Vatican City | 40 | 44 | No |
| Venezuela | *35 | 44 | No |
| Vietnam, Soc. Rep. of | †40 | 0 | —— |
| Wales (see Great Britain) | | | |
| Wallis and Futuna Is. (see New Caledonia) | | | |
| Western Samoa | 40 | 22 | $210 |
| Yemen Arab Rep. (Sanaa) | 40 | 44 | No |
| Yemen, People's Democratic Rep. (Aden) | 40 | 44 | No |
| Yugoslavia | *40 | 44 | $210 |
| Zaire | 40 | 44 | No |
| Zambia | 40 | 22 | No |
| Zil Elwagne Sesel (see Seychelles) | | | |
| Zimbabwe | 40 | 22 | No |

* Dutiable merchandise prohibited in letters or letter packages.

† Restrictions apply. Consult post office.

REGISTRATION is available to practically all countries. The fee is $3.25. Maximum indemnity payable is $25.20. To Canada only, payment of the $3.25 fee will provide indemnity for loss up to $100, and payment of a $3.55 fee will provide indemnity up to $200. Consult post office for further details.

INTERNATIONAL REPLY COUPONS are available at all post offices and are handy to use for small payments. One reply coupon will repay a single rate surface letter from any country.

PAYMENTS to overseas nations may be made by international postal money order or by banker's draft. The international money orders (not acceptable in some nations) are available from many post offices. Banker's drafts are available through most commercial banks. Generally personal checks are NOT acceptable to Mints and Central Banks.

**PLEASE CHECK YOUR POST OFFICE** occasionally to update this chart. These rates are accurate as of June 1982; postal rates are subject to occasional change, and additional restrictions on mail matter are applied by certain nations from time to time.

## Canadian Postal Rates

As a special service, postage rates from Canada are offered in the following brief summary. In mid-1979, Canada converted to the metric system of determining mail weight increments, joining many other foreign countries in "going metric." The following rates, therefore, will not correspond directly to the U.S. postal rates, since metric equivalents are not exact when related to ounces, and the prices are also expressed in Canadian currency, which is not equivalent to U.S. currency (banks can supply the current exchange rate).

The basic first-class letter rate in Canada is for letters up to 30 grams, and is 30¢ within Canada. Postal cards are sold at the basic first-class letter rate of 30¢. The domestic rate within Canada goes to 45¢ for items from 30-50 grams; 60¢ from 50-100 grams; and 20¢ for each additional 50 grams.

The rates for mail from Canada to the United States are no longer identical to Canadian domestic rates. The basic first-class rate is 35¢ for items up to 30 grams. After that, the rate goes to 50¢ for items from 30-50 grams, and 25¢ for each additional 50 grams.

The basic international letter rate to countries other than the United States is 60¢ for items up to 20 grams; 93¢ for items from 20-50 grams; $1.45 for 50-100 grams; $2.92 for 100-250 grams; and $5.60 for 250-500 grams. Aerogrammes are 60¢ each.

The third-class rate is 30¢ for items up to 50 grams, and 15¢ for each additional 50 grams.

Special services, in addition to postage, include: certified mail, $1; insurance, 20¢ minimum (up to $10 indemnity); and registration, $1.85 minimum (up to $100 indemnity).

# Customer Service 24

# Linn's Basic Advertising Policy

Linn's publishers offer advertising space for the purpose of bringing buyer and seller together for their mutual benefit. Years of publishing experience indicate the reader must be able to expect satisfactory service from the advertiser in order to respond to future advertisements. It is by giving such satisfactory service that advertisers can expect to continue productive advertising.

Readers are reminded that all transactions are "two-way streets," and equity must exist for both parties for a satisfactory transaction. Advertisements submitted, which are not in the best interests of the advertiser specifically, and of the trade generally, in the opinion of the publishers, or which may mislead readers, will be rejected.

Customer checks of advertisers are periodically made by the publishers in a practical effort to assure accuracy and reliability of all advertisements. However, it is impossible to guarantee the reader's satisfaction with the advertiser's manner of doing business, and the reader is therefore reminded to exercise common sense in responding to any advertisement.

Remember: There is no Santa Claus in philately! The reader is also urged to exercise patience in awaiting response from an advertiser, making allowances for sufficient mail transit time.

### Return Period

Stamps or philatelic material, which the buyer finds to be in unsatisfactory condition, may be returned to the seller for full refund or replacement if returned as sent. Returns must be made within five days of receipt by the buyer, unless other return periods are specified in the advertisement. Refund, or replacement, will be made by the seller within three days of receipt of the returned item(s).

All trades must be held intact for two weeks following shipment of material sent in exchange, to allow time for receipt and acceptance of material shipped.

### Return Postage on Buy and Trade Ads

All advertisers who do not state "write first" in their ads are expected to return stamps at no expense to the seller or trader. Unless an ad states "write first" or similarly indicates that confirmation is needed before shipping, refusal of packages at the post office may be grounds for suspension of advertising privileges. If over-graded stamps are to be returned at seller's or trader's expense, advertisement must so state.

### Prompt Handling of Orders

Advertisers are normally expected to fill orders within three to five days of receipt of good remittance. In cases where shipment is withheld pending clearance of check (which varies from 5 to 16 days, depending on location), advertisers will so notify the buyer, giving approximate shipping date, unless check clearance terms are stated in the advertisement.

### Layaway Sales

Advertiser must have in his possession, and have good title to, any merchandise offered for sale on any layaway plan.

### Advance Orders

Advertisements for offerings of stamps or philatelic material which are not physically delivered into the hands of dealers at time of placing the advertisements will not be accepted. EXCEPTION: Advertisements will be accepted from Governments or their officially appointed agents or distributors for future issues. Dealers may offer officially announced new issues and new issue services.

## Stamp Descriptions

Stamps offered for sale shall be accurately described. Damaged or repaired stamps should be properly noted in advertisements. Verification by Linn's Customer Checking Service of an advertiser shipping damaged or repaired stamps in response to orders for better grade material will be sufficient cause for declining or suspension of further advertisements.

## Sold Out

In the event an item is sold out, remittance will be returned within 48 hours. The advertiser will not hold the remittance pending arrival of a new supply without obtaining permission of the buyer.

## Authenticity

The submission of an advertisement for publication is considered a warranty by the seller that all items offered are genuine. Any buyer of a fake or spurious item shall be entitled to full refund. Any purchaser who doubts the authenticity of an item may request an opinion from mutually acceptable authority.

It is the responsibility of the purchaser to (A) advise the seller of action undertaken within 25 days of purchase and (B) submit the item to a mutually acceptable authority promptly. Expenses incurred shall be borne by the purchaser except where the lot is other than described, when the dealer shall accept responsibility of the actual cost of the opinion up to $10 or 5 per cent of the sale price (if the cost of the opinion is in excess of $10) with a maximum of $50.

Proof of the inability of a mutually acceptable authority to express a definite opinion is not grounds for the return of an item.

## Complaints

All advertisers will be notified of complaints received in writing from the readers and prompt adjustment by the advertiser, if warranted, and notification to the publisher will be expected as a condition of continued acceptance of advertising. Failure of an advertiser to adjust the cause of a complaint, or satisfactorily explain the same, will be considered sufficient reason for declining or suspending further advertising.

## Copy Regulations

All advertisements submitted are subject to copy regulations contained in the rate card. By submitting advertising, advertiser acknowledges that he is familiar with the advertising contract and copy regulations then in effect. Additional copies will be furnished upon request.

## Customer Checking Service

This checking service has been established to secure verification of certain types of customer complaints received. Collectors living in various parts of the United States, upon instruction from the publishers, place orders for merchandise advertised. The parcels are forwarded, unopened, to the publishers for examination of the contents.

## Reserved Right to Reject Advertising

All advertising is submitted subject to publishers' approval. The publishers reserve the right to reject, or decline, advertising, or suspend advertising privileges for such periods of time as in their discretion they see fit, for any reason whatsoever, irrespective of the validity of reasons for rejection or declination of advertising, or suspension of advertising privileges.

## Liability for Contents of Ads

Advertiser assumes liability for all contents (including text representation and illustrations) of advertisement printed and also assumes responsibility for any claims arising therefrom made against the publishers.

## Verification, Inspection

Acceptance of advertising for any item or service is subject to investigation and verification of the product or service, and of the claims made for it in the advertisement submitted for publication. All such investigations and verifications shall be to the publishers' satisfaction.

## Financial Statement

The publishers reserve the right to require a current financial statement from any advertiser at any time.

## Use of Post Office Box

California law requires complete legal company name and full street address from which the business is actually being conducted. A post office box or phone number is not considered sufficient.

Linn's urges that complete information be included in all ads to promote uniformity and fairness between advertiser and reader.

# Customer Service Department

A carefully organized Customer Service department handles and answers each and every customer complaint received. Operation of this department is costly. However, its effectiveness is very important to you, the reader, and to the bona fide stamp dealer.

Your assurance of good service from a Linn's advertiser (or prompt intervention by our complaint department) will keep you a continued Linn's reader and an active supporter of our advertisers.

If you have a problem with an advertiser we will be happy to assist you in resolving the matter.

May we suggest you follow these basic steps in placing orders and in tracing them:

### Ordering

Be specific in listing what you are ordering, including all pertinent information, such as lot or order number if used, catalog number, price, and from which issue or publication you are ordering. Be sure to list any descriptive information which might identify the stamp such as grade, condition, etc. The dealer may have two similar stamps with different prices. Type or neatly print your order. Be sure that your address is included inside the package. Always keep a carbon, making notes of mailing dates etc., for your own records.

### Order Arrivals

A wait of two weeks prior to inquiry is in order. If you have included a personal check the dealer may negotiate your check and wait for it to clear before shipping. This could require an additional ten days.

If you have not received your order during this time or a post card from the dealer advising of a shipping date, write to the dealer giving full information included in original order, asking for his shipping date. If you are unable to secure a satisfactory response and your merchandise still has not arrived, please forward a letter to Linn's Stamp News, Attention Customer Service Department. List full details, or better yet, send copies of your correspondence if they can be readily obtained.

Be patient in ordering by mail and don't be too quick to blame the dealer for slow delivery. Uncle Sam's mail service is usually fast and efficient, but it is not unusual to experience delays ranging from days to weeks, depending on the area and type of mailing.

### Return Privileges

All Linn's advertisers must offer a five day return privilege. If you are unhappy with the merchandise received, and feel that it is not as advertised, just return it for a full refund (less postage), or for a replacement.

When receiving stamps, open the package immediately upon receipt. Carefully inspect each stamp, comparing the copy received with the carbon of your original order. If it is necessary to return them, carefully package them and return insured or registered.

There may be special instances where the usual five day return privilege is not in force. Some advertisers offer 7, 10 or up to 30 days for returns. When these variations occur they will be listed in the advertisement. In a few instances there may be no return privilege. However, it must be so stated in the ad. An example might be a listing of several poor grade stamps as a lot. The advertiser may indicate these are purchased "as is" and cannot be returned.

### Stamps Lost or Stolen in Shipment

If after following the steps outlined above you determine that your order has been lost or stolen in shipment, ask the dealer to place a "tracer" on the package. Again, patience is in order, as postal regulations require a 30 day waiting period before a tracer can be placed. The post office will contact you to verify that the package did not arrive and will ask you to sign a form indicating it has not. This form will be returned to the dealer for him or her to file an insurance claim.

The dealer is unable to take any steps until this form has been returned. Once this form has been returned he or she is obligated to refund your money or replace the shipment and wait to receive the insurance claim.

### Fake, Altered and Spurious Stamps

What should you do if you think the stamp or philatelic item you purchase through the mail is altered or an outright fabrication: There is nothing more embarrassing than to falsely accuse a dealer or another collector and then find we have been mistaken. It is always best to seek a second authoritative opinion before taking any further action.

After being reasonably sure that your suspicions are well founded, it is advisable to send the material in question to a recognized expert committee, having first advised the seller of your action and secured his agreement to the authority chosen to rule on the item's authenticity. This should be done within 25 days of purchase.

The major expertizing committees are:

American Philatelic Society Expertization Committee, Box 8000, State College, Pa. 16801 (worldwide).

Society of Philatelic Americans Expertization Committee, c/o Gordon Torrey, 5118 Duvall Drive, Washington, D.C. 20016 (worldwide).

The Philatelic Foundation, 270 Madison Ave., New York, N.Y. 10016 (primarily U.S. material).

Friedl Expert Committee, 10 E. 40th St., New York, N.Y. 10016 (worldwide).

Vincent Graves Greene Philatelic Research Foundation, Box 100, First Canadian Place, Toronto, Ont., Canada M5X 1B2 (Canada before 1950).

Royal Philatelic Society, 41 Devonshire Place, London W1, England (Worldwide).

B.P.A. Expertising, Ltd., Box 33, Bognor Regis, W. Sussex PO22 7SR, England (British area).

David Brandon Expert Committee, 77 Strand, London WC2R 0DE England.

National Philatelic Society, 27 King Street, London WC2E 8JD England (Worldwide).

American First Day Cover Society, c/o Edward Siskin, Box 527, Millburn, N.J. 07041.

Croatian Philatelic Society, c/o Dr. H. Rommerskirchen, 415 Krefeld, Nernstrasse 23-25, West Germany (Croatian area).

Germany Philatelic Society, c/o Dr. Werner M. Bohne, Box 328, Syracuse, N.Y. 13201 (German area).

Korea Stamp Society, c/o Harold L. Klein, Box 866, Lebanon, Pa. 17042 (Korea).

Some groups guarantee their certificates; some will indelibly mark any items found to be fraudulent. It is important that the owner carefully read all of the regulations before submitting items for expertization.

Should the expertizer determine that the item is not as advertised, it should be returned, with the certificate, to the seller, who is required to refund the cost of the stamp and the expertization fee, within the guidelines of Linn's Basic Advertising Policy. If the item is shown to be as described, the expertization fee must be paid by the buyer.

Suspected stamps or philatelic material should not be sent to Linn's. The expertization of stamps requires equipment and detailed philatelic knowledge that are best found in the established expertizing committees.

### Responding to Buy Ads

This can be a satisfying experience for both collector and dealer or it can be a difficult transaction when a few basic steps are not followed.

Package stamps securely, since they may receive some rough treatment in the mails. Be sure to insure or register the package for its full value. Remember, you may be paid this amount should the package be lost. Should the dealer's prices be unacceptable to you it is his or her obligation to return to you insured or registered for this same amount.

When preparing your package be sure to include a shipping invoice listing all items sent including catalog numbers, grades, any special features, etc. If you are shipping for an offer, your invoice should include this statement. If you are shipping in response to a specific buy ad be sure to mention which ad, issue date, etc. Dealers may have several buy ads running in different publications. Since deadlines vary from the weekly to monthly publications prices in the ads may differ somewhat.

It is always wise to reexamine your material before sending. In most instances overgraded or misdescribed stamps will be returned to you at your expense.

Read all instructions very carefully. Quantities or conditions may be limited. Remember, dealers are reaching over 90,000 readers. They are not necessarily obligated to buy everything sent to them.

However, they are obligated to return the unneeded items to you, at their expense, unless the ad stated, "write first," if you have followed instructions on grades and quantities.

Many dealers will make commitments by telephone. Such a commitment is binding on both parties under Linn's policy and could be a wise approach in selling your stamps.

# Ordering Stamps

Ordering stamps from dealers is a simple matter. We assume the dealer has advertised or issued a price list. The buyer picks out the stamp or stamps he wants, and then reads the instructions at the beginning of the price list or the end of the advertisement.

If there is a minimum order the dealer will accept, the buyer must reach it or not buy from

that dealer. If the dealer requires an added amount for postage, insurance and handling or whatever, the order must include it.

The instructions may say that a Postal Money Order is required, or a Bank Certified Check, or that a delay will be made to allow a personal check to clear the banks. The buyer will take note of all this, and do as instructed and be prepared to wait for his order, from two to three or four weeks, depending on distance from the dealer and how payment is made.

Half that time will be credited to the check clearing, and the other half to the time it takes for the mail to get the shipment through. This can be up to three weeks or so from coast to coast, after the check clears if that is the method of payment.

Wait at least three weeks before sending a query to the dealer, but it is justified after that time. However, it should be a tactful one and include a return envelope or government post card for reply. There is no reason why a buyer can't write and ask for the date of mailing, so he can check with his local post office. No dealer would get mad at that.

Buying by mail is a two-way proposition, of course. The dealer should hold up his end. Linn's Basic Advertising provides a detailed guide to what standards we believe should be maintained by our advertisers. Failure to adhere to these standards is grounds for the withdrawal of advertising privileges in Linn's.

Finally, to the buyer, do not forget to include your name and full address including ZIP Code when sending the order, both inside and outside the envelope, preferably printed or typed. More disputes have been caused by the buyer's failure to include a legible or any return address than all other causes put together. And, strange as it may seem, some buyers have been known to forget to sign their checks!

Just a few more tips to ensure that transactions go smoothly. If the seller says returns will be allowed for three, five or seven days or any other period, for unsatisfactory merchandise, he means it. If the buyer needs more time to get a stamp authenticated elsewhere, he should ask for it. He would also be wise to ask for a written guarantee of authenticity with the stamp, if it's worth more than a few dollars.

If an advertisement contains the phrase "prices subject to change without notice," in a period of fast rising markets, the buyer should be prepared to get his check returned. If the stamp is one-of-a-kind, he should also be prepared for a "sold-out" answer to his order.

Finally, in some cases it is wise for the buyer to phone the dealer for a confirmation of an order at a given price. The buyer should get the name of the person confirming the order at that price, and how many days he will be allowed to get the payment in.

Most transactions are simple, and most dealers and buyers are well-meaning and honest. There are a few exceptions on both sides. If either buyer or dealer should get "taken" once, they will be suspicious from then on.

# Mailing Stamps

The Postal Service is usually blamed for lost stamps. Most of the time the blame should be placed on the sender.

Mail, on its long and often arduous journey from sender to addressee, is subjected to much handling by many people.

The current mail volume amounts to billions of pieces per year, with many thousand pieces processed each second. With that kind of volume the individual postal employee cannot give attention to each separate piece of mail.

The sender should provide as much protection as possible for his letters and packages. Enclose the stamps on a manila stockcard within a glassine envelope. This may be placed between two pieces of thin cardboard for added protection.

Include a letter identifying the stamp(s) and stating the reason they are being sent. The person who is to examine the stamps should not have to waste time trying to figure out why.

Your letter of transmittal should also include instructions for the return of the stamps and sufficient return postage to provide whatever level of protection you wish.

Registered mail provides signature protection for the contents. That means that anyone handling the package en route must sign for it. Registered mail also provides for a declared value up to the amount specified by the sender (maximum postal liability up to $25,000) upon payment of the proper fee. Registered mail is strictly a first-class service.

A note of caution: USPS liability for loss on registered parcels addressed to foreign countries is limited to $25.20, except Canada, for which the maximum liability is $200.

Insured mail goes via third or fourth-class. It too provides indemnity for declared value but only up to $400. Contrary to popular belief, insuring a package does not guarantee delivery. It guarantees only that the sender will be reimbursed for loss in transit. Further, the sender is not guaranteed to recover the amount declared.

Priority mail may be used for heavier pieces which are charged at the first-class rate, but may be insured at third-class insurance rates, rather than the much higher first-class registration rates.

The Postal Service will often attempt to establish a value for the lost stamps based on findings of a disinterested authority. This is one of the ways by which the Postal Service attempts to protect itself against fraud.

If the stamp has no intrinsic value, it can be sent via certified mail. A receipt is issued to the sender and, for an additional fee, a return receipt can be obtained showing when, where and to whom the mail was delivered.

Both registered and certified mail are traceable from initial mailing to ultimate delivery.

Whatever means of mailing is selected, be certain that the package is securely sealed. An authenticator's nightmare begins with the receipt of a package that is empty because the sender neglected to seal it properly.

Unless special arrangements have been made, limit the number of stamps sent at any one time to three or four. The person to whom you are sending them will also be receiving stamps from many others. He would be forced to ignore your large number of stamps in order to satisfy a greater number of people who have complied with this basic tenet of courtesy. His only alternative to ignoring your stamps would be to ignore all his other correspondents. So, no matter which avenue he chooses, he is automatically guilty of slighting someone.

# Auctions
## Bidding

First rule for bidding in auctions, whether by mail or in person on the floor, is to bid only as high as you know you can pay, unless credit is arranged beforehand, and that is seldom.

Second is to avoid the "shotgun" method, which is bidding on more lots than you actually want, in the hope of getting some of them. This is less likely to happen at floor auctions, although it can, and you may lose out on lots you really want if you have already bought some earlier second choices, simply because your money is all gone.

But it is a danger for inexperienced bidders in mail bid sales. Probably one out of every two old-timers in philately learned his lesson the hard way. He bid on 30 lots in hopes of being high on 10, and found he was successful on 20. This can be embarrassing, at the least. Avoid it.

Knowing what you can afford to spend, then, becomes a grim economic fact of life, and you simply have to expect to become "lucky" enough to be wiped out by your acquisitions.

On the other hand, you must recognize the mail auction in particular as the "patient" route in collecting. You may not win your stamp in the first auction; but continued diligence will eventually deliver it into your collection.

When bidding in mail bid sales, READ THE DIRECTIONS, especially the fine print. Check your bids after you have written them down, to make sure you have the right lot and the bid you want to make. Auctioneers are responsible only for their own mistakes, not yours. Then keep a copy for yourself, for protection if nothing else. Also, you may not remember what you bid and think you have been "hijacked" when you get the results.

Take "estimated values" with a grain of salt, how much salt depending on who wrote the auction catalog. Consider whether stamps are in a rising, falling, or stable market, and how much demand there is for the items you are bidding on. Check the major catalogs and Linn's Trends. You will get a good percentage of high bids on 80 per cent of either or 75 per cent of the printed estimate.

If you want something badly, bid high, especially if the auctioneer will reduce the high bid to a percentage over the second high. You are fairly safe in that case, unless another bidder is doing the same!

Keep in mind that, with a very few exceptions, if you don't get the stamp at your bid, it will come along again in another auction. If you stick to the percentage suggested, sooner or later you will be successful, except in a steadily rising market. In that case, no advice works anyhow.

Mail bid sales and public auctions differ; however, a bidder may submit a bid by mail at either one.

There is an advantage of being present at an auction sale — you can top any other bid. When bidding by mail you speak once and that is it.

Frequently, an auction is conducted by both means: it is held in a hall or room with bidders present, and a list or catalog of items to be sold has previously been sent by mail to any number of persons the seller believes may be interested in bidding.

In the latter case, the mail bidder has one advantage in most auctions. The floor bidder has to top the mail bidder. In other words, in effect, the high mail bid is the starting bid for the auction room. If the amount of that bid is not announced, and the high floor bid is the same amount, the mail bidder gets the lot. Second high mail bid is usually used to start.

Sometimes, the high or second high mail bid is not announced, and the auctioneer starts the bidding just as though there were no mail bid. In that case, the bidding goes up as high as the auctioneer can get it raised, and then it is compared with the top mail bid. If the floor bid is the same or lower, the mail bid gets the lot.

Auctions are sometimes put on by one dealer with his own stock up for sale. Sometimes they are put on by auctioneers who solicit consignments from dealers and collectors, and who have nothing of their own in it. Sometimes the two situations are combined, and a dealer holds an auction with both his and other peoples' stamps.

Most club auctions are of this nature.

In either case, there may be what are called "reserve" or "hold" bids. These are amounts stated by the owner, called "consignor," of the lots as being the lowest bids he will accept for them. Some auctioneers print these amounts, some announce them for floor bidding, and some do not make them known at all.

Whatever is done, if a mail or floor bid does not reach the reserve or hold amounts, sometimes listed as "minimum acceptable bids," then the lot is not sold, and is returned to or retained by the owner.

In some mail auctions, the person responsible will accept what are known as "unlimited" bids, meaning the bidder wants a given lot, no matter what he has to pay for it, and the lot will go to him at a percentage, sometimes 5 per cent, sometimes 10 per cent, over the highest exact figure bid. He may or may not put a maximum amount on his unlisted bid. Some auctioneers consider this unfair to other bidders, and do not allow unlimited bids.

On the other hand, some auctioneers will sell a lot to the high bidder at a price below the bid, if there is a good margin between his bid and the next highest. For example, if a high bidder offers $12 for a given lot, and the next highest is only $8, the high bidder might get it for $9.

There are variations of this type of thing, sometimes the amount saved being transferred to another bid to make it high when otherwise it would not have been. The successful bidder gets more lots for the same amount of money.

Another variation allowed by some auctions is for a bidder to state the total amount he is willing to spend, but bidding more. If his bids are high for more than that amount, the auctioneer will then send him lots costing up to the amount he wants to spend, giving the others to the next highest bid.

Most auctions that furnish a printed or mimeographed list of lots offered for sale, also include the estimated value of each lot. This value is assigned by the person responsible for the auction on the basis of one catalog or another, such as the Scott's Standard Postage Stamp Catalogue or on the basis of prices advertised in philatelic papers and magazines which may be more or less than catalog values.

As a practical matter, in most auctions these values are estimated as high as the auctioneer can find justification for. He will use advertised prices or catalog prices according to which is the higher. In the case of a rare stamp which is in demand, he may even use for an estimated value the price he would like to get for it, regardless of what the catalogs or advertisements say.

These estimated values, however, are never "minimum bids," and are purely guides for the bidder. The stamp may sell for more, or it may sell for less and does so, more often than not. Bidders are told to bid what the given lot is worth to them or what they can afford to pay for it, regardless of what value is assigned to it.

On the other hand, most auctions also have the statement that "unreasonable bids will be refused." A bid that is too low, in the judgment of the seller, will not be accepted, so the estimated value should be taken into consideration to some extent, anyway.

A bid of 50 per cent under estimated value is probably the lowest that would be acceptable, but equally probably would not get many lots, either because of "reserve" prices being higher or because of other bidders. Bids of 30 per cent below estimated value are more likely to be successful, if there are not many bidders for a given lot.

In the case of duplicate mail bids for an item, which is quite likely to happen, the earliest bid gets the lot as denoted by the postmark on the envelope or by the date the bid arrives at "headquarters." The first is fairer, but the second is more likely to be used. That is one reason why auction instructions state to mail bids in early.

It is not customary to send payment with bids, since that would entail returning checks and money orders for unsuccessful bids, and neither bidder nor seller knows in advance how much the buyer will owe. When an auction advertiser asks for cash in advance of the auction date, he lays himself open to suspicion.

However, many auctions, particularly the larger mail and floor auctions where rarities are offered, will usually ask for either a deposit equal to 25 per cent of the total bids by a given bidder, or for suitable references, preferably a bank although a well known dealer or philatelist might be satisfactory. Neither is required if the bidder is personally known to the person conducting the auction but in the larger auctions this rarely happens.

Reasons for this practice, of deposits or reference, is to avoid having to cope with irresponsible bidders who may bid wildly and then not accept nor pay for lots they may have been successful on. That causes unnecessary delay and trouble for the auctioneer and his backers, not to mention the second high bidder who may have committed his money elsewhere since the auction.

Payment is usually required before lots will be mailed to the successful bidder, just as orders from any dealer call for cash in advance.

Auctions, as one professional auctioneer has phrased it, "are not approval sales." On the other hand since mail bidders have to rely on written descriptions, and mistakes in grading or in identification can be made, a period of from three to five days is usually allowed in which a high bidder may return one or more of his lots if they are not satisfactory. He usually has to obtain permission to do this, however. Reputable firms will grant the permission for any good reason, but not for a "whim."

Persons who buy on bids from the floor at auctions usually do not have the return privilege, since they are given opportunity to inspect the lots before bidding and it is their own fault if they do not do so. The mail bidder does not have this opportunity. Reputable auctions carry guarantees that their lots are as described.

No auctions guarantee against mistakes in bidding that might be made by the bidder. So they urge the bidder to check his bids before mailing them, that he has the correct lot number, that he has put down the right price he wants to pay, and so on. It is not necessary to put down more than the lot number, but it helps to prevent mistakes if the bidder also writes down the catalog number or some other feature of the stamp or lot, as well.

Most major auction houses in the U.S. have adopted a split commission, that is both buyer and seller pay a percentage (usually 10 per cent). The commission charged the seller is often negotiable, but that charged the buyer is fixed by law. Once the system is established, individual buyers commissions cannot legally be waived by the auctioneer.

As stated at the beginning of this section, in the United States we have three types of auctions: floor auctions, which may be public or private; mail auctions; and a combination of both.

Small club auctions which are confined to members in attendance, with or without sending auction lists to members absent who may bid by mail, are private auctions and usually are conducted informally and as the auctioneer, a club member, wants to conduct them, or as the members want it done.

Public auctions, with or without mailed catalogs, are subject to the laws of each state, and auctioneers must be licensed. In some states, the auction itself must be licensed or have some sort of "permit." That is why some state conventions confine their auctions to "members only," to make them private and hence not subject to

state laws, which, of course, may or may not be enforced.

The "big" public auctions, with a national mailing list, are formal affairs and carried out with strict legality, and with strict attention to the "usual rules" of auction bidding and auction sales.

This is the type of auction where the top bidder may expect to get a stamp at less than his bid if the second high bid allows enough margin. Smaller auctions have been known to practice this, but not too frequently, and private dealers almost never, in their "mail bid" sales by advertisement, unless they say so.

At most floor auctions larger than club affairs, each potential bidder is given a piece of cardboard with a number on it. When he bids, he can either do it vocally, or raise the cardboard.

The successful bidder's number is written down on the auction chart instead of his name. This saves time, both in identifying people and in writing on the chart. After the auction, the amounts owed are added up by the number of the bidder and he identifies himself with that number.

Some bidders, especially in large auctions, do not want their identities known, and the number system helps to preserve their anonymity.

There is normally no limitation on the bidding of a consignor on his own lots. The consignor who wishes to insure a reasonable price on his lot, and who failed to specify a reserve prior to the sale, or who decides at the last minute to withdraw his material, may thus "buy back" his lots. Under these circumstances, however, the consignor must pay the buyer's fee and can expect, in most cases, to be charged the seller's commission, as well.

## Definitions

**Advance:** Difference between one bid and the next higher, usually not less than 5 per cent accepted.

**Auction:** Process of selling to the person offering the highest price.

**Auction catalog:** Listing of material to be sold; it may be printed or mimeographed separately or appear in a publication.

**Auction rules:** The rules under which the auction is to be conducted, determined by the dealer within the state laws where the auction is held.

**Bid:** The offer to buy at a price stated by the bidder.

**Bidder:** The person who makes the offer, in person or by mail.

**Buy bid:** An offer to buy at an unstated price but at a high enough price to top any stated price offered by another bidder.

**Buyer's Fee:** A fixed percentage buyer's fee, usually 10 per cent of the bid price. Such fees make it possible to lower the commissions charged consignors and so encourage owners to sell their material through auction. Such a split commission has been standard in European auctions for some time, and the system has been adopted by most major U.S. auctioneers during the past few years.

**Commission:** The percentage of the sale price of a lot or consignment paid to the auctioneer for selling it. Generally it is deducted from the total amount realized, the remainder going to the consignor.

**Consignment:** Material submitted to an auctioneer to be sold.

**Consignor:** One who submits the material to the auctioneer to be sold by him.

**Cry an auction:** What the auctioneer does in the process of selling.

**Deposit:** Advance payment, usually 25 per cent, of the total amount of mail bids to ensure the serious intent of the bidder to pay for his successful bids.

**Estimated price or value:** What the auctioneer thinks a given lot is worth, usually based on a catalog value, current retail prices, recent realizations in other auctions, etc. Estimated prices may also be determined by advertised prices or previous auction sales. They are usually printed in the auction catalog opposite the lot. The item may sell for more or less than the estimate which is just a guide to the bidder.

**Execute bids:** Accepting a bid, rating it for whether it is high or not, and arranging for the shipment of successfully bought lots.

**Floor bidder:** A person who attends an auction to bid for himself, or in the case of a dealer, for himself or his client.

**High bid:** The bid that tops all other offers and gets the lot.

**Hold:** A minimum acceptable bid, set by the consignor; the least amount he will accept for the lot.

**Lot:** A given stamp to be sold, or group of stamps, or other philatelic material, to be sold as a unit, which may not be broken up.

**Mail bidder:** A person who submits his highest offer for each lot in advance of the auction sale.

**Minimum bid:** The lowest bid the auctioneer will accept because of the restriction placed by the consignor.

**Nuisance bid:** A bid so low that no reasonable person would accept it; sometimes below the face value of a stamp.

**Prices realized:** A list of the amounts actually paid for the lots on the high bids, after the auction is completed.

**Private auction:** An auction conducted by a club or organization at which members only may bid. It is not subject to state laws applying to public auctions.

**Public auction:** Auction conducted by a licensed auctioneer at which anyone acceptable to the management may bid, subject to state laws regarding auctions. Mail bids may or may not be made, depending upon the prior announcement.

**Reserve:** Same as minimum bid, a lot with a "hold."

**Return privilege:** The right of a successful mail bidder to send a lot back if it is unsatisfactory. Permission must usually be requested, and the time is usually limited to a few days, generally specified.

**Sold to book:** Term used in a combined floor and mail bid auction, meaning that a lot goes to the mail bidder as no floor bidder has topped that offer.

**Sold to order:** Same as sold to book.

**Successful bid:** Same as high bid.

**Terms of sale:** Same as auction rules.

**Unlimited bid:** Same as a buy bid.

**Unreasonable bid:** Same as nuisance bid.

**Unreserved sale:** Same as unrestricted sale.

**Usual rules:** The generally accepted rules for conducting auctions.

**Unrestricted sale:** An auction at which there are no reserve or minimum bids accepted by the seller or auctioneer.

**Work sheet:** The forms used by the auctioneer's clerk to record bids that are successful. In a combined floor and mail bid auction, the work sheets will usually have the high mail bids already entered before they are brought to the floor auction.

## Usual Auction Rules

The following rules are generally the "usual auction rules" referred to by stamp dealers. They are the same as "terms of sale;" however each dealer may vary from these rules for his sales. It is always best to read these for each sale — they are printed in the catalog or advertisement.

1. Unless stated otherwise Mail Bid Sales will close 10 days from publication date.

2. Bid by lot number. No lots broken up. Bid for entire lot.

3. Bids recorded in order received. In case of tie, first bidder gets lot.

4. No "buy" or "unlimited" bids accepted.

5. Shipping, postage, or insurance cost to be paid by bidder.

6. Credit must be established in advance to seller's satisfaction. A 25 per cent deposit sent with bids. Deposits returned within one week after closing date if bids unsuccessful. Deposit is guarantee that high bidder will

honor his bid and is not returnable if bidder fails to do so unless excused by seller; it is otherwise used as partial payment on successful bids. Any deposit is at option of seller.

7. High bidders to be notified (notification must be postmarked no later than 10 days after closing date), payment to be made on notification. (Notification of a successful bid makes a legally binding contract and payment is legally enforceable.) Seller may reject high bid below 50 per cent off catalog value of a lot.

8. All stamps guaranteed genuine and as described. Buyer assumes responsibility for his errors in bidding.

9. No bids accepted from persons under 18 unless signed by parent guaranteeing payment for successful bids.

10. Unsatisfactory lot must be postmarked for return within five days after receipt, but such lots must be returned as a whole, with no part retained.

11. Illustrated lots are not returnable for reasons of centering or other factors apparent in the photograph.

12. Lots containing 10 or more stamps are not returnable.

13. Any exceptions to rules will be so stated in offering advertisement.

"Don't Bid If You Won't Buy"

## Consignments

How to consign stamps to an auction depends on the situation. If it is a local club auction, usually confined to members only, the consignor merely ascertains the club rules and follows them. Either he has to bring or send them in ahead of time, or he brings them to the meeting at which the auction takes place.

If it is desired to consign stamps to a national auction or mail bid sale, the consignor writes first to find out if the auctioneer will accept what he has. That applies whether or not the auctioneer has advertised for consignments. He would be wise to include a return stamped envelope.

Usually the bigger the auction, the better the stamps have to be, either in quality or rarity. Run of the mill stamps will probably never be accepted in a major sale, except as part of a large wholesale or remainder lot. The place to sell that kind is at a local club auction or by advertisement, i.e., the collector should conduct his own mail bid sale, if he doesn't want to sell at fixed prices.

When a consignment has been accepted, the consignor should include in the package a statement of what is in it, or invoice, with reserve if any, and keep a copy himself. He may or may not, as he wishes, send a copy separately to the auctioneer. He would be wise to buy a "return receipt requested" slip for the package, if only for his own peace of mind, as the auctioneer may be too busy to acknowledge right away. For instructions on how to mail the stamps, see that section in this chapter.

Consignments must be sent in some time ahead of the auction date, to allow for processing, that is, describing, listing by lot number, and publishing if an auction catalog is printed.

The larger and more important the auction, the longer time is needed since there are many hundreds of lots and the descriptions are compiled by those responsible for the auction; a catalog is printed, and it must be widely mailed in plenty of time for prospective bidders to study it and mail in their bids.

Small club auctions usually accept the consignor's descriptions, and the bidder takes his chances, but generally can inspect the lots before bidding. This is not possible, with rare exceptions, in mail auction sales.

The exceptions are in the largest auctions where the greatest rarities are offered. In these cases, a prospective bidder whose references are closely checked may sometimes ask to have a stamp sent to him for inspection. That requires that consignments be in even sooner than normal, and the auction lists or catalog be mailed out earlier.

The type of mail auction where this can be done is usually prepared many months in advance, sometimes as long as a year ahead is needed for the preliminary work.

Once the consignor has sent in his material, he then has nothing to do but wait. Occasionally, he will be sent a preliminary or "proof" copy of the auction list, or the part with his consignment in it, so that he can check it for accuracy and satisfactory treatment. This requires more time.

The auctioneer may or may not accept any suggestions the consignor makes. It is the auctioneer's business to sell the lots, and he usually has the final say as to how it can best be done. The responsibility is his, and his judgment is final.

Sometimes a consignor can withdraw some or all of his material, but he should have a very good reason for so doing, and if the auction has already been advertised and his material publicized, he may lay himself open to a law suit, if the auction is a large one. In very few cases should a consignor expect any payment in advance for his lots.

Following the auction, another delay is probable, from 30 days on up, depending somewhat on the size of the auction and somewhat on other factors such as the time available on the part of the auctioneer, and so on. The shortest time lag would be for a purely floor-bid-auction, with no mail bidding.

Reason for this delay is primarily two-fold: first, time necessary to sort out mail bids and determine who is high bidder; second, the time necessary to notify the high bidders, obtain their payments, and then be assured of their satisfaction with the lots.

Consignors are usually not settled with until the money for the entire auction is in hand, and because of the factors just mentioned this may be a month or more, even when there is floor bidding also.

A period of 30 days to a year must be allowed between consignment and auction, depending on the type of auction, and a delay of at least 30 to 60 days between auction and payment to consignor.

This payment will be subject to the commission to be paid the club, auctioneer, or regional organization, or whoever has conducted the auction. The commission may be as low as 5 per cent or as much as 20 per cent, with no hard and fast rule about it. Whatever the percentage is, it will be announced in advance, so the consignor will know what to expect.

# How to Prevent Robberies

Stamp collectors, because of the nature of their hobby, are often marks for burglars. The frequency of robberies for philatelists, as for other collectors of valuable objects, is an unhappy fact of life. Are you protecting your investment the best you can?

**ARE YOUR:**

Doors left unlocked or open?

Doors capable of being opened with a skeleton key, a pen knife, a credit card, or a crow bar?

Windows open or unlocked?

Stamps and other philatelic items insured for their full value?

Outside lights on when you answer the door at night?

Valuables locked in a safe which two people could carry?

**DO YOU:**

Permit strangers to enter your home to use your phone and copy your phone number?

Attend stamp club meetings, shows, conventions, or auctions without necessary security?

Carry with you high priced items and show them around?

Always buy high priced items and let everyone know?

Have a method of operation, a regular schedule of coming and going from your house? Does your family?

Do your shopping on the same day every week, with the same stops, returning home at the same time?

Have the same schedule week in and week out? Could a stranger park his car in your neighborhood and watch your house without you noticing it?

Receive many phone calls where the caller asks for someone who doesn't live at your house?

Have your name on many lists of known stamp collectors?

Go out after stamp meetings, shows, or conventions, to have a drink or a hamburger, always at the same place with the same people?

Pass stamps around among this group and talk about your collection or someone else's collection so everyone can hear about it?

**IF YOU'RE A STAMP DEALER, DO YOU:**

Travel alone, leave your car while you stop and eat, leave your car unlocked?

Leave all your stamps in your car while you check into a motel?

Leave your stamps in your room while you eat or see the town?

Not bother to check into a security room before you check into your hotel room?

Know most hotels have safety deposit boxes for their guests' valuables, some of which will hold two large suitcases? Do you use them?

Have safety deposit boxes, one that you can get into on Saturday and another on Monday?

Have a burglar alarm on your house or store? Have its installers been checked out by the police? Does it have a direct line to the police?

Have a neighbor or relative keep an eye on your house or store while you are on vacation or at a stamp show?

Leave your bourse table unlocked and unattended at a show while you visit other dealers?

Travel with a luggage carrier on top of your car so you can be easily tailed?

Have a bank offering a room or office where you might safely work on your stamps without being disturbed or seen?

Have a bank with arrangements to make night deposits?

Park your car in the driveway after returning home from a show and carry your suitcases in, leaving your stamps in the car?

Travel with other dealers?

Always leave a show during the break time when there's confusion and a shortage of trucks? Who watches your valuables while you hunt a truck?

Have panic buttons at strategic locations in your store?

Have a large enough safe, preferably a walk-in with the walls, ceiling and floor also part of the safe?

Know someone could attach a homing device to your car and follow you for thousands of miles?

Know several cars could be following you, connected by walkie-talkies, interchanging positions so you don't become suspicious?

Think a burglar wouldn't know which stamps to steal? Many are experts in their fields and know which stamps command the highest prices on the market.

Know how long you could remain in business if your stock is stolen while you wait for the insurance company to settle up?

# Auctions

# 25

## Major Sales of the 20th Century

Several great philatelic collections have been brought to the auction block during the 20th century. These collections have contained such rarities as the Black Honduras, the two Mauritius 1-penny orange on cover, the Canada 1851 12p black, Hawaiian Missionaries, France tete-beche issues, United States Postmasters' Provisionals and inverted issues.

The material in these collections have been in the possession of famous philatelists such as Josiah K. Lilly, Col. Edward H.R. Green, Arthur Hind, Alfred F. Lichtenstein, Alfred Caspary, and Count Phillippe la Renotiere von Ferrari.

This listing includes what are believed to be the most prominent auctions to be conducted during the 20th century. The original auction lot numbers are listed. Scott catalog numbers have been provided, unless otherwise stated, for the convenience of the collector.

### Ameer of Bahawalpur

The Ameer of Bahawalpur's Collection was sold by Stanley Gibbons Auctions Ltd., Drury House, Russell Street, Drury Lane, London WC2, England, Dec. 12-13, 1968.

The most notable items in this Sale:

**Lot 60: Mint**

Basutoland official 1934 overprint ½ penny to 6p (S.G. O1-O4). Rare set, original gum. $2,880

**Lot 117: Mint**

Canada 1959 St. Lawrence Seaway 5 cents, center inverted (S.G. 513a) in unmounted mint block of four. $5,160

**Lot 126: Mint**

Ceylon 1912-25 500 rupees (S.G. 329), original gum. $2,400

**Lot 231: Mint**

Jamaica 1919-21 1/-, inverted frame (S.G. 85a), original gum. $4,080

**Lot 238: Mint**

Kenya and Uganda 1912-22 500 rupees (S.G. 63), unmounted mint. $4,200

**Lot 245: Mint**

Kenya and Uganda 1922-27 £20 (S.G. 101), large part original gum. $2,880

**Lot 246: Mint**

Kenya and Uganda 1922-27 £25 (S.G. 102), original gum. $2,880

**Lot 247: Mint**

Kenya and Uganda 1922-27 £50 (S.G. 103) corner control from top left sheet, original gum. $5,280

**Lot 252: Used**

Kenya and Uganda 1954-59 5 cents, "vignette inverted," (S.G. 167a). Lightly postmarked. Royal Philatelic Society certificate. $10,300

**Lot 271: Mint**

Malaya, Straits Settlements 1912-23 $500 (S.G. 215) with sheet margin at right. $4,200

**Lot 279: Mint**

Malta 1919-20 10/- (S.G. 96) original gum, marginal block of four from top of sheet. $2,520

**Lot 321: Mint**

Newfoundland 1919 "Hawker" 3¢ red-brown (S.G. 142), original gum. $5,280

**Lot 334: Mint**

Newfoundland 1927 airmail "De Pinedo" 60¢ black (S.G. 163), original gum. British Philatelic Association certificate. $10,560

**Lot 335: Cover**

Newfoundland 1927 airmail "De Pinedo" 60¢ black (S.G. 163) on large-sized O.H.M.S. cover to Rome with original enclosure. Stamp canceled by "St. John's May 20, 1927" wavyline postmark. Lightly tied with full transit markings, including Trepassy. This envelope was sent from the prime minister's office at St. John's to B.P. Sullivan M.B.E. at the British Consulate in Rome. $4,200

**Lot 458: Mint**

New Zealand 1931-39 35/- (S.G. 544s) corner block of four from bottom right of sheet, original gum. $2,208

**Lot 468: Mint**

New Zealand 1955 Health 3 penny+1p, center omitted (S.G. 744a). Last stamp in an imprint strip of seven from the bottom of the sheet with diagonal paper fold which caused the variety. Stamps are unmounted, mint. $1,968

**Lot 541: Mint**

Papua 1929-30 airmail Ash printing 3-penny (S.G. 120) complete sheet of 40 with diagonal fold which resulted in some of the overprints appearing on the reverse. This sheet gives four pairs showing "overprint omitted" in horizontal pair with normal (S.G. 120a); three vertical pairs showing the variety (S.G. 120b) and eight examples showing "overprint vertical" on back, either wholly or partially (S.G. 120c). $2,400

**Lot 609: Mint**

St. Helena 1961 Tristan Relief Fund 2½penny+3p to 10 cents on 1/- (S.G. 172-175) in marginal pairs, two of which have imprint, unmounted mint. $3,840

**Lot 629: Mint**

Samoa 1914 G.R.I. overprint 1/- on 1-mark (S.G. 111). Diena certificate states, "In my opinion, the stamps and the surcharge are genuine, and original gum in perfect condition." $2,640

**Lot 692: Mint**

Swaziland 1961 decimal surcharge 1 cent on ½ penny, surcharge inverted (S.G. 65a). Unmounted original gum, block of ten which comprises two rows of the sheet, each stamp showing the variety; full imprint and plate numbers. $2,160

**Lot 727: Used**

Togo, British occupation, 1914 10 pfennigs, overprint inverted (S.G. 3a). Marginal block of four canceled on piece with "LOME" circular datestamp showing the variety on each stamp. $2,880

# Robert W. Baughman

The Robert W. Baughman Collection of Imperial Russia and Zemstvo postage stamps and covers was sold during four auction sales March 24-27, 1971, by Robert A. Siegel Auctions, 10 E. 52nd St., New York, N.Y.

The most notable items in the Imperial Russia sale:

**Lot 1: Mint**

Tiflis Local 1857 6-kopeck embossed on white, with margins all around. Clear embossing, fresh original gum. Ex-Stibbe. $7,250

**Lot 25: Proof**

1857 10kop black on wove, frame only, trial color die proof (1P). First impression with imprint of engraver, F. Keppler. Ex-Faberge. $500

**Lot 27: Proof**

1857 10kop black on thin wove, frame only, trial color die proof (1P). Ex-Faberge. $500

**Lot 170: Mint**

1858 20kop blue and orange (3). Horizontal pair, with fresh, brilliant colors, almost centered. $1,100

**Lot 251: Cover**

1863 5kop black and blue (11). Tied by red St. Petersburg postmark on local 1864 cover. $800

**Lot 253: Cover**

1863 5kop black and blue (11). Tied by clear "PETERHOF" postmark on 1864 cover to St. Petersburg. Few mended tears. $575

**Lot 258: Cover**

1863 5kop black and blue (11). Vertical pair, tied by oval "MOSCOW TWO O'CLOCK" postmarks. Two strikes on 1864 cover to SUMY. $1,200

**Lot 297: Mint**

1866 1kop black and yellow, inverted background (19d). Original gum, light crease. $800

**Lot 300: On Piece**

1866 1kop black and yellow, inverted background (19d). Three copies tied on piece. $525

**Lot 319: Used**

1866 10kop brown and blue, inverted center (23b). Used, centered to bottom and lightly canceled. $1,150

**Lot 327: Mint**

1868 20kop blue and orange, vertically laid (24a). Original gum block, partly separated and rejoined. Upper left stamp has thin in top margin. $500

**Lot 330: Mint**

1866 30kop carmine and green (25). Complete sheet of 100, original gum. One stamp with a tiny gum soak. $675

**Lot 342: Used**

1872 2kop black and red, inverted background (26b). Used, centered a bit to right. Ex-Faberge. $1,850

**Lot 348: Used**

1879 7kop gray and rose, watermark hexagons (27c). Used, almost centered. Ex-Rothschild. Signed Friedl. $3,400

**Lot 349: Used**

1879 7kop gray and rose, watermark hexagons (27c). Clear "PERM 1880" postmark. Ex-Goss, Faberge. $2,700

**Lot 357: Mint**

1875 20kop blue and orange "Crossed T" variety (30a). Horizontal pair, original gum. $1,400

**Lot 384: On Piece**

1883 5kop red violet, inverted background (34a). Tied by red postmark on small piece. $1,200

**Lot 395: Cover**

1883 7kop on half of 14kop blue and rose, Kutais Provisional (38A). Tied by "KUTAIS, Aug. 30, 1884" postmark. Royal Philatelic Society Certificate. Ex-Charles Curie. $5,250

**Lot 404: Mint**

1884 3.50-ruble black and gray (39). Complete sheet of 25, original gum. $1,750

**Lot 414: Mint**

1884 7rub black and orange (40). Complete sheet of 25, original gum. Light marginal fold affects one stamp. $1,750

**Lot 522: Mint**

1902 7rub black and yellow, inverted center (70a). Block with right sheet margin, centered slightly to bottom. $3,600

**Lot 750: Cover**

Offices in China 1865-1921 covers and cancellations. Rare early cancels, towns, including Manchuria, consular mail, fumigated covers and Boxer Rebellion. $5,250

**Lot 753: Cover**

Mongolia covers of 1879-1928. Includes Russia, offices, combinations and stamps with Mongolian postmarks. $1,900

**Lot 778: Cover**

Offices in Turkey, 1879 7kop on 10kop carmine and green (19D). Tied by rimless Constantinople postmark on 1880 cover to Odessa. $750

# Arthur W. Bingham Jr.

The Arthur W. Bingham Jr. Collections were sold in two auctions by Robert A. Siegel Auctions, 10 E. 52nd St., New York, N.Y., Nov. 21-Dec. 7, 1967.

The most notable items in Part I:

**Lot 67: Used**

Canada 1868 ½-cent black, watermark (21b). $1,400

**Lot 148: Mint**

Canada 1897 Jubilee $2 dark purple (62) block. $1,350

**Lot 150: Mint**

Canada 1897 Jubilee $3 yellow-bister (63) block. $1,100

**Lot 152: Mint**

Canada 1897 Jubilee $4 purple (64) block. $850

**Lot 154: Mint**

Canada 1897 Jubilee $5 olive-green (65) block, original gum. $2,400

**Lot 173: Cover**

Canada 1899 Victoria 2¢ on two-thirds of 3¢ "Port Hood" Provisional (88C). Tied by "Port Hood Jan.5, 1899" postmark on local cover. $1,800

**Lot 245: Mint**

Canada 1942-43 1¢-$1 War Effort imperforate set (249-262 varieties). $675

**Lot 248: Mint**

Canada 1959 5¢ Seaway inverted center (387a). $1,450

**Lot 256: Mint**

Canada airpost 1935 6¢ red-brown imperf vertically (C5a). Pair within a block of nine, showing the foldover during perforation which made the variety. $1,800

**Lot 317: Used**

New Brunswick 1851 1/- dull violet (4). Margins all around, dot cancel. $1,050

**Lot 328: Mint**

Newfoundland 1861 1-penny reddish brown (16). Margins all around, part original gum. $1,300

**Lot 334: Mint**

Newfoundland 1870 3¢ vermilion (33) block, original gum. $1,150

**Lot 366: Used**

Nova Scotia 1851 1/- reddish violet (6). Large margins, light cancel. $1,150

**Lot 367: Used**

Nova Scotia 1851 1/- violet (7). Margins all around, light cancel. Ex-Ferrari. $1,200

**Lot 385: Used**

Switzerland 1850 2½-rappen black and red without frame (4). Large margins, neatly canceled. $1,300

The most notable items in Part II, United States:

**Lot 193: Cover**

Brattleboro, Vt., 5-cent black on buff (5X1). Tied by red "PAID" with matching Brattleboro postmark on folded letter to New York. $3,750

**Lot 221: Cover**

5¢ red-brown (1) tied by St. Johnsbury, Vt., scarab cancel on folded letter. $3,400

**Lot 462: Cover**

10¢ black (2) horizontal pair tied by red grids,

partial red "U.S. Express Mail Boston" postmark with matching "20" on folded cover to Philadelphia. $2,800

**Lot 465: Cover**

1851 1¢ blue type I (5) position 7R1E. Sheet margin at top, tied by "Windsor, Vt." postmark on local cover. $4,800

**Lot 1033: Mint**

$1 Trans-Mississippi (292) block, original gum. $4,000

**Lot 1035: Mint**

$2 Trans-Mississippi (293) block, original gum. $4,000

**Lot 1037: Mint**

1¢ Pan-American inverted center (249a). $2,000

**Lot 1041: Mint**

2¢ Pan-American inverted center (295a). $8,500

**Lot 1046: Mint**

4¢ Pan-American inverted center specimen overprint (296b). $1,900

**Lot 1064: Mint**

1902-03 $5 dark green (313) block. $1,550

**Lot 1105: Mint**

Bluish papers 4¢ orange-brown-bluish (360). Ex-Green. $4,000

**Lot 1108: Mint**

Bluish papers 8¢ olive-green-bluish (363). Ex-Green. $2,800

**Lot 1231: Mint**

1916 5¢ carmine error, imperf (485). Lower arrow block of 35 with two middle stamps being errors. $3,600

**Lot 1271: Used**

1¢ green (596) Kansas City, Mo., precancel. Probably no more than six copies known to exist. $4,200

# Alvaro Bonilla-Lara

The Alvaro Bonilla-Lara Collection of Costa Rica was sold in one auction by H.R. Harmer, Inc., New York, N.Y., May 1-2, 1961. The highly specialized collection of 14 volumes won first award at CIPEX 1947.

The most notable items in this sale:

**Lot 29: Cover**

1863 coat of arms ½-real blue, 2r scarlet (1, 2). Each tied to cover by grid with No. 1 cancel. $230

**Lot 40: Mint**

1881-82 surcharges. 1 centavo on ½r blue, plate I, pane of 100 (7), original gum, no selvage. $115

**Lot 41: Mint**

1881-82 surcharges. 1c on ½r blue, plate II,

pane of 99 (7). Top right stamp missing, no selvage. $115

**Lot 58: Mint**

1881-82 surcharges. 2c on ½r blue, plate II (9 variety). Block of four. Top left stamp with inverted overprint. Unused, reinforced. $300

**Lot 68: Mint**

1881-82 surcharges with additional overprint "U.P.U." 10c on 2r scarlet (14). Block of nine, unused. $210

**Lot 74: Mint**

1881-82 surcharges with additional overprint "U.P.U." 20c on 4r green (15). Block of four, original gum. Ex-Green. $480

**Lot 98: Proof**

1889 1c to 10 pesos (25-34P). Complete set in black. Thirty-four large die proofs in various stages of printing, some marginal faults. $450

**Lot 99: Proof**

1889 1c to 10p (25-34P). Complete set in black, small die proofs on bond (34 by 39mm). $210

**Lot 100: Proof**

1889 1c to 10p (25-34P). Complete set of small die proofs (26 by 32 millimeters) in original or trial colors. 20c canceled. $270

**Lot 123: Proof**

1892 1c to 10p (35-44P). Complete set in black, small die proofs on bond (34 by 39mm). $210

**Lot 130: Mint**

1892 1c to 10p variety imperf (35-44). Complete set in horizontal pairs, original gum. Ex-Hind. $290

**Lot 135: Proof**

1901-03 1 centimo to 10 colon (45-57P). Complete set in black, small die proofs on bond (34 by 40mm). $150

**Lot 149: Mint**

1901-03 2c vermilion and black, center inverted (46 variety), original gum. Ex-Hind. $550

**Lot 371: Proof**

1936 Map of Cocos Island 4c to 5col (169-76P). In full sheets of 100. Plate proofs on bond in original colors. $210

**Lot 502: Mint**

1941 Soccer Championship 15c to 5col complete set (C57-66). Blocks of four, original gum. 30c vertical crease. 50c, one stamp with tear. $180

**Lot 566: Proof**

1946 Hospital 5c to 5col (Sanabria PP162-74), 26 different bicolored plate proofs on heavy bond. $290

**Lot 685: Mint**

Official 1903 2c yellow-green and black, inverted center (O49 variety), original gum. $210

**Lot 690: Mint**

Official 1903 1col brown and black, inverted center (O55 variety), original gum. $210

**Lot 780: Mint**

Guanacaste 1885 type "b" red overprint (17½ to 18mm) 40c blue (13). Block of four, original gum, reinforced. $360

**Lot 793: Mint**

Guanacaste 1885 type "d" overprint (18½mm) 2c carmine, vertical overprint (20, 24, 28, 32, 36). Partly separated or reinforced plate of 50 of the five different types — d (7), c (13), f (1), g (5), h (15), original gum. $1,250

**Lot 796: Used**

Guanacaste 1885 type "d" overprint (18½mm) 5c blue-violet, partly reconstructed plate of 50 (21, 25, 29, 33, 37). With 24 stamps of the five different types — d (4), e (7), f (3), g (5), h (5), mixed centering. $170

**Lot 797: Mint**

Guanacaste 1885 type "d" overprint (18½mm) 10c orange (22, 26, 30, 34, 38). Partly reconstructed plate of 50, with 43 stamps including blocks of five different types — d (4), e (14), f (9), h (13), mostly original gum. $170

**Lot 808: Used**

Guanacaste 1885 type "g" overprint (19½mm) 5c blue-violet, double overprint (33 variety). $125

**Lot 818: Mint**

Guanacaste 1880-89 type "k" overprint (15½mm) 5c blue-violet (42, 43). Complete layout in bottom right sheet of 50 with types k (25), i (25), original gum. Some paper stuck to back. $125

**Lot 825: Mint**

Guanacaste 1889 overprint 2c blue (47) horizontal overprint type "b". Complete layout of the 50 overprints in two blocks of 25, original gum. $140

**Lot 831: Mint**

Guanacaste 1889 overprint 2c blue, vertical overprint (48, 49, 51, 52, 54). Complete layout of five different overprints in two blocks of 25, comprising types d (15), e (10), f (5), g (13), h (7), original gum. One stamp with rounded corners. $580

## Dr. John A. Buchness

The Dr. John A. Buchness Collection of Lithuania was sold during one auction session, May 19, 1971, by H.R. Harmer, Inc., 6 W. 48th St., New York, N.Y.

The most notable items in the sale:

**Lot 422: Cover**

Forerunners. Used from Poland. 1860 10-kopeck blue and rose, light shade (1). Centered to top left. Tied by four-ring numeral 282 cancel on folded letter to "RIGA." Bears single-circle bi-lingual "KIBARTY" (Lithuania) postmark, and arrival postmark on reverse. $135

**Lot 423: Cover**

Forerunners. 1860 10kop blue and rose (1). Tied on folded letter to "VILNIUS," dated Nov. 7, 1863, by four-ring numeral 282 cancel. Also bearing single-circle "KIBARTY" postmark. Arrival "VILNIUS" with reversed year numeral on back. $130

**Lot 425: Cover**

Forerunners. Used from Russia. 1857 10-kopeck brown and blue, early printing (1). Margins all around, negligible scratch on bottom left corner. Tied by oval dotted numeral "9" cancel on folded cover, dated Sept. 26, 1858, to "RIGA." Also with boxed "TAUROGEN" (Lithuania) and arrival postmarks. $200

**Lot 427: Mint**

Vilnius issue, first printing Dec. 17, 1918. Thin figures. 10-skatiku black (1). Complete sheet of 20, ungummed. $210

**Lot 428: Mint**

Similar lot. $160

**Lot 429: Mint**

Vilnius issue, first printing. Thin figures. 15sk black (2). Complete sheet of 20, ungummed. $160

**Lot 431: Mint**

Vilnius issue, second printing Dec. 31, 1918. Thick figures. 10sk black (3). Complete sheet of 20, ungummed. $270

**Lot 433: Mint**

Vilnius issue. Second printing with thick figures. 15sk black (4). Complete sheet of 20, ungummed. $170

**Lot 466: Mint**

The 1919 Kaunas issue. Error "5" in 15sk, in a complete sheet of 20, position 16 (second setting). Ungummed. $180

**Lot 486: Cover**

The 1919 Kaunas first issue of Jan. 26/Feb. 4 10sk to 30sk (first setting) (9-12). Complete set, tied on cover (folded) to "KOENIGSBERG" by early single-line "GARSDAI" cancel in purple. Manuscript "19.IV.19" marking and German censor marking. $62.50

**Lot 487: Mint**

The 1919 Kaunas issue. First issue, Jan. 26, Feb. 4, 1919. 10sk, 15sk, 30sk, imperf (9, 10, 12 imperf). Corner block of four, ungummed. $155

**Lot 508: Mint**

The 1919 Kaunas third issue of March 5. Complete set in sheets of 160. All possible combinations of se-tenants and a pane of the second Kaunas issue 60sk. $180

**Lot 573: Mint**

Airpost stamps. 1922 3-auksina violet and green (C16). Complete sheet of 108. Full selvages and control No. 12x9-108. Never hinged. Tall "VI" in "1921. VI. 1925" (Position 75). $100

**Lot 577: Mint**

Airpost stamps. 1924 20-centai yellow watermarked (C32a). Original gum. $230

**Lot 594: Cover**

Airpost stamps. 1926 Swallow issue. 1932 Zeppelin sixth South America flight. Three flown registered post cards, franked with 14 stamps and lightly tied, all with appropriate cachets, postmarks and arrival cancels. $270

**Lot 595: Cover**

Airpost stamps. 1926 Swallow issue. 1932 Zeppelin flights. Two flown registered covers, fourth South America flight from "KAUNAS" to "RIO DE JANEIRO," seventh South America flight from "PANEMUNO" to "CURITYBA-PARANA" (Brazil). Franked with 13 stamps and lightly canceled. $180.

**Lot 599: Mint**

Airpost semiofficial. 1933 New York-Kaunas "Darius" flight (Sanabria 85-89). Complete set in blocks of four, lightly hinged. $380

**Lot 600: Mint**

Airpost semiofficial. 1933 New York-Kaunas "Darius" flight. (Sanabria 85a-89a). Complete set in imperforate pairs, lightly hinged. $320

**Lot 603: Cover**

Airpost semiofficial. 1933 New York-Kaunas "Darius" flight (Sanabria 85-89). Complete set of five. Each stamp tied on flown registered cover, also bearing United States 1928 airpost 5-cent stamp. $525

## Caroline Prentice Cromwell

The Caroline Prentice Cromwell Collection of 20th-century British Commonwealth, Canada and Newfoundland was sold during two auctions by H.R. Harmer, Inc., 6 W. 48th St., New York, N.Y., Nov. 25-27, 1957, and Feb. 27, 1958.

The most notable items in Sale I:

**Lot 27: Mint**

Great Britain official 10/- ultramarine (O25) marginal copy, original gum. Philatelic Foundation certificate. $1,900

**Lot 28: Mint**

Great Britain official 1901 £1 green (O26) marginal copy, original gum. Signed W.H.P. with Philatelic Foundation certificate. $850

**Lot 38: Mint**

Great Britain Board of Education 1902-94 1/-carmine-rose and green (O71), original gum. Philatelic Foundation certificate. $1,800

**Lot 151: Mint**

British Central Africa 1907 "MCA" watermark 2-penny violet and dull violet (71), original gum. $800

**Lot 152: Mint**

British Central Africa 1907 "MCA" watermark 4p black and gray-green (72), original gum, marginal copy. $800

**Lot 231: Mint**

Ceylon 1912-25 1,000-rupee violet-red (218), original gum. $1,600

**Lot 282: Mint**

East Africa and Uganda 1912-18 500-rupee red and green (59) marginal copy, original gum. $2,700

**Lot 436: Mint**

Jamaica 1919-21 "MCA" watermark 1/- bright orange and orange, center inverted (83a), original gum. $1,350

**Lot 450: Mint**

Kenya and Uganda 1922-27 £75 purple and gray (S.G. 108), original gum. $1,700

**Lot 451: Mint**

Kenya and Uganda 1922-27 £100 red and black (S.G. 109), original gum. Centered to top left. $1,600

**Lot 532: Mint**

Natal 1902-03 "CA" watermark £20 green and carmine (100), original gum. $6,500

**Lot 805: Mint**

Straits Settlement 1908-11 $500 violet and orange (146), original gum. $4,500

**Lot 812: Mint**

Straits Settlement 1921-32 script watermark $500 orange and dull violet (204), original gum. $1,100

The most notable items in Sale II:

**Lot 244: Mint**

Newfoundland 1910 Guy lithographed 1-cent to 15¢ complete imperf (87-97 imperf). Complete set in original gum, blocks of four; 6¢ type II. $450

**Lot 342: Mint**

Newfoundland airpost April 1919 "Hawker" 3¢ red-brown (C1), full original gum. Initialed "J.A.R." on back. $1,900

**Lot 343: Mint**

Newfoundland airpost April 1919 "Hawker" 3¢ red-brown (C1), full original gum. Initialed "J.A.R." on back. $1,100

**Lot 344: Cover**

Newfoundland airpost April 1919 "Hawker" 3¢ red-brown (C1). Flown cover (side flap missing). The envelope is sealed on back with the usual "Found Open" label. One of three letters sent by the governor of Newfoundland of which another is in the Royal collection. $1,300

**Lot 365: Mint**

Newfoundland airpost May 1927 "de Pinedo" 60¢ black (C4), original gum. $3,300

**Lot 366: Mint**

Newfoundland airpost May 1927 "de Pinedo" 60¢ black (C4), full original gum. "CROM-WELL" block of four. The block is from top left corner of the sheet, positions 1, 2, 11, 12. $17,000

**Lot 370: Mint**

Newfoundland airpost September 1930 "Columbia" 50¢ on 36¢ olive-green (C5). Complete sheet of four, full original gum. $2,100

**Lot 398: Mint**

Newfoundland airpost May 1932 "DO-X" $1.50 on $1 blue (C12a), inverted surcharge, original gum. $900

**Lot 399: Mint**

Newfoundland airpost May 1932 "DO-X" $1.50 on $1 blue (C12a), inverted surcharge, mint sheet of four. $3,400

## Agathon Faberge

The Agathon Faberge Collection of Finland and Poland was sold during two auctions March 14-15, 1940, and the stamps of Russia, Nov. 20-21, 1939, by H.R. Harmer, 131-137 New Bond St., London W1, England.

The most notable items in the Finland and Poland sale:

**Lot 30: Mint**

Finland April 1856 5-kopeck blue. Tete-beche block of four, unused with part gum and with margins all round. Has slight horizontal and two vertical creases. £310

**Lot 32: Mint**

Finland April 1856 5kop blue, a lighter shade. Another tete-beche block of four unused with part gum, with margins all round. One stamp a trifle thinned, vertical and horizontal creases. The former ending in a marginal tear away from the stamp. £215

**Lot 57: Mint**

Finland April 1856 10kop rose. A tete-beche block of six unused with large part gum. Large margins; one corner and one pair slightly creased. £425

**Lot 58: Mint**

Finland April 1856 10kop rose tete-beche block of six. Unused with large part gum. With large margins; one corner and one pair slightly creased. £160

**Lot 76: Cover**

Finland April 1858 5kop blue. A tete-beche pair used on cover, lightly pen marked and tied with "Helsingfors" postmark. One stamp touches one side; otherwise fresh color and appearance. Natural long paper flaw touching both stamps. £115

**Lot 78: Used**

Finland April 1858 5kop blue, laid paper. Lightly pen marked example showing half of the adjoining tete-beche stamp. £125

**Lot 84: Used**

Finland 1866-71 5-penni purple-brown on gray, laid paper, roulette III, variety imperforate between. Horizontal strip of six; several teeth are not complete. £100

**Lot 90: Mint**

Finland 1866-71 5p black on buff error, roulette III (Stanley Gibbons 24). Unused with part gum, centered to left. Points of several teeth are missing. £105

**Lot 123: Used**

Finland 1866-71 8p black on green, variety rouletted 10½ (Stanley Gibbons 50). Teeth perfect and intact all round. Postmarked "FRKO." £72

The most notable items in the Russia sale:

**Lot 167: Mint**

Russia 1858 20-kopeck orange and deep blue, watermarked, and perf 14½, 15. Mint block of four; fine color and embossing; one inside corner perf is short at bottom. Only one other block known. £110

**Lot 194: Mint**

Russia 1858 30kop green and crimson, numeral watermark, perf 14½, 15. Mint block of four with fine color and embossing. A pale blue stamp has just touched left margin of lower stamp. Only one other block known. £100

**Lot 233: Used**

Russia 1866-75 10kop blue and red-brown, horizontal laid paper, center inverted (Stanley Gibbons 21b). Centered to right, lightly canceled. £45

**Lot 235: Used**

Russia 1866-75 10kop, horizontal laid paper. Two singles, both with center inverted, used together on small piece and tied with postmark, "KIBARTY 26. FEB. 1874," slight horizontal crease. £80

**Lot 242: Used**

Russia 1875-79 2kop black and rose, horizontal laid paper, background inverted (Stanley Gibbons 30a). Centered to right, clear cancellation. £40

**Lot 243: Used**

Russia 1875-79 7kop carmine and gray, horizontal laid paper, hexagons watermark (Stanley Gibbons 31b). One perf a trifle short, with clear postmark, "PERM 4 NOV. 1880." Finest of three known copies. £77

**Lot 246: Used**

Russia 1875-79 10kop blue and reddish-brown, horizontal laid paper, with inverted center. One perf short at bottom. Used on small piece, lightly canceled. £34

**Lot 282: Mint**

Russia 1889-94 14kop rose and blue, horizontal laid paper, inverted center (Stanley Gibbons 57a). £40

**Lot 291: Used**

Russia 1902-04 3.50kop gray and black, vertically laid paper, center inverted (Stanley Gibbons 77a). Used and centered to bottom. £40

**Lot 303: Mint**

Wenden 1866 2kop green and rose, entire sheet of 16 (2 by 8) with margins and full gum. The third row comprises tete-beche pair. Sheet has three horizontal creases, one of which just touches one stamp at top. £50

**Lot 304: Mint**

Wenden 1866 2kop green and rose, entire sheet of 16 (2 by 8), mint and in better condition than previous lot, the three creases not touching any stamps. One stamp has thin. £42

## Henry M. Goodkind

The Henry M. Goodkind Collection of airpost issues of the United States was sold in one auction sale, May 6, 1971, by H.R. Harmer, Inc., 6 W. 48th St., New York, N.Y.

The most notable items in the sale:

**Lot 1001: Mint**

Forerunners of airpost. 1877 Buffalo Balloon adhesive 5-cent dark blue, vertical tete-beche pair, original gum, except for hinge removal and thin on one stamp (CL1a). $1,450

**Lot 1002: Cover**

Forerunners of airpost. 1877 Buffalo Balloon 5¢ deep blue, used on flown cover (CL1). Large margined copy at top left bearing a U.S. 3¢ green and cancellation. "Anyone finding this letter will please put it in the nearest Post Office." at top. The Philatelic Foundation Certificate declines opinion. $7,500

**Lot 1003: Cover**

Pioneer flights. Sept. 17, 1911, Rodgers East to West Flight sponsored by the Vin Fiz Co. 25¢ black (Sanabria S2). Tied to a creased, illustrated Vin Fiz card, with a 1¢ green. Used on the stage of the flight from Waco to San Antonio and postmarked on Oct. 22 arrival in San Antonio. $1,700

**Lot 1004: Cover**

Pioneer flights. Ithaca, N.Y., Oct. 13, 1916. "U.S. Aero Mail Service, by Thomas Aeroplane, Oct. 13, Ithaca, N.Y." (American Airmail Society 92). "Ithaca, N.Y. Oct. 16, 1916" machine cancel tying 1¢ to No. 462 card. $300

**Lot 1022: Mint**

1918 airpost. 24¢ carmine-rose and blue, inverted center (C3a). Position 27. $31,000

**Lot 1038: Mint**

1918 airpost. 24¢ carmine-rose and blue, second printing (C3). Centerline block of 12. $360

**Lot 1039: Mint**

1918 airpost. 24¢ carmine-rose and blue, second printing (C3). Margin block of 12. Two plate Nos. 8493 blue, 8492 red, arrow and blue top only. $1,250

**Lot 1056: Mint**

1918 airpost. 24¢ carmine-rose and blue, "grounded plane variety" (C3 var). $650

**Lot 1061: Cover**

1918 airpost. 6¢ orange (C1). Fine, tied on first trip cover by magenta "AIRMAIL SERVICE, WASH., N.Y., PHILA. DEC. 15 7 P.M. 1918 N.Y." postmark. The same type of mark in black dated Dec. 16, 7 p.m. $260

**Lot 1062: Cover**

1918 airpost. 6¢ orange (C1). Stamp centered to left. Tied on first trip cover by "AIRMAIL SERVICE WASH., N.Y., PHILA. DEC. 16 11 AM 1918" in black. $280

**Lot 1071: Cover**

1918 airpost. 16¢ green (C2). Tied on first day cover by "WASHINGTON, D.C., JUL 11 1918" postmark. $3,500

**Lot 1086: Cover**

1918 airpost. 24¢ carmine-rose and blue (C3). Tied on first day cover by "WASHINGTON, D.C. MAY 13, 1918" postmark. Addressed to "Honorable Morris Sheppard, U.S. Senator, Father of the U.S. Air Mail, Washington, D.C." $3,500

**Lot 1087: Cover**

1918 airpost. 24¢ carmine-rose and blue, "grounded plane" variety (C3 var). Tied by "CITY HALL STA. N.Y. JUL. 1" (1924) cancel on cover to "ROCK SPRINGS, WYO." Bears boxed purple cachet, "VIA AIR MAIL On first trip of through schedule involving night flying on a Transcontinental Air Mail Route." $280

**Lot 1113: Cover**

1918 airpost. 24¢ carmine-rose and blue (C3). Bears initials or signatures of those involved in making the stamp. Tied by magenta "WASHINGTON JUL. 25, 1918" postmark on cover to "NEW YORK." Bearing manuscript M.W.B. (Baldwin) engraver, C.A. Huston designer and E.M. Weeks, engraver of numerals and lettering. Also name of sender W.B. Wells, an engraver with the Bureau, to Wm. H. Maple, an engraver with the American Bank Note Co. $380

**Lot 1157: Proof**

1928 5¢ Beacon carmine and blue (C11P). Large die proof (128 by 100 millimeters), sunk on card. Bears signature of Harry S. New and typed "Approved Jun. 18, Postmaster General." $900

**Lot 1165: Cover**

1930 Graf Zeppelin (C13-15). Complete set tied on one first day cover by "WASHINGTON, D.C. Apr. 19, 1930" postmark. Cover bears appropriate round trip cachets of Europe-Pan-American flight. $1,500

**Lot 1226: Cover**

R.F. (Republique Francaise) overprints on U.S. No. 25. Two types on one cover (CM1, 2). Submarine Archimede, type b and type f, on 8¢

olive green (C26), small faults, tied by "POSTE NAVALE 3-4-45" cancel to envelope. "Marine Nationale ..." cachet. $310

## Mr. and Mrs. John H. Hall Sr.

The Mr. and Mrs. John H. Hall Sr. Collection of classic Spain was sold during one auction session, June 10, 1971, by H.R. Harmer, Inc., 6 W. 48th St., New York, N.Y.

The most notable items in the sale:

**Lot 1: Mint**

1850 6-cuarto black, plate 1, type I, except position 9 which is type II (1, 1b). Corner block of nine with full sheet margins at top and left, large margins on other sides. $3,600

**Lot 15: On Piece**

1850 6c black type I (1b). Strips of five and six, canceled on piece by black "CAZERES." Margins all around. $1,500

**Lot 16: Cover**

1850 6c black type I (1b, 3). Horizontal strip of four used with single and pair of 5c red and tied on cover front by "SANTANDER" postmark. Two stamps touching one place, otherwise margins all around. $3,000

**Lot 18: Mint**

1850 12c lilac (2). Large part orginal gum. Signed Friedl. $1,100

**Lot 25: Used**

1850 12c lilac (2). Block of 12. $1,400

**Lot 35: Mint**

1850 6-real blue (4). Original gum. $1,250

**Lot 42: Cover**

1850 6r blue (4). Horizontal strips of 7 and 10 tied by red "CADIZ FEB 1, 1850" postmarks on large envelope (small piece out at bottom and one flap off) to "HAVANA, CUBA." $11,500

**Lot 43: Mint**

1850 10r green (5). Original gum. $2,600

**Lot 44: Used**

1850 10r green (5). Horizontal strip of three. Lightly canceled. $2,400

**Lot 87: Used**

1851 2r red (8). Margins all around. $2,600

**Lot 94: On Piece**

1851 5r rose (9, 6). Horizontal block of 11 and 6c black pair tied on piece. Margins all around. $2,000

**Lot 95: Mint**

1851 6r blue (10). Original gum. Large margins. $2,400

**Lot 98: Used**

1851 6r blue (10). Block of four with margins all around. $3,600

**Lot 99: Used**

1851 6r blue (10). Block of 12 with large margins. $11,500

**Lot 100: Mint**

1851 10r green (11). Margins all around. $1,600

**Lot 119: Used**

1852 2r pale red (14). With light blue cancel. Margins all around. $1,050

**Lot 130: Mint**

1852 6r greenish blue (16). Original gum, margins all around. $1,800

**Lot 131: Used**

1852 6r blue (16a). Large margins and red grid cancel. $1,350

**Lot 147: Mint**

1853 2r vermilion (21). Part original gum. $2,800

**Lot 154: Mint**

1853 6r deep blue (23). Original gum, vertical strip of four. $8,500

**Lot 167: Mint**

1854 2c vermilion on thin white paper (28a). Original gum, marginal block of 16. $1,800

**Lot 291: Mint**

1865 imperforate 19c brown and rose (70). Horizontal pair with large margins all around. Lightly hinged. Ex-Duveen, Hind. $1,800

**Lot 301: Mint**

1865 imperforate 2r salmon (73a). Block of ten (5 by 2). Large margins all around. Lightly hinged. $1,100

## Harrison D.S. Haverbeck

The Harrison D.S. Haverbeck Collection of native Indian States was sold in four auction sessions June 26-29, 1973, by H.R. Harmer, Inc., 6 W. 48th St., New York, N.Y.

The most notable items in the sale:

**Lot 21: Mint**

Bamra 1888 ½-anna rose (2). Block of 74 stamps, plus portions of three others. $2,000

**Lot 25: Mint**

Bamra 1888 8a rose (6). Complete sheet of 80 (10 by 8), unused. $1,800

**Lot 26: Mint**

Bamra 1888 8a rose variety, "Postge" in pair with normal (6, 6a). Ungummed. Royal Philatelic Society Certificate. $850

**Lot 61: Mint**

Bhopal 1876-77 double frame issue ½-rupee red (2a, b, c). Sheet of 20 (5 by 4), showing the BEGAN (position 11), BEGAN (position 19) and EGAM (position 20) varieties. Sideways embossing. The top two rows tete-beche to the bottom two rows. $1,000

**Lot 285: Cover**

Bundi 1894 May. ½-anna slate gray (1). Tied by town cancel. Margins all around. $1,200

**Lot 676: Mint**

Duttia 1896. ½a on black-green (5a), with rosettes in lower corners. Unused, with large margins on three sides and close to slightly cut in at bottom. $850

**Lot 677: Mint**

Duttia 1896. 2a dark blue on lemon (5c), rosettes in lower corners. Unused, margins all round, close at places. $650

**Lot 723: Cover**

Duttia 1917. Handstamped in watercolor 1a blue (30). Vertical pair and a single, with margins to slightly cut in. Tied by "DUTTIAH 22 JL 17" postmarks on back of ½a green entire (Higgins and Gage 4). $1,200

**Lot 1148: Cover**

Jaipur 1904. ½a gray-blue from plate II (2 var). Tied on back of India ½a green entire dated Aug. 7, 1904. Ex-Dawson. $650

**Lot 1203: Mint**

Jammu and Kashmir. The Dak Zaruri 1866 special delivery stamp for official letters. No denomination. Ex-Masson, Dawson. $800

**Lot 1311: Cover**

Jammu 1877 seal provisional. ½a red (Stanley Gibbons 51b). Tied by black seal cancel on back of India ½a blue to "AMRITSAR, OCT. 25, 1877." $550

**Lot 1312: Cover**

Similar cover to "MULTAN, NOV. 19, 1877." $550

**Lot 1349: Mint**

Jammu 1874-76 special printings in watercolor on native paper. ½a to 1a bright emerald green (Stanley Gibbons 68, 69) in complete sheets of four. Ex-Dawson. $1,100

**Lot 1367: Cover**

Jammu 1877 oil colors on thin laid battone paper. ½a red (Stanley Gibbons 84). Two copies, types I, II, tied by square black "JAMMU" seal and pen mark on back of local cover. Royal Philatelic Society Certificate. $550

**Lot 1391: Cover**

Kashmir 1867 (March/April) 1a black (Stanley Gibbons 88). Types II, III, arranged vertically and barely tied by red seal cancel on back of native cover. $550

**Lot 1427: Cover**

Kashmir 1867 1a ultramarine error of color (Stanley Gibbons 93). Types I, II, right stamp slightly cut. Tied by red seal cancel on local cover dated "15 Zulhigga 1283=20 Apr 1867." Philatelic Foundation Certificate. $1,100

**Lot 1428: Cover**

Kashmir 1867 1a ultramarine error of color (Stanley Gibbons 93). Types I, II a trifle faded. Tied by red seal on opened cover. Ex-Masson, Mortimer and Dawson. $1,100

**Lot 1429: Cover**

Kashmir 1867 1a ultramarine error of color (Stanley Gibbons 93). Type V. Tied by red seal cancel. Cover also bears India ½a blue pair, barely tied by "U26" cancel to "UMRITSUR 23 June 1867." Ex-Masson. $700

**Lot 1469: Mint**

Unified series for Jammu and Kashmir. 1878-79 provisional printings. 2a dull ultramarine (Stanley Gibbons 111 var). Unique block of 16 (4 by 4), with rough perfs, types I-XVI. $700

**Lot 1631: Cover**

Poonch 1878. ½a red (Stanley Gibbons 2). Margins all around. Tied by light cancel on back of India ½a blue entire to "CHOYA SAIDAH SHAH" and dated "8 Apr 84." $1,100

**Lot 1632: Cover**

Poonch 1879. ½a red (Stanley Gibbons 2). Large margins. Tied by blurred cancel on back of a stained India ½a green entire to "GUJAR KHAN Jun 9, 85." $1,100

## David Kohn

The "Col." David Kohn Collection of Confederate States covers was sold in two sales by Robert A. Siegel, 10 E. 52nd St., New York, N.Y., Oct. 29-30, 1970.

The most notable covers in this sale:

**Lot 1: Cover**

Charleston, S.C., Dec. 20, 1860, clear postmark tying a United States 3-cent red (26). Small perf faults on cover to "SUMTER, S.C." Secession Day postmark. $325

**Lot 24: Cover**

Charleston, S.C., May 11, 1861. U.S. 24¢ gray lilac (37a), with left straddle margin and centerline, tied by grid and bold red "3" on cover to England. The cover was 20 days in transit and has a red "London, May 31 '61" receiving postmark. Signed MacBride. $450

**Lot 68: Cover**

Postmasters' Provisionals. Columbia, S.C., 5¢ blue on blue quadrille (18XU1 var.) Blue "Columbia, S.C." postmark and a matching "Paid." $290

**Lot 94: Cover**

Postmasters' Provisionals. Spartanburg, S.C., 5¢ black on white, with blue ruled lines (78X1a). Round with wide margins. Tied by bold "Paid." "Spartanburg, S.C., Jul. 6, 1861" postmark. Ex-Brown. $1,150

**Lot 98: Cover**

Postmasters' Provisionals. Unionville, S.C., 5¢ black on bluish white (87X1), margins all around. Stamp not canceled but tied by a light pink discoloration which appears on both sides of the cover. Light "Unionville, S.C.," postmark. Original letter enclosed. $2,300

**Lot 100: Cover**

Postmasters' Provisionals. Walterborough, S.C., 10¢ carmine (108XU2). Envelope, made from an insurance company form, to "Adams Run, S.C." Matching postmark. $400

**Lot 1122: Cover**

2¢ green (3). Large margins. Perfectly tied by "Yorkville, S.C." postmark on homemade envelope, made from part of legal form. Printed political circular enclosed, dated Nov. 14, 1863. $600

**Lot 1124: Cover**

2¢ green (3) horizontal strip of five. Tied by "Georgetown, S.C. Nov. 21, 1862" postmark and manuscript to "Bennettsville, S.C." $650

**Lot 1439: Cover**

Patriotic cover. Huntsville, Ala., June 1, 1861 clear blue postmark and a matching "paid" over "5." First Day of Confederate Postal Service. $1,150

**Lot 1448: Cover**

Patriotic cover. Social Circle, Ga., red "Paid 10" and small 11-star flag to "ARKADELPHIA, ARK." $360

**Lot 1513: Cover**

Unpaid Northern letter. The cover, which went from Boston to Charleston and was forwarded to Greenville, S.C., has the following postal markings: "Boston, Mass., May 28" postmark; a bold "Ship"; an "8" obliterated with grid over "Charleston, S.C., Jun. 4, 1861" postmark; and "Paid" and "5" for forwarding. U.S. rate 3¢+3¢ due for unpaid and 2¢ ship fee. Manuscript "Emily Keith" ship destination. Ex-Antrim. $600

**Lot 1515: Cover**

Blockade cover. Wilmington, N.C., Dec. 3, "5 Paid." "Ship" and manuscript "12" to "SPARTANBURG, S.C." Altered to "5" from the old Union "3 Paid." $600

**Lot 1516: Cover**

Blockade-run cover. "Wilmington, N.C. Apr. 3" postmark, manuscript "Ships-Letter" and "12" (10¢ postage plus 2¢ ship fee) to "SPARTANBURG, C.S.A." $350

**Lot 1519: Cover**

Blockade cover. Charleston, S.C., March 18, 1863. "Steam-Ship" in bold oval, manuscript "12" rate to "SPARTANBURG, S.C." $550

**Lot 1536: Cover**

Prisoner of War cover, South to North, with 10¢ blue (11). Ample to large margins, tied by a brilliant red "Greensborough, N.C. Oct. 23" postmark and manucsript "L" censor mark. Also franked with a U.S. 3¢ rose (65), tied by diamond grid "Old Point Comfort, Va., Jan. 16" postmark. $450

**Lot 1559: Cover**

10¢ blue (12). Strip of three and single, with a couple of tiny faults. Mostly large margins to one just touched. Tied by "Richmond, Va." postmark to "LEWISVILLE, ARK." With manuscript "via Brandon or Meridian, Miss." $475

## Emmerson C. Krug

The Emmerson C. Krug Collection of U.S. covers was sold in one auction by Robert A. Siegel Auctions, 489 5th Ave., New York, N.Y., May 21-22, 1958.

The most notable items in this sale:

**Lot 20: Cover**

5-cent red-brown (1). Margins all around, tied by "Burlington Vt. 5 Jun.24" cancel on small neat cover to Malone, N.Y. $570

**Lot 38: Cover**

5¢ red-brown (1). Margins all around, tied with red 16-bar grid "Hudson Riv. Mail, N.Y." cancel on cover to Kingston, N.Y. $925

**Lot 102: Cover**

10¢ black (2). Margins all around, blue grid not tying, blue "Schenectady, N.Y." postmark on cover to Germany. Numerous transit markings, including "America Ueber Bremen." $750

**Lot 105: Cover**

5¢ red, 10¢ black horizontal strip of three (1-2). Combination usage. Margins all around. Middle stamp creased in strip. Tied on cover to Greenock, Scotland; "Mobile, Ala." postmark and shilling due mark on cover. Backstamps. $1,600

**Lot 117: Cover**

10¢ black (2). Large margins all around, tied criss-cross grid. "Brunswick, Me." postmark on cover to New York. Signed Ashbrook. $780

**Lot 137: Cover**

10¢ black (2) horizontal pair. Margins all around. Tied red St. Louis postmark on cover to Philadelphia. Additional red St. Louis postmark on Whelen correspondence cover. Ex-Moody. $1,075

**Lot 154: Cover**

1851 1¢ blue, type III, position 99R2 (8). Margins all around, showing part of next stamp at left and right. Blue grid cancel. Signed Ashbrook. $950

**Lot 220: Cover**

3¢ bisect covers. 3¢ imperf, bisect use (11c). Vertical two-thirds used as 1¢, tied "Saint Louis, Mo. July 20, 1856" postmark on cover to New York. Address partly changed and cover patched inside. Signed Ashbrook. $775

**Lot 221: Cover**

3¢ bisect covers. 3¢ imperf, bisect use (11c). Vertical third tied "Wrentham, Ms." postmark tying one stamp, and grid cancel tying bisect, marking 10¢ rate to San Francisco. Stamps from plate 5L, manuscript "June 4" within postmark. American Philatelic Society and Philatelic Foundation certificates. $750

**Lot 254: Cover**

3¢ dull red, used in combination with Canada 3-penny red (U.S. 11, Canada 4). Both slightly cut into. Tied Canadian target and the 3p Beaver tied "6d" in circle on cover to New York. "Dundas U.S. 1856" postmark and "Canada 10cts." Prosser correspondence cover. Ex-Caspary. $940

**Lot 395: Cover**

5¢ deep orange-brown, type II, 10¢ green, 30¢ orange (30, 35, 38). Tied red grids, red "New York Paid 9" postmark on cover to France. Rare triple rate. $650

**Lot 584: Cover**

3¢ rose (2), 10¢ green, 90¢ blue (65, 68, 72). Tied with geometric cork cancels on double 53¢ "Heard" correspondence cover from Boston to Shanghai, China. Various transit marks. Ex-Waterhouse. $1,000

**Lot 588: Cover**

10¢ green (2), 12¢ black, 90¢ blue (pair) (68, 69, 72). Tied with dotted cork cancels. Red "N.York Br.Pkt. Paid" and red London transit mark on double $1.06 rate cover to China. $2,400

**Lot 589: Cover**

5¢ red-brown, 10¢ green, 90¢ blue (2) (68, 72, 75). Tied with geometric cork cancels. Red "New York Paid" postmark, magenta manuscript "78" and various transit marks on unusual 13 times 15¢ rate cover to France. Address cut out and patched up inside. $1,100

**Lot 784: Cover**

1869 10¢ yellow, 24¢ green and violet (116, 120). Copies tied by geometric cancels on cover from New York to Chile. Red "12" and "25," manuscript "pr. Alaska." Described in Ashbrook. Philatelic Foundation certificate. $3,400

**Lot 785: Cover**

1859 1¢ buff, 24¢ green and violet (112, 120). Cork cancels "Boston, Mass" postmark on cover to Argentina. Red "8" and blue receiving mark. Ex-Emerson. $1,000

**Lot 788: Cover**

1869 30¢ blue and carmine (121). Copy neatly tied with geometric cancel and "Egg Harbor City, N.J." postmark on cover to Switzerland. Red "New York Br. Transit Paid All" and various backstamps. Signed Ashbrook. Philatelic Foundation certificate. $1,150

**Lot 789: Cover**

1869 30¢ blue and carmine (121). Tied with geometric cancel, red "New York Br. Transit Paid All" postmark on cover to Switzerland. Signed Ashbrook. Philatelic Foundation certificate. $1,050

**Lot 791: Cover**

1869 10¢ yellow, 30¢ blue and carmine (116, 121). Cork cancels and 10¢ tied blue French receiving mark on small cover from Havana, Cuba, to France. Red "New York Paid 12" postmark. Backstamped "Habana" with transit marks. Signed Ashbook and described in his "Special Service." Philatelic Foundation certificate. $1,025

**Lot 792: Cover**

1869 30¢ blue and carmine. France 20-centime blue (U.S. 121, France 33). Tied with bold segmented cork cancel and red "New York Paid 6" postmark, "New Orleans, La." postmark on cover to France. French stamp tied by "532" within dotted diamond cancel. Signed Ashbrook. Ex-Gibson, Ex-Klep. Philatelic Foundation certificate. $1,300

**Lot 793: Cover**

1869 30¢ blue and carmine vertical pair (121). Tied checkered cork cancels, red "New York Paid 24" postmark and blue French transit mark on cover from New York to Paris and forwarded back to New York. Signed Ashbrook. Ex-Seybold. Philatelic Foundation certificate. $1,850

## Col. Hans Lagerloef

The Col. Hans Lagerloef Collection was sold during two auctions by H.R. Harmer, Inc., 32 E. 57th St., New York, N.Y., April 27-May 15, 1953.

The most notable items in Sale I, British Commonwealth and Latin America:

**Lot 97: Used**

British Guiana 1850 cottonreel 4-cent yellow on pelure paper (3), initialed in pencil, cut circular with large margins. Clear impression and neat cancel. $290

**Lot 98: Cover**

British Guiana 1850 cottonreel 4¢ yellow on pelure paper (3), initialed in pencil, cut circular, on small cover to Georgetown. "DEMERARA" cancel, "Febr. 7, 1841," just tying stamp. $290

**Lot 202: Used**

Cook Islands 1902 2-penny chocolate, value omitted (33a) in used block of four. $240

**Lot 268: Mint, used**

Fiji 1871-96 special collection in four albums. Complete mint sheets and mint blocks, used copies showing a study of perf varieties, plate varieties, etc. Also includes a number of rare individual stamps, numerous covers and some proofs. About 6,650 stamps. $700

**Lot 329: Mint, used**

Griqualand West collection of 424 stamps. Property was awarded special honors at the APS convention in 1948. $280

**Lot 343: Mint, used**

India, Native Feudatory States collection in three albums. Early covers, Jammu and Kashmir items, mint blocks and sheets, including Burma 1937 issue to 5-rupees in blocks of four. $420

**Lot 432: Mint**

Mauritius 2-penny blue on bluish (15) unused. Cut close and somewhat faulty. Royal certificate. $250

**Lot 565: Mint**

Natal £1 10/- violet and orange-brown (109), original gum. $195

**Lot 1063: Mint, used**

Transvaal collection of over 1,000 stamps in two albums, written up. All issues well represented with rare stamps, roulettes, inverts, numerous pairs, strips, blocks of four and larger, bisects on pieces and partial cover, combination covers with Cape of Good Hope, Griqualand West, and reference material. $1,100

The most notable items in Sale II, Europe, Asia and Africa:

**Lot 2010: Mint**

Lubeck 2-schilling brown (3, 3a). Complete sheet of 100, including the two errors, original gum. $120

**Lot 2011: Cover**

Lubeck error "ZWEI EIN HALB" (3a) tied by bar cancel to cover front. $125

**Lot 2036: Mint**

Lubeck reprints of 1872 ½s to 4s (3-8 reprints). The five lithographed values in full sheets of 25, original gum. $575

**Lot 2153: Cover**

Thurn and Taxis 1865 roulette 1-kreuzer green, used in combination with Prussia 1867 1kr green (Thurn and Taxis 56, Prussia 23). Two singles tied to cover by "COBURG, Dec. 31, 1867." Ex-Nehrlich. Signed Koehler with his certificate. $185

**Lot 2759: Mint**

Monaco 1885 Prince Charles III 1-franc yellow (9) mint block of four. $150

**Lot 2813: Mint**

Monaco 1919 5fr+5fr dull red block of eight (B8). From top right corner of sheet, hinged in margins. Stamps never hinged. $155

**Lot 2826: Mint**

Monaco 1920 5fr+5fr red, original gum, marginal block of four (B18). Champion certificate. $310

**Lot 2872: Mint**

Reunion 1852 15-centime blue, unused (1). Large margins. $215

**Lot 2875: Used**

Reunion 1852 30c blue (2). Large margins, very lightly canceled. Royal certificate. $270

**Lot 3477: Cover**

Denmark 1851 2-rigsbank daler blue and pair and strip of three of 4-skilling brown arranged in form of horizontal strip tied by "1" to small cover "Copenhagen June 8, 1855" to Koenigsberg (1, 4). The 2rs is slightly cut into. $170

**Lot 3504: Cover**

Denmark 1858 combination cover bearing Denmark 4sk (7) with Prussia 3-silbergroscen yellow (13), with numeral cancel "168" and "HAMBURG" cancel, both tied to small cover to Dresden. Bears "Bahnhof Altona," "Aus Daenemark" and other markings. $180

**Lot 3705: Mint, used**

Russia, Zemstvos specialized collection in eight albums. More than 8,000 stamps and an array of covers. $1,900

**Lot 3723: Mint, used**

Sweden collection presented to Col. Lagerloef on his 70th birthday by the postmaster general of Sweden in 1950 as a token of esteem. The collection is nearly complete from 1919-49, was specially prepared, and has blocks of four of perf issues and strips of three of the coils. The stamps have been hinged and are in a red leather album. $600

## John Lek

The John Lek Collection was sold in five auctions by H.R. Harmer — Sale I in New York; Sale II and III in London, England; Sale IV in New York; Sale V in London, Feb. 9-May 11, 1959.

The most notable items in Sale I, Europe:

**Lot 69: Mint**

Austria newspaper stamps 1851-56 Mercury 6-kreuzer scarlet (P4). Almost full original gum, large margins on all sides. Signed Kohler, Thier, Friedl, "K.C." $4,500

**Lot 349: Used**

Germany, offices in China, 1900 Tientsin handstamped 50-pfennig purple and black on salmon (22). Tied to piece. Signed Kohler. $1,100

**Lot 595: Mint**

Romania, Moldavia 1858 27-parale black, rose (1), unused, good margins on all sides. Signed Diena. $1,350

**Lot 607: Mint**

Romania, Moldavia 1858 wove paper 81pa blue on blue (4), unused, with very large margins on all sides. Signed Kohler. $2,300

**Lot 715: Used**

Switzerland, Geneva 1843 Double Geneva 10-centime black on yellow-green (2L1). Large margins with part of adjoining stamp at left, parts of dividing line at bottom and right, partly close at top clear of design. Red rosette cancel. Signed Friedl. $1,350

**Lot 1007: Cover**

Reunion 1852 15-centime black on blue and 30c black on blue (1, 2). Both copies with small or no margins but not cut into. On small folded letter with double circle postmark "St. Andre, Reunion, July 14, 1852," addressed to Nantes, France. Stamps remained uncanceled at Reunion, the 30c tied on arrival by "COLONIES FRA. MARSEILLE, OCT. 26, 52." Cover bears red "35," double circle "St. Dennis, Reunion, July 13" and Nantes arrival postmark. Ex-Caspary. $4,400

The most notable items in Sale III, British Commonwealth:

**Lot 49: Used**

British Guiana 1858-59 1-cent dull red (4) strip of four with large margins all around showing portions of two adjoining stamps at right. "DEMERARA MR 27 60" cancellation ties strip to lettersheet. $3,000

**Lot 215: Mint**

Great Britain 1840 V.R. 1-penny black (1), original gum, block of six from right sheet showing part of imprint. Large margins all around with natural paper crease at right, mostly in margin. Royal certificate. $1,200

**Lot 217: Used**

Great Britain 1902 I.R. official (O25). Rare Edward 10/-ultramarine. Liverpool postmark. Royal certificate. $2,240

The most notable items in Sale IV, German and Italian Old States:

**Lot 401: Cover**

Mecklenburg-Strelitz 1864 1/- violet (3). Tied to small folded envelope to Neustrelitz, High Military Commission. $625

**Lot 557: Mint**

Saxony 1851-57 ½-neu-groschen black on pale blue (3a). The error of color, part original gum, margins all around. $625

**Lot 690: Used**

Modena 1859 80-centesimo buff (14), large margins with complete frameline on three sides. Canceled by black bars. $1,400

**Lot 728: Cover**

Romagna 1859 6-bajocchi black on yellow-green (7). Margins on all sides, mostly large. Tied by grid to large-size refolded letter "Luga, Nov. 17, 50" to Ferara. Signed in full by both E. Diena and A. Diena. Kohler certificate. $900

**Lot 882: Mint**

Tuscany 1860 Provisional Government 3-lira ochre (23), original gum. Signed A. Diena. $1,550

**Lot 883: Used**

Tuscany 1860 Provisional Government 3l ochre (23), margins on three sides, slight cut into at top right. Canceled by straightline "PER CO(NSEGNA)." $1,000

**Lot 894: Used**

Two Sicilies 1860 Trinacria ½-tornesi deep blue (8), large margins. Lightly canceled. Diena certificate. $1,000

The most notable items in Sale V, German States (part II):

**Lot 2: Used**

Bavaria 1849 1-kreuzer gray-black (3) vertical strip of three on piece with "254" cancellations. $490

**Lot 138: Cover**

Hamburg 1859 4/- yellow-green (1) tied to circular from Hamburg to Lohne (Oldenburg). $420

**Lot 143: Cover**

Hamburg 1859 9/- yellow (1) on envelope to London. $434

**Lot 239: Used**

Oldenburg 1861 ½-groschen moss green (3). Two singles with 3g yellow on piece. Lightly canceled. $812

**Lot 277: Used**

Saxony 1850 3pf brownish-red (1). $518

**Lot 294: Used**

Saxony 1855 10ng deep blue (4) used block of four. $728

## Mortimer L. Neinken

The Mortimer L. Neinken Collection of U.S. classics from 1847-75 was sold in two sales by Robert A. Siegel, 10 E. 52nd St., New York, N.Y., Nov. 19-20, 1970.

The most notable items in this sale:

**Lot 15: Used**

5-cent red-brown (1). Horizontal strip of five, large margins to just clear at left, second stamp from right the "dot in S" variety. Red grids and light brown crayon cancels. $1,000

**Lot 24: Cover**

10¢ black (2). Three large margins, tied by "Steamer 10" in red oval, repeated on the cover. A folded letter (part only), headed "Boston, Mass. Sep. 1, 1847." $2,100

**Lot 71: Cover**

5¢ dark brown (12). Chestnut color, large margins and tied by bold "Philadelphia, Pa., March 24" postmark on folded letter to Halifax, N.S. Philatelic Foundation Certificate. $2,100

**Lot 80: Used**

10¢ green, types I, II, III, IV (13, 14, 15, 16). Combination block of eight. Positions 73-74, 83-85, 93-95L1. Stamps at bottom are type I, in middle type III, etc. Large margins to just in on two. Bold "Fairview, Va." postmark and light manuscript. $1,800

**Lot 140: Cover**

10¢ green types III, IV; 12¢ black (15, 16, 17). Horizontal strip of three of positions 62, 63,

64L1. Latter recut at top and bottom. Used with single 12¢, all paying 42¢ rate to Sweden. All stamps with large margins. Tied by "Peoria, Ill." postmark and by edge of red "Aachen, Franco," via packet from New York, Prussian closed mail, through Hamburg and Helsingborg to Sweden. Red "19" for German credit. Philatelic Foundation Certificate. $3,500

**Lot 200: Used**

12¢ black (17) block of eight. The largest known multiple, positions 22-30, 32-40L1. Ex-Jessup, Tracy. $1,350

**Lot 249: Mint**

10¢ yellow green, types I, II, III (31, 32, 33). Combination block of six, positions 75-76, 85-86, 95-96R1. Stamps at bottom are type I, in middle row type III, at top type II. $3,200

**Lot 251: Used**

10¢ dark green, types I, III (31, 33). Combination block of eight, positions 87-90, 97-100L. "San Francisco, Cal." postmarks. $1,800

**Lot 338: Mint**

24¢ grayish lilac (37a). Block of 12, beautiful color, full original gum, small closed perf tear in one. $1,300

**Lot 355: Cover**

30¢ orange (38). Used with 5¢ brown type II (30A) paying 35¢ rate to Switzerland. Clear "Charleston, S.C., Feb. 25, 1861" postmark, tied by grids and used while South Carolina was a Confederate state. $1,150

**Lot 356: Used**

90¢ blue (39). Reconstructed block of five with the so-called "Shanghai, China magenta pen cancellation." $1,650

**Lot 389: Mint**

1861 1¢ blue (63) complete sheet of 100, with bottom imprint and plate No. 27. Original gum. $1,550

**Lot 429: Cover**

5¢ buff (67). Horizontal strip of three, well centered, right stamp with light bend from cover. Tied by "Stockton, Cal." postmark on orange patriotic cover, with a portrait of George Washington and quote, "to NORTHPORT, CANADA WEST," and red "Chicago, Ill. Paid 15" exchange marking. $900

**Lot 616: Cover**

3¢ red entire (U9). Grid cancel and "Philadelphia, Pa. Aug 17, 1861" postmark. "Old Stamps Not Recognized" and "Due 3" on the cover to "NEW HOPE, PA." Ex-Meroni. $1,200

## John F. Seybold

The John F. Seybold Stamp and Cover Collections were sold in three auctions by J.C. Morgenthau & Co., 87 Nassau St., New York, N.Y., March 15-April 15, 1910.

It should be noted that all catalog numbers given in parentheses are those mentioned in the auction catalog but that Scott catalog numbers have changed since that time and the old numbers are now obsolete.

The most notable items in Part I, U.S., British North America and South America:

**Lot 12: Cover**

New York Postmasters' Provisional 1845 5-cent black horizontal strip of four on a letter canceled "N.Y., Oct. 30 (1845)" and addressed to Cincinnati. The stamps are on a paper that is almost white, and the left-hand stamp is the rare variety with the outer line at bottom. $157

**Lot 18: Cover**

St. Louis Postmasters' Provisional 1845 5¢ on greenish paper, vertical pair on letter "St. Louis, April 8" to Natchez, Miss. Stamps Nos. 1 and 2 of the original plate. $197

**Lot 234: Mint**

1901 Pan-American 2¢ carmine and black with inverted center (295a), original gum. $167

**Lot 301: Used**

Revenue 1871 second issue $500 black, green and red, lightly canceled. $219

**Lot 308: Used**

Revenue 1871 proprietary $5 black and green on violet paper, original gum, lightly canceled. Partial imprint at bottom. $181

**Lot 600: Cover**

Canada 12-penny black (3, G4) canceled in blue, "Hamilton, C.W., Nov. 23, 1853," with red "Canada Paid 20 Cents." Addressed to New York. $515

**Lot 601: Cover**

Canada 12p black (3, G4), large margins top and right, lightly canceled in blue, "Hamilton, C.W., Dec. 8, 1853," addressed to New York with the name cut out. $360

**Lot 666: Cover**

Canada ¼/- purple on cover from "Edmonston, N.B., Nov. 13, 1860" to Quebec. $242

**Lot 724: Piece**

Canada 1/- purple (3) on small piece of original, lightly canceled. $241

The most notable items in Part II, Europe:

**Lot 1084: Cover**

Oldenburg 1/3-groschen green (5). Three copies on one cover from Varel to Delmenhorst, canceled in blue. $162

**Lot 1092: Cover**

Saxony 3-pfennig rose, horizontal strip of three and single used on wrapper addressed to Vienna. The wrapper is canceled "Leipzig July 3, 1850," and the stamps are pen canceled with a cross. $156

**Lot 1162: Cover**

Modena 40-centesimo rose, 80c orange (10, 11) used together on an envelope from Carrara to Philadelphia, March 6, 1880. Bar cancel ties both. $151

**Lot 1236: Cover**

Switzerland, Zurich 4-rappen black, type III, 6rp black, type IV (8, 9) used together to make up 10 centimes rate on front of a cover which is canceled in black, "Greiffensee," and addressed to Uetikon. $315

**Lot 1239: Cover**

Switzerland, Zurich horizontal line 4rp black (10), type III, and right vertical half of 4rp black, type IV, used together to make up 6rp rate on cover from Zurich, Sept. 25, 1849, to Wettschweil. The stamps are canceled in red with the cancellation covering the cut. $725

**Lot 1242: Cover**

Switzerland, Federation Administration 1849-50 (Vaud) 40-centime red and black (12) on cover, Geneva Nov. 12, 1849. The stamp is tied to the cover by a red cancel with Seybold's name stamp on the back. $196

**Lot 1243: Cover**

Switzerland, Federal Administration 1849-50 (Vaud) 4c red and black (12). Horizontal pair on cover canceled "Geneva, Dec. 16, 1849." The stamps have margins on all four sides and light red cancellation. $252

**Lot 1244: Cover**

Switzerland, Federal Administration 1849-50 (Vaud) 4c red and black (12). Horizontal pair on piece of cover canceled "Geneva, Jan. 11, 1850," in red. $241

The most notable items in Part III, British Colonies:

**Lot 1679: Cover**

Mauritius 1859 2-penny deep blue (G30). Two copies of this rarity used together on a cover from Mauritius, Nov. 10, 1859, to Marseilles. Lightly canceled "PAID" in oval. $206

**Lot 2114: Used**

Mauritius 1848 1p vermilion on yellowish paper (G3). Early state of plate, light cancellation. $221

## Theodore Sheldon

The Theodore Sheldon Collection of United States, including autographs and documents, was sold by Mercury Stamp Co., Inc., 10 E. 40th St., New York, N.Y., in three auctions, June 3-5, 1970.

The most notable items in these sales:

**Lot 3: Mint**

Providence, R.I., Postmasters' Provisional 1846 (10X1 (11), 10X2). Complete sheet of 11 5 cents and one 10¢. Philatelic Foundation certificate. $650

**Lot 69: Used**

1869 15¢ brown and blue, type II, inverted center (119b). Lightly canceled. $1,800

**Lot 71: Used**

1869 24¢ green and violet, inverted center (120b). $1,100

**Lot 114: Mint**

1883 Special Printing 2¢ pale red-brown (211B (4), 211C) horizontal strip of six. Center pair imperf between. Top sheet margin and imprint "STEAMER-AMERICAN BANK NOTE CO." $2,000

**Lot 166: Mint**

1901 Pan-American 1¢ green and black, center inverted (294a). $2,300

**Lot 175: Used**

1906 imperf 4¢ brown (314A) tied by characteristic wavy lines cancel to fragment. $1,400

**Lot 177: Mint**

1906 imperf 5¢ blue (315A) center line block of four. $1,300

**Lot 178: Mint**

1909 5¢ blue (317), perf 12 horizontally. Vertical pair. $750

**Lot 277: Mint**

1916-17 imperf 5¢ carmine imperf error (485 (2) ), (482 (98) ). Two errors in full upper left pane of 100 with sheet margins and plate numbers, plus vertical strip of 11 at right and bottom to show center line block, and left and top arrow blocks. $4,500

**Lot 328: Mint**

1930 Von Steuben imperf 2¢ carmine (689a (2) ) block of four with left sheet margin (positions 41, 42, 51, 52 in sheet). $2,600

**Lot 644: Mint**

The Schermack Co. 1906-08 perf type II 5¢ blue pair (315 (2) ). $750

**Lot 680: Mint**

U.S. Automatic Vending Co. perf type III 1914 rotary coil 2¢ carmine pair (459 (2) ). Signed "George B. Sloane" with American Philatelic Society certificate. $1,700

**Lot 785: Mint**

Dated documentary issues. Series of 1951. $30 vertical strip of four (R480 imperf (4) ). $700

**Lot 1084:**

British revenues for use in North America. General issues. 4-penny embossed, die A (RM25) on "18th February 1766" ship clearance document from Pensacola, West Fla. $800

**Lot 1280: Used**

Canal Zone 1906-07 2-cent carmine-red and black (23g), center inverted. $700

**Lot 1362: Mint**

Danish West Indies 1902 green surcharge 2-cent on 3¢ horizontal pair (26, 26a). $900

**Lot 1626: Cover**

Philippines, Spanish-American War. United States military occupation both during and after actual war, 1898-1904. Approximately 225 complete covers plus reference, including some duplicates with a wide range of postmarks, railway post offices, scarce frankings, etc., in stockbook. $1,150

**Lot 1673: Mint**

Philippines 1944 handstamped "Victory" 2-cent rose (463a). Complete booklet pane of six (one 411a) adhering to original interleaving paper. Philatelic Foundation certificate. $700

**Lot 1685: Mint**

Philippines 1944 handstamped "Victory" 12¢ bright blue on 454 (476). $750

**Lot 1711: Mint**

Philippines 1926 Madrid-Manila airpost 16¢ olive-bister, red overprint (C8). Philatelic Foundation certificate. $625

**Lot 1715: Mint**

Philippines 1926 Madrid-Manila airpost 26¢ blue-green (C16). Signed Sanabria with Philatelic Foundation certificate. $625

**Lot 1761: Mint, used, cover**

Philippines Revenue Collection. Aguinaldo issues, 1898-99. The Sheldon Collection of the postage and revenue issues of Gen. Aguinaldo. Comprising seven complete sheets, 26 covers and numerous stamps. Interchangeable uses of postage and revenue stamps, multiples, stampless, reference and rare stamped covers. $1,350

**Lot 1771: Mint**

Puerto Rico. Spanish-American War military covers. The collection of 150 covers, as well as pieces and references. Includes rare military stations, unusual frankings, with some duplication. $600

**Lot 1796:**

U.S. documents, 94 items. Signed letters and autographs, as well as a few other miscellaneous documents, featuring persons portrayed on or concerned with U.S. postage and airmail stamps. Some stamps and other collateral material. $800

## Y. Souren

The stamps of Y. Souren were sold during two auctions by H.R. Harmer, Inc., 32 E. 57th St., New York, N.Y., March 12-15 and Oct. 29-31, 1951 (seven sessions).

The most notable items in Sale I:

**Lot 4: Cover**

Millbury, Mass., Postmaster's Provisional 5-cent black on bluish with "PAID" in red and "MILLBURY, OCT. 30 (1846)," "PAID" and circled "5" postmarks on cover to Augusta, Maine. Stamp is somewhat faulty. One of the few known covers. $1,400

**Lot 265: Mint**

U.S. 8¢ Trans-Mississippi imperf (289a) vertical top margin pair, imperf horizontally, origi-

nal gum. Horizontal crease well above design and thin at bottom. $610

**Lot 312: Used**

U.S. 2¢ Pan-American, center inverted (295a). Used, centered to bottom but perfs clear. Ironed vertical crease, just cracking paper at top and bottom. $625

**Lots 627, 628 combined as 628A: Mint**

U.S. 1917 5¢ carmine imperf error sheet of 400 (482a). Complete sheet includes three of the error stamps, as well as eight error plate numbers "7942," mint. $2,400

**Lot 829: Mint**

U.S. 1918 24¢ carmine-rose and blue airmail, center inverted (C3a). Small thins at top and top left, original gum, also diagonal crease not visible on face. Rather well-centered stamp comparing favorably in appearance with some of the better known copies. $1,800

**Lot 832: Mint**

U.S. 1930 Graf Zeppelin complete (set C13-15), original gum, plate number block of six. First two tops, last bottom 65¢ well centered; $1.30 centered slightly to left, $2.60 very slightly to top. $575

**Lot 1056: Used**

Revenues. U.S. 50¢ blue life insurance (R58a) block of 12 (4 by 3) with left sheet margin, creased and cracked in place. Largest known block. $625

**Lot 1079: Used**

Revenues. U.S. $2 red probate of will (R83a) horizontal pair, large margins three sides, fair at bottom, small defect at top right. $650

**Lot 1271: Mint**

Local stamps. New York City Despatch Post 1842 3¢ grayish (40L1). Upper left corner block of eight (4 by 2), mint. $260

The most notable items in Sale II:

**Lot 92: Mint**

U.S. 1857-61 10¢ green, type I (31), perf 15. Large part original gum, well centered. $560

**Lot 173: Mint**

U.S. 1869 6¢ ultramarine reconstructed block of 24 (115). Complete blocks of eight and 16, full original gum. $800

**Lot 224: Mint**

U.S. 1870-71 24¢ purple (153) without grill. Block of four unused; minor separation, trivial defects at right. Three or four blocks known. $725

**Lot 234: Mint**

U.S. 1888 90¢ purple (218) top marginal block of 20 (10 by 2), imprint and plate No. 23. Full original gum; sheet margin at right. $620

**Lot 536: Mint**

U.S. 2¢ Pan-American, center inverted (295a), original gum. Well centered, minute thin spot and slight gum crease. $1,600

**Lot 538: Mint**

U.S. 4¢ Pan-American (296a) block of four with center inverted. Part original gum, centered, closed tear at bottom and tiny paper scrape, slightly reinforced. Only four blocks of this variety exist, almost all of which are slightly defective. $2,400

**Lot 587: Mint**

U.S. 1909 Bluish Paper 5¢ blue (361) block of four with imprint at top, original gum. Well centered, top left stamp with tiny thin spot. $875

**Lot 629: Mint**

U.S. 1917 5¢ error imperf; 5¢ carmine imperf (482a). This single and double error in a complete mint sheet of 400; full sheet margins with the eight blocks showing plate No. 7942. $2,500

**Lot 636: Mint**

U.S. 1918 24¢ carmine-rose and blue airmail, center inverted (C3a). The bottom arrow pair, positions 95 and 96 in sheet, original gum. Well centered, somewhat creased and left-hand stamp thinning near left margin. $3,300

**Lot 747: Mint**

Revenues. U.S. 3¢ green playing cards (R17a). Uncanceled, margins all around. Large three sides, negligible tiny thinning in outer margin at top, outside of design. $935

## W. Parsons Todd

The W. Parsons Todd Collection of United States was sold in three parts: Sept. 19-20, 1977; Jan. 10-11, 1978; and May 30-31, 1978, by Robert A. Siegel, 120 E. 56th St., New York, N.Y.

The most notable items in Part I:

**Lot 90: Mint**

$3 Columbian (243). Original gum. $10,500

**Lot 91: Mint**

$4 Columbian (244), in a block with partly disturbed original gum. $10,500

**Lot 92: Mint**

$5 Columbian (245). Original gum, left margin block. Minor traces of printing ink on back. $16,500

**Lot 309: Mint**

10-cent brown combination pair of Type I and II (282C, 283). Block with part bottom imprint and plate No. 932 and original gum. Top pair is the variety (282C). $11,000

**Lot 477: Mint**

$5 dark green (313). Top imprint and plate No. 1620 block of six. Original gum and perf strengthening in selvage. $29,000

**Lot 636: Mint**

5¢ blue, bluish (361). Each stamp with light blue "E" backstamp in top imprint and plate No. 4930 block of six. $17,500

**Lot 764: Mint**

10¢ Panama-Pacific perf 10 (404). Top plate

No. 6130 block of six, with trifle disturbed original gum. $11,000

**Lot 932: Mint**

$2 orange-red and black (523). Arrow and double plate number block of 12. $10,000

**Lot 1053: Mint**

10¢ blue (E1). Complete, original gum sheet of 50. $32,500

The most notable items in Part II:

**Lot 370: Mint**

30¢ Columbian (239). Bottom imprint "N" and plate No. 59 block of eight. Original gum. $11,000

**Lot 379: Mint**

$1 Columbian (240). Top imprint "W" and plate No. 93 block of 25. Original gum. $20,000

**Lot 788: Mint**

4¢ orange-brown bluish (360). $7,500

**Lot 999: Mint**

24¢ carmine-rose and blue (C3). Complete sheet of 100 with arrow, double plate number and blue top only. $17,000

The most important items in Part III:

**Lot 330: Mint**

$5 dark green (263). Bottom imprint block. $5,000

**Lot 401: Mint**

$5 dark green (278). Top imprint and plate No. 85 strip of three. Original gum. $5,250

**Lot 969: Mint**

10¢ blue (E1). Bottom imprint and plate No. 495 and right imperforate half arrow block of 15. Original gum. $8,500

**Lot 1265: Mint**

Guam $1 black type II (13), the 1899 overprint, in an original gum block. $7,500

**Lot 1504: Mint**

Philippines 1903 overprints. $2 dark blue (238), in a top imprint and plate No. 1630 block of six. $8,000

**Lot 1505: Mint**

Philippines 1903 overprints. $2 dark blue (238), in a bottom imprint and plate No. 1630 block of six. $6,250

**Lot 1509: Mint**

Philippines 1903 overprints. $5 dark green (239), in a bottom imprint and plate No. 1620 block of six. $27,000

## George Walcott

The George Walcott Collection of used Civil War patriotic covers, compiled by Robert Laurence, 1934, was sold by Laurence Jan. 14-16, 1935.

The most notable items in the collection:

**Lot 145: Cover**

Portraits and campaigns. J.C. Breckinridge.

An adhesive stamp with portrait of Breckinridge in purple, tied with square grid cancel and signed "Breck." under the stamp. The same postmark ties a 3-cent 1857. The late George Walcott paid $300 for this cover. $76

**Lot 163: Cover**

Portraits and campaigns. Lincoln. A cover in black on orange envelope with 1861 3¢ tied. $65

**Lot 164: Cover**

Portraits and campaigns. Lincoln. Cover in black with 1861 3¢ tied on back (second round cover). $60

**Lot 165: Cover**

Portraits and campaigns. Lincoln. Cover in black with an 1861 3¢ tied on back (third round cover). $60

**Lot 166: Cover**

Portraits and campaigns. Lincoln. Cover in black with 1861 3¢ tied on back (fourth round cover). $61

**Lot 167: Cover**

Portraits and campaigns. Lincoln. Cover in black with 1861 3¢ tied on back (fifth round cover). $53

**Lot 169: Cover**

Portraits and campaigns. Lincoln. Cover with "Magnus" in color, "Review of the Army," with 1861 3¢ tied on back. $40

**Lot 227: Cover**

Portraits and campaigns. Lincoln. Cover in black with 1857 tied with blue grid cancel. $40

**Lot 228: Cover**

Portraits and campaigns. Lincoln. Cover with strip of four 1861 3¢ tied with blue Cincinnati cancel. Illustration is the handwriting and signature of Abraham Lincoln. The late George Walcott paid $150 for this cover. $41.50

**Lot 233: Cover**

Portraits and campaigns. Lincoln. Rare cover, "Souvenir of Victory" inscription, "Magnus" in gold, with 1861 3¢ tied on back. $46

**Lot 568: Cover**

Maj. Gen. Grant. Cover in black with "National Union Club" inscription with 1862 2¢ Jackson. The late George Walcott paid $100 for this cover. $49

**Lot 599: Cover**

Adams Express Co. cover in purple. The late George Walcott paid $150 for this cover. $50

**Lot 600: Cover**

Adams Express Co. cover with "Port Royal S.C." $40

**Lot 679: Cover**

Views. Newark, N.J., in color, "Magnus." $53

**Lot 687: Cover**

Views cover, "Magnus," in color with 1861 3¢ tied. View of Chicago. $50

**Lot 688: Cover**

Views cover, "Magnus," in color with 1861 3¢ tied on back. View of Buffalo. $51

**Lot 691: Cover**

Views cover, "Magnus," in color, with 1861 3¢ tied on back. View of Nashville. $51

**Lot 703: Cover**

Battle scenes cover, "Magnus," in bronze, with 1861 3¢ tied on back. $40

**Lot 720: Cover**

Battle scenes cover. "No. 8. Movement of the Armies From Washington." Magnus cover in color with 1861 3¢ tied on back. $50

**Lot 780: Cover**

Camp scenes and hospitals cover. Camp scene with 10 soldiers, "Magnus," in color with 1861 3¢ tied. $41

**Lot 992: Cover**

Caricatures cover in blue, "Dr. Russell at Bulls," Philadelphia, Aug. 27, to Buffalo. $41

**Lot 2116: Cover**

Female Designs. Sitting female surrounded by four flags. Cover by Kimmel in color. This is the fifth of five Kimmel covers which cost the late George Walcott $100 each. $40

**Lot 2381: Cover**

Female Designs. Cover in red, white and blue with a Valentine type enclosure. The late George Walcott paid $150 for this cover. $62

**Lot 2390: Cover**

Eagles and Shields. Cover in color with fancy shield and sitting eagle, inscribed "Liberty, Union, Forever and Ever," with 1861 3¢ tied. $40

Sanitary Fairs. Cover with inscription, "Great Sanitary Central Fair for the Sanitary Commission" from Philadelphia to Boston. Cover is in red on white with a 10¢ Sanitary Commission adhesive. Rare used on cover. $40

**Lot 3114: Cover**

Confederate States Patriotics. Cover, in black on white, with Confederate soldier trampling on U.S. flag. Confederate flag waving at top and Lincoln hanging from tree by his feet with a rail and ax tied around his neck. Postmarked "Marshall, Texas, Paid 10." $77.50

**Lot 3115: Cover**

Confederate States Patriotics. Cover, in black on white, with Confederate flag in color. Postmarked "Tuskegee, Ala. Paid 10." $49

## Marcus W. White

The Marcus W. White Collection of U.S. postal stationery was sold in three sales by Robert A. Siegel, 10 E. 52nd St., New York, N.Y., Dec. 10-11, 1970, to July 15, 1971.

The most notable items in Part I:

**Lot 88: Unused**

1860 Star die. 10-cent green on white (U32). Size 3, knife 2. $1,450

**Lot 306: Unused**

1874 Plimpton issue. 2¢ brown on orange, die

1 (U125), size 4, knife 41, watermark 2, Centennial. $2,600

**Lot 307: Unused**

1874 Plimpton issue. 2¢ brown on orange, die 1 (U125), size 6, knife 43, watermark 2, Centennial. $2,100

**Lot 316: Mint**

1874 Plimpton issue. 2¢ vermilion on manila wrapper, die 4 (W138). Size 161 by 239 millimeters, speciman overprint. $1,500

**Lot 322: Unused**

1874 Plimpton issue. 2¢ vermilion on orange, die 5 (U145). Brown-red, size 4, knife 41, watermark 2. Centennial. Unused. $1,700

**Lot 323: Unused**

1874 Plimpton issue. 2¢ vermilion on orange, die 5 (U145). Brown-red, size 6, knife 43, watermark 2, Centennial. Ex-Barkhausen. $2,500

**Lot 357: Unused**

1874 Plimpton issue. 3¢ green on blue, die 3 (U170), size 5, knife 50, watermark 5, printed return address. $2,200

**Lot 358: Used**

1874 Plimpton issue. 3¢ green on fawn, die 3 (U171), size 5, knife 50, watermark 5, with "Guthrie Center, Iowa" postmark. $1,050

**Lot 366: Unused**

1874 Plimpton issue. 5¢ blue on cream, die 2 (U178A), size 7, knife 34, watermark 2. $600

**Lot 388: Unused**

1874 Plimpton issue. 7¢ vermilion on amber (U186), size 3, knife 41, watermark 2, round gum, Centennial. Ex-Barkhausen. $575

**Lot 446: Unused**

1875 Centennial issue. 3¢ red on white, die 2 (U220), size 4½, knife 44, watermark 2. Ex-Barkhausen. $6,500

**Lot 631: Unused**

Reay War Department issue. 3¢ dark red on amber (UO21). Size 3, knife 29, watermark 2. $4,000

The most notable items in Part II:

**Lot 117: Essays**

2¢ Columbian envelope essays (Thorp 110a-113c). Collection of 14 different complete envelopes, variety of colors, dies, papers and sizes, a few with manuscript numbers. $900

**Lot 244: Used**

1860 Star die. 3¢ red on white, buff, star die entires (U26, U27). $260

**Lot 258: Used**

1860 Star die. 3¢+1¢ red and blue on buff, combination Star die entire (U29). Blue Nov. 29, 1862 "Chicago, Ill." duplex postmark on 7-line embossed corner card. $400

**Lot 261: Used**

1860 Star die. 6¢ red on buff (U31), size 7, knife 3. Grid cancel "Oxford, N.Y." postmark. $700

**Lot 346: Unused**

1870 Reay issue. 3¢ brown on white, error of color (Thorp 259A). Size 3, knife 28, watermark 2. $270

**Lot 588: Unused**

1882-86 issues. 2¢ red on amber, round "O" (U248). Size 3, knife 48. Wells Fargo & Co. frank, type J. $290

**Lot 714: Used**

Official envelope. 6¢ red War Department on white (UO56). Size 8, knife 52, watermark 4, square gum. $900

**Lot 896: Unused**

Entires with advertising collars. George F. Nesbitt and Co. New York type 1 advertising collars on 3¢ pink on white, buff entires (U58, U59). $280

**Lot 1003: Used**

Wells, Fargo & Co., red frank on 10¢ green on buff, Star die entire (U33). Tied by blue target matching "CARSON CITY U.T." postmark and light blue oval "W.F. & CO. ANRORA" (Nev.) cancel. Pasteup with overall multicolor flag patriotic, with 10¢ green, type V (35), sheet centerline at left, tiny nick upper left. Tied by blue target, "Carson City, U.T." postmark. $375

Part III from the collection consisted of large and wholesale lots.

## Robert W. Wiseman

The Robert W. Wiseman Collection of Confederate States of America was sold June 23, 1971, by Robert A. Siegel Auctions, 10 E. 52nd St., New York, N.Y.

The most notable items in this sale:

**Lot 249: Cover**

Postmasters' Provisionals. Danville, Va., 5-cent red on wove, cut to shape (21X1). Ex-Caspary. $800

**Lot 251: Cover**

Postmasters' Provisionals. 5¢ black on dark buff entire (21XU3). Clear "DANVILLE, VA." postmark to "PITTSYLVANIA C.H. Va." Signed "Costales." $625

**Lot 262: Mint**

Postmasters' Provisionals. Pleasant Shade, Va., 5¢ blue (67X1). Position 3, large margins. Signed "W.H. C(olson)." Ex-Lilly. $750

**Lot 269: Essay**

2¢, 5¢, 10¢ black essays on India, by A. Hoen and Co. of Richmond, Va. Mounted on cards. Ex-Dietz. $650

**Lot 338: Cover**

10¢ blue (10). Position 17, type I. Frame lines at left top and right and wide margins at bottom. Tied by "Milledgeville, Ga. Apr. 28" on envelope to Savannah, Ga. $750

**Lot 339: Cover**

10¢ blue (10). Positions 18, 19, types I, II, horizontal pair, combining both frame lines, wide margins at bottom. Tied by "Richmond, Va. Apr. 22, 1863." $800

**Lot 349: Cover**

10¢ blue (10). Position 34, type I, frame lines showing at top left and bottom, wide margins right. Tied by "Mobile, Ala., March 11, 1864" postmark to "MARIANNA, FLA." $400

**Lot 350: Cover**

10¢ greenish blue (10b). Position 35, type I, frame lines show right and bottom, wide margins other sides. Tied by bright red "Monterey, Ala." postmark on blue envelope to "JACKSON, ALA." $550

**Lot 351: Cover**

10¢ greenish blue (10b). Position 36, type I, full frame lines left top and bottom, parts of line at right. Tied by "Culpeper C.H., Va." on cover to "DANVILLE, VA." $400

**Lot 352: Cover**

10¢ blue (10). Horizontal pair, positions 37, 38, types 2, 1, frame lines at left top and bottom, wide margins right, except irregularly close but clear near top right. Tied by "MILLEDGE-VILLE, GA." postmark on official "State of Georgia, Adjutant & Inspector General's Office" envelope with a manuscript "Printed" to indicate it paid ten times the 2¢ printed matter rate. $1,350.

**Lot 355: Mint**

10¢ milky blue (10a). Horizontal strip of four, positions 43-46, type 2, large margins showing parts of frame lines at top and bottom, ample to large side margins. Original gum. $4,000

**Lot 366: Cover**

10¢ deep milky blue (10a). Position 63, type I, huge margins, including three complete frame lines. Tied by "Mobile, Ala., Aug. 10" postmark to Mississippi City, Miss. $750

**Lot 368: Cover**

10¢ milky blue (10a). Position 67, type II, huge margins with three and one-half full frame lines. Tied by "Mobile, Ala., May 8, 1863" postmark to "RICHMOND, VA." Ex-Brooks. $1,000

**Lot 379: Cover**

10¢ blue (10). Two singles, position 89, type II, position 81, type I, used on U.S. 3¢ entire (U26). Each with frame lines on three sides, small margin at top, tied by "Mobile, Ala., Aug. 31, 1863" postmark to "CEDAR SPRING, GA." $1,250

**Lot 384: Cover**

10¢ blue (10). Position 86, type I, frame lines show all four sides. Tied by part of light "Atlanta, Ga." postmark on cover to "FORT MORGAN, ALA." Bold "DUE 10" on the cover. $900

**Lot 385: Cover**

10¢ blue (10). Two singles, originally a pair, position 88, type II, position 87, type I. First with frame lines on three sides, the other with two sides, wide margins all around. Tied by "Mobile, Ala., Aug. 12, 1863" on cover to "CEDAR SPRING, GA." $775

**Lot 393: Cover**

10¢ milky blue (10a). Position 100, type II, frame lines show all four sides including right bottom corner. Tied by "Orange C.H., Va." postmark to "AUGUSTA, GA." $550

# George H. Worthington

Parts of the George H. Worthington Collection of U.S. stamps were sold Oct. 24-25, 1917, at the Collectors Club by Walter S. Scott, auctioneer, cataloged by J.C. Morgenthau & Co., 87 Nassau St., New York, N.Y.

The most notable items in the two sessions:

**Lot 3: Used**

U.S. Brattleboro Postmaster's Provisional 1846 4-cent buff (12). Lightly canceled, "PAID" in red. $575

**Lot 4: Mint**

U.S. New Haven Postmaster's Provisional envelope with 1845 5¢ red (15). Cut to shape and color faded. Rare. $255

**Lot 96: Mint**

U.S. 1893 Columbian 4¢ blue error (233a) block of four. Straight edge at top, original gum. Rare. $255

**Lot 135: Mint**

U.S. carrier official 1851 1¢ blue Franklin (8O1) horizontal pair. Slightly cut into at bottom, original gum. $300

**Lot 201: Cover**

U.S. Philadelphia carrier 1¢ vermilion (8L1) used on original but not canceled; outer line gone at right but large margins at left. Rare. $210

**Lot 206: Used**

U.S. Philadelphia carrier 1851 1¢ black (8L5). Used on small piece of original; red star cancellation. Rare. $220

**Lot 207: Cover**

U.S. Philadelphia carrier 1851 1¢ black (8L6). Printed on margin of 1851 1¢ blue used on original with strip of three 1851 1¢ blue, type II. Stamp with part of design of 1¢ at bottom. $210

**Lot 300: Cover**

Confederate States Athens 5¢ red (3) provisional issue. Lightly canceled. Used on cover from Athens to Macon. $575

**Lot 310: Cover**

Confederate States Autaugaville 5¢ black on white (12b) provisional. Entire envelope which bears cancellation, "Autauaville Ala. Nov. 21." Envelope creased and somewhat soiled. $325

**Lot 311: Used**

Confederate States Baton Rouge 2¢ green (13) provisional. Lightly canceled in black, "PAID," fine margins on all four sides. $500

**Lot 312: Mint**
Confederate States Baton Rouge 2¢ green error "McCormick" provisional (13a). Margins small but design intact except at bottom where it is slightly cut into. $525

**Lot 315: Cover**
Confederate States Beaumont 10¢ pink (18) provisional. Used on original. Stamp pen canceled and close at right. Envelope canceled "Beaumont Jul 7." $410

**Lot 344: Used**
Confederate States Goliad 10¢ gray (48) provisional. Lightly canceled in black. Fine margins on all four sides; slightly thin. $475

**Lot 345: Used**
Confederate States Goliad 10¢ dark blue (50) provisional. Lightly pen canceled, fine margins but face slightly rubbed. Stamp has been creased. $860

**Lot 346: Cover**
Confederate States Greenwood 10¢ black on gray-blue (53) provisional. Used on original, but stamp not canceled. Cover canceled "Greenwood Sept. 21." $810

**Lot 412: Mint**
Confederate States Victoria 5¢ red-brown on green (143) provisional, original gum. $850

**Lot 517: Cover**
U.S. Bakers City Express 2¢ pink (2217) local. Used on original from Cumberland, Md., to Cincinnati. Stamp not canceled and defective at top. $220

**Lot 529: Cover**
U.S. Berford 1849 10¢ puce (2230) local vertical pair and horizontal tete-beche pair. Used together on cover addressed to Valparaiso, Chile, and endorsed on back, "received Mar. 21, 1852." The stamps are not canceled. $370

**Lot 675: Used**
U.S. City Dispatch Post 2¢ pink (2422) local. Lightly canceled in black. $270

**Lot 676: Mint**
U.S. City Dispatch Post 3¢ black on white (2423) sheet of 42, original gum. $245

**Lot 830: Cover**
U.S. New York City Express 2¢ orange (2657) local. Used on original. Lightly canceled in red. $200

# Literature

## Ralph A. Kimble

The Ralph Archibald Kimble Philatelic Library was sold during three auctions (four sessions) by Sylvester Colby, Inc., 545 5th Ave., New York, N.Y. 10017, Dec. 19, 1953, Nov. 13, 1954 and June 24, 1955.

The most notable items in Sale I:

**Lot 30:**
J.W. Scott & Company's "Monthly Price List of Adhesive Stamps," February 1868 (9th edition). Single sheet 17 inches by 7½ inches with three columns. Few slight tears, some light age stains. Rare copy from the first 15 monthly editions. $125

**Lot 31:**
J.W. Scott & Company's "Monthly Price List of Adhesive Stamps," April 1868 (11th edition). Some tears and slight stains. $75

**Lot 44:**
Bacon, E.D., "Catalogue of the Philatelic Library of Earl of Crawford, K.T.," 1911 and 1926 supplement. Bound, red cloth, gilt, bookplate. $75

**Lot 86:**
"Philatelic Literature Society Journal," London, 1908-18 (44 numbers), complete 11 volumes. Cloth bound in five books with wrappers. Title and all plates, plus five supplements and two statutes. $82.50

**Lot 482:**
Bureau Issues Association's "U.S. Plate Number Check List From No. 1 to 21,999," complete with added lists, 500 pages. Buckram bound, one volume. Out of print. $57.50

**Lot 714:**
Woodward, A.M. Tracy, "Postage Stamps of Japan & Dependencies," Shanghai 1928, two volumes, 536 pages plus 243 full plates, some in watercolor. Handmade deckle-edged paper, padded, full leather gold binding. Wooden slip case with cloth binding. No. 38 of limited edition of 100 copies. Autographed. First time offered at auction. $270

**Lot 857:**
Howes, C.A., "Canada, Its Postage Stamps and Postal Stationery," 1911, 398 pages, 15 plates in front pocket. Bound, red cloth. $76

The most notable items in Sale II:

American Philatelic Society, "American Philatelist," 1886-1950, Volumes 1-63 complete, including all early official circulars, member lists, convention proceedings, index. All bound, matched blue library buckram, gold titles. Fifty-eight books. One of the three most valuable reference files in the world. $305

**Lot 149:**
"The Bureau Specialist," 1930-39, Volumes 1-10 complete. Cloth bound. $80

**Lot 227:**
"The Collectors Club Philatelist," New York City, 1922-40, Volumes 1-19. Complete, buckram binding, gold titles. The second of the three most valuable reference files in the world. $130

**Lot 614:**
"Mekeel's Weekly Stamp News," St. Louis, Mo., and Portland, Maine, 1891 to current. Volumes 1-55 (2,608 numbers), complete. Buckram bound in 50 books, black library buckram, gold titles. Volumes 1-3 rare. $210

**Lot 784:**
"Pat Paragraphs," Westfield, N.J., 1931-50, Nos. 1-54. Buckram binding, gold titles in six volumes. $135

The most notable items in Sale III:

**Lot 263:**
Chapman, "Eagle and Maximilian Stamps of Mexico," 1912, 149 pages plus 20 maps and two leaves. Signed copy No. 10 of only 65 printed. $45

**Lot 323:**
Nissen, Charles, "Plating Penny Black Postage Stamp of Great Britain 1840," 1922, 122 pages, illustrated (many added notes). Cloth binding with box, 40 photo plates. $70

**Lot 734:**
"Stanley Gibbons Monthly Journal," London, 1890-1913, Volumes 1-21 (252 numbers), complete Volumes 1-8 bound. Nine volumes three-fourths Morocco leather gilt plus three volumes publishers cloth. Ex-W.R. King Library. $47.50

**Lot 877:**
Col. E.H.R. Green auction catalogs, United States and foreign sales I-XXVIII, except Volume II. Twenty-two are priced. $80

**Lot 914:**
George Worthington auction catalog (Morgenthau, 1917-18), Parts I-VIII. All priced. $66

## Harry M. Konwiser

The Harry M. Konwiser Philatelic Library was sold during one auction by Sylvester Colby, Inc., 545 5th Ave., New York, N.Y. 10017, Oct. 26, 1953.

The most outstanding items in this sale:

**Lot 628:**
"Billig Handbooks." Volumes 1-16 including revisions 2, 3, 4. $47.50

**Lot 641:**
"Mekeel's Handbooks." Lot of 27 different between No. 2 and No. 45. $21

**Lot 649:**
"Stamp Specialist." Complete set of books Nos. 1-20. $41

**Lot 651:**
"Stamp Specialist." Set first through fourth series, 16 books. $20

**Lot 664:**
Earee, "Album Weeds," third edition. Two volumes. Cloth bound. $35

**Lot 667:**
Melville, Fred, "Phantom Philately" (1923), 204 pages (original edition). Cloth bound. $12

**Lot 670:**
Serrane, "Vade-Mecum du Specialiste," "Expert en Timbres-Poste," 1927-29. Two parts bound together. Cloth bound. $21

**Lot 702:**
Knapp, Edward S., "Philatelic Americana," Parts 1, 2, 3, illustrated (1941). $25

**Lot 709:**
Walcott, Col. George, "Civil War Patriotic Covers" (1934). Cloth bound. $16

**Lot 710:**
Walcott, Col. George, "Civil War Patriotic Covers" (1934). Cloth bound (same as previous lot). $16

**Lot 718:**
Jurgens, "Cape of Good Hope Handstruck Letter Stamps, 1792-1853," 141 pages. Cloth bound. $20

**Lot 720:**
Boggs, William, "Canada Postage Stamps." Two volumes, 761 pages, illustrated, wrappers. $19

**Lot 744:**
Boggs, William, "Postage Stamps and Postal History of Newfoundland," 1942, 186 pages. Bound. $14

**Lot 753:**
Ashbrook, "Handbook of the United States 1¢ Stamp, 1851-57," 1938. Two volumes. Bound. $31

**Lot 756:**
Brazer, "Essays of United States Adhesives Stamps," 1941, 236 pages. Bound. $16

**Lot 770:**
Johl, Max, "United States 20th Century Postage Stamps," Volume III, 286 pages. Signed copy, bound. $30

**Lot 832:**
Norona, "Cyclopedia of United States Postmarks and Postal History," 1933, Volume 1. $17.50

**Lot 841:**
Wiltsee, "Pioneer Miner and Pack Mule Express," 1931, 112 pages. Cloth bound. Map and illustrations of covers. $15.50

**Lot 856:**
"Pat Paragraphs," Westfield, N.J., 1933-51, Nos. 16-57. $17

**Lot 857:**
"Philatelic Gazette," New York City, 1910-18, Volumes 1-8. Bound singly. Rare. $42.50

**Lot 863:**
"Stamps," New York City, Volumes 1-26 (16 are complete). Lacks but 27 numbers. Unbound. $28

## John N. Luff

The John N. Luff Philatelic Library was sold during two auctions (three sessions) by Sylvester Colby, Inc., 17 E. 48th St., New York, N.Y. 10017, Feb. 12-13, 1970, and Oct. 13, 1970.

The most notable items in Sale I:

**Lot 201:**
"The American Heritage Series," Volume I, No. 1, September 1949, through Volume XX, 1969, complete. $395

**Lot 202:**
"American Philatelic Congress Books." Com-

plete set from Volume I through Volume XXXI-II. $225

**Lot 246:**
"Collectors Club Philatelist," Volume VII, No. 1 through Volume XXI, No. 4. Privately cloth bound in 15 volumes. Volume XXII (1943) through 1960 unbound. $190

**Lot 268:**
Perry, Elliot, "Pat Paragraphs." A complete set, Nos. 1-58. $275

**Lot 286:**
"Scott's Monthly Journal," Volume I, No. 1, March 1920, through Volume 1969, complete. $190

**Lot 288:**
"S.P.A. Journal," Volume I, No. 1, 1939, through Volume XXXI, August 1969. Includes the "Bulletin" which was the temporary organ of the Society of Philatelic Americans, January and February 1939. Similar to the Meyer holding. $175

**Lot 290:**
Lindquist, H.L., "Stamps." A nearly complete run of this magazine. Volume I, No. 1, 1932, to 1960 privately bound in two types of bindings. Last few years are unbound. $125

**Lot 328:**
"The Ashbrook Service." Set from the original mailing to subscribers. Photos suffer in transition; all important data is as originally issued. $275

**Lot 547:**
Ridgeway, R., "Color Standards and Color Nomenclature," 1912 edition. Cloth bound. $300

**Lot 618:**
"Gibbons Stamp Monthly," Volume I, No. 1, 1890, through Volume XX, No. 240, 1912. Privately bound in 20 volumes. $110

**Lot 662:**
Wilson, Sir John, "The Royal Philatelic Collection," in color. Original puffed Morocco leather edition. $150

The most notable items in Sale II:

**Lot 56:**
"Mekeel's Weekly Stamp News." Complete from Volume XXI through Volume LIII (1939). First five volumes are bound. Also includes over 30 different copies of "Mekeel's News and Trade Circular" starting in 1905, between Nos. 2 and 44. $150

**Lot 56A:**
"Mekeel's Weekly Stamp News." An almost complete run covering the various name changes of the publication from 1894 to the 1940s and 1950s. Many complete volumes bound. Early ones are a bit soiled. Others were bound recently. $165

**Lot 109:**
"Weekly Philatelic Gossip." A cartoon running from 1923 through 1939. $70

**Lot 119:**
"The Ashbrook Service." This is a photocopy set from the original. Photos suffer in transition. All important data is as originally issued. $100

**Lot 277:**
"The Works of Jean de Sperati," four parts. Latter two are supplements. Part III contains nine different examples of his work. $145

**Lot 580:**
"London Philatelist." Almost 300 different between No. 265 (1914) and No. 564 (1938). $150

**Lot 585:**
"Philatelic Journal of Great Britain." Almost 600 different between No. 277 (1914) and No. 789. $100

**Lot 628:**
Robertson, Alan, "Maritime Postal History of the British Isles." Three volumes complete with slip cases. $250

**Lot 657A:**
"British North American Topics." a run of 25 volumes, complete Volumes 1-25. $100

**Lot 827:**
"International Society for Japanese Philately," 1957-1969, nearly complete. $100

**Lot 875:**
Mirabaud and Reuterskiold, "The Postage Stamps of Switzerland, 1843-63," 1899 edition, 266 pages, plus 14 plates. Printed on handmade vellum paper specially prepared for this book. Only 500 copies printed (200 in French, 150 each in German and English). This is No. 77 of 150 English editions. Bound, gilt edge, spine worn. $300

**Lot 876:**
Mirabaud and Reuterskiold, "The Postage Stamps of Switzerland, 1843-63," 1899 edition, 266 pages, plus 14 plates. Copy No. 10 of 200 French editions. Bound, gilt edge. $225

## Philip H. Ward

The Philip H. Ward Philatelic Library was sold during three auctions (six sessions) by Sylvester Colby, Inc., 545 5th Ave., New York, N.Y. 10017, Nov. 27, 1965, June 18, 1966, and Aug. 24, 1967.

The most notable items in Sale I:

**Lot 19:**
"American Philatelic Congress Books," complete set, Nos. 1-30. $100

**Lot 59:**
"Collectors Club Philatelist," Volumes 1-23. Bound. $210

**Lot 60:**
"Collectors Club Philatelist," Volumes 18-34, bound, except 22 and 24; Volumes 35-37 not bound. $100

**Lot 131:**
Ashbrook Service, "Specialized Handbook on U.S.," complete file of this limited reference work with photographs. $475

**Lot 174:**
"Billig's Philatelic Handbooks," Volumes 1-25, complete. $110

**Lot 364:**
Chase-Cabeen, "The First Hundred Years of United States Territorial Postmarks, 1787-87." $105

**Lot 429:**
Ferrari, 14 sales by Broquelet and Gilbert, 1921-25. Complete and priced. $255

**Lot 436:**
Col. E.H.R. Green complete 29 sales, some priced. $110

**Lot 494:**
Sam Page, complete run of his sales, priced. $125

**Lot 525:**
Ridgeway, R., "Color Standards and Color Nomenclature," 1912. Cloth bound. Reference for standardizing colors. $180

**Lot 729:**
Wilson, Sir John, "The Royal Philatelic Collection," in color. Describes and illustrates the late king's collection, now known as the "Queen's Collection." $105

The most notable items in Sale II:

**Lot 34:**
"American Philatelist," a run between 1891 and 1963. Quite complete in the early issues, including some duplicates. $160

**Lot 39:**
"Collectors Club Philatelist," Volume 1922-1954, practically complete. $350

**Lot 60:**
"Postal Markings," Volume I, No. 1, through No. 135, nearly complete. $110

**Lot 474:**
Col. E.H.R. Green, complete 29 sales, some priced. $175

**Lot 553:**
Ridgeway, R., "Color Standards and Color Nomenclature," 1912. Cloth bound, reference for standardizing colors. Pristine and kept away from light for many years. $250

**Lot 862:**
Ward reference Leica color slides of many items from his holdings, totaling slides in a number of slide cases, as well as two new unused cases. $225

The most notable items in Sale III:

**Lot 41:**
"Collectors Club Philatelist," run of 190 different from Volume I No. 3, July 1922, through Volume 41 No. 6, November 1962. $125

**Lot 53:**
"Mekeel's," a group covering various name changes of the publication from 1894 through early 1946. Many complete volumes; about 11 bound. Soiled. $100

**Lots 131A, 131B:**
Ashbrook, S.B. A set of photographs from the "Service" illustrations, and "The Ashbrook Service," complete file for the seven years. Both $425

**Lot 204:**
"The Story of the Zeppelin Weltfahren," two volumes, as told by the albums containing spaces for cigarette cards (photographs). Complete. German text. $255

**Lot 270:**
"Jean Sperati: His Forgeries as Outlined in the British Philatelic Association." $130

**Lot 406:**
Ferrari. A group of 12 of the 14 auction catalogs. $100

**Lot 602:**
Nissen and McGowan, "Plating of the Penny Black 1840." Two volumes with 40 photo plates, 1922 edition. Cloth bound. $120

**Lot 698:**
Woodward, Tracey, "Postage Stamps of Japan and Dependencies," 1922, two volumes. Deckle-edged paper, padded, full leather binding. Wooden slip case with cloth binding. Autographed, 536 pages plus 243 plates. $300

# Copyrights

# 26

## General Information

On Jan. 1, 1978, a completely new copyright statute (title 17 of the United States Code) came into effect in the United States, superseding the Copyright Act of 1909, as amended, and making important changes in the U.S. copyright system. Some of the highlights of the new statute, compiled from circulars issued by the Copyright Office, are listed in this chapter.

### Single National System

Instead of the former dual system of protecting works under the common law before they were published and under the Federal statute after publication, the new law establishes a single system of statutory protection for all copyrightable works, whether published or unpublished.

### Duration Of Copyright

For works created (fixed in tangible form for the first time) after Jan. 1, 1978, the term of protection starts at the moment of creation and lasts for the author's life, plus an additional 50 years after the author's death. In the case of a "joint work prepared by two or more authors who did not work for hire," the term lasts for 50 years after the last surviving author's death.

For works made for hire, and for anonymous and pseudonymous works (unless the author's identity is revealed in Copyright Office records), the duration of copyright is 75 years from publication or 100 years from creation, whichever is shorter.

Works that had been created before the new copyright law came into effect but had neither been published nor registered for copyright before Jan. 1, 1978, have been automatically brought under the statute and are now given Federal copyright protection. The duration of copyright in these works is generally computed in the same way as for new works: the life-plus-50 or 75/100 year terms.

However, all works in this category are guaranteed at least 25 years of statutory protection.

The law specifies that in no case will copyright in a work of this sort expire before Dec. 31, 2002, and if the work is published before that date the term may be extended by another 25 years, through the end of 2027.

For works that had already secured statutory copyright protection before Jan. 1, 1978, the new law retains the old system for computing the duration of protection, but with some changes. The law provides for a first term of 28 years, measured from the date protection was originally secured by publication or registration, with the right to a renewal term of 47 years. Copyrights in their first term must still be renewed to receive the full new maximum term of 75 years, but copyrights in their second term between Dec. 31, 1976, and Dec. 31, 1977, were automatically extended up to the maximum of 75 years without the need for further renewal.

The new law provides that all terms of copyright will run through the end of the calendar year in which they would otherwise expire. This not only affects duration of copyrights, but also the time limits for renewal registrations.

This new Act does not restore copyright protection for any work that has gone into the public domain.

### Termination Of Transfers

Under the old law, after the first term of 28 years the renewal copyright reverted in certain situations to the author or other specified beneficiaries. The new law dropped the renewal feature except for works already in their first term of statutory protection when the new law took effect. Instead, for transfers of United States rights made by an author on or after Jan. 1, 1978, the new Act generally permits the author or certain heirs to terminate the transfer during a 5-year period beginning at the end of 35 years from the date of the grant, or if the grant covers the right of publication, 35 years from the date of publication or 40 years from the date of the grant, whichever is shorter. To terminate, a written notice must be served on the transferee within specified time limits.

For works under statutory copyright protection on Dec. 31, 1977, a similar right of termination is provided with respect to transfers covering the newly added years extending the previous maximum term of the copyright from 56 years to 75 years. Within certain time limits, an author or specified heirs of the author are generally entitled to file notice terminating the author's transfers covering any part of the period (usually 19 years) that has now been added to the end of the second term of copyright in a work.

## Works Of U.S. Government

The new law continues the prohibition against copyright in "publications of the United States Government" but clarifies its scope by defining works covered by the prohibition as those prepared by an officer or employee of the U.S. Government as part of that person's official duties.

## Fair Use

The new law adds a provision to the statute specifically recognizing the principle of "fair use" as a limitation on the exclusive rights of copyright owners, and indicates factors to be considered in determining whether particular uses fall within this category.

## Reproduction By Libraries

In addition to the provision for "fair use," the new law specifies circumstances under which the making or distribution of single copies of works by libraries and archives for noncommercial purposes do not constitute copyright infringement.

For additional information about reproduction of copyrighted works by librarians and educators, write to the Copyright Office and ask for Circular R21.

## Copyright Royalty Tribunal

The new law created a Copyright Royalty Tribunal whose purpose is to determine whether copyright royalty rates, in certain categories where such rates are established in the law, are reasonable and, if not, to adjust them; it also will in certain circumstances determine the distribution of those statutory royalty fees deposited with the Register of Copyrights.

## Notice Of Copyright

The old law required, as a mandatory condition of copyright protection, that the published copies of a work bear a copyright notice. The new enactment calls for a notice on published copies, but omission or errors will not immediately result in forfeiture of the copyright, and can be corrected within certain time limits. Innocent infringers misled by the omission or error will be shielded from liability.

## Deposit And Registration

As under the old law, registration is not a condition of copyright protection but is a prerequisite to an infringement suit. Subject to certain exceptions, the remedies of statutory damages and attorney's fees are not available for infringements occurring before registration. Copies or phonorecords of works published in the U.S. with notice of copyright that are not registered are required to be deposited for the collections of the Library of Congress, not as a condition of copyright protection, but under provisions of the law making the copyright owner subject to certain penalties for failure to deposit after a demand by the Register of Copyrights.

## Manufacturing Clause

The old law required that certain works be manufactured in the United States to have copyright protection here. The new Act will terminate this requirement completely after July 1, 1982. For the period between Jan. 1, 1978, and July 1, 1982, it makes several modifications that narrow the coverage of the manufacturing clause, permit the importation of 2,000 copies manufactured abroad instead of the previous limit of 1,500 copies, and equate manufacture in Canada with manufacture in the United States.

## Background

The effort that led to the general revision of the copyright law began in 1955 with a program that produced, under the supervision of the Copyright Office, a series of 35 extensive studies of major copyright problems. This was followed by a report of the Register of Copyrights on general revision in 1961, by the preparation in the Copyright Office of a preliminary proposed draft bill, and by a series of meetings with a Panel of Consultants consisting of copyright experts, the majority of them from outside the Government.

Following a supplementary report by the Register and a bill introduced in Congress primarily for consideration and comment, the first legislative hearings were held before a subcommittee of the House Judiciary Committee on the basis of a bill introduced in 1965. During the same year a companion bill was introduced in the Senate.

In 1967, after the subcommittee had held extensive hearings, the House of Representatives passed a revision bill whose major features were similar to the bill enacted in 1978. There followed another series of extensive hearings before a subcommittee of the Senate Judiciary Committee, but, owing chiefly to an extended impasse on the complex and controversial subject of cable television, the revision bill was prevented from reaching the Senate floor.

Indeed it was not until 1974 that the copyright revision bill was enacted by the Senate. However, that bill, although in its general terms the same as the measure approved by the House in 1967, was different in a number of particulars. In February 1976 the Senate again passed the bill in essentially the same form as the one it had previously passed.

Thereafter, the House, following further hearings and consideration by the Judiciary subcommittee, passed the bill on Sept. 22, 1976. There followed a meeting of a conference committee of the two Houses, which resolved the differences between the two bills and reported a single version that was enacted by each body. On Oct. 19, 1976, President Gerald R. Ford signed the bill which became Public Law 94-553.

# Registration Procedures

## Application Forms

The old application forms in use before 1978 are no longer acceptable for copyright registration. From now on you will need to submit your applications for copyright registration on entirely different forms.

Most applications will be submitted on one of the following five basic forms:

**Form TX:** for published and unpublished nondramatic literary works.

**Form PA:** for published and unpublished works of the performing arts (musical and dramatic works, pantomimes and choreographic works, motion pictures and other audiovisual works).

**Form VA:** for published and unpublished works of the visual arts (pictorial, graphic, and sculptural works).

**Form SR:** for claims to renewal copyright under the old law.

Three other forms are provided for special situations:

**Form CA:** for supplementary registration to correct or amplify information given in the Copyright Office record of an earlier registration.

**Form GR/CP:** an adjunct application to be used for registration of a group of contributions to periodicals.

**Form IS:** request for issuance of an import statement under the manufacturing provisions of the copyright law.

For more detailed information about all these forms, write to Copyright Office and ask for Circular R1c.

## Changes In Content

The new copyright statute (title 17 of the United States Code) contains a provision (section 409) setting forth in detail a number of items of information that applications for copyright registration are required to contain. The new application forms have been designed to comply with the requirements of section 409. Some of the information they call for is being required for the first time in copyright application forms.

## Changes In Format

The format of the new application forms has also been changed substantially:

**Old format:** The applications in use before 1978 consisted of two parts, both of which were completed by the applicant. The first part was the application proper. The second part, which called for the same information as the first, was issued as the certificate of registration after processing by the Copyright Office.

**New format:** The basic application form now consists of a single sheet, with spaces to be completed on the front and back. Detachable instructions are a part of the form. On the back of one page of instructions is a "Continuation Sheet" for use in those cases where it is necessary to provide more information than the spaces on the single sheet will hold. Applicants are no longer asked to fill out a duplicate form for use as the certificate of registration.

## Changes In Procedures

As part of the various changes in registration procedures, the Copyright Office has reorganized its internal methods for handling applications, including its system for issuing certificates of registration.

**Old procedure:** Under the system in effect before 1978, the Office: (1) examined the application proper; (2) examined the certificate portion of the form to make sure the information was the same as that on the application; (3) added the registration number to both the application and certificate portions of the form; (4) detached the certificate from the application proper, added the Copyright Office seal and signature of the Register of Copyrights; (5) mailed it to the applicant; (6) cataloged the registration from the application proper; and (7) filed the numbered application portion of the form as the Office's official record of the registration.

**New procedure:** Under the system in effect since Jan. 1, 1978, the Office: (1) examines the application (no longer in duplicate); (2) adds the registration number and effective date of registration to the application; (3) catalogs the registration from the application; (4) reproduces (by photocopying process) the application on a preprinted certificate form already containing the signature of the Register; (5) embosses the official seal; (6) mails the certificate (the certified photocopy of the application) to the applicant; and (7) files the numbered application as the Office's official record of the registration.

**What these procedural changes mean:**

It was possible to redesign the application forms without the various problems of having to accommodate the certificate portion as part of the "package";

You are spared the burden of completing the certificate portion of the form;

The Copyright Office is spared the burden of examining the certificate portion and of making sure that it contains the same information as the application;

Since the certificate is a photocopy of the application, the statutory requirement that the "certificate shall contain the information given in the application" will be met in all cases.

The registration is cataloged before the certificate is mailed. This added step necessarily adds to the time between receipt of the application and mailing of the certificate. We hope that the other savings in the procedure will reduce the overall time lag, but there will be some delay.

## Choose Appropriate Form

Most works will fall naturally into one of the first four main classes of copyrightable material. If your work contains copyrightable material falling into two or more classes, choose the one class that is most appropriate for the work as a whole. As a rule, the type of material which predominates in the work should determine the class. Exception: A sound recording must be registered on Form SR.

Form SR may be used, in certain cases, to register both a sound recording and the underlying musical, literary, or dramatic work embodied in the phonorecord. If a literary work or work of the performing arts is being registered, and not the recording of the sounds, Form TX or Form PA respectively should be used, even if the deposit is a phonorecord (disc or tape).

## Use Only Official Form

The Copyright Office stores applications for the duration of the newly extended copyright term, so the application forms must meet archival standards. Because photographic reproductions of these forms may not be of archival quality, applications should only be submitted on the forms printed and issued by the Copyright Office. Application forms are available either with or without the instructions attached.

## Use Ink Pen Or Typewriter

After registration is completed, the application form becomes a part of the official records of the Copyright Office. It should, therefore, be legibly printed in ink or typewritten. Carbons of applications or applications completed in pencil are not acceptable, because they may smear and, in time, become illegible.

## Sending Material

It is important that the application, fee, and complete deposit all be sent together in the same envelope or package. A deposit is not required with Form RE.

## Copyright Fees

When the new law became effective, the entire Copyright Office fee schedule changed. Existing fees were increased and fees for several new services were established. All remittances are to be made in the form of a check, money order or bank draft and made payable to Register of Copyrights.

The Copyright Office cannot assume any responsibility for the loss of currency sent in payment of copyright fees. Anyone planning to submit material from outside the United States should arrange for remittances to be payable immediately in U.S. dollars. Remittance may be in the form of an International Money Order or bank draft. Checks drawn on foreign banks cannot be accepted.

## Registration

The following fees include a certificate bearing the Copyright Office seal.

**For Each Registration:** $10, including supplementary registration.

**Renewals:** $6. For the registration under Section 304(a) of a claim to renewal of a subsisting copyright in its first term.

## Document Recordation

**Basic Fee:** $10, including certification. For the recordation, under Section 205, of a transfer of copyright ownership or other document of six pages or less listing no more than one title.

**Additional Pages or Titles:** 50 cents for each page over six and each title over one.

## Certifications

**Additional Certificate:** $4 for certified copy of the record of registration.

**Other Certificate:** $4, including certifications of photocopies of Copyright Office records.

**Note:** Unless the number and year of registration are furnished to the Copyright Office, there is an additional charge of $10 for each hour or fraction required to locate the record.

## Searches

**Hourly Fee:** $10 for each hour or fraction spent by the staff of the Copyright Office in searching the official records and for the making and reporting of a search.

**Note:** Searches are not made (and are not necessary under the new copyright law) to determine whether a similar work has already been copyrighted.

## Phonorecords Intention

**Fee:** $6 for the filing, under Section 115(b) of a notice of intention to make phonorecords.

## Import Statements

**Fee:** $3 for the issuance under Section 601, or an import statement.

## Receipts For Deposits

**Fee:** $2 for the issuance under Section 407, of a receipt for deposit. This receipt is not available for deposits received for copyright registration. The certificate of registration will include the dates of receipt of deposit.

## Other Fee Provisions

Section 708 contains certain other fee provisions needed because of requirements or services established under the new law. Subsection (a) (11) of Section 708 also authorizes the Register to fix additional fees, on the "basis to the cost of providing the service," for any other special service requiring a substantial amount of time or expense.

If in doubt on any subject, write to the Copyright Office, Library of Congress, Washington, D.C. 20559.

## Deposit And Registration

**Separate Requirements For Deposit and Registration:** The new copyright law makes some important changes in the requirements for deposit and registration in the Copyright Office. The old law combined deposit and registration into a single requirement. In contrast, the new statute regards deposit of copies or phonorecords for the Library of Congress, and deposits of copies or phonorecords for purposes of making a copyright registration, as two separate acts.

**Deposit For The Library Of Congress:** The new law establishes a mandatory deposit requirement for works published with notice of copyright in the United States. In general, the owner of copyright, or the owner of the right of first publication in the work, has a legal obligation to deposit, in the Copyright Office, within certain time limits, two copies (or, in the case of sound recordings, two phonorecords) for the use of the Library of Congress.

Failure to make the deposit can give rise to fines and other penalties, but it does not affect copyright protection. The Copyright Office has issued regulations exempting certain categories of works entirely from the mandatory deposit requirements, and reducing the obligation for certain other categories.

**Deposit For Copyright Registration:** Copyright registration under the new law is generally voluntary rather than mandatory, although copyright owners are required to register their claims in order to obtain certain rights and remedies. Registration for both published and unpublished works can be made at any time during the copyright term by depositing the necessary number of copies or phonorecords (or, in some cases, identifying reproductions) with an application and fee. The Copyright Office has issued regulations specifying the deposit requirements for various categories of works.

**Use Of Mandatory Deposit To Satisfy Registration Requirements:** With respect to works published in the United States, the new law contains a special provision under which a single deposit can be made to satisfy both the deposit requirements for the Library and the registration requirements. The provision requires that, in order to have this dual effect, the copies or phonorecords must be "accompanied by the prescribed application and fee."

## Conditions: Combined Deposits

The Copyright Office has issued regulations establishing the conditions under which a single deposit of copies or phonorecords will satisfy the deposit requirements both for the Library of Congress and for copyright registration.

The copies or phonorecords must be accompanied either by an application for copyright registration or by "a clear written request that they be held for connection with a separately forwarded application."

To be effective as a substitute for an application, the "written request" must appear in a letter or similar document accompanying the deposit. A request or instructions appearing on the packaging, wrapping, or container for the deposit is not sufficient for this purpose.

The Copyright Office regulations make it clear that copies or phonorecords deposited without an application or written request "will not be connected with or held for receipt of separate applications." And, that they will not satisfy the deposit requirements for copyright registration. This means that, if you deposit copies or phonorecords in the Copyright Office without simultaneously submitting an application or written request, the deposit will be sent on to other units of the Library of Congress for its collections or other disposition. Then, if the sender wants to make copyright registration, it will be necessary to deposit additional copies or phonorecords with the application.

Moreover, when sending copies or phonorecords to the Copyright Office in reply to correspondence concerning a pending application, it is important to enclose, with the deposit, either a covering letter, referring to the pending case by number and date, or a copy of the Copyright Office's letter. Otherwise, the copies or phonorecords will be used as deposits for the Library of Congress and not for registration.

## To Insure Dual Use

If you have been sending deposits and applications to the Copyright Office from different points or at different times, the Copyright Office urges you to review your shipping and handling practices and to make the necessary changes as soon as possible.

For further information about the requirements and procedures for deposit and registration, write to the Copyright Office, Library of Congress, Washington, D.C. 20559.

Remember, copies or phonorecords sent to the Copyright Office must be accompanied by an application (or written request) if they are to be used for copyright registration.

# Best Edition Of Work

The Copyright Law requires that copies of phonorecords deposited in the Copyright Office be of the "best edition" of the work. The law states that "The 'best edition' of a work is the edition, published in the United States at any time before the date of deposit, that the Library of Congress determines to be most suitable for its purposes."

When two or more editions of the same version of a work have been published, the one of the highest quality is generally considered to be the best edition. In judging quality, the Library of Congress will adhere to the following criteria in all but exceptional circumstances.

Where differences between editions represent variations in copyrightable content, each edition is a separate version and "best edition" standards based on such differences do not apply. Each such version is a separate work for the purposes of the Copyright Law.

Following are lists of criteria to be applied in determining the best edition of each of several types of material. The criteria are listed in descending order of importance. In deciding between two editions, a criterion-by-criterion comparison should be made. The edition which first fails to satisfy a criterion is to be considered of inferior quality and will not be an acceptable deposit. For example, if a comparison is made between two hardbound editions of a book, one a trade edition printed on acid-free paper and the other a specially bound edition printed on average paper, the former will be the best edition because the type of paper is a more important criterion than the binding.

Under regulations of the Copyright Office, potential depositors may request authorization to deposit copies or phonorecords of other than the best edition of a specific work (e.g., a microform rather than a printed edition of a serial).

## Printed Textual Matter

A. Paper, Binding and Packaging:

1. Archival-quality rather than less-permanent paper.

2. Hard cover rather than soft cover.

3. Library binding rather than commercial binding.

4. Trade edition rather than book club edition.

5. Sewn rather than glue-only binding.

6. Sewn or glued rather than stapled or spiral-bound.

7. Stapled rather than spiral-bound or plastic-bound.

8. Bound rather than looseleaf, except when future looseleaf insertions are to be issued.

9. Slipcased rather than nonslipcased.

10. With protective folders rather than without (for broadsides).

11. Rolled rather than folded (for broadsides).

12. With protective coatings rather than without (except broadsides, which should not be coated).

B. Rarity:

1. Special limited edition having the greatest number of special features.

2. Other limited edition rather than trade edition.

3. Special binding rather than trade binding.

C. Illustrations:

1. Illustrated rather than unillustrated.

2. Illustrations in color rather than black and white.

D. Special Features:

1. With thumb notches or index tabs rather than without.

2. With aids to use such as overlays and magnifiers rather than without.

E. Size:

1. Larger rather than smaller sizes. (Except that large-type editions for the partially sighted

are not required in place of editions employing type of more conventional size.)

## Photographs

A. Size and finish, in descending order of preference:

1. The most widely distributed edition.

2. 8 by 10-inch glossy print.

3. Other size or finish.

B. Unmounted rather than mounted.

C. Archival-quality rather than less-permanent paper stock or printing process.

## Other Graphic Matter

A. Paper and Printing:

1. Archival quality rather than less-permanent paper.

2. Color rather than black and white.

B. Size and Content:

1. Larger rather than smaller size.

2. In the case of cartographic works, editions with the greatest amount of information rather than those with less details.

C. Rarity:

1. The most widely distributed edition rather than one of limited distribution.

2. In the case of a work published only in a limited, numbered edition, one copy outside the numbered series but otherwise identical.

3. A photographic reproduction of the original, by special arrangement only.

D. Text and Other Materials:

1. Works with annotations, accompanying tabular or textual matter, or other interpretative aids rather than those without them.

E. Binding and Packaging:

1. Bound rather than unbound.

2. If editions have different binding, apply the criteria in A.2-A.7 under Printed Textual Matter.

3. Rolled rather than folded.

4. With protective coatings rather than without.

## Phonorecords

A. Disc rather than tape.

B. With special enclosures rather than without.

C. Open-reel rather than cartridge.

D. Cartridge rather than cassette.

E. Quadraphonic rather than stereophonic.

F. True stereophonic rather than monaural.

G. Monaural rather than electronically rechanneled stero.

## Microforms

A. Related Materials:

1. With indexes, study guides, or other printed matter rather than without.

B. Permanence and Appearance:

1. Silver halide rather than any other emulsion.

2. Positive rather than negative.

3. Color rather than black and white.

C. Format (newspapers and newspaper-formatted serials):

1. Reel microfilm rather than any other microform.

D. Format (all other materials):

1. Microfiche rather than reel microfilm.

2. Reel microfilm rather than microform cassettes.

3. Microfilm cassettes rather than micro-opaque prints.

E. Size

1. 35mm rather than 16mm.

## Works Existing In More Than One Medium

Editions are listed below in descending order of preference.

A. Newspapers, dissertations and theses, newspaper-formatted serials:

1. Microform.

2. Printed matter.

B. All other materials:

1. Printed matter.

2. Microform.

3. Phonorecord.

For further information on Copyright Office deposit regulations, write to the Register of Copyrights, Library of Congress, Washington, D.C. 20559.

# Registration for Periodicals

## Information About Authors Required By Law

The new copyright statute requires that all applications for copyright registration submitted after Jan. 1, 1978, include, "in the case of a work other than an anonymous or pseudonymous work, the name and nationality or domicile of the author or authors." Certain other information about the author is also required.

## Form TX For Periodicals

Periodicals, which used to be registered on Form B, are now registrable on a new application form, Form TX. Unlike the old Form B, Form TX calls for the name of the author or authors of the work being registered, and for other information about the authorship of the work.

## Authorship Of Periodicals

An issue of a periodical is considered a "collective work" under the copyright law. Typically, collective works incorporate two different sorts of materials:

**The collective work as a whole.** This includes the elements of compilation, revision, editing, arrangement, and similar authorship that went into putting the work into final form. It also includes any material in the work that was not written independently but was prepared by employees of the periodical publisher as contributions to the collective work. In the case of a periodical issue, the collective work as a whole is usually a "work made for hire," and the "author" is the "employer or other person for whom the work was prepared."

**Independent contributions.** Most periodicals contain individual, self-contained contributions that were written independently, not by employees of the periodical publisher. These contributions are considered to be separately copyrightable works, and the law treats them as different from the collective work in which they appear.

## Space 2 Of Form TX
## For Periodical Issue

**One "Author" Line Must be Completed**

If you are submitting an application for a periodical issue on Form TX, you will need to fill out at least one of the "author" lines in space 2. For registration purposes, it is sufficient for you to complete one line giving information about the author of the collective work as a whole. However, if you wish to, you may also give the names and other information concerning the authors of independently written contributions in the periodical issue — as long as the copyright claimant for the issue as a whole has acquired ownership of all rights originally belonging to each of the authors listed.

**Author of Collective Work as a Whole**

**Name of Author:** If, as is usually the case, the copyrightable authorship in the periodical issue as a whole was "made for hire," the employer or other person for whom the work was prepared should be identified as the "author" in the first line of space 2. The question concerning whether the work was made for hire should be checked "yes," and the blocks concerning birth and death, and anonymous or pseudonymous works, should be left blank.

**Citizenship or Domicile:** Either the citizenship or the domicile of the author should be given. The citizenship of corporations or other business entities organized under U.S. law may be given as "U.S.A."

**"Author of":** In the block headed "Author of" you should give a brief statement reflecting the authorship of the collective work as a whole. A general statement such as "Collective Work" is sufficient for this purpose.

**Author of Independent Contributions**

In addition to the author of the periodical issue as a whole, you may give information about the authors of each of the independent contributions to which the claimant named in space 4 has acquired all rights. This information is optional; in the case of collective works the Copyright Office does not require that all authors and contributions covered by the copyright claim be identified on the application. If you do list individual authors, use a separate line for each author; submit as many continuation sheets (Form TX/CON) as necessary.

As explained in the next paragraph, if your application covers the periodical issue as a whole, you should not list the author of an independent contribution in space 2 unless the claimant identified in space 4 is also the "copyright claimant" (the owner of all rights) in that contribution.

## How To Register A Separately Owned Contribution

Where the owner of copyright in a periodical issue as a whole has not obtained ownership of all rights initially belonging to the author of a particular contribution, it is not the "claimant" of copyright in that contribution. In order to make registration for the contribution in such a case, it is necessary to submit a separate application. The "claimant" identified in space 4 of that application should be the author of the contribution, or a person or organization that has obtained ownership of all of the rights in the contribution that the author originally owned.

## Other Types Of Collective Works

Although this information is aimed primarily at people submitting copyright applications for periodicals, the information applies also to other types of collective works, such as anthologies, collections of essays, and encyclopedias.

## Copyright Office Publications

Most government publications about copyright are available free or at a minimal cost. The Copyright Office distributes free of charge instructional circulars, selected reports on hearings and conferences, its annual report, a general guide to the new copyright law, studies on specific copyright issues, and copies of the law.

Other types of reports and records may be purchased from the Superintendent of Documents or the Library of Congress Photoduplication Service.

Specific instructions on how to order materials that are free of charge are as follows:

Address requests to Register of Copyrights, Library of Congress, Washington, D.C. 20559 and mention the circular number (if known) of the material wanted. Again, the following items are free.

Annual Report of the Register of Copyrights. Copies are available for the fiscal years beginning with 1962. Certain earlier reports also are available.

Before You Submit an Application for Registration of a Claim to Copyright — Circular R1F.

"Best Edition" of Published Copyrighted Works for the Collections of the Library of Congress — Circular R7b.

The Certification Space of the Application Form — Circular R1e.

Computing and Measuring Devices — Circular 33.

Copyright Fees Effective Jan. 1, 1978 — Circular R4.

Copyright Law of the United States of America (1909 Act) — Circular 91. Note: For a copy of the current copyright law please ask for P.L. 94-553.

Copyright Protection Not Available for Names, Titles, or Short Phrases — Circular R34.

Deposit of Copies or Phonorecords Without Accompanying Application or Written Request — Circular R7a.

Duration of Copyright Under the New Law — Circular R15a.

The Effective Date of Registration — Circular R8a.

The Effects of Not Replying — Circular R7c.

Extension of Copyright Terms — Circular R15t.

Highlights of the New Copyright Law — Circular R99.

How to Investigate the Copyright Status of a Work — Circular R22.

How to Open and Maintain a Deposit Account in the Copyright Office — Circular R5.

Ideas, Plans, Methods, or Systems — Circular 31.

International Copyright Conventions — Circular 38c.

International Copyright Relations of the United States — Circular R38a.

Limitations on the Information Furnished by the Copyright Office — Circular R1b.

New Classification System for Copyright Registrations — Circular R1c.

New Copyright Registration Procedures — Circular R1d.

Registration for Periodicals on Form TX — Circular R60a.

Renewal of Copyright — Circular R15.

Repeal of Notice of Use Requirement — Circular R51.

Reproduction of Copyrighted Works by Educators and Librarians — Circular R21.

Reproductions of Copyrighted Works for Blind and Physically Handicapped Individuals — Circular R63.

Requirements for Maintaining a Deposit Account in the Copyright Office — Circular 5a.

Special Library Postage Rate for Books Mailed to the Copyright Office — Circular R30.

Supplementary Copyright Registration — Circular R8.

Trademarks — Circular R13.

## Other Publications

The foregoing represents only a portion of the publications available from the Copyright Office, and only those that may be of value to stamp collectors and hobby writers. For a more complete listing of available material write to the Copyright Office, Library of Congress, Washington, D.C. 20559, and ask for Circular R2.

## Notice Of Copyright

When a work is published under the authority of the copyright owner, a notice of copyright should be placed on all publicly distributed copies and on all publicly distributed phonorecords of sound recordings. The notice is required even on works published outside of the United States.

The use of the copyright notice is the responsibility of the copyright owner and does not require advance permission from, or registration with, the Copyright Office.

The notice for visually perceptible copies should contain the following three elements:

1. The symbol © (the letter C in a circle), or the word "Copyright," or the abbreviation "Copr." and

2. The year of first publication of the work. In the case of compilations or derivative works incorporating previously published material, the year date of first publication of the compilation or derivative work is sufficient. The year date may be omitted where a pictorial, graphic, or sculptural work, with accompanying textual matter, if any, is reproduced in or on greeting cards, postcards, stationery, jewelry, dolls, toys, or any useful article: and

3. The name of the owner of the copyright in the work, or an abbreviation by which the name can be recognized, or a generally known alternative designation of the owner.

Example: © John Doe 1980

The "C in a circle" notice is required only on visually perceptible copies. Certain kinds of works, e.g., musical, dramatic, and literary works, may be fixed not in "copies" but by means of sound in an audio recording. Since audio recordings such as audio tapes and phonograph disks are "phonorecords" and not "copies," there is no requirement that the phonorecord bear a "C in a circle" notice to protect the underlying musical, dramatic, or literary work that is recorded.

The copyright notice for phonorecords of sound recordings has somewhat different requirements. The notice appearing on phonorecords should contain the following three elements:

1. The symbol © (the letter P in a circle); and

2. The year of first publication of the sound recording; and

3. The name of the owner of copyright in the sound recording, or an abbreviation by which the name can be recognized, or a generally known alternative designation of the owner. If the producer of the sound recording is named on the phonorecord labels or containers, and if no other name appears in conjunction with the notice, the producer's name shall be considered a part of the notice.

Example: © John Doe 1980

Note: Because of the problems that might result in some cases from the use of variant forms of the notice, any form of the notice other than the standard ones given here should not be used without first seeking legal advice.

## Position Of Notice

The notice should be affixed to copies or phonorecords of the work in such a manner and location as to "give reasonable notice of the claim of copyright." The notice on phonorecords may appear on the surface of the phonorecord or on the phonorecord label or container, provided the manner of placement and location gives reasonable notice of the claim. The three elements of the notice should ordinarily appear together on the copies or phonorecords. For further information about methods of affixation of the notice, write to the Copyright Office.

The copyright notice is not required on unpublished works. To avoid an inadvertent publication without notice, however, it may be advisable for the author or other owner of the copyright to affix notices to any copies or phonorecords which leave his or her control.

Unlike the law in effect before 1978, the new Copyright Act, in sections 405 and 406, provides procedures for correcting errors and omissions of the copyright notice on works published on or after Jan. 1, 1978.

In general, the omission or error does not automatically invalidate the copyright in a work if registration for the work has been made before or is made within five years after the publication without notice, and a reasonable effort is made to add the notice to all copies or phonorecords that are distributed to the public in the U.S. after the omission has been discovered.

Before 1978, the copyright law required, as a condition for copyright protection, that all copies published with the authorization of the copyright owner bear a proper notice. If a work was published under a copyright owner's authority before Jan. 1, 1978, without a proper copyright notice, all copyright protection for that work was permanently lost in the U.S. The new copyright law does not revive the copyright in those works.

## Notable Dates in American Copyright

**May 31, 1790** First copyright law enacted under the U.S. Constitution. Term of 14 years with privilege of renewal for 14 years. Books, maps, and charts protected. Copyright registration to be made in the U.S. District Court where the author or proprietor resided.

**June 9, 1790** First copyright entry: "The Philadelphia Spelling Book."

**April 29, 1802** Prints added to protected works.

**February 3, 1831** First general revision of the copyright law. Music added to protected works. First term of copyright extended to 28 years with privilege of renewal for 14 years.

**August 18, 1856** Dramatic composition added to protected works.

**March 3, 1865** Photographs added to protected works.

**July 8, 1870** Second general revision of the copyright law. Copyright activities, including deposit and registration, centralized in the Library of Congress. Works of art added to protected works. Translations and dramatizations mentioned. Indexing of the record of registration begun.

**March 3, 1891** First U.S. copyright law authorizing establishment of copyright relations with foreign countries. Periodicals mentioned. Records of works registered, now called the Catalog of Copyright Entries, published in book form for the first time in July 1891.

**January 6, 1897** Music protected against unauthorized public performance.

**February 19, 1897** Copyright Office established as a separate department of the Library of Congress. Position of Register of Copyrights created.

**July 1, 1909** Effective date of third general revision of the copyright law, the basis of the present law. Admission of certain classes of unpublished works to copyright registration. Term of statutory protection for a work first copyrighted in published form measured from the date of publication rather than the date of recordation of the title of the work. Renewal term extended from 14 to 28 years.

**August 24, 1912** Motion pictures, previously registered as photographs, added to classes of protected works.

**July 13, 1914** President proclaims U.S. adherence to Buenos Aires Copyright Convention of 1910, establishing convention protection between the United States and certain Latin American nations.

**July 1, 1940** Effective date of transfer of jurisdiction for the registration of commercial prints and labels from the Patent Office to the Register of Copyrights.

**July 30, 1947** Copyright law codified into positive law as Title 17 of the U.S. Code.

**January 1, 1953** Recording and performing rights extended to nondramatic literary works.

**September 16, 1955** Effective date of the coming into force in the United States of the Universal Copyright Convention as signed at Geneva, Switzerland, on Sept. 6, 1952, which had been proclaimed by the President, and related changes in Title 17 of the U.S. Code.

**September 19, 1962** First of nine special acts extending terms of subsisting renewal copyrights pending Congressional action on general copyright law revision.

**February 15, 1972** Effective date of act extending limited copyright protection to sound recordings fixed and first published on or after this date.

**March 10, 1974** United States becomes the eighth member of the Convention for the Protection of Producers of Phonograms Against Unauthorized Duplication of Their Phonograms which came into force on April 18, 1973.

**July 10, 1974** United States becomes a member of the Universal Copyright Convention as revised at Paris, France, on July 24, 1971.

**December 31, 1974** Ninth in the series of legislative enactments extending all subsisting copyrights in their second term through Dec. 31, 1976.

**October 19, 1976** Fourth general revision of the copyright law signed by the President.

**January 1, 1978** Effective date of the new copyright law.

## Registers of Copyrights

| | |
|---|---|
| Thorvald Solberg, Register | 1897-1930 |
| William L. Brown, Acting Register | 1930-1934 |
| Register | 1934-1936 |
| Clement L. Bouve, Register | 1936-1943 |
| Richard C. Dewolfe, Acting Register | 1944-1945 |
| Sam Bass Warner, Register | 1945-1951 |
| Arthur Fisher, Acting Register | 1951 |
| Register | 1951-1960 |
| Abraham L. Kaminstein, Register | 1960-1971 |
| George D. Cary, Register | 1971-1973 |
| Abe A. Goldman, Acting Register | 1973 |
| Barbara Ringer, Register | 1973 to the present |

## Limitations On Information Furnished By the Copyright Office

The Copyright Office is primarily an office of record: a place where claims to copyright are registered when the claimant has complied with the requirements of the copyright law. We are glad to furnish information about the methods of securing copyright and the procedures for making registration, to explain the operations and practices of the Copyright Office, and to report on facts found in the public records of the Office. However, the Regulations of the Copyright Office (Code of Federal Regulations, Title 37, Chapter II) prohibit us from giving legal advice or opinions.

**The Copyright Office cannot do any of the following things:**

Comment upon the merits, copyright status, or ownership of particular works, or upon the extent of protection afforded to particular works by the copyright law;

Compare for similarities copies of works deposited for registration or give opinions on the validity of claims;

Advise on questions of possible copyright infringement or prosecution of copyright violations;

Draft or interpret contract terms;

Enforce contracts, collect royalties, or recover manuscripts;

Recommend particular publishers, agents, lawyers, "song service," and the like;

Help in getting a work published, recorded, or performed;

Advise on common law or State literary property law;

Interpret or advise with respect to foreign laws and court decisions.

Many requests for assistance require professional legal advice, frequently that of a copyright expert. However, even though the Copyright Office cannot furnish services of this kind, its policy is to be helpful in supplying the information and services it is authorized to provide.

# Famed Philatelists

# 27

# Personalities of the Past

Over the years countless men and women have contributed immeasurably to philately, helping to make it the great hobby it is today, enjoyed by millions throughout the world. The following list of famed philatelic personalities does not include any living person.

## -A-

### Ernest R. Ackerman
### (1863-1931) New Jersey

Congressman from New Jersey, he was serving his 14th term in the House of Representatives at the time of his death and was credited with bringing about much favorable action on legislation of benefit to stamp collectors. His collections included outstanding presentations of U.S. Departmentals on cover, U.S. Proofs and 20th century issues. A collector from boyhood, he recalled late in his life that during an 1883 visit to the national capital he purchased the reissues of the 1869 pictorials, using them on covers addressed to himself.

### William L. Alexander
### (1903-1979) Arizona

Founder of the Western Postal History Museum and the Arizona Philatelic Rangers, William L. Alexander, Tucson, Ariz., was frequently recognized for his efforts in the development of a free philatelic education course for asthmatic and underprivileged children throughout the state of Arizona.

He moved to Tucson in 1959 after retirement from the Gulf Oil Co. He had moved at an early age to Pittsburgh, Pa., from Scotland. Auctions and other activities of the history museum and the Arizona Philatelic Rangers, which he headed, raised more than $100,000 for the National Foundation for Asthmatic Children. On his retirement as a director of the Western Postal History Museum in 1976 he was given the title of director emeritus.

In 1963, he was elected a member of the Arizona Philatelic Hall of Fame and presented a community service award in Tucson in 1969. In addition to his other philatelic associations, he held membership in the American Philatelic Society, the Society of Philatelic Americans, the Collectors Club of New York, the Phoenix Philatelic Association, in addition to the Tucson Stamp Club.

### Spencer Anderson
### (1907-1947) New York

One of New York's best-known stamp dealers during the 1930s and 1940s, working for the Reliant Stamp Company before going into business for himself. His sudden death during the Centenary Philatelic Exhibition (CIPEX) cast a shadow over that event.

### Frank Applegate
### (1879-1964) Oregon

Pioneer student of state revenue stamps, contributing many articles about them to the stamp papers and compiling some of the first catalogs and checklists of such material.

### Stanley B. Ashbrook
### (1882-1958) Kentucky

One of the most distinguished of American Philatelic scholars, famed for his monumental handbook on the 1-cent U.S. stamp of 1851-57 which brought him the Crawford Medal of the Royal Philatelic Society of London in 1937. However, he explored all aspects of the production and use of 19th century U.S. stamps and issues of the Confederate States, producing many articles for philatelic journals on the physical characteristics of stamps and the postal markings found on covers.

# -B-

### Sidney F. Barrett
### (1893-1958) New York

One of New York's leading professionals during the 1940s and 1950s. In the stamp trade for 49 years, he first worked for Eustace B. Power. He later joined Ed Stern as a proprietor of the Economist Stamp Company and opened his own shop in 1951.

### Ralph A. Barry
### (1891-1939) New York

Engineer whose articles on stamp collecting appearing in the New York Herald-Tribune after the 1929 stock market crash attracted favorable attention and led the newspaper's management to engage him to write a weekly column of philatelic news and comment.

### J. Murray Bartels
### (1872-1944) New York

In the collecting of U.S. embossed stamped envelopes the name of Bartels is as esteemed as that of Ashbrook, Chase and Luff to the collector of adhesives. A stamp dealer in Washington, D.C., and Boston before locating in New York, Mr. Bartels took a special interest in U.S. envelopes and postal cards and provided philately with much authoritative literature on this material, particularly after purchasing the comprehensive stock of cut squares and entires assembled by Victor Berthold. His shop in New York City was a species of training school in the stamp trade, for many of New York's leading dealers began their careers there. He contributed many articles to the stamp papers, many dealing with postal stationery, but others providing sound information on the stamps of the Canal Zone, Danish West Indies, Puerto Rico and New York Foreign Mail postal markings.

### C.W. Bedford
### (1884-1932) Ohio

A chemical engineer by profession, Mr. Bedford delighted in the search for plate varieties of U.S. stamps and shared his findings with fellow enthusiasts in the "Shift Hunter Letters" which appeared under his byline in philatelic periodicals during the 1920s and 1930s.

### Julian Blanchard, Ph.D.
### (1885-1967) New York

Doctor Blanchard, a physicist associated with the Bell Laboratories, was one of the founders of the Essay-Proof Society and produced many significant studies on the use of bank note vignettes on adhesive stamps.

### Clarence Wilson Brazer
### (1880-1956) New York

Doyen of specialists on proofs and essays, particularly those of the U.S. and Canada, he was responsible for much of the published literature on this material. He was founder and first president of the Essay-Proof Society.

### John J. Britt
### (1900-1980) New York and Florida

A lawyer by profession and for many years a member of the New York board conducting bar examinations, John J. Britt was the recipient of many philatelic awards during his early residency in New York state and in Florida in later years.

A past president of the Collectors Club of New York, he was the winner of its Lichtenstein award in 1961 for distinguished service to philately. Other honors included the Collectors Club medal and the Bohn award.

An accredited judge, he was internationally known as an exhibitor and won many high honors for his showing of airmails. He served as president of the Aero Philatelists and the Association for Stamp Exhibitions.

After locating in Florida, he was one of the founders of the Hollywood Stamp Club, one of the largest in the country, and also helped establish the School of Philately in that city. He was much in demand as a judge, speaker and master of ceremonies at stamp shows.

In 1974, the John J. Britt Philatelic Foundation was created as a trust to further philatelic knowledge and promote and encourage stamp collecting.

### William P. Brown
### (1842-1930) New York

Pioneer stamp dealer, his activity dated from about 1860 and continued until he closed his Nassau Street shop in New York City in 1920 and retired. Originally a dealer in coins and curios, he was inspired to begin selling stamps at an outdoor stand in City Hall Park, where he displayed stamps pinned to a board from which his customers could take those they wanted. The first of several price lists he published appeared in 1868. During his early years in the stamp trade Mr. Brown handled many adhesives which are rarities today, including a 2-cent Hawaii "Missionary" which he sold to Count Ferrari in Paris for $5!

### Emil Bruechig
### (1903-1947) New York

Alumnus of the Scott Stamp and Coin Company (where many stamp dealers of the 1920s and 1930s learned the ins and outs of the stamp trade) he enjoyed distinction as a specialist dealer in airpost material.

## Franklin R. Bruns Jr.
### (1912-1979) Washington D.C.

Supervisor and curator of the Smithsonian Institution's Division of Postal History, Franklin R. Bruns Jr. was also a nationally known philatelic writer. His journalistic career began in 1932 as stamp editor for the New York Sun. During the succeeding 40 years he developed his own nationally syndicated stamp and coin column. He was also the author of a number of philatelic books.

A native of New York City, he went to Washington in 1951 to assume the position of curator of the Smithsonian Institution's philatelic collection. He also served for a time as director of the Post Office Department's Division of Philately. In 1957, he was named to the original Citizens' Stamp Advisory Committee, and served as the initial curator of the Cardinal Spellman Philatelic Museum, Weston, Mass., serving from 1957 to 1962.

He was again appointed to the Citizens' Stamp Advisory Committee in 1971, and in 1972 returned to the Smithsonian as a research associate. He was elevated to the position of supervisor and curator of the Division of Postal History in 1977.

A guiding spirit in the formation of the American Philatelic Congress, he served as its president from 1944 to 1947, and editor of the organization's official organ, The Congress Books, from 1952 to 1955. He received the society's special service award in 1966. A member of a number of philatelic organizations, he served as a director of the Society of Philatelic Americans and the American Academy of Philately. He also served on the steering committee of INTERPHIL '76.

## Gerald H. Burgess
### (1881-1938) Minnesota

Organizer of a course in stamp collecting at the University of Minnesota in the middle 1930s which is identified as the first such course for which college credit was given in an American educational institution.

## George E. Burghard
### (1874-1963) New York

Specialist in the stamps of Hong Kong and Switzerland, he made pioneer broadcasts on stamp collecting from New York radio stations in the 1920s.

## Al Burns
### (1892-1948) Oregon

Best known as editor of Weekly Philatelic Gossip from 1927 to 1940 and of Western Stamp Collector from 1942 to 1948. While associated with the Rotnem Stamp Company in Minneapolis he was involved in the compilation of its precancel catalogs and during his years as editor of Gossip he was very much involved in the editing and production of the Dworak Catalogue of Air Mail Covers.

## -C-
## Alfred H. Caspary
### (1878-1955) New York

Wall Street personality who quietly assembled a superlative collection of classic stamps of the world which realized a record $2,895,146 when dispersed in a series of 16 auction sales after its owner's passing. Mr. Caspary avoided the limelight, although he served as a judge at the International Exhibition in 1913 and only his most intimate friends knew of his interest in stamps or the extent of his holdings. Although he loaned fine items from his collections for Court of Honor showings in international exhibitions, such as CIPEX in 1947, he did so anonymously and Caspary rarities illustrated in Life magazine's philatelic issue of 1954 were identified simply as items from collections owned by "Pacificus."

## Carroll Chase, M.D.
### (1878-1960) New Hampshire

Because of Doctor Chase's intensive study of its production and use and his publication of his findings, the 3-cent U.S. stamp of 1851-57 may be described accurately as the United States postal adhesive which has given more solid pleasure to serious philatelists than any other. Beginning his studies of this first U.S. 3¢ stamp early in the century, he assembled thousands of copies and devoted many hours to their study. His initial monograph, published by the American Philatelic Society in 1909, reported his first efforts to plate the issue. Eventually he was able to complete this plating and his handbook detailing this work received the Crawford medal of the Royal Philatelic Society of London in 1930.

Doctor Chase, who was a pioneer in radium therapy, lived in France for many years and produced monographs on French stamps and the postal markings of French railroads. Returning to this country just before World War II he took up the study of the territorial postmarks of the United States, collaborating with Richard McP. Cabeen in a series of articles in the American Philatelist which were published as a handbook in 1953.

## James M. Chemi
### (1912-1976) Arizona

A professional newspaperman by vocation, James M. Chemi became the first full-time paid editor of the American Philatelist when the official publication of the American Philatelic Society was put on a full time basis in 1965. He began his professional career with the Philadelphia Inquirer in 1934 and during World War II he served in the European Theatre of Operations. For 11 years following the end of that conflict he was on the staff of the Kansas City Star, joining the Phoenix Gazette as sports make-up editor in 1957. When David Lidman relinquished the editorship of the American Philatelist in

1960, Mr. Chemi took over that post on a part-time basis, and five years later became the first full-time editor.

He was the recipient of the John N. Luff award and was elected a member of the Arizona State Philatelic Hall of Fame, serving two terms as president of the Phoenix Philatelic Association. A founding member and trustee of the American Philatelic Research Library, he was also serving as president of the APS Writers Unit No. 30 at the time of his death. He was an accredited judge in the categories of Great Britain and Colonies, France, British North America, Topicals, General and Literature.

In 1960, he organized the first Arizona Philatelic Workshop and helped to reactivate the Arizona Federation of Stamp Clubs in 1969. He was an avid supporter of juniors in philately and along with his other activities compiled two philatelic columns each week for the nonphilatelic press, appearing in Phoenix newspapers.

### Hugh M. Clark
### (1886-1956) New York

Editor of the Scott Catalogue from 1936 to 1946, he was intimately involved in its production for a dozen years before that. A young stamp dealer in Chicago during the early years of the century, Mr. Clark joined the staff of the Scott Stamp and Coin Company in 1912 and became its proprietor in 1935. Trained in the fine art of philatelic catalog editorship by John N. Luff, he gradually relieved Mr. Luff of much of the routine work of producing the annual editions so that there were no problems when Mr. Luff died in 1938.

Mr. Clark's major contribution to the Scott Catalogue was the development of the new system of catalog numbers introduced in the 1940 edition. Under Mr. Clark's administration of the Scott organization, publication of the Scott Specialized U.S. Catalogue and the Scott Air Post Catalogue began and a variety of new albums were introduced. Failing health made it necessary for Mr. Clark to restrict his activities and in 1946 he sold Scott Publications, Inc., to Gordon Harmer, who was proprietor until its sale in 1960 to Esquire, Inc. Mr. Clark was active in organized philately and was a prime mover in the establishment of the Philatelic Foundation in the 1940s.

### Charles B. Corwin
### (— 1891) New York

One of the founders of the American Philatelic Association (now the American Philatelic Society) in 1886 and a leading spirit in the establishment of the Collectors Club in 1896, Mr. Corwin was one of the first collectors in this country to take watermark and perforation varieties seriously. He had the distinction of being the first collector in history to pay more than $1,000 for a single postage stamp when he bid $1,010 for the 2-cent British Guiana "Cottonreel"

of 1851 when the DeCoppet collection was dispersed at auction by John Walter Scott.

## -D-
### Louise Boyd Dale
### (1905-1967) New Jersey

First woman to be invited by the Philatelic Congress of Great Britain to sign its Roll of Distinguished Philatelists. Daughter of Alfred F. Lichtenstein, she inherited her father's feeling for stamps and mastered the fine art of philately under his tutelage. Chairman of the Philatelic Foundation, she headed its Expert Committee for many years. She was the first woman to serve as a member of the jury at an international philatelic exhibition at FIPEX in 1956.

### Hiram E. Deats
### (1870-1963) New Jersey

Last survivor of the group which organized the American Philatelic Association (now the American Philatelic Society) Sept. 14, 1886. He began collecting about 1880 and selected the development of the U.S. postal service as the subject for his graduation thesis at Princeton University. His purchase of U.S. Treasury Department waste paper in the 1890s put him in possession of information on the production of U.S. Revenue stamps which he used in the writing of what is known as the Boston Revenue Book. He is also famous in philately as the discoverer of the unique Boscawen, N.H., Postmasters' Provisional stamp of 1845.

### August Dietz Sr.
### (1870-1963) Virginia

As the doyen of specialists in the stamps and postal history of the Confederate States of America he was known affectionately as "The General" by members of the Confederate Stamp Alliance, the organization of collectors of Confederate States material in whose formation he played an active role. His Postal Service of the Confederate States of America, published in 1929, is an established reference book and editions of his Confederate Catalogue and Handbook, which began appearing in 1936, are an invaluable source of information.

"General" Dietz, who came to this country from Germany as a young man, was a skilled lithographer and printer, heading a publishing firm in Richmond which was famous for the quality of books appearing with its imprint. Not only did it publish books written by its proprietor, but also a variety of books and monographs of interest to philatelists, as well as the monthly Stamp and Cover Collector's Review, edited by Mr. Dietz.

### A.V. Dworak
### (1879-1931) Kansas

Proprietor of a printing establishment which published a variety of philatelic literature, notably the periodical, Weekly Philatelic Gossip and the Dworak Catalogue of U.S. Air Mail Covers, Mr. Dworak was a skilled printer and a stamp collector. He launched a journal known as Philatelic Gossip in 1915, publishing it monthly until weekly publication began in 1923. The airmail cover catalog developed from information on the expanding U.S. airmail service appearing in the Weekly in the 1920s. After Mr. Dworak's death his widow, Dorothy E. Dworak, carried on the business and Philatelic Gossip, with Al Burns, Charles S. Thompson, Charless Hahn and Harry Weiss as editors. The publication appeared weekly until 1960.

# -H-

## Mannel Hahn
### (1895-1954) Illinois

Prolific contributor to the stamp papers in the 1930s and 1940s, he produced the chapter on postal markings in Stanley Ashbrook's handbook on the 1¢ U.S. 1851-57. Trained as an engineer, he was a flier during World War I, holding a pilot's license signed by Orville Wright. His publications include a handbook on U.S. postal markings of 1847-51 and the how-to-do-it book, So You're Collecting Stamps, published in 1940.

## Henry E. Harris
### (1902-1977) Massachusetts

Recognized by many as the "Grand Master of Philately," Henry E. Harris was the founder in 1916 of the H.E. Harris and Co., a business that developed into "The World's Largest Stamp Firm." He started the Boston-based company at the age of 14 years, carrying on the business from the family home, first in Washington and later in Boston. At the time he sold the business to General Mills in 1973, what had once been a one-man operation in a bedroom had a payroll of approximately 400 permanent employees.

In 1933, he conceived the idea of packaging stamps for sale in packets in chain and variety stores. The following year, he came up with the marketing coup of offering stamps as premiums, and in three years was credited with distributing more than four hundred million stamps.

A legal victory that prevented Canal Zone postal authorities from reprinting the Thatcher Bridge commemorative "error" brought him the Luff award from the American Philatelic Society in 1966. He also received a special citation in the same year from the Society of Philatelic Americans. In 1976 he was presented the American Stamp Dealers' Association Service to Philately award.

## Clarence W. Hennan, M.D.
### (1894-1955) Illinois

A collector since boyhood, this Chicago physician became intensely interested in U.S. precancels in the 1920s and wrote about them extensively. Later he became interested in the stamps of Curacao and produced a specialized catalog

and formed an important collection of Haiti. President of the American Philatelic Society from 1931 to 1933, he was active in the American Philatelic Congress, heading it in 1951.

## Arthur Hind
### (1856-1933) New York

Wealthy manufacturer of upholstery plush, he began the building of a fabulous collection of the world's postage stamps after buying his doctor's collection as an investment in 1891. He was a heavy buyer of rarities during the Ferrari sales in Paris in the 1930s, making headlines by paying the highest price ever paid for a single postage stamp when he acquired the unique 1¢ British Guiana provisional of 1856 for the equivalent of $34,000 in U.S. funds. This showpiece and other rarities from his albums were the cynosure of the 1926 International Philatelic Exhibition in New York City. After Mr. Hind's death the U.S. material in his collection realized $244,810 at auction sales in New York City. The balance of the collection, with the exception of the British Guiana rarity, was sold to a syndicate which realized the equivalent of $680,544 at a series of auction sales in London in 1934 and 1935.

# -J-

## Lucius J. Jackson
### (1915-1978) Vermont

A well-known authority in the field, Lucius J. Jackson had been owner and publisher of Stamp Wholesaler for more than 41 years at the time of his death in August 1978. Although probably best known for his interests in the publication field, other philatelic accomplishments include his role as a founder of the Cardinal Spellman Philatelic Museum Corporation. He was a member of the Collectors Club of New York and a life member of the American Stamp Dealers' Association.

Mr. Jackson took over publication of the Stamp Wholesaler, in the summer of 1937 from Ray D. Fisher. Established by Harold C. Theba, the first issue, designed to serve principally the wholesale stamp trade, had appeared in April a year earlier. It ceased publication after seven issues.

In his 25th anniversary issue, Jackson noted that Fisher had acquired the magazine from Theba for $5, but after five issues suspended publication and sold out to Jackson for the same price.

## Max G. Johl
### (1901-1957) Connecticut

Thread manufacturer whose specialized interest in U.S. postage stamps of the 20th century inspired many articles in the stamp papers about his discoveries with eventual publication of handbooks which provide authoritative material about those issues. The first of these handbooks, covering U.S. stamps from 1901 to 1922, was produced in collaboration with Beverly S. King. After Mr. King's death the series was continued by Mr. Johl and its fourth volume, covering commemoratives of the 1930s, received the Crawford medal in 1938. The first volume of the series was revised by Mr. Johl after modification of U.S. regulations restricting the picturing of postage stamps made possible publication of adequately illustrated philatelic reference works. In 1947 Mr. Johl authored a two-volume handbook on U.S. commemoratives which received the American Philatelic Society's Luff award in 1950.

### Albert I. Jones
### (— 1956) Indiana

Pioneer in the serious collecting of U.S. precancels whose checklist of known varieties printed in Mekeel's Weekly Stamp News in 1898 was one of the first such listings published.

# -K-
### Col. Ralph A. Kimble
### (1893-1974) Michigan

Editor of the American Philatelist from 1936 to 1951 with leave of absence during World War II for service in the U.S. Army. He was active in the philatelic life of Chicago during the 1920s, organizing some of the first radio broadcasts calculated to stimulate interest in stamp collecting. His writings include books on stamp collecting, stamps as an investment and U.S. commemoratives which were published by Grosset and Dunlap in the early 1930s. His impressive philatelic library, one of the largest ever formed by an individual, was dispersed by Sylvester Colby in a series of auction sales in the 1950s.

### Beverly S. King
### (1879-1935) New York

Engineer whose interest in 20th century U.S. stamps led to his collaboration with Max G. Johl in the writing of articles about these stamps. Mr. King's death in a traffic accident ended the collaboration, but Mr. Johl continued the articles under his own byline and they eventually appeared in a series of four handbooks published by H.L. Lindquist.

### Eugene Klein
### (1878-1944) Pennsylvania

Philadelphia professional whose activities included purchase of the unique sheet of the 24¢ U.S. airmail invert of 1918 from W.T. Robey of Washington, D.C., and its sale to Col. E.H.R. Green. He was founder and first president of the American Philatelic Congress, contributed many articles to the stamp papers and published the definitive handbook on the postal markings of U.S. inland waterways.

### Harry M. Konwiser
### (— 1960) New York

Best known for his U.S. Stampless Cover Catalogue, listing postal markings of the era before stamps came into use and prepayment of postage became mandatory. Student of postal history and a prolific writer for the stamp papers, his publications include monographs on Colonial postal service and the postal service of the Texas Republic and the American Stamp Collector's Dictionary.

# -L-
### Alfred F. Lichtenstein
### (1876-1947) New York

First president and later chairman of the board of the Ciba Corporation, manufacturer of dyestuffs and pharmaceuticals, Mr. Lichtenstein ranks as one of philately's greatest proponents and valued enthusiasts. Described as a philatelist in the fullest sense of the term, he collected stamps and devoted many hours to the study of them and the circumstances under which they were issued, developing an intimate knowledge of philatelic art which was unrivaled. Only the finest specimens satisfied him and his collections represented the superlative in condition.

His specialized presentations of Mauritius, British Guiana, Canada, the Cape of Good Hope, Switzerland, the United States and other countries received many awards in international competition. At the 1926 international show in New York City his Uruguay received the grand award as best in the show and his Newfoundland, Nova Scotia and Cape of Good Hope received gold medals.

He began collecting as a schoolboy in Brooklyn and had amassed impressive holdings in 1917 when he paid $445,000 for the outstanding collection formed by George Worthington, Cleveland industrialist, which had received major awards at the 1913 international exhibition in New York City. Mr. Lichtenstein took what he wanted from the Worthington collection and turned the balance over to J.C. Morgenthau for sale at auction.

Mr. Lichtenstein joined the Collectors Club in 1911 and was one of its most generous patrons, financing many of its projects, including the acquisition of its permanent home at 22 E. 35th St. in New York City. Just before his unexpected death in 1947 he was a prime mover in the establishment of the Philatelic Foundation. As a tribute to his standing as a philatelist, the Court of Honor at the Centenary International Philatelic Exhibition (CIPEX) was dedicated to Alfred F. Lichtenstein, and the Collectors Club gave his name to its annual award for distinguished contributions to philately by living philatelists.

### Harry L. Lindquist
### (1884-1978) New York City

Although Harry L. Lindquist is probably best known as the founder of Stamps magazine, he served in many capacities in the philatelic world, as well as in other fields in which he had an interest. As a youth, he developed a taste for many hobbies, especially stamp collecting. He also collected minerals, fossils and other natural history specimens that abounded in his home area of the Upper Peninsula of Michigan. At the age of 17 he was editor of the magazine of the American Society of Curio Collectors.

When the family moved to Chicago, he began meeting some of the famous philatelic personalities he had read about and the field of philately dominated his interests. He joined the Chicago Philatelic Society and later edited its monthly publication. Moving to New York, he began publishing Stamps magazine, the first issue appearing under date of Sept. 17, 1932.

Mr. Lindquist served on the first Citizens' Stamp Advisory Committee, and also served as president of the People to People Hobby Committee, Inc., appointed by President Eisenhower in 1956 to promote friendship and understanding between Americans and citizens of other lands.

A life member of the Collectors Club of New York, he served as the group's president 1927-30. He was an honorary member of many philatelic societies and held regular membership in others, including the American Philatelic Society and the Society of Philatelic Americans. Over the years he participated in more than 800 radio broadcasts, promoting the hobby, and he made 52 broadcasts over the Armed Forces Radio. In 1952, he founded the National Federation of Stamp Clubs, and was its active president for a number of years.

### George Ward Linn
### (1884-1966) Ohio

Philatelic publisher and editor, famed for the vigor of his writings. With decided opinions on most philatelic subjects, he voiced them in language which even those who disagreed with him admitted was never dull. Son of a country printer, Mr. Linn's first essays in stamp paper publishing were produced in his father's shop in connection with a stamp business he had started. Developing an interest in philatelic literature, Mr. Linn made a pioneer effort to launch a philatelic literature society in 1910 and held literature auctions in 1911 and 1912. When interest in Revolutionary issues of Mexico dominated the philatelic scene in the second decade of the century, Mr. Linn produced a monograph on the Coach Seal issues of Sonora which is still authoritative.

Linn's Stamp News, first published in Dayton, Ohio, and later in Columbus, Ohio, adopted a tabloid newspaper format when its office was moved to Sidney, Ohio, in 1943. Mr. Linn retired in 1965 and moved to Florida, Carl P. Rueth succeeding him as editor of the Weekly until 1969 when he sold the newspaper to Amos Press Inc. Mr. Linn's publishing efforts include a

checklist of philatelic publications in English in 1909, a catalog of the patriotic covers of World War II and a definitive monograph on the "Paid" markings found on the 3¢ U.S. 1851.

### Frances C. Locey, M.D.
### (— 1932) Virginia

Navy medical officer whose interest in the postal markings of naval establishment postal installations led to his creation of the system for classifying U.S. Navy Postmarks bearing his name.

### John N. Luff
### (1860-1938) New York

Probably the most distinguished of American philatelic scholars, whose competent editorship of the Scott Standard Postage Stamp Catalogue during the first three decades of the 20th century made it one of the world's most prestigious philatelic reference books. He was one of the first Americans invited to sign the Roll of Distinguished Philatelists when the Philatelic Congress of Great Britain created it in 1921.

Active in organized philately, Mr. Luff was president of the American Philatelic Society from 1907 to 1909 and served two terms as president of the Collectors Club, in whose formation in 1896 he had been a prime mover. He served as a judge at international exhibitions in Europe in the 1920s and was chairman of judges at the 1936 show in New York City.

The Luff Reference collection, which he formed to provide a basis for the listings in the Scott Catalogue during Mr. Luff's editorship, became an asset of the Philatelic Foundation when it was established after World War II. Mr. Luff was a prolific writer in the stamp papers and his major production in hard covers is the handbook on 19th century U.S. stamps, based on articles appearing under his byline in the American Journal of Philately at the turn of the century.

## -M-

### F. Van Dyk MacBride
### (1893-1961) New Jersey

Investment banker whose presentations of the U.S. 1869 series and 19th century Valentines received many awards in stamp shows, but he is best known in philately for his activity as a specialist in Confederate States material. He was a founder and past president of the Confederate Stamp Alliance and a prolific contributor to its journal. He joined the American Philatelic Society in 1908, after exhibiting as a 14-year-old collector at one of its conventions and in 1947 produced a monograph, which was published in the American Philatelist, on Barnabas Bates, leader of the campaign for postal service reform in this country which led to issue of the 5¢ and 10¢ U.S. stamps of 1847.

### Mrs. Catherine L. Manning
### (1881-1957) Washington, D.C.

Curator of the National Stamp Collection at the Smithsonian Institution in the national capital during the last two decades of her life. Beginning her business career soon after the turn of the century in John Bartels' stamp shop in Washington, she joined the Smithsonian staff on a temporary basis to mount stamps the U.S. Post Office had received from the Universal Postal Union and had turned over to the Smithsonian. Mrs. Manning spent the next forty years building the National Postage Stamp Collection.

### Dr. James J. Matejka Jr.
### (— 1979) Illinois

A general practitioner in Chicago for 39 years, Dr. James J. Matejka Jr. was a world-renowned philatelist and had a major role in the hobby as a collector, a judge and a commissioner for international exhibitions. Shortly before his death, he was honored by being asked to sign the Roll of Distinguished Philatelists at the Congress of the British Philatelic Federation, the highest honor in international philately.

He was a member of the Citizens' Stamp Advisory Committee for eight years. He served as U.S. commissioner to international shows in Belgium and Czechoslovakia, and as an international judge of philately in Taiwan, Berlin and England. His personal collections of Newfoundland Airmails, Czechoslovakia, United States and Austria were outstanding.

Among his numerous philatelic affiliations were: Society of Philatelic Americans (past president), American Philatelic Society, Royal Philatelic Society of London, Collectors Club of New York, Collectors Club of Chicago, charter member of the Cardinal Spellman Philatelic Museum. A member of the American Philatelic Congress, and past president of the American Air Mail Society, he was a co-founder and life member of COMPEX — Combined Philatelic Exhibition of Chicagoland.

### Charles Haviland Mekeel
### (1864-1921) Missouri

Dominant figure in American philately in the 1890s whose C.H. Mekeel Stamp and Publishing Company is said to have placed stamp collecting in this country on a dollar rather than a penny basis. The firm, established in 1890 with a capitalization of $100,000, carried on an aggressive trade in stamps, published three editions of a general catalog of stamps of the world and a variety of albums and became headquarters for Mexican stamps after the firm made a deal with a revolutionary government and acquired the holdings of Mexico's dead letter office. Acquisition of the fabulous Louisville find of St. Louis "Bears" was another of its coups.

Mr. Mekeel, who had published a stamp paper as a boy in Chicago in 1881, began publishing the American Journal of Philately in 1883 after moving to St. Louis, and published it monthly until 1895. In 1891 he launched Mekeel's Weekly Stamp News and in 1896 began publishing the Daily Stamp Item. Mr. Mekeel kept the daily coming out for a year, but confided to his friends that he was some $5,000 out of pocket as a result.

The Mekeel Company experienced financial difficulties in 1897 and in a reorganization Mr. Mekeel's brother, Isaac A. Mekeel took over the Weekly and published it as an in-depth journal. After Isaac's death in 1913, Charles E. Severn, Willard Otis Wylie and Charles Jewett organized the Severn-Wylie-Jewett Company to continue its publication. C.H. Mekeel left St. Louis after 1900 and located in Virginia where he launched and published the Albemarle Stamp Collector.

### William Claire Menninger, M.D.
### (1899-1967) Kansas

Probably the most distinguished of the many medical men who found stamp collecting a satisfying avocation. One of the country's leading psychiatrists, Dr. Menninger began collecting as a boy and never lost his enthusiasm for the hobby. He sought the stamps of all countries in postally used condition, stamps of the U.S. regularly used on cover and stamps with medical subjects.

### Walton I. Mitchell, M.D.
### (1878-1960) California

Though best known as editor of the Official Catalogue of U.S. Bureau Precancels, Dr. Mitchell was a distinguished student of postal stationery of the world, particularly postal cards and the Revenue stamps of Canada. A physician in practice in Kansas and Colorado before locating in California in the 1920s, Dr. Mitchell's studies made possible publication of the first catalog of Bureau Precancels in 1925 and he edited annual editions of the catalog until failing eyesight made it necessary for him to discontinue the activity in the late 1950s.

### Edwin Mueller
### (1891-1962) New York

A professional in Austria for many years, associated with the distinguished Otto Friedl and administrator of the impressive WIPA exhibition in Vienna in 1933, Mr. Mueller came to this country in 1938 and established the Mercury Stamp Company in New York City. His special field was 19th century Europe with emphasis on Austria and imperforate stamps. His published works include the monograph on Austrian postmarks which he published in Vienna in 1927, a bilingual specialized catalog on Austria, published in 1927, and a monograph on the prestamp postmarks of Austria which appeared in 1950.

## -N-
### Saul Newbury
### (— 1950) Illinois

Chicago department store executive who formed a collection of 19th century Brazil featuring the "Bull's-Eyes" of 1851 which earned many major awards in international competition. He later assembled the collection of 19th century U.S. which received the grand award at the Centenary International Philatelic Exhibition (CIPEX) in 1947.

## -O-
### Max Ohlman
### (1881-1957) New York

Nassau Street professional for many years, holding auction sales in which many collections were dispersed during the 1920s and 1930s. Franklin D. Roosevelt was one of his clients and while the late president was serving as New York's governor, Mr. Ohlman sponsored his application for membership in the American Philatelic Society.

### Ross O'Shaughenessy
### (— 1954) California

One of San Francisco's stamp dealers at the turn of the century and the only one to resume business after the 1906 earthquake and fire. A pioneer collector of Western Express covers and related material.

## -P-
### Elliott Perry
### (1884-1972) New Jersey

Inspired to take up stamp collecting by the appearance of the Columbian commemoratives in 1893, Mr. Perry spent his life in philatelic activity, functioning as a full time stamp dealer after 1915. While his most spectacular achievement was his successful plating of the 10¢ U.S. stamp of 1847, something Luff and other students had feared was impossible because of the dearth of material available for study, he made significant contributions to philatelic understanding of 19th century postage and revenue stamps and their use. Notable are his studies of the distribution of the 1847 stamps to post offices, the demonitization of the 1857 series in 1861, issues of Sanitary Fairs and U.S. Locals and Carrier stamps. He produced many articles for the stamp papers, using the pseudonym Christopher West on some of his contributions, and published a house organ, Pat Paragraphs, in which he recorded facts developed by his research.

### Thomas Doane Perry
### (1878-1958) New Jersey

Wood products engineer, playing a significant role in the development of the plywood industry,

Mr. Perry's philatelic interests centered on U.S. embossed stamp envelopes and he made signal contributions to the literature of envelope collecting.

### Sidney G. (Sid) Pietzsch
### (— 1978) Texas

A newspaperman by profession, the interests of Sidney G. (Sid) Pietzsch in philately carried him into extensive writings in the hobby, both for the philatelic and nonphilatelic press. He began his writing career as editor of the University of Texas humor magazine, later returning to his hometown of Beaumont, Tex., to work as a reporter and as city editor of the Beaumont Journal.

After serving in the Army during World War II as a public information officer, he returned to the newspaper business, joining the staff of the Dallas Morning News. He also served as administrative assistant to former Dallas Mayor and Congressman Earle Cabel, retiring in 1971.

For five years previous to his death, his writings for Linn's Stamp News included the popular feature Cinderellas, and compilation of the first Linn's Basic Knowledge For The Stamp Collector. He compiled a stamp column for the Dallas Morning News, along with other writings. He was a member of most major philatelic organizations as well as several local clubs.

### Bertram W. H. Poole
### (1880-1957) California

Emigrating to this country from England in 1900, Mr. Poole located in Los Angeles where he operated a stamp shop and found time to produce many articles on stamps and stamp collecting for the stamp papers. Many of these articles were published in some 30 pamphlet handbooks by Mekeel's Weekly Stamp News. He was one of the first professionals to call attention to the interest of subject matter (topical) collecting. Late in his life he assembled a Philosophy of Collecting presentation which was exhibited at the National Philatelic Museum in Philadelphia and was described in a handbook appearing with the museum's imprint.

### Eustace B. Power
### (1872-1939) New York

Professional who is said to have restored sanity to U.S. collecting by publication in the 1920s and 1930s of a series of Philatelic Horse Sense pamphlets in which he detailed a common-sense approach to the collecting of U.S. adhesives. Born in England, Mr. Power came to this country in the 1890s and was associated with J.C. Morgenthau in Chicago before coming to New York, where he managed the U.S. branch of Stanley Gibbons Ltd. of London for a time before going into business under his own name.

# -R-
## Joseph S. Rich
### (1860-1931) New York

A collector from the age of 16, Mr. Rich was a dominant figure in American philately for more than half a century. One of the proprietors of the Scott Stamp and Coin Company from 1895 to 1913 he was intimately involved in the production of the Scott Catalogue as it assumed stature as a major reference work. One of the founders of the Collectors Club, he was active in its affairs until his death. Mr. Rich had a special interest in U.S. Telegraph stamps and his 1897 monograph on them, revised by his son for publication by the Society of Philatelic Americans in 1946, is a standard reference book.

## Stephen G. Rich
### (1890-1958) New Jersey

A leading spirit in half a dozen philatelic organizations, a publisher and contributor to nearly all the stamp papers of his era, Stephen G. Rich is probably the best-known philatelic personality of the years before and after World War II. Son of a proprietor of the Scott Stamp and Coin Company, Mr. Rich grew up in a philatelic atmosphere and philatelic activity dominated his life. He was active in the American Philatelic Society, the Collectors Club, the Society of Philatelic Americans, the France and Colonies Philatelic Society, the Precancel Stamp Society and New Jersey stamp clubs. He published a dozen editions of the Mitchell-Hoover Bureau Precancel Catalogue and three editions of Harry Konwiser's Stampless Cover Catalogue, as well as the monthly Precancel Bee and Postal Markings journal. He was a prolific writer, his byline appearing in the stamp papers over articles dealing with almost every aspect of philatelic activity with special emphasis on his particular interests: the stamps of France, Poland's first adhesive and South African philately.

## Franklin Delano Roosevelt
### (1882-1945) New York

Because he was an enthusiastic collector and was always willing to talk about his interest in stamps and stamp collecting, Mr. Roosevelt is generally believed to have done more than anyone else to give the hobby of philately the prestige it enjoys in this country. No one could say that stamp collecting was a juvenile activity when the president of the United States let it be known that he regularly spent happy hours working with his stamp collections.

It was while he occupied the White House that federal statutes limiting the illustration of stamps were changed, making possible publication of more useful albums, catalogs and philatelic literature.

Mr. Roosevelt developed an interest in stamp collecting as a youngster and continued a collection formed by his mother. His enthusiasm for the hobby continued and by the time he was elected governor of New York his collection filled many volumes. Though he was interested in all stamps he had a special affection for the issues of Hong Kong, Haiti, Argentina, Venezuela and British colonies in the Caribbean.

Following his death his heirs decided to sell most of his collections and the property was appraised at $80,000 by the late George B. Sloane, Nassau Street professional. However, Mr. Roosevelt's stamps brought $221,000 when sold at auction in 1946. Certain collections which were retained by the late president's family are on exhibit in the Roosevelt Library in Hyde Park, New York.

# -S-
## Waller A. Sager
### (1929-1977) California

Leading spirit in the Collectors of Religion on Stamps Society (COROS) and editor of its journal, COROS Chronicle, for 23 years, his more significant contributions to the literature of topical collecting include monographs on stamps illustrating the life of Martin Luther, U.S. stamps with religious subjects and Christmas stamps.

## Nicolas Sanabria
### (1890-1945) New York

A native of Venezuela, Mr. Sanabria came to the United States in 1922 and went to work in Victor Weiskopf's stamp shop. In 1927 he went into business for himself, specializing in airmail material and launching the catalog of airpost stamps bearing his name.

## John Walter Scott
### (1842-1919) New York

Generally identified as the Father of American Philately, Mr. Scott came to this country in 1861, bringing with him a stamp collection he had assembled as a youth in England. Within a decade he was one of New York City's foremost stamp dealers, had issued the first of the detailed price lists which were to develop into the Scott Standard Postage Stamp Catalogue, had held the world's first auction sale of postage stamps, and had published the first of the more than 30 stamp albums bearing his imprint.

In 1886 he sold his prosperous business, including the right to use the Scott name, to George C. Calman and went back to England. Returning to the United States in a few years, Mr. Scott resumed activity as a stamp dealer where he was a dominant figure on the philatelic scene until his death in 1919. He was one of the founders of the Collectors Club in 1896 and at the time of his death was president of the American Philatelic Society.

## George I. Silberberg
### (1911-1982) New York

George I. Silberberg, founder of Philatelic Hobbies for the Wounded and chairman of Hobbies for All Ages, died in New York City, Feb.

14, 1982. His voluntary crusade to rebuild the spirits of those ill and confined grew out of a personal tragedy in 1942, when his legs were severely crushed in an accident.

Mr. Silberberg was a member of the American Philatelic Society, the Society of Philatelic Americans, the Bronx County Stamp Club, and the American Stamp Dealers' Association. He was also an honorary member of many school clubs which he visited on a trip around the world.

Retiring as an engineer in 1960, Mr. Silberberg continued as president of Philatelic Hobbies for the Wounded and chairman of Hobbies for all Ages. He also served as vice president of the Grand Street Boys' Foundation and vice president of the Grand Street Boys' Association (New York).

### James N. Sissons
### (1914-1980) Ontario, Canada

A leading Canadian philatelic authority, James Normart Sissons, was credited with having sponsored Canada's first postage stamp auction in 1946. He was president of J.N. Sissons Limited, a stamp auction firm in Toronto. He was the founding president of the Canadian Stamp Dealers' Association.

A native of Pennsylvania, Mr. Sissons went to Toronto as a child and entered law studies in Canada. His interest turned to stamps, however, and his philatelic career began before his law studies were completed. He was a leading auctioneer in Canada and was described by some as "the world's foremost authority on Canadian stamp collecting."

### Charles E. Severn
### (1872-1929) Illinois

A contributor to Mekeel's Weekly Stamp News from its beginning in 1891, Mr. Severn became proprietor of the periodical when the Mekeel organization was reorganized in 1897 and was its editor until he retired in 1926. He was one of the Americans invited to sign the Roll of Distinguished Philatelists when it was created in 1921 by the Philatelic Congress of Great Britain.

### George C. Slawson
### (1905-1969) Vermont

Student of stamps, postal stationery and postal history whose publications include the catalog of postal stationery of U.S. possessions brought out in 1958 by Van Dahl Publications, and Postal History of Vermont, appearing in 1969 with the imprint of the Collectors Club's Theodore E. Steinway Memorial Publications Fund.

### Hugh M. Southgate
### (1871-1940) Washington, D.C.

Most of what collectors know about the production of U.S. stamps during the 1920s and through the 1940s stems from Mr. Southgate's rapport with responsible personnel at the Bureau of Engraving and Printing during that period. A dedicated philatelist, trained as an engineer, Mr. Southgate enjoyed the friendship of Bureau personnel at a time when the introduction of the rotary press and other sophisticated equipment was revolutionizing U.S. stamp production. He was alert to every development there and communicated his observations to the philatelic world through articles in the stamp papers.

Mr. Southgate was a leading spirit in the organization of the Philatelic Plate Number Association in 1926 and four years later, when this organization expanded its activity to cover everything produced in the Bureau and assumed the style of Bureau Issues Association, Mr. Southgate was named president and held that office for a decade. His services to philately brought him the Washington Philatelic Society's Michael Eidsness award in 1939.

### Francis Cardinal Spellman
### (1889-1967) New York

A collector since boyhood in Massachusetts, His Eminence built an exceptional collection of mint U.S. singles and added Vatican City issues to his interests while stationed in Rome before returning to New England. In his numerous global travels as a bishop, archbishop and cardinal, he acquired collections from every corner of the earth.

Coming to New York, he led the campaign for the Al Smith stamp. When he was named a cardinal in 1946, he donated his entire collection to Regis College, where it first was housed in the college library. Subsequently, through a contribution by a personal friend and benefactor, a special building was designed to become the Cardinal Spellman Philatelic Museum, constructed on the campus.

His collection was first displayed at the 1947 CIPEX international stamp show at Grand Central Palace, New York. After that it was displayed at numerous international shows in Europe, Argentina, the Philippines and other nations.

### Theodore E. Steinway
### (1883-1957) New York

Member of the distinguished family of piano manufacturers, Mr. Steinway has been identified as the "Renaissance Man" of American philately because of the scope of his philatelic interests and enthusiasms. Though his collections of Hamburg and other German States and the "Sydney Views" of New South Wales demonstrated his scholarship adequately, he formed outstanding presentations of stamps with "on the nose" postmarks and stamps with musical subjects and ignored no aspect of philately.

Joining the Collectors Club in 1912, he was one of its most generous patrons, providing the funds for its purchase in 1922 of the outstanding philatelic library formed by Chief Justice Suppantschitsch. It was because of his interest in philatelic literature that the Collectors Club established the Theodore E. Steinway Memorial Publications Fund after his passing. He was a judge at many international exhibitions and was chairman of the jury at the Centenary International Exhibition (CIPEX) in 1947.

## Byron F. Stevens
### (1903-1970) Illinois

Student of the stamps of Mexico and a leading spirit in the formation in 1935 of the specialist organization now known as the Mexico-Elmhurst Philatelic Society, Inc.

## Kent B. Stiles
### (1887-1951) New York

American philately's most active publicist, producing regular columns of news and comment about stamp collecting for many years in popular periodicals such as American Boy, Youth's Companion and Boy's Life, producing a syndicated column appearing in many newspapers and serving as stamp news editor for the New York Times during the last two decades of his life. He was one of the editors of the Scott Monthly Journal from its beginnings in 1920, producing many features dealing with the stories suggested by stamp designs and the personalities portrayed on postal adhesives. His Stamps, An Outline of Philately, was published by Harpers in 1929 and his Geography and Stamps was brought out in 1932 by McGraw-Hill.

## David C. Stump
### (—1982) Pennsylvania

David C. Stump, Devon, Pa., a past president of the American Philatelic Congress, Inc., and a founder of the Perfins Club, died Jan. 5, 1982. Active for years in philatelic circles, he edited the Congress Book from 1964 through 1971 in addition to serving the APC Council.

Mr. Stump edited the Perfins Club Bulletin for 15 years, was the group's treasurer for 20 years, and served as president from 1976, resigning the latter position shortly before his death. A past president of the Philatelic Press Club, he served as vice president of INTERPHIL '76, and as chairman of the Association International des Journalistes Philatelique.

An engineer by profession, Mr. Stump served with the Pennsylvania Railroad for 42 years, retiring as an official of that railroad. He was a graduate of the Pennsylvania Military College, receiving a degree in civil engineering. He did post-graduate work at the University of Pennsylvania, University of Maryland and Purdue University.

## -T-
### John K. Tiffany
### (1847-1907) Missouri

St. Louis business man and pioneer collector who was one of the organizers of the American Philatelic Association (now the American Philatelic Society) and its president from 1886 through 1896. He wrote a history of U.S. stamps which was published in the French language by Moens in Belgium in 1883 and in the English language in this country in 1887.

## George T. Turner
### (1906-1979) Washington, D.C.

A past curator of the Smithsonian Institution's Division of Philately, Mr. Turner was perhaps America's leading philatelic bibliophile. He amassed a philatelic library of immense scope and was instrumental in the publication of several works, most notably Sloane's Column, a collection of columns by philatelic writer George Sloane.

He was a graduate of Cornell University with bachelor's and master's degrees in chemistry. He left a 27-year career in business to head up the Post Office Department's Division of Philately in 1958. He retired in 1962, devoting his time to stamp collecting pursuits.

He was chairman of the Sixth International Philatelic Exhibition in 1966, and was a director of the American Philatelic Society from 1951-61 and from 1971-75. He served as vice president of the organization from 1961-65, and was its director of international affairs from 1975-78. He was a signatory of the Roll of Distinguished Philatelists in 1978.

## -V-
### Daniel W. Vooys
### (1914-1978) New York

A collector of philatelic literature in his association with the hobby, Mr. Vooys was serving as president of the American Philatelic Research Library at the time of his death. He joined the American Philatelic Society in 1937 and served two terms as president of the association from 1969-73. He founded the Philatelic Literature Association in 1942 and was instrumental in merging that group into the present American Philatelic Research Library.

Mr. Vooys was inducted into the Writer's Hall of Fame in 1975 and received the Luff Award for meritorious contributions to philately by living philatelists in 1956 and again in 1978, on the weekend of his death.

The 1956 award was for exceptional contributions to philately, while the 1978 award was for outstanding service to the APS. Deeply interested in financial policies of the APS, he served as a member or chairman of the Finance Committee for almost 25 years. He was also a major financial benefactor of the APRL. He represented the APS at a number of FIP (Federation International de Philatelie) congresses, the first APS president to attend such sessions.

## -W-

### Philip H. Ward Jr.
### (1890-1963) Washington, D.C.

A member of the American Philatelic Society for almost 60 years, Philip H. Ward Jr. was a widely known dealer and philatelic columnist.

An electrical engineer by profession, he was a former president of the Ward Electric Co. in Philadelphia, Pa., until his retirement in the late 1950s.

He joined the APS in 1906 and for some years was a columnist for Meekel's Weekly Stamp News. He embarked on an autograph collecting project at the age of 10, a project that later developed into one of the world's finest assemblages of presidential letters and American historical documents.

Reportedly, it was a letter from former President Grover Cleveland, sent in response to one sent by Ward to Mr. Cleveland, about the turn of the century, that was the start of his collection.

### P. M. Wolsieffer
### (1857-1934) New York

Prominent figure in the stamp trade, operating retail shops and staging auctions in Philadelphia and New York City in the years after World War I. He is said to have begun operating as a stamp dealer in Chicago at the age of 12 and was one of the Windy City's leading dealers before shifting his operations to Philadelphia. He is famed as the inventor of the approval card.

### Willard Otis Wylie
### (1862-1945) Massachusetts

Editor of Mekeel's Weekly Stamp News from 1927 to 1940 and a dominant figure in American philately during the first four decades of the 20th century. He began writing for Mekeel's in 1902 while carrying on a stamp business in Boston. Later he became a proprietor of the Philatelic Era. This periodical was consolidated with Mekeel's in 1922 and the Wylie-Severn-Jewett Company was set up to publish it. Mr. Wylie and Charles E. Severn shared editorship of the weekly until Mr. Severn retired.

### William W. Wylie
### (1905-1982) Nebraska

William W. Wylie, one of the nation's outstanding philatelic journalists, died March 25, 1982 in Omaha, Neb. Born in Burdett, N.Y., he was the recipient of many philatelic awards, including the Luff Award presented by the American Philatelic Society in 1979.

A member of the Arizona Hall of Fame, the National Writers Hall of Fame and the Writers Unit No. 30 of the APS, he also held memberships in the Bureau Issues Association, the Society of Philatelic Americans, the Precancel Stamp Society, the United Postal Stationery Society and the Collectors Club.

A journalist by profession, working for newspapers in Kansas, Missouri and New York, he turned to writing for the philatelic press. He joined the staff of Western Stamp Collector in 1948 and continued that association for some 20 years.

Joining the Scott Publishing Company, he served as editor of the Scott Monthly Journal until the publication was sold by Duane Hillmer. On his retirement from active writing, Mr. Wylie continued his philatelic work by acting as a consultant to the PhilaMatic Center at Boys Town (Neb.) until he was hospitalized in 1978.

## -Z-

### Helen Kingsbury Zirkle
### (1902-1976) Pennsylvania

A graduate of Bryn Mawr College, Mrs. Zirkle took up stamp collecting in 1945 and, since she had spent her youth in Japan, took a special interest in East Asian material. She was one of the founders of the International Society for Japanese Philately and was its secretary-treasurer for many years. Besides definitive monographs on the stamps of Korea and Manchukuo, she produced the Philately article in the Encyclopedia Britannica and a series of articles on the problems of the newcomer in stamp collecting.

# Philatelic Honor Roll 28

## Eminent Contributors

Outstanding service awards have been established by a number of philatelic organizations to recognize individual contributions to the hobby. Identification of these accolades are listed first, followed by the individuals who have received the honors.

### APC Service Award
Established in 1959 by the American Philatelic Congress for outstanding service to that organization.

### APS Hall of Fame
Established by the American Philatelic Society in 1941 to recognize deceased individuals for significant contributions to philately.

### Angers Award
Award in the name of George W. Angers, a past president of the American Air Mail Society, made from time to time for outstanding contributions to aerophilately.

### Arizona Hall of Fame
An honor roll, primarily honoring achievements in philately in that part of the world, established by the Phoenix Philatelic Association in 1961.

### Barr Award
American Philatelic Congress award in the name of Jere. Hess Barr, one of its founders.

### BIA Hall of Fame
Established by the Bureau Issues Association to honor deceased members who had made outstanding contributions to the association and the collecting of U.S. postal paper.

### Bohn Award
Award in the name of Richard S. Bohn, a leader in Aero-Philatelists, Inc., for outstanding contributions in airpost collecting.

### Broken Pen Award
Established in 1970 by the Writer's Unit of the APS as an accolade for activity as a philatelic writer.

### Champion of Champions
Winner in the annual World Series of Philately, held in connection with the annual meeting of the APS, at which top award winners in more than 20 state and regional exhibitions are in competition.

### Conrath Award
Made from time to time by the American Air Mail Society in the name of Walter Conrath, one of its founders, for service to aerophilately by a member of the society.

### Crawford Medal
Award established in 1923 by the Royal Philatelic Society of London, made in the name of the Earl of Crawford, distinguished philatelic bibliographer, for a significant contribution to philatelic literature.

### Cryer Research Award
Award established in 1981 by friends of Jim and Corita Cryer "to honor the individual who has contributed at the highest level to philatelic research in U.S. philately in both traditional and postal history fields." It carries with it a $1,000 cash prize.

### Distinguished Topical Philatelist
A hall of fame for outstanding contributions in the field of subject matter (topical) collecting, established in 1952 by the American Topical Association and expanded annually.

### Eidsness Award
Made by the Washington Philatelic Society from time to time in the name of "Mike" Eidsness, for many years in charge of philatelic activities of the U.S. Post Office Department.

### Erani P. Drossos Award
American Philatelic Congress award established in 1981. The article judged as the best in the Congress Book receives this award.

### Klein Award
American Philatelic Congress Award made in the name of its founder, Eugene Klein, Philadelphia professional.

### Lagerloef Award
Established by the Society of Philatelic Americans in 1938 in the name of Hans Lagerloef, a distinguished patron of the society. Made annually for outstanding service to the society and to philately.

### Lichtenstein Award
The accolade of the Collectors Club, New York, made annually in the name of Alfred F. Lichtenstein, distinguished philatelist and patron of philately, for outstanding service to philately by a living philatelist.

### Lindenberg Medal
Award for meritorious literature by the Berlin Philatelic Club in the name of Carl Lindenberg, distinguished European philatelist.

### Luff Award
Established in 1940 by the American Philatelic Society in the name of John N. Luff, dean of American philatelists during the first decades of the 20th century. It is made at two-year intervals for meritorious contributions to philately by living philatelists.

### McCoy Award
American Philatelic Congress award in the name of Walter R. McCoy, a leading spirit during his early years.

### Mexico Hall of Fame
Established in 1969 by the Mexico-Elmhurst Philatelic Society, International, to identify individuals who have made outstanding contributions to the collection and study of the stamps and postal history of Mexico.

### Newbury Award
The Chicago Philatelic Society accolade for outstanding service to philately by a living philatelist in the Chicago area. It carries the name of the distinguished Chicago philatelist Saul Newbury.

### PNW Distinguished Philatelist
Member of a hall of fame established in 1960 by the Northwest Federation of Stamp Clubs to honor residents of the Pacific Northwest who made significant contributions to philately in that part of the world.

### Roll of Distinguished Philatelists
Established at the 1920 Philatelic Congress of Great Britain with the late King George V as the first signatory to a scroll on which the signatures of outstanding philatelists are added annually.

### Writer's Hall of Fame
Accolade for distinguished philatelic writers of the past and present established in 1974 by the Writer's Unit of the American Philatelic Society.

Contributions to the stamp collecting hobby have brought many individuals honors from philatelic institutions and organizations. It is admitted that this Honor Roll is subject to extensive expansion and this is contemplated in future editions of Linn's World Stamp Almanac. The year of an honoree's death, when known, is indicated in parentheses following the name.

## — A —

**Abt, Henry (1962)**
Luff Award, 1958

**Aisslinger, Horst**
Roll of Distinguished Philatelists, 1981

**Alexander, William L. (1979)**
Arizona Hall of Fame

**Alkema, Ward**
Lagerloef Award, 1962

**Alley, William R.**
Conrath Award, 1975

**Altmann, Solomon**
Klein Award, 1968

**Amos, William T.**
Broken Pen Award, 1975

**Andersen, Stig**
Roll of Distinguished Philatelists, 1980

**Andrews, Dr. Melvin J.**
Distinguished Topical Philatelist, 1966

**Angers, George W.**
Conrath Award, 1943

**Angers, Margaret**
Angers Award, 1963

**Apfelbaum, Earl P.L.**
Luff Award, 1962
Writer's Hall of Fame, 1979

**Ashbrook, Stanley B. (1958)**
Charles Severn Memorial Award, 1936
Crawford Medal, 1937
Luff Award, 1940
Roll of Distinguished Philatelists, 1950
APS Hall of Fame, 1959
Writer's Hall of Fame, 1974

## — B —

**Bacon, Edward Denny**
APS Hall of Fame, 1972

**Bailey, Stewart T.**
Lagerloef Award, 1965
**Barkhausen, L.H. (1963)**
APS Hall of Fame, 1963
**Barnet, Alexander A.**
PNW Distinguished Philatelist, 1969
**Barnum, W. Hamilton (1941)**
APS Hall of Fame, 1942
**Barovick, Fred**
Lagerloef Award, 1961
**Barr, Hugh (1960)**
APS Hall of Fame, 1963
**Barr, Jere. Hess (1955)**
APS Hall of Fame, 1955
**Barrett, Sidney F. (1958)**
APS Hall of Fame, 1958
**Barry, Ralph A. (1939)**
APS Hall of Fame, 1941
Writer's Hall of Fame, 1976
**Bartels, J. Murray (1944)**
APS Hall of Fame, 1946
**Bartley, Deane C. (1970)**
PNW Distinguished Philatelist, 1966
**Bash, John K.**
Mexico Hall of Fame
**Bates, Jack B.**
PNW Distinguished Philatelist, 1966
**Becker, Rev. S.C.**
Distinguished Topical Philatelist, 1953
**Beltmann, Clarence**
Distinguished Topical Philatelist, 1968
**Berolzheimer, D.D. (1952)**
APS Hall of Fame, 1955
**Bertalanffy, Dr. Felix D.**
Writer's Hall of Fame, 1978
**Berthelot, Lucien**
Roll of Distinguished Philatelists, 1972
**Best, Hil F.**
Lagerloef Award, 1947
**Billings, R.R.**
Mexico Hall of Fame
**Binks, Bury C.**
PNW Distinguished Philatelist, 1960
**Birkinbine, John II**
McCoy Award, 1969

**Bjaringer, Tomas**
Roll of Distinguished Philatelists, 1978

**Blake, Maurice C.**
Roll of Distinguished Philatelists, 1962

**Bledsoe, Arthur (1974)**
Lagerloef Award, 1951

**Blizil, George A.**
Luff Award, 1962
**Bloch, Herbert**
Luff Award, 1968
Lichtenstein Award, 1968
Roll of Distinguished Philatelists, 1968
J.W. Scott Award, 1979
**Blogg, Cecil A. (1971)**
PNW Distinguished Philatelist, 1961
**Blumenthal, Frank H.**
Conrath Award, 1975
**Boehret, Jessie and Diane**
McCoy Award, 1982
Drossos Award, 1982
**Boggs, Winthrop S. (1972)**
Crawford Medal, 1947
Luff Award, 1952
Lichtenstein Award, 1958
Roll of Distinguished Philatelists, 1959
APS Hall of Fame, 1974
Writer's Hall of Fame, 1974
**Bojanowicz, M.A.**
Roll of Distinguished Philatelists, 1966
**Boker, John R. Jr.**
Roll of Distinguished Philatelists, 1964
Lichtenstein Award, 1967
Luff Award, 1978
**Bolaffi, Dr. Giulio**
Roll of Distinguished Philatelists, 1981
**Bonilla-Lara, Alvaro**
Roll of Distinguished Philatelists, 1967
**Bourgraf, George (1964)**
Distinguished Topical Philatelist, 1953
**Brandeberry, Robert B.**
APC Service Award, 1964
Phoenix Award, 1968
**Branz, Hermann**
Roll of Distinguished Philatelists, 1982
**Braunstein, Ila**
Bohn Award, 1966

**Brazer, Clarence W. (1956)**
Eidsness Award, 1942
Luff Award, 1946
APS Hall of Fame, 1956

**Brenke, Donald B.**
ATA Distinguished Topical Philatelist, 1979

**Brett, George W.**
Phoenix Award, 1964
Luff Award, 1978
Writer's Hall of Fame, 1979

**Britt, John J. (1980)**
Collectors Club Medal, 1960
Lichtenstein Award, 1961
Bohn Award, 1962

**Brookman, Lester (1971)**
Luff Award, 1946 and 1948
Roll of Distinguished Philatelists, 1950
APS Hall of Fame, 1972
Writer's Hall of Fame, 1974

**Brown, R.D.**
Arizona Hall of Fame

**Bruns, Franklin R. Jr. (1979)**
APC Service Award, 1966
Lagerloef Award, 1972
Distinguished Topical Philatelist, 1976
Writer's Hall of Fame, 1979

**Bryant, Roger A.**
Bureau Issues Association Hall of Fame

**Buhler, Josua I.**
Roll of Distinguished Philatelists, 1964

**Bulkley, Grant**
Arizona Hall of Fame

**Burghard, George E. (1963)**
Roll of Distinguished Philatelists, 1963

**Butler, A.R.**
Roll of Distinguished Philatelists, 1975

# — C —

**Cabeen, Richard McP. (1969)**
Newbury Award, 1953
Luff Award, 1966
APS Hall of Fame, 1971
Writer's Hall of Fame, 1974

**Calder, Sen. James A.**
Roll of Distinguished Philatelists, 1947

**Caldwell, Judge David (1953)**
APS Hall of Fame, 1953

**Campbell, Lt.Col. Fred H.**
Distinguished Topical Philatelist, 1964

**Campbell, H.M.**
Roll of Distinguished Philatelists, 1969

**Canman, Richard W.**
Newbury Award, 1967

**Caroe, Sir E.A.G., CBE**
Roll of Distinguished Philatelists, 1972

**Carver, Fred E. and Margaret**
PNW Distinguished Philatelists, 1960

**Casey, Brother Camillus, O.S.F.**
Distinguished Topical Philatelist, 1967

**Caspary, Alfred (1955)**
Roll of Distinguished Philatelists, 1953
APS Hall of Fame, 1977

**Cate, Richard W.**
Arizona Hall of Fame

**Chafter Bey, Ibrahim**
Roll of Distinguished Philatelists, 1950

**Chaloner, Henry (1963)**
APS Hall of Fame, 1964

**Chase, Dr. Carroll (1960)**
Roll of Distinguished Philatelists, 1924
Crawford Medal, 1930
Lindenberg Medal, 1931
Luff Award, 1944
Lichtenstein Award, 1954
APS Hall of Fame, 1960
Writer's Hall of Fame, 1974

**Chemi, James (1976)**
Luff Award, 1964
Rosen Medal, 1971
Arizona Hall of Fame
Writer's Hall of Fame, 1974
APS Hall of Fame, 1977

**Christian, C.W.**
Broken Pen Award, 1973

**Clark, Emerson A.**
Luff Award, 1980

**Clark, Hugh M. (1956)**
Eidsness Award, 1940
SEPAD Merit Award, 1946
Roll of Distinguished Philatelists, 1947
APS Hall of Fame, 1957

**Clark, Lawrence S.**
McCoy Award, 1970

**Clark, Theresa M. (1954)**
APS Hall of Fame, 1954

**Clary, Joseph M.**
Luff Award, 1964

**Cleveland, Ennis C. (1965)**
Distinguished Topical Philatelist, 1960

**Cohn, Ernest**
McCoy Award, 1979
Barr Award, 1982

**Cole, Ezra**
Luff Award, 1970

**Conrath, Grace**
Conrath Award, 1951

**Conrath, Walter J. (1942)**
APS Hall of Fame, 1942

**Cooper, Jal (1972)**
Distinguished Topical Philatelist, 1958

**Corless, Robert E.**
Arizona Hall of Fame

**Costales, Eugene**
Luff Award, 1974

**Coyne, Bernard V.**
Arizona Hall of Fame

**Cratsenberg, Charles C.**
Luff Award, 1961
Arizona Hall of Fame
Broken Pen Award, 1972

**Crustin, J.H.E.**
Roll of Distinguished Philatelists, 1972

**Cummins, Edna**
Distinguished Topical Philatelist, 1973

## — D —

**Dale, Louise Boyd (1967)**
Roll of Distinguished Philatelists, 1956
Lichtenstein Award, 1962
APS Hall of Fame, 1968

**Davidson, Robert**
APC Service Award, 1969

**Davis, Bernard**
SPA Honorary Life Member
Luff Award, 1958

**Davis, Dr. Holland A. (1955)**
Luff Award, 1954
APS Hall of Fame, 1956

**Deats, Hiram E. (1963)**
Roll of Distinguished Philatelists, 1933
APS Hall of Fame, 1963

**DeBeer, W.S. Wolff**
Roll of Distinguished Philatelists, 1954

**Degler, Claude W.**
Wisconsin Hall of Fame, 1976

**De Violini, Barbara W. (1981)**
Broken Pen Award, 1978

**DeVoss, Col. James T.**
Luff Award, 1952 and 1958
McCoy Award, 1959 and 1966
Barr Award, 1959
APC Service Award, 1965
Champion of Champions, 1969
Lichtenstein Award, 1978
Roll of Distinguished Philatelists, 1981

**Diamant, Charles S. (1972)**
Distinguished Topical Philatelist, 1972

**Diamond, Alfred**
Lagerloef Award, 1946

**Dickason, Donald E.**
Conrath Award, 1971

**Diena, Alberto**
APS Hall of Fame, 1978

**Diena, Dr. Enzo**
Roll of Distinguished Philatelists, 1977
Lichtenstein Award, 1979
Luff Award, 1981

**Dietz, August (1963)**
Lindenberg Medal, 1938
Luff Award, 1940
Lichtenstein Award, 1955
APS Hall of Fame, 1964
Writer's Hall of Fame, 1974

**Dinshah, K.D.**
Distinguished Topical Philatelist, 1971

**Ditzler, Robert E.**
Arizona Hall of Fame

**Doane, Edith R.**
Barr Award, 1961 and 1968
Klein Award, 1967
McCoy Award, 1968
Writer's Hall of Fame, 1978

**Doane, Percy G. (1945)**
APS Hall of Fame, 1946

**Domanski, Vincent Jr. (1968)**
Lagerloef Award, 1966
APS Hall of Fame, 1968

**Dromberg, D.A.**
Roll of Distinguished Philatelists, 1977

**Dunn, John**
ASDA Service to Philately Award, 1976

## — E —

**Edmunds, Larry**
Lagerloef Award, 1967

**Eisendrath, Joseph**
Conrath Award, 1961
Bohn Award, 1969

**Elliott, Howard H. (1963)**
APS Hall of Fame, 1964

**Engstrom, Victor E.**
Champion of Champions, 1975

**Erle, Everett**
Writer's Hall of Fame, 1976

**Esten, Sidney R. (1965)**
Distinguished Topical Philatelist, 1957

**Evans, Albert**
Arizona Hall of Fame

## — F —

**Faries, Belmont**
Lagerloef Award, 1969
Rosen Medal, 1971
Writer's Hall of Fame, 1975

**Faulstich, Edith (1972)**
APS Hall of Fame, 1973
Writer's Hall of Fame, 1974

**Fechner, Catherine D.**
Distinguished Topical Philatelist, 1953

**Fergus, W. Lee (1972)**
Newbury Award, 1964

**Field, Francis J.**
Roll of Distinguished Philatelists, 1968

**Finch, Wilfred J.**
Arizona Hall of Fame

**Fine, Harry L.**
Arizona Hall of Fame

**Fisher, H.W.**
Roll of Distinguished Philatelists, 1981

**Fitzgerald, Edwin G. (1972)**
Arizona Hall of Fame

**Flagg, May**
Arizona Hall of Fame
**Flath, Edward J.**
Distinguished Topical Philatelist, 1958
**Fleishman, Leo**
Arizona Hall of Fame
**Flower, Rollin E. (1961)**
APS Hall of Fame, 1961
**Fortgang, Morris (1960)**
APS Hall of Fame, 1961
**Foster, Charles**
Writer's Hall of Fame, 1979
**Fox, William**
ASDA Service to Philately Award, 1976
**Foxworth, John E. Jr.**
Phoenix Award, 1969
**Fraser, R. Thurlow**
PNW Distinguished Philatelist, 1973
**Freedner, O. Frank (1964)**
Distinguished Topical Philatelist, 1962
**Fricke, Charles A.**
Barr Award, 1964
Luff Award, 1981
**Fricke, Ellsworth C.**
Arizona Hall of Fame
**Fromaigeat, Dr. J.**
Roll of Distinguished Philatelists, 1974
**Fuerst, Thomas**
Newbury Award, 1978

— G —

**Garabrant, Mr. and Mrs. Melvin**
Distinguished Topical Philatelists, 1973
**Gartner, John**
Roll of Distinguished Philatelists, 1976
**Gatchell, L.B. (1970)**
Conrath Award, 1944
APS Hall of Fame, 1971
**Gebhart, Robert**
ASDA Service to Philately Award, 1976
**Gerrish, William E.**
APS Hall of Fame, 1981
**Glass, Sol (1973)**
Luff Award, 1954
APC Service Award, 1967
BIA Hall of Fame
APS Hall of Fame, 1974
**Goodkind, Henry M. (1970)**
Bohn Award, 1961
Lichtenstein Award, 1963
Roll of Distinguished Philatelists, 1966
APS Hall of Fame, 1975
Writer's Hall of Fame, 1975

**Goodwin, Dr. James**
APS Hall of Fame, 1954
**Gordon, Robert S.**
Phoenix Award, 1966
**Green, Brian and Patricia**
Barr Award, 1970
**Green, Mrs. Doris M.**
Roll of Distinguished Philatelists, 1970
**Green, Jack H.**
Distinguished Topical Philatelist, 1977
**Greene, Vincent G.**
Roll of Distinguished Philatelists, 1963
Lichtenstein Award, 1964
**Griffenhagen, George B.**
Barr Award, 1969
Distinguished Topical Philatelist, 1970
**Groet, John (1966)**
Distinguished Topical Philatelist, 1954
**Grunin, Louis**
Champion of Champions, 1972
**Guggenheim, Max**
Director, INTERNABA Exhibition, 1974
Roll of Distinguished Philatelists, 1976
**Guzzio, George T.**
Distinguished Topical Philatelist, 1974

— H —

**Hackett, Mrs. Margaret R.**
Distinguished Topical Philatelist, 1956
**Hahn, Charless**
Newbury Award, 1972
**Hainlen, Dr. E. Willis (1972)**
Distinguished Topical Philatelist, 1967
**Hamilton, Col. Charles S. (1968)**
APS Hall of Fame, 1969
Mexico Hall of Fame
**Hargest, George E.**
Luff Award, 1980
**Harmer, C.H.C.**
Roll of Distinguished Philatelists, 1969
**Harring, Robert (1978)**
Conrath Award, 1966
**Harris, Adm. Frederick R. (1949)**
APS Hall of Fame, 1950
**Harris, Henry E. (1977)**
Luff Award, 1966
ASDA Service to Philately Award, 1976
APS Hall of Fame, 1979
**Harrison, Horace**
Luff Award, 1974
**Hart, Creighton C.**
Luff Award, 1970

**Hatcher, James B.**
Writer's Hall of Fame, 1974
**Hatfield, A.**
Roll of Distinguished Philatelists, 1925
**Havemeyer, John T.**
Mexico Hall of Fame
**Haverbeck, Harrison D.S.**
Lichtenstein Award, 1966
Roll of Distinguished Philatelists, 1970
**Heiman, Irwin M.**
APS Hall of Fame, 1978
**Heinmuller, John F.V.**
Conrath Award, 1955
**Helzer, James**
ASDA Service to Philately Award, 1976
**Hennan, Dr. Clarence W. (1955)**
Newbury Award, 1951
Lichtenstein Award, 1953
APS Hall of Fame, 1956
**Hennig, Bernard**
Lagerloef Award, 1968
Newbury Award, 1968
Roll of Distinguished Philatelists, 1982
**Henry, C. Charlton (1936)**
Roll of Distinguished Philatelists, 1929
**Herst, Herman Jr.**
Luff Award, 1961
Broken Pen Award, 1971
Writer's Hall of Fame, 1974
**Hicks, William W. (1966)**
APS Hall of Fame, 1967
**Hill, Sir Rowland**
APS Hall of Fame, 1941
**Hilton, Hugh**
Arizona Hall of Fame
**Hitt, Henry C.**
PNW Distinguished Philatelist, 1960
**Holcombe, Henry W. (1973)**
Writer's Hall of Fame, 1979
**Holmes, H.R.**
Roll of Distinguished Philatelists, 1953
**Holmes, Dr. L. Seale (1961)**
Writer's Hall of Fame, 1978
**Howes, Clifton A. (1936)**
Roll of Distinguished Philatelists, 1921
**Hunziker, Hans**
Roll of Distinguished Philatelists, 1979
**Hurt, E.F.**
APS Hall of Fame, 1953
**Husak, Jerome K.**
Distinguished Topical Philatelist, 1952
Wisconsin Hall of Fame, 1976

**Hutcheson, Robert J.**
McCoy Award, 1963

## — I —

**Ichida, Dr. S.**
Roll of Distinguished Philatelists, 1971
Lichtenstein Award
**Ihms, James**
Arizona Hall of Fame
**Isaacs, Mark R.**
Newbury Award, 1979
**Ishikawa, Ryoshei**
Champion of Champions, 1978

## — J —

**Jackson, Lucius (1978)**
Writer's Hall of Fame, 1979
**Jacobs, Burleigh**
Wisconsin Hall of Fame, 1976
**Jacobs, Ernest R.**
Newbury Award, 1958
**Jacobson, Gerald A.**
Lagerloef Award, 1959
**Jacquemin, Ralph E.**
Arizona Hall of Fame
**James, Milo**
Arizona Hall of Fame
**Janecka, Joseph J. Jr.**
Newbury Award, 1975
**Jarrett, Fred**
Roll of Distinguished Philatelists, 1935
Writer's Hall of Fame, 1977
**Johl, Max G. (1957)**
Crawford Medal, 1938
Luff Award, 1950
Roll of Distinguished Philatelists, 1957
APS Hall of Fame, 1957
Writer's Hall of Fame, 1974
**Johnson, Harvey E. (1975)**
Distinguished Topical Philatelist, 1960
**Johnson, Adm. Jesse (1980)**
Conrath Award, 1953
**Jones, Homer L.**
Distinguished Topical Philatelist, 1952

## — K —

**Kaiser, J.B.**
McCoy Award, 1953
**Kante, Robert F.**
Distinguished Topical Philatelist, 1978
**Kaub, Vernon**
Wisconsin Hall of Fame, 1976
**Keenan, Charles J.**
Distinguished Topical Philatelist, 1952

**Kehr, Ernest A.**
Conrath Award, 1946
Distinguished Topical Philatelist, 1954
Lichtenstein Award, 1974
Roll of Distinguished Philatelists, 1975
Luff Award 1976
Writer's Hall of Fame, 1977

**Keller, Peter G. (1972)**
APS Hall of Fame, 1973

**Kelly, Denwood**
Luff Award, 1976

**Kenworthy, Waldo V. (1966)**
Newbury Award, 1947

**Kimble, Col. Ralph A. (1973)**
Luff Award, 1944
Writer's Hall of Fame, 1975

**King, Beverly S. (1935)**
APS Hall of Fame, 1941

**King, Oliver**
Arizona Hall of Fame

**Kingdom, George D.**
Conrath Award, 1947

**Klein, Eugene (1943)**
Eidsness Award, 1938
APS Hall of Fame, 1944

**Kleinart, Herman**
Conrath Award, 1979

**Klemann, J.J.**
Angers Award, 1965

**Knapp, Edward S. (1940)**
APS Hall of Fame, 1941

**Koeppel, Adolph**
Klein Award, 1963

**Kohl, Richard F.**
Angers Award, 1976

**Konwiser, Harry (1960)**
APS Hall of Fame, 1961

**Korotkin, Fred**
Distinguished Topical Philatelist, 1962

**Kovarik, Frank J. (1974)**
Luff Award, 1961
Newbury Award, 1965

**Kronstein, Dr. Max**
Angers Award, 1966

**Kufahl, Lester E.**
Distinguished Topical Philatelist, 1972

**Kuyas, Tevfik**
Roll of Distinguished Philatelists, 1980

## — L —

**Lane, Maryette B.**
Luff Award, 1970
Phoenix Award, 1971

**Langois, M. Pierre**
Roll of Distinguished Philatelists, 1967

**Lapham, Raymond, W.**
Grand Award, TIPEX, 1936

**Lee, R.A.G.**
Roll of Distinguished Philatelists, 1965
Lichtenstein Award, 1980

**Leigh, Dr. Southgate**
Angers Award, 1967

**Levett, John H.**
Roll of Distinguished Philatelists, 1979

**Lichtenstein, Alfred H. (1947)**
Grand Award, Second International
Philatelic Exhibition, 1926
Roll of Distinguished Philatelists, 1927
Grand Award, Midwestern Philatelic
Exhibition, 1928
Chairman of Judges, National Exhibition,
New York City, 1934
President and Jury Chairman, TIPEX, 1936
Chairman, CIPEX, 1947
APS Hall of Fame, 1948

**Lidman, David**
Newbury Award, 1945
Luff Award, 1946
Phoenix Award, 1961
APC Service Award, 1962
APS Writer's Unit Medal, 1972

**Light, Theodore**
Newbury Award, 1970

**Lindquist, Harry L. (1978)**
Roll of Distinguished Philatelists, 1947
Luff Award, 1948
Lichtenstein Award, 1957
Writer's Hall of Fame, 1974
APS Hall of Fame, 1979

**Lindsay, James Ludovic**
APS Hall of Fame, 1941

**Linn, George W. (1966)**
APS Hall of Fame, 1967
Mexico Hall of Fame
Writer's Hall of Fame, 1974

**Lipschutz, M. Michel**
Roll of Distinguished Philatelists, 1968

**Livingston, Lyons F. (1972)**
Writer's Hall of Fame, 1978

**Long, Russell A.**
PNW Distinguished Philatelist, 1968

**Longinotti, Helen**
Lagerloef Award, 1955

**Love, L. Cecil (1977)**
Newbury Award, 1969

**Lowe, Robson**
Luff Award, 1980
Writer's Hall of Fame, 1980

**Luff, John N. (1938)**
Roll of Distinguished Philatelists, 1921
APS Hall of Fame, 1941
Writer's Hall of Fame, 1974

**Lundy, Mrs. J.W.**
BIA Hall of Fame

**Lybarger, Donald F. (1970)**
Luff Award, 1950
APS Hall of Fame, 1971

## — M —

**MacBride, F. Van Dyk (1961)**
Luff Award, 1952
APS Hall of Fame, 1962

**McAlister, Clare**
Distinguished Topical Philatelist, 1957

**McCoy, Mrs. Ethel B.**
APS Hall of Fame, 1981

**McCoy, Walter R. (1952)**
APS Hall of Fame, 1952
BIA Hall of Fame

**McIntyre, Walter A.**
BIA Hall of Fame

**McKenzie, Vernon L.**
McCoy Award, 1960

**McNaught, Kenneth John**
Roll of Distinguished Philatelists, 1978

**Manning, Lester F.**
Conrath Award, 1964

**Marriott, John B.**
Keeper of Queen's Collection
Roll of Distinguished Philatelists, 1972

**Marston, C.L.**
PNW Distinguished Philatelist, 1965

**Martin, Donald W. (1952)**
APS Hall of Fame, 1952

**Martin, George M.**
PNW Distinguished Philatelist, 1962
Luff Award, 1974

**Mason, Edward H.**
APS Hall of Fame, 1949

**Matejka, Dr. James J. Jr. (1979)**
Newbury Award, 1959
Conrath Award, 1963
Lagerloef Award, 1970
Roll of Distinguished Philatelists, 1979
APS Hall of Fame, 1981

**Mekeel, Charles H. (1921)**
APS Hall of Fame, 1972

**Melville, Frederick J. (1940)**
APS Hall of Fame, 1941
Writer's Hall of Fame, 1980

**Melvin, George H.**
PNW Distinguished Philatelist, 1972

**Messenger, John L.**
Roll of Distinguished Philatelists, 1979

**Metzong, Debs**
Arizona Hall of Fame

**Meyer, Charles E.**
Lagerloef Award, 1963

**Meyer, Henry A.**
APS Hall of Fame, 1969

**Michael, A.L.**
Roll of Distinguished Philatelists, 1978

**Minkus, Jacques**
ASDA Service to Philately Award, 1976

**Mitchell, Milton**
Lagerloef Award, 1974
United Nations Philatelist of the Year, 1974

**Moorefield, Emily (1975)**
Lagerloef Award, 1958

**Morgan, A.L.**
Roll of Distinguished Philatelists, 1978

**Morgan, Mrs. E.L.**
Roll of Distinguished Philatelists, 1976

**Morgenthau, Julius C.**
APS Hall of Fame, 1978

**Morison, Gordon**
ASDA Service to Philately Award, 1976

**Mueller, Barbara R.**
McCoy Award, 1955
Luff Award, 1956
Wisconsin Hall of Fame, 1976
Writer's Hall of Fame, 1978
Lichtenstein Award, 1980

**Mueller, Edwin (1962)**
APS Hall of Fame, 1974

**Muller, Frank**
Angers Award, 1978

**Murch, Robert W.**
Barr Award, 1960 and 1963
Conrath Award, 1961
Phoenix Award, 1974

**Musser, H. Clay**
Phoenix Award, 1962
Luff Award, 1966

**Myee, John N.**
McCoy Award, 1957

**Myer, Henry A. (1968)**
Lagerloef Award, 1950
Hanford Trophy (Garfield-Perry Philatelic
Society), 1965
APS Hall of Fame, 1969

**Myers, Archie**
SEPAD Merit Award, 1946

**Myers, Blake M.**
Champion of Champions, 1981

## — N —

**Nahl, Dr. Perham C.**
Conrath Award, 1968

**Nathan, Mel C.**
Phoenix Award, 1963

**Neinken, Mortimer**
Eugene Klein Award, 1961 and 1964
Luff Award, 1962
Lichtenstein Award, 1971
Cryer Research Award, 1981

**Nelson, Hildegarde**
Arizona Hall of Fame

**Newbury, Saul (1950)**
Grand Award, CIPEX, 1947
APS Hall of Fame, 1950

**Newcomer, Ewald J.**
PNW Distinguished Philatelist, 1967

**Norona, Delf (1974)**
Barr Award, 1962
Writer's Hall of Fame, 1974
APS Hall of Fame, 1975

**Nouss, Henry O. (1978)**
Lagerloef Award, 1957

## — O —

**O'Brien, Emma**
Arizona Hall of Fame

**Odenweller, Robert P.**
Barr Award, 1971
Champion of Champions, 1973

**Oesch, Robert S.**
Distinguished Topical Philatelist, 1965

**Oriol, Rafael**
Conrath Award, 1957

**Owen, Arthur E. (1944)**
BIA Hall of Fame

**Owens, Mary Ann**
Distinguished Topical Philatelist, 1969

## — P —

**Pack, Charles Lathrop (1933)**
Roll of Distinguished Philatelists, 1921
Crawford Medal, 1923
Collectors Club Medal, 1924
APS Hall of Fame, 1941

**Palmer, Derek**
Roll of Distinguished Philatelists, 1977

**Papa, Inez**
Lagerloef Award, 1971

**Patrick, Douglas A.**
Writer's Hall of Fame, 1976

**Payne, Edwin R. (1959)**
PNW Distinguished Philatelist, 1960

**Pearce, Basil C.**
Phoenix Award, 1970

**Pearson, P.C.**
Roll of Distinguished Philatelists, 1974

**Pelander, Carl E. (1966)**
APS Hall of Fame, 1966

**Pennycuick, Kenneth**
Roll of Distinguished Philatelists, 1980

**Perry, Elliott (1972)**
Luff Award, 1944
APS Hall of Fame, 1973
Writer's Hall of Fame, 1974

**Perry, Thomas Doane (1958)**
McCoy Award, 1956
Writer's Hall of Fame, 1977

**Peterson, Henry**
Distinguished Topical Philatelist, 1966

**Phillips, Charles J. (1940)**
APS Hall of Fame, 1941

**Pierce, Charles J.**
Wisconsin Hall of Fame

**Plancquaert, Jules L.J.**
Roll of Distinguished Philatelists, 1975

**Plant, Anna (1971) and Paul J.**
Luff Award, 1968

**Pollock, Dr. Herbert C.**
Newbury Award, 1955

**Polson, M.P.**
Distinguished Topical Philatelist, 1959

**Poole, Bertram W.H. (1957)**
Writer's Hall of Fame, 1977

**Pritzlaff, Mr. and Mrs. A.H. Jr.**
Distinguished Topical Philatelists, 1964

**Purves, J.R.W.**
Roll of Distinguished Philatelists, 1980
APS Hall of Fame, 1980

## — R —

**Ragatz, Lowell**
APS Hall of Fame, 1979

**Ranschaert, Cyril C.**
Distinguished Topical Philatelist, 1969

**Ray, Samuel**
Newbury Award, 1966

**Rayl, H.F.**
Distinguished Topical Philatelist, 1965

**Reeves, Ben (1964)**
Lagerloef Award, 1949
Newbury Award, 1954

**Reiner, Ignatz**
Lagerloef Award, 1953

**Rice, Stanley R.**
Bohn Award, 1968

**Rich, Stephen G. (1958)**
Lagerloef Award, 1948
APS Hall of Fame, 1959
Writer's Hall of Fame, 1974

**Richards, C.R.**
APS Hall of Fame, 1945

**Richert, Harvey**
Wisconsin Hall of Fame, 1976

**Richter, John H.**
Distinguished Topical Philatelist, 1963

**Ricketts, William R. (1956)**
Roll of Distinguished Philatelists, 1921

**Rider, John F.**
Roll of Distinguished Philatelists, 1969

**Ringstrom, Sigge**
Roll of Distinguished Philatelists, 1977

**Risueno, Manuel M.**
APS Hall of Fame, 1976

**Rivolta, Dr. Achille**
Roll of Distinguished Philatelists, 1968

**Robbins, Phillip R.**
ASDA Service to Philately Award, 1976

**Roosevelt, Franklin D. (1945)**
APS Hall of Fame, 1945

**Rowe, Basil L.**
Angers Award, 1972

**Rueth, Carl**
Phoenix Award, 1965

**Russo, Anthony C. (1974)**
Newbury Award, 1957

**Ryan, Gary S.**
Roll of Distinguished Philatelists, 1980

— S —

**Salisbury, Dr. Gregory B. (1968)**
APS Hall of Fame, 1969

**Salm, Arthur**
Roll of Distinguished Philatelists, 1980

**Sampson, Edward (1978)**
Luff Award, 1972

**Sanabria, Nicolas (1945)**
APS Hall of Fame, 1951

**Schag, Gustave**
McCoy Award, 1961

**Schatkes, Dr. Joseph**
Roll of Distinguished Philatelists, 1963

**Schilling, Wilbur H.**
Champion of Champions, 1971

**Schoberlin, Melvin H. (1977)**
Writer's Hall of Fame, 1979

**Schrader, Col. Otto**
Newbury Award, 1962

**Schulze, William H. and Anna**
Newbury Award, 1961

**Scott, John Walter (1919)**
APS Hall of Fame, 1941
Writers Hall of Fame, 1974

**Scott, Walter S.**
APS Hall of Fame, 1950

**Seigle, Daniel R.**
ASDA Service to Philately Award, 1976

**Sellers, F. Burton**
Lichtenstein Award, 1977

**Selzer, Howard**
Lagerloef Award, 1973

**Severn, Charles E. (1929)**
Roll of Distinguished Philatelists, 1921
APS Hall of Fame, 1941

**Severn, Mrs. Evelyn (1941)**
APS Hall of Fame, 1942

**Seymour, J.B.**
APS Hall of Fame, 1951

**Shaner, James B. Jr.**
American Philatelic Congress Service Award, 1961

**Shoemaker, Laurence D.**
Luff Award, 1950

**Shreve, Forrest**
Arizona Hall of Fame

**Sievers, Walter W.**
Distinguished Topical Philatelist, 1956

**Sievert, Louis K. (1960)**
Distinguished Topical Philatelist, 1959

**Silver, Philip**
Bohn Award, 1965
Roll of Distinguished Philatelists, 1978
Luff Award, 1979,
Angers Award, 1980
Lichtenstein Award

**Simon, Dr. Ludwig L.**
Champion of Champions, 1974

**Singley, Richard L.**
Conrath Award, 1945

**Sloan, Louis**
Lagerloef Award, 1956

**Sloane, George B. (1961)**
APS Hall of Fame, 1962

**Slough, J. Burton**
PNW Distinguished Philatelist, 1963

**Small, Lester E.**
PNW Distinguished Philatelist, 1975

**Smeltzer, Chester**
Luff Award, 1948

**Smith, Donald W.**
Distinguished Topical Philatelist, 1976

**Smith, Dorothy F.**
Distinguished Topical Philatelist, 1970

**Smith, Dr. Gerald B.**
PNW Distinguished Philatelist, 1964

**Smith, Rev. James L.**
Arizona Hall of Fame

**Smith, John J.**
Conrath Award, 1955

**Smith, Ruth J.**
Conrath Award, 1959

**South, George**
Roll of Distinguished Philatelists, 1974

**Southgate, Hugh M. (1940)**
BIA Hall of Fame
Eidsness Award, 1939
APS Hall of Fame, 1941

**Spaulding, Robert M.**
Writer's Hall of Fame, 1975

**Spellman, Francis Cardinal (1967)**
APS Hall of Fame, 1968

**Springer, Arthur**
Arizona Hall of Fame

**Spurgeon, Edgar W. (1970)**
Distinguished Topical Philatelist, 1961

**Stanley, Marcel**
Roll of Distinguished Philatelists, 1971

**Stanley, Willard F.**
Distinguished Topical Philatelist, 1955

**Starr, Maj. James (1947)**
Roll of Distinguished Philatelists, 1947
APS Hall of Fame, 1949

**Staub, Louis N.**
Bohn Award, 1970

**Steeg, Adolph (1959)**
APS Hall of Fame, 1960

**Steinway, Theodore E. (1957)**
Roll of Distinguished Philatelists, 1947
Chairman of Judges, CIPEX, 1947
Lichtenstein Award, 1952
APS Hall of Fame, 1958

**Stern, Capt. M.F.**
Distinguished Topical Philatelist, 1963

**Stevens, Byron F. (1970)**
Mexico Hall of Fame

**Stevens, Clark H.**
Phoenix Award, 1975

**Stevens, Warren C.**
McCoy Award, 1965

**Stewart, William R.**
Writer's Hall of Fame, 1978

**Stiles, Kent B. (1951)**
Writer's Hall of Fame, 1976

**Stilpen, George**
Writer's Hall of Fame, 1974

**Stone, Daniel A.**
Mr. Stamp Collector Award, ROMPEX, 1976

**Stone, Robert G.**
Gerard Gilbert Award, 1948
McCoy Award, 1958 and 1962
Lichtenstein Award, 1981

**Stone, William C. (1939)**
APS Hall of Fame, 1947

**Stowell, John W. (1955)**
APS Hall of Fame, 1957

**Strait, Walter G.**
Newbury Award, 1946

**Stuart, Elmer**
Newbury Award, 1952

**Stump, David C. (1982)**
American Philatelic Congress Service Award, 1970

**Swanker, Dr. Wilson A.**
Distinguished Topical Philatelist, 1955

# — T —

**Tapling, Thomas Keay**
APS Hall of Fame, 1941

**Tatelman, Judge Edward I.P.**
Klein Award, 1962
Luff Award, 1964

**Taylor, J. Pascoe**
PNW Distinguished Philatelist, 1976

**ter Braake, Alex**
Barr Award, 1965 and 1967
Klein Award, 1970
McCoy Award, 1971
Luff Award, 1972
Phoenix Award, 1972

**Theobald, John (1973) and Lillian**
Arizona Hall of Fame

**Thiele, R.R.**
PNW Distinguished Philatelist, 1960

**Thomas, Frederick B.**
Phoenix Award, 1967
Luff Award, 1972

**Thomas, John**
Distinguished Topical Philatelist, 1968

**Thompson, Cyrus R.**
Luff Award, 1981

**Thorp, Prescott Holden**
Crawford Medal, 1945
Writer's Hall of Fame, 1974

**Tiffany, John Kerr (1907)**
APS Hall of Fame, 1941

**Topping, William E.**
PNW Distinguished Philatelist, 1970

**Tower, Rev. William R. (1950)**
APS Hall of Fame, 1951
**Towle, Charles L.**
Klein Award, 1969
**Townsend, W.A.**
Roll of Distinguished Philatelists, 1969
**Trefonas, George P.**
APS Champion of Champions, 1979
**Tucker, Shirley C.**
Distinguished Topical Philatelist, 1961
**Turner, George T. (1979)**
American Philatelic Congress Service Award, 1968
Luff Award, 1976
Lichtenstein Award, 1976
Roll of Distinguished Philatelists, 1978
Writer's Hall of Fame, 1980

**— V —**

**Van Dahl, Al (1954)**
APS Hall of Fame, 1954
PNW Distinguished Philatelist, 1960
Writer's Hall of Fame, 1974
**Van Dahl, Arlene**
PNW Distinguished Philatelist, 1960
**Van der Willigen, Dr. A.M.A.**
Roll of Distinguished Philatelists, 1973
**Van Handel, Ray**
Wisconsin Hall of Fame
**Vining, J. Edward (1955)**
Lagerloef Award, 1944
**Vooys, Daniel W. (1978)**
Luff Award, 1956 and 1978
Writer's Hall of Fame, 1975
Second Hall of Fame Citation, 1980
**Vrendenburgh, Walter**
Lagerloef Award, 1954

**— W —**

**Wagner, C. Corwith**
McCoy Award, 1954
**Wanderer, Fred E.**
PNW Distinguished Philatelist, 1977
**Ward, Philip H. (1963)**
APS Hall of Fame, 1966
**Ware, William R.**
Conrath Award, 1973
**Warm, Lynne S.**
Champion of Champions, 1980
**Warns, Dr. M.O.**
Conrath Award, 1948
**Warren, Arnold H.**
Luff Award, 1968

**Watt, Myrtle (1977)**
Distinguished Topical Philatelist, 1975
**Webb, Sophia**
Distinguished Topical Philatelist, 1971
**Weinberg, Irwin**
Broken Pen Award, 1979
**Weiss, Harry (1966)**
APS Hall of Fame, 1967
Writer's Hall of Fame, 1975
**Wellburn, Gerald**
Roll of Distinguished Philatelists, 1951
Grand Award, Canada Centenary Exhibition, CAPEX, 1951
PNW Distinguished Philatelist, 1960
**Wellman, Earl H.**
Newbury Award, 1973
**Wetmore, Ruth**
Distinguished Topical Philatelist, 1975
**Wickersham, Gen. C.W.**
Chairman of Jury, FIPEX, 1956
Roll of Distinguished Philatelists, 1956
Lichtenstein Award, 1959
**Wilde, Donald E.**
Arizona Hall of Fame
**Wilkinson, Sam III**
Distinguished Topical Philatelist, 1977
**Willard, Edward L. (1973)**
Broken Pen Award, 1970
Klein Award, 1971
**Williams, L. Norman**
Writer's Hall of Fame, 1980
**Williams, Maurice**
Writer's Hall of Fame, 1980
**Williamson, Omega**
Arizona Hall of Fame
**Wilson, Sir John**
APS Hall of Fame, 1976
**Winick, Lester E.**
Distinguished Topical Philatelist, 1978
**Wolfe, Fred S. (1978)**
Phoenix Award, 1976
**Wolffers, Richard**
ASDA Service to Philately Award, 1976
**Wolsieffer, Philip M. (1954)**
APS Hall of Fame, 1941
**Wolter, K.K.**
Roll of Distinguished Philatelists, 1976
**Wood, Kenneth**
PNW Distinguished Philatelist
Distinguished Topical Philatelist, 1979
**Woodward, Tracy**
Crawford Medal, 1929

**Worthington, George H.**
Grand Award, International Exhibition,
New York City, 1913

**Wright, Allyn H.**
Distinguished Topical Philatelist, 1952

**Wunsch, Dr. Charles W.**
Broken Pen Award, 1974

**Wunsch, Mrs. Margaret**
Champion of Champions, 1970

**Wurtz, Margaret M.**
Distinguished Topical Philatelist, 1974

**Wylie, Willard O. (1944)**
APS Hall of Fame, 1945
Writer's Hall of Fame, 1977

**Wylie, William W. (1982)**
PNW Distinguished Philatelist, 1960
Arizona Hall of Fame
Writer's Hall of Fame, 1974
Luff Award, 1979

**Wynn, William T.**
Conrath Award, 1971

— Y —

**Yag, Otto (1982)**
Arizona Hall of Fame
Mexico Hall of Fame

**Yant, Hilda P.**
Lagerloef Award, 1964

**Yant, Robert (1973)**
Lagerloef Award, 1960

**Yort, Svend (1981)**
American Philatelic Congress Service Award,
1963
Master of Philately Award of the Academy
of Philately, 1970

**Young, Winnifred H.**
PNW Distinguished Philatelist

— Z —

**Zinsmeister, J. Elmer and Marian**
Newbury Award, 1956

**Zinsmeister, J. Elmer (1968)**
Lagerloef Award, 1945

**Zinsmeister, Marian C.C.**
Lagerloef Award, 1952

**Zirkle, Mrs. Conway (1976)**
American Philatelic Congress Service Award,
1960
Klein Award, 1965

# Stamp Columnists  **29**

## Nonphilatelic Press

Following is a list of names and addresses of columnists who write for the nonphilatelic press. The title of the column appears below the name of the columnist. The listing following the name indicates the publications in which the column appears and the frequency of publication.

**BLAUVELT, Mrs. Lea**
21207 S. Avalon Blvd., No. 33
Carson, Calif. 90745
  (Stamping Around the World)
Copley News Service
P.O.Box 190
San Diego, Calif. 92112
Column has national
  syndication
**BROWN, George W.**
Asbury Park Press
Press Plaza
Asbury Park, N.J. 07712
  (Stamps)
Asbury Park Press
Press Plaza
Asbury Park, N.J. 07712
Column appears on Sunday
**BRUNS, James H.**
7215 13th Ave.
Takoma Park, Md. 20912
  Denver (Colo.) Post
  St. Petersburg (Fla.) Times
  Syracuse (N.Y.) Herald-
    American
  Albany (N.Y.) Times-Union
  Newark (N.J.) Star-Ledger
  Washington (D.C.) Post
  Column appears on Sunday
**BRYAN, Al**
330 Hancock St.
Findlay, Ohio 45840
  (The Philatelist)
The Findlay Courier
701 W. Sandusky St.
Findlay, Ohio 45840
Weekly column

**BRYANT, Harry G.**
Box 196
Patterson, N.Y. 12563
  (Bits and Pieces)
Pawling News Chronicle
East Maple Avenue
Pawling, N.Y. 12564
Column appears occasionally
**CARR, Richard**
Business Desk
Fort Lauderdale News
Fort Lauderdale, Fla. 33302
  (Richard Carr on Stamps)
Fort Lauderdale News
  and Sun-Sentinel
P.O. Box 14430
Fort Lauderdale, Fla. 33302
Column appears on Sunday
**CHAFETZ, Donald**
P.O. Box 225
Mt. Freedom, N.J. 07970
  (Stamps)
Morris County Daily Record
800 N. Jefferson Road
Parsipanny, N.J. 07054
Weekly column
**CONSTABLE, George N.**
70 W. Fourth St., Box 25
Mansfield, Ohio 44901
  (With the Collectors)
News Journal
70 W. Fourth St., Box 25
Mansfield, Ohio 44901
Column appears on Sunday
**DAVIDSON, Warren E.**
P.O. Box 5337

Sarasota, Fla. 33579
  (The Stamp Collector)
Sarasota Journal
P.O. Box 1719
Sarasota, Fla. 33578
Weekly column
**DECKER, David G.**
50 W. Fifth
Oswego, N.Y. 13126
  (World of Stamps)
Palladium-Times
140 W. First
Oswego, N.Y. 13126
Weekly column
**DETJEN, Gustav Jr.**
154 Laguna Court
St. Augustine Shores, Fla. 32084
  (The World of Stamps)
Civic Advocate
213 Deltona Blvd.
St. Augustine, Fla. 32084
Monthly column
**DONALDSON, Joe**
310 LaSalle Expressway
Niagara Falls, N.Y. 14305
  (Stamp News)
Niagara Gazette
310 LaSalle Expressway
Niagara Falls, N.Y. 14305
Weekly column
**ESRATI, Stephen G.**
1801 Superior Ave.
Cleveland, Ohio 44114
  (Stamps)
The Plain Dealer
1801 Superior Ave.

Cleveland, Ohio 44114
Column appears on Sunday

**FARIES, Belmont**
11713 Chapel Road
Clifton, Va. 22024
(Stamps)
Boston Globe
Boston, Mass. 02107
Column appears on Sunday

**FLORIDA, Dr. Robert E.**
Box 14, Brandon University
Brandon, Manitoba R7A 6A9
Canada
(Corner on Stamps)
Winnipeg Tribune
Box 7000
Winnipeg, Manitoba R3C 3B2
Canada
Biweekly column

**FREDERICK, Robert H.**
276 Dowd Road
Elyria, Ohio 44035
(Stamp Facts)
The Chronicle-Telegram
225 East Ave.
Elyria, Ohio 44035
Column appears on Sunday

**GASQUE, James**
The Sunday Sun
Baltimore, Md. 21203
(Stamps)
The Sunday Sun
Baltimore, Md. 21203
Column appears on Sunday

**GOODRICH, Ronald L.**
P.O. Box 981
Worcester, Mass. 01613
(The Stamp Corner)
The Worcester
Sunday Telegram
20 Franklin St.
Worcester, Mass. 01613
Weekly column

**GREENE, J.R.**
33 Bearsden Road
Athol, Mass. 01331
(Stamp-ing Around)
Athol Daily News
Athol Press Inc.
Exchange Street
Athol, Mass. 01331
Weekly column

**HAHN, Charless**
370 Walnut St.
Winnetka, Ill. 60093
(Stamps)
Chicago Sun-Times
401 N. Wabash Ave.
Chicago, Ill. 60611
Column appears on Sunday

**HALTER, Jon C.**
1325 Walnut Hill Lane
Irving, Tex. 75062
(Stamps and Coins)
Boys' Life Magazine
Monthly column

**HASSELL, Wayne**
1765 Juno Ave.
St. Paul, Minn. 55116
(Stamps in the News)
St. Paul Pioneer Press
55 E. 4th St.
St. Paul, Minn. 55101
Column appears on Sunday

**HATHAWAY, Bradford A.**
87 Aucoot Road
Mattapoisett, Mass. 02739
(Stamps)
New Bedford Standard-Times
P.O. Box D-912
New Bedford, Mass. 02742
Biweekly column
The Cape Cod Times
319 Main St.
Hyannis, Mass. 02601
Weekly column

**HIGGINS, R.R.**
1901 Taylor Road
Columbus, Ind. 47201
(The Stamp Man)
The Columbus Republic
333 Second St.
Columbus, Ind. 47201
Biweekly column

**JOYCE, Edward R.**
5552 Riverton Road
Jacksonville, Fla. 32211
(Stamps-Coins)
Times-Union Journal
1 Riverside Ave.
Jacksonville, Fla. 32201
Column appears on Sunday

**KEHR, Ernest A.**
P.O. Box 1
Richmond Hill, N.Y. 11419
(Stamps)
Newsday
Long Island, N.Y. 11747
Column appears on Sunday

**KENT, David A.**
P.O. Box 13
New Britain, Conn. 06050
(Stamps)
The Hartford Courant
285 Broad St.
Hartford, Conn. 06115
Column appears on Sunday

**KING, Dick**
Topeka Capital-Journal
616 Jefferson St.
Topeka, Kan. 66607

(Stamping Around with
Dick King)
Topeka Capital-Journal
616 Jefferson St.
Topeka, Kan. 66607
Column appears on Thursday

**LEVINE, Dr. Earl J.**
120 N. Ohio Ave.
Wellston, Ohio 45692
(Stamps and Stuff)
Tri-State Trader
P.O. Box 90
Knightstown, Ind. 46148
Weekly column

**LORENSON, Russell J.**
550 N. Ashe St.
Southern Pines, N.C. 28387
(Stamps and Coins)
The Pilot
Box 58
Southern Pines, N.C. 28387
Weekly column

**LUTGENDORF, Alex L.**
5260 W. Sweetwater Drive
Tucson, Ariz. 85745
(Through the World
of Stamps)
Green Valley News and Sun
P.O. Box 567
Green Valley, Ariz. 85614
Column appears every
other Wednesday

**MacKENDRICK, Russell**
Box 390
Manchester, Conn. 06040
(Collectors' Corner)
Manchester Evening Herald
Herald Square
Manchester, Conn. 06040
Weekly column

**MARTIN, James**
Box 279
Greenville, Calif. 95947
(Stamps)
Sacramento Bee
Box 15779
Sacramento, Calif. 95813
Column appears on Sunday

**MASSE, Denis**
P.O. Box 1212
Place d'Armes Station
Montreal, Quebec
Canada H2Y 3K2
(Notes Philateliques)
La Presse
7 St. James St.
Montreal, Quebec
Canada H2Y 1K9
Column appears on Saturday

**MONTAGNES, James**
11 Burton Road
Toronto, Ont., Canada M5P 1T6

(Stamps)
Toronto Star
1 Yonge St.
Toronto, Ont., Canada
  M5E 1E6
Column appears on Saturday

**MOSES, Alfred J.**
P.O. Box 3547
Riverside, Calif. 92519
(Stamps)
(Stamp Talk)
Collectors News
P.O. Box 156
Grundy Center, Iowa 50638
Monthly column

**NAWYN, Bert**
298 Brown Ave.
Paterson, N.J. 07508
(World of Stamps)
Hawthorne Press
417 Lafayette Ave.
Hawthorne, N.J. 07506
Weekly column

**NICHOLS, Jim**
Dayton Daily News
Dayton, Ohio 45401
(Stamps)
Dayton Daily News
Dayton, Ohio 45401
Column appears on Sunday

**PACKARD, Jim**
2207 Brookhaven Road
Richmond, Va. 23224
(Stamps and Coins)
Richmond Times-Dispatch
333 E. Grace St.
Richmond, Va. 23219
Weekly column

**PELLERIN, Andre**
Le Nouvelliste Ltee
500 St-Georges
Trois-Rivieres, Quebec,
  G9A 5J6 Canada
(Les Timbres)
Le Nouvelliste Ltee
500 St-Georges
Trois-Rivieres, Quebec
  G9A 5J6 Canada
Weekly column

**PUGH, Kenneth W.**
134 20th St.
Brandon, Manitoba R7B 1L4
  Canada
(Special Delivery)
The Brandon Sun
6th Street and Rosser Avenue
Brandon, Manitoba R7A 5Z6
  Canada
Column appears on Saturday

**READ, Mike**
Philatelic Editor
The Houston Post

Houston, Tex. 77001
(Stamps)
The Houston Post
Houston, Tex. 77001
Weekly Column

**REASON, Delbert C.**
P.O. Box 97
Shirley, Ind. 47384
(Collectors Corner)
The Courier-Times
P.O. Box 369
New Castle, Ind. 47362
Weekly column

**RECHNER, Bernadine M.**
P.O. Box 75
Prospect Heights, Ill. 60070
(Stamp Notes)
The Herald
Paddock Publications
217 W. Campbell
Arlington Heights,
  Ill. 60006
Column appears on Sunday

**ROHLING, Eugene M.**
P.O. Box 1535
Casper, Wyo. 82602
(Stamps)
American Collector
P.O. Drawer C
Kermit, Tex. 78745
Monthly column

**ROTHBLUM, Morris C.**
103 Leconey Circle
Palmyra, N.J. 08065
(Stamps and Coins)
Courier-Post
Camden, N.J. 08101
Column appears on Sunday

**SHEEDY, T. J.**
4105-40th St.
Red Deer, Alberta,
  Canada T4N 1A4
(Philatelic pot-pourri)
Red Deer Advocate
P.O. Box 520
Red Deer, Alberta,
  Canada T4N 5G3
Weekly column

**SMITH, H. Arthur III**
128 Voorhees Ave.
Pennington, N.J. 08534
(Stamps)
Trenton Times Newspapers
500 Perry St.
Trenton, N.J. 08605
Weekly column

**SPAHICH, Eck**
1512 Lancelot Road
Borger, Tex. 79007
(Stamps and Coins)
Borger News-Herald
P.O. Box 5130

Borger, Tex. 79007
Weekly column

**STEGEMEYER, F. Lee**
Box 4082
West Palm Beach, Fla. 33402
(About Stamps & Coins)
Cincinnati Enquirer
617 Vine Street
Cincinnati, Ohio 45202
Palm Beach Post
Drawer T
West Palm Beach, Fla. 33402
Miami News
Box 615
Miami, Fla. 33152
Weekly column

**STERN, Henry B.**
3982 Bayberry Lane
Seaford, N.Y. 11783
(Jewish Week Stamp Collector)
Jewish Week
No. 1 Park Ave.
New York, N.Y. 10016
Weekly column
(The Stamp Collector)
Jewish News
60 Glenwood Ave.
East Orange, N.J. 07017
Weekly column

**TAUB, Peter B.**
55 Exchange St.
Rochester, N.Y. 14614
(Peter B. Taub)
Rochester Times-Union
55 Exchange St.
Rochester, N.Y. 14614
Monday through Saturday

**TOWER, Samuel A.**
The New York Times
229 W. 43 St.
New York, N.Y. 10036
(Stamps)
The New York Times
229 W. 43 St.
New York, N.Y. 10036
Column appears on Sunday

**TURNER, Leon**
174 Base Line Road E
London, Ont., Canada N6C 2N9
(Stamps)
The London Free Press
P.O. Box 2280
London, Ont., Canada N6A 4G1
Weekly column

**VASKAS, Edmund J.**
20 Franklin St.
Worcester, Mass. 01613
(With the Collectors)
The Evening Gazette
20 Franklin St.
Worcester, Mass. 01613
Weekly column

**WENDT, Robert L.**
P.O. Box 10308
Winston-Salem, N.C. 27108
(Stamp Album)
Clemmons Courier
Clemmons, N.C. 17012
Pacific Stars & Stripes
APO San Francisco,
Calif. 96503
Weekly column

**WERST, John P.**
285 W. Second St.
Moorestown, N.J. 08057
(Speaking of Stamps)
Burlington County Times
Willingboro, N.J. 08046
Bucks County Courier Times

Bristol, Pa. 19007
Column appears on Sunday

**WINICK, Les**
Chicago Tribune 4th Floor
435 N. Michigan Ave.
Chicago, Ill. 60611
(Stamps)
Chicago Sunday Tribune
435 N. Michigan Ave.
Chicago, Ill. 60611
Weekly column

**WOLINETZ, Harvey D.**
14 Cloverdale Lane
Monsey, N.Y. 10952
(Stamp Column)
The Jerusalem Post
Box 80

Jerusalem, Israel
Weekly column

**ZIMMERER, Carl E.**
610 Wataga Drive
Louisville, Ky. 40206
(Stamps and Coins
in the News)
The Courier-Journal
Louisville, Ky.
Column appears every Sunday

**ZOLLMAN, Joseph L.**
P.O. Box 632
Long Beach, N.Y. 11561
(Stamping Grounds)
Features Associates
San Raphael, Calif. 94901
Weekly column

# Repairs, Regumming Reperfing

# 30

By Earl P.L. Apfelbaum, Inc.
2006 Walnut Street
Philadelphia, Pa. 19103

Alterations are made on stamps to improve their appearance. When sold as such they marginally increase the value of the item over an unaltered specimen.

However, most altered stamps are not sold as such. Rather, they are sold by unethical collectors and dealers as perfect specimens, at the huge premiums that perfection demands.

The morality and legality of the issue is clear: there is nothing wrong with a repaired, reperfed, or regummed specimen of a stamp if it is sold as such. But it is unethical as well as illegal to sell an altered specimen as a perfect stamp.

Many altered stamps are sold as perfect. Sometimes this is the result of stupidity on the part of dealers and collectors, but more often than not it is simple ignorance.

The methods of determining whether or not alterations have been performed on a stamp are as follows. This should be used as a guide only, however.

Experience is indispensable as some stamps that look unaltered really are and a few that manifest the characteristics discussed are in fact unaltered.

## Repairs

There are many types of repairs — filled thins, closed tears, ironed out creases, added margins. All can be told by use of the watermark tray.

It is important to use as good a wetting agent in the tray as is safe with the particular printing on the stamp involved.

**Filled thins** — Thins decrease the value of a stamp. A repairer will fill a thin with liquid paper, egg white, or another compound so that to normal sight it appears as if there is no thin in the paper.

In the tray, a filled thin looks lighter, usually much lighter than the surrounding paper as the material used to fill the thin is usually far denser than the surrounding paper mesh.

**Closed tears** — Tears are closed with various forms of epoxy or glue. In the tray they show up as a thin dark line or a thicker lighter line.

Such inclusions can occur naturally in paper though, so it is important to confirm possible closed tears by use of a magnifying glass (10X) on the design portion of the stamp.

A tear, closed or otherwise, will break the printing — a pulp or natural inclusion will not.

**Ironed out creases** — A crease will affect the value of a stamp. Sometimes the crease is ironed out to make the stamp appear as if it is not creased at all.

A stamp is wetted and heat is applied to hide the effects of a crease to the unaided eye.

In the tray, ironed out creases appear as straight lines, like regular creases, except that the boundaries of the crease have begun to spread.

**Added margins** — A margin or margins can be added to improve the centering of a stamp.

As this is extremely extensive repair work, it is usually very easy to determine by looking for the lightness (in the tray) due to thicker paper where the added margin is joined to the main of the stamp.

More sophisticated repairers will add all four margins to a stamp, especially an imperforate stamp where such extreme premiums are paid for margin size.

The stamp is shaved to a fine thinness and backed onto a larger piece of paper similar to matting a print.

The work can be detected by a hint of a dark rectangle in the tray comprising the original stamp and some deft work with a magnifying glass around the margins.

Cancellations, if any, are made to extend to the margin. When done expertly, such work is very difficult to detect and quite beautiful to behold.

## Regumming

Qualified professionals and amateurs rely on two factors to ascertain if gum is original or not — color and tone of the gum and its relationship to the stamp's perforation teeth.

The color and tone method takes a great deal of experience. An experienced collector or dealer just gets a feel for how the gum on a certain stamp should look.

The perforation teeth method is more empirical. When a postal service prints a stamp it is gummed before it is perforated. When a regummer plies his trade the gum is applied after perforating and will inevitably tend to congeal ever so slightly on and over the perforation tips.

It is important to remember though, that a slight amount of gum running to the tips of the perforations when seen through a magnifying glass is normal in many older stamps, especially those stored in mounts or humid climates.

A collector should be suspicious if he sees through his magnifying glass the gum extending a tiny bit beyond the perforation teeth, but such evidence is not alone grounds for conviction.

## Reperforating

Stamps are reperforated to disguise a straightedge side. Such a straightedge could be the result of printing method, as in the flat press U.S. stamp to about 1930, or can result from damage.

In any case, reperforated perforation holes usually are misaligned from their opposite holes. They tend to be flat at the edges, unlike a true perf hole which shows slight fraying from where it was torn from the stamp next to it.

Often, the holes tend to be slightly larger or smaller than the holes on the sides of the stamps.

## Summary

In all this discussion, rest assured that the reperfers, regummers and repairers of the world are well aware of the flaws of their trade, and like any artisan, ethical or not, are taking steps to refine their trade and make it more difficult to determine their work from the unaltered.

There is little danger of repairs or reperfing on most post-1940 issues. Regumming is only a problem on issues where large premiums are paid for perfect gum.

# Index

# — Mc —

# — M —

**NOTES**

**NOTES**

**NOTES**

**NOTES**

**NOTES**

**NOTES**